FROMMER'S
EUROPE
ON $25 A DAY

by Arthur Frommer
with sightseeing commentaries
by Hope Arthur

1985 Edition

Published by Frommer/Pasmantier Publishers
A Division of Simon & Schuster, Inc.
1230 Avenue of the Americas
New York, New York 10020

ISBN 0-671-52473-9

Manufactured in the United States of America

*Although every effort was made to ensure the accuracy
of price information appearing in this book,
it should be kept in mind that prices
can and do fluctuate in the course of time.*

CONTENTS

MAPS

PREFACE TO THE TWENTY-EIGHTH YEARLY EDITION OF EUROPE ON $25 A DAY

TWENTY-EIGHT YEARS AGO, under its earlier title, this book made its first appearance on the travel shelves of the nation's bookstores—and provoked something close to a minor riot. "Impossible!" cried one class of readers, as they spotted its name. *"Europe on $5 a Day?"*

"Is he crazy?" countered another. "I did it on $2 a day."

Now controversy was expected when this book appeared. But no one—not even my most Bohemian advisers—anticipated complaints that I had *over*priced the cost of a European vacation. And yet there came such letters: gentle, chiding letters, suggesting that the guide to a really low-cost vacation was yet to be written; regretful letters, stating it was such a shame I had missed that cute little hotel in Madrid where a room-plus-three-meals cost—at that time—$4.10 a day.

Among the hundreds of letters that readers have written, letters of the disappointed variety were happily few in number. But I mention the minority reaction to *Europe on $25 a Day* to prove a point. Twenty-five dollars a day is no miracle budget for life in Europe. There is nothing fantastical about this book, or about the recommendations it contains. Mention its title to a European—or to an experienced American tourist—and they will ask what all the fuss is about.

Do you still doubt it? Do you wonder that travel on a strange continent can cost a fraction of the amount you'd spend in the United States? Thousands of Americans have come, seen, and been convinced. For an opening bit of proof, try the following letter from an Army captain and his wife, who were equally doubtful:

"Frankly, we took a rather jaundiced view of your book because of the sharp contrasts it offered to American vacation prices. Nevertheless, we took it with us on our first trip to Paris, which we regarded as the supreme test. We bought $400 in francs here in Nuremberg prior to departure, drove to Paris and back in our own car, stayed seven days, followed your book almost completely, and returned with $50 in francs. . . . Our room at the Hotel Voltaire on the Left Bank cost $18 a night for the two of us, and while it was three flights up, it was a charming place with a little balcony that opened onto the Seine. We have a friend who is studying at the Sorbonne, and as we walked with him to lunch one day, we passed a sidestreet on which we recognized the Restaurant St. Michel from your book. We ate for $5 apiece among students and artists, and we had a wonderful time. Our friend, who has been in Paris for over a year, was amazed as to how we could have discovered such a true Parisian hangout. . . . There were superb meals at the other restaurants you mentioned—meals that couldn't be found in the U.S. at three times the price—so as far as we're concerned, they can keep the Tour d'Argent and Maxim's."

The mail was literally filled with such experiences. There was, for instance, the middle-aged lady from Portland, Oregon, who found that she could stay near her beloved Tate Gallery in London, in a quaint and comfortable boardinghouse-hotel packed with other art enthusiasts, for only $12 a night. There were the honeymooners from Atlanta, Georgia, who had breakfast in bed for 10 francs ($1.25) in Nice. There was the co-ed from Radcliffe who was able to purchase a full-course meal in the price paradise of Madrid for less than she'd pay for an ice-cream sundae at home.

To me, communications like these convey the best travel news of the year. They are evidence that after decades of fear and bewilderment, Americans are finally and forcefully "wising up" about Europe.

In the years that followed the war, a legend spread about the cost of a European vacation. The story went that a heavy curtain had descended over the continent—a curtain composed of crisp, green travelers' checks. These checks came in wads thick as your fist, and they were said to peel away like the leaves of Fall. Believing the tale, Americans trudged without protest to the most expensive hotels and restaurants in Europe, reacted in horror and disgust when the bills came in, and created bad vacations for tourists to budget $50 a day for their trips to Europe, the average European tourist—the Frenchman, the Englishman, the Swiss—was enjoying a far better vacation at the rates and standards prescribed in this book. Fifty dollars a day for life in Europe? Why, some Europeans at that time considered themselves lucky to earn $50 a week!

But the most pitiful part of the average American vacation was not its price. By the mere act of overpaying, Americans robbed themselves of all the thrill and flavor of Europe. Invariably, they bought themselves into the most dreary hotels and restaurants—the most elegant bores—the most gold-plated clip joints—that Europe had to offer.

Who needs it? Who needs suffer the pink-and-porcelain "recreation lounges" of a de luxe class European hotel? Who needs the waltz competitions and the planned picnics of a Biarritz resort? Who but an ancient Victorian would prefer the cathedral quiet of the Restaurant Ritz to the briskness of a sidewalk Paris bistro? It is the tourist who lives inexpensively on a European vacation, who lives relaxed, who seeks out the European side of European life—it's that person who enjoys a European trip.

An ever-growing number of Americans have caught on to this secret of European travel. You'll spot them at the airports as they eagerly swap stories of the exciting low-cost finds of their European tour. They engage in no endless monologues about an unending succession of overcharges and cheats. For them Europe was a fulfilling experience, because they dared to live as the Europeans do, and in return, encountered warmth and friendship wherever they went. The size of this group is reflected by the success of the first twenty-seven editions of *Europe on $25 a Day,* and by the fact that it has now eclipsed in sales a better-known guidebook whose author believes that the best way to belittle a European hotel is to say that it "reeks of local color."

I've tried to keep faith with the readers of *Europe on $25 a Day* in this twenty-eighth edition. Europe has again been revisited, hotels reviewed, meals re-eaten, and at least four pairs of my shoes worn out. The result is a completely revised, expanded and up-to-date version of a book that has now carved out its own established niche in the world of travel, and will be issued, similarly revised, in every year to come. For aiding me to do this, my thanks go out to the tens of thousands of persons who gave such an eager, exciting reception to the earlier editions of *Europe on $25 a Day*. In their disdain for ostentation and their love of people, they are the truest diplomats our country has, and they have my everlasting admiration and affection.

I hope the readers of this new edition will enjoy the book as much as I've enjoyed researching and writing it. Travel, after all, is a marvelous thing. It's a time of your life when all the habits and obligations of daily existence are hurled aside, and the scope of your needs becomes no bigger than a suitcase. You emerge from familiar routine into a world where everything is unexpected, where even your language can no longer serve as a handy crutch. In that kind of setting, all the minutiae of life can fall away, an individual can finally know what he or she is all about—and find freedom.

To the discovery of that spirit of freedom, this book hopes to contribute.

Have a good trip!

New York, N.Y.
October, 1984

A FINAL NOTE FROM A.F.: I could not send this 1985 edition to press without acknowledging the untiring efforts of my associate, Nikolaus Lorey, in reviewing the accuracy of each factual assertion in this book. His contributions to this revision—in discovering new establishments worthy of recommendation; in commenting on current operations of existing recommended establishments; and his dogged, punctilious attention to detail and precision, the hallmark of this book—have been absolutely invaluable to me.

To my
beloved
Hope

Europe on $25 a Day

The title of this book refers to a self-imposed allowance of $25 a day for basic living costs in Europe—that is, room and all three meals. That limit is normally maintained by spending no more than $12 to $14 per person for a double-occupancy room, $2 for breakfast, $3.50 for lunch, $4 or $5 for dinner. In countries where a free breakfast is provided with the room charge (England and Holland), the allocation for hotels can rise to $18-or-so for a single room, $26 to $30 for a double.

The cost of transportation within Europe, of sightseeing and entertainment, is not included in the $25 figure. Because of that, this book is not a guide to mere subsistence-level living, but deals instead with clean and comfortable accommodations that can be used with safety by persons of all ages and by both sexes.

A Modest Proposal

Numerous readers have written in to complain that this book, in its successive yearly expansions, has become too bulky for easy use in Europe. Some have suggested that I print it on perforated pages, or issue the book in three-ringed, loose leaf binder form, or simply split it into three or more separate volumes. Adoption of any of these proposals would necessarily require a substantial increase in the retail price of *Europe on $25 a Day*, which is to me inconsistent with its theme and philosophy.

May I suggest the following? Each of our chapters begins on a right-hand page, and ends on a left-hand page. If you will carefully bend back the pages at the opening and end of a chapter, you will find that you can easily tear out that chapter intact, and then stuff it into pocket or purse for use in the city it covers. Although this may seem a somewhat mercenary suggestion on my part (because it results in the systematic destruction of this book), it is, I submit, a better idea than to adopt a format costing $16.95 or more per copy.

A Note to Readers

In the last edition of this book, I wrote that *Europe on $25 a Day* hoped to become "a clearing-house for the low-cost hotel and restaurant finds of its readers." As the pages of this edition indicate, hundreds of readers were delighted to take the hint. Their cost-saving choices and schemes make up the sections entitled "Readers' Selections" now found in each chapter.

In part, this book will continue to be a joint enterprise. If you've discovered an establishment which belongs on these pages, then write a letter about it to Arthur Frommer.

A Small Disclaimer

Many thousands of hours of research are each year directed to ensuring the accuracy of prices appearing in this book and, for the most part, we believe that we've succeeded in obtaining reliable up-to-date data. Nevertheless, prices do change in the course of time, and proprietors of establishments sometimes do change price policies in the course of a travel season. Therefore, it's fairly obvious that we cannot guarantee that each and every such price will remain unchanged during the lifetime of this edition.

Readers should also note that the establishments described under Readers' Selections or Suggestions have not in many cases been inspected by the author and that the opinions expressed there are those of the individual reader(s) only. They do not in any way represent the opinions of the publisher or author of this guide.

EUROPE ON $25 A DAY

The Reason Why

THIS IS A BOOK for American tourists who
a) own no oil wells in Texas
b) are unrelated to the Aga Khan
c) have never struck it rich in Las Vegas
and who *still* want to enjoy a wonderful European vacation.

This is also a book for Americans who would like, on their overseas trip, to see Europe and Europeans, and not simply other Americans.

Rarely has a travel book contained such information. For proof, let's examine a few.

I have one of the better-known European guidebooks before me as I write. This tome states that one really can't consider staying in Paris at hotels other than the Ritz, the Crillon or the Plaza Athenée (at $150 for room and bath). It recommends the elegant Tour d'Argent and Maxim's for your evening meal. It shudders at any form of European train transportation other than First Class. It maps out, in other words, the short quick road to insolvency that most American tourists have been traveling for years.

But money and economy are not the only areas in which the normal sources of travel information fall short. More often than not, the high-priced hotels and restaurants they recommend are the least European, least interesting and most disappointing accommodations available to you.

Across the street from Terminal Station in Rome, for instance, stand three great continental hotels. These are the "name" establishments to which all the travel books and vacation pamphlets direct the American tourist. They attract no one else. Walk into one of these spots on a summer night in Rome, and you might just as well have never left home. English fills the air. Bridge games go on in the lobby. For $90 a day in the Eternal City, you have bought the equivalent of a Legion convention in Detroit.

Three blocks away, of course, are a host of smaller Italian hotels and pensions—uncrowded, quiet and inexpensive. These are the lodgings patronized by European tourists, who find rooms within them, clean and comfortable rooms, for prices ranging around $14 per person per night. Americans never hear of them. Because most guidebooks assume that every American carries with him gunny sacks of gold, Americans continue to crowd into the least satisfying hotels in Rome, while Europeans vacation comfortably, at one-fourth the price, just three blocks away.

Contrasts such as these, repeated all across the continent of Europe, have convinced me that there is a crying need for one American guidebook devoted to the inexpensive hotels, the inexpensive restaurants, the inexpensive methods of touring Europe. Such a book would collect, in one volume, all the "finds" of the continent: a Left Bank restaurant in Paris where a superb three-course dinner costs $5.50; a hotel in Florence, fronting the Arno River, where sunny and spacious rooms rent for $10 per person.

These finds exist, in abundance, in nearly every city of Europe. They exist because of the hard, unalterable fact that prices, wages and costs in many European countries are at least a third below those of the United States. It is a fact—check it if you will—that an experienced secretary in London can earn less than $180 a week. An apprentice architect in Italy earns $200 a week. Yet these people travel, and travel well. They are able to vacation on limited funds because they know the rules of European living, and they know where to stay and where to eat.

The smart American can do the same. *I say that most of the major cities of Europe can still be traveled, adequately and well, for living costs per person (that is, room and board) of no more than $25 a day. I say that the same budget vacations which once thrilled the pre-war tourist are still available to the American who is willing to think and plan for himself.*

The items to be had for these cut-rate costs are surprising in their quality. Twenty-five dollars a day is no mere survival budget: no one expects you to eat picnic lunches or sleep in a tent. The recommendations set forth in this book are designed for normal vacation living: tasty and filling restaurant meals, clean and comfortable hotel beds.

An inexpensive European vacation requires more, though, than lists of restaurants and hotels. You'll need transportation information, currency tips, menu translations, entertainment advice—a flock of other suggestions and aids. Here's how *Europe on $25 a Day* intends to set forth that information:

■ **Chapter 1** expounds on the general theories of budget living in Europe—the broad rules and principles to be followed wherever you go. This chapter sets the stage for the more detailed information on specific cities which follow later. It must be read in advance of those later chapters, because it explains the terminology that will be used and the assumptions that will be made.

■ **Chapter 2** offers my wife Hope's advice on the articles of clothing that ought to be packed for a low-cost trip to Europe. You would not think that the contents of a suitcase affect your expenses—but they do, vitally.

■ **Chapter 3** deals with the problem of getting to Europe. All the best price-cutting schemes are discussed—standby seats and "budget" fares, "apex," "super-apex," and the "public charter." The chapter then ends with a fast look at the cost of sea transportation.

■ **Chapter 4** contains a concise railway timetable of the major European expresses, giving their hours of departure and arrival in every major European city. The chapter also includes some hints on the science of European train travel—which you'll discover is quite an art.

■ **Chapter 5** discusses auto rentals. We'll discuss the cheapest methods of traveling by car in Europe, and all the other ramifications of this complex, tricky subject.

■ **Chapters 6 through 26** are devoted to the major tourist centers of Europe: London, Paris, Brussels, Copenhagen, Stockholm, Oslo, Amsterdam, Munich, Vienna, Venice, Florence, Rome, Nice, Salzburg, Innsbruck, Zurich, Geneva, Berlin, Athens, Madrid and Lisbon. For each of

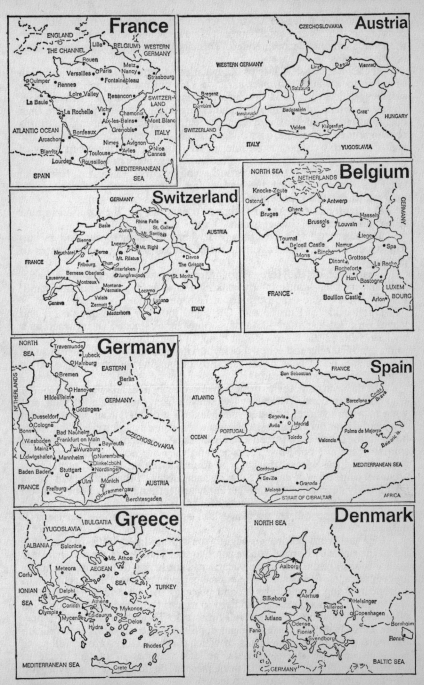

these 21 cities, *Europe on $25 a Day* provides specific data on best buys in restaurants, hotels and entertainment. The book also tells you how to reach the establishments recommended. The city chapters are accompanied by maps.

■ **Chapter 27**—"A Tale of Many Cities"—fulfills a long-time ambition of mine to expand *Europe on $25 a Day* into a comprehensive, self-sufficient guide that need not be supplemented by another travel book. Here, we briefly survey sleeping and eating accommodations in more than one hundred smaller or more remote European cities, setting forth our recommendations of the best budget hotels and restaurants in each. The inclusion of this chapter is an interim step toward the day when many of these cities will be the subjects of individual chapters in this book.

■ **Chapter 28** provides capsule vocabularies in seven European languages—short lists of the words and phrases you'll need to make yourself understood, plus phonetic pronunciations of the same.

■ **Chapter 29** offers translations of the menus you'll encounter in nine European countries. Enough said.

■ **Chapter 30** tells you how and where to change your dollars into foreign currency. It ends with a set of tables showing current rates of exchange.

Nearly all of the foregoing information was gathered in a basic, firsthand manner—on foot—by walking and searching, notebook in hand, through most of the urban centers of Europe.

I first came to Europe as a G.I., and took my three-day passes and leaves on a lot less than $25 a day. Many times since, I've returned as a civilian, with a little more cash on hand, but with the same aversion to clip joints, padded bills and other classic tourist traps. Europe has never lost its thrill for me, and I have never found that a bulging wallet is the key to an enjoyable European vacation.

On the contrary, the Europe I love is chiefly unavailable to the tourist who does overspend. Whenever I've strayed from the budget formula, and gone to a grand hotel or eaten in a Maxim's-type restaurant, I have soon discovered that my vacation has become self-conscious, fettered, and really quite dull. These high-priced establishments—created for the unthinking tourist—they are not "my" Europe, and they are not the Europe of all those Americans whose trip was a profound, living experience, rather than an unvarying series of guided tours and snapshots. If these comments seem insufferably dogmatic (and they certainly are!), then I simply hope that you will put me to my proof, and discover for yourself that traveling on a budget is not only done out of necessity, but—more important—because it is desirable.

One last word before we begin. You will find very little in this book about the sights of Europe you've come to see. That doesn't mean that your author looks upon a European vacation as consisting of nothing but hotels and restaurants. It is precisely because I believe that the daily mechanics of European living should take second place to the art and culture of that continent, that this book tries so hard to render those mechanical details as effortless as possible. That's a full-time task. Though occasionally I may break loose from the crass financial details, I make no effort to duplicate the more descriptive guidebooks of which the bookstores are so full.

And now we start—with the general theories of budget living in Europe, the broad rules and principles to be followed wherever you go—and to be studied before you leave!

Chapter I

RULES OF THE GAME

The Basic Theory

THERE ARE RULES to traveling inexpensively in Europe. There are subtle ways of conducting yourself which should never vary, regardless of the particular European country in which you happen to be. Even such common habits as your attitude towards baths and breakfast can mean the difference between a budget vacation and a bankrupt one.

Sounds silly? Let's test the statement by examining an unheard-of travel topic—the theory of baths—which can cut your costs by amazing amounts on every day of your European trip.

BATHS IN EUROPE: When an American registers at a European hotel and is asked if he wants a private bath with his room, his normal reaction is to answer, "Of course." By so doing, he immediately increases the cost of his hotel by about 50%, and yet obtains essentially the same bath he could have had by answering "No." The reason is as follows:

Few Europeans regard a bath or shower as a daily necessity. The usual practice overseas is to start the day with a simple splash in the sink. Because of this, very few rooms in the lower-priced European hotels are equipped with private bath; and consequently, the rental charge for those rare rooms with bath is unusually high. I know of a large six-story hotel in high-priced Munich with over a hundred rooms, of which only nine have private baths. The rooms without bath in this hotel cost a reasonable $12 a night per person; the few rooms with bath cost $20 and up. The story is the same all over Europe—baths cost money. And moreover, insistence on a private bath will often make it impossible for you to stay in some of Europe's most delightful, and least expensive, budget lodgings—guesthouses and pensions, particularly—that sometimes have no rooms at all equipped with private bath.

This doesn't mean, however, that you must forego baths to travel inexpensively in Europe; you need only know where to take them. Virtually every hotel or other lodging in Europe maintains a room per floor solely as a private bath. To use that room, you ring for the chambermaid. She draws the bath, piles out large towels for your use, and you then pad across the hall in robe and slippers and splash away. In Germany, this costs 2 marks (80¢). In Italy it costs about $1. By adding this charge to your hotel bill, you can have a room *and* bath for $9.60 per person, instead of a room *with* bath for $16. The room is the same in either case. The saving results from the simple act of walking across the hall.

Rule 1 of your European travels is, therefore, never to ask for a private bath with your hotel room. It is impossible to travel cheaply in Europe otherwise. The prices listed for hotel rooms in later chapters of this book are all for rooms without baths, but all in hotels or pensions where baths are available for a slight supplemental charge.

BREAKFASTS: Where and how you eat breakfast in Europe is another key to successful budget living. We start with these facts:

Outside of England and Holland, Europeans confine their morning meal to the so-called continental breakfast, which consists of nothing but coffee and pastry or rolls. Poverty is not the reason. To a European, gorging on eggs, bacon and oatmeal at this hour would be nothing short of barbaric.

This will have an important effect upon your costs. Because European restaurants aren't geared to provide large breakfasts, the American-style meal of eggs-plus-all-the-trimmings will cost a small fortune. The same restaurant that serves a reasonably priced lunch or dinner will charge an outrageous sum for breakfast.

On the other hand, because the continental breakfast is so standardized and mass-consumed, it costs very little—provided you eat it in the right place. In France, for instance, nearly every cafe, bar or pastry shop sets up a coffee machine and a box of croissants (delicious, moon-shaped rolls) in the morning hours. This breakfast is identical to the one you'd be served in a restaurant or hotel dining room. The difference is that the coffee-and-croissants purchased in a Paris bar will cost about $1.20, while precisely the same meal will run to $3 or $4 in a hotel or restaurant. A similar price paradox exists in the rest of Europe, too.

All this adds up to the following tips. First, never enter a restaurant for breakfast in Europe. You'll find the same small continental breakfast available elsewhere (in bars and cafes) at one-third the price. Second, if you must have a large breakfast, try filling up on two or three continental breakfasts in place of the eggs and bacon. The latter will wreck your budget. If you can't stand that much coffee and that many rolls, try obtaining the additional foods at places other than restaurants. On my own trips to Italy, I usually take the continental breakfast in a bar or cafe, then stroll over to a market place for fruit and cheese—all for a few pennies. Try any of these alternatives. But whatever you eat, and however you do it, don't go to a restaurant for breakfast.

Disregard this advice in Holland and England, though. There, breakfast should always be eaten in the dining room of one's hotel, because the price of a Dutch or English hotel room always includes a *free* breakfast— and it's a whopper. For no extra price, you can have your fill of eggs, bacon, porridge, kippers, toast, jam and tea. More about this subject in our chapters on Amsterdam and London.

RESTAURANTS: Although succeeding chapters of this book provide specific names and addresses of good, inexpensive restaurants, there will still be times and occasions when you yourself must find a place to dine. Certain general restaurant tips are thus in order. Remember, first, never to patronize an establishment which doesn't display a menu in its window. That way, you can't possibly be overcharged once inside, or be handed a menu whose prices differ from those quoted to local residents.

Try, in addition, to discover restaurants which offer fixed price meals—that is, several courses for one lump sum, as opposed to the "à la carte" meal where you pay a separate sum for each individual dish. The cost of the fixed price dinner is considerably lower. Ask your waiter whether his restaurant serves a fixed price (in France, the "prix fixe," in Italy, the "prezzo fisso") dinner, for in many restaurants the fixed price menu will not automatically be handed to you. Search the menu for a possible cover charge. Particularly in France, you may find that the cover has catapulted the price on what had seemed to be a reasonable meal.

And finally, give thought to occasionally dispensing with a restaurant visit altogether, in favor of a do-it-yourself meal purchased from a grocery and eaten in a park or your hotel room. The delicatessen and food counters of Europe not only offer a means for saving money, but a chance to sample exotic and unforgettable foods. Indeed, once you've seen the colorful display cases of a French "charcuterie" (delicatessen), or the Chianti-selling-for-pennies in an Italian wine shop, you'll realize that picnic meals in Europe can be a supreme, but budget-priced, adventure.

FINDING A HOTEL: This, of course, is the make-or-break task of every one of your stops; the right choice, at the right price, can make the difference between your hating a city and loving it. Therefore, don't leap to find a hotel. However tired you may be from the trip, it is vitally important that you make a careful and deliberate study of several hotels before alighting at one. An hour spent at this job can result in several full days of pleasant consequences.

For the major cities of Europe, we've tried to eliminate most of the work by providing you with specific hotel descriptions and recommendations. For other cities not yet included in this book, the following is our "standard operating procedure":

Don't embark on the search laden with luggage. Either check your bags at the airport terminal or train station, or else leave them (and your travelmate) at a restaurant or cafe while you go out to look. Obviously, you need mobility and ease to make a proper selection.

Never rent a room sight unseen. On approaching each hotel, ask to see the rooms, and then check the bath and toilet facilities on each floor. Show a healthy regard for price. Let it be known that you are willing to proceed down the street if rooms are unavailable in your price range.

Naturally, you needn't become a disagreeable horse-trader in these dealings, or regard every hotel as an enemy to be out-foxed. Remember only that in renting a room, you are making a purchase which, multiplied by the days of your stay, can amount to a hefty sum. The choice should receive the same thoughtful care that any equivalent purchase would get. By analogy, no self-respecting British tourist would step to a hotel counter, learn that a room is available, and then immediately check in, as so many American tourists are quick to do.

Check, too, to determine whether any extra charges are to be added to the basic room rent. Are taxes included? Is breakfast included? Is breakfast at the hotel obligatory? If breakfast at the hotel is not taken, is a penalty charge added to the hotel bill? (This amazing practice is actually far more prevalent at de luxe hotels than at budget ones.) If any difficulty in communication exists between you and the hotel clerk, have him write the price of your room on a piece of paper, and keep the notation for later proof.

Properly and courteously done, these requests will not even slightly offend a European hotel management. Instead, they will evoke a measure of respect similar to that which the champions of budget travel—the British—have been receiving for years.

NEVER JUDGE A HOTEL BY ITS COVER:

One final note about judging a budget hotel: never be deterred by the exterior appearance of the hotel or by its lack of all those streetside touches that mark most American hotels—i.e., marquees, ground-floor lobbies, smartly designed entrances. Many excellent European hotels just aren't built that way—and to prove my point, let me use an analogy.

There are millionaires in Italy who live in buildings that resemble, from the outside, an 18th century warehouse; their walls are crumbling, ancient, peeling, cracked. Yet walk inside and you'll discover elegance unheard of—for Europeans value the architecture of the past and would never think of remodeling the exterior of a genuine period building.

The same with hotels. One particular budget choice of ours in Florence occupies the second floor of a loggia-enclosed building, constructed in the 18th century. Peer into the entrance and all you'll see is a dark, stone staircase, without decoration or amenities of any sort. But walk upstairs, and suddenly you'll be in a perfectly clean, charming and sunny hotel, whose rooms are as comfortable as any in Italy. You simply can not judge a European hotel by its exterior.

Then, too, some European hotels and pensions are located on the second and third floors of business buildings. The excellent Hotel Hemmet in Stockholm, for instance, looks—from the outside—like a collection of lofts, housing fly-by-night offices. But once again, walk upstairs and you'll find chintz curtains and a cozy lounge and rooms that would satisfy a D.A.R. member.

Always reserve judgement until you have actually seen the rooms. Get used to inspecting hotels that carry no outside markings other than a small plaque. Remember that you are in the Old World, whose surroundings and outlook are different from ours—and rejoice in that fact!

HOTEL RESERVATIONS:

Do you need them? That depends on your own personal inclinations and travel habits, and upon a balancing of advantages against disadvantages.

The advantages of advance reservations are obvious. You arrive in a European city and immediately check into a hotel without fuss or bother. In some cities, at certain periods of the year, that can save a lot of hotel searching.

The disadvantages are equally obvious. By making advance reservations (which often require deposits), you necessarily must accept a fixed and unalterable schedule for your travels in Europe. You cannot, mid-trip, decide to lengthen or shorten your stay in a particular city without affecting the reservations you've made in other towns. And, of course, you must go through the process of writing ahead to many hotels, some of which may answer that they're fully booked.

For those who do want the certainty of a room at a particular hotel, there are several general rules to follow. First, remember that these are budget hotels, and that the cost of conducting an air-mail correspondence over reservations is a relatively heavy one for them. You must accompany your reservations request with "International Postal Response Coupons" available at any U.S. Post Office. Do not send American stamps, which are useless to a European hotel owner. Second, you must state an exact date of arrival and departure, and not simply an "on or about" estimate. And finally, be prepared to pay an advance deposit on your reservation, to be forfeited if you don't show up on the exact date you've stated (a hotel may hold your room vacant on that date, and thus lose the chance for other business).

For those readers who'd prefer to follow a looser schedule and itinerary, without reservations, I've tried to ease the task in the formulation of our hotel recommendations. In seeking hotels for this book, I seek clusters of hotels, so that if one hotel is full, readers may simply walk to another hotel, a few feet away. Although, in that manner, you may not end up in your preferred choice, you'll usually find a suitable budget hotel without too much difficulty, depending on the city and the time of year.

HOW TO USE THIS BOOK: We move from these general rules to specific details in the upcoming chapters ahead devoted to cities. It's important that you know the form in which these facts will be presented.

Your housing needs come first. In those cities, particularly the southern European cities, where a $20 budget is achievable, we'll provide names and addresses of hotels, pensions or guesthouses where double rooms are available for from $16 to $18 without breakfast, for slightly more with. In more expensive cities—namely, the northern cities of Europe—where a budget tourist must devote up to $25 a night for basic living costs, we'll recommend guesthouses and hotels charging $14 to $16 *per person* for a double room. And we'll list establishments, too, offering single rooms at budget rates. In each case, the prices listed are for rooms without private baths. Except in Spain and Greece, where prices are so low that even the other variety is available at our level, insistence on a private bath will destroy the utility of this book.

Most city chapters also contain a list of at least a dozen good, but inexpensive, restaurants—the type charging (depending on the city) from $4 to $5 for an adequate meal. The aim, remember, is Europe on $25 a day, which means hotel for from $12 to $14 per person (using double occupancy rooms), breakfast for $2, lunch for $3.50, dinner for $5. But every city chapter will also sneak in a section entitled "Starvation Budget," showing you how to make it on a lot less. For comic relief, there'll be an occasional paragraph called "The Big Splurge," revealing the whereabouts of "luxury" meals that may run as high as $7 or $10.

Finally, this twenty-eighth edition of *Europe on $25 a Day* contains many hundreds of "Readers' Selections"—a term which refers to hotel and restaurant recommendations mailed in by readers. I have no doubt but that these choices may provide some of the most satisfying meals and rooms of your trip. At the same time, I cannot personally vouch for any of them, because the establishments listed as "Readers' Selections" are only those which I've been unable to see and try for myself. Rather than postpone their mention for a subsequent edition, I've included them now, untested except by the reader making the choice. But that's no small recommendation. Take it from me that the readers of this book are the most interesting, discerning and elite travelers of all who cross the Atlantic.

How much do the prices in this book change in the period before revised editions are issued? Not much at all. The point, you see, is to recommend hotels and restaurants which cater mainly to European tourists. These people simply won't tolerate sharp revisions in price, and their number is still far greater than the number of Americans who come overseas. In those few instances where European establishments have over-reacted to their mention in this book, they have been mercilessly yanked from this edition. That Parisian restaurant which put a copy of the book in its window, doubled its prices, and printed a separate menu in English, just won't be found in these newly revised pages.

The $25-a-Day Travel Club—How to Save Money on All Your Travels

In this book we'll be looking at how to get your money's worth in Europe, but there is a "device" for saving money and determining value on *all* your trips. It's the popular, international $25-a-Day Travel Club, now in its 22nd successful year of operation. The Club was formed at the urging of numerous readers of the $$$-a-Day and Dollarwise Guides, who felt that such an organization could provide continuing travel information and a sense of community to value-minded travelers in all parts of the world. And so it does!

In keeping with the budget concept, the annual membership fee is low and is immediately exceeded by the value of your benefits. Upon receipt of $15 (U.S. residents), or $18 U.S. by check drawn on a U.S. bank or via international postal money order in U.S. funds (Canadian, Mexican and other foreign residents) to cover one year's membership, we will send all new members the following items:

(1) *Any two* of the following books

Please designate in your letter which two you wish to receive:

Europe on $25 a Day
Australia on $25 a Day
England and Scotland on $25 a Day
Greece on $25 a Day
Hawaii on $35 a Day
India on $15 & $25 a Day
Ireland on $25 a Day
Israel on $30 & $35 a Day
Mexico on $20 a Day
New York on $35 a Day
New Zealand on $20 & $25 a Day
Scandinavia on $25 a Day
South America on $25 a Day
Spain and Morocco (plus the Canary Is.) on $25 a Day
Washington, D.C. on $35 a Day
Dollarwise Guide to Austria and Hungary
Dollarwise Guide to Canada
Dollarwise Guide to the Caribbean (including Bermuda and the Bahamas)
Dollarwise Guide to Egypt
Dollarwise Guide to England and Scotland

Dollarwise Guide to France
Dollarwise Guide to Germany
Dollarwise Guide to Italy
Dollarwise Guide to Portugal (plus Madeira and the Azores)
Dollarwise Guide to Switzerland and Liechtenstein
Dollarwise Guide to California and Las Vegas
Dollarwise Guide to Florida
Dollarwise Guide to New England
Dollarwise Guide to the Northwest
Dollarwise Guide to the Southeast and New Orleans
Dollarwise Guide to the Southwest
(Dollarwise Guides discuss accommodations and facilities in all price ranges, with emphasis on the medium-priced.)

Dollarwise Guide to Cruises
(This complete guide covers all the basics of cruising—ports of call, costs, fly-cruise package bargains, cabin selection booking, embarkation and debarkation and describes in detail over 60 or so ships cruising in Alaska, the Caribbean, Mexico, Hawaii, Panama, Canada, and the United States.)

How to Beat the High Cost of Travel
(This practical guide details how to save money on absolutely all travel items—accommodations, transportation, dining, sightseeing, shopping, taxes, and more. Includes special budget information for seniors, students, singles, and families.)

The New York Urban Athlete
(The ultimate guide to all the sports facilities in New York City for jocks and novices.)

Museums in New York
(A complete guide to all the museums, historic houses, gardens, zoos, and more in the five boroughs. Illustrated with over 200 photographs.)

The Fast 'n' Easy Phrase Book
(The four most useful languages—French, German, Spanish, and Italian—all in one convenient, easy-to-use phrase guide.)

Where to Stay USA
(By the Council on International Educational Exchange, this extraordinary guide is the first to list accommodations in all 50 states that cost anywhere from $3 to $25 per night.)

A Guide for the Disabled Traveler
(A guide to the best destinations for wheelchair travelers and other disabled vacationers in Europe, the United States, and Canada by an experienced wheelchair traveler. Includes detailed information about accommodations, restaurants, sights, transportation, and their accessibility.)

Marilyn Wood's Wonderful Weekends
(This very selective guide covers the best mini-vacation destinations within a 175-mile radius of New York City. It describes special country inns and

other accommodations, restaurants, picnic spots, sights, and activities—all the information needed for a two- or three-day stay.)

Bed & Breakfast—North America
(This guide contains a directory of over 150 organizations that offer bed & breakfast referrals and reservations throughout North America. The scenic attractions, businesses, and major schools and universities near the homes of each are also listed.)

(2) A one-year subscription to The Wonderful World of Budget Travel

This quarterly eight-page tabloid newspaper keeps you up to date on fast-breaking developments in low-cost travel in all parts of the world bringing you the latest money-saving information—the kind of information you'd have to pay $25 a year to obtain elsewhere. This consumer-conscious publication also features columns of special interest to readers: **The Traveler's Directory** (members all over the world who are willing to provide hospitality to other members as they pass through their home cities); **Share-a-Trip** (offers and requests from members for travel companions who can share costs and help avoid the burdensome single supplement); and **Readers Ask . . . Readers Reply** (travel questions from members to which other members reply with authentic firsthand information).

(3) A copy of Arthur Frommer's Guide to New York

This is a pocket-size guide to hotels, restaurants, nightspots, and sightseeing attractions in all price ranges throughout the New York area.

(4) Your personal membership card

Membership entitles you to purchase through the Club all Arthur Frommer publications for a third to a half off their regular retail prices during the term of your membership.

So why not join this hardy band of international budgeteers and participate in its exchange of travel information and hospitality? Simply send your name and address, together with your annual membership fee of $15 (U.S. residents) or $18 U.S. (Canadian, Mexican, and other foreign residents), by check drawn on a U.S. bank or via international postal money order in U.S. funds to: $25-A-Day Travel Club, Inc., Frommer/Pasmantier Publishers, 1230 Avenue of the Americas, New York, NY 10020. And please remember to specify which *two* of the books in section (1) above you wish to receive in your initial package of members' benefits. Or, if you prefer, use the last page of this book, simply checking off the two books you select and enclosing $15 or $18 in U.S. currency.

A second, vital, pre-trip activity involves the choice of what to take. It may be hard to believe that the contents of your suitcase can affect the cost of your trip, but they do, materially. My wife Hope has devoted a great deal of time and thought to that subject, and her comments on packing are the subject of our next chapter.

Chapter II

PACKING TO SAVE MONEY

By Hope Arthur*

1. Basic Freedom—Luggage
2. What to Take in Summer
3. What to Take in Winter
4. The Suitcase Itself
5. Sending You Packing

MOST OF THE chapters of this book deal with the low-cost facilities, attractions and accommodations that you'll encounter within Europe itself. I've been asked to deal with the "home front"—the packing and preparations before you leave. And that's no minor topic. It may be hard to believe that the contents of a suitcase can affect your travel costs, but they do, vitally. The tourist who carries heavy luggage and a complete wardrobe to Europe spends a great deal of money unnecessarily. Here's why:

1. Basic Freedom—Luggage

THE BURDENS OF BAGGAGE: A light suitcase means freedom. To emerge from a train or plane in Europe with bundles and boxes in every hand means porters, means taxicabs, means that the first hotel you pass must be the hotel in which you'll stay. To jaunt along with a light suitcase is to avoid all these costs, to use buses instead of cabs, to make your hotel choice slowly, carefully, and without desperation. With all the increase in mobility and decrease in fatigue which a light load entails, you can simply walk out when the clerk at the hotel counter quotes too high a price—and seek another hotel.

Don't sneer at this freedom. The traveler whose arms are bursting from their sockets with weight is a prisoner. It costs her or him dollars simply to get from train to hotel; it costs him or her tiring effort simply *to move,* and shopping around for a suitable hotel is out of the question.

A light suitcase means spiritual freedom, too, and an ability to

*Mrs. Arthur Frommer

concentrate on Europe in preference to mundane, daily needs. With too many clothes, and too many parcels, you'll spend hours unpacking and arranging your apparel when you check into a hotel. You'll spend hours packing them away again as you prepare to leave. You'll awake on the morning of departure, spend frantic and precious time in packing and wrapping, and finally collapse in sweat on your outgoing plane or train. Moreover, you'll have a disorderly, bursting suitcase—cluttered with dirty and unwashed clothes—in which to search for items on the trip itself.

Remember, too, that these problems increase as your European trip continues. However heavy your suitcase may have been as you left the U.S., it'll be twice as heavy as you go along. At every stop of your trip, you'll pick up mementos, gifts, books, papers, maps, souvenirs. Unless you've had a one-third-empty suitcase to begin with, you'll be festooned with extra parcels and packages near the end. You'll loop them over your shoulder, you'll squeeze them under your arm, you'll carry some with your little finger—and you'll approach each new city and each new hotel search in a mood of desperation. The first hotel you examine will have you at its mercy.

Make the choice. Decide to live and experience Europe, or choose instead to have an outfit available for every conceivable and far-fetched occasion. Decide to be a frenzied, harried clothes-horse, or a carefree, unburdened world traveler.

If you make the right decision, you'll do the following when it comes time to pack. You'll first buy the lightest suitcase available. You'll then fill it with the skimpiest set of clothing your courage will allow. Having done that, you'll then remove half these clothes from the suitcase, and depart on your European trip. You won't, for instance, take eight complete changes of underwear. You'll realize that four are enough, since you'll have to wash out those T-shirts yourself, in any event. You'll recognize how depressing it is to cart a suitcase of dirty clothes over half the continent of Europe.

If you've made too many eliminations of clothes before you start, you can always remedy the overzealousness in a European store. But don't worry. Whatever you take will be much too much.

2. What to Take in Summer

FOR WOMEN: After many summers of disregarding my own advice, I've finally settled on the wardrobe listed below as perfectly sufficient for a woman going to Europe for four to six weeks. (Only going for a week or two? Eliminate "L," some of the "R's" and "U.")

A. 4 pairs of nylon panties (you can rinse these out as you travel)
B. 4 pairs of pantyhose and 2 pairs of knee-hi's (and if you don't wear stockings in summer, more power to you; but take at least 1 pair for surprise special occasions or sudden unexpected changes in the weather)
C. 2 panty girdles (of quick-drying material) if you use them
D. 2 slips of any quick-drying synthetic material (only 1 for a short stay)
E. 2 bras of nylon or other quick-drying synthetic material
F. 1 cardigan sweater (which can double as a "knock-about" sweater or a wrap for cool evenings)
G. 1 pair of jeans, or solid-color, all-purpose pants

H. 1 pair of sandals (for walking, beachwear and bedroom slippers)
I. 1 pair of good, sturdy walking shoes (sensible heels a must!)
J. 1 pair of dressy shoes
K. 1 bathing suit and bathing cap
L. 1 wash 'n wear daytime dress
M. 1 traveling suit (pants or skirt or both)
N. 2 blouses (drip-dry) or 2 synthetic knit shirts
O. 1 all-purpose outfit (wonder fabric) which can double for afternoon and evening: possibly a decolleté dress with a jacket, or a long dark skirt that can double with sporty or dressy (but washable) tops
P. 1 pair of pajamas (or nightgown)
Q. 1 lightweight robe (or use your raincoat)
R. Jewelry, scarves and accessories, so you won't go mad wearing the same 3 basic outfits in different combinations day in and day out
S. Cosmetics and toiletries
T. 1 all-purpose rain-proof travel coat, which you can carry onto your plane
U. Your "traveling to" Europe outfit—just wear something you like. I'd wear the traveling suit. But whatever you decide, make sure it's something comfortable because you may find yourself wrapped up in it for several hours while you're "plane–ing" the Atlantic.

Note for the young, or the young at heart: Please know how gratifying it is to me to have seen the style of traveling change. Today hordes of kids—ranging in age from teens to 40's—are backpacking, whether they're actually youth-hosteling or not! Most of the young American gals that I see in Europe dress in jeans or a long skirt; these two items in combination with a couple of well-chosen tops complete the *entire wardrobe,* which is carried easily in a backpack. And for my money (and time) that, friends, is the way to travel!

As you can see the above list relies heavily on drip-dries. Look for labels reading nylon, Dacron, Orlon, polyester, Arnel, Banlon, Lycra, Spandex, Qiana, or my own favorite, Trevira (slightly more expensive, but sensuously silky, and wears like iron). Concentrate on clothing made of crease-resistant materials, and in simple, easy-to-care-for designs. Avoid pleats and ruffles (unless they are the permanent kind, with no ironing), and leave at home those lovely light, wispy dresses that need constant care and attention to look fresh.

There's been a slight shift of emphasis on my part from lightweight, cotton-like drip-dries (which are still highly recommended, especially for hot, humid climates) to synthetic knits or silky nylon jerseys (i.e., Banlon or Trevira, both so like matte jersey), which I've found to be marvelous for travel. They pack beautifully. No matter how you roll or bunch them up, they scarcely ever seem to wrinkle, and if they do, you need only hang them up for an hour or so to regain the original shape. (More difficult cases will sometimes come around if you'll take them to the bath down the hall, and steam them there while you shower or bathe.) And, they simply never seem to get soiled or dirty-looking, especially if you choose dresses in dark shades.

At first glance, you might think that synthetic or wool knits (which I like) are too heavy to be comfortable or packable (winter travelers excepted, of course). But even in this respect, they proved quite adaptable. I traveled extensively with a bare-backed sleeveless black synthetic knit dress, with a jacket that had long sleeves. Without the jacket, the dress was quite comfortable, even in the hottest climates. With the jacket, the outfit was heaven-sent for the chilly weather you'll sometimes experience in Europe, even in summer. Similarly, a knit suit with both skirt and pants is a marvelously versatile travel outfit.

Fashion here and there: Pants suits are as acceptable in European cities as they are here. Follow this rule of thumb: if it's an outfit you'd wear in your own nearest large city, feel free to wear it in a large European city (rural districts sometimes require more propriety in dress). One vital exception: churches (particularly in Italy and Spain) will not admit women wearing shorts or short-short skirts, frown on overly casual attire as being disrespectful, and may require that heads and/or shoulders be covered as well.

A final hint: Plan your wardrobe so that the clothes you take can be mixed and matched into a number of different combinations. By adding scarves and jewelry, the possibilities can be further multiplied. (I used to dream about designing the perfect travel outfit, one that would zipper or tie to create six or more different combinations—but I think a woman from California has beaten me to it; hers, however, is expensive.)

FOR MEN: The packing list can be even more severe, and still be perfectly sufficient. If you seek comfort and economy on a summer trip, then this is all you need take (in addition to whatever you wear on the plane) for a six- to eight-week trip. (Shorter visits, of one or two weeks? Eliminate "L," "M," and "N," the latter if you wear jeans on the plane, or "O" if you travel in a suit.)

A. 3 pairs of drip-dry undershorts or briefs
B. 3 drip-dry undershirts, if you wear them
C. 4 pairs of socks (all of quick-drying materials)
D. 1 handkerchief (if you're a sport)
E. 1 sweater
F. 2 drip-dry sport shirts (or synthetic knits, or nylon jerseys)
G. 2 drip-dry dress shirts (the cotton look, or nylon tricot)
H. 1 pair of dress shoes
I. 1 pair of rubber-soled walking shoes, or comfortable all-weather boots or shoes
J. 1 light bathrobe (or wear your raincoat)
K. 1 pair of pajamas
L. 1 sport jacket
M. 1 pair of durable, but smart-looking, slacks
N. 1 pair of jeans or chinos
O. 1 summer suit
P. 1 raincoat
Q. 2 neckties (the extra one's in case of spots)
R. 1 bathing suit
S. Toilet and shaving articles (adapted for European use, if electric).

Don't take another thing! We've based these lists on long, disastrous experience—on days without number when the weight of our suitcases caused a weight in our hearts. Believe me, you won't mind repeating a travel outfit when the returns in lightness and freedom are as great as this.

Our suggested summer wardrobes (which include articles you'll wear on the trip) will add up to much less than the current baggage allotment on an economy flight to Europe. (For new baggage regulations, please see "The Suitcase Itself," below.) They'll leave plenty of room in your suitcase for all the gifts and articles you'll pick up in Europe, and they'll permit you to carry exactly one light suitcase, and no other parcels of any kind, on your European trip.

3. What to Take in Winter

FOR WOMEN: Winter, of course, means special packing problems. It can be quite cold in Europe, even in Spain and Italy, and you must be prepared with heavy, sturdy, woolen clothing. And that means that you must be even more stern with yourself. Because your bulky winter clothes will weigh more and take up more room, you must take far less. You simply cannot afford to fill your suitcase with any nonessential item. Trudging through snow with a heavy suitcase is even worse than trudging in the hot sun. Here are my suggestions for a woman's winter wardrobe for a four- to six-week stay (for short trips, eliminate "H," "N" and "W"; combine "J" and "K"):

A. 4 pairs of nylon panties (2 pairs, if you're taking pantyhose)
B. 4 pairs of warm woolen or heavier nylon pantyhose, or knee-hi stockings (take a least 1 heavy warm pair)
C. 2 panty girdles (quick-drying), optional
D. 2 slips (nylon, of course); eliminate 1 for short stay
E. 2 bras (also quick-drying)
F. 1 pair of warm, woolen black pantyhose
G. 1 heavy woolen cardigan sweater
H. 1 long-sleeved pull-over sweater, preferably something you can combine with the cardigan, if need be
I. 1 pair of heavy corduroy or woolen slacks
J. 1 pair of all-purpose nasty-weather snow boots
K. 1 pair of good sturdy walking shoes
L. 1 pair of dressy shoes
M. 1 pair of warm bedroom slippers
N. 1 woolen or wool-knit daytime dress, or skirt and top
O. 1 heavy woolen traveling suit
P. 1 jersey or synthetic-knit blouse or shirt
Q. 1 wool-knit or silk-jersey dress which can double for afternoon and evening wear
R. 1 pair of heavy, warm flannel pajamas
S. 1 very warm robe
T. Jewelry, scarves and accessories
U. 1 super-warm coat, rain-proofed, and preferably with a detachable lining
V. Cosmetics and toiletries
W. Your "traveling to" Europe outfit

FOR MEN: The following should be adequate for a four- to six-week visit (for a shorter stay, combine "K" and "L," and eliminate "M"):

- **A.** 3 pairs of shorts
- **B.** 3 T-shirts
- **C.** 4 pairs of socks (of which two should be heavy woolen ones)
- **D.** 2 handkerchiefs (1 for short stays)
- **E.** 1 heavy sweater
- **F.** 2 sport shirts (1 in wool or flannel)
- **G.** 2 drip-dry dress shirts
- **H.** 1 woolen bathrobe
- **I.** 1 pair of heavy, warm flannel pajamas
- **J.** 1 pair of dress shoes
- **K.** 1 pair of heavy walking shoes
- **L.** 1 pair of galoshes
- **M.** 1 sports jacket
- **N.** 1 pair of heavy, warm woolen slacks
- **O.** 1 winter suit
- **P.** 1 heavy coat, water-repellent
- **Q.** 2 neckties
- **R.** Toilet and shaving articles

Spring or fall wardrobe? Strike a happy medium between our summer and winter suggestions, and also take into account the area in which you'll be traveling. Climatic patterns around the world have been changing drastically, but generally, if you'll take the kinds of clothing that would be suitable in New York or Chicago during these seasons, you'll be covered for most areas in Europe.

4. The Suitcase Itself

For carrying these clothes, you'll want to buy the lightest suitcase available: either a plastic suitcase, or, even better, one made of fabric. Cloth luggage is fairly durable, comes in handsome designs of varying sizes, and is feather light. Equally important, it's the cheapest on the market and yet offers the greatest amount of space. You'll value the expandable nature of a fabric suitcase when you start to cram in all the little odds and ends you just couldn't resist picking up along the way! (On my last trip I used a cloth case without *any* frame, and was amazed and delighted at how fresh and wrinkle-free my clothes remained. But beware "the hook" at some European baggage claim areas!)

Here's the latest news on baggage allowance for air travelers. Since 1981, your luggage is weighed in at airports not by weight only, but also by the amount of space it occupies. (This ruling is in effect for all European destinations, but each airline makes slight individual modifications: if necessary, check with your carrier before departure.) Each economy-flight passenger may check aboard two pieces of luggage free of charge, but with space restrictions as follows. Total dimensions of each individual suitcase, which you calculate by totaling (adding) length, width and depth, must not exceed 62 inches (some airlines restrict the second piece to 55 inches). In addition to the two cases you may check through to your destination, you are also allowed to board the plane with a "carry-on" bag, not to exceed 45 inches. This bag must be small enough to fit under the seat in front of you. Again, if in doubt, check with your individual carrier.

These space allowances are generous. I just measured, and our own largest case (a three-suiter) is only 52 inches total; even our "carry-on" totals only 42 inches, three less than the usual allotment. New weight allowances are generous too. Each suitcase checked aboard must not exceed approximately 62 to 70 pounds (depending on the carrier). But take care: for excess baggage penalties, now computed by space *and* weight, can still run high if you over-pack.

Regardless of new airline regulations, and strictly for your own comfort, do try to be a one-suitcase traveler. If you're a couple and feel that one suitcase per person just will not do, then, instead of getting another valise, buy a Valpak (a fold-over, soft wardrobe case) as your third piece of luggage. You simply hang your clothes inside, lock the clothes rack, zip it up, fold the case and—presto—you have a suitcase with a convenient carrying handle. Most Valpaks also contain extra inner pockets for shoes, underwear, or other soft goods, and they have loads of useful extra space on the bottom and along the sides. All in all, these foldable bags are the best gadgets I know for keeping wrinkles and creases out of traveling clothes.

Consider seriously the new "carry-on" type luggage: a smallish case with handy outerzippered compartments, which slips under an airplane seat. If you can cram all your things into this small case, you'll save lots of time upon arrival, especially if you happen to be flying a stretch-jet or 747!

Most luggage stores sell collapsible luggage carts with small wheels—an indispensable and money-saving aid, especially for those long walks in airline terminals. Or you can buy wheels and attachable straps. There are also suitcases available with permanent ball bearings on the bottom, and a snap-on guiding strap at one side; they're supposed to glide.

The latest, most chic case on the market is our old friend the backpack: a bag made with shoulder straps (some also have waist ties; others convert from one- to two-shoulder use)—and thus the Establishment has finally caught on to the luxury of traveling light and free.

5. Sending You Packing

Whenever possible, carry all liquids in flexible lightweight plastic bottles. Then place all "spillables" in a zippered or well-sealed plastic bag to avoid accidents in case of leakage. If you must take along a glass container, such as a perfume bottle, avoid spillage by sealing the cap of the bottle with a layer of candle wax (but consider switching to solid-state cologne or perfume, which is light-weight and practical, and now available in some very nice fragrances).

Roll into scroll-like shapes whatever is rollable: underwear, slips, bras, and so forth—all things that don't have to be wrinkle-free. In that manner, these items can be placed along the sides of your suitcase easily, or into the most unusual cracks and crevices (you'll discover plenty of them while packing). For items that do wrinkle, a layer of tissue paper or, more durable, a sheet of plastic (the kind that comes from the cleaners) placed above and below the garment (and one in the folded crease) will prove to be a surprising wrinkle-preventer. Place garments into your suitcase in the shape they should be in, with buttons loosely buttoned, top and bottom (except for men's jackets); and alternate piling, with the top of one piece of clothing placed over the bottom of another.

I must mention here that Arthur uses neither tissue paper nor plastic sheets. He packs all his clothing "raw," and it always travels well. He does know a secret kind of male way to flip a coat or jacket inside out so that it always emerges from a suitcase fresh as a daisy. Something like this: fold back, shoulder to shoulder, then flip. Try as I may, I cannot master it. Good luck to you—I'm stuck with tissue paper.

Finally, conserve space. Don't let anything go to waste. A handbag should be jammed with small articles, shoes jammed with socks, and so on.

One packing method which I've never found satisfactory is the use of plastic bags to compartmentalize the contents of your suitcase—but some travelers swear by this system. The theory is that you have a different plastic bag for each category of clothing—i.e., that you place all underwear in one bag, all nightwear in another, and so forth, thus enabling you to extract each item as needed, without disarranging the remaining contents of your suitcase. When I tried the plastic bags, it seemed to me they filled with air and thus added unnecessary bulk to the case. I also found it a patience-tryer and a time-waster to be constantly sorting things out.

What to do instead? I like the layered principle of packing, which simply enables you to flip along the edge of your case to get what you need.

FOR MEN ONLY: A Reader's Unbeatable Suggestions . . . "To keep your clothes in tip-top condition while traveling, here are some common sense rules which always yield excellent results. Socks should be placed inside the sleeves of jackets, to keep the shoulders and sleeves of a jacket crease-free. Also, leave the laundry cardboard inside your shirts, and place them inside your flat-folded jacket, again to retain the jacket's shape. Ties should be folded in half. If they get creased, the crease usually winds up under your collar so no-one will notice. For protection, your toiletries kit should be placed directly beneath the carrying handle of your case with a buffering layer of clothing between the kit and the case. Shoes should go at the bottom of your suitcase, at the opposite side away from the handle. They will then act as a buffer against shocks and jostling" (David Gideon, New York, New York).

ODDS AND ENDS: Since you will probably be doing your own laundry, you must take at least one plastic bag with a zipper, for carrying wet clothes or wash cloths from town to town. Also recommended is Woolite, the cold water soap. Take as many packets as you think you'll need—one packet will do for a full washbowl of laundry. . . . Since most European budget hotels do not provide soap, you will also need a plastic soap dish with a lid, and, of course, soap. Towels are provided everywhere, so you needn't worry on that score. . . . If you like sleek, well-polished-looking shoes, try convenient (in traveling packets) Mr. Shine, available at drugstores or notions sections of large department stores. . . . To repeat a point that cannot be overstressed, invest heavily in drip-dry shirts and underwear—the type that can be washed in lukewarm water, and hung up overnight to dry. Eliminate the clothes that require a fancy cleaning-and-pressing job. Unless you do, you'll spend enormous sums for cleaning and laundry, you'll be continually inconvenienced, and you'll end up—in our worst nightmare—lugging a suitcase full of useless, dirty clothes. . . . To drip-dry your clothes in a hotel room that lacks a private bath, or in a hotel that has no laundry room, start by blotting up the excess moisture with a towel (towel-drying), and/or spread newspapers or plastic "sheets" below to catch the dripping.

What do you do when the hotel will not allow laundry to be washed in your room? First, understand their point of view: some hotels recommended in this book have precious antique wooden floors that would be ruined by water spots; others have proprietors so super neat and clean that the very idea of washing clothes in the *hand* basin is an affront to their sensibilities! Second, inquire politely of the management if there is a facility in the hotel for doing your laundry, i.e. a real laundry room, a private w.c. of the management's, a basement. Third, have you considered the "midnight dip"? And if all else fails, pack it up and head for the nearest cheapest laundromat.

On the art of drip-drying: I write this only because so many readers have complained that drip-dry clothing doesn't really work. It does, with the proper care. Here's how. You'll get the best results with clothes that are really dripping wet—the theory being that the weight of the water "irons" the clothes. But even if you can't enjoy the luxury of heavily sodden dripping, you can still do well if you'll remember (1) to separate the material so that the back does not cling to the front and (2) "hand iron" the material—smooth the garment out (or puff it out from underneath) in those areas where it might wrinkle or bunch up. Always button the top buttons, and put collars down and cuffs in shape. In other words, mold the garment into the shape in which you'd like to see it dry. Take a few extra seconds to perform these simple tasks, and you'll nearly always enjoy better than decent results.

Should you require the services of an English-speaking doctor while traveling to exotic places, you can always call the local American Embassy for suggestions. *OR* you can join IAMAT (International Association for Medical Assistance to Travelers) by making a donation. Your tax-free contribution entitles you to a card identifying you as a "member" (valid for one year), a booklet listing IAMAT Centers all over the world, and a wealth of interesting information on global health-related matters. IAMAT physicians all over the world charge the same fees: $20 for an Office Visit, $30 per House (or Hotel) Call or Night Call (from 8 p.m. to 8 a.m.); while Sundays and local holidays are $35. If you're interested, make your check payable to IAMAT, 736 Center Street, Lewiston, NY 14092.

How about taking pharmaceuticals, water-purifying pills, and the like? Don't. You'll soon discover that Europe is civilized, that there are pharmacies everywhere, and that all these items can be picked up on the spot—when and if needed (except personal prescription medicines, of course). Furthermore, the water, milk and food in all major European cities is today as safe as anywhere you can name.

FOR WOMEN ONLY: Handy neat little luxuries are those small, compact packets, filled with washcloth, shower-cap, little capsules of cold-water detergent, and a portable rubber clothes line (complete with tiny clothespins) capable of being tied and hung up anywhere. These packets are practically weightless, and they can be purchased in any drug or department store. . . . Purse-sized Wash 'n Dri towelettes for quick semi-dry washing, can be a lifesaver in any number of travel emergencies (I always carry a cleansing cream as well). . . . Glamour gals will take Andrea nail polish remover pads and the overly fastidious may even carry individualized packets of spot remover. . . . A pocket-sized plastic case, containing a tiny toothbrush and a small tube of toothpaste, is also a great comfort on long plane or train trips. These are available at most drugstores. . . . For the young or vain: hotel rooms usually have sinks which are adequate for washing hair. If you must shampoo often and need to carry a hairdryer, don't forget to include an electricity converter. Several good hair-care products are available for travel, including blow-driers and curling irons equipped with currency-adapters: try **Braun, Norelco** or **Wik's Interconti 1000,** which is encased in a lightweight, handy and quite attractive black traveling case. A simpler solution? Try a neighborhood beauty parlor, or do as I do: look in the local telephone directory for the nearest beauty school (always the cheapest place in town for a wash and set).

READERS' SUGGESTIONS: "I recently returned from four exciting months in Europe. The trip was marvelous because I was totally free. Before I left I bought a nylon backpack; frame, padding and all for only $30. In it, I had one long skirt for dress and for romping around, a white blouse, sweater, toothbrush, wash cloth, and a pair of sandals. I also had my jeans, T-shirt and hiking boots, which I wore most of the time. Whenever I got tired of these things, I'd buy something else, wear it once or twice and send it home. I really didn't need anything else. Believe me, it's the only way to travel" (A student, San Francisco, California). . . . "From observations in expensive restaurants, hotels and La Scala Opera, I noticed many European men wearing grey (medium to darkish) suits. Therefore, one well-tailored medium-grey suit should take a man anywhere. And I would not recommend sport shirts at all—any man over 25 looks like a hick in one in public, and the European caricatures of an American man show him with a sport shirt hanging out. Neckties, and shirt inside of pants while in cities, please" (Stephen Beattie, West Orange, New Jersey). . . . "I always travel with a grey suit, 1 pair of tan slacks, and a blue blazer. I get four completely different outfits out of this combination, which keeps me looking well dressed even on quite long trips" (David Gideon, New York, New York). . . . "We travel light since porters are expensive and often nonexistent. A B-4 bag (softside with outside pockets) plus an oversized plastic flight bag with shoulder strap. That's it for *two*. And invariably we find we have toted things we didn't need. My wife carries our documents and heaven knows what else in a large shoulder-strap handbag. Our motto: Don't travel with more than you can carry" (Norvelle H. Sannebeck, Michoacan, Mexico). . . . "After having used your books for four years, I want to advise your readers on what I feel is the perfect luggage for a summer in Europe: a flight bag measuring approximately 15″ × 10″ × 5″! All my travel needs can be placed in it: 1 extra outfit, 1 pair of shorts, sweater, sweatshirt, windbreaker, raincoat, swim-suit, toilet articles, etc., towel, and a cut-down copy of 'Europe' on top. When the plane lands in Europe I grab my bag and arrive at my hotel before most of the passengers have located all their luggage!" (William D. Poriz, Norman, Oklahoma). . . . "Instead of one large suitcase, it's much easier to take two very small ones. Often you can leave one somewhere and just take half your clothes with you when off on a shorter excursion. Wheels on suitcases are a must if you travel alone" (Nancy Wasserman, Cambridge, Massachusetts; note from HA: several readers have been enthusiastic about the advantages of carrying two small bags. But to keep my traveling life simple, and packing chores minimal, I'll stick to one case. My oversize handbag will do nicely for shorter jaunts. Men who don't carry purses might like to try duffle or airline bags). . . . "Flight attendants will hang folding Valpak cases in a coat closet if you unfold the case. Hang belts over clothes on one hanger, don't roll them up or they'll take as much room as shoes" (Delos V. Smith, Jr., Hutchinson, Kansas). . . . "For a carry-on bag I used a picnic-type insulated bag, which was great for carrying food on trains, ideal for picnics, and also for food kept in our room. I'd also like to recommend packing a folding umbrella, the kind that fits into a large handbag" (Dorothy R. Astman, Levittown, New York). . . . "I do very much disagree with your suggestions of attachable wheels for women's or anybody's suitcase. All you encounter is stairs, stairs, stairs, and with the additional weight of heavy wheels plus straps" (Ms. Sandra Tanner, Madison, Wisconsin). . . . "If you'll be traveling in the fall, winter or spring, when rain can frequently be expected, take along a pair of Ripple Sole shoes. One walks over the puddles, not through them, and the weight and bother of overshoes are avoided. Usually the uppers of these shoes, not made for 'elegant' wear, are sturdy enough, and lend themselves to waterproofing" (Stephen H. Frishauf, New York, N.Y.). . . . "The best shoes to take are Famolare 'Get-Theres,' the ones with the wavy bottoms. They held up under the worst walking conditions, were comfortable, and looked good with dresses, pants and bathing suits. Could be the only shoes you need take on a trip" (Carla Miller, Jacksonville, Florida). . . . "Pack articles which might break, small ones that is, in the toes of that extra pair of shoes every traveler should carry" (Mary Jenkins, Wilmette, Illinois). . . . "I'd like to suggest putting liquids in plastic bottles filled nearly ¾ full. Then squeeze the bottle gently—putting the top on tighter so there's still a 'dent' in the bottle as you let go. This prevents spilling nearly 100%. I am a stewardess and can vouch for many miles in pressurized airplanes which usually invite leaks! We learned this in stewardess training and it's invaluable" (Joellen Ayers, Redondo Beach, Calif.). . . . "Aluminum film containers, available at photo supply shops, are the cheapest and best non-breakable receptacles for odds and ends like pills, small amounts of lotion and loose seashells. Get the plastic snap-on lid, the metal screw-on lid will rust" (Lauren Friedman, Bronx, N.Y.). . . . "I always carry fold-up slippers in my purse, so that I can slip them on while riding on a plane or on long bus or train trips" (Ms. Billie Brooks, Inglewood, California). . . . "On a guided tour when I had a room without bath for a week, I took along a sponge in a plastic bag and in the evening I soaped it well, washed from head to feet, standing on a newspaper or paper bag, rinsed off, and that was that!" (Andrew J. O'Laughlin, Nice, France). . . . "Suggest to your readers that they pack opera glasses: these are wonderfully handy if you are theatre lovers, as we are, and must sit with the gods" (Christie J. Bentham, Scarborough, Ont., Canada). . . . "First, it's a must for people traveling through the hotter countries to take a plastic snap-on cover for soda bottles. We found them indispensable, especially throughout Italy; they're also helpful on those long train trips, and good for wine bottles, too. Another item we brought from home was one of those multi-use pocket knives—the kind with blades, openers, scissors and even spoon and fork. It's small, and oh, so handy for the many times we bought our lunch ingredients at a delicatessen and then needed something with which to cut cheese or meat" (Gloria Ruggiero, Astoria, N.Y.). . . . "We found a small travel kit of a mug and an immersion heater invaluable for that odd cup of coffee or tea. We would heat the water in the mug, brew the tea or coffee, pour it into a yogurt container, then boil more water for the second cup" (Bella and Fritz Goldschmidt, Welkom, Orange Free State, South Africa; note from HA: immersion heaters have been around for a long time. Although they're small and compact and I used one when we were traveling with our infant daughter, I haven't felt the need to take one with me since. However, for people like my mother, who cannot open her eyes in the morning until she has that first cup of coffee, I guess they're a must. And with the price of a cup of coffee going up, up, up (!) the immersion heater could be a real $-saver, and very handy for those "picnic" lunches and suppers. If you take one, be sure it's adaptable for European use). . . . "This is for those of you who are traveling light and must do a little washing every night. Throw your laundry in the bath tub and let it soak right along with you, while you are bathing. Then all it takes is a quick sudsing in the lavatory, as the presoaking has hastened the job along" (Mrs. John Frerichs, Girard, Kansas). . . . "To drip-dry shirts or blouses, button all buttons and pull placket at both ends simultaneously to 'iron out' wrinkles. Button cuffs and pull flat. You can hang drippers from light or cabinet over wash basin. I find it useful to carry tiny postal scales, small Scotch tape, a dozen air mail letters with no stamps, tiny scissors and nail clippers, and stick nonperspirant" (Delos V. Smith, Jr., Hutchinson, Kansas). . . . "Club soda is good for removing stains on clothes; Scotch tape is great for removing lint, and also for taking up a fallen hem line. In an emergency, toilet-paper rolls make excellent hair rollers, and Scotch tape can be used in place of bobbie pins. These cardboard rollers may also be used as funnels when oil or water must be put into a rented car. A nylon slip over your pillow-case will preserve a hair setting, and a lamp shade can hold that wig" (Mrs. M. Del Pizzo, Miami, Fla.). . . . "Perhaps the most versatile item I took to Europe was a raincoat with a zip-out lining. In a pension, it doubled as a bathrobe for those walks down to the shower. On an all-night train, I used the lining as a pillow and the coat itself for a cover. On picnics, it served as our tablecloth. At the bull fights it served as a cushion; very necessary on those rock or concrete seats. At the beach, you can change your clothing underneath one. Finally, it kind of came in handy when it rained!" (Mark G. Simkin, New City, New York). . . . "Being in the Army, my husband and I have had ample opportunity to travel in Europe and Scandinavia, and we have yet to find a use for bathrobes and slippers. When one needs to go out into the hall for any reason, we find our coats and shoes just as easy to use over our nightclothes and sometimes preferable. Robes and slippers simply take up valuable space, and add more weight to the suitcase. In lieu of slippers we both carry heavy woolen socks which can, and often need, be worn in bed as Europeans tend to conserve on heat" (Mrs. Mark Stetson, Orleans, France).

READERS' PRODUCT SUGGESTIONS: "Please, please, let the world in on the glories of Baggies—both sizes. For a little over $1 one has disposable cosmetic cases, wet clothing carriers, sweater bags, jewelry cases, soap dishes, make-up savers, food containers for picnics (or whatever), beer tops (saves the carbonation), and a great item in which to wrap odds and ends which are to be mailed home. Take the cardboard roll out of the Baggies, compress them, and bingo—instant traveling. The one (and only) item which we couldn't locate in Europe was cheap, good quality plastic, and when the toothbrush container broke, the soap dish got lost, and the hose snagged if thrown in the suitcase, Baggies saved everything. I'm taking both large (sweater and shoe bags) and small Baggies this time" (Leoni Zverow, Chicago, Illinois). . . . "Glad Bags, which now come in two sizes, have been indispensable to us shutter bugs in protecting cameras, lenses, etc., from water and dust in inclement weather. Only Glad Bags have fold over closure" (Mary Jenkins, Wilmette, Illinois). . . . "On my last two trips I discovered the wonder of Handi-wipes. One Handi-wipe, cut in two pieces, makes a wonderful throw-away wash rag. Obtainable at any supermarket" (Mrs. Jas. C. McQueen, Dallas, Tex.). . . . "We found most helpful ear plugs and eye shades, since we are light sleepers. The best of the former we have found are the plastic 'Mack's Pillow Soft Earplugs' that fit over but not into the ear canal. They cost about $2 for 4 plugs from McKeon Products, Inc., 121 Elm Park, Pleasant Ridge, Michigan 48069—if not available at your local pharmacy. The same concern has eye-shades or sleepshades for $4. Under conditions of noise and bright light, these two items are life-savers" (J. Calvin Keene, Canton, New York; note from HA: McKeon informs us their ear plugs are useful for protection while swimming, too). . . . "If your feet have a tendency to ache, Dr. Scholl's arch supports are wonderful. I wear them all the time when walking" (Nell J. Masters, Atlanta, Georgia). . . . "For rainy days, be sure to take the little toe rubbers that you can slip over any type heel. They were very difficult to find, but certainly well worth the effort" (Billie Brooks, Camarillo, California). . . . "Listerine mouth wash can also be used on cuts and insect bites" (Mrs. M. Del Pizzo, Miami, Fla.). . . . "If you want to drip-dry clothing in a hotel room that lacks a private bath without soaking the floor, pack in your suitcase a square of sturdy plastic. Mine was about 54 inches square, and folded flat to almost nothing. (It was sold in a dime store for a tablecloth, I think.) I spread it underneath my clotheslines, folded the sides over to form a sort of pool, and found that no water could escape. I also took along a sponge to mop up the first deluge. (I loved my braided rubber clothesline, which eliminated the need for clothespins)" (Phyllis Brush, Ipswich, Massachusetts). . . . "In a room with only a washbowl I wash out clothes, squeeze them as dry as possible and hang them on hangers in the closet, with a newspaper below to absorb the water" (Andrew J. O'Laughlin, Nice, France). . . . "Here's a drip-dry tip that proved invaluable to me (after I had stained a floor with wet newspapers). I cut a piece of medium weight plastic (18" × 36") from an old shower curtain, and use it with four paper clips. I cup the corners of the plastic and secure each one with a paper clip: it makes a perfect pan to catch the drips. Usually I lay a used towel in it—no noise, and just wring out the towel later and use it to wipe out the pan" (Ms. Harriett Ross, Bredeston, Fla.). . . . "I found that a wrap-around dress worked equally well as a daytime casual dress and as a robe for trips down the hall to the w.c. I would suggest that two extra plastic hangers are essential for washing out items, but finding a place to hang them is sometimes difficult. We took a large plastic garbage bag, and used it for the dirty clothes on our way home" (Marion J. Durham, Flagstaff, Arizona). . . . "1) Very useful items which take no space in your suitcase are safety pins, rubber bands, and paper clips. 2) Take a small cup, preferably a folding cup, and a bottle opener for those mineral water bottles on train trips" (Roberta and Jack Sarfatt, La Jolla, California). . . . "My best hint for this section is the purchase before leaving of a crazy little device for hanging wet garments—better than all the clotheslines and pins. It is a hanger with one head and about ten arms that fold in or out like an umbrella, with a little clip on the end of each arm. That way, you can hang about ten items from one spot and they all dry overnight. It is compact and folds easily into a corner of the suitcase, and was my life-saver in small rooms. (Mrs. Gene A. Rudolph, Los Angeles, California). . . . "A drip-dry shirt or dress dries much faster and with fewer wrinkles if it is hung from an inflatable plastic travel hanger. We were given one 7 years ago, and I use it now even at home. When not in use, the air is released and the hanger is folded into a small pocket" (Shirley Stein, Downers Grove, Illinois). . . . "Want that nice touch of fabric-softened clothing without toting a gallon jug of softener on your travels? 'Bounce' (a product of Procter & Gamble) is ultra-lightweight 9 × 11″ sheets of nonwoven rayon impregnated with fabric softener. Although specifically designed to be added in an automatic dryer (each sheet does a full washload), it can also be added to the final rinse water of drip-dry items. Each sheet is already partially scored into seven strips and can be divided for 'just this much' in a hand basin. I found it particularly good on Qiana, Arnel, and other 'man-mades' that tended to wrinkle and create static electricity. A small strip of Bounce took care of both of these problems. The product seems expensive, but considering the mileage one gets out of just one sheet, the cost is negligible. An extra bonus: when packing, if you layer the sheets among your clothing, it will give you fresh scented clothes, because 'Bounce' contains a light fragrance that even men wouldn't object to. Great!" (Carole Sebastian, St. Louis, Missouri). . . . "For a recent trip to the Orient, I purchased a 'Monaco' windup razor made in Monaco, of all places. It shaves adequately and the advantages are obvious" (Norvelle H. Sannebeck, Michoacan, Mexico; note from HA: according to Winston's Sales and Service Co., 143 East 60th Street, New York, N.Y. 10022, which used to sell the "Monaco," these wind-up razors are no longer available in the U.S.; they recommend instead the Eltron Mobile Battery Shaver, made by Braun, and retailed at $50, including 2C batteries good for approximately 30 shaves; additional batteries can of course be purchased). . . . "A hint I have to pass on to you and your readers concerns soap. It was always a fussy bore to wrap up a sticky piece of soap that inevitably dripped and got even more gooey. Then I discovered 'Badedas,' a liquid soap that comes in tubes and, more recently, small plastic bottles. It can be used for showers, baths, and as a shampoo. They also make a lighter solution for young children. At any rate, if Badedas is not available, try to purchase any liquid soap in plastic bottles. Such a blessing!" (Denyse Tessensohn, Singapore; note from HA: in the U.S., "Badedas" is "Vitabath"). . . . "Rather than carry bar soap and a plastic dish on trips, I find it much more convenient to carry just a tube of shaving creme, which I find covers all my needs. Perhaps some of your readers will be as delighted as I was to find that shaving creme works just as well as soap, and by providing for my bathing as well as shaving needs, this one tube eliminates the need to carry soap, soap-dish and the bulky aerosol shave cream can" (John J. Bartko, Ph.D., Bethesda, Maryland). . . . "Handy items I am packing: a wash-and-wear lightweight wig (saves time in hairdressers), and a tube of shaving cream for hair washing—no spillage, lightweight and doubles as toilet soap and toothpaste!" (Ms. Yvonne Foster, Claremont, Perth, W. Australia). . . . "Clairol makes rollers to take on trips, 'Set to Go' (five rollers). Check the bottom of the rollers to make sure they work on 115 *and* 220, some of them do not. When you get to Europe, all you have to do is snap on an adapter plug (either a three-prong for England or the round two-plug for the Continent). You do not need an adapter for the current. American hairdryers blew out every adapter we had—we finally just bought a British one" (Carla Miller, Jacksonville, Florida). . . . "I spray my outer clothes, coats, hats, scarves and dresses with Scotchgard Fabric Protector to make them water repellent. It works very well on everything but knit fabrics. Scotchgard is manufactured by the 3M Company of St. Paul, Minn., and can be purchased in our supermarkets and hardware stores. Woven woolens, cottons and synthetic fabric take kindly to Scotchgard and I'm enthusiastic about using it. It seems to make dresses more crease resistant as well as water repellent" (Ruth Graham, Gr. Barrington, Massachusetts; note from HA: only fancier supermarkets carry Scotchgard, which sells for around $8.50 for 16 ounces). . . . "Anyone from Backpack to Ferrari set should have a Health Kit with First Aid booklet, prescriptions and medicines they take regularly, copies of prescriptions for eyeglasses if not an extra pair, their hospitalization insurance cards, aspirin, thermometer, motion-sickness drug, diarrhea and laxative remedies, nail scissors, tweezers, bandages, gauze, tape, sleep aids and No Doz, antacid, sunscreen—you can squeeze all into a cosmetic pouch. I like bug spray, quinine, Viaforma, and disinfectant when in the tropics. I never *open* most of them unless to dose my friends, (Delos V. Smith, Jr., Hutchinson, Kansas; note from HA: all of these items can, of course, be picked up when and if needed at European pharmacies, which are everywhere; why lug them along?).

STARVATION BUDGET: "All year long I shop for very, very cheap undergarments in discount stores. I take one bra and slip for every three days: panties for every other day. After wearing them for the allotted time, I simply discard them. No more washing, hoping it will dry before leaving the next morning. I wear a black dress and take a black cardigan sweater (wear also), and a black skirt—I take no other clothes (the skirt and sweater would serve as an outfit if something drastic happened to my one dress). I take one nightgown, two bright scarves, wear a dark one around my neck to keep my dress clean; and take a dress-up set of jewelry, wearing a day set. I wear dress-shields, take a bath every night, and thus am as clean and dainty as women who drip-dry and worry about excess baggage. No one has ever noticed what I was doing. As for my make-up, I take small jars, small bars of soap, old washcloth, etc., with just enough to last through the trip and discard before returning home (I also take folding rain boots, raincoat and umbrella). All the above fits into a large tote with zipper, which I carry on board the airplane with me (my large handbag holds maps, tickets, etc.). This system has adequately supplied me for as long as three weeks without any problems. Basically, it is a disposal trip. Naturally, my return flight finds me with the lightest luggage of all!" (Ms. Sandra Pearce, Morristown, New Jersey).

"*Every* travel book advises us to take too much to Europe. For a two- or three-month summer trip, I do not take a suitcase at all. I take only the give-away airplane bag and my purse.

"I wear a dark, flared, lined rayon suit, long-sleeved, with a dark lace shell. This becomes an evening gown, train travel dress, restaurant costume, or sightseeing outfit, as the occasion demands. *I do not take another outfit.* (If I were the active sports type, I would take a cheap nylon shift, which would double as a night gown.) I do not take a change of underwear—just what I have on. I wash it every night and blot it dry with a hotel towel. I wear very comfortable, dark, pump-type shoes for dress-up. My travel outfit is completed with a package veil-and-ribbon hat, dark gloves that live quite a bit of the time in my pocket, and a coat that serves as raincoat and robe. My shoes are rubber soled for damp sidewalks and a purse-size plastic scarf keeps my head dry.

"In the flight bag I pack (everything in plastic bags) a pair of dark, comfortable rubber-soled walking shoes; tiny knit bedroom slippers; plenty of medium-sheer hose of the same color; a skimpy nightgown; soap, toothpaste, toothbrush, dusting powder and cold cream (the cosmetics in small amounts and in plastic containers); a fancy dark sweater for an evening wrap, variety in daytime wear, or simply warmth; a needle, thread, small pair of scissors; a moderate supply of the vitamins and medicines that I use; and last but not least, a current copy of Frommer's *Europe on $25 a Day.*

"I keep most of my travelers' checks, my return passage, my health card and my passport in a fool-proof money belt that I made myself. Of course, if I know that I will need any of these things during the day, I put them into my purse before leaving the hotel.

"My purse is a sturdy shoulder bag with a good catch. I never lay it down anywhere. In it I keep a compact, comb, lipstick, Chapstick, pens, Kleenexes, a little notebook, a money changer, and coin purse. I carry bills and travelers' checks in zippered compartments. People who take a lot of stuff do not use it, anyway" (Name withheld, Hollywood, California).

I hope you will send me more of your own packing discoveries (to Frommer/Pasmantier Publishers, 1230 Avenue of the Americas, New York,

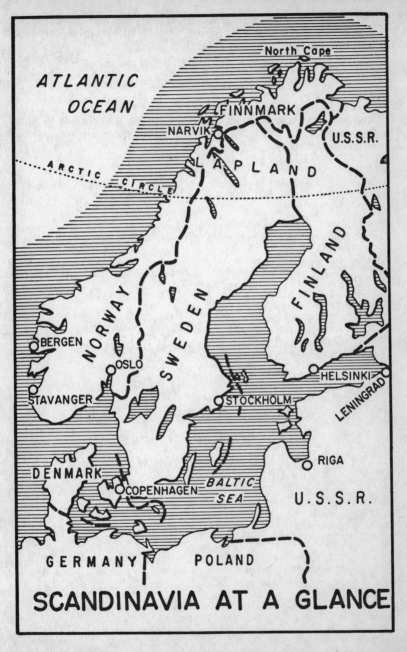

SCANDINAVIA AT A GLANCE

NY 10020), so that we may further test and amplify the "easy travel" tricks advanced in this chapter. Pending those letters, I'll stick to my theme song: take only one suitcase, and keep it light!

—**Hope Arthur**

And now that your suitcase is suitably packed, we're ready to start. The first problem of a European vacation is getting there. For suggestions, see our next chapter.

Chapter III

GETTING THERE

**Super Apex
and Assorted Gimmicks**

**1. Charters to Europe
2. Stand-By Seats (London only)
3. The "Cheap Airlines"
4. Super-Apex Fares**

MY VERY FIRST TRIP to Europe was made in the aluminum bucket-seat of an Army transport plane, filled with dank canvas knapsacks. Yet even under those unpromising conditions, the sight of the coast of Europe—which I had longed for years to see—was one of the great thrills of my life. Suddenly to be passing over tiny squares of manicured fields, above farm villages with ancient church steeples, and then to see the familiar landmarks of large cities, was like re-living a thousand novels and picture books.

Since that first Atlantic flight, I've repeated the process on many occasions and under radically changed circumstances—the last time in a mammoth, wide-bodied jet equipped with movies and fully reclining chairs. And yet, even as the supposedly blasé many-time traveler, I felt the same surge of excitement as the loudspeaker said that the line of surf in the distance was the coast of Europe. To leave one's job and one's cares behind, to step on a plane and hurtle overnight to an entirely different way of life, is an experience that never goes stale.

You've probably gathered from the above that I greatly enjoy the act of flying to Europe, and still become thrilled over the prospect of a trans-Atlantic flight. But how do the costs work out, and what are the best fares? That's a more sobering subject. The price of flying to Europe has never been more difficult to comprehend and compute.

PLANE ECONOMICS: Time was when this chapter on transportation to Europe could consist of a few simple charts setting forth standard rates to various European capitals. Prior to 1980, all major airlines—other than Icelandair—belonged to the International Air Transport Association (I.A.T.A.), which prescribed fares and periodically revised them, on a uniform basis for all its members. As a result, all I.A.T.A. airlines charged the same fares to the same cities.

Then came along a new U.S. President and his appointee to head the Civil Aeronautics Board, Dr. Alfred Kahn, and deregulation of international air fares began on a cataclysmic scale. Today, I.A.T.A. no longer prescribes uniform fares for international flights, and the setting of fares is either a matter for individual airline decision (in the case of Holland and the other Benelux countries) or for bilateral negotiations between the U.S. and various European governments, country by country (in the case of most other European nations). To many destinations, an airline now proposes a fare structure. Another airline then files a competing and different fare structure. A process of jockeying occurs, which may, or may not, result in a uniform price structure for all airlines flying to that particular country. The process of deregulation has continued and in fact the CAB itself is slated to go out of existence in early 1985. Although some of its legal functions on behalf of consumers have been transferred to other governmental agencies, at this writing (fall 1984) it's not yet clear which functions will cease altogether.

Moreover, the structure of trans-Atlantic air transportation now encompasses more than one type of airline. While, on the one hand, there are the traditional companies flying from U.S. and Canadian cities to the European capitals—the KLMs, the TWAs, the British Airways, and so on—there are now, as well, an array of lesser carriers—the People Expresses and Virgin Atlantics, the Capitols, the Arrow Airways—offering entirely different trans-Atlantic air fares, at different levels and subject to different conditions. Both groups—the old and the new—keep introducing, withdrawing, revising air fares until just shortly before the spring/summer/fall "season" to Europe begins, when prices jell for a time, only to undergo further revisions in mid-season. Therefore, a travel guide published in January 1985, as this one will be, cannot hope to set forth accurate air fares for the year ahead. It would even be difficult to tell you what *were* the levels in 1984!

Rather, what we can do is to list the *categories* of air transportation and air fares available to you, and to discuss the means for ascertaining prices when the time comes for actually purchasing the fare. These categories—in more-or-less ascending order of price—are: (1) charters; (2) stand-by fares; (3) "cheap airlines"; and (4) super-apex fares.

1. Charters to Europe

Except from Newark, on limited scheduled service, charters provided the cheapest means of traveling to Europe in 1984, for rates of around $399 to $499 from East Coast cities, round-trip. Indications are that this resurgence of trans-Atlantic chartering activity will continue in 1985, not at the unusually high levels experienced in 1977 (when many hundreds of trans-Atlantic charter flights were operated), but on a substantial frequency, nevertheless.

Thus, **Wainwright Travel,** a major firm strangely headquartered in Bethlehem, Pennsylvania, has already announced 1985 charter programs from New York, Philadelphia and Baltimore to several European cities at round-trip rates of around $449 (London) to $499 (Paris). A New York charter operator named **Travac,** 1270 Broadway, New York, NY 10001 (phone 212/563-3303) is planning to add London to its charter offerings of Paris, Amsterdam, and Zurich; round-trip charter seats will sell for around

$529 between New York and Zurich. The official U.S. student travel organization, the **Council on International Educational Exchange (C.I.E.E.),** 205 East 42nd St., New York, NY 10017 (phone 212/661-1414), will once again, from April through October of 1985, offer weekly charter departures from New York to Paris at prices of around $499, round-trip, on flights that permit you to remain in Europe for several weeks. **Spantax**—a major charter airline of Spain—will be advertising round-trip "air only" rates of between $449 and $499, for flights between New York and Madrid. And there will be other extensive charter programs offering, if you wish, the purchase of air seats only, from **Tourlite** (516 Fifth Avenue, New York, NY 10020, phone 212/575-8888) and **Homeric** (595 Fifth Avenue, New York, NY 10020, phone 212/838-9630) going to Greece, from **Arthur Frommer Holidays, Inc.** (*that's* a top firm!), 770 Broadway, New York, NY 10003 (phone 212/598-1800), to several European destinations, from **International Weekends of Boston,** and from **Carefree David** of Miami.

Where do you ferret out the dates, departure cities and prices for charter transportation between North America and Europe? You consult two sources of information. One is simply the Sunday travel section of your local newspaper, or, if you reside in a small town, the Sunday travel section of the nearest large-city newspaper. You can be sure that if a major charter program is scheduled to operate from that city, it will be advertised in that newspaper.

A far more comprehensive source of information is the monthly **Jax Fax,** magazine of the air chartering industry, published from 280 Tokeneke Road, Darien, Connecticut 06820. Travel agents all over the nation subscribe to Jax Fax for its exhaustive listing of every charter scheduled to depart from every major U.S. city in the next six months. But you needn't yourself subscribe to Jax Fax to obtain that information. Simply visit a nearby travel agency, and ask courteously whether you may quietly peruse their current copy of Jax Fax on the premises. Since the same travel agent can then book you aboard that charter, and earn a commission for doing so, he or she will usually be happy to oblige!

2. Stand-By Seats (London Only)

These provide an almost equally inexpensive means of crossing the Atlantic, but they are available (with one minor exception) only to and from London. Except for the occasional offer of stand-by facilities on the flights of Capitol Air to Brussels, it is currently only the airlines flying to London that offer drastically reduced prices for seats sold only on the day of departure, subject to availability. Readers willing to hazard the risks— the disappointment and inconvenience of occasionally waiting two or three days for an available departure flight, of then hanging about in London for some time before an available return seat turns up—were able to fly round-trip between New York and London for around $558 in the summer of 1984, and should be able to do so for about the same in the summer of 1985. And stand-by seats to London are also available, at slightly higher rates, from the dozen or so other cities in the United States from which direct air transportation to London is available.

Who offers the stand-bys? From New York: British Airways, Air India, Pan Am, TWA. From other cities: some of the above airlines, as well as Delta, Northwest, British Caledonian, American Airlines, Arrow Airways.

Consult a travel agent, or simply phone any airline that flies to London from a city near you.

Although some airlines eliminate their stand-by facilities in winter, all usually reinstate them from April to December.

3. The "Cheap Airlines"

A third, and almost equally inexpensive, method of flying cheaply to Europe is to fly there on an airline that, until recently, did not operate scheduled flights to Europe and is therefore not yet well associated in the public mind with particular European destinations. To enter that market, these new airlines are presently offering trans-Atlantic air crossings for less than is charged by the so-called "flag carriers" or other major airlines servicing certain European points. Just as deregulation of the aviation industry caused several new "cheap airlines" to emerge on the domestic scene—People Express, New York Air, Muse Air, Midway Metrolink, Mid-Pacific Air—the same lifting of regulations has permitted a number of airlines to operate scheduled flights at cheap prices between North America and Europe. These "new" airlines are, in the main, the formerly so-called "supplemental carriers" that once were limited by C.A.B. regulations to the operation of charter flights only, but can now—and do—operate scheduled flights almost anywhere they choose.

(And incidentally, the only thing "cheap" about these airlines is their price structure, not their service or standards. They fly the same planes as the major carriers, adhere to the same standards, usually hire the same calibre of personnel. A common error made by some timid travelers is to assume that a lesser-known carrier is somehow less safe than a better-known one; there isn't an iota of statistical evidence to support that belief).

Among the "cheap" airlines to Europe:

People Express Airlines, Newark International Airport, Newark, New Jersey, phone 212/772-0344, and **Virgin Atlantic Air,** Newark International Airport, Newark, New Jersey, phone 212/243-1464 or 201/624-6855, both of which operate cut-rate flights between Newark and London for a maximum coach fare of $189 each way (as of the date of writing), which sometimes descends as low as $159 each way. Flights utilize Gatwick Airport outside London, and are heavily booked.

Capitol Air, 230 Park Ave., New York, NY 10169 (phone 800/CAPITOL), flies from several U.S. cities to Brussels and Zurich, at prices lower than the competition. My guess is that they'll be offering an unrestricted round-trip fare of around $599 in the summer of 1985.

World Airways, Oakland International Airport, Oakland, CA 94614, phone 800/772-2600, services the route between Baltimore and London/Frankfurt, at rates that undercut the normal fares between the Washington, D.C. area and Europe.

TransAmerica Airlines, P.O. Box 2504, Oakland Int'l Airport, Oakland CA 94614 (phone 800/227-2888), a member of the giant TransAmerica conglomerate, flies several times each week to both Shannon and Amsterdam, again for less than is normally charged to those two cities. In winter, their round-trip rate is $529 for both cities. This will probably ascend to around $599 in summer of 1985.

Finally, the growing **Arrow Air,** headquartered at Miami International Airport, Miami, Florida, but phone 212/520-2525 or 516/222-2680, flies between Tampa and London, and between Denver and London, at rates considerably below the normal charge.

And there are still other "cheap airlines" about to enter the trans-Atlantic scramble. Look for their ads, or look up their numbers, then phone and inquire.

4. Super-Apex Fares

If you can't find an acceptable charter, if a stand-by possibility causes concern, and if no "cheap airline" flies from or near your city, then you'll want to purchase a "super apex" fare, of the sort offered by every airline (although sometimes under different names). The "apex" in "super apex" stands for "advance purchase excursion," and simply means that you must purchase your ticket at least 14 to 21 days in advance of departure (incurring a $50 penalty if you cancel thereafter), and that you must stay in Europe for an excursion period of at least 7 days, but for no more than 180 days.

Currently, super-apex air fares to such destinations as London, Paris, Lisbon, Madrid, Amsterdam, Brussels and Rome range—in the peak summer months—from $549 (round-trip between New York and London), to $599 (Spain), to $799 (Rome). Nearly every industry observer expects them to rise by about 10% as we approach the summer of 1985. Since these are hefty sums, it behooves you to search out (a) a charter, or (b) a cheap airline, and, failing that, to purchase your ticket well in advance, and at least by 14 or 21 days in advance of departure, in order to qualify for a super-apex fare.

TIPS ON SHIPS: So much for planes; we come now to the subject of sea transportation to Europe. But that form of travel, sad to say, must quickly be dismissed for budget-minded travelers. Even before the cost of oil caused heavy "fuel surcharges" to be added to the price, the charge for a one-way summer crossing in the most basic of sea accommodations had already topped $500. Even before the fuel crisis, shipline after shipline had announced that they were ceasing to operate trans-Atlantic. Thus, a memorable form of travel is no longer a realistic one for budget tourists to Europe, although it remains a "once-in-a-lifetime" experience for our more affluent readers.

FREIGHTERS: And for the most part, you can forget about these, too. With the exception of occasional ships leaving from Norfolk or Newport News, Virginia, the average freighter charges only about $50 less than the single normal passenger liner for the one-way trip across the North Atlantic. Indeed, some freighters offer such luxurious accommodations to their eight or ten passengers that they actually charge *more* than the passenger liners. But even when you can save $50, you'll nearly double your travel time (most freighters take from 8 to 10 days to cross the Atlantic) and you'll also place yourself at the mercy of erratic and sporadic sailing schedules (some passengers wait a week in New York for their freighter to finally leave).

This is not to say that a freighter-crossing isn't a unique and satisfying experience. As a passenger, you'll receive unbeatable service, you'll have the run of the ship, and you'll form a fast camaraderie with the entire crew. If you have unlimited time, and want a relaxed, informal crossing, you might do well to take a freighter berth. One reader wrote me:

"For those few of us who are making the trip on money saved just prior to resignation from a job, and who, therefore, are limited only by monetary considerations, to spend the fourteen days required to move from New York to Copenhagen on a small Danish ship is to arrive in Europe partially Europeanized and completely exhausted from the daily social life that Danish crews and passengers seem to consider normal. More practically, for $550 you will receive accommodations that no passenger ship can furnish in even their luxury berths, and a completely personalized treatment from crew and agent. Of course no one who is subject to seasickness should attempt such a voyage, but for any others with unlimited time I heartily recommend this means of travel—especially if the ship is Danish."

Now you have the pros and cons. My own opinion remains as before, that if you are the normal vacationer, who wants to leave and return on a set date, and take only five or six days for the trip, you'd best pass up the freighters, for their financial advantages are slight.

We'll continue to assume you're going by plane. Logical starting point is John F. Kennedy Airport, New York. Want to start living like a $25-a-day'er? The 40-minute airlines bus to Kennedy charges a stiff $7 per person, to which you must also add the cost of getting to the air terminal (on 37th Street and 1st Avenue) to pick up the bus. The much-advertised "train to the plane," using IND 6th Avenue subway stations, scarcely does better: $6 each way. And a taxi from Manhattan to Kennedy Airport costs a minimum of $24 or $26, plus tip. To beat the system, take the IND subway ("E" or "F" train) to the Union Turnpike Station (90¢); then change, at the subway exit, to a Q-10 bus (90¢), which wanders through the borough of Queens for half an hour, but then shoots straight to the international departure area at Kennedy Airport in ten more minutes. Total cost is $1.80, and total elapsed time is 1 hour and 15 minutes, as compared with the 40 minutes you'd be in an airlines bus or taxi.

Once you've arrived, whether by charter, cheap airline, stand-by or super-apex, you must then travel from city to city in Europe by rail, bus or car *only*. The cost of air transportation within Europe has become so prohibitively high that no budget traveler can any longer consider it. But this, in a sense, is all to the good, as it is land transportation that affords the best experience of Europe, and enables you to encounter average Europeans in a friendly and intimate fashion. Therefore, in planning the itinerary for your trip, you might immediately consult the next two chapters—our rail transportation chapter for the cost of point-to-point train fares or a Eurailpass, or else our auto chapter for the cost of car rentals and car leases. The days of the "multi-stopover" air ticket, at an affordable price, are conclusively over in Europe, and budget tourists proceed from place to place by surface transportation.

Chapter IV

EUROPEAN TRAINS

With Important Class Distinctions

THE LIFE OF EUROPE is mirrored in its trains. You haven't really savored the essence of the Continent until you've chugged along in a second-class compartment and shared the sausage-and-Chianti of an Italian family, or carried on a bouncing conversation in broken French, or simply leaned back and observed the European in his holiday-traveling mood. On most other occasions in Europe, the tourist is likely to be a frenzied animal, divorced from a truly human contact with the population. In a train, this remoteness falls away. A moment occurs when the sights and sounds of Europe become intimate and related to people—and that, to me, is a thrill which no monument or museum can ever provide.

Now, assuredly, the joys of a tiring train trip will not enthrall all the readers of this book. But there will be times and occasions when you can't or won't want to fly from city to city in Europe. You have to consider the science of European train transportation—which is just that, a science. It even has a key formula which, for the budget tourist, goes something like this: *Always travel second class in a major European express.* Here's why:

THE BIG DIFFERENCE: European trains tend to bunch themselves into two categories: magnificent and awful. There is no middle variety. In the first group, you'll find a type of European train which provides superb, lightning-like service. Only around forty of these trains exist, and they can be recognized by the fact that they carry names as well as numbers: the **Simplon-Orient Express,** the **Gondoliere,** the **Golden Arrow,** for instance. No one could want better train service than these provide. They normally run overnight, stop only in the largest cities, and cut hours from your travel time. Schedule your trips and your connections for the named, international trains, and traveling can be a cinch.

THE MONEY QUESTION: Riding on the great international expresses can have an important effect upon your costs, too, enabling you to buy an inexpensive railroad ticket at no sacrifice to physical comfort. Here's why. You will quickly learn that European trains carry both first- and second-class accommodations. A first-class ticket costs 33% to 50% more than a second-class fare. But while a second-class ticket on a major international express will purchase a perfectly comfortable, well-padded seat, a second-class ticket on the wrong type of European train can often lead to disaster.

By traveling on the international expresses, you can purchase money-saving second-class tickets, and protect your sacroiliac at the same time.

As for traveling first class in Europe, well, that's very unwise. The difference in quality between first- and second-class seats in a major international express is infinitesimal—a matter of one or two inches of extra padding, at most. The people who travel first class are also much less interesting types—but we won't go into that. The major gain to be realized from traveling second class is a financial one; it can reduce your transportation costs within Europe to a most reasonable expense. For European trains are moderate in price—and less expensive than those in the United States. You may change your notions about the cost of a European vacation when you learn that the long train trip down the boot of Italy from Venice all the way to Rome costs only $22 (second class). In early 1985, a one-way, second-class ticket for trips between the major cities of Europe totalled up as follows:

AMSTERDAM to: Paris, $43; Copenhagen, $74; London, $55; Vienna, $98; Brussels, $20; Frankfurt, $43; Rome, $117; Venice (via Basel), $102.

LONDON to: Brussels, $60; Edinburgh, $71; Glasgow, $63; Dublin, $70; Paris, $70; Amsterdam, $55.

PARIS to: Brussels, $24; Amsterdam, $43; Madrid, $93; Copenhagen, $110; Frankfurt, $49; Munich, $73; Zurich, $49; Rome, $86; Cannes, $77; Lourdes, $62; Marseille, $63; Nice, $79; Strasbourg, $37.

ROME to: Florence, $12; Naples, $9; Genoa, $20; Venice, $22; Milan, $25; Amsterdam, $117; Barcelona, $82; Brussels, $108; Frankfurt, $83; Geneva, $50; London, $157; Madrid, $118; Munich, $46; Nice, $29; Paris, $86; Vienna, $53; Trieste, $22; Zurich, $51.

MADRID to: Barcelona, $38; Toledo, $5; Valencia, $22; Lisbon, $33; Paris, $93; Rome, $118; Seville, $30.

BARCELONA to: Marseille, $38; Nice, $53; Paris, $79; Rome, $82; Lourdes, $41.

FRANKFURT to: Amsterdam, $43; Brussels, $36; Copenhagen, $73; Innsbruck, $52; Milan, $57; Naples, $92; Paris, $49; Rome, $83; Venice, $66; Vienna, $56.

MUNICH to: Amsterdam, $74; Brussels, $69; Copenhagen, $98; Innsbruck, $16; Milan, $32; Naples, $54; Paris, $73; Rome, $46; Salzburg, $13; Venice, $36; Vienna, $32; Zurich, $37.

PRICE CUTS: In addition to their initially low costs, nearly all the European railways offer money-saving plans of one sort or another. While some of these are fairly worthless come-ons, it may be that a particular plan will fit your travel needs. Here's a fast rundown:

Netherlands Railways, to begin the survey, offers a ticket good for eight consecutive days of unlimited travel throughout the Netherlands, for 158 guilders ($52.66) in first class, 107 guilders ($35.66) in second class. Write to Netherlands Railways, 576 Fifth Ave., New York, N.Y. 10017.

BritRail Travel International promotes a scheme of "BritRail Passes" entitling the bearer to unlimited rail travel throughout England, Scotland and Wales, provided that the pass is purchased prior to departure, in North America (through either a travel agent or BritRail Travel International, 630 Third Avenue, New York, N.Y. 10017). You can buy a BritRail Pass either for first-class travel ($147 for 7 days, $219 for 14 days, $272 for 21 days, $317 for one month) or for second-class travel ($107 for 7 days, $162 for 14 days, $205 for 21 days, $243 for one month), and there's also a second-class economy Youth Pass (for those aged 16 to 25) costing $93 for 7 days, $144 for 14 days, $183 for 21 days, $215 for one month. For a supplement of about $25 to these rates for one-way, or $50 for round-trip, a Britrail Seapass will enable you to travel between London and the Continent by train and Sealink ship or Hoverspeed Hovercraft.

French National Railways offers an unlimited mileage scheme called "France Vacances," and what a scheme it is! In addition to endless rail transportation within France for either 7 days ($170 first class, $115 second class), 15 days ($220 and $150), or 30 days ($345 and $230), it also throws in a 2-day Paris Métro pass for the 7-day card (first or second class), or a 4-day Paris Métro pass for holders of the 15-day cards and a 7-day Métro pass for holders of the 30-day pass. The Métro pass is also valid on Paris buses. French National Railways also grants a 30% reduction on train fares to couples with at least three children under the age of 18. Finally, a "Carte Couple," valid five years from date of issue, but only sold in Europe, enables the second party of a couple to pay half-fare when the first party pays the full fare. For further information contact the French National Railroads, 610 Fifth Ave., New York, N.Y. 10020 (phone 212/582-2110); 360 Post St., San Francisco, Calif. 94100; 11 East Adams St., Chicago, Ill. 60603; 9465 Wilshire Blvd., Beverly Hills, Calif. 90212; or 2121 Ponce de Leon Blvd., Coral Gables, Fl. 33134.

Swiss Federal Railways, slickest train company in Europe, offers the choice of either an unlimited mileage pass, or else a voucher entitling you to a 50% price reduction whenever you do buy a railroad ticket in Switzerland. The former is called a "Swiss Holiday Travel Card," can be purchased in the U.S. or at both airports (Geneva and Zurich) as well as at major rail stations in Switzerland, and is available for either 4 days ($63), 8 days ($74), 15 days ($90) or one month ($124) of second-class travel. The latter can be bought either pre-departure (from any Swiss National Tourist Office) or at major railroad stations in Switzerland, and is valid for either 15 days ($27) or one month ($34), during which time you can buy as many tickets as you want, at half price. Finally, women over the age of 62, and men over 65, can purchase a Swiss half-fare pass valid for an entire year, for only $61. Write to the Swiss National Tourist Office, 608 Fifth Ave., New York, N.Y. 10020.

Spanish Railways offers a form of discount coupon for its passengers from abroad. You purchase 17,000 pesetas ($113) worth of coupons, which are valid for 20,000 pesetas ($133) worth of rail travel—approximately a 15% reduction. The coupons are accepted as currency in every sort of train operated in Spain. Consult the Spanish National Tourist Office, 665 Fifth

Ave., New York, N.Y. 10022 (phone 212/759-8822). Actually, it sometimes pays to travel by plane in Spain, whose excellent Iberia Airlines charges only $47 for the long trip from Madrid to Seville.

Italian Railways are so cheap to begin with that they offer few discount plans; but one that you might want to consider is an unlimited rail pass within Italy (the *Biglietto Turistico di Libera Circolazione*) costing $72 for 8 days, $87 for 15 days, $102 for 21 days, $127 for 30 days, second class. Write to CIT, 666 Fifth Ave., New York, N.Y. 10103 (phone 212/397-2667).

Austrian Railways sells an "Austria Ticket" for young people under 26 valid for either 9 or 16 days of unlimited, second-class rail transportation in Austria, at a cost of either 950 schillings ($51.35) for 9 days, or 1,350 schillings ($72.97) for 16 days. Also it offers discounts of approximately 25% for groups of ten or more, traveling together; while senior citizens (women over 60, men over 65), regardless of nationality, travel at half-fare by buying a special identification card for 160 schillings, or $8.64 at train stations in Austria. **Germanrail** offers a Tourist Card for rail transportation on all passenger trains within the Federal Republic of Germany for periods of 9 days ($120 in second class, $165 in first) or 16 days ($155 and $215). This Tourist Card is also valid on all S-Bahn trains (suburban city railways) in Hamburg, the Ruhr area between Köln and Dortmund, in Frankfurt, Stuttgart and Munich, and on the airport shuttle trains in Frankfurt and Düsseldorf. Other bonuses include reduced rates or free transportation on certain river boats and buses. At 300 railway stations, Germanrail offers free rental bikes to Tourist Card holders. Men over 65 and women over 60 are entitled to a 10% discount with a special *Seniorenkarte,* costing 100 marks and valid for one year. Tourist Cards and other rail information can be obtained at 747 Third Ave, New York, NY 10017 (phone 212/308-3100). The Germanrail office will also provide information for Austrian Railways.

Finally, there's a particular cost-saving device that virtually all the European railways offer, and you'll want to consider it:

EURAILPASS:
This valuable, simple-to-use railroad pass is one of the most ingenious travel ideas in years. All the European railways, other than the British, have together created a single ticket—the **Eurailpass**—good for *unlimited* first-class rail travel throughout all of Europe (other than the British Isles) for a specified period of time. A 15-day Eurailpass costs $260, a 21-day Eurailpass $330, a one-month Eurailpass $410, a two-month Eurailpass $560 and a three-month Eurailpass costs $680. Children under 12 go at half fare and children under 4 travel free. Anyone under the age of 26 can purchase a **Eurail Youthpass,** entitling them to unlimited *second-class* transportation for one month for $290, for two months $370.

Assume that you've planned a two-month trip through Europe, and that you hope to do a great deal of traveling during that time. Purchase a Eurailpass or Eurail Youthpass *before* you leave for Europe—they are sold all over the world, except in Europe. With one, you can board any train you wish, as often as you wish, flash the pass at the conductor, and take any seat in any first-class compartment on the train. You needn't buy a single other ticket, or pay any supplemental or reservation charges. Theoretically, a man with a Eurailpass could spend 60 straight days on a train—all for $560. A student can do the same, second class, for only $370.

The extent of your savings with a Eurailpass will depend upon the length of your expected itinerary. I doubt that a one-month tourist (especially one willing to dispense with first-class seats) would normally do enough traveling to make the purchase worthwhile. But the two-month tourist—and particularly the tourist who's over for a longer Grand Tour—will give this gimmick a great deal of thought.

TRAIN HINTS: Finally, a few general railroad rules: First, never discard your train ticket after it has been marked or punched by the conductor. Some European railroad stations require that you later present your ticket in order to leave the station platform at your destination. On an overnight trip, you'd do well to inquire concerning the availability of second-class couchettes. These are compartments equipped with six lightly padded ledges along the wall, on which you can stretch out full-length to sleep. They would horrify Mr. Pullman, but they're dirt cheap and a god-send to persons who can't sleep sitting up. To vary the routine of a long second-class trip, simply walk into the dining car and order a beer. You'll be able to sit there, in a cushioned chair, for hours; for in Europe, no one would dream of asking you to move on.

On an overnight trip, be sure to purchase a bottle of mineral water or soda before boarding the train. Rarely does a European train carry a drinking water fountain or spout, and the dining car may be closed. As you'll soon discover, the experienced European traveler comes loaded with hampers of food and drink, and munches away through the trip. In nearly every major European city, an English-speaking railway information office can provide you with additional data on schedules, prices and policies. Phone numbers are as follows, in: London (834-2345); Paris (261-5050); Brussels (523-8134); Amsterdam (255-5151); Copenhagen (1417-01); Stockholm (255-060); Oslo (421-919); Munich (412-04-05); Vienna (1552) (Westbahnhof); Vienna (1553) (Südbahnhof); Rome (463-941); Nice (616-165); Zurich (211-5010); Madrid (733-3000); Athens (821-3882).

READERS' TRAIN SUGGESTIONS: "The most direct crossing from England to the continent is via BritRail. Harwich to Hook of Holland takes six to eight hours, and there are two crossings daily. Cost from London: $55, first class, $35 second class, while overnight berths are $8 to $54 (deluxe cabin)" (John O. Wall, Palo Alto, California). . . . "Here's a scenic and inexpensive way for Eurailpass holders to leave Vienna. They are entitled to a free steamer ride from Vienna to Passau, and can stay on the boat overnight for as little as 400 schillings. The boat departs at 8 a.m. and arrives in Passau 1:15 p.m. the following day." (Mr. & Mrs. Robert Clever, Chambersburg, Pennsylvania). . . . "A hint for rail travelers to travel by night to save a night's lodging and arrive early enough to find plenty of vacant rooms upon your arrival (especially in Scandinavia)" (Robert Hults, New York, New York). . . . "Readers should be aware that it is possible to reserve seats on second-class trains. The cost is about $1 and buys some important advantages. First, of course, is the fact that one can arrive at the station at the last minute and have a definite place to sit—the alternative being to arrive an hour (sometimes) ahead of time and search for a seat. Secondly, from what I have observed, there is no guarantee that you'll have a seat if you haven't reserved one. Anyone who has spent the night in the corridor of one of these trains will certainly appreciate what it means to have a seat. The seating situation is most acute during July and August and on weekend travel" (Leonard I. Krauss, Union, New Jersey).

SCHEDULES: In order to plan your European trip, you'll now need a timetable of the major European expresses. That data follows on the next several pages. It requires some explanation.

The schedules are broken down to show the trains which depart from major European cities on your tour. With very few exceptions, only the major international expresses are listed—the fast, crack trains. But not every international express is here, because many of these famous trains have only First Class accommodations. You can be sure that if a train is mentioned in *Europe on $25 a Day,* it has second-class seats or second-class "couchettes."

Below we have listed the departure and arrival times of the major international connections, in effect between June 2 and September 28 in 1985.

Unless otherwise stated, these trains make their runs every day of the week and in every season. The abbreviation "lv" means "leaves"; the abbreviation "ar" indicates a train's arrival time. Usually, we'll give the train's departure time from all of the cities in the country from which it sets out, and provide its arrival time in the various cities of the countries to which it goes. Thus, the schedule of the Orient Express—"lv Paris 11:15 p.m.; lv Strasbourg 4:24 a.m.; ar Stuttgart 6:50 a.m.; ar Munich 9:31 a.m.; ar Salzburg 11:25 a.m.; ar Vienna 3:36 p.m."—indicates that the Orient Express leaves Paris at 11:15 p.m. daily, goes to Strasbourg, from which it then departs at 4:24 a.m.; arrives in Stuttgart at 6:50 a.m., in Munich at 9:31 a.m., in Salzburg at 11:25 a.m., and finally pulls into Vienna at 3:36 p.m.

If you plan to travel more extensively on the European and British railroads, you may want to secure the latest copy of the Thomas Cook Continental Timetable of European railroads and rail map of Europe. This comprehensive 500+ page Timetable details all of Europe's mainline rail services with great detail and accuracy. Both are available exclusively in North America from Forsyth Travel Library, P.O. Box 2975, Shawnee Mission, KS 66201. The timetable costs $15.95 plus $1 postage, and the rail map is $6.95, plus $1 postage. If purchased together the map and timetable are only $21.95 plus $1 postage.

Meanwhile, we start our schedules with the trains leaving from London.

TRAINS LEAVING LONDON

London-Paris: Trains depart from Victoria Station. Lv London 9:45 a.m.; ar Paris 5:50 p.m.; lv London 2:30 p.m.; ar Paris 10:28 p.m.; lv London 9 p.m.; ar Paris 8:53 a.m.

London-Amsterdam: Your best train for this trip leaves London (Liverpool Street Station) at 7:40 p.m., arrives Amsterdam at 9:03 a.m. A second train departs the same station at 9:40 a.m., arrives Amsterdam at 9:32 p.m. (summer only).

London-Brussels: Train leaves London (Victoria Station) at 9:15 a.m. and 1:15 p.m., arriving Brussels (Midi Station) at 5:43 and 9:43 p.m.

London-Copenhagen: Lv London (Liverpool Street Station) daily at 2:25 p.m.; lv Harwich 4:30 p.m.; ar Esbjerg at 1 p.m. the next day; ar Copenhagen 7:17 p.m.

London-Cologne-Munich: Lv London (Victoria Station) 9:15 a.m., ar Cologne 10:19 p.m.; ar Munich 6:55 a.m.

London-Edinburgh: Lv London (King's Cross Station) daily except Sundays at 8:00 a.m., ar Edinburgh 12:17 p.m.; lv London at noon, ar Edinburgh 4:47 p.m.; lv London 11:20 p.m., ar Edinburgh 7:05 a.m.

TRAINS LEAVING PARIS

SIMPLON EXPRESS: Paris-Lausanne-Milan-Venice-Trieste

Lv Paris (Gare de Lyon) 6:50 p.m.; ar Lausanne 12:10 a.m.; ar Milan 3:57 a.m.; ar Venice 6:57 a.m.; ar Trieste 9:27 a.m. Takes passengers only for stations beyond Milan.

ORIENT EXPRESS: Paris-Munich-Vienna

Lv Paris (Gare de l'Est) 11:15 p.m.; lv Strasbourg 4:24 a.m.; ar Stuttgart 6:50 a.m.; ar Munich 9:31 a.m.; ar Salzburg 11:25 a.m.; ar Vienna 3:36 p.m.

NAPOLI EXPRESS: Paris-Torino-Genoa-Pisa-Rome-Naples

Lv Paris (Gare de Lyon) 8:39 p.m.; ar Modane 3:25 a.m.; ar Torino 5:35 a.m.; ar Genoa 8:10 a.m.; ar Pisa 10:30 a.m.; ar Rome 1:55 p.m.; ar Naples 4:52 p.m.

THE NORD EXPRESS: Paris-Hamburg-Copenhagen

Lv Paris (Gare du Nord) 5:10 p.m.; lv Liège 8:57 p.m.; ar Cologne 10:33 p.m.; ar Hamburg 3:12 a.m.; ar Puttgarden 5:07 a.m.; ar Copenhagen 9:17 a.m.

Paris-Frankfurt: Trains depart from the Gare de l'Est: Lv Paris 7 a.m., ar Frankfurt 1:21 p.m.; lv Paris 1:42 p.m., ar Frankfurt 8:24 p.m.; lv Paris 5:15 p.m., ar Frankfurt 11:08 p.m., lv Paris 11 p.m., ar Frankfurt 7:28 a.m.

Paris-Brussels-Amsterdam: All trains leave from the Gare du Nord. Lv Paris 7:48 a.m.; ar Brussels 10:48 a.m.; ar Antwerp 11:45 a.m.; ar Rotterdam 1:07 p.m.; ar The Hague 1:31 p.m.; ar Amsterdam 2:15 p.m.

Lv Paris 10:23 a.m.; ar Brussels 1:16 p.m.; ar Antwerp 2:07 p.m.; ar Rotterdam 3:25 p.m.; ar The Hague 3:50 p.m.; ar Amsterdam 4:34 p.m.

Lv Paris 2:38 p.m.; ar Brussels 5:36 p.m.; ar Antwerp 6:31 p.m.; ar Rotterdam 7:50 p.m.; ar The Hague 8:09 p.m.; ar Amsterdam 8:57 p.m.

Paris-London: The following trains leave from the Gare du Nord: Lv Paris 7:55 a.m.; lv Dover 12:20 a.m.; ar London 1:50 p.m. Lv Paris 11:30 a.m.; lv. Calais 3 p.m.; ar London 5:31 p.m. Lv Paris 2:23 p.m.; ar London 9:03 p.m. (via Boulogne).

Paris-Barcelona: Trains leave Austerlitz Station. Lv Paris 9:33 a.m.; lv Toulouse 5:15 p.m.; ar Port-Bou 8:45 p.m.; ar Barcelona 11:33 p.m. Lv Paris 9:25 p.m.; lv Toulouse 5:10 a.m.; ar Port-Bou 9:05 a.m.; ar Barcelona 1:05 p.m.

Paris-Madrid: Lv Paris (Austerlitz Station) 5:50 p.m.; lv Bordeaux 10:21 p.m.; lv Irun 2:01 a.m.; ar San Sebastian 2:18 a.m.; ar Burgos 6:35 a.m.; ar Madrid 10 a.m. Alternatively, lv Paris (Austerlitz Station) 10:15 p.m.; lv Bordeaux 3:59 a.m.; lv Biarritz 6:33 a.m.; lv Irun 8:55 a.m.; ar San Sebastian 9:21 a.m.; ar Burgos 1:42 p.m., ar Madrid 5:37 p.m.

Paris-Luxembourg: Trains leave from the Gare de l'Est: Lv Paris at 7:16 a.m., 11:03 a.m. and 6:52 p.m., arrive Luxembourg at 11:18 a.m., 2:44 p.m., and 11:28 p.m. respectively.

Paris-Rome: Trains leave from the Gare de Lyon. Lv Paris 6:47 p.m., ar Torino 3:01 a.m., ar Genoa 4:53 a.m.; ar Pisa 6:59 a.m., ar Rome 10:05 a.m. (Termini).

Paris-Nice: The famous "Train Bleu" (first class sleepers only) lvs Paris (Gare de Lyon) 9:46 p.m.; lv Cannes 7:16 a.m.; lv Nice 7:55 a.m.; ar Monaco 8:21 a.m.

The normal Paris-Nice train (both 1st and 2nd class coaches) lvs Paris 9:41 a.m.; lv Lyon 2:08 p.m.; lv Marseille 5:33 p.m.; lv Cannes 7:31 p.m.; ar Nice 8:07 p.m.

Paris-Geneva: Lv Paris (Gare de Lyon) at 7:34 a.m., 10:41 a.m., 2:32 p.m., and 9:13 p.m., arriving Geneva at 11:08 a.m., 2:25 p.m., 6:16 p.m., and 10:57 p.m., respectively. This is the famous "TGV High Velocity" train.

Paris-Zurich: Lv Paris (Gare de l'Est) 10:40 p.m.; ar Basel 5:39 a.m.; ar Zurich 7:09 a.m.

Lv Paris (Gare de l'Est) 5:06 p.m.; ar Zurich 10:57 p.m. Another train leaves Paris at 7 a.m., ar Basel 11:56 a.m., ar in Zurich at 1:09 p.m.

TRAINS LEAVING BRUSSELS

OSTEND-VIENNA EXPRESS: Brussels-Cologne-Frankfurt-Vienna
Lv Brussels (Nord Station) 6:40 p.m.; lv Liège 7:48 p.m.; lv Aachen 8:48 p.m.; ar Cologne 9:27 p.m.; ar Bonn 9:59 p.m.; ar Frankfurt midnight, ar Passau 5:52 a.m.; ar Vienna 9:50 a.m.

Brussels-London: Trains leave from the North Station. Lv Brussels 7:59 a.m.; ar London 3:03 p.m.; lv Brussels 12:05 p.m.; ar London 6:58 p.m.; lv Brussels 11:41 p.m.; ar London 7:09 a.m. All via Dover.

Brussels-Rotterdam-Amsterdam: Trains leave from Midi Station. Lv Brussels 11:04 a.m.; lv Antwerp 11:47 a.m.; ar Rotterdam 1:07 p.m.; ar The Hague 1:31 p.m.; ar Amsterdam 2:15 p.m.

Lv Brussels 1:29 p.m.; lv Antwerp 2:09 p.m.; ar Roosendaal 2:36 p.m.; ar Rotterdam 3:21 p.m.; ar The Hague 3:50 p.m.; ar Amsterdam 4:34 p.m.

Lv Brussels 5:52 p.m.; lv Antwerp 6:33 p.m.; ar Roosendaal 7:03 p.m.; ar Rotterdam 7:50 p.m.; ar The Hague 8:09 p.m.; ar Amsterdam 8:57 p.m.

Brussels-Paris: Trains leave from the Midi Station. Lv Brussels 8:04 a.m.; ar Paris 10:50 a.m.; lv Brussels 10:10 a.m.; ar Paris 1 p.m.; lv Brussels 2:07 p.m.; ar Paris 4:55 p.m.; lv Brussels 7:12 p.m.; ar Paris 10:06 p.m.

Brussels-Luxembourg: Lv Brussels (Gare du Nord) 7:16 a.m.; ar Luxembourg 9:49 a.m.; lv Brussels 12:12 p.m.; ar Luxembourg 2:44 p.m.; lv Brussels 2:15 p.m.; ar Luxembourg 5:10 p.m.; lv Brussels 3:37 p.m.; ar Luxembourg 6:10 p.m.; lv Brussels 6:02 p.m.; ar Luxembourg 8:47 p.m.

TRAINS LEAVING AMSTERDAM

HOLLAND-ITALY EXPRESS: Amsterdam-Milan-Florence-Rome
Lv Amsterdam 7:51 p.m.; lv Utrecht 8:24 p.m.; ar Cologne 11:39 p.m.; ar Basel 5:28 a.m.; ar Lucerne 7:37 a.m.; ar Milan 12:00 p.m.; ar Florence 4:33 p.m.; ar Rome 8:07 p.m.

THE LORELEY EXPRESS: Amsterdam-Cologne-Basel-Milan-Rome
Lv Amsterdam 8:58 a.m.; ar Cologne 12:02 p.m.; ar Mainz 1:57 p.m.; ar Basel 5:36 p.m.; ar Lucerne 7:10 p.m.; ar Milan 11:35 p.m.; ar Rome 7:58 a.m.

HOLLAND-SCANDINAVIA EXPRESS: Amsterdam-Copenhagen
Lv Amsterdam 8:02 a.m.; ar Hamburg 1:54 p.m.; ar Puttgarden 3:47 p.m.; ar Copenhagen 7:29 p.m.

NORTH-WEST EXPRESS: Amsterdam-Hamburg-Copenhagen-Stockholm
Lv Amsterdam 8:02 p.m.; ar Hamburg 2:09 a.m.; ar Puttgarden 4:17 a.m.; ar Copenhagen 8:09 a.m.; ar Helsingborg 9:35 a.m.; ar Stockholm 4:47 p.m.

HOLLAND-VIENNA EXPRESS: Amsterdam-Cologne-Frankfurt-Nuremberg-Vienna
Lv Amsterdam 5:21 p.m.; ar Cologne 8:42 p.m.; ar Frankfurt 11:07 p.m.; ar Nuremberg 0:55 a.m.; ar Vienna 8 a.m.

Amsterdam-Munich: Lv Amsterdam 9:19 a.m.; ar Cologne 12:49 p.m.; ar Munich 8:33 p.m.

Amsterdam-London: Lv Amsterdam 9:32 a.m.; ar London 7:18 p.m.; lv Amsterdam 9:08 p.m.; ar London 9:14 a.m.

Amsterdam-Brussels-Paris: Lv Amsterdam 7 a.m.; ar Antwerp 9:17 a.m.; ar Brussels 9:49 a.m.; ar Paris 1 p.m.
Lv Amsterdam 10:55 a.m.; ar Antwerp 1:15 p.m.; ar Brussels 1:46 p.m.; ar Paris 4:55 p.m.
Lv Amsterdam 3:54 p.m.; ar Antwerp 6:12 p.m.; ar Brussels 6:43 p.m.; ar Paris ¹0:06 p.m.

TRAINS LEAVING COPENHAGEN

THE NORTH EXPRESS: Copenhagen-Hamburg-Cologne-Paris
Lv Copenhagen 9:10 p.m.; ar Hamburg 3:08 a.m.; ar Cologne 8:16 a.m.; ar Aachen 9:02 a.m.; ar Liège 10:10 a.m.; ar Paris 2:34 p.m.

NORTH-WEST EXPRESS: Copenhagen-Hamburg-Amsterdam-London
Lv Copenhagen 10:10 p.m.; lv Puttgarden 2:05 a.m.; ar Hamburg 3:51 a.m.; ar Amersfoort 9:04 a.m.; ar Rotterdam 10:21 a.m.; ar Hook of Holland 10:42 a.m.; ar London 7:18 p.m.

SCANDINAVIA-HOLLAND EXPRESS: Copenhagen-Hamburg-Bremen-Amsterdam
Lv Copenhagen 9:25 a.m.; lv Puttgarden 1:10 p.m.; ar Hamburg 3:01 p.m.; lv Bremen 4:26 p.m.; ar Amsterdam 9:32 p.m.

Copenhagen-Stockholm: Lv Copenhagen 6:34 a.m.; ar Stockholm 4:25 p.m.

Copenhagen-Vienna: Lv Copenhagen 1:10 p.m.; ar Hamburg 6:26 p.m.; ar Passau 6:14 a.m.; ar Vienna 9:50 a.m.

TRAINS LEAVING STOCKHOLM

Stockholm-Oslo: Lv Stockholm at 6:55 a.m.; ar Oslo 1:25 p.m.; lv Stockholm daily at 3:25 p.m.; ar Oslo 9:44 p.m.; lv Stockholm daily throughout the year at 11:10 p.m.; ar Oslo 7:55 a.m.

Stockholm-Copenhagen: Lv Stockholm 7:08 a.m.; ar Copenhagen 3:21 p.m.; lv Stockholm 1:08 p.m.; ar Copenhagen 9:51 p.m.; lv Stockholm 9:08 p.m.; ar Copenhagen 6:21 a.m.; lv Stockholm 11:08 p.m.; ar Copenhagen 8:21 a.m.

TRAINS LEAVING OSLO

Oslo-Copenhagen: Lv Oslo 7:40 a.m.; ar Copenhagen 5:05 p.m.; lv Oslo 11 a.m.; ar Copenhagen 8:51 p.m.; lv Oslo 10:40 p.m.; ar Copenhagen 9:07 a.m.

Oslo-Stockholm: Lv Oslo 8:40 a.m.; ar Stockholm 3:00 p.m.; lv Oslo 3:55 p.m.; ar Stockholm 10:30 p.m.; lv Oslo 10:35 p.m.; ar Stockholm 6:55 a.m.

TRAINS LEAVING MUNICH

THE ISAR-RHONE EXPRESS: Munich-Zurich-Berne-Geneva
    Lv Munich 9:08 a.m.; lv Lindau 11:41 a.m.; ar St. Margarethen 12:08 a.m.; ar Zurich 1:50 p.m.; ar Berne 3:13 p.m.; ar Lausanne 4:22 p.m.; ar Geneva 4:58 p.m.

THE ITALICUS: Munich-Innsbruck-Verona-Florence-Rome
    Lv Munich 7:20 p.m.; lv Innsbruck 9:42 p.m.; ar Verona 2:15 a.m.; ar Florence 5:28 a.m.; ar Rome 9:05 a.m. (summer only).

THE BRENNER EXPRESS: Munich-Florence-Rome
    Lv Munich 11:20 p.m.; ar Bolzano 4:02 a.m.; ar Verona 6 a.m.; ar Bologna 7:47 a.m.; ar Florence 9:12 a.m.; ar Rome 12:45 p.m. At Verona, you can change to trains departing within the hour for Venice or for Nice.

Munich-Hamburg-Copenhagen: Lv Munich 10:51 p.m.; ar Hamburg 8:09 a.m.; ar Puttgarden 10:15 a.m.; ar Copenhagen 2:09 p.m.

THE BAVARIA: Munich-Zurich
    Lv Munich 4:03 p.m.; lv Lindau 6:37 p.m.; ar St. Margarethen 7:04 p.m.; ar Zurich 8:37 p.m.

TRAINS LEAVING VIENNA

VIENNA-OSTEND EXPRESS: Vienna-Frankfurt-Brussels-London
    Lv Vienna (Westbahnhof) 8:50 p.m.; ar Passau 12:30 a.m.; ar Frankfurt 6:25 a.m.; ar Cologne 8:48 a.m.; ar Aachen 9:47 a.m.; ar Liège 10:49 a.m.; ar Brussels 12:05 p.m.; ar Ostend 1:14 p.m.; ar London 6:58 p.m.

THE ORIENT EXPRESS: Vienna-Munich-Paris
    Lv Vienna (Westbahnhof) 3 p.m.; lv Salzburg 6:52 p.m.; ar Munich 8:34 p.m.; ar Strasbourg 1:51 a.m.; ar Paris 6:44 a.m.

Vienna-Paris: Though the Orient Express offers your best bet for this trip, two other trains make the run via Munich and Strasbourg: Lv Vienna on the "Mozart" at 8 a.m.; ar Paris 11:10 p.m. Lv Vienna on the "Wiener Walzer" at 6 p.m.; ar Paris 9:37 a.m.

Vienna-Venice: The Romulus Express (departing at 7:55 a.m.; arriving in Venice at 4:54 p.m.) is your best train for this trip, but there are three other trains which leave Vienna daily for Venice. All depart from the Südbahnhof. For instance, lv Vienna 9 p.m.; ar Udine 4:06 a.m.; ar Venice 5:54 a.m.

Vienna-Belgrade: Lv Vienna (Südbahnhof) at 9 a.m.; ar Zagreb 4:19 p.m.; ar Belgrade 11:02 p.m.; lv Vienna 10:50 p.m.; ar Zagreb 5:05 a.m.; ar Belgrade 10:13 a.m.

TRAINS LEAVING ROME

THE PALATINE EXPRESS: Rome-Torino-Paris
    Lv Rome 6:45 p.m.; lv Pisa 9:51 p.m.; lv Torino 1:53 a.m.; ar Paris 10:07 a.m. Sleepers and couchettes only.

ITALY-HOLLAND EXPRESS: Rome-Cologne-Amsterdam
Lv Rome 9:35 a.m.; lv Florence 1:32 p.m.; lv Milan 6:05 p.m.; lv Lucerne 10:40 p.m.; ar Basel 12:15 p.m.; ar Cologne 6:17 a.m.; ar Utrecht 9:08 a.m.; ar Amsterdam 9:38 a.m.

THE BRENNER EXPRESS: Rome-Florence-Innsbruck-Munich
Lv Rome 5:48 p.m.; lv Florence 9:04 p.m.; lv Bologna 10:34 p.m.; lv Verona 12:17 p.m.; ar Innsbruck 4:46 a.m.; ar Kufstein 5:53 a.m.; ar Munich 6:57 a.m.

THE SIMPLON EXPRESS: Rome-Florence-Venice-Trieste-Belgrade
Lv Rome 9:50 p.m.; lv Florence 1:36 a.m.; lv Venice 5:27 a.m.; lv Trieste 9:53 a.m.; ar Ljubljana 2:10 p.m.; ar Zagreb 4:29 p.m.; ar Belgrade 10:43 p.m.

LORELEY EXPRESS: Rome-Florence-Milan-Lucerne-Basel-Cologne-Amsterdam
Lv Rome 10:23 p.m.; lv Florence 1:56 a.m.; lv Milan 7:10 a.m.; lv Lucerne 11:44 a.m.; lv Basel 1:16 p.m.; ar Cologne 7:17 p.m.; ar Amsterdam 10:28 p.m. Note: the Loreley now carries couchettes and sleepers only, no coaches.

Rome-Florence: The following is only a partial listing of the many departures available to you: lv Rome 9:35 a.m., ar Florence 1:22 p.m.; lv Rome 10:38 a.m.; ar Florence 2:50 p.m.; lv Rome 1:55 p.m., ar Florence 4:46 p.m.; lv Rome 4:20 p.m., ar Florence 7:20 p.m.; lv Rome 5:15 p.m., ar Florence 8:17 p.m.

Rome-Nice: Lv Rome 10:55 a.m.; lv Genoa 5:45 p.m.; lv Ventimiglia 9:25 p.m.; lv Monaco 9:50 p.m.; ar Nice 10:19 p.m. Lv Rome 10:48 p.m.; lv Genoa 5:58 a.m.; lv Monaco 9:47 a.m.; ar Nice 10:02 a.m. At other times, take any train that goes to Ventimiglia or San Remo, where you can make connections for Nice.

Rome-Switzerland: Lv Rome 7:58 p.m.; lv Florence 1:09 a.m.; ar Brig 6:27 a.m.; ar Montreux 8:04 a.m.; ar Lausanne 8:26 a.m.; ar Geneva 9:08 a.m.
Lv Rome 7:15 a.m.; lv Florence 11:27 a.m.; lv Milan 5:15 p.m.; ar Brig 7:45 p.m.; ar Montreux 9:15 p.m.; ar Lausanne 9:37 p.m.; ar Geneva 10:13 p.m. On this trip, a change of trains must be made in Milan.

TRAINS LEAVING NICE

Nice-Rome: Lv Nice 8:19 a.m.; ar Ventimiglia 9 a.m.; ar Genoa 12:37 p.m.; ar Pisa 3:37 p.m.; ar Rome 7:55 p.m.
Lv Nice 8:18 p.m.; lv Monaco 8:37 p.m.; ar Ventimiglia 9 p.m.; ar Genoa 12:03 a.m.; ar Pisa 2:52 a.m.; ar Rome 7 a.m.

Nice-Zurich: Lv Nice 8:23 p.m.; lv Cannes 9:07 p.m.; lv Marseilles 11:54 p.m.; lv Avignon 1:25 a.m.; ar Geneva 7:43 a.m.; ar Lausanne 8:30 a.m.; ar Berne 9:38 a.m.; ar Zurich 10:54 a.m.

TRAINS LEAVING ZURICH

KOMET EXPRESS: Zurich-Basel-Hanover-Hamburg
Lv Zurich 8:57 p.m.; lv Basel 10:20 p.m.; lv Hanover 5:53 a.m.; ar Hamburg 7:59 a.m.

BAVARIA EXPRESS: Zurich-Munich
Lv Zurich 9:19 a.m.; ar St. Margarethen 10:43 a.m.; ar Lindau 11:13 a.m.; ar Munich 1:45 p.m.

Zurich-Rome: Lv Zurich 11:04 a.m.; lv Lugano 2:13 p.m.; ar Milan 3:40 p.m.; ar Florence 8:45 p.m.; ar Rome 12:20 p.m.
Lv Zurich 9:04 p.m.; ar Florence 5:21 a.m.; ar Rome 8:53 a.m. (Termini).

Zurich-Paris: Lv Zurich 6:57 a.m.; ar Basel 7:56 a.m.; ar Paris 12:59 p.m. Lv Zurich 10:42 p.m.; ar Basel 11:42 p.m.; ar Paris 6:48 a.m.

Zurich-Nice: Lv Zurich 7 p.m.; lv Berne 8:16 p.m.; lv Geneva 11 p.m.; ar Grenoble 1:28 a.m.; ar Avignon 4:26 a.m.; ar Marseille 5:52 a.m.; ar Cannes 8:38 a.m.; ar Nice 9:14 a.m.

Zurich-Innsbruck-Salzburg-Vienna: Lv Zurich 9:26 a.m.; ar Innsbruck 1:24 p.m.; ar Salzburg 3:36 p.m.; ar Vienna 7 p.m. Lv Zurich 12:26 p.m.; ar Innsbruck 4:19 p.m.; ar Salzburg 5:36 p.m.; ar Vienna 9 p.m. Lv Zurich 2:26 p.m.; ar Innsbruck 6:19 p.m.; ar Salzburg 7:36 p.m.; ar Vienna 11 p.m.

TRAINS LEAVING MADRID AND BARCELONA

IBERIA EXPRESS: Madrid-Biarritz-Bordeaux-Paris
Lv Madrid (Chamartin) 12:40 p.m.; lv Burgos 5:04 p.m.; lv San Sebastian 8:56 p.m.; lv Hendaye 10:28 p.m.; ar Biarritz 11:36 p.m.; ar Bordeaux 2:01 a.m.; ar Paris (Austerlitz Station) 6:51 a.m.; an alternate train leaves Madrid (Chamartin) at 6:10 p.m., arrives Paris 10:33 a.m.

HISPANIA EXPRESS: Barcelona-Lyon-Geneva-Berne-Zurich
Lv Barcelona 7 p.m.; lv Cerbere 10:48 p.m.; ar Geneva 7:25 a.m.; ar Lausanne 8:30 a.m.; ar Berne 9:38 a.m.; ar Zurich 10:54 a.m.

LUSITANIA EXPRESS: Madrid-Lisbon
Lv Madrid (Atocha) 11:10 p.m.; lv Valencia de Alc. 6:45 a.m.; lv Marvao 6:19 a.m.; ar Entroncamento 8:10 p.m.; ar Lisbon 9:35 a.m.; alternatively leave Madrid (Atocha) 10:15 a.m.; arrive Lisbon 7:05 p.m.

TRAINS LEAVING ATHENS

HELLAS EXPRESS: Athens-Belgrade-Salzburg-Munich
Lv Athens 7 p.m.; lv Thessaloniki 4:50 a.m.; ar Gevgeli 5:15 a.m.; ar Belgrade 5:05 p.m.; lv Zagreb 11:40 p.m.; ar Ljubljana 2 a.m.; ar Salzburg 8:21 a.m.; ar Munich 10:10 a.m.

VENEZIA EXPRESS: Athens-Belgrade-Trieste-Venice-Milan
Lv Athens 9:10 p.m.; lv Thessaloniki 6:52 a.m.; ar Belgrade 6:48 p.m.; lv Ljubljana 4:25 a.m.; ar Trieste 9 a.m.; ar Venice 11:07 a.m.

The major alternative method of surface travel through Europe is the rented car—the subject to which we turn next.

Chapter V

INEXPENSIVE AUTO RENTALS

For Do-It-Yourself Travel

IF THIS IS your first trip to Europe, and you're anxious to cram in a great many different cities and countries, then car travel is not the mode for you—it will necessarily limit the number and variety of your stops in Europe. For, while distances on a European map may seem short, they are deceptively short. Excepting only a few major highways in France and Germany, the normal European road will not permit you to travel as fast as you might in the United States. And if you're to cross mountains on your ride, you'll crawl. The route from Munich to Venice may seem like a short one—but it's over the Alps!

But having painted the foregoing gloomy picture, and having conceded all the drawbacks, I can now with good conscience assert the following stubborn proposition: no one has seen Europe who has not traveled in it by car. The life should be tried: not, perhaps, on a first trip to Europe, when you'll want to see a great many cities, in a number of countries—but ultimately, when you're content to examine at leisure a particular country or area through which you've earlier passed.

How can that be done at the least cost? There are a number of alternatives. We'll first discuss the general principles, and then go on to provide specific names and addresses for specific planning.

OUTRIGHT PURCHASE: A most obvious step, but a serious one. Still, if you've already been planning the purchase of a European car, merely put off the purchase until you arrive in Europe. The normal European small car costs at least $400 less overseas than here. The cost of then shipping the car back to the United States (New York) is (for the smaller cars) about $350. Even when U.S. import duty and excise tax are added, you may end up saving some money on the purchase price; but your greatest saving stems from the fact that you will have paid nothing for the use of the car in Europe—a saving of $600 and more.

MONTHLY LEASES: If you plan to stay in Europe at least a month, and expect to do a substantial amount of driving during that month, then your next best course is to lease (rather than rent) for a flat monthly charge that includes unlimited mileage privileges. Such a one-month arrangement presently costs around $587 for a Fiat 127, $860 for a comfortable Volkswagen Rabbit, and $1,220 for a larger Opel with automatic transmission. Firms usually include full insurance coverage with this arrangement at no extra charge. The only disadvantage in leasing is that delivery and return arrangements tend to be less flexible than with car rental.

SHORT-TERM RENTALS: For periods of less than a month, of course, you'll have to rent a car at a daily or weekly rate. That amounts, for autos of the Volkswagen Rabbit or Renault 5 class, to around $197 per week, if you want unlimited mileage privileges; from $21 per day, plus 21¢ per kilometer (there are about 1.6 kilometers to a mile). Either way, you'll pay about $29 per day for your car (not including gas or added value tax). Most expensive country for auto rentals? Switzerland. Least expensive? Denmark, Spain, Portugal, England, and Luxembourg. By picking up your car in Madrid or London, you can save up to $80 (on a 30-day rental) over what you would have spent by renting the car in most other European cities.

Prices vary considerably not only from country to country, but from firm to firm. Various plans, too, are offered by car rental companies, so do check carefully to find an offer that suits your particular budget and transportation needs.

WHEN AND WHERE: In months other than May through September, you can safely wait until you arrive in Europe to make your car arrangements. The local auto firms will greet you with open arms—off-season. In the summer months, the situation can get tight in certain cities and at varying times; although even then, it's often possible to find an available car simply by appearing on the spot. Moreover, you'll find that the rates you'll obtain from the local and lesser-known agencies in Europe are sometimes cheaper than those offered by U.S.-based firms.

Nevertheless, readers who want absolute certainty in their travel arrangements would do well to contact any one of a number of American agencies that deal in European car hire. And, of course, if you plan the more serious step of purchasing a car overseas (either with or without guaranteed repurchase plan), then you should definitely make all the arrangements, at least a month in advance, in the United States.

The "ShipSide Showroom"

But you needn't even bother making such long-in-advance arrangements for the purchase of a car—if you fly to Amsterdam. For there, on the grounds of Amsterdam Airport, you'll find a showroom of all the best-known European cars, attended by salesmen who will sell you one on the spot! This quite unique operation is known as the **"ShipSide Showroom"** (although it's at an airport, not at a dock), and its U.S. representatives are **ShipSide Car Delivery, Inc.,** 576 Fifth Ave., New York, N.Y. 10036 (phone 212/869-4484), whose brochure about on-the-spot purchase of a European car is quite fascinating (write, and they'll send it to you).

You can pay ShipSide with travelers' checks, certified check, or even personal check (although you'll have to wait for the bank's clearance on the latter form of payment); once payment is made, you can pick up the car immediately—and drive away. ShipSide has been known to complete all the arrangements within an hour after the customer's plane has touched down on the field! Of course, they're also able to have special-make cars available for you, if you can give them advance notice.

As we pointed out before, the purchase of a tax-free European car, in Europe, may involve an initial saving. That, coupled with the absence of car taxes, and supplemented by other reductions brought to you by ShipSide, can result in your paying a little less for a European car purchased in Europe than for one purchased in the United States or Canada, even when you include the cost of shipping it back home and paying duty on it. And, of course, you have increased that saving by having the car for all your transportation needs in Europe. That latter benefit can amount in value to $600 and more.

Where and from Whom to Rent

On the straight rental of a car, keep in mind that rental prices vary according to the European city in which you pick up the auto. Currently, the lowest car-rental rates in Europe are offered in Copenhagen, Madrid, Lisbon, London, and Luxembourg.

All the major car rental agencies are of course represented in the major European cities, and several of them—Hertz, Avis, National, Automaggiore, Kemwel, others—maintain rental desks in the arrival halls of Europe's major airports, where they can often provide you with cars even if you haven't reserved ahead. For names and addresses of U.S.-based firms where you can rent cars for use in Europe, see our section below called "U.S. Firms Offering Car Rentals."

The Amazing Mr. Hildebrandt

Now let's talk about the rental of a car that comes equipped with tent, sleeping bags, gas stoves, cooking utensils—and all the other paraphernalia you'll need to join the growing number of persons who are using the vast network of campsites in Europe for their overnight accommodations. Here you'll want to turn to an "underground hero" of budget travel in Europe, a Copenhagen tailor named **Hendrik Hildebrandt,** who, from his tailor shop at 61 Studiestraede in Copenhagen (phone 12-06-43), began renting a spare car or two a few years ago, and progressed to the point where he now controls a large fleet of autos (equipped with tents and/or trailers) which he continues to rent from the same tailor shop! He has no overhead to speak of, offers the continent's lowest prices for cars with camping equipment, and may even sell you a suit while he's at it.

Hildebrandt will make delivery of a new 1985 car, thus equipped, directly to you at depots in Amsterdam, Brussels, Frankfurt, Luxembourg, or Copenhagen, at a delivery charge of only $50 in Amsterdam, Brussels, Frankfurt and Luxembourg (none in Copenhagen), and with no later collection fee for picking up the car in those same cities. He achieves this feat by having the cars delivered and picked up by Danish university students, who thus obtain free transportation on their own vacation travels to those cities. Normally, his charge for the rental to two persons of a 1985 Opel Corsa or Ford Fiesta, the delivery charge for Amsterdam, Brussels, Frankfurt or Luxembourg plus unlimited mileage, complete insurance, two-person tent that is physically attached to the car, two sleeping bags, car atlas, camping guidebook, and membership in the International Camper's Union is approximately $461 for two weeks, $645 for three weeks, $814 for four weeks, and $25.70 per day for each day in excess of the first four weeks;

the charge is only slightly more when three or four persons use the car (additional tents and sleeping bags are then provided). But beyond that, Hildebrandt will give a 10% discount off these prices to anyone who writes him mentioning this book.

For readers desirous of renting a 1978–82 model Volkswagen camper-bus (capable of sleeping up to four people), Hildebrandt has that, too, at prices of around $840 for two weeks, $1,260 for three weeks, $1,680 for four weeks, including unlimited mileage, value added tax, delivery and collection, and again a 10% discount to readers of this book. For readers who have heard of the new Opel Kadett "Campette" (with seats that unfold within seconds into a double bed with polyfoam mattress and curtains), Hildebrandt has a supply. And for readers who would simply like to rent a car without trailer or tent from Mr. H. (Opel Corsa or Ford Fiesta, unlimited mileage, and pick-up and delivery in Amsterdam, Copenhagen, Brussels, Frankfurt and Luxembourg), the cost is $342 for two weeks, $486 for three weeks, $628 for four weeks, with a 10% discount off those prices to readers, and an additional 10% discount on off-season rentals ending before May 1 or starting after September 24. If, incidentally, you'd prefer to collect or drop off the car in Vienna, Zurich, London or Rome, the supplemental charge is $140. And if you'd like a daily rental only, the Opel Corsa is available from Hildebrandt for only $8.90 a day plus 14¢ per kilometer, with 10% off to readers of this book. Rates can change if changes occur in the future value (post December, 1984) of the U.S. dollar vis-à-vis the Danish kroner. For further information on the availability of upgraded cars, or for a brochure, or to make your booking, write Hendrik Hildebrandt, Share-a-Car, Inc., 61 Studiestraede, Copenhagen 1554, Denmark (phone 12-06-43).

A Discounted German Rental

Readers traveling to Germany may want to know, instead, that the country's largest privately owned auto-rental firm, Sixt/Budget, 2 Dr. Karl von Linde Strasse, Pullach near Munich, phone 089-791071, has offered a 10% discount off their normal rates to bearers of this book. Sixt has offices in the ten largest German cities, and at several airports, too, but you'd best phone or write for the discount to the Chief Reservations Manager, Frau Neudeck, at the Munich headquarters.

U.S. Firms Offering Car Rentals

If, in preference to all these alternatives, you'd like to deal with a U.S.-based firm for your European car rental, then you can contact one of a number of major U.S. companies that now do nothing but the rental of cars (or sale of cars) to U.S. tourists vacationing in Europe. Among the largest of these companies are: **Europe by Car, Inc.,** 1 Rockefeller Plaza, New York, N.Y. 10020 (phone 212/581-3040 or nationwide 800/223-1516), which also maintains offices in Los Angeles (9000 Sunset Blvd.), and Seattle (510—4th & Pike Building (phone 206/624-5357), with unlimited mileage rental rates starting at $89; and **Auto-Europe, Inc.,** P.O. Box 500, Yorktown Heights, NY 10598 (phone 914/962-5252 and outside of New York state 800/223-5555). And for the purchase of specific makes of cars, you might want to deal directly with: **Renault USA, Inc.,** 499 Park Ave., New York, NY 10022 (toll-free phone 800/221-1052; in New York City, phone 212/980-8500); **Volkswagen Bristol Motors, Inc.,** 506 E. 76th St.,

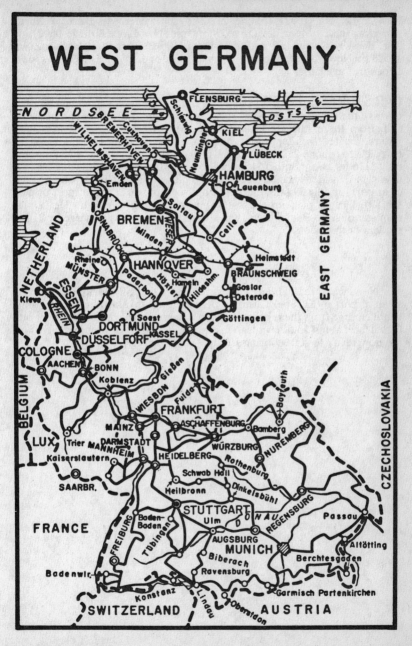

New York, NY 10021 (phone 212/249-7200); **Mercedes-Benz of North America, Inc.,** 1 Mercedes Drive, Montvale, NJ (phone 201/573-0600); or **The Kemwel Group** (all makes of cars), 106 Calvert St., Harrison, NY 10528 (in New York state phone 800/942-1932, or elsewhere, 800/431-1362). Brochures available.

CAR STORAGE IN NEW YORK: A thought, now, for readers who plan

to drive their own cars to New York and pick up a Europe-bound plane or ship from there: the cheapest storage garage in the U.S. is **Auto Baby Sitters,** located in a large gray building at 827 Sterling Place, Brooklyn, N.Y. 11216 (phone 212/493-9800), which charges $32 a week, $64 a month, only $116 for two months, $156 for three months, for keeping your car in a dry, clean, inside storage place, and will pick up the car from you at a pier or airport for only $9 (and thereafter deliver it to you at that airport or pier for $9). They'll pick up the car from your hotel, free. Mr. De Toma, manager of Auto Baby Sitters, will also reduce the storage charge by $1 for readers of this book.

Now, we're really ready to begin. Your plane will shortly touch down at an airport in Europe. Customs clearance will take a short while. Soon you'll emerge from the terminal exit, to a staging area where an airport bus (usual fare: about $3.50) waits to take you to the heart of your first city. You are now ready to start touring Europe—on $25 a day.

Chapter VI

LONDON

Breakfast Is Included

LONDON, TO SOME, is an imposing place, to be respected rather than enjoyed. To me, this city is as unpretentious as the smallest country hamlet. When London is known and absorbed, it remains in the mind not as a memory of monuments and museums, but of utterly simple and sympathetic sights: the galleries at Covent Garden filled with students rapt upon a Frederick Ashton ballet; the calm and smoky innards of a corner pub; the clusters of children in Kensington Park; the cheese-and-ale parties in the one-room skylight flats of Chelsea.

All you've heard to the contrary, Londoners are among the friendliest people of Europe, and London itself is an inviting town. It has charm and a politeness of attitude, in such abundance, that few travelers fail to extend their stay, once they've arrived. Can you live in London on $25 a day? To answer that question, let's examine some human statistics.

PRICES AND WAGES: I have a friend in London who is a graduate of the Old Vic Company, and a recognized, steadily employed actor in the theatres of the West End. His salary averages to barely more than £125 ($175) a week, less tax. On that sum, he maintains not merely a proper standard of living, but a constant round of entertaining and much-too-frequent pub-crawling. I know a reporter who works for one of Britain's top weekly magazines. She averages £140 ($196) a week. She dresses well, shares a comfortable flat near Holland Park, and is considered in England to be quite adequately paid. For these two people, a ten-dollar bill has the purchasing power of nearly fifteen dollars over here, and neither of them would be shocked, surprised or in any way nonplussed by the standards prescribed in this book.

You would expect one of the oldest democracies on earth to possess a price structure with a broad, mass appeal—and it does. Despite the surface elegance of England, the entertainment, eating and housing facilities of that nation are actually far more concentrated in the middle- and lower-class areas than in the United States. Low-cost chain restaurants, moderate hotels and inexpensive night-spots are astonishingly abundant, at prices that would shame their American counterparts, because they are geared to the low (for America) wages of the overwhelming bulk of the British population. Because of that, the tourist who can't find a satisfying meal for $4, or a satisfying room with breakfast for as little as $12 per person, just isn't half trying.

You'd like proof? Read on.

1. Getting Around

You set out on your search for hotels utilizing one of the best subway and bus systems in the world; it not only whizzes you about comfortably and at relatively low cost, but also transports you from London's Heathrow Airport to the very center of town for only $2.80. Upon arrival at Heathrow, look for signs pointing the way to the "underground": there, a subway of the Piccadilly line takes you in 45 minutes to numerous stations in the heart of London for £2 ($2.80). At London's other airport, Gatwick, you again find a train station in the center of the arrival terminal, this time taking you by British Rail to Victoria Station in downtown London for £3.30 ($4.62).

Once settled into accommodations, and embarking on in-city travels, you'll find London's subway system to be a revelation: quiet, comfortable, clean, efficient, with upholstered banquettes, no less, all at fares that range from 40p to 80p (56¢ to $1.14), the average ride probably requiring a 50p fare. You must hold on to the tickets you purchase, and present them to an attendant upon exiting the station, as proof that you've paid the right amount for the trip you've taken. While London's double-decker bus system is more rarely used by tourists, it's equally comprehensive, and similarly priced; this time, you buy your ticket from the conductor—often, a dignified Jamaican—inside the bus.

Because you will probably be making such a heavy use of subways and buses, and rarely taking the rather expensive taxis, it is highly advisable to purchase an unlimited London Transport pass for one, three, four or seven days of travel on all the subway lines and all the red buses within the 80 square miles of central London. These are called **London Explorer Tickets;** they're sold at numerous main underground stations (you'll see signs), and cost: one day, £3 for adults, £1.30 children; three days, £8 for adults, £3 children; four days, £10.50 for adults, £4 children; seven days, £13 for adults, £5 children. Unless you're an unusually sedentary tourist visiting but one site per day—and obviously you're not—you will realize substantial savings with the London Explorer Ticket, and should definitely buy one; it will also transport you to and from Heathrow Airport (provided you're within the validity period of your ticket), and that alone saves you £2.

On Sundays in London, all subway tickets (except to Heathrow) cost a maximum of 40p for a single journey, 60p round trip. Sunday is obviously the day for heavy sightseeing. For free subway and bus maps, apply at the **National Tourist Information Office** next to the main entrance of Victoria Station, or to "London Transport Enquiry" windows in the Piccadilly Circus Station, Oxford Circus Station, or at the station in Heathrow Airport from which you take the train into town.

Incidentally, so good is London's subway system that it really doesn't matter where you stay in London; you're rarely more than 15 comfortable minutes away from any major location.

2. Budget Hotels

These can be obtained for at least a third less than you'd pay in an American city. And that outlay results not only in a room, but in breakfast as well! The first thing to know about budget-priced British hotels is that most of them include a free, enormous morning meal in their room charges. Served each day at stated hours in the hotel's dining room, it costs nothing and it's a whopper—the kind that would be priced at least at $4 in the U.S. And so, when a London guesthouse quotes a nightly rate of, say, $14 per person, they mean that room *and* breakfast will come to $14 per person—an exceptional value.

Consequently, to stay on a budget in London, you can go to as high as $16 per person in your room charges ($32 for a double), because that charge includes a large breakfast (usually with unlimited servings). But $16 is stretching it a bit, and we've scoured the city for rooms costing considerably less. Here are the results:

ROOMS WITHOUT BATH FOR £5.50 TO £9 ($7.70 TO $12.60): We introduce you here to the institution of the British bed-and-breakfast house—classically, a four-story Georgian town house originally built, somewhere after the turn of the century, to house a single middle-class or upper middle-class family. In the typical tale, that family or its successors later fell upon hard times and were forced to take in transient visitors to whom they supplied: bed and breakfast. Naturally, the rooms are without private bath, the structure lacks an elevator or large lobby, and there isn't a bellboy or a doorman in sight. What there is, instead, is unpretentious comfort, intimacy, human contact with proprietors and other guests.

In London, as in other large English cities, clusters of bed-and-breakfast houses are found in every major section. But in London, wherever bed-and-breakfast houses are clustered, their rates tend to average between £9 and £11 ($12.60 and $15.40) per person per night. To find the establishments charging less, you've got to phone the places that tend to stand alone, of which the dozen-or-so establishments that follow (all personally selected in the summer of 1984) are typical:

Near Victoria Station

Douglas Private Hotel, 84 Warwick Way (phone 834-5636), less than seven minutes on foot from important Victoria Rail and Coach Station, is a three-floor, 25-bed guesthouse operated by an amiable couple, Sarah and Nigel Drew, which charges only £9 ($12.60) per person per night for its several double rooms, including a breakfast of fruit juice, cornflakes, bacon and eggs, toast and tea or coffee. Guests enjoy free showers, the use of a lounge with color TV, and a small kitchen in which to prepare their own tea at other times of the day. From the station, cross Eccleston Bridge, continue into Belgrave Road, and the fifth sidestreet turning right is Warwick Way.

Windsor Guest House, 36 Alderney St. (phone 828-7922), on a side road that crosses Warwick Way about 200 yards from Douglas Private Hotel, occupies an ideal location and is probably the best bargain near Victoria. Twelve no-frills but perfectly acceptable rooms on three floors, for which owner, Mr. Pardihan, charges only £8 ($11.20) per person in doubles, £7.50 ($10.50) per person in twin, £7 ($9.80) per person in quads, including a substantial breakfast and free showers. Single rooms are not available.

In Chelsea

Near the home of brooding Thomas Carlyle, a short ride from Victoria Station, **Happy House,** 73 Oakley St. (phone 352-6610 or 352-5599), has, inexplicably, no name on the door, but if you'll simply ring the bell, owners Roy or Eleanor Torrens will greet you, in my experience, with a smile. Their charge is only £7.50 ($10.50) per person for one of their dozen twin rooms, including a full English breakfast that features: eggs any style with bacon, brown or white bread, marmalade, butter, coffee or tea. Extra bonuses: a small kitchen with pots and pans for free use; a coin laundry (80p per load); color TV and small laundry in the multi-purpose lounge. From Victoria Station, take either bus 11 (a five-minute ride to the Chelsea Town Hall stop), or the "underground" (subway) to Sloane Square (one stop, then walk up King's Road for several blocks to Oakley Street, next to a fire station). And if you get lost, ask for the celebrated house of Thomas Carlyle. Another nearby landmark in full view: Albert Bridge crossing the Thames into Battersea Park.

Near Paddington Station

London House Hotel, 81 Kensington Gardens Square (phone 727-0696), is a rather large guesthouse (82 rooms) located on a leafy square of Edwardian buildings that will remind you of *Upstairs, Downstairs* times over 80 years ago. Its special charge, to readers of this book only, is £9 ($12.60) per person per night, including continental breakfast with free second and more helpings—a pledge assured by charming Mrs. Coombes, the manageress, born in Hungary. Although it's close to both the Paddington and Bayswater underground stations, it's best reached by underground to Bayswater. Leaving the station, turn left into Porchester Gardens, and the first street on your right is Kensington Gardens Square.

South of the Thames

Abbeville Guesthouse, 89 Abbeville Rd., Clapham Common (phone 622-5360), has been operated for 25 years by Mr. and Mrs. Coleman—he's also a London taxi driver—who charge only £7 ($9.80) per person, with full English breakfast. You'll particularly like room 8 in the attic, with its view on a school garden. Take the underground to Clapham Common, leave at the south exit, walk along Southside Street for about 100 yards, turn left into Crescent Lane (not Grove), a curved street which, after 300 more yards, crosses Abbeville Road.

Edwards Guesthouse, next door at 91 Abbeville Rd., Clapham Common (phone 622-6347), rents rooms with wall-to-wall carpeting for a similar £7 ($9.80) per person, including full English breakfast, but with an extra charge of 10p for a hot shower. Mr. and Mrs. Powell are the hard-working owners who keep their house clean as a pin.

Mary Ward's Guesthouse, 98 Hambalt Rd., Clapham Common (phone 673-1077), around the corner from the first three Clapham Common houses listed above, is also the smallest (four double rooms) of our recommendations, and also one of the most simple (one room has no wash basin), but charges only £5.50 repeat £5.50 ($7.70) per person per day, including a morning meal of cereal with all the milk you want, two slices of bacon and one fried egg, as much toast as you can eat, coffee or tea. Mrs. Ward is able to charge such low rates because she does all the work herself, and believes a small profit is sufficient. Three hurrahs for her!

Helix Lodge, 51 Bonham Rd., Brixton (phone 274-7166), also charges an amazingly low (for London) £5.25 ($7.35) per person, without breakfast, for a room with coin-operated gas stove and cupboard filled with cutlery, plates, pots—even a bottle opener. Mr. and Mrs. Harrington, he originally from India, she from Malta, have been the owners and managers since 1964, and their house is 15 minutes on foot from the Brixton underground station, itself four stops and 40p from Victoria Station.

The best for last: in the south London area a five-minute walk from the Elephant and Castle tube station, three stops from Charing Cross, the remarkable Mr. Terry Driscoll (who deserves a knighthood) maintains a 45-year-old experiment in international understanding at his 200-room **Driscoll House** at 172 New Kent Road (phone 703-4175), catering to as many as 30 nationalities at any given time. All 200 rooms are singles, and all rent, to both men and women, at £50 ($70) per person per week, *including* breakfast *and dinner* every day, as well as use of four color TV rooms, table tennis lounge, eight pianos, a sewing room and laundry. There are medical and law students staying here, civil servants, teachers and tourists: while priority is obviously given to long-term guests, a great many one-week and two-week visitors find frequent vacancies, and participate in the activities—excursions to theatres and important sights—organized by Mr. Driscoll, who has, in his 45 years here, accommodated among others 1,251 guests from the United States, 106 from Sri Lanka, 1,746 from India, 1 apiece from Sikkim and Qatar, all at rates that are obviously intended to permit low-income international travelers to enjoy a dignified, comfortable stay in London. Why shouldn't Mr. Driscoll receive a knighthood?

Back North of the Thames

Finally, in quiet, residential surroundings, with laundromat, shopping center, free public library, and the grave of Karl Marx nearby, **Mrs. Jo Purcell,** 26 Dartmouth Rd. (phone 485-5903), rents three twins and four single rooms for *long-stay* travelers wanting to do their own preparation of meals: each such room is equipped with coin-operated gas and electric ranges (20p being sufficient for the average meal), in addition to all the kitchen utensils you'll need. Weekly rates, believe it or not, are only £19 ($26.60) per person, bed linen is changed once a week, and at these prices you'll need to pay for the heating of your room on cold days, using a coin-operated gas heater that requires only £2 for a full week of heat. One bathroom (with tub, not shower) on each of the two floors; fellow guests are a savvy crew of Americans, New Zealanders, Canadians and Australians (one of whom has been staying there, as of mid-1984, for 18 months), and tube stop is Tufnell Park, seven stops and 60p from Leicester Square. From the subway exit, walk uphill on Dartmouth Park Avenue for about 400 yards, turn left after St. Mary's Church, then right into Laurier Street after 50 more yards, and after 50 additional yards, you'll see Dartmouth Park Road to the right. There's no name on Mrs. Purcell's door; simply ring the bell.

ROOMS WITHOUT BATH FOR £9.50 TO £14 ($13.30 TO $19.60): Though clean and perfectly proper, the bed-and-breakfast houses listed under the previous price category are obviously those in which the frills are missing. Of slightly higher standard and comfort—some, in fact, quite lovely and with character—are the more traditional London guesthouses found in at least five distinct districts of town. These are:

Near Russell Square

Found but a short walk from Russell Square, a lovely little park within walking distance of the British Museum, the theatres of London, and Soho, **St. Athans Hotel** at 20 Tavistock Place (not to be confused with Tavistock Square), phone 837-9140, is a 40-room guesthouse famous for its English breakfast of cereal, eggs, bacon, ham and sausage, fried tomatoes, toast, butter, marmalade and tea, all personally served in a cozy basement breakfast room by owner Hans Geyer, wearing white apron (he also operates a small budget restaurant, "Hans' Place," in the same building). 1985 rates, guaranteed to bearers of this book, are £11.50 ($16.10) per person in double rooms, £10 ($14) per person in triples, £9 ($12.60) per person in quads, £18 ($25.20) single, including that famous breakfast for all, but in rooms without private bath, yet with free showers down the hall. To reach the St. Athans, take the London subway to Russell Square, whose station exit is on Bernard Street, cross Bernard Street into Herbrand Street, and a couple of hundred yards along, you'll find Tavistock Place.

THE BRITISH POUND ("£"), presently worth approximately $1.40, is divided into 100 pence ("p") worth 1.4¢ apiece. £1.50 means one pound and 50 pence; £10 are ten pounds; 10p are 10 pence. To calculate the very rough value of English prices, simply multiply by 1½, and you'll be only slightly off.

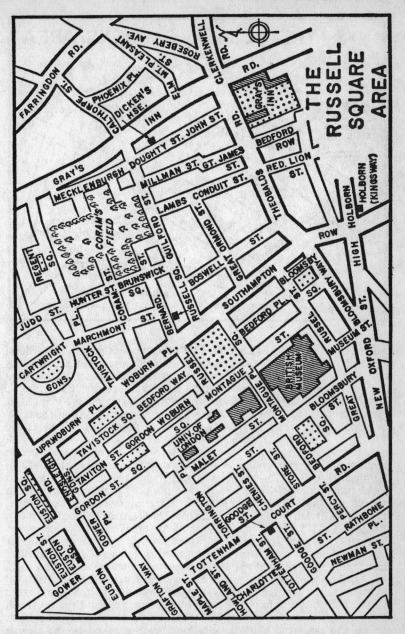

The Incomparable Cartwright Gardens: Now, if you'll walk from Tavistock Place to the end of Marchmont Street, you'll encounter the most attractive and pleasant street of budget hotels in the Russell Square area, which faces a tree-lined, dead-end square on which are spotted tennis

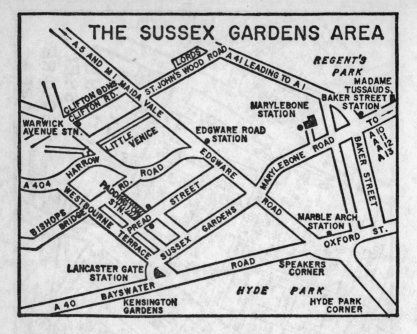

THE SUSSEX GARDENS AREA

courts of the University of London. That's the famous **Cartwright Gardens,** on which there's a two-block crescent of handsome nineteenth-century town houses (they feature cut-glass windows and chandeliers, red-carpeted entrance hallways), every one of which is today a top-notch budget hotel. The roomiest of these is the 43-room **Harlingford** (phone 387-1551) at 61 Cartwright Gardens, which has both a TV lounge and a lounge without TV for people who prefer conversation, and which charges £12 to £17.50 ($16.80 to $24.50), the latter for a single, per person, for bed-and-breakfast; while nearby are two other favorites of frequent visitors to London: the 26-room **Avalon,** at 46 Cartwright Gardens (phone 387-2366) charging £11 to £14 ($15.40 to $19.60) per person—including breakfast, and whose proprietors, Mr. and Mrs. Taylor, not only provide showers at no extra charge, but will direct you to nearby tennis courts costing 60p an hour; and **Jenkins Hotel,** the latter at 45 Cartwright Gardens (phone 387-2067), charging £11 ($15.40) per person, for bed-and-breakfast, in double rooms. Especial kudos go to Jenkins Hotel, which can turn a pleasant London stay into a memorable one; two budget-minded members of Parliament live here during sessions, and the air crackles with intellectual debate; then, too, Mr. and Mrs. Williams—who manage the Jenkins—are superb hotel proprietors. . . . Fourteen pounds ($19.60) single, £12 ($16.80) per person double, bed-and-breakfast, is charged by the rather stylish **Crescent Hotel,** 49 Cartwright Gardens (phone 387-1515); all prices including breakfast, service and tax. And a fractionally lower rate is asked by the **George Hotel,** 60 Cartwright Gardens (phone 387-1528), £13 to £15 ($18.20 to $21) per person for bed-and-breakfast, with central heating in winter and reduced rates for children.

Bloomsbury and Gower Streets: A cluster of cheaper hotels, in almost as pleasant a setting, is found at the far side of Russell Square (an easy walk from the Russell Square tube exit) on the famous **Bloomsbury Street,** which bears that designation for about a hundred yards, and then becomes **Gower Street.** Both names are identified with a brilliant period of pre-World War I British intellectual history (Sidney and Beatrice Webb, George Bernard Shaw, Virginia Woolf), and you'll find book publishers, university buildings, philanthropic societies and schools all along the length of the street.

The higher-priced budget hotels are on Bloomsbury Street (for which the nearest underground stop is Tottenham Court Road), in an exquisite series of Georgian town houses. One of these, the **Gresham Hotel,** 36-38 Bloomsbury St. (phone 636-1067), built in 1880, charges from £10 to £12 ($14 to $16.80) per person, depending on the size of the room, is directly around the corner from the British Museum. The **Morgan Hotel,** at 24 Bloomsbury St. (phone 636-3735), charges £12 ($16.80) for the same deal, is highly recommended, as is the **Regent House Hotel** at 28 Bloomsbury St. (phone 636-4888), with roughly similar rates per person in double rooms. All three hotels are located just next to tiny Bedford Square, a well-known publishing center which intersects Bloomsbury Street and Gower Street. Or try the **Cosmo-Bedford House Hotel,** 27 Bloomsbury Square (phone 636-4661 or 636-0577), where Irishman Michael Fitzgerald rents his 35 rooms for £14 ($19.60) single, £22 ($30.80) twin or double, and £28 ($39.20) for triples. Lounge with color TV, free showers and English breakfast included. Ideal location, very quiet surroundings.

On the other side of Bedford Square, Bloomsbury Street becomes Gower Street, and the hotel prices descend as you move deeper into the area of the University of London. The exceedingly friendly **Arran House Hotel,** 77 Gower St. (phone 636-2186 or 637-1140), is my choice here, because of its colorful, ex-British Army-officer-proprietor (Maj. W. J. Richards), who puts you at ease and charges £10.50 ($14.70) per person, breakfast included, for a broad variety of rooms. Numerous readers have liked the rose garden out back, the military etchings and other touches in the breakfast room. Try, also, the 23-room **Staunton Hotel,** 13–15 Gower St. (phone 636-5583), in a 200-year-old building with interesting winding staircases and outgoing, almost effervescent in attitude proprietors, Mr. and Mrs. Morgan (£9.50 per person in twin rooms, including full English breakfast); the **Ridgemount Private Hotel,** 65 Gower St. (phone 636-1141), £9 ($12.60) per person for bed-and-breakfast in a centrally heated establishment operated by a warm-hearted Welsh couple, Royden and Gwen; the **Jesmond Hotel,** 63 Gower St. (phone 636-3199), £10 ($14) per person in a double, £9 ($12.60) in triple or four-bedded rooms for bed-and-breakfast; **Maree Hotel,** 25 Gower St. (phone 636-4868), £11 to £13.50 ($15.40 to $18.90) per person; and **Gower House,** 57 Gower St., £9.50 in a double room, £8.50 per person in a four-bedded room, including breakfast served by the proprietors themselves. At the last of these Gower Street hotels, you'll be directly across the street from the Royal Academy of Dramatic Art ("R.A.D.A."), where the greats of the British stage, from John Gielgud to Albert Finney, have trained. The Borg brothers and their respective wives operate Gower House, and offer washing and ironing on the premises; phone 636-4685 to learn about vacancies.

By the way, a station called "Goodge Street" is the closest underground stop to the Gower Street hotels.

Bedford Place (Big Splurge Only): A far more elegant street running off Russell Square is a solid row of white Georgian town houses, with

Bloomsbury Square (a park) at one end, Russell Square at the other. Unfortunately, only one hotel here—the relatively plain **Thanet**, at 8 Bedford Place (phone 636-2869)—is within our budget range, with bed-and-continental-breakfast rates throughout the year of £11 ($15.40) per person (in double rooms). The proprietors here are tourists themselves, having used our guide, *England on $5 & $10 a Day,* on their honeymoon early in 1965! Four other quite lovely hotels—the **Wansbeck,** 5 Bedford Place (phone 636-6232), £12 ($16.80) per person in twin rooms; the **Bedford House,** 1 Bloomsbury Place (phone 636-0577), £10 for bed-and-breakfast; the **Haddon Hall,** 40 Bedford Place (phone 636-0026), £13.50 per person twin, £15 single, a Georgian gentleman's town house, now offering reduced rates for children; and the large **St. Margaret's Hotel,** 26 Bedford Place (phone 636-4277), £14.50 ($20.30), per person bed-and-breakfast, all included—are beyond our usual limits, but might be tried in an emergency. The nearest underground stop for all five hotels is: Holborn.

Sussex Gardens

A second, major hotel area in London is a single, but many-blocks-long, avenue called **Sussex Gardens,** which is almost continuously lined with bed-and-breakfast houses charging somewhat less than the going rate around Russell Square. The hotels here are so numerous that it's hard to imagine you won't find a vacancy, even at the peak of the summer season when Russell Square will very definitely present difficulties. Side streets off Sussex Gardens—particularly the guesthouse-crammed **Norfolk Square** near Paddington Station—offer further possibilities and even cheaper rates.

V.A.T.: Like other nations in the European Community, England assesses a "Value Added Tax" ("V.A.T."), currently 15%, on hotel rates. And like the hotels in those European nations, all English hotels of the budget category now include the tax in their published rates, as do restaurants. Thus, there's nothing further to be added to the hotel and restaurant prices set forth in this chapter.

Sussex Gardens lies just off Edgware Road, and Edgware Road leads, in a short walk, to Marble Arch and Hyde Park. The best tube stops are Paddington Station (for reaching the buildings on Sussex Gardens numbered 100 or higher) or the Edgware Road station of the Metropolitan line (for the numbers under 100), from which any passerby will point the way to Sussex Gardens. A particular advantage of Sussex Gardens, for readers with cars, is that it has an inner parallel road on which there's unrestricted parking.

The most numerous Sussex Gardens budget hotels are those closest to Edgware Road, these normally charging £9 to £14 ($12.60 to $19.60) per person for bed-and-breakfast. They include the **Red Court Hotel,** 14 Sussex Gardens (phone 723-6378), £9 per person; manager is a Maltese/Australian named John Louis Bayada; **Cameron Hotel,** 10 Sussex Gardens (£12 for room and breakfast, phone 262-1538); **Cambridge House,** #36 (phone

723-9936), £11.50 per person, double; the exceptionally friendly **Haven Hotel,** #8 (phone 723-2195; £13 single, £11.50 per person double), whose wonderfully friendly and gregarious landlady, Bridget Giles, likes receiving families with children; **Stuart House,** 30 Sussex Gardens (phone 723-2486), £11 to £13 per person; and **Nayland Hotel,** 134 Sussex Gardens (phone 723-3380), charging £12 to £14 ($16.80 to $19.60) per person, including a big English breakfast, and operated for the past 30 years by various members of the Naylor family, whose experience is evident in the personal attention and service they provide.

But the best Sussex Gardens hotels (nearly always £9.50 to £12 a night for bed-and-breakfast) are the group of houses that bear numbers 120 to 148. They're located along a particularly nice stretch of the avenue, and most of them welcome families with children. Try, for instance, the **Tyburn Hotel,** 148 Sussex Gardens, phone 723-5096 (in a slightly higher price category, but which promises to charge from £9.50, $13.30, to readers of this book, and will cook bacon in the American style—"burned"). One proprietress along this block recently wrote me that she has "come to know and respect American likes and dislikes: no basement rooms, no top floor, showers, lots of towels, scrambled eggs, burnt bacon!"

Farther along the street, our choices include: **Lyndon House Hotel,** 84 Sussex Gardens (phone 262-2387), £8.50 ($11.90) per person, including full English breakfast, long recommended in this guide and long a favorite of students in London; and two doors away, **Cornwall House,** 82 Sussex Gardens (phone 262-2941), £12 ($16.80) per person for bed-and-breakfast. Try, too, the **Margam Private Hotel,** 120 Sussex Gardens (phone 723-0528), bed-and-breakfast for £10 per person; and finally, the comfortable **Berkeley Court** at 94 Sussex Gardens (phone 723-4801), charging £13 for singles, £11.50 per person double, including breakfast.

If these, however, are full, then you still have at least 30 other hotels on Sussex Gardens from which to make your choice; and consequently, if you've arrived in London in June, July or August, you might save quite a bit of time by simply heading for this hotel-packed area, sans further ado.

READER'S HOTEL SELECTIONS (SUSSEX GARDENS AREA): "Our **Tregaron Hotel,** 17 Norfolk Square, W.2 (phone 723-9966), will charge £9.75 per person in 1985 for bed, breakfast and V.A.T. We shall be most pleased to accommodate your readers and shall do all in our power to help them and make them comfortable" (W. George, London, England; note by AF: the **Ashley Hotel,** next door to the Tregaron at 15 Norfolk Square—phone 723-3375—is under the same management, charges the same rates).

Nearby Norfolk Square: The pickings are even larger, and cheaper, on nearby **Norfolk Square,** a block from Sussex Gardens and a block, in the other direction, from Paddington Station. Its greatest recommendation is that most of the hotels here sport multi-consonant Welsh names or are owned by Welshmen, characteristically warm and hospitable. Why so many Welshmen? "If we ever get homesick," one proprietor explained to me, "we can hop a direct day-trip to Wales from Paddington Station." Try: the 38-room **Falcon Hotel,** 11 Norfolk Square (phone 723-8603), charging £9.50 per person in a double, £11.50 single (its owner, Mr. Rees, one of those outgoing Welshmen, has installed showers and a color TV in every room); the **Border Hotel,** 14 Norfolk Square (phone 723-2968) charging £11 per person in double rooms (Mr. and Mrs. Davies, who hail from Port Talbot, are the proprietors); the unusually comfortable (large rooms, soft carpeting) but reasonably priced **St. George Hotel,** 46 Norfolk Square (phone 723-3560), charging only £10 per person in double rooms, including full English breakfast, only £12 single; and the **Tudor Court Hotel,** at 10 Norfolk Square (phone 723-6553), charging £10 per person, and featuring full central heating.

Cheapest of the Norfolk Square establishments is the **Bristol Hotel,** 38 Norfolk Square (phone 723-0114), which sometimes calls itself a youth hostel, but actually caters to all age groups. Unusually attractive for a hostel, it charges £5 ($7) per person in a crisply new blue and white dorm-style room, £6.50 ($9.10) per person in a double, always including a continental breakfast and use of kitchen facilities. Managers Gale Heaven and Elizabeth Palmer also operate the similarly priced **Avon Hotel,** a few doors away at 50 Norfolk Square (phone 723-4921), where weekly rates are as little as £25 ($35) per person in a double-decker bunk. Capacity is about 110 beds in all at the exciting Bristol and Avon.

Victoria Station—Belgrave Road

Another solid line of bed-and-breakfast houses—less crowded in summer than those around Russell Square or Sussex Gardens—is found on Belgrave Road, just a few hundred yards behind Victoria Station (which is itself behind Buckingham Palace and relatively near to Westminster Abbey and the houses of Parliament). Because of their location, and not because the street itself, or the houses, are more attractive than others we've named, most of the Belgrave Road establishments charge a bit more per person than do their counterparts on Sussex Gardens or around Russell Square. At the same time, it's hard to deny that the location is good; you're only a few short blocks from Victoria Coach Station (the city's major bus terminal, from which tours depart for outlying areas of England), a three-minute walk from Victoria Rail Station.

Probably your best bet here for finding rooms is at the big (109 beds) **Easton Hotel,** 36 Belgrave Rd. (phone 834-5938), which consists of three tan-and-white town houses joined together as one hotel, and where the charge is £10 ($14), bed-and-breakfast per person, in double rooms, £13.50 in singles.

Dozens of other quite similar hotels line Belgrave Road, including the homey **Corona Hotel** at 87 Belgrave Rd. (phone 828-9279), £14 ($19.60) per person for bed-and-breakfast, in a twin room with hot and cold running water, well managed by Mr. and Mrs. Chandock and family, who also offer several family rooms, such as one with four beds, at £10 ($14) per person; and **Central House Hotel,** 37 Belgrave Rd. (corner of Gloucester Street), phone 828-0644, owned by the helpful Mr. Jani, who charges £10.50 ($14.70) per person in twin-bedded rooms. But those of our readers who arrive in London in winter will particularly like the **Victoria Private Hotel,** 23 Belgrave Rd. (phone 834-7965), which is one of the several budget establishments around here to have central heating! The charge is £12.50 per person, bed-and-breakfast; manager is Mr. S. J. Shah.

Overflow digs in the Belgrave Road area? Walk one block over to the parallel **St. George's Drive,** and look in at **St. George's Hotel** at 107 St. George's Drive, phone 834-0210 (spotless, pastel-colored doubles with central heating, a lovely little chandelier and good English breakfast for £9 per person in a number of rooms).

Additional hotels on nearby Warwick Way: the **Vegas Hotel,** 104 Warwick Way (phone 834-0082), charging £9 ($12.60) per person in a twin room with full English breakfast; the **Surtees Hotel,** 94 Warwick Way (phone 834-7163), and the **Brindle House Hotel,** just off Warwick Way at 1 Warwick Place North (phone 828-0057), £10 per person.

Ebury Street—The Big Splurge

The London area known as "Belgravia," wedged between Sloane Square and Victoria, is a plush precinct frequented by film stars, politicians, and socialites that nevertheless possesses a moderately priced street of guesthouses—Ebury Street (underground stop is Victoria)—marvelously convenient to Buckingham Palace and Victoria Station. You'll get the flavor when you walk into **Alison House Hotel,** 82 Ebury St. (phone 730-9529), and are handed a welcoming glass of sherry by proprietors Frank and Alison Haggis; they may even walk you around the corner to Chester Square to point out the homes of neighbors Julie Andrews, Christopher Plummer, Sir John Gielgud, and Stewart Granger! The charge is a high but moderate £12 to £16 ($16.80 to $22.40) per person for a twin-bedded room with a "burster" of an English breakfast. **Lewis House,** at 111 Ebury St. (phone 730-2094), charges slightly less for bed-and-breakfast, and here you're in the former residence of Noel Coward, possibly sleeping in his very bedroom. Mr. and Mrs. Lewis are warm-hearted and extremely capable guesthouse managers. They also offer a large bed-and-living-room suite, easily housing four, with private bath and w.c., for £13 per bed in 1985, including breakfast. Alternatives include **Harcourt House,** 50 Ebury St. (phone 730-2722), and **Ebury House,** 102 Ebury St. (phone 730-1350), both charging £14 ($19.60), per person per night.

Near King's Cross Station

And now, a last hotel district, where you'll find the city's largest collection of low-cost bed-and-breakfast houses, but in one of the less interesting areas of London. Its main virtue is that it's largely undiscovered by overseas tourists, and patronized—thus far—almost entirely by English visitors.

Several blocks to the north of Russell Square, on Euston Road, are two major railroad stations of London—St. Pancras and King's Cross—and in front of the King's Cross station are three more-or-less parallel and somewhat shabby streets—Birkenhead, Crestfield, and Argyle—that lead in a short walk to the far more attractive Argyle Square. It is on these three streets and square that more than 50 budget-type guesthouses can be found, in less than a two-minute walk from the King's Cross/St. Pancras tube exit. Though, once again, this area can't compare in attractiveness or location with Russell Square, Sussex Gardens or Belgrave Road, it is one of the few such sections where single persons traveling alone in summer can fairly easily find single rooms—a commodity virtually unobtainable at that time in the other establishments we've named.

Best bargain in the King's Cross area is the 34-room **Ferndale Hotel** at 21 Argyle Square (phone 837-4974), whose proprietor, Maurice Castle, not only promises the excellent rates referred to below, but also absolutely swears that the breakfast included in those rates will begin with cornflakes or juice, then go on to two eggs with bacon, tomatoes, sausages and "fried

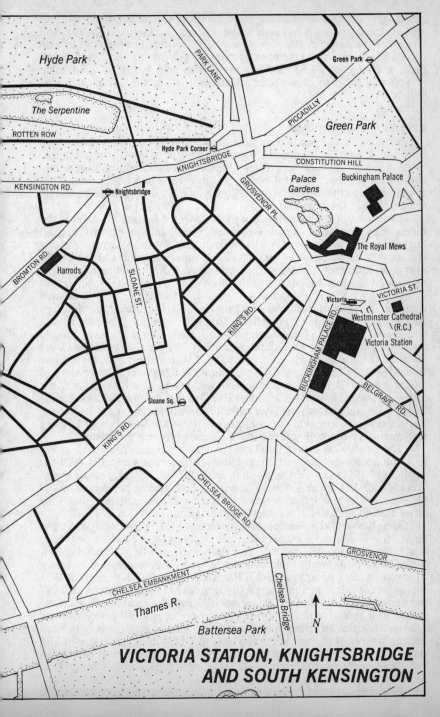

VICTORIA STATION, KNIGHTSBRIDGE AND SOUTH KENSINGTON

bread" (try it), and will include up to three cups of coffee per person, as well as tea, if you want it, toast, butter and marmalade. And showers will be free. How much in 1985? A superb £7.50 ($10.50) per person in twin or double rooms, a supplement of only £4 ($5.60) for third and fourth beds, a charge of £9.50 ($13.30) for singles with breakfast. But some of you will have to climb four and five flights in this elevator-lacking building!

Elsewhere in London

Thus far, we've focused on areas in the city where budget hotels are clustered. There are, of course, numerous budget hotels that stand alone. Since many of these are particular stars, they call for careful consideration. But remember that you must phone first to determine whether rooms are available; for at the selections that follow, you can't always count on finding other hotels in the same block.

First, one of the best bargains in London for budget travelers is the increasingly popular **Coleman Group of Hotels,** four six-story Georgian town houses with large and airy, adequately furnished rooms, and a remarkably friendly and efficient staff, all supervised and trained by the energetic Margaret Coleman. She promises V.I.P. treatment and the following 1985 rates for bearers of this book only: £9 ($12.60) for singles, £8 ($11.20) per person in doubles or twins, £7 ($9.80) per person sharing triples and quads, all inclusive of a "proper" English breakfast, with free added helpings of tea and coffee. The four stars of this mini chain: **Crossroads Hotel** at 55 Gloucester Road (phone 935-2579), near Marble Arch and Baker Street tube stations, managed by Trudi; **Gloucester Court Hotel** at 47 Gloucester Place (phone 935-8571), managed by Jeffrey; **Rena House Hotel,** 34 Craven Hill Gardens (phone 723-2438), near Marble Arch, Paddington or Baker Street tube stations, managed by Trish; and the **Coleman Lodge Hotel,** 31–33 Craven Hill Gardens (phone 723-2438), near Paddington, Queensway or Bayswater tube stations, managed by Kerry. For suggestions, compliments or complaints write directly to Margaret Coleman—like any top hotelier, she's receptive to such comments.

The Queensway Court Hotel, 36 Queensway (phone 229-5184), caters to a young crowd. Newly decorated and spotless rooms cost £14 ($19.60) single, £10 ($14) per person double, and £9 ($12.60) per person triple. Weekly rates are much lower. The nearest tube station is Queensway. If Queensway Court is full, manager Mr. Mace will accommodate you at his other establishment at 33 Cranley Gardens (same prices).

Mrs. Bedford's Guesthouse, 39 Gunterstone Rd. (phone 603-3551), has been a top selection for many, many years. It has eight rooms: one single, five twins (ask for #1, which has wall-to-wall carpets, corner windows, bidet, hot and cold water) and two family rooms with four to five beds (try to book #2, very cozy, four beds). Rates guaranteed until the end of 1985 for readers of this book only: single (a tiny one) £7 ($9.80), twin £8 ($11.20) per person, multi-bedded £6 ($8.40) per bed, including a cooked breakfast, served in a basement dining room. Kids under 12 pay half price, showers are free. Located near the West Kensington subway stop (turn right after leaving station, then turn left), and next to an idyllic mini-park, with old trees, lots of benches, a water fountain and micro-pond, with two ducks usually swimming in the middle. Managed by Mrs. Bedford, with the help of Mr. Cotter. An extremely friendly place.

Elsewhere in town, in the Earls Court area, the widely known **Hunter's**

Lodge, 38 Trebovir Rd. (phone 373-7331), whose exceptionally pleasant hostess, Mrs. Frerichs, immigrated from Rhodesia, charges only £10.50 ($14.70) for singles, £8 ($11.20) per person for twins, £6 ($8.40) per bed for multi-bedded rooms (of which there's one with seven beds for women, and one with six beds for men, both with private shower), and there is a six-bedded dormitory in the basement, with private shower and w.c., ideal for families or small groups, for £6 per person. All these prices include a cooked breakfast. Short walk from the Earls Court station.

Finally, on a site only 300 yards from where the queen lives at Buckingham Palace, the red-bricked **Red Shield House,** a Salvation Army hotel at 66 Buckingham Gate (phone 222-1164), charges £8 ($11.20) per person in rooms with hot and cold running water, £7.50 ($10.50) in rooms without, including cooked English breakfast of cereal, eggs any style, toast, marmalade, butter, and, within reason, unlimited helpings of coffee and tea. Hosts are Major and Mrs. Groom, who emphasize that tourists are perfectly welcome, just as they are in a somewhat cheaper **Red Shield House,** also in a red-brick building, at 37 Hunter Street, corner of Tavistock Place near the Russell Square tube station. At this second Salvation Army establishment, singles are £8.80 ($12.32), doubles £7.70 ($10.78) per person, triples £7 ($9.80) per person, a single family room (for two adults, two children) £6.50 ($9.10) per person. Major J. Moir imposes an 11 p.m. curfew here, a small enough price to pay for hospitality priced at these levels.

READER'S HOTEL SELECTION (BAYSWATER): Note by AF—Bayswater is an area directly north of Kensington Gardens, between Notting Hill Gate and Paddington. "We found a very friendly small bed-and-breakfast place called **Dean Court Hotel,** 57 Inverness Terrace (phone 229-9982), a few minutes walk from Oxford Street in the Bayswater area. For £5.50 per person in a dorm-like room, we had toast, corn flakes and a huge English breakfast which sustained us for most of the day. We were made extremely welcome by the Australian and New Zealand staff. We highly recommend it" (Sue Allen and Anne Walker, Greymouth, New Zealand; note from AF: The 75-bed Dean Court Hotel, in 1985, charges £9.50 ($13.30), for singles; £16 and £17 ($22.40 and $23.80) for doubles and twins; and can take up to 20 men and 20 women in multi-bedded share rooms for £5.50 ($7.70) per person, including cooked breakfast, free showers, free tea throughout the day, and use of kitchen facilities. When last visited, everyone on the premises other than the owner was from Australia or New Zealand; he alone was British. Location is a one-minute walk from Bayswater tube station, on a quiet residential street).

READERS' HOTEL SELECTIONS (KENSINGTON): Note by AF—Kensington is an area south of Hyde Park; readers' finds are as follows: **"Western House Hotel,** 8 Holland Rd., Kensington (phone 603-3099), charges £7 to £9 per person for bed-and-breakfast, and is within walking distance of the underground station, Kensington High Street. I think it's more interesting to take the bus into the center of town, however, and both #73 and #9 stop close by. The owners must spend a little more for the food they serve, because the breakfast was excellent and very appetizing. They will burn the bacon if you ask them to" (Edward Pietraszek, Chicago, Illinois; seconding recommendations from Steve and Mary Aujmuth, Niles, Illinois, who report that "the couple who run the Western House are an enjoyable pair who carry on a lively repartee while serving breakfast"). . . . "By chance, I hit upon the **Vicarage Private Hotel,** 10 Vicarage Gate, Kensington (phone 229-4030). I'm in my second month here now, and I like the place more and more. Unlike many London hotels, the Vicarage has many single rooms (approximately £12 a day). The ample breakfast will carry you through a full day of sightseeing. The location is superb— Kensington Gardens is just a block away—and the Circle, Central and District Underground stations are just five minutes away. A two-minute walk will get you to a couple of large shopping areas, where you'll find two laundromats—a Godsend for the weary traveler with a suitcase of dirty clothes" (C.J. Kennedy, San Francisco, California; enthusiastic seconding recommendations from Mrs. Ursula Duffy, Suitland, Maryland; note from AF: 1985 per-person rates are £12, $16.80, in a single; £10, $14, in a double; £8, $11.20, in a triple; £7, $9.80, in a quad room, including breakfast. The friendly hosts are Martin and Eileen Diviney.)

READER'S HOTEL SELECTION (NEAR VICTORIA STATION): "The well-run, tidy and pleasant **Hotel Simone House,** 49 Belgrave Rd. (phone 828-2474), a ten-minute walk or £1.50 taxi ride from the rear of Victoria Station, provides a lovely English breakfast in its room rates, and yet charges only £12 ($16.80) single, £19 ($26.66) double, £25 ($35) triple, with free showers down the hall. Owner is Mr. Pelly, quite friendly" (Mr. and Mrs. Steven Anderson, American Fork, Utah).

READERS' HOTEL SELECTIONS (FARTHER OUT): The rates decrease in locations of few minutes by tube beyond the ones we've discussed, as witness: "The accommodation with **Jimmy and Tove Farrelly,** 98 Park Avenue North, Willesden Green (phone 452-4085), was our best find in all of Europe: our bedroom was beautifully decorated with comfortable beds and a color TV for our personal use; the bathroom was immaculate; and we awoke to the smell of bacon and eggs and couldn't wait to go downstairs to sample our full English breakfast. All this, in 1985, for £9 ($12.60) per person single, £7 ($9.80) per person twin, including breakfast, with children under six staying free" (Cheryl and Tony Singleton, Johannesburg, South Africa; note by AF: I visited this residence in mid-1984, and found it to be both charming and of good value. Take the tube to the Willesden Green station (nine stops up from Oxford Circus), turn right into St. Paul's Avenue, and after a few hundred yards turn right after the filling station. Park Avenue begins after you have passed under the railway bridge). . . . "I discovered **Mario's Guesthouse** at 69 St. Georges Ave. (Northern Line—Tufnell Park stop; phone 607-6386), London N7, where there are ten rooms, some with three and four beds apiece. Mario charges only £9 per person, including a large and delicious breakfast, a cup of tea whenever you come in, and great conversation. This is no hotel—it is a home, and you truly feel a part of it" (Carol Boss, Far Rockaway, New York). . . . "Our find makes some of your cheaper places look expensive. The house is in an outer London suburb, Hendon, about 30 minutes from Leicester Square by tube on the Northern Line. It's Mrs. L. M. Taylor's **"Solana,"** at 18 Golders Rise, Hendon, NW4, phone 202-53-21. £14 ($19.60) acquired a warm double room with comfortable beds and adjacent toilet and bathroom. Breakfast is included. Smokers, however, are apparently not welcome, as the many signs in the house emphasize" (Dr. J. Szer, East Bentleigh, Victoria, Australia).

READER'S BIG SPLURGE SELECTIONS (VICTORIA STATION): "Ms. Rhoda Barker, proprietress of the **Woodwill House Hotel,** 107 Ebury Street (phone 730-2574), at a perfect location in elegant Belgravia, near Victoria Station, is determined to provide the best service of any hotel in the area. All her rooms are attractively furnished, with color TV; tiled bathroom with free shower and tub are down the hall; breakfasts are large and hearty; and she provides free laundry service for guests, in addition to booking theatre tickets and tours. Every night, a tray of tea and cookies awaited us upon our return in the evening. The building was the residence of the late Sarah Churchill, and autographed pictures of celebrities adorn the breakfast room. 1985 rates, including full English breakfast: £13 ($18.20) per person double" (Milton F. Allen, San Francisco, California).

Summer Hotels

During the limited period of July 1 to September 30, the famous London School of Economics (home of the influential Socialist economist, the late Harold Laski) makes its three student residence halls available to tourists of all ages, at a per-person per-day rate (including full English breakfast) of £10 ($14) in July, but only £8 ($11.20) in August and £6.50 ($9.10) in September, plus Value Added Tax of 15%. You ask for the "hall bursar" in phoning the three large establishments, which are: **Carr-Saunders Hall,** 18 Fitzroy St. (phone 580-6338), having 130 singles, 10 doubles, near the Warren Street subway station, hall bursar is presently Mr. Tibbles; **Passfield Hall** on Endsleigh Place (phone 387-7743), having 98 singles, 38 doubles, 13 triples, near Euston Square station, hall bursar is Ms. Martin; and **Rosebery Avenue Hall,** 90 Rosebery Ave. (phone 278-3251), with 163 singles and 16 doubles, near the Angel underground station, hall bursar is Ms. Zanfal. All rooms, from my own sample observation, are pleasantly furnished in modern style, and each facility has TV lounge, a cafeteria and inexpensive launderette on the premises, while Carr-Saunders Hall offers 78 "flats" as well, equipped with private bath—an amenity you don't receive in normal rooms. Considering location, comfort and rates, these are top opportunities for you, barely diminished by the fact that linen is changed, and rooms cleaned, only once in your stay, when you first "let" the room or flat.

LAST RESORT: If you can't find a room at any of the hotels we've listed (which is highly unlikely), then there are two old-standby establishments in London which you might try. Both of them are relatively large and usually have vacancies, but neither is as highly recommended as the hotels previously listed. They are, with addresses and phone numbers: the 370-room (of which 251 are singles!) **Mount Pleasant Hotel** at 53 Calthorpe Street (phone 837-9781), a longish walk from Russell Square, charging £16 ($22.40) single, £13 ($18.20) per person double, for rooms without bath, but with radio and telephone, and with full English breakfast included, all in a relatively modern building; and, much lower in category, but acceptable if you are desperately seeking a room: the 86-bed **Hotel Northumberland** at 9 Euston Road (phone 837-286), opposite King's Cross Station, charging only £10 ($14) single, £8.50 ($11.90) per person twin, £7 ($9.80) for a third bed, breakfast included, without private bath of course, but with free showers. . . . And if these final listings don't work, then apply for aid, first, to the **National Tourist Information Center** next to the main entrance of Victoria Station (they charge £2 for making such a booking); or else go to the privately owned **Hotel Bookings International, Ltd.,** either at their desks in Heathrow Airport, or by phoning 459-1212. Usually, however, no such searching is necessary: merely head for Sussex Gardens, Norfolk Square, King's Cross or Victoria in the spring and summer months, or for Russell Square in off-season.

A last observation, in which I go way out on a limb: generally speaking, I think you'll find that English hotels, in all price ranges, are not as good as those on the continent, and—except for their phenomenal, free breakfasts—fail to offer values comparable to those found in Holland, Germany, Scandinavia—even Italy and France. But the important point to remember is that the inexpensive English guesthouses share these defects to no greater an extent than do most first class English hotels.

Some readers, for instance, have complained that their guesthouse rooms had a Dickensian gloom about them, with heavy mahogany fixtures, and brown woolen drapes. Other readers have written in that their breakfast bacon was underdone, and the eggs greasy. Fact: the hotels in the elegant Mayfair section serve underdone bacon and greasy eggs.

When in London, expect these things, and revel in them. For England would not be England if the interiors of hotels were decorated in Scandinavian-type pastels. And what would the stories of Sherlock Holmes be like—if it weren't for the fog!

One thing of which you can be sure in England: that if, in dealing with hotel personnel, you comport yourself with the dignity and restraint that Englishmen expect, you'll get back an unprecedented amount of politeness, amiability and warmth that will more than make up for the ancient fixtures and decorations of most budget-priced London hotels.

HOTELS AND GUESTHOUSES SEEKING MENTION: "Our **Don Ludwig Student House,** at 372 Gray's Inn Rd., almost opposite King's Cross Station (phone 837-5318), is designed for young people up to the age of 30, and charges only £3.50 per person per night, including linen and tax, in fully carpeted dormitories. We offer, in addition, a TV lounge, washing, ironing and cooking facilities, but we do not serve breakfast" (The Warden, Don Ludwig House, International Students and Youth Centre). . . . "At the **Jill Doldrina Student House,** 285 Pentonville Rd. (phone 278-5385), the charge will be £3.50 ($4.90) per person per night, £22 ($30.80) per week, bed only, including bed linen and V.A.T. Accommodation is provided in small dormitories with a maximum of five people in a room; nearest Underground station is King's Cross" (Warden, Jill Doldrina Student House).

LONDON ROOMS FOR LENGTHY STAYS:

Apart from renting your own apartment or one-room flat ("bedsitters," the Londoners call the latter), the most pleasant and often the cheapest way to stay in London for several weeks is with a private family, whose names are often available from the **National Tourist Information Center** next to the main entrance of Victoria Station. Most of the year, they'll provide you with advice and also make the bookings for minimum stays of one week, at rents of around £45 a week, per person, breakfast included.

Or, you can find a low-cost room or flat for weekly rental by purchasing a copy of the *London Weekly Advertiser,* sold for 30p on all major newsstands in London, which contains numerous listings of "Furnished Flats to Let," mainly in the £50-a-week (per person) category. Need a roommate? Call **Share-a-Flat Ltd.,** Empire House, 175 Piccadilly (phone 493-1265), which will seek to match you up with someone of similar age and background; their rates average £55 a week outside the center, £60 in central London, always per person. For a much cheaper room or flat, consult the bulletin boards you'll find outside some London subway stations, where local residents often list their rooms—a description of one such notice area appears in our "readers' selections" section that follows.

A multi-room apartment in London, for temporary rental? Try the housing firm of **James and Jacobs,** 94 Jermyn St., St. James's, London S.W.1 (phone 930-0261), which maintains a long current list of furnished flats for rent. Minimum period of rental is three months; rents start at about £130 per week for one-bedroom flats.

READERS' SELECTIONS AND OFFERS FOR LENGTHY STAYS: "The best bargain accommodation, available all-year-round, is a private room in which you stay on a weekly basis. Even in fashionable Hempstead, NW3, it should not cost more than £40 per week. How to find them? Take the underground to the Earls Court Road stop. When you get out, look in the shop windows around the station; you will find plenty of addresses, but take only those with inner London telephone numbers to make sure you get a room in the right area. Generally speaking, you will find addresses on the boards of any London suburban sweet or grocery shop" (Ditmar Grünewald, Mainz, Germany; note by AF: the largest and best known of the bulletin boards offering rooms is a vast one at 214 Earls Court Road, near the Earls Court Road subway station, entree to the area sometimes known as 'London's bedroom,' in a tiny arcade leading to a stationery store; it also carries ads of items for sale, rides to be shared, jobs to be had at £2 an hour). . . . **"London Tourist Holiday Flatlets** are perfect for readers who plan to stay in London for several weeks. They are at 117 Sydney Street, London S.W.3, and are operated by a Mr. Wiggins and Mr. Kauntze, who charge from £45 a week for a nicely furnished single with full kitchen; doubles are also available for £50. Phone 589-1103" (Robert Johnson, Sacramento, California). . . . "For £90 ($126) per week, or less than $10 per person per day, we rented a fully furnished, bright, clean, carpeted apartment that included not only a sparkling kitchen and bathroom, but a big color TV and ironing board *cum* iron. The two charming and cooperative ladies who manage the **Crawford Holiday Flats,** 33 Crawford St. (phone 402-6165), near the Baker Street underground, within easy walking distance of Oxford Street, booked us in the £90 studio flat, but placed on us on arrival in a £130 one-bedroom flat for four weeks at the lower rate because the studios were being redone" (Alan Gilbert, Glendale, California).

3. Starvation Budget Lodgings

Now for the dorms, which we'll review in very quick fashion: **Gayfere Hostel,** 8 Gayfere St., S.W.1 (phone 222-6894), provides dormitory accommodations for young travelers (both sexes), charges £3.75 ($5.25) per night, £22 ($30.80) per week in high season, including tax and linen, does not provide breakfast, but offers free kitchen facilities in the basement. Total 29 beds on three floors. It is well located on a quiet Georgian street behind Westminster Abbey (and therefore enforces a strict 11:45 p.m. curfew). Take the underground to Westminster, turn right, walk toward Millbank, and again turn right in Great Peter Street to Gayfere, passing an enormous two-piece Henry Moore sculpture named "Knife Edge" at Abingdon Street Garden.

And then there are five official youth hostels in London, with over 900 beds, of which the most modern structure is the **King George VI Memorial Youth Hostel,** Holland Walk (phone 937-0748), a tree-shaded complex of buildings in historic Holland Park. To find it, take the subway to Holland Park station. Turn at the first left, then right, and walk through the cast-iron gate at the white wall into Holland Park. Cross the park; you'll find the hostel at the other end of the park. Perhaps a bit easier to reach is **Earls Court Youth Hostel,** 38 Bolton Gardens (phone 373-7083), near Earls Court tube station, with 110 beds; while farther out are the **Carter Lane Youth Hostel,** between St. Paul and Blackfriars tube stations (phone 236-4965), with 300 beds; the **Hampstead Youth Hostel,** 4 Wellgarth Rd., in northern London, near the Golders Green tube stop (phone 458-9054), 220 beds; and, finally, **Highgate Youth Hostel,** 84 Highgate West Hill (phone 340-1831), with 60 beds, and nearest tube station is Archway. All such hostels are open only to members of the Youth Hostel Association (which sells its Hostel Card on the premises for £8.25) and charge £4.50 per night if you are over 20; £3.50 if you are a "Junior," that is age 16 to 20; and £2.75 if you are even younger than that, for dormitory-style accommodations (usually five to 14 cots per dorm), although there are a few family-type rooms available. Curfew: at 11:30 p.m.

READERS-ON-THE-STARVATION-BUDGET: "A clean and proper place to stay, yet for only £5.50 ($7.70) a night per person, is **O'Callaghan's Nightly Tourist Accommodation** at

205 Earls Court Rd. (phone 370-3000 or 373-9153), across from the tube station" (Linda Rorke, Montreal, Quebec; note from AF: Total 24 beds on three floors, no breakfast served, but free hot water all the time to make tea or coffee—kettle is provided in each room. Two showers, one bathroom, three w.c.'s. To find it: leave Earls Court tube station, cross the street, walk up 50 yards to the right, and you are facing the door. . . . In addition to several approving letters from readers, a note from Mr. O'Callaghan himself confirms the rate, and states that "young people are very welcome." Additional plusses include free showers, a lounge with TV set, and no curfew). . . . "Anyone under the age of 28 is advised to try the **Saney Guruji Hostel,** 18a Holland Villas Rd., W.14 (phone 603-3704), which offers dormitory-style accommodations to both men and women for exactly £4 ($5.60) per night, not including breakfast. Cooking facilities are available, and you can get a key giving you a chance to come in as late as you wish. Terrific, friendly atmosphere" (Stuart Lewis, Albany, New York; note by AF: Saney Guruji is operated by "International Co-operative and Socialist Youth Hostels, Ltd.," and nearest tube station is Holland Park, on the Central Line). . . . "Scouters, Scouts and Cubs can now find accommodations at **B. P. (Baden-Powell) House,** Queen's Gate, South Kensington, S.W.7 (phone 584-7030), and I think that it may be possible for women to stay there, too. There is a good cafeteria as well, and this is quite certainly open to qualified persons and their guests, of either sex. I stayed there for about a week, and found it quite a good place—though the noise of traffic in Cromwell Road, below my bedroom windows, was rather troublesome. The rate per person per night, including breakfast and V.A.T., is £8.50 ($11.90) in a multi-bedded room, £13.50 ($18.90) in a twin, and £16 ($22.40) in a single room (with ladies and married couples undoubtedly being placed in the single and twins). B. P. House is quite near the Gloucester Road underground station" (C. P. Wright, Ottawa, Ontario, Canada; note by AF: Rates given are for non-scouts. Members of the scouting movement—including female scouts, who are also welcome—pay about 20% less).

READERS-ON-THE-SUB-STARVATION-BUDGET: "The **Office of the Youth Hostels Association,** which will accommodate you throughout England and Wales for about $5.50 a night average, is at 14 Southampton St., London W.C.2, phone 836-8541" (Rosemary Jordan, Oxford, England). . . . "I suppose that most of your readers go to more expensive places than our tented hostel, but we must have had thousands of Americans enjoying the atmosphere of our place last summer. **Tent City,** Old Oak Common Lane (phone 743-5708); underground train to East Acton, open from June through late August, consists of 10 large tents (men's, women's and mixed) in which there are 320 beds; you use your own sleeping bag or hire our bedding; come at any time to leave your baggage and sleep; pay only £2.50 ($3.50) a night; and reach the hotel from Heathrow Airport by taking direct bus 105 to East Acton" (Barnaby Martin, Tent City Limited, 11 Ellesmere Rd., Twickenham, Middlesex).

With a room acquired, we turn now to the question of meals—a tricky subject, but not from the standpoint of cost:

4. Low-Cost Meals

THE CHAINS: London is unlike the other capitals of Europe in its attitude towards food. Outside of England, meals are occasions, and cooking is an art. The restaurants in Rome and Vienna and Paris are restaurants—and not mass-production, plate-lunch joints. In London, on the other hand, chain restaurants abound, standardized places, serving fast meals, cheap.

With great despair, this book recommends that you eat in these inexpensive chains while in London, and save your money for the better meals available in France and Italy. Cooking is a lost art in Great Britain. Your meat-pie-with-cabbage will turn out to be just as tasteless for $3 in a chain restaurant as it will for $9 in a posh London hotel. At least for one meal a day, stop in at any of the major British chains—the **Pollys,** the **Wimpys, Strikes, Oodles**—they're scattered all across the city, and you needn't spend more than $3.50 at any of them.

The "Pots"

A string of trendy restaurants, with the word "Pot" in their titles (and don't go getting any ideas), offer budget dining with a flair, at only a few pence more than you'd pay at the chains. Best located of the Pots is **The Stockpot,** 6 Basil St., a block from the famous Harrod's department store (a sightseeing attraction in its own right). It serves a thick minestrone for 40p (56¢), five or six thoughtful main courses (like ham and chicken fricassee or stuffed pimiento) for £1.20 ($1.68), omelettes for less, desserts for 50p, milk for 30—and warns that "there is a minimum charge of £1." Another Stockpot at 98 King's Road, also known as the **Chelsea Kitchen,** caters to a trendy young crowd and the owners of the boutiques lining King's Road. Same approximate rates: about £2 ($2.80) for main courses, 40p for coffee, 60p for "sweets" (desserts). Still a third slew of Pots, under totally independent, unrelated ownership, can be found along and off Earls Court Road; they include the **New Hotpot** (at 314 Earls Court Road, serving omelettes for 90p, roast chicken for £1.35). Despite the competing titles, these Pots also promote a common theme: traditional English and some European dishes in a fresh, country-like atmosphere, without tablecloths or linen napkins, but with young continental girls as waitresses and prices that permit you, with care, to stay below £3 ($4.20) for an attractive, tasty meal. This is economy with dignity, and we bless the unknown founder of the Pots.

The Spaghetti Houses

The Pots, however, enjoy hot competition from the only slightly more expensive Spaghetti Houses, of which there are presently 14 in London. Italian residents flock here in numbers because the pasta dishes, with their thick sauces, are as good as in Italy, and radically different from the sorts normally found in the U.S. and England. At a typical **Spaghetti House,** 77 Knightsbridge, two short blocks from the Hyde Park Hotel, four blocks from Harrod's department store, various large pasta plates with superb sauces, enough for a meal, are £2.30 ($3.22), and a side cup of tea is 35p, while large and attractive "salad platters" (with meat) start at £2.50. But these prices are available only downstairs, in the self-service *tavola calda* portion of the Spaghetti House. A second Spaghetti House, the **Tavola Calda,** is found at 4 Victoria House near the end of Southampton Row, just off Vernon Place, two blocks from the Holborn underground station; and here the cheap area is on the ground floor. Closed Sundays. Slightly more expensive is the original **Spaghetti House** at 15 Goodge St., off Tottenham Court Road, just behind the University of London, where the decor is so fanciful—fake Italian farmhouse style, in green and red—that you might even schedule a stop for a special night out. Here, you can spend as little as $6.50 for an excellent meal, in contrast to other Spaghetti Houses where careful à la carte ordering can keep the check to $5 and less.

Four final Spaghetti House selections include **"Spaghetti-Land"** at 10 Blenheim St. near the Bond Street Tube Station (freshly made minestrone for £1, various pasta dishes for £1.60 to £2.40); the nearby (50 yards) **Luigi e Paolo,** at 21 Woodstock St. (spaghetti Bolognese £1.65), with two outside tables; **"Spaghetti House,"** at 30 St. Martin's Lane near Leicester Square (spaghetti Napoli or Bolognese for only £1.60, stuffed peppers for £1.90); and **Buttery Grill,** at 32 Rathbone Place, off Oxford Street near Tottenham Court Road (spaghetti, rigatoni and risotto dishes for £1.65, $2.31).

THE NON-CHAIN BUDGET RESTAURANTS: Another type of budget eatery in London is more difficult to describe. They have no distinguishing characteristics, except for the fact that they are individually owned, extremely plain and simple, tiny in size, serve English food only, and are refreshingly cheap. But the only way to find these budget havens is to have their addresses, which are now set forth. And to keep everything clearly separated, by location, we'll number the paragraphs that lead off the listings in particular areas of London:

(1) Near **Piccadilly,** the prime examples of these eateries are found on **Denman Street,** just off the bottom of Shaftesbury Avenue, a few feet from Piccadilly Circus. Thus, all the best-known English specialties are available at moderate cost at the **New Piccadilly Restaurant,** 8 Denman St., which charges £1.90 ($2.66) and under for most meat plates with two vegetables, and is open seven days a week. The straightforward **"Café-Restaurant"** (that's its name), nearby at 2 Denman Street, offers similar rates (£2 for most meat plates with vegetables, 75p for desserts, 50p for soup) and is an always reliable, eat-it-on-the-run, Piccadilly Circus dinery.

Even lower in price, better furnished, and with a larger variety of dishes, the **Three Lanterns Restaurant,** 5 Panton St., is just off Piccadilly Circus, and has over 100 seats on two levels. It serves daily except Sundays at least five £1.85 ($2.59) dishes, such as, for example, chicken casserole or curried beef with rice, plus three kinds of vegetables. And if these filling plates should still leave you hungry (which is doubtful), you can enlarge your meal to a three-course lunch or dinner by adding soup of the day (40p) and a sponge pudding with custard (55p). Tea is 25p, coffee 35p, ice cream 40p, a roll with butter 25p. It's the best value you can get, near one of the most famous squares in the world.

(2) Opposite the exit of the **Earls Court Road** subway station, at 183 Earls Court Rd., is an **ABC Self-Service Cafeteria** with lunchtime prices (50p for soup, £1.40 for steak pie and vegetables, 25p for tea, 50p and up for desserts) that can't top $3 for two courses. Try also the several eateries on Hogarth Road, almost directly opposite the Earls Court Road tube station, and on Kenway Road, a block away.

(3) Near **Victoria Station,** the **Green Cafe** at 16 Eccleston St., managed by a hard-working Italian family, is one of the best value-for-your-money choices in this area. At seven small tables in a corridor-like room, it serves a daily "plat du jour" (actually, a two-course meal, like roast lamb preceded by soup) for £2.30 ($3.22), a club sandwich with a cup of tea for £1.35 ($1.89), spaghetti bolognese for £1.

Across the street from Victoria Coach Station, corner of Buckingham Palace Road and Elizabeth Street, **The Well,** at 2 Eccleston Place, proclaims that "all the food served is prepared on the premises on the same day." Luncheon—the quick type—is usually about £2.50 ($3.50) in price— an example being steak-and-kidney pie with a vegetable salad. But it's at supper time that the Well moves into high gear. That's when you find a delicious onion soup for 75p, brisket of beef for £2.40 ($3.36), various "sweets" (desserts), of the sort rarely found in a budget location, for 80p, a "nice cup of tea" for 25p. Ordering the beef, you'll feast for about $6, tip included, but you can easily limit the check to $5. This extremely friendly place is owned by a nonprofit religious organization that donates all tips you may leave to charity. Closed Saturday and Sunday.

Roughly in the same area, about 300 yards from the queen's dining room at Buckingham Palace, but this time at 66 Buckingham Gate, across from the impressive St. James Hotel, the 50-seat **Red Shield Restaurant,** managed by the Salvation Army and open Monday to Friday for lunch only from 11:30 a.m. to 1:30 p.m., offers remarkable value: soup 30p, roast beef with Yorkshire pudding, potatoes and two vegs, £1.90 ($2.66), desserts 30p, eggs and chips 90p ($1.26), tea 14p, coffee 18p, in 1985. Go to the counter, order and pay for your meal, then sit down and wait to be served. It's the best budget eatery in the center of London, and perfectly appropriate for use by tourists.

(4) Off **The Strand** at 49 Bedford St., a side street of that famous thoroughfare, the **Strand Café** serves up tomato soup for only 40p, roast lamb with vegetables for £1.45, fish 'n chips for £1, steak pie with two vegetables for 85p, a big cheese-and-ham omelette with chips for £1.10, coffee for 30, milk for 20. Plain and strictly matter-of-fact in setting and mood, it still provides the best inexpensive food in this relatively expensive part of London.

(5) Near the **Bond Street** tube station, the **Widow Applebaum** at 46 South Molton St. is recommended here only for its take-away sandwiches, which cost considerably more if you eat them on the premises. But you may decide to sit outside at one of the white tables and watch this busy thoroughfare as you drink a cup of tea (60p) or coffee (70p). This is where celebrity guests of nearby Claridges Hotel buy their pastrami sandwiches for £1.65, salt beef (akin to our "corned beef") sandwiches for £1.80, various salads for 80p apiece.

(6) In the **Russell Square** area, two other proprietary restaurants of this sort are clustered on Southampton Row, just below the Square. The better one is the somewhat pricey **Trattoria Verdi,** at 110 Southampton Row, which can be visited on a budget basis only for lunch (when soup is 90p, main courses £3.30), and somewhat less expensive is the nearby **Green Parrot,** at 146 Southampton Row, where a set, three-course lunch (soup, meat with two vegetables, a sweet and coffee) is £2.80, exactly.

A small **Red Shield Restaurant** only 150 yards from the Russell Square tube stop, at 37 Hunter Street corner of Tavistock Place, operated by the Salvation Army, opens on Sundays only, from 12:30 to 1:30 p.m., to serve a three-course lunch for £2.20 ($3.08). It is perfectly recommendable.

(7) An inexpensive eatery in the posh **Knightsbridge area,** immensely popular, is the **Upstairs Restaurant** at 8 Basil Street, a country-style dining room with wood tables, whitewashed walls and leaded windows. You can help yourself to all you can eat from the "Salad Bowl"—an array of meat salads, rice molds, egg dishes, cold casseroles, etc.—for £3.75 ($5.25), including a sweet from the trolley. Or you can make your selections (once again, all you want) from the "Copper Hot Plate," where the likes of creamed chicken, beef Stroganoff, vegetables, and potatoes are the featured fare. Including dessert, the latter meal costs £4.50 ($6.30). Open for lunch only, noon to 3, closed Sundays.

(8) For health food fans, a highly recommended stop is **The Nuthouse,** 26 Kingly St., off Regent Street, near **Oxford Circus** and behind the Liberty Store. Here, there's an interesting choice of £1.75 ($2.45) dishes, such as ratatouille, lasagne with cheese, mixed vegetable casserole; and a wide choice of salads—minced vegetables, all kinds of beans, wheat, lentils, carrots and the like—costing 95p (small bowl) and £1.60 (very large bowl).

Coffee is 35p, cakes and pies 55p, and one can also buy homemade bread, sugar-free jam, fruit and fresh vegetables, nuts and many other health food items. Open Monday to Friday 10:30 a.m. to 7 p.m., Saturday to 5 p.m.

READERS' RESTAURANT SELECTIONS (NEAR SIGHTSEEING ATTRACTIONS): "It is often difficult to find a restaurant for a snack on a Sunday in the vicinity of Trafalgar Square, and I would like to recommend the very quiet and restful **Buffet inside the National Gallery,** where one can sit as long as one likes over a 20p cup of tea and a sandwich" (Ms. R. E. Seaton, Bath, Somerset, England; note from AF: The restaurant, completely rebuilt in 1980, seats 180 people and is open from 10 a.m. to 5 p.m. Monday to Saturday, 2 to 5 p.m. Sunday, serving coffee for 28p, chocolate 25p, salads 65p and a choice of hot dishes from £1.60 to £2. . . . "I hope you will allow a mere Englishman to make a recommendation in regard to his own country. During a recent rare visit to London, I was struck by your lack of budget food opportunities in the neighborhood of the Tower of London. By a happy chance my wife and I came across the small budget establishment of Mr. Novani, at the **Minories Restaurant,** under the railway arches about 150 yards north of the Tower. There, at 105A The Minories, we had a splendid three-course meal with coffee for £2.45 ($3.43) a head, of British home cooking of a standard rarely met with these days, in an atmosphere much more redolent of homely Amsterdam than of overdeveloped London. Although we were obviously not big spenders, we were welcomed by the owner and made to feel we had known him for years" (M. G. Habberley, Powys, Wales). . . . "On a sunny day at the Tower of London, plan to have lunch on the riverfront directly in front of the complex. Walk out to the wharf, turn left and there's a snack bar, built into the base of Tower Bridge, selling hamburgers, hot dogs, fries, soft drinks and beer. It's pleasantly set among trees with a plastic covered arbor overhead" (Barbara P. Willson, Jamestown, North Carolina). . . . "Next door to the Westminster tube station, **Grandma Lee's** is a cafeteria serving delicious sandwiches on thick 'Canadian' bread, with side orders of cole slaw and potato chips. Lettuce, tomato, cucumbers and cheese were on my turkey sandwich, making it a meal, for £2, $2.80. Tea is 45p. The 'special' sandwich, with several kinds of meats and cheeses, goes for £2.20, $3.08. . . . This is handy for before or after a visit to Parliament or Westminster Abbey" (Kay Ellen Thurman, St. Louis, Missouri; note from AF: open seven days a week, Grandma Lee's upper floor looks directly out onto Big Ben—a view extraordinaire).

A READER'S HIGH TEA SELECTION: "Everyone visiting London should have a proper **English tea** some afternoon, and our favorite place for tea is **Harrod's department store** (underground stop: Knightsbridge). Every day, from 3:30 p.m. to store-closing, there is a fantastic tea served in the fourth floor **restaurant.** The waiters bring you tea and milk, and you help yourself from a huge table covered with every conceivable kind of cakes, pastries, lovely scones with Devonshire cream as thick as butter, and strawberry jam. You can eat all you like, and you might not want dinner that night. All this for £4 ($5.60)" (David Finkel, Lewisburg, Pennsylvania).

Indian Restaurants

For a budget-minded traveler, the best change of pace from English cooking is provided by the many inexpensive Indian restaurants that have sprouted all over London, many of them offering hot curry dishes for as little as £1.70 (and that one plate is all you'll be able to finish); add rice, a beverage and tip, and you'll generally spend $4.50-or-so for a memorable, spicy meal that brings tears of satisfaction (both physically and symbolically). To spend even less, order a half portion of curry, or one plate of curry and two plates of rice for two persons—which is still more than you'll be able to finish.

Here's where you'll find them:

In the **Sussex Gardens** area, a really excellent Indian restaurant is the

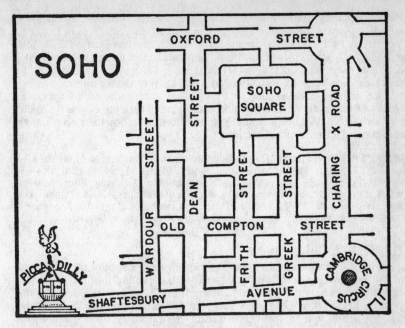

SOHO

Golden Shalimar at 6 Spring St., just off Sussex Gardens near Paddington Station. Open daily including Sundays from noon to midnight, with normal low prices for Indian food (except for your opening course of soup, for which they inexplicably charge 90p—it's a top of 80p elsewhere), courteous Indian waiters, and the right to order half-portions of some menu items, for half the menu price—an opportunity that should be seized whenever you eat in an Indian restaurant. Nearby, and with slightly lower prices, is the **Taqdir Indian Restaurant,** at 8 Norfolk Place (near Praed Street), to which you might want to alternate visits; Taqdir is open seven days a week, and serves a complete, three-course Indian lunch (soup, meat or chicken curry, dessert) for only £3.10 on weekdays.

In the **Russell Square area,** an exceptionally cheap Indian restaurant is the **New Madras,** at 51 Marchmont St., where a spicy, thick mulligatawny soup (which you ought always to choose for openers in an Indian restaurant) is 80p ($1.12), a full order of meat curry is £2 ($2.80), a vast side plate of rice is 60p (84¢), and mango chutney is 40p. It might be wise, again, to order half portions of the beef or lamb curry at the New Madras, £1.25 ($1.75), since you can always order more if they fail to fill you (unlikely). On **Tavistock Place** in the Russell Square area, the slightly more attractive **New Shahbhag Restaurant,** at 52 Tavistock Place, charges a bit less (£2.10 for the beef curry), and actually encourages the ordering of half portions (£1.05).

Around **Earls Court Road,** the curry king is **Sri Hatta,** at 10 Hogarth Rd., the street opposite the Earls Court Road subway station (£2 for most beef curries, £1.80 for chicken curry, 80p for mulligatawny soup).

And finally, near Piccadilly Circus, the moderately priced curry restaurants cluster on **Rupert Street** (from the Eros Statue, walk down Coventry Street for two short blocks and turn left on Rupert), where the

West End Curry Centre and the **New Curry Centre** both offer inexpensive and filling plates, though at higher plate prices than elsewhere in London. Vegetable curry is £1.60, meat curry £2.20, chicken curry £2.15, and mulligatawny soup costs 80p at both the New Curry Centre (18 Rupert St.) and the West End Curry (34 Rupert St.). Order tea, not coffee, to conclude, and keep Rupert Street in mind for pre-theatre dinner.

Of course, don't assume that all Indian restaurants are inexpensive; some of the slicker ones charge substantially more than the £2 you'll want to pay for curry. And don't hesitate to ask Londoners for their own Indian recommendations in other sections.

READER'S INDIAN RESTAURANTS: "Indian food enthusiasts should head for the area around Paddington Station, where two good (and cheap) Indian restaurants are located. Probably the best is the **Taqdir Restaurant** at 8 Norfolk Place, between Praed Street and Sussex Gardens, where an order of beef curry, rice, and a pitcher of water costs only £2 ($2.80), and vegetable curry can be had for £1.80. The other is the **Golden Shalimar,** 6 Spring St." (S. C. Gruber, Huntington Beach, California).

The Fish 'n Chips spots

Fast disappearing from London's food scene, because of the rising cost of fish and competition from new fast-food outlets, the fish 'n chips stores can still provide you with a quality meal for $3.50, tea included. At the popular **Friar Tuck,** 113 Lupus St. about 300 yards from the Pimlico tube station, people queue up outside during "frying times," which are weekdays from 11:30 a.m. to 2:30 p.m. and from 5 to 10 p.m., Saturdays from 11:30 a.m. to 2:30 p.m. only, and what results are (take away prices): cod for 80p, plaice for £1, haddock for £1.10, chips for 30p, fish cakes (delicious) for 20p, soup for 24p, steak and kidney pie for 75p. If you choose to sit down and eat, these prices will increase. Tuck is my own personal favorite for fish 'n chips in London. Alternatively, try the larger and slightly costlier **Kings Cross Fish Bar** at 290 Pentonville Rd., a short walk from the Kings Cross underground station, charging 30p for chips, £1 for haddock, £1.85 for scampi and chips, only 35p for a portion of cod roe. Near Earls Court tube station, at 9 Kenway Rd., the small **Hi-Tide Fish 'n' Chips Restaurant** charges £1.40 for cod and chips, £2.20 for scampi and chips, 80p for a steak and kidney pie, £1.25 for a quarter southern fried chicken, and 15p for bread and butter. And remember: fish 'n chips shops are fading fast, enjoy them while you may!

READERS' FISH-AND-CHIPS: "In London's Cartwright Gardens area, the **North Sea Fish Bar and Restaurant** is excellent for fish. Cod and chips, £1.60, and cod only is 90p. The food is steaming hot and good. That's at 8 Leigh St., intersection of Leigh and Sandwich Streets, just off Marchmont" (Marie J. Moreau, Lakeside, California). . . . "Since many people in England earn £60 ($84) or less during a week, you know there must be economical places to eat. Just a short block or so from Victoria Station, at 81 Wilton Rd., one should try the **Seafresh Restaurant.** Haddock and chips, £2" (John L. Gatfield, Napa, California; enthusiastic seconding recommendation from Don and Shirley Ward of Unionville, Ontario, Canada, who hail "the tastiest fish eaten in all our travels through Britain").

SOHO—FOR HIGHER-PRICED EATING: At some point, now, you'll want to vary English fare with still other instances of foreign cooking, and for that, the area to visit is fabulous **Soho**—a jumble of foreign restaurants,

dives and bars, resembling a cross between New York's Greenwich Village and San Francisco's Fisherman's Wharf. Soho is located just north of the theatre section, within an easy walk from Piccadilly. Although its prices are somewhat higher than those we've been considering, it's still hard to spend more than $6.50 here, and quite easy to spend much less.

The main thoroughfare of Soho is Frith Street, on which you'll find a score of international restaurants. I like, in particular: **The Asia Indian,** 44 Frith St. (chicken curry with rice and chutney for about $3.50); and the **Osteria Larinna,** 48 Frith St., £3.50 ($4.90) for an excellent, three-course Italian dinner (an especially good value), the same for lunch, plus 25p for bread and butter, and 10% for service.

The most popular (because it's popularly priced) of the Chinese restaurants in Soho is **Wong Kei,** at 41 Wardour Street, where the quality of the food is first class, the service quick, and you can eat well for about $7, including service, Jasmine tea, and all kinds of soya sauces placed on the tables for free helpings. Sweet-and-sour soup at 70p (98¢) and roast duck with numerous accompaniments (an atypically high £3.75, $5.25), are two recently sampled (1984) dishes among the 131 items listed on the menu card. And whereas some Soho restaurants close on Sundays, Wong Kei is open seven days a week.

READER'S BIG SPLURGE SELECTION: "Just around the corner from the many bed-and-breakfast selections on Ebury Street, the restaurant known as **The Tent,** 15 Eccleston St., serves a fixed-price, three-course meal, including wine, tax and service, for exactly £10 ($14). It includes a wide assortment of 'starters' (artichoke vinaigrette, shrimps and celery salad), many high quality entrees (always including several well-cooked vegetables), a phenomenal assortment of desserts from a trolley wheeled to your table. A real find!" (Jackie, Lloyd and Kristen Barnes, Sunnyvale, California).

PUB LUNCHES: One other mealtime subject requires special attention, because it involves the most popular lunchtime restaurant of the average Englishman—the pubs. Nearly every pub in London serves either hot or cold food at lunchtime, some of them elaborately, others by merely placing a serving bowl, containing a single food item—hot macaroni and cheese, for instance—onto the bar.

The food at pubs is surprisingly tasty and consists of the best British specialties—such items as "Scotch eggs" (a hard-boiled egg surrounded by ham and veal, and enclosed in a dough crust), a veal pie (a cutaway chunk of bread, with a hard-boiled egg and veal inside it), or meat "salad" (roast beef with a touch of greens; tomatoes and cole slaw), and all accompanied by a pint of beer (mild or bitter or "half-n-half"). None of these items should run to more than £1.50 at a pub, and an entire pub lunch shouldn't exceed £3. If you'll eat standing up (the sit-down meals in a pub are always more expensive), and are prepared to gain your acceptance in the pub by being quiet and unobtrusive, you'll partake of a wonderful English experience, and you'll have some of the best meals available in London. Where are the pubs? They're everywhere—and they carry quaint names like **"The Lamb & Flag,"** or **"The King's Head,"** or **"The Museum Tavern,"** the latter being opposite the British Museum and one of the best in town (offering six different draft ales at a pound a pint; closed Sundays). Some pubs tip you off to the existence of their hot plates by displaying cryptic references to "hot pork and platter dishes," as does **The Salisbury Buffet,** a pub on St. Martin's Lane, corner of St. Martin's Court, in the heart of the theatre district. A pub in the Sussex Gardens area? Try the **Fountains Abbey,** at 109 Praed St., a block from Paddington Station, where a homemade steak-and-kidney-pie with mashed potatoes costs £2 ($2.80). A luncheon-serving pub on Earls Court Road? Try the **Bolton Pub,** 326 Earls Court Rd. (corner of Old Brompton Road). More pubs? On the Strand, next door to #408, is the **Nell Gwynne Tavern,** a pub with cold luncheon counter. Behind Victoria Station, near our hotel choices on Belgrave Road, is **St. George's Tavern,** 14 Belgrave Rd. (corner of Hugh Street), where homemade steak-and-kidney pie is £1, a Scotch egg costs 80p ($1.12) and portions of potato salad, cole slaw or baked beans also 80p.

A typical pub meal? Hope usually has a Scotch egg, potato salad, and tomato juice; I have a slice of meat pie with mustard, and a glass of lager. Total cost for both of us: £3.50, or $4.90.

READERS' PUB COMMENTS: "A note on pubbing: most English pubs are divided into first and second class. The first section, with appropriate clientele and higher prices, is called 'Saloon Bar' or 'Lounge Bar'; the second-class section, also with appropriate clientele and lower prices, is called 'Public Bar' or just plain 'Bar.' The cheapest beer, and I think the best, is 'ordinary bitter.' The pub is a superb institution, steeped in tradition as a congenial neighborhood retreat. Go to one, talk to the customers, converse with the barkeep—this is the way to see and know the British. Warning: all pubs close at 11 p.m. One pub with an attractive gimmick is **The Sherlock Holmes,** at 10 Northumberland Ave., on the left-hand side, and one block toward the Thames from Trafalgar Square; it has a Holmes tableau and much memorabilia. Another pub that the English tourists (that is, the country people who come to visit the big city) all go to see is **The Prospect of Whitby,** in the dock section, alongside the Thames; it displays a colorful nautical exhibit. That's a half hour from the West End, however; take the Underground to Whitechapel, and change there for Wapping. Or you might try asking any Englishman where a good pub can be found; he'll be most happy to tell you" (John H. M. Austin, New Haven, Connecticut; note from AF: The Sherlock Holmes was mentioned in *The Hound of the Baskervilles,* and the upstairs restaurant is reconstructed to resemble Holmes's study in Baker Street. The Prospect of Whitby, offering live entertainment most nights, is London's oldest riverside pub, dating from 1540. Two other pubs worth a visit are the **Edgar Wallace,** 40 Essex Street, with its exhibits on the life and work of the famous detective author, donated by his family, and the **Gilbert and Sullivan,** 23 Wellington St., the last galleried coaching inn, with the famous Act of Parliament Clock in the downstairs bar. It was known to Charles Dickens, who mentions it in *Little Dorrit*).

WHEN IN DOUBT: Order steak-and-kidney pie in London, which invariably comes with two vegetables, rarely costs more than £1.80, often costs less. It's a tasty and inexpensive dish, even in the higher-priced restaurants.

5. The Top Sights

We turn now to the real reasons for your trip to London. To see everything of interest in this vast, sprawling capital would take a decade. To make even a more-or-less thorough tour of the more important buildings and museums will take two weeks. For readers with less time available, there is a basic minimum of four indispensable sights that must be seen.

THE TOWER OF LONDON: For this, the most profound experience of your London stay, schedule an entire weekday afternoon—and never, never go on Sunday, when it's badly crowded. Rather, immediately after a weekday lunch, enter the London Underground and take a train of the Inner Circle or District lines to the Tower Hill Station, which is a two-minute walk from the fabled **Tower of London,** on the banks of the Thames. Admission to the grounds in summer is £3 for adults (but only £2 from October through March), £1 for children, and there's an extra 80p charge for entrance to the underground building that houses the Crown Jewels. That $5.32 will plunge you into the turbulent, bloody world of British history, which surrounds you with intense reality as you wander into the stone apartments of Sir Walter Raleigh, his place of imprisonment for 12 years; and see the room in which the Little Princes were smothered; the scaffold site of the execution of queens and nobles; and finally, the "Armories" in the important White Tower, in the very center of the tower complex, where the armor of King Henry VIII is mounted atop a white horse. In the grounds wander the famous "Beefeaters" (they've heard the gag about the gin hundreds of times) and the ravens with clipped wings, who are symbols of the tower. Don't allow yourself to be shortchanged for time, and don't—again—go on Sunday.

THE BRITISH MUSEUM: In this massive building on Great Russell Street (the nearest tube stations are Holborn and Tottenham Court Road), Britain preserves and displays its most awesome State documents and manuscripts: the original Magna Carta, the log-book of Admiral Nelson and his half-finished letter to Lady Hamilton, written just before he died; the first draft of the dream-inspired "Kubla Khan" by Samuel Coleridge; a deed to William Shakespeare; a host of other papers that will send chills up your spine. And here, too, is kept the plunder of Britain's imperial era: the famous Rosetta stone and the stunning Elgin Marbles from the front of the Parthenon. There is no admission charge, and there are, in addition, free lectures Tuesday through Saturday at 1:15 p.m., as well as gallery talks presented at 3 p.m., Monday through Saturday, by a staff that sometimes includes ex-university dons, who each day deal with a different subject: "Everyday Life in Assyrian Sculpture," "Karl Marx in England," "The Boer War." Don't miss a visit to the museum, and to start things off, ask the guards to direct you to the British Library and the Elgin Marbles. The building is open from 10 a.m. to 5 p.m., Monday through Saturday, and from 2:30 to 6 p.m. on Sundays.

MADAME TUSSAUD'S: And next, to see frighteningly lifelike wax replicas of the people whose lives are reflected in the British Museum, go to the celebrated waxworks of **Madame Tussaud** (on Marylebone Road, near the Baker Street tube station), where figures of the world's most famous personages, past and present (they have astronaut Neil Armstrong, John F. Kennedy, John McEnroe, Telly Savalas, Elvis Presley, too) are grouped into amusing and fascinating tableaux—all so real that when you stare into the face of Pablo Picasso or Winston Churchill, you'll think he's staring back and about to open his mouth! All quite eerie, not to be missed, and the admission charge is £3.40 ($4.76) for adults, £1.90 ($2.66) for children, which includes the right to visit "the Chamber of Horrors" where Jack the Ripper is the star attraction. Open daily *including* Sundays, from 10 a.m. to 6 p.m.

PARLIAMENT: Finally, Hope and I make it a point, on each of our visits to London, to attend a session of the House of Commons, in the great Palace of Westminster; because the ritual, the pageantry and the brilliant debate of this most famous of legislative bodies is an inspiring experience that reinforces one's belief in democracy.

To gain entrance without standing in line, you'll need a ticket from the American Embassy—but that's really too much of a chore to consider. Except for debates of exceptional importance, you'll rarely have to wait more than an hour for admission, and you can spend this time sitting on a cushioned ledge in the hall that leads to the visitors' galleries.

Sessions of the House of Commons begin at 2:30 p.m. from Monday to Thursday, at 9:30 a.m. on Friday, and often last late into the evening (except cn Fridays, when they usually end at 3 p.m.; August and September are usually, but not always, the months of recess). Visitors who do not possess tickets from their Embassy or from an M.P. are admitted to the galleries beginning at around 4:15 p.m., at 10 a.m. on Fridays. Keep in mind, as you watch the session, that amplifiers are ingeniously concealed in the woodwork at your shoulders. Therefore, if you lean back slightly, rather than lean forward, you'll be able to hear perfectly.

Best time for avoiding a wait in line to enter Parliament? Around 6 p.m., when the crowd thins out—the only disadvantage being that the more important opening speeches of debates are usually concluded by that time. The tube station for Parliament is Westminster; the phone number for its information office, providing last-minute information on scheduled debates, sessions and the like, is 219-4272.

Incidentally, it is usually a bit easier to attend sessions of the House of Lords, where the ritual and pageantry are decidedly more impressive than in the Commons, as is the chamber itself. Sessions of the Lords begin at 2:30 p.m. Monday to Wednesday and 3 p.m. on Thursday (the Lords take a long, long weekend) and end about 8 p.m. Visitors are admitted from the beginning of the sitting; go to the same entrance as for Commons, and then ask a policeman for further directions.

THE OTHER SIX: The Tower of London, the British Museum, Parliament, and Madame Tussaud's—those are among the ten top sights of London we think you'll want to see. The other six: Westminster Abbey; the National Gallery (and Trafalgar Square); Buckingham Palace (Changing of the Guard), the Mall and Hyde Park Corner; the Tate Gallery; the Victoria and Albert Museum, with its across-the-street neighbor, the Science Museum; and St. Paul's Cathedral. Details, and methods of touring, are now coming up:

6. Tours & Sightseeing Notes

TOURS: The most fabulous value in all European city tours is the £3.50 ($4.90), two-hour, 20-mile **"Round London Sightseeing Tour"** offered by "London Transport," the official city bus company with departures from both the south side of Piccadilly Circus (you'll see a special stand), from Marble Arch (near Speaker's Corner in Park Lane), and from Grosvenor

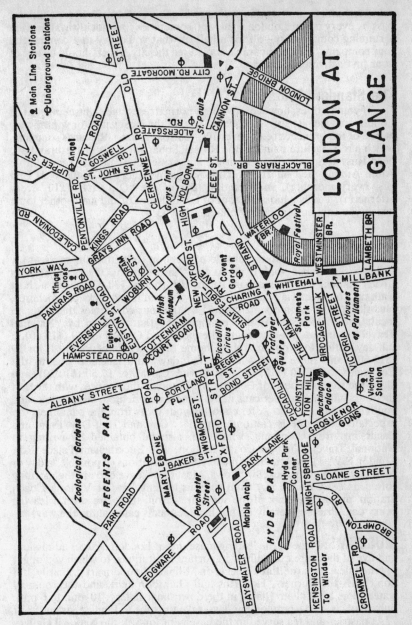

LONDON AT A GLANCE

● Main Line Stations
⊖ Underground Stations

Gardens near Victoria Station; you'll soon find the departure point for the bright red buses. They operate every day of the week throughout the year except on Christmas Day, every hour on the hour from 9 a.m. to 8 p.m. in summer, until 5 p.m. in winter, charge £3.50 for adults, £2.15 for children, pass by every major London sight, and sometimes (but not always) provide a running commentary—all for a half of what you'd pay to a commercial tour company. An incomparable way to see the city, which should be one of your first activities in London.

The Standard Tours

If you'd prefer, however, to take a normal, escorted sightseeing tour of London and vicinity, you'll probably receive the most value for your money at one of the branches of the over 100-year-old **Frames-Rickards** company, which has departure points in the Russell Square area (at 11 Herbrand St., near Russell Square Tube Station), and at Seymour Street, near Marble Arch. Among their offerings for 1985 are a morning tour of the West End (£8, every morning), an afternoon tour of the "Old City" (£10, every afternoon), a daily panoramic tour of London for £6, and many other tours which you can learn about by phoning 837-6311.

Outside of London

For the cheapest tours outside of London (operated summers—May through September—only), go to the "Information Office" at **Victoria Coach Station,** 164 Buckingham Palace Rd. (phone 730-0202), just a short walk up from Victoria Railroad Station, and you'll find racks of brochures, plus ticket sales counters maintained by the tour companies that cater to local, *British* tourists. As one example, the tours offered by **"National Travel"** include a full-day trip to Blenheim and Oxford for £9 ($12.60), a full-day outing to Woburn Abbey, home of the Duke of Bedford, for £9 ($12.60), and more than a dozen half-day tours, such as one to the Cotswolds for £7.50 ($10.50), to Warwick Castle for £7.50 ($10.50), and along the Kentish coast for £8 ($11.20). Compare those prices with those of the tours offered to Americans in the American-oriented, large hotels, and you'll get quite a shock. After choosing your tours from the pamphlets (an especially good one is National Travel's "Day and Half-Day Tours and Excursions from London," which can also be obtained by writing to National Travel, Victoria Coach Station, 164 Buckingham Palace Rd., London S.W. 1), you can then make your reservations (if possible, a day or so in advance) at the ticket windows. Most tours leave early in the morning (often as early as 8 a.m.) from the bus-loading bays at Victoria Coach Station, and at the peak of the summer season, there are several leaving every day. Prices generally do not include meals eaten along the way.

MUSEUMS: None of the leading museums of London charges admission, and five of them are exceedingly important institutions, to which you ought to schedule a visit: the **Tate Gallery,** on Millbank (modern art primarily, but don't miss the Turners, Hogarths and Gainsboroughs, and the room of watercolors by William Blake, in the downstairs gallery; 10 a.m. to 6 p.m. on weekdays, 2 to 6 p.m. on Sundays, take the tube to Pimlico, or bus 88 or 77A; pastries and tea served in the basement for $2); the **National Gallery** on Trafalgar Square (housing the classic paintings, both ancient and contemporary, including Leonardo, Titian, Rubens, Monet, Degas and Picasso; 10 a.m. to 6 p.m. on weekdays, 2 to 6 p.m. on Sundays; take the tube to Charing Cross); the **Wallace Collection,** on Manchester Square (17th- and 18th-century French and other paintings; miniatures, sculpture, ceramics, furniture and armor; 10 a.m. to 5 p.m. on weekdays, 2 to 5 p.m. Sundays; tube to Bond Street); the **Victoria and Albert Museum,** corner of Cromwell and Exhibition Roads (sculpture and applied arts, a magnificent assortment; 10 a.m. to 5:50 p.m. weekdays, except Fridays; 2:30 to 5:50 p.m. Sundays; take the underground to South Kensington, and walk several blocks north); the **Science Museum,** on Exhibition Road (across from the Victoria and Albert, 10 a.m. to 6 p.m. on weekdays and Saturdays, 2:30 to 6 p.m. on Sundays). There are, of course, many, many others; if you've time for only two, make them the National Gallery and the Tate; but go to the British Museum ahead of all.

FREE SIGHTS: "**Speaker's Corner**" at Hyde Park (near Marble Arch) is a Sunday must. Soapbox orators of every variety: Communists, violent racists, vegetarians. They undergo the finest heckling in the world, a vicious repartee, by professionals who've known the speaker for years and vice-versa. Take the underground to Marble Arch. . . . **Old Bailey,** the famous criminal courts building of London, opens its public galleries at 10:15 a.m. and 1:45 p.m. on weekdays. Leave your camera at the hotel (they're not permitted here), take the underground to St. Paul's and look for the public gallery entrance on Newgate Street. Lesser crimes are tried at the **Bow Street Magistrate's Court,** 10 a.m. to 4:30 p.m., for which the underground stop is Covent Garden. . . . Civil law courts open their public galleries from 10 a.m. to 4 p.m. on weekdays, when court is in session; tube stop is Temple. . . . Changing of the guard? It takes place daily at 11:30 a.m. in front of **Buckingham Palace;** and to reach the palace, take the underground (Circle, District or Victoria Line) to Victoria, the Piccadilly Line to Hyde Park Corner, or the Piccadilly or Victoria Lines to Green Park. . . . The **London Stock Exchange,** Old Broad Street, maintains a free visitors' gallery, 10 a.m. to 3:15 p.m., weekdays, and provides guides, plus explanatory movies. Nearest underground station is Bank. . . . Finally, you needn't be reminded to visit **Westminster Abbey,** where all but two of England's sovereigns were crowned; see Hope's description (and take the underground to Westminster). . . . And, while the crypt at **St. Paul's Cathedral** (take the underground to St. Paul's) charges 70p admission and shouldn't appear in this section, nevertheless, it's here that you'll see the famous ornate funeral carriage of the Duke of Wellington, and memorials to many other British greats, such as Nelson—all of which exercise a strange fascination, and shouldn't be missed.

SOME ORDER TO YOUR TOURING: The vastness of London makes this a large task; perhaps the best course is to choose one particular feature of London life, and thereafter concentrate on either "Royal London" (Buckingham Palace, the Mall, the Tower, the Horse Guards, Changing of the Guard), "Literary London" (Dickens's House, Carlyle's House, Sherlock Holmes's Baker Street, the Cheshire Cheese, the Old Curiosity Shop), "Legal and Financial London" (the City, Inns of Court, the Stock Exchange, the Guildhall), "Residential London" (Belgravia and Mayfair), or any of a dozen other aspects of this phenomenon of cities—you won't run out of "aspects" to see. "When a man is tired of London," said Samuel Johnson, "he is tired of life; for there is in London all that life can afford."

My wife, Hope, has tried her hand at suggesting methods of touring London that deal with attractions other than those I've described before.

We'll turn to her discussion now, and then go on to excursions outside of London.

7. Hope's London

"During World War II when bombs fell on the city, there was discovered in the rubble a little red flower that had not been seen since London's Great Fire in 1666: the people named it 'London Pride' and Noel Coward wrote a song about it. In the section that follows, we'll try to discover the sources of 'London Pride.'

A PROUD AND ROYAL TOUR: "After visiting Parliament as Arthur suggests (subway stop is Westminster), cross the street to **Westminster Abbey,** which is the nation's most impressive example of early English Gothic architecture and the most awesome burial place you are ever likely to see. Everyone who was anyone in England either has a memorial or is actually entombed here, from Chaucer to Churchill. Most English kings and queens are buried here, too, and since 1066, when William the Conqueror was crowned King of England within these walls, the Abbey has provided the setting for practically every coronation. The building itself, which was polished and regilded for its 900th birthday in December, 1965, is a spectacle of gold leaf, stone and stained glass. Definitely pay the £1.30 admission price ($1.82, free on Wednesdays from 6 to 8 p.m.) to see the Royal Chapels (not open to view on Sunday) and Tombs, the Coronation Chair (with the famous Stone of Scone under the seat), and Henry VII's Chapel, a magnificent 16th-century fane with filigreed, fan-vaulted ceiling and banners of the Knights of the Bath. I think you'll find especially thrilling the tombs of Queen Elizabeth I, the Little Princes who were killed in the Tower (Edward V and Richard, the Duke of York), and Mary Queen of Scots (her monument is decorated with Scottish thistles). The Abbey is open daily from 8 a.m. to 6 p.m. (Wednesdays till 8 p.m.; except when a service is being conducted) and admission to the nave is free. *Extra:* a favorite secret spot of mine—peaceful and atmospheric—is the Cloisters behind the Abbey, which also include the Chapter House and the Abbey Treasures Museum. For details, see Readers' Selections.

"Now, head north (back in the direction of Westminster Tube Station) toward Trafalgar Square for a walk along **Whitehall,** which used to be the site of Whitehall Palace but is now famous as the street of British government offices. Make a short detour to your left, near the Cenotaph, to have a look at **No. 10 Downing Street,** a modest little three-story brick building with only two solitary 'Bobbies' keeping watch in front, which serves as London residence for the English Prime Minister. Compare it to our White House!

"A little further on, also on your left, is the colorful **Horse Guards;** you can't miss it—two guards in splendid uniforms on horseback, stationed in front of a quaint-looking tower. If you arrive at 11 a.m. (10 a.m. on Sundays), you'll see a Changing of the Horse Guard, which takes place half an hour before the equally elaborate ceremony at Buckingham Palace. A shorter, simpler 'inspection' takes place at 4 p.m. every day. If you like, you can walk through the Archway and see the **Horse Guard Parade,** a wide open yard used for the ceremony of the 'trooping of the colors' on the Queen's official birthday.

"London's latest, major sightseeing attraction, opened to the public for the first time in 1984, is located near here: the so-called **Cabinet War Rooms,** an underground complex of 150 units, of which 16 rooms are now available for visiting, used by Winston Churchill and staff during the most critical times of World War II. You'll see the great man's bedroom and private office, the world map still bearing the colored pins with which he charted the course of the war, the trans-Atlantic phone used for his frequent conversations with President Franklin Roosevelt. All this is found under the new Public Offices on the corner of Horse Guards Road and Great George Street, open daily except Monday from 10 a.m. to 5:30 p.m., for an adult admission of £2 ($2.80), only £1 ($1.40) for children.

"Directly across the street from the Horse Guards is the **Banqueting House,** all that is left of the old Whitehall Palace, and now open from 10 a.m. to 5 p.m., Monday to Saturday, from 2 to 5 p.m. on Sundays, for an admission charge of 50p (children 25p). It was designed by Inigo Jones, completed in 1622, and has a ceiling of nine panels painted by Rubens. Here King Charles I stepped through a second floor window onto a scaffolding to have his head cut off; William and Mary accepted the Crown of England; and many other events of historical interest occurred on the site.

"Now, continue on your walk to **Trafalgar Square** where you'll see, directly across the Square, the **National Gallery** already mentioned by Arthur; if you're curious to know how London looked more than a century ago, the trip to Trafalgar Square and the National Gallery (gaze at the top of the Square) will give you an idea. Arriving at this spot also provides the opportunity to nip into the **National Portrait Gallery** located directly behind the National Gallery on St. Martin's Place and Charing Cross Road. Admission is free, and the gallery is open from 10 a.m. to 5 p.m. on weekdays, Saturdays till 6 p.m., and from 2 to 6 p.m. on Sundays. I recommend the National Portrait Gallery to you as a kind of picture book history. There are paintings of everyone from the 15th century onwards, including the present Prince and Princess (Lady Diana) of Wales, and while the paintings themselves are for the most part not worth mentioning (notable exceptions: Holbein's Henry VIII, the Rubens sketch of the Earl of Arundel, superb self-portraits by Gainsborough and Reynolds, the portrait of the Brontë sisters by their brother Branwell), they are bound to appeal to the gossip in you.

SOME HISTORICAL WALKS: "You might next like to see a session of the **Royal Courts of Justice** (tube stops are Temple or Aldwych), which is open when Courts are in session on weekdays from 10:30 a.m. to 4 p.m. Directly across the street are two of the Inns of Court called 'The Temple,' which contain the **Middle Temple Hall,** and **Temple Church.** The former was built in 1570 and is a glorious Tudor Hall with crests everywhere and ornamental armor and guns; it is believed that the Shakespeare Company performed *Twelfth Night* here in 1601, and the hall does have the feeling of jolly old England. Admission is free; hours are 10 a.m. to 12 p.m. and 3 to 4 p.m. (but the hall is occasionally closed to the public when in use). Temple Church, open daily from 10 a.m. to 4:30 p.m., is a gabled Gothic building that was badly damaged during the war but has been faithfully restored. The nave was completed in 1185 and has stone effigies of knights and earls (Crusaders) on the floor.

"From the Temple, walk through Inner Temple Gate; directly opposite the Gate is Chancery Lane; walk about half way up the first block and you'll find on your right the **Public Record Office** with its small museum, admission free and open Monday to Friday from 1 to 4 p.m. This is a history student's dream, for here you can see the famous Domesday Book (William the Conqueror's list of all the property in his new realm, drafted for him in 1086), a copy of the final version of the Magna Carta, royal autographs, letters of Ben Jonson, Bacon, Milton, and many others too numerous to mention.

"Now turn back to **Fleet Street,** turn left and walk up the street about two blocks, because you ought now to pay a visit to **Dr. Johnson's House,** at 17 Gough Square (watch for a sign on your left pointing the way); admission £1 (50p for students and children), open from 11 a.m. to 5:30 p.m., 5 in winter, closed Sundays. It was in this house that most of the work on his magnum opus was done, and you can actually see a copy of the first edition of Dr. Johnson's famous Dictionary here (visit the Dictionary Garret where Johnson's copyists worked), along with portraits of most of the people connected with Johnson, and all manner of Johnson memorabilia.

"After your visit to St. Paul's (tube stop: St. Paul's), make a short detour to the **Church of Saint Bartholomew the Great,** open daily till dusk and located near Smithfield Market (from the tube station find a street called Little Britain and walk along nearly to the end; there are two entrances to the church, one on Little Britain itself, or turn right into a street called Cloth Fair). This lovely Norman structure, built in 1123, is the oldest parish church in all of London. Next, walk back toward the tube station and ask for Wood Street, which leads into Gresham Street, and at the junction of Gresham and King Streets you'll find **The Guildhall,** built in 1425, admission free, open Monday through Saturday from 10 a.m. to 5 p.m. The Guildhall is the Civic Hall of the City of London, and while a very correct English friend of mine tells me it's been restored and is therefore not strictly authentic, I find here a wonderful sense of the way London must have been 500 years ago. In any event, part of the interior of the porch, part of the hall, and the crypts are genuine 15th century, and the hall itself is wonderfully stone-Gothic with stained glass windows and includes a statue of Winston Churchill, Gog and Magog, and the official standards of lengths.

THE HOUSES OF SOME MEN TO BE PROUD OF: "For £1 (75p for
students, 50p for children), you can visit **The Dickens House, Library and Museum** at 48 Doughty St. (subway stop: Russell Square, then walk three blocks up Guilford Street, away from Russell Square, or buses 19 or 38 to John Street), open daily except Sundays and bank holidays from 10 a.m. to 5 p.m. Charles Dickens lived here from 1837 to 1839, during which time he wrote most of *The Pickwick Papers, Oliver Twist,* and *Nicholas Nickleby,* and thus became a very famous and celebrated man while still in his mid-twenties. The house is just the kind of place you'd expect Dickens to live in, and is filled with personal mementos, family portraits, photographs, the desk and chair used during the last years of his life, and pictures and crockery celebrating famous Dickens characters.

"Real Dickens enthusiasts will also want to pay a visit to **The Old Curiosity Shop,** 13–14 Portsmouth St. (tube stop—Holborn; come out on Kingsway, turn left and walk about three blocks to Sardinia Street, turn left again and Portsmouth is the first street in on your right), open every day of the year, except Christmas, from 9:30 a.m. to 5:30 p.m. Lovers of Little

Nell and her Grandfather will remember this tiny old Tudor shop, built in 1567, from the graphic pages of Dickens's novel *The Old Curiosity Shop.*

"Next, you might go to Apsley House, town house of the first Duke of Wellington, now known as **The Wellington Museum,** 149 Piccadilly, near the entrance to Hyde Park (tube is Hyde Park Corner; open every weekday except Monday and Friday from 10 a.m. to 6 p.m. and Sundays from 2:30 to 6 p.m., admission 60p). It contains many priceless paintings, relics and honors collected by the Duke, conqueror of Napoleon—in the vestibule, for instance, stands Canova's gigantic nude statue of Napoleon, a rather sardonic touch. The dining table and chairs in the dining room were used by the Duke at his annual victory celebrations or Waterloo Banquets, as he called them, and the ornate silver and gilt centerpiece was given to him by the Prince Regent of Portugal. There are some interesting political cartoons in the basement.

"If you plan to take a walk around **Chelsea** (London's former Bohemialand), and I heartily recommend that you *do* if you have the time, then at 24 Cheyne Row (located off Cheyne Walk between Albert Bridge and Battersea Bridge) you'll find the charming old (built in 1708) **House of Thomas Carlyle,** open daily, except Mondays and Tuesdays, from April 1 to October 31, from 11 a.m. to 5 p.m., Sundays from 2 to 5 p.m., and charging a £1 admission fee to adults, 50p to children. Carlyle lived here for nearly 50 years, from 1834 to 1881, and left a strong imprint on the place; all the furnishings and decorations are just as he and his wife placed them; you can feel his presence. You'll see photos, drawings, and paintings of Mr. and Mrs. Carlyle, as well as letters, books, pens, pipes and spectacles, the attic room in which he worked, his desk, and a very touching letter from Disraeli. The surrounding neighborhood is delightful, too, with its lovely old Georgian and Victorian houses and many famous landmarks, such as **The Chelsea Old Church** and **The Chelsea Royal Hospital.** As you walk through Chelsea (which ignores the seasons, and somehow always looks green), keep your eyes peeled for those little round blue disks identifying famous London sites, because for a couple of hundred years there were more famous and illustrious writers and painters living (and dying) in Chelsea than anywhere else in London. (Nearest tube stop: Sloane Square, then a fairly long walk; or from the West End, take buses 11, 19 or 22 to Chelsea Town Hall—which puts you closer to the heart of the neighborhood; to get to Carlyle's House from here, take the first street on your left, Oakley Street, then the first street on your right, Upper Cheyne Row, to Cheyne Row, first street on your left.)

SOME EXTRAS: "Be sure to save time for **Covent Garden** (tube stop is Charing Cross), where the historic wholesale marketplace has now been converted into a modern shopping and restaurant center, called **The Market,** housing select shops selling everything from groceries, herbs and spices to natural cosmetics and shoes, toys, books, crockery, pottery, and fashions. Restaurants range from coffee and sandwich shops, wine bars, an English-style brasserie, and a pub (the 'Punch and Judy,' with a terrace overlooking the piazza), to more fashionable eateries between the arcades of the shops. Forty renovated original wrought-iron trading stands from the old flower market make up the new 'Apple Market,' now a sort of high-class flea market. Open Monday to Saturday from morning to 8 p.m. and definitely worth visiting.

"Also have a look at **St. Paul's Covent Garden** (directly opposite), a small church designed by Inigo Jones, where Ellen Terry and many other notables are buried, and whose portico provided the setting for the opening scene of the film of G. B. Shaw's *Pygmalion*. (The square between the church and Covent Garden Market provides an hospitable space for street buskers, rock bands, and many other types of lively outdoor entertainments —it's a jumping place.) . . . Archaeology pros and amateurs: there are 'digs' in London! All along the Thames-front, from near and around London Bridge to Blackfriars, archaeologists have been uncovering ancient artifacts (from as far back as Roman London), and considerately dating (with clear signs and maps) the revealed structures for the curious. Volunteers are welcome, and on-site workers are extremely friendly and knowledgeable. This summer, when I visited the Mermaid site where I saw medieval ruins from the 13th and 14th centuries (now covered up), I was told by the chief archaeologist that the current excavations were the largest and most important of their type in the country. They have provided a uniquely detailed picture of the development and quality of London waterfront life. Digging will continue for the next six years. For current information on where to locate sites, call the London Tourist Board, phone 730-0791. . . . London's magnificent **Harrod's department store** in Knightsbridge, especially its ground floor, is a sightseeing attraction in its own right and shouldn't be missed. . . . A worthwhile purchase by tourists remaining in England long enough to justify it is an **'Open to View'** ticket, which costs $20, is valid for 30 days from the first day of use, and admits the bearer to over 400 varied attractions. In London: Banqueting House, Carlyle's House, the Tower of London, and Westminster Abbey. Outside London: Hampton Court Palace, Kew Palace, Stonehenge, Windsor Castle, Harvard House and Shakespeare's Birthplace in Stratford-upon-Avon, Woburn Abbey, Edinburgh Castle and Palace of Holyrood House in Edinburgh. If interested, mail a check or money order to Britrail Travel International, 270 Madison Avenue, New York, N.Y. 10016, and you'll receive an 'O.V.' ticket, along with a booklet describing the attractions at which it can be used."

READERS' SIGHTSEEING TIPS: "The new Egyptian Gallery at the **British Museum** simply has to be seen to be believed. The tremendous collection is shown off to its best in a large, airy, well-lit gallery" (S.D. Borisky, Charlottesville, Virginia). . . . "One of the oldest rituals in London, the **Ceremony of the Keys,** takes place at 9:30 p.m. at the Tower of London. It's free, and very impressive, but only a limited number of people can watch it. You must write in advance to the Resident Governor, HM Tower of London, EC3N4AB, enclosing SAE, giving a preferred date and an alternate date, and specifying the number of people in your party" (Janet Zimmerman, Pittsburgh, Pennsylvania). . . . "We enthusiastically recommend the **London Walks,** whose topics include 'Ghosts of the West End' and 'Dickens' London.' The price is £1.50 (children under 16 free) for a 2- to 2½-hour walk with a very knowledgeable guide" (Steve & Dolores Bartholomew, Warsaw, Poland; note by AF: there are more than 40 London walks, among them "Jack the Ripper," "In the footsteps of Sherlock Holmes," "London and the Monarchy"; phone 882-2763 for current information). . . . "The best collection of French Impressionists and post-Impressionists outside of France, is to be found at **The Courtauld Institute Galleries,** which are part of London University (located in the Warburg Building, on Woburn Square at the corner of Torrington Place—Tube: Goodge Street, Russell Square or Euston Square; admission is 50p for adults, 25p for children, open 10 a.m. to 5 p.m., Sundays from 2 to 5 p.m.). If you include a stop here on your itinerary, I assure you, you're in for some thrilling surprises" (Robert Rogers, New York, New York). . . . "We spent a delightful day exploring **Kensington Gardens**—the Round Pond, Broad Walk, Sunken Garden, Orangery, etc. Our excursion gave us the chance to visit the

State Apartments in Kensington Palace, where we were most taken by Queen Victoria's bedroom (where she first learned she was to be Queen), and the Ante-Room, which contains Victoria's doll house and other toys. Open weekdays from 9 a.m. to 5 p.m., and Sundays from 1 to 5 p.m., admission £1—tube stops are Queensway, Bayswater or Kensington High Street" (Mathew Marshall, New York, New York). . . . "Brass-rubbing enthusiasts needn't travel miles to deserted and desolate country churchyards. Just go to the **London Brass Rubbing Centre** at St. James Church, Piccadilly, where you will be given all the materials you need to make brass rubbings from their exhibition brasses of medieval knights, ladies, merchants and priests. A staff member will show you how if you've never done a rubbing before, and charges start at 50p and go to £8, depending on the size of the rubbing. The London Brass Rubbing Centre is open Monday to Saturday, 10 a.m. to 6 p.m., and on Sundays from noon to 6 p.m. After you've done your brass rubbing, you should pay a visit to St. James Church itself. Set back from the hustle and bustle of Piccadilly, and behind its own courtyard with gardens and a fountain, this famous Wren church includes some of the finest work of the British master woodcarver, Grinling Gibbons"; note from AF: There is another interesting Brass Rubbing Center at the historic church of **All Hallows,** near the Tower of London, open from May to October, with the finest collection of memorial brasses in town. Beneath All Hallows is a little known but fascinating small museum which features the pavement of the Roman villa on which the church was founded, together with other items both gruesome and glorious from All Hallows' past. As the neighboring church to the Tower, it used to receive the headless bodies after executions; from its tower the diarist Samuel Pepys watched the Great London Fire burn towards his home; the Blitz of World War II revealed a Saxon wall in the church, older than the Tower. These and many other fascinating historical snippets make a visit to All Hallows worthwhile. . . . At **St. Margaret's Church,** sandwiched between the Abbey and the Houses of Parliament, I was amazed and delighted to re-discover that any and every corner of London is alive with evocative material of historical significance. Beginnings are somewhat shrouded in the fog of time; it is known that the site was inhabited as long ago as the Roman era, because a Roman sarcophagus was found in the church yard (it's currently on view at the entrance to the Abbey's Chapter House). St. Margaret's is (since 1614) the parish church of the House of Commons. It was here that Thanksgiving services were held at the endings of World Wars I and II; here that Sir Winston and Lady Churchill were married in 1908. Also, Sir Walter Raleigh was executed (1618) right outside the church, and his remains are buried underneath the high altar—with the exception of his head, which his widow took charge of (the West window inside the church is a memorial to Raleigh). Famous parishioners at St. Margaret's have included Oliver Cromwell, Chaucer, Samuel Pepys, John Milton (who delivered sermons here; he also has a window memorial with an inscription by John Greenleaf Whittier), and William Caxton, who was recently honored in London for having introduced printing in England (he's commemorated by a brass memorial). Another real curiosity is the East window, originally made in Flanders on the occasion of the marriage of Catherine of Aragon in 1501 (at age 15) to Arthur, the Prince of Wales. Five months after the wedding Arthur died and the lovely but unlucky Catherine married his brother, Henry VIII; the rest, as they say, is history" (Laib Bell, Evanston, Illinois). . . . "Hope, don't shortchange **Westminster Abbey!** Your readers should know about **the Cloisters** behind the Abbey, with its charming inner courtyard garden. And the **Chapter House,** one of the oldest remaining sections of the Abbey and the first meeting hall for the House of Commons (open daily, except Sundays, from 10:30 a.m. to 6:30 p.m., winters closing at 3:30 p.m., admission is 60p). And what about the **Westminster Abbey Treasures** containing a fascinating collection of funeral effigies, Henry V's sword and saddle, and the ring Elizabeth I gave to Essex? The Treasures are open daily from April through September from 10:30 a.m. to 4:30 p.m. Admission is 30p for adults, 10p for children under 16" (Corky Rissman, Chicago, Illinois). . . . "Those in the mood for the grisly and the ghoulish might try London's newest 'experience': the **London Dungeon,** at 34 Tooley Street, in an old vaulted warehouse beneath London Bridge Station (take the Northern Line on the underground to London Bridge stop). Note that a cobweb covered board suspended from the shadows lists the fates of those who have gone before you—69 fainted, 12 are semi-mad, four totally insane—and the management 'accepts no responsibilities for subsequent nightmares.' Featured are realistic tableaux of Great Britain's criminal and horrific past from the Dark Ages to the end of the 17th century, including Morgan le Fay, Merlin, a murdered Thomas à Becket and Charles I at his beheading. As you pass through the shadowy, candlelit halls, you hear from the darkness the sound of witches' chants and bats, a lone menacing drum beat, a sword being sharpened. Definitely not for the nervous or for very young children. For other daring souls, the London Dungeon is open daily from 10 a.m. to 6 p.m., with an admission of £3.50 for adults, £2 for children" (Kathy Pasmantier, London, England). . . . "If you find yourself in the area of Lincoln's Inn Fields, near the Old Curiosity Shop, be sure to drop in at #13, **Sir John Soane's Museum,** open Tuesday through Saturday from 10 a.m. to 5 p.m., with free admission. Soane was an architect (he did the Bank of England) and collector extraordinaire; and he designed and lived in this house for 25 years, till his death in 1837. Soane was an innovative and imaginative classicist, and architects visit the museum in droves—but even if you're not an architect, the house is so bizarre and amusing (with its Monk's Parlour, Crypt, decorated hallways, mirrored domes, etc.), it's worth a visit. And the collections are fascinating, including an Egyptian sarcophagus; Greek and Roman architectural fragments and vases; busts and statuary (and plaster casts); ceramics, architectural models; William Hogarth's series of paintings, 'The Election' and 'The Rake's Progress'; landscapes by Turner; drawings by Piranesi; and all manner of the collector's mania—too numerous to mention, but lots of fun to look at" (Mrs. Lou Levy, Augusta, Georgia). . . . "The **Imperial War Museum,** across the river in Lambeth Road (tube is Lambeth North or Elephant and Castle), contains a wealth of memorabilia on the two World Wars; the display on the origins of World War I is superb. Hours are: 10 a.m. to 5:50 p.m., Mondays through Saturdays, 2 to 5:50 p.m. on Sundays, and admission is free. The new **National Army Museum,** on Royal Hospital Road in Chelsea, is an excellent presentation of the evolution of British military tactics, leadership, uniforms and equipment, keyed to specific wars, campaigns and opponents" (Harry Roach, Willow Grove, Pennsylvania; note by AF: among the Imperial War Museum's latest acquisitions: the campaign caravans of Field Marshal Montgomery, Lawrence of Arabia's rifle, a German V1 and V2, two 15-inch Naval guns, a captured Argentine position from the Falkland Islands). . . . "A visit to the **RAF Museum** at Hendon (underground to Colindale and a short walk—turn left out of station and follow signs) provides a fascinating account of aviation history and the Battle of Britain" (John and Mary Banbury, Breckenridge, Colorado).

8. London Excursions

At least once during your stay, you'll want to venture outside the city boundaries to one of the following, major sights of England—most of them no more than an hour-or-so away:

(1) **Hampton Court Palace:** This, to me, is the most interesting of all England's "stately homes." Built by Cardinal Wolsey over 400 years ago, and then "presented" by him to King Henry VIII, it is the most mammoth Tudor structure ever built, and contains such eye-openers as an indoor kitchen where an entire ox could be roasted whole. The State Apartments here are open from 9:30 a.m. to 5 p.m., the grounds (including the Maze, for a small fee) until 9 p.m., and a single admission of £2 ($2.80) in summer, £1 ($1.40) in winter, admits you to virtually everything. Either take the train from Waterloo Station in London to Hampton Court, or else a #718 Green Line Coach (bus) from Victoria Station to Hampton Court; the trip takes 40 minutes and passes through Chelsea, Putney, and Kingston-upon-Thames.

(2) **Windsor Castle:** The largest inhabited palace in the world, which is open to visitors even when the Queen is in residence there; it stands in an

1,800-acre park. Open 10:30 a.m. to 5 p.m. (from 1:30 to 5 p.m. on Sundays) for a £1 admission charge; you reach it either by train from Waterloo or Paddington Station, by Green Line Coach bus 704 from Hyde Park Corner, or by Green Line bus 718 from alongside Victoria Station. The school of Eton, incidentally, is a short walk from the castle, and is usually combined with a visit to it.

(3) **Brighton:** This invigorating seaside resort, on the English channel, is only an hour by train (and £6.10 for a single day round-trip excursion) from London's Victoria Station. Or, you can take a bus from Victoria Coach Station (two hours, because of many stops).

(4) **Greenwich:** The famous Thames River port of London, where "Greenwich Mean Time" is fixed, it houses the impressive Royal Naval College (which you can visit free), the National Maritime Museum (again free but closed Mondays), and the clipper ship *Cutty Sark* (£1). Take a train there from Charing Cross Station, on The Strand; round trip fare is £1.60 ($2.24). Or better yet, take a Thames river boat (phone 730-4812 for information) in summer from Charing Cross Pier to Greenwich; they leave every 20 minutes from 10:20 a.m. to dusk, take 50 minutes each way, and charge £2.80 round-trip.

(5) **Kew Gardens:** Site of the Royal Botanic Gardens (admission 10p), it can be reached simply by taking the subway (District Line, Richmond train) to Kew Gardens.

(6) **Cambridge:** It's only 56 miles from London, and can best be reached by train (from Liverpool Street or King's Cross Stations) in about 1½ hours. Round-trip day excursion: £6.80.

(7) **Oxford:** Nearly 64 miles from London, and again easily accessible (about 1½ hours) by train from Paddington Station. One-way fare is £6.30, round-trip day excursion only £6.70, total.

(8) And, of course, **Stratford-upon-Avon,** 121 miles and two hours by train from London's Paddington Station, for a round-trip day excursion fare of £11.30.

As you've seen, London possesses no fewer than six major railroad stations: **Euston** (servicing trains to and from Coventry, Birmingham, Liverpool, Manchester, Glasgow); **King's Cross** (Hull, Leeds, Edinburgh); **Paddington** (Oxford, Penzance, Plymouth, Bath, Bristol, Cardiff, Exeter); **Victoria** (Dover, Brighton, Gatwick Airport); **Waterloo** (Portsmouth, Southampton, Bournemouth); and **St. Pancras** (Nottingham).

READERS' EXCURSION RECOMMENDATIONS: "As we did not have time for more than a one-day excursion out of the London area, we decided to go to **Salisbury.** British Railways runs day excursions to just about anywhere in England, out of any London railway station. You can take any train, at any time, with a few rare exceptions. As long as you leave London and arrive back on the *same day,* you can ask for an excursion fare ticket and save plenty. Example: it costs only £9.40 round-trip to Salisbury on the day excursion, compared to an ordinary one-way price of £9. If you don't ask for the excursion, of course, you are stuck" (Barbara and Bob Budnitz, Cambridge, Mass.; note by AF: the British Railways hand out a red-colored pamphlet that describes scores of "day excursions"—the British call them "cheap-day returns"—offered by them; it's often pleasant, early on a summer morning, simply to go to Waterloo Station and choose your destination and excursion on the spot; especially recommended is the one-hour journey to Brighton, which costs only £6.10, round-trip, second class, on a "day excursion"). . . . "Visitors to London can get to **Stonehenge** easily, quickly and cheaply by catching the 1 p.m. train to Salisbury from Waterloo Station. A Hants & Dorset bus will meet you at theSalisbury station at 2:38, take you to the ruins, and get you back to the station in time for the 4:40 train which gets to London at 6:14. Railroad, bus fares, and Stonehenge admission came to £14.50 (£7.25 for children). The same British Rail Excursion Ticket includes a trip to Old Sarum (the Norman castle and cathedral ruins) and Salisbury Cathedral if you can get to Waterloo Station at 9:05 a.m." (Josephine Blair, No. Babylon, New York). . . . "We highly recommend the hour-long boat ride down the Thames River to **Greenwich** (£1.80 one way, £2.80 round trip), during which the boat captain calls out points of interest, and which allows you to walk around Greenwich to see the clipper ship *Cutty Sark* and the naval museum" (Walter J. Dwyer, Woodside, New York; note by AF: in summer, there are departures every 30 minutes from Westminster pier to Kew, site of the Royal Botanic Gardens and Kew Palace, round-trip fare of £2.80, to Greenwich and the *Cutty Sark* round-trip £2.80, and—at less frequent intervals—to Hampton Court Palace home, first, of Cardinal Wolsey, and then of Henry VIII, round-trip for £4.80; phone **Thames Launches,** operator of the cruises, at 930-8294 . . . "A cheap-day return ticket (that's a round-trip ticket in English lingo) to **Brighton** costs exactly £6.10, with trains leaving from Victoria Station at 9, 10, 11 a.m. and 12 and 1 p.m., arriving there in 55 minutes. Return trains to London leaving in the afternoon and evening are as follows: 3:45, 4:45, 5:45, 6:45, 7:45 and 8:45 p.m. Brighton is so close to London that I personally would recommend it only as a one-day excursion and not for an overnight stay. An interesting note about Brighton is that many plays, before arriving on the London theater scene, try out there. Perhaps some of your readers will be lucky enough to catch one. . . . The cheap day round-trip ('return') ticket to **Oxford** costs exactly £6.70, and the trip takes one hour and five minutes. Trains leave from Paddington Station 15 minutes after the hour starting at 8 a.m. Trains from Oxford leave at 2:25 p.m., 3:35, 4:15, 6:35 and 8:41 p.m. Oxford is such a small college town that all the major sights and colleges can be seen and enjoyed on your own with a map that you can get at the railroad station. The Enquiry Office will give you a free map which outlines a two hour walking tour and, believe me, this is really going at it leisurely. . . . A cheap day 'return' (round-trip) ticket to **Cambridge** costs only £6.80. Trains depart from Kings Cross station at 9:05 a.m. and 11:35 and return from Cambridge at 3:40 and 5:40 p.m. Departures from Liverpool Station are 8:36 a.m., 9:36, 10:36 and 12:36 p.m. and return to the same station at 2:40, 3:55, 4:40 & 6:40 p.m. from Cambridge. A walking tour of the college at Cambridge can be made in about two hours. Heading back to the railroad station after seeing all the colleges in Cambridge, you'll find on either Hill or Station roads, the fabulously cheap restaurant in the **Great Northern Pub,** where three-course luncheons cost around £3.50 ($4.90). It was a perfect way to wind up the trip. . . . There are very frequent trains leaving for **Greenwich** each day and the cheap day 'return' (round-trip) tickets cost £1.40 ($1.96) and leave from Charing Cross station. An afternoon trip here is better than one in the morning because, of the three major sights, the Royal Naval College does not open its doors until 2:30 p.m." (Edward H. Pietraszek, Chicago, Illinois). . . . "An easy way to go to **Stonehenge** is to take the train from Waterloo Station to Salisbury, a bus from Salisbury to Amesbury, and then a little bus going to Shrewton, which drops you about a mile from Stonehenge, to which you have a beautiful walk on a 'Public Footpath.' It cost about a third as much as taking a tour from London" (Dorothy Gamble, Glendale, California). . . . "Recent English sovereigns, including Edward VIII awaiting Mrs. Wally Simpson, are buried in St. George's Chapel crypt. The effigies on top are made at the time of the first death in the couple: the Queen Mum had a cast of her face made after George VI's death and so she will look the same age as him for eternity. Mention should be made of the cruise of the docks in **Greenwich,** and the Brighton Pavilion of the Prince Regent; a fun spot, and more important than the beach at Brighton" (Delos V. Smith, Jr., Hutchinson, Kansas).

9. Evening Entertainment

THE THEATRE: London offers playgoing in its most exciting, comfortable and inexpensive form. At least 40 plays or musicals are always running and all but the top two or three hits have available seats up to five minutes of curtain time, which is 7:30 or 8 p.m. in most London theatres. The highest-priced orchestra seats (here they're called "stalls") in the best theatres rarely cost more than £12 ($16.80), but you needn't pay more than $7 in the "upper circle" (first balcony); and you can do it for less. "Slip seats" (side circle) for performances at the new National Theatre on the South Bank can be had for as little as £3.50. My idea of a London vacation is to see a play a night. They're the city's top attraction, and they can be managed on the tightest budget.

In fact, if you are extreme theatre buffs, as Hope and I are, you can hustle to as many as three plays in one day in London. That's because on certain matinee days, some London theatres schedule their afternoon performances for 3 p.m., others for 5:30 or 6 p.m. On one memorable Saturday in London, we saw Alec Guinness in *Ross* at 2 p.m., Ralph Richardson in *The Complacent Lover* at 5 p.m., and Sir John Gielgud in *The Ages of Man* at 8 p.m. We did it by eating sandwiches at numerous intermissions throughout the day and evening (sandwiches and tea are sold in most London theatres), and by then taxi-ing to the next theatre in the five-or-so minutes between performances. I certainly don't recommend this tiring fanaticism, but merely set it forth, as an example of the attraction that London theatre can have. . . . Try to avoid buying your tickets at brokers. Since nearly all theatres have available seats, there's no need to incur the added commissions.

London theatres with especially cheap seats: the **Globe Theatre,** with upper circle seats for £6 ($8.40); the **Apollo Theatre,** charging the same; the 110-year-old **Criterion Theatre,** again the same; the **Theatre Royal Haymarket,** with gallery seats for £5.90 ($8.26); the renowned **Aldwych Theatre,** with "top circle" seats for £7, less at matinees; the **Comedy Theatre,** balcony for £6 ($8.40); the **Shaftesbury,** balcony for £4; the **Wyndham Theatre,** £6 ($8.40) for balcony seats; more than a dozen other theatres (the **Queens,** the **Phoenix,** among them) which offer good first balcony or upper circle seats for £6.50 ($9.10).

And do use the half-price ticket offerings of the **Leicester Square Theatre Ticket Booth** in a Jack-and-Judy-puppet-show-type structure in the park area of the square. They sell day-of-performance seats at all London theatres (subject to availability) for 50% off plus a 75p fee, from noon to 2 p.m. for matinees, from 2:30 to 6:30 for evening performances, Monday through Saturday. Students and senior citizens with identification can also receive large discounts by presenting themselves half an hour before performance time at the theatres which identify themselves with a circled "S" in their ads. That's also subject to availability, of course.

A READER'S COMMENT: "Any bright tourist should take advantage of the British theatres—every night! You can appear 10 or 15 minutes before curtain time at any theatre of your choice and you can always find a 'single' priced at just about $7 and often less" (Anne Fomin, Dearborn Heights, Michigan).

DISCOTHEQUES AND DANCING: London's inexpensive night life is centered in a number of rock clubs which sprout and die much too rapidly for this once-a-year book to keep up with them. They're listed, though, in a weekly magazine called *Time Out* (60p), to be picked up at any London newsstand. . . . For disco dancing, you ought definitely to make at least one visit to the phenomenal **Empire Ballroom** on Leicester Square (get off

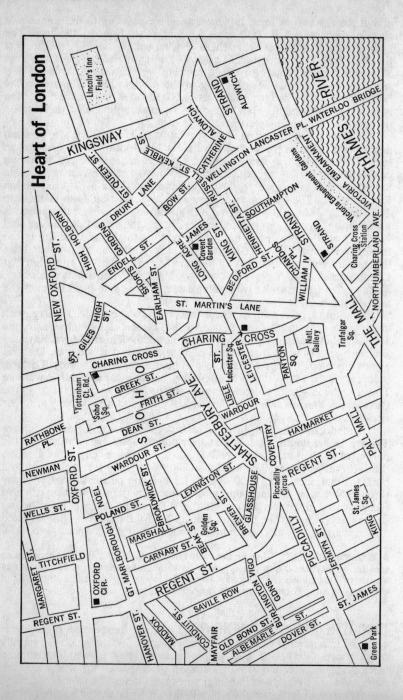

Heart of London

at the Leicester Square or Piccadilly tube station), a gigantic dance hall and legitimate pick-up spot for London's unmarried young people, with space for over 2,000 celebrants. This is one of the top tourist attractions of London: hundreds and hundreds of single men and women (on a Saturday night), flashing colored lights, a famous revolving globe of light-reflecting mirrors, continuous bands on a revolving stage. The action extends from 8 p.m. to 2 a.m., Monday through Thursday (admission is £3 before 10 p.m., £3.50 thereafter); on Friday and Saturday, from 8 p.m. to 3 a.m. (£4 before 10 p.m., £5 after). Sunday hours are 8 p.m. to 1 a.m., with an admission fee of £2.50 for the entire evening. You're under no obligation to pay a single thing more, after you've purchased your entrance. A somewhat older crowd patronizes the once-renowned **Lyceum** on Wellington Street, off The Strand, which has been somewhat pushed into the shadows by the new Empire Ballroom. At the Lyceum, Edwardian "music hall variety" is currently featured on Tuesday and Sunday (£3), "international discotheque" on Monday and Saturday (with admission of £2.50 Mondays, £4 on Saturdays).

READERS' ENTERTAINMENT TIPS: "London offers some wonderful dance spots. **Camden Palace,** near the Morning Crescent tube stop, caters to London's young avant-garde population. Crowded but fun; the dance floor is supplemented by a three-tiered bar with food served on the top floor. **Peppermint Park** on Upper St. Martin, near the Leicester Square tube stop, is an attractive restaurant with medium-priced food and disco dancing after midnight; reservations required on weekends" (Nina Kessler and Marion Freedman, New York, New York). . . . "For real, down-to-earth nakedness, there are a dozen or more strip shows in the Soho area, where admission is generally £3; the best of these (for those interested in this particular art form) are on and about Dean Street" (Henry S. Sloan, New York, New York; note by AF: though admission to some strips is only £3, an additional "membership" fee of £2 is often assessed once you're inside; the shows themselves—which normally consist of motionless posing by the girls—are not up to Jersey City or Baltimore standards). . . . "The best concert buy I know anywhere is for the **'Proms'** at The Royal Albert Hall.** This is a series of daily concerts in July, August and September, featuring superb soloists and orchestras in a gigantic oval auditorium that alone is worth the price of admission (£2). Find out the time of the concert in *What's On In London,* then take the Underground to South Kensington, arriving 90 minutes in advance, ask the way to the Royal Albert Hall (about three blocks), and join the queue for the 'Arena.' On the way, stop at a bakery and pick up some food, because everyone takes his supper and eats it while waiting in line. Once in the auditorium, you will discover that the 'Arena' is the bottom of the hall, a flat area with no seats and a fountain in the middle. This is where the orchestra seats would be if they had any—which means that if you are willing to stand, you can get within six feet of the conductor, or if you wish to sit you'll still be only some 25 feet away. The Arena audience is young, intense, and often informally dressed. 'Doing the Prom' is a wonderful experience; count it high among the attractions of London" (John H. M. Austin, New Haven, Connecticut). . . . "Ballet Tip: If you're eager to see a ballet or opera at Covent Garden and are told 'All sold out,' don't despair. Just drop by the theatre about 45 minutes before curtain time and join the discreet line forming to the left of the main entrance. Everything from boxes to standing room are offered, strictly fairly, to the first person in line and then so on down the line if he decides to wait and see what else comes up. We never failed to get in, even when Nureyev and Fonteyn were dancing" (Dr. and Mrs. Kenneth Korven, Susanville, California; note by AF: The Royal Opera House at Covent Garden is usually closed in August).

OFFBEAT LONDON: Every night throughout the year, London sees a succession of protest meetings, forums and fests by society's dissenters. If you'll buy a copy of the weekly *New Statesman* (50p), and turn to the back page, you'll find advertisements of free lectures, films and discussions, ranging in subject from politics to vegetarianism, and sponsored by organizations running the gamut from the Bertrand Russell Foundation and the Fabian Society, on the left, to the Empire Loyalists on the right; non-political meetings deal with spiritualism, theosophy, what-have-you. These events provide a marvelous opportunity for meeting interesting Englishmen and women, and the setting is somehow conducive to easy introductions and quick friendships. . . . Roulette, anyone? London, amazingly enough, has become one of the world's major gambling capitals, as you may have deduced from the casino scenes in James Bond movies. While all the casinos are run as clubs for members only, all offer temporary membership to visitors from overseas who register at the clubs at least 48 hours before they plan to play, and the cheapest of the clubs—**Charlie Chester's Casino,** 12 Archer St. (near Piccadilly Circus)—charges a fee of £5 to sporting bloods from abroad for the right to try its roulette, black jack, and Las Vegas dice. Open daily including Sundays from 2 p.m. until 4 a.m. . . . Most sophisticated movie theatres in London, attracting a dedicated audience of movie buffs: the **Academy Cinemas,** 165 Oxford St. (phone 437-2981 or 437-5129); these are three adjoining auditoriums, of which one is reserved for club members only; the other two play unusual films, such as Kon Ichikawa's *Tokyo Olympiad.*

A READER'S SUGGESTION: "An interesting way to put in an evening and meet the Londoners is to visit the **Centurions' Arms Club** at 7:30 p.m. on Wednesday (except in August) at St. Martin-in-the-Fields Church, near Trafalgar Square. Tea is served and a program follows. In April, when I was there, they presented a travel film; in October, they had a program from the musical conservatory—excerpts from the *Marriage of Figaro* sung in English. Visitors are welcome" (J. Y. Guinter, Chicago, Illinois; note by AF: a Saturday afternoon event at St. Martin-in-the-Fields, called the **International Club,** caters more specifically to overseas visitors, meets from 4 to 6 p.m., except in August, and charges entrance of 20p, which includes refreshments; the Saturday activity is perhaps more suitable for readers than the Wednesday evening gathering of 'Centurions').

10. London Shopping

The major attraction here, of course, is men's clothing—for this country is one of the few in the world where men are generally better dressed than women! If you have at least two weeks in London, then you should quickly choose a reputable-looking tailor and have him custom-make a suit; it will wear for life, and it will cost half the price of a similar job in the United States. If you don't have the time available, then your best bet for an inexpensive, but well-designed, ready-made suit or jacket is one of the large men's chains, of which a typical one is Montague Burton, Ltd.

You'll see stores with the sign **"Burton"** at over six locations in London, the most central of which is the Burton's at 114 Regent Street, just a block off Piccadilly, where the second floor is packed with racks selling Harris tweed sports jackets for £63 ($88.20), ready-made suits from £60 ($84). I picked up a heavy, woolen sports jacket for exactly £50 ($70) that would easily have cost $120 in the U.S. While this may have been a particular bargain, the normal prices at Burton's should not vary upwards by any great amount.

Women's woolen sweaters are a second good buy in London—

particularly the ones on sale at **Marks & Spencer department store** ("Marks & Sparks," the British call it) at 458 Oxford Street. Hope and I recently found Shetland wool cardigans selling there for £14 ($19.60) that would have cost at least $40 in the States. We found heavy button-down sweaters selling for £17 ($23.80) that would certainly cost much more over here.

Finally, another of the bargains of London are books—purchased at the famous **Foyle's** (world's largest bookstore, stocking more than four million volumes), on Charing Cross Road (#119), where the hard-cover prices are generally half those of the United States. In fact, some books are priced so low that even the cost of shipping them home will not appreciably affect your saving. And it's wonderful fun to browse through the store.

FLEA MARKET!: On weekends in London, the city's big open-air markets roar into operation, and if you're an indefatigable shopper, with a fair amount of endurance, you'll return with unusual values.

The Saturday market is held on **Portobello Road,** in the Notting Hill section (take the underground to Notting Hill Gate), but is limited mainly to antiques, silver, metal bric-a-brac of every kind. The larger and more varied market takes place Sunday morning (but continuing till about 1 p.m.) on **Petticoat Lane,** which is known as Middlesex Street the rest of the week. This time, take the underground to either Liverpool Street, Aldgate or Aldgate East, and be prepared to encounter huge, jostling crowds, plus everything you can name in the way of cheap or second-hand articles for sale.

READERS' SELECTIONS: "Hints for weary and wary travelers: Carry an umbrella wherever you go in London. I found it convenient to buy one of the foldup kind in a slip case (and I could pack it in my suitcase easily, too); as a man, I hooked it into my trouser belt at the side. They cost about £5 in the stores, but the street vendors sold exactly the same umbrella for either £3 or £4" (Professor Arthur M. Sanderson, Tampa, Florida). . . . "Now that the 'Romantic Look' is highly fashionable again, a must-see for every woman or girl going to London is the moderately priced **Laura Ashley** shop at 7–9 Harriet St., phone 235-9797 (it's located near Harrod's, in Knightsbridge). If you hanker for 'English Ethnic,' or have always secretly yearned to look just like one of Kate Greenaway's illustrations, this is the place for you! Always crowded, this is a 'no-frills,' all clothes-hanging, open-to-view, on pipe-racks (on two sizeable floors) establishment. Not much elegant service or individualized attention, but at these prices ($45 to around $70 for long cotton gowns; frilly 'gypsy' skirts $26 and up) who cares? Many good sales here, too" (Arthur Landow, Brooklyn, New York). . . . **"Reject China Shop** at 34 Beauchamp Place, just off Brompton Road near Harrods, carries second and third sortings (rejects) of fine English china, and the selections change daily. Prices range from £1.25 for a small china animal, to £800 for a dinner service" (Dr. and Mrs. Albert O. Girz, Ann Arbor, Michigan). . . . **"Hamley's** on Regent Street, is a fascinating, 6-story-high toy store, and has an excellent selection of dolls for collectors" (Carole Carter, Universal City, California; note from AF: the *Guinness Book of World Records* claims Hamley's is the largest toystore in the world). . . . "Pipe smokers should not fail to pick up some of the pipe bargains offered at **Selfridge's Smoke Shop** during the summer. English-made briar pipes from about £8 ($11.20)" (T. K. Moy, Hempstead, New York). . . . "Shopping area: anywhere in England, but especially in London, a marvelous purchase is the famous lemon soap, **Bronnley Lemons.** Available in boxes or individually, in three sizes, they are found in most department stores and drug stores (chemists). They cost pennies over there (£1.20 for a bar of toilet soap, £1.85 for bath soap), and a fortune here in specialty gift shops. A highly recommended purchase" (Dr. & Mrs. Kenneth Korven, Susanville, California). . . . **"The Railway**

Lost Property Shop, on the second floor of 359 Oxford St., across from the Dolcis Shoe Store and open during regular shopping hours, sells hundreds of second-hand trunks, bags, suitcases, umbrellas, rucksacks, belts and the like at bargain rates. I bought a practically new suitcase here in summer 1984 for £4 ($5.60)" (Nick Lorey, Velden, Austria).

11. London Miscellany

BICYCLE RENTAL: **Savile's Cycle Stores,** 97 Battersea Rise, Battersea (phone 228-4279), charges £14 the first week, £10.50 for subsequent weeks. Closed Wednesdays and Sundays; bring your passport if you plan to rent. Alternately, but at a higher price, try **Rent-a-Bike,** Student Centre, Old Palace Barracks, Church St., Kensington (phone 937-0726), charging £3.50 a day, only £13.50 per week, for a three-speed, small wheel, foldaway, quite fabulous. . . . Care for a moped instead? With helmet, basket in front, security lock and insurance coverage? **M and D Rent-a-Ped Ltd.,** 29 Orde Hall St. (near Russell Square, no phone), will provide, at £7.50 ($10.50) per day, plus a refundable deposit of $50. Included are 50 miles of free petrol. And if you hire for a week, two days are free.

TIPS: Buy a copy of *What's On In London* (50p), or *Time Out* (60p), available at all newsstands, the moment you arrive. This weekly pamphlet provides details on every current entertainment attraction in London. . . . If you feel like a movie in London, then consider one of the several **"Classic Repertory Theatres"** (addresses are listed in *What's On In London*). The "Classics" play nothing but the best of the old films—the Greta Garbo epics, masterworks like *The Informer*—and charge only £2.50 ($3.50) for admission, less if you go in before 3 p.m. . . . Need a druggist after 6 p.m.? **Boots,** on Piccadilly Circus, is the most conveniently located late-night chemist in London. . . . Nicest walk in London: down the Mall, from Trafalgar Square to Buckingham Palace. . . . A swimming pool in chilly London? The best one is the indoor **Oasis,** corner of High Holborn and Endell Streets, directly across from the Shaftesbury Theatre. Open daily, with both swimming (80p on weekdays, plus 20p for the rent of the towel) and hot baths (30p for the baths, 6p for soap). And there's a heated outdoor pool (open May to September) and an inexpensive cafeteria in the same building. To get here, take the underground to the Holborn or Tottenham Court Road stations. . . . Best advance reading for London: Dickens, any novel he ever wrote. . . . Always order tea in London. It's incomparable. . . . Used, pre-1968 London taxicabs are available from **London Cab Co.,** 1 Brixton Rd. (phone 735-7777), from £2,000 upward. At the same address is a **Taxi Museum,** free entrance, displaying taxicabs from 1907 to the present day. . . . London with children: phone 246-8007 for a recorded message on special London events and attractions for children. And for a memorable children's visit, try **Pollock's Toy Museum** at the corner of Scala and Whitfield Streets, next to Tottenham Court Road. Open daily except Sundays from 10 a.m. to 5 p.m.; 20p for children, 50p for you. "If you love art, folly, or the bright eyes of children, speed to Pollock's," wrote Robert Louis Stevenson. . . . In addition to the lectures we've described at the British Museum, talks are offered at 1 p.m. on Wednesdays and Thursdays at the **National Gallery,** Trafalgar Square; Tuesdays, Thursdays and Saturdays, at 3 p.m., at the **Natural History Museum;** Tuesdays and Wednesdays at 1:15 p.m., and Saturdays at 3 p.m., at the **Victoria and Albert**

Museum. . . . Need a babysitter? Try **Childminders** (phone 935-9763) or **Universal Aunts** (phone 730-9834). . . . **Banks** open weekdays from 9:30 a.m. to 3:30 p.m. In an emergency try Harrods, which operates a bank service from 9:30 a.m. to 5 p.m. Monday to Saturday, until 7 p.m. on Wednesdays. . . . For serious problem-solving try (whichever is appropriate) the **U.S. Embassy**, 24 Grosvenor Square (phone 4999000); **Australian High Commission**, Australia House, Strand (phone 438-8000); **Canadian High Commission**, McDonald House, 1 Grosvenor Square (phone 629-9497). . . . **Central Post and Parcel office** is located at St. Martin's Place, just off Trafalgar Square, open daily 24 hours; the **International Telephone Bureau** at 1 Broadway next to the St. James Park tube station stays open from 9 a.m. to 7 p.m. daily.

READER'S TRANSPORTATION TIPS: "One soon finds that bus travel in the British Isles is simple, efficient, and often 40% less than travel by rail. For example, from the Victoria Coach Station on Buckingham Palace Road, London to Edinburgh is £10 ($14), leaving day and night. To Dublin, coach to Liverpool is £8.50 ($11.90), steamer from there to Dublin £31 ($43.40). To Dover, where you get a steamer for the continent, the ride is £5 ($7). Compare these rates with fares asked by British Railways" (Thomas A. Giltner, Dallas, Texas).

READER'S TIPS: "The privately owned Turkish baths of London can be quite expensive, as at the Savoy, but this need not be so. The city of London operates many municipal baths and charges as little as £5 (which includes what they call a soap shampoo in which an attendant will soap you from neck to foot) for use of the steam and dry rooms and 'plunge pool.' In the Bayswater area of London there is the **Porchester Hall Turkish Baths,** Porchester Road (U-Royal Oak), phone 229-3226, open from 9 a.m. until 7 p.m. for men, Monday, Wednesday and Saturday, and alternate days (except Sunday, the closed day) for women" (Edward H. Pietraszek, Chicago, Illinois).

STUDENT AND YOUTH TRAVEL: For young people planning rail travel

throughout Britain, or from London to the continent, or within the continent, the name **Transalpino**—Europe's largest youth rail operator—is an important word to be treasured. In London, its offices are at 71–75 Buckingham Palace Rd. (phone 834-9656), across the street from the main entrance to Victoria Station, and they're visited each day in summer by literally thousands of customers, who receive attention from nearly 20 bilingual clerks. Provided only that you're under the age of 26, and regardless of whether you're a student, you'll receive discounts of up to 50% on European rail tickets purchased from Transalpino, whose hours are weekdays from 9 a.m. to 5:30 p.m., Saturdays from 9:30 a.m. to 12:30 p.m. (with shorter opening times in winter). Although we've scattered Transalpino addresses through other chapters of this book, it's helpful to look them up in whatever major European city you're visiting.

THE LAUNDERETTES OF LONDON: These are available in great

profusion. In the **Russell Square** area, try "Red and White Laundries," 78 Marchmont St., open daily including Sundays from 8 a.m. to 10 p.m.: £1 for the machine, 30p for the dryer, 30p for soap. In the **Earls Court Road** area, near the former West London Air Terminal, there's a similarly priced serve-yourself laundry at 5 Kenway Rd. (which boasts it's the only launderette in London open 24 hours a day, 365 days a year), another at 4 Hogarth Place (directly opposite the entrance to the Earls Court Road tube

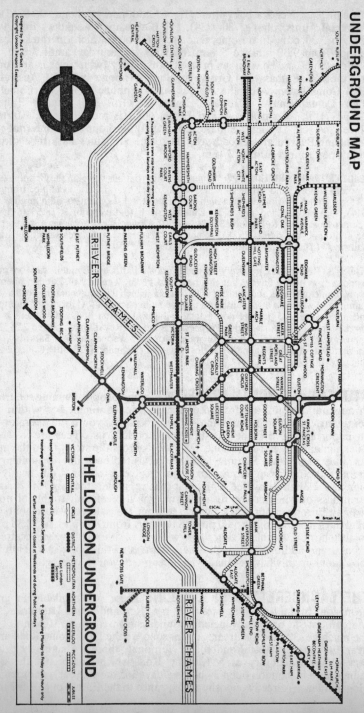

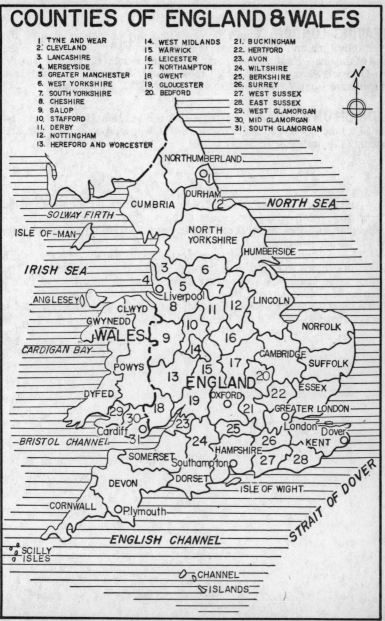

COUNTIES OF ENGLAND & WALES

1. TYNE AND WEAR
2. CLEVELAND
3. LANCASHIRE
4. MERSEYSIDE
5. GREATER MANCHESTER
6. WEST YORKSHIRE
7. SOUTH YORKSHIRE
8. CHESHIRE
9. SALOP
10. STAFFORD
11. DERBY
12. NOTTINGHAM
13. HEREFORD AND WORCESTER

14. WEST MIDLANDS
15. WARWICK
16. LEICESTER
17. NORTHAMPTON
18. GWENT
19. GLOUCESTER
20. BEDFORD

21. BUCKINGHAM
22. HERTFORD
23. AVON
24. WILTSHIRE
25. BERKSHIRE
26. SURREY
27. WEST SUSSEX
28. EAST SUSSEX
29. WEST GLAMORGAN
30. MID GLAMORGAN
31. SOUTH GLAMORGAN

station). Near **Paddington Station,** you'll find the **Wash Inn Self-Service** at 14 Craven Rd., half a block from the station and open seven days a week. Convenient to Victoria Station: **Ashbourne Laundry,** 93 Pimlico Rd.

LEAVING LONDON: Simply descend into any subway station of the Piccadilly Line and take the first train (they run every 10 minutes) to the end of the line—Heathrow Airport, 50 minutes and £2 (£2.50 by bus) away. To Gatwick Airport, from which most charter flights leave, you take a direct train from Victoria Station for exactly £3.30, second class.

LONDON ON A BUDGET: You've seen it can be done. Bed and breakfast for $12, luncheon for $3.50, dinner for $4.50, with subway rides at 60¢, and evening theatre seats for $7.50.

———————

And now the stop is Paris, land of François Mitterand, Truffaut and the "prix fixe" meal, where prices are high, but "finds" are everywhere— important, low-cost finds that can enable you to keep room-and-meals costs to $25 or under a day.

The trip from London to Paris is most pleasantly made by plane, which costs little more than the same trip by train and channel steamer. The planes leave London Airport every hour, arrive an hour later at Paris's Charles de Gaulle Airport, from which a bus to the city costs less than $4. Just a short while after leaving London, you're in the place of which you've always dreamed—the City of Light—Paris.

Chapter VII

PARIS

Life in the Latin Quarter

THE PRICES OF PARIS are perhaps the most talked-about topic of European travel. Let's put the matter in a little perspective. Been to New York lately? At their very worst, Parisian prices are no higher than those of New York, even for the most luxurious of purchases. A meal at New York's "21," Caravelle, or Lutèce costs just as much as the world-renowned repasts to be had at Paris's Maxim's, Fouquet's, or Tour d'Argent.

Let's move a step farther. In the middle-class area, Parisian prices are much lower than their New York counterparts. The highest-priced seat at Paris's thrilling Comédie Française costs 85 francs ($10.66). Compare that with the $40 you'd pay for a Broadway show.

And now for the comparison most pertinent to this book: the prices paid by the average Parisian for his or her basic, low-cost needs are so much lower than those in New York that they would set eyes to blinking. The level of those prices permits even a low-salaried Frenchman to live in a most enjoyable French manner. He eats and imbibes regally, because he avoids the glitter of the Champs Elysées, just as you'd avoid Park Avenue. Scattered throughout Paris are incredible values for the tourist on a budget.

Don't, therefore, be fazed by the legend—illogical as well as untrue—that the cost of visiting Paris is simply beyond human means, and that Paris has lost all its charm, as a result. This is still the haven for the adventurous, the resourceful, and the young in heart—the capital of Europe—a city of breathtaking beauty, pervaded throughout with an exciting intellectual atmosphere. It can't be missed, and it needn't be. Can you live enjoyably in Paris on $25 a day? With care, with a proper approach, and with a sort of pinpoint accuracy in choosing your hotel and restaurants, you can. Here's how.

1. Orientation

If you have traveled to Paris by scheduled flight, you'll arrive at **Charles de Gaulle Airport,** from which everyone will advise you to take the Air France bus into town (to the Porte Maillot City Air Terminal) for 30 francs ($3.75) each way. Be it known that the **Roissy Rail bus-train** ride from the airport to Paris's Gare du Nord (look for signs or ask) is both quicker and cheaper (20 francs, $2.50). Same alternative, same saving, is available at **Orly Airport,** where international charter flights land: airport bus to the Invalides Terminal near the Eiffel Tower costs 27 francs ($3.37), while **Orly Rail** to the Boulevard St. Michel station on the Left Bank is 20 francs ($2.50).

THE TRAIN STATIONS OF PARIS: Trains arrive at no fewer than six different, major stations. They are: **Gare du Nord** (for connections with London via Calais-Dover, and Brussels, Amsterdam, Munich, and Vienna); **Gare de l'Est,** a few hundred yards away from the Gare du Nord (for Luxembourg, Strasbourg, Frankfurt, and Zurich); **Gare de Lyon,** located on the Right Bank (for Lyon, Grenoble, Marseille, Nice, Rome); **Gare d'Austerlitz,** on the Left Bank, across the Seine and about 300 yards from the Gare de Lyon (Orleans, Bordeaux, Madrid, Lisbon); **Gare de Montparnasse,** on the Left Bank again (to and from Versailles, Le Mans, Rennes, St. Malo, Brest); and **Gare St. Lazare,** on the Right Bank, half a mile from the Opera (for Cherbourg, Le Havre, Dieppe). Each of these stations has a nearby Métro station bearing the same name. For general train information, phone—day and night—261-50-50.

THOSE MAGNIFICENT SUBWAYS ("THE MÉTRO"): For in-city travel: the Métro. "Three things are cheap in Paris," goes an ancient adage, "bread, wine—and the Métro." Once you get the hang of it, the Paris subway system will become your very best touring aid, inexpensive and efficient. There are 14 subway lines, all criss-crossing each other like the grids on a map. To reach your destination, you must usually make at least one change *(correspondance):* you go up one line and then across another, or across one and then up another. This seems complicated, but the task is eased by a lighted board on the wall next to the ticket booth in most Paris Métro stations. You press a button opposite the name of the station to which you want to go. Immediately, the board lights up, showing the two lines you must take to reach your destination. It becomes clear instantly. Paris subway fare (second class) is 5 francs (about 62¢) to any point in the city; but a book *(carnet)* of ten subway tickets is only 30 francs, reducing the cost of each such ticket to only 3 francs (38¢)—always buy the book of ten tickets.

While there are also buses in Paris (same 5-franc fare, reducing to 3 francs if you buy ten at a time), their routes aren't generally geared for tourist purposes, and they are not heavily used by tourists. Take the Métro

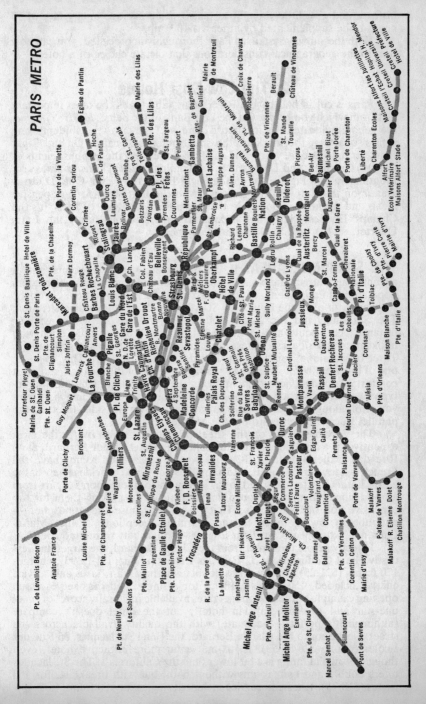

PARIS METRO

instead, and give little thought to taxis, whose average in-city fare of $5 needs to be supplemented by at least a 10% tip.

With the subway system of Paris thoroughly appreciated, you can now turn to the geographical considerations that dictate choice of a hotel:

2. The Low-Cost Hotels

Paris is cut in half by the River Seine, and that's the most important fact from which you begin. On the Left Bank of the Seine, *la Rive Gauche,* are generally located the inexpensive areas of the city—the students' and artists' quarters, the markets, the small hotels and cafes. On the Right Bank, *la Rive Droite,* you'll find the broad avenues, the establishments of Messrs. Givenchy and Dior, and the screaming prices. This isn't always so: Montmartre and Pigalle are on the Right Bank, the swank Quai D'Orsay area is on the Left. But in general, go to the Left Bank for inexpensive meals and accommodations. Go there also for a real taste of Paris; it's the Champs Elysées which has become commercial and hard; the Latin Quarter, on the Left Bank, retains its honesty.

THE SORBONNE AREA: If, in particular, you're a young and/or adventurous tourist, and want to live in a section jammed with the student population of Paris, then take the Métro to the **St. Michel station.** Go up the steps and you're on the Boulevard St. Michel—heart of the university area. The Sorbonne and the Ecole des Beaux Arts are all within walking distance. The Boulevard St. Michel itself is a broad avenue lined with bookstores and sidewalk cafes. Walk up the boulevard as it goes uphill. Three blocks along, you'll find the Rue des Ecoles. Turn left. This, to me, is one of the great hotel streets of Paris. It has some of the cleanest and most comfortable budget accommodations in the city—priced, true, at splurge-type levels in the section closest to the boulevard, but descending in price as you stroll along and particularly as you head down the side streets to the parallel Rue du Sommerard or Rue Monge.

The very best hotel on the street (although it's also by far the most expensive) is a big splurge selection called the **Hotel Claude Bernard,** at 43 Rue des Ecoles (phone 326-32-52), whose upper-floor rooms have tall French windows which open onto a small balcony, and provide a view of the entire Latin Quarter. But, sad to say, every one of those rooms (apart from an odd single) is now equipped with private bath, making them far too expensive for our standards. That's a pity because the atmosphere— undoubtedly owing much to the charming receptionist, Mlle. Marie-Laurence, who speaks excellent English—is unusually warm and friendly.

Directly across the street from the Claude Bernard, the larger and less costly **Hotel California,** at 32 Rue des Ecoles (phone 634-12-90), charges 170 francs ($21.25) for a bathless double with breakfast, taxes and service charge included, 150 francs ($18.75) for a single, and thus serves as an opening example of the low budget rates available in literally scores of small one-star and two-star Parisian hotels; but the hotel doesn't compare (although it's perfectly adequate) with the quality available across the street. Next door to the Claude Bernard, the **Hotel St. Jacques,** 35 Rue des Ecoles (phone 326-82-53), is, to me, a far more attractive hotel, even though its official rating is a bit lower than the California's. The St. Jacques offers double and twin rooms without bath, but with breakfast, for 150 francs ($18.75), taxes and service included; singles for 100 francs ($12.50).

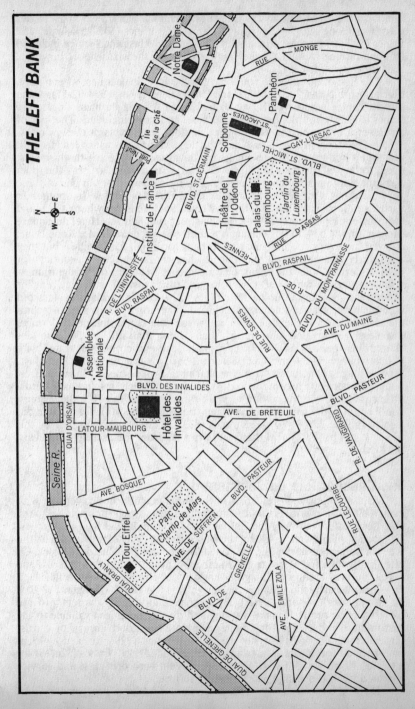

THE LEFT BANK

Similar rates are offered by the **Hotel des Carmes,** a block away at 5 Rue des Carmes (phone 329-78-40), which charges 110 francs ($13.75) single, 180 francs ($22.50) double or twin with shower, breakfast and service included (for indifferent rooms). Three single rooms on the sixth floor, however, rent for only 90 francs!

The first major avenue you'll cross is the Rue St. Jacques, where half a block downhill at #73 you'll find the **Hotel Diana** (phone 354-92-55), a fine budget choice where you'll pay 80 francs ($10) for a bathless single, 140 francs ($17.50) double, breakfast, service, and taxes included. The lack of an elevator in this clean and well-kept six-floor hotel explains the low rates.

A few steps on, you'll pass the Rue de la Montagne, which leads uphill, in about a hundred yards, to a truly medieval section of Paris that remains, even today, a quarter for impoverished writers and artists—the poet Verlaine wrote his famous "Il pleure dans mon coeur . . ." in one of these very buildings. But keep walking along the Rue des Ecoles. In another 20 yards, you'll pass, on the left, the tiny Rue des Bernardins where a new and elevator-equipped hotel at #42 on the street is called the **Hotel du Square Monge,** phone 634-13-00. During a recent visit, its owner, Mr. René Baur, showed me every room. They are perhaps too small for families, but they are utterly clean and well maintained, they contain bidets and outlets for both American and European electric razors (a touch of thoughtfulness you'll appreciate when you travel through other towns), and they rent for 210 francs ($26.25) double, 160 francs ($20) single, with breakfast but without bath, service and taxes included. The hotel receives high recommendation. Across the Rue des Ecoles from the Hotel du Square Monge, the newly renovated and refurbished **Hotel Plaisant,** at 50 Rue des Bernardins (phone 354-74-57), in a small dead-end corner decorated with plants, charges 185 francs ($23.12) for a bathless double room, breakfast, service and tax included. It has a charming proprietress, Madame Brethous, and perfectly acceptable rooms, some with balconies that look onto a little square. If you're willing to walk farther down the Rue des Ecoles, you'll come to the somewhat basic, but friendly, **Hotel Minerve,** 13 Rue des Ecoles (phone 326-81-89); 185 francs ($23.12) double or twin, but by this point, you'll probably feel that you're too far from the exciting Boulevard St. Michel.

The Cheaper Rue du Sommerard

A less expensive hotel street in the same neighborhood, yet one with even a bit more charm, is the Rue du Sommerard, which runs parallel to the Rue des Ecoles, between the Boulevard St. Germain and Rue des Ecoles. To reach it, again walk uphill on the Boulevard St. Michel until you pass the Rue du Sommerard on your left, one block before the Rue des Ecoles. Or else simply take the Métro to the Maubert-Mutualité stop, which is also the closest subway station to the great majority of Rue des Ecoles hotels.

The star attraction here is the sprightly, little **Hotel Marignan,** 13 Rue du Sommerard (phone 325-31-03), whose multilingual owners provide babysitters on request, make washing and ironing facilities available to the customers, send cables for you, and maintain a good library of tourist information. The cost for all this is 160 francs ($20) for a double or twin-bedded room (breakfast and service included), 210 francs ($26.25) for a triple, 90 francs ($11.25) for a single—again with breakfast and service included in all those charges. Showers are free.

Down the block, a close runner-up (and it's a large hotel) is the **Hotel**

Wetter, 9 Rue du Sommerard (phone 634-20-90), which charges far too much for singles, but only 180 francs ($22.50) double, 215 francs ($26.87) triple, all prices including breakfast and taxes. The Wetter's owners, M. and Mme. Lacroix, speak only a bit of English, but their daughter is fluent—a high recommendation for this friendly hotel, whose prices are moderate for rooms of fair quality. If the Wetter is full, walk in the other direction to the much cheaper, and equally popular (mainly among students), starvation budget lodgings of the big **Grand Hotel de la Loire** at 20 Rue du Sommerard, whose English-speaking proprietors—M. and Mme. Victor— receive high praise in a number of recent letters to me. They charge, in 1985, 50 francs ($6.25) single, 65 francs ($8.12) double, 85 francs ($10.62) twin. The hotel has 50 rooms on six floors, but no breakfast is served. Phone 354-47-60.

Off and on the Boulevard St. Michel

Right at the corner of Boulevard St. Michel and Boulevard St. Germain, is the **Hotel Cluny Square,** 21 Boulevard St. Michel (phone 354-21-39), 200 yards from the Métro stop St. Michel; reception desk is on the second floor (there are 28 rooms on four floors), up a spiral stairway. This is one of the great values in town: 65 francs ($8.12) for a single, 90 francs ($11.25) double, 130 francs ($16.25) twin; 15 francs ($1.87) for an optional breakfast, the same for a shower. You'll enjoy the cultivated Quartier Latin atmosphere radiated by the (some-English-speaking) manageress, Madame Goutel.

If you'd prefer to stay closer to the Seine, at the base of the Boulevard St. Michel, and are willing to spend substantially more, then, as you leave the St. Michel Métro exit, look to the left and you'll see two tiny streets: Rue de la Harpe and Rue de la Huchette. At #1 Rue de la Harpe, the **Hotel d'Albe** (phone 634-09-70) charges a top of 280 francs ($35) for breakfast for two, service charge included, in twin-bedded rooms with shower (elevator building, telephones in all the spanking-clean rooms), and is the hotel par excellence for readers who like to be surrounded by color and excitement.

Still another cluster of inexpensive hotels in the $17 range are found on the **Rue Cujas** (two blocks past the Rue des Ecoles, on the left off the Boul' Mich) and around the corner on the **Rue Victor Cousin.**

Top choice here is the **Hotel de la Sorbonne,** 6 Rue Victor Cousin (phone 354-58-08), where a nicely decorated double with phone but no bath is 140 francs ($17.50), breakfast, service, and taxes included. But also highly recommended is the attractive **Hotel Cujas,** 18 Rue Cujas (phone 354-58-10), offering singles with shower for 90 francs ($11.25), doubles and twins for 140 francs ($17.50). All rooms at the **Hotel Saint-Michel,** next door at 19 Rue Cujas (phone 354-47-98), have bath or shower. Rates, *sans* breakfast, are 135 francs ($16.87) single, 250 francs ($31.25) for doubles or twins with complete private bath.

READERS' HOTEL SELECTIONS (BLVD. ST. MICHEL AREA), LEFT BANK: "You have overlooked one of the nicest small hotels in Paris, the **Grand Hotel de Lima** at 46 Blvd. St. Germain (at the corner of Rue des Bernardins), phone 634-02-12. It is immaculate, always warm, and there is always an abundance of hot water. The breakfast coffee is superb, and you get three grand cups of it! Notre Dame Cathedral is a block away, and it's conveniently close to all of the attractions in the student quarter. I lived at the hotel for an entire winter, spring and early summer while I was writing travel stories for the *Houston Post,* and I cannot recommend it enough. The manager, M. Massot, speaks English and has lots of opinions on various matters and an appealing frankness in discussing them with you; his wife is helpful and considerate, and the small staff of maids is efficient. A small single room (with lavatory and bidet) costs 160 francs; doubles cost 190 francs; and doubles with showers are 220 francs. The prices include all service and taxes, and it's only 18 francs more for a good breakfast of rolls, jam, butter, and coffee, which is served either in your room or in a cheerful dining room" (Mary Anne Haynes, New York, New York; note from AF: Nearest Métro stop is Maubert-Mutualité). . . . "At the family-operated **University Hotel**, 160 Rue Saint-Jacques (phone 354-76-79), in the Latin Quarter, all rooms are very clean and rustically furnished with oaken armoires and double beds and are equipped with lavatory and bidet. If you arrive in the tourist season and find your room located on the fifth or sixth floor (no elevator), the fantastic view will be worth the climb. The hotel is ideally situated for sightseeing. The famous Mouffetard Market, the Luxembourg Gardens, the Pantheon, Montparnasse, Notre Dame, and the Centre Pompidou are all within walking distance. And the Sorbonne, that 800-year-old university, is a scant 50 yards away. Two Métro stops are nearby, also" (Tim Farley, Paris; note from AF: 1985 rates here are 75 to 120 francs, $9.37 to $15, for singles, 130 to 150 francs, $16.25 to $18.75, for doubles, 140 to 160 francs, $17.50 to $20, for twins, including breakfast. The higher rates apply to the lower floors of this six-story building. Nearest Métro stops: Luxembourg and Maubert-Mutualité).

ST. GERMAIN DES PRÉS:

Although the Sorbonne area has more moderately priced hotels than any other district in Paris (and thus provides you with the optimum chance of finding a budget room in the summer months), nevertheless, the district can't compare in color and charm with the bustling area around the Ecole des Beaux Arts, near the Seine. How would you now like to live la vie bohème, and plunge into a world of art galleries and studios, palettes and beards? Walk down the Boulevard St. Germain to the breathtakingly beautiful **Eglise** (church) **St. Germain des Prés,** and turn right on the Rue Bonaparte, to the Seine. As you approach the river, you'll pass the Rue Jacob. And if you turn right on the Rue Jacob, you'll come to the Rue de Seine. These are the three blocks for budget hotels in this area: the Rue Bonaparte, the Rue Jacob, and the Rue de Seine. The Métro stop for all three is called St. Germain, and as you consider stopping there, keep in mind that the hotels in this district (the 6th arrondissement, around the St. Germain des Prés church) are of a slightly higher quality and price than those in the preceding section (the 5th arrondissement, around the student-packed Boulevard St. Michel); they also cater to a somewhat older age level than do the hotels near the Boulevard St. Michel.

Several hotels on these blocks offer especial values for their rooms with private bath. On the Rue Jacob, for instance, the redecorated, now stylish, and elevator-equipped **Hotel des Deux Continents,** at #25 (phone 326-72-46), offers doubles with private shower for 260 francs ($32.50), doubles with bath and w.c. for 295 francs ($36.87), inclusive of breakfast and all else.

In the very same area, on the Rue Bonaparte, but this time on the other side of Boulevard St. Germain, the **Hotel Bonaparte,** 61 Rue Bonaparte (phone 326-97-37), is a turn-of-the-century-type establishment, with elegance, chic, and enormous rooms, and average room charges of 250 francs ($31.25) for a double with bath, two breakfasts included, 225 francs ($28.12) single. Many ladies stay here and love it; don't be discouraged by the small and incongruous service station on one side of the street—around the corner is a lovely little square. A scant block from the church, and right near the famed Café Flore, the **Hotel Montana,** 28 Rue St. Benoit (phone

548-62-15), rents bathless doubles for 175 francs ($21.87), doubles with private shower for 240 francs ($30), those rates not including breakfast.

Throughout this section, inexpensive restaurants abound, and there are markets, cafes, theatres—much life. The late Jean-Paul Sartre lived one block from the St. Germain Métro stop.

THE LUXEMBOURG GARDENS:

THE LUXEMBOURG GARDENS: For families traveling with children, the top hotel section in Paris is just below the beautiful Luxembourg Gardens (still on the Left Bank), where there are enclosed playing areas, with attendants, and an atmosphere of peace and charm. And on a quiet street called Rue Madame, which runs just parallel to the gardens, families have flocked for many years, with good results, to **Regent's Hotel** at 44 Rue Madame (phone 548-02-81), in a completely new building, modern and sparkling clean, and with elevator. At Regent's, you'll pay 275 francs ($34.37) for a double with shower, two breakfasts included.

To reach any hotel in this area, take the Métro to the St. Sulpice or St. Placide stop. You'll find that you're only a short walk away from the bustling St. Germain des Prés, and yet in a calm residential section.

PLACE DE L'ODÉON:

PLACE DE L'ODÉON: As our last Left Bank hotel area, we've chosen a locale for older readers who'd like to be near the excitement of the Left Bank, but who wish to stay in quiet, and relatively dignified, surroundings. That prescription is filled by the stately Odéon, a square dominated by the marble Théâtre de France, which is one of the three state-run theaters in Paris. Only three blocks away is the Boulevard St. Michel; but here it's a different world.

On one side of the square, the **Michelet Odéon,** 6 Place de l'Odéon (phone 634-27-80), is a beautiful budget hotel, but one in which nearly every room is now with shower or bath, for which the charge is 310 francs ($38.75) double, including breakfast, service and tax. Perfect for that occasional splurge. On the streets that run off from the Odéon, the cheaper hotels are on the Rue Casimir-Delavigne, where two generally lower-cost choices, both close to the square, are excellent for older tourists: the **Hotel des Balcons,** 3 Rue Casimir-Delavigne, phone 634-78-50 (doubles with breakfast for 165 francs, $20.62, and every room possessing a balcony); and the **Hotel St. Sulpice,** 7 Rue Casimir-Delavigne, phone 326-94-44 (doubles with bath and w.c. for 250 francs—$31.25—including breakfast and service). The Métro stop for all the above choices is, of course, Odéon.

READERS' HOTEL SELECTIONS (AREA OF THE ODÉON), LEFT BANK: "A lovely pension near the Place de l'Odéon is the **Hotel des Ecoles,** 19 Rue Monsieur-le-Prince, operated by the delightful Mr. Boissier. We had a room for two for 200 francs ($25), including a fantastic free breakfast of baguettes and croissants" (Dr. and Mrs. John Dabel, Dover, Delaware). . . . "At the **Grand Hotel des Etrangers,** 2 Rue Racine (phone 634-26-50), just off the Boulevard St. Michel a block from its intersection with the Boulevard St. Germain, a clean, bathless double, large, costs 200 francs a night, including breakfast. Fluent English spoken by the management" (Richard and Jean Hjorth, Cherry Hill, New Jersey).

CHAMPS ELYSÉES—ARC DE TRIOMPHE:

CHAMPS ELYSÉES—ARC DE TRIOMPHE: Most of the older readers of this book, however, will probably prefer to live in an area closer to the shopping districts of the Right Bank, and less infused with students. While the Odéon and Ecole des Beaux Arts area on the Left Bank will appeal to some, there are several different Right Bank sections—the Arc de Triomphe area, the streets near the Palais Royal and the Louvre, the area of the Opera, and others—which should suit these wants with precision.

The most plentiful cluster of budget hotels on the Right Bank is found—surprisingly enough—in a small area just two and three short blocks from the Arc de Triomphe. If you want to be sure that you'll find an available room on the Right Bank without much searching, then this is the section to visit.

Walk up the Champs Elysées to the Arc de Triomphe. That monument stands on a plaza now formally named the "Place Charles de Gaulle," but popularly known as **L'Etoile**—so called because it forms the axle of twelve broad avenues, which radiate out like the spokes of a wheel. The inexpensive hotels are to be found at the right of the Arc de Triomphe, as you face it from the Champs Elysées, and they are mainly on the side streets which intersect the spoke-like avenues.

Rue Troyon, Rue Brey

Walk away from the Arc de Triomphe down the Avenue de Wagram. After two blocks, you'll see the Rue Troyon. Here, at #10, **Hotel Troyon** (phone 380-14-09), equips all rooms with shower or bath and private w.c., yet charges only 160 francs ($20) for singles, 220 francs ($27.50) for doubles, and—for families or small groups—390 francs ($48.75) for one of six large, 4-bedded rooms. One block farther down Avenue de Wagram, the Rue Brey turns up and there the Hotel Wagram and Hotel Tilsitt, at numbers 3 and 23, are top choices in this normally expensive Arc de Triomphe district. **Hotel Wagram** (phone 380-15-52), is the better of the two, charging 200 francs ($25) for one of 15 bathless twins (the remaining 30 doubles are with bath and w.c. and too costly for our needs). **Hotel Tilsitt** (phone 380-39-71) is much smaller and more basic, but still quite acceptable, at a rate of 160 francs ($20) for a twin without bath, breakfast included.

Downhill on the Champs Elysées

Other hotel-bearing streets just off from the Champs Elysées itself, a few hundred yards before you reach the Arc de Triomphe. The side streets to the left of the Champs, as you approach the Arch, house the expensive ones. The narrower and more bustling shopping streets to the right of the Champs provide a few good budget choices. On the Rue de Colisée, for instance, just 30 yards from the Champs Elysées, the **Hotel Royal,** at 7 Rue du Colisée (phone 359-32-40), has clean, but compact, double rooms with bath for 265 francs ($33.12) a night; and though it's on the busiest little side street you can imagine, its location is a superb one, just a few feet from a Métro exit on the Champs Elysées (which I believe is the Franklin Roosevelt stop).

IN PIGALLE: Near the heart of this sometimes raucous area, whose reputation is worse than the reality of it, and on a quiet and rather charming side street that suggests the middle-class character of the neighborhood in former times, stands the **Hotel de Navarin et d'Angleterre,** 8 Rue Navarin (phone 878-3180), whose proprietress—Mme. Ginette Maylin—is unusually cordial to visiting Englishmen and Americans. As summer of 1985

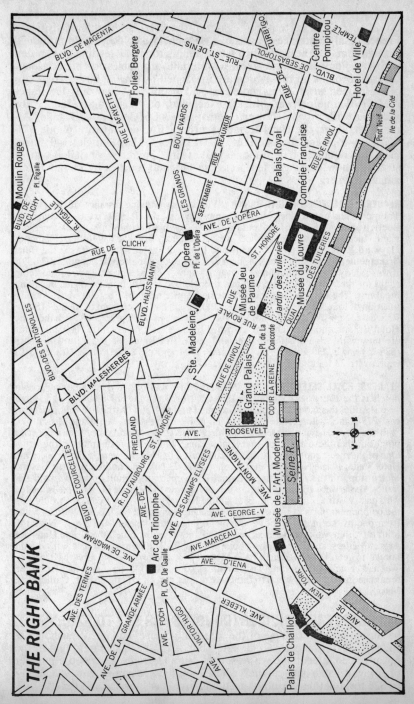

THE RIGHT BANK

BLVD. DE MAGENTA

Folies Bergère

RUE—ST.DENIS

RUE DE SEBASTOPOL

BLVD. DE SEBASTOPOL

RUE DE TURBIGO

TEMPLE

Centre Pompidou

Hotel de Ville

Pont Neuf

Ile de la Cité

RUE LAFAYETTE

BOULEVARDS

RUE REAUMUR

Palais Royal

Comédie Française

RUE DE RIVOLI

Moulin Rouge

BLVD. DE CLICHY · Pl. Pigalle

R. PIGALLE

RUE DE CLICHY

LES GRANDS

4 SEPTEMBRE

AVE. DE L'OPERA

Opéra

Pl. de L'Opéra

ST. HONORE

Musée du Louvre

Jardin des Tuileries

DES TUILERIES

QUAI

BLVD. HAUSSMANN

BLVD.-DES BATIGNOLLES

Ste. Madeleine

RUE ROYALE

RUE

Musée Jeu de Paume

RUE DE RIVOLI

BLVD. MALESHERBES

Pl. de La Concorde

Grand Palais

COUR LA REINE

Seine R.

FRIEDLAND

BLVD. DE COURCELLES

ST. HONORE

AVE.

ROOSEVELT

AVE. DES CHAMPS ELYSEES

AVE. MONTAIGNE

Musée de L'Art Moderne

R. DU FAUBOURG ST. HONORE

AVE. DE

AVE. GEORGE-V

AVE. DE WAGRAM

Arc de Triomphe

Pl. Ch. De Gaulle

AVE.MARCEAU

AVE. D'IENA

NEW YORK

AVE. DE

AVE. DES TERNES

AVE. DE LA GRANDE ARMEE

AVE. FOCH

VICTOR HUGO

AVE. KLEBER

AVE.

Palais de Chaillot

N

S

E

W

approaches, Mme. Ginette is busily redoing rooms and lobby, which is a pity, because the current impression of the hotel is like that of visiting a French family: entrance consists of a glass-enclosed office, an old-fashioned sitting room, a typically French family dining room, all leading to a garden with two immense acacia trees, a waterfall, and tables for breakfasting. Guests in rooms on the garden are awakened by singing birds. There are old-fashioned guest rooms, no elevator. For this you'll pay only 175 francs ($21.87) double or twin, breakfast included, only 210 francs ($26.25) for a double with private shower. Métro stop is St. Georges or Pigalle. Almost next door, the **Hotel Royal Navarin,** 7 Rue de Navarin (phone 878-5173), is good for the overflow, at 90 francs ($11.25) single, 140 francs ($17.50) double, 160 francs ($20) twin, breakfast included, in a structure now bearing a few welcome Oriental touchès by its new Vietnamese owner.

READERS' SELECTIONS (RIGHT BANK): "Within easy walking distance of the Arc de Triomphe, and only a block off the Champs Elysées, the **Hotel D'Artois,** 94 Rue de la Boetie (phone 225-76-65), gave us a double room with bidet and toilet for $36 a night. Included were tax, services and continental breakfast" (Robert Shannon, Hayward, California). . . . "My wife and I were delighted with our stay at the **Hotel Britannique,** 20 Avenue Victoria, near Boulevard de Sebastopol (phone 233-74-59). It was run by a most helpful and engaging famly. We had a huge, light, comfortable room for three with a double bed and a single bed for 320 francs a night, including breakfast. The hotel is conveniently located, quite near the Chatelet Métro stop (a junction of four Métro lines), on the Right Bank, a half-block from the Seine" (Sayre P. Schatz, New York, N.Y.; note by AF: I have seen photographs of the handsome Hotel Britannique, which has been owned by the Perret family since 1860; all rooms are now with private bath, shower and color TV. Rates for 1985 are 210 francs ($26.25) single, 230 francs ($28.75) double, 250 francs ($31.25) twin, 320 francs ($40) triple, with 20 francs extra for an optional breakfast).

READERS' HOTEL SELECTIONS (THE MARAIS, RIGHT BANK): "A jewel among Parisian hotels is the **Hotel des Celestins,** 1 Rue Charles V (phone 887-87-04). Near Métro stop Bastille, this modest hotel is clean, quiet and well run. Attractive rooms for two cost 275 francs with private bath" (Mrs. L.D. Eykelboom, Meridian, Miss.). . . . "Although you have a subsection entitled 'Don't Miss the Marais,' you neglect to point out that there are some marvelous, cheap hotels and restaurants in this area. One of the nicest rooms my husband and I stayed in while we were in Paris was in the **Hotel Stella,** 14 rue Neuve St. Pierre (phone 272-23-66). This hotel is near the Bastille Métro stop, off the Rue de St. Antoine. For a charming double room, we paid 150 francs. Baths were 16 francs extra, per person. And the Rue de St. Antoine is loaded with pastry, wine, cheese, and meat shops. For very satisfying meals, we would buy the component parts at these stores—often supplemented by deliciously fresh fruits from one of the many street vendors who lined both sides of the street. Near the Marais (within walking distance), we found another great hotel, the **Grand Hotel des Arts et Métiers,** at 4 Rue Borda (phone 887-73-89). The best way to reach this quaint hotel is to get off at either the Arts & Metiers Métro stop or the Republic Métro stop. We had a delightful room, with small balcony, for 145 francs—which included breakfast in bed! Baths were 16 francs extra, per person" (Gale Glazer, Cambridge, Mass.).

SIX SCATTERED CHOICES (DOUBLES FOR $17 TO $26):

Finally, because a high percentage of the foregoing choices charge as much as $22 single, $30 for a bathless double (but scan the text carefully for the lower-priced selections), we've sought out and briefly described a number of always reliable budget hotels whose rates have remained, for 1985, at $17 to $26 for a bathless double, including breakfast, service and tax.

Left Bank

Hotel des Grandes Ecoles, 75 Rue du Cardinal-Lemoine (phone 326-7923), has unusual character, and an unusual location in a lovely garden off the street: one enters through high wooden gates and then passes along a cobbled lane to the garden. Simple but practical rooms, new beds, nice proprietors, relaxed clientele; you'll need advance reservations for this one. Bathless doubles are 140 francs ($17.50); triples 175 francs ($21.87), singles aren't available.

Hotel du Centre, 24 bis Rue Cler (phone 705-5233); Métro: Ecole Militaire; is located above one of the colorful food shops that line the Rue Cler, itself one of the major market streets of the 7th arrondissement. Once you've climbed to the upstairs reception area, you'll find a gaily decorated lounge that more nearly resembles the foyer to a private apartment than to a hotel. There are 29 rooms here, small but clean, and renting for 110 francs ($13.75) single, 185 francs ($23.12) double, and 15 francs extra for breakfast.

Hotel de la Loire, 39 Rue du Moulin-Vert (phone 540-6688), Métro: Alesia or Plaisance, in Montparnasse, is an ideal choice for visitors seeking unusually quiet surroundings. In this three-floor structure without elevator, rooms are tastefully furnished, with wall-to-wall carpeting, and consist of singles 95 francs ($11.87), doubles *grand lit* (double bed) 115 francs ($14.37), twins 130 francs ($16.25), double *grand lit* with shower and private w.c. 225 francs ($28.12), same but with twin beds 208 francs ($26), same but with three beds 265 francs ($33.12), breakfast 20 francs ($2.50) extra. The charming owner speaks little English, but employs English-speaking help in the busy summer season.

READERS' HOTEL SELECTIONS (NEAR AIR TERMINAL INVALIDES, LEFT BANK): "I was searching for a hotel near the 'Aerogare,' the Paris Air Terminal (behind les Invalides), from where I could later on take my return trip to New York. Five hundred yards away, I hit upon the **Comète Hotel,** 159 Rue de la Comète, phone 705-0853. As I inquired, the most friendly and helpful proprietress said she charges 135 francs ($16.87) for a single room, including breakfast. This price seemed very satisfactory, as other hotels around the Gare du Nord (where I had to stay first) charged around 160 francs. This happened in the first week of July. And when I returned to Paris at the end of August and took a room at the Comète, to my surprise I was charged only 120 francs for the single room with breakfast. Friends of mine to whom I recommended the hotel occupied a large double room with shower and toilet for 220 francs; seemingly because the tourist season was regarded as over" (Peter N. Abbott, New York, New York). . . . "The oddly named **Pretty Hotel,** 8 Bis Rue Amelie, phone 705-46-21, is family run, with Miss Alice Leroux-Girard carrying on a tradition which goes back to the end of World War II. Henry Miller stayed here once! Staff is extremely nice; breakfast good, location near the Latour-Maubourg stop in the Aerogare des Invalides area. A gem. The best part? Their 57 rooms are 110 francs single, 135 francs double, including breakfast. This hotel saved us financially in Paris." (A.J. and M.B. Rockmore, San Francisco, Ca.).

READERS' HOTEL SELECTION (LEFT BANK, EIFFEL TOWER AREA): "The **Grand Hotel Leveque,** 29 Rue Cler (phone 705-49-15), near Métro stop Ecole Militaire, on a picturesque, pedestrian, open-street market near the Eiffel Tower, charges only 105 francs ($13.12) single, only 150 francs ($18.75) for a double, has a very friendly, English-speaking management" (Lynne Coumier, Windham, New Hampshire).

Right Bank (near Gare du Nord)

Arriving with the boat train at dawn or late at night, exhausted and not in the mood for a Métro trip, you may find the location of the **Hotel Paradis,** at 9 Rue de Paradis (phone 770-18-28), 350 yards from the Gare du Nord, appealing. Room-and-breakfast rates, guaranteed till the end of 1985 by owner M. Massine: 160 francs ($20) for a double, 190 francs ($23.75) for a twin, 225 francs ($28.12) double with shower and w.c., 280 francs ($35) twin with shower and w.c.

Right Bank (near Gare de l'Est)

And near this popular station, in a welter of hotels not all of which are nearly as suitable inside as they may appear from without, two comfortable budget hotels, personally checked in the summer of 1984, are: **Hotel Liège-Strasbourg,** 67 Blvd. de Strasbourg (phone 770-10-57), five floors, an elevator, and double rooms with private w.c. ranging from 155 francs ($19.37) to 262 francs ($32.75) in price; and **Hotel de Londres et d'Anvers,** 133 Blvd. Magenta (phone 285-28-26), six floors with elevator, offering rooms without bath for 130 francs ($16.25) single, 170 francs ($21.25) double or twin, 205 francs ($25.62) triple, not including breakfast (20 francs—$2.50) or showers down the hall (18 francs—$2.25, per optional shower). The latter, managed by André Tritsch, beautifully fluent in English, is no more than five minutes on foot from the station.

READERS' HOTEL SELECTIONS (NEAR RAILROAD STATIONS, RIGHT BANK): "Right opposite the Gare de l'Est and about 20 feet from the Métro station, **Hotel de Champagne et de Mulhouse,** 87 Boulevard de Strasbourg (phone 607-51-26), is a fine choice for the middle-bracket visitor. Rates for a room with shower and w.c., breakfast included, are 195 francs single, only 245 francs double, and everything is very clean" (Tino Christofilis, Nassau, Bahamas). . . . "A well-located hotel—the **Little Regina Hotel,** 89 Blvd. de Strasbourg (phone 607-86-73), Paris 10e, right opposite the Gare de l'Est—offers a small single room, without bath—wonderful comfortable bed—for 145 francs ($18.12), breakfast, service and tax included. M. Corbel, who speaks English, owns this with his charming mother" (Mrs. Christine Mead, London, England). . . . "My family and I found the rooms to be well-furnished, clean, and very moderately priced (190 francs for a double without shower, 245 francs for a double with shower) at the **Helvetia Hotel,** 28 bis Boulevard Diderot (phone 343-25-19), only 1½ blocks from the Gare de Lyon. And breakfast is included in the rates" (Andrew Hickerson, age 12, Kowloon, Hong Kong).

PARISIAN PENSIONS: Readers who plan a fairly lengthy visit to Paris may want to consider staying in a family-operated pension, where they can take meals along with their room. Among the establishments offering those arrangements are the well-recommended: **Résidence "Littré,"** 44 Rue d'Assas (phone 548-89-72), charging weekly rates of 950 francs ($118.75) per person for room and two meals, with wine included; it's within view of the Luxembourg Gardens; **Pension Pédron Ladagnous,** 78 Rue d'Assas (phone 326-7932), 150 francs, or $18.75, per person for room and demi-pension; **Les Marronniers,** 78 Rue d'Assas (phone 326-37-71), offering accommodations to tourists (minimum stay: 4 weeks), demi-pension boarders for 165 francs ($20.62) per day; vegetarian cuisine can be arranged; **Residence LaFayette,** 24 Rue Buffault, phone 878-73-57 (Métro: Cadet), with charming, sunny rooms, 140 francs ($17.50) per person, demi-pension

—monthly stays are asked! Three of these pensions—Littré, LaFayette, and Ladagnous—accept tourists only between July 1 and September 30, although Ladagnous sometimes grudgingly accepts a foreign visitor in the winter months, too. Another well-recommended establishment, **Residence Cardinal,** 4 Rue du Cardinal Mercier, phone 874-1616 (in the area of the Place Clichy, near raucous Pigalle), offers rooms with two meals for 2,700 francs per person per month (and Scott Fitzgerald lived here in the '20s).

STARVATION BUDGET HOTELS: And now we descend in price.

Cleanliness fetishists among our starvation budgeteers will like the big **Hotel des Bains,** 33 Rue Delambre, which runs directly off the broad Boulevard Montparnasse, near the intersection of the Boulevard Raspail, Métro: Vavin, ten yards away (phone 320-85-27), which happens to be a public baths building as well as a hotel. There is no end to the hot showers (7 francs) available here! Actually, the very clean, very proper hotel is physically separate from the baths, and the rooms—all of which are doubles—resemble what you'd find in the ordinary species of hotel. Twenty of the rooms rent for 120 francs ($15)—that's for *two* people, remember! —while ten larger ones go for 180 francs ($22.50), service and tax included (with breakfast an extra 12 francs per person). A single drawback for shy people is that none of the rooms has twin beds, but are equipped instead with what the French call *un lit* (bed) *matrimoniale* (a large one).

Perhaps the largest cluster of cheap-but-decent hotels in Paris ($6 to $8 per person, per night) are found on the romantic **Ile St. Louis**—that little island in the Seine that seems to be annexed to the larger Ile de la Cité, on which Notre Dame stands. On the adjoining Ile de la Cité, the **Hotel Henry IV,** 25 Place Dauphine (phone 354-44-53), charges 73 francs for singles, 102 francs double or twin, 140 francs triple, 160 francs for four, including breakfast and service. M. Balitrand is the English-speaking owner; he requires a $25 deposit for reservations.

READERS' SELECTIONS (STARVATION BUDGET): "Le Foyer International des Etudiantes, 93 Blvd. St. Michel, phone 354-49-63, houses women throughout the year (male students in summer only) for 65 francs per person a night, breakfast extra, in twin-bedded rooms, for a minimum stay of five nights. That's in the heart of the Latin Quarter, near the Luxembourg Gardens, and the accommodations are neat and comfortable with shower" (Jeannine Beaudoin, Paris, France). . . . "A fantastic find in Paris—the bargain of our trip—was Hotel Castex, 5 Rue Castex (phone 272-31-52), near the Bastille Métro stop. Not only were the rooms clean, comfortable, and cheap, but the owner (who speaks no English) was nevertheless very helpful. All rooms were 85 francs, whether for one person or two (thus, 42.50 francs each)" (Jonathan Rudensky, Belle Harbor, New York; note from AF: This astonishing rate has been reconfirmed for 1985, but breakfast will be extra, at 15 francs per person).

3. Students in Paris

The most exalted citizens of France are students—and that's a category applied as easily to a sophomore from Rutgers as to an existentialist from the Sorbonne. Any student, whether French or foreign, studying in Paris or simply there on vacation, can take advantage of literally dozens of government-operated, or government-subsidized, student hotels, and of more than 30 student restaurants, in Paris, whose prices (about $9 for bed and breakfast, around $3.30 for meals) are among the best values in

Europe. Generally (but not always), you'll need proof of full-time student status, best obtained by requesting an International Student Identity Card (which costs $8) from the **Council on International Educational Exchange (C.I.E.E),** 205 East 42nd St., New York, New York 10017 (phone 212/661-1414), or 49 Rue Pierre Charron, Paris 8e (phone 359-2369). Write first for the application form which, properly filled out and submitted with payment, will later result in your receiving the all-important card. With one, you can then proceed to obtain your housing and meals in Paris by contacting any one of the following three organizations:

THE O.T.U.: First, and best of all, visit or phone the **Organisation pour le Tourisme Universitaire** (O. T. U.), 137 Boulevard St. Michel, next to the Port Royal Métro stop (phone 329-12-88) the moment you arrive in Paris. Ask for Mademoiselle Ritz. She'll assign you a single room in a centrally located student hotel or residence, requiring only that you stay a minimum of five days and that you have arrived between July 1 and September 20. Should you need such assistance either very early or late in the day (O.T.U. is open only during normal office hours), or on Sundays or holidays, visit or call La Maison des Eleves Ingenieurs Arts et Metiers, 33 Boulevard Jourdan (phone 253-51-44), nearest Métro stop Cité Universitaire. It too will book you into student accommodations, again in single rooms, for 65 francs ($8.12) per night. Even if you don't plan to use O.T.U.'s accommodation service, you should drop in to pick up their list of student restaurants serving meals for $3 (hors d'oeuvres, entree, dessert and beverage) and to obtain current information on where student meal tickets can be gotten (one student restaurant at which these are always available is the big **Mabillon,** at 3 Rue Mabillon, near the St. Germain des Prés Métro stop, where an average of 4,000 lunches and suppers are served on weekdays. Open Monday to Friday from 11:30 a.m. to 2 p.m. and 6 to 8 p.m. Others, more likely to be open in August and September, include the **Censier,** 5 Rue Censier; the **Cuvier,** 8 bis Rue Cuvier). There's also a bulletin board here that simultaneously offers car rides and the like, and also portrays the hijinks of Parisian studentdom: "Jeune étudiant Canadien cherche une jeune fille qui veut faire l'auto-stop en Suède."

CITÉ UNIVERSITAIRE: Contrary to popular impression, the O.T.U. will not book you into any of the buildings of Paris's famous **Cité Universitaire** —that vast complex of 37 student residences situated at the side of the Parc Montsouris, 10 minutes out from the Latin Quarter. Rather, O.T.U. utilizes centrally located and scattered student hotels, in the heart of the central city.

If you'd prefer to live in this total student community—whose 37 buildings, each surrounded by gardens, are nothing less than the "city" their title proclaims—then write to the **Foundation Nationale de la Cité Universitaire,** 19 Boulevard Jourdan, Paris 14e, which accepts foreign students and teachers during the period from July 1 to September 30 (minimum stay, two weeks). Specify your dates of arrival and departure in Paris, and whether you require a single room or will agree to share a twin-bedded room. They'll house you in one of the 37 "Maisons" of the Cité (if you write at least a month in advance), and charge you only 60 francs ($7.50) per person per day in a double room, 70 francs in a single;

meals generally run around 24 francs ($3). The Cité possesses over 4,300 rooms, and its major congregating spot during the summer is La Maison Internationale, with its game room and lounges, restaurants, gymnasium and tennis courts; this was built by John D. Rockefeller, Jr., and is a sister institution to the "international houses" he founded at Berkeley, Chicago and Columbia Universities; mammoth cafeteria inside, where meals are 24 francs. An alternate name for the institution you'll be visiting: Cité Internationale de l'Université de Paris; I've heard of students appearing on the spot for accommodations, without reservations (Métro stop is Cité Universitaire), but that's tricky: phone 589-68-52, first.

ACCUEIL DES JEUNES EN FRANCE: A final, room-finding, student and youth-helping organization, **Accueil des Jeunes en France,** with offices at 119 Rue St. Martin (directly across from the Centre Pompidou; Métro: Châtelet or Les Halles) and at 16 Rue du Pont Louis Philippe (near the Ile St. Louis; Métro: Hôtel de Ville), operates a youth accommodations service every month of the year, weekdays from 9:30 a.m. to 7 p.m. At either office, and for only 55 francs ($6.87) per night, including breakfast, you'll be assigned a cot in a two- to four-bedded room at one of four major student hostels located at 11 Rue du Fauconnier, 12 Rue des Barres, 6 Rue Francois Miron, and at 6 Rue de Fourcy, or at a low-cost tourist hotel or youth center, all within easy walking distance of both Accueil des Jeunes offices. Although the Accueil advises you to apply in person, they have occasionally been known to respond to a call: phone 277-87-80 for the 119 Rue St. Martin branch (situated near the two ventilation pipes of the Centre Pompidou), and phone 278-04-82 for the branch at 16 Rue du Pont Louis Philippe.

STUDENTS' STARVATION BUDGET: The **Association des Etudiants Protestants de Paris,** 46 Rue de Vaugirard (phone 633-23-30), Métro stop is Luxembourg or Odéon (in the Sorbonne area), accepts foreign students of both sexes throughout the year, charges only 50 francs ($6.25) in four- to five-bedded dorms, 55 francs in a double, 65 francs in a single, breakfast and free showers included. Minimum stay of five days; office remains open on Sundays from 10 a.m. to noon, too. On the right bank, near the Louvre (Métro stop is Palais Royal), the **Foyer Jacques de Rufz de Lavison,** 18 Rue J. J. Rousseau (phone 508-02-10), takes student-age foreigners of both sexes, from June 1 to September 30, for 65 francs per person, including breakfast, in either single, double, triple or quadruple rooms (80 beds total). This one sports a courtyard garden, and is beautifully located, just off the Rue de Rivoli. Sharing this superb location, accepting students *all* year round and offering 200 beds is the **Centre International Louvre,** 20 rue Jean-Jacques Rousseau (phone 236-88-18), where arrangements are provided on a demi-pension basis at 95 francs ($11.87) per day, or full pension at 130 francs ($16.25). There are three to six beds per room. Management is top-notch, and the mix of nationalities makes for a polyglot's paradise.

OTHER STUDENT FACILITIES: Not to be compared with the Cité Universitaire, but still a cut above the quality of most other student accommodations, in central Paris, is **La Maison des Clubs Unesco,** with two hostels (160 beds); one at 13 Rue de Vaugirard, 20 yards from the Boulevard St. Michel (phone 326-50-78); the other, same name, at 43 Rue de la Glacière, also on the Left Bank (nearest Métro stop Glacière, phone 336-00-63), for both men and women. Sixty-five francs ($8.12) per person in two- to eight-bedded rooms, breakfast and shower included. Simpler, much cheaper, and very central, near the Folies Bergère (Right Bank), is Paris's **YMCA** (**UCJG** in French), at 14 Rue de Trevise (phone 770-90-94), charging 85 francs ($10.62) per night for bed and two meals (half-board).

4. The 12 Best Budget Restaurants: Full Meals for $4.12 to $5.87, Wine Included

Finding an inexpensive restaurant in Paris is much harder than finding an inexpensive hotel. The French place much more emphasis on food than we do, and devote much more of their budget to it. There will be times in Paris when you will wonder where the non-millionaires could possibly eat.

But there are inexpensive restaurants in Paris, and the quality of their cuisine, at the prices they charge, makes for an astonishing value. If you'll follow our street directions, and plan to be in certain locations at meal-times, you'll experience what can only be described as miracles in budget eating. They fall into three price categories: the unbelievable finds serving three-course meals for $4.12 to $5.87; the numerous cafeterias where three courses and beverage can be had for about $4 to $5 (and individual plates for less); the bistros (little family-operated restaurants) where you can obtain full meals for $6.50 to $8.

Category One follows now. There are, I can say with foot-weary certainty, precisely 12 of these little wonders (for I've searched, oh how I've searched). And since their prices and typical French cuisine are all fairly similar, I'll devote—in most instances—more space to describing where they are than what they're like.

ON AND OFF THE "GRANDS BOULEVARDS" (RIGHT BANK): (1)

Le Drouot, 103 Rue de Richelieu (Métro stop is Richelieu-Drouot): To find this first "little wonder," you should know that the term "Grands Boulevards" refers to the single avenue that starts out at the Opera as the Boulevard des Italiens, then changes its name successively into the Boulevard Montmartre, Boulevard Poissoniere, Boulevard Bonne Nouvelle, Boulevard St. Denis, Boulevard St. Martin. It's a broad, bustling thoroughfare, lined with movie theatres, variety music halls, stores and shops, that progressively gets poorer, and therefore more interesting, as you stroll along it—and to stroll along it is the advice of a famous Yves Montand recording, in which he tells you there are *tant de choses à voir* (so many things to see) here, including, I might add, Communist Party headquarters, decked out with red flags. If, from the Opera, you'll walk for five minutes down the Boulevard des Italiens, to that point where the avenue veers right and becomes the Boulevard Montmartre, you'll find the famous Le Drouot, upstairs, at the corner of Boulevard des Italiens and Rue de Richelieu (it's 20 yards down on the Rue de Richelieu; revolving doors, a small green sign, and a blackboard listing plates of the day, are all you'll see). Upstairs, you'll emerge into a large room decorated in 1920s modern, where hundreds of non-tourist Parisians dine on appetizers priced at 6 francs, on main courses with vegetables (cassoulet parisien, rognons sauté aux champignons, many others) that average 18 francs, and on cheese or other desserts—many of which are priced between 6 and 7 francs. Meals for $5, which includes a 12% service charge, are easily possible. Open from 11 a.m. to 3 p.m., from 6 to 9:30 p.m., every day of the week throughout the year, and much less crowded at night than it is at lunch.

(2) **Restaurant Chartier,** 7 Rue du Faubourg Montmartre: Walk one block farther along the "Grands Boulevards" (here, the Boulevard Montmartre) until you come to the Rue du Faubourg Montmartre; turn left and in 30 yards, on a colorful open market street, you'll see a courtyard, at the end of which is a mammoth, wood-paneled former library (you can still see the index card files) housing the Restaurant Chartier. Here, if you can imagine it, the charges are even lower than at Le Drouot and the setting more picturesque. And thus, if you'll have pâté de campagne (6 francs) or a tomato salad (6 francs) to begin, then a plate like langue de boeuf sauce piquante (beef tongue in a spicy sauce, with potatoes, 18 francs) and yaourt (yogurt) for dessert (5 francs), you'll pay a total of about 35 francs including wine, but plus a 12% service charge. Open every day of the week, for both meals.

NEAR THE COMÉDIE FRANÇAISE (RIGHT BANK): (3) Ma
Normandie, 11 Rue Rameau, decorated and furnished in "Normandie" style, serves a 3-course prix-fixe menu for 36 francs ($4.50), this time including wine (red, white or rosé) served in brown pitchers, or a bottle of cider—a typical product of Normandy. The available choices are listed on a blackboard hanging on a wall opposite the entrance, and provide as many as five selections for your appetizer, as many as five main plates (including coq au vin, choucroute and other mouth-watering French specialties). From the Comédie Française, walk up the Rue Richelieu until you find the Rue Rameau on your left, four short blocks up. Open Monday to Friday only, from 11 a.m. to 2:30 p.m.

IN MONTPARNASSE (LEFT BANK): (4) Chez Wadja, 10 rue de la
Grande Chaumiére, off the Boulevard Montparnasse (near Métro stop Vavin), has been operated for over 40 years by a Polish immigrant family. They serve a delicious 36-franc ($4.50), three-course menu, wine included, and a variety of other dishes, such as a large salad bowl (six kinds of vegetables, 12 francs ($1.50), lapin with a nouvelle cuisine sauce, french fries and green beans for 35 francs ($4.37), Ritz-quality, and—you should try it—a homemade cheesecake for 8 francs, $1. While the Wadja is fairly large, it is open weekdays only (noon to 2:30 p.m. and 7:30 to 9:30 p.m.) and is so popular that you may not get a seat if you arrive after 1 or 8 p.m.; come early.

NEAR THE EIFFEL TOWER (LEFT BANK): (5) Restaurant le Com-
merce, 51 Rue du Commerce: In the general area of the Eiffel Tower, but a bit too far to be reached on foot (it's really closer to the back of the Parc du Champ de Mars, behind the tower; closest Métro to the restaurant is Emile Zola; the station called Commerce is also nearby), this is another of those large miracle restaurants, where appetizers or hors d'oeuvres are 5 to 6

francs, main courses are 18 francs (in most cases), desserts are 5 to 7 francs. My last visit, I had celeri rémoulade (6 francs) to begin, petit sale aux lentilles (a marvelously cheap Parisian dish, found everywhere—corned beef with lentils, in sauce; here, 18 francs), then a mousse au chocolat for dessert (7 francs) for a total of exactly 31 francs plus 12% service. Location is on another of those colorful market streets, appropriately enough called Rue Commerce, and the restaurant is open every day of the year.

ON THE RUE ST. DENIS (RIGHT BANK): (6) Du Grand Cerf, 145 Rue St. Denis (Passage), near Métro stops Etienne Marcel and Réaumur-Sebastopol, charges only 33 francs ($4.12), including wine, Pepsi or beer, for a three-course meal that permits a choice among 8 appetizers or soups, 14 main courses with vegetable, 8 dessert listings (including 4 types of cheese), and bread. Spanish owner, Mr. Pepito, must think himself in Madrid rather than Paris! Open daily except Sundays for both lunch and dinner, this 39-seat eatery is an exceptional choice except perhaps for its location, smack in the heart of a red-light district (if you're concerned about such things).

IN THE STUDENT QUARTER (LEFT BANK): (7) Stop Cluny, 94 Boulevard St. Germain near the Boulevard St. Michel, is strictly a cafe and no relaxed restaurant, but its offerings are large in variety and cheap: ten different sorts of omelettes for 10 to 16 francs, nine different salads for 19 to 20 francs, several *plats du jour* for 32 francs ($4), and three-scoop ice cream desserts for less than a dollar. In June of 1984, my hamburger steak with pepper sauce and giant accompanying heap of spaghetti, with a glass of red wine, totalled 38 francs ($4.75), service included.

(8) **Le Petit Vatel,** 5 Rue Lobineau, is probably the smallest low-cost restaurant in Paris: 15 chairs and stools, all painted violet, in a dining room the size of a spread bedsheet, with a connecting kitchen so tiny the young female cook could, without moving, stir the soup-pot on the stove with her left hand and serve you at your table or board with her right. It's open Monday to Friday from noon to 2:30 p.m. and 7 to 9 p.m. The prices, in 1985, allow you to eat a three-course meal (the dishes are chalked on the wall), wine included (red only, however), for 39 francs, or $4.87. Example: salad, soup or a large artichoke as a starter (8 francs each), chicken, sausage or hamburger or stew or fish, with fries or vegetables (19 francs per), as main course, followed by fromage or gâteau (8 francs per serving), and a glass of wine (4 francs), total 39 francs. This no-frills pocket-sized restaurant is worth a visit. To find it quickly, walk into Rue Mabillon from the St. Germain des Prés Métro stop, then turn into second street left, where the market is.

OFF THE BOULEVARD ST. GERMAIN (LEFT BANK): (9) Owned and managed with great dedication by Mr. Michel Jussot, **Auberge In**—which stands for *aubergine,* eggplant in French—at 34 Rue du Cardinal Lemoine, is a very special vegetarian restaurant. There is always one plat du jour (daily special) selling for 32 francs ($4)—an example is polenta with vegetables—and always a three-course prix fixe menu at 47 francs ($5.87), which might include soup, cooked rice with fresh green peas, white cheese

and a glass of carrot juice. Auberge In has two large dining rooms (each seating 50), one for nonsmokers and teetotallers, the other, with a separate entrance around the corner, for smokers (wine is served in the latter, too). Monsieur Jussot, who speaks English well, will be happy to answer questions about cuisine or to discuss his unique methods for the organic cultivation of vegetables. Learn while you eat.

NEAR THE CENTRE POMPIDOU (RIGHT BANK): (10) **Le Petit Gavroche** (named after a character in Victor Hugo's *Les Misérables),* at 15 Rue St. Croix de la Bretonnerie, a small side street off the Rue Maubourg, serves a three-course lunch (11:30 a.m. to 2:30 p.m.) or dinner (7 to 11:30 p.m.), daily except Sundays, for only 35 francs ($4.37), and it permits you to choose one of three hors d'oeuvres, one of five plats du jour, then cheese or dessert (homemade cake or mousse au chocolat), all of excellent quality. The two wall posters condemning alcoholism shouldn't stop you from ordering a quarter-liter of the local red wine—as everyone does—to accompany your meal for an extra 70 U.S. cents. If the six ground-floor tables are taken, walk upstairs where there are twelve more.

(11) **Tout au Beurre**, 5 Rue Mandar, just off the Rue Montmartre, is always crowded with employees of the area seeking out its 40-franc ($5), three-course, prix fixe meal, served daily except Sunday; there is no à la carte menu. Rather, you choose from no fewer than 18 hors d'oeuvres, from 10 different plats du jour, then choose either cheese or dessert, and receive a small bottle of wine or mineral water thrown in. You eat best in the upstairs room, then pay the standard 41 francs as you leave, to the patron behind the counter. It's obvious that the main courses here—boeuf bourguignon, pepper steak, pot au feu, calves liver, tripe—are the kind rarely found on the prix fixe menus of low-cost establishments, and that quite obviously accounts for the immense popularity of Tout au Beurre.

NEAR THE CHAMPS ELYSÉES: (12) **Chez Melanie** at 27 Rue du Colisée, near the Franklin D. Roosevelt Métro stop, is probably the finest value in this entire high-priced district, a small, family-run restaurant on the fourth floor of an apartment house less than a minute from the Champs Elysées. It's worth the inconvenience to be squeezed onto 50 seats in two small dining rooms, because the food is well-prepared, quickly served, and costs only 38 francs ($4.75) for a three-course prix fixe lunch starting with hors d'oeuvres, followed by a plat garni (example: roast veal with green beans), then cheese or dessert, wine, and *pain à volonté* (as much bread as you wish). And service is included. Entering the house at no. 27, you step into a tiny courtyard, then ascend 60 steps of a narrow staircase to the Melanie. Remember, always, that it is open for lunch only, and weekdays only.

And there you have the 12 wonder restaurants of Paris. Have I missed any?

5. The Cafeterias of Paris: Full Meals for $4 to $5

Much to the horror of the super-gourmets, Paris has begun to sprout with cafeterias—that's right, cafeterias in Paris, but cafeterias with a special French flavor, like little flasks of wine ($1) at the end of the serving line.

The food served in these cafeterias is like no cafeteria fare you've ever encountered—it's tasty, attractive to look at, and well planned—for even when the French aren't trying, they do awfully well. Best yet, the cafeteria food is marvelously low-priced; you can see what you're buying and you can easily put together a meal for about $4 to $5. Finally, you can eat quickly, instead of dawdling for an eternity in the typical Parisian bistro. For your basic meals in Paris—the ones priced at the above levels—go to a cafeteria. They're scattered all over the city, rarely more than five minutes from any major location.

Not all the cafeterias, however, are similarly priced; they range from a number of wonderfully cheap (and generally independent) establishments charging 12 to 20 francs for main plates, to the generally higher-priced chain of Jacques Borel cafeterias, which can usually be recognized by the words "Auberge Express" in their titles. We've sought out only the cheaper cafeterias, and we'll now attempt a geographical rundown of them.

In the **Sorbonne** district, a typical choice is the **Latin-Cluny Self-Service,** 98 Boulevard Saint Germain, corner of Boulevard St. Michel, where I recently stuffed on hors d'oeuvres (6 francs), followed by a casserole dish of roast chicken, surrounded by parsley, potatoes, mushrooms and a delicious sauce (all for 24 francs). Total with wine: only slightly more than $4. No cover charge; no tipping. Other typical dishes: a small steak with french fries (20 francs), Frankfurt sausages with ham and sauerkraut (9 francs), cheese for 4.50 francs, a little jar of yogurt for 4 francs. And those are fairly representative prices, which you can expect to prevail in the lower-cost category of Parisian cafeterias.

In the area of the **Arc de Triomphe** (200 yards away), the **Cafeteria** (no other name) in the basement of 39 Avenue de Wagram, open only for lunch, Monday through Saturday, prices its vast selection of main plates at an average of only 28 francs ($3.50), charges 4 to 8 francs for salads, only 4.50 francs for a quarter liter of wine, only 1.80 francs (22¢) for coffee.

Behind the major **department stores,** upstairs at 73 Rue de Provence (near the corner of the Rue de la Chaussée d'Antin), **La Biella** is a bit more expensive than its cafeteria colleagues on the Left Bank: hors d'oeuvres range from 5 to 12 francs; a number of main courses are priced at 18 to 29 (although some are a franc or more higher). Closed Sundays.

On a side street midway along the **Champs Elysées,** and only a few steps in from it, the **Self Elysées,** 67 Rue Pierre Charon, specializes in chicken, but has other dishes available; and offers typical-to-higher self-service prices (23 francs for steak frites, 15 francs for an omelette, 18 to 28 francs for most other main plates).

In the **American Express** area, the large **Self-Service Rallye-Opera,** on the second floor of 35 Boulevard des Capucines, exactly one block up the Rue Scribe from American Express itself, serves a complete meal at lunch—hors d'oeuvres, entree, cheese or dessert, and bread—for 36 francs ($4.50). To reach the Rallye-Opera, walk down the Rue Scribe from Am Ex to Boulevard Capucines, and don't confuse the cafeteria with the more expensive Restaurant Rallye, around the corner at Rue Daunou.

One block from the **Folies Bergère,** the super choice is the **Super Self Service Montmartre,** 16 Faubourg Montmartre (subway stop is Rue Montmartre); moderate prices, including an immense beefsteak with french fries for 19 francs, other main plates for less, and a full, three-course, prix fixe meal for only 34 francs ($4.25). This is one of the largest and best of the cafeterias.

In the area of the **Louvre,** almost directly opposite the Tuileries Métro stop, the **Self-Service des Tuileries,** 206 Rue de Rivoli, between the Rue du 29 Juillet and Rue St. Roch, is another excellent cafeteria, but with prices a trifle higher than those in similar spots (main courses with vegetables for 24 to 34 francs).

Near the **Bastille** (Métro stop is Charonne) is the best find of all: the 500-seat **Self-Service Restaurant de l'Armée du Salut** (Salvation Army), 94 Rue de Charonne, patronized not by *clochards* but by average, middle-class French folk, among whom single ladies, families, backpackers will be fully at ease. Open seven days a week from 11:45 a.m. to 12:45 p.m. and from 6:30 p.m. to 8 p.m., it's a spacious place, friendly to outsiders, and so very moderately priced that you can enjoy a giant meal for 33 francs ($4.13) by choosing an hors d'oeuvre for 5 francs, then one of five main dishes or entrées for 18 to 20 francs (veal steak, goulash, fried sole, curried pork, with french fries, spaghetti or salad), cheese for 4 francs, beverages for 5 francs, a roll for 60 centimes, butter for 80 centimes.

There are many others you'll discover in other areas. At all of them, you can eat for the same $4 to $5 price.

6. The Bistros of Paris: Full Meals for $6.50 to $8

But now, for your more leisurely meals, priced in the $6.50 to $8 range, we'll take up the subject of the Paris bistro—those little restaurants scattered around the city, where the art of French cuisine is often as well practiced as on the Champs Elysées. The best finds for a budget vacation are the bistros serving prix fixe meals—a set three- or four-course meal for one lump sum. Since these restaurants concentrate on the dishes they've included in the prix fixe, the cooking is apt to be very good, often better than the quality you'd find in a more expensive à la carte house. No self-respecting artist, student or other cost-conscious Parisian would eat in any but a restaurant offering prix fixe meals. I've scoured Paris for them, and have come up with the following finds:

BOULEVARD ST. MICHEL AREA—LEFT BANK: We start in the same area recommended for your best hotel buys: the Sorbonne district, near Boulevard St. Michel. Get out at Métro stop St. Michel. Look to your left and you'll notice the small Rue de la Harpe. At 35 Rue de la Harpe (also near the Cluny Métro stop) stands **La Petite Hostellerie,** a typically tiny and inexpensive bistro, with good food and a friendly-to-Americans staff. Its budget prix fixe meal consists of three delicious courses and costs 48 francs ($6). Wine is 8 francs ($1) extra. Open daily except Sunday, throughout the year.

For a somewhat more exotic meal, proceed up the Boulevard St. Michel, to Rue des Ecoles (our street for hotels), turn left, and in another block, you'll find the tiny Rue Champollion. The **Restaurant Champollion,** at 3 Rue Champollion, is also a tiny place, but the quality and moderate cost of its French-Russian food have begun to attract persons from all over the Sorbonne area. The chef, Mr. Zylberman, is the son of the Russian emigré who founded it in 1930; his three-course prix fixe meal is 54 francs ($6.75), including service charge; and his borscht (which you can order on the prix fixe) is a soup specialty that tastes like nectar. By the way, don't be scared away by the line of people that almost always blocks the door; the line is composed of Sorbonne students trying to get into the cheap movie theatre *next* door.

And now, if you're confident enough to attempt an à la carte restaurant, which has no prix fixe but remarkably cheap rates, then your destination should again be the Rue de la Harpe (that little street that runs off the Boulevard St. Michel, near the Seine), where you'll find **Les Balkans,** at 3 Rue de la Harpe, another enormously popular Left Bank establishment charging 20 to 32 francs ($2.50 to $4) for most main courses with vegetables. Generally, your meal here—carefully chosen—will run to less than $6.50; and if you're lucky, you can have the meal at a sidewalk table. You can also try another (and less crowded) branch of the **Restaurant Les Balkans** at 33 Rue St. Jacques (corner of Boulevard St. Germain). It may be my imagination, but I've always enjoyed the food at the St. Jacques branch of Les Balkans more than at the Rue de la Harpe location, even though the menus and prices are identical.

ST. GERMAIN DES PRÉS—LEFT BANK:

In another Left Bank section—near the Ecole des Beaux Arts—you'll find several budget restaurants of a particularly wonderful flavor. The **Restaurant des Beaux Arts,** 11 Rue Bonaparte, across the street from the school, is anyone's conception of how a French restaurant should look: open kitchen in view of the diners, buxom waitresses, an intense, disputatious clientele. And a three-course, prix fixe dinner, including wine and service, for 48 francs ($6, see upper right hand corner of menu); à la carte prices totaling about $8 for a complete gourmet meal of excellent food.

On the other side of the Boulevard St. Germain, near the 17th-century church of St. Sulpice, is the restaurant **Lou Pescadou,** 16 Rue Mabillon, serving two prix fixe menus at 35 and 54 francs ($4.37 and $6.75), wine and service included. In good weather you can dine al fresco under a bright red awning, savoring the typical sidewalk bistro atmosphere that abounds here.

A lighter and cheaper meal, in the area of the St. Germain des Prés church, can be had at **A la Bonne Crêpe,** 11 Rue Gregoire des Tours (the little alleyway that leads into the Rue de Buci from the Boulevard St. Germain), where 24-or-so francs brings a prix fixe dinner that always includes crêpes (thin pancakes surrounding an inner ingredient of various sorts) as the main course. The meal comes with a bowl of cider, of all things, and the prix fixe total includes service charge. Heavily crowded with young people. Closed Sundays for lunch. . . . Nearby, **Au Vieux Casque,** 19 Rue Bonaparte, typically Rive Gauche, charges 48 francs ($6) for a three-course prix fixe, including wine and service.

NEAR THE PALAIS ROYAL—RIGHT BANK:

If you're art minded and want to camp near the Louvre, you'll find a surprising number of good restaurants nearby. Walk the short distance from the Louvre to the Palais Royal. Alongside the Palais Royal runs the little Rue Montpensier, and next to it, runs the Rue Richelieu—two narrow little streets. At 23 Rue Montpensier, there's a narrow little restaurant which calls itself the Unbelievable—**Restaurant L'Incroyable**—where a prix fixe meal of hors d'oeuvres, meat, vegetables, cheese, fruit or dessert, wine and bread, costs 38 francs ($4.75), service included. There's another entrance to L'Incroyable, by the way, through a small arcade at 26 Rue Richelieu. Serves only from noon to 2:30 and from 6:30 to 9; closed Sundays, and the month of August. In the same general area, near the Tuileries Gardens, **Au Petit Bar,** at 7 Rue du Mont Thabor, charges a similar price for the same kind of meal.

NEAR THE ARC DE TRIOMPHE—RIGHT BANK: And amazingly

enough, this next elegant section has its occasional budget standouts:

L'Etoile Verte, at 13 Rue Brey, third side street to the left from Avenue Wagram (walking down from the Arc de Triomphe), serves rather remarkable three-course meals for only 40 francs ($5), wine included, with à la carte choices only slightly more expensive. My own recent meal consisted of a tasty vegetable soup, coq au vin (first class), and a small bottle each of rosé wine and Perrier water, for a total of 46 francs ($5.75), bread, service and tip included. Forty tiny checkerboard-sized tables, covered with paper napkins (on which the waitress will write your order). Open seven days a week from 11 a.m. to midnight.

Off the Champs Elysées, at 45 Rue de Berri, **Mamie Suzette** is a crêperie that serves a three-course, crêpe-oriented lunch or dinner for only 36 francs ($4.50): soup, a crêpe with garnishings, salad and dessert; it all makes for a refreshing and fully adequate meal. Closed Saturdays and Sundays.

OFF THE CHAMPS ELYSÉES—RIGHT BANK: Can you eat cheaply

near the Champs Elysées? You can, with a sort of pinpoint accuracy in choosing your restaurants.

Walk downhill on the Champs Elysées to the Rond-Point, and turn into the Rue Jean-Mermoz. At no. 19 Rue Jean-Mermoz, the restaurant **Chez Germain** serves a plat du jour for 30 francs ($3.75), with wine an extra 7 francs (87¢) per quarter liter. Or, walking downhill on the Champs Elysées from the Arc de Triomphe, turn left on the third side street down, Rue Washington, to no. 13. There, the tiny **Chateaubriand** serves one-plate meals for only 28 francs ($3.50), but without wine. Your best chance for finding a seat is at dinner time, not at lunch. Closed weekends.

THE FRENCH FRANC: At the present time the French franc is exchanged at the rate of approximately 8 French francs to the dollar. That makes the franc worth 12.5 U.S. cents, the basis for all dollar prices appearing in this chapter.

---

7. Starvation Budget Meals

A RIDICULOUSLY CHEAP RESTAURANT ODDITY: Appropriate

fanfare should now be heard for the astonishing **Restaurant Casa Miguel,** 48 Rue St. Georges (which runs off the Rue St. Lazare near the Gare St. Lazare, on the Right Bank; Métro: St. Georges): Cheapest restaurant in all of France (it's listed in the Guinness Book of Records), that's what this next one is—a curiosity for whose continued prosperity (and survival) I pray each night. Open seven days a week (except on Sunday evenings) throughout the year, from noon to 1 and 7 to 8 p.m., it charges only 6 francs for a three-course meal with wine, but then shyly adds that *service non compris*. For a total of 6.60 francs (82¢), including the service, you choose from five different appetizers, but from a single main course, and select either cheese or fruit at the end. And you enjoy all this in a pleasant little room of eight tables covered with pink-checked oilcloths, under a sign reading: "Mangez mieux, mangez plus, Economisez." Is it a stage setting? A Russian plot? The work of a saint returned to earth?

But let me, in the manner of a former President, make one thing perfectly clear: Restaurant Casa Miguel is not of the quality of our "little wonder" restaurants earlier described; those are for tourists of every station, offering superb local color and ample food for the price. At Casa Miguel, portions are small (but you can order second helpings of anything for from 2.50 to 3 francs), and main courses consist of couscous au mouton (Algerian rice with lamb) on Sundays, Mondays, Wednesdays and Thursdays, of lamb with green beans or roast pork sausage, *saucisse de Toulouse,* on Tuesdays, of macaroni bolognaise on Fridays, and of lentils with lamb or pork sausage on Saturdays. But if all you have is 6.60 francs (82¢), what a find!

LA SOUPE POPULAIRE: For emergencies only, you'll want to head for **La Soupe Populaire,** a Salvation Army type soup kitchen at 4 Rue Clément, to sample a *complet*—a bowl of soup, followed by a plat du jour (meat and vegetables), including bread—for a mere 3 francs (37¢), daily except Sundays, from noon to 12:30 p.m., in very spartan surroundings with only 40 seats. Obviously this is only for people in fairly desperate straits but nevertheless to be considered if you're down to your last few sous. Look for the queue that forms up a few minutes before noon, and note how some customers carry the food out in pots and other containers which they've brought to La Soupe. Location is central, off the Blvd. St. Germain next to the Mabillon Métro stop.

A CHANGE OF PACE—COUSCOUS: Way back when, in the days of my first trips to Paris, couscous was a relatively rare food item, served only one or two days a week in tense Algerian restaurants, catering to an almost exclusively Algerian clientele. One evening, on my once-a-week visit to eat couscous, I arrived at one of these spots just minutes after the chef had been machine-gunned by fellow Algerian nationalists for some political misdeed.

Today, couscous—a sort of grainy Algerian rice, over which are poured meat and various sauces—is served daily all over Paris, and—with the advent of an enlightened French policy toward rebellious colonies—eating it isn't dangerous at all. The largest cluster of good, cheap couscous restaurants is found on the Left Bank, on the **Rue Xavier Privas,** a tiny street running off the Rue St. Severin, which itself runs off the Rue de la Harpe, near that point where the Boulevard St. Michel meets the Seine: Ask a gendarme.

The Rue Xavier Privas—"couscous street," to me—houses six different couscous restaurants charging 10 to 15 francs for appetizers (a tomato salad is good for openers) and from 32 to 44 francs for couscous and meat—enough for a sumptuous meal. These are, in ascending order of price, **Au Meilleur Couscous** at 10 Rue Xavier Privas (only 12 francs for tomato salad, 33 francs for couscous); **Le Latin** at 22 Rue Xavier Privas (22 and 35 francs for same); **La Belle Etoile** at 15 Rue Xavier Privas (32 francs for couscous, a tiny place); **Au Village** at no. 14; and (most expensive of all) **Au Bon Couscous** at no. 7. One couscous is more than enough for two—no one ever finishes it alone—and with the couscous, you drink—you guessed it—Algerian wine.

THE RESTAURANT OF THE ALLIANCE FRANÇAISE: One of the best food bargains of Paris is this immense establishment at 101 Boulevard Raspail (Métro: St. Placide), open weekdays only from 11:45 a.m. to 2:15 p.m. and from 6 to 8 p.m.; but officially, it's supposed to be used only by persons studying the French language (no one checks). That requirement attracts a large number of the many thousands of students from 135 nations who come here each year to bravely confront French irregular verbs and Molière, and you'll see students from nearby Luxembourg seated next to students of all ages from as far afield as Zambia, Ruanda and Malawi. They're served a first-class, three-course menu for the remarkable price of 24 francs ($3). Thus does France, through its officially subsidized Alliance Française, conquer the hearts, minds—and stomachs!—of additional multitudes each year.

CHARCUTERIES: A final way to eat cheaply but well in Paris is to purchase picnic ingredients for do-it-yourself meals (consumed in your hotel room or in a park) at a Parisian charcuterie (delicatessen). But to call a charcuterie a delicatessen is to do this unique institution a severe injustice. They are more properly gourmet appetizer shops, selling subtly flavored pâtés, salads, cheese, pickled snack items, and the like, and they're heavily patronized by French housewives, who demand reasonable prices. Some addresses of typical charcuteries? The city's best, in my opinion, is the **Pou**, at 16 Avenue de Ternes, two short blocks down from the Avenue Wagram, and therefore only a short walk from the Arc de Triomphe. Closed Mondays. Runner-up, in the area near the Tuileries Gardens, is the **Cours des Halles** at 304 Rue St. Honoré, near the Rue des Pyramides. Nearer the Palais Royal and the Au Louvre department store, there's a typical charcuterie at 136 Rue St. Honoré, and another at 41 Rue Richelieu. Again on the Right Bank, at 1 Rue Montmartre, the **Bruneau** opens daily at an astonishing 4 a.m., closes at 7 p.m. Monday through Friday, 6 p.m. Saturday and 11:30 a.m. Sundays. And on the Left Bank, near the Panthéon, you'll find charcuteries all up and down the Rue St. Jacques, the best being at 198 Rue St. Jacques.

8. Some Final Food Tips

Wherever you eat in Paris, several rules of thumb will keep your costs down. (1) Order soup as your opening course; it's invariably priced at 6 or 7 francs, unfailingly good. (2) When in doubt, choose an omelette as your main course; French chefs coax marvelous results out of just-plain-eggs, and rarely charge more than 15 francs ($1.88), often as little as 12 francs, for the omelette of your life. (3) Alternatively, keep in mind that old standby, *steak frites,* a small, thin steak with a mound of french fries made only as they do here, and invariably priced between 20 and 25 francs. It is always available in every restaurant and cafeteria, although it must often be specifically requested and individually prepared for you in a cafeteria. (4) Eating in an à la carte restaurant, never order a separate vegetable (*legume*) with your main course unless you're utterly famished; even though the menu may not mention it, your main course will already be *garni* (accompanied by vegetable or potatoes), and the order of a separate dish will simply result in an uneaten portion. (5) Try ordering yogurt (*yaourt*) as your dessert, just as the French do. It costs only 4.50 or 5 francs, it clears the palate, and is, as Commander Whitehead would say, "curiously refreshing." (6) Finally, never let your eyes overeat in a cafeteria. Skip the appetizer, and order only a main course and dessert—usually, in Paris, that will be as much as you'll want or are able to finish.

READERS' RESTAURANT SELECTIONS (BIG SPLURGE VARIETY): "No visitor to Paris should miss a meal at the **Cafe Procope.** A special menu meal at lunchtime comes to 45 francs, though the dinner menu is a steep 85 francs, including service charge. The 45 francs buys the best food available in Paris, and the restaurant is atmosphere plus. The plaque at the door tells the reader that the 'café' was founded in 1686, and has been frequented by such diverse Parisians as Napoleon I, Voltaire, Benjamin Franklin, and Diderot. It is located at 13 Rue de l'Ancienne Comédie, a tiny street near the Métro Odeon—be sure to eat upstairs" (Robert M. Gill, Blacksburg, Virginia; note by AF: Procope is closed throughout all of July). . . . "On a side street off the Champs Elysées (Rue de Berri), the Chinese restaurant **A La Pivoine Chinoise,** 47 Rue de Berri, charges 46 francs per person for a French omelette with vegetables, fish in sauce piquante with rice, beignet de pommes, and beer. Closed Sundays. Paris, je t'aime!" (Lasse Andersen, Aabyhoej, Denmark).

READER'S RESTAURANT SELECTIONS (BUDGET VARIETY): "**Restaurant My-Vi,** 6 Rue des Ecoles near Métro stop Cardinal Lemoine, serves Vietnamese and Chinese specialties, and must be one of the cheapest restaurants in Paris. A delicious and filling prix fixe menu was 33 francs ($4.12), wine included" (Matti Anttila, Duncan, Canada).

READERS' EATING TIPS: "My money-saving trick in Paris was to shop for my lunch in the little food shops where the Parisians go. A baguette of crisp, hot bread, a cheese or bit of pâté, some of those superlative strawberries, and demi-bottle of wine, and lunch was eaten in my room at a total cost of about $3 (American). To do this, one *must* speak at least basic French, but I feel one should try this anyway. If one does, the people seem more helpful and friendly and their smiles are warmer, even though they may be smiling at one's bad French. This trip was, without a doubt, one of the most marvelous things in the life of a fifty-ish grandmother, which I am, and I am planning to return next year, God willing" (Mildred H. Devlin, San Francisco, California). . . . "Tell your readers always to seek out the *marchés,* or open air markets appearing regularly once or twice a week at the same spot in Paris (e.g., there is one on Av. Pres. Wilson in front of the Musée d'Art Moderne every Wed. and Sat. morning). Besides, being colorful and fun, they offer absolutely the best bargain and freshest foods: fruits, vegetables, cheeses, etc., all offered in a hurly-burly atmosphere, a tradition that goes back to the dawn of the first city and shows no sign of dying in Paris. Here your readers can get everything they need for a fabulous picnic except the wine and the bread. And you can also buy thread, underwear, flowers and *bas-collants* (panty hose). The original one-stop shopping center! One warning: bring your own shopping bags" (Susan DeSimone, Paris, France). . . . "One good way to save money, or to permit yourself to afford a splurge, is to eat lunch in your hotel room. The basis, of course, is the wonderful French bread, which should be picked up fresh. The names, weights and prices of the various loaves are as follows: Gros Pain, 1 kilogram 6.50 Fr; Baguette Longue, 250 gr. 1.85 Fr; Parisien, 500 gr. 2.65 Fr; Petit Parisien (vulgarly called Bâtard), 250 gr. 1.80 Fr; Ficelle (small and round; nearly all crust), 100 gr. 1.40 Fr; Petit Pain, a 2½-oz. size that is ordinarily enough for one person, a complete small crusty loaf, 70 gr. 1.10 Fr; and a section of a longer loaf, about 60 gr. cut off a longer one, 0.70 Fr. . . . If one prefers a dark bread, it may be obtained (of a very fine quality) from a number of health food stores; if wrapped in a moist towel, will keep for almost a week, quite fresh. . . . Then, as a pièce de résistance, one should eat cheese. I began with one variety at a time, eating it until I got tired, first Brie, then Camembert, then taking up the smelly 'classic' cheeses, Pont l'Eveque and Livarot, and so on. A French cheese store presents an almost innumerable variety. Finally, after six months of cheese every day for lunch, I finally got tired of all cheese and took up cold cuts. A fine place is **Charcuterie de Seine** at 81 rue de Seine 6e; that store has a fine assortment at fair prices, for that is where the penny-conscious French housewives shop. . . . As for wine, one can easily afford a quality above the vin ordinaire; for 8 or 9 francs one can get wine with the words *Appellation Controlée* ('Registered Label') on the label; that was as good a quality as I could appreciate. With cheese one should drink white wine. If a novice, one may wish a somewhat sweet wine such as Montbazillac, or Entre Deux Mers" (Pauline Hadley Maud, New York City). . . . "What we usually do is buy our own food and eat right here in our hotel room for *less* than half the price we'd pay in restaurants. *And no service charge!* The food itself is nine times out of ten of better quality, as well. In Paris, the delicatessens are of a standard 'par excellence' and plentiful. Let me give you just one example of a typical 'homemade' meal: half a hot chicken costing 25 francs for two big double portions. A good French vin ordinaire costs 11 francs per bottle, which is enough for two meals. Half a French bread costs about 1 franc. Instead of chicken, you may have sausages or wonderful French meat loaves, all of which are beautifully and tastefully prepared. The above portions are big and can obviously be cut down considerably, but they are what we consider a good meal" (R.A. Dyker, Johannesburg, South Africa). . . . "Throughout our trip, we had no difficulty in finding nice, clean and inexpensive eating places. We also like to buy the good breads they have over there and have our evening snack in our room—with cheese, fruit, etc.; what could be better!" (Woodrow and Letress Berryhill, Phoenix, Arizona). . . . "A *Croque Monsieur,* consisting of ham and melted cheese on toasted bread, is a typically Parisian snack, and is available for 14 francs at cafes and street vendor carts. There is also a *Croque Madame,* which adds a fried egg on top, but is rarely seen" (Martha Brooks, Bryrup, Denmark). . . . "At the corner of Rue St. Jacques and Rue Gay Lussac, **Super Mams,** an establishment somewhat reminiscent of the corner grocery stores of the United States, is a place not be missed. Here everything is priced by the piece: 12 slices of packaged cheese 9 francs; 2 or 3 slices of ham 8 francs; containers of milk at 2.50 francs; wine around $1.50; assorted crackers, sardines, fruit, etc. Across the street is a bakery. All in all a meal for three people could be assembled here for as little as 35 francs, no more than 40. Thus, after a hard day at the museums, you're ready to relax with a picnic lunch in a Parisian park." (Patrick Dougherty, Canton, Ohio).

9. Daytime in Paris

THE TOP TEN SIGHTS: The very best way to sightsee in Paris is simply at random, wandering wherever your fancy takes you, witnessing the colorful day-to-day life of the Parisians, and savoring the unexpected scenes and delights that every quarter of the city holds in abundance. But if you're determined to do it in an organized fashion, you'll need a quick checklist of the more important sights. We'd rate them as follows: (1) First, the Arc de Triomphe and the Champs Elysées (Métro station for the Arc is Etoile, for the Champs Elysées go to Franklin D. Roosevelt); (2) then, Notre Dame (Métro is Cité); (3) Sainte Chapelle (Cité); (4) the Louvre and the Jeu de Paume (Métro is Palais Royal for the Louvre, Concorde or Tuileries for the

Jeu de Paume); (5) Invalides, the Tomb of Napoleon, and the Army Museum (Métro is Invalides); (6) the Eiffel Tower (Métro is Bir-Hakeim or Trocadéro); (7) Sacré Coeur and Montmartre (Métro is Abbesses); (8) Versailles (Métro to Pont de Sèvres, then bus 171); (9) the galleries and studios of the area of St. Germain des Prés—from here, walk down the Rue Bonaparte toward the Seine; and (10) the Pantheon and the Latin Quarter (Métro is St. Michel, then a walk). Here's how to tour them:

ESCORTED SIGHTSEEING: Commercial sightseeing is expensive in Paris and readers will note that I've set forth numerous suggestions for do-it-yourself touring. Still, if you'd like a preliminary, escorted ride through the city, then you'll want to know that the wildest and most comprehensive tour of Paris is run by a company called **Cityrama,** which owns a fleet of double-decker buses almost entirely covered in glass—each is an apparition straight from a Jacques Tati movie. The customers sit in easychair-type seats, to which are attached earphones hooked up to a magnetic tape recorder, carrying a tour commentary in seven different languages. You dial your own language—just like at the U.N.—and then hear a canned commentary as the bus travels a prearranged route. The tour lasts three hours, costs 137 francs ($17.12), and leaves at 9:30, 10, 11 a.m. and at 1, 2 and 3:30 p.m. from 4 Place des Pyramids, which is off the Rue de Rivoli, near the Louvre, directly opposite the Tuileries Métro stop.

During your visit, you ought not to miss a boat tour of Paris, along the Seine, which costs less than the bus does. The **Bateaux Mouches** tour boats run from 10 a.m. to 11 p.m.; the fare is 20 francs ($2.50). Boats depart from a dock on the Right Bank, next to the Pont de l'Alma (Métro stop is Alma Marceau). Boat tours offer fantastic opportunities for camera addicts (the gargoyles of Notre Dame, the bridges of the Seine), and you'll be left with a striking impression of how awesomely beautiful Paris really is.

TIPS FOR INDEPENDENT SIGHTSEEING: Virtually all the museums and monuments of Paris (including the Louvre and Fontainebleau) are closed on Tuesdays, when you ought to take that trip to Versailles or Chartres. For consistent money-saving, schedule your visit to the Louvre for Sunday, when no admission is charged. . . . You can sit all day at a sidewalk cafe in Paris for the price of a cup of coffee; it's considered bad form for a waiter to ask you to move on. Watching the passing parade on the Champs Elysées in this manner is about the best form of entertainment in Paris—and it's free. . . . For a refreshing dip in the hot summer months, schedule an afternoon at the **Piscine Deligny**—a swimming area in the **Seine River,** Left Bank, next to the **Pont de la Concorde.** Four francs to check belongings, 21 francs to swim. . . . Most thrilling sights of Paris? The **Jeu de Paume,** a small museum on the grounds of the Tuileries Gardens, Place de la Concorde, housing the most famous impressionist paintings of the 19th century, which still aren't permitted in the Louvre. Closed Tuesdays; admission 13 francs, 6 francs on Sundays, free to young people under 18; don't miss the upstairs Van Goghs. . . . The **Eiffel Tower,** of course. Subway stop is Trocadéro, and the cheapest ascent (to the tower's first level) is 9 francs by elevator, 7 francs on foot. . . . The **Tomb of Napoleon** (an indispensable visit). . . . The **Musée de l'Armée,** behind the tomb (10 to 6 daily; closed January 1, May 1, November 1, and December 25; 12 francs). . . . **Montmartre,** at dusk. . . . The **Rodin Museum** (9 francs ad-

mission, 4.50 francs on Sundays), on the Left Bank, 77 Rue de Varenne (Métro stop: Varenne), filled with works by the greatest sculptor since Michelangelo. Free entrance on Wednesdays, closed on Tuesdays.

SOME SIGHTSEEING MISCELLANY: The eight-franc visit to the

Sewers of Paris (*les Egouts de Paris*) is the continent's weirdest tour, on which you'll not only view a 200-meter section of the famous Paris sewer (shades of Jean Valjean!) but also peruse an actual midget museum devoted to the history of the Paris sewer system (only in France). Entrance is from a stairway on the southeast sidewalk of the Alma Bridge (Pont de l'Alma) across the Seine, at the corner of the Quai d'Orsay on the Left Bank. Take the Métro to Alma-Marceau, then cross the bridge to the Place de la Résistance. In 1984, visits were permitted between 2 and 5 p.m. every Monday, Wednesday, and the last Saturday of every month. I'm hoping that, with Gallic logic, the schedule remains unchanged in 1985. . . . The open-air food markets of Paris, open every morning except Monday, are a fascinating sight as well as a valuable source of inexpensive picnic lunches and eat-them-in-your-room snacks. Try those on the Rue Mouffetard (Left Bank, Métro is Censier-Daubenton), the Rue de Buci (Left Bank, Métro is Odéon), the Cité Retiro (Right Bank, Métro is Madeleine), or the Rue Lepic (Right Bank, Métro is Blanche). . . . A do-it-yourself trip to **Versailles** costs a fraction of what the commercial tours charge. Simply take the Métro to the Pont de Sèvres exit (it's marked "Coté Pont de Sèvres"), where you'll find the waiting place for municipal bus no. 171 (it's almost always there as you emerge from the subway). The bus takes 15 minutes for the ride to Versailles, charges 12 francs (but you can pay with three Métro tickets taken from your carnet of 10, and thus spend only 9 francs). While you can also take a 6.50-franc train from the Gare Montparnasse to Versailles (free for Eurailpass holders), that leaves at scheduled times only and goes not to the gates of the palace (as bus no. 171 does) but to the railroad station in Versailles, where you'll have to take another bus to the palace grounds. Bring a picnic lunch for a meal on the unbelievably magnificent grounds, and then—for the touring portions of your outing— simply attach yourself to any of the large groups being taken around. When the tour is over, don't fail to visit also the Petit Trianon and the Bergerie—the latter a simulated farm where Marie Antoinette and her court cavorted as shepherds, herders, and the like.

VERSAILLES VIA EURAILPASS: "By far the best way for Eurailpass holders to get to **Versailles** is as follows: there is a commuter line to Versailles which has a train leaving every 15 minutes from a small station directly connected to the Invalides Métro station. It's a local line, but run by the S.N.C.F. (the French railways) and therefore free to Eurailpassers. One debarks at the Versailles-Rive Gauche station, turns right on coming out of the station, and proceeds along the street. Turn left at the first main street, and you will see the palace just ahead. This route is much faster than bus no. 171 and costs not a centime" (Mr. and Mrs. Roger Beare, Ottawa, Ont., Canada). . . . "Cheaper and faster than the bus to Versailles is the commuter railroad which goes along the left bank of the Seine. It looks exactly like the Métro and costs 10 francs. Changes from ordinary Métro to commuter system are at the Métro stations: **Invalides** and **Javel**, just follow the signs: 'S.N.C.F.—Versailles-Rive Gauche.' This commuter train ends up just 200 yards in front of the palace. Please do not confuse it with ordinary trains which stop miles from the castle!" (Matthias Risch, Munich, Germany). . . . "Chartres and Versailles can both be visited the *same* day if train departure is made from the Montparnasse station. This should be good news for those traveling by train and pressed for traveling time! Of course Eurailpasses are valid. The train destined for Chartres makes a scheduled stop at Versailles. We suggest going to Chartres first and stopping at Versailles on the return trip. (When leaving Versailles to return to Paris, a choice by train is available either via the SNCF Versailles station, from which the train goes to the Paris Montparnasse station, or via the Versailles SNCF Rive Gauche station whose train goes to the Paris Invalides station.) We saved additional time by returning via Invalides station. However, check the train schedule for your particular plans. Trips to Fontainebleau can also be made by train, free of charge, by Eurailpass holders" (C. W. Page, Bethany Beach, Delaware). . . . "On the way to or from Versailles, one may get off the bus or Métro at Pont de Sèvres and visit the Sèvres factory and museum for five francs. They also operate an outlet store for their fine chinaware products" (Douglas King, West Germany).

THROUGH MEDIEVAL PARIS WITH HOPE: To gain the best appreciation of Paris, a study of its origins and medieval history is most important. My wife Hope has developed a description of some fascinating sights, which follows now:

"The city was originally a village on the Ile de la Cité, in the middle of the Seine, where Notre Dame now stands. As an introduction to its mood, wander through the old section of the Ile between the cathedral and the Quai aux Fleurs, which used to be the Old Cloister and School area of Notre Dame, and where you'll see markings of the old Roman wall, the site of the home (on the Quai) of philosophy's most torrid, tragic lovers, Heloise and Abelard, wonderful medieval-looking alleys and homes, and the charming flower market of Paris.

Notre Dame

"**Notre Dame** itself, that grey stone Gothic marvel, begun in 1163 and now the very soul of Paris, is most often associated with Maurice de Sully, Bishop of Paris, under whose reign it was begun, and Viollet-le-Duc, who did a major restoration job on the cathedral in the 19th century—unfortunately the original architect remains an anonymous genius. In touring it, don't hit and run. Notre Dame is beautiful from every angle and it's worthwhile and satisfying to walk all around taking a good long look—sit for a moment in the small park in back to get the best view of the awesome flying buttresses of the Apse.

"Note especially the magnificent carved portals (almost the beginning of sculpture) and the famous Gothic Rose Window (begun in 1230), which became models for so much that was to come. As you face the cathedral, the central portal is known as 'The Last Judgment'; on your right is 'St. Ann's Portal'; and on your left, the only door with a gable, 'The Portal of the Blessed Virgin Mary'—all intricately and cunningly carved. Inside Notre Dame (open every day from 8 a.m. to 7 p.m.), you'll want to see those two vivid Rose Windows at the intersection of the transept; both date from the 13th century but the rose-toned window has been greatly restored, while the predominantly blue-toned glass opposite, on your left, is almost totally intact. Also in the transept on the right side is the 14th century statue, 'The Virgin of Notre-Dame de Paris.' And all around the Chancel is a quaint and lovely series of 14th century haut-reliefs, done in stone with gold, depicting scenes from the life of Christ. Unless you're very religious, skip the Treasury, which is not very interesting, is closed on Sundays, and also requires a 9-franc entrance fee. But if you can make it, it's quite a thrilling view from the **Tower of Notre Dame** (252 steps to the Grand Gallerie, another 90 or so more up to the South Tower), and worth the 12-franc ticket (half price on Sunday); open every day except Sunday from 10 a.m. to 5:30 p.m., entrance around the left on Rue Cloître-Notre-Dame, inside an iron fence (look for a sign reading *Tours,* which means 'Towers' in French).

"After your visit to the cathedral, don't fail to spend a few extra minutes at the nearby Conciergerie, 1 Quai de l'Horloge, near the Pont au Change, and then at the Sainte Chapelle (in the Palais de Justice), both on the Ile (Métro stop for the Ile is Cité). Both of them charge 12 francs (6 francs on Sundays, and every day for students), and both are open every day except Tuesday. Hours to visit the Conciergerie are from 10 a.m. to 6 p.m.; Sainte Chapelle's winter hours are 10 to 11:45 a.m. and 1:30 to 4:45 p.m. (10 a.m. to 5 p.m. in summer). The Conciergerie closes on Fridays in winter only.

The Conciergerie

"Once part of a medieval palace, the Conciergerie later became a prison to which most of the famous victims of the French revolution—Marie Antoinette, Robespierre, Danton and Madame du Barry—were sent to await their executions. A guided tour (French only) leaves every 20 minutes (no extra charge for this, but tip the guide), and as you wait in the dark, damp and very forbidding Gothic foyer, you'll be able to imagine how it must have felt to be led away from here to the guillotine. You'll then be taken through the Salle St. Louis (or Salle des Gens d'Armes), an enormous and impressive Gothic stone chamber, where you'll see the dining room and kitchen of the old palace, and the shaving room for prisoners who were about to be executed—and finally, you'll see cells that housed some of the personages named above.

Sainte Chapelle

"Just around the corner from the Conciergerie is the Sainte Chapelle (chapel), a stained-glass flower of the Middle Ages, with windows as alive and shimmering as a rainbow—an infinity of Biblical scenes, and a lovely rose window too. This was built in the 13th century by St. Louis (King Louis IX, the Crusader King, who was later canonized) to house the Crown of Thorns and a piece of the Cross that Louis purchased in Constantinople. Surprisingly, for those like me who have always looked upon the Middle Ages as a dark and brooding time, the chapel is made almost entirely of glass, and inside (on the upper floor) it is so light and airy that you almost have the feeling of being in the open air.

The Pont Neuf and the Square du Vert Galant

"From here, you can rest awhile in the Square du Vert Galant, a charming tiny green park that is a ten-minute stroll away from Sainte Chapelle. Simply walk to the tip of the Ile (at the opposite end of the island from Notre Dame) until you find the equestrian statue of Henry IV (the Vert Galant himself—a fond nickname of the people for a king who was a noted ladies' man). Go down the stairs behind the statue, and you'll find the park, which is shaped like the 'prow' of the Ile, underneath the Pont Neuf. The Pont Neuf itself is the oldest bridge in Paris, and has a row of cunning heads carved along it; bearded and very hairy heads they are, too, some with the most comical expressions.

The Musée de Cluny

"From the Ile de la Cité, proceed now to the Left Bank, where you'll be able to visit the outstanding medieval museum of Paris: the Musée de Cluny at 24 Rue du Sommerard or 6 Place Paul-Painlevé (Métro stop is Odéon on St. Michel)—a magnificently fanciful 15th century Gothic structure which houses a display of medieval painting, sculpture (including original pieces from the facades of Notre Dame and Sainte Chapelle), jewelry, religious and ecclesiastical relics, enamels, furniture, tools and household articles from the Middle Ages, as well as its most famous exhibit, the 'Lady and the Unicorn' tapestries. And as if all this were not reason enough to visit the Cluny, the 'cherry on the top' is the ruins of old Roman baths, located in the basement (where the exhibits have been expanding to include columns and sculpture from the Gallo-Roman era). Open daily except Tuesdays from 9:45 a.m. to 12:30 p.m. and from 2 to 5:15 p.m.; a top sight but with a stiff 9-franc admission fee to visitors other than students, so go only on Wednesdays when entrance is free or on Sundays when you can get in for 4.50 francs.

"Now we move to the Right Bank, for a visit to the Marais.

THE MARAIS: "Marais (or marsh-lands), supposedly the second oldest inhabited area of Paris (populated after the people outgrew the Ile), is now a working-man's living quarter with a large Jewish section (look for the colorful Rue des Rosiers), and is one of the most fascinating places in which to wander—not only because of its rather exotic present character, but also because it is dominated by the spirit of beloved King Henry IV, and has some of the finest old mansions in Paris. A good plan is to start with the **Place de la Bastille** (Métro stop: Bastille:), walk from there to the **Place des Vosges** and its **Victor Hugo Museum** (making a small detour to look at the **Hotel Sully** before entering the Place), and then on to the **Museum Carnavalet,** and the **Palais Rohan-Soubise.**

Place de la Bastille (Métro: Bastille)

"Prepare, first, for a surprise; what you will see as you emerge from the Métro is a cheery, busy, carnival-like, enormous traffic circle—a miniature Place de la Concorde—with nothing left to remind you of the grim prison except some tracings along the pavement that outline where the Bastille used to stand. In the center of the vast plaza stands the airy, delicate-looking, monumental **July Column,** which the adventurous tourist used to be able to climb, being rewarded at the top with splendid views of Paris. Now, alas, the structure is permanently closed to the public.

Place des Vosges

"Now to reach the important **Place des Vosges** (a genuine 17th-century square, built by Henry IV), you take your life in your hands and cross the traffic circle opposite the little stone ticket building of the July Column, to the Rue St. Antoine, walk away from the Column for four blocks, turning right on Rue de Birague (to reach the **Hotel Sully,** described below, continue a bit further along the Rue St. Antoine), and a few feet ahead you'll spot the entrance to the Place des Vosges. Inside is a large square and a strolling arcade with a very active kiddies' park in its center. The buildings today are all dulled oranges and yellows and were crumbling until the recent restoration program began; but the lush Renaissance spirit of Henry IV's pet project shines through nevertheless. The king was assassinated before the Place was completed but still it had its share of distinguished tenants; among them were Richelieu (no. 21), Corneille, Descartes, Pascal and Molière.

Maison de Victor Hugo

"Not the least distinguished resident of the square was the genius Victor Hugo, who lived at 6 Place des Vosges, now the **Victor Hugo Museum** (open from 10 a.m. to 5:40 p.m. every day except Monday; entrance fee is 7 francs, half price for students, free on Sunday), housing a collection of 19th-century illustrations for Hugo's novels (you'll recognize those from *The Hunchback of Notre Dame*), a few Daumiers (caricatures on the staircase), a virtual gallery of drawings by Victor Hugo himself (450 to be exact: landscapes, castles, portraits); and costumes-pictures-manuscripts of many of his plays. But for me, the most personal and therefore the most interesting part of the Maison is the third floor—the apartment occupied by the writer from 1832 to 1848, where you get a keen sense of the flamboyant spirit of the artist and the fantastic range of his talents: you'll see the incredible Chinese dining room decorated and furnished by Hugo himself, and the intricately carved wooden bench (and two sideboards) that he personally designed. And, in addition to his writing desk, there's the usual death mask of the man of the house in his bedroom.

Musée Carnavalet

"The **Musée Carnavalet,** nearby at 23 Rue de Sévigné (open every day except Monday from 10 a.m. to 5:40 p.m.; entrance, sad to report, has escalated to 9 francs, but is still half price to students), but with free entrance on Sundays, is just a hop, skip and a jump from the Place des Vosges (or take the Métro to Saint-Paul); to walk there, head diagonally across the square from the Victor Hugo Museum to the Rue des Francs-Bourgeois, which leads to the Rue de Sévigné. The museum is devoted to the history of Paris commencing at the end of the 16th century (antique street decorations, artists, famous people, events of Paris—especially rich material on the Revolution), and contains too many interesting relics to look at, let alone list. The mansion itself is also worth a visit: built in 1545 and decorated by the famous sculptor Jean Goujon (note the elegant sculptures on the façade and in the cour d'honneur), then touched up in 1655 by the celebrated François Mansart, it's a graceful stone building with a fastidiously manicured inner courtyard whose focal point is a statue of Louis XIV (a petit Versailles). Madame de Sévigné lived here from 1677 to 1696; she's the lady who wrote to her daughter and you can see some of her letters in the museum. Also inside, don't miss the model of the Bastille (on the ground floor); numerous mementos of Marie Antoinette and Louis XVI (locks of their hair, his shaving articles, games used by their children in prison, and some of the furniture from their cell at Temple); the palette of Daumier; Napoleon's field kit; and an astonishingly tiny glove worn by the Emperor (small hand, large ambition?).

Hotel de Sully

"If you had the fortitude *not* to turn right at Rue de Birague (for the Place des Vosges), but continued along the Rue St. Antoine, you'll be rewarded at number 62 with the **Hotel de Sully,** recently cleaned and restored and wedding-cake lovely. Sully, as you know, was Henry IV's brilliant Minister of Finance who spent most of his days living in spartan simplicity until he retired and broke out into the kind of splendor you'll see in his Hotel. This petit palais opens its doors to the public on Wednesday, Saturday and Sunday at 3 p.m. for a one-hour guided visit (conducted only in French), and the price is rather high: 19 francs for adults, 14 for children. If you are lucky enough to be in Paris during a Festival du Marais (in June, but not every year), you may see a concert here. Students or specialists may be interested to know that the Hotel de Sully is the information center for all Historic Monuments of France. Programs of daily activities (which include listings of all cultural events: sound and light shows, festivals of dance, music and poetry, etc.), information on guided visits (tariff usually runs around 19 francs, in French—guided two-hour walking tours available daily at 3; lower rates for groups and 30% off for students), maps, etc., available on request. During the tourist season (sometimes from mid-June to mid-July only), they also sponsor nightly visits of the illuminated Marais, with rendezvous usually at 9:30 in front of the Métro station St. Paul or from the Eglise Saint Gervais—a two-hour walking tour for 26 francs (20 francs for students). Still, it costs nothing to view the Hotel and its lovely courtyard from the outside, and it's worth making the side trip to see it.

National Archives in the Palais Rohan-Soubise

"The **Palais Rohan-Soubise,** home of the **National Archives** since the days of Napoleon and now also housing the **Musée de l'Histoire de France,** is a *short* five-block walk from the Musée Carnavalet, and located at 60 Rue des Francs-Bourgeois (at the intersection of Rue des Archives—nearest Métro is Hotel de Ville or Rambuteau). The Palais Soubise itself is worth seeing—a delightful, cream-colored, stone manor house flanked by classic porticos forming a long cobblestone courtyard (with old garret windows peeping over the wall) which invites you into the early 18th-century building housing the Museum of the History of France. (Incidentally, the architect had the good taste to include the turreted door of the 14th-century Clisson Mansion in his design for this palace—you can see it around the corner on Rue des Archives.) The museum, open every day except Tuesday from 2 to 5 p.m. for a 4-franc entrance fee (2 francs on Sundays, free on Wednesdays), displays original documents (letters from such as Henry IV, Richelieu, Voltaire, Marie Antoinette, Napoleon, etc.), and rare objects illustrating the history of France from earliest times on. But the most intriguing parts of the museum (and reason enough to visit here) are the two 18th-century rococo suites of the Princess Rohan-Soubise: the Chambre de Parade, with its royally outfitted red-canopied bed, gilded walls and crystal chandelier; and the even more impressive (and perfect in its way) Salon Ovale, which is absolutely filled with gold —little gilded cherubs, inset wall paintings, mirrored and decorated to the teeth, but most pleasing. The surrounding neighborhood is fascinating, too, and full of history. If you have enjoyed what you've seen of the Marais and would like to know more about it or see more of it, pick up the excellent little brochure (with a marked map) called 'Le Marais' from the above-mentioned information center at the Hotel de Sully.

CENTRE NATIONAL D'ART ET DE CULTURE GEORGES POMPIDOU (BEAUBOURG): "This new, ultra-modern controversial cultural center, located on Rue Beaubourg, and often referred to casually as the **Centre Pompidou** or **Beaubourg** (Métro: Hotel de Ville, Rambuteau or Chatelet), has fast become the most popular attraction in Paris, a beehive of activity that exudes gaiety and a freshness of spirit, an audacious poem to technology, with all the 'guts' of the building on the outside. One rides up to the exhibition floors on an escalator encased in an outside futuristic see-through tube, and the view of the city from the top terrace is spectacular. But the fun starts even before you enter the building, in the outdoor square filled with all manner of street entertainers (dog acts, jugglers, magicians, snake-charmers, etc.), somewhat like a circus (and in fact, when I was last here, there *was* a circus encamped in the square, which may or may not be a permanent fixture). Inside, the scope of activities is broad and ambitious, almost as active as the happenings outdoors, and one can wander and see a lot before an admission ticket becomes necessary. There's a Library (including the latest in audio-visual), an Industrial Design Center, Children's Workshops (and a huge climbing nest for the kids outside), Music Center, Cinema, concerts, plays, and special exhibitions. And, of course, this is the new headquarters for the **Museum of Modern Art,** whose collection—in greater space—looks much better than before. Open daily, except Tuesdays, from noon to 10 p.m., and Saturdays and Sundays from 10 a.m. to 10 p.m. You can buy a 27-franc (*Laissez Passer*) Discovery Ticket valid for the entire day and admitting you to everything.

LE FORUM DES HALLES: "Built on the site of the now demolished, once celebrated, early-morning food market of Paris, **Le Forum des Halles**—a gigantic and partially underground shopping center—has become the latest sightseeing attraction of Paris, following its opening in late 1979. Two hundred shops and boutiques, sixteen restaurants purveying everything from french fries to lobsters, one dozen movie theatres, a wax museum, banks and hairdressers, create a crazy melange, and the architectural style is a mixture of marble and neon, the engine and boiler-room of a trans-Atlantic liner, the Plexiglass gangways of Aéroport Charles de Gaulle, the sculpture of Niki de St. Phalle, all connected by escalators and elevators, stairways and streets. On weekends, an estimated 200,000 Parisians and tourists go window-shopping here, sometimes shouting *merveilleux* or *horrible* as they glimpse a particular display. The rather expensive Le Forum is not recommended for shopping—at least not to readers of this book—but it's a must for students of modern society, an urban experiment that stirs the senses. Take the Métro to Les Halles or Chatelet.

KEY TO THE NUMBERED REFERENCES ON OUR PARIS MAP:
1—Arc de Triomphe; 2—Basilique du Sacré-Coeur; 3—Bibliothèque Nationale; 4—La Bourse; 5—Catacombes; 6—Cathédrale de Notre-Dame de Paris; 7—Sainte-Chapelle; 8—Georges Pompidou National Center (Beaubourg); 9—École Militaire; 10—Église de la Madeleine; 11—Église Saint-Pierre de Montmartre; 12—Les Égouts (Sewers); 13—Grand and Petit Palais; 14—Hotel des Invalides; 15—Institute de France; 16—Jardin des Tuileries; 17—Jardin du Trocadéro; 18—Marché aux Fleurs; 19—Musée Carnavalet; 20—Musée de Cluny; 21—Musée de l'Armée; 22—Musée de l'Histoire de France; 23—Musée de l'Orangerie; 24—Musée des Arts Décoratifs; 25—Musée de Jeu de Paume; 26—Musée Grevin; 27—Musée National d'Art Moderne; 28—Musée Rodin; 29—Musée Victor Hugo; 30—Palais Bourbon; 31—Palais de Chaillot; 32—Palais de Justice; 33—Palais de l'Élysée; 34—Palais du Louvre; 35—Palais and Jardins du Luxembourg; 36—Palais-Royal; 37—Panthéon; 38—Palais Opéra; 39—Place de la Bastille; 40—Place de la Concorde; 41—Place du Tertre; 42—Place Vendôme; 43—St-Etienne-du-Mont; 44—St-Germain-des-Pres; 45—St-Julien-le-Pauvre; 46—St-Séverin; 47—St-Sulpice; 48—Sorbonne; 49—Tour Eiffel; 50—Val-de-Grâce.

MORE BEAUTY MARKS OF PARIS: "Don't, of course, miss the gardens of the **Palais Royal** (built by Cardinal Richelieu), with their lovely shops and apartments (Métro stop is Palais Royal, directly opposite the Louvre). The French Revolution was ignited here by Camille Desmoulins at the now-demolished Cafe Foy. . . . And schedule a stroll through the **Luxembourg Gardens** (Métro stop is Odéon or St. Sulpice), which is like walking through a Seurat painting. . . . Attention all interior decorators, designers, scenery designers, and antique collectors: you will love the **Musée des Arts Décoratifs,** 107 (and be sure you *enter at 107*) Rue de Rivoli (Métro: Palais Royal); entrance is 10 francs (but only 5 francs to students with valid I.D.'s); open from 2 to 6 p.m. weekdays except Tuesdays, which has rooms full of furniture and trappings tracing the history of decoration not only in France, but in Europe and the Orient as well (also watch for exciting special exhibitions, which usually are worth the admission). . . . The **Petit Palais,** Avenue Alexandre III or Avenue Winston Churchill (Métro: Champs Elysées—Clemenceau, directly across the bridge from Invalides), has an interesting collection of antiques, mostly objets d'art of the 13th to 19th centuries (including stamps, books, dishware, 18th-century furniture), some sculpture, a small Flemish collection, some drawings by Rembrandt and Van Dyck, several Monets, Renoirs, Degas, Cezannes, Rodins, Daumiers, Bonnards, Vuillards, and a whole roomful of Courbets. The inner circle of the museum contains the picture gallery, the outer one houses everything else, and there's a nice garden in the center in which one can rest. Tariff is 9 francs; free on Sundays, students can always get in for half price; hours are from 10 a.m. to 5:40 p.m. every day except Monday. . . . The **Galeries Nationales of the Grand Palais,** directly across the street, are used for temporary exhibitions of national character. Open daily, except Tuesday from 10 a.m. to 8 p.m., for an entrance fee of 15 francs, 12 francs on Saturdays. This is not to be confused with the **Palais de la Découverte,** housed in another section of the Grand Palais, and described below.

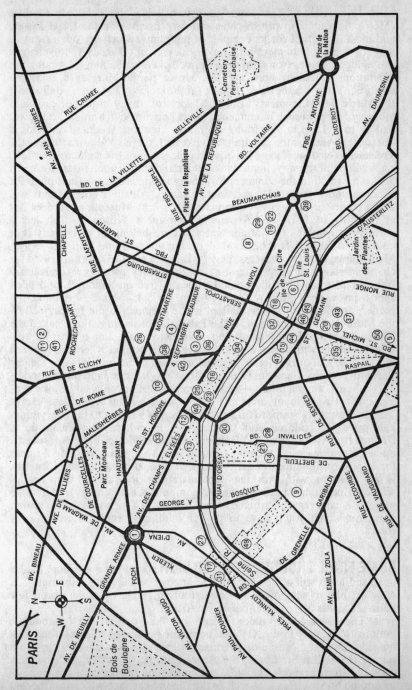

FOR THE KIDS: "The junior tourists will like the **Palais de Chaillot** (Métro: Trocadéro), with its cafes and park fronting on the Eiffel Tower, and most important for its complex of museums, which are open from 10 a.m. to 5 p.m. (summers till 6) every day except Tuesdays, for charges averaging 10 francs (some offer half-price tickets on Sundays). Among the institutions clustered here are the **Musée de la Marine** (a maritime exhibition); the **Musée de L'Homme** (anthropology, 10 francs admission); the **Musée des Monuments Français** (historical survey in plaster casts and models of large French monuments; hours here are 9:45 a.m. to 12:30 p.m. and 2 to 5:15 p.m., 9 francs entrance, free on Wednesdays, closed Tuesdays). And for the children who like fish, there's the **Aquarium of the Trocadéro Gardens** (facing the Tour Eiffel, go down the stairs to your left, signs will point the way) housed in a cold, dark grotto, open from 10 a.m. to 5:30 p.m. (6:30 in the summer) for a 5-franc admission fee (half price for children under ten, and special family rates). All the while, parents will undoubtedly enjoy themselves more at the nearby **Museum of Modern Art of the City of Paris** (11 Avenue du President Wilson), which has a permanent exhibit of paintings and sculpture belonging to the city (not quite up to the standard of *the* Modern, but good—some Matisses, Dufys, Modiglianis, Utrillos, Picassos, Légers, Braques and Gris): it's also used for changing shows of very interesting contemporary painters. Admission 9 francs, half price for children and students (free on Sundays), and open every day except Monday from 10 a.m. to 5:45 p.m. . . . Around the corner, at 2 Rue de la Manutention, in the premises formerly occupied by the Museum of Modern Art, is the **Palais de Tokyo** (sometimes called the Musée d'Art et d'Essai), displaying an attractive collection of *Post* Impressionists, along with some works that were left behind when the Modern moved to Beaubourg. Here you'll see paintings by Seurat, Pissaro, Signac, Bernard, Maillol, Gauguin, Bonnard, Toulouse-Lautrec, and some wonderful Vuillards, among others—a collection that not only fills an historic gap, but creates a pleasant ambiance all its own. Open every day, except Tuesday, from 9:45 a.m. to 5:15 p.m., it charges 9 francs to see everything, half price for children and students. . . . Elsewhere, the **Palais de la Découverte,** Avenue Franklin Delano Roosevelt (Métro: F. D. Roosevelt), open every day except Monday from 10 a.m. to 6 p.m., charging 7 francs for admission (children under 3 admitted free, older kids pay 5 francs), is an institute with working demonstrations in various branches of science (including space problems, computers and energy). All done with great flair, very much in the French manner. There is also a planetarium here, for which you'll have to pay an additional entrance charge of 8 francs.

SOME FINAL THOUGHTS ON TOP SIGHTS: "First a warning: Ladies in spiked heels will not be admitted to ancient buildings or museums. . . . Now I'd like to set down, for easier touring, some extra data on a few must-see sights already mentioned by Arthur.

"The **Hotel des Invalides** (Métro: Invalides or La Tour Maubourg), built in 1670–74 by Louis XIV as a home for pensioned soldiers—and now housing the grand Musée de l'Armée (open every day from 10 a.m. to 6 p.m.); the Eglise St. Louis (the Army Church, decorated with banners captured from France's enemies, and containing mementos from Napoleon's tomb at St. Helena, as well as the funeral carriage which transported his remains to Paris), and the Eglise du Dome (an elegant, classical structure by Mansart, whose golden dome is a Parisian landmark)—is considered one of the finest buildings in the city. But the main reason why visitors flock here is that the Church of the Dome contains **Napoleon's Tomb** (open every day from 10 a.m. to 6 p.m., for an entrance fee of 12 francs, which also admits you to the Army Museum). Nineteen years after his death, Napoleon's wish to return to Paris was finally carried out (note the following words inscribed over the entrance to his tomb: 'Je désire que mes cendres reposent sur les bords de la Seine, au milieu de ce Peuple Français que j'ai tant aimé'), and he was buried with great pomp and ceremony along the banks of the Seine in this magnificent grey and white stone church. His tomb is sunken (one floor below, to get there use the staircases on either side of the rococo gold altar—you'll spot it as you enter), but is dead center in the middle of the building directly under the cupola, and has a balustrade around it permitting you to gaze down on the gigantic rust-colored porphyry tomb (inside Napoleon is encased in six caskets!). Around the tomb are twelve enormous, almost identical stone maidens, holding laurels or keys commemorating Napoleon's most famous battles. On the main floor, sharing the glory, are Napoleon's relatives and generals (to your left, as you enter, the most ornate gilded chapel is a memorial to Napoleon's son, the King of Rome, whose actual remains were lowered in 1969 and placed in a crypt at the foot of a statue of Napoleon in holy robes, facing the emperor's tomb), and a few chosen heroes of France, such as Turenne, Vauban, and World War I's Maréchal Foch. Don't overlook the adjacent **Army Museum,** probably the best of its kind in the world; its collections evoke the military and political history of France and all nations, from the Paleolithic era through World War II. Armor, weapons, cannon, flags, banners and uniforms through the ages, all very colorfully displayed and quite fascinating. Also, coming directly from his tomb, with Napoleon in the forefront of the mind, you'll find some astonishing exhibits on him: on the ground floor (in the building to your right, when approached from the Dome Church) is the standard flag room; but upstairs on the first floor you'll find Napoleon's tent, his death mask, his portable battle library, his sword, famous hat and great-coat (now crumbling a bit, but very recognizable), and a number of personal objects used by him on Elba and St. Helena—including his death bed, and one of the emperor's favorite horses, stuffed and decorated with his parade saddle. But skip the old Musée des Plans-Reliefs, which can be of interest only to the most technical military strategists.

"The **Rodin Museum** (Métro stop: Varenne), at 77 Varenne, is located directly across from the side of Invalides (you will exit from the Dome Church to Avenue de Tourville, make a left to the Boulevard des Invalides, left again and cross the street; Varenne is the first street on your right), and is open every day except Tuesday from 10 a.m. to 5 p.m. (summers till 6) for an admission price of 9 francs; try to go on Sunday for only 4.50 francs. (Young people under 18 enter free, and students 18 to 25 pay half-price). The museum is housed in the enchanting dark grey stone Hotel Biron, a mansion surrounded by grounds which grow into a small park behind the house, providing a luxuriant background for Rodin's sculptures. To your right, as you enter the cobblestoned inner courtyard, is Rodin's most famous work 'The Thinker,' to your left the intriguing composition 'Les Bourgeois de Calais,' and the fantastic unfinished work 'The Gate of

Hell' (of which 'The Thinker' is a central figure), which was partly inspired by Dante's *Inferno* and is a stunning depiction of the agonies of mankind. Rodin is usually regarded as a poet of romantic or sexual love (i.e., 'The Kiss' or 'The Eternal Spring'), but when you look around this museum, which once was his home and has originals or replicas of nearly everything he did, you begin to sense another side—a brooding imagination concerned with tragic thought as well (note, for example, the evocative 'Obsession' or 'Main Sortant de la Tombe,' 'The Good Genie' and 'The Bad Genie,' as well as 'The Gate of Hell'). Two of my favorites (both on the second floor) are the nude study of Balzac rising from a tree-trunk (which caused a furor when it was first shown); and the tender, young, striving wholly upward-moving 'L'Enfant Prodigue.'

"The **Jeu de Paume** (Place de la Concorde, open every day except Tuesday from 9:45 a.m. to 5:15 p.m.—tickets on sale till 4:45; admission is 13 francs, 6 francs on Sunday, always free to young people under 18), already mentioned by Arthur, is devoted to Impressionist paintings (Manet's famous 'The Picnic,' Degas, Renoir, Van Gogh, Monet, Cezanne, Gauguin) and is not, on any account, to be missed. But directly behind the Jeu de Paume, and often overlooked, is the little **Museum of the Orangerie** (also part of the Louvre, it is used mostly for special exhibitions), which gave me a surprise and thrill on a trip or two ago to Paris. I had come to see a special showing of the works of Vuillard, and wandered unaware into two large oval rooms on the ground floor which contained Claude Monet's painfully beautiful, absolutely other-worldly, shimmering 'Les Nymphéas' (right, the famous 'Water Lilies')! This is a rare experience; beg or borrow, but see it if you can. Except for a portion of 1985 when it will be closed for reconstruction, the museum is open every day, except Tuesday, from 10 a.m. to 8 p.m. (Wednesdays till 10 p.m.), for an admission charge of 10 francs, 6 francs on Saturdays, 6 francs for students, and 3 francs for children. But if you're not particularly interested in this month's 'Orangerie Special,' you can see only the 'Salles de Nymphéas' for 5 francs on weekdays (half-price on Saturday), from 10 a.m. to 5:15 p.m. (of course, your general admission ticket to the Orangerie *includes* admission to 'Les Nymphéas,' even with an evening purchase; save the ticket and come back with it the following day): there's a separate entrance on the Seine side—inquire at the main desk.

"Still another 'must' for art lovers is the now quite celebrated **Marmottan Museum,** which was transformed from a seldom visited collection of Renaissance and Empire furnishings (and a few Monets) to a major attraction by the acquisition in 1971 (through a bequest by his son) of 65 of Claude Monet's paintings. The exhibit, in a specially built wing of the museum, entitled 'Monet and His Friends,' includes the work of other famous Impressionists (portraits of Monet by Renoir, works by Pissarro, Sisley, Delacroix, others), and is probably the largest collection of Monet anywhere in the world—the impact is stunning. Downstairs, the large canvases are breathtaking: there are some renowned oils as well as the famous world of blue and purple water lilies, casting a mysterious spell of infinity caught; and several unfinished paintings which look surprisingly avant-garde. Unfortunately, the Marmottan, at 2 rue Louis-Boilly (just off the Bois de Boulogne), is not very centrally located—best take the Métro to La Muette; it's a pleasant walk from the station and signs will point the way. The museum is open from 10 a.m. to 6 p.m. every day except Monday, for a 15-franc admission fee, while students pay half-price.

"Just a word about the **Louvre** (it'd be rather pretentious to try to say more), open every day except Tuesday from 9:45 a.m. to 5:15 p.m., for a 13-franc admission, half price for persons under 25 or over 60, free to those under 18, and free to all on Sundays (Métro stops are Palais Royal or Louvre). This may be the world's greatest museum, but it surely is one of the world's hardest museums to see. You can't possibly cover all of it, but the more time you have, the greater will be your reward. I have never recommended this before, but for the Louvre, it might not be a bad idea to invest 14 additional francs in one of the guided tours the museum provides (in English and French, duration 1 hour, 15 minutes) every day except Tuesday and Sunday at 10:30 a.m. and 3 p.m. (or the Bureau of Information will give you explanations, in French, of what you'll see in the painting galleries). Of course, everyone knows about and wants to see the 'Venus de Milo,' 'Winged Victory,' and Da Vinci's masterwork, the 'Mona Lisa,' but there is much more here—over 125 works classified 'masterpieces'! The Greek and Roman Antiquities present a stunning collection (watch for fragments and pieces from the Parthenon); there is so much in the Department of Paintings and Drawings I can't even begin to talk about it (but please try to see the Rembrandts—four of his great self-portraits and 'Bathsheba,' among others). In the room of 'Mona Lisa' are more excellent Da Vincis near the door, Veronese's stunning 'Marriage at Cana,' Giorgione's haunting 'The Concert,' and Titian's 'Man with the Glove.' To the right of the 'Winged Victory' are famous Botticelli frescoes from the Villa Lemmi; there are unusually complete collections of Egyptian and Oriental antiquities; sculpture; and objets d'art (including the 'Galerie Apollon' with the Crown Jewels, Napoleon's crown, Louis XV's crown, and a ring of St. Louis). Bon Appetit! And make it a long feast.''

READERS' SIGHTSEEING SUGGESTIONS: "You'll have to add the **Catacombs of Paris** ('Les Catacombes de Paris,' 1 bis Place Denfert-Rochereau, Paris 14e; 10F admission) to your list of weird tours. It is open daily except Mondays. Arrive with your boots on about thirty minutes early and be prepared for a macabre one-hour hike through limestone tunnels. The tomb entrance bears the inscription 'Arrête, c'est ici l'empire de la mort.' As you pass below this admonition, you will view the remains of literally millions of Parisians, whose bones were placed here when certain cemeteries were needed for other purposes. Begun as a tomb near the end of the 18th century, the catacombs became the final resting place for many of the victims of the French Revolution. . . . At Pont d'Austerlitz on the Seine, you'll find the **Jardin des Plantes** (Place Valhubert, Paris 5e), one of the oldest public gardens and zoos in Paris. In the park itself, there are experimental flower gardens, a huge tropical hothouse (afternoon tours available), a zoological museum and plenty of benches for enjoying this beautiful little uncrowded oasis in the heart of Paris. The excellent **Menagerie** (12F adult admission) is full of exotic animals and is maintained as part of the science center of the University of Paris. This zoo is smaller and not as crowded as the much larger, more publicized zoo at the Bois de Vincennes, Avenue de Saint Maurice, Paris 12e" (A. Emerson Smith, Columbia, South Carolina). . . . "Terrific fun for kids: the **Jardin d'Acclimatation,** the Children's Amusement Park in the Bois de Boulogne, which charges a 6-franc entrance fee to all over the age of 3, and is open from 10 a.m. to 6 p.m. (Métro is Les Sablons). Nearby, and fun for you (kids might enjoy it, too), is the new **Musée National des Arts et Traditions Populaires,** open daily except Tuesday from 10 a.m. to 5 p.m. Eight francs to enter, free for kids under 18, and half price for everyone on Sunday: entrance is around the corner from the Jardin, on Avenue du Mahatma Gandhi" (Mrs. Lou Levy, Springfield, Illinois). . . . "It's an easy and worthwhile excursion from Paris to see the historic **Basilique St. Denis** (legend has it that St. Denis was buried here, and the present church had its early beginnings in 475); take the Métro to St. Lazare, then change to Métro line no. 13 to Carrefour Pleyel (watch the light-up signs on the platform, do not go to Clichy, it's the last stop on the line; then, just at the Métro exit, take bus no. 153 or no. 142 to the church. This is not only the first great Gothic church and therefore the model for much that was to follow (e.g., Chartres, etc.), but it was also the burial place of all the kings and queens of France (from Dagobert on). Unfortunately, most of the bodies were exhumed during the French Revolution, but the tomb sculptures were saved—and they are fascinating, because from the time of Phillippe III (late 13th century) the royal likenesses were done from actual death masks. Also, the Romanesque Crypt does contain the tomb of the Bourbons, where the bodies of Louis XVI, Marie-Antoinette and Louis XVIII are buried. You must wait for a guide to take you through and the cost is 10 francs—open for visiting from 10 a.m. to 6 p.m. daily, except Tuesdays or when a religious service is in progress" (Pauline Rissman, Miami, Florida). . . . "The best panoramic view of Paris is to be had—free—from the roof garden of the **Samaritaine Department Store** at the Pont Neuf. Go to the no. 2 store, take the elevator to the 9th floor, and walk up one additional flight; you'll find the railing decorated with illustrated maps indicating landmarks, and the use of a telescope will cost 40¢ depending on the scope. An inexpensive outdoor cafe on the roof itself makes this a good midafternoon stop-off. And Samaritaine is one of the city's biggest and most complete department stores" (Mr. and Mrs. Arthur Lake, Paris, France). . . . "An afternoon's entertainment that no female in Paris should miss is the high fashion couturier showings. They start every afternoon at 3 p.m. at all the houses. Many of the smaller houses require no reservation or appointment—just appear at 3 o'clock. Each house presents its line in its own way, and each is a fascinating experience, all for the price of a little ingenuity—if you don't give in to expensive temptation!" (Ann Fomin, Dearborn Heights, Michigan). . . . **"Pigalle Street** is filled with clip joints; readers should be advised against going to see any of the Parisian striptease shows on or near Pigalle. But it does offer perhaps the most interesting free entertainment in Paris. Merely wander up and down the streets and alleys and *look*" (Nathanial R. Risenberg, Madison, Wisconsin). . . . "The **Marché aux Puces** (flea market) at the Porte de Clignancourt is open on Saturdays, Sundays and Mondays, and advertises itself as the biggest in the world; everything is to be had there at varying prices, from carrousel horses of the 19th century to sandals, Chinese vases, books, old coins, clothing, campaign supplies, chickens, and hours of free entertainment watching people try to think of a practical use for the old brass thingamajig they've got their hearts set on buying" (Victoria Rippere, Paris, France). . . . "The most impressive new sight in Paris is the **Monument to the Two Hundred Thousand Who Died in the Concentration Camps.** It is reached by crossing the Pont de l'Archevêché, directly behind Notre Dame—the monument is located in the Square de l'Ile de France. There is a flight of stairs at the tip of the square which leads down to the major part of the edifice, and the sculpture inside the crypt-like building and the poetry on its walls are an experience I shall not forget. Nor will I forget the inscription you read as you leave; 'Pardonne, Mais N'Oublie Pas'" (Mrs. Henrietta Rothaizer, Flushing, New York). . . . **"La Crypte Archéologique,** under the Parvis of Notre Dame, which was first opened to the public in early 1981, offers a wonderful look at the Roman ruins under the plaza in front of Notre Dame. Open 10 a.m. to 4:30 p.m. every day, for an admission of 11 francs" (Dorothy Tinkhoff, Olympia, Washington; note from AF: the remains of the largest structure of its kind on earth, which include a Roman wall built 300 B.C., and remnants of the Merovingian cathedral of Saint-Etienne dating back to 500 A.D., are all artfully displayed in this underground crypt and very worth seeking. Admission is 11 francs to visitors over 25 years of age, only 7 francs for younger folk). . . . "I would advise others to steer clear of the Place de l'Opera area if they're looking for local atmosphere. One of my favorite devices was to plan to be near the Galeries Lafayette or Au Printemps department stores around lunch time and have a tasty and inexpensive light lunch in one of the innumerable small restaurants in that vicinity. Camembert on a baguette with white wine is delicious, followed by a fresh fruit and black coffee" (G. LaPorte, Brooklyn, New York). . . . "Definitely try to visit **Notre Dame Cathedral** on Sundays. To hear the organ and choir is the experience of a lifetime." (A.J. and M.B. Rockmore, San Francisco, California). . . . "At 74 Champs Elysées is Galerie de Laridge, and at the underground is a very beautiful water-clock" (Rogerio Vieira, Rio de Janeiro, Brazil; note by AF: This water-clock is an interesting sight, worth a short visit if you are strolling along the Champs Elysées. It's kept in motion by a complex system of glass tubes filled with colored liquids, utilizing the changes of barometric pressure. The artist who built this time-machine was no doubt trying to create a perpetual motion machine).

EXCURSIONS INTO THE ILE DE FRANCE: "A visit to Paris is incomplete without a visit to at least one of the towns or chateaux of the Ile de France, some of which rival those of the Loire Valley itself. Such points may be reached quite conveniently by frequent trains from Paris. An excellent day excursion takes you to the chateau of **Rambouillet**, a favorite residence of General De Gaulle; **Maintenon**, the exquisite home of Mme. de Maintenon; and the cathedral of **Chartres**—in that order, and all for 74 francs. Maintenon is my favorite of the French chateaux (and I saw some 20 in the Loire Valley alone)—and a walk through the little town provides a charming rural French vista. But an early start is necessary to see all three sights. My advice is to forget Rambouillet and to visit simply Maintenon and Chartres. Another excursion would be to the race track, chateau, and museum of **Chantilly.** And from Chantilly one can take a bus to **Senlis**, a gem of a French town with cathedral, chateau, and ancient Roman ruins. Anyone wishing to spend a night in rural France would do well to do it in Senlis. Total cost of a ticket to both towns is only 42 francs round trip. A final fascinating rural town is **Provins,** an ancient walled city famous for its roses, which was once more important than Paris itself. Rail fare is 82 francs round trip" (Robert M. Gill, Blacksburg, Virginia). . . . "Consider an excursion to the village and chateau of **Chantilly,** about 26 miles from Paris. Take the Métro to the Gare du Nord, stop and hop on one of the frequent trains to Chantilly. If you're feeling energetic, you can walk from the train station to the chateau (about 20 minutes); otherwise, take the bus marked Chantilly-Senlis, which leaves the station every hour or so. If time permits, have a meal at the **Lion D'Or** on the road to the chateau. Fixed price menu for 37 francs, including regional specialties such as rabbit. And be sure to try some of the famous Chantilly cream" (Mr. and Mrs. Dennis Halloran, Madison, Wisconsin). . . . "**Chartres Cathedral** is a must! Trains run from the Montparnasse Station at 37 francs each way" (Steven and Linda Cades, Edison, New Jersey. Note from HA: Trains leave almost every two hours (check R.R. schedule; take the Métro to Montparnasse) and a fast train will reach Chartres in one hour. This Romanesque-Gothic cathedral, with its differing spires, flying buttresses, and magnificent sculpture around the entire edifice, is awe-inspiring and not to be missed. The Treasury and the Towers are open from 10 to 11:30 a.m. and 2 to 6 p.m. weekdays, and there are guided tours of the Cathedral itself, conducted in English, at 12:15 and 2:45 p.m. on every day in summer. Inside, you will be able to see the Crypt (the oldest part of the cathedral) and muse upon the 167 windows: each tells a story, and most are different from one another. Some look like glittering celestial postage stamps: all are gorgeous). . . . "A worthwhile side trip, via Eurailpass (otherwise costing 266 francs, round trip), is to **Mont St. Michel.** Trains leave fairly frequently from the Montparnasse station bound for Avranches, where you can catch a train for the town nearest to the Mont. From here, it is about five minutes by bus, on an inexpensive ticket" (John Kuehnle, Painted Post, New York).

A READER'S EXCURSION TO MALMAISON: "Anyone interested in Napoleon (and Josephine) can easily make the short excursion costing 114 francs, round trip, to **Malmaison,** the 'relax-away' home that General Bonaparte and his wife bought a few years after they were married. Located in Rueil-Malmaison, about 10 miles outside Paris: take the new R.E.R. subway line from Auber or L'Etoile to the La Defense station (and *not* to Rueil-Malmaison, too far from the chateau), then take Bus #158A to Chateau Malmaison, which is a short walk from the bus stop. (When you exit from the Métro, the bus stop is right there, just *be sure* you are waiting in the correct place for #158A—the bus ride costs 6 francs and takes about 15 minutes). Malmaison, which incidentally was built on the grounds of what used to be a leper

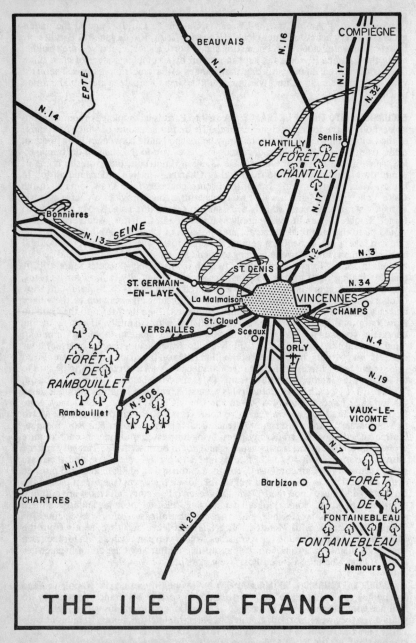

THE ILE DE FRANCE

colony (hence, the name), is open every day except Tuesdays and legal holidays from
10 a.m. to 12 noon and 1:30 to 5:30 p.m. (winters they close one hour earlier), and
the price of admission is 8 francs, and half-price for everyone on Sundays. This small
charming gray stone chateau, with a manicured garden in front and sizeable park in

the rear, is full of history—many important institutions and documents were created here; it was to Malmaison that Josephine retired after her divorce, and here she died; it was to this home that Napoleon returned from Waterloo, etc. And since the home contains the possessions of Napoleon and Josephine and most of the original furnishings, the spirit of this famous couple lingers evocatively about the place—especially Josephine's. Of the more formal rooms on the ground floor (the classical vestibule, drawing rooms, elegant dining room with golden state serving dishes, music room, Napoleon's library), probably the most striking is the Council Chamber, which is decorated like a military tent (the one where Cassius met Brutus flashed across my mind). Upstairs, among many important mementos (fancy dress clothes worn by the emperor, including his coronation robe, a table made to commemorate the victory at Austerlitz, the well-known painting 'Bonaparte Crossing the Alps' by David, dishware, etc.), most interesting to me was Josephine's sumptuous red-draped bedroom, with her ornate Empire bed (golden swans form the sides of the headboard), and filled with personal objects such as her slippers, hats, shawls, sewing table and her portable 'toilette.' You also see her bathroom (a plumbing feat, I guess, in its day). A guide is included in your entrance fee and you must wait for him to take the tour (French speaking only); a small tip is expected" (Pauline Rissman, Chicago, Illinois). . . . Note by HA: "Avid Napoleon enthusiasts will also want to make an excursion to the famous **Fontainebleau,** so intimately associated with the emperor: he made his famous farewell to the troops in the grand White Horse courtyard here; signed his first abdication from the Fontainebleau study (you'll also see his bedroom, Josephine's bedroom, and much more). And of course, the grounds and the chateau (dating back to St. Louis in the 13th century, and added to helter-skelter by succeeding monarchs) are gorgeous. Here one finds not only exciting historical associations, but also many rooms of sumptuous art-work—of special note, the 'Salle de Bal' and 'Gallery of Francis I.' Trains for Fontainebleau leave from the Gare de Lyon (early a.m. departures, late p.m. returns—check the train schedules); round-trip fare is 56 francs for a 2nd class ticket. When you arrive at the town of Fontainebleau, you'll find buses to your left as you exit from the station; they leave every 15 minutes for the chateau and cost one franc: Entrance to the palace, which is open daily except Tuesday from 10 a.m. to 12:30 p.m. and 2 to 5 p.m., costs 8 francs, half-price on Sunday."

10. Evening Mischief

The nightlife of Paris is available to you in infinite variety, but it's most cheaply pursued by simply sidewalk café-sitting, as the world and demi-monde passes by before you. Spend one evening on the Champs Elysées, another at one of the congregating points on the Left Bank (St. Germain des Prés, Boulevard St. Michel), but avoid three of the more expensive sidewalk cafés of Paris: the Café de la Paix near the Opera, the Café des Deux Magots and the Café de Flore near St. Germain des Prés. Contrasting with them in price is the huge café **La Coupole** on the Boulevard Montparnasse (Left Bank, Métro is Vavin), where coffee costs 8 francs and can suffice for an entire evening of café sitting (closed in August).

VARIETY MUSIC HALLS: And then try an evening of French vaude-ville, liberally sprinkled with topless showgirls. The **Elysées-Montmartre** theatre, 72 Blvd. Rochechouart (Métro stop is Anvers or Pigalle), specializes in such strippers, presents a 9:15 p.m. show nightly except Sundays, has some back orchestra seats for 85 francs, balcony locations for 70 francs, standing room for 45 francs. Its counterpart on the Left Bank, the **Bobino Music Hall** in Montparnasse, 20 Rue de la Gaité (Métro stop is Gaité or Edgar Quinet), places a greater emphasis on musical acts, including rock bands, girl singers, and the like. Here, standing room is only 60 francs, balcony is 110, and the show begins at 8:45 p.m. on all nights other than Monday, when the theatre is closed (Sunday matinee at 4). The big pop stars, and occasional musical extravaganzas, appear at the large **Olympia Music Hall** on the Blvd. des Capucines, near the Madeleine, where some seats sell for 60 to 85 francs.

THE THEATRE AND NIGHTCLUBS: Three, in particular, are musts for your Paris stay. The renowned **Comédie Française,** first, for its stylized productions of the French classics—Molière, Racine, Corneille. Most of its performances start late—at 8:30 p.m.—and side gallery seats can be had for as little, believe it or not, as 18 francs, while the gallery de face and second balcony have excellent views for 31 and 45 francs. To purchase the cheapest seats, go to the little sidewalk ticket office (*au petit bureau*) located not at the front of the theatre, but alongside it, on the Rue Montpensier. It opens half an hour before each performance and dispenses third and fourth gallery seats for 18 francs. Located on the Place du Théâtre Française, next to the Palais Royal, the Métro stop for the Comédie Française is Palais-Royal. . . . Next, the Paris **Opéra** which, unfortunately, is closed from July 14 to September 15. Orchestra seats sell for a maximum of 280 francs; but descend rapidly from there, and are available for as little as 20 francs in the upper locations; a surprising number of seats can often be picked up the day before the performance (during the box office hours, from 11 a.m. to 6 p.m.). For information on what's playing, call 742-5750; English is spoken. Métro is, of course, Opéra. If tickets are unavailable, try the lighter operas (*Marriage of Figaro, Madame Butterfly, La Bohème*) at the **Opéra Studio de Paris** (formerly the Opéra Comique, closed in summer), 5 Rue Favart (off the Grands Boulevards; Métro is Richelieu-Drouot), where the maximum price is 80 francs ($10), and numerous good seats can be picked up for between 20 and 30 francs.

I don't recommend that you see the **Folies Bergère,** because I think you'll find the production has become sloppy and the nudity de-emphasized. But knowing that no one will take this advice, I do at least recommend that you get the cheapest admission possible, which is a seat in the second gallery (*fauteuils galeris deuxième série*) for 140 francs ($17.50), as compared with the 300 francs ($37.50) charged for top orchestra locations. The Folies, with those elaborately plumed and costumed beauties parading before lavish stage sets, are located at 32 Rue Richer (Métro stop is Cadet), and there's a show every evening except Monday at 8:45 p.m.

LES CAVES: These are the smoky basement nightclubs in which the impecunious of Paris nurse a single drink for hours on end. The youngest students go to the **Caveau de la Huchette,** 5 Rue de la Huchette, for a 50-franc entrance fee (female students pay 35 francs) which includes the right to buy the first drink inside for only 10 francs. . . . Serious, and older, jazz addicts like the **Trois Mailletz,** 56 Rue Galande, which is off the Rue St. Jacques, a block from the Boulevard St. Michel, near the Seine, 10 francs entrance, 25 francs per drink at the bar; top, avant garde bands which begin playing at 9 p.m.; closed Mondays and late July and August. Don't go unless one of the big names (Memphis Slim, Bill Coleman, Don Byas, Slide Hampton) is playing. . . . The older folks (or even young, tired ones) will enjoy the **Caveau des Oubliettes,** a few steps from the Trois

Mailletz (go to 11 Rue St. Julien le Pauvre, in the courtyard of the 12th century Church of St. Julien le Pauvre, you'll see signs), where there's a homey show of French folk-singing, and reasonable admission and drink prices. It's great fun and your only charge is a 60-franc drink, which allows you to see the show, presented from 9 p.m. to 2 a.m. Afterwards, a guide takes you farther into the depths to see chastity belts, instruments of torture, and the holes (*oubliettes*) through which medieval prisoners were once dropped into the Seine. . . . In the area of the Ecole des Beaux Arts (near the St. Germain des Prés), the top student *cave* is **Le Riverbop**, 67 Rue St. André des Arts (40 francs weekend entrance, drinks from 10 francs, mostly jazz and little dancing; closed Sundays, Mondays, and the month of August), followed by the more expensive and elegant **Le Caméléon**, 57 Rue St. André des Arts (dancing downstairs), where the entrance fee is 45 francs and drinks are 22 francs apiece. Open Thursday through Saturday only. . . . And finally, there's now a Right Bank *cave*, the **Slow Club**, 130 Rue de Rivoli (near the Louvre), where entrance is 50 francs, but drinks are only 8. Teenagers and students in their early 20s are the clientele; many, many singles of both sexes. The action begins at 9:30 p.m., closed Sunday and Monday. . . . Remember, all these spots are the basements of ordinary-looking cafés; the excitement doesn't begin until you walk downstairs.

Just plain ballroom dancing, for older tourists? That takes place daily at the big **La Coupole**, 102 Boulevard du Montparnasse (downstairs) on the Left Bank, from 4:30 to 7 p.m. and from 9:30 p.m. to 2 a.m. Drinks at night are 55 francs, service included, but that's all you'll need to pay for a full evening of dancing to a live band, among couples and stags in their 30s and 40s. Take the Métro to Vavin.

SOUND AND LIGHT: Finally, an impressive evening show that for years has been presented only for a French-speaking audience. Now, in 1985, the illuminations, music and dramatic commentaries of the *Son et Lumière* "Sound and Light" presentation in the courtyard of **Les Invalides** (Métro is La Tour Maubourg or Invalides) are available in an English language version at 9:30 and 11:15 p.m. from Easter to October (but only at 11 p.m. in June, July and August). The charge is 30 francs ($3.75) per person, 15 francs for children under 12, the show is called "Shades of Glory," and the "shades" are those of Louis XIV, Napoleon, L'Aiglon, and Rouget de l'Ile, whose words you'll hear as lights play upon different sections of the historic structure built by the architect of Versailles. It's a special sort of evening entertainment for a visit to Paris, and about the cheapest evening show you'll find in the city.

11. Paris Miscellany

PARIS SHOPPING: The first floor of the Louvre, off the main entrance, houses a museum store which sells reproductions that (1) aren't usually bought in the United States: and (2) sell for several times the price, when they are. We bought an unsigned Bernard Buffet lithograph of the Ile de la Cité for $15. We saw the very same lithograph, bearing the penciled signature of Buffet, selling for $165 in a gallery on Madison Avenue in New York. We bought a blue-and-white reproduction of a recent Matisse study (now on the foyer wall of our apartment) for $10. It isn't sold in the U.S., and it would cost $25 if it were. . . . In ouying perfume in Paris, your aim is to find a "parfumerie" offering the greatest discount off already low list prices. Contrary to all the touts in the American Express area, these places are not found on the second floor of abandoned warehouses in Montparnasse. Some of the most elegant stores offer the greatest discounts. Try Paul's on the chic Rue de Rivoli, at 210 (take the Métro to the Tuileries stop). You'll get the maximum legal reduction, and you'll be treated with honesty and with respect. . . . For cheap articles of French-styled clothing (jazzy sports shirts, scarves) go to the **Prisunic,** which is a giant dime-store on the right-hand side of the Champs Elysées as you walk toward the Arc de Triomphe (corner of Rue la Boetie). Shirts for $14, scarves for $5, bikinis for $11. . . . Elsewhere, the **Museum of Modern Art** in Paris (recently moved to the new Georges Pompidou Center of Art and Culture, near the old Les Halles) has good, very modern reproductions (Klee, Léger) for 65 francs ($8.12).

The chief shopping attraction of Paris is, of course, women's dresses, but those are stratospherically priced in the custom-made shops. I think you'll find something quite comparable, but vastly less expensive, on the third floor of the **Galeries Lafayette,** which Hope and I think is the best department store in the world. On its third floor, Galeries Lafayette sells copies of all the renowned designs, and prices them so well that, during one sale, Hope picked up a Saint-Laurent-type trench coat for 400 francs ($50). There are numerous racks of ladies' suits selling for 450 francs ($56.25), and there are coats that shriek with chic at prices substantially lower than American women usually pay for comparable items. Everything in the store is the highest fashion, including even the cheapest items, such as the hats and bathing suits that sell on its ground floor; and to relieve the fatigue, there's an open-air café on the roof (*Super Terrasse*) with gaily colored awnings and garden-type tables, and moderate prices for lady-like snacks.

READERS' SHOPPING SELECTIONS: "I should like to suggest that you include in your sources for inexpensive goods the **Laboratoire de la Chalcographie du Louvre.** It is located on the third floor of the stairway on the riverside entrance to the Louvre, just a few yards from the main selling room. It is open also on Saturday. The Laboratoire makes reprints from old engraving plates, and sells some for as little as 50 francs ($6.25). They also have a catalogue listing all the 16,000 plates from which they make engravings. The subjects comprise maps; etchings from reproductions of paintings of the 17th and 18th centuries; scenes of Paris, Versailles, etc.; buildings, architectural details, etc., etc. What is particularly interesting is that at such low prices you get an authentic actual print, of which only the paper is modern. Some of these prints are on sale at much higher prices in bookstores, antique shops, etc. Once framed, they cannot be distinguished from the real thing. They make inexpensive, beautiful gifts, which take little or no place in one's baggage and can be sent by mail" (G. A. Loewenthal, SHAPE, APO 55, New York, New York). . . . "While in Paris we felt we must buy some Paris fashions but were on a Chicago budget. We had given up, until we found a small odd-lot clearance shop, **Unishop Shopping,** 50 Rue de la Verrerie, Paris 4, phone 277-54-42, that had only the fine quality women's fashions, many originals included. My wife's black lace formal, an original, was among those on the 80-franc rack. You take it from there" (Capt. Dean A. Hansen, West Germany).

A FINAL NOTE: Readers staying in Paris for at least a month will want to take French language lessons at the renowned **Alliance Française,** 101 Boulevard Raspail (nearest Métro is Notre Dame des Champs or Saint Placide), phone 544-3828, where you can enroll any week throughout the year, and where the fee is only 600 francs ($75) plus 100 francs enrollment charge, for a daily, two-hour course. The school also operates a 25-franc restaurant mentioned earlier and numerous social events, and is one of the best places around for meeting people in Paris. . . . Tired of those interminable waits to cash travelers' checks at American Express? A French money-changer, across the street and then a few doors up at 9 Rue Scribe, has no line—and sometimes gives a better exchange rate, to boot! . . . A long thin loaf of that wonderful French bread (*baguette longue*) costs only 2 francs at any neighborhood bakery. Buy sandwich ingredients ⸱t a nearby charcuterie, and you've beaten the high cost of living in Paris. . . . And ordering wine in any French restaurant, ask for a *rouge ordinaire* or a *blanc ordinaire;* all of them carry ordinary table wine, which you'll find to be surprisingly tasty and cheap. . . . In any Paris cafeteria, a small loaf of crusty French bread (*petit pain*) is 1.60 francs, a small bottle of red wine is 6 to 8 francs, and a big slab of luscious country pâté, pickle on the side, is about 12 francs. Spread the pâté on the bread, slice and arrange the pickle, imbibe it all with the wine, and you have an ever-satisfying 22-franc ($2.75) meal. . . . In Parisian groceries, the price affixed to meats and vegetables is the price per kilo (2.2 pounds), and that's usually more than you'll want. Two hundred grams (*deux cent grammes, s'il vous plaît*) of lunch meat or pâté will usually suffice for two or three persons, 150 grams for two.

READERS' TIPS: "The **Alliance Française** (101 Blvd. Raspail) can be one of the most frustrating places to walk into. Here is information on where to go and what to do. When you arrive, with a view to enrolling in a course, proceed through the main entrance doors (opposite the newsstand) and go up the stairs to the first floor (French first floor, that is), turn right and go to Room 11. In this room behind the desk are the only officials who speak English. Here you will be given a test and some forms to fill out. (Don't be afraid of the test. It's the only basis they have for placing you.) The test is used primarily for the grammar courses so if you want conversation also or instead, please make this known. Further, they will require your passport and two photos. Near the school on Boulevard Raspail, there are photo machines which charge three francs for the necessary pix. These pictures will be used when you pay, which is done after registration, on the main floor. Before you know it, you're a student in Paris. If all the commotion disturbs you when you arrive and you're frustrated because you can't speak to anyone and don't understand the signs, wait for someone carrying the *Herald Tribune*. He or she will have been through it all and will have the answers" (Ken Caunce, Ontario, Canada). . . . "Readers should be aware that enrollment at **Alliance Française** entitles them to student discounts at theatres, cinemas, parks and museums in Paris. If you have your student card from Alliance Française (or an International Student ID card), be sure to ask '*Avez-vous un rabais pour les étudiants?*' ('Do you have any student discounts?') whenever an admission fee is charged. Many establishments do not openly advertise these student discounts; so, always present your card and ask for a discount. Discounts at parks and museums run about 30%" (A. Emerson Smith, Columbia, South Carolina). . . . "It was in Sweden that I heard about the **Accueil Franco-Nordique,** 18 Avenue Carnot, 75017 (phone 227-21-67), which specializes in placing Scandinavian girls in French homes. Girls have their choice of working 2 hours for room, or 4 hours for room and board, or 5 hours for room and board and pocket money. The work usually consists of simple housework and child care which enables the girl to practice her French while living as a member of a French family. This agency will now accept American girls who wish to live in Paris to study the language and the French way of living. They would be grateful if girls would include international reply stamps with their letters, though, as this is a non-profit organization which cannot pay high mailing costs (later there is a $40 fee). There is also a club the agency sponsors to promote activities between the au-pair girls and the French young people. The agency is willing to help girls with any problems that might arise, and in my case definitely helped me to adjust to a different environment" (Janice Frederickson, Glenview, Illinois).

OTHER FROMMER GUIDES: Europe on $25 a Day has now been supplemented by five other $$$-a-Day guides and seven Dollarwise Guides dealing with individual European countries or areas: **Ireland on $25 a Day, Greece on $25 a Day** (including Istanbul and Turkey's Aegean Coast), **Spain and Morocco (plus the Canary Islands) on $25 a Day, England and Scotland on $25 a Day, Scandinavia on $25 a Day, Dollarwise Guide to England & Scotland, Dollarwise Guide to France, Dollarwise Guide to Italy, Dollarwise Guide to Switzerland & Liechtenstein, Dollarwise Guide to Austria & Hungary, Dollarwise Guide to Germany,** and **Dollarwise Guide to Portugal, Madeira & the Azores.** In contrast with the book you are now reading, which deals primarily with 21 major European cities, each of the above guides treats in depth one particular country or area, and sets forth hotel, restaurant and sightseeing suggestions for literally scores of individual cities and tourist destinations in that country or area. The Frommer Books can be obtained at most bookstores, or by mailing the appropriate amount (refer to the last page in this guide) for each book to: Frommer/ Pasmantier Publishers, 1230 Avenue of the Americas, New York, New York 10020.

THE OTHER WAY TO ORLY: "At Orly, walk past the Air France buses, and just after you'll find buses operated by the city of Paris, whose fare is only three subway tickets (9 francs) or 15 francs cash. The buses leave every ten to fifteen minutes and take you to Place Denfert Rochereau (Métro: Denfert Rochereau). From there, you can take the Métro to wherever you like. (The Hotel des Bains and Grand Hotel des Ecoles are within walking distance.) Service begins at about 6 a.m. and lasts until late at night. Transportation can be acquired in any direction (from Orly to Rochereau or vice versa). Besides, you'll be glad to see that you're mingling with stewardesses and Parisians, and not simply other tourists" (Alan Minz, Montreal, Que., Canada). . . . "The S.N.C.F. (French National Railway) now has a cheap and convenient rail connection between Orly Airport and the S.N.C.F.-Pont St. Michel Métro stop. A bus called 'S.N.C.F. Aerogare' departs from Orly Airport about every 20 minutes. It connects with a train which runs to the Pont St. Michel Métro stop (which is quite central). Eurailpasses are accepted. From Pont St. Michel, one can then make Métro connections to almost anywhere in Paris. This rail route is much cheaper and more convenient that the Air France bus service" (John Albin Broyer, Edwardsville, Illinois; note from AF: for cheap (5 Métro tickets), rapid, city bus transportation to **Le Bourget** or **Charles de Gaulle Airports,** take bus no. 350 from the Gare de l'Est (which is also a Métro station), or (to Charles de Gaulle only) bus no. 351 from Place de la Nation (also a Métro). For Orly, as outlined above, take bus no. 215 from Place Denfert-Rochereau).

PARIS ON $25 A DAY: With continental breakfasts for $2, hotels for $9 per person, and meals prix fixe, you can easily keep basic costs to a reasonable figure. Since all these items can be found, with a little effort, for lesser sums, there's room for leeway in your travel budget—even in high-priced Paris.

After Paris it's time to stretch out on a warm, sunny beach, with the blue Mediterranean lapping at your feet. The French Riviera is next—on $25 a day.

Chapter VIII

NICE

Bikini Land without the Bite

THE FRENCH RIVIERA is a never-never land for many American tourists. Tales of outrageous prices, of extortion-type menus and hijacking hotel bills, have all combined to scare the more cautious traveler away. Any substance to these fears?

In resort towns like Juan-les-Pins or St. Jean-Cap-Ferrat, yes. These are the haunts of international high society—the Jackie Onassis set—and prices are wondrous to behold. But Nice is different. Endowed with all the beauty of the Riviera—the palm trees, the Mediterranean, the sun—Nice is nevertheless a city, and not simply a cluster of elegant hotels, snuggled around a small bay. If you'll take time to learn the layout of that city, you can live moderately in Nice, just as do many middle-class French citizens, who flock here for their summer vacations and live on costs that approximate $25 per day.

1. Orientation & Getting Around

In all the years that I've been visiting and exploring Nice, I have never once used a bus or taxi for travels within the city—it's that concentrated and small in area. For trips outside Nice, one uses the train for locations along the coast, as they leave with extraordinary frequency and take but a short while for the ride to Monaco (in one direction), to Cannes and St. Tropez (in the other). For trips inland, into the mountains of Provence (the French département in which Nice is located, buses depart from the **main bus terminal** next to the Place Masséna, and the staff in your hotel will advise you of routes and schedules.

Far more important is that you learn about the price differences between seaside and train station locations in Nice:

2. The Many Budget Hotels of Nice

NEAR THE RAILROAD STATION: To understand the hotel situation in Nice, look at our map, and imagine that you are walking from the railroad station to the sea. As you near the water, hotel prices increase; at the waterside, hotel prices become astronomic; if you stay near the railroad station, hotel costs are entirely moderate. While there are one or two outstanding exceptions to this rule, the bulk of our hotel selections will be found in the station district.

Don't assume, though, that staying in a hotel near the top of the map will keep you from the all-important bathing and sunning facilities of the town. Nice is packed into a relatively small area, and the railroad station is about a 20-minute walk from the beach. Furthermore, the station section is as quiet and clean as any other in the city.

The street which runs in front of the railroad station is the Avenue Thiers, and running perpendicular to it are a series of little side-streets—the treasured locales of my favorite budget hotels in Nice. The hotel to which I head happens to be one of the plainest and most basic in the area—don't stop there if you require creature comforts. But the **Hotel Darcy,** 28 Rue d'Angleterre (phone 88-67-06), not only has rock-bottom, third-class prices for its 25 rooms on four floors—68 francs ($8.50) single, 90 francs ($11.25) for *grand-lit* doubles, 130 francs ($16.25) for triples, 162 francs ($20.25) for quads, breakfast included—but its present owners, Monsieur and Madame Santonci (and their teenage daughter Arielle, who learned English in Pennsylvania) have guaranteed these prices, for holders of this book only, until the end of 1985. The Darcy has for years served as a virtual clubhouse for its $25-a-day guests, the owners acting as translators, information dispensers, ticket agents, and confidants. Whenever Hope and I look in on the Darcy, we are invariably besieged by young couples and students, all begging us to sing the praise of the hotel. We fully agree.

THE FRENCH FRANC: Presently exchanged at the rate of 8 francs to one dollar, the French franc is therefore worth about 12.5¢.

There are immediate, nearby alternatives to the Darcy, if the Darcy is packed: first, the 29-room **Hotel Novelty** at 26 Rue d'Angleterre (phone 87-51-73), with nearly identical rates for clean, sunny and typically French rooms, well maintained by the English-speaking owner, Mr. Fillatreau; and then, the much better, impressive former mansion that's now the **Hotel Belle Meunière,** at 21 Avenue Durante (phone 88-66-15), two short blocks from the Darcy, and with a gravel courtyard in front for parking. At the latter, bathless doubles can run as high as 125 francs ($15.62), again with breakfast, service and tax included.

Up in Quality

Back in the more familiar area of second-class accommodations, the older tourists will find an exceptional value in the sunny, pleasant, and elevator-equipped **Hotel D'Orsay,** at 20 Rue Alsace-Lorraine (phone 88-45-02), just two short blocks down from the station, and slightly to the east of it. Eighty francs for a bathless single with breakfast, 130 francs ($16.25) for a double, in a clean and quiet building. If the D'Orsay is full, the **Hotel Normandie,** around the corner at 18 Rue Paganini (phone 88-48-83), can take the overflow (but for about $5 per person more, as virtually all rooms here are with private shower).

For readers who can't take another step, the 61-room **Hotel des Nations,** 25 Avenue Durante (phone 88-30-58), is located in front of the railroad station (but faces a large garden on the other side), and has always found favor with $25-a-day'ers. Average rates of 125 francs ($15.62) for a single with breakfast, but without private bath; 170 francs ($21.25) for a double with two breakfasts, and with service and taxes included. While the superficial impression of the hotel, from the railroad station, is not a good one, once inside you'll not only look out upon the aforementioned garden, but find a quiet reading room, surprisingly quiet bedrooms, and parking space for your car. A good budget choice.

Along the Avenue Thiers, which runs in front of the station, there's a great variety of budget establishments, some with rock-bottom prices, but none as well recommended as those listed above. The **Hotel Lyon-Milan,** at 5 Avenue Thiers (phone 88-22-87), typical of the station hotels, charges 90 francs ($11.25) for one person, 120 francs ($15) for two, 150 francs ($18.75) for a three-person room, breakfast, service and taxes included, and the hotel is clean and well maintained by an owner who has traveled in the United States. . . . The **Hotel Rochambeau,** 27 Avenue Thiers (phone 88-96-18), charges 145 francs ($18.12) for their bathless doubles (with breakfast); and at the other end of the street, the **Hotel de Berne,** 1 Avenue Thiers (phone 88-25-08), will quote only slightly higher rates: 165 francs ($20.62) double, including breakfast.

NEAR THE SEA: Now we'll take up those rare exceptions to the rule that moderately priced hotels are to be found only in the station area. One block from the sea, directly behind the swank hotels of the Promenade des Anglais ("Europe on $200 a Day"), the little Avenue de Suède houses three exciting finds: the **Hotel le Meurice,** 14 Avenue de Suède (phone 87-74-93), which charges 155 francs ($19.37) for a bathless double room, breakfast, service and taxes included: the 14-room **Hotel Canada** at 8 Rue Halévy (off the avenue, 100 yards away), managed by a young Dutch couple who charge 90 francs ($11.25) for a bathless single, 120 francs ($15) for a bathless double, plus 16 francs ($2) extra per person for breakfast, and the recently upgraded **Hotel Harvey,** 18 Avenue de Suède (phone 96-16-43), which asks a splurgy 245 francs ($30.62) for its double rooms *with* private bath (and that includes breakfast, service and tax), but only 200 francs ($25) for doubles with private shower and breakfast, with supplementary beds priced at 75 francs ($9.37), including breakfast, for the third or fourth person in a twin-bedded room. Lobby of the earlier mentioned Meurice is on the second floor of its building (take the elevator), and rooms are cool and almost antiseptically clean; while the more expensive Harvey was thoroughly redone in recent years by its new and charming owners, the English-speaking Passeris, who installed air conditioning and an elevator. If all three hotels are filled, then try the cute, little **Hotel Paris-Nice,** again only a block from the beach (but at 58 Rue de France, phone 88-38-61), with rates of 165 francs ($20.62) single, 210 francs ($26.25) for a good double with private bath, with new carpeting, breakfast, service and taxes included. That's just behind the deluxe Hotel Negresco.

TWO AREAS FOR OLDER READERS: The Rue Paul Déroulède, just off the Avenue Jean Médecin (Nice's main boulevard), and only a few short blocks from the beach, is an oasis of quiet and calm, with fewer humans and activity than you might find elsewhere, and two top budget hotels: the **Hotel d'Italie,** 9 Rue Paul Déroulède, phone 88-35-90 (as pleasant as they come, and highly recommended; 165 francs ($20.62 for bathless doubles, 14 francs extra for a shower, but breakfast and all else included), and the older and even slightly elegant (it has a drawing room lifted straight from the time of Napoleon and Josephine) **Hotel Athena,** 11 Rue Paul Déroulède (phone 88-03-19), where all rooms have private bath and rent for 125 francs ($15.62) per person in double rooms, breakfast, service and tax included. Both hotels are virtually in sight of the sea, and perfect for our quiet-living readers; they are, indeed, perhaps the best of Nice's moderately priced hotels, in this middle range.

Two other relatively inexpensive hotels are found about halfway between the station and the sea—both near the intersection of the Boulevard Victor Hugo and the Rue Grimaldi. These are: the **Nouvel Hotel,** 19 bis Boulevard Victor Hugo (phone 87-73-60) and the **Hotel King-George,** 15 Rue Grimaldi (phone 87-73-61). Because of their location, both charge highest second-class prices: 145 francs ($18.12) for a bathless double at the Nouvel, 230 francs ($28.75) for a double with private bath or shower at the King-George. The Nouvel should be your first choice.

ON THE SEA: If you insist on a room that is actually on the sea, about the best you can do is the small white villa with adjoining garden that constitutes the **Hotel Eden,** 99 bis Promenade des Anglais (phone 86-53-70), five blocks along the sea from the world-famed Hotel Negresco. Proprietors M. and Mme. Prone like having U.S. guests (and that's a fact) and charge only 115 francs ($14.37) for two bathless singles, 230 francs ($28.75) for doubles or twins with private shower, 275 francs ($34.38) for triples with shower, including breakfast in each instance. If you're traveling alone, try to rent the single room near the reception desk, from which the Mediterranean is in plain view. . . . Cheaper than, but almost as suitable as, the above, but 50 yards away from the sea, is the larger and therefore more easily booked **Hotel Magnan,** on Square Général-Ferrié (phone 86-76-00), a modern, elevator-equipped, six-story building in which most rooms have balconies looking onto the Mediterranean, and nevertheless rent for 200 francs ($25) a night, double, breakfast for two and private shower included. At the Magnan, you can put on bathing suits in your room, then—in beach robes—walk the 50 yards to the Promenade des Anglais and the sea. A high recommendation.

SEVERAL SCATTERED CHOICES: Hotel **Ann-Margareth**, at 1 Avenue St-Joseph, a small side street off Avenue Gambetta (the sixth, coming from the train station), phone 88-72-23, is among the stand-outs of the two-star Nice hotels, with 30 bathless rooms. Singles without bath: 85 francs ($10.62), doubles 110 francs ($13.75), triples 130 francs ($16.25), quads 150 francs ($18.75), breakfast included; some rooms with private facilities for 30% more. Ideal if you like quiet surroundings.

Hotel Meublé Célimène, 65 Rue de France, 200 yards off 33 Promenade des Anglais, and next door to the Musée Masséna (phone 88-61-51), rents a total of ten rooms, all on the second floor (there is an elevator), at the remarkable rate of 85 francs ($10.62) for a double with shower, 110 francs ($13.75) with private w.c.! Each room is equipped with a kitchenette, which can be used for a daily supplement of 12 francs, or $1.50 (complete with pots, pans and refrigerator); and preference is obviously given to guests staying a week or longer—phone first, as this place is heavily booked.

Hotel de la Victoire, 43 Avenue Jean Médecin (phone 88-02-05), is a small, no frills (only 14 rooms) but very friendly place, which charges 85 francs ($10.62) single, 130 francs ($16.25) double, breakfast included.

OTHER FROMMER BOOKS: Europe on $25 a Day, has now been supplemented by five other $$$-a-Day guides and seven Dollarwise Guides dealing with individual European countries or areas: **Ireland on $25 a Day, Greece on $25 a Day, Spain and Morocco (plus the Canary Islands) on $25 a Day, England and Scotland on $25 a Day,** and **Scandinavia on $25 a Day, Dollarwise Guide to England & Scotland, Dollarwise Guide to France, Dollarwise Guide to Italy, Dollarwise Guide to Germany, Dollarwise Guide to Switzerland & Liechtenstein, Dollarwise Guide to Austria & Hungary, Dollarwise Guide to Portugal, Madeira, & the Azores.** In contrast with the book you are now reading, which deals primarily with 21 major European cities, each of the above guides treats in depth one particular country or area, and sets forth hotel, restaurant and sightseeing suggestions for literally scores of individual cities and tourist destinations in that country or area. The Frommer Books can be obtained at most bookstores, or by mailing the appropriate amount (refer to the last page in this guide) for each book to Frommer/Pasmantier Publishers, 1230 Avenue of the Americas, New York, New York 10020.

Hotel Wilson, 39 Rue de l'Hotel-des-Postes (phone 85-47-79), is plain but clean, and in a superb location within short walking distance of the central Place Masséna. Seventeen rooms on the third floor of an elevator-lacking apartment building in which doubles rent for only 85 francs ($10.62), singles for only 65 francs ($8.12), no breakfast, with additional beds at 15 francs and showers for 6 francs. Proprietress Madame Zerbib speaks just enough English for communication.

HOTELS, STARVATION-BUDGET STYLE: Hotel Alp Azur, 15 Rue

Michel Ange (phone 84-57-61), is a five-story building without elevator, but in a quiet location 15 minutes on foot from the station (toward the Old City), and well managed by English-speaking M. and Mme. Fernez. They charge only 95 francs ($11.87) for a double room, 105 francs ($13.12) for a twin, 120 francs ($15) triple, with a supplement of 12 francs ($1.50) per day for guests wishing to rent a kitchenette. Take bus no. 1, 2 or 22 from the Avenue Malaussena (near the station) to Michel Ange (third stop).

Hotel Radio, 6 Rue Miron (phone 62-10-65), consisting of 40 rooms in a six-floor, elevator-equipped building, charges only 90 francs ($11.25) for a double room with one large bed, 100 francs ($12.50) twin, 140 francs ($17.50) triple, 170 francs ($21.25) quad, including breakfast served in an attractively furnished room on the second floor. Madame Ghnassia is the English-speaking manageress.

Hotel du Centre, 2 Rue de Suisse (phone 88-83-85), with elevator, is ideally situated near the Avenue Jean Médecin and the station, and can service your starvation-budget needs if you're able to rent one of its bathless rooms (the majority are with shower); the former include such stunning values as a one-large-bed double room for only 115 francs ($14.37), including breakfast, served to your room by manageress Madame Cipollon. The nearby **Hotel Gilbert,** 14 Rue Pertinax (phone 85-16-60), is for single travellers, who can obtain there a single room without bath for only 65 francs ($8.12), breakfast included.

Hotel les Orangers, 10 bis Avenue Durante (phone 87-51-41), managed by a charming English-speaking couple, Jocelyne and Marc Servole, deserves special mention. Two hundred yards from the railway station, it has 12 rooms (with one to six beds) on three floors, and these (guaranteed) 1985 rates: only 48 and 57 francs ($6 and $7.12) for singles, 85 to 130 francs ($10.62 to $16.25) for doubles or twins, 160 francs ($20) for triples, 200 francs ($25) for quads, the same (in total) 200 francs for a five-bedded room, only 260 francs ($32.50) for a six-bedder! Each room is equipped with a hotplate, pots, pans and cutlery, and a supermarket is around the corner for supplies. If the Servoles are full (and they've housed hundreds of readers over the years), they'll help you find alternate accommodations in Nice, no matter how many phone calls that requires.

READERS' HOTEL SELECTIONS: "For those anxious to escape the downtown din, I recommend the **Hotel Helios,** 54 Boulevard de Cimiez (phone 53-04-55). A single room was 130 francs, including breakfast and free showers. The hotel is situated on a hill above Nice, with a bus route providing frequent and quick transportation" (Dale C. Dalton, Sunnyvale, California). . . . "The **Central Hotel,** 10 Rue de Suisse (phone 88-85-08), offers charmingly furnished rooms at low prices—110 francs double, including breakfast. And location is quite near the railroad station" (Vincent and Nancy Traina, Studio City, California; Harriet Baumgarten-Schultz, Portland, Maine; note by AF: 1985 rates of this no-frills but clean and central place are: 80 francs, $10, single; 110 francs, $13.75, twin; 140 francs, $17.50, triple, including a good breakfast served in your room by the owner Madame Norma Cornacchini). . . . "At the **Hotel Le Clemenceau,** 3 Avenue G. Clemenceau (phone 88-61-19), we enjoyed a spotless double room with comfortable beds, and the freshest continental breakfast we had in months, all for 110 francs ($12.94). This is near the station and the beach and is managed by the former director of another of your recommendations, who still has the 'touch'" (Dr. and Mrs. Robert Giller, San Marino,

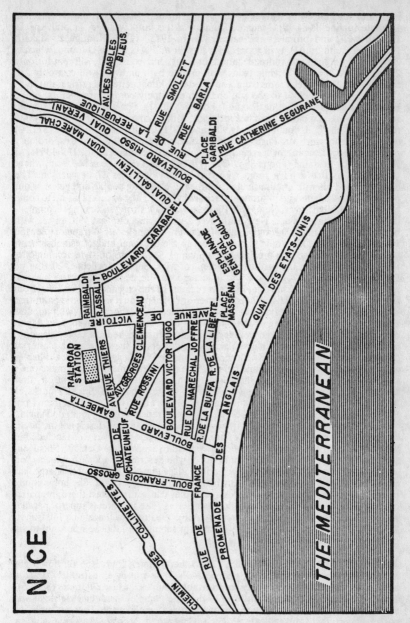

Map of Nice showing streets including: AV. DES DIABLES BLEUS, RUE SMOLETT, RUE BARLA, RUE CATHERINE SEGURANE, PLACE GARIBALDI, AV. DE LA REPUBLIQUE, BOULEVARD RISSO, QUAI VERNAI, QUAI GALLIENI, QUAI MARECHAL, BOULEVARD CARABACEL, RAIMBALDI, R. ASSALT, BOULEVARD DE VICTOIRE, AV. GEORGES CLEMENCEAU, RUE ROSSINI, RAILROAD STATION, AVENUE THIERS, RUE DE CHATEUNEUF, GAMBETTA, BOUL. FRANCOIS GROSSO, CHEMIN DES COLLINETTES, RUE DE FRANCE, BOULEVARD VICTOR HUGO, RUE DU MARECHAL JOFFRE, AVENUE DE RUE R. DE LA BUFFA, R. DE LA LIBERTE, BOUL. FRANCOIS, PROMENADE DES ANGLAIS, PLACE MASSENA, ESPLANADE GENERAL DE GAULLE, QUAI DES ETATS-UNIS, NICE, THE MEDITERRANEAN

California; note by A.F.: In 1985, Le Clemenceau will charge 85 francs single, 110 francs double, 130 francs triple, 160 francs for four persons, all rates including breakfast, and all for large, cheerful rooms with high ceilings and terracotta floors). . . "We were surprised, in 1984, to pay only $26 for a double with private bath and kitchen (with fridge) at the nicely located **Hotel Durante,** 16 Avenue Durante (phone 88-84-40). Madame Dufaure of this hotel was very helpful, speaks English well, and promises the same rates in 1985" (Cora Rodriguez, Makati, Phillipines; note by AF: twin rooms with shower and w.c. at the Durante, which is 200 yards from the main railroad station, in a park-like courtyard, will rent for only 200 francs—$26 in 1985, while twins with private bath and w.c. will cost only 210 francs—$26.25; all such rooms come equipped with kitchenette and refrigerator. . . . "A beautiful hotel close to the station, with extremely cordial proprietors, is the **Hotel Lyonnais** at 20 Rue de Russie (phone 88-70-74). For an immaculate double room with sink and bidet, breakfast included, with clean towels every other day and toilet across the hall, you'll pay only 90 francs ($11.25) in 1985, 100 francs ($12.50) with private shower! Mr. Pages and his family, the proprietors, are extraordinary people" (Peggy Boman, Switzerland). . . . "We must recommend the **Hotel Prior,** 5 Rue d'Alsace-Lorraine (phone 88-20-24), right off the Avenue Jean Médecin, where the two of us had a huge room with two double beds, for $7 per person. The concierge and his wife are unusually friendly and charming people and acted as our personal travel agents and information bureau in Nice. They were a pleasure to come home to" (Marilyn Silver, New Hyde Park, New York); strong seconding recommendation from Judith Weiner, New York, N.Y., who points out that 1985 prices with breakfast will be only 100 francs double (there are no singles), 130 francs triple, 150 francs quadruple. This would appear to be an almost ideal budget establishment, with a pleasant terrace for breakfast or lounging. . . . "Pension-style accommodations are available in the private apartment of **Mrs. Sophie Koelichen,** 20 Rue de France (phone 88-26-70), whose flat is located on the main floor of the famous, historical Palais Marie-Christine, in the very heart of the city and a block away from the Promenade des Anglais. While the exterior is sumptuous, with a little palm-tree square in front, the interior has been converted into apartments with modest appointments, but including everything that is necessary for a pleasant stay. Upon our arrival, we found a large double bedroom with twin beds, a table, a vanity, night-tables, armchairs and chairs. There were flowers on the table and a platter of oranges to welcome us. Mrs. Koelichen (or Madame Sophie as everyone calls her) is an unusually warm and hospitable person, who does her utmost to help make one's stay pleasant and home-like. She allows young people to use her kitchen, thus enabling them to save on food and repeatedly invited us to tea. She has stacks of letters from grateful tourists and students from all over the world, many of them from the U.S. and Canada, where she is called 'our dear French Mother,' 'our good angel,' 'our loved friend.' She charges 140 francs for two and while breakfast is not included, she will serve one upon request. We strongly feel that she deserves to be included in your book" (Prof. Monique Wagner, Wayne State University, Detroit, Michigan, seconded by Mrs. T. Rubnikowicz of London, who describes Madame Sophie as "an ex-Polish aristocrat, who formerly owned the Palace in which she now has a large flat. She is always gay, and speaks so many languages I have lost count. She helps young people with their shopping to save costs, and they can get breakfast there, prepared by her, or they can cook something for themselves. The location is superb, parallel with the Promenade des Anglais"; note by A.F.: 1985 rates will again be 140 francs, $17.50, for one of Mrs. Koelichen's three twin rooms—in a house where up to six persons can be accommodated).

APARTMENTS AND FURNISHED ROOMS. "The **Liberty Hotel,** 5 bis Rue Berlioz (right near the Promenade des Anglais, phone 88-59-23), is run by an extremely friendly and helpful manager who lets large, comfortable doubles for just 130 francs ($16.25). Each room has a delightful feature: a kitchenette complete with electric stove and sink and all the pots, pans, crockery and cutlery you would want. This can cut living costs wonderfully" (Mr. and Mrs. P. Hirst, Chatswood, N.S.W., Australia; note by AF: scores of young Americans, in particular, stay each year at the Hotel Liberty, and fill its guest book with enthusiastic appreciations. On a recent summer day, Hope and I met five football-types from San Jose State College who were all living in one double room at the Liberty, for a total of 150 francs (only 30 francs per person) per night—and cooking their own meals!). . . . "As it is situated on the inner court of a pedestrian mall, the **Hotel Rex,** 3 Rue Masséna (phone 87-87-38), is extremely quiet.

And since it is only three short blocks from the sea, you save money on bus fares—everything is convenient (the old town, bus station, Prisunic and markets). All rooms are with private showers, some with kitchenettes, some with balconies, and doubles in 1985 will rent for 130 francs ($16.25), with kitchenettes an extra 20 francs ($2.50) per day; proprietress is the charming, vivacious Mme Claude Verna" (Aaron B. Everett, St. Peter, Minnesota). . . . "Try 'housekeeping' to beat the August prices for rooms in Nice. At the **'Primavera,'** 3 Avenue Auber (phone 88-44-23), just half a block north of Blvd. Victor Hugo on the west side of the street, one can obtain bathless rooms, double, for low cost, depending upon how well you negotiate with the proprietors. We paid $14 double, with the proviso that we wouldn't cook *too much* (though we could heat morning water for shaving and coffee). Pots and pans are provided for breakfast and snacks" (John and Florence Lane, Salt Lake City, Utah; note by A.F.: in 1985, double rooms here will rent for 100 francs in July and August, 85 francs all other months, while singles will sell for 90 francs in July and August, 80 francs all other months; another *meuble* in Nice, offering kitchen facilities, and superior to the Primavera, is the **Hotel-Meublé Flor-Amy,** at 13 Rue d'Italie, phone 88-56-92, charging 45 to 60 francs per person).

HOTELS—THE BIG SPLURGE: With its skilled and multi-lingual staff, large lobby with antique furniture, functioning elevator, and especially its attractive rooms with television, phone, radio, private bath and w.c., the 80-room **Hotel Napoleon,** 6 Rue Grimaldi (phone 87-70-07), is to me the best of the 30-or-so three-star hotels of Nice, offering considerable value at 245 francs ($30.62) single, 335 francs ($41.87) twin, plus 22 francs ($2.75) per person for optional breakfast. Location is also ideal, no more than 150 yards from the sea and the Promenade des Anglais. For those occasions when you'd like to break loose into something more elegant than you've thus far been experiencing on your trip, this is the place.

A VERY SPECIAL HOSTEL: Despite its name, the 150-bed **Relais International de la Jeunesse** at Avenue Scuderi, no house number (phone 81-27-63), takes persons of all ages into a structure built by volunteers of no particular political or religious affiliation, who simply advocate friendship between people of good will; when I last visited, I saw one guest who looked 80 years old! Location is one of the city's best residential districts adjoining a private park and open-air swimming pool; rooms are clean and airy housing three to 20 persons apiece in double decker beds; each room has private bath and w.c.; and yet prices are only 35 francs ($4.37) per night, including breakfast, while lunch or supper—hors d'oeuvre, meat dish with vegetable and salad, fruit or cheese—is 29 francs ($3.62), with wine 8 francs ($1) extra per liter. A single drawback to the Relais is an 11 p.m. curfew, but considering the open-minded international ambiance, the setting and the price, that's a small concession to pay. Take bus #15 from Place Masséna to the Scuderi stop (20 minutes and 4.50 francs away), turn left into the winding Scuderi Avenue, walk for about 500 yards passing imposing villas, palm trees and other exotic vegetation, and you'll find the Relais, which is also called "Clairvallon," to your right, where the big cypress trees are.

THE OFFICIAL YOUTH HOSTEL: Nice's one and only official youth hostel, **Auberge de la Jeunesse,** at Route Forestière (no house number), phone 89-23-64, has a total capacity of 60 cots, 30 each for men and women, and charges 35 francs ($4.37) per night, a Spartan breakfast included. On a hill in the outskirts overlooking the town, the hostel is best

reached by bus no. 14 to Mont Alban. But phone first, between 7 and 10 a.m., as no one will reply during other times of the day.

A GEOGRAPHICAL NOTE: The main street of Nice, formerly the Avenue de la Victoire, was renamed the Avenue Jean Médecin in recent times, after the gentleman who was mayor of Nice from 1928 to 1965. Avenue de la Victoire may occasionally still be referred to as such by the citizens of Nice.

We turn to food:

3. Nice Restaurants

Loosen your belt, take a deep breath, and pitch in: Nice is a gourmet's paradise, at low (for France) prices. This is mainly because the fixed price (prix fixe) meal in Nice is no rarity, but the general rule. In a city with over 120 restaurants, there are less than ten that offer only à la carte selections. And, while a Parisian restaurant normally serves three courses on its prix fixe, the restaurants in Nice often throw in four. This, remember, is the city where the French come to relax: the meals are huge and delicious.

Moreover, the *most* you need pay for one of these three-course feasts (except in the first class or deluxe restaurants) is 58 francs ($7.25)—and there are spots in town that charge 38 to 40 francs ($4.75 to $5) for almost the same meal! Hope and I have had at least one course at each, and can advise that there's only the subtlest of difference between the highest and lowest-priced (although there's often a course or two lacking in the under-30-franc places). We'll discuss them in descending order of price, and suggest that you carefully note whether the charge includes wine.

FOR 58 FRANCS ($7.25): Costliest of our choices, but well worth the splurge, is **La Taverne de l'Opera** at 8 Rue St. François de Paule, next to the famous Opera House and even better known Flower Market, only 200 yards from the azure sparkle of the Mediterranean Sea; you can eat either indoors or out. And what you receive for 58 francs ($7.25) is an appetizer, main course with vegetable, and dessert, as well as your choice of wine, beer or mineral water, with service charge included in the price.

The Luxury Cafeterias

Two modern cafeterias, located in super-modern shopping centers, provide a contrast but an equally high-quality meal, for the same 58 francs ($7.25). The air-conditioned **Cafeteria Nice Etoile** occupies the second floor of a futuristic complex of shops at 30 Avenue Jean Médecin, corner of Blvd. Dubouchage, reached by an external elevator shaped like a Montgolfier balloon (or by escalator), serves *plats du jour* (daily platters) for only 16 francs ($2), and prices its other dishes—such as minestrone soup for an appetizer, cheese for dessert, in such a way as to enable you to create a three-course meal, with wine, for precisely 58 francs ($7.25). Closed Sundays. A similarly styled **Cafeteria Le Montreal** at 11 Rue Maccarani, off the Place Grimaldi only 300 yards from the sea, is found on the second floor of a new shopping center building called Espace Grimaldi which houses 16 boutiques and a ladies' hairdresser. Here, the blackboard actually lists two daily three-course meals for 45 francs ($5.62) and 50 francs ($6.25), an example of the latter being spaghetti with meat sauce as your appetizer, roast chicken as the main plate, ice cream for dessert. In this busy part of the new city of Nice near the beaches, you'll see numerous other restaurants with slightly higher prices, but this is one of the best choices. Closed Sundays.

FROM 42 TO 45 FRANCS ($5.25 to $5.63): Restaurant Arc-en-Ciel

(Rainbow), at 6 Place Wilson, is a rather distinguished restaurant patronized by upper-middle-class residents (and where you'll seldom see tourists), which charges—either because of that reason or despite it—only 42 francs ($5.25) for a three-course meal at either lunch or dinnertime. It consists of an hors d'oeuvre to start, meat or fish with vegetable or salad, and dessert. While wine is not included, a small pitcher big enough for two is only 8 francs ($1). Closed Friday evenings and Saturdays. Walk up the Rue des Postes behind the Galeries Lafayette department store; Place Wilson is the square with enormous trees, a small park complete with fountain and children's playground equipment.

Restaurant Le Coquet, 18 Rue Pertinax, open weekdays only, is a rather simply furnished place, but one that serves above-average food to the shopkeepers and store clerks employed in the area, to whom it prices its three-course meal, wine included, at always under 45 francs ($5.63). And you can choose the specialty plats du jour for only 27 francs (the frequent customers do)—like *tripes Niçoises,* a highlight of the cuisine of Provence, served with stewed tomatoes.

Restaurant Acchiardo, 38 Rue Droite, in the heart of the old city, open every day of the week, serves delicious *plats du jour* for 30 francs ($3.75), like loup du mer—steamed whitefish with aioli sauce—and potatoes, carrots and celery, my own happy selection in the spring of 1984. Adding half a bottle of local wine, and cheese for dessert, a filling meal will cost less than 45 francs ($5.63). While you may be the only non-French eating here, the bright waitresses understand English.

Restaurant La Petite Biche, 9 Rue Alsace-Lorraine, is a small, sidewalk-tables bistro whose fixed-price, three-course meal, costing only 44 francs ($5.50), almost always starts with a flavorsome fish soup, goes on to grilled pork or fried chicken with salad, and ends with cheese or ice cream for dessert. Wine is 8 francs ($1) extra.

FOR 38 TO 40 FRANCS ($4.75 TO $5): Star of this price category,

and one of the largest restaurants in this central area of new Nice, is the important **Restaurant du Soleil** at 7 bis Rue d'Italie, corner of Rue de Russie. Open seven days a week from mid-morning until late at night, it charges only 38 francs ($4.75) for a three-course meal, includes wine in the price (and service charge, too), and typically selects salade Niçoise as your opener, then roast turkey with french fries (*pommes frites*) for the next course, then an apple tarte (*tarte de maison*) as your dessert, all accompanied by a quarter liter of red, rosé or white wine. Not only is the 38-franc price guaranteed until the end of 1985, but owner Roger Germain will grant you an additional discount of 2 francs per person if you display this book to his wife, his son or himself!

Restaurant de Paris, in the station area at 28 Rue d'Angleterre, is nearly as good as the Au Soleil (above), and charges 40 francs ($5), wine included, for a three-course meal that might begin with mussels, omelette or grapefruit, then go on to a quarter roast chicken with french fries or vegetables, conclude with fruit or crème caramel, and include wine, beer or a Coke as your included beverage. The English-speaking Mr. Eubaz is the owner, and he opens for both lunch and dinner every day but Mondays.

Here's another stand-out. At the clean, airy, popular and always crowded **Restaurant Maire,** upstairs at 10 Rue Suisse, in the very heart of Nice, monsieur the owner sits behind the cash register coolly surveying all, and the three, good-looking blonde waitresses with napkins over their left shoulders, are his daughters and daughter-in-law. They dispense three-course meals for just 40 francs ($5), and you can choose from five different first courses (which usually include the classic quiche Lorraine appetizer), 15 main courses and five types of dessert! Open from 11:30 a.m. to 2 p.m., from 6 to 9 p.m., and closed on Saturdays.

Finally, **Restaurant Chez Palmyre** is our 40-franc choice in the Old City of Nice, at 5 Rue Droite. Widely popular, although it has only eight tables (all covered in red-and-white-checked oilcloth), the food here is so good that you'll have to endure a short wait in line unless you come early. Three courses (five or six choices of appetizer and entree, plus fruit, cheese or yogurt for dessert) cost only 40 francs ($5), with wine 6 francs extra. Open seven days a week, for lunch starting at noon, for dinner starting at seven.

UNDER 30 FRANCS ($3.75): The 320-seat **Flunch** at 7 Rue Halévy, within sight of the Promenade des Anglais and the Meridien Hotel, is the largest self-service restaurant in Nice, offering an immense selection of plates (from minestrone to Cordon Bleu), at remarkable prices: a blackboard near the serving counter every day lists a suggested three-course meal (one example: tomato soup, cheese omelette, salad, ice cream and beverage) for under 30 francs ($3.75)! A second Flunch, with identical policies, has recently opened near the train station. Both are open seven days a week, from 11 a.m. to 2:30 p.m., and from 6 to 10 p.m.

THE CHEAPER MEALS: Funds depleted? Then turn to our "Starvation Budget" section, or else head—but only in the direst of emergencies—for the **Restaurant Municipal,** at 1 Rue Guigonis, in the old city, near the Place St. François. This is Nice's city-owned people's restaurant, officially open only to local residents, but they may be willing to serve you lunch (not dinner), from 11:45 a.m. to 1 p.m., and the price for a two-course menu, with no choices about it, is 10 francs ($1.25). And after that, head for the nearest telegraph for funds to return home (or to the **Accueil de Nuit,** 14 Rule Jules-Gilly, also in Old Nice, where you can stay for free, demi-pension!).

PICNICS AND PAN BAGNAT: As we've pointed out before, the mid-day meal in the restaurants of Nice is the "expensive" one; the evening meal sometimes plummets in price. To beat the relatively high cost of lunch, and to eat sensibly at the same time, you'll occasionally want to consider a do-it-yourself picnic. And the place for those picnic ingredients is the unusually inexpensive grocery section (look for the sign "Libre Service

Alimentation") of the **Prisunic Department Store** on the Avenue Jean Médecin, corner of Avenue Maréchal Foch, where huge chunks of cheese are 5 francs, a container of milk 5 francs, enough lunch meat for three large sandwiches is 12 francs, and cucumber or carrot salad or tomatoes provençales sell for 21 francs the kilo (2.2 lbs)! In a restaurant, you'd pay 18 francs for a large bottle of brand-named mineral water; here the same bottle sells for 7 francs. A huge quart-and-a-quarter of good red wine is 8 francs; even a full quart bottle of Coca-Cola is only 6 francs. And, of course, vast loaves of French bread sell for 2.20 and 3 francs—and under.

The Prisunic is also where you may be introduced to Nice's famous fill-you-up-for-hours sandwich, a picnic lunch in itself called the *pan bagnat*. Best described as a salade niçoise inserted into a six-inch-diameter roll, a pan bagnat (enough, believe me, for lunch) sells for 10 francs ($1.25) at a ground floor counter found just as you walk through the corner entrance of the Prisunic. That may be the city's cheapest price for pan bagnats, which are found in snack bars, bakeries and charcuteries (delicatessens) all over town. A pan bagnat near the sea? Try the **Station Uvale,** a snack stand selling them for 12 francs, on the Rue Halévy, 20 feet from the Promenade des Anglais.

READERS' RESTAURANT SELECTIONS: "Self-Service Cafe de Paris, 42 Rue Pastorelli, has excellent cold hors d'oeuvres, several of which along with cheese, bread and wine, cost 16 to 20 francs. Hot dishes are also good quality and reasonably priced, and the sidewalk cafe atmosphere is unique for this kind of establishment" (G. Wehrenberg, Kent, Washington). . . . "Another self-service cafeteria in Nice is the **Café de Paris** at 42 Rue Pastorelli, just off the Avenue Jean Médecin, where hors d'oeuvres start at 4.50 francs, meat plates at 11 francs, desserts at 5 francs, drinks at 4.50 francs, although most items sell for more than those minimums. This is quite similar to the cafeterias in Paris" (Pauline Rissman, New York, New York). . . . "The **Restaurant d'Angleterre**, at 25 Rue d'Angleterre, serves soup, a main plate (perhaps a meat course with vegetables) and a dessert for 44 francs. Wine is 8 francs more. They also offer a daily platter for 28 francs" (Susan Pollak, Brunswick, Maine).

4. On a Sub-Starvation Budget

For your most decent rock-bottom dining, you'll need to walk about half an hour from the center of Nice, but you'll save at least 15 francs per meal by dining at the **Restaurant Universitaire,** 3 Avenue Robert Schuman, during the ten months (September through June) when it's in operation. Head down the Rue de France, turn right into the Boulevard François Grosso, cross under highway bridge, then left into the winding road (that's the Avenue Robert Schuman), passing palm trees, a small restaurant, a yellow wall bearing student inscriptions (*liberez Corsica*), and then, on your left, the Restaurant Universitaire. Step inside to the *caisse* (cashier), request a *tarif passager* meal ticket for 24 francs ($3)—no student card required—and you'll receive a three-course meal, plus an orange, in the cavernous, 600-seat basement dining hall. Watch the hours, which are from 11:30 a.m. to 1:30 p.m. for lunch, 6:30 to 8 p.m. for dinner, Monday through Saturday only.

SUB-STARVATION BUDGET: Europe on $3 a day? In Nice, it's possible, but only suggested if you're really down and out. The **Restaurant**

Municipal, 1 Rue Guigonis (in the old city), is a city-owned people's restaurant charging only 10 francs ($1.25) per two-course meal, and open Monday through Friday from 11:30 a.m. to 1 p.m.

If a turnout of pockets doesn't produce even 10 francs, despair not. Just head for the spartan but clean dining room at the **Fourneau Economique,** 1 Rue du Choeur (also in the old city), where Catholic nuns dish out hot soup and a plat du jour daily except Thursdays and Sundays from 11:30 a.m. to 1 p.m., for free.

And while you're thinking of ways to earn some cash, or waiting for a check from home, you can get a bed and half-board (just enough to survive) at the **Accueil de Nuit,** 14 Rue Jules Gilly (old city). The first three nights are free, after that you can stay for eight more nights paying 10 francs ($1.25) per night. Accommodations are dormitory style; men and women are accepted; apply between 6 and 7 p.m.

5. Hope's Museums of the Riviera

There's more to Nice and vicinity than sunning and swimming. Hope has contributed the following report on the culture of the Côte d'Azur.

IN THE AREA NEAR NICE: "Rainy days on the Riviera can be richly rewarding if you spend them visiting some of the fast-growing number of museums that dot the area. With Nice as your base, you can take a train or bus to nearly every point of interest; the train for coastal locations, the bus for the inland hills.

"The train station in Nice you already know; the bus depot called 'Gare Routière' is behind the Place Masséna, between Avenue Felix Faure and Avenue Jean Jaures, and has large blue and white signs clearly indicating different destinations; buses leave with some frequency, and you can pay on board. Whatever the weather, you should bend every effort to get to the following:

Foundation Maeght—Saint Paul

"The **Marguerite and Aimé Maeght Foundation,** built by the well-known gallery owner and art lover on his estate just outside Saint-Paul (a quaint looking, but really swinging, old walled city which you should take time to explore), is part of an eventual art center, and undoubtedly was a most revolutionary advance in museum design. I urge you to see it—the site is like a happening in total beauty. Every element of it is placed organically —the breathtaking natural setting is used as a background for sculpture, and in turn, the trees, plants, and flowers take on the aspects of works of art; the two white concrete arcs (that look like the tops of nuns' hats) on the roof of the building are incorporated into the symbol which guides you to the museum; the front 'lawn' is scattered with delightful modern sculpture that seems as though it had grown in the garden—gigantic bronze, steel and lead flowers sharing space with the trees. And the interior is no disappointment either (the setting is blunt stone walls and terra cotta floors), with many of the 'old' masters represented—Giacometti (the largest collection I've ever seen, and most impressive), Braque, Matisse, Chagall, Bonnard, Leger, Miró, Calder; and perhaps equally important, a really superb presentation of what's fun and 'now' in modern art—Adami, Bury,

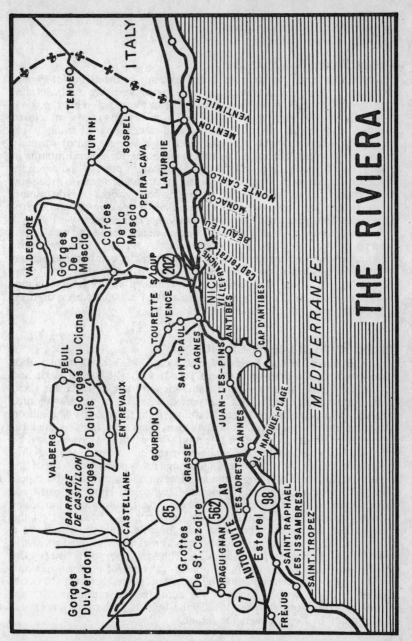

Chillida, Rebeyrolle, Riopelle, Tapies. Plus a fascinating library of originals, all for sale, including Chagall, Steinberg, Miró, and more: it's a small gallery within the gallery. This be-in of modern art is available to you for a very well-spent 18 francs (12 francs for students), from 10 a.m. to 12:30 p.m. and 3 to 7 p.m. every day of the week, non-stop!

Musée Picasso—in Antibes

"Another 'must' on your list should certainly be the **Grimaldi-Picasso Museum,** on the ramparts of Antibes (ten minutes from Nice on a fast train; from the station walk to the port, turn right, and signs will point the way); open daily from 10 a.m. to noon and 3 to 7 p.m. (winters till 6 p.m., closed Tuesdays and the month of November), and charging 10 francs. This ancient, granite castle (built on the ruins of a Roman camp) formerly known as 'Chateau Grimaldi,' was Picasso's home for several months in 1946. It now houses a large collection of the master's pottery and paintings (some exhibited tastefully next to ancient pillars and fragments) that you have probably never seen before (including some works of wry humor; fawns, sprites, centaurs), and you are not likely to see anywhere but here. Although the museum exhibits the works of other contemporary artists, it is truly a celebration of Picasso—and a rare experience I hope you won't miss. (You might also enjoy a stroll around the quaint old part of the town near the ramparts; and archaeology buffs *only* may want to look in at the **Bastion Andre's Archaeological Museum**—open 9 a.m. to noon and 2 to 7 p.m. (closed Tuesdays and the month of November), for 6 francs—whose collections are billed as '4,000 years of history': i.e., what's been dredged up from the sea in and around Antibes.

Musée Fernand Leger—in Biot

"The **Musée National Fernand Leger,** located in the small town of Biot (near Antibes), and open daily except Tuesdays from 10 a.m. to noon and 2:30 to 6:30 p.m. (winters, 2 to 5 p.m.) for a 5-franc entrance fee (2.50 francs for students), is difficult (but not impossible) to reach without a car—the train deposits you a good distance from the country-like hill on which the museum stands. It's a healthy hike; catch a bus or ask some local people to point you in the right direction. But when you arrive you'll be delighted, for you'll find a rich, white-carpeted, marble and stone, spankingly modern museum which offers a thorough retrospective showing of this important modern (including some striking ceramics, mosaics and tapestries), who specializes in large, machine-like images. Here you can trace Leger's work at various stages in his development, noting with particular interest in some rare compositions the influence of African art on the artist—I get the distinct impression that Leger's intention was to be a modern primitive, to paint with new eyes (breaking with old forms) the latest totems of his society: the machines. The final room you'll visit (on the second floor) is almost entirely devoted to canvases of modern man and industry, the only exception being the artist's occasional reversion to circus themes, with his special fondness for acrobats and musicians. It's an impressive collection, starting outside the building, where an enormous mosaic mural by Leger covers the facade.

Le Trophée des Alpes—at La Turbie

"The **Trophy of the Alps** is a spectacular and partially reconstructed Roman ruin (and the only surviving monument of its kind), built in 6 B.C.

to commemorate the conquest of the Alps by the Emperor Augustus (thus Rome joined Gaul and Germania to Italy, guaranteed her security, and opened the historic route from the Mediterranean coast, spreading Roman civilization to the ancient world). At the highest point of the Roman artery, La Turbie, the Trophy was erected; on its face is an inscription honoring Augustus and listing the 45 conquered hostile tribes—this has been called the first page of French history—and on either side are reconstructed bas reliefs. It's presumed there were originally statues between the pillars on the upper level, and a statue of Augustus or a decorative trophy at the very top of the monument; as you look, try to imagine them. Behind the monument is a small museum displaying pillars and fragments found at the site, a model showing how the original Trophée looked (it must have been gorgeous), and exhibits illustrating the process of restoration. Behind that, the terrace affords panoramic views of Monaco and the entire coast. The Trophée, open from 9 a.m. to 5 p.m. for a 7-franc entrance fee (but free for children and students), is located directly above Monaco, but can be reached by bus from Nice (a 45-minute trip, cost is 13 francs; but service is limited—there are buses leaving at 7 a.m. and 11:15 a.m., last bus back to Nice from La Turbie is at 6:10 p.m.—to be sure, best pick up a schedule at the bus station); the ride along the Grande Corniche is breathtaking, and, as you approach La Turbie, the view of the Trophée is one you will long remember and treasure.

IN NICE: "You can sun on the beach with a clear conscience, rather than spend any time at the **Musée des Beaux Arts,** at 33 Avenue des Baumettes (dedicated to Jules Chéret, a rather interesting, vivacious painter with a distinctly '20s style), because there is not much here, in my opinion, that is really first rate, apart from an occasional impressionist and several ceramics by Picasso. Admission is free. The following are of more interest.

Villa des Arènes—Cimiez

"Way up in the hills of Nice (take city bus no. 15 or 17 from Place Masséna, just across the street from the Galeries Lafayette, or from 'Magenta,' a 7-franc ride), you'll find the **Villa des Arènes,** which houses both the **Matisse Museum** and the **Museum of Archaeology** (open in summer from 10 a.m. to noon and 2:30 to 6:30 p.m., closed Sunday mornings and all day Mondays; in winter open from 2 to 5 p.m., closed Mondays and the entire month of November; admission is free). The first, of course, houses an interesting collection of Matisse's paintings, drawings, studies, models (including those for his chapel in Venice), and some of the famous 'cut-outs.' It's a profound sensory pleasure to view this artist's work in the setting in which he actually painted because, as you enter the museum still tingling with the unique Riviera atmosphere in your mind's eye, you'll realize you are seeing nature as he saw it—and suddenly you'll appreciate why he chose to paint in the vivid colors of his most familiar works. And in a small room of Matisse's furniture, it's fun to recognize actual items you've seen portrayed so often in his paintings. The Archaelology Museum on the first floor (no extra charge) displays a nice little collection of artifacts found at or near the site—ceramics, coins, sculpture, tools and jewelry. Outdoors, all around, are the ruins of Cimiez (founded by the Romans under Augustus in the first century B.C., the town later became the Roman capital of the Maritime Alps), which, like a park, stay open most of the day—and the 1st-century Amphitheatre is used for public performances for a month during the summer Cimiez Art Festival. But you must pay an additional franc to wander the 'streets' of the archaeological site, and inspect the Roman baths (all first to third centuries).

Musée Chagall

"Above Nice on the way to Villa des Arènes (you can make a day of it in the hills; again take bus no. 15 or 15-A, a 4.80-franc, ten-minute ride; ask the driver for 'Chagall' or look for the 'Dr. Moriez' stop, walk uphill in the same direction the bus is going, and around the first bend you'll see a sign pointing the way) is the **Musée National Marc Chagall** (open daily, except Tuesdays, from October 1 to June 30 from 10 a.m. to 12:30 p.m. and from 2 to 5:30 p.m., July 1 to September 30 from 10 a.m. to 7 p.m., for a 9-franc entrance fee, 4.50 francs for children). The museum itself, a squat white stone modern building in a park-like setting, is pleasantly light and airy inside, and all the works exhibited (which were donated to France by the Chagalls) deal with Biblical subjects—but, because it's Chagall, that's a much livelier experience than one might anticipate. Note, particularly, the three large stained-glass windows, the several rooms of grand-scale canvases (e.g., *Moses and the Burning Bush, The Sacrifice of Isaac,*) and a room of stunning paintings illustrating *The Song of Songs*—all in lush tones of purples and reds, both hot and cool.

Musée Masséna

"The **Musée Masséna,** which fronts on the Promenade des Anglais just across the street from the Hotel Negresco (although the entrance is around the block at 65 Rue de France), open every day except Monday from 10 a.m. to noon and 2 to 5 p.m., free entrance, is devoted mainly to regional art and objects pertaining to the history of Nice. This elegant villa, built in 1900, was the former home of Victor Masséna (a grandson of Napoleon's Marshal), and was donated to the city by the Masséna family in 1919, on the condition that it be maintained as a museum of local history. Its first floor consists of the original accessories), and some sculpture and paintings of Napoleon's family—an amusing classic statue of Napoleon as a man emperor, a portrait of Josephine, and a copy of Canova's bust of Pauline Borghese, Napoleon's sister—the Massénas were apparently very proud of the Napoleonic connection. But head immediately upstairs to the second floor for the star attraction of the museum: two rooms full of light-hearted Dufys, which alone make the visit here worthwhile. A third room contains pictures of other painters who lived around Nice, including Monet and Renoir, some primitive Niçois paintings and sculpture from the 15th century, and objects relating to the Masséna family, Napoleon and Nice. The third floor has more on the history of Nice (including a room devoted to Garibaldi, who was born in Nice, in 1807), and an exhibition of applied arts—jewelry, furniture, church reliquaries, swords, armor, guns, and the like.

La Tour Bellanda

"Located at the end of the Promenade des Anglais (or the Quai des Etats Unis; walking east from the center of town) is **La Tour Bellanda,** a popular tourist attraction because it offers not only a lovely winding park (with a chateau, ruins of the ancient fort-palace, later cathedral, on top—this is where the town of Nice began) and a small **Naval Museum,** but also, because it is actually a small mountain, with a marvelous view of Nice. I suggest you take the elevator up (4 francs to ride up; another 4 francs to ride down; or 6 francs for the round-trip) and walk down, stopping on your way to see the Naval Museum (open every day except Tuesday from 10 a.m. to noon and 2 to 7 p.m., free entrance, the park is open summers til 8 p.m., but the elevator closes at 7). The little museum has all kinds of maritime memorabilia reflecting the naval history of Nice, but the most fun is a high-powered telescope which you can train on the city to check the local action."

READERS' SIGHTSEEING SUGGESTIONS: "Please do not neglect to mention Nice's other fine museums such as the **Musée Barla** (natural history), 60 bis Boulevard Risso, unique for its collection of artificial mushrooms [Note by HA: closed Tuesdays and from mid-August to mid-September, open 9 a.m. to noon and 2 to 6 p.m., free entrance, and located across the street from the Flea Market]; and the **Musée du Vieux Logis** at 59 Avenue St. Barthelemy. The modern **Church of Ste. Jeanne d'Arc** is on the Avenue Borriglione and has interesting frescos by Kelmenţief. The **Russian Orthodox Cathedral,** famous for its iconostasis (an ornamented screen bearing sacred images), is on Blvd. du Tzarewitch. There are small galleries and many other corners of interest as well" (Dr. and Mrs. A.M. Cooper, Fresno, California). . . . "You might take a look at the **Palais Lascaris** at 15 Rue Droite in the Old City of Nice, open from 9:30 a.m. to noon and 2:30 to 6:30 p.m. (winters till 6 p.m. on Wednesday, Thursday, Saturday and Sunday); free entrance. Lascaris, built in 1648 and restored in 1706, is now a fading baroque patrician mansion with mostly Provence-style furniture (all of which had to be replaced, since everything disappeared during the French revolution). The ceilings are attributed to the 17th-century Carlone; and on the ground floor there's an antique pharmacy which was founded in 1738. It was an amusing experience to me because some of the decorations here are so garish they were almost like 'Pop Art.' Lascaris is also the headquarters for 'visites Commentés du Vieux-Nice,' several tours of old Nice, which are usually scheduled daily at 10 a.m. and 3 p.m., and are free" (Pauline Hadley, New York, New York). . . . "To combine a pleasant outing with a cultural feast, take a one-day joint excursion to Beaulieu-sur-Mer and Saint-Jean-Cap-Ferrat. At Beaulieu you'll find a lovely beach, and the **Foundation Theodore Reinach's Villa 'Kerylos'** (open daily, except Monday, from 3 to 7 p.m. in the summer, for a 12-franc admission price), a remarkable reproduction of a Greek villa of the 4th and 5th centuries B.C.—around the Age of Pericles. Reinach, an archaeologist, scholar and numismatist, built and lived in the house for 18 years—and all the furniture (except a few Roman and Egyptian chairs) and decorative elements are as exact a duplication of a wealthy ancient household as Reinach's scholarship, with the help of imported craftsmen, could accomplish: the construction of the building alone cost eight or nine million *gold* francs. I never dreamed anything like this existed—from the tranquil inner courtyard, mosaic floors and precious marbles, the painted walls and beamed ceilings, the dining room with a reclining chaise for the master of the house, to the shower, and the sunken marble bath—all conspire to make one feel like a privileged visitor to the villa of an ancient, aristocratic Greek. Reinach chose this gorgeous spot by the water because it reminded him of Greece ('Kérylos' means 'Bird of the Sea'); it's just opposite Cap Ferrat, and from here you can see the **Villa-Musée Ile-de-France,** the former home of Madame Ephrussi de Rothschild. It's filled with Madame Rothschild's vast collections—precious tapestries (Aubusson, Gobelins); Regency, Louis XV and Louis XVI furniture (including pieces that belonged to Marie Antoinette); a priceless porcelain collection; objets d'art from the Far East; Fragonard, Boucher, and some impressionist paintings. To give you some idea of the sumptuousness of this villa, just imagine using a Gothic confessional to cover a service entrance (as Madame did)! And the surrounding gardens are magnificent. Open from 3 to 7 p.m. in the summer (winters, and that's through June 30, from 2 to 6 p.m.), and admission is 25 francs for the museum and the gardens, 10 francs for the gardens only. Note: both the above museums are closed Mondays, and have annual closings during the month of November. And to wander around Cap Ferrat, with its beautiful port, elegant mansions, and lovely little beaches is a sheer delight" (Pauline Rissman, Miami, Florida). . . . "The lofty old 'top of the mountain' walled (formerly part of the fortress) village of **Roquebrune** (above Cap Martin), with the remains of an 11th-century Carolingian castle (open from 9 a.m. to noon and 2 to 7 p.m. for a 5-franc admission: just the prison and a few sparsely furnished chambers are all that's left now, but there's a nice view from the top), is a charming medieval town with narrow up-and-down, completely covered streets. The ancient character of the village is so intact, it's a heady experience to walk through it (seems to be a gathering of artists and craftsmen here too, taking inspiration from the spot); but it's quite difficult to reach without a car" (Angela Marto, New York, New York). . . . "If you find yourself in Monaco (and who won't?), you might like to visit the **Exotic Garden,** which is cut out of the side of a mountain, and has the largest (and probably the tallest) assortment of cacti one is ever likely to see—I began to feel I was walking through Rousseau's painting *The Dream.* Open from 9 a.m. to 7 p.m. in summer, 9 a.m. to 6 p.m. the remainder of the year, for a 19-franc entrance fee (9.50 francs for children), this may be one of the last sightseeing bargains left in Monaco (which has become such a tourist trap). For the same admission you can also see **The Grotte** (underground caves which were a prehistoric dwelling pace, with stalactites and stalagmites—you must wait for a guide to take you through, though) and **The Anthropology Museum** (with finds from the Grotte and the nearby area—tools, bones, etc; an interesting exhibit on prehistoric art; a Roman collection: and skeletons known as Grimaldi negroids and Cro-Magnon men). Oh, and there's a beautiful view of Monaco and its port from the terrace. You can catch a bus directly to Nice from the Jardin; across the street from the tobacco shop is the 'Nice Arret,' but the last bus for Nice from here is a 7 p.m." (Adam Slote, New York, New York). . . . "The Riviera trains are relatively cheap and run fairly frequently all along the coast. But for a ride on the breath-taking Moyenne Corniche (middle road) or Grande Corniche (high road), take the bus, and do stop at **Eze,** a medieval village perched 1,200 feet over the water just off the Moyenne Corniche. Charming, no carts, all footpaths only, and a spectacular view" (Phil and Maryjane Bradley, Watertown, Massachusetts). . . . "The **Nice Tourist Office,** on the Avenue Thiers (to your left as you leave the station), is staffed with friendly, young, English-speaking French girls who, aside from answering all your questions about Nice and surroundings, will give you a free map of Nice, a list of museums and other informative brochures. Open Monday to Saturday, 8:30 a.m. to 12:30 p.m. and 2 to 6:00 p.m." (Michael Mendelsohn, New York, New York; note by AF: a second branch of the Nice Tourist Office, maintaining the same hours, is at 5 Avenue Gustave V, next to the Casino Ruhl near the Promenade des Anglais—the large Air France office is in the same block).

6. Tours & Excursions

For organized sightseeing tours your best bet is the large, bustling office of **Santa Azur,** at 11 Avenue Jean Médecin (phone 82-38-78), which owns its own buses, and passes on no middleman's fees to you. Their basic tour of Nice departs at 9:30 a.m., costs 45 francs, while other tours go daily to Monte Carlo (2 p.m., 60 francs), to the perfume factories at Grasse (2 p.m., 60 francs), and to other key locations along the Riviera, including the fabled St. Tropez (92 francs). . . . On your visit to Monaco, try to catch the noontime changing of the guard at Prince Rainier's palace. Like a fairy tale.

Nice should be made your headquarters for forays along the Riviera. That way, you'll be able to dart to high-priced Monaco or Cannes in the day, but return to a budget-priced pad in low-cost Nice at night. The train takes exactly 22 minutes to make the trip to Monaco, costs 10 francs one-way, leaves about once per hour. But caution: the last train leaves Monaco for Nice at 10:53 p.m. The trip to Cannes takes 34 minutes, costs 19 francs one-way, and leaves at half-hour intervals. . . . You'll want to make at least one run to Monaco by bus, along the incredibly beautiful Moyenne Corniche. Buses depart from the Gare d'Autobus, approximately every hour from 7 a.m. to 7:30 p.m. Monaco features: the Casino at Monte Carlo (entrance fee of 25 francs, but no admission charge to the room of "one-armed bandits"; passport essential; sober dress—tie and jacket— usually required), the palace of Prince Rainier, a yacht basin often filled with the pleasure craft of Greek millionaires, and the famous Musée Oceanographique, world's largest marine museum (entrance 30 francs, half price for children). You may have no present liking, for the subject of sealife, but you'll soon pick it up at this place; a fascinating, weird series of exhibits. . . . Whatever you do, don't stay overnight in Cannes, the most expensive city on the Riviera, totally lacking the hordes of prix fixe restaurants and budget hotels found in Nice. . . . On a day excursion to Cannes, however, try to get to the island of Ste. Marguerite, a mile away, to view the fort built by Richelieu, where you can still see the cell where the Man in the Iron Mask was held prisoner for 11 years by Louis XIV. . . . And if you have a car, drive eight kilometers beyond Cannes on the sea road to the village of La Napoule and its **Henry Clews Museum.** Both Hope and I look upon our accidental visit to this museum (the former villa of the underrated American sculptor) as one of the high points of our trips to Europe. Admission is 5 francs (2 francs for students and children) to view the lifework of an amazing, offbeat mind. Open daily except Sunday from 5 to 6 p.m. (guided tours).

On our most recent trip to Nice, Hope and I spent an afternoon in **Vallauris,** the village in which Picasso developed his own unique style of ceramic designs. The entire town has now turned to pottery-making, and offers mountains of cheap pottery to visiting tourists, but the chief attraction of Vallauris is the **National Picasso Museum** (open daily from 10 a.m. to noon and from 2 to 5 p.m.), 5 franc entrance, students and visitors older than 60 years half price, which has a stunning impact, and the pottery store of **Madoura,** the only shop in town licensed to sell copies of Picasso's own pottery designs (some plates go for as little as 500 francs). The trip is made via train from Nice to Golfe Juan (30 minutes, 14.50 francs per person) and by then taking a 3 franc bus from Golfe Juan to Vallauris. I mention it here only as an example of the many interesting, one-day excursions you can make from Nice—to Cannes, to Juan Les Pins, or to the fabulous St. Tropez, for example—all of which will cost you nothing if you have a Eurailpass, and very little even if you don't.

READERS ON AN OUTING: "We rented two motorized bikes for three days and with these we surveyed all of Nice, traveled to Cannes, Vallauris, Monte Carlo, Monaco, and all the villages along the coast. We strapped food packs to our bikes and had all the freedom of time and place which public transportation doesn't allow. And for the leery—it is easier than pedaling a bike!" (Gordon and Lori Burghardt, Chicago, Illinois). . . . "From Nice, I took a bus to the Italian border, then traveled by S.A.T.I. bus to Rapallo on the Italian Riviera—a journey I recommend most wholeheartedly. Total cost for the Nice-Rapallo bus trip (two tickets) is about 95 francs, one way. It was comfortable, the driver was an expert at his job, and the couriers most efficient. No resort, however small, was omitted, so it was in effect a grand tour of the Cote d'Azur and the northern Italian coast" (Edward A. Creed, Salisbury, Rhodesia). . . . "Please mention another worthy side trip out of Nice, to the strikingly small chapel at Vence, executed by Henri Matisse" (Marianne Durand,

San Francisco, California). . . . "Buy a Niçoise sandwich—a 'pan bagnat'—and a bottle of wine at a side street delicatessen, and take the bus to Monaco for the changing of the guard at 11:45 a.m. Then have lunch on a bench overlooking the sea" (Arthur F. Damon, Roseville, Minnesota).

7. Evening Entertainment

There is, of course, no really inexpensive way to while-away the evening in a Riviera gaming hall. But the casinos at Nice offer perhaps the least pressured forms of gambling of all the European rooms of this type. Certainly you'll spend less here, and you'll do it more enjoyably, than in the fabled, but disappointing, Casino at Monte Carlo, where the crowds are monstrous and the croupiers grim. At the **Ruhl Casino** on the Promenade des Anglais in Nice, entrance fee is only 40 francs, and chips are as little as 20 francs apiece at most of the roulette tables. Play it cool, study the game well before you plunge, and tip the croupiers if you win a pile of chips: if you do, they'll call it your way on the disputed plays. . . . Keep in mind that you'll be made to present your passport on entering: don't leave it at the hotel. . . . Care to know a time-honored (if somewhat boring) method for winning (I don't guarantee it) at roulette? Write down the numbers 1, 2, 3, 4, 5 in a column, then bet the total of the top and bottom number (1 and 5 = 6 chips) on a 2-1 chance (odd or even, red or black). If you win, cross out the top and bottom numbers (1 and 5). If you lose, place the number of the chips you lost at the bottom of the column, and again bet the total of the uncrossed-out top and bottom numbers (this time, 1 and 6), crossing out those numbers each time you win. Unless your luck is unusually bad and you lose several bets in a row (thus pushing this progression to unacceptable limits), you'll eventually cross out all the numbers and retire a winner, having depleted the French economy by about $4.

8. Nice Miscellany

Nice has several coin-operated laundromats! **Taxi-Lav,** at 22 Rue Pertinax, is just a block-and-a-half from the Avenue Jean Médecin, near the railroad track end: 11 francs for 4 kilos washed and dried, open from 7 a.m. to 8 p.m., Monday through Sunday. In the Old City (*Vieux Nice*), the same facilities and rates are available at **Lavazur,** 2 Rue Rossetti, just off the small church square of this colorful quarter, and at the **Lavomatique,** 11 Rue du Pont Vieux.

LA MER: Unlike the beach at the Lido in Venice, long segments of the beach at Nice are admission free—as, for example, nearly the entire stretch of beach to the east of the Ruhl Plage (in front of the Meridien Hotel). Where a hotel controls a particular stretch, the price of admission is 12 to 15 francs, including a cabin, showers, etc. . . . It costs 3 francs to sit in a beach chair on the Promenade des Anglais.

TRANSPORTATION: No need to rent a car; try a motorized bicycle (*un Moped Ciao*) instead. These can be had at **Loca 2 Roues,** 29 Rue Gounod (phone 87-20-07), in the station area, open weekdays from 9 a.m. to noon and 2 to 7 p.m., renting mopeds for 42 francs per day, 240 francs per week, inclusive of helmet and insurance. Normal bicycles are available, too, as are far more elaborate motorbikes, up to 125 ccm, renting for 215 francs and requiring a refundable deposit of from 1,000 to 2,000 francs. The smaller

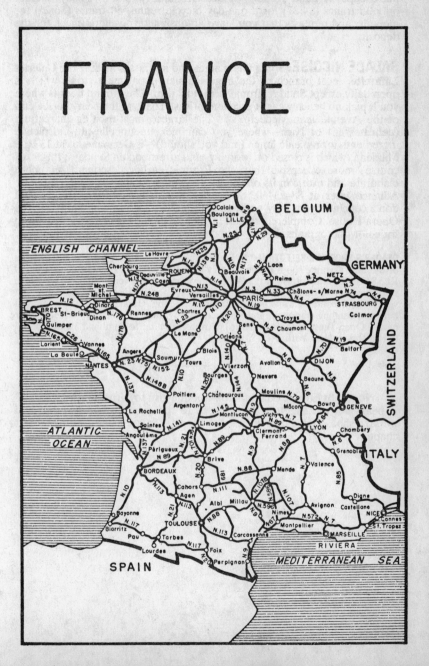

but cheaper **Arnaud** agency, 4 Place Grimaldi (phone 87-88-55), charges only 35 francs ($4.37) for a one-day bicycle rental, 50 francs ($6.25) for mopeds, and requests that you leave an unsigned traveller's check for the deposit.

SALADE NIÇOISE:
Some final names and addresses include the **Galeries Lafayette,** local branch of the huge Parisian department store, which is open daily except Sunday, from 9 a.m. to 7 p.m. The ground floor is where you'll pick up beach wear at excellent prices. That's at the near-the-sea end of the Avenue Jean Médecin. . . . The largest, most exciting charcuterie (delicatessen) of Nice—where you can pick up unbelievably attractive ingredients for a picnic lunch (and you should)—is **Germanetto**, at 13 Rue Masséna, which is closed on Mondays and afternoon on Sundays; this is, of course, more expensive than the Prisunic earlier described, but more elaborate and exotic in its offerings. . . . For reputable babysitters, phone **Alliance Inter** at 88–23–60, or **Service Etudiants** at 96–73–73. . . . And don't conclude your stay without visiting Nice's flower market, near the Opera House. Completely rebuilt in 1982, it provides the perfect backdrop for color photographs, and is open daily except Mondays from 6 to 11 a.m.

READER'S SHOPPING SELECTION: "In France one naturally thinks of perfume, and one of the best perfume shops in the country is **F. Poilpot, Aux Parfums de Grasse,** 10 Rue Saint Gaetan (aptly near the famous flower market). Over 65 different scents are sold here at 10 francs per glass flask; they're prettily displayed like fruits and vegetables in containers and boxes in front of the shop. Upon request, the owner will help you combine various brands to create a fragrance just for your personality or mood. Open Tuesday through Saturday from 9:30 a.m. to noon and 3 and 7 p.m." (Yetta Reich, New York, New York).

No trip to Europe is complete without a visit to surprising Amsterdam! It bears not the slightest resemblance to the musty image of tulips and wooden shoes that you've been led to expect—as you'll discover in our next chapter.

Chapter IX

AMSTERDAM

The Surprising City

AS I STEPPED OUT of the airport bus, on my very first trip to Amsterdam, I expected to see a rather sleepy city, populated by plump, red-cheeked people who spent their time strolling along quaint canals.

What a surprise I had in store!

■ In no more than a few hours, I had passed restaurant after restaurant where dark-skinned, turbaned waiters were serving exotic dishes of the East Indies to residents and tourists alike.

■ I had walked through a massive amusement area—the famous Rembrandtsplein—where literally scores of cafes and cabarets were offering the kind of entertainment you expect to find only in Paris—but available here for one-third the price!

■ I had sat at sidewalk cafes in the student section where bearded young scholars were arguing the merits of op art and underground films.

■ I had seen the shops of chic couturiers standing side-by-side with open-air herring stands, at which lovely Dutch co-eds, in the most modern hairstyles, were dipping chunks of raw fish into bowls of chopped onions and chomping away!

■ I had quaffed beer in a café on the 13th floor of a skyscraper overlooking the port of Amsterdam, and then descended in an elevator to an area, several square miles in size, where scarcely a building had changed since the 17th and 18th centuries!

Amsterdam—as you've undoubtedly grasped from the above exposition—is a city of fantastic surprises, a place crammed with sights and activities that seem to bear not the slightest resemblance to the picture of tulips, cheese, and wooden shoes that most visitors expect to find.

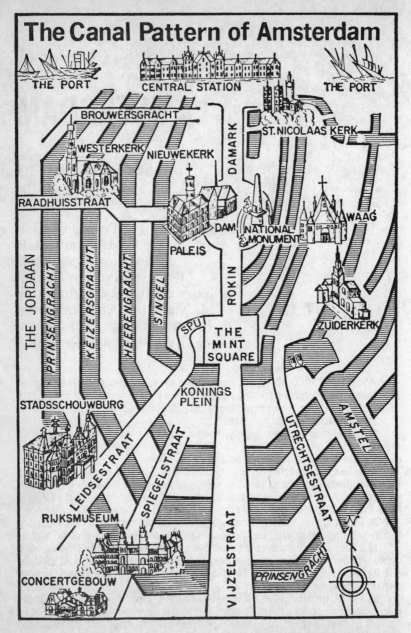

The Canal Pattern of Amsterdam

That's not to say, of course, that the famed quaintness of Amsterdam doesn't still exist. There will be times when you round a corner to come upon one of the city's 50 canals, and to view one of its 1200 bridges, and as you gaze upon the vista of quiet waters that flow between an unbroken line of trees and gabled old mansions, you will catch your breath at the sheer beauty of it all. And indeed, the massive central section of Amsterdam, whose architecture has been maintained unaltered for centuries, has been called "the largest open-air museum in the world."

But the predominant impression of Amsterdam is that of an active, throbbing, cosmopolitan city. It is, of course, one of the chief trading ports on the continent, to which dozens of ships each month, from Indonesia, Dutch Guiana and other exotic lands, wend their way, through the North Sea Canal and then into the harbor at the heart of the city. These, together with all of the trains and planes that every day pour into Amsterdam, in staggering numbers, make it a true crossroads city—a Europe in miniature —and therefore an unbelievably exciting place.

1. Orientation & Transportation

Amsterdam, in its physical aspect, is almost entirely a product of the so-called "Golden Age" of the Netherlands—that period in the 17th century when Holland surged to the near-pinnacle of world power, after its victory over Spain in the brutal Eighty Years War. It was during this period that the merchants of Amsterdam—then the dominant element in the city—laid out a pattern of gently curving, concentric canals that occupy the central section of Amsterdam and constitute the city's particular glory today.

The canals run in a fairly regular pattern that makes it quite easy to orient yourself. Starting at the Central Station, the first of the canals is the **Singel.** Then comes the **Herengracht** (Gentlemen's Canal), then the **Keizersgracht** (Emperor's Canal), and finally the **Prinsengracht** (Prince's Canal). Along these canals the merchants of 17th-century Amsterdam constructed what seem today like endless lines of gilded, patrician mansions and homes. These have, in recent years, been occupied by business firms, but their façades are absolutely untouched—and it is in this most beautiful centuries-old setting that you'll want to spend most of your time in Amsterdam.

Crossing through this pattern of parallel, concentric canals, like the spokes of a wheel, are avenues, the most important of which is the **Damrak,** which starts at the **Central Station** and heads straight to the **Dam Square,** site of the Royal Palace, the Nieuwe Kerk (New Church), and National Monument. From the Dam Square, this street becomes the **Rokin,** and veers a bit as it heads to the **Mint Square** (Muntplein), where the famous old Mint Tower of Amsterdam stands, and where the Amstel River begins. Near the Mint Square is the **Rembrandtsplein** (Rembrandt's Square), one of the two major entertainment areas of Amsterdam; a bit farther out, and to the west, is the **Leidseplein** (Leidse Square), the other entertainment section of Amsterdam, and site of the Stadsschouwburg (Municipal Theatre). And beyond this central area is a slightly more modern section where you'll find the three great art museums of Amsterdam—the renowned **Rijksmuseum,** the **Vincent van Gogh,** and **Stedelijk Museum**—as well as the famous home of its much acclaimed orchestra, the **Concertgebouw.**

TRAINS AND PLANES: By train, you'll arrive at Amsterdam's one-and-only "Centraal Station" after a trip of 12 hours from London's Liverpool Station (via Harwich and the Hoek of Holland), 2¾ hours from Brussels, 5¾ hours from Paris, 12 hours from Copenhagen, 7 hours from Frankfurt,

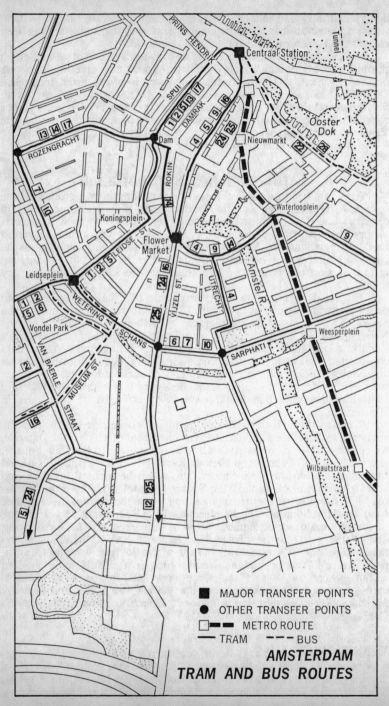

**AMSTERDAM
TRAM AND BUS ROUTES**

1¼ hours from Rotterdam, 45 minutes from the Hague. By air, you arrive at the superb Schiphol Airport—most efficient and comfortable airport of Europe—on a landing field 13 feet below sea level, where the hulks of ancient warships once greeted the eye when the giant lake above it was drained many years ago. (Schiphol means "Ship's Hole"). A KLM bus brings you quickly into town for only 9 guilders ($3). But on the return trip to Schiphol, you'll find it easy to save about $1 per person by boarding yellow bus no. 143 from the Victoria Hotel opposite the Central Station for only 6 guilders ($2); it leaves at 20-minute intervals from 6 a.m. till late at night.

STREETCARS OF AMSTERDAM: Though the city enjoys several bus lines and a rapidly increasing subway system, it is the trolleys of Amsterdam that serve most tourist needs. You can buy tickets for their use either aboard the trams or from automatic dispensers near most stops, and you have a choice of purchasing either unlimited-travel tickets for durations of one day (7.85 guilders), two days (11 guilders) or three days (13 guilders), or a six-strip ticket *strippenkaart* for 4.75 guilders ($1.58)—most trips within the central area of Amsterdam requiring that you use two of the six strips. Unless you plan a heavy, repeated use of the trolley system, I'd confine myself to simply buying a six-strip strippenkaart.

The Trolley Routes

Every tram bears a number which indicates the route it follows. There are, in all, 15 such routes (and therefore 15 numbers), ten of which travel to and from the Central Station.

Trams 1 and 2 start at the Central Station, go down the Nieuwe Zijds Voorburgwal over to the Spui, then turn down the Leidsestraat and travel the entire distance of that street to the Leidseplein; they cross the Leidseplein, but then take different routes; tram 1 goes down the Overtoom, while tram 2 heads in the direction of the Rijksmuseum, via the le C. Huygenstraat, then turns into the Willemsparkweg, goes along that street to Koninginneweg, and then proceeds the entire length of that street. Both trams also make the same trips in the opposite direction. To summarize their key stops: take either tram 1 or 2 to go to the **Leidseplein;** take tram 2 to go to a location near (but not at) the **Rijksmuseum;** take either tram to go to the **Central Station.**

Trams 16, 24 and 25 also start at the Central Station, but travel down the Damrak and the Rokin to the Mint Square. At this point, they proceed straight down the entire length of the Vijzelstraat, cross the Singelgracht, and then take different routes. Tram 16 goes past the Van Moppes diamond factory, then over to Museumplein, and then down the entire length of De Lairessestraat, passing near the Amsterdam Hilton Hotel. Tram 24 turns into Beethovenstraat, and afterwards proceeds to the Zuid (south) Station of the Schiphol Airport railway line (25). Tram 25 heads down Ferdinand Bolstraat into Churchill Laan, and then down that lovely residential street. All three trams, of course, make the same trips in the opposite directions.

Trams 4 and 9 also start at the Central Station, and travel down the length of the Damrak and Rokin into the Mint Square. At this point, both turn down the Reguliers Breestraat into the Rembrandtsplein, but then take different routes: tram 4 turns down the Utrechtsestraat to the

Frederiksplein and the Rai; tram 9 leads across the Amstel River past the Waterlooplein, then turns and travels in the direction of the Artis Zoo. **Tram 7** (which you can pick up on the Leidseplein) heads straight to the zoo. All trolleys make the same trip in the other direction. To sum up the highlights: take tram 4 or 9 to reach the **Rembrandtsplein;** take tram 4 for the **Frederiksplein;** take tram 9 for the Artis Zoo; take the metro for the **Amstel Station.**

Finally, **tram 13 and 17** start at the Central Station, travel along the N.Z. Voorburgwaal until they pass the Raadhuisstraat, turn into the Raadhuisstraat, ride past the Westerkerk (West Church), near which the Anne Frank house is located, and then continue on the Rozengracht out into the modern Western sector of the city. Then they make the return trip. Point to remember: to reach the Anne Frank house from the Central Station, take tram 13 or 17.

2. Amsterdam Hotels

With the trolley routes in mind, you can now find a room for your stay, in some of the most delightful lodgings that Europe offers:

CANAL-HOUSE HOTELS: The budget hotels of Amsterdam are like no others on earth. Located chiefly in canal houses of 17th- and 18th-century construction, they go up, not out. So narrow are these buildings that their stairways are like a ship's—thin little ledges that require a banister for support. On the outside of each house, you'll see an iron beam with pulley that juts over the roof. That's for hauling furniture and other heavy items—which simply can't be carried up the steep stairs!

But don't let the stairway situation discourage you; older tourists are always placed on the ground or lower floors, and younger or more vigorous ones will look upon the stairs as a sightseeing attraction!

Some other features of the budget hotels in Amsterdam: each of them serves a gigantic, free breakfast—just as the British hotels do—except that here the emphasis is not on bacon and eggs, but on cheese, ham, several different kinds of Dutch bread, butter, and milk. Always remember that every quoted hotel price, at a budget hotel in Amsterdam, includes a whopping big morning meal. And that price is often quoted as a per person rate—rather than for single or double rooms. A hotel in Amsterdam will often charge either 26, 28 or 30 guilders per person, regardless of whether you occupy a single or double room.

We've grouped our hotel choices in Amsterdam according to price, beginning with the more expensive "big splurge" hotels, and then proceeding downwards, guilder-by-guilder. Obviously, our lowest-priced categories are composed of the very oldest canal houses, with the steepest stairs; but as we ascend in price, the stairs will flatten out (a little), the rooms will grow in size, and you'll discover that Amsterdam offers some of the best hotel values in Europe.

35 to 45 Guilders ($11.66 to $15) per Person, Breakfast and Service Included

On the canals: We begin our search along the great, concentric canals that form the inner portion of Amsterdam: the Singel, Herengracht (Gentlemen's Canal), Keizersgracht (Emperor's Canal), Prinsengracht (Prince's Canal), and Stadhouderskade. Loveliest and most elegant of these (and with the most consistent 17th-century architecture) is the patrician Herengracht, on which a former recommendation of ours—the stylish **Hotel Ambassade,** 341 Herengracht (phone 26-23-33)—has sadly departed the budget scene through embellishments, refurbishing and price increases that now render most of its rooms just a touch too high for our budget. But on that same elegant canal, and quite charming with its potted plants and other authentic touches, is the superbly located but pricey **Hotel Hegra,** 269 Herengracht (phone 23-53-48), built in 1656 no less, with 11 rooms, of which two bathless ones rent for 38 guilders ($12.66) per person, with breakfast and service included, 50 guilders ($16.66) for the nine rooms with private shower. This, again, is on an awesomely beautiful waterway, and bears numerous features of traditional Dutch decor and architecture. If the Hegra can't take you, then, on the almost-as-lovely Prinsengracht, nearby, you'll find a very adequate and less costly substitute in the **Hotel Prinsenhof,** 810 Prinsengracht (phone 23-17-72), with its beautiful, big, old rooms with beamed ceilings and wall-to-wall carpets. The price here is 35 guilders ($11.66) per person in double rooms, 50 guilders single, and the breakfast features four kinds of bread, a boiled egg, cheese and jam. No rooms with private bath or shower, but of course you can't expect that in a 17th-century merchant's house. And don't hesitate to stay in the cozy, top-floor rooms, to which your luggage will be transported via pulley!

On the quiet Leidsegracht (the Leidse Canal), a short walk from the important Leidseplein (Leidse Square, one of the two major entertainment areas of Amsterdam), you should be well-pleased with the **Hotel de Leydsche Hof,** 14 Leidsegracht (phone 23-21-48), where most rooms rent for 40 guilders per person (with nearby baths and showers always available at no extra charge), including service charge and tax. A beautiful oak staircase here, unusually large wood-paneled rooms, and baby cots available (with special prices for children, too). Highly recommended. Nearby, the **Hotel de Lantaerne,** 111 Leidsegracht (phone 23-22-21), is an alternative choice if the de Leydsche Hof is full. Here, a full 40 rooms are priced in 1985 at 48 guilders ($16) for singles, 75 guilders ($25) for twins, 100 guilders ($33.33) for triples, always with full Dutch breakfast included, and free showers down the hall. From the Central Station, take trolleys no. 1 or 2 to the Leidseplein stop and simply walk through the Marnixstraat from there.

Het Witte Huis Hotel, at 382 Marnixstraat (phone 25-07-77), offers 24 inexpensive rooms (8 singles and 16 doubles) at 40 guilders ($13.33) single, 35 guilders ($11.66) per person double or twin, 30 guilders ($10) per person in triples and quads, including a remarkable breakfast of coffee, tea or milk, an egg, cheese, ham, sausage, marmalade, chocolate-spread and four types of bread (two slices of white, one each of brown and biscuit bread). Owner is a Mr. Kogels, helpful and kindly.

There are other canalside establishments that compete quite closely, beginning with several on that stretch of the broad canal that encircles the inner city of Amsterdam and is called the Stadhouderskade; on it, near the Heineken Brewery but almost equally near to the Rijksmuseum, is a solid old home with stained glass doors, a marble entrance, and red Persian carpets, all housing the once-elegant, now moderately priced, **Hotel Linda,** 131 Stadhouderskade (phone 72-56-68), where 45 guilders ($15) per person brings you the works including service charge (but without private bath), in rooms that are, if anything, overfurnished. If the Linda is full, as it often is, try the barely less expensive (44 guilders per person) **Hotel l'Esperance** at 49 Stadhouderskade (phone 71-40-49), whose managers, Mr. and Mrs. De-Zeeuw, have been unusually cordial to readers, and provide large, carpeted, cheery rooms. For both hotels, take tram no. 16 or 24 from the Central Station.

One of the tiniest of the city's canal houses, but full of warmth and fellowship, is the **Hotel van Hulssen,** 108 Bloemgracht (phone 26-58-01), a few steps away from several earlier recommendations. While the van Hulssen hasn't the style of the higher-priced houses, the charm of its proprietor—Mr. Loak van Onna, a consummate Dutchman—makes up for much—and Mr. van Onna's charge is only 38 guilders per person, including breakfast, service and tax. A few doors away, Mr. van Onna's second hostelry, the 25-bed **Hotel van Onna,** at 102 Bloemgracht (phone 26-58-01), reflects some of the same intimate warmth of this ancient section of Amsterdam (it also offers central heating), charges the same 38 guilders per person in singles, doubles or triples, all inclusive. Take tram no. 13 or 17, four stops (and five minutes) from the Central Station.

On the Prinsengracht, at no. 328, about 25 minutes' walk from the Central Station, is the 38-room (that's large for a canal house) **Hotel Wiechmann** (phone 22-54-10), whose American owner, Ted Boddy (from Oklahoma), has somehow taught his Dutch wife to speak English with an absolutely authentic U.S. accent! His charge for bed, breakfast and service in most rooms is 45 guilders per person (but there are some smaller rooms for 38 guilders, some with private shower for 55 guilders, and two large family rooms on the top floor with four beds each costing 160 guilders, private shower included), and his breakfast is one of the best in Amsterdam: Dutch currant bread, white bread, wheat bread, a rusk, honey cake, a soft-boiled egg, a slice of breakfast cheese, coffee or tea, and of course plenty of butter, jam or marmalade. The establishment, as you'd expect, is quite popular, and you'd be advised to reserve more than three weeks in advance, although a phone call on the day before your arrival can also sometimes turn the trick.

Off the Canals: The land-locked choices, in this price category, begin (in order of preference) on the Damrak, a few steps from the Central Station. I particularly like the **Hotel van Gelder,** up a seemingly endless flight of near-perpendicular stairs at 34 Damrak (phone 24-78-79); you'll be surprised at how nice the hotel is, once you've reached its upstairs lobby. Per person rate is 38 guilders ($12.66) a night, including breakfast, service and tax, in all months other than the winter ones. Several other budget hotels are a few doors in either direction.

In a quiet, residential neighborhood beyond the Rijksmuseum, the 23-bed **Hotel Casa Cara** at 24 Emmastraat (phone 72-31-35) receives high marks for cleanliness, rates and careful management by a charming, young couple, Mr. and Mrs. Van Ingen. They charge 44 guilders ($14.66) single, 65 guilders ($21.66) for a double, 130 guilders ($43.44) quad, including a hearty Dutch breakfast and free showers. Take tram no. 2 or 16 from the center, to the Emmastraat stop.

Finally, an entire group of 35-to-45-guilder hotels is found in a string of Victorian-looking, apartment-house-type buildings on the Jan Luykenstraat, which runs along the side of the Rijksmuseum, and is a perfect location for tourists wishing to spend a good deal of time at that institution. The 160-bed **Hotel Acro,** 42 Jan Luykenstraat (phone 72-55-38), is one of the best of these, with heavily furnished, large rooms (most with radios) and a dining hall in "Old Dutch style." Most rooms here rent for exactly 35 guilders per person, double, and there are eight-bedded dorms costing only

26 guilders ($8.66) per person, with breakfast and all else included. Astonishingly, too, there's an elevator. Highest recommendation. Alternatively, try the **Hotel Museumzicht,** 22 Jan Luykenstraat (phone 71-29-54), which charges 38 guilders per adult (all included) for some of its rooms; or the nice **Hotel Aalders,** 15 Jan Luykenstraat (phone 72-01-16), whose much costlier rooms (several are quite large) are generally 48 guilders per person, breakfast included. Other hotels on the same street offer rates that hover about the 45 guilder mark, and all these hotels can be reached via the no. 2 tram from the Central Station.

34 to 42 Guilders ($11.33 to $14) per Person, Breakfast and Service Included

Hotel de Gouden Kettingh, a canal house at 268 Keizersgracht (phone 248-287), is not only named after a jewel (Gouden Kettingh meaning Golden Chain), but is indeed a gem that is sparkling clean. Eighteen tastefully furnished rooms, of which the bathless variety rent for 50 guilders ($16.66) single, 75 guilders ($25) double, including Dutch breakfast, while rooms with private bath rent for far more (add 50%). The owners—a charming, young couple—are extremely friendly and helpful, speak good English and keep a goldfish as a pet next to the reception desk. Take streetcar no. 13 from the Central Station to the Western Church stop; from there it's a five-minute walk. Highly recommended.

Another house somewhat more basic than some we've named, but with exceptionally genial proprietors (Mr. and Mrs. Peter de Vries), is the **Hotel Keizershof,** 618 Keizersgracht (between Leidsestraat and Vijzelstraat, phone 22-28-55), which charges 34 to 36 guilders per person per night (double occupancy), breakfast, service, and free showers included. Again the hotel is in a 17th-century building, this time furnished with piano, TV, soft leather chairs—and with a peaceful, little beflowered backyard— particularly suitable for older tourists.

The **Hotel Fantasia,** at 16 Nieuwe Keizersgracht (phone 23-82-59), built nearly 300 years ago, is still another large canal house, as canal houses go, located only 50 yards from the broadest and most beautiful portion of the Amstel River, near the famous Skinny Bridge *(de Magere Brug)*. It has 19 rooms that can accommodate up to 40 or 45 persons, and most of them rent for 38 guilders per person, including breakfast, service, and tax. This is an excellent hotel for *groups*.

For family travelers to Amsterdam, the **Hotel Kap** at 5B Den Tex Straat (phone 24-59-08) in the Leidseplein-Rijksmuseum area, offers several four-bedded rooms at 42 guilders ($14) per person, into which they'll place additional children at much-reduced rates. I saw a family of seven in residence in May of 1984. The price includes a Dutch breakfast with egg any style other than poached; the bonus features include a scale next to the ground floor staircase, on which you can check your weight, free.

Much farther out, in a pleasant and quiet residential area near the Zoo, the **Hotel Olszewski** at 89 Plantage Muidergracht (phone 23-62-41), is owned and managed by a friendly but somewhat strict retired police officer of Polish descent, Viktor Olszewski, who rents bathless rooms (showers are free) at 42 guilders ($14) per single, 35 guilders ($11.66) per person double, 38 guilders ($12.66) per person for twin beds, all in well-furnished and impeccably clean rooms—but ones in which you can't hold a noisy party at night (you'll be asked to leave the next day)! There's also a 1:15 a.m. curfew. And downstairs, the lounge and bar are decorated with flags, badges and postcards from fellow police officers all over the world. Here's one for readers seeking order and security in a turbulent world.

32 to 38 Guilders ($10.66 to $12.66) per Person, Breakfast and Service Included

An entire collection of extremely cheap hotels (again with near-perpendicular stairs, but satisfactory rooms) is found in an almost unbroken line, composed of half a dozen establishments, on the Raadhuisstraat—which is a three-minute walk from the Dam Square, between the Herengracht and the Keizersgracht. My favorite here is the **Hotel Westertoren,** 35B Raadhuisstraat (phone 24-46-39), owned by a young Dutch-American couple (he's from Boston), Alan and Sigrid Grusd, both excellent hosts who make a point of explaining the history and layout of the city to their guests. Their charge per person is 38 guilders per night; and their hotel is best for use in the off-season, when the central heating and the Dutch TV are both on full blast, and Alan and Sigrid can give you their full attention and advice. The several other hotels on this street charge, with some exceptions, slightly more—as, for example, the **Hotel Clemens,** 39 Raadhuisstraat, phone 24-60-89 (32 guilders per person for bed and breakfast); the **Hotel Ronnie,** 41 Raadhuisstraat, phone 24-28-21 (33 guilders for bed, breakfast, service and tax); the **Hotel Pax,** 37c Raadhuisstraat (phone 24-97-35; English-speaking owners, and similar in price—28 guilders per person, but without breakfast—to the others).

30 to 33 Guilders ($10 to $11) per Person, Breakfast (sometimes) and Service Included

Now the price is again lower, but the location is the lovely Herengracht, where the **Hotel Groot,** an old canal house at 137 Herengracht (phone 23-14-38), charges only 30 guilders ($10) per person, and provides reasonably acceptable rooms, as well as central heating and a family atmosphere. Recently, the Groot's new management sent me an inch-thick batch of Xeroxed pages from their guestbook, recording poems and paeans of praise: "It's Great at the Groot." "We had a few Hoots . . . At the Hotel Groots." "We got quite a fright . . . When we saw the first flight . . . But . . ." So, with fingers crossed, I've restored the inexpensive Groot to these pages, in hope that previously grumpy attitudes of the management have improved.

Again in the heart of the city, but for young tourists mainly, the magnificently located and much better **Hotel de Beurs,** at 7 Beursstraat (one block from American Express, just off the Damrak), phone 22-07-41, with 130 beds, is primarily a 33 guilders ($11) per-person establishment (including free showers, but without breakfast). Beds here are cots (but with good, innerspring mattresses), and most are arranged three to six to a room; but the hotel is light and cheerful, the proprietress is a motherly woman who keeps a color TV set in the lounge of the hotel, downstairs; and the location (just a short walk from the Central Station) is a marvelous one, even though not on a canal.

Try, too, the little **Hotel Brian** at 69 Singel (phone 24-46-61), which charges 30 guilders per person for top floor rooms, with bacon-and-egg breakfast included, no less. Here, there's only cold running water in the rooms, but unlimited hot water in the bathrooms, and the hotel itself is as much a scene as a hotel: Bob Marley posters in the lobby, rock music playing, and hip young owners in *High Times* T-shirts.

THE SPECIALTY HOTELS: There remain to be considered the specialty hotels of Amsterdam:

A Hotel for Ministers

The **Hospice San Luchesio,** 9 Waldeck Pyrmontlaan (phone 71-68-61), which can be reached by taking tram no. 2 to the Amstelveenseweg stop, is a modernistic, big-windowed building built in 1961 by the Third Order of Saint Francis for the accommodation of both Roman Catholic and Protestant clergymen (and their families), as well as members of religious orders. It has 25 rooms (11 singles, 14 doubles), each with private shower, a recreation room—and seven altars for daily Mass! The cost per person, including breakfast: 36 guilders ($12).

Hotels for Students

There are many of these, for Amsterdam ranks with Paris in the variety and number of its student housing facilities—indeed, no other city in Europe touches these two in that regard. And leading the list is the modern (and therefore relatively expensive—32.50 guilders per person for triple or four-bedded rooms with "semi-private" shower) **Hans Brinker Stutel** at 136 Kerkstraat (phone 220-687), which surely must rank among the continent's finest student lodgings. Ingeniously re-created out of a former in-city monastery, in a marvelously central location just a five-minute walk from the Leidseplein, the Stutel has a capacity of 250 beds, in a configuration that places one private shower between every two rooms. If you're concerned about such things, you'll have to carefully lock the door to the adjoining room before stripping to the buff! There's a large garden with a terrace, a restaurant, a late night student bar, ten dormitory rooms in which rates descend to 27 guilders and less, and a large student travel office across the street. Rates include breakfast, service and tax.

The largest of the student lodgings (second in preference only to the Hans Brinker Stutel) is the **Hotel Cok,** 1 Koningslaan (phone 79-66-53), an imposing mansion on grounds of its own, 15 minutes by trolley from the Central Station (take tram no. 2 from the station, which passes directly in front of the door and stops a block away). Inside, the rooms are not nearly as imposing—with some sporting double-decker beds—but there are 180 beds available, which rent in 1985 for only 30 guilders ($10) per person in seven- to eight-bedded rooms, including breakfast, service and all taxes. Next door at 34 Koninginnenweg is a spectacular new annex (the self-styled "Young Budget Hotel," brightly decorated) with 200 additional beds renting for the same price, but with considerably upgraded, modern facilities—in terms of quality and comfort, it's the best student deal in town. A cheaper dormitory-type establishment is the **Hotel Adolesce,** 26 Nieuwe Keizersgracht (phone 26-39-59), where students pay 14 to 25 guilders ($4.66 to $8.33) per night for one of 130 available bunks, breakfast and service included.

Much of the overflow from these two major establishments goes to the generally less expensive **Kabul Budget Hotel** at 42 Warmoesstraat (phone 23-71-58), only 100 yards from the front of the Central Station, in a far more congested area of Amsterdam, and on a narrow, narrow street. Here, multibedded rooms are 17 to 27 guilders a night (depending on the number of beds in them), breakfast is 5 guilders extra, and there's a pleasant self-service restaurant and recreation room. . . . A final, pleasant surprise: the student hotels of Amsterdam require no special student international identification card or other student credentials: if you look like a student, you get in!

ROOMS IN PRIVATE HOMES: As you've seen from our earlier discussion, scattered hotels in Amsterdam offer rooms with breakfast for less—sometimes considerably less—than 30 guilders ($10) per person, but the great majority charge from four to eight guilders more. Therefore, to keep your costs in an acceptable budget range, your next alternative is to seek a room in a private home. Those in central city tend to charge 27 to 30 guilders for bed-and-breakfast, those farther out tend to drop the price somewhat (see our "Readers' Selections" for several such examples).

Thus, in her well-located canal house, **Mrs. Huser,** at Tweede Kostverlorenkade 21 on the first floor (phone 16-92-56), provides you with your own private entrance, and also includes showers in her price of 27 guilders ($9) per person, including a large Dutch breakfast with boiled egg. One of her rooms overlooks a picturesque canal bordered by willow trees, where white swans slowly float around and patient fishermen wait for a catch; another is a single room, equipped with kitchenette. When you phone Mrs. Huser, whose English is excellent, she'll respond: "Take streetcar no. 13 and leave after bridge no. 9 (the Elisabeth Wolff Straat stop)". . . . Care for a houseboat? **Mr. H.J. Steens,** at Ark Oase, opposite Da Costakade 216 (phone 16-76-14), rents two rooms of his spacious boat, on a canal in the center of town, for 28 guilders ($9.33) per person, including a Dutch breakfast served in the large and very comfortable living room. While the two floating bedrooms are themselves rather small, their location is central (in the museum area)—and when, after all, did you ever live on a houseboat before? Take streetcar no. 17 to the Bilderdykkade stop, where you'll find the bearded Mr. Steens and his houseboat, home to hundreds of enthusiastic guests over the past ten years. . . . For a room overlooking a windmill, phone **Mrs. Sloof,** at 84-11-66. She lives with her husband at Willem de Zwijgerlaan 353, reached in 20 minutes by boarding bus no. 21 at the Central Station. Rate per person, breakfast included, is 30 guilders ($10) for a superbly furnished room which Mrs. Sloof has been renting for 25 years, not for the money, she says, but for the chance to meet and talk with international visitors. . . . Closer to the center of town, five minutes from the Leidseplein and museum areas, at Eerste Helmerstraat 55 HS, phone 12-61-76, **Mr. and Mrs. Krieghenbergh,** an amiable middle-aged couple (she speaks some English, he none), can take up to six guests in one twin-bedded room (29 guilders per person) and one four-bedded room (25 guilders per person); the four beds take up so much space in the room that you can hardly move about!

READER'S HOTEL SELECTIONS (23 Guilders): "At the **Hotel Schröder,** 48 B. Haarlemmerdijk (phone 26-62-72), a few minutes' ride via bus no. 22 from the Central Station, we received our best room in two months of traveling in Europe. And the price of 23 guilders per person included the huge breakfast one expects in Amsterdam. The establishment is run by a wonderful couple who are only too happy to help you plan your day in their wonderful city" (Robert Rothenhaus, Long Island

City, New York; note by AF: the Schröder, in a letter confirming the 23 guilder rate for 1985, says it hopes to become the "least expensive hotel in Amsterdam").

READERS' HOTEL SELECTIONS (33 to 37.50 Guilders): "At the **Hotel Schirmann,** 23 Prins Hendrikkade (phone 241-942), rooms are simple but clean, come with private shower and w.c., yet rent for only 37.50 guilders per person, no breakfast. A two-minute walk from the railroad station" (Donald Lamont, Downsview, Ontario, Canada). . . . "The charming **Hotel Gé Byleveld,** 109 Nicolaus Maesstraat (phone 79-23-01), whose host is marvelously friendly and helpful, is decorated with a mélange of antiques, potted plants, oriental rugs, fresh flowers—all of which contribute to a cheery, comfortable stay with some of the color and feeling of old Amsterdam. The charge is 35 guilders ($11.66) per person for singles and twins, including breakfast served on a beautiful verandah, and location is good, near the Concertgebouw. A stay here absolutely made our European trip!" (Dr. Mary Merrill, Santa Rosa, California). . . . "The well-located **Hotel Abba,** on the second and third floors of 12 Overtoom (phone 18-30-58), has immaculate, cheery rooms, an up-to-date atmosphere, and the most charming young owners we've met in Europe: Dick and Edith Heckes. A double with sink, shower down the hall, breakfast and service included, was an unbelievable 33 guilders per person. From the Central Station, simply take tram no. 1 to the Overtoom stop, directly in front of a Mercedes Benz dealer" (Laura Pearre, Charlottesville, Virginia).

READERS' HOTEL SELECTIONS (39 to 45 Guilders): "On two visits I have enjoyed staying at the **Hotel Smit,** phone 76-63-43, 24 P. C. Hoofstraat, next door to the Museum Hotel. For 88 guilders ($29.33) we had a double room with bath plus lavish breakfast, including egg and orange juice" (Mrs. Frances Vogel, Glenview, Illinois). . . . "Never have we found a hotel so clean, anywhere in the world, as the **Hotel Wijnnobel** at 9 Vossiusstraat (phone 72-22-98), near the Rijksmuseum. Twin rooms for 82 guilders ($27.33), triples for 112 guilders ($37.33), quads for 140 guilders ($46.66), including a giant Dutch breakfast (with one egg per person) brought to your room at any time you wish. And an owner so very willing to help with ideas and directions. But there is no lift, and the usual steep stairs" (Martin and Jezy Levinson, Alghero, Sardinia). . . . "**Centralpark West Hotel,** 27 Roemer Visscherstraat (phone 852-285), behind the Marriott Hotel, is managed by an American, offers big, spacious rooms overlooking a park, 55 guilders single, 77 guilders twin, 120 guilders quad, and 185 guilders for a baseball-field-sized quintuple room, always including continental breakfast. We hated to leave" (Ann Redfield, Miami, Florida). . . . "I spent five nights at the **King Hotel,** Leidsekade 85, phone 24-96-03, where a single room cost me 48 guilders a night, including breakfast and service charge; doubles are 39 guilders per person. This included an ample breakfast brought to my room. The hotel is about a three-minute walk from the Leidseplein, where you'll find the American Hotel, Opera House, restaurants and shops, and it's about a ten-minute walk from the Rijksmuseum. My single room was very small, but it was comfortable, and the doubles I saw were large and tastefully furnished. Stairs here were *very steep,* but the climb was made completely worthwhile by the cordiality of the host and his wife" (Grace Ewing, Jamaica, New York; note by AF: several other readers' endorsements were received for the King Hotel). . . . "We are staying at the **Hotel Impala,** Leidsekade 77 (phone 23-47-06), 38 guilders per person all year round, including service, breakfast and free showers. The breakfast is magnificent—an egg, cheese, bread, jam, butter and many cups of coffee. The hotel is run by an amiable young couple, and the place is immaculate. Our room has a fabulous bay window, plus another huge window, and would be perfect for a family. Our windows overlook the junction of two canals, around the corner from the Leidseplein" (Philip W. Sultz, Amsterdam, Netherlands; note by AF: other hotels on the Leidsekade, all in the 38- to 42-guilders-per-person range, include the **Hotel Kooyk,** 82 Leidsekade (whose proprietor is particularly kind and helpful to "lost sheep" Americans; his dining room is decorated with photographs of film stars of the 30's; phone 23-02-95); this is just around the corner from the big American Hotel and the action and color of the Leidseplein). . . . "**Hotel De Ijtunnel,** at 145 Prins Hendrikkade (phone 230-430), is extremely well located near the railroad station, has numerous rooms all with private facilities, for which it charges 45 guilders per person, including a large and delicious breakfast, possesses an annex a few doors away, and is capably operated by Mr. and Mrs. Grishaver; a wonderful place, well heated in winter" (Pauline Hadley, New York City). . . . "We had such a pleasant stay at the **Hotel Belga,** 8 Hartenstraat (phone 24-90-80), Amsterdam, we feel we should recommend it to other travelers. We were there in summer, when a double room without private bath cost 44 guilders per person, including breakfast and free use of the shower. The owners, Mr. and Mrs. Vreugd, speak English very well and are eager to advise on sightseeing and to provide helpful tips on the best places to shop. There are about ten cheerful rooms, always filled with fresh flowers from Mr. Letteboer's rooftop garden, and unpretentiously but comfortably furnished. Of course the famous Dutch breakfast is served, and to greet you in the morning there are the Letteboers' two finches and canary, who keep you company from their perches on the wall. The location, although only a few minutes' walk from the Dam or the Anne Frank House, is quiet, and you can hear the wonderful bells of Amsterdam chime through the day" (Mr. and Mrs. Robert L. Feldman, Alexandria, Virginia). . . . **"Hotel 7 Bridges,** 31 Reguliersgracht (phone 23-13-29), a short distance from the Rembrandtsplein, overlooking a beautiful canal, is a real bargain at 65 guilders ($21.66) for a double room, 90 guilders ($30) triple, plus 4 guilders ($1.33) for breakfast—and all in the very heart of the city! Owner Pierre Keulers is a delight. Take streetcar 16, 24 or 25 to the Keizersgracht stop, and walk from there" (Michael Ross, Los Angeles, California). . . . "The manager of the **Hotel Maas,** a canal house hotel at 91 Leidsekade (phone 233-868), was the most helpful hotel manager I've encountered in years. The charge was 45 guilders for singles, 70 to 75 twin, 110 triple, with showers for free, and location is just around the corner from the Leidseplein, in the heart of Amsterdam" (Maureen Stepanoff, West Leederville, Western Australia). . . . **"Hotel Asterisk,** 16 Den Tex Straat (phone 262-396), is perfect for families with young children, with babysitters available, rooms offered on the ground floor, and four-bedded rooms with private bath, and four large Dutch breakfasts, renting for 160 guilders ($53.33). Easily reached by streetcars 16, 24 or 25 from the Central Station to the Wetering Square stop" (Mrs. C. Passmore, Horsham, West Sussex, Great Britain); note from AF: The price for this four-bedded room, without babysitting service, is 160 guilders, in 1985.

PRIVATE HOMES THAT READERS HAVE LIKED: "By far our best accommodations were at the residence of **Mrs. Ursula Schoniau,** 134 Jan Evertsenstraat (phone 122-527). Her rooms are spotless, as is the rest of her home, and are rented for 26 guilders ($8.66) per person per night, including a delicious breakfast. Mrs. Schoniau takes a very personal interest in the happiness of her guests, gave us an orientation to Amsterdam, and then let us use two of her three bicycles to see the city as we pleased" (Dr. Robert M. Friedman, Oakland, California; note from AF: Ursula Schoniau does part-time voluntary work for a non-profit organization aiding social underdogs; she's an outstanding lady with a rare sense of responsibility for social problems. Take streetcar no. 13 from the Central Station to the Mercatorplein stop, where you'll find that no. 134 is in a shopping street next door to a butcher shop. One of Mrs. Schoniau's three rooms is a single). . . . "The home of **Eugene Heuvel,** 147 Nieuwe Kerkstraat (phone 22-79-14), offers private rooms for 25 guilders per person. This is the best buy in town and Eugene vows it will remain that way. The rooms are clean, cozy, carpeted and comfortable. We had at no extra charge, a large Dutch breakfast, complete with eggs, ham, tomato, bread, jam, peanut butter and a bottomless pot of tea. The nicest part was Eugene's warmth, his knowledge of Holland and our feeling of being at home. Great location, too. Take tram no. 9 from Central Station to the first zoo (Artis in Dutch) stop" (Glenn Kesselhaut and Brian Coven, West Orange, New Jersey). . . . "We stayed with **Mr. and Mrs. C. P. Riphagen** in their private home at 27 Nich. Japiksestraat, and fell in love with this family who speak English, offer a delicious breakfast, hot shower, and treat you like one of the family. All for 23 guilders per person. Call 151520 and take tram no. 1 to Johan Huizingalaan (the tram driver will be glad to tell you when to get off). Walk down a flight of stairs, turn left, and go past the Algemene Bank. Continue past Peter's Snackbar (which is, by the way, a very good place to eat) and the Laundry Mat until you reach Nich.

Japiksestraat; you will see a Texaco service station across the street. Turn right and walk up this street to no. 27 (the name C. P. Riphagen is on the door). You will be glad you did!" (Woodrow and Letress Berryhill, Phoenix, Arizona; subsequent seconding recommendation from C. W. Page, Bethany Beach, Delaware, and Paul Trinkkeller, Pacific Palisades, California). **"Mrs. Charlotte Wormer** runs a congenial and pleasant pension at 91 Marco Polostraat (phone 12-64-82), just ten minutes by tram no. 7 or 13 from the Central Station, charges 28 guilders per person, and provides a phenomenal breakfast of bacon, eggs, cheese, tomatoes, cucumbers, ham, toast and coffee" (Cecilia Ruvalo, Hialeah, Florida; Molly Gerkin and three other co-eds from Oklahoma State University). . . . "I stayed in a place that is not in your book, but they would like to be. The owner is the nicest person in Holland: **Mrs. Borg-Hagg,** 24/ Admiralengracht, phone 189-382. (Martin Vogt, Gosnells, Western Australia; note from AF: To reach Mrs. Borg-Hagg, take streetcar no. 13 from the Central Station, get off at Marco Polo Street, about 12 stops, and walk one minute to the house. The helpful lady rents two twin rooms, for 30 guilders per person, including a cooked breakfast).

READERS' SELECTIONS JUST OUTSIDE AMSTERDAM: "The **Herman van Empels** are not only the best 'bargain' (25 guilders per person, including breakfast, service, and tax) we have found in our travels, but also the best hosts. The address is Mathijs Sterklaan 13, Halfweg-Zwanenburg, phone 02907-5235, 15 minutes by bus (no. 85, on the road to Haarlem) from the center of Amsterdam. Not only are the beds comfortable and breakfast plentiful, but the personal attention they give their guests is noteworthy, and the fresh-ground, fresh-brewed coffee is the best by far we encountered on the continent. Many of our friends go there and are as enthusiastic as we are, particularly as the van Empels go 'All Out' for their guests, especially Americans, and it is fun to meet people of all nationalities in their homey living and dining rooms. They are very generous with outstanding TV programs and often will show color slides, and help plan scenic days of interest. They have even picked up and returned guests to the airport, and there is a bus nearby to Amsterdam" (Mrs. Thorburn S. McGowan, Storrs, Connecticut; also D. S. Rintoul, Hong Kong; William E. Brewer, Indianapolis, Indiana; Florence Stark, Desert Hot Springs, California; note by AF: Mr. van Empel has confirmed that he will continue to charge only 25 guilders in 1985, and points out that his house is only 10 km. from the center of Amsterdam, and thus particularly suitable for readers with cars). . . . "Our first choices in hotels in Amsterdam were filled due to a busy Easter and tulip-time week-end. At that point a man, who had approached us before, reappeared and offered rooms at his private home near Volendam. We were wary of this tactic, but, in desperation, said we'd take a look. The quaint lakeside community of Volendam delighted us, as did our stay with the perfectly charming family of **H. Rikkers,** Iepenlaan 16, Volendam (N.H.), phone 02993-63933. He speaks English, his wife makes an excellent try. She also serves a huge Dutch breakfast and on our arrival—too late for restaurants—she made an appetizing dinner for us. In the evenings we were served coffee or drinks in the family living room, were helped with our plans for excursions within the Netherlands. This family was certainly worth getting to know and I highly recommend their home to readers who want to be part of the community life of this warm village. I almost forgot: the price for 1985 is only 23 guilders per person." (Sue Ann Allen, Flint, Michigan).

We'll now assume that you're ensconced in an Amsterdam hotel and are ready to eat—an activity that, in this town, can involve some gratifying surprises.

3. Restaurants & Meals

To begin with, the restaurants deal in the most exotic cuisine of Europe. There are, for instance, Indonesian restaurants here, by the dozen, where you'll see residents at work on a 20-dish dinner called "rijsttafel"; there are just as many Chinese-Indonesian restaurants where secretaries and office boys dart in for a normal lunch of "nasi goreng," with a "loempia" on the side! In even the most elegant restaurants, smoked eel pops up as one of the most popular opening courses, and for snacks throughout the day, you'll discover the ubiquitous but unique sandwich shops *(broodjeswinkels)* of Amsterdam, serving ground raw meat on a soft bun! There are so many of these food surprises in Amsterdam—including a cocktail drink called "Advokaat" which you eat with a spoon!—that there's scarcely time for a three- or four-day visitor to sample them all.

How to organize this information? In preparing a recent guide to Amsterdam, I ate my way through more than 100 of the city's restaurants and peered over the shoulders of diners in about 30 more. I've concluded that the only coherent plan for presenting my restaurant suggestions is to group them according to the meal of the day in which they specialize. And thus, we'll deal first with breakfast, then with lunch, then with snacks, and then with dinner, concentrating always on establishments that offer budget-priced meals.

BREAKFAST IN AMSTERDAM: The first meal of the day presents no problem in Amsterdam—it is always served in your hotel, is nearly always included free in the cost of your hotel room, and is always the most incredibly large morning feast you've encountered: several sorts of Dutch breads and rolls, huge hunks of butter, marmalade, slices of luscious Dutch cheese, at least one slice of meat, sometimes a boiled egg, followed of course by tea or coffee. This is the typical Dutch breakfast, and most tourists are unable to eat again until evening. I'm told that even larger breakfasts are served in the south of Holland, but I for one find that hard to believe!

LUNCH: What do the Dutch eat for lunch? Well, most of them eat a *second* breakfast! By that, I refer to the famous institution of the *Hollandsche Koffietafel* (Dutch coffee table), and although it may be unfair to refer to it as a "breakfast," it is essentially an expanded version of what you've had upon arising: several different kinds of bread, slices of cheese, butter, slices of meat—usually supplemented, this time, by a single small hot dish, such as a hot meat croquette or a bowl of soup, followed by either milk or coffee or tea. For that percentage of traditionally minded Dutch who lunch on a koffietafel, the custom is to put off a big hot meal until evening. And if that seems strange, then let it be known that the Dutch have the highest longevity rate in the world, which many attribute to their eating habits. Nor will the custom seem so strange if you will remember that many people in other countries—most particularly, the citizens of the United States, England and Scandinavia—also have a cold meal at lunch—consisting usually of sandwiches.

Restaurants Serving the Hollandsche Koffietafel

A large percentage of the restaurants in Amsterdam include a koffietafel on their lunch-time menu, even when they specialize in hot meals. It's rarely difficult, therefore, to find a koffietafel, and it's also good to remember that a koffietafel is an inexpensive lunch to have. Typical of what you'll receive and pay is the koffietafel served at the moderately priced **Koffiehaus Blom**, 117 Nieuwendijk, a short walk from the Central Station, which charges 9 guilders ($3), for an enormous koffietafel lunch that includes a hot meat croquette and milk or coffee. In other restaurants throughout the city, the koffietafel is occasionally referred to by its alternate name, a twaalfuurje (a 12 o'clock bread-lunch), costs 8 guilders (including service charge), and consists of a thick slice of bread with ham, an equally thick slice of bread with roast beef, Russian salad, and a choice of coffee, tea or milk. Try **Singeltje,** facing the plant-and-flower-shops at 494 Singel, corner of Koningsplein, for precisely such a meal. Still other establishments serve a Brabantse koffietafel for 9 guilders (exactly $3, including service), which includes most of the above items plus an egg, an extra slice of bread, and a second glass of coffee or milk.

Sandwich Shops (Broodjeswinkels)

Even more prevalent than the restaurants serving koffietafels, are the unusual sandwich shops of Amsterdam (broodjeswinkels), where again a large percentage of the population—perhaps a third—take their cold lunches, consisting usually of two or three *broodjes* (sandwiches) and a glass of milk. And if that sounds rather unexciting, then you haven't tasted a Dutch sandwich! Prepared on a buttered soft roll, liberally sprinkled with salt, its ingredients consist of a full half-inch to an inch of thinly sliced (and therefore unusually tender) meat, including some of the most delicious rare roast beef in the world. Or you can have a broodje tartare—ground raw hamburger on a soft bun—or a broodje warm vlees, which is a hot meat sandwich, covered with a heavy, brown gravy and eaten on a plate with a fork and knife. The variety of ingredients spread out before you is enormous and appealing, but the most significant aspect of a Dutch sandwich lunch is its cheapness: many of the broodjes cost only 3 guilders ($1), and only the unusual varieties, or those involving hot meats, rise to more than 3.50 guilders ($1.16). Two broodjes and a glass of milk make an excellent, quickly served lunch—perfect for a fast-moving tourist—and that repast should rarely cost more than 8 guilders ($2.66). Warning: order only one or two broodjes at a time; you'll be surprised to discover how filling they are. The greatest danger, and worst temptation, to tourists in Amsterdam is overeating!

Where do you find broodjeswinkels? Everywhere—you can scarcely walk for a block without passing the invitation to enjoy *belegde broodjes* (diverse sandwiches). The most numerous chain of shops is that operated by the brilliantly named **Broodje van Kootje** (try pronouncing it), most of whose *broodjes* cost 3 or 4.50 guilders, including service and tax, and whose shops are located at 12 Rembrandtsplein, 20 Leidseplein, and 28 Spui. Here, if you'll order a big, hot meat croquette on a buttered roll (2.50 guilders), and a glass of milk (2 guilders), the total—including service—will be 4.50 guilders ($1.50), and who can eat more than that? The largest of the broodjeswinkels is **Van Dobben** at 5 Korte Reguliersdwarsstraat (just ten yards off the Rembrandtsplein), but the one with the largest and most attractive selection of ingredients is—to my mind—the **Plein 24,** at 24 Leidseplein. Another unusually good sandwich shop—where you will always find hot meat sandwiches with gravy, along with other varieties—is a place that is actually called (in English) the **"Sandwich Corner,"** and which stands at no. 1 Kromme Elleboogsteeg, a tiny alley that runs off the Rokin, near the Dam Square. (It's closed on Sundays.) Here, the broodjes range from 3 to 4 guilders. A typical Frommer feast, that leaves me perfectly well filled: one *broodje* croquette (3 guilders), plus two glasses of milk

(4 guilders). Total, including service charge: 7 guilders ($2.33). Never over-eat!

At any broodjeswinkel, the best buy, bar none, is the hot meat croquette (kroket) broodje selling for never more than 3 guilders ($1). It's phenomenal in taste. And incidentally, the price for milk *(melk)* or coffee *(koffie)* at most broodjeswinkels is 2 guilders (66¢). You'd be well advised to drink the superb Dutch milk, which is consumed in staggering quantities in Holland—perhaps another explanation for the long life spans of the Dutch.

Uitsmijters

Another item offered at most sandwich shops and restaurants—and which many Amsterdammers consume for lunch—is an *uitsmijter* (pro-nounced "out-smay-ter," it means "bouncer"), a plate consisting of two buttered slices of bread, topped with either ham or roast beef, atop which is then a fried egg or two! You'll learn very quickly that it is unusually filling (consumed with a glass of milk)—and relatively cheap (usually no more than 7 to 9 guilders, ($2.66, to $3). Places serving uitsmijters: virtually every sandwich shop in town, plus the well-located **Honeds' Bakhuisje,** 39 Kerkstraat, off the Leidsestraat; the large cafe-restaurant of the **American Hotel,** 28 Leidseplein (ham or cheese uitsmijter for 8.50 guilders, meat or cheese croquettes for 3.50); the **Sandwich Corner,** 1 Kromme Elle-boogsteeg (see above, uitsmijters for as little as 5 guilders).

Bami Goreng, Nasi Goreng

And now, lest we leave the impression that everyone in Amsterdam eats a cold lunch, we'll turn to an especially popular, noontime warm dish. Although many Amsterdammers have a normal meat-and-potatoes meal for lunch, several thousands of them head instead for an Indonesian or Chinese-Indonesian restaurant and order a heaping plate of bami goreng or nasi goreng. While these items are available for dinner, too, they carry a much lower price tag at lunch, when they are consumed in great quantity. Indeed, in nearly a dozen restaurants, you can have a three-course bami goreng or nasi goreng meal (starting first with chicken soup—*kippensoep;* then *loempia*—eggroll; then the bami goreng or nasi goreng) for about $2.75 to $3.50.

And what are these strangely named concoctions? In their purest Indonesian state, bami goreng is a heaping plate of buttered noodles mixed with little strips of meat, while nasi goreng is a plate of rice with meat. But the Dutch have added other embellishments: a fried egg atop the pile, a slice of ham or pork underneath, some crisper noodles along the side, the whole garnished with lettuce and pickles. It tastes better than it sounds, it provides a whopping big meal that you won't be able to finish, and it is—as we noted—unusually cheap.

Every Indonesian and Chinese-Indonesian, and even a few Dutch, restaurants serve an inexpensive bami goreng or nasi goreng meal at lunch, and we'll list a few, categorized according to the area of town in which they're found.

On the tourist-heavy **Damrak,** leading up from the Central Station, you'll discover the **Wah Nam Restaurant,** 32 Damrak, serving *kippensoep* (chicken soup), eggroll, nasi or bami goreng, and coffee, all for a relatively high (for Amsterdam) 8 guilders at lunch (a more elaborate nasi or bami goreng dinner in the evening costs 16 guilders).

But on the less expensive **Nieuwendijk,** a shopping street that runs parallel to the Damrak, the **Chinese Canton Restaurant,** 65 Nieuwendijk, charges only 7 guilders (including service) for a three-course nasi or bami goreng lunch, as do one or two other establishments (the **Lin Fa** at no. 149 Nieuwendijk, for example: 8 guilders) on that stretch of the Nieuwendijk that is closer to the station.

Again running parallel to the Damrak, but on the other side, the narrow **Warmoesstraat** is the site of several restaurants serving three-course nasi goreng meals for as little as 8 guilders, and I'd particularly invite you to try the rather basic **Tsuan Sheng,** at 83 Warmoesstraat (only 7.50 guilders for lunch), whose prices at night are also remarkably cheap: 6.50 guilders for a nassi rames, 7 guilders for a nassi rames special—an abbreviated rijsttafel—highly recommended.

On the **Damstraat,** which runs off the Dam Square, the place to visit is the **Dragon City Restaurant,** 18 Damstraat, where the lunchtime meal (served only from noon to 3 p.m.) consists of kippensoep, bami or nasi goreng, coffee or tea, and costs exactly 9 guilders.

In the area of the **Stedelijk Museum,** the **Restaurant De Orient,** 21 Van Baerlestraat, a fairly expensive place, nevertheless charges only 9.50 guilders ($3.16) for a fairly elegant, two-course nasi or bami goreng dinner. Open daily from 4:30 to 11:30 p.m.

On the **Oude Zijds Voorburgwal,** a short walk up from the station, the **Restaurant Tai Pang,** 47 O.Z. Voorburgwal, charges 8 guilders for a three-course b-or-n goreng lunch (including soup, eggroll and coffee), 14.50 guilders for four courses at night.

And finally, for your most numerous collection of restaurants serving this inexpensive specialty, head for the **Binnen Bantammerstraat,** fairly near the railroad station, which forms the heart of Amsterdam's district of Chinese restaurants. There you'll find at least four restaurants (including the **Ling Nam,** 3 Binnen Bantammerstraat; the **Azie,** 9 Binnen Bantammerstraat) serving a three-course lunch of this sort for 10.50 guilders, including service and tax.

AFTERNOON SNACKS: Around four hours after lunch, you'll be ready for the favorite afternoon snack of the Amsterdammers—a raw herring, eaten with a toothpick, from the counter of an open-air stand! While other European cities specialize in hot sausage stands, scattered around town, Amsterdam offers herring stands instead—and after eating your first raw Dutch herring, covered with chopped onions, you'll understand why. I don't care how many other species of herring you've had—marinated, creamed, pickled, salted—there's nothing so good as a raw Dutch herring, for which the charge is usually 4 guilders ($1.33) at the famous open-air herring stands of Amsterdam.

There are, quite literally, at least a score of herring stands in the central part of Amsterdam, never far from where you may be (ask a resident to point one out). If you're lucky, you'll arrive at the stand while a true Dutchman is "imbibing" the succulent fish. Notice how he grabs it daintily by the tail, holding it high above his mouth, and then devours from the bottom up. For you, the owner of the stand will cut the skinned and gutted fish into four pieces, give you a wooden pick with which to pick the pieces up, and a bowl of diced onions into which to dip the fish. The best time for herring is late April or May, when the first catch of *nieuwe haring* comes in. The quality remains high throughout the end of September but begins to disappear as the winter months set in. Whatever your normal attitude is towards herring, don't miss an opportunity to taste the Dutch variety—it's incomparable, a major surprise of amazing Amsterdam.

DINNER: But now we arrive at the normal, hot-meal-serving restaurants of Amsterdam, to which most people go at night (although they can obviously patronize them at lunchtime, as well). These include restaurants of every nationality and kind—Dutch, French, Spanish, Italian, you name it—but the most unusual, and the ones for which Amsterdam is particularly famed, are the Indonesian and Chinese-Indonesian restaurants serving rijsttafel. You can't pass through Amsterdam without sampling this glorious meal at least once!

Rijsttafel Restaurants

Rijsttafel (literally, "rice table") is a meal the Dutch discovered during the days of their empire in the Dutch East Indies (now Indonesia); it consists of a central, large dish of rice, surrounded by as many as 20 (that's right, 20) other small dishes, each including a serving of unusually prepared and often fairly spicy, meat or vegetables. One or two at a time, you transfer the contents of the little dishes onto the big pile of rice, eat the rice and its condiments together, and then cool your red-hot throat with big draughts of cold Dutch beer. Not all the dishes are as spicy as I may have implied, however, and the more cautious eaters can put together a rijsttafel meal that is memorable and unique—even though not spicy.

What's in the little dishes that surround your main bowl of rice? To describe them best, I should describe the best-known of Amsterdam's rijsttafel restaurants, which is the famed but expensive **Bali**, 95 Leidsestraat (two short blocks below Leidseplein). It charges exactly 49.50 guilders ($16.50) per person, including service and tax, for a 22-dish rijsttafel consisting of rice, soup, pork in soya sauce, meat in madura sauce, steamed meat, liver in a special sauce, eggs in sauce, sweet potatoes, bean sprouts, roast pork on sticks, fried bananas, stuffed omelette, bamboo shoots, shrimp bread, mushrooms, java sauce, soybean cakes, vegetables in peanut sauce, cucumber in sour sauce, mixed sour vegetables, fruit in a sweet-and-sour sauce, and fried grated coconut. And now you know what a rijsttafel is!

No budget tourist, however, need pay as much as the Bali asks, because other restaurants in town—particularly those on the famous **Binnen Bantammerstraat**—offer a nearly equivalent rijsttafel for far less money. Simply ask a resident for the location of the Binnen Bantammerstraat, which is a street in the area to the southeast of the railroad station. There you'll discover, in one block, no fewer than six restaurants serving rijsttafel. Try, in particular, the **Kong Hing**, 11 Binnen Bantammerstraat (16.50 guilders for a 14-item rijsttafel); or the **Ling Nam**, 3 Binnen Bantammerstraat (14.50 guilders for 14 items). I should prefer one, but after having eaten at each at least twice, can't decide which I like best! Friendly, unpretentious atmosphere—and good rijsttafel—at both.

Abbreviated rijsttafels? The tiny **Restaurant Madoera**, 86 Reguliersdwarsstraat (just 75 yards off the Rembrandtsplein), serves 12 items for 22.50 guilders, while the swankier **Restaurant Indrapoera**, directly on the Rembrandtsplein, at 40, serves 19 items ("Rijsttafel Populair") for 29 guilders ($9.66).

A slightly more expensive version of these multi-item dinners can be had at the tiny, but well-located, **Kow Loon,** 498 Singel, on the street of the Amsterdam flower market, just 50 yards away from the Nieuw England Department Store and the beginning of the Leidsestraat. Here, a 13-item rijsttafel is only 19 guilders, 20 items 25 guilders. An important budget bonus: from noon to 4 p.m. and again at night from 9:30 to 10:30 p.m., the Kow Loon serves a still different abbreviated, but filling, version of a rijsttafel, called "nasi ramas," for only 12.50 guilders ($4.16): a stick of barbecued pork next to a mountain of rice, over which are poured a number of rijsttafel ingredients.

(Incidentally, this "nasi ramas speciaal" is offered by nearly all the Chinese restaurants of Amsterdam, and is, as we've mentioned, a stripped-down version of a rijsttafel—poured directly onto a vast mound of rice, and lacking the excitement of the 15-or-so separate dishes in which a normal rijsttafel comes. It also consists of not more than six items. Still, it's a cheap alternative or follow-up to the standard rijsttafel).

Finally, on the Nieuwendijk (that shopping street that parallels the Damrak), you can have a 14-dish rijsttafel for 17 guilders at the somewhat plain, but utterly authentic, **Lin Fa Restaurant,** 149 Nieuwendijk; a ten-dish rijsttafel for 14 guilders at the **Fong Won Restaurant,** 85 Warmoesstraat (also running parallel to the Damrak); and a nine-item rijsttafel, at dinner only, for 15 guilders, at the **Restaurant de Orient,** 21 Van Baerlestraat (near the Concertgebouw and the Stedelijk Museum; open daily); all including service and tax, but plus the cost of your beverage, of course.

THE NORMAL MEALS: Now we move into the less exotic areas of Dutch cuisine. And because we've listed a great many lunchtime spots where you can eat well for $3.50 to $4 (the restaurants serving Hollandsche Koffietafels, for instance; the sandwich shops; the Chinese-Indonesian restaurants with their bami goreng and nasi goreng), we can now afford to splurge a bit—surveying, first, the restaurants offering full lunches and dinners for about $9, including tax and service, returning then to the more normal budget-type establishment where dinner is $4.50 and under.

CURRENCY RATES: As we go to press the Dutch guilder is valued at approximately 3 to the dollar, which makes each guilder worth about 33 U.S. cents. Although you should recheck these rates at the time of your own trip to Holland, they shouldn't vary too greatly from the 3 to 1 ratio that presently exists.

Super-Splurge Meals for $9 and $9.50

First a lunchtime splurge, then an evening selection. Nearly 300 Amsterdammers meet for lunch each day in the vast and traditionally styled restaurant of the landmark **American Hotel** on the Leidseplein, one of the city's two major entertainment squares; they do so because of the restaurant's reputation for quality meals at moderate prices, quickly served, in a dignified setting. A daily-changing, two-course "menu" (example: creamed tomato soup with croutons, followed by fried river trout with parsley potatoes) sells for 28 guilders, just over $9, and à la carte choices total to about the same for two courses and beverage.

For an interesting evening meal costing around $9.50, you might next try the picturesque **Holland's Glorie Restaurant,** 220 Kerkstraat (right off Vijzelstraat), which I call the "poor man's Five Flies." The reference is to Amsterdam's expensive and famous "Five Flies" restaurant, which has one of the most authentic 17th-century interiors in Holland. This budget counterpart—Holland's Glorie—bears a startling resemblance to its wealthier brother, with stained glass windows, mahogany walls, pewter mugs, and all the other accoutrements of 17th-century life—an exciting atmosphere, to which you might even take someone you're trying to impress! You might order a delicious beefsteak Grand Mère (with mushrooms, ham, onions and sauce) for 21 guilders. Soup of the day is 4 guilders ($1.33) and desserts are 4 and 5 guilders. It's easy to eat well for a flat $9.50 (and sometimes less) in one of the most stunningly decorated dining rooms in all of surprising Amsterdam. Open evenings only, from 5 to 10 p.m., but seven days a week.

Meals for $8

A cheaper splurge? **Honed's Bakhuisje,** 39 Kerkstraat (just off the Leidsestraat, near the Leidseplein), our top recommendation in this category, is an ornately decorated little place (stained glass windows and Delft china on the walls) where there's always one two-course dinner for 24.50 guilders ($8.16), including service charge: soup, meatballs, potatoes, vegetable, pudding. The daily *dagschotels* (blue-plate specials) are 16 to 22 guilders, and are piled with food four inches high; there's nothing dainty about these longshoreman's type suppers (served from 6 p.m. to midnight), but they'll fill you for hours. Closed Sundays except during summer.

(Incidentally, most main plates at Honed's—as at most other restaurants in Amsterdam—carry huge portions of meat, gravy, potatoes, and are almost impossible to finish. Therefore, unless you're famished, it's wise to skip the appetizers and soup at this and other restaurants in Amsterdam—a practice that will considerably reduce the cost of your meals.)

Meals for $4.50-and-Less

The more typical, and lower-priced restaurants, include some exciting finds, among which are the following:

(1) The cafeteria of the **Hema Department Store** (second floor), 174 Nieuwendijk, near the Damrak, is the cheapest self-service restaurant in town, where you can stuff yourself for $3, and yet a beautiful, modern and clean room that provides for fairly pleasant, although strictly utilitarian, dining. Prices are almost unprecedented by Amsterdam standards: 1.50 guilders for milk, 1.60 guilders for coffee, only 7.50 guilders ($2.50) for plates such as calves liver with potatoes and applesauce, or for other daily special platters, 4.50 guilders ($1.50) for two luscious meat croquettes with french fries, 4.50 guilders for platters of hard boiled eggs, tuna fish, and potato salad (large enough for two to share). Here's an institution that's always reliably cheap for reasonably well-prepared food, but is open—quite obviously—only until 6 p.m., and is closed Sundays.

(2) **Keuken van 1870,** 4 Spuistraat (a short walk up from the Central Station near the plush Sonesta Hotel) is probably the cheapest of Amster-

dam's sit-down restaurants. Opened over 110 years ago as a soup kitchen for the poor, this non-profit establishment has developed into a perfectly acceptable budget eatery, seating around 100 people in a large mensa-type dining room, charging the following: two-course menu of the day 11 guilders ($3.66); meat-and-vegetable stew with mixed salad (an enormous meal by itself) 7.50 guilders ($2.77), omelettes 5 guilders; coffee, tea and milk for 1.40; Coke 1.80; beer 2, and yogurt 1.90 guilders. Open Monday to Friday from 11 a.m. to 7 p.m., weekends from 4 to 8 p.m. The manageress-waitress, Frau Ria, speaks English, and you'll find English menu cards on each table.

(3) The **Eethuisje Cantharel,** 377 Kerkstraat (20 yards from Utrechtsestraat), which is open from 5 to 10 p.m., charges 8 to 15 guilders ($2.66 to $5) for most of its vast meat plates with potatoes and vegetables. Even if you're not a student, you can enjoy a bountiful meal of liver, vegetables and potatoes for 12 guilders. Plastic tablecloths, of course, but with gaily muraled walls. Closed Sundays.

(4) The **Egg Cream,** at 19 St Jacobs Straat, a short and narrow street connecting Voorburgwal and Nieuwendijk, 250 yards from the Central Station, is a favorite vegetarian eatery of Dutch employees working in this busy area. Here at any of the seven wooden tables, lighted by Tiffany lamps, a daily lunch will cost 7.50 guilders ($2.50)—soup, sandwich, salad, coffee or milk—followed by homemade cakes (chocolate, apple, rhubarb, lemon, etc.) 3.50 guilders, and a large choice of juices (apricot, pine-apple, apple, pear, carrot, prune, etc.) 2.50 to 3 guilders per glass. If you buy take-out food, you'll save the 10% service charge. Open seven days a week, from 11 a.m. to 7:30 p.m.

(5) **In De Oude Goliath,** at Kalverstraat 92, directly on the pedestrians-only shopping street, is actually the restaurant of the Historical Museum, but is open to the general public; it's named after the enormous, 20-foot statue of Goliath carved out of a tree, with a tiny David next to him, both built in the 17th century for a Dutch amusement park. Daily dishes and salad bowls are 9.75 guilders ($3.25), various soups (with a roll) 6 guilders ($2), pancakes 6.75 guilders ($2.25), and tea, served between 2:30 and 4:30 p.m., at 2 guilders (66¢) for a cup. Open Monday to Saturday from 9:30 a.m. to 5 p.m., Sunday from 1 to 5 p.m.

(6) **Moeders Pot,** 119 Vinkenstraat, in the Haarlemmer Square area, serves giant daily platters for 10 guilders ($3.33), and provides a mixed salad with each platter for no extra charge. Opens at 5 p.m., closed Monday, a small place with an intimate and pleasant atmosphere.

(7) **De Bast,** 9 Huidenstraat, near Spui and Herengracht, is a trendy, vegetarian restaurant whose price structure just barely fits here: 14 guilders ($4.66) for a filling "grain of the day" plate—as, for example, millet with leeks and milk, preceded (optionally) by soup for 3.50 guilders. Open daily except Sundays from noon to 8:30 p.m.

(8) **De Lantaarn,** 64 Tweede Const. Hugyensstraat (just ten yards off the Overtoom), another typical little *eethuisje* (eating house), with very good food, for which the charge averages 9 guilders a plate; soup is 3 guilders. Within walking distance (just barely) of the Leidseplein; you'll notice it by the little green lantern that hangs outside, but don't confuse De Lantaarn with De Groene Lanteerne in the area of the Central Station. Open 4:30 p.m. to 11 p.m. only, closed Saturdays. Highly recommended.

(9) **Mr. Hot Potato,** 44 Leidsestraat, corner of Keizersgracht, sells 30 varieties of baked potato platters, ranging from one with butter or cream,

priced at 2 guilders (66¢) to a deluxe, 5.50 guilders ($1.83) spud served with shrimp salad. Filling, and a good value.

(10) **Nordzee,** 122 Kalverstraat, in the pedestrian zone area, is a self-service fish restaurant where a steamed cod fillet with mashed potatoes and butter sauce is 7.75 guilders ($2.58). Fried fishburgers—especially popular with children—are considerably less in price. Conveniently, the restaurant is open seven days a week until 8 p.m.

(11) **The English Fish and Chip Shop,** 63 Utrechtsestraat, off the Rembrandtsplein, is a tiny place managed by an actual young Englishman from Yorkshire, Garry McKirdy, who sells fish and chips for 6 guilders ($2), chips alone for 1.60 guilders, homemade pies and sausages at 4 guilders apiece. Meals for $3.50 and less are easily do-able.

(12) **Salerno,** at 1 Admiral de Ruyterweg, five minutes from the Westerkerk (West Church), is without doubt the finest of the budget-priced Italian restaurants of Amsterdam, managed by Signor Vittorio Scarpa with typical Italian temperament and know-how; his lasagne al forno (14 guilders, $4.66) is as good as the kind served in Naples or Rome. Large bowl of spaghetti: 9 guilders, $3; roast chicken with fried potatoes: 9.50 guilders or $3.16.

Finally, for a meal that will cost about $3, walk over at lunchtime to the **Valkenburgerstraat** near the Waterlooplein (the daily flea market of Amsterdam) where you'll find stands selling a cup of filling, hot erwten soep (pea soup) for 2.50 guilders, a bag of french fried potatoes for 2 guilders, and a portion of raw herring for 4 guilders. Delicious!

DRINKING IN AMSTERDAM: All the normal soft and hard drinks are of course available in Holland, including the incomparable, world-famous Dutch beers. But you'll want to try the Dutchman's favorite aperitif, a gin drink called *genever*—which all the world knows as "Dutch gin." It packs a wallop, it needs a little time to get accustomed to, but it grows upon you! And it's cheap; normally about $1.25 per shot; in a nightclub therefore, you'd be well advised to keep ordering only genever (chased, perhaps, by beer).

Genever, by the way, is available as either *jonge genever* (young genever) or *oude genever* (old genever); the young kind has less of the distinctive perfumed taste of the other, and is usually more palatable to tourists trying this drink for the first time. Some tourists, for whom genever may be too strong an item, can try another unusual drink called "Advokaat"—a heavy, spiked, egg-nog-type substance which you eat with a spoon. Prior to World War II, I'm told, Advokaat was about the only drink a proper lady would be caught imbibing; during the war, however, the women switched to genever and drink it today in about the same quantity that U.S. women devour dry martinis.

THOSE INCOMPARABLE CROQUETTES: This, now, is our final food tip: when in doubt in Amsterdam, order *croquetten* (meat croquettes). Breaded and crisp outside, creamy and smooth inside, and served with a plate of french fried potatoes covered with a tangy, tartar-type sauce, they are a Dutch classic—and they are always cheap, even at the most expensive of restaurants (expect to spend a maximum of 7.50 guilders for two croquettes, french fries and sauce). At restaurants up and down the Kalverstraat (the walking street), just off the Dam Square, two meat croquettes with bread are 6 guilders; with french fries as well—7.50 guilders; go to the swank counter-restaurant of Amsterdam's Schiphol Airport, and you'll pay scarcely more than 50 Dutch cents extra. And at the **Sandwich Corner,** 1 Kromme Elleboogsteeg, that amazing little snackbar on the alley that runs off the Rokin, a croquette sandwich can be had for only 3 guilders without french fries, for 4 guilders with. At least for a snack, and even for a meal, have a Dutch croquette!

READER'S RESTAURANT SELECTION: "At the remarkable **De Boemerang,** 171 Weteringschans (about three blocks from the Heineken Brewery, not far from the Rijksmuseum), I had the best mussels I have ever tasted. A mussels dinner overflowing with the little delicacies is only 15 to 22 guilders, depending on type, and one particular combination of mussels with three sauces is highly recommended for 17.50 guilders" (Mel Small, Royal Oak, Michigan).

AMSTERDAM'S STUDENT FACILITIES: We've already reviewed the
student hotels of Amsterdam, in our general section on housing. For student meals, another large group of institutions exists for your benefit but the very best of them is the **Mensa Academica Tangram,** at 3 Damstraat, just off the Dam Square, behind the Krasnapolsky Hotel (an ideal location, easy-to-find). Here, on three spacious floors in standard, self-service cafeteria style, three-course student meals are served for either 5 guilders ($1.66) or 8 guilders ($2.66), every day of the week, from noon to 7 p.m. Student I.D. cards are *not* required. At two other semi-official student mensas—**H 88** near Westermarkt and the Anne Frank House, and **De Welsper** near the Waterlooplein—similar rates and hours prevail; but Tangram, with its generous helpings of top quality dishes, remains your best bet.

4. Starvation Budget

For dormitory accommodations in Amsterdam, look at our section on specialty hotels, which discusses student hotels that are not strictly limited to students; and add to that list the **Christian Youth Hostel "Eben Haëzer,"** 179 Bloemstraat, phone 24-47-17, which offers dormitory accommodations (and a midnight curfew) for just 13.50 guilders a night. Take streetcar no. 13 or 17 from the Central Station to the Marnixstraat stop, or else simply walk from the station (15 minutes) to the corner of Rozengracht and Marnixstraat, then glance about for Bloemstraat.

Amsterdam's official youth hostel, open only to international youth hostel members (you can join on the spot for 30 guilders, $10), is the **Vondelpark** at 5 Zandpad (phone 83-17-44), next to the Vondel Park and near the Rijksmuseum (only a few hundred yards away). In hostel tradition, the accommodations are dormitory in style, extremely cheap (16 guilders, $5.33—for bunk-and-breakfast), and marred only by a 1 a.m. curfew. This is a big one, with 310 beds, a restaurant on site serving three-course meals for 11 guilders ($3.66). Take streetcars no. 1 or 2 to the Leidseplein, and walk (five minutes) from there.

BUDGET ALLEY: Near the Central Station, there's a street, which I call "Budget Alley," because it's packed with starvation budget-type restaurants and accommodations. Beginning at the station, the street is called Martelaarsgracht; as it passes the Nieuwendijk, it veers to the right and changes its name first to Hekeleved and then to Spuistraat. As you walk along, you'll pass the famous **Quick Snackbar** mentioned below. And then there's the **Nieuwe Nieuwestraat,** which I call "French Fried Potato Street," a little alley off the Nieuwendijk, where you'll find at least seven shops selling large paper cones of freshly made fries served with mayonnaise-like sauce, for 2.50 guilders (83¢). Some of the shops have chairs outside; my favorite is no. 26, called **De Belegde Bol,** where you can choose from meat balls (2 guilders), croquettes and at least 50 varieties of sandwiches (as little as 2.20 guilders). Anywhere along this street a filling lunch with milk, tea, or beer included, should cost you no more than $2.

READERS-ON-THE-STARVATION BUDGET: "We stayed at the Christian youth hostel called **The Shelter** at 21 Barndesteeg (phone 25-32-30), right in the red light district! Our accommodations were in segregated dormitories (according to sex), for which we paid 14 guilders per person, including breakfast. Very clean; good showers; youth hostel card not necessary; strict curfew rules (midnight); no mixing of men and women; and a pervasive but utterly non-pressured religious attitude, with Bible-study groups offered, gifts of prayer books, etc. There's also an excellent and inexpensive restaurant here serving delicious homemade vegetable soup for 1.50 guilders, daily platters for 6 guilders, many more tasty foods. All within ten minutes' walk of the railroad station" (Mrs. Gregory Brandis, Danbury, Connecticut). . . . "After intending to stay for only five nights, I ended up staying ten, because of the incredible time I had at the **International Budget Youth Hostel,** at 76 Leidsegracht, where no youth hostel card is necessary, and families are accommodated to the same extent as young single people! Location is only a two-minute walk from the central Leidseplein; rates are only 20 guilders ($6.66) per night in a quad (there are doubles and triples, too), and optional breakfast for 5 guilders brings you ham and eggs—absolutely delicious. The person behind all this is owner Nick Fisser, who worked as a dairy farmer in New Zealand before opening this hostel in 1983" (Karen Mazer, Quebec, Canada).

SUB-STARVATION BUDGET: A meal for $2? All over Holland, you'll

encounter automat-type stores (they're called *automatieks)* selling hot food items individually displayed in little glass cases that you open by inserting a coin. Amsterdam has the largest—and most astonishing—of these in its **Quick Snackbar,** which is located at 50 Nieuwendijk, corner of Martelaarsgracht, in the area near the Central Station (the Nieuwendijk, as you'll remember, is that inexpensive shopping and jukebox street that runs parallel to the important Damrak). One entire side of the Quick is a wall of glass display cases containing literally scores of different sandwiches, hors d'oeuvres, various hot meat croquettes and the like, all priced at 2 guilders (66¢) per item. Three items—which should always include one of those creamy breaded Dutch croquettes—cost a total of $2, and make an entirely filling meal! Open seven days a week from 6:30 a.m. to midnight.

Other automatieks with similar prices but not so large a selection: at 102 Leidsestraat, just off the Leidseplein; nearby at 47 Kerkstraat, just off the Leidsestraat; at 332 Spuistraat, just off the Spui.

ALTERNATIVE AMSTERDAM: Thus far, our recommendations in this

chapter have been of fairly traditional tourist facilities. But there's another type of tourism here. As every savvy traveler knows, Amsterdam remains the world's capital for young people pursuing an alternative life style—and if you're among them, hats off to you! For such travelers Amsterdam offers special lodgings, special restaurants, special nightspots and markets—even special advice centers for when things go wrong.

Public Sleep-Ins

At the bottom of the scale (and it's quite a bottom indeed) are the emergency "Sleep-Ins"—old and dilapidated warehouses fitted out with cattle-like pens, in which young people are invited to lay their sleeping bags on metal bunks with foam rubber mattresses, six or twelve to a pen, boys and girls indiscriminately. If the Nativity Scene comes to mind, that's exactly the image. "What if you want some privacy?" I asked one long-haired couple. "You get in the same sleeping bag," came the calm reply.

In the summer of 1984, Amsterdam maintained an 850-bed **"Sleep-In"** costing 10 guilders ($3.33) a night at 28 Mauritskade (phone 947-444), 250 yards from the Weesperplein metro station (third stop after Central Station), in the Waterlooplein area, and the word is in, just as we go to press, that the same structure, same rates, will be maintained in 1985, June to September only. The extremely basic "Sleep-In" should not be confused with the better multi-bedded dorms of the Kabul Student Hotel mentioned earlier in this chapter and offered as a less expensive (17 guilders) alternative to the Hans Brinker Stutel.

Far superior to the Sleep-Ins is the 13.50-guilder-a-night **Christian Youth Hostel "Eben Haezer"** at 179 Bloemstraat (phone 24-47-17), mentioned earlier in this chapter, or the attractive **Stadsdoelen** youth hostel at 97 Kloveniersburgwal (phone 24-68-32), the latter charging 16 guilders ($5.33) per person, breakfast included, in its 20-bedded dorms. A mellow place, with good vibes and attractive rooms, a non-institutional ambience, the Stadsdoelen requires a youth hostel card, unfortunately, which they'll sell on the spot for 30 guilders ($10). A last hostel, not quite as attractive, is the **Jeugdhotel Waldeck** at 27 Groenburgwal (phone 24-84-29), charging 18 guilders per night for a dormitory bed, breakfast included, and offering dinner for 7 guilders. . . . Frankly, why endure a Sleep-In when such places as the Eben Haezer are available for about $1 more?

Sleeping in the Vondel Park near the Leidseplein is no longer permitted, although Amsterdam's hippie groups continue to gather there by day.

Privately owned Sleep-Ins

For a still-reasonable 18 guilders ($6) a night, you should like the 16 dorms, 120 double decker beds, and 15 free showers of the typical, three-story canal house called **Fat City Student Hotel** at 157 O.Z. Voorburgwal (phone 22-67-05); that's in the very heart of the red light district, but there's no cause for concern: owner Frans, a Dutchman, is strict about keeping the hostel free of unsavory elements. The 18-guilder price includes breakfast, and the large, ground floor bar overlooks the town's cheapest discotheque, to which guests of the hostel are admitted free. An incidental note: toilets here are the cleanest I've seen in any hotel in Amsterdam. From the Dam Square, turn into Damstraat and, crossing the first bridge, you'll see Fat City.

Again in the heart of the inner city near the train station, **Bob's Youth Hostel** at 92 N.Z. Voorburgwal (phone 23-00-63), contains 100 double decker beds on four floors, for which the charge is 17 guilders ($5.66) per bed, with sheets and showers included. Opened in late 1978 by a man from Morocco named Bob El-Moutamid (his English is perfect), it quickly became popular for three reasons: central location, new mattresses, a friendly staff. An annex, called **"Bob II,"** around the corner at 46 Spuistraat, offers another 110 beds at the same rate.

A houseboat known as **"Wu-Wei,"** moored opposite 145 Hendrikkade, five walking minutes from the Central Station, provides still other accommodations in this category, in two dorms with 10 and 20 beds (not cots) apiece, and in several twin-bedded cabins. Rate per night ranges from 14 to 22 guilders ($4.66 to $7.33), showers are free, and a coffee shop lounge with bike rental facilities completes the amenities, in a setting of brand-new furniture, total cleanliness, peaceful atmosphere. *Wu-Wei,* in Chinese, means "doing without doing" or "action without action," and expresses the Zen philosophy of the charming young couple who own and manage this unusual sleepery. Phone 23-87-64 to inquire about vacancies.

Finally, **Studentenhotel 88,** at 88 Herengracht (phone 24-44-46), open from the end of May to early September, is noted not simply for its 16-guilder ($5.33) price (dormitory cots, including breakfast) and excellent, canalside location, but also for its basement dining room (open to all), which serves three-course meals (soup, main dish, fruit), weekdays only, for 5 guilders ($1.66).

Eat-Ins

Amsterdam's alternate food? It's macrobiotic, vegetarian, organic—macrobiotic at the **Kosmos,** 142 Prins Hendrikkade near the train station (but for members only), and at **The Garden,** 75 Weteringschans, a macrobiotic restaurant and tea house serving healthful meals from 10 a.m. to 10 p.m. There's a book and herb shop upstairs. At each of these, 7.50 guilders should result in vast platters of grains, vegetables, fruits.

Be-Ins

The really mind-boggling features of Amsterdam's youth scene are, however, its unique, mind-stretching nightspots, famous—or infamous—throughout the world. Two names lead the list: the immense **Paradiso** at 6 Weteringschans, two blocks from the Leidseplein (open Wednesday, Thursday, Friday and Saturday from 8 p.m. to 1 a.m., 8 guilders admission), which features far-out rock, and all the pharmacology associated with light shows and far-out rock; and **Kosmos,** the "Center of Meditation," at 142 Prins Hendrikkade (phone 267477), near the train station, open Monday through Friday from 6 p.m. to midnight, 9 guilders entrance (less for members), where the purists pursue various forms of transcendental experience: both Western and Eastern yoga, astrology, herbs, tarot, magic, zen, a co-ed sauna, and kabbala. Downstairs, in a basement restaurant, you can balance your yin and yang with a macrobiotic meal (lentil soup, a rice-bean-soya-seaweed-lettuce-cabbage-nuts-raisin dish, then an apple, for 9 guilders, $3, and if you only want the meal, without the other activities, you'll be refunded your entrance charge). Several other competing establishments run the leaders a hard race, of which the most important is

Melkweg ("Milky Way"), at 234a Lijnbaansgracht, behind the Opera House, off the Leidseplein (experimental theater, live music, films, and workshops); it's housed in an old milk factory, charges 5 guilders for membership and 7.50 guilders per admission, and is open Wednesday through Sunday from 6 p.m. to 2 a.m., when its offerings consist of folk, rock, jazz, classical and dance concerts, as well as theatre, and a market of little shops. A restaurant on the premises serves light meals and snacks.

And Help

And to round out the institutions, there's a **Youth Advisory Center** *(Jongeren Advies Centrum)* at 30 Amstel, phone 242-949, around the corner from the Rembrandtsplein, for legal, financial and spiritual scrapes; a number of public bathhouses for the unwashed (200 Da Costakade, 5 Marnixplein, 3 Fronemanstraat); a "free-market" on the Leidsebosje off the Leidseplein, daily except Sunday from 9 a.m. to 7 p.m., where anyone at all can sell handicrafts and art. Whatta scene!

5. Tours & Daytime Sightseeing

Both day and night, there's far too much to see and do here. To provide you with even a minimum list requires that we describe two basic tours and 15 indispensable sights, of which about ten can be packed into a three-day stay.

A CANAL BOAT RIDE: The very first thing to do in Amsterdam? Why, that's to take a ride along the canals and into the harbor of Amsterdam, in one of the many glass-sided canal boats that operate throughout the year. No better way exists to see all the essential features of the city, and to see them in only an hour and a quarter of time. The boats pass alongside the façades of old patrician homes on the Herengracht and other canals; they show you the picturesque "Skinny Bridge" *(Magere Brug)* on the Amstel, and the furniture hooks on top of the canal houses; they pass dozens of other important sites; and finally, they sail out into the vast harbor of Amsterdam, past freighters from exotic lands, and past drydocks where gigantic ships have been lifted from the waters for cleaning and repairs. Throughout, the witty, learned (and sometimes pretty), guides keep up a running commentary on the attractions you pass along the way. How much for this entire tour? Exactly 9 guilders ($3) per person.

The departure docks of the several companies that run these tours can be spotted by a sign reading *Rondvaart* (round-trip), which you'll see displayed at several waterside locations in town. All charge the same 9-guilder price; all offer departures throughout the day, generally at half-hour intervals; all run essentially the same tour; and all of the following companies can be counted on for an excellent hour ride: **Holland International,** whose boats leave from the bottom tip of the Damrak, just opposite the Central Station, and which offers departures almost every ten minutes in summer; **Reederij Plas,** also on the Damrak, a bit farther up from the Station; **P. Kooij,** on the Rokin, near the Spui, and just a block away from the Mint Tower (here they take snapshots of you as you enter the boat, and have the finished photos ready for your inspection—and possible purchase—at the end of the one-hour trip); **Nord-Zuid,** 25 Stadhouderskade, opposite the Park Hotel. In the summer, beginning around May 15, the *rondvaart* companies run nighttime canal tours as well, so that you can see the city's 17th-century canal houses in their illuminated state—one of the great sights of Europe.

A MOTORCOACH TOUR OF THE CITY: Other aspects of Amsterdam can best be seen by bus. For a traditional tour of the city, lasting 2½ hours, there are motorcoach departures every day of the week at 10 a.m., from a number of tour offices located up and down the Damrak. These begin by edging their way through the narrow streets of the original city, passing the Montelbaan Tower, Rembrandt's House, the Waag and the Nieuwmarkt, the Portuguese Synagogue, and a score of other famous sites (many of which are described later in this chapter); they then pass into the plush residential sections of Amsterdam near the Hilton Hotel, drive through the Leidseplein and the Rembrandtsplein, stop for a visit to a diamond cutter, where you're shown the polishing and shaping of stones, and then end with a lengthy guided tour of the Rijksmuseum. The price for all this is a standard 32 guilders ($10.66), including all entrance fees, and among the companies offering these trips, I particularly like **Holland International Travel Office,** 7 Damrak (10 a.m. and 2:30 p.m. departures, 32 guilders) and **Key Tours,** 19 Dam (10 a.m. and 2:30 p.m. departures, 32 guilders).

AMSTERDAM BY BIKE: One reason why Holland has suffered only slightly from any energy shortage is that virtually every Dutchman and Dutchwoman (from age 5 to 80) travels and commutes by bicycle along the country's absolutely level terrain. So why not do the same? An easy-to-find bicycle rental firm is housed in the basement of the Central Station (to the right, facing the main entrance, in the brown-brick wing). Open seven days a week from 5:30 a.m. to 5:30 p.m. (until 5:30 p.m. on Saturday and Sunday), it's called **Rent-a-Bike,** and it charges only 6 guilders ($2) a day, 30 guilders ($10) per week, after you've made a refundable 200 guilders ($66) deposit.

A more organized form of bicycle touring, **Ena's Bike Tours,** (phone 015-143797), is the creation of an enthusiastic group of young people (Ena Govers is their senior tour leader) who purport to "show you Holland by bike," along carefully selected scenic country lanes through farmland and quaint Dutch villages. En route, visits are made to a working windmill that dates to 1741, a farm where cheese is still produced by hand (a refreshing treat that gives you energy for the rest of the ride), and a lake with excellent swimming facilities (a boat ride is part of the tour). You can bring a picnic lunch or dine at a restaurant by the lake. Tours leave daily, June 1–October 1 at 10 a.m. from various points in Amsterdam and return at 5:30 p.m. Total cost: 30 guilders ($10), which includes the bike, the cheese farm and windmill visit, and the boat ride. Call for reservations, and you'll enjoy a delightful experience.

THE REMBRANDTHUIS (THE HOME OF REMBRANDT): Now we start the visits that you'll make on your own. One of the important ones is to the home of Amsterdam's most celebrated citizen, Rembrandt Harmenszoon van Rijn, who first came here as a young art apprentice in 1623, and spent the remaining 46 years of his life in this very city, where he created nearly 500 paintings, 287 etchings, and 1,400 ink and pencil sketches—all with such genius that he is now ranked with El Greco, Raphael and Velasquez as one of the greatest artists of all time. A few remarks about the early fame of Rembrandt will help set the scene for a visit to his home.

Rembrandt had established himself, at the age of 26, as one of the city's most successful painters. Commissioned by a Professor Tulp to paint a group of surgeons attending a dissection, he succeeded so well in his "The Anatomy Lesson of Dr. Tulp" (now hung in The Mauritshuis in The Hague) that other portrait commissions poured in by the dozens. Around the same time, he met and married a plump, pretty blonde from Friesland named Saskia van Uylenburgh, whose dowry amounted to 40,000 florins (guilders); there followed eight years of extravagant living which culminated on the day that Rembrandt saw and fell in love with a magnificent three-story home on the Jodenbreestraat, of a splendor that few artists could normally aspire to. He purchased it on credit, incurring a heavy and continuing debt, and several years later discovered that the citizens of Amsterdam were no longer purchasing his paintings!

Part of the reason for Rembrandt's economic decline was his own increasing mastery, which made him increasingly unwilling to follow the art fashions of the time. In 1642, for instance, he was commissioned by a certain Captain Banning Cocq to do a group portrait of a company of the Civil Guard of Amsterdam—a "corporate" portrait for which each person portrayed in the painting would contribute a portion of the artist's fee. Normally, these paintings gave equal prominence to each contributor, and showed them standing or sitting in one or two uniform lines. But Rembrandt had a greater vision, and portrayed the men in a moment of action, as they assembled for a parade upon the visit of Maria de Medici (the widowed queen of France) to Amsterdam. The resulting painting—the Rijksmuseum's great "Night Watch," which some acclaim as the greatest painting of all time—portrayed a number of these civilian-soldiers in shadows, obscured others entirely, cut off the bottom of one face with an outflung arm. The men of Captain Banning Cocq's troop were furious, and their enraged outcries caused all Amsterdam to look upon the portrait as a failure. From that moment, paintings by Rembrandt were no longer in favor, the fortunes of the artist declined, and crushing interest payments on his expensive house soon placed him in bankruptcy. Rembrandt moved from the Jodenbreestraat to the poorer Rozengracht, and for the rest of his life was forced to evade his creditors by working as the employee of an art firm formed by his son, Titus, and his mistress (Saskia having died), Hendrickje Stoffels.

Knowing all this, I think you'll experience both a chill and a thrill to visit the magnificent **Rembrandthuis,** at 4 Jodenbreestraat, whose interior is an almost exact reproduction of the style of the 17th century. The visiting hours are from 10 a.m. to 5 p.m. on weekdays and Saturdays, from 1 to 5 p.m. on Sundays, and the admission is only 2.50 guilders (83¢) for adults, 1.50 guilders (50¢) for children; you can reach the house by taking tram no. 9 at various points in town, or simply by walking for ten minutes from the Dam Square (head down the Damstraat, which then becomes Doelenstraat, then Hoogstraat; as you pass the Zuiderkerk—South Church—you'll encounter St. Antoniesbreestraat, which you follow for 1½ blocks to the Rembrandthuis; it stands almost on the corner of the Zwanenburgwal canal). Inside are displayed more than 200 of Rembrandt's etchings (one of the largest collections of them in the world), numerous of his sketches, and his etchings press. But for paintings by this awesome genius, you must now turn to the Rijksmuseum, for which the Rembrandthuis serves to whet the appetite!

THE RIJKSMUSEUM: This is certainly one of the greatest (if not the greatest) art museums in the world. It was originally housed on the upper floors of the Royal Palace on the Dam Square, was then transferred to the Trippenhuis on the Kloveniersburgwal in 1818, but then, in 1885, acquired its own home in this massive building at 42 Stadhouderskade, which was designed by P. J. H. Cuypers. He also designed the Central Station in Amsterdam, and you'll notice similarities between the two buildings.

The hours of the Rijksmuseum (that means "National Museum") are from 10 a.m. to 5 p.m. on weekdays and Saturdays, from 1 to 5 p.m. on Sundays and holidays, closed Mondays, and admission is 6.50 guilders ($2.16) for everyone except those under 18 or over 65, who pay only 3.50 guilders ($1.16) apiece. Immediately upon entering, go straight to the second floor, where you'll see signs directing you on an itinerary of rooms that eventually leads to the large gallery housing the "Night Watch." Initially, as you walk through these rooms, you'll encounter Dutch art of the 16th century; later the breathtaking 17th century begins, represented by such marvels as Frans Hals' "The Merry Toper," Ruysdael's "The Mill at Wijk bij Duurstede," the witty paintings of Jan Steen, countless others. Then, four rooms before the "Night Watch," there appear paintings by the "school of Rembrandt," beginning first with several works by his most famous students and apprentices—Gerard Dou, Ferdinand Bol, Govert Flinck, Nicolaes Maes—and followed then by three glorious rooms of paintings (any museum in the world would be lucky to have one) by the master himself: a famous Self Portrait; a portrait of his mother; and of Saskia; Titus; "The Oriental Potentate," "The Jewish Bride" (done in tones of gold and red that seldom are even barely captured in reproductions, and slathered on with blobs of paint a quarter of an inch thick); and finally, "The Syndics of the Drapers' Guild" (more popularly known as the "Staalmeesters"), another famous regents' piece (or corporate painting) done by Rembrandt late in his life, and designed to be hung in the old Cloth Hall of Amsterdam. The chief reputation of the Cloth Guild, by the way, was for honesty—an attribute reflected in a stern refusal ever to let a flawed bolt of cloth be shipped out of Amsterdam. Notice how Rembrandt captures this quality in his painting, which depicts the Staalmeesters at a meeting, as they gaze out at a questioner from the floor.

Now, in the next and larger hall, there finally appears: the "Night Watch," in which Captain Banning Cocq and Lieutenant van Ruytenburgh (the latter clad in a brilliant yellow jerkin with gold braid) go striding forth eternally into the fame that Rembrandt's masterpiece alone brought them. Keep in mind that the painting has been considerably cut down from the original; if you'll examine a small 17th-century copy displayed at one side of the room, you'll see how the original first looked. It is thought, too, that the painting is not of a night scene at all, but that successive layers of protective varnish—now removed—once darkened the canvas much beyond Rembrandt's intention; the purists argue that "Night Watch" is a misnomer, and simply call the painting "The Company of Captain Frans Banning Cocq and Lieutenant Willem van Ruytenburgh." To appreciate the leap in art that "Night Watch" represents, look at the dull, uniformly lighted regents painting by van der Helst, which is hung to the left of the "Night Watch" itself.

When you have seen the "Night Watch," don't prepare to leave the museum, because something equally good is still to come. That's found at the opposite end of the room from the "Night Watch," where a short half-flight of stairs leads to several further rooms in which the small, cameo-like masterpieces of the great Jan Vermeer (together with several lesser, but excellent, small paintings of Pieter de Hooch and Gerard ter Borch) are hung: "A Street in Delft," "A Maidservant Pouring Milk," "Woman Reading a Letter," "The Love Letter"; only 36 paintings remain of the work of Vermeer, and these four are among the greatest of them. Contrast their silent, exquisitely composed style with the slashing, strong emotion that flows from Rembrandt's portraits; the results, in any event, are enthralling, and you'll surely want to pick up reproductions of the paintings (16 guilders for a one foot by eight-inch plasterboard) at the sales desk of the Rijksmuseum, also on the second floor.

After you've returned to the room that houses the "Night Watch," you can walk down a long "Gallery of Honor" where works of great foreign artists—Goya, Tintoretto, Veronese, among them—are hung. Downstairs, on the ground floor, are prints, etchings and watercolors of several different periods, together with a good deal of 18th- and 19th-century art—but none of it comparable to the magnificent oils upstairs. The Rijksmuseum also houses a Department of Sculpture and Applied Art (furniture, Delftware, engraved glass, etc.), a print room of graphic art, a museum of Asiatic art (in the basement), and an art library. Schedule at least two hours for this remarkable institution, and be prepared to return time and again.

THE STEDELIJK (MUNICIPAL) MUSEUM: Within easy walking distance of the Rijksmuseum is the second great gallery of Amsterdam, which occupies a position in modern art that is akin to the status of the Rijksmuseum in classic art; indeed, with the possible exception of the Museum of Modern Art in New York, I know of no other museum of modern art that even remotely compares to the **Stedelijk** in Amsterdam.

In summer, the Stedelijk displays its entire permanent collection: a priceless, almost unequalled array of Chagalls, Picassos, Monets, Cezannes, Matisses and Mondrians, mixed and matched with the post-1945 output of the current reigning modernists: Appel, De Kooning, Dubuffet, and some unusually far-out local examples of Pop Art, Nouveau Réalisme, and Color Field painting. In winter, much of the permanent collection is sent into storage, and the space is devoted to sculpture, as well as graphic and applied art. In either season, the items on display are a provocative reflection of the modern world, that enlarge and uplift your spirit. All this is found at 13 Paulus Potterstraat, Tuesday to Saturday from 10 a.m. to 5 p.m., Sundays and holidays from 1 to 5 p.m., closed on Mondays, for an admission of 5 guilders ($1.66) adults, free for escorted children 6 and under, 2.50 guilders for kids ages 7 to 17. The combined cost of $3.82 for visiting both the Rijksmuseum and the Stedelijk is probably the finest art bargain in the world!

Until recently, the paintings at the Stedelijk that caught most visitors by surprise were an incredibly numerous collection of Van Goghs on the second floor—more than 200 individual paintings and sketches by the great Dutch impressionist. Now these 200 works have been supplemented by 500 more and all moved next door into a remarkable new museum that has quickly become the city's third major attraction and one of the world's greatest galleries:

THE RIJKSMUSEUM VINCENT VAN GOGH:

It was completed in the 70s, a cubistic structure open to daylight—because Van Gogh painted in daylight—containing 200 paintings, 500 drawings, by the tortured Dutchman who became a giant of modern art. Van Gogh was born in the Dutch province of Noord-Brabant in 1853, received his upbringing and later his art education in Holland, and died by his own hand in 1890, in Auvers-sur-Oise, France, at the age of 37. It was perhaps inevitable that the Dutch would construct this superb museum and acquire for it nearly half of everything he painted. Here are the incomparable originals of scenes you've seen in reproduction all your life: "Portrait of My Room at Arles," "Sunflowers," "The Zouave," "Corn Field with Crows," "The Armchair," "Boats on the Strand"—and that bitter indictment from Van Gogh's earlier period, "The Potato Eaters" (De Aardappeleters). There are so many that they nearly overwhelm the senses. And here, too, is a library of literature on Van Gogh, a bookshop, a cafe, an atelier in which visitors are encouraged to pick up a brush and themselves attempt a painting. Admission is 6.50 guilders ($2.16), and the National Museum Vincent Van Gogh, at 7 Paulus Potterstraat, is open Tuesday through Saturday from 10 a.m. to 5 p.m., Sundays from 1 to 5 p.m., closed on Mondays. Take tram no. 2 or 16 from the Central Station.

A VISIT TO A BREWERY:

Next: a free tour on which you'll receive food and drink—and one that you should take. For, while the citizens of such countries as Germany or Denmark will argue loud and long over whether Holland produces the world's best beer, no one will dispute that Amsterdam offers the best free brewery tours in Europe! In other cities, the breweries take you through their premises, and then give you free beer. But in Amsterdam, they give you free beer, cheese and "nibb-its" crackers! Typical of what's offered is the free visit to the great **Heineken's Brewery,** 78 Stadhouderskade (a short walk over from the Rijksmuseum), which you can make by appearing at Heineken's weekdays only, at either 9 a.m. or 11 a.m. in June, July and August, and at 10 a.m. all other months. You'll receive an informative guided stroll through all areas of the huge plant (including the fascinating, clanking bottling works) and then be led into a richly furnished beerhall where tables have been set with beer (generous servings, within reason, can be had), cheese, toothpicks for the cheese, and those savory "nibb-its." It's all unusually convivial and pleasant.

Incidentally, although the brewery itself receives no admission charge, a one guilder (33¢) contribution to UNICEF (the United Nations Childrens Fund) is currently requested.

A VISIT TO A DIAMOND CUTTER:

Diamond cutting is another major industry of Amsterdam, and here no one disputes that the Dutch are among the most skilled diamond cutters in the world. They're also the most friendly, and offer free tours of their diamond cutting factories, regardless of whether you plan to purchase a diamond at the end of the tour. Although you'll need invitations to visit some of the city's diamond works, these are readily available at most hotels, and can always be picked up—in a last resort—at the main office of the **VVV,** facing the Central Station.

The largest of the diamond cutting factories is **A. Van Moppes & Zoon,** 2 Albert Cuypstraat, corner of Ruysdaelkade (a short walk from Heineken's Brewery, an only slightly longer walk from the Rijksmuseum), which conducts thousands of visitors each year on a thoughtfully planned tour of all phases of diamond cutting, shaping and polishing; they also display the world's smallest diamond, along with replicas of the world's most famous diamonds—the "Hope Diamond," the "Shah of Persia," the "Jubilee." Visits can be made from 9 a.m. to 5 p.m. daily; closed Sundays in winter. Among the many other companies offering free diamond exhibitions are **Cordes Slijper,** 4 Weesperplein (4th floor, room 78–81), whose visiting hours are from 9 a.m. to 5 p.m. on weekdays; **Bernard Schipper,** 38 Kalverstraat (this being a jewelry store primarily, but with a small diamond cutting room next door); **Gassan Diamond House,** 17–23 Nieuwe Achtergracht (weekdays, 9 a.m. to 5 p.m.; Saturdays and Sundays, 10 a.m. to 5 p.m.; a major establishment located near the Weesperplein, and reached by bus 56); and **Holshuysen-Stoeltie,** 13 Wagenstraat (from the Rembrandtsplein, walk a few feet down Amstelstraat, then turn left into Wagenstraat; this last-named spot is unusually pleasant and patient in explaining the entire process; weekdays and Saturdays 9 a.m. to 5 p.m., Sundays in summer from 10 a.m. to 5 p.m.). None of Amsterdam's diamond cutters will coerce you actually to buy a diamond, but you'll enjoy the world's lowest prices for diamonds if you do.

And now, a different—and most important—sort of Amsterdam experience:

THE HOME OF ANNE FRANK: "In spite of everything, I still believe that people are really good at heart. If I look up into the heavens, I think that it will all come right, that this cruelty too will end, and that peace and tranquility will return again."   —From *The Diary of Anne Frank*

Those words were written in Amsterdam by a 14-year-old girl who had just spent two years hiding in the secret annex of a building at 263 Prinsegracht. With her were her parents, an older sister, two family friends—the Van Daans—and their teenage son, Peter, and a dentist named Dussel. On August 4, 1944, the Gestapo broke into their secret hiding place, and sent the entire group, along with other Dutch Jews, to extermination camps at Auschwitz and Bergen-Belsen. Only Otto Frank, Anne's father, survived. When he returned to Amsterdam after the war, he found a diary that Anne had maintained throughout the two years of the family's concealment. It is one of the classic volumes of literature produced in this century, and it has made a shrine out of the building at 263 Prinsengracht (around the corner from the West Church—the "Westerkerk," where a tenderly tiny memorial statue of Anne by Mari Andriessen was unveiled by her father in March, 1977, at the Raadhuisstraat side of the church, near Prinsengracht) to which thousands of tourists now pay visits of tribute each year. None of us should ever pass through Amsterdam without making a similar pilgrimage—both to recall the terrible events of World War II, and also to gain inspiration from Anne's immortal and unflagging spirit.

The building is open weekdays from 9 a.m. to 5 p.m., Sundays from 10 a.m. to 5 p.m., for an admission fee of 4 guilders (2.50 guilders for children aged 12 to 18). Inside, you walk behind a bookcase that conceals a stairway to the clandestine upstairs apartment, then into the now-bare rooms where the family lived, and along the wall, protected by glass, you'll see the yellowing clippings which teenage Anne pasted there—a photo of Deanna Durbin, a news item about the little princesses—Elizabeth and Margaret— of England. The effect is searing, heartbreaking, infuriating beyond belief. Downstairs, regularly changing exhibitions deal with present-day racism and political repression. The Anne Frank House can be reached by trolleys no. 13 and no. 17. You'll want to support the Foundation's work by signing on as a member; but in any event, you'll want to visit the Anne Frank House on your stay in Amsterdam.

OUR LORD IN THE ATTIC: This is the world's most unusual church, a product of that Reformation period in the 1600s when Catholic worship was in disfavor in Amsterdam, but still tolerated and connived at by the civic authorities. The compromise they reached was a semi-clandestine form of Catholic services, conducted at times in the attics of normal houses! This particular attic church, which actually occupies the top floor of the three adjoining buildings at 40 Oude Zijds Voorburgwal, represents the highest form of this covert church architecture: a miniature-sized and quite beautifully furnished cathedral, capable of accommodating as many as 200 worshipers, all concealed within three very typical, 17th-century houses. Because the downstairs portion of the canal house has also been perfectly preserved, with its original furnishings and paintings, the entire establishment is known technically as the "Museum Amstelkring," but all the world knows of its upstairs church as "Our Lord in the Attic" *(Ons' Lieve Heer op Solder)*. You can visit weekdays from 10 a.m. until 5 p.m., on Sundays from 1 to 5 p.m., for an admission charge of 2 guilders (66¢); and you should, because the oddness of this situation, combined with the ornateness all around, provides a fascinating glimpse into the spirit of the Dutch "Golden Age."

CANAL MANSIONS: Ever cared to know what one of those 17th-century canal mansions looks like inside? Most of them are today operated as offices, but two have been turned into museums whose chief interest is the glimpse they give you into 17th-century life.

The first, **The Theatre Museum,** 168 Herengracht, houses such stage items as old props, busts of famous Dutch performers, and sketches and models of early stage scenery. But it is chiefly fascinating for its interior, which is that of a sumptuously decorated merchant's home, with marble floors and walls, frescoes, and little plaster figures decorating the ceiling. Open weekdays from 10 a.m. to 5 p.m., weekends from 11 a.m. to 5 p.m., with admission of 1.50 guilders (50¢); half price for children 14 and under.

The second of these establishments, the **Willet-Holthuysen Museum,** 605 Herengracht, is simply devoted to displaying the contents of the very typical patrician mansion that it is. This one provides a perfect introduction to the mood of elegant, old Amsterdam: the interior is more sedate, less flamboyant than that of the Theater Museum, and the household exhibits include glassware, china, tapestries and paintings, some lovely items in gold, silver and ivory, even an old sea chest. Open Tuesday through Sunday from 10 a.m. to 5 p.m., except on Sundays, when it opens at 1 p.m.; the admission is 1.75 guilders (58¢), one guilder for kids 16 and under. To get here, take trolleys no. 4 or no. 9. Something on the same order is the **Museum van Loon,** 672 Keizersgracht, a patrician mansion built in 1671 and now completely restored to its late 18th-century state. Open Mondays only from 10 a.m. to noon and 1 to 5 p.m., for a three-guilder admission charge.

THE BEGIJNHOF: The most enthralling spot in Amsterdam? Without hesitation, I say the **Begijnhof** (Beguine Court), an oasis of beauty that 90% of all tourists miss because it's located behind unmarked and closed (but usually unlocked) doors and walls just 20 yards away from the bustling Kalverstraat, the main shopping street of Amsterdam! (If they are locked, simply turn the corner to the other entrance on the Spui.) Walk down the Kalverstraat until you pass a tiny side street (the Begijnensteeg) between numbers 130 and 132 on the Kalverstraat; then walk to the end of Begijnensteeg, and enter the gate at the bottom, at which point you'll gasp in surprise as you suddenly find yourself in the quiet 18th century, in a perfectly preserved grass-covered quadrangle that is flanked on all sides by 18th-century dwellings inhabited today by elderly lady pensioners. The Begijnhof is the best-known of the many *hofjes* scattered through Amsterdam—a *hofje* being a little plaza of homes built by socially conscious, wealthy families of the 1600s and 1700s, as "housing developments" for the poor of Amsterdam. In a courtyard are an English Presbyterian, and a Roman Catholic, church, both of which merit a visit; but most important, simply stand silently in the quadrangle and drink in the view. Wouldn't it make a marvelous movie set?

THE WAAG: Not everything in Amsterdam was built in the 17th century! Smack in the center of the Nieuwmarkt Square is the 15th-century **Waag** (a weighing house for merchandise), whose circular interior, with surprising nooks and crannies, is as delightful as its circular, turreted exterior would indicate. Since 1926, the building has housed the **Jewish Historical Museum** (ceremonial religious objects of great splendor, owned by Amsterdam's once-large Jewish population) on its ground and first floors. A fee of 1.75 guilders (58¢)—one guilder for kids—admits you to the museum which is open on weekdays except Mondays from 10 a.m. to 5 p.m., on Sundays from 1 to 5 p.m.; it may move to the Synagogue at Waterlooplein in late 1985.

THE HOUSE OF MR. TRIPP'S COACHMAN: Don't go out of your way to see this next spot, but if you happen to be near no. 26 Kloveniersburgwal, take a look at the narrowest house in Amsterdam. It was built by a wealthy 17th-century merchant named Tripp, whose coachman had been overheard to say: "I'd be happy if I had a house as wide as your front door." So, Mr. Tripp built him a house as wide as Mr. Tripp's front door!

READER'S SIGHTSEEING SUGGESTIONS: "Urge everyone to visit the **Royal Palace** on the Dam. For only 1.50 guilders you can see the palace and an audio-visual program on the history of Amsterdam." (Tamara L. Blok, Lisse, Netherlands; note from AF: The palace is open to the public from June to mid-September, daily from 12:30 to 4 p.m.).

WALKS AROUND TOWN: In the last analysis, the most interesting way to see Amsterdam is on your own two feet, by merely wandering at random through a city whose every streetcorner seems to hold a surprise. And what

if you get lost? Well, first, it's almost impossible to get lost in Amsterdam—because you can always simply ask a bystander (in English) to tell you where you are. And if you still get lost, you simply hop aboard any trolley marked "Central Station" and thus return to the center of town.

To aid you in your wanderings, however, we'll set forth two suggested walking tours—one of the oldest sections of the city and one of a relatively newer area. Neither tour should take more than three hours, and each can be done in considerably less. Both start from the **Dam Square,** at the side of which is the **Royal Palace** built in 1648.

A Foot Tour of the Oldest Sections

From the **Dam Square,** walk to the **Damstraat,** at the side of the Krasnapolsky Hotel, and then start walking down the Damstraat, gazing at the old canals you'll pass along the way. One block down, the Damstraat becomes the **Oude Doelenstraat,** then the **Oude Hoogstraat;** three blocks along you'll cross the **Kloveniersburgwal** canal. Turn down that canal for one block into the **Nieuwmarkt Square,** where you'll be able to visit the **Waag** (Weighing House). Then, from the Nieuwmarkt, walk along the **Sint Antonies Breestraat,** which leads you eventually to the **Rembrandthuis** (Rembrandt's House) on the **Jodenbreestraat.** Now you'll be in the center of the old Jewish section of Amsterdam; from here (after visiting the Rembrandthuis) walk three further blocks down the Jodenbreestraat, and then down **Lazarus Straat** to the **Portuguese Synagogue,** which is only one block from the **Waterlooplein**—a big, old square that used to be the setting for Amsterdam's daily-except-Sunday flea market (a sight you can still see on the Valkenburgerstraat, reached via a tunnel entrance from the Waterlooplein). From the Waterlooplein, cross the **Amstel Bridge,** and then walk along the banks of the Amstel (where ships are passing and gulls are circling overhead) to the **Mint Tower.** And from the Mint Tower, walk down the **Rokin** back to the Dam Square.

A Foot Tour of "Modern" Amsterdam

From the Dam Square, walk down the famous **Kalverstraat**—which is Amsterdam's main shopping street, and which winds all the way to the **Mint Tower.** At the tower, detour one block down the **Reguliersbreestraat** to the **Rembrandtsplein,** circle that entertainment area, then return to the tower. And then, from the Mint Tower, walk along the flower market on the banks of the **Singel,** which in one block leads to the **Koningsplein.** From the Koningsplein, walk one block to the **Leidsestraat,** and next walk the entire length of the Leidsestraat (passing the **Herengracht, Keizersgracht** and **Prinsengracht**) to the **Leidseplein.** At the **Leidseplein,** cross the bridge at the end of the square, and then walk down the **Stadhouderskade** to the **Rijksmuseum.** After visiting the Rijksmuseum, end your tour by walking over to the colorful **Albert Cuypstraat** street market—a fascinating and indispensable last stop.

6. Nighttime Entertainment

The most surprising aspect of Amsterdam is its nightlife. No other capital of Europe has so high a per person ratio of cafes featuring variety acts, exotic dances, jazz, and other after-dark divertissements—and it's all so unexpected! Somehow, nothing you have ever read about "quaint" Amsterdam quite prepares you for the sight of the dozens of sophisticated cafes on the Rembrandtsplein, or the bright lights of the Leidseplein, or the frenetic action on the Zeedijk.

And the best thing about the nightlife of Amsterdam is that it is unusually cheap. On weekday nights—and in some establishments, even on weekends—there is seldom a need to pay more than the price of a single inexpensive drink for the right to dance or to view a nightclub show. Because of that, the citizens of Amsterdam don't go to just one nightspot on their evenings out—they skip from one to another! So, if you've ever wanted to play the part of a nightclub-crawling playboy, this is your chance!

Of course, in addition to the cafes and cabarets, all the more sedate forms of evening entertainment are on hand as well. We'll deal first with the normal theatres and presentations, and then turn to the delights of the Rembrandtsplein, Leidseplein and Zeedijk.

THE CONCERTGEBOUW: The crowning glory of Amsterdam's evening cultural life is the great **Concertgebouw** orchestra, which you may have encountered on one of its innumerable concert tours throughout the world. But to hear this orchestra in its own hall (the Concertgebouw building, on the Museumplein), which is one of the most acoustically perfect in the world, is a major opportunity that shouldn't be passed up. The orchestra's performances are concentrated in its September-through-May season, but there will be other weeks—particularly during the time of the yearly "Holland Festival" (in 1985, from June 1 to July 23)—when you will also see its performances advertised; when that happens, run, do not walk, to get tickets. These cost a maximum of 40 guilders ($13.33) at the height of the Festival fervor, and can be had for as little as 18 guilders ($6) on other occasions.

THE STADSSCHOUWBURG: The opera house of Amsterdam is the **Stadsschouwburg** (Municipal Theatre) on the Leidseplein, where various national theatre groups and ballet companies (the "Haagse Comedie," the "Nieuw Rotterdams Toneel," the "National Ballet") alternate with the important "Nederlandse Operastichting"; unfortunately, the theatrical performances are in Dutch, but you will definitely want to attend the operas, which are almost always presented in the French, German or Italian of their original composition. I won't pretend that the "Nederlandse Operastichting" is one of the greatest of the world's opera troupes, but it puts on a lusty show, whose enjoyment is heightened for me by the relatively intimate size of the opera house itself. Compare a performance of *Faust* or *Rigoletto* here with one presented in the cavernous Metropolitan Opera House in New York—and see which you like best! Compare the prices, too, and you'll receive a gratifying surprise: the most expensive orchestra seats are 38.50 guilders ($12.83), there are excellent loge and front balcony locations for 19 guilders ($6.33), and seats in the second gallery go for only 10 guilders—the latter price being exactly $3.33. Ballet performances are much less. Performances, which begin at 8 p.m., are well advertised in the papers and in *This Week in Amsterdam* (which you'll find at newsstands all over town), in addition to being prominently displayed on posters in front of the opera house itself (a building you'll pass on the trolley at least several times a day); generally, the box office is open for seven days before each performance, from 10 a.m. to 3 p.m.

THE THEATRES: Elsewhere in town are numerous, excellent theatres—the **Nieuwe de la Mar,** the **Kleine Komedie,** the **Bellevue Theatre,** many others—but as their performances are usually in Dutch, they aren't of special interest to tourists. One, however—the colossal **Theatre Carré,** on the Amstel River, a single long block from the Amstel Hotel—specializes in musical revues that will entertain you as much as they will any resident of Amsterdam. Here you'll be able to see—among others—the top stars of the Dutch music-hall and variety theatre (Paul van Vliet, Herman van Veen, in particular) in a lengthy succession of dances, sketches and songs that require a knowledge of the language only at times. Weekday performances, which start at 8:15 p.m., cost only 15 guilders for the gallery, 17 to 25 guilders for the balcony, 30 guilders for the better orchestra locations, but balcony seats are perfectly adequate in the vast, unobstructed, horseshoe-shaped hall.

THE MOVIE THEATRES: Here, now, is an area of evening entertainment in which you'll have no language problem. For, unlike the movies presented in France, Italy and Germany, where voices are dubbed into the local languages, all films shown in the Netherlands are presented in their original languages, with written Dutch sub-titles superimposed. On every night of your stay, you'll be able to choose from more than a score of mid-town movie houses showing American, British, and French films. Like other entertainment in Amsterdam, the admission prices are moderate (from 10 to 14 guilders in the most expensive movie theatres, but generally averaging about 10 guilders in the neighborhood locations); and the shows go on at 2:30, 6:45 and 9:30 p.m. on weekdays, at 1:30, 3:45, 7 and 9:30 p.m. on Saturdays and Sundays (although these times vary a bit with individual theatres). The big **Tuschinski** theatre, on the Reguliersbreestraat (just off the Rembrandtsplein), occasionally throws in a stage show, too, as does the elegant **City Theatre** on the Kleine Gartmanplantsoen (just off the Leidseplein).

NIGHTCLUBS AND CABARETS: Now comes the action. The nightclub industry in Amsterdam is one of the most unusual in the world, in that it is intended to provide—and is priced to provide—entertainment at not much greater cost than you would incur in a bar or tavern. On Mondays, Tuesdays, Wednesdays and Thursdays, there is scarcely ever an admission charge to any Amsterdam nightclub, and even on the weekends, the normal entrance fee is only 10 guilders ($3.33)—provided that a fee is charged at all. After that, your only expense is for drinks, which can cost as little as 4 guilders (if you order genevers or beers), and rarely goes higher than 10 guilders or so for brandy or highballs. On that price per person per drink, you can dance—and see an entire show.

The Bright Lights

There are three basic nightclub-and-cafe areas in Amsterdam: the **Leidseplein;** the **Rembrandtsplein** (with its adjoining **Thorbeckeplein**); and the so-called "sailor's district" around and along the Zeedijk (which we'll

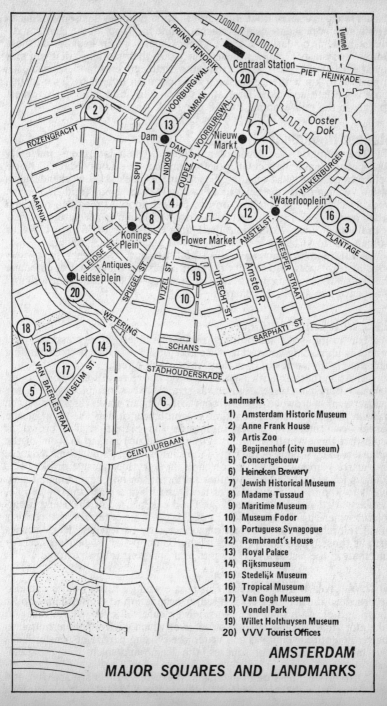

Landmarks

1) Amsterdam Historic Museum
2) Anne Frank House
3) Artis Zoo
4) Begijnenhof (city museum)
5) Concertgebouw
6) Heineken Brewery
7) Jewish Historical Museum
8) Madame Tussaud
9) Maritime Museum
10) Museum Fodor
11) Portuguese Synagogue
12) Rembrandt's House
13) Royal Palace
14) Rijksmuseum
15) Stedelijk Museum
16) Tropical Museum
17) Van Gogh Museum
18) Vondel Park
19) Willet Holthuysen Museum
20) VVV Tourist Offices

AMSTERDAM
MAJOR SQUARES AND LANDMARKS

discuss later, in a separate section). Of the first two, the Leidseplein houses the slightly more sedate establishments, while the spots on the Rembrandt-splein (and particularly on the Thorbeckeplein) go in heavily for those Dutch "ecdysiasts" (ladies who sinuously doff their clothing) that you may have heard about. With respect to all the establishments in these areas, it's important to know their exact hours of operation (which we'll set forth); some open late and close late, others open early and close early, others operate in the mid-evening, from 8 p.m. to 2 a.m.

Student Nightclubs

The youngsters of Amsterdam—those in their late teens and early 20s—patronize one particular spot for dancing: The **Lucky Star,** 28 Korte Leidsedwarsstraat (just off the Leidseplein), is packed on weekend nights with its younger clients, then attracts a barely-older group (mid 20s) on the weekdays. There's action here on two midget floors to recorded rock and other music, and a bar observation post which allows spectators to view both floors at once. Admission: the Dutch equivalent of 75 U.S. cents for women, about $1.50 for men, with beer or genever for 3 guilders.

Amsterdam's famous **Paradiso** and **Kosmos,** two other immensely popular nightspots, are so very different from the traditional discotheque that we've discussed them in a separate section—"Alternative Amsterdam" —appearing earlier in this chapter.

Bars with Entertainment

For losing your inhibitions, ridding yourself of aggressions, and generally immersing yourself in noise and music, there are two outstanding bars among the scores of bars that Amsterdam offers.

The one that can always guarantee the above results is the celebrated **Bamboo Bar,** 64 Lange Leidsedwarsstraat (two short blocks from the Leidseplein), a crowded, smoky room with African masks displayed on the walls, a pianist (who bears a strong resemblance to Mao Tse-tung) in one corner, two mariachi players alongside the pianist, and a crowd of somewhat tipsy Amsterdammers (20s, 30s and up) ranged in front of the pianist, usually singing at the top of their lungs. There's no room to dance, and scarcely enough space to consume the very inexpensive drinks (4.50 guilders for genever and most other potions); the only remaining alterna-tive is to join in the fun and meet the Dutch! Not a place for shy people. Less crowded is the **Carrousel,** 20 Thorbeckeplein (off the Rembrandt-splein), where drinks are 10 to 15 guilders, and the entertainment consists of a live orchestra, not to mention topless lady bartenders. Here, scenes such as those which always erupt at the Bamboo Bar, *sometimes* occur— and that, in the last analysis, is up to you and your fellow patrons.

SIDEWALK CAFE SITTING: This next evening activity (which can also be practiced during the day) is a major occupation in Amsterdam—and a cheap and pleasant one, too. No sidewalk cafe will ever require that you take more than a single cup of coffee, over which you're then permitted to linger the entire evening as you watch the passing parade in Amsterdam's two major entertainment squares: the Rembrandtsplein and the Leid-seplein.

Of the two, the Rembrandtsplein possesses a bit more activity, and here the cafes, with their sidewalk table areas, are lined almost solidly along two sides of the square. On the Leidseplein, the major outdoor cafes are those operated by the American Hotel and the Cafe Moderne, but the three most exciting ones are the **Hoopman Bodega,** the **Cafe Reynders,** and the **Cafe Eylders,** all three on the Korte Leidsedwarsstraat, just off the Leidseplein, alongside (but across another small square from) the Opera. Of these, the **Cafe Reynders** is the outstanding student cafe of Amsterdam, heavily patronized by Amsterdam's version of the hippie, along with their surprisingly pretty, hair-to-the-waist companions. Obviously, there's no minimum, no cover charge, and drinks average 3.50 guilders ($1.16), for which you can sit and meet people all evening. The Cafe Eylders is a slightly more polished version of the Reynders, and the Hoopman Bodega is a somewhat more elegant bar, patronized by some fairly elegant older people; its prices are about 20 Dutch cents higher than those charged at the Reynders and Eylders for jonge genever (3 guilders) and beer (3.50 guilders). During the winter, all three establishments continue full blast, but without the sidewalk tables.

THE SAILORS' QUARTER: One final nightlife area deserves consideration, because it represents a phenomenon that is fast disappearing from Europe, and that continues to exist in its classic form only in Amsterdam, Hamburg, and a few other cities: a full-fledged, rip-roaring, wide-open sailors' entertainment area, which in Amsterdam comprises the district on and near the winding **Zeedijk.** Here there are not merely dozens of bars, but scores of them—sporting such names as "Casa Blanca," "City Lights," "Sailor's Place," "Salon Mexico," "Skip O Hoy Bar"—and it's a highlight of your European trip to stroll alongside them, peering into the taverns, and then walking along the equally bawdy streets nearby (particularly, the Oude Zijds Achterburgwal and the Oude Zijds Voorburgwal). For those of you who would like to do this area in an organized manner, I suggest the following evening foot tour:

From the Krasnapolsky Hotel on the Dam Square, walk down the narrow Warmoesstraat until you come to the bottom of the Zeedijk, near the Central Station. Then walk up the entire length of the Zeedijk, until you reach the Nieuwmarkt. From the Nieuwmarkt, walk across the Barndesteeg to the Oude Zijds Achterburgwal, and walk down the Oude Zijds Achterburgwal to its end, near the station; then cross over to the parallel Oude Zijds Voorburgwal and walk up that canal until you reach the Damstraat, where you can turn in again to the Dam Square. Did you ever expect to find *this* in Amsterdam?

7. Excursions from Amsterdam

After you've spent three-or-so days in the city, you'll want to tack on some extra time for all the many one-day excursions that can be made to places near Amsterdam—to **The Hague** and **Rotterdam,** for instance, or to the tulip fields of Keukenhof, or to Leiden, Haarlem, Arnhem, Delft—or to a dozen other spots. If I had time, however, for only one excursion from Amsterdam, I'd make it to a site associated with the former Zuiderzee—either to the stupendous **Enclosure Dike** (Afsluitdijk) that transformed the Zuiderzee into a peaceful lake (the Ijsselmeer), or to **Marken** and **Volendam**—two picturesque fishing villages on the Zuiderzee—or to the newly built, planned cities that now stand on "polders" carved out from that body of water. It's fascinating to contrast these new towns, created from the sea, with the centuries-old ports of the Zuiderzee, now deprived of their former importance as major shipping centers. In some of these—primarily on the island of **Marken** and in the village of **Volendam,** both of them less than 40 minutes from Amsterdam—the inhabitants still wear the traditional ancient clothing of The Netherlands: the men in black, bell-bottom trousers, tight black jackets, and tight visored caps; the women in broad aproned dresses reaching to their feet, with white lace caps, and curls that hang down straight on both sides of their faces. And all, of course, in wooden shoes!

Marken was once an island in the Zuiderzee, inundated at least once a year; many of its houses are therefore on stilts that enabled them to ride out the floods. Volendam is an equally picturesque fishing village whose residents wear costumes and carry on traditions that differ in subtle ways from those prevailing on Marken. Although Marken is still almost entirely surrounded by water, a dike—atop which is a highway—now connects it to the mainland; and sadly, the construction of the Markerwaard Polder will soon make it a normal, landlocked town. Try and see it now, in its glorious island state!

THE SITES ON THE ZUIDERZEE: To visit these sites inexpensively, you can use several alternative forms of transport.

First, you can make these excursions on your own, by car. From Amsterdam to Marken and Volendam is a half-hour's ride, once you've crossed the Ij by ferry. And if you're a good driver, you can reach **"Den Oever,"** one of the terminal points of the Afsluitdijk (Enclosure Dike), in less than an hour more. Crossing the dike takes about 30 minutes (but allow a 20-minute stop at the tower monument, for a birdseye view of the entire phenomenon), and you can then spend three-hours-or-so driving south along the other side of the Zuiderzee (now the Ijsselmeer), visiting the planned city of Emmeloord, and viewing the most recently drained polders. This entire circular tour of the Zuiderzee can quite easily be made in a day. Or, if you prefer to go directly to the polders from Amsterdam, you can drive east along the bottom of the Zuiderzee and then head north toward Emmeloord. A glance at a good highway map will make the routes instantly clear to you.

If you do not have a car, you can still make the trip to Marken and Volendam on your own by taking one of the fabulous **"NZH"** bus rides there for a round-trip price of exactly 16 guilders ($5.33). The ride starts from a point on the Prins Hendrikkade near the large church (the one with the cupola and two towers) diagonally across from the Central Station, with departures at 30-minute intervals throughout the day, starting at 9:30 a.m., daily from April 1 to September 20. From there, you'll be taken by bus through a tunnel under the Ij River, and then through actual polderland to the quaint, old town of Monnickendam, from which you take a boat to Marken. From Marken, when you're ready to return, you take another boat to Volendam, and then—after strolling about for as long as you wish—you catch another bus back to Amsterdam. All for 16 guilders.

Guided Tours to Marken, Volendam, and the Enclosure Dike

If you'd prefer to make these trips in a group, and with a guide, then simply visit the offices of any of the tour operators in Amsterdam, for whom the Marken excursion is a major business item. **Holland International Travel Service,** at 7 and 10 Damrak (phone 22-25-50 and 25-30-35), operates tours to Marken twice a day, at 10 a.m. and 2:30 p.m., and charges 38 guilders ($12.66) per person. Tours last a total of four hours, go first to Marken, a former island, then proceed to Volendam, a fishing village and visit a real Dutch cheese farm before returning to Amsterdam. And in case you prefer to visit Volendam by public transportation, take bus no. 110, departing every 30 minutes, all year round, from opposite the Nikolaas Church, across the Central Station.

Most of the Amsterdam tour companies also operate guided tours to the Enclosure Dike, but only on Tuesdays and Thursdays from June 1 to September 30; the all-day excursion costs 55 guilders ($18.33), not including lunch. These tours visit another major point of interest along the way—the Friday morning cheese market in the town of **Alkmaar.** You may, however, want to consider the trip to Alkmaar on your own, via the next surprising method of transport: a Cheese Express (see below):

The Kaasexpres (Cheese-Express) to Alkmaar

Alkmaar, where a world-famous cheese market is held on Friday mornings in summer, less than an hour from Amsterdam, is a picturesque Dutch town replete with canals, lovely old houses, and a major square in which the cheese market takes place. On Friday mornings, from May through September, the square erupts into a frenzy of color and activity, as white-suited cheese porters, each wearing a red, blue or yellow hat according to the guild to which he belongs, go trotting across the square carrying sleds of stacked cheeses. Ranged around the square are literally thousands of tourists, for whom the Netherlands Railways has arranged unusually inexpensive transportation, via a special **"Cheese Express"** (the *Kaasexpres)*. It leaves Amsterdam's Central Station at 9 and 9:26 a.m. on Fridays from mid-June through early September, arrives in Alkmaar at 9:32 and 9:55 a.m., and costs only 14 guilders ($4.66) round-trip, second class. Aboard the train, women volunteers in traditional costumes pass out free cheese.

If you can't be in Amsterdam on a Friday, but do happen to be there on a Thursday from mid-June to mid-August, you can take advantage of a similar deal—the **"Schagermarkt-Expres"**—to visit the West Frisian Market in the town of Schagen. Farmers and their wives from miles around, in traditional West Frisian dress, come here to make purchases and to participate in or watch exhibitions of West Frisian folk dancing. The special train to Schagen leaves the Amsterdam Central Station at 9:26 a.m. on Thursdays from June 30 to September 1, arrives in Schagen at 10:19 a.m., and costs 21 guilders ($7), round-trip, second class.

Care for a Wednesday tour? On that day from June 15 to August 15, a train leaves the Amsterdam Station at 8:41 a.m., arrives in the 600-year-old town of Hoorn at 9:38 a.m., depositing you at a market of clog makers, net menders, potters and other fascinating folk, who set up a profusion of stalls and sell their wares and services while groups of folk dancers and musicians perform. This one costs 15 guilders ($5) round-trip, and the return can be made via almost hourly trains to Amsterdam throughout the day.

THE OTHER TOWNS: Unfortunately, we haven't the space to go into detail about the many other Dutch towns within one-day excursion range of

Amsterdam. But you may be interested in the transportation procedures for getting to two of them—The Hague and Rotterdam.

To reach The Hague from Amsterdam, you can—as a first alternative —simply take the train: they depart at least every hour (and sometimes more often) from the Central Station, take slightly under an hour for the trip, and cost 22 guilders ($7.33), round-trip second class. For only 5 guilders ($1.66) more (a total of 27 guilders) you can also take a Netherlands Railways' "Day Excursion" from Amsterdam to The Hague and Scheveningen, on a ticket that not only includes your round-trip transportation to and within The Hague, but also covers admission to Madurodam and the Pier at Scheveningen. Pick up your ticket for this trip at the Central Station.

There are, in addition, a number of full-day escorted bus tours to Rotterdam, The Hague and Delft, and half-day tours simply to The Hague and Delft which all the major tour operators in Amsterdam (their offices are located up and down the Damrak) offer for approximately the same price 57 guilders ($19) for the full-day version, 40 guilders ($13.33) for half a day. The former invariably begin at 10 a.m., drive first to Aalsmeer (where you visit the flower auctions, several hot-houses, and a wooden-shoe-making factory), and then head to The Hague, where stops and visits are made at the Peace Palace, the Binnenhof, the Royal Palace, and the Huis ter Bosch ("House in the Woods," a summer residence of the Queen), Madurodam, and Scheveningen. After lunch, the bus then proceeds to the beautiful canal city of **Delft** (one of the best preserved of the old Dutch towns), where you pay a visit to the Royal Delft Ware Factory "De Porceleyne Fles," that famous manufacturer of Delft Blue China (since 1653). And some of the tours, on the return trip to Amsterdam, even manage a stop in **Leiden** and **Haarlem** (in which latter city they visit the renowned Frans Hals Museum).

From Amsterdam to Rotterdam, excellent superhighways permit a good driver to make the trip in just slightly more than 75 minutes; by train from Amsterdam's Central Station, the second-class, round-trip fare is around 31 guilders ($10.33), and there are hourly departures. On a Netherlands Railways "Day Excursion" from Amsterdam to Rotterdam (operated daily from April 1 to September 30), the price is 44 guilders, and that includes a "Spido" boat trip through the harbor area, and admission to the Blijdorp Zoo.

Cities nearer to Amsterdam? Hope likes Haarlem, and here's her report:

HOPE IN HAARLEM: "The easiest half-day excursion you can make is to the evocative old city of Haarlem, chartered in the 13th century, and now best known to tourists for its **Frans Hals Museum.** Trains leave Amsterdam's Central Station every 15 minutes, take 15 minutes for the trip, cost 7.60 guilders ($2.53) for the round-trip, and provide some bonus pastoral scenes of grazing cows along the way. Once there, allow ample time to wander and savor the atmosphere, which is especially heady in the immediate vicinity of the museum: an area of narrow old cobble-stoned streets with rows and rows of gabled houses, interspersed with charming antique shops. If the historic beauty of the street of Groot Heiligland (the Frans Hals is at 62) doesn't make you dizzy with the sensation that you've stepped into a 17th-century etching, then the 'Grote Markt,' the city square, is sure to get to you. On it, you'll find the City Hall, a part of which was originally begun in the 13th century as a palace for Dutch nobility (if you arrive before 2 p.m., and if you're lucky enough to be in Haarlem on a day when no marriages are being performed, you may get a chance to see the 14th-century 'Gravenzaal'—Hall of the Counts, among many points of interest *inside* the Hall); St. Bavo Church (the 'Grote Kerk'), an enormous, imposing, dark stone, medieval structure (15th and 16th centuries—Frans Hals, and other dignitaries, are buried here), with a famous 18th-century organ (open weekdays 9 a.m. to 5 p.m., entrance fee 1 guilder, 50 Dutch cents for children); and 'De Hallen,' an affiliate museum of the Frans Hals, with temporary exhibitions of both old and new art. (Not far from the Grote Markt, at Spaarne 16, is **The Teylers Museum,** the oldest in Holland, with a varied and interesting collection of fabulous fossils, gems and minerals, bones and skeletons, pre-historic-looking insects or lizards with monstrous jaws and teeth, historical scientific instruments—and, just for good measure, a couple of rooms of paintings and drawings, including some by Rembrandt, Raphael, Michelangelo and Claude Lorrain. Open daily, March through September, Tuesday tnrough Saturday from 10 a.m. to 5 p.m., winters till 4 p.m. and Sundays from 1 to 5 p.m., for an admission of 2.50 guilders, 1.25 guilders for children.)

"But the key visit is to the Frans Hals Museum; immediately upon stepping off the train, cross the street in front of the station, look for the stop marked 'Perron D,' board bus #2 or #70—direction Schalwijk (fare is 1 guilder), and ask the driver to let you off at the proper stop and point you in the direction of the museum: 62 Groot Heiligland, open weekdays from 10 a.m. to 5 p.m., Sundays from 1 to 5 p.m., admission of 2.50 guilders from March through October, free from November through February. (If you need further help, you'll find a VVV office to the right as you exit from the station.)

"You may agree with me that the Frans Hals is a strangely moving experience. For here one enjoys that all too rare combination, the perfect marriage between setting and subject matter. The building, which opened its doors as an old men's home, is an almost perfectly preserved, early 17th-century mansion, with a beautiful formal garden in its inner courtyard. The structure itself stirs the imagination, with its rooms so reminiscent of the very scenes that inspired the School of Haarlem painters during the 17th century (Frans Hals not the least among them). Of course, all of these gentlemen (Jan Mostaert, Jacob van Ruysdael, Adriaen van Ostade, Jan Steen, Adrien Brouwer, Cornelis Dusart, among others) are represented here, along with Dutch and Flemish artists who were not of the Haarlem school. Also on display are rooms of period furniture, china and silver, coins and medals, a replica of an ancient pharmacy, and a cunning antique doll house with tiny dogs, dishes on the table, and the most minuscule playing cards imaginable.

"The star attraction remains Hals himself, and two particular masterpieces: 'Governors of the Old Men's Home at Haarlem' and 'Lady Regents of the Old Men's Home at Haarlem,' which I would travel a lot farther than the distance between Amsterdam and Haarlem to see! Both were done in 1664, when the artist was over 80! In his last years, after a successful career, Hals found himself alone and impoverished (the art histories tell us he was fond of the good life, and incurred too many debts), and relegated to living on a subsidy from the town: 200 guilders a year, and three cartloads of peat! For these paintings, his last commission, the governors of the home must have reckoned something like this: 'Let old Frans Hals earn his keep by painting our picture,' and the rather sardonic results are now before you—the women with their dry, monkey-like faces, the men younger but ineffectual looking. One of the older guards tells me that Manet came to the Frans Hals Museum when *he* was a very old man, and sat for hours in the room of The Governors.

Farther Afield

"A much longer trip is to the **Kröller-Müller Museum** in Otterlo, which sophisticated museum devotees acclaim as one of the world's best; but reaching the museum is exhausting, and totally impractical in winter, unless you have a car: one hour by train first to Arnhem (29.50 guilders round-trip), then another 40 minutes by bus to the museum (take the bus marked 'Hoge Veluwe' in front of the railway station, 14.50 guilders round-trip including admission to Hoge Veluwe Park—buses leave on the hour, *almost* every hour, check the posted schedule). (But warning: this direct bus operates only from June to September; other months one must bus to Otterlo, then taxi or hike for about 20 minutes to the museum.) Take only an 'Intercity' train to Arnhem, leaving Amsterdam's Central Station every hour at 17 minutes past and 13 minutes to the hour, or an international 'D' train bound for Germany and leaving Amsterdam at 8:19 a.m.; all other trains to Arnhem are locals or take an indirect and interminably long route.

"Still, if you've got the stamina and time, you'll find here an exquisite collection amassed, for the most part, and donated to the public by Mrs. Kröller-Müller, who spent a good deal of her time musing on the possibilities of interplay between architecture, art and nature. It is the juxtaposition of these elements which make this one of the world's outstanding museums: a quiet forest surrounds you, inside the museum the paintings are displayed with good taste and good lighting, and the 'Sculpture Garden' (late 19th century to the present, including Henry Moore, Barbara Hepworth and Dubuffet), which covers 11 acres of ground with nature as a backdrop, is unbelievably moving and beautiful. (Incidentally, white bicycles are provided free of charge by the park, so you can pedal around the collection or through the woods comfortably for as long as you wish.) As if all this were not enough, the Kröller-Müller also happens to have a large collection of priceless Van Goghs. To be exact (according to their catalogue), there are 89 paintings and 187 drawings here—many famous and familiar, but also some little-known, and extremely offbeat, early work. Since it was Mrs. Kröller-Müller's intention to assemble a collection that would illustrate the development of painting from the 19th century on (though there are early Dutch and Flemish masters here, too, and Lucas Cranach), the Impressionists are quite well represented. Required viewing for museum builders and curators, the Rijksmuseum Kröller-Müller charges no admission (but there *is* a charge to enter the park: 6 guilders for adults, 5.50 guilders extra for a car, 2.50 guilders for children 16 and under, no charge for bicycles or motorcycles though; on the bus your admission fee is included in the fare) and is open on weekdays except Mondays from 10 a.m. to 5 p.m. (Sculpture Park closes at 4:30, and is closed completely in winter), and Sundays from 1 to 5 p.m. (Summers from 11 a.m.; Sculpture Park from 11 a.m. to 4:30 p.m.)."

READERS' WHIRLWIND EXCURSIONS: "If you are rushed for time, our suggestion is not to take the separate day excursions to The Hague and Rotterdam respectively, but simply to purchase a round-trip train ticket from Amsterdam to Rotterdam. Go direct to Rotterdam, get a city map at the Information Desk, and walk out of the station 200 yards straight downtown, then turn left into the famous shopping boulevard where no cars are allowed. After this, proceed to the Euromast and then return to Rotterdam Station, where you take the train to Amsterdam via The Hague. At The Hague, stop off and proceed with tram #8 outside the station to the Peace Palace. Stop off here for one of the organized tours (5 guilders), then again take the #8 tram to Scheveningen, and walk around the seaside resort for about a half-hour. Then take tram #9 to the miniature town of Madurodam, stop there for an hour, then take tram #9 back to the train station, and return to Amsterdam—all on one ticket at a third of the price of the two excursion trips. But to do it all in one day, you must leave at 8:30 a.m. and move fairly fast" (Lenard G. Lever and Ben-Zion Surdut, Cape Town, South Africa). . . . "Upon arriving in The Hague, take tram #9 opposite the train station to the Mauritshuis—one of the best small museums in Europe, with mouthwatering Rembrandts and Vermeers. Continue on tram #9 to Madurodam; we spent nearly an hour and a half there, but you could do it in less; continue on tram #9 to Scheveningen, and walk to the end of the Pier. If it's a warm day, there will be thousands on the beach—a colorful scene—and you can swim or lie on the beach too, if you like. Then return on tram #8, which passes the Peace Palace. Continue on tram #8 to the Central Station, and take a train that stops in Haarlem (they run about every 15 minutes). Follow Hope Frommer's instructions for reaching the Frans Hals Museum, which we found most rewarding. Then return to Amsterdam. We did this entire trip without hurrying or feeling rushed, and were back in Amsterdam shortly after 5 o'clock" (Mr. and Mrs. Paul Redin, Oklahoma City, Oklahoma; note by AF: at window #13 of the train station in Amsterdam, buy a 'day excursion' to The Hague for this trip (27 guilders), which includes round-trip transportation for the day to The Hague, stopovers on the way, unlimited tram transportation in The Hague, and admission to Madurodam and to the Pier at Scheveningen. Trains to The Hague run every few minutes, with one particular express leaving Amsterdam at 8:59 a.m., arriving The Hague at 9:26 a.m.).

READERS ON BIKES: "The high point of my entire journey was a bicycle trip through the Dutch countryside, near Leiden, leaving from the Hans Brinker Stutel (student hotel) in Amsterdam. We went by car to Leiden and then spent about three or four hours bicycling through some very charming countryside, including windmills, canals, etc. We also stopped for lunch (sandwiches) and ate in a field. If readers are interested in this, I suggest they contact in Amsterdam Miss Anja Nort, a totally charming and informative guide. Her address is 11 Brouwersgracht, phone 252-014" (Ronald Merkin, Brooklyn, New York). . . . "At the **Waterlooplein Flea Market,** you can purchase bicycles for as little as 80 guilders. The dealer who sold me a bike for that sum promised to buy it back for 50 guilders. After riding around the canals for a week, I returned the bike and the total cost was only 30 guilders, compared with the daily rental of 6 guilders!" (Kerry Pattison, Westwood, California).

8. Amsterdam Miscellany

SHOPPING: The **Tax-free Shopping Center** at Amsterdam International Airport—biggest and best in Europe—is the chief shopping draw of this surprising city. A survey conducted several years ago by *Life* magazine confirmed that "Amsterdam Airport is possibly the best in Europe for a variety of dutiable items at the lowest prices. Dutch gin and Bols Geneva are available for $3.50 a bottle, Dutch Schimmelpenninck cigars $7.50 per 25, less than half the price of the cheapest Havanas. Perfume prices are as good as those in Paris, in some cases a few cents less. Precision goods are among the cheapest in Europe."

Liquor, particularly, is a stunning value at Amsterdam Airport— priced last year at only $7.50 a quart for such brand-name Scotch as Johnnie

Walker Red Label, Vat 69, Haig & Haig, Grant's, White Horse, others. That compared with the $10 you'd pay for the same bottle in Copenhagen, the $11 to $12 you pay in London, Brussels or Frankfurt, and the $11-and-up charged in New York.

In the city itself, low-cost diamonds and prints are the top buys. Obviously, we'll pursue the latter item only. A wide variety of really superb reproductions and posters are sold at a store called **Kunsthandel Verkerke,** on the important avenue, Leidsestraat, no. 12, just two blocks from the Leidseplein square. A particular rack of prints sell here for 30 guilders ($10) apiece; another 10 to 15 guilders; and there are small reproductions for 5 and 6 guilders ($1.66 to $2) on the walls. A similar collection, with some different items (Marc Chagalls, especially), is available in the $5 range at the second-floor shop in the **Stedelijk Museum,** the magnificent modern art gallery at Paulus Potterstraat 13. Rembrandts, on foot-square slabs of beaver-board, average 12 guilders at the **Rijksmuseum,** Stad-houderskade 42. These lay easily in your suitcase; the others must be rolled into a long cardboard tube. . . . Elsewhere in town, there are establishments which sell Dutch wooden shoes not as souvenirs, but for actual use by Dutchmen! My favorite is **A.W.G. Otten,** 102 Albert Cuypstraat (between Bolstraat and le van der Helsstraat), which stands right in the heart of the colorful Albert Cuypstraat street market. Here, large, adult-sized wooden shoes cost only 25 guilders ($8.33) a pair, smaller ones only 20 guilders ($6.66), and there are also sold the rubber or leather inners that real people, wearing wooden shoes, use. I doubt that you can find better, or cheaper, wooden shoes anywhere else in town. . . . For hand-painted Dutch tiles, try the shop of an old gentleman named **Kramer,** at 64 Nieuwe Spiegelstraat (between Prinsengracht and Kerkstraat), where authentic, non-imitation, 18th and 19th century blue tiles sell for 25 to 50 guilders apiece; this is the best selection of tiles I've found in town. . . . Don't, by the way, fail to visit the Amsterdam "flea market." In most other cities, the "flea market"—an assemblage of pushcart vendors selling second-hand goods of every type—takes place but one day a week. In contrast, Amsterdam's flea market, on the nondescript **Waterlooplein,** operates every day of the week except Sunday; its offerings include old clothes, books, records and paintings, all kinds of food, furniture and antiques. See it even if you're not planning to buy a thing. . . . Elsewhere, on the **Albert Cuypstraat,** starting at the corner of Ferdinand Bolstraat, two blocks from the Heineken's Brewery, a several-square-block-long street market also takes place daily but Sunday, and is one of the city's top sightseeing attractions. The goods here are merely cheap, not second hand, but they're just as varied as those offered on the Waterlooplein: ties, socks, vegetables, herrings, clothes, corsets, flowers, fish, hardware. Don't miss it. The pushcarts are colorful, the shoppers even more colorful and volatile, and the entire setting is a picture straight from Breughel!

FINDING A SELF-SERVICE LAUNDRY: Look for the sign "Wasserette" or sometimes even "Launderette." They charge around 8 guilders ($2.66) for the washing and drying of one machine-load (5 kilos) of laundry, and generally maintain hours of from 8 a.m. to 8 p.m. on weekdays. Four centrally located "wasserettes": at #12 Oude Doelenstraat (best in town), a continuation of the Damstraat, about 1½ blocks from the Dam Square; at 9 Ferdinand Bolstraat (near the Heineken's Brewery); at

375 Kerkstraat (near Utrechtsestraat); at 59 Elandsgracht (near the Leidseplein).

SOME FINAL FACTS ABOUT AMSTERDAM: The famous "Get in Touch with the Dutch" program, operated by the **VVV** (Amsterdam's Tourist Association) from its main office near the Central Railway Station (phone 26-64-44), will give you the name and address of a Dutch family (if you wish, someone who shares your business, profession, or other interests) to whose home you can drop over for a visit. Contact the **VVV** in advance of, or on the day of, your arrival in Amsterdam, as these meetings take a day or so to arrange; in either event, you'll have to appear in person at the **VVV** office to make the final arrangements. . . . Amsterdam's student activities? They're operated by the **N.B.B.S.** (Netherlands Office for Foreign Student Relations) out of an office at Dam 17 (phone 23-76-86), open 9:15 a.m. to 5 p.m. weekdays, 9:45 a.m. to 2 p.m. Saturdays. Here's where you'll learn about student discounts on charter flights and trains. . . . Bicycle rentals? Since Holland is almost entirely flat, it's the perfect land for cyclists (who can even make an excursion to Marken and Volendam from Amsterdam). For motorbikes, the chief supplier is **Heja Rijwiel-en Brom-fietsbedrijf,** 39 Bestevaerstraat (phone 129-211), charging 21.50 guilders a day (depending on the model), 129 guilders per week; it also rents bicycles for 6.50 guilders per day, 32.50 guilders per week. From the station, take tram no. 13, or bus no. 33, to reach Heja's showroom. . . . In case you've been wondering, the population of Amsterdam is between 700,000 and 800,000, while the bicycles owned by that population exceed 500,000! I'm told that a used bike can be bought at the Amsterdam flea market (on the Waterlooplein) for the equivalent of $30. . . . For cheap indoor swimming in Amsterdam (3 guilders), the address is 19 Heiligeweg (the **Zwembad Heiligeweg),** just off the pedestrians-only shopping street called Kalverstraat. . . . The city has over 50 different canals, between 1000 and 1200 bridges (and that makes Venice "the Amsterdam of the South")! The population of the Netherlands itself exceeds 14,000,000. . . . Restaurant tipping: A service charge—usually 15%—is automatically included in your bill (as is tax), and there is no obligation to leave anything other than the very small change which you'll receive back (i.e., a few 10-Dutch-cents-pieces). Most Dutchmen don't even do that!

Brussels, the capital of glorious Belgium, is 2½ hours by train from Amsterdam. To the land of Rubens and Van Eyck, of steamed mussels and 300 varieties of beer, of medieval splendors and Europe's finest food, we'll head next on this $25-a-day tour.

Chapter X

BRUSSELS

The Triumph of Miniver Cheevy

THERE IS A SQUARE in the heart of Brussels, called La Grand' Place, which instantly reveals the character of this city. It's a spectacular sight: I know of none other in Europe to equal it—neither Princes Street in Edinburgh, nor the Duomo in Milan, nor the Place de la Concorde. This is a square whose major structures are the ancient and untouched Guild Halls of the Middle Ages. Each is festooned with a brilliantly colored medieval flag, and the cornices of the buildings are covered in pure gold leaf. Stand in this square, and you will be thrillingly transported to the world of Breughel and Van Eyck, of Memling and Bosch. But—

You will find that you need advance preparation for your visit to Brussels, for its sights are not of the easy, Eiffel-Tower-type variety. They reflect the great but unfamiliar (to most Americans) culture and history of Flanders—that meeting place in Europe of the Latin and Germanic peoples—and they are mainly associated with the equally unfamiliar period of the High Middle Ages, when great trading cities flourished, Flemish painters achieved supreme masterworks, Gothic cathedrals were built, and mankind achieved feats of art and commerce rarely again duplicated. *Read* before your trip to Brussels: read about the Flemish "primitives," about the builders of the cathedrals, about the later Protestant revolution in Belgium against the inquisitorial methods of Spain's Philip II. With advance knowledge, you'll see beneath the surface of things, and count your Belgian sojourn among the highlights of your European trip.

In Brussels, you'll want to see: the **Musée de l'Art Ancien,** Rue de la Régence, housing the most magnificent collection of Flemish art in the   world (open daily except Monday from 10 a.m. to 5 p.m.; admission 18¢); the **Palais de Justice,** on the Place Poelart, an incredibly massive stone structure, whose courtyard affords a panoramic view of Brussels below (admission is free); the **Hotel de Ville,** on the Grand' Place, a superb example of Gothic architecture with only one flaw: an off-center door in the main tower (an apocryphal legend, almost certainly untrue, has it that the architect committed suicide when he discovered his mistake); the battlefield of **Waterloo,** just outside the city (take bus "W" from Place Rouppe to Waterloo, the last stop); and finally, the statue which all the ladies from Dubuque deplore: the **Manneken-Pis,** which isn't vulgar at all in its Brussels setting (just behind the Hotel de Ville, off the Grand' Place). Other spots of interest are listed in a booklet which you can obtain from the Brussels Tourist Office at 61 Rue du Marché-aux-Herbes (phone 513-18-40), just off the Grand' Place.

And before you leave Brussels, you'll want to make an indispensable excursion: to medieval Bruges, 1¼ hours away by train, stopping perhaps in Ghent along the way, saving another day to visit Antwerp, the city of Peter Paul Rubens.

First, though, you'll need to know how to get around:

1. A Quick Orientation

Arriving by air, at Brussels' **Zaventem Airport,** you'll immediately discover the world's most convenient railway connection, a train station in the center of the arrival terminal (downstairs), from which thrice-hourly locomotives speed you to both the North and the Central stations of downtown Brussels, in 18 minutes flat, for only 70 francs ($1.27) each way. Buy your tickets in the terminal before boarding the train, and get off at the North Station for hotels in the area of the Place Rogier, but stay on till the Central Station for everywhere else.

Brussels possesses no fewer than three major railroad stations, all on the same line: the **Gare du Nord** (North Station), **Gare Centrale** (Central Station), and **Gare du Midi** (South Station); some trains stop at all three; virtually all stop at least at two of the stations. The Gare Centrale is the one just up the hill from the Grand' Place, in the very center of the city, and will become best known to you; but the Gare du Midi, in the midst of a bustling, poor and heavily ethnic area of the city, is Brussels' most important station, servicing most of the great international trains. In advance of arrival or departure from Brussels, you should always carefully check to make sure you're going to, or leaving from, the right station.

Taxis are expensive and unnecessary; subways—the newly completed **metro**—are the way to go. They cost only 40 francs per ride, only 220 francs for 10 rides (thus only 40¢ per ride) if you buy a 10-ride ticket. The trolley system is now a part of the subway system, sometimes even running underground into the subway tracks, and the whole ingenious pattern of travel within Brussels is clearly set forth on maps posted at each station; it quickly becomes familiar.

And now that you have your bearings, it's time to search for a moderately priced hotel. Brussels has a more than sufficient number of them, but of a somewhat lower quality than you'll find for the same price in other European cities. Thus forewarned, be assured that you can still live well on a budget in Brussels, as follows:

2. Budget Hotels

NEAR THE GRAND' PLACE: Nearly everyone traveling to Brussels wants to stay near the **Grand' Place,** close to the colorful restaurants and medieval atmosphere of the narrow streets that jut off the main square, but sadly there's no real quality budget-priced establishment in the streets immediately adjacent to the square. Directly in front of the Central Station, and just around the corner from the Grand' Place, the 50-room **Hotel La Madeleine** at 22 Rue de la Montagne (phone 513-73-92), above a restaurant of high quality, offers comfortable rooms of the standard we've come to enjoy in other cities, at only slightly higher-than-budget rates: 770 francs ($14) for bathless singles, 1000 francs ($18.18) for singles with private shower, 1500 francs ($27.27) for twins with private bath or shower—and all of the twins are so equipped. Breakfast is not included. Similar rates, similar amenities, and a few double rooms without bath, are found at the nearby **Hotel Elysee,** 4 Rue de la Montagne (phone 511-96-82).

Much less expensive, lower in category, but still close to the Grand' Place (from which it's about 300 yards, in fact) is the 20-room, elevator-equipped **Hotel Pacific,** 57 Rue Antoine Dansaert (phone 511-84-59), recommended to me by a great many readers before my own visit to it; owner-manager Madame van Overstraeten and her two sons have apparently been friendly to a great many overseas visitors. Their rates, including breakfast-with-an-omelette: 600 francs ($10.90) single, 800 francs ($14.54) double or twin, 1200 francs ($21.81) for a so-called "quadruple" (which is actually two large beds—*grands lits).* The midnight curfew here is a single drawback, the location a great plus. **Hotel Ruche-Bourse** at 1 Rue Gretry (phone 218-58-87), basic but acceptable, should be tried for its fairly similar rates, if the better Hotel Pacific is full; it's over a budget-priced restaurant, a three-minute walk from the splendor of the incomparable Grand' Place.

NEAR THE GARE DU MIDI (AND LESS EXPENSIVE): Now walk out of the Gare du Midi (South Station) one block to your right, and you'll be on a square (Place Bara), off which runs the Avenue Clemenceau; this is at the end of the long main street of Brussels known successively as the Boulevard Adolphe Max, Boulevard Anspach, and Boulevard M. Lemmonier, and therefore away from the bright lights and activity that converge near the Place Rogier; but the area is easily accessible to that action by underground trolley. We mention it because, at 1 Avenue Clemenceau, the **Hotel Clemenceau** (phone 521-45-38) is a particularly appealing, homey, and comfortably furnished guesthouse that prices its rooms at 600 francs ($10.91) per person in a single or double room, breakfast, service, and tax included. While there is no elevator at the Clemenceau (and there are five floors), there is a little lounge, and paintings everywhere. Note that showers not included in the room fee cost an additional 50 francs, and the front door is locked at 11:30 p.m. The rock-bottom **Hotel du Merlo** at 2 Avenue Fonsny (phone 538-15-69), next to the station, has bathless singles for 300 to 380 francs ($5.45 to $6.90), doubles for 490 to 750 francs ($8.90 to $13.63), the higher rates in each range being for rooms on the first three floors, the lower prices for rooms on the fourth floor. And if you'll agree to climb to the fifth floor, you'll enjoy the romantic atmosphere of rooms

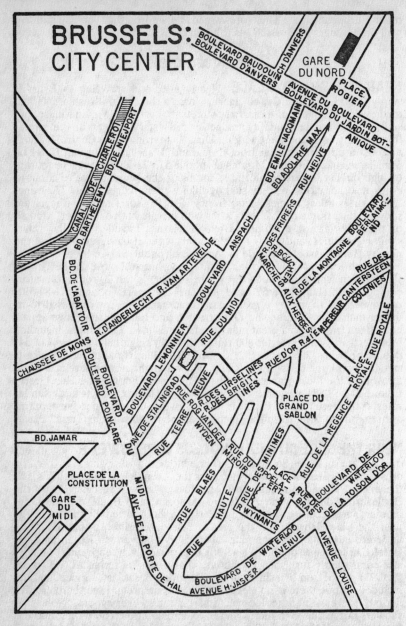

looking out *sur les toits de Bruxelles* for only 220 francs ($4) per person in a double, 100 francs ($1.81) single. For all guests, an optional breakfast is served in the ground-floor café, next to the three billiards tables, for 100 francs ($1.81) per person. A simple, but entirely clean and proper, place.

The area of the Gare du Midi is, as you'll quickly see, one of the poorer sections of Brussels, site of a fascinating open-air market on Sunday mornings attended by the city's large Turkish and Moroccan community of "guest workers." If, as it is to me, this is "your type of place," then you may want to consider three final Gare du Midi selections, all personally visited in the summer of 1984: the five-floor **Hotel de France,** 21 Blvd. Jamar (phone 522-79-35), charging 800 francs ($14.54) single, 920 francs ($16.72) double, 1300 francs ($23.63) triple, always including breakfast; the **Hotel Jamar,** next door at 11 Blvd. Jamar (phone 522-01-04), whose every room is with private shower and w.c., and yet costs (with conti-nental breakfast included) only 750 francs ($13.63) single, 970 francs ($17.63) twin, 1400 francs ($25.45) triple; and finally, around the corner, the three-star **Hotel de Paris,** 80 Blvd. Poincaré (phone 523-81-53), at which all rooms are with bath and w.c., and rent (including breakfast) for 950 francs ($17.27) single, 1300 francs ($23.63) double, 1750 francs ($31.81) triple. Nearest trolley stops: Lemonnier or Gare du Midi.

Three Old Standbys

Finally, a large second-class hotel (140 rooms) nearby, is the **Van Belle,** 39 Chaussée de Mons (phone 521-35-16 or 521-35-40). This hotel throws in a free buffet breakfast with its all-inclusive rates, in 1985, of 850 francs ($15.45) for bathless singles, 1,150 francs ($20.90) for bathless doubles, 1,550 francs ($28.18) for doubles with bath. (There's a special 5% discount on these prices to holders of this book). Located three trolley stops (take streetcar 101) from the Gare du Midi, this is the always reliable budget hotel of Brussels: Each room is attractive and unique, windows sparkle and floors are waxed to a high gloss. And if the Van Belle is full, the management will try very hard to find alternate accommodations for you in the same area. . . . More conveniently placed, but more heavily booked, is the large **Hotel du Rhin,** only steps off the Place Rogier at 90 Rue St. Lazare (phone 217-06-86). This is the classic group hotel of Brussels, and rates reflect that function: 500 francs ($9.09) per person in a triple room, 450 francs ($8.18) per person quad, 550 francs ($10) per person in a bathless double, 650 francs ($11.81) per person twin, 800 francs ($14.54) single, always with breakfast included, and all for tastefully furnished accommoda-tions, some of them enhanced by oil paintings done by the owner's talented Japanese son-in-law, Mr. Shimohara. These are specially reduced rates for readers of this book. . . . And still a third, well-located choice is the 25-room **Hotel International** at 344 Rue Royale near the Sainte Marie Church, high on a hill to the side of the Gare du Nord. A hotel of surprisingly good quality for the low prices it charges (large lobby, elevator, good furnishings), it asks only 1250 francs ($22.72) for twins without bath, breakfast included; only 1700 francs ($30.90) for a triple *with* private bath and breakfast for all; only 860 francs ($15.63) for bathless singles, again breakfast included. Alexandre Zoumis, fluent in English (because he moved here from South Africa), is the new owner/proprietor for this top budget choice. Take tram 62 from either the Gare du Nord or Gare du Midi.

PEACE AND QUIET:
For older tourists, the most elegant section of Brussels is the **Porte Louise,** where you'll find the quiet Rue de Suisse, just two blocks off the Avenue Louise. Here, a superb pension with 13 rooms, charging 550 francs ($10) for bathless singles, 650 francs ($11.81) for singles

with shower, 750 francs for singles with bath ($13.63), 750 francs ($13.63) for bathless twins, 950 francs ($17.27) for a twin with bath, always including breakfast, is the **Pension Les Bluets,** 24 Rue de Suisse (phone 538-44-28), with garden and large, old-fashioned rooms, perfect for readers seeking restful accommodations. *Bluets* is the name of a blue prairie flower, and the English-speaking owner, Madame Mente, grows lovely lilacs in the garden. An alternate in the same area, if Les Bluets is full: the **Residence Osborne** at 67 Rue Bosquet (phone 537-92-51), charges these 1985 rates for its 15 rooms on three floors: single (one only) 580 francs ($10.55), twin 850 francs ($15.45), triple 1200 francs ($21.82), quad 1600 francs ($29.09), with breakfast. Nearby, the even more exciting and much larger **Hotel-Pension Astor,** 9 Rue Capitaine Crespel (phone 511-60-86), a beautifully furnished townhouse closer to the activity of the Porte Louise, is also recommended —particularly for families. Madame Forlini, who has been managing this 13-room establishment since 1960, charges 1985 rates, with breakfast always included, of 630 francs ($11.45) single, 870 francs ($15.81) twin, 1400 francs ($25.45) triple, 1700 francs ($30.90) quad, the last-named room with private bath. . . . To reach Les Bluets from the Porte Louise, walk down the Avenue Louise to the Rue Jean Stas, and follow that street to Rue Suisse. To reach the Osborne, walk one block from Les Bluets. To reach the Astor (one of the best of the lodgings recommended in this chapter), simply head for the new Brussels Hilton on the swank Avenue de la Toison d'Or, only 50 yards away; then, from the Hilton, look for the little Rue des Drapiers, which curves into the Rue Capitaine Crespel.

There are three other recommendable Porte Louise and Avenue Louise choices:

First, **Hotel de Boeck,** 21 Rue Veydt (phone 537-40-33), two blocks off the Avenue, one block behind the large Ramada Hotel, which features 40 very large rooms (some with bathrooms as spacious as the bedrooms), TV and reading lounges, and a London-born manager, Eric Gibbs, who charges 850 francs ($15.45) for bathless singles, but only 1100 francs ($20) for bathless twins or doubles, only 1,350 francs ($24.54) for twins with private bath. Showers-down-the-hall, for those staying in bathless rooms, are free.

Similarly priced, and of similar standard, the **Richmond House Hotel,** 21 Rue de la Concorde (phone 512-62-59), is elevator-equipped and has a pine-paneled dining room and elegant reception room with carved and gilded ceiling, marble fireplace and crystal chandeliers. Rooms have an assortment of furnishings with an emphasis on rattan and bamboo. Rates for bathless doubles, including breakfast and free showers, are 975 francs ($17.72), tiny singles begin at 750 francs ($13.63), and larger singles are 950 ($17.27) francs.

And then there's the rather basic **Residence Berckmans,** 12 Rue Berckmans (phone 537-89-48), a no-frills hotel ideally suited for backpackers, with these low rates guaranteed to the end of 1985 to holders of this book: 500 francs ($9.09) single, 700 francs ($12.72) twin, 950 francs ($17.27) triple, plus 100 francs ($1.81) for an optional breakfast (with an egg or cheese). Showers cost 40 francs extra. There are 26 rooms—each connected by intercom with the street door—on three floors.

A newcomer in this edition is **Hotel Leopold III,** 11 Square Joséphine Charlotte (phone 762-82-88), consisting of 15 rooms on three floors, no elevator, in a quiet, residential part of Brussels, seven subway stops (40 francs) from the Gare Centrale. Bathless singles, with breakfast, 795 francs ($14.45), "grand lit" doubles 1175 francs ($21.36), twins 1275 francs ($23.18), triples 1800 francs ($32.72), quads 3,000 francs ($54.54), with showers for free. Subway stop is Joséphine Charlotte; turn right after leaving it. Located near a small park with a monument, no. 11 is the building with rosebushes in the small garden. Its owner, Jan Leemrjise, speaks excellent English.

READERS' HOTEL SELECTIONS: "The 17-room **Hotel George V,** 23 Rue 't'Kint (phone 513-50-93), offers a friendly, relaxed, home-like ambience, and a delightful proprietor who is colloquially fluent in both English and French. Bathless singles are 680 francs, doubles 950 francs, with breakfast included" (Lloyd Seaver, Oakland, California). . . . "**Hotel à la Grande Cloche,** 11 Place Rouppe (phone 512-61-40), a short walk from the Grand' Place, is highly recommended, safe, quiet, and endowed with a most friendly and helpful manager, Cristea Michel. It also charges, in 1985, only 1200 francs ($21.81) for a double, 1,050 francs ($19.19) single, inclusive of continental breakfast served in the delightful restaurant attached to the hotel, downstairs" (Marty and Joan Maynard, New York, New York).

3. Starvation Budget Rooms

Despite their title, the **Student Homes** of the Free University of Brussels, available to visitors from July 15 to September 30 each year, are rented to students and non-students alike, of any age, and offer one of the great values in European lodgings: individual rooms with complete bathrooms, assembled around a common living room with refrigerator, for only 280 francs ($5.09) per day, including breakfast, for persons under 26 or over 60 staying for more than five days, 330 francs ($6) for lesser stays. For middle-aged types over 26 or under 60, the rate is 390 francs ($7.09), although I'm told that age limits and price distinctions aren't too strictly observed. The nearby "mensa" (no age limits there), located in a bunker-like construction next to Block F, serves a filling, three-course meal (soup, main dish, dessert) for just 160 francs ($2.90). But all this is fairly far out at the Oefenplein campus, or specifically at "Studen-tenwijk Oefenplein," 1 Triomflaan (phone 641-28-31). From the Central Station, take metro no. 1 to the Pétillon stop (7 minutes, 40 francs), go out through the Volontaires exit, turn right into Avenue des Volontaires, walk to the end of the street (about half a mile), then cross the Chaussée de Wavre into Avenue Henri Schoofs, where you'll see the large, modern campus with blue signs pointing to the reception office.

4. The Remarkable Restaurants of Brussels

Although it's one of the more expensive cities of Europe, the town nevertheless enjoys a substantial number of budget eating places where you'll dine magnificently, at reasonable cost (for the Belgians love to eat). We'll deal first with the normal, sit-and-be-served restaurants where you can eat for $4 to $6, then with the self-service restaurants that charge slightly less, and then with the slightly better restaurants where you can try the food specialties of Brussels—particularly, mussels *(moules)* and *carbonnades flamandes*—for from $7 to $9.50 (appetizer and dessert included).

$4 TO $6 RESTAURANTS: To bring order into this first category, we'll group our choices geographically.

Around the Grand' Place

Both on and off the awesome Grand' Place are at least two little bistros where fixed-price, two-course meals cost 280 to 380 Belgian francs ($5.09 to $7.60)—with individual plates for less. To orient yourself in the Place, note that the City Hall is on one side, the Maison du Roi on the opposite side; and that of the other two sides, one has a higher elevation than the other—this we'll refer to as the "top side" of the Grand' Place. Directly on the Grand' Place, at the "top side," is a quaintly decorated cellar restaurant which you'll scarcely be able to find until you nearly fall into it. **Au Caveau d'Egmont et de Horne,** 14 Grand' Place (named after two martyred noblemen of medieval Brussels, but better known as "Au Caveau") is one of the premier budget restaurants of the city, serving generously portioned, two-course meals for either 200, 240 or 270 francs ($3.63, $4.36 or $4.90), depending on their ingredients, offering an omelette with ham for only 120 francs ($2.18), a beefsteak with french fries for 235 francs ($4.27), and that outstanding specialty of Brussels: *moules/frites* (a huge serving of mussels with french fries) for 340 francs ($6.18). M. and Mme. Boitel have managed Au Caveau for 35 years. Open noon to 3 and 6 to 9:30 p.m.; closed Mondays and Tuesdays.

Less crowded in summer, but simply because it's a block (about 50 yards) from the famous square, is the **Snack Les Deux Cloches,** 23 Rue des Eperonniers, on a narrow street that also runs off the Grand' Place. Here, in a short, narrow room attended by uniformed waiters with epaulets, five daily platters—*les plats du jour*—are 190 francs ($3.45) apiece, omelettes of various sorts are 120 francs ($2.18), and a popular, filling salad bowl (chicken, corn, lettuce, cucumber, carrots, tomatoes and bacon) 180 francs ($3.27). A surprisingly comfortable restaurant for such moderate (in Brussels) rates. Open noon to 10 p.m. Closed Sundays.

Near the Place Louise

In this area, which is a bit more elegant than other parts of Brussels, the always reliable eatery is the **Restaurant La Fringale,** at 5 Rue Jourdan, just off the Avenue Louise; from the Place Louise, walk down the Avenue Louise for only one short block and then turn right. Here, in fairly slick, bar-restaurant surroundings, there are excellent and filling plates—meat courses with salad and french fries for 300 francs ($5.45)—priced within the range we seek, as well as a daily changing two-course meal (soup or appetizer, then plate of the day, such as filet of sole with steamed potatoes) for 300 francs ($5.45), and three courses (add dessert and coffee) for 420 francs ($7.63), including tax and service charge (the service charge is always included, in Belgian restaurants, and obviates the need to tip). Monsieur le patron, Marcel, has long been mentioned in this book, and now speaks English! But La Fringale is open weekdays only—take care—and is closed from late July to mid-August.

SELF-SERVICE MEALS FOR $4.50 TO $5.50: Here, now, are some of the finest food values of Brussels, to be found in the low-priced

self-service cafeterias of the city's major department stores. As in the rest of Belgium, Brussels' giant emporiums place great effort into their upper floor cafeterias, and two particular stores with branches all over town—**"Innovation"** and **"Sarma"**—offer especially fine dishes at moderate rates. The largest of the "Inno's" is on the Rue Neuve, the long shopping street that's barred to cars, starting from near the Place Rogier (one block in) and continuing to the Place de la Monnaie, site of the Brussels opera house. Inno maintains a giant cafeteria on its third floor, open Monday through Saturday until as late as 8 p.m., where it sells daily platters ("plats du jour"—such as the delicious carbonnades flamandes, a brown beef stew cooked in beer) for 190 francs ($3.45), with all sorts of side dishes enabling you to eat for a total of $4.50 to $5.50—and you eat well at those prices. At the various "Sarma's" scattered about, even cheaper prices prevail for platters piled up, and consisting of such items as veal cutlet with steamed potatoes, pepper sauce and green peas, for only 185 francs, the array of plates ranging from 150 to 230 francs ($2.72 to $4.18). In the summer of 1984, my own steak tartare with toast, a mixed salad bowl, and glass of excellent red wine came to a total of 185 francs ($3.36).

A CURRENCY NOTE: Prices in this chapter have been converted into dollars at the rate of 55 Belgian francs to one dollar. If that rate should change by the time of your arrival in Brussels, then dollar equivalencies in this chapter may be slightly off, although prices set forth in francs will remain the same.

Self-Service on the Avenue de la Toison d'Or

"Upper" Brussels—the area along the elegant, modern Avenue de la Toison d'Or and Avenue Louise overlooking the older parts of the city—is scarcely where you'd expect to find a budget cafeteria, yet there's one here that vies with the department stores as a low-cost leader. **Mister G.B.** at the Porte de Namur, in the arcade of the big AG Building skyscraper standing at the Porte de Namur, is an ultra-modern, tastefully decorated cafeteria whose prices belie its luxurious interior: as little as 180 francs for several main courses, 38 francs for soup, 65 francs for dessert, all permitting—through careful selection of daily specials—a $5.14 meal. Other "Mister G.B.'s" are located in residential shopping centers elsewhere in Brussels (and next door to the large Bon Marché Department Store at Place Rogier), but this one was obviously meant to be the showplace of the chain. A high recommendation, for an eatery open seven days a week, from 11:30 a.m. to 8:30 p.m.

THE $7 TO $8 RESTAURANTS: And now, for your extra special culinary treats, return to the Grand' Place and search out the tiny Rue Chair et Pain, which runs off the Place, just at the side of the Maison du Roi (which is itself opposite the City Hall). A short walk along the Rue Chair et

Pain, crossing the Rue Marché aux Herbes, and the street changes into the famous, colorful, and bustling **Petite Rue des Bouchers,** which then runs into the diagonal **Rue des Bouchers.** These two medieval-like streets, both less than 50 yards-or-so from the Grand' Place, are almost uninterruptedly lined with picturesque Belgian restaurants, in virtually every price range. Indeed, as you initially walk down the Petite Rue des Bouchers, you'll pass at least four of them—Le Bigorneau, La Filibuste Joyeuse, Le Mouton d'Or, the expensive Aux Armes de Bruxelles—where you can eat, with care, for from $10 to $13. But if you proceed to the intersecting Rue des Bouchers, you'll find—immediately ahead of you—my favorite $8 restaurant in Brussels: **Chez Leon,** 18 Rue des Bouchers, serving that incomparable food specialty of Brussels, which, fittingly enough, is mussels!

Steamed mussels—a dish that is variously called moules marinières or moules casserole, and which consists of mussels steamed in a vegetable broth—are available in any period other than May through mid-July. They can be ordered in Brussels simply by asking for "un speciale." Upon uttering those words, you'll receive an iron pot full of mussels and broth, with a side dish of french fried potatoes—all of which is a complete meal in itself, and is so considered in Belgium. Indeed, the serving is so large that it's always advisable to order one *speciale* for two persons.

Un speciale will cost exactly 360 francs ($6.54), at Chez Leon, but that serving is, once again, more than sufficient for two persons, and should be ordered for two persons! With it, you'll need a beer for 70 francs ($1.27). Alternatively, you can order ten other varieties of moules as well as mussels soup for 210 francs ($3.81).

And now let's repeat an important budget tip: order one speciale for two persons (and a smaller dish for the second person), or else moules casserole for one of you, and the less expensive moules provençales—moules with a tomato and cheese sauce—for the other.

You can, of course, have mussels with french fries for 340 francs or less at other restaurants, such as **Au Caveau d'Egmont** (previously mentioned, 280 francs for moules and frites), but Chez Leon is by far the giant in the field—in 1984, Chez Leon consumed more than 200,000 kilos of mussels!

A similarly priced meal on a street just off the Grand' Place? At **La Coquille d'Or,** 7 Rue de la Colline, amid oilcloth tablecloths, lace-curtained windows, comfortable oak and leather chairs, a three-course prix-fixe—soup; then the plat du jour, roast chicken with french fries and salad or goulash; and dessert—is just 330 francs ($6). . . . And for a $4.81 meal served directly on the Grand' Place, you'll like the comfortable **Restaurant Le Chêne,** 37 Grand' Place, where three courses cost a prix fixe total of exactly 265 francs. It's wise to select the three-courser that includes carbonnades flamandes (braised beef cooked in beer)—an item that ranks second only to mussels as a favorite of the citizens of Brussels.

STARVATION BUDGET: In the United States, as readers of *New York on $35 a Day,* and *Washington D.C. on $35 a Day,* have discovered, a sub-starvation-budgeteer can usually walk into a Chinese restaurant, order a bowl of rice for $1, and then flavor the rice with the free soya sauce found on every table. In Brussels, the trick is to have french fries (the Belgians make the world's best french fries) with béarnaise sauce—a meal in itself for as little as 55 francs ($1). In the cafeteria of almost any department store, if you'll take a plate of french fries (50 francs), then specifically request the béarnaise sauce, *une portion de sauce béarnaise, s'il vous plait*—they'll give you a small portion for 15 francs, and precede it all with soup (32 francs), you'll have quite a passable, if starchy, meal for under $1.80.

Mayonnaise with Your French Fries

Even smarter, though, is to head for the spots that provide Belgian-style mayonnaise (almost a sauce béarnaise, and almost as tasty) with your incomparably delicious, Belgian french fries. The restaurant of the **Sarma Department Store,** which charges 50 francs for french fries and 10 francs for sauce béarnaise (taken from pots at the side of the dining room), is one such place; as is the **Self-Service Colmar** (see the offerings at the end of the serving line), as is **Mr. G.B.** at the Porte de Namur. And if you think I'm balmy about the prospects of a meal of french fries with Belgian mayonnaise, try it—just once!

The Perfectly Acceptable Practice of Eating with the "Army"

Finally, an excellent three-course meal is available for only 140 francs ($2.54), both at lunch and supper, at the no-frills dining room of the **Armée du Salut** (Salvation Army), 27 Rue Bodeghem, where the setting and atmosphere are definitely not à la Ritz, but where it is perfectly safe and acceptable to eat (and that advice applies to both sexes). At least a dozen normally dressed, middle-income residents appear here each meal. This is on a small side street near the Place Anneessens, a few minutes on foot from the Grand' Place. Open seven days a week, from noon to 1:30 p.m. and again from 6:30 to 7:45 p.m., the method of operation is self-service, and a typical three-course meal might consist of soup, then a quarter of a roast chicken with vegetable, followed by a dessert such as chocolate cream or fruit. Plastic table tops, of course.

Picnicking

Picnic meals in Brussels? Go to the open-air market in the **Place St. Catherine,** in the vicinity of the Bourse; or, if you're more fastidious, try the self-service grocery in the basement of the **City 2** shopping complex at the head of the Rue Neuve near the Place Rogier.

THE BIG SPLURGE: If you're now in the mood for a $14 dinner, you'll do well at the **Restaurant au Coq au Vin,** 62 Rue Marché au Charbon, four blocks from the Grand' Place, which charges exactly 700 Belgian francs for soup, a magnificent wagon laden with hors d'oeuvres, main course, and dessert (but that price does not include wine—a large bottle of a good vin du Patron, enough for four people, will cost about $8). It's a thoroughly native-type restaurant, perfect for a big splurge in Brussels, but always packed with Belgians, and usually requiring a reservation—phone 513-23-68. Closed Sundays and the month of August.

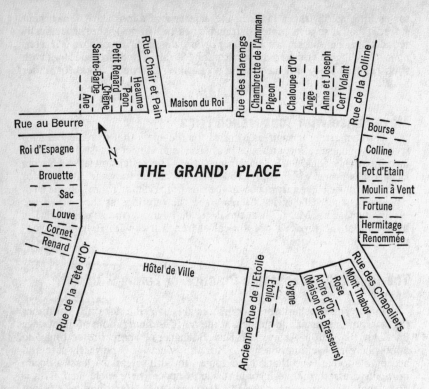

THE GRAND' PLACE

Rue Chair et Pain · Heaume · Paon · Chêne · Petit Renard · Sainte-Barbe · Âne

Maison du Roi

Rue des Harengs · Chambrette de l'Amman · Pigeon · Chaloupe d'Or · Ange · Anna et Joseph · Cerf Volant · Rue de la Colline

Rue au Beurre

Roi d'Espagne
Brouette
Sac
Louve
Cornet
Renard

Bourse
Colline
Pot d'Etain
Moulin à Vent
Fortune
Hermitage
Renommée

N

Rue de la Tête d'Or

Hôtel de Ville

Ancienne Rue de l'Etoile · Etoile · Cygne · Arbre d'Or (Maison des Brasseurs) · Rose · Mont Thabor · Rue des Chapeliers

READER'S RESTAURANT SELECTION: "Just 10 minutes by foot from the Grand' Place, I stumbled into **La Tartinette,** at 126 Rue du Midi, operated by an English-speaking Vietnamese who serves you through a round window that looks like a ship's porthole. Here, one can have the dish of the day, usually served with rice or potatoes, for only 150 francs, a filling soup for 40 francs, sandwiches or omelettes for 45 francs. But this is open weekdays only" (L. D. Lacson, New York, New York).

5. Youth & Student Facilities

YOUTH HOSTELS, YOUTH RESTAURANTS: Brussels possesses four major youth hostels, of which one—the **Jan Brueghel,** at 2 Rue du St. Esprit (phone 511-04-36), just at the side of the Eglise Notre Dame de la Chapelle, where Jan's father, the great Pieter Brueghel, is buried, all less than a quarter mile from the Central Station—is one of the finest hostels in all of Europe, a four-story masterpiece of modern architecture that somehow blends the most futuristic shapes and angles into a perfect, complementary fit with the 17th-century buildings alongside—why can't all modernists protect the physical environment in this way? All in red brick, but with modern Scandinavian-style pine furniture, carpeting, modern washroom facilities, an elevator, various lounges, and a large ground-floor cafeteria, the Brueghel offers both singles, twins and quad rooms, as well as one or two dormitories, at 1985 rates, including continental breakfast, of 450 francs ($8.18) single, 380 francs ($6.90) per person twin, 300 francs ($5.45) per person quad, 275 francs ($5) in the dorms. You'll need a youth hostel membership card, sold on the spot for 700 francs ($12.72), but if you don't want to buy one, the Brueghel will sell you a one-day card for only 100 francs ($1.81); and they'll sell the card to persons of all ages, although they give priority to young people in the summer months. A ground-floor cafeteria, mentioned earlier, sells three-course meals at both lunch and dinner for only 220 francs ($4). Because the hostel tries to close at mid-day for cleaning, try to arrive before 10:30 a.m. or after 4:30 p.m. From the station, simply walk along the Boulevard de l'Empereur until you reach the Rue du St. Esprit.

Close runners-up to the Brueghel, because of their atmosphere (delightful), and not in terms of physical facilities, are two older, well-located facilities, of which my preferred choice would be the **"SleepWell"** (more formally known as the Auberge du Marais), at 27 Rue de la Blanchisserie (phone 218-50-50), a tiny walk from the Place Rogier near the Gare du Nord, a few steps off the famous, pedestrians-only shopping street, the Rue Neuve. Here, in a happy older building covered (inside and out) with murals of the sort you'd find in a college dorm, staffed by French- and English-speaking young people (the Brueghel is a Flemish hostel, where you'll hear only English and Dutch), you'll pay a lower-priced 330 francs ($6) for one of three single rooms, 250 francs ($4.54) for an available twin or two, 225 francs ($4.09) for a bunk in the two five-bedded dorms maintained for young ladies or the 10-bedded dorms maintained for men. Breakfast (rolls, butter, coffee), use of showers, a reading room, bar and canteen, are included in the price. Walking tours of Brussels—called "Bruxelles sur le Pouce"—are sometimes conducted from here by English-speaking Belgian students in July and August. And the SleepWell does not require a hostel card, nor does it impose any maximum age limit at all upon its guests.

Of almost identical standard, this time up on the hill overlooking the Botanical Gardens at the side of the Gare du Nord, the equally popular **"CHAB"** (Centre d'Herbergement de l'Agglomération de Bruxelles), at 6 Rue Traversière (phone 217-01-58), is another of those youth hostels that theoretically operates only for those under the age of 30, but no one checks, and no one requires youth hostel membership either. Found on a street possessing all sorts of youth facilities (including a "Sleep Theatre" housing overflow guests on the floor of an auditorium in summer months, a far-out, youth-type restaurant, "L'Ecole Buissonnière," selling three-course meals with a glass of superb Belgian beer, for 260 francs ($4.72), CHAB also offers private rooms, as well as dorms, in its stairs-only building, and charges 450 francs (just under $8.18) in its few singles, 380 francs ($6.90) per person in doubles, 350 francs ($6.36) in its many three- and four-bedded rooms, only 250 francs ($4.54) in just plain dorms, with breakfast always included in the price.

Cheapest of all, but least central, is the former monastery that became, in 1970, the **Maison Internationale,** open all year at 205 Chaussee de Wavre (phone 648-97-87), near Place Luxembourg/Porte de Namur, and reached from the Gare du Nord by bus no. 38 to the Chaussée de Wavre stop, or from the Gare du Midi by bus 20 or 21 to the Quartier Leopold stop. Here, no fewer than 35 single rooms rent for 350 francs ($6.36), breakfast included; twins for 300 francs ($5.45) per person; and behind the building, in a large park, a comfortable youth camping site is available for those with their own sleeping bags, for only 160 francs ($2.90) a night, with breakfast thrown in. Europe on $5 a Day!

STUDENT HOUSING, STUDENT FLIGHTS: Acotra, at 38 Rue de la Montagne (phone 513-44-80 for lodgings, 512-55-40 for travel), upstairs, near the Grand' Place, is where students are sent for student lodgings in Brussels, and for student flights and trains; you might as well head directly there, weekdays from 9:30 a.m. to 5:30 p.m., Saturdays from 9 a.m. to noon.

6. Sightseeing Notes

DAYTIME SIGHTSEEING: Apart from the Grand' Place and Waterloo, the one indispensable visit in Brussels is to the great **Musée de l'Art Ancien** (the Classical Art Museum), at 3 Rue de la Régence, about 30 yards from the Place Royale, which opens every day except Monday from 10 a.m. to 5 p.m., charges the amazing admission of only 10 francs (18¢) all times other than Wednesdays and weekends (when it's free), and houses probably the most breathtaking collection of Flemish art in the world. The "ancient" paintings are on the upper floors, where you should patiently wend your way to the rooms housing the surrealistic masterpieces, centuries ahead of their time, of Hieronymus Bosch (1450 to 1516); they actually depict men bombing villages from flying-fish-airplanes! Nearby, you'll see the renowned *Landscape and the Fall of Icarus* and *Kermesse Flamande* of Pieter Brueghel, his equally famous *De Kindermoord (Murder of the Innocents),* and at least a dozen *Temptations of St. Anthony* done by both Brueghel the elder and younger, by Van der Heck and others. Mainly, you'll want to concentrate on Brueghel's scenes of Flemish village life, in which literally scores of individually drawn peasants enliven each canvas; but there are as well in this stupefying museum a number of Rubens and Van Dycks (including a Van Dyck portrait of the sculptor who created the *Manneken Pis)*—and even a few Dutch painters (Rembrandt, Hals, Steen), too. . . . The major works (Ensor, Magritte, Delvaux) of Brussels' important **Museum of Modern Art** were housed until recently on the ground and lower floors of the Musée de l'Art Ancien, while the Modern Art Museum at 1 Place Royale, up the street, underwent complete reconstruction. That work should be complete by the time this edition appears, and a vastly improved, greatly expanded Musée de l'Art Moderne will be holding forth again at 1 Place Royale; its collection is an important one, and should not be missed.

A BEER MUSEUM: You'll receive a free glass of cool pilsner beer (the kind selling for 60 francs at one of the open-air cafés on the Grand' Place) by simply paying the 20-franc admission charge to the **Maison des Brasseurs** at 10 Grand' Place. That fee admits you (after you've first rung the bell near the large, brown, and closed door) to a small basement museum of brewers' implements having an unbroken link to one of the old Guilds. You'll hear an amusing, ten-minute tape recording of the industry's history (presented in 20 languages, even Chinese), and then you'll receive your beer! Open weekdays from 10 a.m. to noon and 2 to 5 p.m., Saturdays from 10 a.m. to noon, closed Sundays.

. . . AND A MUSEUM OF LACE: Lace, after beer, is the second great product of Brussels. In fact, lace is to Brussels as glass is to Venice, chips to silicon valley. From the 16th through the early 19th centuries, Belgium was the world's leading producer of lace, and Brussels **Musée des Dentelles,** 6 Rue de la Violette (a block from the beer museum and the Grand' Place), honors that once-major industry that operates in reduced but still prominent fashion today. If you plan to purchase lace at any point of your Belgian stay, you should first hone your skills by visiting the three floors (with elevator) of the Musée des Dentelles (Museum of Lace), perusing the varieties of lace and learning something of its manufacture. Hours are 10 a.m. to noon and 1 to 5 p.m. on weekdays, 10 a.m. to noon only on weekends, for an admission charge of 50 francs, except on Sundays when entrance is free.

7. Hope in Brussels

While I traipse through the hotels and restaurants of Brussels, my wife Hope likes to stick to the Grand' Place. Here's her report on the specific sights to be seen, both here and in other areas of town:

AROUND THE GRAND' PLACE: "This magnificent square, described earlier by Arthur, began its life as a market place, and is still used for that purpose to this very day—come early in the morning and you'll see the stands. But the most thrilling time to visit the square is at night, particularly when the town puts on its own 'Sound and Light' show by flashing colored beams across the Hotel de Ville and playing Bach or Beethoven over concealed loudspeakers.

"Wherever you go in Brussels, you'll be drawn back to the Grand' Place like a magnet, and the feeling is not to be resisted, because there are three major attractions in the area: the Hotel de Ville, the Maison du Roi, and the old Church of Gudule, nearby.

Hotel de Ville

"The **Hotel de Ville,** or Town Hall, is the oldest (begun in 1402), largest, and most imposing structure on the Grand' Place, and also one of the finest examples of Gothic architecture in Europe. It's open to visitors Tuesdays through Fridays from 9:30 a.m. to 5 p.m., Saturdays from 10 a.m. to 4 p.m., closed Sundays and Mondays. For 50 francs admission (90¢) you'll be taken on a guided tour of the interior, which includes the splendid, red-and-gold Council Room, the Mayor's room filled with paintings of old Brussels, the 'Salle Gothique' festooned with tapestries of the Guilds, and the beam-ceilinged Marriage Chamber with its old tile floor and shields of the Guilds. While all of these are immensely impressive, I get a particular thrill from reading the two framed posters on either side of the door to the main lobby, which contain defiant proclamations of the two wartime

Mayors (Bourgermasters) of Brussels—Adolphe Max and F.J. van de Meulebroeck—during the occupation of the city by German troops in World Wars I and II. Both counsel the citizens to remain calm and give no aid to the enemy—especially to any puppet government official who might be appointed by occupying forces. And one ends with the ringing words: 'Je suis, je reste, et je resterai le seul bourgmestre legitime de Bruxelles.'

Maison du Roi

"Located directly opposite the Hotel de Ville is the **Maison du Roi**, constructed in the 16th century, restored faithfully to the original in the 19th century, and now the historical Municipal Museum of Brussels (open from 10 a.m. to 4 p.m. on weekdays; Saturdays and Sundays from 10 to noon, and charging admission of 50 francs. Apart from its historical and archaeological relics relating to the city (altarpieces, ceramics, porcelain, tapestries, and, most interesting to me, sculptures and pieces of sculpture from the Hotel de Ville, the Maison, and the Churches of N. D. du Sablon, N. D. de la Chapelle, and St. Michel Cathedral), it displays paintings (a Brueghel on the first floor) and puppets, and an amusing exhibit on the third floor (to the right of the staircase) of some of the costumes, decorations, and honors that have been bestowed upon the Manneken Pis! There are scores of models here of that symbol of *l'esprit ironique* of Brussels (a cherubic-looking little boy in bronze: his 'duty' immortalized in a fountain), all costumed in different uniforms, including one of the Foreign Legion, into which he was inducted with the following words:

> *'Petit bonhomme légendaire*
> *Illustration de la cité*
> *Te voici donc incorporé*
> *Dans la Legion Etrangère.'*

St. Michel Cathedral

"The official cathedral of Brussels, **St. Michel Cathedral** (still called **St. Gudule** by the natives, although in 1962 it was discovered that St. Gudule never existed) is only a short walk from the Maison du Roi. The church, begun in the ninth century, is a large grey stone cathedral with twin towers that took over 300 years to build (from in the 15th century). Its impressive main entrance is opened only on state occasions (the doors being too old and delicate for constant use) like the marriage of King Baudouin and Queen Fabiola—but a visit through the side door will be more than worth your time; note the baroque wooden pulpit, which was carved from a single tree trunk; and more important, the exquisite stained glass windows which experts in church architecture say are among the finest in the world.

THE SABLON: "The charming and fashionable district of Sablon, located off the Place Royale, near the Museum of Ancient Art (two blocks down, and cross the street), has as its centerpiece the gardens of the **Place du Petit Sablon** (right off Rue de la Régence), created to honor two victims of the long arm of the Spanish Crown, the Counts Egmont and de Hornes, whose statues are the focal points of the park. (The Place, a small green square, is enclosed by a charming wrought iron fence which is decorated with Gothic-looking pillars, each one supporting a different statuette, representing the ancient Guilds—a closer look will reveal which Guild you're looking at. And the surrounding neighborhood has some restored houses dating back as far as the early 16th century.) . . . Music-makers or music-lovers might like to drop in at **The Brussels Museum of Musical Instruments,** on a corner of the square at 17 Place du Petit Sablon, open Tuesday, Thursday and Saturday from 2:30 to 4:30 p.m., Wednesday from 5 to 7 p.m., Sunday from 10:30 a.m. to 12:30 p.m. There's free admission on all days of operation, and guided tours can be arranged; both European and non-European musical instruments are displayed. . . . Afterwards, you can cross the Rue de la Régence to the Place du Grand Sablon where you can see the interesting, flamboyant Gothic church **Notre-Dame au Sablon** (very romantic looking at night when it's lit up), whose interior has vaulted stone ceilings, but is nevertheless decorated in the rococo manner. On Sundays, some very elegant antique stalls set up shop in front of the church—and the surrounding neighborhood is filled with antique shops, too. . . . While in the neighborhood, do have a look at the King's 'office,' **The Royal Palace** (once a royal residence, but the present King lives elsewhere), a grand Louis XVI-style building filled with marble, shimmering chandeliers, Goya tapestries, royal family portraits, silver, china, and featuring interesting changing special exhibitions. Open daily, except Monday, from 10 a.m. to 4 p.m. (from August 1 through September 14); admission free.

MAROLLES: "Below the Palais de Justice, off and around the Rue Haute, is the rougher, more medieval, Brueghel-like section of Brussels (matter of fact, Brueghel the Elder lived at #132). Turn off at Rue du Renard or Rue de la Rasière to get to the quaint cobblestoned Place du Jeu de Balle—and go particularly on Sunday mornings when the Place becomes the lively **Flea Market of Brussels** (good bargains too, amid piles of junk: a pair of antique wooden bellows for $15!). . . . After you finish exploring the neighborhood, you can walk up the Rue Haute toward the center of town where, in about five blocks, you'll come to the lovely Roman-Gothic **Church of La Chapelle** (which is actually closer to Notre-Dame au Sablon); begun in the 12th century, the sides of the church are especially beautiful, and Pieter Brueghel is buried in one of the chapels.

SMALL EXCURSIONS: "The **Royal Museum for Central Africa,** 11 Leuvensesteenweg, Tervuren (open daily from 9 a.m. to 5:30 p.m., 10 a.m. to 4:30 p.m. in the winter, free admission), is located on the outskirts of Brussels in Tervuren Park (an exquisitely sylvan retreat), and is a 30-minute, 40-franc (72¢) ride from the center of town (take the metro at Gare Centrale to Montgomery, ask for a 'ticket de transit' and use it to board tram #44 at Montgomery, then get off at the end of the line, and signs will point the way). You'll find it an interesting trip, through some of the most elegant residential districts of Brussels, then the forest; and the museum itself offers some of the best African art to be seen anywhere. It's a large and unusually comprehensive collection, encompassing everything to do with the life and culture of Central Africa. You start, of course, with zoological and agronomical exhibits, then go on to a fine collection of minerals, and a gallery on the prehistory of Africa; but more interesting are the vast sections devoted to crafts and customs (especially the ceramics and woven goods of great beauty), and to African art, revealing a surprising diversity in the various Central African cultures: a wealth of material. There are also two galleries dealing with the opening up of Central Africa (including personal artifacts of Stanley and Livingstone) and (probably a bit of nostalgia for local residents) the history of the Belgians in Africa.

The Home of Erasmus

"A last visit, for students of the early Renaissance, is to the House of Desiderius Erasmus—the great humanist and Latin scholar—which is located a fair distance (20 minutes) from the center of town, at 31 Rue du Chapitre, Anderlecht (take the metro to St. Guidon, and look for the museum near the cathedral). The interior of this substantial home has been maintained in its original state, is filled with carefully preserved books translated and annotated by the famous philosopher, and has numerous other relics of the time. Admission is 20 francs; hours are from 10 a.m. to noon and 2 to 5 p.m., every day except Tuesday and Friday.

"*Tip:* Unless you have considerable time in Brussels, you can safely skip **The Royal Art and History Museum,** and the much-touted **Antoine Wiertz Museum-Gallery** (both of some interest, but out-of-the-way places and not worth the effort); you'll do better to spend that extra time in those two unforgettable Belgian cities—Bruges and Ghent."

8. Tours & Excursions

TOURS: Sightseeing buses operated by a number of tour companies (a typical one is De Boeck at 8 Rue de la Colline) leave from the corner of Rue de la Colline and Rue des Eperonniers on a comprehensive series of tours, including three daily sightseeing trips through the city proper, each costing 450 francs ($8.18). Tours depart at 10 a.m., noon and 3 p.m., go to all major attractions, including the site of the 1958 World's Fair. For 480 francs ($8.72), you can take a lengthier tour (departing daily at 3 p.m.) into the outskirts of Brussels, visiting the Museum of Central Africa in the park of Tervuren, then stopping at Waterloo to see the famous "Lion's Mound" (where the popular Prince of Orange was wounded in that famous battle), then to the World's Fair Site, and back along all the sights of the city itself. And finally, for the supreme sightseeing experience of Belgium—the awesome medieval cities of Ghent and Bruges (the latter with its city canals, its regally floating swans, and magnificent museums of Gruuthuse and St. John's Hospital)—there is the popular, 800-franc ($14.54) all-day tour of Flanders, leaving daily at 9 a.m. My own preference is to make this full-day excursion—the indispensable side visit on a stay in Brussels—on one's own, by train to Bruges (1¼ hours away) or to Ghent (40 minutes away)—see our discussion later in this chapter. But if you're inclined to escorted motorcoach sightseeing, you'll find that the Bruges/Ghent full-day'er is one of the lowest-priced of all the 7-hour tours in Europe.

READER'S SELECTIONS: "Instead of taking an expensive guided excursion to Bruges, I went to the railroad station and bought a ticket for 'un beau jour à Bruges et au littoral.' This included, for about $9, round-trip fare from Brussels to the seashore via Bruges, a ticket of entry to the city museum in Bruges, and a ticket for a ride on the canals of the little city. I was in Bruges the whole day until about 4:30 p.m.; then I took the train to Blankenberge, swam, ate an enormous pile of 'moules'; returned to Bruges, where I walked around for an hour looking at the lit-up monuments; and finally took the train back to Brussels. Such 'Beau Jours' are available for many other excursions and a list of them is available in any railroad station" (Peter J. Feibelman, New York, New York; note by AF: ask specifically, at the ticket window, for *Une journée à la mer,* a day at the seashore, which permits you during the summer months only—July to mid-October—to buy a round-trip, one-day ticket to any seaside location in Belgium, for the one-way fare there—an average of 500 francs, $9.09).

READERS-ON-AN-EXCURSION: "No one should leave Belgium without making a trip to **Antwerp,** but don't plan your trip for a Monday, when many of the main attractions are closed. This is a marvelous city, where you may even want to spend several days. There is so much to see. The train for Antwerp leaves from the Gare Centrale every 30 minutes. If you take the express train, the trip is only 30 minutes. The local train can take as much as an hour to get there so it is worth waiting ten minutes for the express, on which a round-trip ticket is about 420 francs ($7.63). You can also drive to Antwerp easily, passing the World's Fair Grounds and then the Royal Residences. Coming into Antwerp you will see the first tank to come into the city for the liberation from the Germans during World War II. Follow the signs to the Central Station and park your car there. Everything is in walking distance.

"On the back of the map you'll receive at the Tourist Office, you'll find a list of things to see in the city. The following are musts: **Rubens House** (Rubens was one of the few artists of the time who was recognized as a great during his lifetime. Consequently, he lived like a rich man of the time. His house is fascinating, and the admission is free)! **Open Market** (The open market place is right down the street from Rubens House; it is where the produce market is held on Saturdays. This is really fascinating to see, and a great place to meet the people. If you want some fresh fruit to munch on, what better place can you find to buy it?); **Grote Markt** (This is the Grand' Place of Antwerp. It is not as grand as the one in Brussels, but a must to see. It typifies the city. The statue and fountain in the center of the square is of Brabo, the hero of an old legend. According to the story, the site of Antwerp was inhabited by the giant Antigoon. He extracted a tribute from all who navigated the river and cut off the hand of those who refused to pay. The giant was finally killed by the Roman soldier Brabo, who cut off the giant's hand and threw it in the river. And thus the name of the city 'Ant,' from the word hand and 'Werpen,' from the verb to throw. The throwing of the hand is portrayed here); **The Steen** (This old turreted castle now houses the Navigation Museum. It also provides a good view of the harbor—the second largest on the North Sea. If you have the time, you can take a boat tour of the harbor, which is operated by the Flandria Line and leaves from just to the left of the Steen. And if you are ready for a snack, the frites stand at the foot of the ramp to the Steen sells excellent french fries. The section between the Steen and the cathedral is also an excellent area to try the local specialty, mussels); **The Cathedral** (You should plan your visit to the cathedral for after lunch. The famous triptychs by Rubens are closed in the morning to protect them from the strong sunlight which shines on them); **Plantin-Moretus Museum** (This museum houses a complete antique press and engraving plant. In the 16th century, it was the finest printing and engraving shop in Antwerp. Plantin's work was carried on by his son-in-law Moretus and his heirs for three centuries); **The Zoo** (The zoo is beside the Central Station. It is reputed to be one of the finest in Europe. And if you are looking for nightlife, try the places on the side streets off the **Grote Markt** or the Koningin Astrid Plein by the Station" (Judy Nesbit, Kohlenweg, Germany).

"**Bruges** (Brugge) is a city of the past living in the present. By train it's about an hour from the Gare Centrale in Brussels. From the station walk to the Market Square on the other side of town; the little old streets are delightful. Then walk to the adjoining Burg Square, which is surrounded by four buildings representing four different centuries. One of them is the **Chapel of the Holy Blood,** the most famous building in Bruges, housing the relic which was brought from the Holy Land in the 12th century (it is displayed on Friday mornings). On Ascension Day you can see the Procession of the Holy Blood, a spectacular sight which attracts people from all over the world. . . . Next I would suggest that you take a canal tour of the city. There are several departure spots. After the tour, head toward **Notre Dame Church.** Charles the Bold and Mary of Burgundy are both buried here and there is a beautiful marble Madonna by Michelangelo. By this time, it should be about lunch time. There is a picturesque little restaurant across the street where, for about $4.50, you can have, for example, an omelette, french fries and a Coke, or 'tomates crevette' (tomatoes stuffed with little shrimp—a really typical Belgian dish worth trying) and a Coke.

Around the corner is the **Memling Museum.** From here continue on to the **Beguinage.** Inside, to the left of the gate, is the Beguinage house which is open to visitors. . . . In your walk through the city you should see ladies sitting out in old costumes making lace. This is a fascinating art, you can't leave Belgium without a piece of this world famous lace. The shops near the Beguinage are good ones. From here you are not too far from the railroad station. There are maps posted all over the city, so you should have no trouble finding your way around" (Judy Nesbit, Kohlenweg, Germany).

"Another must is a stop at **Ghent.** This can be done on the way back from Bruges if you get an early start. From the railroad station take the train to the center of town, where you should be sure to see the famous polyptych *The Adoration of the Mystic Lamb,* by van Eyck, in a chapel of the **Cathedral of St. Bavo.** The guard will supply an explanation in English. He will also close it so that you can see the outside panels. You should see the rest of this cathedral, the 12th-century castle of the Counts of Flanders, and the views from St. Michael's Bridge and from the Belfrey" (Judy Nesbit, Kohlenweg, Germany; note by AF: trains for Bruges and Ghent leave the North Station nearly every 30 minutes throughout the day, at a charge of 500 francs ($9.09) round-trip).

"Some of your readers may enjoy the university town of **Louvain** (Leuvén), 20 minutes from the North Station in Brussels (for a round-trip fare of 200 francs—$3.63). It features an entirely new and architecturally interesting university a few kilometers outside the 'old' Louvain; the loveliest town hall in Europe (say I), a few minutes' walk from the station; and a worthwhile cathedral." (J. Auth, Toledo, Ohio).

THE INDISPENSABLE ONE-DAY EXCURSION: To Bruges, approximately one hour away by train costing 500 francs, round-trip. And don't even dream of also stopping in Ghent (which deserves its own trip); Bruges has enough to occupy you for a week. A fully developed, almost fully preserved 14th- and 15th-century Flemish city, perhaps the most beautiful on earth, reflecting the vigor and taste of a long-ago time, it will change all your opinions about those supposedly dark days of the Middle Ages.

WATERLOO!: Suddenly, as you drive out of Brussels on the road to Charleroi, signs begin appearing that bear crossed sabres accompanied by the numerals, "1815." They contain, and need, no identifying words. June 18, 1815, was the date of Waterloo, the battle that decided the destiny of Europe; and the signs point to the village of Waterloo in the suburbs of Brussels, beyond which is the still untouched plain—several square miles in size—that witnessed the brutal clash between the forces of Napoleon and the armies of the Allies, under the Duke of Wellington.

I can't anticipate what your reaction to these farmlands will be, but my own visits there have been among the more soul-stirring occasions of my life—an idiosyncrasy that may date back to the days when I played with tin soldiers who wore uniforms like those of Napoleon's troops. Today, there exists little on the battleground except the gigantic, pyramid-like "Lion's Mound," from the top of which you gaze out upon the fields and plains where once these armies clashed. Below are a number of garish carnival-like "museums" that play nickelodeon-type films of the event (admission: 50 francs; the soundtrack is in French, but you won't mind), as well as the genuinely interesting circular building that houses a panoramic painting of a scene at the height of the battle.

That—and a few scattered monuments and ruined farmhouses—is all there is. And yet, so help me, I can't approach this vast and silent place without feeling a subtle tremor and without hearing the imagined sounds of a cavalry charge, and the shouted orders of Marshals Ney and Blucher, or the crackling muskets of a square of English infantry. Read a history of Waterloo—there are several books sold on the site—and perhaps you too will share the sentiments of Victor Hugo, who lived near here (in the Hotel des Colonnes) to gather battle data for scenes in his *Les Miserables,* and then wrote:

> *Quarante ans sont passés, et ce coin de la terre,*
> *Waterloo, ce plateau funèbre et solitaire,*
> *Ce champ sinistre . . .*
> *Tremble encore d'avoir vu la fuite des géants!*

> (Forty years have passed, and this corner of earth,
> Waterloo, this solitary and funebral plain,
> This sinister field—
> Still trembles from having seen the fall of giants!)

To get to Waterloo on your own, take Bus "W" from the Place Rouppe (leaving every half hour, for a one-way charge of 66 francs), but stay on past the village itself until you reach Mont St. Jean and the "Lion's Mound"—center of the battlefield. Best, of course, is to drive there; and next best course is to take a tour.

9. Evening Entertainment

The only always-satisfying means of evening entertainment in Brussels is to grab a chair at a sidewalk café in the Grand' Place and drink in the beauty of the floodlit, golden buildings that ring the square. It's amazing how much one can discover about these buildings by staring at them for hours on end, and that—strangely enough—is a pleasant and moving task. A coffee on the Grand' Place is 60 francs, but for that you can sit forever.

The outstanding café of the Grand' Place is called, appropriately enough, the **Café de la Grand' Place.** It's located at the bottom side of the Place (corner of Rue au Beurre), has no identifying number, but can be spotted by the gilded head of a Cardinal out front or by the unbelievably picturesque decor inside—which is that of a typical, 15th-century Belgian inn. That means that there are posts and timbers, and rough-hewn walls of wood, a center fireplace with a roaring fire, leather bladders suspended from the beams, and a stuffed, full-size horse at the stairway leading to the *estaminet* (old tavern) on the second floor. Don't fail to roam throughout the entire establishment, including the smoky *bier kelder* downstairs; to do all of this requires the purchase of as little as a single beer (60 francs), a glass of wine (75 francs) or a coffee or tea (50 francs); in particularly cold weather, you can spend a wonderfully dreamy evening by the fire, sustained by a *vin chaud* (heated wine) for 85 francs. . . . Brussels's historic puppet playhouse, the **Theatre Toone,** is found at the end of a tiny blind alley called the Impasse Schuddeveld, next to no. 21 Petite Rue des Bouchers (the colorful restaurant street near the Grand' Place). "Spectacles" nightly except Sunday at 8:30 p.m., 125 to 250 francs for seats, dialogue in French with a distinct Brussels accent. "Toone" is named after Antoine, founder of the theatre in 1830. . . . After absorbing the beauty of the Grand' Place, you'll want to walk to the *Manneken-Pis.* Simply head behind the City Hall straight down the Rue Charles Bols for two short blocks.

For disco in Brussels, the leading club—in fact, *le dernier cri,* according to many Bruxellois—is **Le Club 25** at 25 Rue Henri Maus, a short walk from the Grand' Place. No admission, but you'll pay 100 francs ($1.81) per soft, 180 francs ($3.27) per hard drink, in this complex of three dance floors—one of stainless steel, complete with disc jockey, laser beams, smoke effects, and psychedelic lights. Open seven days a week, 2 p.m. to 2 a.m. . . . This time just for listening, with no dancing, is the jazz tavern called **Pol's Bierodrome,** at 21 Place Fernand Cocq, in the uptown *(haut de la ville)* area of the Brussels Hilton, up the Avenue d'Ixelles from the Porte de Namur. Officially designated as Chapter 1152 of the organization called "Friends of Jazz," Pols features live jazz combos, in a dark and smoky college-beerhall-type setting whose walls are covered with college pennants and photos of jazz greats. I've never been there at night, but the charwoman who showed me through one afternoon assured me it was *"pas cher, monsieur"*—no admission, average 150 francs ($2.72) per drink.

One last, and relatively unexpected, form of evening entertainment is provided by Brussels's **Musée du Cinema** (Cinema Museum), in the Palais des Beaux-Arts, 9 Rue Baron Horta (phone 513-41-55), which shows classic films in their original languages (René Clair, John Ford, David Lean, Billy Wilder) every evening at 6:15, 8:15, and 10:15, silent films in a different screening room at 7 and 9 p.m., and charges only 30 francs (55¢) per showing.

10. Brussels Miscellany

An easy-to-find laundromat: **Self-Service Lav-O-Net,** at 23 Rue du Marché, just around the corner from the Rue des Croisades (off the Place Rogier). For less than $2.50, you can do five kilograms of laundry.

———————————

Coming up: a high-point of your tour. From Brussels we move to colorful Italy, and to the "Eternal City"—Rome.

Chapter XI

ROME

The Arithmetic of a Roman Holiday

ROME NEEDS NO BUILD-UP in this book. A vast number of Americans saw *La Dolce Vita* and have ached to get here ever since. They won't be disappointed. The excitement of Rome has an almost physical impact as you step from the train. You immediately know that this is a capital—a pulsating center of creation and activity, whose ideas and tastes are felt round the world.

But keep in mind two very basic facts about Rome. First, this is not a city which can be covered in two or three days of touring. Rome is too large, too varied, too abundant with sights. If you're to realize anything from your stay, you must schedule several more days to it than you devoted to other comparable European towns. Second, this is not an easy city in which to keep costs down—although it doesn't approach Paris in that respect. Nevertheless, you can be clipped unmercifully if you wander by mistake into the wrong hotel or restaurant. If you're to live on $25 a day in Rome, you must set out now to orient yourself in the city. We'll start with the spot where it all begins.

1. Orientation

TERMINAL STATION: Your train will arrive in Rome at Terminal Station—a big ultra-modernistic building that's a city in itself. If you've been rumpled by the ride, then all you need do is walk downstairs to the **Albergo Diurno** "day hotel," where you'll find baths and showers, a barber shop, women's hairdresser, cleaners, and many other conveniences open seven days a week from 7:20 a.m. to 8:40 p.m.

The station can be overwhelming to a stranger so here are some hints to help orient yourself. Ticket and information windows are usually either temporarily closed or have long lines. You can save time by purchasing your train tickets at either the tiny Transalpino booth near track 22, open seven days a week from 8:30 a.m. to 9:30 p.m., or at the main Transalpino office, open Monday to Saturday from 9 a.m. to 1 p.m., at 8 Piazza Esquilino, a few hundred yards away near the Santa Maria Maggiore Church. At both offices, you'll receive quick, professional service from English-speaking personnel.

For free hotel bookings, go to the EPT-booth (Ente Provinciale Turismo) near track 4, open seven days a week from 9 a.m. to 7 p.m., or to the main EPT-office at 7 Via Parigi (a few hundred yards away, near Piazza Repubblica, next door to the Grand Hotel), open Monday to Friday from 8:30 a.m. to 1:30 p.m. and from 2 to 7 p.m. You can also obtain free maps and brochures here.

SUBWAYS AND BUSES: Rome has three subway lines. The oldest, completed nearly 30 years ago, runs from Termini Station to Ostia Lido, for 900 lire (56¢). By getting off at Ostia Antica, two stops before Ostia Lido, you'll find excavations that rival Pompeii. Ostia was a well-developed port in the days of ancient Rome during the reign of Emperor Claudius, particularly—and archaeologists are still digging in a huge area of the imperial city. Entrance to the grounds (closed Mondays) is 2,000 lire, and you can enjoy a picnic lunch while contemplating the ruins. Important: only the trains leaving Termini at 8, 9, 10 and noon stop at Ostia Antica.

The two new subway lines, A and B, were completed in 1980, after 20 years' construction. Line A goes from Via Ottaviano, near St. Peter's, via the Spanish Steps, Piazza Barberini, Piazza della Repubblica, Termini Station, Piazza Vittorio Emanuele (not the monument) and San Giovanni to Cinecittà. The B line connects Termini Station with San Paolo fuori le Mura via Via Cavour, the Colosseum, Circo Massimo and Garbatella. A one-way ticket on A and B costs 500 lire (31¢); tickets are sold at automats inside the 22 stations, and at nearby newspaper stands.

The city's green and yellow buses, some of them double deckers like the #64 that goes to the Vatican City, also charge 500 lire per ticket. Purchase them at the ATAC kiosk in front of Termini Station. No tourist tickets or one-day tickets are available, but you can save time by purchasing several tickets at once.

The plaza in front of Termini Station is a starting point for many of these green and yellow coaches: to get to the Vatican area (where we'll recommend several hotels), take bus 64, which is also marked "San Pietro." For transportation to American Express, which is just next to the Spanish Steps (a central point), take bus 77 or 78 (and get off at Largo

Goldoni). And for the Colosseum, take bus 27 or 792, changing later to bus 118 for the Baths of Caracalla. At night, the bus marked "Roma-Tivoli," (1,400 lire one-way) leaving from a little depot near the station (we'll describe its location further on), goes to the illuminated Fountains of Tivoli and the Villa d'Este—and that means that nearly all the major sights of Rome are serviced by the buses leaving from Terminal Station.

TO AND FROM THE AIRPORTS: Rome's large international **Aeroporto Leonardo da Vinci,** located 18 miles away near the Mediterranean Sea, is connected to the city air terminal at Termini Station by buses that operate 24 hours a day, running every 15 minutes from 7:15 a.m. to 9 p.m., and once an hour after that time. A one-way ticket, purchased at ticket windows, not from the driver, is 5,000 lire ($3.12). Rome's second airport, **Ciampino,** is used exclusively for charter flights and is best reached by taking subway A from Termini Station to Cinecittà (500 lire), and a bus from there (1,000 lire) to Ciampino.

2. Moderately Priced Hotels

For your rooms in Rome, we'll deal first with hotels, then with the far less expensive, usually far more attractive, pensiones.

Three areas in Rome possess most of the good budget hotels: the streets on both sides of Terminal Station; the section to the south of the Vatican; and the area in front of, and behind, the Spanish Steps (the American Express area). Each of these sections, in turn, possesses several particular hotels that star: the **Bramante** in the Vatican area; the **Albergo Frattina** near American Express (both third class); the **Y.M.C.A.** and the **Touring,** next to the station (both second class). Most of the latter, of course, are in the Big Splurge category only; from $31 to $35 for a bathless double room without breakfast, by the time all taxes and supplements are totaled up; from $17 and up for a single. But each of them is either surrounded by, or near to, other less expensive second-class establishments ($23 to $29 for a double, all included), and even less costly, but still satisfactory, third-class houses ($9 to $10 per person). Each is also the focal point for a cluster of attractive and less expensive pensiones, which we'll describe in a later and separate section of this chapter, and which provide the true budget lodgings in Rome.

THE VATICAN AREA: We'll assume, first, that you crave peace and quiet, even at the cost of being across the river from the downtown theatres and cafes. This area is, of course, the most subdued section of Rome, lovely and restful. Take bus 64 from the train station or air terminal, which comes directly here.

You'll alight at the broad boulevard, the Via della Conciliazione, which leads to St. Peter's. Fifty yards away, the **Hotel Bramante** at 24 Vicolo delle Palline (phone 654-04-26), provides the best of moderately priced lodgings in the Vatican area. The building itself is an historic one, begun in the 14th century; from the backyard garden, where breakfast is served in summer, you can see a medieval escape wall used by popes and other dignitaries to walk unseen from Vatican City to the safety of the fortress-like Castel Sant'Angelo. Today, a proud Roman named Publio Mariani, who was born

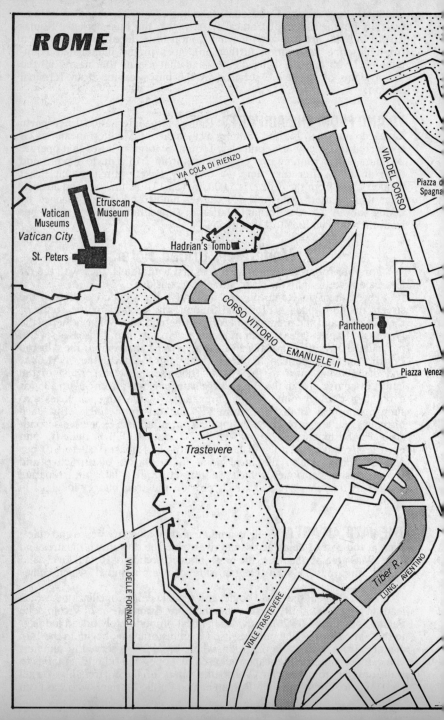

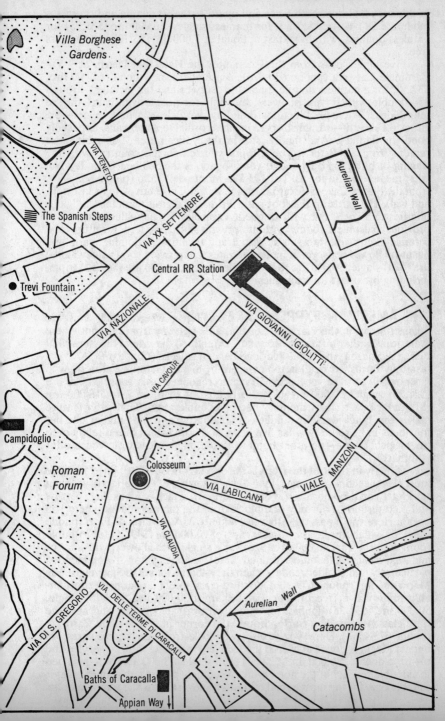

in this very building, both owns and operates the Bramante and charges a moderate 28,000 lire ($17.50) for bathless singles, 50,000 lire ($31.25) for bathless doubles, with breakfast optional at 5,000 lire ($3.12) and showers free.

Five long blocks from the Bramante, the **Hotel San Pietro,** at 9 Via Cardinale Cassetta (phone 630-876), is a modern, new hotel (60,000 lire, $37.50, for a bathless double, breakfast, service and tax included, around $50 double with private shower), but only for people with cars—they're long blocks. A crisply functional building, very clean, whose owner—Sr. Ernesto Felicetti—is English-speaking and cordial to Americans. Especially good for families. And finally, still in the Vatican area, but a bit more remote from St. Peter's (you'll think yourself in the country, with the singing of birds the only sound you'll hear), is the 300-bed **Casa Tra Noi** (that means "house for us") at 113 Via Monte del Gallo (phone 632-954); from the Piazza Cavour next to Castel S. Angelo, take bus 34 to its last stop, and walk 150 yards up the foot path. Primarily a group hotel for religious pilgrims and such, but with frequent vacancies for individuals, the Casa provides balconied rooms without private bath, modern furniture and ceramic floors, elevators and restaurant facilities, adjoining park and beautiful flower beds, yet at moderate rates that provide good value: 32,000 lire ($20) single, 56,000 lire ($35) double or twin, 76,000 lire ($47.50) triple, including breakfast for each guest.

THE AMERICAN EXPRESS AREA:

Here's where you'll find the Spanish Steps, at the Piazza di Spagna, a block away from the spot where Americans gather once a day for mail. Directly to the side of the steps, at 9 Piazza di Spagna, the **Hotel-Pensione Lago di Alleghe** (phone 679-5174) is a tastefully furnished small hotel managed by Signor Georgio Valdroni, who has pledged to offer special 1985 rates to readers of this book: 34,000 lire ($21.25) single, 50,000 lire ($31.25) double or twin, an extra 18,000 lire ($11.25) for each supplementary bed in a double room. That latter feature makes this hotel ideal for families or small groups: room number one has four beds in it, room two has five beds, and both rooms face directly onto the magical piazza—no other hotel in Rome, high-priced or low, can offer you that!

Directly in front of the steps is the swank Via Condotti, lined with the most elegant shops of Rome. If you'll walk down the Via Condotti and then turn left, you'll be on the Via Mario de Fiori, which is a bustling, narrow and picturesque street only one block from the famous square where you began. Here you'll pass the **Albergo Condotti,** 37 Via Mario de Fiori (phone 679-4769), high third class; all-year rates of 70,000 lire ($43.75) for a double room with shower, 40,000 lire ($25) for a single with shower, with service and tax included; a quiet, refined hotel, with elevator, recommended particularly to our older readers; then the **Albergo Piazza di Spagna,** 61 Via Mario de Fiori (phone 679-3061), a third-class hotel that has been considerably improved in recent years, and charges 30,000 lire ($18.75) single, 50,000 lire ($31.25) double, for rooms with private shower; and next the third-class **Albergo San Carlo,** around the corner at 93 Via delle Carrozze (phone 678-4548). Here, you're only two blocks from American Express, in budget lodgings priced at 50,000 lire ($31.25) including shower, service and tax for a double, 36,000 lire ($22.50) for a single, 18,000 lire for a third bed in a double room; but the hotel is an exceedingly plain establishment that is suitable only for the most casual of tourists; nevertheless the rooms upstairs (there's an elevator) are surprisingly better than the dreary entrance would lead you to expect. A last and much better hotel of the middle category, nearby, is the more modern, third class **Albergo Homs,** 20 feet off the Via Mario de Fiori, on the small Via della Vite (#72; phone 679-2976), 64,000 lire ($40), service and tax included, for a double room, 37,000 lire ($23.12) for a bathless single. And how well they maintain these rooms is revealed by the fact that the Homs is a particular favorite among Scandinavian and Swiss tourists! Rated in order of quality, this group of hotels would begin with the Lago di Alleghe, then continue with the Homs, followed by the Condotti, then the San Carlo.

Two other fairly simple hotels in this area are the **Albergo Frattina,** 107 Via Frattina (phone 679-2071), 35,000 lire ($21.87) single, 52,000 lire ($32.50) double, all for rooms with private shower; and the nearby **Pensione Firenze,** second floor of 7 Via Bocca del Leone (corner of Via Frattina), phone 679-86-61, managed by English-speaking Signor Parisi. 35,000 lire ($21.87) single, 64,000 lire ($40) double, breakfast included, for rooms with private shower and w.c. . . . The strange thing is that few Americans know of the existence of this hotel area, just two and three blocks below American Express.

THE ITALIAN LIRA: For the purposes of this chapter, we've converted Italian lire into dollars at the rate of 1,600 lire per dollar—the approximate "floating" rate of the lira as of the time of writing. Thus, 100 lire have been assumed to equal 6.2¢ U.S.

Atop the Spanish Steps

Still a second area in the American Express section begins at the very top of the Spanish Steps. Ascend the steps and you'll immediately spot the swank Hotel Villa Hassler, which stands at the beginning of the Via Sistina, a rather elegant shopping street. But walk down the Via Sistina for a hundred yards, and turn right into Via Francesco Crispi, where, at 49, you'll find a fairly reasonable alternative in this increasingly swanky area, in the 25-room, second-class **Hotel Elite** (phone 678-0728); in 1985, its rates for rooms with private bath (and all of them are) are 50,000 lire ($31.25) single, 75,000 lire ($46.87) double, 22,000 lire ($13.75) for supplemental beds, including continental breakfast. Perfect location, spotless rooms, professional service, all supervised with a watchful eye by the owner, Signor Maurizio, who speaks English better than most of us. Highly recommended. Next block down, the **Pensione Scalinata di Spagna,** 17 Piazza Trinità dei Monti (phone 679-3006), has added a private shower to every double room, surged in popularity and renown, and now charges 44,000 lire ($27.50) per person for bed-and-breakfast; if you do wish to stay in this trendy location, make reservations far in advance.

Various streets that run off the Via Sistina, 50 yards or so from the Spanish Steps, possess less costly third-class choices. For example, you can walk from the Via Sistina into the Via Gregoriana which, despite its exterior appearance, is one of the most fashionable streets in Rome.

Lodgings at the **Pensione Suisse,** 56 Via Gregoriana (phone 678-3649), cost 32,000 lire ($20) per person for bed-and-breakfast, 26,500 lire ($16.56) per person for a twin with private bath, 19,000 lire ($11.87) per person for a large, four-bedded family room, again including breakfast; and there's a sunny, beflowered roof garden here for relaxation, reading and letter-writing. Mrs. Jole Ciucci is the English-speaking owner, the recipient of numerous written commendations from satisfied guests, who usually remark about the particularly friendly and personal atmosphere. Signora Ciucci has been listed in this book for more than a decade, and never once in that time have I received a critical letter from any reader about her or her pensione. She enjoys her work, has a big heart, and charges reasonable rates.

Between Piazza di Spagna and Piazza del Popolo

There's a final gem of a choice available to you nearby, if the ones we've listed in this area seem packed. From the Piazza di Spagna, walk down the Via Babuino halfway to the Piazza del Popolo, then turn left down the tiny Via Laurina. At 34 Via Laurina, smack in the midst of art galleries and studios: the modern-art-filled **Hotel Margutta** (phone 679-8440), with rooms that all come equipped with private bath or shower, and yet at moderate prices that range between the second- and third-class categories (30,000 lire, $18.75, per person, double occupancy, breakfast, service, bath, and taxes included).

TERMINAL STATION AREA: Here, of course, is the most numerous concentration of hotels in Rome. We'll deal, first, with a particularly outstanding choice in the area to the right of the station, and then with an entire cluster of budget finds grouped in the area to the left. The area to the right (as you leave) is, to my mind, far more pleasant and also endowed with better budget values than you'll find on the left side of the station.

To the Right of the Station (as You Leave)

First, as you leave Terminal Station, turn right and walk three short blocks along the Via Marghera to the Via Varese and the exciting **Hotel Venezia,** 18 Via Varese (phone 494-01-01), one of the foremost stars of this book, where Mrs. Diletti (she's Swiss) has five floors and 65 rooms of an elevator building, and offers special rates to $25-a-day'ers only: 30,000 lire ($18.75) per person in a double room (breakfast, service and taxes included), 28,000 lire ($17.50) per person in a triple, 25,000 lire ($15.62) per person—breakfast and service again included—in a four-bedded room. She is a cordial lady; her hotel is kept impeccably clean; and it occupies a nice, quiet area, despite the nearness of the station.

If the Venezia can't take you (and I hope it can; this is a low-budget wonder, with brightly furnished rooms, outlets for American razors, a fresh and friendly atmosphere), then walk one short block along this excellent hotel street (the Via Varese) to a string of generally higher-priced but relatively moderate hotel-pensiones at 6, 8 and 10 Via Varese. The **Albergo Montagna,** at 10 Via Varese (phone 495-3329), leads the trio, with its peaceful inner courtyard dotted with chairs and umbrella-topped tables, its carpeting on marble steps, and rates of 55,000 lire ($34.37) for a bathless double, two breakfasts included, which are then discounted by 10% to bearers of this book. The **Hotel Select** (phone 49-11-37), next door at 6 Via

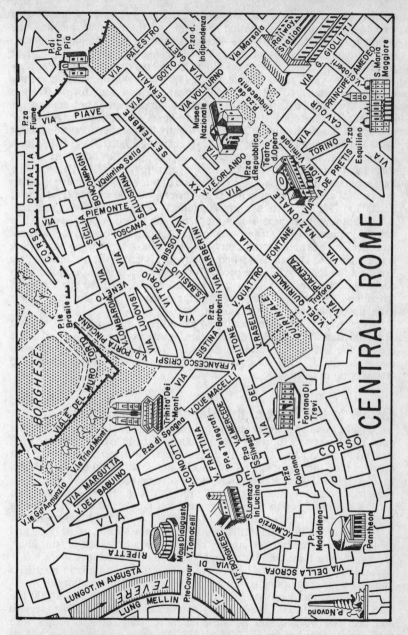

Varese has bathless doubles for 50,000 lire ($31.25) with breakfast, service and taxes included, and the **Hotel Astoria Garden** (phone 49-53-653) at 8, charging 33,000 lire ($20.62) single without bath, 75,000 lire ($46.87) double with bath, breakfast and service included, are of the same high quality, peaceful variety (all with inner gardens, polite old porters dozing next to softly tuned-in television sets), and all three establishments—the Montagna, Select, and Astoria—are particularly recommended by me to older budget tourists, although readers of any age should first seek space at the Hotel Venezia. Finally, you might like to seek space at the **Pensione Varese** at 26 Via Varese (phone 495-2694), whose 40 rooms are currently owned and managed by the Fanelli brothers, and rent for 46,000 lire ($28.75), without bath, but with breakfast, service, free showers and tax included. The fratelli Fanelli lived for 16 years in Melbourne, Australia, and speak Aussie-English. Or try the slightly lower-priced **Pensione Ascot** at 22 Via Montebello (phone 474-1675), charging 35,000 lire ($21.87) for a double, including free showers, service and tax, but not breakfast. A few steps away, on the third floor (there is an elevator) of 34 Via Palestro, the **Pensione Danubio** (phone 474-3608), is one of our best recommendations in this central area, not merely for its low prices—20,000 lire ($12.50) single, 33,000 lire ($20.62) twin, breakfast included—but because it's organized in a way that few Roman pensiones are: a bulletin board displays worthwhile details on museums and transportation; a city map is provided the moment you check in; bus and metro tickets are sold at the desk; evening babysitting is available; and laundry is washed, dried and folded on the premises (7,000 lire for a full load). All this is probably due to Patricia (from London, with cockney accent and all), wife of proprietor Mario; because she's anxious that female guests feel safe, she bars the pensione, so she says, to male chauvinists, playboys and Casanovas. Drat!

Now is as good a time as any to repeat that this area to the right of Terminal Station (as you leave the station) is infinitely to be preferred to the area to the left of the station; it's quieter, less hot and dusty, and more budget-oriented, with several of the cheapest trattorias (family-owned restaurants) in town.

Farther to the Right of the Station (as You Leave)

Again as you leave the main entrance of Terminal Station, turn right onto the street that borders the big plaza in front of the station, walk straight ahead on that street, along the plaza, until you come to the first turning, then turn right again for a block, and you'll be on the little Piazza Indipendenza. There, at 23c Piazza Indipendenza (phone 464-921), stands a modern, seven-story building housing the **Y.M.C.A. Hotel**—but it's not a "Y," it's a hotel, open to men, women and families alike, and offering moderately priced values. In addition to its 110 rooms, the hotel operates a large restaurant downstairs (12,000 lire for minestrone, roast veal and spinach, cheese, fruit or ice cream; 5,000 lire for a breakfast of fruit juice, an egg, rolls or toast with butter and coffee), an even cheaper snack bar, a gym, sauna, TV lounge, a huge lobby with interesting bulletin boards, a billiards room, ping pong room, and a play area for little children!

Rooms without private bath or shower rent at the Y for 30,000 lire ($18.75) single, 52,000 lire ($32.50) double, including breakfast, service and tax. For women and families, the hotel rents double rooms with semi-private showers for 62,000 lire ($38.75), again with breakfast and all else included. And for families, the hotel disposes of several "apartments," which consist of two double rooms, an anteroom, a private bath and a toilet, and which rent—total—for 130,000 lire ($81.25) a night. To obtain any of these accommodations, particularly in summer, write well ahead for reservations, or phone the number given above upon your arrival in Rome; the Y hotel is always heavily booked.

If the Y is full, look across the square to the crumbling, unattractive façade of the **Hotel Salus,** 13 Piazza Indipendenza (phone 495-0044); swallow hard as you recall that key rule of budget travel, "disregard the façade of hotels"; walk inside; and voilà! (or *ecco!*), there's a relatively modern interior with a good lounge (sporting an Italian TV set), and large, clean (if undecorated) rooms renting for 36,000 lire ($22.50) double, 26,000 lire ($16.25) single, not including breakfast, which is 4,500 lire more.

In the same area, at 31 Via Castelfidardo, **Pensione Asmara** (phone 474-2894) may not impress you from the outside but the prices of the impeccably clean rooms on the third and fifth floors certainly will. Twins are 30,000 lire ($18.75); additional beds 14,000 lire ($8.75); showers are free; and the amiable owner, Signora Silva Mantovani, speaks English quite well and will kindly give you a house key if you plan to come home late.

To the Left of the Station (as You Leave)

There are other budget hotels on the other side of the station, although these tend to be more expensive and less desirable than the hotels and pensions we've listed for the above area (see our pension descriptions further on). As you leave the main entrance, this time turn left, and you'll immediately see a number of expensive first-class establishments: the **Hotel Mediterraneo,** the **Massimo D'Azeglio.** But avoid those. Keep walking to the streets behind these edifices, and you'll find whole clusters of second- and third-class choices.

In this area, the best of the second-class hotels are the big **Albergo Nord Nuova Roma,** 3 Via Giovanni Amendola (phone 465-441), which has 180 rooms, and the magnificently furnished **Hotel Diana,** 4 Via Principe Amedeo (phone 475-1541), both listed here only for the purpose of warning you that virtually every room in these supposedly second-class structures has now been equipped with private bath, and thus soars way outside our price range. (When you glimpse the spectacular interior of the Diana particularly, you'll share my own regret over this bit of progress). Only several doors away from the Diana, however, at 34 Via Principe Amedeo, is a more moderately priced and yet thoroughly reliable second-class establishment called the **Albergo Touring** (phone 465-351), whose fairly small and plain lobby is no indication at all of the quite serviceable rooms it offers upstairs. A capable management offers prices of 58,000 lire ($36.25), taxes and service included, for a twin-bedded room without bath; but better still, the Touring operates a much plainer hotel called the **Annex** at 2 Via Principe Amedeo (phone 471-911), charging 26,000 lire ($16.25) single, 43,000 lire ($26.87) for a bathless double, including service and tax. Both the main building and the annex are recommended by me.

A far less expensive alternative to the Touring, and only one block from the station, is **Albergo Termini** at 77 Via G. Amendola (phone 46-36-67); its refreshingly low hotel rates are 30,000 lire ($18.75) for a double room, 18,000 lire ($11.25) single, but without breakfast (although free showers are included).

And Elsewhere

Want a room near the Colosseum? Try the fourth-class **Albergo Perugia,** 7 Via del Colosseo (phone 679-7200), where the most expensive bathless double room runs about 22,000 lire ($13.75) per person per night, but not with breakfast, and where the Roman Forum is only a short distance away.

Or, if you prefer rooms with bath, the most economical choice in this same very historical area is the **Hotel Alba,** 12 Via Leonina (phone 48-44-71), at the corner of Via Cavour. Twenty-five rooms, spread over three floors, are all well-kept by the owners—three charming brothers, Quirino, Giulio, and Romeo—who have graced the walls of the house with their collection of art by young Roman painters. A twin room here, with breakfast included, is 33,000 lire ($20.62) per person.

READERS' HOTEL SELECTIONS: "**Pensione Adriatic,** 25 Via G. Vitelleschi (phone 656-9668), can be reached by taking bus 64 from the main train station. (When you get off at the end of the line on Borgo Sant'Angelo right near St. Peter's, you go under a portal, continue on Via Porta Castello until you reach the main intersection with Via G. Vitelleschi and turn left.) Here, double rooms are only 30,000 lire (10,000 more with bath), single rooms without bath 20,000 lire, with service and tax included. And Lanfranco Mencucci, the proprietor, his wife, and son Marino, take great pride in their hotel and see to it that the rooms and bathrooms are kept clean and attractive. We make frequent trips to Rome, and will continue to stay at the Adriatic because the Mencucci family always makes us feel at home" (Judy Scarpella-Walls, Bowling Green, Kentucky). . . . "One wonderful hotel no one in your book mentioned was the **Memphis,** at 36a Via Avignonesi (phone 485-849), on a narrow street near the Piazza Barberini (we were told about it by a Danish family over lunch one day). We went and looked it over. A double room *with* private shower, breakfast, service and taxes included, is 60,000 lire ($37.50). Clean as a pin, with a small lobby and elevator. She said it would be cheaper out of season and by the week" (Mrs. Howell Evans, Nashville, Tenn., plus recommendations from other readers as well, who point out that all rooms here have private shower and toilet, and rent for 35,000 lire ($21.87) single, 60,000 lire double, breakfast, service and tax included). . . . "I want to recommend highly the **Pensione Cristallo,** 114 Via Montebello (phone 475-9810), where bed alone in a very clean double room was 13,500 lire per person. The Cristallo is in the station area. Signora Maria Boccone, the proprietress, treated us like her own children; she helped us plan our sightseeing in Rome, and a trip to Greece. When we decided to hitchhike to Brindisi, she not only planned the best route for us, but held all our extra clothing and luggage free of charge" (Judith De Leo, Brooklyn, New York). . . . "**Hotel Pincio,** 50 Via Capo le Case, phone 679-1233, located between Via del Tritone and the Spanish Steps, definitely deserves to be recommended. Its owners, Renato Carosi and his wife Olga, have spent quite a few years in England, so there is absolutely no language barrier. Rates, which include breakfast, are single 27,000 lire, double 51,000 lire, breakfast included" (Mrs. Karen L. Prisco, Bogota, New Jersey).

THE BIG SPLURGE: A bright, young Italian named Guido Agnolucci and an American named Marvin Hare teamed up some years ago to open a pension in Rome that would cater to the thoughtful tourist—people anxious to absorb the highest cultural lessons of the city. To give their establishment a name no one would ever forget, they called it the **Pensione Texas.** You'll realize how perfectly inappropriate that monicker is when you enter this tastefully decorated, duplex apartment at 47 Via Firenze (phone 485-627), just two short blocks from the important Via Nazionale. Whenever 6 p.m. approached last summer, Hope and I felt a genuine urge to rush back to the Texas to hear the exciting conversation that fills the cocktail-lounge of the pension (our fellow guests, among others: a member of the Minneapolis Symphony, and his wife; a professor from the Nationalist Chinese University on Taiwan). How much for all this culture, comfort and charm?

Forty-two thousand lire ($26.25) per person for a bathless room (that's for one of the Texas's several budget rooms), *with* breakfast and one other large meal (demi-pension), taxes and service included, at the height of the summer season—an excellent value, justifying this just-once departure from normal budget limits. A few years ago the Texas took over the **Pensione Seven Hills** (phone 484-846), downstairs in the same building, where they offer the same demi-pension arrangements (that is, bed and two meals) for 42,000 lire ($26.25) per person in twin-bedded rooms without bath, tax and service included. Guests at the Seven Hills—which is operated with punctilious care, in the manner you'd expect from Messrs. Hare and Agnolucci—are permitted to use the cocktail lounge of the Texas, upstairs. Rooms with bath are also available, as are increasingly frequent offers of a bathless room with breakfast only—no other meal—for 50,500 lire ($31.56) per person. Next door to the Texas, at 38 Via Firenze (phone 460-368), the **Pensione Americana Nardizzi** is less insistent on the demi-pension requirement, asks 50,000 lire ($31.25) double without bath, 60,000 lire ($37.50) with shower, including breakfast, service and tax in each case, all for large and well-furnished rooms enjoying a nice view over Rome. Signor Nardizzi speaks English well, and will treat you like a V.I.P. if you're a user of this book. In the same building (38 Via Firenze), **Pensione Oceania** (phone 475-0696), managed by Armando and Luisa Loreti, a very friendly husband-and-wife team (Armando speaks some English), rents 12 impeccably clean rooms. Singles with shower and w.c. for 40,000 lire ($25); doubles without bath, 57,000 lire ($35.62); doubles with shower, 72,000 lire ($45); doubles with shower and w.c., 77,000 lire ($48.12); 22,000 lire per bed for third and fourth beds (if you need one of these, ask for the largest room, 8); breakfast is always included in the price. And the name "Oceania"? It reflects the sympathies of the Loretis for Australians and New Zealanders, who often find their way here.

One of the most modern budget hotels in Rome, **Albergo Villafranca,** 9 Via Villafranca (phone 491-152), enjoys a location close to Terminal Station and the air terminal. Leaving the station at the side entrance facing Via Marsala, walk up Via Vicenza: Via Villafranca is the fifth street going left. This huge, six-floor, 140-bed, elevator-equipped establishment is managed by Signor Salvatore Schifano, who speaks excellent English. His offerings: single rooms for 32,000 lire ($20); doubles or twins 55,000 lire ($34.37); triple rooms 75,000 lire ($46.87); quadruple rooms 88,000 lire ($55); breakfast included; showers free. On clear days, one has a beautiful panoramic view of the Castelli Romani area from the roof garden, where you can sit and relax and drink a Coke or a small bottle of wine (2,500 lire each). And on not so clear days, you may want to sip an excellent dry martini at the well-stocked cocktail bar (near the reception desk and the restaurant, where three-course meals cost 18,000 lire, wine included). An alternative to the Villafranca if the latter is full, and located just around the corner from it, is the even more modern **Hotel Canada** at 58 Via Vicenza (phone 49-57-85). Although its 1985 bed-and-breakfast rates will be 38,000 lire ($23.75) for singles, 60,000 lire ($37.50) for doubles or twins, 69,000 lire ($43.12) for triples, 85,000 lire ($53.12) for quads, owner Signor Pucci has promised a 10% discount from these rates to bearers of this book in 1985, thereby placing the Canada just about on a par with prices of the Villafranca.

Now we move to a category of generally less expensive accommodations:

3. Roman Pensiones

The Roman pensione is always on the upper floor of an apartment house or office building and is apt to have surprisingly large and comfortable rooms. For the "king" of pensions, turn to "The Big Splurge," and read about the **Texas.** For the best of the lower-priced establishments, walk one long avenue block from Terminal Station to the Piazza Repubblica, the site of a lovely fountain—the Fountains of Esedra—which are beautifully illuminated at night. The business building at 47 Piazza Repubblica houses four particularly good pensions.

On the third floor is the **Pensione Esedra** (phone 463-912), best of the four, whose manageress is the genial and lady-like Mrs. Moretti. She does not require that you take meals. Her prices for 1985 will be 19,000 lire ($11.87) for her only single room, all taxes and service included, 18,000 lire ($11.25) per person for a double, including a continental breakfast, 2,000 lire for a bath, 1,600 lire for a shower. Despite the location of this pension on a busy plaza, it is remarkably quiet—and the rooms are as comfortable as you'd wish. In certain front locations, you'll want to lie abed for hours, simply watching the lights play on the dramatic Fountains of Esedra.

In the same building as the Pensione Esedra (same address, second floor), the **Pensione Terminus** (phone 461-505), is somewhat more commercial in aspect, and higher in price, but offers especially large rooms and comfortable public facilities. Just before presstime, the management wrote that "in view of [our] preference for American tourists," they would abide by the following reduced prices for anyone flashing them a copy of this book on registering and staying for five nights or more: double rooms for 21,000 lire ($14.37) per person, including breakfast, service and taxes; triples for 19,000 lire ($11.87) per person. There's an ornate large dining room in which you'll take the morning meal, and the food is prepared with care. . . . Cheaper, of lesser standard, and one floor higher up, is Signor Imperoli's **Pensione Eureka** (phone 47-55806), where—if you don't mind no-frills accommodations and plain surroundings—you'll pay only 22,500 lire ($14.06) single, 32,000 lire ($20) for twins, 40,000 lire ($25) for triples, 48,000 lire ($30) for a large room with five cots. All prices include continental breakfast, served in a dining room seemingly the size of a football field and with a full view of the Esedra Fountain. Finally, if the first three pensions of 47 Piazza Esedra are full, you'll want to go upstairs (top floor) to the **Pensione Wetzler** (phone 475-1994) of "Mama Clara," charging 15,000 lire ($9.37) per person for dorm-type rooms of two to four cots apiece. Mama Clara has been applying her warm personal touch to the Pensione Wetzler since 1960, which helps one to overlook the rather basic furnishings. Ask to have a glimpse of the roof garden where she maintains various plants, including lemon and orange trees set in old bathtubs. Mama Clara will allow guests to dry laundry there or to take photographs that use the lovely skyline of Rome as backdrop.

Off the Piazza della Repubblica

Just next to the building that houses the pensions Esedra, Terminus, Eureka and Wetzler, around the corner, you'll find the beginning of the important Via Nazionale, which sweeps downhill for several hundred yards. All along its length, but particularly near the Piazza della Repubblica, are inexpensive pensions. At 13 Via Nazionale, my favorite is the

Pensione Millefiori (phone 475-0108), on the third floor, operated by charming Signora Nedda Santi, who speaks English well and French and Arabic perfectly (she managed a hotel in Alexandria, Egypt, before moving to Rome many years ago), and charges 42,000 lire ($26.25) for a bathless double, including breakfast; some of her 12 rooms have three or four beds, for which she adds a supplement of 15,000 lire ($9.37) per bed. The building itself is almost next door to St. Paul's Within the Walls, Rome's American Episcopal church.

If the Millefiori is full, then you might try, three blocks to the side of Piazza della Repubblica (take bus 64 from Terminal Station and get off at the third stop), the much-higher-priced **Pensione Hannover,** 4 Via XX Settembre (phone 461-162), which offers on-season prices to readers of this book only, of exactly 38,000 lire ($23.75) per person for room and breakfast, service and taxes included, and has unusually quiet rooms, some of which overlook the stately Prince Barberini Gardens, and all of which enjoy a distant view of St. Peter's. The owner, Mr. Richard Hernes (who was born in Poland), speaks excellent English. You ought to know, too, that the clientele often includes Protestant church groups from the U.S.—which should give you an idea of its character. Well-recommended for older readers.

In the American Express—Spanish Steps Area

Here, the unhesitating choice is the warm and friendly **Pensione Erdarelli,** 28 Via Due Macelli (phone 679-1265), whose five floors have just been freshly redecorated, yet without a significant increase in rates, which are special to readers of this book: 30,000 lire ($18.75) per person, breakfast, service and taxes included, in a double room; 35,000 lire ($21.87) in a single, and no insistence at all on taking meals other than breakfast. The pension is only two short blocks from the Spanish Steps; all rooms are brightly and colorfully furnished, some have balconies, all have telephones, the building is elevator-equipped, and the Italian family who operate the pension (and place fresh flowers everywhere) are a sheer delight. Run, do not walk.

Across the Tiber

On the Vatican side of the Tiber, far from the hustle of downtown, the second class **Pensione Fabrello-White** (phone 360-44-46) is a thoroughly refined pension, which stands in a quiet location, on the third floor (via elevator) of an old ducal palace at 11 Via Vittoria Colonna. Its charges— quite moderate for such a cultivated atmosphere, and always including breakfast—are 33,000 lire ($20.62) single, 28,000 lire ($17.50) per person double, only 25,000 lire ($15.62) per person quad. Signor Renato Marchi is the amiable, English-speaking owner; his terrace breakfast room affords a panoramic view of Rome's skyline, including the Trinità dei Monti church atop the Spanish Steps.

Via Veneto and Elsewhere

A pension on the swank Via Veneto? I've scoured this lush, expensive area of Rome and, much to my own surprise, found two moderately priced pensions on my last visit. One is at 24 Via Sicilia, a side street tucked away from the activity of the Via Veneto, where the **Pensione Sicilia-Daria** (phone 493-841) offers rooms all equipped with private bath or shower, heavily decorated with bric-a-brac and Italian antiques, with plants and pictures everywhere. A gracious English-speaking manageress is in charge. The rooms themselves are rather small, but they are all with private bath and rent for 60,000 lire ($37.50) single, 90,000 lire ($56.25) double, including breakfast, service and tax, which are astonishing prices by the $100-a-night (and up) standards of the Via Veneto, just steps away. There's a not terribly attractive entrance to the building, but a good, modern elevator, and older readers should be well pleased with both the location and the amenities.

The most numerous collection of pensions? They're on the Via Principe Amedeo, between the Via Gioberti and the Via Cavour—at least 30 of them (eight alone are in the building at 9 Principe Amedeo), the best being the four establishments in 76 Via Principe Amedeo, followed by those at 62, 67 and 79. Try, for instance, Signora Regina Charles' **Pensione Tony,** 79d Via Principe Amedeo (phone 736-994), charging 17,500 lire ($10.93) single, 23,000 lire ($14.37) double, 28,000 lire ($17.50) double with private shower. Or try the **Pensione Giorgina** next door at 67 Via Principe Amedeo (phone 476-118), fourth floor, where large doubles are 32,000 lire, triples 38,000 lire, 4-bedded rooms 44,000 lire. That's only a block from the railroad station (to the left, as you exit from the main entrance) and you'll have to shop around to find a pension that suits you.

PENSIONS SEEKING MENTION: "The coming season will be my twenty-second as owner-director of **Forti's Guest House,** 7 Via Fornovo, corner Via Cosseria (phone 382-431). Already recommended by the American, Belgian, German, Norwegian, Greek and Portuguese automobile clubs, our pensione is regularly used by the South African, Japanese and Pakistan embassies to host newly assigned personnel and their families until they find permanent housing. The American, Australian and Nigerian embassies have also sent official representatives and nationals desiring comfortable, quiet, economical accommodations in clean family atmosphere. Basic prices are: 23,000 lire for a single with continental breakfast, 40,000 for a double with breakfast, 50,000 for full pension. All prices include service and tax. We also have several triple rooms from 55,000 including breakfast, for three persons. Our location is excellent. Via Cosseria is a private street with ample free parking only one block from the Tiber (on the Vatican side) between Viale Giulio Cesare and Viale delle Milizie in Prati. We are only 20 yards from bus lines leading to Termini (99 and 78), Via del Corso and Caracalla (90) and about 50 yards from the line 30 for St. Peter's and the Vatican museums. We are in a quiet residential area removed from the noise and the confusion of downtown Rome, yet only minutes from all historic and scenic points of interest" (Charles Cabell, Rome, Italy; note from AF: Forti's can now also be reached by taking the A subway line from Termini Station to the Lepanto stop).

READERS' PENSION SELECTIONS (NEAR TERMINI STATION): "**Locanda Lazioli,** on the third floor of 33 Via Quintino Sella (phone 465-227), offers everything you could want in a low-cost lodging (including free elevator and advice and assistance from Signora de Santi), and rates of only 14,000 lire per person per night in double or triple rooms, plus 3,000 lire for breakfast. Five minutes from the Central Station" (Kaulesh B. Shah, Bombay, India; warmly seconded by Sandra Leana, Freeport, Grand Bahama). . . . "**Locanda Aurora,** 39 Via Magenta (phone 495-7613), two blocks from the railroad station, was the cleanest and most comfortable of our travels, and its proprietors—Mr. and Mrs. Gigliesi—the most cordial. Twenty-eight thousand lire ($17.50) for a double room" (Mr. and Mrs. Paul Sieczkowski, Omaha, Nebraska, seconded by Catherine Ronconi, San Lorenzo, California, and by Mr. and Mrs. Gary Goldetsky, Minneapolis, Minnesota). . . . "We're enthusiastic about the home of **Signora Antonelli,** 20 Via Quintino Sella, telephone 460-617, where the 1985 charge is only 15,000 lire ($9.37) per person in a double, 18,000 lire ($11.25) in a single. Look for 'scala A, interno 9.' In Rome, which has become increasingly expensive, we managed to stay under $15 a day" (John Reynolds, East Orange, New Jersey; note by AF: this "Affittacamere" is centrally located, in the area between Piazza della Repubblica and Via Veneto). . . . "The owners of the **Pensione Sonya,** at 58 Via Viminale (telephone 475-9911), are a wonderful family named Velletrani, who treat you as one of them. Their pension is immaculately clean, well-located (near the station), and close to buses. . . . These people were so terrific I had to leave Rome. They didn't tell you where the bus stop was, they *walked* you to it. And one day, when I was going to the beach for the day (Lido, according to your instructions), they packed an unbelievable lunch for me and my Japanese friend! Their token of hospitality! Price was 28,000 lire, single, with everything (breakfast, tax and service) included. Running water and bidet in the room, bathrooms available very close by" (Irma Mitchell, Sherman Oaks, California). . . . "I would strongly recommend the **Pensione Andreotti,** at 55 Via Castelfidardo, phone 483-553, just three short blocks to the right of Termini Station, on the first three floors of the building, with 36 rooms, and free showers on every floor. 1985 rates will be: singles 30,000 lire, doubles 42,000 lire, breakfast 5,000 lire. Mr. and Mrs. Andreotti speak English and treat everyone like family" (Jacqelyn J. Vollmer, Jacksonville, Florida). . . . "At the **Pensione Assisi,** 27a Via dei Mille (phone 49-53-813), double rooms in 1985 are priced at only 32,000 lire ($20), but without breakfast. As you leave the right side of Terminal Station, turn right and walk for one block, then turn left on the Via Milazzo and walk for two blocks. The pensione is over a grocery store" (Philip S. Mayer, Indianapolis, Indiana). . . . "At the **Pensione Primerose,** 104 Via Montebello (phone 474-3393), we had an unbelievably large and clean room, in especially quiet surroundings (eight rooms look out on a quiet convent garden), yet only four short blocks from the train station—turn right as you leave the station to the first main street, then left two blocks. Twin rooms rent for only 30,000 lire ($18.75), multi-bedded rooms for only 13,500 lire ($8.43) per person, breakfast (optional) is 4,500 lire extra, showers are free, but there are no single rooms. Reception desk is on the second floor, reached by a 50-lire coin elevator" (Marilyn Bakken, Seattle, Washington).

READER'S PENSIONE SELECTION (NEAR PIAZZA NAVONA): "**Pensione Lunetta,** 68 Piazza del Paradiso (phone 656-1080), is very plain, but offers an unbeatable Roman atmosphere, and is quite inexpensive: 26,000 lire for twins ($16.25), 37,000 lire ($23.12) for triples, 48,000 lire ($30) for quads, but without breakfast. Showers, however, are free" (Jamie Newland, Leamington, Ontario, Canada).

GET THEE TO A NUNNERY: There is yet a third type of accommodation

available to you in this city, in the form of convent quarters—and I am utterly serious. Several religious orders in Rome help support themselves by taking paying guests. Several others do so merely to be of service. In both instances, the rooms offered are spotlessly clean and proper, and the prices charged for room and all three meals are almost within our limits. Families, particularly, should give these a try.

To illustrate: in the area of the Vatican, where numerous such institutions abound, a convent known as the **Casa N.S. di Fatima,** 4a Via Gianicolo (phone 654-3349), charges 38,000 lire ($23.75) for room and all three meals, 36,000 lire ($22.50) for room and two meals, but boards women and families only, for whom it has nearly 60 beds. Highly recommended (but with a 10:30 p.m. curfew); take bus 64 from the railroad station to Ponte Vittorio (at the side of St. Peter's) and walk from there. Nearer to the Vatican than the above-named is the convent of the English-speaking **Franciscan Sisters of the Atonement** (from Graymoor, New York), 105 Via Monte del Gallo (phone 63-08-72), charging 30,000 lire

($18.75) per person for room and all three meals ("full pension") in the summer of 1985; location is to the left of, and behind, St. Peter's on a steep hill—again best for readers with cars, but also reachable by bus 34 from Piazza Cavour. Nearby, the **Sisters of the Immaculate Conception** at 38 Via Monte del Gallo (phone 630-863) charge 34,000 lire ($21.25) per person for room and two meals a day, but do not speak English. They have singles, doubles and triples—a total of 80 beds—but also impose an 11:30 p.m. curfew. A final and much more expensive convent-run establishment is the well-located **Foyer Unitas Casa** (operated by the Dutch order known as the Ladies of Bethany, particularly for non-Catholic visitors to Rome), which has space for about 24 guests at 26,000 lire ($16.25) per person for bed and breakfast, in the Pamphili Palace (elevator to fourth floor) on the Piazza Navona, entrance at 30 Via di S. Maria dell' Anima, phone 656-5951 or 654-1618. True to their birthplace, the sisters offer large Dutch breakfasts (cheeses, jams, good crusty rolls) and particularly spacious and well-furnished rooms. It's not at all necessary to have a private bath, as all showers and public bathrooms are sparkling clean and always available. Closed during some summer weeks; best write ahead for reservations.

READER'S CONVENT SELECTION: "**Istituto Piccole Suore Sacra Famiglia,** 92 Viale Vaticano (phone 319-572), almost opposite the entrance to the Sistine Chapel, is run by nuns and reasonably priced at 16,000 lire ($10) per person per night" (Mrs. Willard Rhodes, Highland, New York).

A READER'S SELECTION FOR GROUPS: "I made my nth trip to Italy this summer as chaperone to high school students. We stayed at the **Centro Universitario Marianum,** near the Church of St. John Lateran (30 Via Matteo Boiardo, phone 757-4241). Immaculate rooms with toilet facilities, shower, spacious atmosphere, friendly personnel—and the food! Not once were we able to eat all that was offered! And good! All for 25,000 lire ($15.62) per person per day, including all three meals" (Mary Ferro, New Haven, Connecticut; note by AF: Marianum is under religious auspices, but accepts groups of any kind, with no questions as to religion asked).

STUDENT IN ROME: For you, the street to seek out is the Via Palestro, several short blocks to the right of Terminal Station, as you leave it, traditionally the site of Italy's official student organization, including the new **Relazioni Universitarie** organization at 11 Via Palestro (phone 47-55-265); "R.U." currently performs many of Italy's student travel functions, including the selling of student charter flights, and will assist arriving student travelers to find low-cost rooms, meals and tours in Rome. This fairly quiet thoroughfare has known so many student travelers over the years that pensions along it (and there are many of them) have specialized in offering rates as low as 11,000 lire ($6.87) per person per night, sometimes by creating multi-bedded rooms. Numerous Via Palestro pensions will, in fact, charge 11,000 lire ($6.87) and less in 1985: among them, try the cordial and English-speaking **Student Home Michele,** 35 Via Palestro (phone 474-3383), 10,000 lire per person, and management by a friendly brother-and-sister team; the **Locanda Bolognese,** 15 Via Palestro (phone 485-848), doubles for 11,500 lire ($7.19) per person, singles for 13,000 lire; **Locanda Marini,** 35 Via Palestro (phone 482-333), only 10,000 lire per person.

If you'd prefer an actual student hotel, then try phoning the important youth hostel called **Ostello per la Gioventù del Foro Italico,** 61 Viale Olimpiadi (phone 396-4709), on the Lungotevere Maresciallo Cadorna

(Piazza Maresciallo Giardino), with its 25 dormitories and 18 bedrooms (men on the ground floor, girls upstairs), where everyone pays 11,000 lire per night (sheets, hot water, showers and breakfast included), 8,000 lire for lunch or dinner. At the Ostello, you'll need an International Youth Hostel Card, but they'll sell you one on the spot for 26,000 lire.

For extremely cheap student meals in Rome, the modern **University Mensa,** Via Cesare de Lollis 20, is officially open to Italian students of Rome University only, but since the limitations aren't always observed, you might try one of their 1,300 lire (81¢) menus, three courses with beverage. Open Monday through Saturday from 11:45 a.m. to 2:45 p.m. and from 6:45 to 9:45 p.m., the Mensa offers two choices of meals, posted on a board, for which tokens are sold next to the entrance. Adjoining the Mensa is a Cafeteria, definitely open to all, selling sandwiches for 800 lire, salads for 1,200 lire. Take bus 492 or 115 from Termini Station, asking the driver to drop you off at the Casa dello Studente stop, after a five-minute drive; or walk there: from Termini Station, first up Via Marsala to Piazzale Sisto V, then along Via dei Ramni, which, after a few hundred yards, leads into Via Cesare de Lollis (the total walk will require about 20 minutes).

4. Starvation Budget

You won't be many days in Rome before you hear talk of a 184-room hotel called the **Albergo del Popolo** "Hotel of the People," which charges only 12,000 lire a night ($7.50) per person for single—that's right, single—rooms (and it rents only singles). The Popolo happens to be one of those amazing European establishments which is nominally under the auspices of a charitable organization (in this case, the Salvation Army), but is maintained as a normal tourist hotel, with nothing charitable about it—the Mission hotels in Scandinavia are of the same type. Although it is located in a workingmen's quarter of Rome, at 41 Via Apuli (phone 49-19-39 or 49-05-58), just off the Via Scalo San Lorenzo (behind Terminal Station), the hotel is a modern and quite pleasant building that was erected only a few years ago, and that sports a peaceful garden.

For years, the del Popolo has accepted male tourists only, but recently it opened a small next-door annex at 39 Via Apuli accepting women at a charge of only 7,000 lire ($4.37) per night in tiny cubicles containing a cot apiece; a similar annex at 40 Via Apuli accommodates men for only 6,000 lire ($3.75), but in dorms; both annexes are closed for cleaning from 9 a.m. to 3 p.m. Even in the men-only section, the del Popolo is a thoroughly proper and well-maintained tourist hotel, whose 12,000 lire rates for privacy-affording single rooms make it one of the best starvation budget finds of this book. From Terminal Station, take bus 415 or 492, and ask the conductor to let you off at the Quartiere San Lorenzo. Or, if you'd prefer to walk from Terminal Station (bearing in mind that it is a *long* walk), leave the station at the Marsala exit, walk up Via Marsala for half a mile, crossing the medieval triple-arch into Via di Porta San Lorenzo (the street with the long Roman brick wall), passing the round tower with the external stairway. The fourth street after this tower, turning right, is Via dei Marsi, and Via Apuli is the second street on your right. This is a substantial stroll (about 25 minutes), but an easily followed route. You will, I think, find it edifying and exciting to live in a typical quarter of Rome, where tourists rarely go.

Starvation budget pensions? They're found in the streets to the immediate right and left of Terminal Station, particularly on the Via Palestro (which is lined with them), the Via Montebello, and the Via

Principe Amedeo (where there are nearly two dozen). On the latter street, I particularly like the **Soggiorno Cortorillo,** 79a Via Principe Amedeo (phone 731-6064), where if you're lucky, you can get one of the large single rooms (with a picture window and sink with three faucets—hot, cold and specially chilled) for 18,000 lire, a double for 13,000 lire per person. Breakfast will be brought to your room by Signora Cortorillo—a warm gracious lady who speaks not a word of English—for another 4,500 lire, and you'll be lucky to finish it. Take the stairs on the right side of the building to the fifth floor. Other pensions in the same building—such as **Aldo Pezzotti's** on the second floor (phone 73-11-561, and take the stairs to your left)— charge 14,000 lire per person in a double room, only 17,000 lire single.

READERS-ON-THE-STARVATION BUDGET: "For only 10,000 lire ($6.25) per person in a double, 8,000 lire ($5) in a four-bedded room, you'll be given spacious, clean accommodations at Signor and Signora Rossi's **Locanda Otello,** 13 Via Marghera (phone 490-383), fourth floor, half-a-block from the side entrance to the central train station" (Hiroko Ishikawa, Tokyo, Japan; with seconding recommendations from Mary Scent, Melbourne Beach, Florida; Fausto Trubano, Natick, Massachusetts; and Ruth Ann Kelleher, Canal Zone, Panama). . . . "We frequently travel to Rome and always stay at the 15-room **Pensione Di Rienzo** for 15,000 lire ($9.37) per person. That's at 79a Via Principe Amedeo (phone 73-48-74), two blocks from the station; Mr. Di Rienzo speaks some English" (Lorraine Callahan and Carole Ann Murphy, New York City, New York). . . . "I paid only 12,000 lire ($7.50) for a single room at a pension called **'Tina'** at 13 Via Magenta, phone 49-55-297, near Terminal Station. While this is a basic place, which does not include breakfast in the price (which is set at only 11,000 lire ($6.87) per person for a double room), the location is central, there's no curfew, and the young owner is a friendly chap who speaks excellent English" (D. J. Ames, Highton, Victoria, Australia).

5. Low-Cost Restaurants

Rome is a difficult town in which to find budget restaurants. There are only three small areas in this entire large city where you'll discover anything resembling a cluster of good, low-cost eating spots. But there are, in addition, a number of isolated budget restaurants; and there are, finally, the unique stand-up counter establishments called "Rosticcerias-Tavola Calda." We'll start with the cheapest of the cheap, and then gradually ascend in price.

THE BUDGET AREAS: Of these there are several—we'll deal with them in roughly ascending order of cost:

To the Right of Terminal Station (as You Leave)

The largest cluster, and the very cheapest, of Rome's budget restaurants is found in the streets in the area to the immediate right of Terminal Station, as you exit from the station. **Ristorante da Pippo,** at 77 Via Montebello in this area, offers a tasty, three-course meal (an example would be spaghetti carbonara, followed by veal scaloppine, then salad and fruit) for 9,500 lire ($5.93). Closed Thursdays. **Trattoria da Benedetto** at 44 Via Vicenza, a few steps down from street level, offers a superb and overflowing dish of fettuccine with cream sauce, and accompanied by a glass of wine, for less than 4,000 lire ($2.50). But cheapest of all is **Osteria da Salvatore,** at 39c Via Castelfidardo, corner of Via Montebello, which charges only 7,000 lire ($4.37) for a full menu turistico (three courses, including bread, wine and service), specializes in fish dishes, and has recently added a 8,000 lire ($5) high quality menu whose price is emphatically guaranteed until the end of 1985: zuppa di verdura, tortellini pomodoro, or spaghetti carbonara to start, then scaloppini vitello, bistecca milanese or pork chops with vegetable and salad, a quarter liter of white wine, bread and service included. One could also have a filling à la carte meal here—like spaghetti, two fried eggs, wine, bread—for 5,000 lire. Salvatore, Rocco and Carmine, the three brothers who operate the Salvatore, are quite eager to please holders of this book. Closed Tuesdays. Verily, this area—which you can find on even a condensed city map—is Rome's best for rock-bottom-priced meals, with Osteria da Salvatore leading the list of sit-down restaurants: you can't eat better, for less, at any other establishment to the left or the right of Terminal Station.

To the Left of Terminal Station (as You Leave)

Here, the pickings are fewer (in the budget range, that is), but you might nevertheless try the tiny **Trattoria Angelo,** 104 Via Principe Amedeo, two short blocks to the left of the train station as you leave; it's a cool, calm little spot, and Angelo is a friendly restaurateur who charges 13,000 lire ($8.12) for a menu turistico consisting of three courses, bread, wine, cover and service charge. Closed Wednesdays. Nearby, the **Trattoria Alfredo** at 126a Via Principe Amedeo, charges a similar 13,000 lire ($8.12) for its own menu turistico, and is open daily except Sunday. Better-located, cheaper, but perhaps not as good, is the **Rosticceria Picca** at 7g Via Principe Amedeo, where the menu turistico is only 11,000 lire, and Roman gnocchi (4,500 lire) are served on Thursday. À la carte, you'll pay 2,400 lire for soup, 3,800 lire for pasta dishes (most Italian meals start with either soup or pasta), 4,500 to 6,000 lire for main dishes with vegetables.

Near American Express and the Spanish Steps

A single phenomenon makes this an area for moderately priced restaurants: the price war presently raging between the **Hostaria il Cantinone,** 21 Via Vittoria (15,000 lire for a three-course meal, including service and wine), and the **Trattoria Porcellino,** across the street at 16a Via Vittoria (which charges the same 15,000 lire for a somewhat similar meal, either at lunch or dinner); both restaurants offer moderately low prices for à la carte selections as well. How to find them? Well, the Via Vittoria, site of the epic gladiatorial contest, is stuck among the collection of small streets in front of the Spanish Steps, in the direction of the Via del Babuino (that is, on the other side of the steps from American Express). You can reach either by walking to the end of the Via Bocca di Leone and turning left, or by doing likewise on the Via Mario de Fiori. Or, from the Spanish Steps, walk one block down the Via Del Babuino and turn left.

Near the Piazza Venezia

The main square of Rome is the Piazza Venezia, at the head of which stands the monstrous Victor Emmanuel Monument—Mussolini delivered his major speeches from the balcony you'll see at the side of the square. If you'll walk from here to the nearby Corso Vittorio Emmanuele, and head down the avenue to the Largo Argentina, another square, you'll soon discover on the Largo, at 67 Corso Vittorio Emmanuele, Rome's largest delicatessen-type restaurant—**Il Delfino**—which has a marvelous array of spit-roasted chickens, hors d'oeuvre counters, pizza ovens. Walk into the big, hot, crowded room to the left (where the prices are the least expensive), sit at one of the bare tables, and order a pizza capricciosa (5,000 lire), which is a pizza covered with at least four different ingredients—a big pizza, enough for a full meal. There is soup for 3,000 lire, pasta for 4,000, meat dishes for 3,000 (chicken) to 6,000 (steak), but the pizza capricciosa is the outstanding find. Closed Mondays.

Fountain of Trevi

A second cluster of moderately priced restaurants is found on the little streets that branch off from the Fountain of Trevi, with its magnificent pool into which you toss a coin, and make a wish, to insure your return to Rome.

I'd head for the **Piazza Fontana di Trevi** for at least one meal in Rome—the surroundings are fabulous, and the fame of the fountain has caused almost a dozen trattorias to spring up. These come in two types: the restaurants on the plaza itself, which charge $14 and up for a prezzo fisso meal (at least three courses); the restaurants on the little streets that branch off from the plaza, which charge $10 and less, for the same three-course prezzo fisso meal. These streets are looking away from the fountains, from left to right: the Via del Lavatore, the Via di S. Vincenzo, the Via delle Muratte, and the Via de Crociferi.

Hope and I particularly like the **Hostaria Trevi,** 42 Via del Lavatore (just a few feet from the plaza), where for 17,000 lire ($10.62) apiece, we recently ordered and received a well-cooked prezzo fisso meal, including wine and service: two large bowls of minestrone, then veal with vegetables, cheese for dessert. Closed Sundays. But two doors up, at 40 Via del Lavatore, stands the budget standout of the Trevi Fountain area—a more modern eatery called **Al Picchio,** which offers four fixed-price meals: for 9,000 lire (vegetable soup, veal cutlet with roast potatoes, beverage, bread), for 10,000 lire (spaghetti, roast chicken and potatoes, beverage and bread), for 11,000 lire (spaghetti, beefsteak with potatoes, beverage and bread), and for 12,000 lire (vegetable soup with noodles, pork chops, potatoes, fruit salad, beverage and bread), always with service included. Look for the semi-basement eating room, down three steps. Closed Mondays.

Probably the best medium priced restaurant in the area ($8.12—13,000 lire—for its meals) is the **Trattoria Quirino,** 84 Via delle Muratte, which is slick and clean, and yet not overly commercial. Closed Saturdays. And on the Via de Crociferi, you'll find a number of other recommended spots, including **La Toscana** at 13 (about $10 for dinner), closed Mondays.

And if a full meal is too much, why not go to **Pizza Pazza,** at 20 Via dei Greci, a side street off the Via del Corso halfway between the Spanish Steps and the Piazza del Popolo, where you can buy some very unusual varieties of pizza (with squash or potatoes?) for 1,600 lire ($1) a slice. Three pieces could save you a more expensive tab in a trattoria. To find the place, look for the Mozart Hotel. Pizza Pazza (which means Crazy Pizza) is across the street.

Near St. Peter's

With but a few exceptions, the meals around here come relatively high; but the variety of choice is great. In the streets to the right of St. Peter's (as you face it) are clustered a whole host of trattorias that cater to the pilgrims and visitors who throng to Vatican City. These include: **Da Romolo alla Mole Adriana,** at 19 Via Fosse di Castello, two short blocks to the right of Via della Conciliazione (closed Mondays); and across the street, on 11 Via di Porta Castello the less expensive **Trattoria e Pizzeria Federico,** closed Fridays. Da Romolo offers no fixed-price table d'hôte meals, but its à la carte platters—lasagne verdi con sugo for 4,500 lire, risotto al ragout for 4,000 lire—are a delight. Aldo and Marco are the owner and headwaiter, respectively. Federico serves a 13,000 lire ($8.12), three-course lunch or dinner of spaghetti or soup, followed by meat or fish, bread, fruit, and a glass of wine, beer, orange drink or (*mirabile dictù*) Coca-Cola. Both establishments serve pizza made on the premises—4,500 lire for a large serving—after 6:30 p.m.

READERS' RESTAURANT SELECTIONS (VIA NAZIONALE AREA): "At **Ristorante Quattro Fontane,** 128 Via Quattro Fontane, a delicious three-course meal is 13,000 lire ($8.12), including a choice of five first courses, five main courses with salad and potatoes, and fruit and ice cream for dessert, plus wine and bread" (Diane Martin and Lynda Holden, Minneapolis, Minnesota). . . . "Please tell your readers about **Cafe Aureli,** the best food buy in Rome, located at Via Quattro Fontane 38, right off Via Nazionale. Up front it's a café and pastry shop, but in the back, there's a fabulous self-service cafeteria, serving a wide selection of delicious food at unbeatable low prices. The meals are superb in quality and the servings are huge" (Eva and Bernard Stevens, Northbrook, Illinois).

READER'S RESTAURANT SELECTION (NEAR THE PANTHEON) "Directly facing the Pantheon, is the **Ristorante Dai Tre Amici,** 7 Via della Rotonda, an outstanding Roman restaurant. It's impeccably clean and attractive, with linen tablecloths and fresh flowers on the tables, and the service is most attentive. I had a menu turistico there of delicious boneless chicken breast, marinated and then broiled, preceded by homemade minestrone and accompanied by potatoes, *fresh* fruit cocktail, hot bread, and a quarter liter of wine, all for 15,000 lire, including tip. I cannot recommend the place highly enough" (Ronald A. Audet, Portsmouth, Virginia).

A READER'S BREAKFAST TIP: "In Italy, the usual continental breakfast of two hard rolls with marmalade and a cup of coffee costs $3.50 to $4.50 in a hotel. Try the Italian method instead: buy your espresso and brioche (much more tasty than hard rolls) at one of the numerous stand-up coffee bars for about a dollar. If you should happen into an establishment that has a place to sit down, that brings the price up about 20%" (Jean Johnston, Poughkeepsie, New York).

A READER'S PICNIC TIP: "For picnic lunches near St. Peter's: the **Borgo Pio,** a street to the right of St. Peter's as you face it, has many food shops along its length that sell all sorts of picnic fare (cheeses, salamis, ham, rolls, olives, pickles, etc.) at low prices. Some stores sell these items prepackaged, thereby eliminating all language problems. It is easy to assemble a lunch for $6 or less—a quick procedure, and a good change from the heavy Italian fare" (John E. Westcott, Jr., Bethesda, Maryland).

MEALS—THE BIG SPLURGE: A big splurge in food? Maurice Chevalier once called the **Trattoria Romolo** an *"endroit de rêve."* This is a garden restaurant, set in the courtyard of an old Renaissance home, near the Aurelian wall, at 8 Via di Porta Settimiana (far side of the Tiber). Launch your meal with spaghetti alla boscaiola (spaghetti with tuna, mushrooms and cheese) for 6,500 lire ($4.06). Go then to abbachio al' cacciatore (11,000 lire), followed by insalata mista (3,500 lire) and top it all off with charlot for 4,000 lire (charlot being a sponge cake covered with whipped

cream, chopped-up cherries and grated peanuts). Total cost is 25,000 lire ($15.62), including service, for an unequalled dinner. Closed Mondays.

More easily found, and considerably cheaper, are the splurge-type restaurants on the Via della Croce, just off the end of the Piazza di Spagna (and thus near the Spanish Steps), where the choice is between the **Trattoria da Gigi**, at 99 Via Belsiana, between Via della Croce and Via delle Carrozze, a small restaurant, where a delicious dish of paglia e fieno alla ciociara accompanied by a bottle of red or white Frascati will come to a grand total of $8, and the **Re Degli Amici**, at 33b Via della Croce, where $12 will suffice for a two-course meal with wine and service included. Closed Mondays. Just down the street, at 39 Via della Croce, the **Fiaschetteria Beltramme** is heavily patronized by a local Roman clientele who find that they can construct a tasty, filling meal from the à la carte menu for less than 16,000 lire ($10): spaghetti al sugo di vitella (spaghetti covered with a delicious white sauce of cream and veal juice) for 4,500 lire, boiled beef tongue or a quarter roast chicken for 5,000 lire, parmesan cheese (the soft type, to be eaten with a piece of white bread) for 2,400 lire, all of it accompanied by an excellent red Chianti or white Castelli wine for 4,000 lire per liter.

READERS WHO HAVE SPLURGED: "We find there is really only one restaurant which best combines excellent cuisine and the gracious atmosphere of old Rome with the traveler's budget. It is **Le Tavernelle**, 48 Via Panisperna, centrally located near the Via Nazionale and the Piazza Venezia, and closed Mondays. Our meals there are among our fondest memories of Rome and typify the hospitality which distinguishes Rome from other European capitals. The owner, Goffredo, is a true continental host, charming and courteous as only a Latin can be. His three-course prezzo fisso meal (wine and service included) is 16,000 lire ($10), but his specialty is cannelloni, which, being our favorite dish, we sampled all over Italy and found to excel at Le Tavernelle—at the price of 5,500 lire ($3.43)" (Betty Woodside, El Paso, Texas, and Mary M. Addison, Klamath Falls, Oregon).

READERS' TIPS: "Do you ever advise your readers of the simplicity of assembling sandwiches on one's own? For instance, on a side street in back of the Due Macelli, which runs into the Via Mercede, many Italians (and at least two Americans I can name) frequently stopped into the bakery for a bun or two which the bakerman sliced, moved down the block to the small grocery which is almost half butcher shop, very clean and of excellent variety, stated the number of grams of cheese or salami or cooked ham or other cold meat which they wished sliced and placed in the buns, and then moved back to the wine shop in between the two and ordered a glass of cold wine, all of which could be carried out to a pleasant garden area in back or eaten at the counter. This repast can be made into a really sumptuous picnic by the addition of Krik Krok potato chips, olives, pickled onions, peppers and other delicatessen items from the butcher counter, and it would be difficult to spend more than $6 per person" (Dr. and Mrs. A.M. Cooper, Fresno, California). . . . "I do not think you emphasize strongly enough how important it is to bargain in not only Rome but all of Italy. It is not unusual or hard to get a quarter or even a third off the asking price in some cases. Furthermore, this does not refer only to a few products but rather most. I found even the ice cream men would bargain!" (Dale Watts, Dearborn, Michigan). . . . Some food notes from AF: first, you should know that a trattoria is usually simply a small restaurant, smaller and less pretentious than a ristorante, although that isn't always the case. Inside, food items are normally grouped under the titles antipasti appetizers, zuppe soups, asciutte pasta dishes such as spaghetti, carne meat. Hardly any budget-minded Italian begins, though, with antipasto, but instead with soup or pasta, and so should you. The typical Italian meal consists of either soup or pasta, then a main course, then fruit for dessert. But you're under no obligation to order all three courses, and you might definitely consider skipping the first one especially on hot days; a simple dish of fresh melon with thinly-sliced prosciutto ham ("prosciutto melone") accompanied by a small bottle of mineral water, can often provide the most refreshing sort of lunch, particularly if you plan to stroll the Palatine Hill in the broiling sun afterwards.

6. Rome's Specialty Restaurants

RESTAURANTS FOR OCCUPATIONAL GROUPS: Every union, every military branch, has its own restaurant in Rome—and many of them are open to the public. In the area of Terminal Station, you'll find two particularly good examples—the **Dopolavoro Ferroviario Mensa Tavola Calda,** "Restaurant of the Railway Workers," the best, is at 88 Piazza dei Cinquecento, on the first floor of the building with a Panasonic sign on top, to the immediate right of the station as you exit from it. It charges 5,500 lire for main meat courses, 1,800 lire for vegetables, 2,400 lire for pasta dishes with sauce, 800 lire for fruit, 800 lire for cover. A full menu turistico is 11,500 lire ($7.18), including wine. Order your dishes at the Cassa (cashier) first, then consume them at pleasant little tables in a spacious hall. Open noon to 9 p.m., seven days a week. Cheaper, but for servicemen only, is the military restaurant operated directly in the station (lower level); enter it from the Via Giovanni Giolitti at the side of the station, at that point where you see a sign reading *"Posto Sosta e Ristoro per Militari";* it's about 100 yards down the side of this immense building at #44 on the street. While preference here is given to Italian soldiers and airmen, military of other nations are occasionally also served, at prices that average 3,000 lire for main courses, 800 lire for fruit, from 1,400 to 2,800 lire for soup and pasta. Closed Fridays.

RESTAURANTS IN TRASTEVERE: The most typical part of Rome, so the Romans say, is Trastevere, in the southwest section of the city, on the left bank of the Tiber. For centuries, artists and writers have worked and lived here, inspired by the special atmosphere and excellent cuisine; today, as happens with Greenwich Village-type places, Rome's most elegant restaurants are also to be found in Trastevere. But among them is the miraculously low-priced **Mario's,** at 53 Via del Moro, where à la carte charges (there is no fixed-price menu) are so very reasonable—pasta for 1,500 lire, at least 19 main courses, for 2,000 to 3,500 lire ($1.37 to $2.18)—that you can easily put together a three-course meal including wine for 6,000 lire or else simply choose the fixed price meal, one of the cheapest and best in the city for only 6,500 lire ($4.06). Or you can eat for considerably less by ordering a large bowl of minestrone (vegetable and noodle soup) for 1,200 lire, two fried eggs and a ciriolina (a large white bread roll, a specialty of Trastevere bakers) for 1,400 lire, grilled liver with onions for 2,500 lire. Forty-two-year-old Mario presides over all, aided by Mamma Clelia, wife Vanda, sister Lina, brother Giorgio, son Massimo, and sister-in-law Rosalba. From Terminal Station, take bus 75 or 170 to the Ponte Garibaldi, alight at the first stop after the bridge, then turn right and walk toward the Ponte Sisto—halfway along, on your left, you'll find Mario's (which also displays a yellow telephone disc over its door). Inside, in true Trastevere spirit, the second dining room carries works by promising Roman artists, including a painting by Semyonov, and a sculpture named "Battle," by Rioli (he has his studio around the corner) worthy of any art gallery. Open Monday to Saturday from 12 to 4 p.m. and 7 to midnight, closed on Sunday and for a two-week holiday in August. Our highest recommendation in Rome.

Except for the Student Mensa discussed elsewhere in these pages, the very cheapest restaurant in all of Rome is a lunchtime only (noon to 2 p.m.) establishment known as the **"Cucina Economica,"** 9lb Via della Lungaretta, in Trastevere, heavily supported by various Catholic church organizations which distribute free meal tickets for it to the needy of their parishes. Despite that, this religious "Peoples' Kitchen" quite readily accepts, even encourages, a tourist clientele, although the shyer folk among that clientele simply order a takeaway half-chicken for 3,000 lire ($1.87), which they cart to their hotel room or a nearby park bench—the same half chicken that would cost double that in a deli or rosticceria. The tourists who do stay to eat pay only 1,000 lire (62¢) for an appetizer of risotto al pomodoro, 1,500 lire (93¢) for a quarter roast chicken, 300 lire (18¢) for a glass of wine, and thus spend well under 4,000 lire ($2.50) for a three-course lunch (including a fruit dessert). From Terminal Station, take bus 75 or 170, get off just after the bus crosses the Garibaldi Bridge, and you'll find Via della Lungaretta to be the first street turning right from Viale Trastevere— the Cucina is under a sign reading "Circolo San Pietro" over the street-level door. Closed Sundays.

ROSTICCERIAS: Generally, however, your most effective money-saving method is to eat at cafes and bars in Rome that carry the sign Tavola Calda (hot table), sometimes preceded by the word Rosticceria. Normally, these are stand-up eating spots, although quite a few have tables and chairs in the back. They nearly always feature a glass counter with trays of hot and cold food from which you can choose, and they are perfect for fast-moving tourists. You can have either a large hors d'oeuvre sandwich, or a bowl of pasta, or a plate of hot meats, with rolls, and you can order the marvelous cappucino—the nearest Italian equivalent of our coffee (1,500 lire)—to top it off. If you do take snacks in a rosticceria, in preference to the normal two-hour Italian meal, you'll feel light and relaxed for your touring activities, and you'll rarely ever encounter prices that strain a modest budget.

Care to have the addresses of a few typical rosticcerias? Just next door to the Hotel Pincio, at 53 Via Capo le Case (near American Express and the Spanish Steps), you'll find **Fuligni,** a rosticceria-tavola calda where I often eat—always for less than $6. Just off the Piazza del Popolo, at 11 Via Flaminia, an elaborate tavola calda shop is the well-known (and somewhat high-priced) **Ristorante-Rosticceria Catena.** And among the largest of the tavola calda/rosticcerias, easy also to find, is the modern **Self-Service Tavola Calda Orsetto,** at 64 Piazza dei Cinquecento, corner of Via d'Azeglio (in front of Terminal Station and directly to the left of it, as you exit). Here, dishes displayed upon a long counter include soup for 2,000 lire ($1.25), main courses with vegetables for 5,500 lire ($3.43), pasta for only 2,700 lire ($1.68). A sample recent meal: minestrone soup, roast beef and spinach, baked custard for dessert, accompanied by red wine, all totalling 9,000 lire ($5.62).

PORCHETTA ROMANA: Ever try a porchetta romana (spiced roast pig) sandwich? It's as typical of Rome as pizza is of Naples, and will cost you only 1,500 lire, plus 600 lire for a quarter liter of wine, if you buy it at a tiny shop about the size of a train compartment, called **Vino e Porchetta Romana,** and located at 2f Via del Viminale (between Via Giovanni Amendola and Via Principe Amedeo, near the big square in front of Terminal Station). Owner, Signor Franco Fioravanti, is busy all day selling his tasty and filling sandwiches, as well as separate orders of porchetta alone (2,200 lire for 100 grams) and his excellent wine in one-liter bottles (2,300 lire). I'm told the turnover is one roast pig per day. Closed Sundays.

7. Tours & Sightseeing

THE ORGANIZED TOURS: So vast is Rome, and so infinite its sights, that the basic city tours are cut into four parts, each lasting half-a-day, and each costing from 24,000 to 30,000 lire ($15 to $18.75). Tours 1 and 2 generally split up the town between them (24,000 lire each); tour 3 takes in the Vatican Museum, Sistine Chapel, and Spanish Steps (30,000 lire); tour 4 goes to the outlying sections, including the Old Appian Way, the Catacombs, the Quo Vadis Chapel, and so on (28,000 lire). Among the companies offering these escorted rides, I like **Carrani Tours,** an Italian outfit with intelligent, multi-lingual guides, whose offices are at 95 Via Vittorio Emmanuele Orlando (phone 460-510 or 474-2501), opposite the plush Grand Hotel. They offer a discount of 10% off any tour purchased by a reader of this book (flash them a copy), a discount of 20% for taking two tours, and also operate all the standard one-day and two-day excursions to Capri, Sorrento, and other near-Naples sites, as well as to Florence. Tours start at 9 a.m. and 3 p.m.; ladies planning to visit churches and cathedrals should wear long-sleeved dresses.

A FREE TOUR: Europe's most amazing tours are operated in Rome, every month except August, by a small group of multi-lingual Dutch nuns, wearing ordinary street clothes, who constitute the **Foyer Unitas** and operate out of the beautiful Pamphili Palace, which faces the Piazza Navona (the exact entrance being at 30 Via di S. Maria dell' Anima, Rome, phone 656-5951 or 654-1618). The tours, to begin with, are absolutely free. And they are offered primarily to *non*-Catholic visitors—not for proselytizing reasons, but simply on the grounds that there are plenty of Catholic organizations in Rome that will take care of Catholic tourists. The tours operate Mondays, Tuesdays, Fridays and Saturdays, at 9:30 a.m. The procedure for you is simply to stop by at the above address and express your interest—the sisters will then tell you what's scheduled, or even inquire as to what you'd like to see.

What's the catch? Well, these are not ordinary tours. They are for a special kind of tourist, who has a serious and intense interest in the history or culture of Rome—and is willing to examine particular sites *in depth*. The sisters may spend an entire morning, for instance, showing you one building, or one particular area, of the Vatican. They'll spend hours discoursing about the history and background of one of the Roman catacombs, another morning taking you through the Vatican Museums (for which there's an extra charge of 3,000 lire). They will not rush from place to place, and they will make no concessions to the tourist who simply wants a fast TV-type briefing on the art of a particular century.

Obviously, I hesitated long and hard about disclosing the existence of these tours—despite their budget aspect. Please, please stop by *only* if you are quite certain that you are willing to give the kind of serious attention that these fine women deserve. If you do, you'll receive a profoundly educational experience that costs not one lira—except for a modest contribution (500 lire) toward the guide's expenses. For the work of these sisters—communicating the glories of Rome—is their vocation and the reason for their organization.

LOW-COST SIGHTS: The Colosseum, of course, which charges no admission for entrance to its ground floor, and no admission at all to visit any part of the ruins on Sundays (from 9 to noon only). Following that, drive out as far as you have time to go along the ancient **Appian Way** (Via Appia Antica, not to be confused with the modern Via Appia Nuova). It's here that you'll pass the several largest Christian catacombs. Most interesting and significant of these are the **Catacombs of Saint Sebastiano** (once the burial place of both St. Peter and St. Paul), which are the second catacombs you'll pass as you proceed along the Appian route. The monks charge 2,000 lire ($1.25) for a multi-lingual guided tour, and operate them every day of the year except on Thursdays and on Christmas, New Year's Day and Easter Sunday. If you haven't a car, take bus 118 from the Colosseum to reach the catacombs.

The **Vatican Museums,** with the **Sistine Chapel** and **Raphael Rooms** (admission fee of 3,000 lire for all three, except on the last Sunday of each month, when admission is free; closed the first three Sundays each month, and holidays), are also musts. Remember that they are at the rear of the Vatican, a long walk from the front of St. Peter's, and that they close for the day at 1 p.m. (although St. Peter's itself stays open until 5). Downstairs in St. Peter's, a number of glass-sided coffins containing bodies of the popes are on view.

The figures inlaid on the floor of St. Peter's show the length of other famous cathedrals, thus giving you an indication of the enormous size of St. Peter's.

In the Villa Borghese Gardens, you won't want to miss the fabulous **Museo Borghese** (sometimes called the "Galleria Borghese"), admission 2,000 lire, with its treasures of paintings, sculpture and furnishings. On the first floor, there are works by the great sculptor Bernini (his famous "Rape of Persephone" is here); on the second floor is Raphael's "Descent from the Cross," together with several Titians and a whole array of paintings by my own favorite, the master Caravaggio. And, of course, Canova's erotic sculpture of Paolina Borghese (sister of Napoleon) on the ground floor. Open daily except Mondays from 9 a.m. to 2 p.m., Sundays until 1 p.m.

Finally, the grandest sight in Rome, to my mind, is the **Campidoglio** (Capitoline Hill), the sight of which has caused many a tourist actually to weep over its sheer beauty. The steps and approaches were designed by Michelangelo; the plaza displays one of the few classic bronze statues in existence—the Emperor Marcus Aurelius on horseback—which was discovered several centuries ago on the bottom of the Tiber, where it had been thrown by Roman-hating barbarians. When Michelangelo was asked to design a pedestal for the statue, he answered, "I am not worthy." If the horse itself seems somewhat oddly proportioned, it is because (some experts think) the statue was made to stand at a great height, which would have corrected the perspective view.

Try, if you can, to visit the Campidoglio at night, when the sounds of the city are stilled, and the bronze of the statue takes on a dull glow. Then go to the back of the hill, which overlooks the Roman Forum from the very best vantage point in town, and offers a quiet, half-illuminated view of these magnificent ruins that will cause you to reflect upon the rise and decline of great civilizations. Wandering through the Roman Forum, in the daytime, costs 2,000 lire.

CHECK LIST: Because there is so much to see and do in Rome, it occurred to me that it might prove helpful to provide a fast summary of the indispensable sights for a first-time visitor. If there were only ten visits for which I had time in Rome, I'd make them: **(1)** St. Peter's and the Vatican Museum (including the Sistine Chapel and the Raphael Rooms); **(2)** the Colosseum; **(3)** the Roman Forum (preferably at night); **(4)** the Campidoglio (Capitoline Hill), again at night; **(5)** the Via Veneto, in Spring, Summer or Fall; **(6)** the Villa d'Este, in Tivoli, on the outskirts of Rome (best at night); **(7)** the Appian Way and the Catacombs; **(8)** the Baths of Caracalla; **(9)** the Pantheon; and finally, **(10)** the Piazza Navona, with its three Bernini fountains. And as my final send-off to Rome, I'd go to the **Restaurant Tre Scalini** on the Piazza Navona and I'd have its specialty—a tartufo (ice cream covered with whipped cream, cherries and bitter chocolate chips), which costs 6,000 lire if you sit at the outside tables, but only 5,000 lire if you have the same tartufo inside. Closed Wednesdays.

8. Hope's Rome (A Postscript)

Aghast and appalled, however, that I could pare down the sights of Rome to ten (which is a pretty monstrous thing), Hope has asked for equal time to discuss a few others, all in aid of readers who may have more than the normal five-or-so days to spend here. This is her report:

"Rome defies organization. It's a city layered with history, like the skins of an onion—you peel off the top layer and immediately find another, ad infinitum. It seems to me that the most exciting approach to Rome is through the spectrum of history, visiting the sights chronologically as much as possible.

THE ETRUSCAN MUSEUM: "You can make a good start with the Etruscans, at the **National Museum of Villa Giulia** (The Etruscan Museum), just at the other end of the park from the Galleria Borghese, 9 Piazzale Villa Giulia (open daily except Mondays from 9 a.m. to 2 p.m., Sundays from 9 a.m. to 1, Wednesdays from 2 to 6:30 p.m., entrance of 2,000 lire, free on Sunday), which displays the world's finest collection of Etruscan sculpture, jewelry, pottery and household goods.

"Who were the Etruscans? That's the $64,000 question! Nobody really knows where they came from or even exactly when or where they landed in Italy (at some point, they settled in Tuscany, bringing with them a highly developed culture). According to legend, they were one of the three tribes (the Latins, Sabines and Etruscans) living on the hills of Rome, who ultimately banded together for protection. And Etruscan kings are actually thought to have ruled Rome for at least a century, about 100 years after the legendary founding of the city by Romulus and Remus (753 B.C.). Whatever their origins, it is clear that they beautified and improved wherever they went, and what is known today about their civilization is based on what has been found of their art, which is astonishingly advanced and 'modern' (I saw one vase that I'd swear was a Picasso). Most artists, anthropologists, and archaeologists would never pass through Rome without making a pilgrimage to the Etruscan Museum; don't miss Room VII, which houses what experts consider to be the most important find of the museum (the 'Apollon'); and don't miss the famous 'Sarcophagus of Caere' in room IX on the first floor.

HISTORICAL STATION BREAK: "With the expulsion from Rome of the Last Ancient king, in 509 B.C., the era of the Roman Republic was launched. It lasted for nearly 500 years—through the vicissitudes of the invasions of the Gauls and the sacking of Rome by them in 390 B.C.; the two Punic Wars; and the attack by Hannibal—until Julius Caesar became dictator, and the colorful era of the Roman emperors (Julius Caesar, Augustus Caesar, Tiberius, Caligula, Claudius and Nero) began. To have a marvelous glimpse into those times, try the:

PALATINE HILL: "The **Roman Forum** and the **Palatine** form the very heart-line of ancient Rome, and are also the very best buys in town—a 2,000-lire ticket admits you to both sites, daily except Tuesday, from 9 a.m. until two hours before sunset; enter from the Forum on Via dei Fori Imperiali (and head for the Arch of Titus to find the right path up the hill). The Palatine is one of the most stirring spots in all of Rome for appreciative eyes (there are scholars who spend months here). For this is where the Roman Empire had its beginnings—on this hill Romulus ploughed the acres that became the first city; later the emperors erected their palaces here, in the choicest locations, overlooking the Forum. And the ruins, which indicate buildings of staggering proportions, sumptuousness, culture, comfort and beauty, give you an insight into *la dolce vita* of the average Roman emperor and upper-class citizen. You'll see the Baths of Septimius Severus; the Stadium of Domitian; the Domus Augustana (official palace built for the imperial family); the Flavian Palace; the Temple of Cybele; the Palace of Tiberius. But whatever you see, don't miss the House of Livia (which is believed to have been the House of Augustus), with frescoes inside that are 2,000 years old and absolutely thrilling (if necessary, ask the guard to open the doors for you)! For maximum enjoyment I suggest you buy a map to guide yourself through.

NATIONAL ROMAN MUSEUM: "The local citizens know this as the **Museo delle Terme;** it's located on the Piazza della Repubblica, directly across from Terminal Station, in the Baths of Diocletian. Entrance is a very well-spent 1,500 lire and hours are daily except Mondays from 9 to 2, on Sundays from 9 to 1. Don't miss such famous pieces of Roman sculpture and art as 'The Pugilist' (a copy from the Greek original) in Room IV (which earns its title of 'The Room of Masterpieces'), the 'Head of a Young Girl' in Room IV, the 'Marble Altar of Ostia' in Room VII, and the 'Fragments of the Secular Games' held under Augustus Caesar and Septimius Severus; and don't fail to allow plenty of time to explore all the treasures of Roman statuary and mosaics.

BASILICA OF SANTA MARIA DEGLI ANGELI (THE BATHS OF DIOCLETIAN): "Just next door to the Terme Museum (walk down the street to your right as you exit from the Terme) is the best-preserved hall of the **Baths of Diocletian,** which were converted by Michelangelo into the Church of Santa Maria degli Angeli. Constructed in the fourth century A.D., this was one of the largest baths of its kind, with staggering proportions that make our modern-day saunas seem puny indeed (of course, the Roman baths were social gathering spots as well, where concerts and lectures were often held). Entrance is free; the hours vary, so check them in *This Week in Rome.*

THE CAPITOLINE MUSEUM: "Arthur has already referred to the great Campidoglio, on one side of which is the **Capitoline Museum,** with the **Conservatori** on the other. You'll want to spend most of your time at the Capitoline (daily except Mondays from 9 a.m. to 2 p.m., on Tuesdays and Thursdays from 5 to 8 p.m., and on Saturday evenings from 8:30 to 11 p.m.; free on Sundays, 1,500 lire otherwise), which will provide you with a rare and wonderful opportunity to put faces on the ancient Romans. There are several rooms devoted to busts of 'just plain folks' from the Imperial era, and other rooms containing the better-known heads of Roman emperors and other celebrities of the time. And don't miss the mosaics from Hadrian's Villa, the famous statue of 'The Dying Gaul,' and the equally renowned 'Boy Extracting a Thorn from His Foot' (the latter two being copies from the Greek). All of these—except 'the Boy'—are in the Capitoline; he's in the Conservatori."

THE PANTHEON: "The **Pantheon,** at Piazza della Rotonda (take buses 26, 87 or 94), is the only complete major building of ancient Rome left standing—and it's one of the greatest free sights in the world. From it, you'll get a good idea of how to fill in the details of other Roman buildings that have only a column or two remaining. Built by Agrippa in the time of Augustus Caesar (around 27 B.C.) as a temple to the gods Venus and Mars, it was originally a rectangular structure. Later, all but the front columns and portico were destroyed by fire, and when it was rebuilt under the Emperor Hadrian (130 A.D.), it was constructed as the inspiring round architectural wonder that you see today. The painter Raphael is buried here (among many other dignitaries). Since the sole source of interior light is from a hole in the impressive dome, the Pantheon stays open only from 9 a.m. to 5 p.m., and is closed from 1 to 2 p.m.

TAKE AN IMPERIAL WALK: "Start at the **Colosseum,** where it's worth your while to take some time to contemplate the size and grandeur of this magnificent structure—imagine it covered with marble and filled with thousands of ancient Romans shouting thumbs up or thumbs down! Look below into the pits where lions, Christians, and general provisions were kept. Across the street is the **Arch of Constantine,** and the **Roman Forum;** to your left is the **Palatine.** Continue your walk up the Via dei Fori Imperiali (heading in the direction of the Victor Emmanuele Monument), and when you are nearly past the Roman Forum, across the street, to your right, you'll see **Augustus's Forum;** farther along and to your left is **Caesar's Forum;** and farther still is **Trajan's Forum,** with its magnificent **Trajan's Column,** covered with winding bas-reliefs depicting Trajan's victory over the Daci. Across the street is **Trajan's Market** (entrance at 94 Via IV Novembre), which you can visit for 1,000 lire every day except Monday, from 9 a.m. to 1 p.m. and 3 to 6 p.m., winters, 10 to 4 p.m. (Sunday from 9 to 1 p.m., free admission); it will give you a good idea of how vast and impressive the ancient Roman markets were.

THE CHURCH OF ST. CLEMENT: "And finally we come to the Christian era. If you'd like to experience in a most direct way what it must have felt like to be an early Christian in Rome, make a visit to the lower depths of the **Basilica of St. Clement,** on the Via S. Giovanni in Laterano, a street at the side of the Colosseum. Even if you later visit the massive catacombs outside the city, you'll have a more intense experience here, because you are allowed to wander through the maze of underground rooms (which include a 1st century house and 4th century church) by yourself, without benefit of a guide. It's sinister and dark, with the spooky sound of rushing waters beneath the ground on this early meeting place of Christians and worshippers of Mithra (a vigorous, masculine cult that venerated the God of Light—or the Sun). The church itself, medieval and made of stone in that distinctive yellow-orange earth color that you see only in Rome, has a mosaic in the apse which dates from the 12th century, and is run by Irish Dominican fathers, whose charge of admission to the excavations is 1,500 lire, and hours of entrance are from 9 a.m. (Sundays from 10) to noon and 3:30 to 6 p.m. Take the subway *Metropolitana* to the Colosseum, walk to your left around the Colosseum to Via S. Giovanni in Laterano (the second street on your left), and then walk down the street for two blocks.

CHURCHES IN ROME: "This is like talking about coals in Newcastle, and I certainly won't attempt to provide a complete listing of all the major churches in Rome, but merely point out the most important or interesting ones to see. Generally the churches open around 7 a.m., close from noon to 3:30 or 4 p.m., and open again until sunset. The very most important sightseeing attractions, like St. Peter's and the other main cathedrals, are an exception and remain open all day long.

The Big Four

"The four main cathedral churches of Rome, after St. Peter's, are the **Church of St. John Lateran, Santa Maria Maggiore,** the **Church of St. Paul,** and **San Lorenzo Outside the Walls.** The limited scope of this book does not permit a detailed description of **St. Peter's,** but the Church of the Vatican State stands on one of the most beautiful and harmonious squares in the world (by Bernini), and the interior, created by such as Michelangelo, Raphael, Bernini, Bramante and others, deserves careful scrutiny. Immediately to your right as you enter is Michelangelo's spell-binding 'Pietà'; it breathes! The Dome was also done by Michelangelo; the Papal Altar and Canopy, and the exuberant 'Gloria' Apse, are by Bernini. Next in importance is **S. Giovanni in Laterano** (located very near St. Clement; just continue to the end of Via S. Giovanni in Laterano), the oldest church in Rome (built on pagan ruins, and incorporating many styles), and given to the popes by the Emperor Constantine—it's often referred to as *the* cathedral of the world. Among the treasures of the church are a piece of the table of the Last Supper (facing the Apse door); a part of the original altar on which St. Peter said mass; and a great bronze door (now in the middle of the main entrance) from the Senate House of the Roman Forum. . . . Across the square are the **Scala Santa** or Holy Stairs (located in a building which used to serve as residence and private chapel of the popes), which consist of twenty-eight steps from Pontius Pilate's villa brought to Rome by St. Helen (Constantine's mother); it is supposed to be the stairway that Christ ascended when he was condemned to death. Pilgrims from all over the world come here to do penance by climbing up the steps on their knees, receiving years of absolution for their efforts. Interesting for a short visit is the **Church of St. Maria Maggiore** (located a few blocks from the railway station, off the Via Cavour). Built on the site of the so-called 'Miracle of Pope Liberio' (snow fell here in August), it has the Holy Crib, and a beautiful ceiling made of the gold that Columbus brought back from the New World. Unless you're on a pilgrimage, you may not wish to see **San Lorenzo Fuori le Mura** (St. Lawrence Outside the Walls, located alongside Rome's Monumental Cemetery; take bus 492 from the Piazza della Repubblica at the corner of Via Nazionale), which does not offer as much of interest as other major basilicas. But **San Paolo Fuori le Mura** (St. Paul's Outside the Walls) is outstanding: a 20-minute ride from central Rome on bus 170 (catch it along Via Nazionale, or take the Metropolitana), and remarkable for its sheer size—second only to St. Peter's in Rome. This great basilica, with the remains of the apostle under the Confessional Altar, was almost completely destroyed by fire in 1823. What remains of historical importance are a 5th century mosaic on the Arch of Triumph, a Tabernacle of Arnolfo di Cambio over the Main Altar, and to the right of the Main Altar, a superby sculptured Pascal Candelabrum dating from 1170 (also, take a look at the lovely 13th century Cloisters here). What's 'new' in the basilica and of special interest are the unique alabaster windows which suffuse the church with soft and romantic lighting; and the 271 mosaic portraits (all around the upper wall) of all the popes since St. Peter. If the main door of the church is closed, enter around the side. And finally, between St. Maria Maggiore and the Colosseum, or at the bottom of Via Cavour (go up a long stairway), on the Piazza St. Pietro, there's **San Pietro in Vincoli** (St. Peter in Chains), which does have St. Peter's chains, but is notably chiefly because it houses the unfinished tomb of Pope Julius II by Michelangelo, with his magnificent 'Moses.'

JUST FOR FUN: "And now, if you're feeling in a prankish mood, you might next head for the **Coemeterium Capuccinorum** (Capuchin Church) at the bottom of the Via Veneto (#27) near the Piazza Barberini, where the monks have made decorations out of the skeletons of their dead brothers. Walk up the church steps, enter through the side door of the monastery and this will lead you directly into the bone cellar where every inch of the ceiling is decorated with bones. Even the lamps are made of bones and skulls. It's like a Hitchcock nightmare, with mummified monks bowing graciously amid the rubble of pelvi and tibia. Open from 9:30 a.m. to 12 and from 3 to 6 p.m., and entirely free, except for a small donation which you'll want to make.

SOME FINAL DATA: "While the **Vatican Museums** charge a high 3,000-lire entrance fee (and are free only on the last Sunday of each month!), there is more here than one can possibly see on a single visit. I suggest you take the elevator to the top floor and work your way down. In addition to the Sistine Chapel and the Raphael Rooms, there is also the Pio-Clementino Museum (ancient Greek and Roman sculpture) adjacent to the

Belvedere Courtyard (with four corners of masterpieces, including the 'Apollo' and the famous 'Laocoon and His Sons'), and the stunning ancient Greek fragment 'The Torso of Belvedere'; the Egyptian Museum; the Etruscan Museum; the Borgia Apartments; the Pinacoteca, a picture gallery with a fine collection; a missionary museum; and much more. Keep in mind that the museum is closed the first three Sundays of each month, and holidays (otherwise, open 9 a.m. to 1 p.m.). Close to St. Peter's and the Vatican and dominating the skyline, is the imposing **Castel Sant' Angelo,** charging an entrance fee of 1,500 lire, open daily except Mondays, from 9 a.m. to 2 p.m., on Sundays until 1. The castle is a large, dreary, maze-like building, full of history, but you'll have to climb a very long ramp and interminable stairs before you get to where the action is. Built originally in 139 by the Emperor Hadrian as his mausoleum, it has through the ages served many and varied purposes—as a fort, a papal refuge (there's a tunnel connecting the castle to the Vatican), and a prison (among its inmates were Cellini and the notorious Cenci family). There are numerous points of interest in the castle (weapon and uniform exhibits, etc.), but don't miss, in particular, the ornately decorated Pauline Hall, Perseus Room, or the Library on the third tier. There are also excellent views of Rome from the high terraces of the castle, and a place for light refreshment at the top. If you have spare time in Rome, spend it in the enchanted **Piazza della Bocca della Verità** (on the Tiber opposite the Ponte Palatino, within hiking distance of the Campidoglio Hill, the Palatine, and Circo Massimo).' Nearby are the arches underneath which the Cloaca Maxima once dumped its sewage into the Tiber, and on the piazza itself are two ancient buildings: the **Temple of Fortuna Virilis,** a small square temple with Ionic columns built at the end of the second century B.C.—it is the oldest, 'still in one piece' (miraculously) building of its kind in Rome—and the younger (100 B.C.), round, and graceful **Temple of Vesta.** These two structures, seen together, are majestic spellbinders. As for the piazza itself, it's named after the 'Mouth of Truth,' a stone mask which supposedly has the power to bite off the hand of a liar. If you're anxious to test your integrity in this way, you'll find the mask on the porch of the **Church of Santa Maria in Cosmedin** (8th century, built on pagan ruins, with ancient columns inside; it, too, is worth a short visit). From the **Pincio,** at the edge of one side of the Borghese Park, you'll have a beautiful view of Rome. Directly below, on the **Piazza del Popolo,** the **Church of St. Maria del Popolo** (completed in the 15th century) has many treasures, including the Chigi Chapel designed by Raphael, and two enthralling paintings by Caravaggio (to the left of the main altar).

A SHORT TRIP TO TIVOLI: "Tivoli, where you can visit the **Villa d'Este** and **Hadrian's Villa** (in Italian, Villa Adriana), is about 45 minutes outside Rome—from Via Gaeta, a little street off the Piazza della Repubblica, near Terminal Station, take the coach marked "Autobus Per Tivoli" for a round-trip fare of 2,800 lire. Buses run nearly every half hour, but check the timetable coming back or you'll wind up spending the night in Tivoli. The most efficient way to make the tour is to take the bus all the way into Tivoli and see the Villa d'Este first, then take bus 2 or 4 from town to Hadrian's Villa (bus 2 deposits you closer to the entrance).

"The **Villa d'Este,** built by Cardinal d'Este in the 16th century on the site of what is virtually an oasis in dry territory, is the grandest happy playground of water you'll ever see. The tiered garden of trees and near-tropical vegetation, interspersed with every conceivable size and type of water fountain, has a most delightful and intriguing effect. It also happens to be a great engineering feat, for the 500 varied fountains are run strictly through the aid of nature. No gadgets or pumps whatsoever were used. (Like the saying, there's water everywhere, but only one fountain is safe to drink from, so be careful.) Hours are from 9 a.m. to an hour before sunset every day, for a 2,000 lire entrance fee.

"The **Villa Adriana** is open every day except Monday from 9 a.m. till about an hour before sunset (summers as late as 8 p.m.; admittance up to 1 hour before the villa closes), and again charges 2,000 lire for entrance, but is free on the second and fourth Sundays, the first and third Saturdays, of each month. The misnamed villa, which was Hadrian's hideaway, turns out actually to be a small-sized town where the emperor tried to re-create architecturally all the beautiful places he'd seen in the world. Work was begun in 118 A.D., and it is thought that the emperor himself closely supervised the designs. Among many other ruins, you'll see the Circular Portico or Maritime Theatre, a small circular apartment completely surrounded by water (it's thought that Hadrian came here for quiet contemplation), which is in sufficiently restored condition to allow you easily to fill in the gaps; and the marvelous Canopus, an artificial valley with a gorgeous pond decorated with statues, surrounded by small apartments close to the Bath, and bounded on one side by the small museum at the side of the pond, which houses statues that once stood on the Canopus (many archaeologically interesting pieces found on this site have been moved elsewhere—lots are in Roman museums). In its time, the Villa Adriana must have afforded its residents a kind of luxury undreamt of today. It's still an enchanted place."

READERS' SIGHTSEEING SUGGESTIONS: "No one should leave Rome without visiting **New Rome.** This is the section called EUR, and is reachable by taking the metropolitana (subway) to the Esposizione (West or East) stop. There is a splendid view, with the wonderful sports stadium at the top of the hill, a magnificent sculpture garden, and lakes and play areas all around it. On the other side is a modern rendition of the Colosseum which is used as a state office building, a magnificent new cathedral, and dozens of beautifully landscaped private homes. New Rome was started by Mussolini as a showplace of Fascism, and completed by the Republic as a showplace of Italian architecture and design, and it is every bit as charming as Old Rome. For the young, sturdy readers, there are small paddle boats for rent at the modest charge of 2,500 lire an hour on the artificial lake in front of the stadium. An hour's paddle will give you a cool, enjoyable, ever changing view of some of the most beautiful scenery south of Tivoli" (Burt Wolfson, New York, New York). . . . "The best museum for students of Latin and Ancient History is the **Museo di Civiltà Romana,** 15 Piazza G. Agnelli, in the new section of E.U.R., easily accessible by subway. There are separate rooms devoted to Caesar, Cicero and Virgil" (Mrs. Doris M. Bacon, East Aurora, N.Y.; note by AF: hours are 9 a.m. to 2 p.m., daily except Monday, admission 1,000 lire). . . . "Add to your visit to **St. Peter's,** the 2,000 lire elevator ride to the roof, to view those splendid statues that edge the roof. Then continue your ascent of the dome itself by a winding stair for a magnificent view of Rome and the Vatican gardens. You can also get onto a lofty balcony overlooking the interior of St. Peter's" (Thomas S. Mortimer, Silver Spring, Maryland). . . . "Please stress **Trajan's Market** a bit more—it's the only one place in Rome where, thanks to reconstruction, a visitor can have a sense of what it was like to walk down a Roman street in a market district. It's also very quiet and has few visitors, and is a good place to escape the bustle and noise, or eat a picnic lunch" (John Goldrosen, Chapel Hill, North Carolina). . . . "A tip for tourists who go to the **Sistine Chapel:**

bring along small opera glasses, as the ceiling is very high. These would also be useful on the tours of the gorgeous palaces all over Europe to study more closely the ceiling paintings" (Mrs. Paul Lauzon, Pittsfield, Mass.). . . . "The last Sunday of the month the **Sistine Chapel** and **Museums** are open free. The guards at the Vatican may tell you otherwise, but don't believe them. Go and find out for yourself. I asked two different guards for directions. Both told me the chapel and the museums were closed, so I missed seeing them. A friend later told me they were indeed open and free" (Ms. Anne Lipp, Boyds, Maryland; note by AF: The friend was right). . . . "Anyone who has read Kenneth Clark's *Civilization* will want to see Bernini's 'St. Teresa in Ecstasy,' which many pinpoint as the embodiment of high Baroque. The sculpture is to the left of the main altar in the **Church of Santa Maria della Vittoria** on the Piazza San Bernardo (across the street from Saint Susanna's)" (Janice к. Bellace, London, England). . . . "The Metro Underground, main entrance in the Termini, costs 500 lire, stops at the Colosseum and the Basilica of St. Paul. Literature buffs may wish to get off at the Piramide stop to visit the **Protestant cemetery** for the grave of John Keats, without his name but with the epitaph he wished: 'Here lies one whose name was writ in water'" (James L. Rohrbaugh, Seattle, Washington). . . . "The graves of Keats, Shelley, and John Addington Symonds, in the Protestant cemetery, deserve a visit by those interested in the 'English Rome'" (Lawrence Poston, Lincoln, Nebraska). . . . "Most visitors to **Piazza Venezia** in Rome look up at the famous balcony where Mussolini made the world tremble with his terrifying threats, but very few know it is possible to enter for a few lire through a side entrance on the left into a quiet, beautiful courtyard, up steps trod by numerous heads of state and finally into a huge palace salon which Mussolini used as his office. It gives you an eerie, spooky feeling" (Professor Carlo Vacca, Framingham, Massachusetts). . . . "If you are going to **Tivoli** from Rome on any conveyance other than a tour bus, try and stop at one of the travertine quarries along the road. They have been worked for two thousand years and a visit is free. The one where we stopped was quarrying 25-ton chunks for a new opera building. The foreman's English and my Italian were both nonexistent, but we got along fine and he was most friendly and happy to explain as best he could, and show us where to stand for the best view" (Daniel M. Kappel, Poughkeepsie, New York). . . . "A 'do-it-yourself' walking tour: from **Terminal Station,** walk first to the **Colosseum,** then to the **Roman Forum,** then up the **Spanish Steps** to the **Villa Borghese.** After visiting the museum there, take a #30 bus from in back of the zoo to **St. Peter's.** From there, a #64 bus back to **Terminal Station.** Warning: this is only for the hardy" (Roselyn Yung Yap, Cambridge, Mass.). . . . "All the ruins are best seen at night, when fantasizing is possible" (Mark Estren, Middletown, Connecticut).

READERS ON SCOOTERS: "We rented a scooter from **Scoot-A-Long** at 302 Via Cavour, near the Coliseum, for the low cost of 36,000 lire ($22.50) a day, plus gas. Then we went to Naples for the day, leaving in the morning and returning at night after a wonderful day of sightseeing" (Janice Wakellin, Rome, Italy). . . . "A fine place for renting licensed motor scooters is the **Scoot-A-Long Agency,** 302 Via Cavour, tel. 678-0206, for approximately 36,000 lire ($22.50) a day, less on a weekly basis. This is more expensive than a car for the daily rate, *but* there is no kilometer charge and that is where you save money. It's also a heck of a lot more fun and convenient for parking in overcrowded Rome. We used both car and then scooter and much preferred the latter" (Dana A. Regillo, Lexington, Mass.). . . . "My wife and I rented a Vespa for one month from the **Scoot-A-Long** office, and traveled on it through Italy, Southern France, Spain, Morocco, Algeria and Tunis. That's quite an inexpensive way to travel, and we had little difficulty with the scooter" (William D. Jeffrey, Chicago, Illinois).

9. Evening Entertainment

TERME DI CARACALLA: Open-air opera at the Baths of Caracalla (bus #93 takes you there) is one of the great summer events of Europe. The opera stage is set amid the gigantic ruins of the former Roman bath house, and the setting is spectacular—for certain productions, the ruins are actually employed as part of the scenery. Performances are scheduled almost nightly in July and August, with tickets ranging downward from a high of 9,000 lire, to 5,000 lire, the 5,000-lire seats being perfectly satisfactory; they can be purchased in advance at the Rome Opera House (off the Via Firenze) from 10 to 1 and from 4 to 6:30. Try, of course, to get to any of the performances, but if a production of *Aida* is scheduled, then rise from a sick bed to be in attendance, because you'll see a spectacle that's equaled by no other opera company. A near-army of extras fills the stage during the triumphal march of the second act, and an elephant or else a brace of horses comes charging in at the climax. With all this, the voices may seem overlooked, but the overall effect is stupefying.

ROME AT NIGHT: The discotheques and nightclubs are atrociously expensive, and many visitors simply devote the evening hours to a leisurely, late meal. Apart from that, the most popular form of evening entertainment in Rome is to sit at a sidewalk cafe on the Via Veneto, and watch the passing parade—a wonderfully varied procession of chic women, tailored men, types and characters of every sort. The cafes charge no more than 3,200 lire for a coffee, and a coffee will last you an hour or even two. An interesting sidelight: each year on the Via Veneto, one or two particular cafes become mystically selected as the places to sit. Their sidewalk tables are then fully packed, while the cafe next door —the same prices, same decor—is empty and forlorn. The next year, an Italian movie star may take a liking to the sidewalk tables of the formerly forlorn cafe, and the situation is instantly reversed. I sometimes wonder how Via Veneto cafe owners sleep at night; in 1984, Doney's and Rosati's were the favored spots, but who knows what next year will bring? In any event, be sure to spend a few evening hours simply sitting there over a $2 (3,200 lire) coffee; you'll be glad you did.

One other suggestion for evening activities: go to a museum. There is at least one major museum open every weekday night in Rome, between the hours of 8:30 and 11 p.m. That permits you to keep up with your sightseeing schedule in Rome, and to do it at the best time of day. While these late-hour evenings vary—and must always be currently checked—the **Capitoline Museum** and **Conservatori** atop the Campidoglio Hill (one of which is devoted to paintings, the other to sculpture, with one 2,000-lire ticket admitting you to both), most definitely stay open late on Saturday evenings, from 8:30 to 11 p.m. and daily except Mondays and Saturdays from 5 to 8 p.m.

10. Excursions

READERS ON AN EXCURSION: "From Rome, it is simple for readers to make their own trip to Pompeii, Sorrento and Capri. Take the early train to Naples (11,000 lire; round-trip fare between Rome and Naples is 22,000 lire) and in Naples walk two blocks to the Circumvesuvio station. Here, obtain a ticket to Pompeii and stop off at Pompeii for at least 1½ hours to visit the museum and the ruins; then take the Circumvesuvio train to Sorrento, and use Sorrento as your overnight base in preference to going to the much higher priced island of Capri. After breakfast, take the ferry from the harbour to the Blue Grotto and Capri. In Capri ride the funicular to the top level and make good use of the buses which take you, inter alia, to Marina Piccola (where you can swim—don't forget to go inside the Canzone del Mare where there is a lovely swimming pool); and to Anacapri, where you can take a cable car to the top of the mountain and enjoy a panoramic view of the island. To return to Naples, you can take a boat from Sorrento (1 hour)" (Lenard G. Lever and Ben-Zion Surdut, Cape Town, South Africa). . . . **"Rome-Naples-Sorrento-Capri:** This 4-day trip was one of the high points of our travels this year. From Rome to Naples, take the train from Terminal Station at 8 a.m.—24,000 lire, round-trip, second class—2½ hours to Naples. There, about 100 yards in front of the station, is a Garibaldi statue and the street car lines run on Corso Garibaldi. Take bus 49 to the National Museum to see the wonderful friezes, statues, bronzes and mosaics from Herculaneum and Pompeii—the best works from both places are here. Now take bus 54—on the left one block as you leave the museum, to Portici, then bus 225, from the same stop at Portici to Herculaneum (Ercolano in Italian). Here, don't hire a guide but wander and let the custodian for each section tell you about their sections—in broken English but very understandable. Plan on about two hours, for the things they can show you are very interesting. Then take bus 225 to the train station, at Naples. Spend the night at Hotel Mignon—7 Corso Novara—two blocks on the right as you leave the station. (This hotel compares with the Pensione Texas in Rome.) They charge 45,000 lire for an excellent double without bath, but with breakfast and all else included, 35,000 lire single.

"In the morning, take the Circumvesuviana from the station at 339 Corso Garibaldi—same place where you take the bus to the museum—buy a ticket to Sorrento (1,200 lire) and get off at Pompeii. Again make friends with the custodians in each block and they will show you unusual sights for a small tip. Then get back on the train and continue to Sorrento.

"At Sorrento, you can buy a round-trip ticket to Capri for 6,800 lire that includes the boat direct to the Blue Grotto. The boat waits while you transfer to a rowboat for 3,000 lire and your pass (without the pass it's an additional 2,000 lire). See the grotto, and then the boat will take you to Marina Grande, the big port. See the island, then in the afternoon the same boat takes you back to Sorrento. To get back to Rome on any day but Sunday, take the bus from the main square near the Campidoglio. On Sundays, you'll have to take the Circumvesuviana to Naples and the train from Naples to Rome" (Mrs. E. R. Toporeck, Santa Barbara, California).

11. Markets & Shopping

FLEA MARKET: Though nearly every major European capital has a Sunday flea market, I like the one in Rome best. It's cheaper than its Paris equivalent, provides better bargaining opportunities (offer only 50% of the asking prices, and stick to your guns), and has a far wider selection of articles—everything from 17th-century candelabra to secondhand toothbrushes!

For those unfamiliar with the term, "flea market" refers to a big open field in Rome on which merchants, every Sunday, set up make-shift booths, or spread a blanket on the ground, for the sale of every conceivable secondhand article—clothes, old gramophones, wooden Sicilian statues, old busts and medals of Mussolini, fraying-at-the-edges etchings and posters, antique door-knobs. If you bargain properly, you can stock up on amazing values, limited only by your estimate of what you'll be able to stuff in your suitcase. Naturally, you'll be heartbroken over having to pass up the bulkier items that are too heavy to lug across Europe. Hope still dreams of the two 6-foot-long torches-on-a-pole (painted pale blue and yellow, the kind that lean out from a wall, at an angle), which we couldn't carry away from our last trip to the Rome flea market. They were priced at $30 apiece; they would've gone for $150 or more at the furniture auctions in New York.

The flea market in Rome is located at the Porta di Portese (bus 57 from Terminal Station goes within three blocks of it; get off at the stop called "Ponte Sublicio"), in the Trastevere section—ask anyone to point the way. The flea market is open only once a week, on Sunday, from 6 a.m. to 1 p.m., when it closed punctually. It's such an exciting, colorful sight that you'll want to see it, even if you don't plan to buy a thing.

THE DAILY MARKET: The huge and bustling **Piazza Vittorio Emmanuele** (to the side and behind the railway station, within walking distance of it) is the daily grocery-and-clothes market of Rome, an open-air fiesta of such exotica as you'll never find at the A&P: live chickens, pigeons and rabbits, tripe, octopus, mortadella (a kind of pork sausage), all sorts of other cheeses, live fish, ten types of olives, canaries, kidneys, cheap shoes, pants and ladies blouses (on the far side), an area inside for eating the picnic meals you'll pick up here (try 1,000 lire of sour olives, then cheese and bread), and a children's playground to boot. Don't miss.

ADDITIONAL SHOPPING TIPS: On weekdays, go instead to the Spanish Steps, where you'll find the Via Condotti, then walk down the Via Condotti until you come to the little open square that is the **Piazza di Fontanella Borghese.** Nearly every booth and pushcart in this open-air market is devoted to the low-cost sale of old books, etchings, posters and reproductions. You must bargain, sticking to 50% of the offering price.

Rome's most popular (and popularly priced) shopping mall is the **Via Cola di Rienzo** in the Vatican area, running from the Piazza del Risorgimento to the Ponte Margherita that crosses the Tiber (and best reached by taking the subway to either the Lepanto or Ottaviano stop). Walking up and down this one-mile-long street, you'll pass literally dozens of shoe, leather, souvenir, and glove shops, supermarkets, pharmacies and small department stores, all considerably cheaper than their counterparts in the central areas of Rome.

12. Rome Miscellany

HOURS: Rome closes down tight from noon to 4 p.m., when people return home for their biggest meal of the day and a snooze. They go back to work at 4 p.m. and stay hard at it until 8 p.m. This will significantly affect your eating hours, for no restaurant really begins serving meals until 1 p.m. (for lunch) and 7 p.m. (for dinner). Don't show up before those times, or you may have to wait unattended in an empty restaurant. You'll find, by the way, that the habit of a noon-day siesta in sunny Rome is a marvelous way to stay refreshed during the remaining, cooler periods of the day. And since all stores and museums close down for those four hours, it's fruitless to spend the time on your normal sightseeing rounds.

ODDS AND ENDS: No Italian restaurant serves spaghetti with meat balls, and no one here has heard of biscuit tortoni. . . . The pasta dishes are eaten by discerning Italians only at lunch time; the evening meal is a lighter one, and begins with soup, not pasta. . . . The funniest travel story I know, is a true one, and concerns an American couple who asked the owner of a pension in Rome to recommend a tourist attraction which they might visit. He advised them to see the Roman Forum. They returned two hours later, white with anger, grim and trembling. "I had no idea you Italians were so nationalistic," said the wife. "Our first day in Rome, and you send us to see what the American bombs did." . . . Read *I, Claudius,* by Robert Graves, and you'll be able to create a wonderful fantasy-world about the ruins and sights in Rome. Or, for a more contemporary view, read H. V. Morton's magnificent *A Traveler in Rome.* The city requires advance preparation and study for its maximum enjoyment. . . . One of the time-honored methods of touring the city for a pittance is to take a bus ride on the "Circolare Sinistra" bus that starts at Terminal Station and makes a loop through the city, ending at Terminal Station, for 500 lire. The CS bus has now been redesignated as bus 30; walk 50-or-so yards to the front of the station, turn left, and you'll see its pick-up point.·. . . Alternatively, you can bear in mind that bus 64 (which is often a double-decker) starts at Terminal Station, goes down the important Via Nazionale into the Piazza Venezia, turns over to the Largo Argentina, and then crosses the Tiber to St. Peter's, a trip with a goal. But remember that the museum areas of the Vatican are closed after 4 p.m. . . . And look for that little bus station at the corner of Via Gaeta and Largo Giovanni Montemartini, behind the Museo delle Terme (near the Piazza della Repubblica). It's from here that a bus leaves every half-hour for Tivoli, for a one-way fare of only 1,400 lire. Once at Tivoli, it'll cost you 2000 lire to enter the gardens. . . . A gentle warning: Rome's 500 lire bus fare is, at the moment, the biggest bargain in town, but not if your pocket is picked on the bus; keep your wallet where you can feel it. . . . The international hospital of Rome, with many English-speaking doctors, is **Salvator Mundi,** 67 Viale Mura Gianicolensi (phone 586-041). Ask for the Directress, Sister Delores, who is especially helpful. . . . **Baby Parking,** a day-night nursery at 16 Via Santa Prisca (phone 577-8638), near the Piazza Venezia, will take care of your toddlers up to the age of ten, for 6,000 lire per hour, plus cost for transportation. . . . In months when the Pope is in Rome (usually every month other than July and August), papal audiences are held on Wednesdays at 11 a.m., at a new audience hall near St. Peter's. You can obtain a ticket to attend either at the Bishop's Office for United States Visitors to the Vatican, at 30 Via dell' Umiltà (phone 672-2256), one block from the Trevi Fountain (the office preferring that you write ahead, adding the zip code 00187 to their Rome address), or at the easily found headquarters of the English-speaking Paulist Fathers, in the **Church of Santa Susanna,** at 14 Via XX Settembre on the Piazza S. Bernardo (near the Piazza della Repubblica); their hours are daily from 9 a.m. to 12 and 4 to 7 p.m.; go there to reserve a ticket; pick up the ticket between 4 and 6 on Tuesday. If you can't attend a Wednesday audience, you can see the Pope—but from a much farther distance—at noon on most Sundays, when he appears promptly at the strike of the hour upon a high balcony overlooking the square of St. Peter's Basilica, to deliver a short sermon to an applauding crowd below. That's almost every Sunday, in fact. . . . For help with serious problems contact the following **embassies:** U.S.A., 119 Via Veneto (phone 4674); Canada, 27 Via G. B. Rossi (phone 855-341); Australia, 215 Via Alessandria (phone 841-241); Great Britain, 80 Via XX Settembre (phone 475-5441). . . . Note that banks are open weekdays only from 8:30 a.m. to 1:30 p.m.; stores are generally open from 9 a.m. to 2 p.m., and from 4 to 7 or 8 p.m.

A LAUNDROMAT IN ROME? I've found two outstanding spots, of which the most handy is the **Lavanderia Automatica,** at 11 Via Montebello, just off the Via Volturno, which is to the right of Terminal Station as you leave it; 9,000 lire for 5 kilos of wash, including drying. **Lavanderia a Gettoni** at 38 Campo dei Fiori charges the same 9,000 lire ($5.62), but is in the less handy Piazza Navona area, and open weekdays only, until 5 p.m.

AMERICAN G.I.'S: Numerous facilities are available to American military on leave in Rome at the **USO,** 2 Via della Conciliazione. The center is open daily from 9 a.m. to 7 p.m., runs low-priced tours of the city, helps arrange papal audiences, offers information, aid and advice, and throws in nursery, kitchen and shower facilities. Phone 656-4272 for further details.

READER'S COMMENTS: "There is a suggestion I would like to see printed somewhere, for women traveling alone, or in the company of other women, or with their young children, as I was doing in Latin countries. That is, not to be insulted by, or to ignore, the open admiration that the Latins have for the female. They admire beauty in everything, be it a woman, a tree, a ripe fruit or vegetable. When they speak to a stranger at the Piazza della Repubblica or Via Veneto or Piazza San Marco, they are not being fresh. Hopeful perhaps, but they never intend to be rude. They are curious, intrigued and sincere in their admiration. Time and again, throughout Italy and France, I saw American women asserting their virtue by repulsing the Latin, when all he wished was a little warmth of conversation. The woman is not respected for her behavior; she is considered cold, unpleasant and unfeminine, and conclusions are drawn that we American women are all this way. I believe it would be safe to say that should the woman prove to be simpatica, the Latin would not object if events developed beyond the conversation, and in fact would bring all his charm into play to bring this about. If, however, this is not agreeable to the woman, she may politely refuse (this may be necessary several times, a bit firmer each time) and that will be that. The pride of the Latin seems stronger than the desire. If the woman refuses smilingly, she wins his respect and a true admirer who leaves with a pleasant memory of an enjoyable interlude and with his dreams intact" (Mrs. Harlan Hall, Baton Rouge, Louisiana). . . . "In Italy, a money belt is an absolute must. If you have anything valuable in your pockets, pin them shut with a safety pin. If you value your camera, better leave it home. Italian tourist robbers are pros. They even strip off wrist watches" (Earl Clark, Port Angeles, Washington).

READERS' MISCELLANEOUS SUGGESTIONS: "Mailing a package anywhere in Italy can be a real hassle unless you know what you are doing. You might go to a *cartoleria* and buy a special string, paper, and seal to wrap up your parcel with. These items aren't expensive (you might get the string free) but it is the only packaging accepted by the Italian post" (Ms. Anne Lipp, Boyds, Maryland; note by AF: a *cartoleria* is an Italian stationery shop). . . . "I would like to see your book include a warning to readers about gypsies in Rome. They gather in small groups, and grab people walking past them. These attacks all too often result in their stealing wallets from pockets and handbags, and don't underestimate their skill! Avoid them if at all possible by crossing the street. They are particularly notorious in the areas of the Vatican and Railway Station, and their main prey is unsuspecting tourists. Beware!" (Mrs. J. A. Williams, Shalimar, Carada, Australia). . . . "I would like to make a suggestion to those on their way to Rome. You mention the Salvatore Mundi Hospital as having English-speaking staff. I found myself with a sprained ankle far away from the Salvatore Mundi, so I walked into the **American Embassy** at Via

Veneto, where I was given a list of physicians, dentists, hospitals, and pharmacies that have English-speaking staff. The embassy people were very nice and kind and will gladly find a doctor near your particular location. I hope this suggestion comes in handy!" (Alison Bracker, Sherman Oaks, California).

The awesomely beautiful city of Florence—capital of the Italian Renaissance—is about 2½ hours by train from Rome, the same by car. Florence is the next stop in our tour of Italy.

Chapter XII

FLORENCE

City on the Arno

AFTER THE FRENZY of Rome, this is a city for reflection. The museums of Florence have a near monopoly on the artistic masterpieces of the Renaissance. The treasures here are so thick that Raphael's priceless "Madonna of the Chair" is casually stuck away in a little nook of the galleries of the Pitti Palace.

This is also a city for buying gifts. You'd do well to delay your European shopping until you've seen the leather goods stalls in the Florence straw market or the jewelry shops on the Ponte Vecchio. Items which sell for $30 and more on New York's Fifth Avenue are priced here at less than ten bucks. If you've followed the $25-a-day regimen on the earlier part of your trip, you should have enough stashed away by now for a gift-buying splurge. Here's how to continue living on a budget—in Florence.

1. Orientation

Since almost no one arrives in Florence by air, and because the train station is within walking distance of most of our hotel choices, there's no major transportation cost on arrival. And once ensconced in your hotel or pensione, you'll discover that virtually all else in this relatively small city is within an easy stroll. If you ever do decide, on occasion, to take the bus somewhere (and that's unlikely in this walkers' city), be forewarned that bus fares (400 lire) aren't sold on the bus; rather, they must be purchased in advance from bus ticket offices, called **ATAF** (of which the easiest to find is in the central station, in the Casina della Rose snack bar next to the tracks;

alternatively, they're available at most newspaper stands or tobacco shops—*tabacchi)*. But it's on your own two feet that you'll first be seeking accommodations in this glorious city of art:

2. Florence Hotels

We'll discuss hotels in ascending order of price, beginning with the very cheapest. For Florence has some of the least costly hotel "finds" in Europe—so many of them, in fact, that it really isn't necessary to move as high as the second-class category—although there are some pretty superb choices in that classification, too.

You ought to know, preliminarily, that some of our selections are pensions—those tiny European hotels that offer meals along with their rooms (some, however, do not require that you take the meals). In Italy, the normal pensione consists of a single floor of an apartment house or office building, almost always upstairs; and you must reserve judgment until you've actually ascended in the elevator and inspected the accommodation. Particularly in Florence—which is an ancient city, historic, and with virtually no modern buildings—the inside appearance of most pensions is far better than their shabby 18th-century exteriors would indicate. Some of them offer amazingly large rooms, with balconies, parlors, all sorts of added features. To prove it, we'll immediately proceed to discuss the areas in which you'll find these choices, and then the choices themselves:

THE VIA FAENZA: The most startling proof that outward appearance can deceive, is found on a street called the Via Faenza, which is only three short blocks from the railroad station. If, from the station, you'll walk up the Via Nazionale for two blocks and turn left on the Via Faenza, you'll soon find a rather nondescript building at 56 Via Faenza that once was a monastery, now houses several stores on its ground floor, and will fill you with apprehension as you near it. Yet upstairs are five pensions whose owners, amenities, atmosphere—and price policies—are among the most charming in all Europe!

THE ITALIAN LIRA: For the purposes of this chapter, we've converted Italian lire into dollars at the rate of 1,600 lire per dollar—the approximate "floating" rate of the lira as of the time of writing. Thus, 100 lire have been assumed to equal 6.2 U.S.¢. Though you can expect further fluctuations by the time of your own stay in Italy, the variance should not be substantial.

The stars of 56 Via Faenza (although they have close competitors) are the three lovely Azzi sisters (Alba, Marga and Armanda), who operate the **Pensione Azzi** on the second floor (phone 21-38-06), where they dispense a kind of hospitality that is straight from the pages of Louisa May Alcott—this establishment, with its typical Florentine furnishings and cozy rooms, is the Italian equivalent of that mood. The rooms are of course impeccably clean, and—because they are in the back of the building, away from the street—unusually quiet. For such rooms, with all service charges and taxes included, the charge is only 16,500 lire ($10.31) single, 27,500 lire ($17.18) double, 38,000 lire ($23.75) for a group of three. A terrace with beautiful flowers, plants, and vines is open to all, and a refrigerator is available free to store food or drinks. Hot showers are 1,000 lire, cold 500 lire extra.

On the same floor, the **Locanda Armonia** (phone 211-146) has proprietors—Alighiero and Artea Pedani—who have their own qualities to commend them. They hand you a free map of Florence as you register, tell you to regard their establishment as your "second home," and intervene on your behalf to *salvare la situazione* with troublesome railway officials, tour operators, auto mechanics, and other tourist banes; they'll even watch your children when you go out for the evening. For tastefully furnished rooms, the charge here is exactly 13,000 ($8.12) per person in a double room, service and taxes included, 10,000 ($6.25) per member of the group for three or more sharing the same room. English is spoken by both hosts.

One flight up, proprietor Agostino di Stefano of the **Locanda Anna** (phone 298-322) does not speak English, but he refuses to let that be the slightest deterrent to the warmest sort of welcome, in rooms with marble floors and frescoed ceilings, with fresh cut flowers in the lounge, clean towels every other day, and an occasional piece of cold watermelon, which Agostino will sometimes hand you as you return from a hot day in the museums. Here the rate is a uniform 17,500 lire per person (service included) in twin rooms, 15,000 lire per person for groups of three, including breakfast; and again the rooms and bathrooms are scrupulously clean. . . . The other occupants of 56 Via Faenza are the **Pensione Merlini** (phone 212-848), whose furnishings would be the envy of any antique collector (26,000 lire ($16.25)) double, and breakfast, 4,500 lire extra, served on a terrace decorated with frescoes by American art students, and the **Locanda Marini** (phone 284-824), which is as friendly as the rest (and also offers the same rates of 26,000 lire ($16.25), double, without breakfast, 12,000 lire per person in triples or large four-bedded rooms). The Marini has recently inspired a flood of admiring letters from readers.

If these are full, then try the almost equally pleasant **Locanda Marcella,** next door at 58 Via Faenza (phone 21-32-32), some of whose rooms have a beautiful view out over Fiesole, and whose owner, Signor Noto Calogero, is a warm and welcoming gentleman whose rates are 16,000 lire ($10) single, 13,000 lire ($8.12) per person in doubles, triples and quadruples, all without breakfast. Due to flood damage, the stairway here is one of the worst (in appearance) you'll ever see; but upstairs you'll emerge into a well-furnished home atmosphere. In the same building, the **Locanda Mia Cara,** 58 Via Faenza (phone 216-053), charges a remarkable 14,000 lire per person in doubles or twins, plus 4,500 lire for breakfast (but nothing for showers), is one of the cleanest of the cheapest, and has a hardworking manager, Mr. Noto Pietro. . . . Or walk over to Mario Noce's **Locanda Mario,** one flight up at 89 Via Faenza (phone 212-039), which consists of nine beautifully furnished rooms with shining brown ceramic floors. Although it's by far the most expensive locanda on the street 42,000 lire ($26.25) double or twin, 53,000 lire ($33.12) triple, inclusive of a super breakfast and free showers), a great many readers seem to regard those rates as justified by the comfort and impeccable cleanliness of the Mario. Come to think of it, we receive more letters of praise about the Mario than for any other locanda in Florence. . . . Or have a look at **Locanda Nella,** 69 Via Faenza (phone 284-256), 12,000 lire per person in a triple or four-bedded room, including breakfast brought to your room on a copper trolley; or at **Tony's Inn**, 77 Via Faenza (phone 217-975), where Antonio and Rosemarie Lelli (she's from Toronto, he's a professional photographer) rent high-ceilinged rooms for 38,000 lire ($23.75) double, for not much more triple or quad.

A final, of somewhat splurgey, standout on the Via Faenza: the 24-room **Hotel Nuova Italia**, at #26 (phone 287-508), with its modern furniture throughout and wall-to-wall carpeting in every room. Singles 30,000 lire ($18.75), doubles 45,000 lire ($28.12), supplementary beds 14,000 lire ($10), and non-obligatory breakfasts 7,500 lire ($4.68). Signora Elida Viti, the Italian version of a Jewish mother, watches over all, assisted by her son Luciano and his wife Eileen. And how could the daughter-in-law be named Eileen? Eighteen years ago, she vacationed here with her family from Montreal, staying at a pensione chosen from this book—then called *Europe on $5 a Day* (happy days!). There she met the son of the pensione owners, Luciano Viti, and (you guessed it) they married.

If all the establishments on the Via Faenza are full (which is unlikely), then ask for directions to the Via Fiume, a block away from Faenza, and only one block from the side of the station itself. The **Albergo Petrarca**, at 20 Via Fiume (first floor, phone 26-12-09), is a cheerful little place in an elevator-equipped building, whose proprietor speaks a bit of "hotel English" and charges 44,000 lire ($27.50) double, including breakfast, service and tax for two.

NEAR THE DUOMO: This is the next general neighborhood in which I'd continue my search. The cathedral square of Florence *(Piazza del Duomo)* stands almost in the very center of the city, and the Duomo itself—with its exotic, pink-white-and-green-marble exterior, and its famous Ghiberti doors, which Michelangelo said were "fit to stand at the gates of Paradise" —is an important focal point of your touring activities. For one thing, the Academy Museum *(Accademia)*, at the Piazza San Marco, is only a few short blocks away, and it's here you'll find the original "David" by Michelangelo—which you cannot, under any circumstances, fail to see.

Off this square, on the second floor of 3 Via dei Conti (a side street off the Via de Cerretani; phone 21-52-16), the highly recommended but somewhat pricey **Pensione Centrale** rents ten extremely large rooms of the former patrician residence ("Palazzo Malaspina") it occupies. Including breakfast, service and tax, its high-season rates are 36,000 ($22.50) single, 56,000 lire ($35) double or twin, 24,000 lire ($15) for an extra bed in a double room—the rooms being especially suitable for travelling families. There's a friendly and English-speaking staff, and although you'll initially glimpse an enormous marble staircase, there's also an elevator. . . . A less expensive alternative to the Centrale, in a nearby location: **Pensione Sally**, 3 Via dei Servi (phone 284-519), whose managers are the Sergio Avellinos. They charge 35,000 lire ($21.87), breakfast included, for a double room, 28,000 lire ($17.50), breakfast included, for one of their very large singles, and the situation of their "hotel" is magnificent, just a few feet from the Duomo. Stairs only; a fairly forbidding exterior; but large rooms.

PIAZZA SS. ANNUNZIATA: The lodging for worshippers of the Renaissance is the surprisingly spacious **Hotel Morandi**, at 3 Piazza SS. Annunziata, phone 212-687, on a square so picturesque and unchanged that if you were to take away the autos, you'd instantly be in another age. There are loggias on three sides. Directly across from the hotel is the famous foundling hospital of Florence (oldest in Europe and the first Renaissance structure in Florence) with its arches designed by Brunelleschi and with the world-famous *putti*—or swaddling babies—of della Robbia. In the square stands a statue of Ferdinand de Medici, and two beautiful fountains of Pietro Tacco. The entrance to the Etruscan Museum is also in this square. And, of course, the baroque-style Church of SS. Annunziata is an important Florentine site—a place to which the brides of Florence, by custom, bring their wedding bouquets.

Now the Hotel Morandi itself is in an ancient—and at times, rather formal—building, but it has an elevator, and the rooms inside have character (beamed ceilings, among other things) and are quiet; and finally, the prices are good: room-*and*-breakfast ranges from 22,000 to 28,000 lire ($13.75 to $17.50) per person per day, depending mainly on whether you occupy a double or single room; discounts are granted to groups or families occupying rooms with three and four beds. Highest recommendation.

PIAZZA DI SANTA MARIA NOVELLA: We move now to two higher-priced and fairly large third-class hotels, located only two blocks from the railroad station, on or near the famous and often pictured Piazza di Santa Maria Novella—a huge, quiet square with two giant obelisks in its center, classic loggia on one side, the Church of Maria Novella on the other—really an awesome sight. Directly on the square, the always serviceable, if unexciting, **Hotel Universo,** 20 Piazza Santa Maria Novella (phone 212-184), is elevator-equipped and charges 23,000 lire single, 42,000 lire ($26.25) double, including breakfast, service and tax. Dreary entrance and corridors, but quite satisfactory rooms.

In previous editions of this book, I gave a high recommendation to the beautiful **Hotel Croce di Malta,** which is half a block off this square, on the Via della Scala, and has its own open-air swimming pool. Unfortunately, the Croce di Malta has equipped so many of its rooms with private bath, that it no longer fits within our price range. Therefore, Hope and I just recently walked several feet farther away from the square to a building that had often intrigued us, where we now discovered the **Hotel Aprile,** at 6 Via della Scala (phone 21-62-37)—and it's a worthy successor to the Croce di Malta. A low, three-story building, the Aprile turns out to be nothing other than a former palace belonging to the Medicis (and once called the Palazzo del Borgo), completely remodeled, with 30 very fine rooms, plus lounges and a garden. From April through October, the Aprile charges 37,000 ($23.12) per person in a bathless room, including breakfast, service and taxes; and although that's above our limits, the hotel and its amenities are really quite outstanding: there are marble tiled corridors with blue-and-yellow gilt doors, etchings on the walls, tastefully decorated rooms. Those with private bath and private facilities are 43,000 lire ($26.87) per person, breakfast and all else thrown in.

NEAR THE RAILROAD STATION: For your most plentiful supply of budget rooms, the street where you'll always find something is the little **Via Panzani,** located off the Piazza Unità Italiana, almost directly in front of the railroad station. You'll have to carry your luggage less than a hundred yards before you come upon it; and then, stretching before you for a solid two blocks, you'll pass an unbroken line of third- and fourth-class hotels, all with tiny lobbies, and most with stairs only; but some with surprisingly decent and comfortable rooms (not, however, to be compared with selections in other areas of town).

In the third-class category, you'll probably find the best rooms at the **Lombardia,** 19 Via Panzani (phone 21-52-76) (doubles for 35,000 lire, not including breakfast); or at the **Gioconda,** 2 Via Panzani, phone 21-31-50 (twins with private shower for 48,000 lire, service and taxes included, doubles without shower for 37,500 lire, singles 31,000 lire, breakfast 5,000 lire); and the less expensive—but still third-class rated—**Polo Nord,** 7 Via Panzani (phone 287-952), charging 17,500 ($10.93) per person, service, taxes, and free showers included.

HIGHER-PRICED—ALONG THE ARNO: This is the river that courses

through Florence, and that caused the tragic flood of November 4, 1966. So thoroughly unchanged are the buildings and famous bridges along it, that in winter and spring—when the river is full—the resulting scene looks as though it were lifted unaltered from the famous painting that shows Dante first espying Beatrice, as she walks with companions at the river's edge. Generally, this is also the most expensive area of Florence, but there are some budget exceptions in it.

The best of these is the **Pensione Adria,** 4 Piazza Frescobaldi (phone 21-50-29), which is just across the Ponte San Trinità (one of the world's most beautiful bridges), on the far side of the Arno. An eccentric elevator will transport you slowly (but safely) to the top floor, where Giuliana Nardi rents comfortable bedrooms at 28,500 lire ($17.81) for singles, 48,000 lire ($30) twins, including breakfast served in a glass-covered loggia-lounge overlooking historic Florence.

Not directly facing the Arno, but near it (and near the Berchielli), is one of the best bargains in town: Signora Ada Cestelli's four-room **Albergo Cestelli,** 25 Borgo Santi Apostoli (phone 214-213), at which the kindly proprietress offers very special rates to readers of this book only (guaranteed up to the end of 1985): 19,000 lire ($11.87) for a small double; 30,000 lire ($18.75) for each of two enormously large double rooms with mammoth beds à la Medici and antique furniture; 35,000 lire ($21.87) for the only room with bath; all rates including breakfast. Third and fourth beds are available at a supplement of 35% to the twin rate. From the central station, walk up the Via Tornabuoni to Piazza Santa Trinità, and then turn left into the narrow Borgo Santi Apostoli.

FAR SIDE OF THE ARNO: For readers who seek a quiet location, or need

parking space for their car, the large **Pensione Silla,** 5 Via dei Renai (phone 284-810), is an appropriate choice. It's operated by a genial, English-speaking gentleman named A. Silla, and offers a fixed-price policy to readers of this book: 28,000 lire ($17.50) per person in a bathless double room, with breakfast, taxes, and service charge included, 35,000 lire ($21.87) per person for the same with private bath. A large and luxurious summer terrace is available for guests; in fact, you'll be flabbergasted, I think, to find such comfort and tasteful decoration behind such battered walls. Best of all, the building occupies a residential location, with virtually unlimited parking space on the street below (a crucial feature for motorists in Florence), yet close to everything important—but if you do park here, take all valuables out of the car.

NEAR THE PIAZZA DELLA SIGNORIA:
The best known site of Florence is, of course, the Piazza della Signoria, in front of the Palazzo Signoria, Florence's City Hall, where stands the well-known copy (not the original) of Michelangelo's "David." It is here, too, that you'll find the renowned Uffizi Gallery; and all of this is but a block-or-so from the Ponte Vecchio (the famous covered bridge of Florence) and the Arno River.

In the area around the Piazza are found several relatively large, relatively old, second-class hotels. They strain the budget somewhat, but they are each well suited for older tourists who'd like a touch of history and 19th-century atmosphere in their hotel—but at moderate cost.

Typical among this group, and to be considered only on a big splurge basis, is the venerable **Hotel Porta Rossa**, 19 Via Porta Rossa (phone 287-551), at the corner of Via Monalda, one block from the Arno. Built around a medieval tower dating back to the 13th century, the Porta Rossa has been officially listed as a hotel since the year 1386! Now completely modernized, its lounge facilities are spacious, with heavy leather chairs that make you feel cool and relaxed on the hottest day, and the tastefully furnished rooms are unusually large (because it is such a very old hotel). Singles 36,000 lire, including service charges and tax; bathless doubles 48,000 lire, with service and tax. Breakfast: 6,500 lire extra, per person.

In the same area, only one short block from the Piazza della Signoria, is a big (probably largest in its category) and somewhat costlier third-class hotel that is again one of the oldest in Florence (its dining room was once the Parliament chamber of Florence; the age of the building means that its bedrooms are, once more, unusually large). That's the **Hotel Columbia-Parlamento,** at 29 Piazza San Firenze (phone 21-34-00), corner of Via dei Leoni and Borgo dei Greci, with 92 rooms renting for 50,000 lire ($31.25) double, 36,000 lire ($22.50) single, including service and taxes, but not breakfast (8,000 lire, $5, extra); there's an elevator, after you walk up the first flight of stairs to the huge dining room, with its frescoed ceilings and portraits of Garibaldi; you may want to sightsee through the dining room, even if you aren't staying at the hotel.

Finally, two blocks from Piazza della Signoria, at 7 Via Dei Pepi, next to Piazza Santa Croce and 100 yards from the home of Michelangelo (Casa Buonarroti at 70 Via Ghibellina), **Pensione La Locandina** (phone 24-08-80) offers a $1 per day discount to bearers of this book, off a price of $55,000 lire ($34.37) for a lovingly furnished, antiques-filled double room with private shower and w.c., including breakfast for two served in a dining room with parquet floor, large original open fireplace, the largest chandelier in Florence, and window curtains fit for Buckingham Palace. Unfortunately, there are no single rooms in this extremely stylish and serene pensione located on the second floor of a 14th-century mansion. Signora Roberta and Signor Nanni are the current proprietors, both English speaking.

THE SHOPPING AREA:
An alternative choice in the same central area, the **Hotel-Pensione La Residenza,** 8 Via Tornabuoni, phone 284-197, is located on the most fashionable street of Florence, which is lined with

elegant stores, good for window-shopping only. But La Residenza itself is fairly moderately priced, and is again an excellent buy for older tourists. It's on the second, third and attic floors of a 14th-century building, no less; the lounges and rooms are beautifully furnished and upkept by an attentive staff, supervised by the bilingual Gianna Vasile; and it offers special prices for readers of this book who display a copy upon entering: 39,000 lire ($24.37) for bathless singles, 62,000 lire ($38.75) for bathless doubles, with breakfast, service and taxes included. The management will normally want you to take half-pension, however, which is priced (again for readers only) at exactly 57,000 lire ($35.62) per person for bathless rooms, at 62,000 lire ($38.75) per person with private bath or shower. Excellent food; discounts for families traveling with children; two large lounges; television, roof garden; elevator; garage service; and bar. . . . In the very same shopping area, but much less expensive, the 81-bed **Albergo Firenze,** 4 Piazza Donati (phone 214-203 or 268-301), is surely one of the best bargains in Florence in the economy category, charging only 22,000 lire ($13.75) for bathless singles, 34,000 lire ($21.25) for bathless twins, 42,000 lire ($26.25) for twins with private w.c., 5,000 lire for breakfast ($2.50), 2,000 lire ($1.25) for showers. Four floors, no elevators, rather plain but very clean, and in quiet surroundings, a few steps from the central Piazza della Repubblica (from which you walk down the Via del Corso for about 50 yards until you see the tiny courtyard of the hotel to your right). While owner Signor Rocchini speaks only basic English, he knows enough to service your needs.

READERS' PENSION SELECTIONS: "**Pensione Kursaal,** on the second floor of Via Nazionale 24N (phone 496-324), just a few blocks from the station, is capably managed by Signor Franco Bellini, extremely clean, well furnished, conveniently located, and especially impressive for its lovely bed linens. The charge in 1985 will be 22,000 lire ($13.75) single, 33,000 lire ($20.62) double, 43,000 lire ($26.87) triple, 53,000 lire ($33.12) quad, not including optional breakfast which is 6,000 lire ($3.75) extra" (Bill and Carline Gayde, Royal Oak, Michigan). . . . "Signor Antonio Minoia's **Soggiorno Satellite,** top floor of 14 Via Fiume (phone 294-796), just around the corner from the railroad station and off the noisy main streets, offers many extras in the way of old Florence atmosphere: high ceilings in large, spacious rooms, lovely antiques in reception and breakfast area, spotlessly waxed floors and clean beds, an elevator, rooms with French doors leading to balconies with views of distant hills over Florence rooftops, fresh air stirring, birds singing—what a treat after a hot, noisy day in the city! Double rooms with breakfast for 40,000 lire ($25); singles for 26,000 lire ($16.25), and free showers" (Mary L. Radcliffe, Cottonwood, Arizona; similar raves from Stephen Hellman, Department of Political Science, York University, Ontario, Canada, who points out that the Satellite's rooms, "given their internal location, are extremely quiet—something of a rarity in Florence during the summer. Several rooms even offer a marvelous view of an old courtyard framed by the nearby hills of Fiesole"). . . . "I certainly hope you'll find room to include Signora **Aldini's Locanda,** 13 Via Calzaioli (phone 214-752), which is just a half block from the famous Duomo, and where a room for three, with breakfast in bed, and a shower in the room, was a mere 40,000 lire ($25). Such a pleasant atmosphere surrounded this home it would be a shame to overlook it" (Susan Lynn Boettcher, Lawndale, California, seconded by Monica Lidral, Rhinelander, Wisconsin: all double and triple rooms are with private bath, yet will rent in 1985 for only 40,000 lire ($25) double, 56,000 lire ($35) triple, 70,000 lire ($43.75) quad, breakfast included). . . . "**Pensione Manuelli,** Via Martelli 6 (phone 270-893), conveniently located near the Duomo and Baptistery, has beautifully kept rooms with charming touches, for which it charges 33,000 lire ($20.62) for two, per night. On the third floor of an elevator-equipped building; its proprietress is a gentle, gracious lady; and no meals except breakfast are served, thus giving one the opportunity to enjoy the many fine Florentine restaurants" (D. J. Abbate, Wolcott, Connecticut). . . . "**Locanda**

Marilena, 20 Via Fiume (phone 261-705), is only a block from the railroad station, yet charges only 29,000 lire ($18.12) for a lovely and spacious double room. Breakfast, however, isn't served" (Wendy Furman, Cerritos, California). . . . "**Pensione Joly,** in a pensione-packed building at 20 Via Fiume, is central but quiet, and charges only 38,000 lire ($23.75) for a twin-bedded room, breakfast for two included" (Carlos Eduardo Shmerkin, Buenos Aires, Argentina). . . . "Of all the pensions and hotels listed in your chapter, **Soggiorno Stella Mary,** 17 Via Fiume (phone 21-56-94), is closest to the railroad station, less than five minutes away on foot. Very friendly people, with very little English, but they enjoy helping foreigners with their phrasebook Italian. Rates are only 27,000 lire ($16.87) for doubles, 11,000 lire ($6.87) per person in quads, showers 2,500 lire ($1.56) extra; while the elevator—one of the largest I've seen—requires a 10-lire coin! Make sure you equip yourself with one" (Sam and Robin Cope, Auckland, New Zealand). . . . "**Pensione Gioia,** 25 Via Cavour (phone 282-804), is a jewel of a place—a home away from home. Excellent meals, large, beautiful rooms, a warm host and hostess (Mr. and Mrs. Carlo Tatini, son Carlo and daughter Carla) that I shall long remember and hope to see again in the near future. Doubles without bath will be 35,000 lire ($21.87) in 1985. What a family! What a place!" (Elvira C. Weeks, New York City). . . . "An absolute gold mine was the **Pensione Gioia,** Via Cavour 25, where we had an immaculate room. We were in walking distance of the magnificent Piazza Duomo and the unbelievable shoppers' paradise, the flea market. The family which ran this pension not only took us into their lodgings, but into their lives. They guided us everywhere and even called ahead to Rome when we were ready to leave Florence and booked us hotel reservations for the upcoming holiday weekend. They also had a van which picked up guests arriving on late evening trains into Florence. This is our third trip to Europe and I must say the Pensione Gioia is one of our treasured finds" (Dr. and Mrs. Barry Levy, Pompano Beach, Florida). . . . "We drove out to the hill suburb of Fiesole and found the **Hotel 'Villa Bonelli,'** Via Francesco Poeti, N. 1 (phone 59-513), one of the finest places, ideal for anyone visiting Florence. Cool and pleasant, new and very modern in every way; we found nothing to equal it anywhere in Italy. Bus service to Florence is excellent (about a 20-minute trip), making it practically the same as living in the city" (A. E. Roper, Middletown, Ohio; note by A.F.: the famous, cool Fiesole is an Etruscan city built before 500 B.C., several hundred meters above Florence. To get there, take the #7 bus from the central railway station square in Florence, 20 minutes away. The Villa Bonelli, will be charging 40,000 lire ($25), single with bath and w.c., 55,000 lire ($34.37) double, 67,000 lire ($41.87), for a double with private bath, always including breakfast, in 1985, with supplementary beds 24,000 lire (in rooms with bath), or 20,000 lire (without bath), including breakfast served in a charming dining room with panoramic view. We've received a great many letters of praise for the Villa Bonelli and its English-speaking owners, the Boninsegni brothers. From the Fiesole bus stop (400 lire fare, one way), walk uphill along the main road for 500 yards, then turn right into the narrow Via F. Poeti, or phone the Boninsegni brothers who will pick you up free in their car).

READERS' SELECTIONS FOR READERS WITH CARS: "Arriving by car in the middle of the maddening traffic of the city, I decided to stay outside of the center in a quiet and sane section, characterized by broad boulevards, yet within walking distance of all the attractions. And I found the **Pensione Losanna,** 9 Via Alfieri (phone 245-840), to be spacious, clean, quiet—and with virtually unlimited parking space. The English-speaking proprietor charges 24,000 lire ($15) for singles without bath, but including breakfast and service; 37,000 lire ($23.12) for doubles without bath, including breakfast and service; 46,000 lire ($28.75) for doubles with private bath. I enjoyed my stay here and the reprieve it offers from the Florentine bustle" (Mrs. Herbert Miller, New York City; note by A. F.: several other recommendations for the Losanna, including one from Michael Meade of Hays, Kansas, who writes: "As you know, Florence can be very noisy in the center. Here, all the rooms face on a garden. . . . The Losanna's proprietor and his wife are a charming couple from Calabria who have lived a number of years in Australia and speak English well. I'm sure you'll find Signor Vicenzo Campagna as pleasant and helpful as I did"). . . . "We were very happy at the **Pensione Alfa,** 9 Via Alfieri (phone 24-58-25), where we had plenty of hot water, enjoyed good street parking nearby, and were well treated by the young proprietors, an Englishman married to a Florentine. Rates are only 30,000 lire ($18.75) for a large bathless double, plus 7,000 lire (quite high) for an optional breakfast—and you won't be pressed to take breakfast at the pension. What's more, prices for showers are waived to readers of your book!" (Jean H. Paschen, Glenview, Illinois). . . . "We decided to stay outside the town and were directed to the **Albergo Trieste,** at 16 Via Campo Sportivo (phone 44-33-49) in Sesto Fiorentino. It was a wonderful bargain for a new, well-furnished clean double with bath—all for 38,000 lire ($23.75). The same room without bath would have been only 29,000 lire ($18.12). There is a direct bus service to Florence every 20 minutes" (Gita Gopalakrishnan, Calcutta, India).

THE BIG SPLURGE PENSIONS: Two particular pensions deserve special mention and special consideration by readers willing to spend just a bit more for their accommodations.

Directly on the Arno River near the Ponte Vecchio, the **Pensione Quisisana,** 4 Lungarno Archibusieri (phone 216-692 or 215-046), is serviced by a burnished-wood elevator that takes you into a heavily furnished, labyrinthine, 37-room apartment whose interior resembles that of Rembrandt's home in Amsterdam. There's punctilious polite service by a staff of white-jacketed stewards and rates of 60,000 lire ($37.50) for bathless doubles, breakfast, service and taxes included.

Smaller and more lightly elegant, and again on the Arno, is the **Pensione Bretagna,** 6 Lungarno Corsini (phone 263-618), whose parquet floors, crystal chandeliers, gilt and embroidered furniture, are constantly being polished or swept by a crew of white-aproned, black-uniformed maids; every room, even the bathless ones, has a bidet in it; and there's a lovely balcony off the drawing room that looks out over the Arno. Here the charge for bathless rooms is 30,000 lire ($21.42) single, 56,000 lire ($35) double, but that includes continental breakfast, as well as service and taxes.

3. Starvation Budget Rooms & Meals

There are important finds for the indigent in Florence, too. First we'll consider the rock-bottom rooms and then the rock-bottom meals.

Cheapest of the cheap, in tutta la città, is the privately operated 154-bed **Santa Monaca Hostel** at 6 Via Santa Monaca (phone 26-83-38), which charges only 9,000 lire ($5.62) per person per night, plus 1,500 lire every four days for the rental of a linen sleeping bag. Better than a youth hostel, but not as good as a pensione, it takes both men and women, whom it places in rooms with 6 to 20 beds, imposes a midnight curfew and closes the dorms from 9:30 a.m. to 6 p.m. for cleaning, offers free showers but no meals, and stays open all year around. Europe on $10 a Day! That's on the far side of the Arno; from the station walk to the Piazza Santa Maria Novella, then down the Via dei Fossi, cross the Arno bridge (Ponte alla Carraia), walk up the Via dei Serragli, and the third street to the right is Via Santa Monaca. Personally measured walking time: 12 minutes.

STARVATION BUDGET MEALS: For meals, Florence offers two exceptionally low-cost dining halls, of which the most important is the 500-seat **Student Mensa** of the University of Florence, at 25a Via San Gallo, about three short blocks from the Piazza Indipendenza. Walk inside, into the courtyard, where you'll see a neon sign reading "Bar"; walk up the 41 steps at that point, and you'll find the huge Mensa, serving equally huge meals (ask for the "Pasto Completo") for 4,000 lire (three courses), including wine—you can't possibly spend more than $2.50. Hours are noon to 2:15 p.m., and 6:45 to 8:45 p.m., Monday through Saturday, and the posted regulations (which are not always observed) require a student card.

Unfortunately, the Mensa closes from August 1 to September 15. When that happens you'll want to seek another budget haven, but one that has no student affiliation, called the **Casa di San Francesco,** which is maintained by a religious order, at 2 Piazza SS. Annunziata. Pay 8,500 lire ($5.31) at the door, then walk inside to partake of pasta, a main course with salad or vegetable, plus fruit and wine. You'll dine among a wonderful melange of students and old people, priests and workingmen; and you'll simply have to point at what they're eating to order from the waitress—there's no menu. Don't wear your newest and most expensive clothes. Serving times are from noon to 2:30 p.m., for lunch only. Closed Saturdays and Sundays.

READERS-ON-THE-STARVATION-BUDGET: "The tidy **Locanda Enza,** 47 Via San Zanobi (phone 490-990), within walking distance of the train station, charges 29,000 lire ($18.12) for a double without bath, is managed by a dynamic young couple who speak excellent English" (Stephen C. Becker, Asbury Park, New Jersey).

READERS-ON-THE-SUB-STARVATION BUDGET: "The Youth Hostel called **'Villa Camerata'** is located at 2/4 Viale A. Righi (phone 601-451), in a fine park at the last stop of bus #17 B, and can house as many as 430 persons. Since I live in Florence, I am not allowed to spend my nights there, but many people have told me that this is one of the best in Europe. The fee per night is 11,000 lire (including sheets), and if you do not have a membership card you can buy one there for 24,000 lire (valid all over the world)" (Giuseppe M. Massaro, Florence, Italy; note by A.F.: the stunningly beautiful youth hostel of Florence, a mammoth villa of the 15th century surrounded by a large park and garden, on the outskirts of Florence, has from 12 to 20 beds per room, takes both men and women, but requires that you have a youth hostel card, obtainable in the U.S. from American Youth Hostels, Inc., 1332 Eye St., NW, Washington, DC 20005, for $14 per year if you're over 18, for only $7 if you're under 18 or older than 60. Rates are 11,000 lire ($6.87) per person, breakfast included; and there's an evening curfew of 11:30 p.m. Important warning: if you arrive in summer, always phone first to this immensely popular place before embarking on the long bus ride, and don't appear before 2 p.m.—the time when new arrivals are accepted. And finally, don't be dismayed to discover that from the bus stop (in front of the huge park of the hostel), you'll need to walk about half a mile along a winding alley to reach the hostel).

4. Moderately Priced Restaurants

The budget restaurants of Florence are scattered throughout the city, in every major district. We'll discuss them by area, in roughly ascending order of cost:

NEAR THE RAILROAD STATION: You'll find some real stars here, beginning with the restaurant of the railway workers' union—patronized by many middle class Florentines—on the street that runs along the side of the railroad station. It's called the **"Mensa DLF,"** is located at 6 Via Luigi Alamanni, operates only from noon to 2:30 p.m., and from 7:15 to 9 p.m., and charges 1,600 lire for soups, 1,800 to 2,400 lire for pasta of various sorts, 3,100 to 4,800 lire for most main courses, 800 lire for fruit. Leave the station from the side of the telephone office (look for the sign "Telefoni"),

walk down the steps, turn right, pass the ground floor supermarket and the florist, continue walking, always keeping the long grey wall to your right, and after about 300 yards you will have reached the Mensa DLF.

Three normal commercial restaurants hereabouts: the superb little basement restaurant called the **Trattoria Enzo e Piero**, at 105r Via Faenza, which charges exactly 11,000 lire ($6.87) for a true menu turistico (three courses, including bread, wine, cover and service)—it's always crowded, but worth the wait, closed Sundays; 200 yards away, at 34r Via Faenza (which is not to be confused with 34n), the **Trattoria Guido,** charging the same 11,000 lire ($6.87) for a tasty menu turistico (but one that does not include wine), served in spotless surroundings, closed Wednesdays; and, farther up from the station, the exciting **Taverna Medici**, 61r Via Cavour (corner of Via Guelfa), which is patronized by some of the nicest people in Florence, and operates a self-service section downstairs, where main courses are 3,000 to 4,500 lire, vegetables, 1,200 to 2,000 lire, pastas 3,000 lire, cheese and ice cream 2,200 lire (you'll pay 20% more for the same items on the ground floor). In the station itself, you'll quickly spot a counter restaurant identified as a **Self-Service,** which serves a huge bowl of spaghetti for 2,800 lire, or a sizable hunk of pizza alla napoletana for 3,000, or pizza Margherita for 3,300, any one of which is enough for a full meal.

BEHIND THE UFFIZI GALLERIES:

The only cluster of moderately priced restaurants in Florence is found at the side of and behind the Uffizi Galleries, on two little streets—the **Via dei Neri** and more particularly, on the **Via dei Leoni.** For value received, these can scarcely be equalled throughout the rest of Europe. On Via dei Leoni alone, there are four restaurants serving three-course prezzo fisso meals for 12,500 to 13,000 lire ($7.81 to $8.12)—and two of them include a quarter of a liter of wine in the basic price. They are: the **Ristorante Montecatini,** Via dei Leoni 6 (13,000 lire, which includes cover charge and tip); the **Buzzino,** Via dei Leoni 8 (13,000 lire, including wine, service charge and cover); the **Trattoria Roberto,** which is on a continuation of Via dei Leoni, called Via dei Castellani, No. 4r, near the river (12,500 lire for soup or pasta, main course with vegetables, fruit or cheese, a quarter of a liter of chianti, and bread; closed Wednesdays). Again on the Via dei Leoni, at #14, the **Trattoria Alfredo,** charges 13,000 lire for yet another three-course meal, including service and wine (closed Wednesdays). And even if you order à la carte at these places, you can still get away for very little. At the Buzzino, I recently had spaghetti, roast chicken, cheese, and wine for 13,000 lire ($8.12). Sample à la carte meals at the Ristorante Montecatini: cotoletta alla Milanese for 6,000 lire ($3.75); spaghetti for 3,200 lire ($2); minestrone for 2,600 lire ($1.62).

Which of the four seem outstanding? I vacillate between Alfredo's and the Roberto, but usually end up going to Roberto's. If you're approaching this area from the river, try the nearby Roberto, which is where most of the museum guards at the Uffizi eat. If you're walking down the Via dei Leoni from the Piazza della Signoria, try Alfredo's. But if you're feeling flush and willing to blow an extra 1,000 lire, then try the attractive Montecatini, and order either its *ravioli fatti in casa* (home-made ravioli, a specialty) for 4,000 lire, or its *petti di pollo dorati* (chicken in an egg batter, a Florentine specialty) for 5,200 lire.

Cheapest place to eat à la carte in this area? That's at **Trattoria da Benvenuto,** 47 Via dei Neri, where the spaghetti is only 3,000 lire ($1.87), fried fish with green sauce 5,000 lire ($3.12), zucchini salad 2,200 lire ($1.37), a quarter liter of red wine 1,000 lire (62¢), cover charge 1,200 lire, and service 12%. Finest individual dishes? The risotto alla Fiorentina, available at most ristorantes hereabouts—it's a delicious rice-and-tomatoes treat; the chicken cacciatore; the tender gorgonzola cheese called "verde dolce."

And where do you go if you simply want a light snack or something less than a full meal? Well, in the same area, a small rosticceria at 74r Via dei Neri sells tasty sandwiches for 2,000 lire ($1.25); a frigittoria at 8 Via de Neri specializes in pizza for 2,500 lire; and a baby-sized wineteria (simply called "vino" and no larger than a telephone booth) at 70r Via dell' Anguillara, a side street off the Via dei Leoni, sells 25 different kinds of local wines at 400 to 600 lire (31¢ to 37¢) per glass, as well as rye bread sandwiches for 600 to 900 lire. This place is crowded if more than one client is inside, and nobody minds if you drink your glass of orvieto sole or chianti controllato on the sidewalk—you won't be the only one.

ON THE PIAZZA DELLA SIGNORIA: Your one "expensive" meal—preferably in the evening—should be taken at the **Ristorante Orcagna,** the big outdoor establishment on the Piazza della Signoria. Prices here are not the cheapest, but with care a meal can be had for about $9. Recommended feast? Start with the luscious tortellini with meat sauce (*tortellini al sugo di carne*) 4,000 lire, then order liver à la Venice *(fegato alla Veneziana)* 6,500 lire, and have a tomato salad (it's a huge one) on the side, 3,000 lire. Total: 13,000 lire, plus bread and cover charge of 1,200 lire, plus 12% service, for a grand total of 14,800 lire ($9.25). And there's also a three-course prezzo fisso here for 14,000 lire ($8.75), wine included. The view is worth the price: This is the square on which the most successful copy of Michelangelo's "David" stands, along with Cellini's famous "Perseus Holding the Medusa's Head" and other masterworks of sculpture, magnificently presented in the world-renowned square.

A SPECIAL TREAT—NEAR THE DUOMO: Food with fellowship! Because **La Botteghina Rossa,** at 24r Via degli Alfani, five short blocks from the Duomo and Borgo Pinti, possesses only two long tables with 24 seats apiece, you have no choice but to meet your fellow communal diners, an interesting mixture of local artists, students, low and high society. They flock here for an astonishingly copious 9,000 lire ($5.62) three-course menu that includes free wine and mineral water, hors d'oeuvres (curried rice, olives, sardines, beans-onions-tomato salad, minced carrots, spiced pickles and caviar, to name just a few), followed by pasta with meat sauce, then, for the main course, grilled fish or a meat dish. Served on Limoges or Rosenthal china, the food is so plentiful that you probably won't even touch the (free) bread. Stately Señora Ferdinanda Martini Monti vedova Dini Foschi, who watches over all with aristocratic mien, has personally guaranteed the 9,000 lire price until March of 1986 to anyone showing a copy of this book upon entering. Hours are limited: evenings only, from 5 to 8:30 p.m.; if you arrive later than 6 p.m., you probably won't find a seat! Closed Sundays.

SELF-SERVICE RESTAURANTS: There are two large ones in Florence, the better of which is called **Self-Service Restaurant,** and is located upstairs at 5 Via Pecori, near the Via Vecchietti, 1½ blocks from the Duomo. From the Baptistery of the Duomo, walk down the Via Pecori; the first side street you'll pass will be the Via dei Brunelleschi, the second is the Via Vecchietti; between these two, on the Via Pecori, look up and you'll spot a self-service sign—entrance is up a plain stairway between a purse store and the subscription offices of the newspaper, *Corriere della Sera*. Once upstairs, you'll find crowds of Florentines (mainly at lunch, less so at dinner), who pack away servings of pasta (2,800 lire), soups (1,900), main courses with vegetable (most of them 5,000 lire), desserts (fruit 900, sweets 1,800 lire). Some budget rules for cafeteria dining in Italy: make your main course pasta with meat sauce, rather than meat and vegetables—you'll save 600 to 700 lire; choose ordinary wine, not the brand name; choose, pay for, and eat one course at a time—then go back (if you can) for more; the eyes of many tourists are bigger than their stomachs, and funds are wasted on selections that can't be finished. Open 11:45 to 3 p.m. and 6:45 to 10 p.m.; closed Saturday.

The other major cafeteria? That's the **Self-Service Giannino in San Lorenzo,** next door to the ristorante of the same name, at 31r Borgo S. Lorenzo—50 yards up from the Via Panzani, and just around the corner from the Medici Chapels and the San Lorenzo Church. Prices somewhat higher (main courses for 5,000 lire, pasta or soup for 3,000) than at our preferred self-service spot. Closed Tuesdays.

PASTA, PASTA, PASTA: A final oddity: **Spaghetteria,** at 26r Via dell' Oriuolo, corner Via San Egidio, about 500 yards from the Piazza della Repubblica, which serves 35 different kinds of spaghetti, tortellini, ravioli, risotto and gnocchi, all at the uniform price of 5,000 lire ($3.12) per large helping, including a roll and service. Open daily except Wednesdays from 11 to 3 and 7 to 9 p.m.

PREZZO FISSO VS. À LA CARTE: Which should you seek? In Italy, the price of a prezzo fisso (table d'hôte) meal may seem high in comparison with the à la carte cost of individual plates; however, persons dining à la carte must usually pay a cover charge of 1,200 lire and a service charge of 12%. Since these items are *included* in the price of a prezzo fisso meal, the prezzo fisso can often bring a price advantage to you. On the other hand, the prezzo fisso meal may not include the restaurant's most attractive specialties. So which should you choose? Hmmm. . . .

READERS' RESTAURANT SELECTIONS: "The **Piccadilly Pizza** at 43 Via Por S. Maria, a block from the Ponte Vecchio, serves huge, thick slices of pizza with 12 different choices of topping—ham and artichoke, onions and mushrooms, sausage and peppers, etc.—for 2,400 lire, with cold drinks for 1,500 lire. A quick, delicious lunch for under $2.50" (Prof. S. Friedland, Brooklyn, New York; note by A.F.: In addition to selling unusually flavored ice cream cones for 1,500 lire (93¢)—such as *uva* (grape), *mulatta* (chocolate with almonds)—Piccadilly Pizza offers a specialty known as *mangia e beve* (literally: eat and drink), which consists of fresh lemon juice and vegetable and fruit salad, all served in a large beer mug with spoon and straw, for 3,500 lire ($2.18). Excellente! And open daily except Mondays from 11 a.m. to 10:30 p.m. . . . "A self-service restaurant, the **Grande Italia,** 25 Piazza della Stazione, is just opposite the railroad station, on the corner of the Piazza Stazione and the Via Nazionale. It is clean and roomy, the food is cheap and hot, and there is a wide variety of selections to choose from. I was in Florence in January with two other brothers, and we ate here all the time (except on Fridays, when the restaurant is closed). A typical à la carte meal price for pasta, chicken with chips, bread and a bottle of wine is 11,500 lire" (Brother Dunstan Henry, Marcellin College, Auckland, New Zealand). . . . "We found a super restaurant near the Santa Monica Student Hostel. It's called **La Mangiatoia,** 8r Piazza San Felice, and offers the most scrumptious pizzas (1,800 lire), and spaghetti dishes. We ate there every night that we were in Florence and were fascinated by the rapid turnover of the pizzas" (Susan Wells, Durban, South Africa; note by AF: La Mangiatoia, literally, "The Eatery," is a unique pizzeria-trattoria-tavola-calda-rosticceria. Spaghetti dishes 2,900 lire, meat dishes 5,000 lire. Located 150 yards behind Pitti Palace, coming from the Arno River side, and closed Mondays).

READERS' BIG SPLURGE SELECTIONS: "A restaurant to which I was introduced some years back during my student days in Florence, and which I recommend especially for their dazzling and delightful selection of antipasti, is **Ristorante Da Pennello,** also simply known as "Casa di Dante" by its regular clientele because of its proximity to the house in which Dante was born. Location is at 4r Via Dante Alighieri, and for a full-course, big splurge meal, you pay 25,000 lire ($15.62), which includes the right to fill your plate with as many of the 20-plus delicious antipasti as it can hold. Next is your pasta dish, naturally, followed by your main course including vegetables, and the meal is topped off with your choice of the heavenly pastry cakes (dolci). Wine and service are included in the price, as is a warm and friendly atmosphere, one in which you are treated as one of the family" (Rodney Chonka, Vineyard Haven, Massachusetts; note by AF: Da Pennello is closed Mondays and all of August). . . . "One tourist attraction I was surprised not to find in the chapter on Florence, and which every American student studying in Florence knows about, is **Vivoli,** at 7 Via Isola dei Stinche, near Santa Croce. It is here that one finds the best ice cream in the world, bar none! This world-renowned ice cream parlor—where an ice cream cone costs 2,500 lire, $1.56—is a definite must for every visitor to Florence. Of course, there are other good gelaterias in Florence, but none compares to Vivoli" (Rodney Chonka, Vineyard Haven, Massachusetts).

READERS' FOOD TIPS: "Do mention the lovely, marble market building diagonally across from the Medici Chapels. Ask for the **Public Market** if you miss it. Open mornings from about six to noon. The place for a portable feast and a glimpse of Italy in action. Marble stalls stacked with rabbits neatly arranged, their pink ears in a pile, fruit sellers with barrels of olives, lovely pears, grapes, whatever is in season, butchers with sausages fat and slim, all nicely spiced, and counters of cheeses—you can buy just one slice, and sample many—a separate section for fish, and much more. A shopping idea: buy a few tubes of anchovy paste, maybe a couple of catsup and mayonnaise. All packaged like toothpaste. Cheap, non-breakable, and they won't leak if you open them" (Dr. and Mrs. Kenneth Korver, Susanville, California; note by A.F.: the advice to consider an occasional picnic lunch in Florence is an excellent one, and if you're not near a large market, simply look for the delicatessens bearing the words "salsamentaria" or "gastronomia" in their titles. At one of the most expensive of these on the Piazza San Marco, Hope and I recently purchased a bottle of chianti for 5,000 lire, an enormous roll (big enough for two) for 500 lire, a hunk of soft, white cheese, two large slices of lunch meat, and two tomatoes covered with *salsa verde* (green sauce) for an additional 5,000 lire, making a total of 10,500 lire, or about $3.28 apiece, for a refreshing, wine-accompanied lunch that we ate in a nearby cool, green park).

THE BIG, BIG SPLURGE: It costs 25,000 lire ($15.62), but it's a feast you'll long remember, at the **Ristorante Il Latini,** 6r Via Palchetti, where Narcisio Latini and his sons Giovanni and Torello operate one of the busiest trattorias in town: three small rooms with about 100 seats, where you'll be lucky to find a chair between noon and 3 p.m. or from 7:30 to 10:30 p.m. (closed Mondays). One way of arriving there: from the Arno, walk up the Via Tornabuoni, turn into the second street to your left (Via della Spada),

again the first to your left (Via Federighi), and 50 yards to your left again is The Latini, buzzing with activity: the old man standing behind the counter, watching with an eagle eye, shouting orders, talking to four persons at once, placing telephoned orders to his own farm in the famous Chianti valley about 20 miles from Florence, and never losing control over the wonderful chaos. If you crave atmosphere, this is the place. Some 50 hams (they sell for $80 apiece) hang from the ceiling, walls are covered with colorful pictures, and wine, mineral water, and aromatic white and dark bread can be taken *a volantà,* meaning as much as you like—they're already included in the $15.62 banquet, which also includes: (1) an aperitivo (local sweet wine); (2) an antipasto (one slice of crude ham, same type as dangles from the ceiling, and two slices of local sausage); (3) homemade noodles, or one of five other first dishes; (4) a plate with four different cooked or roast meats (pork, chicken, veal and rabbit) on it, or one of seven other specialties of the house; (5) fruit and ice cream, or a choice of five local cheeses; (6) one cup of espresso; and (7) a small glass of sweet wine served with almond biscuits.

THE FOOD OF FLORENCE—A RECAP: Summarizing the lengthy and possibly confusing discussion just ended, here's a quick listing of Florence's finest food values: (1) The 4,000 lire ($2.50) menu, wine included, of the **Student Mensa** at 25A Via San Gallo, closed Sundays and from August 1 to September 15; (2) The self-service meals for 7,500 lire ($4.68) and less at the **DLF Mensa**, 6 Via Luigi Alamanni next to the train station, open daily; (3) The 9,000 lire ($5.62) feast—not a meal, a feast!—with wine, at the unique **Botteghina Rossa,** 24R Via degli Alfani, closed Sundays; (4) The two-course luncheons, with beverage, for 8,500 lire ($5.31) at the **Casa di San Francesco,** 2 Piazza Sant' Annunziata.

5. Tours & Sightseeing Notes

MUSEUMS: Florence has over 40 museums and art galleries, and none of them asks admission on Sundays. The two giants are, of course, the **Uffizi Galleries** and the **Pitti Palace** (both closed Mondays), charging a high but deserved, 3,000 lire ($1.87) in the case of the Pitti Palace, 3,000 lire ($1.87) at the Uffizi, on their admission days. They contain priceless collections of the world's greatest art, and require slow, unhurried, reflective visits for maximum enjoyment.

One other Florentine museum—the **Accademia** near the Piazza San Marco (from the Duomo, walk down the Via Ricasoli to reach it)—may alone be worth your entire trip to Europe. For here, in a magnificent setting, stands the original of Michelangelo's "David"; and when you've seen it, you'll realize how inadequate are the weatherworn copies scattered elsewhere in Florence. Here, too, are several unfinished sculptures of Michelangelo, all the more fascinating because they give you a glimpse into the method of their creation. Admission charge of 3,000 lire on weekdays when the hours are 9 a.m. to 2 p.m., Sundays 9 a.m. to 1 p.m. Closed Mondays.

READERS' MUSEUM SUGGESTIONS: "The Gallery of Modern Art in the **Pitti Palace** contains a super collection of all-Italian artists representing at least the first 30 years of this century; it may one day be the outstanding Italian collection representative of our times" (Victor Henry Matson III, Torrance, California). . . . **"Casa Buonarroti,**

70 Via Ghibellina, should be on the list of Michelangelo lovers. This house, once occupied by a nephew of the sculptor, is now a museum (closed Tuesdays) charging 3,000 lire entrance. In addition to four original figures by Michelangelo, there is a large collection of his anatomical and architectural sketches. For those who have already admired his Pietas in the Duomo and the Accademia, the museum has reproductions of the other two, which are in Milan and Rome. Wonderful if you like to compare" (Marianne Durand, San Francisco, California). . . . "One note about museums: scout around to the far end of the Pitti and knock (hard) at the door of the carriage museum. We had a most interesting tour by the lady caretaker who somehow managed to make us understand, even with our limited Italian. The carriages are beautifully preserved and very colorful" (Christie J. Bentham, Scarborough, Ontario, Canada). . . . "While wandering around the cathedrals of Florence, we realized that we should take a pair of lightweight binoculars to see the detailed work on the domes. Our enjoyment of such wonderful structures as the Baptistery was immensely enhanced. . . . No guide book mentions a visit to the **Jewish Synagogue** on 4 Via L. C. Farini, whose entrance is through a garden. It is an excellent example of Moorish architecture, built in 1882, and the woman who opened the door for us modestly stated: 'This is the most beautiful synagogue in all of Europe.' We think she's right! The synagogue is open daily from 9 a.m. to 7 p.m. in summer, from 9 a.m. to 6 p.m. in winter, and admission is free" (Victor Honig, San Francisco, California; note by AF: On the third floor of the synagogue, the museum, free entrance, displays impressive pieces of religious art). . . . "The **History of Science Museum,** at 1 Piazza Dei Giudici, directly behind the Uffizi, is filled with 16th- and 17th-century clocks, microscopes, telescopes, surveying instruments, models of the universe, all sufficiently beautiful to be enjoyed simply as works of art, but also providing insight into the minds that developed the art, architecture and science of Florence. . . . Galileo Galilei's right index finger is displayed in a small glass container" (Alan Wagshal, New Haven, Connecticut; note by AF: The Science Museum is open Monday to Saturday from 9:30 a.m. to 1:30 p.m., Monday and Friday also from 3:30 to 7 p.m.).

TOURS: C.I.T., at the corner of Piazza della Stazione and Piazza della Unità Italiana, offers two separate half-day motorcoach tours of Florence, including visits to the Medici Chapels, the Uffizi Galleries (except on Mondays), and the breathtaking Piazzale Michelangelo, on a hill overlooking the city. Price for each half-day is 30,000 lire.

The same company operates a 27,000 lire ($16.87), half-day tour to Pisa—but that's a trip which can be duplicated on your own for less cost and with a much greater range of activities. Simply take a round-trip ride by train from Florence to Pisa (10,800 lire, second class). When you arrive in Pisa, take the bus marked "Duomo" from in front of the railroad station (round-trip bus ride, 800 lire). Then buy a 3,000 lire admission ticket to the Leaning Tower. For about $9.12, you'll have visited the key attraction of the commercial tours, and you'll be able to spend as much time in Pisa as you like.

Incidentally, the round-trip fare to Venice from Florence is 32,600 lire, and a train leaves every two hours or so.

READERS-ON-AN-OUTING: "For a wonderful side trip from Florence, spend a day in Siena. For 10,000 lire ($6.25), you can buy a round-trip bus ticket from the SITA company located near the train station on Via S. Caterina di Siena. The trip takes 1½ to 2 hours, but for the shorter journey, make sure you take the bus indicated as 'via superstrada.' Buses go in both directions several times a day, and the bus leaves you a ten-minute walk from the heart of Siena. The 'musts' to see in Siena are the Palazzo Pubblico (with its towering Campanile—3,000 lire to climb—which offers a fantastic view of the entire area), the Duomo (which ranks with the finest in all of Italy), and the Museo dell' Opera del Duomo (2,000 lire), containing magnificent paintings by

Duccio" (Lewis and Deanna Rappaport, Brooklyn, New York). . . . "For only 10,000 lire, you can make a round trip by bus returning the same day, from Florence to **San Gimignano,** the most medieval, fortified town you can imagine on Italian soil. The bus follows part of the same route as the 12 noon Sita bus to Siena, but you continue after a short pause at Poggibonsi in another bus" (Oscar Gilson, Munich, Germany). . . . "Most of the Italian cities have bus lines following a scenic circular route, on which a ride costs as little as 500 lire. From the railway station in Florence, bus lines 13 and 19—Circolare Sinistra and Circolare Destra—cover some of the most admirable sights for only 400 lire" (Karl Heinz Ries, Hannover, Germany). . . . "Walk to the coffee house in the **Boboli Gardens,** where you can sit forever with a 1,800 lire Coke and look over the whole of Florence and on to the hills beyond Fiesole" (Polly Cobb, Blacksbury, Virginia).

FLORENCE MISCELLANY: Got only a day to spend in Florence? Early in the morning, get set at the **Piazza della Signoria,** dash into the **Palazzo Vecchio,** then the **Uffizi Galleries** next door, cross over the **Ponte Vecchio,** glancing at its shops, examine the **Palazzo Pitti** and the **Boboli Gardens,** have lunch; retrace your steps to the **Baptistery,** go into the **Duomo,** walk up the **Bell Tower,** enter the **Medici Chapels,** and then—as dusk falls—head up to the **Piazzale Michelangelo,** overlooking the city, for a Florentine sunset. . . . Then, after you've decided to spend a week in Florence, be certain to visit the **Church of Santa Croce**—the "Pantheon of Tuscany"—with its memorials to Dante, Galileo, Michelangelo. In 1965, the city celebrated the seventh centenary of Dante (whom it exiled); in his *Divine Comedy,* Dante glorified Florence, but not the Florentines, for whom he invented exquisite tortures in hell. . . . Pass up, however, the shops and "leather factories" on Santa Croce Square—they're among the most expensive in Florence. . . . A fairly recent addition to the sights of Florence: the home of Elizabeth Barrett and Robert Browning **(Casa Guidi),** 8 Piazza S. Felice (Via Maggio, near the Pitti Palace), which has now been restored to its original state after 100 years of disuse and is open to the public (2 to 6 p.m., Monday through Thursday, Easter to September). Now, here's my wife Hope for a closer look at the glorious art treasures of Florence:

6. Hope's Florence

"Many of us first fully realized what Florence meant to us in those anxious days following the flood of November, 1966. I, for one, was almost physically ill at the thought that anything in Florence might be damaged or lost. And I felt moved beyond measure when hundreds of Europeans and Americans (especially younger ones) converged on the city to save its priceless treasures of literature and art.

"Florence is so very important and dear to us because it is in the very fabric of our civilization; it provides the roots of what we are today. The home of the Renaissance, of Michelangelo, Dante, Leonardo Da Vinci, the Medicis, Donatello, Cellini, even Machiavelli—it is a simply overwhelming city which at times seems almost too much to cope with: walk into even the tiniest church, and you'll find something vital to see. Obviously, on a short stay, you'll want to concentrate on the major areas and sites that Arthur has described; but if you have the extra time, then don't overlook the following:

AROUND THE DUOMO: "On the Piazzas del Duomo and S. Giovanni, which is really one large plaza and a focal point of the city, you'll find the

Cathedral of Santa Maria del Fiore (the Duomo); **Giotto's Tower;** and the **Baptistery**—all done in that dramatic multi-colored marble of Tuscan style.

The Baptistery

"A good place to start is at Lorenzo Ghiberti's famous doors (on the side of the **Baptistery** directly opposite the cathedral), christened for all time by Michelangelo when he first saw them and exclaimed, 'These doors are fit to stand at the Gates of Paradise!' The glittering gilded doors were 27 years in the making and depict scenes from the Old Testament. The second door at the entrance to the Baptistery is by Andrea Pisano, and depicts the life of John the Baptist, the patron saint of Florence (to whom the Baptistery is dedicated). The final door is an earlier work of Ghiberti's illustrating the New Testament.

"Now you must not fail to go inside the Baptistery to see the colorful 13th-century mosaics which cover the ceiling (they're by Cimabue, Andrea Tafi, Apollonio Greco, others)—don't miss the 'Inferno of Hell,' above you to the right of the main entrance, with the terrible horned monster gobbling up little people. Hours are 9:30 to 12:30 and 2:30 to 5:30.

The Cathedral of Santa Maria del Fiore

"The first architect for the cathedral was Arnolfo di Cambio (whose name has been associated with the Palazzo Vecchio and Santa Croce); but the real masterwork of the Duomo is Brunelleschi's soaring dome—a daring concept in its time, built with double walls but without any support from the floor below. Under the dome are stained glass windows made by Ghiberti, Donatello and Uccello; the painting on the dome itself is 'The Last Judgment' by Vasari and Zuccari. Also inside this rather stark and bare cathedral are some very nice stained glass windows, many of them by Ghiberti; decorations by Luca della Robbia; and a couple of incongruous and military-looking equestrian frescoes—one by Paolo Uccello, the other by Andrea del Castagno. You can climb up to the gallery of the dome for 2,000 lire, from 8:30 a.m. to noon and 2:30 to 5:30 p.m. Recently opened to the public here: the ruins of the pre-existing, 10th-century S. Reparata cathedral once standing on this site, now viewed below the ground floor. It's open 9:30 to 12:30, 2:30 to 5:30, for a 2,000 lire entrance fee.

The Campanile

"Giotto spent the last three years of his life working on the campanile; he died in 1337 before it was completed. Although his work on the Florentine Gothic tower was then carried forward by Andrea Pisano and Francesco Talenti (with contributing work from Luca della Robbia), the structure is always referred to as **Giotto's Tower.** Note especially the fine bas-reliefs around the tower, attributed to Pisano, della Robbia, and Arnoldi (all copies: the originals are now in the Museo del Duomo). For 2,000 lire, between the hours of 8:30 a.m. and noon and 2:30 and 5:30 p.m. you can climb to the top of the tower for good views of the cathedral and Florence.

Museo dell' Opera del Duomo

"Directly behind the cathedral, at Piazzo Duomo #9, is the **Museo del Duomo** (or Museo dell' Opera di Santa Maria del Fiore, as it's sometimes

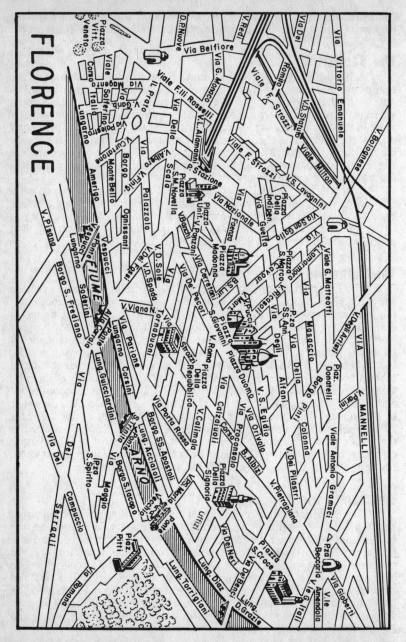

called): open daily from 9:30 a.m. to 1 p.m. and from 2:30 to 5:30 p.m., for a 2,000 lire entrance fee. Easily overlooked by tourists, this quiet, airy, little museum contains all the art works and furnishings that used to be in the cathedral. Even in the ticket office there's a bust of Brunelleschi, and over the doors two glazed terracottas by the della Robbias. In the second inner room (to your left) you'll find the remains of the old façade of the cathedral (destroyed in 1587), including work by the original architect Arnolfo di Cambio, a weather-worn but noble 'St. John' by Donatello, and Nanni di Banco's intriguing 'San Luca.' Upstairs in the center room are some unusually powerful statues by Donatello and Nanni di Bartolo, and some work which was removed from the Campanile in 1941 (by the aforementioned artists; as well as some attributed to Maso and Giovanni di Giuliano da Poggibonsi); but the special treats are the marble choirs of Luca della Robbia and (opposite) Donatello—Luca's choir has been removed down to eye-level for better viewing. Della Robbia's singing gallery is based on the 150th Psalm of David ("Praise the Lord in song and gladness . . .") and you'll smile when you see it—for it's filled with realistic bambinos having such a good time making music: the work is infused with joy and mischief. Directly across the way, Donatello's choir is equally delightful and a good contrast to della Robbia—here, the highly stylized little cherubs explode in dance, running wild with exuberance. In the room to the left there has been assembled the cycle of bas-reliefs from the first and second stories of the Campanile (removed in 1965; mostly attributed to della Robbia and Alberto Arnoldi). Another priceless and fascinating masterpiece, in the last room on the second floor, is the silver altar piece with stories from the life of St. John the Baptist—a joint effort by Betto di Geri and Leonardo di ser Giovanni, and perhaps Paolo and Michele di Monte (and others), with a wonderful central statuette of John the Baptist by Michelozzo. (I wonder, did Edward Albee get the idea for his play 'Tiny Alice' here? All the little figures in the wonderfully alive altar piece seem imprisoned, but nevertheless leading independent lives of their own.) Among many other points of interest is Donatello's exotic wooden statue of Mary Magdalen. But, most important of all is Michelangelo's other, unfinished 'Pietà,' made when he was more than 75 years old; the figure of Nicodemus (or Joseph) is supposed to be a self-portrait of the artist, old, tired and nearly blind. Legend has it that Michelangelo later sought to destroy the work, and it is generally accepted that the figure of the young girl (Mary Magdalen) is a subsequent addition and not the work of the master.

The Medici-Riccardi Palace

"Close to the Duomo (from the main entrance of the cathedral, face the Baptistery, turn right to Via de Martelli, proceeding one block to a pile of dark stones resembling a squat fortress) is the **Medici-Riccardi Palace** at 1 Via Cavour, commissioned by Cosimo il Vecchio (and built by Michelozzo, Brunelleschi's pupil, between 1444 and 1464); this was home to Cosimo the Elder and Lorenzo the Magnificent. Across the courtyard, there's a second-floor baroque gallery with Giordano's frescoes illustrating the 'Apotheosis of the Medici Dynasty'; and, the best for last: a chapel with magnificent frescoed walls by Gozzoli (the artist included the Medici and some of the local citizens in the scene). Open daily from 9 a.m. to 7 p.m. (Sundays 9 a.m. to 1 p.m.), free admission. Closed Wednesdays.

The Medici Chapels

"The **Church of San Lorenzo,** at 9 Piazza San Lorenzo, is across the street from the Medici Palace; upstairs in the Cloister of San Lorenzo is **The**

Laurenziana Library, built for the Medici by Michelangelo. All the way around the church, on Piazza Madonna, is the entrance to the **Medici Chapels** (3,000 lire admission, open from 9 a.m. to 7 p.m. weekdays, Sundays from 9 a.m. to 1 p.m., closed Mondays); go to the 'New' Sacristy first, which contains Michelangelo's tomb for Lawrence the Duke of Urbino (with the figures of 'Dawn' and 'Dusk') and his tomb for Giuliano the Duke of Nemours (with the figures of 'Night' and 'Day'). Chairs are provided for comfortable contemplation, and the longer you look at the works, the greater they'll appear. The other chapels, decorated to their baroque teeth, are almost jolly in their aspect, with six enormous tombs lining the walls; there are two rooms behind the altar containing treasures and religious relics, very much in the Italian manner (bones of saints entwined with pearls in golden cases, etc.).

The Church of Santa Maria Novella

"Not far from San Lorenzo is the **Church of Santa Maria Novella** (walk up Via del Giglio or Via Melarancio), on the striking Piazza Santa Maria Novella, with its church cloister that charges 1,000 lire to enter (9 a.m. to 2 p.m. weekdays, 8 a.m. to 1 p.m. on Sundays, when admission is free; closed Fridays); the Florentines are casual in pointing out that the church contains works by Lippi, Ghiberti, Ghirlandaio, Brunelleschi, Giotto and others; the cloister dates from the 14th century, and contains a particularly magnificent room called the 'Spanish Chapel.'

STARTING AT PIAZZA DELLA SIGNORIA: "Now head for the Piazza della Signoria, the landmark square of Florence where you are probably already spending a great deal of your time. It hardly seems necessary to advise you to take a good look at the lovely Loggia, a virtual outdoor sculpture gallery; in front of the fountain with the huge white statue of Neptune (by Ammannati) is a small round disc marking the spot where Savonarola was burned in 1498 (ironically, he was executed here, in the same Piazza where he had previously burned such heretical objects as books and pictures); and of course you already know that the great Uffizi Gallery is right next door to the Palazzo.

"Now I suggest you take a quick tour through the **Palazzo della Signoria** (better known as the 'Palazzo Vecchio'; open from 9 a.m. to 7 p.m. weekdays, for 3,000 lire, and on Sundays from 8 a.m. to 1 p.m. for free, closed Saturdays), to get some feeling of the place where many of Florence's most historic events occurred, and also to learn how the other half lived (Cosimo I de Medici resided here for ten years). Of special interest is the Hall of the 500 built during Savonarola's term, and there are excellent views of the city from the top floors and tower.

The Uffizi

"The **Uffizi,** or 'offices,' built in 1560 by Duke Cosimo Medici to house the city administration alongside the Piazza della Signoria, were converted a few years later into a museum that today receives more than 1,000,000 visitors per year, more than to any other museum in Italy except those of the Vatican. And no wonder: here are exhibited some of the finest works of genius that Western civilization has produced: Giotto's 'Madonna' (painted in 1310), Botticelli's 'Birth of Venus' and 'Allegory of Spring' (painted in 1486), Leonardo Da Vinci's 'Adoration of the Magi,' Cranach's 'Adam and

Eve,' Michelangelo's 'Holy Family,' Titian's 'Flora,' Rosso Fiorentino's charming 'Cherub Playing a Lute,' Tintoretto's 'Leda and the Swan,' Caravaggio's 'Medusa,' Rembrandt's 'Self Portrait as a Young Man,' Canaletto's 'Ducal Palace in Venice,' Raphael's 'Self Portrait,' the enchanting Medici 'Venus,' to name but a few. All these can be seen on the third floor! The Uffizi is open weekdays except Mondays from 9 a.m. to 7 p.m., Sundays and holidays from 9 a.m. to 1 p.m. for an entrance charge of 4,000 lire ($2.50), and you might conclude your visit with a stop at the cafeteria, not necessarily to eat anything, but simply to enjoy a breathtaking panoramic view of the Piazza della Signoria, the Ponte Vecchio, Il Duomo, and, on that distant green hill, Fiesole.

The Church of Orsanmichele

"Very close to Piazza della Signoria (exit kitty-corner to the Palazzo Vecchio to Via Calzaioli, one of the main shopping streets of Florence) is the little 14th-century **Chiesa Di Orsanmichele,** which was originally built to do double duty as a church and storehouse for grain. Inside, the church has vaulted Gothic arches, lovely stained glass windows, and frescoed walls and ceiling dating from the 14th and 15th centuries. But the star attraction, which you'll spot immediately if you enter from the Via Calzaioli, is the colorful sumptuous Tabernacle by Andrea Orcagna (14th century)—be sure to ask to see it with lights on, revealing that every inch of it is filigreed and sculpted. In the niches all around the exterior of the church you have a history of Florentine sculpture from the 14th to the 16th century: each statue was sponsored by one of the medieval guilds (on Via Calzaioli, facing the entrance, to your left, is 'St. John' by Ghiberti and to your right 'St. Thomas' by Verrocchio; the medallions above are by Luca della Robbia). Open weekdays from 9 a.m. to 2 p.m., closed Sundays, entrance is free.

Palazzo Bargello

"Located between the Duomo and the Piazza della Signoria, at 4 Via del Proconsolo, is the **National Museum** (or Bargello Palace: the former home of the 'People's Representative,' then a prison, and finally an office for the 'Bargello,' or Chief of Police), in another romantically medieval building with astonishing treasures: Michelangelo's 'Bacco,' his 'Madonna Teaching Jesus and St. Giovanni to Read,' 'Brutus,' and the unfinished 'Martyrdom of St. Andrews'; as well as Ammannati's famous 'Leda and the Swan,' Gimbologna's statue of 'Mercury,' Donatello's sculpture of 'St. George,' works by Cellini and Giovanni della Robbia. Open weekdays from 9 a.m. to 2 p.m. (2,000 lire), Sundays from 9 a.m. to 1 p.m. (with free entrance on the second and last Sunday, and on the first and third Saturday of each month) closed Mondays.

Casa Buonarroti

"Now, as you exit from the Bargello, walk up the street and turn right on Via Ghibellina; at #70 you'll find the **Casa Buonarroti,** the graceful house that Michelangelo bought and designed for his nephew, and which his heirs turned into a museum. For admirers of the master, it's worth a short visit, since here one finds four large early statues and two marble reliefs; drawings; plans; and the largest collection of his small-size models.

There's a small gallery of works by other artists assembled by later members of the Buonarroti family. Admission is 2,500 lire; open daily except Tuesdays, from 9 a.m. to 1 p.m.

The Church of Santa Croce

"From the Casa Buonarroti, it's only a short walk to the Franciscan **Church of Santa Croce,** the Pantheon of Florence (containing actual tombs or monuments to such as Michelangelo, Dante, Machiavelli, Galileo, Rossini). But to me the most interesting features of the interior of the church are the restored Giottos, some work of Donatello, and the Pazzi Chapel by Brunelleschi (seriously damaged by the flood, but now completely restored). Previously the entire church was covered with frescoes by Giotto and Cimabue, but when the altars were built these were painted over with whitewash! So what you see now is the restored work of Giotto (in the first two chapels to the right of the main altar), or rather the artist's designs, like an outline, without his original color. In the first chapel on the right are 'Scenes in the Life of St. Francis' (in the little picture of the death of St. Francis, the guards are anxious to point out the figure of one kneeling friar who took this opportunity to pick up St. Francis's robe and check on his stigmata!); the other chapel contains stories of St. John. On the left, in the Bardi Chapel, is the wooden crucifix by Donatello, and his striking bas-relief of the Annunciation is on the right side of the church, just a few steps from Machiavelli's tomb. The entrance to the Cloisters (which now contain the church's museum, and a leather factory and showroom) and to the Pazzi Chapel is on your right at the back of the church.

AND ELSEWHERE: "The **Museum of San Marco,** often referred to as **The Angelico Museum in The Convent of St. Mark,** because it's a virtual monument to the work of Fra Angelico, the museum is located near the Academy Gallery (from the Piazza Duomo, walk up Via Ricasoli to the Piazza San Marco). The monastery provides a remarkably beautiful and evocative setting for Fra Angelico's works. In the Hospice (first room on your right as you enter) is the largest collection of Angelico's movable paintings in Florence: Old and New Testament scenes, ornate, detailed and yet somehow simple and mystical (note the very explicit and gory tortures of Hell in his 'Last Judgment')—it is said that for Fra Angelico painting was the same as praying. The Chapter contains Angelico's large and impressive fresco of 'the Crucifixion,' a very fine and interesting work although somewhat formal and idealized; while on the staircase leading to the upper floor, there's the Refectory of the Guest Room with one of Domenico Ghirlandaio's depictions of 'The Last Supper': this has his usual amount of realistic detail, with Judas seated in the foreground in front of Jesus, and a cat on the floor. At the top of the stairs you'll be stopped in your tracks by one of the most famous and beautiful of Angelico's masterpieces, 'The Annunciation.' The monks' cells in the dormitory on the second floor were either painted by Fra Angelico himself or by his assistants under his direction; and to me the work upstairs is even more exciting than what we've seen before—less ornate, simpler and somehow freer. The final must-see attraction of San Marco is the cell of its former Prior, the fanatic enemy of the flesh, Savonarola. Located at the end of the corridor, the cell contains a stark portrait of Savonarola by his convert Fra Bartolomeo, his sleeping chamber, notebook, rosary, and remnants of the clothing worn by him at his execution. For your 2,000-lire entrance fee, you'll have a memorable experience at San Marco: open daily except Monday from 9 a.m. to 2 p.m.; Sunday from 9 a.m. to 1 p.m.

The Pitti Palace

"Cross the bustling Ponte Vecchio (the bridge nearest the Piazza della Signoria) and walk straight up Via Guicciardini to the **Palazzo Pitti,** which is not a whit the 'itty-bitty-Pitti' you might have been expecting, but looks more like a great stone penal institution. Begun in 1458 (from plans by Brunelleschi) for the rich banker Luca Pitti (later occupants included the Medici family and the House of Savoy), the palace now contains a complex of museums: the Palatine Gallery (star attraction); the monumental Apartments; the Silver Museum; the Gallery of Modern Art (on the second floor); the Carriage Museum; and the Boboli Gardens (open from sunrise to sunset in the summer). Do not miss the Palatine Gallery (entrance through the main door), despite the fact that the place itself is so ornate and the lighting so poor that it's hard to see the paintings. Everybody knows about the outstanding Raphaels collected here (his most famous round panel 'Madonna of the Chair'; the splendid master portraits of 'Angelo and Maddalena Doni'; and 'Tommaso Inghirami,' to mention a few), but there is also a large collection of works by Andrea del Sarto; Fra Bartolomeo's beautiful 'Deposition from The Cross' and 'San Marco'; some superb works by Rubens including 'The Four Philosophers' and his famous 'Isabella Clara Eugenia' (who looks something like Bette Davis dressed up for a role in *The Bells of St. Mary's*) and also his usual large cartoons; Tintoretto; Veronese; some absolutely stunning portraits by Titian—'Pope Julius II,' 'The Man with the Grey Eyes,' and 'The Music Concert'; a curiously sensual and ascetic portrait of 'Cardinal Bentivoglio' by Van Dyck; and work by the fascinating mystic Dosso Dossi. By the way, this is a wonderful place to look at the backgrounds in the pictures—you'll be stunned to notice in many cases it's the same countryside you see outside Florence today (those rolling hills and gorgeous trees were not a product of fanciful imagination, but were painted from reality!). The Royal Apartments are ornate, gilded and chandeliered—and also contain some interesting portraits of the Medici. Open weekdays, except Mondays, from 9 a.m. to 2 p.m., for a 3,000-lire entrance fee; Sundays from 9 a.m. to 1 p.m., free entrance. The Museo degli Argenti is open daily except Mondays—the Royal Apartments open Tuesday, Thursday and Saturday."

A READER'S SUGGESTION FOR AN EVENING OF ART HISTORY: "Kirk van Durer, a New Yorker in his early thirties who studied at Columbia University, presents lectures on the Florentine Renaissance five evenings a week, from 8:30 till 10 p.m., on the top floor of the Penthouse Galleria at 20 Borgo San Lorenzo in the heart of the city, between the Duomo and the Central Market. The charge is 5,000 lire to readers of your book. The talks are supplemented with color slides, while classical music (Palestrina) plays softly in the background; before the lecture, the audience meets on the terrace for a preliminary (and free) glass of wine. This was one of my most pleasant evenings in Europe, and extremely valuable; I had no real grasp of the art of Florence before attending this talk" (Diana Peters, Modesto, California; with numerous seconding recommendations from other readers, including Dr. John Hanelow, Professor of History at Cairo University: "Kirk van Durer was informed and articulate; his explanation and exploration of the sequential progression of artistic thought and cultural broadening from the Byzantine period through Giotto was enlightening," and Nanette S. Laughlin, Huntsville, Alabama: "He provided perspective and brought the Renaissance to life; the lecture was delivered in concise style, amusing, always absorbing. And there was a beautiful terrace with wine and a lovely view on the cathedral and Giotto's tower").

7. Evening Entertainment

SIGHTS AND SOUNDS: There's little decent nightlife in Florence, particularly in summer when residents take off for the cool hills of Fiesole. Best thing to do is simply stroll or relax in the **Piazza della Repubblica,** and listen to the open-air bands. . . . An evening of semi-inexpensive dancing can be had, however, at the enormous (it holds as many as 1,000 persons) "audio-visual, multi-media environment dance hall" of **Space Electronic,** at 37 Via Palazzuolo, which charges a total of 10,000 lire for entrance and one drink, from 3,000 to 4,000 lire for the second drink, and will sometimes lower the admission to 7,000 lire for bearers of this book. A creation of four avant garde architects—Signori Birelli, Caldini, Fiume and Galli—who have exhibited at the Museum of Modern Art in New York, the Space Electronic is what the name implies: a crazy collage of machines and artifacts, ranging from an open parachute over the dance floor to TV cameras that film you as you dance atop a stainless steel floor. Open daily in spring and summer from 9 p.m. to 1 a.m., open Tuesday through Sunday only in winter. From the Piazza S. Maria Novella, walk down the Via dei Fossi, and the first street to your right is the Via Palazzuolo.

The Red Garter

I hesitate to recommend one final Florentine nightspot (open year round) because it is so very American in both form and substance that one wonders why anyone should travel several thousands of miles to visit it. You'll know its character from its name: the **Red Garter,** at 33r Via dei Benci (off the bottom of the Piazza Santa Croce), pursues the roaring twenties theme, with banjos and straw hats, schooners of tap beer, and a wooden-barn, sawdust-covered-floor interior that's an exact replica of hundreds of beer-and-booze hangouts on the campuses of our U.S. colleges. To round out the scene (an Italian sociologist was taking notes during my last visit), at least two-hundred-or-so U.S. collegians turn up here every night in summer (from 8:30 p.m. on, daily) to belt out multiple choruses of "This Land is My Land," just as if they were back at old Iowa U. Why did they ever leave home? It costs 8,500 lire to enter, which includes the first drink.

READERS' ENTERTAINMENT SUGGESTIONS: "Opera in Florence at the **Teatro Comunale,** 16 Corso Italia (box-office phone 216-253), is excellent—our second gallery seats were 4,000 lire—and the opera hall is new and beautiful" (Evin C. Varner, Jr., Clinton, South Carolina). . . . "There are open-air concerts, like those in the Vienna Rathaus, in the courtyard of the **Palazzo Pitti,** two nights a week during the summer. The artists are young Italians, some good, some not so good; still, the atmosphere is quite charming, and some performances are surprisingly worthwhile. Seats cost 4,000, 2,000, or 1,500 lire (the last are unnumbered and rather far back); students with international identity cards get half price on the first two categories only" (Mark Estren, Middletown, Connecticut). . . . "I would like to suggest the **Piscina Bellariva** (public Olympic swimming pool) in Florence for weary tour-worn travelers who have several days to spend in this lovely city. The pool can be reached by bus 14 from the station or Piazza del Duomo (400 lire), and admission charge is 3,000 lire, which includes a dressing stall in the bath house. Snack bar and juke box are provided, plus beautiful surrounding landscaping with umbrella tables, footbridges, and the like" (Alayne Brown, Arlington, Virginia).

8. Florence Miscellany

THE LAUNDROMATS OF FLORENCE: I've found three of them—the **Lavaget** at 110r Borgo Ognissanti (8,000 lire for the machine, including detergent and dryer; open 8 a.m. to 12:30 p.m. and 2:30 to 7 p.m. Monday to Friday, 8 a.m. to 12:30 p.m. on Saturday), an unnamed "washerette" at 1 Via XXVII Aprile, corner of S. Reparata, a block from the Piazza San Marco (same prices; attendants will operate the machine while you dash out to see Michelangelo's "David," in the Accademia, nearby); and a **Lavamatic** in the area of the Piazza della Signoria at 46r Via dei Neri.

SHOPPING IN FLORENCE: The most interesting market in Florence for sightseeing purposes is the huge **Mercato Centrale,** open from 7 a.m. to 1 p.m., at the Piazza del Mercato Centrale, near the station. The outdoor stands on the Via dell' Ariento (which starts at the Via Nazionale), and the vast indoor market itself, should both be seen.

The not-to-be-violated rule for a female shopper in Europe is to resist all temptations until she arrives in Florence. Whatever other women's items you may see in Europe, or in Italy, Florence has them better. Beautiful ladies' gloves, shoes, handbags—elegantly styled but cheap. Throughout the city, you'll find ladies' glove stores, among others, selling gloves for $6 per pair that would be the desperate envy of any far-higher priced American women's store.

As for leather goods—whether men's or women's, household or personal—again, wait until you get to Florence. Magnificent Florentine men's leather wallets are available for $6, leather cigarette cases for $5; leather change purses and glass cases with intricately worked designs, for $4 apiece. Ashtrays covered with leather, and with modern, ceramic mosaics inside, can be had for $6, leather notebooks for $3.50. Where to find them?

Before buying leather of any sort in Florence, you'd do well to visit the **Scuola del Cuoio** (school of leather) inside Santa Croce Church. Simply walk past the imposing tombstones of Michelangelo, Dante, Machiavelli and Rossini, turn immediately right after the Ugo Foscolo statue, walk through the wooden door between the two church windows, and there you'll find the skilled craftsmen at work, in a showroom displaying practically everything that can be made of leather. Manager Signor Gori, and his three daughters who assist him are happy to answer questions. The **Straw Market** in Florence (selling leather, as well as straw products, and open daily from 9 a.m. to 7 p.m.) should then be visited for the experience of its bustling, bargaining atmosphere. But the same items sell for much less in the open-air market of pushcarts and stalls along the streets surrounding the **Mercato Centrale,** near the railroad station, which happens to be the place where Florentines themselves—and very few tourists—shop. Walk, for example, along the **Via dell' Ariento,** which begins at the Via Nazionale near the station: you'll find ladies' gloves for 9,000 lire ($3.75), black leather briefcases for 6,000 lire ($3.75), stylish black leather suitcases for 20,000 lire, ladies' blouses for 12,000 lire, and—best bargain of all—mohair sweaters offered at varying prices (often, only $10), but always unusually cheap. Another way to approach this market area is via the **Piazza San Lorenzo,** behind the San Lorenzo Church, which itself is near the Duomo. Here, too, are dozens of stalls with many of the items that sell for more at the Straw Market or in the subsidiary tourist market in the courtyard of the Uffizi Galleries. And when you buy here, bargain! You ought never to purchase anything in Florence except at a 20% (or greater) discount off the first price quoted to you.

Finally, the reproduction stands (there are six of them) next to the entrance of the Uffizi Galleries have excellent art bargains, including several foot-square details of Botticelli's "Rites of Spring" and "Venus," mounted on hard beaver board, for 18,000 lire ($11.25). These can be laminated when you get back to the States, and placed on the bathroom or kitchen walls of your home.

Used paperback books? The **Paperback Exchange Store** at 31r Via Fiesolana, closed Sundays, displays 20,000 English-language titles, useful for stocking up on reading material for the remainder of your trip. Hours are 9 to 1, and 3:30 to 7:30 p. m.

READERS' SHOPPING SELECTIONS: "If you like **Pucci** go to his shop which is in his Palazzo. Even if you don't buy anything, it's something to see. Elegant!" (Irwin Katz, Mamaroneck, New York; note from HA: Marquis Emilio Pucci's Palazzo is at Via di Pucci 6, in the vicinity of the Duomo. In his second-floor boutique (walk up the marble staircase covered with a soft blue carpet, then turn left), you'll find occasional bargains (scarves for 6,000 lire, multi-colored velvet purses for 12,000 lire) mixed among the expensive merchandise. And if you turn right, you can peep into the famous showroom). . . . "We went to dozens of leather factories, but **Fibbi Brothers,** at 21r Corso dei Tintori, had the best selection, best qualities and best values. Employees all speak English, and are unusually helpful. For gold jewelry, our best find was **Il Regalo,** 32b Via San Giuseppe, near Santa Croce; they had better prices than on the Ponte Vecchio" (Eileen Zarick, New York City; note from AF: despite the high cost of gold, Il Regalo was, in the autumn of 1984, selling small gold bracelets for $40, gold chains for $55. An annex known as the "Florentine Jewelry Center," directly facing Santa Croce Cathedral, has similar products at identical rates). . . . "Mailing a package anywhere in Italy can be an extremely difficult task unless you know what you are doing. You must go to a *Cartoleria* (stationery shop) and buy a special string, paper, and seal to wrap up your parcel. These items aren't expensive (you might get the string free) but they are the only packaging accepted by the Italian post" (Anne Lipp, Boyds, Maryland).

STUDENT SERVICES: Centro Turistico Universitario (phone 29-65-86),
at 12r Via San Gallo, across the street from the Student Mensa, supplies reduced-price student or youth tickets for air, rail, bus and ship, including those all important ducats for the Brindisi-to-Greece ferry.

ADVANCE READING: Irving Stone's best-selling biography of Michelangelo, *The Agony and the Ecstasy* (available in an inexpensive Signet paperback edition), can make all the difference in your stay. For Michelangelo was a Florentine, and many of the major episodes of his life—which the book describes in great detail—took place in the very buildings and square which you will view today.

Nearly half the statues made by Michelangelo now stand in Florence: at the Accademia, in the Medici Chapels, in the Casa Buonarroti (Michelangelo's family name being Buonarroti), in the Duomo, and in the Bargello. A painting of his hangs in the Uffizi Galleries. When you have

read the fascinating background of these masterpieces, which is related to the turbulent times of Renaissance Florence, you'll receive an unparalleled thrill from seeing them before your very eyes.

CODA: All the ancient bridges of Florence, other than the Ponte Vecchio, were destroyed by the Germans in their senseless defense of the city in 1944. On the Palazzo Vecchio there is now affixed a tiny plaque whose proud inscription gave me a particular thrill, which I would like to share with you. The inscription reads: "On the 11th August 1944, Freedom, the Sole Dispenser of Social Justice, Not Granted but Reconquered, At the Cost of Destruction, Torture and Blood, Thanks to the Rising of the People and to the Victory of the Allied Armies, Has Taken Her Place in this Palace of our Fathers, Amid the Ruins of our Bridges, Forever."

————————

Coming up: another high-point of your tour. It's off to Venice, just four hours away by train.

Chapter XIII

VENICE

Don't Go Near the Water

1. Orientation
2. Budget Lodgings
3. Low-Cost Restaurants & Meals
4. What to See & Do
5. Evening Entertainment
6. Venice Miscellany

VENICE IS A fantastic dream. To feel its full impact, try to arrive at night, when the wonders of the city can steal upon you, piecemeal and slow. At the foot of the Venice railway station, there is a landing from which a city launch embarks for the trip up the Grand Canal. As you chug along, little clusters of candy-striped mooring poles emerge from the dark; a gondola approaches with a lighted lantern hung from its prow; the reflection of a slate-grey church, bathed in a blue spotlight, shimmers in the water as you pass by. This is the sheerest beauty, and it is a moment that no one should miss.

In the daytime, the city becomes a commotion of people and exotic sights. There's no need to buy your entertainment in Venice. You'll want nothing more than to stroll and window shop along its narrow streets; or to listen to a band concert in the Piazza San Marco; or to sail through the canals on a 75¢ vaporetto ride. In considering your basic costs, remember that Venice caters to many more French and German tourists than to Americans, and there are thus numerous moderate hotels and restaurants scattered throughout the city. By living where the Europeans live, you can thrive in Venice on entirely moderate costs.

1. Orientation

GETTING TO VENICE: The main and only railway station, **Stazione Centrale Santa Lucia** (named after a Christian martyr buried in a glass coffin at San Geremia church, a few blocks away), connects Venice with the mainland of Europe via a four-mile stone bridge crossing the Adriatic lagoon. If you're coming from Florence, travel time to Venice is four hours, from Rome eight hours, from Munich nine hours, from Vienna nine hours and from Paris 17 hours. The rail information office, between tracks five and six, is open from 8 a.m. to 8 p.m. If you prefer to phone, the number to call is 71-55-55.

Venice's airport, **Aeroporto Marco Polo,** named after the famous explorer who allegedly introduced spaghetti to Italy from China, is eight miles away on the mainland. An Alitalia bus (2,000 lire, $1.25) and a public bus (1,000 lire, 62¢) connect with the Piazzale Roma air terminal.

GETTING AROUND VENICE: And now, the transportation question, to be answered quite simply: you walk. In Venice, cars are prohibited, buses and streetcars don't exist, and the only form of public conveyance is a sea-going, canal-traversing boat that comes in three selections: **vaporettos** holding 350 persons, for your main trips up and down the Grand Canal (average fare of 1,200 lire, 75¢); **motoscafos,** a smaller, sleeker vessel (about 100 passengers) servicing the narrow side-canals, such as the Rio Nuovo connecting Piazzale Roma and Accademia (average fare of 1,500 lire); and the **motonave,** a large, double-decker boat holding about 900 passengers, used mainly for the non-stop shuttle runs between St. Mark's and the Lido (1,200 lire). If you plan to take more than six trips a day on a combination of any of these, it's advisable to buy a day ticket for 8,000 lire ($5), available at the clearly marked ticket booths near the 30 or so boat stops. All these water boats operate every ten minutes from 6 a.m. to midnight, except the motonave going to the Lido, which departs every 20 minutes from St. Mark's, from 6:45 a.m. to 9:05 p.m., and in the other direction, from the Lido to St. Mark's, from 7 a.m. to 9:20 p.m. Detailed timetables are posted near each stop.

Gondolas? They're around in great quantity, but prohibitively expensive: an average of 40,000 lire ($25) for the first 50 minutes, 20,000 lire ($12.50) for each additional 25 minutes, and even then you should carefully agree on the price before stepping aboard.

THE ITALIAN LIRA: For the purposes of this chapter, we've converted Italian lire into dollars at the rate of 1,600 lire per dollar—the approximate "floating" rate of the lira as of the time of writing. Thus, 100 lire have been assumed to equal approximately 6.2 U.S.¢. Though you can expect further fluctuations by the time of your own stay in Italy, the variance should not be substantial.

2. Budget Lodgings

HOTELS, PENSIONE AND LOCANDE OF VENICE: More than 250 establishments—classified by the Italian government into four categories of hotels (first to fourth) and two categories of pensions (pensione and ultra-cheap locande)—compete quite strenuously and slash their rates for the tourist in off-season, but then raise those rates to alarmingly high (for Italy) levels during a short, four-month high season of summer. At that time of the year, when Venice receives the great bulk of its visitors, all categories of hotels in Venice charge considerably more than their counterparts in Rome, Naples and Florence.

Most of these hotels are clustered in two areas—near the railroad

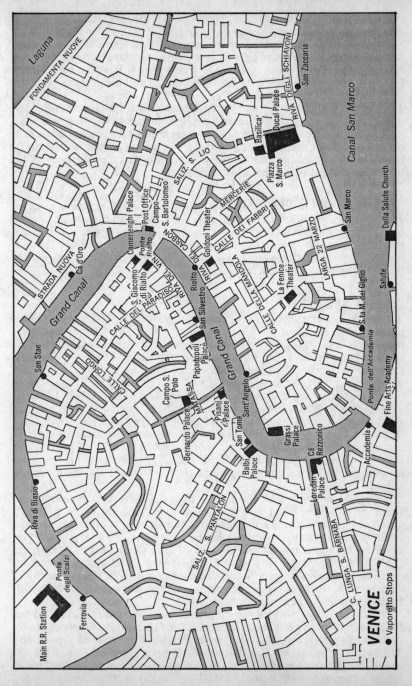

Laguna

FONDAMENTA NUOVE

San Zaccaria

RIVA DEGLI SCHIAVONI

Ducal Palace

Basilica

Canal San Marco

SALIZ. S. LIO

Piazza S. Marco

MERCERIE

Camerlenghi Palace

Post Office

Campo S. Bartolomeo

CALLE DEI FABBRI

San Marco

Della Salute Church

Ponte Rialto

Goldoni Theater

STRADA NUOVA

Cà d'Oro

Grand Canal

CALLE DEL PARADISO

CALLE DEL DI RIALTO

RIVA DEL CARBON

Rialto

RIVA DEL VIN

San Silvestro

CALLE DELLA MANDOLA

LARGA 22 MARZO

La Fenice Theater

S. ta M. del Giglio

Salute

San Stae

CALLE LONGO

Papadopoli Palace

CALLE DELLA MATASSA

Grand Canal

Sant'Angelo

Ponte dell'Accademia

Fine Arts Academy

Campo S. Polo

Bernardo Palace

Pisani Palace

San Tomà

Grassi Palace

Accademia

Balbi Palace

Cà Rezzonico

Loredan Palace

SALIZ. S. PANTALON

Riva di Biasio

C. LUNGA S. BARNABA

Ponte degli Scalzi

VENICE

• Vaporetto Stops

Main R.R. Station

Ferrovia

station *(Ferrovia)* and around St. Mark's Square (Piazza San Marco). In a short trip to Venice (say, of one or two nights' duration), or arriving with heavy luggage, I'd stay in the station area, where all hotels are within easy walking distance, enabling you to dispense with expensive porters or always crowded vaporettos. Once installed in your lodgings near the stazione or Piazzale Roma (site of the immense, station-area parking garage), you can then walk to the sights of St. Mark's in only 15 minutes.

Conversely, on a lengthier stay in Venice of three nights or more, I'd put up with the travel difficulties of lugging your bags to the historical area of St. Mark's. Once you've sweated your suitcase over innumerable small bridges and down narrow streets, with no vehicle (other than a vaporetto) to aid you, you'll find yourself in the very heart of this unreal city, with all the important sights less than 500 yards away.

FERROVIA (RAILWAY STATION): As you leave Venice's modern railway station, look left. The street you see is the **Lista di Spagna,** almost continuously lined with hotels of a moderately costly second-class and third-class category. Yet on this convenient Lista di Spagna, and on the first two side streets that cross it, are nine very suitable budget lodgings with prices in the range we seek for Venice.

Lista di Spagna

Hotel Terminus, 116 Lista di Spagna (phone 71-50-95), is the hotel nearest to the stazione, just after the church—a sizable, second-class hotel with fairly high rates. But Manager Mario Indri has offered a special concessionary price to readers of this book, throughout 1985, of 24,000 lire ($15) per person, in a bathless double room, breakfast included, and that's a bargain in costly Venice for an establishment of this sort.

A hundred yards farther on, the considerably cheaper **Locanda Carretoni,** 130 Lista di Spagna (phone 71-62-31), is an extremely simple, family-style cross between a hotel and a pensione, with only 15 rooms, but there's no better value than the Carretoni on the entire street. It charges only 17,000 lire ($10.93) for single rooms, 30,000 lire ($18.75) for twins, from 12,000 down to 10,000 lire ($7.50 to $6.25) per person for rooms with three to five beds each, with a supplementary charge of 1,500 lire for every shower you take.

Casa Nives Ottolenghi, 180 Lista di Spagna (its entrance on a tiny side street behind the Hotel Continental, phone 71-52-06), vies with the Carretoni. Here is another Venetian star, the apartment of Signora Nives, in which five attractive rooms are rented as doubles, triples or quads (but never for single occupancy) for only 32,000 lire ($20) double, 44,000 lire ($27.50) triple, 55,000 lire ($34.37) quad—breakfast not included or available and therefore to be had at a café downstairs. While little English is spoken here, location and rates make this an unbeatable address for backpackers and other unpretentious folk.

A few more steps along this excellent hotel-and-breakfast street, **Hotel Minerva** at 230 Lista di Spagna (phone 715-968), and **Hotel Guerrini** at 265 Lista di Spagna (phone 71-51-14), both charge (at the peak of the season) 40,000 lire ($25) single, 70,000 lire ($43.75) twin, 85,000 lire ($53.12) for triples, 100,000 lire for quad rooms, breakfast included; and both rent some rooms with private bath for only 10,000 lire ($6.25) per person more. Both, in the highly exact Italian system of hotel classification, are rated fourth-class hotels, but are akin to what most of us would call second class in quality.

Calle Priuli

Leaving the station and walking along the Lista di Spagna, the first cross street on your left is the narrow Calle Priuli, on which the **Hotel Dolomiti,** 72 Calle Priuli (phone 71-51-13), a four-story building with no elevator, provides the highest quality in the low-cost range, at a charge of 32,000 lire ($20) per person in a twin-bedded room, 25,000 lire ($15.62) per person if you take one of the four family rooms with four beds each. Breakfast, included in those rates, is served in a large, ground-floor room with the shining-clean kitchen in full view.

Considerably more basic, but acceptable as a very last resort, is the **Alloggi Orsaria,** across the street at 103 Calle Priuli (phone 71-52-54), and managed by a friendly old lady whose favors to readers—tea on a rainy afternoon, helpful suggestions—go way beyond the normal hotel amenities. She imposes a 10:30 p.m. curfew only because she cannot afford to hire a night porter. Five hostel-type rooms, with two beds apiece, rent for 17,000 lire ($10.62) per person per night, no breakfast.

Both the Dolomiti and the Orsaria have fairly forbidding exteriors, a characteristic of most Venetian hotels found on these opera-setting streets, but please keep an open mind until you've seen the rooms; and don't be discouraged by the unusual narrowness of the street—most streets in Venice are like that!

Calle Misericordia

Again as you continue down Lista di Spagna, the second side street to the left is Calle Misericordia, so narrow that you can barely walk it with an open umbrella! It provides one moderately priced and two cheaper selections:

The always-reliable **Hotel Atlantide,** 375A Calle Misericordia (phone 71-69-01), is a four-story structure with functioning elevator(!); it quotes a bed-and-breakfast basis of 36,000 lire ($22.50) single, 64,000 lire ($40) for a twin room, 84,000 lire ($52.50) for a triple, 108,000 lire ($67.50) quad, with free showers for all guests, and breakfast (included in the price) served in a small backyard against a setting of panoramic murals painted by various international art students.

Across the Calle, at #358, the smaller, 13-room **Albergo Santa Lucia** (phone 71-51-80), all of whose rooms are on the ground floor, is an ideal accommodation for older folks averse to negotiating stairs. You'll recognize the structure by its flower-decorated stone terrace with sun chairs, all filled with roses, oleander, ivy and birds singing in trees—a rare sound in Venice. And you'll like the old-fashioned way in which breakfast is served, with coffee and tea poured from sterling silver pots. For all this, the rates are quite reasonable (for Venice): 31,000 lire ($19.37) single, including breakfast; 49,000 lire ($30.62) twin with two breakfasts; 68,000 lire ($42.50) triple with breakfasts; 100,000 lire ($62.50) quad room with breakfasts. Owner Signora Emilia Gonzato does not speak English, but her son, Gianangelo, does.

Finally, at the end of the Calle, **Pensione Villa Rosa,** #389 (phone 71-65-69), is not quite of the standard of the other Misericordia hotels, but may have vacancies on the day you're there. Twenty-seven rooms, three floors, night porter, and the following prices, always with breakfast included: 30,000 lire ($18.75) single, 48,000 lire ($30) twin, 66.000 lire ($41.25) triple, 80,000 lire ($50) quad, 3,000 lire ($1.87) for showers.

If you arrive in Venice in July or August, you may have to trek to a number of the station-area hotels to find a vacancy, but somehow, you will always find one. Still, check your bags at the station first (800 lire for 24 hours), then find the room, then return for your bags—and in that manner, the whole process can lose its terror.

Calle San Leonardo

The Lista di Spagna, after crossing the bridge with four obelisks called "Ponte delle Guglie," changes its name at the next long stretch, leading finally to St. Mark's, and is called Calle or Salizzada San Leonardo. There, after 250 yards, to your right at #1814, is **Archie's House,** operated by a unique couple, Arcadio (Archie) Baghin and Chuen-Lih, his Taiwanese wife. They rent seven very large, high-ceilinged rooms, barely but adequately furnished, for 18,000 lire ($11.25) per person in twins, 17,000 lire ($10.62) per person in triples, 15,000 lire ($9.37) in quads, without breakfast; there being no single rooms. If you don't mind no-frills accommodations, this centrally located pension—an easy walk from the station, ten minutes by foot to St. Mark's—can be an enjoyable experience, as witness its collection of guest books filled with praise. Prices are reasonable, and the manager is a 38-year-old doctor of philosophy who speaks eight languages, and patiently answers questions on Venice and the world in general. If you travel in fours, try to rent room 2, with a loggia-like stone balcony for watching the colorful life of Venice. Archie's is open from mid-April through October only. The phone number is 72-08-84.

PIAZZA SAN MARCO AREA: Now, how about a hotel on the little inner canals of Venice, along alley-like streets that look like a set from Othello? If you don't mind searching and asking for directions, then take the vaporetto to the Piazza San Marco stop, and start looking for the **Albergo Atlantico,** located less than a hundred yards from the Piazza, at 4416 Calle del Rimedio (phone 709-244), on the canal of the Bridge of Sighs; from St. Mark's Square, walk down the Calle Larga San Marco till you pass the little Calle va al Ponte de l'Anzolo, and turn into that tiny street, then turn left just before the Trattoria alla Canonica, and then right on Ramo de l'Anzolo, where you'll find signs pointing to the Atlantico—a huge, labyrinthine building whose large stone rooms are all newly furnished, and most of whose windows and balconies have views of the Bridge of Sighs—no other hotel in Venice can claim that! The 1985 rates for all this, in high season: 36,000 lire ($22.50) per person in double rooms, breakfast included, 32,000 lire ($20) per person triple, 30,000 lire ($18.75) per person in an enormous four-bedded room; probability of a 10% discount to bearers of this book who present a copy on registering to English-speaking owner Laura Innocenti.

If the Atlantico is full, try first the nearby **Locanda Riva,** 5310 Ponte dell' Anzolo (phone 27-034), whose kindly owner, Isidoro Salmaso, charges 28,000 lire ($17.50) single, 50,000 lire ($31.25) double, 20,000 lire ($12.50) per person for a triple or four-bedded room, with breakfast included. But if that, too, is full, you can then seek out the utterly spotless private home accommodations of the remarkable **Signora Teresa Gobbato** at 4406 Calle del Rimedio (phone 702-866), about 150 yards from St. Mark's Square. She has 15 beds to rent, and they go for only 21,000 lire ($13.12) per person double, 20,000 lire ($12.50) per person triple or quadruple. Your landlady, once again, is Signora Gobbato, but ring the bell with the name Kantz on it. If the Signora has no space for you, she'll send you to the nearby **Alloggi Gino,** 4412 Calle del Rimedio (phone 70-62-32), where Signor Garavello rents five rooms (some with four beds) for an average rate of 20,000 lire ($12.50) per bed per night.

For Older Readers

Not far from the Piazza San Marco, but on the other side, is the Teatro La Fenice (Venice's opera house), at the peaceful Fenice Square (although the approach to this area is through narrow streets, the square itself is one of the most attractive in Venice). And running off this square are pleasant little lanes on which you'll find elegant, small third-class hotels, all quiet, and all patronized by knowledgeable middle-aged persons and other extremely genteel folk. The top choice here is the beautifully furnished **Hotel Ateneo,** Campo San Fantin (1876 Calle Minelli), phone 700-588, whose 1985 charges are 39,000 lire ($24.37) for a single without bath, 75,000 lire ($46.87) for a bathless double, 85,000 lire ($53.12) double with bath, with breakfast, service and taxes included. Individual room air-conditioners are also available, at an extra charge of 5,000 lire ($3.12) per room per night. Follow the Calle de Ca'Giustinian Orsato from the theatre to find the hotel. In the very same area, the similarly priced **Hotel Kette,** 2053 San Marco (phone 70-77-66), offers a special rate to readers of this book only, of 68,000 lire ($42.50) for a bathless double room—their official price rising substantially higher.

Fairly similar amenities and prices—35,000 lire ($21.87) per person in double rooms, 40,000 lire ($25) in a single, including *breakfast,* service and tax—are found in the smaller **Albergo San Fantin,** one flight up in an apartment-like building at 1930A Campiello della Fenice (phone 31-401).

CA'FOSCARI OR SAN TOMÀ AREA: As you'd expect, Venice's best
hotel values are found on the non-San Marco side of the Grand Canal, and we've recommended numerous low-cost pensiones and locande there— much cheaper than the establishments listed thus far—in our low-budget section appearing later in this chapter. Of better quality in this same area—Ca'Foscari or San Tomà—is the **Albergo Iris,** at 2910A San Polo (phone 22-882), next door to the pleasant, outdoor Ristorante al Giardinetto, with 75 beds, of which 50 are in a new wing, with new entrance, marble steps, and new furniture. Rates are 38,000 lire ($23.75) single, 68,000 lire ($42.50) double, but they include shower, breakfast, service and tax. Take vaporetto 1 to San Tomà (station 10), then walk up the narrow street, take the first turn to the left, then first to the right, facing the canal, and soon you'll spot the sign posted by Livio and Flora Fullin, who operate both the pensione and the restaurant (where they serve meals to guests taking demi-pension arrangements). Try for the new wing.

RIVA DEGLI SCHIAVONI: Back now to the costlier choices. Just beyond
the Piazza San Marco on the Grand Canal, you'll often pass a broad quay

called the **Riva degli Schiavoni,** which can be further recognized by the large statue of a man on horseback in the center of the quay. In this setting, a few steps away, the **Casa Paganelli,** 4182 Riva Schiavoni (alternate entrance at 4687 S. Zaccaria), phone 24-324, is a surprisingly modern, 38-bed pension charging 69,000 lire ($43.12), breakfast, service and taxes included, for a double room. And for similarly priced, pleasant and clean rooms nearby, walk from the Riva degli Schiavoni along the Canal, back in the direction of the Piazza San Marco, where soon you'll see a narrow street, the Calle delle Rasse, which runs between the two buildings of the swank Hotel Royal Danieli. Turn in, and ten yards up, at 4551 Calle delle Rasse (phone 28-814; vaporetto is S. Zaccaria, #16), you'll espy the **Hotel Commercio e Pellegrino,** which never requires that you take meals, and which charges exactly 84,000 lire ($52.50) for a double *with* bath, breakfast, service and taxes included, 49,000 lire ($30.62) lire for a single on the same arrangement.

ON THE GIUDECCA CANAL: Here you'll find two unique Venice institutions that catered to a highly intellectual sort of British tourist until British economic woes diminished the flow of English tourists to Venice. The **Pensione la Calcina,** 780 Zattere (phone 27-045), and the **Pensione Seguso,** 779 Zattere (phone 22-340), are both highly attractive hotels, the latter in marble with Venetian antiques and Murano glass, but neither would normally be thought to be well located—unless you crave an absolutely quiet situation away from commerce, drenched in sunlight and space, and directly facing the broadest segment of the Giudecca Canal. Charges at the Calcina are 65,000 lire ($40.62) for a double without bath, but with two breakfasts included; at the costlier Seguso, half-pension is required, at a charge of 64,000 lire ($40) per person, in bathless rooms. Although the Zattere is serviced by a different vaporetto than the one that makes the trip up the Grand Canal, you can still reach it in the normal manner by going to the Accademia stop, and walking across the narrow neck of land from there. In fact, both the Seguso and the Calcina are only 200 yards from the Accademia Bridge on the Grand Canal; walk over that bridge and in a trice you're at the Piazza San Marco. Try the Calcina first, whose middle-class English atmosphere, with lace curtains on the windows, may prove a respite from the exotica of Venice.

IN THE FONDAMENTA NUOVA AREA: An oddity ends our hotel discussion. Ideal for families, small groups, basketball teams and choirs, who will enjoy rooms the size of museum exhibition halls, is the **Hotel Madonna dell' Orto,** at 3499 Cannaregio (phone 71-99-55), its foundations dating back to the 14th century. Originally the dwelling of a rich Venetian merchant of Marco Polo times, it later housed the Napoleonic embassy, then the governor of the Austro-Hungarian Empire, before its later conversion into a nunnery in 1918, after which it became a hotel. All 40 rooms have terrazzo floors, high stuccoed ceilings, antique furniture, solid walnut doors and balconies, and are so large that your voice will echo if you speak loudly enough. There are, to top things off, so many corridors, halls, cellars and secret doors that a ghost which reputedly wanders through the hotel is undoubtedly a tourist who got lost there years ago! Breakfast is served in a garden (complete with grotto used as a bar) and atop the structure is a spectacular terrace overlooking Venice. The price? 58,000 lire ($36.25) for a bathless twin room, inclusive of breakfast, 26,000 lire ($16.25) for each additional bed with breakfast—and you can add quite a few to the average room. From the station, take the circolare #5 motoscafo to the Madonna dell' Orto stop (one leaves every 15 minutes from 6 a.m. to 9 p.m. on the 12-minute trip, 1,200 lire); from there walk through Ramo Terzo Piave and, passing a drugstore called Despar, to the canal facing the hotel.

READER'S HOTEL SELECTION: "We were lucky to find the **Hotel Basilea,** 817 Rio Marin, phone 718-477, rated as a third-class hotel but with service I have not seen equaled in America; the charge for a double room, including breakfasts, service and taxes, is 66,000 lire ($41.25), slightly more—84,000 lire ($52.50)—for a double with private bath and breakfast; 38,000 lire ($23.75) for a single including breakfast and service" (Charles Hooper, Dallas, Texas; note by A.F.: this is a very short walk—two bridges—down the Rio Marin, across the Grand Canal from the railroad station).

READERS' PENSIONE SELECTIONS: "May I recommend the beautiful **Casa Frollo,** Island of Giudecca #50, phone 22-723, just across the Grand Canal from the Piazza S. Marco, and only a few steps from the motoscafo stop 'Le Zitelle' (motoscafo stop 5, second stop from S. Marco). The house is 16th century, with a superb large breakfast room with authentic old furniture, whose windows as well as a number of rooms overlook an incomparable two miles of Venetian scenery, including San Marco and La Salute. The pensione is well run by the very friendly blonde Venetian, Mrs. Flora Soldan, and is a meeting place for quiet people and for artists. I met an American writer (lady) who stayed there for more than one month. Unlike other Italian hotels, it has no television or radio set in the hall nor in the breakfast room, so that you can stay there reading or talking, as you like. It also has a nice garden, for sunbathing. Have a look at the kitchen: you'll see a fantastic old collection of copper kitchenware. Rates for 1985 are 35,000 lire ($21.87) in bathless singles, 64,000 lire ($40) for bathless doubles, breakfast included, and as no other meals are served, there is no need for demi-pension arrangements. The view of Venice's skyline from the seven enormous breakfast-room windows is unique" (Emilio Fumagalli, Milano, Italy; note from A.F.: access to Casa Frollo from the train station is via boat #5, on the linea circolare).

READERS' SELECTIONS (MESTRE): "Instead of staying in high-priced Venice (the most expensive town in Italy, on-season), our Italian friends in Sorrento advised us to stay in Venice-Mestre, outside of Venice. Therefore, we stayed at the **Hotel Venezia,** Piazza 27 Ottobre (phone 972-400), Venice-Mestre. It was only 15 minutes by bus from our hotel entrance to the end of the Venice causeway and the start of the Grand Canal. We had no problem with luggage, garage, etc. And, we had a double room without bath for 46,000 lire ($28.75), taxes and service included with breakfast at 5,000 lire ($3.13) per person extra (singles were available for 27,000 lire)" (Mark and Ruth Marron, Hayward, California; note by A.F.: we've had numerous other recommendations for the modern, 100-room Venezia, whose rooms with private bath are in the budget range, too; there apparently is a Pam supermarket directly opposite the Venezia, serving price-fixed meals for 12,000 lire—more typical of Italian prices than what you'll encounter in Venice). . . . "My wife and I stayed two nights in mid-October at the **Locanda Corso** in Mestre, on the third floor of a new ten-story building, half-a-block south from the Ambasciatori (Ambassador) Hotel, at 231 Corso del Popolo, phone 93-00-75. Our room had all new furniture, comfortable beds, a balcony, polished marble floors, and a spotless tiled bathroom was next door. The cost for a double room with service charges included (for two) was only 38,000 lire ($23.75). One of our best finds in Europe" (John J. Chalmers, Alberta, Canada; strong seconding recommendation from Mrs. Frank L. Meyer, Vista, California). . . . "I hit a train strike on the way in from Vienna, so the train stopped in Venezia Mestre and was not allowed into Venice itself. Remembering what several readers had said, I decided to stay in Mestre, and booked into the **Hotel Centrale,** 14 Piazza Donatori del Sangue (telephone 985-522), which proved to be the most modern hotel I stayed in in Europe. The hotel has 105 rooms (230 beds), all modern conveniences, free showers, a staff of bellboys and the like. I got clean towels every day and the maids even folded my dirty wash when I happened to leave it out! The cost? Only 34,000 lire ($21.25) for a single—a price unheard of in Venice proper. Breakfast is 6,000 lire additional, delicious and brought to your room on request. Commuting to Venice? Bus 7 stops right smack in front of the hotel, takes 15 minutes for the trip to Venice, costs 500 lire, 31¢. Other conveniences of the hotel (small things in America, but greatly appreciated in Europe): phone and hot and cold running water in all rooms; pullcords on the curtains; U.S.-style toilet facilities. And the staff will even mail your postcards and letters for you!" (Mark Estren, Middletown, Connecticut). . . . Note from A.F.: Arriving in Venice without a reservation during peak season (July through September), you might want to forego a lengthy hotel search by simply staying in Mestre and commuting from there (five miles, 500 lire) into Venice proper. Less expensive than the readers' selections appearing above are: **Locanda Maria Luisa,** 2 Via Parini (phone 93-19-68) (15,000 lire, $9.37, per person in twins, 12,500 lire, $7.81, per person quad, free showers, kind proprietress but with very little English); **Locanda Dina,** next door at 4 Via Parini (phone 92-65-65) (same rates); and **Locanda Al Veronese,** 94a Via Cappuccina (phone 92-62-75) (again same rates). Higher category and only 150 yards from the station as you leave it: **Hotel Trieste,** 2 Via Trento (phone 29-94-62) (25,000 lire, $15.62, per person for bathless rooms, including breakfast and free showers).

READER'S SELECTION (LIDO): "The **Pensione Villa Parco,** located in Lido at 1 Via Rodi (phone 760-015), is a proof positive that the 'exclusive' Lido section doesn't necessarily have to cost an arm and a leg. This is a charming family pensione which has recently been renovated, and rates are 50,000 lire ($31.25) for a double, including breakfast. The Parco has a beautiful shaded garden and is located in a very quiet section right near the beach. In case you are arriving by car, they have a parking lot which is absolutely free to all guests" (Berne Thompson, New York, New York; recent seconding recommendations from other readers; note by AF: the 21-room Villa Parco is owned by Signora Giulia Cipollato, who also owns a private "capanna" on the famous Lido beach, available to guests for 4,000 lire ($2.50) per day. She is fluent in English. From the Lido boat station, take public bus B or C for three stops to "Quattro Fontane," near a small bridge, and you'll immediately see the Parco upon leaving the bus).

THE LOWER-PRICED ROOMS: As we enter 1985, Venice's most

comfortable low-budget value for men is a modernistic, little Hilton-like place called the **Domus Cavanis** (sometimes known as the Istituto Cavanis), at 912A Accademia (phone 87-374), diagonally across the narrow street from 989 Accademia (the only street number you'll be able to spot); from the main side of the Grand Canal, walk over the Accademia Bridge to the renowned Accademia museum, then walk up the street alongside the museum to find the Domus, on your right. Operated by a religious organization, managed by gentle, white-haired Padre (Father) Luigi Toninato, equipped with an elevator, with stylish Scandinavian-modern furnishings, and a large breakfast room lounge, and open to foreigners (males only, but of all ages) only in summer, the Domus has more than 70 rooms, renting for 18,000 lire ($11.25) per person in doubles or triples, not including breakfast. That's for plain rooms, of course, with narrow beds; but some rooms even sport a small balcony! Don't, of course, confuse this recently built portion of the Domus with its older wing.

If you're a female budgeteer, try the **Domus Ciliota,** next door to 2976 Calle de la Muneghe (phone 704-888), two short blocks from the Campo S.

Stefano (nearest vaporetto is stop 13), and therefore only five minutes on foot from the Piazza San Marco, on the main side of the Grand Canal. A large rust-colored building operated as a school in winter (it has the pace and tone of a convent), this one accepts foreigners in July and August only, and specializes in women and families. About 50 rooms in all, for which the charge is 28,000 lire ($17.50) single, 36,000 lire ($22.50) double, no breakfast; from the huge Campo S. Stefano, walk two short blocks down the Calle de la Boteghe until you see Calle de la Muneghe on your left—the Ciliota is 30 yards down the street, on your left.

A third and primarily student hotel, but again for women only, is the **Casa della Studente Domus Civica,** at 3082 S. Rocco (phone 24-332), three short blocks from the Campo S. Rocco and its famous Scuola S. Rocco. This establishment, operated by the Associazione Internazionale al Servizio della Giovane, but accepting women under 25 in summer, is on the quieter, cheaper and non-tourist side of the Grand Canal, and the building is considerably more comfortable than the usual hostel of this sort. You'll pay 16,000 lire ($10) per person, in double rooms; and you'll encounter an 11:30 p.m. curfew. Highly recommended. From the train station, walk over the large stone bridge (Scalzi) crossing the Grand Canal, turn into the first street to your left, continue walking, cross another small bridge, and you'll be at Domus Civica in ten minutes.

THE LOCANDAS OF VENICE:

Beneath the fourth-class category of Italian hotels is still a lower subdivision known as "locanda," but if the thought causes you to quake—it shouldn't. I've found, after examining several in Venice, that they scarcely differ from the more simple forms of pensions; and indeed, several of them have actually replaced the "locanda" in their title with the words "pensione" or "casa"—boarding house. Yet because of their category, they charge as little as 36,000 lire ($22.50) for a double room, service included. A typical example is the **Locanda Semenzato,** 4363 Calle Bembo (phone 27-257), just off the S.S. Apostoli, which charges just that for a double room on its third floor, only 60,000 lire ($37.50) for a family room housing four. Take the vaporetto to the Ca' d'Oro stop (#6), walk up Traghetto Street to Strada Nuova, follow that to the right until you reach the Campo S.S. Apostoli, and when you're in front of the church that you'll soon see, take the first turn on the left (the square building to your right is one of the few Lutheran-Protestant churches in Italy), pass the coffee shop and the pharmacy, and then turn into the first narrow street to the left. And add 5,000 lire per person for breakfast. Phone first. . . . Alternatively and around the corner from the Ca' Foscari university building (pass a bridge to reach it), the **Locanda Ca' Foscari,** at 3888 Calle della Frescada (phone 25-817), is managed by Signora Meneghetti and her English-speaking son Walter, offers 30 beds in one single, three double, and several triple and four-bedded rooms, at the reasonable rates (for Venice) of only 20,000 lire ($12.50) single, 32,000 lire ($20) double, 46,000 lire ($28.75) triple, 56,000 lire ($35) quadruple. Breakfast is 5,000 lire extra. Nearest vaporetto stop: San Tomà, #10.

It should be stressed again that this area of Ca' Foscari, between the San Tomà and Ca' Rezzonico vaporetto stops, on the non-San Marco side of the Grand Canal, is considerably less expensive, and less touristic, than across the way. From the Calle Larga Ca' Foscari, for instance, walk down the Crosera to the Calle S. Pantalon, and on that last named street, you'll find several establishments (such as the one at #3737) selling delicious portions of fried fish (which you eat on the spot) for 5,000 lire per portion. Or, from the Campo (Square) San Barnaba, and the Ca' Rezzonico stop, walk down the Calle Lunga, and you'll pass trattorias selling full meals for 14,000 lire and less. This is where the Venetians go to eat, and cost-conscious travelers will join them.

Back, though, on the main side of the canal, and only 200 yards from St. Mark's Square, the **Locanda Silva,** 4423 Fondamenta del Rimedio (phone 27-643), offers 25 clean rooms in a surprisingly quiet location, all under the calm management of Signor Ettore and his daughter Sandra (the latter acting as interpreter). Their charge, which *includes* breakfast, is 24,000 lire ($15) single, 38,000 lire ($23.75) double, 58,000 lire ($36.25) for a room with three beds. The Silva is just around the corner from the central tourist office of Venice (E.P.T., Ente Provinciale per il Turismo), and you can find it by following the yellow E.P.T. signs posted at various house corners in the Calle Larga San Marco and on the Piazza San Filippo e Giacomo.

If you arrive in Venice by car and use the parking lot near Piazzale Roma, then **Locanda Stefania** at 181 Tolentini (phone 70-37-57), 200 yards away and requiring no seagoing transportation, might be a good choice. Seventeen rooms, all multi-bedded, all on the second floor of an old apartment building, and with frescoes on the ceiling. Twins are 33,000 lire ($20.62), triples 46,000 lire ($28.75), a few very large quads with private shower are 72,000 lire ($45), and breakfast is 5,000 lire more. From the Piazzale Roma, walk over the bridge next to motoscafo stop #2, pass the big Park Hotel, cross a second bridge, and there you'll be. Serenading gondolas pass right by the rooms that front on the water, on most summer evenings.

Locanda Belvedere, Riva Sette Martiri (phone 85-148), on the water-front near Arsenale and Giardini Pubblici, offers a spectacular, panoramic view onto the lagoon, the Lido, San Giorgio Maggiore, the St. Mark's area and Salute Church. Twenty rooms on three floors rent, breakfast included, for 25,000 lire ($15.62) single, 44,000 lire ($27.50) twin, 20,000 lire ($12.50) per person in quads and five-bedded rooms. And showers are free. From the station, take vaporetto 1 to Arsenale, or motoscafo 5 to Tana.

A last locanda, in the Via Garibaldi area (nearest vaporetto stop, #18, is Giardini), at 269 Castello (phone 70-42-03), in a new building with modern furniture and spectacular Murano lamps, is the **Santa Anna;** it's operated by a particularly friendly Venetian family named Vianello, and if you'll phone Signor Bruno Vianello from the station, he'll send over son Walter (23 years old) to meet you at the Giardini vaporetto station—he speaks English. Doubles 40,000 lire ($25), triples 48,000 lire ($30), breakfast included.

TWO RELIGIOUS HOSTELS: Cheaper than the average locanda are two religious hostels, of which one is under Catholic auspices, the other a Protestant house.

Istituto San Giuseppe, at 5042 Castello (phone 25-352), a private Catholic kindergarten operated by nuns, accepts up to 50 tourists, male and female, from July 1 to September 30, in bathless twin rooms renting for 18,000 lire ($11.25) per person per night, without breakfast. This is in a unique central position, and easy to find: walk through the Clock Tower

(Torre dell' Orologio) at St. Mark's Square into the Merceria, then take the second turn right, pass the movie theater and souvenir shop, cross the small square called Campo della Guerra, then walk over the bridge (called Ponte della Guerra): the opaque glass door in the marble arch right after the bridge is the Istituto's entrance. Ring the small brass bell, and a nun will greet you with a smile.

Foresteria della Chiesa Valdese, at 5170 Castello (phone 86-797), consists of two very large, high-ceilinged rooms on the second floor of a palazzo built in 1590, one with 12 double-decker beds for men, one with 16 for women; before falling asleep, you can admire the paintings on the ceiling. Price is 12,000 lire ($7.50) per person, free showers included, and there's no evening curfew; but Signor Riccardo Bensi—the Protestant official in charge—will ask that you be in by 9 p.m. on your first night there. If, after that, he ascertains that you're the proper sort (he won't, for instance, allow "noisy people" to remain), he'll provide you with a house key, and you'll make your own hours. Again, a central location: walk first to the Istituto San Giuseppe (see above), but keep walking straight ahead after the Ponte della Guerra, cross another bridge and the Campo Santa Maria Formosa, then walk into the Calle Lunga, at the end of which is another bridge (Ponte Cavagnis) leading directly to the Foresteria at #5170. Open all year.

THE YOUTH HOSTEL: Venice's youth hostel, the **Ostello Venezia,** a fortress-like red-brick building at 86 Zitelle (phone 38-211), on the Giudecca Island facing the lagoon next to the Zitelle motoscafo stop, was completely modernized and expanded in recent years to accommodate up to 300 guests in large, airy, 30-bed dorms, girls on the first floor, boys on the second floor, each floor containing eight showers, nine wash basins and eleven toilets. Provided you have a hostel card (which you can purchase on the spot from manager Paolo Berni for 24,000 lire), you will pay only 10,500 lire ($6.56) per night for your bed, breakfast included. Downstairs is, also, the best budget restaurant in Venice, which can be patronized by non-hostel-card-holders as well—even adults, if they wish!—who pay only 7,000 lire for a menu consisting of spaghetti or soup, meat dish with vegetable, a piece of fruit and a roll. Beer or wine are 1,000 lire extra, and hours are from 7:30 to 9 a.m., noon to 2 p.m., and 6 to 8 p.m. To reach the hostel, either from the railroad station or St. Mark's Square, take motoscafo 5 (1,500 lire) to the Zitelle stop.

3. Low-Cost Restaurants & Meals

Italian restaurants dish out huge, filling portions of the food they serve. You'll find that one or two courses, chosen from any à la carte menu, are all you'll need or want for at least one of your daily meals in Venice. By limiting that meal to a sensible two courses, you'll also keep eating costs around $4 or $5, and still emerge with bulging Bermudas.

Thus, for example, a large plate of spaghetti with meat sauce—a full meal—costs 4,000 lire ($2.50) in most Venetian restaurants. Antipasto, enough for a light lunch, ranges around 4,500 lire. A meat plate with vegetables is rarely more than 6,000 lire ($3.75). If you eat more than this, you'll feel the effects as you stagger out into the broiling midday sun to continue your touring activities.

In the evening, of course, you'll want a full dinner, and for that purpose, the prix fixe meal—several courses for one lump sum—is the item to find. Here, it's called the "pranzo a prezzo fisso," and it's huge: spaghetti or minestrone, followed by meat course and vegetable, followed by salad, with cheese or fruit for dessert, and often with wine or bread included in the price of the meal. In France, as you'll recall, similar meals average slightly under $9. In most Italian cities, they're easily found at numerous restaurants for 11,000 to 13,000 lire ($6.87 to $8.12). In tourist-happy Venice, as you'd expect, the normal prezzo fisso dinner is a higher 14,000 to 16,000 lire ($8.75 to $10), although we'll find a few restaurants charging considerably less.

Also in Venice, you'll encounter the most frequent new Italian variation on the prezzo fisso meal, called the "menu turistico." Since a prezzo fisso can vary considerably in the number of items provided on it (either two or three courses, with or without beverage, with or without service charge), the Italian tourist authorities recently came up with a new designation—menu turistico—which must, by law, refer to a three-course meal with beverage, service charge and bread included; when you order a menu turistico, at a certain price, there mustn't be a single penny added to that price on your bill. The official regulations read: "The tourist menu consists of a first course, a second course with vegetables, then cheese or fruit or a sweet for dessert, and ¼ liter of wine or a glass of local beer or other aerated beverage, or a half bottle of mineral water. The price includes bread, cover charge, service charge and taxes." For present purposes, keep in mind that a menu turistico is often different from a prezzo fisso—it contains more items and fewer surprises.

The magic words "prezzo fisso" or "menu turistico" can be spotted all over Venice, but they're most easily found in the area of the railroad station: at the Mensa DLF, and along the street called Lista di Spagna.

THE MENSA DLF: From the railroad station, walk down the station steps almost to the water, then turn immediately right for 100 yards, and you'll spot a modern building at 19 Fondamenta S. Lucia that houses the **Mensa Dopolavoro Ferroviario** (Mensa DLF for short), which shares honors with the youth hostel restaurant and the stand-up Rosticceria S. Bartolomeo as the top budget restaurant of Venice. Here, in a mammoth L-shaped dining room, you select your dishes from a self-service counter, where you'll find soup or pasta for 2,500 lire, main courses for 4,000 lire, vegetable or salad for 1,400 lire, a quarter liter of wine for 800 lire—meaning that you can compose a full-course meal similar to a prezzo fisso for 8,700 lire—2,500 lire less than you would pay in the waiter-equipped dining room next door (the cafeteria is open for lunch only, from noon to 2:30 p.m., but seven days a week). Operated by the railway workers union, Mensa DLF caters to just about every secretary, shopgirl and gondolier in the area. Why aren't our railway workers this enlightened?

ON THE LISTA DI SPAGNA: Another major area for budget restaurants serving menu turistico meals is along the **Lista di Spagna,** the street which runs from the left of the railroad station. The first of these, which can be seen from the station steps, is the **Trattoria Povoledo,** 122Q Lista di Spagna, serving spaghetti or soup, then veal cutlet Milanese, salad, cheese or fruit, wine, and large chunks of fresh Italian bread, for exactly 13,000 lire ($8.12). This is almost directly across the street from the more easily found Trattoria Bella Venezia (see below), and is highly recommended—not only for its food, but for its backroom garden, which faces directly on the Grand Canal. Closed Fridays. . . . Only slightly more expensive are the meals (on a menu turistico) to be had across the street for 14,000 lire ($8.75) at the **Trattoria Bella Venezia,** 129 Lista di Spagna. This, by the way, is a beautiful place, with clean tablecloths and flowers, and cool air, even in the midday sun. Excellent food and friendly waiters, but not the standout that the Trattoria Povoledo is, and closed on Thursdays. . . . The well-recommended **Trattoria Nuova,** 189 Lista di Spagna, closed Fridays, charges 13,000 lire for its menu turistico, and the **Trattoria Tre Gobbi,** 148 Lista di Spagna, wants 14,000. . . . To lower this cost, keep walking up the Lista di Spagna, and in a couple of blocks you'll reach the little square called Campo San Geremia, on which you'll see the **Ristorante Vittoria,** closed Thursdays, offering three courses plus service for 9,500 lire ($5.93), but without beverage. . . . These, by the way, are the prices charged at the height of the summer season: they're often less in other months.

And if, on the Lista di Spagna, you'd prefer a simple plate of spaghetti or a pizza, then try **Gino's,** 158 Lista di Spagna, for its 4,000 lire ($2.50) spaghetti bolognese; or **Beau Brummel,** 160A Lista di Spagna, for its large, 5,000 lire ($3.12) pizzas. The latter may be munched at one of five street-level wooden tables, as you watch crowds of Venetians and foreign tourists pass by.

BEYOND THE LISTA DI SPAGNA: As you walk to the end of the Lista di Spagna (around the Campo San Geremia), this broad (for Venice) street continues as a major thoroughfare under other names, which in turn are grouped under the heading "Strada Nuova"—the street continues nearly to the Rialto Bridge, and along its length you'll find other budget restaurants that generally undercut the Lista di Spagna establishments by from 1,000 to 3,000 lire. Thus, for example, at 2232 Strada Nuova, the **Trattoria Da Luciano** (closed Sundays) serves a three-course prezzo fisso—including everything except beverage—for 11,000 lire ($6.87); another trattoria at 5619A Campiello Riccardo Selvatico offers the same repast for 10,000 lire (closed Mondays); and for 1,000 lire more, around the corner from the last-named spot, and on a tiny canal at 5597 Calle Dolfin, you'll find the best of these eateries—the **Trattoria al Vagon**—charging 11,000 lire ($6.87) for its summer season meal, wine included.

PIAZZA SAN MARCO: More prezzo fisso meals near the Piazza San Marco? There are a number of good ones, but mainly in the $9 to $12 price range. At the right of the stunning Ducal Palace, along the Canal, you'll see the very swank Hotel Royal Danieli. It's composed of two buildings. Between those buildings is a little alleyway called the **Calle delle Rasse.** Walk down that lane for fifty yards, and you'll pass no fewer than three prezzo fisso restaurants offering meals for 14,000 lire ($8.75)—the best of them being **Ristorante Nuova Grotta,** at 4538, where you might order the zuppa di pesce, fish soup, or the spaghetti alle vongole, pasta with clam sauce. The price ascends to a high 16,000 lire (including beverage and service—it's a menu turistico) at **Ristorante La Gondola,** 4610 Calle Rasse,

which you might try and where the zuppa di verdura is especially good. Nearby, at 4620 Calle delle Rasse, the small, self-service **Rosticceria Scarpa** is an alternative for quicker meals, such as a plate of pasticcio di lasagne for 2,800 lire ($1.75), or delicious hot sandwiches baked in oil (mozzarella in carrozza), for only 1,000 lire (62¢).

At the end of Calle delle Rasse, you'll be on a square called Campo S. Filippo Giacomo (Giacomo Square). Off the Giacomo Square, you'll find a tiny alleyway called the Calle degli Albanesi, which runs parallel to Calle delle Rasse and whose only inhabitant seems to be the large and pleasant **Taverna dei Dogi,** 4250 Calle Albanesi, closed Tuesdays, serving a three-course big-splurge meal, wine and service included, for 18,000 lire ($11.25); on that meal is an incomparable specialty of Venice—fritto misto dell' Adriatico, sometimes known as frittura dell' Adriatico—which are tiny, goldfish-sized fish fried in batter, and something you really should try. The picturesque dei Dogi is highly recommended.

Alternatively, if you either walk or take the vaporetto one stop beyond the first Riva degli Schiavoni stop, in the direction of the Lido, you'll quickly find the **Calle della Pescaria,** site of the **Trattoria alla Bronza** (serving a true menu turistico for 12,000 lire; sidewalk tables), and **Trattoria alla Doccia** (seafood specialties; menu turistico 11,000 lire). The 11,000 lire ($6.87) trattoria here—the Doccia—is undoubtedly one of the cheapest in the San Marco area, but the location is a good five-minute walk from St. Mark's along the canal going towards the Lido (watch the side streets on your left, one of which is the Calle della Pescaria). Nearby, at 3983 Bragora, a small fish restaurant called **Friggitoria Caratteristica Veneziana** is slightly less expensive than the restaurants on the Calle della Pescaria: menu turistico for 10,000 lire, polenta 1,800 lire, fried octopus or grilled fresh sardines for 6,000 lire, two glasses of white wine 900 lire. There is no other place in Venice where you can eat fish specialties for less money. Location: just around the corner from Trattoria alla Doccia, about 20 yards away.

NEAR THE RIALTO: In this busy, central market area, **Antico Dolo,** 778 Ruga Vecchia, is a small trattoria specializing in the most classic, local dishes of Venice, priced extremely low and thus attracting a clientele of nearby market personnel—you'll be the only tourist eating here. My own two courses with wine (including a roll and service charge), in the summer of 1984, totalled 6,700 lire ($4.18), and consisted of pasta fagioli (a thick beans-and-noodles soup flavored with oregano), 2,000 lire ($1.25), to begin; a main course of trippa pomodoro (tripe in a tomato sauce), 3,000 lire ($1.87), and a quarter-liter of white wine, 800 lire (50¢), pumped from a 50-liter glass container covered with straw (a damigiana). Signor Piero, wearing a white jacket, is the proprietor-chef, and also waits on tables. From St. Mark's, cross the Rialto Bridge, and walk straight on, passing the many colorful stands, until you reach the first street turning left; this is the Ruga Vecchia. Only a lamp, and no sign at all, identifies the unique and agreeably priced establishment at #778. Closed Sundays.

TRATTORIA BRUNO: A budget stand-out on the *other* side of the Grand Canal, the **Trattoria Bruno,** 2754 Calle Lunga, is just a few yards off the Campo S. Barnaba, and offers a remarkable meal of pasta, followed by meat or seafood with one vegetable and one roll for 12,000 lire ($7.50), including beverage and service charge. In this white-tiled little eatery with modern art on the walls, the selection of dishes is a surprisingly wide one, the food unusually tasty, and the location—away from the more heavily touristed areas of Venice—is probably the explanation for the atypical prices. Operated by a charming Venetian, Italo Libralesso; closed Sundays.

VENICE'S SELF-SERVICE RESTAURANTS:

Yes, there are a few of them, and to adaptable tourists, they offer good value, but one is unlike any cafeteria you've ever seen: stand-up only (sometimes you eat your meal right on the ten-yard-long display counter), very plain in appearance, but with delicious food. Operated by the three Rizzo brothers—Gianni, Renato and Paolo—its name is **Rosticceria S. Bartolomeo,** and it's at 5423 Calle della Bissa (just off the Campo San Bartolomeo, which is itself just a few steps from the Rialto Bridge; cross the bridge to the San Marco side, walk 30 yards to the Campo San Bartolomeo, and on the Campo, take the underpass to the left marked "Sotoportego de la Bissa"). The restaurant opens for dinner at 5 p.m. It offers no fewer than 11 different risotto dishes (vast mounds of rice flavored and topped by other ingredients) for 3,000 lire ($1.87). Other massive plates of more varieties of pasta than you ever dreamed possible are 2,600 lire ($1.62) (try pasta e fagioli, a Venetian specialty), sandwiches are 900 to 1,200 lire, a rugged glass of plain white or red wine is 500 lire; meat dishes are comparatively expensive, but still as little as 5,500 lire ($3.43) for much more than you can possibly eat. As in any Italian self-service place, order and eat the pasta (or the risotto or the gnocchi) first, before you select your meat course, as chances are you won't be able to finish the pasta alone! This is my own favorite among all the rosticcerias of Venice, and highly recommended for readers with adventure in their blood. Closed Mondays.

Somewhat smaller, but better located, and operated on the very same principles by the very same family, is a semi-cafeteria called **Rosticceria al Teatro Goldoni,** at 4747 Calle dei Fabbri, next to the Campo San Luca, only 200 yards from St. Mark's Square (on the square, walk over to the famous Café Quadri, where starts the Calle dei Fabbri). The four pezzi forti (most popular dishes) here are (a) the pasticcio di lasagne al forno and gnocchi di patate con ragout, two pasta appetizers for 3,000 lire ($1.87) apiece; (b) baccalá con polenta, a filling fish platter with hot ground corn, a specialty of northern Italy, for 5,000 lire ($3.12); (c) mozzarella in carrozza, a delicious hot sandwich filled with mozzarella cheese, only 850 lire (53¢), and (d) the piatto del giorno, actually a two-course menu with wine and a roll, all for only 8,500 lire ($5.31). Closed Wednesdays.

A third self-service restaurant, which opened in 1982, faces the Canal Grande near Rialto Bridge at the side where the vaporetto and motoscafo stops are. The **Rialto Self-Service,** at #4174, has 180 seats in three air-conditioned dining rooms, and is open from noon to 2:45 p.m. and 7 to 9:30 p.m., closed Sundays. It offers an unusually large selection of 25 hors d'oeuvres, averaging 2,500 lire ($1.56), 14 pasta and rice dishes in the 3,000 lire ($1.87) range, 30 main entrees, ranging from fried sardines for 3,800 lire ($2.37), to stewed rabbit ragout for 5,000 lire ($3.12). Wine, beer, and soft drinks are available for 1,600 lire ($1); a three-course-with-wine menu turistico costs 11,000 ($6.87). And while you are there, you may notice a small marble sign on the house next door (it's the mayor's office), with the name "Elena Piscopia" inscribed on it. This Venetian lady, born in 1646, passed exams in 1678 to become the first female doctor of philosophy in Europe.

A Students' Self-Service

At 2839 Ponte dei Pugni on Campo San Barnaba, next to the canal where Katherine Hepburn was doused in the movie "Summertime," the self-service **Trattoria ai Padovani** is heavily frequented by students from the nearby Ca' Foscari University, attracted by filling meals with beverage priced at only 7,500 lire ($4.68). I tried it in the summer of 1984, and had a memorable lasagne al forno, followed by a quarter roast chicken with french fries, and two glasses of red wine, at that price. An accompanying bonus is the classical music which proprietor Signor Giovanni plays over a loudspeaker throughout each meal. Closed Saturdays.

SOME THOUGHTS ON VENETIAN MEALS: The kitchens of most trattorias and ristorantes close at 10 p.m.; if you need to eat at a later time, go to the Piazzale Roma near the train station—that large and very unpicturesque square of garages—where the **Trattoria al Bolognese** (at #462) serves a 14,000 lire ($8.75) pranzo à prezzo fisso (spaghetti alla bolognese, veal cutlet bolognese—veal slathered with melted cheese and ham, swimming in olive oil—and fruit or cheese) until nearly 11 p.m. Closed on Saturdays. . . . Some specialties of Venice, which you shouldn't miss: spaghetti alle vongole (spaghetti with clam sauce, usually 4,500 lire), zuppa di pesce (fish soup, 6,000 lire), and especially frittura mista or frittura di pesce—tiny fish of the Adriatic, fried in crisp batter, and so delicious (and cheap) that the waiter will nearly bestow congratulations as you order it. . . . Everywhere on menus, you'll see risotto di pesce, risotto de fegatini, risotto de . . . , all of which refer to a vast mound of rice, covered with sauce, and interspersed with ingredients pesce (fish) and fegatini (chicken livers) named above.

STARVATION BUDGET MEALS: They're available for only 6,000 lire ($3.75), and consist of three courses and a roll, with beverage (a glass of wine, beer, mineral water or lemonade) included, at the 500-seat **Mensa dell' Istituto di Architettura** at 2480 San Polo, Monday through Saturday, noon to 2:30 p.m. and 6:30 to 8:30 p.m., from January through the 19th of July, and then from September 16th onward. While technically for students of Venice's large architectural institute (a high school with university status), nobody will object if you simply quietly join the queue—unless you're carrying a suitcase, that is! Pay first at the cashier's box, then step in line for your tray, and later take a seat at one of the long tables. But first you'll need to find this slightly difficult address: take vaporetto 1 to the San Tomà stop, walk to the Frari church square, then over the bridge with the white marble handrails (Ponte dei Frari), turn left (along the canal), passing over a second, smaller bridge, pass a police station (the yellow building), and the Mensa is in the first street turning right. And if you lose your way, ask for the Archivio di Stato; the Mensa is next door.

Another important haven for persons of all ages, and a major inflation-fighting institution (especially important in Venice, where restaurants charge far more than in Florence or Rome), is the **Mensa Universitaria** at 3861 Dorsoduro, next to Ca' Foscari, a short (three minutes') walk from the Ca' Rezzonico vaporetto stop. Open to everybody—repeat, everybody—in all months other than August, from Monday through Saturday from noon to 2 p.m. and from 7 to 8:30 p.m., this is a typical Mensa restaurant on the third walk-up floor of a massive stone building that also houses the Venetian fire department (whose red fire boats are easily glimpsed). Students of Ca' Foscari pay only 1,000 lire (62¢), while non-students pay 7,000 lire ($4.37), for: a choice of spaghetti, vegetable soup (minestrone) or risotto, followed by a plate of beef, chicken or rabbit stew, with a choice of one out of three vegetables and salad, followed by fruit, with beverage (beer, wine or a Coke) and unlimited bread included. Quality of the ($4.37) meal is as fine as that of any $8.75 menu turistico served elsewhere in town. Don't miss. And if any question should arise about your right to use the Mensa, simply walk over to its Administrative Office at 3144 Fondamenta Rezzonico, 200 yards away (near a small bridge leading to and from San Barnabà, open Monday through Saturday from 8 a.m. to 2 p.m.), and they'll phone over to give the green light.

Incidentally: if, instead of taking the vaporetto to Ca' Foscari, you'd prefer to walk, then: either cross the Accademia Bridge (coming from San Marco), turn right, and ask for Ca' Foscari; or cross the Rialto Bridge (again coming from San Marco), turn left, and ask for Ca' Foscari. From St. Mark's Square, walking time to the famous Mensa is 15 minutes via Accademia, 25 minutes via the Rialto Bridge.

READERS' RESTAURANT SELECTIONS: "There is a very cheap, simple but clean and efficient **vegetarian restaurant** (the **Piccola Cucina Serprado**) at 230A Lista di Spagna (not far from the railway station). Very good for huge plates of spaghetti, rice, or all types of egg dishes and one of the few places where you can get boiled eggs" (Mr. and Mrs. H. B. Valman, London, England). . . . "**Trattoria Self Service Ai Gond-olieri,** at 106 Calle Priuli, is a reasonably priced and genuinely Venetian tavola calda near the station, where you needn't pay cover charges or feel obliged to order a full meal, and can simply point to what you want. This is just around the corner, after leaving the railway station, to your left" (Philip T. Rank, Rome, Italy).

THE PICNIC CENTER: Do-it-yourself meals? Take the vaporetto to the Ca' d'Oro stop, then take a gondola directly across the canal for 400 lire (you'll see a couple of beat-up boats that ply this shuttle route). You'll arrive at the Rialto Marketplace—a colorful collection of grocery stalls, meat and fish stands, offering exotic and delicious foods. Bread, fruit, cheese, olives and prosciutto, which makes a good picnic lunch, cost very little when purchased here. But open only from 7 a.m. to 2 p.m., Monday to Saturday.

A RECAP: To summarize, the city's best food values are: the astonishing 7,000 lire menu at the **Mensa Universitaria** near Ca' Foscari; the 7,000 lire menu served in the ground floor restaurant of the Venice Youth Hostel **Ostello Giudecca;** the two-course, 8,500 lire menus at **Rosticcerias San Bartolomeo** and **Al Teatro Goldoni;** and the 7,500 lire menu, wine included, offered by **Trattoria ai Padovani** at Campo San Barnaba.

4. What to See & Do

TOURS: The best tour of Venice is the one you can take by yourself. Venice is a relatively small city; it can be covered almost entirely in two days of walking. It's fun simply to wander—through streets so narrow your outstretched hands can touch the buildings along each side—to gaze in stores where eels and octopus are the merchandise. Then take a marathon vaporetto ride: start at the railroad station and glide up the Grand Canal to the Lido at the other end. That takes an hour and costs 1,200 lire (75¢) on vaporetto 1, or 40 minutes and 1,500 lire (93¢) on express vaporetto 4, and provides your best all-around look at the city.

But don't confine your sightseeing to the Grand Canal; you haven't really seen Venice until you've also made the trip around the outside of the city, via the equally important Giudecca Canal. From the San Zaccaria station (#16) near St. Mark's Square (and also near vaporetto stop #15, but not to be confused with it), **Motoscafo Circolare** (Circular Motorlaunch) #5 makes an entirely circular tour of the city—one boat goes clockwise, the other counterclockwise—and leaves at 15-minute intervals until 11 p.m. From San Zaccaria, #5 Destra goes first to San Giorgio, then through the Giudecca Canal to the railway station and the Ghetto, and then, after stopping at the Fondamente Nuove and passing the cemetery island of San Michele (where Igor Stravinsky is buried), it reaches famous Murano with its glass factories and glass blowers. The trip takes one hour and 10 minutes, and costs 1,500 lire. Coming back, you can board Motoscafo 5 from Murano (the Museo stop), and return directly for another 1,500 lire to San Zaccaria near St. Mark's Square. Or, you can make the entire circular tour without ever leaving the boat for 3,000 lire—the cheapest 2½-hour sightseeing tour in the world!

MURANO, BURANO AND TORCELLO: If you're the most avid sort of sea-goer, you might also want to consider an extension trip that you can make from the Fondamente Nuove to the island of San Erasmo for 3,000 lire, round-trip, lasting nearly two hours. But you take this one only for the boat ride and rest; peaceful vegetable gardens are all that await at San Erasmo. A far more interesting cruise, and an excellent value, is the 20,000-lire tour (escorted) operated by the Serenissima Company to the three major islands of the Venice lagoon: Murano (for its glass factories), Burano (for its lace factories), and Torcello (for its church, oldest in Venice). The boats leave twice a day, at 9:30 a.m. and 2:30 p.m., from a dock almost directly in front of the Bridge of Sighs, near San Marco Square (look for the sign reading "Escursione alle Isole"). You'll return at 1 p.m. or 6 p.m. having visited all three islands at a cost that is less than some tour companies charge for the Murano visit alone.

THE LIDO: Swimming in the Adriatic, at the beaches along the Lido, is another thrill that cannot be missed. The key to doing it is the camerini— little dressing rooms along the shore which you are required to rent in order to use the beach; you cannot simply undress on the sands (as in Coney Island). The two largest Lido beaches, managed and operated by the city administration, are the **Bucintoro,** just to the left at the end of the Gran Viale Santa Maria Elisabetta (walk down six wide steps to reach the ticket counter), and the **San Niccolò,** a mile farther down to the left, reached by walking along the straight promenade, or by taking bus "B" for 500 lire. Both these beaches are open in summer from 9 a.m. to 7 p.m. and charge a uniform 7,000 lire ($4.37) for a cabin for two, with a 3,000 lire ($1.87) supplement for additional persons, up to a maximum of four. Children under 14 pay 1,500 lire (93¢), and there is a 3,000 lire ($1.87) deposit for the cabin key, refunded when you leave and hand it back. Self-service restaurants on the beaches, facing the Adriatic sea, are no more expensive than their counterparts in Venice: 4,000 lire ($2.50) for a big helping of spaghetti with tomato sauce, 1,200 lire (75¢) for a small bottle of red wine. I especially like to sit in the Onda Azurra restaurant on Bucintoro beach; both the view and the quality of the food justify a trip to the Lido, weather permitting.

To reach the famous Lido, take boat 6 from its dock opposite the Royal Danieli Hotel (near the Piazza San Marco and the Bridge of Sighs); this is a large, doubledecker vessel that makes the trip nonstop in about 15 minutes, charges 1,200 lire, and leaves every 20 minutes. When you land at the Lido, you'll find the public bus "B" waiting to take you (for 500 lire) out to the public beach (last stop), which is just to the side of the San Niccolò beach, and which charges no admission at all. Before boarding that bus, you might first want to seek out the Standa Department Store on the Lido's main street—Viale S. M. Elisabetta—where you can buy inexpensive picnic ingredients, even on a Sunday.

MURANO ALONE: Finally, you ought not to leave Venice without first taking a side excursion to the island of Murano, whose factories turn out the famous glassware of Venice, spidery, rainbow-hued and sold at mile-high prices throughout the rest of the world. Don't, however, take one of the organized 20,000-lire tours to the island. Either board motoscafo 5 to Murano from St. Mark's Square (1,500 lire) or take the same boat from the Fondamente Nuove, at a round-trip cost of 3,000 lire. The factories of Murano then admit visitors free for a glass-blowing exhibition, hoping they'll stay to buy glassware in factory showrooms. But you needn't delay your purchases of Venetian glass that long: many, many trips there, and the confirming comments of numerous readers, support the conclusion that Murano prices for glass are often higher than in Venice itself (that's how you indirectly pay for the factory visit!) Do, however, pick up a pedestal ashtray for around 8,000 lire. They shimmer in water-like tones of blue and rose, and will forever remind you of the look of Venice.

READERS' SIGHTSEEING SUGGESTION: "The **Ancient Ghetto** in Venice is the 'original' ghetto, in that the word itself comes from the Italian for 'foundry,' once nearby. It today possesses five very old, elaborate synagogues which can be visited by applying to the office of the Jewish community at 1188A Ghetto Vecchio (phone 71-50-12), within easy walking distance of the railway station. Services and tours (there's a museum) are scheduled from 10 a.m. to 12:30 p.m. and from 3:30 to 6 p.m., daily except Saturdays and Sunday afternoons, but it would be wise to check in advance. Extremely interesting" (Ruth Gruber Fredman, Rockville, Maryland).

HOPE'S VENICE: The soul of Venice is, of course, its art and architecture. Hope has briefly itemized, in the report that now follows, the outstanding churches and museums that a first-time visitor will want to see:

"The lush, sumptuous fantasy that is Venice was never meant to be a tourist attraction, nor did the Italian government construct it (as one American lady once suggested) to compete with our Disneyland! To understand the overwhelming richness of the city's external aspect, you must know that in the 15th century, Venice was the capital of one of the world's greatest empires, and the undisputed ruler of the Adriatic, a natural gateway for trade between East and West. What you see today are vestiges of the proud and wealthy 'Serene Republic' (*La Serenissima*), and that peculiar (to Venice) merging of the sensual East with the Christian West.

"Some of my happiest hours have been spent simply wandering at random in Venice and I recommend that aimlessness to you because, in a way, the entire city of Venice is a kind of bizarre museum in which deliberate visits to specific museums and sights seem almost superfluous. But believe it or not, the interiors of some Venetian 'palazzos' are just as exciting as their exteriors, and therefore well worth a specific trip.

AROUND THE PIAZZA SAN MARCO: "The major attractions of Venice are centered around the Piazza San Marco, where a never-ending stream of visitors comes to pay tribute to the medieval beauty of this unique square.

St. Mark's Basilica

"You'll of course want to explore the inside of the voluptuously Byzantine-Romanesque-Gothic Church of San Marco, which stands on the square of the same name, and has always been intimately associated with the history and political life of the town (in the early days it was the Doge's Chapel; meetings were held and proclamations were heard there). Legend has it that in 828, four Venetians (a monk, a priest, and two merchants) conspired to 'rescue' the remains of St. Mark from an Alexandrian Church, and smuggled the sacred relic to Venice. Thus it was that St. Mark replaced the Greek St. Theodore as patron of the city, and the citizens vied with each other in donating gifts for the final resting place of the saint (now under the high altar, in front of the gorgeous Pala d'Oro).

"But it is the glittering mosaics of the church, which took 700 years to complete, and which literally cover its interior and explain its nickname 'Church of Gold,' that are really the outstanding feature here. (A favorite with the experts, and easily overlooked, is the exotic little mosaic rendering of 'Salome's Dance' in the Baptistery—first door on your right as you enter; look directly above.) For a better view of the mosaics, pay an extra 1,000 lire and go up to the gallery—from this vantage point you can begin to distinguish detail, see the bizarre pattern of the floor, and get a better appreciation of the church as a whole.

"That 1,000 lire also admits you to the gallery, where you'll have a nice view of the piazza below, and to the Museo San Marco (liturgical treasures—tapestries, robes, rugs, the lion of St. Mark's). There, one can visit the four famous bronze horses brought to Venice in the 13th century from Constantinople, and now on display in the basement. They were moved from their original position on the church gallery to protect them from pollution.

"Entrance to the church, which is open from 9:30 a.m. to 4:30 p.m., is entirely free. But there is a charge of 1,000 lire for those wishing to see the Pala d'Oro, the staggering jewel-encrusted golden altarpiece (with 2,486 jewels!) in the Presbytery; and the Treasury, which was begun in the 13th century with Crusaders' plunder from Constantinople, and contains many sacred relics. I'd see them.

The Palace of the Doges

"The interior of the pink-shimmering, oriental-looking palazzo where the Doge lived, and which was also the home of the government and the courts, is almost as rich as its exterior, with its cunningly carved columns, famed 15th-century Porta della Carta—the main entrance to the palace where the Doge's proclamations were posted—and the splendid inner courtyard which, because of the double row of Renaissance arches on the palace, looks rather like a sugary stage setting, topped off by the elegant Giant's Staircase. Inside you'll see wood-paneled courts and meeting rooms richly decorated by the cream of Venetian painters (Veronese, Titian, Carpaccio and Tintoretto), an actual chastity belt (complete with spikes, the first I've ever seen!) in the Armory Museum, the cells of prisoners formerly incarcerated here, and the Bridge of Sighs—over which you'll actually walk. Of special interest historically is the Room of the Council of Ten (the dreaded Star chamber of an otherwise admirable and efficient, albeit strictly patrician government) with its adjacent vestibule, the Sala della Bussola, containing the last complete 'lion's mouth'—a container (like a small door in the wall) into which secret denunciations of suspected enemies of the state were placed for quick action by the Council. The most impressive room (among many riches) architecturally is the vast and open Great Council Hall (constructed with no supporting pillars), enhanced by Tintoretto's masterpiece 'Paradise' (above the Doge's chair) and a spectacular 'Glorification of Venice' by Veronese in the oval on the ceiling—the portraits of the Doges all around the top of the room were also done by Tintoretto (whose portrait of Doge Faliero, you'll notice, has been painted out in black: he was a traitor, beheaded in 1355). Open in summer from 8:30 a.m. to 6 p.m. daily, entrance fee of 3,000 lire, 1,500 lire for students.

The Campanile

"From the top of the straight and simple red brick bell-tower, you'll have a really splendid view of Venice and vicinity. On a clear day you can see the Lido and all the way out to the sea. Open summer from 10 a.m. to 7:30 p.m.; take the elevator to the top for 1,200 lire.

The Correr Museum

"Also located on St. Mark's Square, directly opposite the Basilica, this rather interesting museum contains a first floor section dealing with Venetian history (costumes, coins, replicas of boats, paintings of sea battles, weapons), and an outstanding second floor art gallery displaying some wonderful primitives (look for Cosmé Tura's 'Pietà,' among many others), as well as more sophisticated work by Bellini, Carpaccio (including his famous 'Two Courtesans'), Canova, and Lorenzo Lotto, to mention a few. Entrance fee of 2,000 lire; viewing hours from 10 a.m. to 4 p.m., Sundays from 9 a.m. to 12:30 p.m. Closed Tuesdays.

AND ALONG THE CANALS: "The art treasures of Venice can be seen in the city's glorious palazzi, scuole, museums, and galleries, many of them as impressive architecturally as they are notable for the renowned masterpieces they house. We'll highlight only some of the most important.

Ca' Rezzonico

"The Ca' Rezzonico (which you reach by taking the vaporetto to stop #11, called Ca' Rezzonico) is an 18th-century palazzo, now a museum containing articles relating to 18th-century Venetian life—furniture, paintings, various artifacts. The collection itself is fairly good and if you're curious to see what living in an 18th-century palazzo was like, this is a pleasant way to do it. You'll definitely want to see the charming mezzanine apartment once occupied by Pope Clemente XIII, and at another time the home of Robert Browning. Entrance fee of 1,000 lire; hours from 10 a.m. to 4 p.m.; Sunday mornings 9:30 a.m. to 12:30 p.m. Closed Fridays.

Scuola di San Rocco

"This is a vast monument to the work of Tintoretto, the largest collection of his paintings anywhere (and some of the largest canvases I've ever seen)—a must for all art lovers. You'll find, among many impressive works, 'The Slaughter of the Innocents' (on the ground floor, with seven other New Testament scenes), which is so full of dramatic urgency and energy that figures seem almost to tumble out of the frame; and, in the center of the ceiling of the Great Hall upstairs, the mystical and powerful 'Miracle of the Bronze Snake' (the paintings on, or near, the staircase are not by Tintoretto). You can reach the scuola on foot from the Ca' Rezzonico, or else take the vaporetto to stop 10—San Tomà. Entrance charge of 2,500 lire; hours in summer from 9 a.m. to 1 p.m. and 3:30 to 6:30 p.m.

St. Mary's of the Frari Church

"A few steps from the Scuola di San Rocco, the Frari Church is particularly impressive because it houses the melodramatic and grandiose tombs of two famous Venetians—Canova and Titian—and also because there hangs, behind the High Altar, Titian's 'Assumption of the Virgin' and in the left nave his 'Virgin of the Pesaro Family'; you'll also see Bellini's triptych, 'Madonna and Child' (through a door on the right, in the Sacristy), and an almost primitive-looking wood-carving by Donatello of 'John the Baptist.' Entrance is 500 lire; hours are from 9:30 a.m. to 12 p.m. and 2:30 to 6 p.m., winters till 5 p.m.—but no visiting during services.

Ca' Pesaro (Gallery of Modern Art)

"Farther up the Grand Canal, past the Rialto (take the vaporetto to stop 5, S. Stae), the Ca' Pesaro Gallery has an exciting array of master-works by Chagall, Klee, Rouault, Rodin, Moore, Kandinsky, Bonnard. And all of this is supplemented by the equally exciting opportunity to see what the inside of one of those Baroque, beside-the-water palazzos (which this is) looks like. Entrance of 2,000 lire; hours from 10 a.m. to 4 p.m.; from 9:30 a.m. to 12:30 p.m. Sundays, free.

Ca' d'Oro

"Close to Ca' Pesaro, but on the opposite side of the Canal, is Ca' d'Oro (or Gallery Franchetti, vaporetto stop is Ca' d'Oro), the best preserved (15th century) and most impressive of the patrician Venetian palazzos; entrance to the museum is directly opposite the vaporetto stop, and the street number is 3932. You'll first pass through a cool green courtyard and emerge into one of the most glorious rooms I've ever seen, with ornately decorated beamed ceiling, colorful mosaic floor and rose walls. The atmosphere conjures simultaneous visions of Othello, Machia-velli, and the Renaissance. A graceful outside stairway takes you to second-floor exhibits where you'll see furniture, tapestries, medals, and the art gallery (there's Titian, Tintoretto, Carpaccio, Mantegna's famous 'St. Sebastian,' a Van Dyck and works by lesser Flemish and Dutch masters), but the main point of interest is the palace itself.

Galleria dell' Accademia

"The Academy of Fine Arts (vaporetto stop 12, Accademia) is the definitive treasure house of Venetian painting, exhibited chronologically from the 13th to the 18th century. Many Carpaccios (keeping company with Titian, Veronese, Tintoretto, etc.), Giorgione's fascinating 'The Tempest,' and a magnificent collection of scenes of Bellini, Bastiani, and Mansueti in Room XX—my own favorite among the many rooms. You can't make a better 2,000-lire investment than this gallery, and on the first and second Sundays and fourth Saturday of each month, the entrance is free. Open from 9 a.m. to 2 p.m., Sunday 9 a.m. to 1 p.m., closed Monday.

The Guggenheim Collection

"The best for last. The home of the late Peggy Guggenheim (Palazzo Venier dei Leoni, #701 Dorsoduro, a short walk from the Accademia) is open to the public (from around April 1 through October) for an admission fee of 4,000 lire (2,000 for students) daily except Tuesdays from noon to 6 p.m. (free on Saturdays from 6 to 9 p.m.)—and if you miss this place, you can kick yourself! The collection inside is best described by Herbert Read in his foreword to a souvenir book available on the premises: 'The collection of 20th-century paintings and sculpture formed by Peggy Guggenheim is the only one in Europe to have a systematical historical basis. It embraces all the major movements which since about 1910 have transformed the very concept of art and which can now for the first time be seen in a unified perspective.' There are works by Picasso, Chagall, Leger, Braque, Dali, Jackson Pollock (almost a dozen of his canvases), and many others too numerous to mention. As a sidelight, you receive from this visit an idea of what a wonderful life hers must have been, surrounded by great art. One exhibition room, a dining room with the great Cubist paintings, was obviously used for living purposes as well; and another room, formerly Ms. Guggenheim's bedroom, contains a spectacular bed with silver headboard by Calder, and also paintings by Pegeen, Ms. Guggenheim's deceased daughter. The home, once more, is open to the public daily except Tuesdays; and I say: 'Hats off to you, Ms. Guggenheim, you were a woman of great soul!'"

A VISIT TO THE GONDOLA FACTORY: Several hundred of the unique black gondolas now in service in Venice, including the one owned by the late Peggy Guggenheim, were built by a 72-year-old master craftsman and greatest living gondola expert, Cavaliere Giovanni Giuponi, who entered the profession 62 years ago as an apprentice to his father. Cavaliere Giuponi's tiny shipyard, one of three in Venice, still manufactures four or five gondolas each year, and the proud cavaliere is happy to show you around. He requires three to four months to construct a gondola, which is made of seven different types of wood, has a life expectancy of 20 to 25 years, and costs approximately 16 million lire (about $10,000), of which 10% goes for the ferro alone, the famous metallic bow or nose.

Best visiting hours for the "shipyard" are from 9 a.m. to noon, Monday through Friday. To get there, walk over the Accademia Bridge to Zattere, then board a ferry-vaporetto (the stop is in front of the Gesuati church, the boat leaves every ten minutes, and charges 800 lire one-way—buy the ticket at the newspaper stand) for a five-minute ride to Giudecca island. There, turn left and walk along the waterfront, over the little bridge called "Ponte Piccolo," into the first very narrow street turning right called "Calle Stretta Ferrando," pass the club of the Communist Party (you can't miss the red flag), and ring the bell at house number 410A. Either Signor Giuponi or his assistant will let you in to a pocket-sized factory that has accounted for a large percentage of the 500-or-so gondolas gracefully floating on the canals of Venice.

After your visit, I'd suggest you walk back to the Giudecca waterfront, turn right over the large iron bridge called Ponte Longo and over another smaller bridge, passing the Redentore Church to the Zitelle boat stop; from there, take motoscafo circolare 5 (there's a boat every 15 minutes) back to St. Mark's. This ten-minute, 1,500-lire trip provides a spectacular panoramic view of the Campanile, St. Mark's Church, and Doge's Palace.

5. Evening Entertainment

CONCERTS AND THEATRE: Three times a week, but on varying days (watch the posters), the municipal government offers free band concerts in the Piazza San Marco, at 5 p.m. Sundays and 9 p.m. the other two days. Your theatregoing should be confined to the jewel-like **Teatro la Fenice** (mainly grand opera, occasionally classic dramas), and to the loggione seats of that theatre (second gallery, costing 6,000 lire). Weekdays, performances start at 8:30 p.m., Sundays at 3:30 p.m., and a few loggione are sometimes available a few minutes before starting time. If they aren't, then standing room (palchi) is 5,000 lire, and well worth it. Casts are composed of Italy's finest singers, particularly in the summer months when Milan's La Scala Opera shuts down.

PAINLESS NIGHTSPOTS: There are two, and only two, methods of inexpensive nightclubbing in the Venice area, and the first is to visit **Discoteca New Life** at 124 Lista di Spagna, in the area of the Venice railroad station. This is the place to meet young, single and unaccompanied Venetian girls, who are attracted to the spot in quantity by the management's policy of charging an entrance fee of only 8,000 lire, which *includes* the right to a whiskey, beer or aranciata (orange soda)—the only drink you need imbibe to spend an entire evening in this haven—and thus, you have a total expense of $5 for dancing, liaisons and drink. Following Italian custom, the second drink costs considerably less (4,000 lire). Open seven days a week from 9 p.m. to 1 a.m., with two dance floors, psychedelic lights, and live musicians alternating with the discs.

Venice's other budget nightspot, the **New Club 22,** is on the Lido, at 22 Lungomare Marconi, and is open during the summer months from 9 p.m. to 4 a.m. daily, in all other months on Saturday and Sunday evenings only; it charges 8,000 lire for entrance (which includes the right to one drink), but only 5,000 lire for every successive drink; the action occurs on an elevated platform above the sandy Adriatic beach, where patrons dance. To find the club, walk up the Gran Viale from the boat stop until you reach the sea front, then walk right along the coast line, passing the Grand Hotel des Bains (where much of the motion picture *Death in Venice* was filmed), until you reach New Club 22, on your left.

6. Venice Miscellany

STUDENTS IN VENICE: For youth-oriented charter flights, cheap student ship tickets to Egypt, Greece and Spain, cheap student train tickets to northern climes, try **CTS** (the so-called Centro Studenti) at 3252 Fondamenta Tagliapietra, near Ca' Foscari, phone 705-660, open Monday through Friday, 9:30 a.m. to 12:30 p.m. and 3:30 p.m. to 7 p.m., Saturdays 9:30 a.m. to noon.

THE SELF-SERVICE LAUNDRIES IN VENICE: The most easily found is the **Lavaget,** at 1269 Cannaregio (al Ponte delle Guglie—at the Guglie Bridge). From the railroad station, walk down the Lista di Spagna until you come to the bridge at Cannaregio, walk over the bridge and immediately turn 20 yards left. Three-and-a-half kilos of laundry will cost you 10,000 lire at the Lavaget, and that includes detergent and drying. Hours are Monday through Friday, 8:30 a.m. to 12:30 p.m. and 3 to 7 p.m., closed Saturdays and Sundays. . . . Nearer to St. Mark's Square: **Lavanderia a Gettone Gabriella,** at 985 Calle Colonnette, where four-and-a-half kilos of laundry, washed and dried, are 10,000 lire. This time, walk from St. Mark's Square through the clock tower into the Merceria (the main shopping street), then turn left, walk over the bridge into Calle Fiubera, make your first right and first left. And if you get lost, ask for the Hotel Astoria: Gabriella is in the block behind this small hotel. Open Monday through Friday, 8:30 a.m. to 12:30 p.m. and 3 to 7 p.m., closed Saturdays.

VENICE MISCELLANY: While the game of trick-the-tourist is a highly developed art in Venice, developed over decades, sometimes tourists overreact and suspect everyone. In fairness to the men who run the vaporettos, let it be known that they *do* have a right to require that you pay 1,000 lire for every large suitcase you bring aboard. See why it pays to travel light? . . . The same applies to the seemingly wily behavior of the waiters at the Piazza San Marco, who will sometimes charge 3,000 lire, at other times 5,000 lire, for a cup of espresso. They're not pocketing the difference, the 2,000 lire is a music tax; to avoid it, order **and** pay for your drinks while the band is **not** playing. . . . That's not to say that the outdoor cafés at the Piazza aren't expensive; they are, and the cheapest thing you can have is a cup of espresso. . . . The stalls at either end of the Rialto Bridge offer your best shopping buys; their prices for scarves, ties and women's wool sweaters are easily a third less than elsewhere in the city, and the stall owners will bargain, occasionally knocking 1,000 lire off the price. . . . The greatest free sight in Venice is simply the Piazza San Marco, a world in itself. . . . Parking your car at one of the big garages near the Piazzale Roma costs an average of 16,000 lire ($10) per day, for all but the very large cars. . . . In Venice, never ask what an item or a service costs: simply hand the man the lowest amount of change your courage will allow, and look confident—it works! Crossing a canal on a shuttle-gondola, I recently gave 600 lire to the gondolier and it was accepted. A Venetian who got on after me handed him only 400 lire for the same ride, apparently the standard charge! . . . The city tourist information office, called **Ente Provinciale per il Turismo (E.P.T.),** is on St. Mark's Square under the arcades of the Procuratie Nuove, all the way across from St. Mark's Cathedral. Opens Monday to Saturday from 9 a.m. to 12:30 p.m. and 3 to 7 p.m., closed Sunday, it is staffed with English-speaking hostesses who will answer most of your questions about Venice. . . . Although there's a **British consulate** at 1051 Dorsoduro (phone 27-207) near the Accademia Bridge, the nearest **U.S. consulate** is in Trieste, 9 Via Roma (phone 040/68-728). . . . Running short of cash? **Banks** stay open from 8:30 a.m. to 1:30 p.m. weekdays; shops and stores are open usually from 9:30 a.m. to 12:30 p.m. and 3 to 7:30 p.m. Monday through Saturday. . . . If you want to mail a package or letter, head for the **Central Post and Parcel Office** in the courtyard of the old palace Fondaco dei Tedeschi, next to the Campo San Bartolomeo near the Rialto Bridge (San Marco side); open 8:30 a.m. to 6 p.m., until noon on Saturdays. The **International Telephone Office** is also located in the same building, remaining open seven days a week until midnight.

READERS' SHOPPING SELECTION: "**Roberta di Camerino,** which operates a luxury shop for ladies' fashions and accessories on New York's Fifth Avenue, maintains its headquarters in Venice, with a fantastically decorated store at 1255 San Marco, next to the Post Office. Her dresses, handbags, and umbrellas are $100-a-day, but if you buy one of her foulards, 90 by 90 centimeters, 50,000 lire ($31.25), or select one of her beautiful cotton scarves, 50 by 50 and 70 by 70 cm, 10,000 lire ($6.25), as I did in 1984, you've enjoyed a real bargain, even if you are a $25-a-day traveller. And if—after browsing through the upstairs showroom—you do not buy anything—the experience is still worth the effort. Opening hours are 9 a.m. to 1 p.m. and 3:30 to 7 p.m., Monday to Saturday" (Julie Chan, New York City).

Venice, to be savored, should be sipped in small doses—it can become a little too rich for the blood. Three or four days make a perfect visit; and then it's off to Vienna. Prior to departure from the Venice railroad station, you can buy a box lunch for the journey (cestino da viaggio) in the station restaurant. The carton contains a serving of roast chicken, french fries, cheese, fruit, bread and a little flask of wine—all for 8,000 lire ($5). A short nap or a pleasant novel, a meal made of the box lunch, and soon your train approaches the imposing capital of the once-great Austro-Hungarian empire, the city of the blue Danube.

Chapter XIV

VIENNA

Strauss and Strudel

THIS IS A CITY of ever-present nostalgia. The trappings of the old Austro-Hungarian Empire are faded by now, and the great baroque buildings of Vienna are weatherworn and chipped. The city is no longer the powerhouse of Central Europe—and its charm has increased for that very reason. Having witnessed so much turbulence in their time, the Viennese are willing to chuck the ambition and concentrate on life. The mood all around is like an old Nelson Eddy film, a gracious and slow, courtly and polite. It can be the relaxing midpoint of your European tour.

Your accommodations in Vienna can also be the very best of your trip, for the quality is high in the low-cost pensions. But care is still needed, and pitfalls exist. Here's how to live in Vienna on moderate costs:

1. Getting Around

You begin by avoiding taxis (as costly as in New York) and learning to use the abundant streetcars, subways and buses, for which an unlimited, three-day pass—valid on all three means of transportation—costs only 83 schillings ($4.48); they are sold at the information offices of the main subway stations, or at the two main railway stations: the **Südbahnhof** (from which trains go to Graz, Klagenfurt, Italy, Yugoslavia and Greece) and the **Westbahnhof** (servicing Salzburg, Munich, Zurich, Budapest, Warsaw). Individual subway or bus tickets cost 18 schillings (97¢). Coming in from the airport, you again eschew the taxis ($22) and use $3 buses going to the two main stations or to the City Air Terminal Stadt park, near the Hilton Hotel.

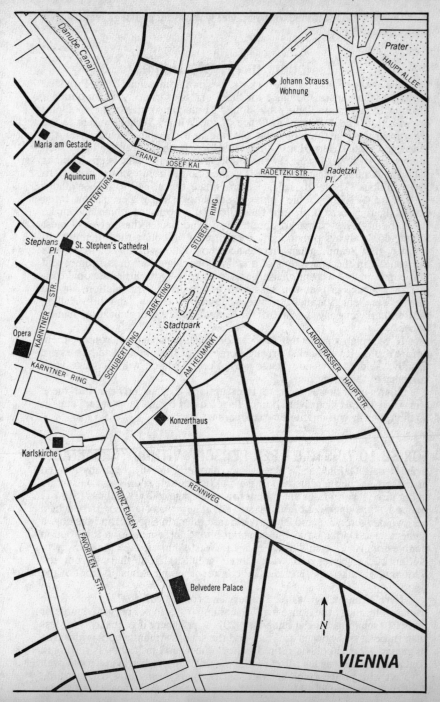

Prater
HAUPT ALLEE

Danube Canal

◆ Johann Strauss
Wohnung

◆ Maria am Gestade

FRANZ JOSEF KAI

RADETZKI STR.

Radetzki Pl.

■ Aquincum

ROTENTURM

STUBEN RING

Stephans Pl.

■ St. Stephen's Cathedral

PARK RING

Stadtpark

KARNTNER STR.

SCHUBERT RING

AM HEUMARKT

LANDSTRASSER HAUPT STR.

■ Opera

KARNTNER RING

◆ Konzerthaus

■ Karlskirche

RENNWEG

PRINZ EUGEN

FAVORITEN STR.

■ Belvedere Palace

↑
N

VIENNA

And thus, properly attuned to the budget way of life, you begin your search for lodgings:

2. Rooms in Private Homes

The cheapest accommodations are the non-commercial ones. Provided only that your stay in Vienna is for three nights or more, you can obtain a room with a private family by simply contacting an extremely helpful organization: the Information Office of the **Wiener Verkehrsverein** in the *Opernpassage* (the underground passage and shopping center near the renowned State Opera House—the Staatsoper), where Frau Gerlinde, who speaks English very well, is the information clerk. She keeps copious listings of families accepting tourists in their homes at rates averaging 220 to 250 schillings ($11.89 to $13.51) for a single room, 340 to 440 schillings ($18.37 to $23.78) double, plus 40 schillings ($2.16) per person for a non-obligatory breakfast; and the office will phone the home and make the booking for a charge of about $1.50. The homes themselves, I must admit, don't always provide an experience in "Meeting the Viennese" in the way that Scandinavian private accommodations often do; the rooms are usually in the apartment of a widow desiring additional income, and you come and go as you please but—ordinarily—with little personal contact. My advice is that you first seek to obtain accommodations in one of the excellent Viennese pensions described below, and only failing that should you pay a visit to the tongue-twisting organization named above.

If you plan to use the services of the Opernpassage, contact them before 4 p.m. if you seek a private home; after that time all addresses are usually "sold out." And, by the way, Frau Gerlinde will exchange your currency at the going bank rate.

There are, however, several exceptions to that advice, and these consist of 12 specific private homes ferreted out on my most recent stay in Vienna, which you might very well contact yourself.

FOR $8.10 TO $13.51 PER PERSON, WITHOUT BREAKFAST:

Frau Renate Gajdos, at 28 Pressgasse (phone 57-74-16), centrally located near the Karlsplatz, rents two single and five double rooms and one single in her large second-floor apartment for an average of 200 schillings ($10.81) per bed, which includes breakfast served on heavy oak tables with benches; her two daughters, 26 and 27 years old, are fluent in English, and the dog, a lassie named Dania, barks but does not bite. Supplement for a third bed in double rooms, 175 schillings. From the Westbahnhof, take the subway to Kettenbrückengasse, and walk (three minutes) from there. From the Südbahnhof, take bus 13 or 59A, the latter stopping almost in front of the door.

Herr Bruno Elbel, at 62 Seuttergasse (phone 826-82-72), rents three rooms of his nice little house for 175 schillings ($9.45) per person, double or twin; 210 schillings single; but adds a 20% supplement if your stay is for less than three days. Showers are free, and the small swimming pool is also free to guests. Herr Elbel is a retired police officer, and his hobby is staying in contact with colleagues all over the world; witness his living room wall covered with police emblems and sheriffs' stars from Texas to Australia! Take the subway to Hütteldorf, and walk from there (you'll pass the Lainzer

Tiergarten populated by deer and wild boars—free entrance); or else drive past Schönbrunn Castle to the Elbel home.

Herr Rupert and Frau Erika Koch, at 49 Steinböckengasse (phone 94-81-35), on the outskirts of Vienna near the West exit of the Salzburg Autobahn, are a blessing for traveling families: they rent five rooms, including two children's rooms, and a tiny, Scandinavian-style washroom (where showers are free) in bright colors and so clean you could eat from the floors. The price is 220 to 250 schillings ($11.89 to $13.51) per bed, 30 schillings extra for (an optional) breakfast brought to your room in a basket, all plus a 20% surcharge if you stay for less than three nights. Assets include a quiet location, beautiful garden, and inexpensive grocery next door. Mrs. Koch speaks English, French and Italian. Take streetcar #49 to the final stop called Hütteldorf, from which the house is a 20-minute walk.

Frau Marie Kossowski, at 6/14 Czerningasse (phone 26-43-94), near the Praterstern, rents a twin-bedded room for 240 schillings ($12.97), a triple for 260 schillings ($14.05), a four-bedded room for 330 schillings ($17.83), breakfast extra, in a simple and plain, no frills apartment where only basic English is spoken. From the Südbahnhof take streetcar "O" to the Franzensbrücke stop; from the Westbahnhof, take subway U1 to Nestroyplatz.

Frau Theresia Tichy, at 17 Scheugasse (phone 64-22-02), is a kind, grey-haired lady who lives alone in a small house where she rents three of her rooms (two to four beds in each) at 150 schillings ($8.10) per person, plus 40 schillings ($2.16) extra for an optional breakfast that includes boiled egg and homemade marmalade. Two of the rooms are communicating and ideal for families or a small group. Scheugasse is near the Südbahnhof: take the U-Bahn to Keplerplatz and walk around five minutes from there. As for Frau Theresia, she speaks very little English, but somehow understands you, and you will, with patience, understand her.

Frau Hilde Wolf, at 7 Schleifmühlgasse (phone 574-90-94), is an English-speaking lady who loves books, which are everywhere in sight, even in the rooms she rents: for 220 schillings ($11.89) single, 320 schillings ($17.29) double, a supplement of 100 schillings for a third and fourth bed. The double rooms are particularly spacious and crammed with fin-de-siècle furniture. Breakfast is 40 schillings ($2.16) more, and Frau Wolf assures me that readers of this book can have second (and more) helpings of coffee, bread, butter and marmalade at no additional charge. Schleifmühlgasse is a typical, old-Vienna street, near the central Karlsplatz and the Naschmarkt, the popular market area. From the Westbahnhof, take streetcar 58 or 52 to Getreidemarkt and then subway U 2 one stop to Karlsplatz and one stop by tram 62 or 65 to Schleifmühlgasse; from the Südbahnhof take the "O" streetcar to Südtirolerplatz and change there to the U-Bahn going to the Taubstummengasse stop.

Frau Antonia Kaller, 5/15 Uchatiusgasse (phone 72-30-022), a Viennese lady of the "old school," who speaks some English, rents four doubles for 165 schillings ($8.91) per person, including free showers; she charges 30 schillings ($1.62) extra for an optional breakfast. The rooms, with fin-de-siècle furniture and Persian carpets, are large enough for a third and fourth bed, for which a supplement of 150 schillings ($8.10) is charged. The location is very central, near the Hilton city air terminal. Take streetcar #52 from Westbahnhof, #0 from Südbahnhof, and get off at the Landstrasse stop.

Herr Dietrich Knöll, 59 Anzengrubergasse (phone 97-22-14), who lives in a small house on the northern outskirts of Hütteldorf, offers three rooms—one single, one twin, one triple—for 170 schillings ($9.18) per bed including free showers. If you wish, Frau Knöll, who was born in Budapest, Hungary, will prepare a 30-schilling breakfast (with egg, cheese, etc.) for you. Everybody here understands and speaks English, including Frau Knöll's thirteen-year-old daughter, Barbara. Ask Mr. Knöll for travel instructions, and don't confuse Anzengrubergasse with Anzengruberstrasse, which is in another district.

Frau Barbara Koller, 11 Schmalzhofgasse (phone 57-18-003), is especially recommended for small groups or large families: she rents five adjoining rooms with a total of 10 beds, and charges 220 schillings ($11.89) per bed, inclusive of breakfast and free showers. The rooms have modern furniture, are on the third floor (no elevator). Located near the Westbahnhof you can either walk 10 minutes, or take the streetcar #58 to Zieglergasse stop; from Südbahnhof take streetcar #58 to the Westbahnhof, and stay on as already discussed.

Frau Adele Grün, 1 Gonzagagasse (phone 63-25-06), near Schwedenplatz, in a very central and quiet area of Vienna, offers three large rooms in her old, but lavishly furnished apartment, for 250 schillings ($13.51) per bed; showers are 25 schillings ($1.35) extra. Frau Grün speaks fairly good English, has relatives living in the U.S. and claims to have received ambassadors among her frequent guests. The apartment, #19, is on the fourth floor—but reached by two super-modern elevators. And if the house phone doesn't answer, try her office number: 63-62-73.

To get there from the Westbahnhof, take streetcar #52 to the Ring and board streetcar #2 going to Schwedenplatz; from the Südbahnhof board streetcar D to Schwarzenbergplatz and change to streetcar #2 going to Schwedenplatz.

PRIVATE HOMES THAT READERS HAVE LIKED: "As you leave Vienna, driving east, you pass the Prater amusement park, and then cross the Danube on the new bridge (Reichsbrücke). The street you are on as you come off the bridge is called the 'Wagramerstrasse,' and at #18, on your right, is a Gästehaus run by **Frau Elisabeth Werner** (phone 23-57-12), which is so new and comfortable that it is graded Class 'A.' This is a private home with a modern annex built in the back. The rooms are comfortable, and there is off-the-street parking, in a locked parking lot. Frau Werner's price is 200 schillings ($10.81) without shower, 230 schillings ($12.43) with shower per bed per night, for a stay of three nights or more. If you stay less than three nights, there is an extra charge of 25% per bed per night. It was a very pleasant stay" (Mr. and Mrs. Murray Rubin, APO, N.Y.; strong second from Elizabeth Dickinson, Palm Springs, California, and from Doris R. Lawrenz, Skokie, Illinois). . . . "For 200 schillings ($10.81) I had bed and breakfast (enormous) and stayed with the nicest family in the world, **Mr. and Mrs. Walter Lorenz.** They live at Schwarzenbergplatz 10, Wien IV, phone 651–28–14. The family has room for about three people. I was treated as a member of the family and utterly spoiled" (Joanna Fisher, Khandallah, Wellington, New Zealand). . . . "One of our most pleasant stays while in Austria was that spent in the home of **Frau Magdalena Stadler,** Dobrowsky-Gasse 9 (off Triesterstrasse 255, one of the main roads leading into the city once you leave the Autobahn coming from Graz), phone 67-52-82. This is a quiet suburb and only a short bus ride from the center. Their son, Robert, speaks excellent English and was a big help in acquainting us with the city. The Stadlers offer one single room, 180 schillings ($9.72); five doubles, 330 schillings ($17.83); and one triple, 495 schillings ($26.75), central heating and hot water. Breakfast, included in the price, consists of fresh rolls, butter, jam, coffee, tea, milk, or hot cocoa, and is served in a pleasant room overlooking the garden" (Nicholas Evangelos, North Andover, Massachusetts). . . . "We arrived in the middle of the Festival, and were placed in the apartment of **Frau Grete Balaban** at 1 Jacquingasse, Wien III (phone 78-42-323 or 72-30-054), where for 300 schillings—$16.21—per couple, my parents, husband,

and I had two adjoining bedrooms and an adjoining kitchen and bathroom. Baths were extra. Frau Balaban was an exceptionally nice person and most helpful. She advised us of the places we had to see in her beloved city and how to get to them. Our stay coincided with a Middle East crisis, which caused us much worry. Frau Balaban gave us all the news that she had heard on the radio and was herself most concerned about it. I would highly recommend her place to a $25-a-Day'ers who are interested in meeting the local residents. Frau Balaban suggests that people write her in advance to assure a vacancy for them" (Mrs. Joan Deifell, Edinburgh, Scotland). . . . "We had the good fortune to stay in the home of **Maria Traxler,** 4 Stadiongasse (phone 43-22-15), two blocks from the parliament. We paid 240 schillings for a double, but what made our stay so pleasant, was the delightful company of Frau Tutzi, as she is affectionately called by her boarders. At 77, she is a wonder who does more than is required or expected of her. In October, she provided us with an assortment of outer clothing to wear to ward off the cold and early snowfall! She has one room which sleeps two, another four beds, and she prefers girls. We found her environment to be safe, warm, and most enjoyable" (Suzanne Arthur, 9901 Richmond Ave., Houston, Texas; note from AF: 1985 rates are 120 schillings, $6.48 per bed per night). . . . "We stayed at a small apartment ten minutes from the center of town, owned by **Hans Masak,** who speaks English, and his wife. They live in the apartment next door to the one we were in, at 129 Wiedner Hauptstrasse (phone 55-69-553). Accommodations for two people were 400 schillings and included breakfast and an equipped kitchen and private shower" (Jan Steen and Elisa Cirieco, Los Angeles, note by AF: The location is near Südtiroler Platz, in the vicinity of Südbahnhof; if you will phone Herr Masak either at home or at work (83-25-81) before arriving, he will pick you up in his car at station or airport). . . . "We suggest you include **Frau Gally Hedwig,** 25/10 Arnsteingasse (phone 83-04-244). This lady met us at the station and is truly an Arthur Frommer Special, i.e., she fits the description that so many of your readers give! She charged 275 schillings for two persons in a huge room with two single beds, down quilts (wintertime), and a small room where we could cook, provided with pots, plates and flatware. She also gave us a map, suggested places to see, and explained the trolley system to us—certainly a tourist agency in her own right! Only a ten-minute walk from the Westbahnhof" (Milburn and Mary-Ann Thompson, Louisville, Kentucky; note from AF: to find Arnsteingasse, walk up Mariahilferstrasse from Westbahnhof (going in the direction of Schoenbrunn); it's the eighth street on the left. . . . "Please include the home of **Herr Johann Ribisch,** 51 Bahnlaende (phone 685-6622). He has five lovely guest rooms, all with sinks and hot water. We paid 330 schillings for a comfortable room and the price included hot showers and breakfast (all the coffee I could drink). Herr Ribisch is enormously helpful. Before we set out for our first day of sightseeing, he gave us a set of maps, explained the street plan of the city, made a few suggestions about things we might want to see first and sold us our three-day passes for the Vienna transport system" (Bob and Lee Sheldon, San Jose, California; note by AF: this address is in the Oberlaa district of Vienna, roughly halfway between the city center and Schwechat Airport. . . . "We highly recommend the home of **Frau Hilde Wolf,** 22 Bahnhofstrasse, about one block from the Hütteldorf station of the No. 4 subway (U-Bahn), phone 82-95-952 or 94-35-733. For 150 schillings per person per night, we had a very large, clean room with double beds, free use of the shower, the best breakfast we had in Europe, always inclusive of either egg, cheese or meat along with bread, butter, jam and tea, and the use of the clothesline and clothespins in the backyard for our laundry. For an extra 50 schillings, Hilde will meet you at the train station and take you to her house. She has two guest rooms in her house, but she and her family live five minutes away. She comes every morning to clean the room, then she goes home and you have the place to yourself for the rest of the day and evening" (Helen and John McFarland, Charleston, Illinois).

3. Hotels & Pensions

Apart from apartments and homes, budget-priced lodgings of a non-private nature are available in substantial quantities here. They are, however, scattered—not clustered—over large areas of the city. In one neighborhood, you may find a rock-bottom hotel standing beside a moderately priced one, which is itself across the street from a relatively expensive hotel; it's hard, in other words, to find a single block or area in which the budget establishments are lined in a row.

Therefore, in order to give some geographical unity to our discussion, we've had to mix together establishments of differing cost—dealing, in one area, both with hotels that charge $26 a night for a bathless double, without breakfast, and with those that charge as much as $35 double, without breakfast, as well. It's important, as a result, not simply to assume that the following establishments are all uniformly priced, but to examine carefully the specific 1985 rates that I'll quote for each one. We have, however, divided our recommendations to deal separately with pensions and hotels:

THE VIENNESE PENSIONS: These provide your most reliable, consistently inexpensive rooms. In the many years spent researching this book, I have never found a slovenly Viennese pension, or received more than a scattered complaint about any of them.

Off the Graben

The best located of the Viennese pensions (and with slightly higher quality than our other selections) are the **Pension Nossek,** at 17 Graben (phone 52-45-91), and the **Pension Aclon,** at 6 Dorotheergasse, phone 52-54-73 (just off the Graben), both in that quite lovely area to the side of St. Stephen's Cathedral, in the very center of the inner city. The **Nossek** is the more elegant of the two: its bathless singles rent for 275 schillings ($14.86), bathless twins for 600 ($32.43), family rooms with 4 beds for 820 schillings ($44.32), breakfast and free showers included; and its owner-manager is a Doctor Cremona, who lived for 20 years in Ohio and speaks American-style English. The **Aclon** is nearly as nice as the Nossek, and charges a slightly cheaper 550 schillings ($29.72) for doubles with bath and w.c., 800 schillings ($43.24) for three-person or four-person family rooms, always with breakfast included, but a costlier 400 schillings ($21.62) for one of its three bathless singles. Location of the latter is only a few feet from the Nossek, on a slightly noisier block; to find it, turn off at 10 Graben into Dorotheergasse, a small alleyway of a street.

A nearly budget-priced choice in this area, is the **Pension Pertschy,** at 5 Habsburgergasse (phone 52-38-67), just a few steps off the Graben, four tiny blocks from the Stephansplatz, and more precisely located on the first, second, and third floors (there is an elevator) of an ancient "palais" built in 1725 and now an official historical landmark. The ceilings are high and vaulted, the floors a rich warm wood, and to get from room to room, you walk along an enclosed catwalk on a balcony that traces around the courtyard; the Pertschys themselves are a nice young couple with two sweet girls (and a boy), who encourage families to come, and understand the problems of traveling parents. Mr. Pertschy lived in Canada for 10 years and all the family speak perfect English. How much for all these features? 640 schillings ($34.59) for a double room, breakfast, service and taxes included, which is almost as low a price as Vienna goes nowadays for such pleasant accommodations; 460 schillings ($24.86) for singles, 780 schillings ($42.16) for triples, 920 schillings ($49.72) for four in a room—again, with breakfast, service and taxes included. All rooms are with private shower or bath. Central heating in winter; highly recommended.

A capsule summary of the geography of these pensions: walking down the Graben toward St. Stephen's Cathedral, the streets running off the Graben on the right are in this order: Habsburger (Pension Pertschy), Bräunerstrasse, Dorotheergasse (Pension Aclon), Spiegelgasse, Seiler-gasse, and you are at Stephensplatz. The Pertschy and Aclon are just steps off the Graben, while the Nossek is right on it.

Also in the Inner City

The small, five-room **Stadtpension,** 3A Annagasse (phone 52-49-04), is beautifully situated off the Kärntnerstrasse, halfway between the Opera House and St. Stephen's. Here the rooms are large, simple, homey and clean and some are big enough to accommodate three or four beds. Frau Hoffman, a perky woman with a good command of English, keeps the pension running and the attention personal. Singles are 310 to 380 schillings ($16.75 to $20.54); doubles 450 to 600 schillings ($24.32 to $32.43); triples 770 schillings ($41.62), breakfast, service and taxes included. The pension is on the first floor of an elderly apartment building—walk in, walk up the first long flight of stone steps, turn right, and there you are.

In the Alserstrasse Area

A street in Vienna that is packed with pensions (but in differing price ranges) is Alserstrasse, which passes next to the University of Vienna; the lowest-priced of the establishments here is the **Pension Vera,** Alserstrasse 18 (phone 43-25-95), where you'll be charmed by the warmth of your reception and the old-fashioned rate for your room—230 schillings ($12.43) single, 450 schillings ($24.32) double, breakfast and service included (and though it's a fairly basic, but friendly, place, it's recommended for travelers of all ages). Prices and quality ascend sharply, however, in the other pensions on the street, until they reach a budget limit at the **Pension Zenz,** 21 Alserstrasse (phone 42-52-68). During the summer of 1985, a double room at the Zenz, with two breakfasts, a private shower, all taxes and service, will cost 550 Austrian schillings—$29.72. Eliminate the shower, and the price is 500 schillings ($27.02). A single, again with shower, breakfast and taxes, will be 320 schillings ($17.29). The clientele   ? Well, the medical profession won't appreciate my giving away the name of this one; it's a favored stopping-place for American M.D.'s attending lectures at the famous Vienna University Hospital (where Freud once worked), across the street. They receive wonderfully big and spotless rooms; furnished with heavy wood pieces, well-oiled and cared for. . . . If the Zenz can't take you, try the nearby **Pension Astra** at 32 Alserstrasse (phone 42-43-54), with its fairly similar rates of 315 schillings ($17.02) single, 490 schillings ($26.48) double, breakfast included; and don't form the impression, upon entering, that you've wandered into a railroad station or museum hall—this is how some houses in Vienna were designed a hundred or more years ago! Upstairs the rooms are quiet and clean, the proprietress—Frau Gaby Brekoupil—extremely cordial. Phone first for vacancies.

Just 2½ blocks off Alserstrasse, the **Pension Columbia,** at 9 Kochgasse (phone 42-67-57), is another establishment back in the lower-priced category of the Pension Vera: 180 schillings ($9.72) per person, breakfast, service and taxes included, in triple rooms, 220 schillings ($11.89) per person in a double. Plenty of hot water, and a pleasant, English-speaking host (Mr. Naschenweng) who gets very concerned lest his guests fail to see all that's worth seeing in his beloved Vienna. Possibly more comfortable than the Vera, if not as well located.

And, finally, there's the 84-bed **Hotel Thüringerhof,** 2 Theresiengasse (phone 42-81-98), where English-speaking manager Herr Rolf Wilhelm charges 260 to 320 schillings ($14.05 to $17.29) single, 450 schillings ($24.32) double, including free showers and continental breakfast plus an egg or sausage. To find the Thüringerhof, walk to the end of Lazarettgasse and cross the Währinger Gürtel.

Near the Town Hall and University

Comparatively central (bus #8, tram #2 or subway No. 2 (Rathaus stop) from the Westbahnhof), and within walking distance of the Ring and the Rathaus, is the **Pension Edelweiss,** 61 Lange Gasse (phone 42-23-06), where 14 rooms are all rather spacious, airy, high-ceilinged, and therefore quite pleasant. Rates include breakfast, service and tax, and, for 1985, are 350 schillings ($18.91) single, 500–560 schillings ($27.02 to 30.27) double, 650 schillings ($35.13) triple. Mrs. Pertschy, the manageress, speaks excellent English. From the Westbahnhof, take streetcar #5.

Close by at 49 Lange Gasse, the **Pension Zipser** (phone 42-02-28) is a really superb choice, with 50 rooms, many of which overlook lovely gardens and even have balconies for making the most of the view. Large clean rooms, all with double doors for extra quiet, go for 330 schillings ($17.83) single, 600 schillings ($32.43) double, and 600 schillings ($38.91) triple, with breakfast, service and taxes included.

Alternatively, and on the same block, the newly furnished **Hotel Rathaus,** 13 Lange Gasse (phone 43-43-02), offers extra large rooms for these rates: single 320 schillings ($17.29), single with shower and w.c. 420 schillings ($22.70), double 530 schillings ($28.64), double with shower and w.c. 700 schillings ($37.83), with breakfast, service and taxes included.

The **Pension Amon,** Daungasse 1 (phone 42-01-94), is also located near the university and is a 12-room pension which takes on personality from its English-speaking owner, Mr. Amon, who hunts for a hobby and decorates the hallways and lounge with the trophies. The rooms are comfortable, if old-fashioned, and Mr. Amon is a willing dispenser of tips on where to go and what to see in town. Singles cost 330 schillings ($17.83), doubles are priced at 430 schillings ($23.24), triples at 550 schillings ($29.72), with breakfast, service and taxes included.

Near the Mariahilferstrasse

Walking from the Opernring up Mariahilferstrasse, one of the two main shopping streets of the city (the other being the more elegant Kärntnerstrasse), in an excellent, central location, you'll find the tiny 30-bed **Pension Reimer,** 18 Kirchengasse (phone 93-61-62), a somewhat basic spot, whose proprietress, Margarete Mattis, speaks only a smattering of English. But her price for a single (service included) is this time only 240 schillings ($12.97), for a double 400 schillings ($21.62), for a triple only 520 schillings ($28.10), and four beds in a room go for 780 schillings ($42.16) and this one is with shower. Breakfast is an extra 40 schillings. Rooms are large, clean, with modern furniture, neat but sparsely decorated; there's a comfortable TV lounge for the use of guests (and the owners' tykes), and the entire establishment is a homey, pleasant place, if a bit plain. Try it.

Near the Südbahnhof

A fine pension (one of our stars, in fact), and within walking distance of the Südbahnhof, the **Pension Esperanto,** 53 Argentinierstrasse (phone 65-13-04), rents 11 neat rooms with country-style iron bedsteads and gleaming wood floors. Frau Hildegard Hahn, who requires that you stay for a minimum of three days, is the efficient owner; English is well-spoken; and singles are priced at 230 schillings ($12.43), doubles at 460 schillings ($24.86), service, taxes and breakfast included. From the station's main exit, cross the tram rails, walk left up Wiedner Gürtel, and you'll find Argentinierstrasse to be the second turning right.

READERS' PENSION SELECTIONS: "For 420 schillings ($22.70) a day, we stayed at the Pension Lindenhof, 4 Lindengasse, tel. 93-04-98, in a huge double room with a good breakfast; baths extra. The owner, Mr. Georg Gebrael, speaks English and is always ready to help or provide information on Vienna. His pension occupies the second floor of an old building a block off Mariahilferstrasse" (Valentin Gomez, Buenos Aires, Argentina; note from AF: In 1985, the Lindenhof will rent single rooms for 250 schillings ($13.51), doubles for 420 schillings ($22.70), multibedded rooms (three to five beds) for 200 schillings ($10.81) per person, always with breakfast included; shower or bath 20 schillings extra. Location is behind the large Herzmansky department store at Mariahilferstrasse). . . . "Pension Am Operneck, 47 Kärntnerstrasse, (phone 52–93–10), offers an excellent location diagonally across from the Opera House and on one of Vienna's most popular shopping streets. An immaculate, high-ceilinged, bathless single, with a large double bed, costs about $20 a night, breakfast included" (Chris Buba, Secane, Pennsylvania; George Schaefer, Forest Hills, New York; John K. Ries, Brooklyn, New York). . . . "A high recommendation for Pension Andreas, 11 Schlösselgasse (phone 42-34-88), in the university area behind the Rathaus: friendly, English-speaking manager; rates of only 580 schillings ($31.35) for a bathless double with two breakfasts and free showers" (Dr. Douglas Hernandez, Maracaibo, Venezuela).

VIENNA'S BUDGET HOTELS: Now we move to the larger ones. We'll deal first with the "B" class hotels (doubles without breakfast for $28 to $38), then with the "C" class establishments, whose charge for a double is usually $27 and under.

The "B" Class (Second-Class) Hotels

To start with a big, big splurge, the **Hotel Austria,** in the very center of town at 3 Wolfengasse (phone 52-67-24), near St. Stephen's Cathedral, is among my favorite Viennese hotels, even though its minimum prices for bathless rooms with breakfast, service, and taxes included (520 schillings, $28.10, single; 770 schillings, $41.62, double), are considerably higher than I usually like. But for several years now, manager Herr Walter Koschier has offered to grant a 12% discount to anyone producing this book, and so far as I know, he's kept to his pledge (the book, however, *must* be shown on arrival and not suddenly produced upon check-out—that's a tax technicality). You will, I think, be well-pleased with this hotel: the staff spares no effort to be helpful (tickets to the Opera, tours), and there's no hanky-panky with the prices when the final bill is prepared. To reach the hotel from the Westbahnhof, take the *stadtbahn* (city train) to Schwedenplatz; from the Südbahnhof, take tram D to the Ring, then change to tram #1 or 2 going to Schwedenplatz. And then walk to Wolfengasse, which is a tiny lane off the Fleischmarkt—Vienna's meat market in medieval times. Arriving by cab, your best bet is to ask not for Wolfengasse, but for "Fleischmarkt 20"—that being the corner building from where one turns into the tiny lane. . . . A final word about the discount offered at the Hotel Austria; it's available only to readers who have not booked their rooms through travel agents (including the information people at the railroad stations), to whom the hotel would have to give still a second discount.

In a far cheaper range, the **Hotel Kongress,** at 34B Wiedner Gürtel (phone 65-91-65), directly across from the Südbahnhof (South Railway Station), is rather a plain hotel, with old-fashioned furnishings and nondescript decor, but with elevator, clean linoleum floors, a friendly and English-speaking staff, and neat, comfortable rooms. Rates are 390 schillings ($21.08) for bathless singles, 600 schillings ($32.43) for bathless doubles, including breakfast. And all rooms have hot and cold running water. Recommended.

Near the Westbahnhof

All of the above choices, as you've seen, are scattered around town. About the only "cluster" of budget hotels in Vienna is found in the area of the **Westbahnhof** (West Railroad Station), where you may very well arrive. These include, first, the handy and handsome **Hotel Mariahilf,** at 121B Mariahilferstrasse (phone 57-36-05), which is within walking distance of all the downtown activities, and where you won't be disappointed—as many big-splurge-type readers have confirmed (it's not to be confused with the tiny Pension Mariahilf, at 49 Mariahilferstrasse). Price per person for bathless double rooms is exactly 300 schillings ($16.21), breakfast, service and taxes included, 310 schillings ($16.75) for singles, all included. There are 30 such bathless singles, which means good hunting for the lone traveler. . . . But if you'd like to stay even closer to the Westbahnhof, then try the newly refurbished **Hotel Westbahn,** 1 Pelzgasse (phone 92-14-80), directly across from the station, where doubles with bath are 750 schillings ($40.54), buffet-breakfasts, service and taxes included; or the recently renovated 83-room **Hotel Fuchs,** at 138 Mariahilferstrasse, phone 83-12-01 (exit from the Westbahnhof down the steps to the right; the hotel is a short walk from the station), where bathless doubles go for 590 schillings ($31.89), including breakfast.

"C" and "D" Class Hotels

Thus far, we've dealt primarily with "B-class" hotels in Vienna—the "B" designation being the Austrian equivalent of the "2nd Class" category used in other countries of Europe. The best of the "C" and "D" class hotels—with bathless double rooms averaging $27 a night (though some run higher, some lower)—are the following:

Hotel Wolf, 10 Strozzigasse (phone 42-23-20), in the Josefstadt district, a charming, quiet area of the city within ten minutes' walking distance of the Ring. A medium-sized hotel, two floors only, with no elevator, but where the furnishings are modern, rooms are spotless, floors are linoleum, decorations are neat and simple, and English is perfectly spoken by the helpful manager who goes out of his way to give budget travelers tips on cheap restaurants nearby. All 53 rooms, single, double and triple, are priced from 260 to 310 schillings ($14.05 to $16.75) per person (depending on the size and location of the room), breakfast, service, taxes and free use of the showers, included. From the south station, take bus # 13; from the air terminal (at the Hilton) take subway No. 4 to Karlsplatz and change to tram "J"; from the west station, take tram # 8 and change to # 46 downtown.

The **Goldenes Einhorn,** 5 Am Hundsturm (phone 55-47-55): Another personality place, packed with Old Vienna atmosphere. It's a tiny, two-story, 26-room hotel in a little old-fashioned building with white stucco walls and arched hallways, potted plants in alcoves, and the usual cat-walk-style, enclosed balcony overlooking a courtyard and hung with plants and vines. The Viennese lady who tends the hotel speaks English, and is delightfully cordial and courtly in her manners. Rooms are spotless, pleasantly filled with the usual mixture of modern and antique furnishings, and rates are: 195 to 220 schillings ($10.54 to $11.89) for singles, 390 to 440 schillings ($21.08 to $23.78) for doubles, service and taxes included. The top-priced double comes with a bath, the majority are share-bath; the hotel is located in a quiet residential area, about a ten-minute train ride from the Opera House.

Two "Park Hotels" Charging $18.10 to $22.70 Double, Including Breakfast

Two very special selections offer good value and reasonable rates, but both are located in the outskirts (although within city limits).

Haus Starkfried, at 15 Starkfriedgasse (phone 47-15-28), is a nonprofit, 190-bed, student-style hotel, recently built in a beautiful park area containing swimming pool, many rare trees, a chapel and mosque. It rents single rooms for 200 schillings ($10.81), doubles for 335 schillings ($18.10), including breakfast. From central Vienna, take streetcar 41 to Ludwiggasse (last stop, a 20-minute trip) and then walk five minutes to this comfortable choice.

Europahaus, at 429 Linzer Strasse (phone 97-25-38), is one of several structures making up the Miller-Aichholz Castle, built in 1750 by the famous architect Fischer von Erlach, whose better-known masterpiece in Schönbrunn Palace. Originally owned by industrialists who supplied Empress Maria Theresa's army with uniforms and such, it changed hands several times, became French occupation army headquarters in 1945, and was then ceded to the Austrian government which used it as a conference center for political studies. Today, it is an all-year-around hotel offering singles with shower and w.c. for 300 schillings ($16.21), bathless doubles for only 420 schillings ($22.70), breakfast included. In 1982, an annex was added, with smaller but perfectly acceptable rooms costing 140 schillings ($7.56) per person in triples, 160 ($8.64) in twins, breakfast and free showers included. From the Ring, board streetcar 49 or subway No. 4 and 35 minutes later get off at the last stop called Hütteldorf.

A Modern Budget Hotel

So far, we've quoted rates only for bathless rooms; the city's largest array of moderately priced rooms *with* private shower is found at the gigantic (948 beds) modern student residence known as **Haus Döbling,** 85 Gymnasiumstrasse (phone 34-76-31), which is operated for tourists of all ages from July 1 to September 30 at a rate of 350 schillings ($18.91) single, 600 schillings ($32.43) double, breakfast included. Döbling is well stocked with English-speaking personnel, operates a budget restaurant where two-course meals cost 90 schillings, and can be reached from the Westbahnhof for 18 schillings by first taking the S-Bahn to Nussdorferstrasse and then streetcar 38 for two stops.

4. Rooms for the Starvation Budget

Some of the cheapest, but most atmospheric, accommodations in Vienna, are offered at the **Hostel Ruthensteiner,** at 24 Robert-Hamerling-Gasse (phone 83-46-93 or 83-08-265), corner of Haidmannsgasse, about a ten-minute walk from the Westbahnhof; this one is run by a charming young couple, Erin and Walter Ruthensteiner, and since Erin is an American girl from Pittsburgh, you know the management will understand you! There are three dorms (two with four beds and one with eight beds), in which a total of 80 beds rent for an amazing 120 schillings ($6.48) per night, while accommodations in either single, two-bedded or three-bedded rooms cost 150 schillings ($8.10) per person per night. No age limit, no curfew. Latest addition to the Ruthensteiner is a micro-snackbar next to the ground-floor reception desk, where you are served, through a tiny window not much larger than this book: coffee for 10 schillings (54¢), rolls for 27¢ and portions of butter and marmalade for 32¢ each. Showers are free.

THE AUSTRIAN SCHILLING: In this chapter on Vienna, we've assumed the exchange rate of the Austrian schilling to be approximately 18.50 to the dollar, thus making each schilling worth approximately 5.4 U.S.¢.

VIENNA'S YOUTH HOSTELS: The major hostel, open all year, is the **Jugendgästehaus** Hütteldorf at 8 Schlossberggasse (phone 82-15-01), a five-minute walk from the last station of the U-Bahn (No. 4), called **Hütteldorf-Hacking.** Its rates are a refreshing 100 schillings ($5.40) per night including breakfast, from 50 to 60 schillings for lunch and dinner. If you're over the age of 25, you'll be asked to present a youth hostel card. A second youth hostel, **Turmherberge Don Bosco,** 12 Lechnerstrasse (phone 73-14-94), open from March to November, accepts men only. There are a total of 50 doubledecker beds in seven rooms on seven floors of a bell-tower, priced, in 1985, at 50 schillings ($2.70) per bunk per night. Take streetcar #18 from Süd- or Westbahnhof to Stadionbruecke stop; from there it's a few minutes on foot. Again, a Youth Hostel card is a must.

THE LOW-BUDGET HOTELS: Extra-cheap hotel rooms? The 140-bed **Auge Gottes,** 75 Nussdorferstrasse (open only from July 1 to September 30), phone 34-25-85, charges 200 schillings ($10.80) per person per night (including free showers and breakfast). And keep in mind that people of all ages, students or not, can now enjoy the astonishing rates of the **Student Home of the University of Vienna** (Studentenheim des Asylvereines der Wiener Universität), open July 1 to September 29 at 30 Porzellangasse (phone 34-72-82); 100 schillings ($5.40) per person per night. It's reached via the "D" tram (Sundays via the 36 tram), or by U-Bahn No. 4 to the Rossauerlände stop. **Jugendgästehaus Gatterburg** at 55 Döblinger Haupt-strasse in the University area (phone 36-25-23), is an alternate, at 140 schillings ($7.56) single, 230 schillings ($12.43) twin, 30 schillings ($1.62) for breakfast; but open only from July through September.

READERS-ON-THE-STARVATION-BUDGET (ROOMS): "I am the owner of a boarding house (rooms with breakfast), where numerous young people, other university teachers with family, have enjoyed their stays in Vienna, near the Vienna Woods. The cheapest rooms we can offer are double-rooms and cost Austrian schillings 300 ($16.20) for two persons. Of course we have also better ones, with private bathroom too, which are more expensive. Breakfast costs 30 schillings—per person—and is generally very appreciated by my guests for both quantity and quality" (Adolf Kestler, **Pension A. Kestler,** Rodaun, Ketzergasse 356, phone 88-32-12; note by AF: to reach Mr. Kestler's haven, take the Stadtbahn, S-Bahn, or local train, from the Westbahnhof and get off at Hietzing, then board trolley #60 and leave at the last stop, Rodaun. Total cost: 18 schillings).

5. Student in Vienna

For you, first stop should be the **Austrian Student Travel Office** at 13 Reichsratstrasse (phone 42-15-61), behind the Rathaus in the University area, which operates a **Student Accommodation Service** throughout the year; staff here will make direct bookings for student visitors in several hotels they control where prices average 200 schillings ($10.81) per person in one-, two-, or three-bedded rooms with running water and the use of community showers, or about 240 schillings ($12.97) in somewhat more sophisticated accommodations.

Also available at the Student Travel Office: information on student discounts for sightseeing, plays and concerts, cheap student flights within Europe, and special discounted tours. Office hours are 9:30 a.m. to 5:30 p.m., weekdays only.

Closer to the center of town, at 10 Führichgasse (near the Opera), the same Student Travel Office operates a small student buffet (messhall) serving two-course menus ranging in price from only 38 schillings ($2.05) (for soup, spaghetti with meatballs) to 50 schillings ($2.70) (for soup followed by wiener schnitzel), and platters—such as baked ham with two poached eggs—for 33 schillings; it is open seven days a week from 10 a.m. to 8 p.m., Sundays from 11 a.m. to 2:30 p.m., and serves only the higher-priced menu on weekends. Officially for students only, the Mensa employs no one at all to check student credentials, and thus attracts a broader clientele.

As for lodgings that are just for you, try first the modern student hostel known as the **Heim der Musikhochschule,** at 8 Johannesgasse (phone 52-05-050 or 52-62-150), quite centrally located, between the Opera and St. Stephen's, which charges a high 300 schillings ($16.21) per night in a single room, 250 schillings ($13.51) per person double, but only 200 schillings ($10.81) per person triple or quad, including breakfast; it's open, in 1985, from July 1 through September 30, and offers 190 beds.

6. Low-Cost Restaurants

Frankly, finding a budget meal in low-cost Vienna is no great accomplishment; but that relatively simple task will become almost effortless if you keep in mind certain categories of low-cost restaurants.

THE BILLATERIAS: The best spots for your basic, low-cost meals (the hurried and unextraordinary ones) are a string of self-service restaurants called **Billaterias** (after the German word *billig,* meaning cheap), where you can put together multicourse meals for less than $3.50. Such a repast during one recent summer (1984), included leberkäse with mashed potatoes as the main course, at 45 schillings ($2.43). Vienna possesses several Billaterias, of which the two at **5 Babenbergerstrasse** (two short blocks from Mariahilferstrasse, a ten-minute walk from the Opera) and at **6 Singerstrasse** (where the Billateria is known as the "Stadtkeller," and is located near St. Stephen's Cathedral) are the most central. At both, soup costs 15 schillings (81¢), main courses with vegetables 35 to 42 schillings ($1.89 to $2.27), Hungarian goulash, french fries and salad 45 schillings ($2.43). Open daily, except Sundays, from 7 a.m. to 10 p.m.

THE NASCHMARKTS: More, but not much more, expensive than the Billaterias are the **Naschmarkt Restaurants,** one at the famous **Schwarzenbergplatz,** the other at **85 Mariahilferstrasse,** and the third at **1 Schottengasse.** The basic philosophy of this chain is to attract as many customers as possible by offering a large spectrum of dishes, from junk-food to wiener schnitzel by candlelight: pizzas (served at a pizza-paradies-counter) cost 36 to 66 schillings ($1.94 to $3.56); two daily menus offering three courses (soup, main dish, dessert) are priced at 48 and 62 schillings ($2.59 to $3.35), the latter including half a roast chicken; a filling dish of sausages with sauerkraut and mashed potatoes, costs 39 schillings ($2.10), and various soups, including the bean variety, spiced with peppers, are 28 schillings ($1.51). Each ultra-modern establishment seats 200 and is open seven days a week, from 11 a.m. to midnight. Looking for the Schwarzenbergplatz-Naschmarkt? You'll find it next door to McDonald's, near the Imperial Hotel, and 200 yards from the Russian War Memorial, the one with the fountain.

THE BEISELS: What's a beisel? It's a small, plain, pub-style place with no identifying characteristics other than the occasional appearance of the words "Gasthaus," "Gaststätte" or "Gastwirtschaft" in its title, and the fact that it's family-operated and modest in price for good, home-style food; 65 to 75 schillings ($3.51 to $4.05) for two-course luncheons, from 70 to 80 schillings ($3.78 to $4.32) for main courses at night. A typical and highly recommended beisel in the inner city is **Gastwirtschaft R. and K. Körber** at 4 Schulerstrasse, corner of Domgasse, directly behind St. Stephen's, where Rudolph and Kornelia Körber specialize in schweinebraten with knödel (60 schillings), in wiener schnitzel (an enormous portion) with salad (66 schillings), and in a usually accompanying quarter-liter of white wine for 15 schillings. (They do not speak English, but should you have language problems while ordering, they'll invite you to walk into the kitchen behind the beverage counter, where you can point to the dishes you intend to eat.) Incidentally, this is a favorite eating place of the *fiakers,* the famous Viennese horse-taxi drivers stationed around the Stephandom. You're sure to recognize them by their black bowler hats, which they keep on even while eating. Open Monday through Friday from 8 a.m. to 7 p.m. Closed Saturday and Sunday. Similarly priced is the **Stadtbeisl** at 21 Naglergasse, near the Freyung, which serves an excellent goulash with "knödl" for 100 schillings ($5.40); the beisel known as the **Pantherbräu** at 10 Judenplatz (full-course meals for 70 schillings, wiener schnitzel with mixed salad for 90 schillings, $4.86); and **Riedl's Wiener Beisl** at 24 Berggasse, corner of Porzellangasse, in the University area near the Sigmund Freud museum, of which half is pub, half a simple restaurant, serving cold platters for as little as 28 to 36 schillings. The latter is open weekdays only, from 9 a.m. to 9 p.m. And then there's the **Gasthaus Mayerhofer,** at 29 Ungargasse, near the Stadtpark, where main dishes are only 40 to 50 schillings ($2.16 to $2.70). A small place, it has the reputation of serving especially good *heuriger* wine (a dry white, made from grapes harvested the year before) for 23 schillings. Open weekdays only, until 10 p.m. Monday through Thursday, until only 4 p.m. on Friday. Or there's **Pronto,** Vienna's newest and smallest "standing-up beisel," at 2 Spiegelgasse, right off the Graben next to Stephansplatz, where salads (vegetable and fruit), spaghetti carbonara, and meat stews all cost around 60 schillings ($3.24). Squeezed between two boutiques, Pronto, with a dining room too narrow to park a golf cart, is packed with at least 30 customers at lunch and supper hours. To find space to move (and eat) try to eat lunch before noon or after 2 p.m., and avoid the 5 to 7 p.m. crush; it's open Monday to Friday 11 a.m. to 9 p.m., Saturday 11 a.m. to 8 p.m.

A final beisel: the **Müllerbeisel,** at 15 Seilerstätte, a street running parallel to the Kärntnerstrasse, less than five minutes on foot from the Stephansplatz. Here, if you're sick and tired of wiener schnitzel (which costs 100 schillings at the Müllerbeisel), you can order such exotic (for Vienna) plates as fried squash with sauce tartare or stewed eggplant in meat sauce (65 schillings, $3.51), or a *kesselgulasch für zwei personen* for 140 schillings ($7.56). Served to your table in a big copper pot, it's more than enough for two persons (who thus pay $3.78 apiece), and could even suffice for four persons (who would pay only $1.89 apiece)!

THE REMARKABLE SANDWICH BARS: Vienna possesses two unusual sandwich shops, famed throughout the city, where a near-banquet of hot and cold items can be put together for a moderate outlay. Where else but at **Pic-Pic,** 4 Bräunerstrasse (a small side street off the Graben, near the Pestsäule Monument), for instance, could you eat all the following for only 75 schillings ($4.05): a ham-and-egg club sandwich plus a plate of bean soup with a roll plus a glass (krügel) of draught beer plus a delicious apfelstrudel followed by a cup of coffee? Fifty varieties of sandwiches sell at Pic-Pic, for either 5, 8 or 10 schillings; a take-away lunch of three sandwiches and a Coke, all in a yellow plastic bag, are only 60 schillings ($3.24); a tiny, eight-liter glass of beer called a *pfiff* (whistle), designed for ladies, is priced at only 5 schillings (27¢); and the wine listed at 16 schillings for a quarter liter is the same brand used at the glamorous Hotel Sacher. Closed

Saturday afternoon and Sunday; get here before noon or after 2 p.m. to insure a seat. . . . Pic-Pic's competitor is the older **Trzesniewski** at 1 Dorotheergasse (a side street parallel to the Bräunerstrasse), where exotic open sandwiches are offered for 7 schillings (hot ham or anchovies with mushrooms on delicious fresh bread). Beer or apple cider is another 7 schillings, a glass of authentic Polish vodka (ask for a *stamperl*) at 15 schillings, and Trzesniewski is highly recommended not merely for its values (see "Readers' Selections" for additional description), but for its typical Viennese atmosphere. Closed Sunday.

THE CELLARS AND THE WINE HOUSES: To find other budget meals, look for the "keller" restaurants; and for even cheaper meals, eat in the wine houses.

The cheapest keller restaurant? That's the **Melkerstiftskeller,** at 3 Schottengasse, where a full, several-course meal costs 96 schillings ($5.18) (open only from 4 p.m. to midnight, closed Sunday and holidays). The most modern keller? That's easily the **Schottenkeller,** operated by Wienerwald, 6 Freyung (across the street from the Naschmarkt Restaurant on Schottengasse), which offers rich and chunky chicken soup with noodles for 40 schillings ($2.16) and tasty filling plates from 68 schillings ($3.67) for Hungarian goulash with steamed potatoes, to 110 schillings ($5.94) (for super-schnitzel with mixed salad and fried potatoes). The most atmospheric keller? The **Zwölf Apostelkeller** at 3 Sonnenfelsgasse, where you descend two flights of stairs to sit in the underground catacombs of Vienna dating back to the 13th century, and snack on a "Liptauerbrot"—a spicy cheese mixture spread on a thick slab of rye bread for 13 schillings, and washed down with a cool "Veltliner," a mug of white wine, for 16. Plates range from only 22 to 46 schillings. The most rustic keller? Try the **Alter Rathauskeller,** at 8 Wipplingerstrasse, near the Hoher Markt, a few minutes from Stephansplatz. Generations of Viennese have eaten in this room, where the city of Vienna offers banquets to visiting dignitaries (of a fairly low level). Walls are decorated with old rifles and hunters' trophies, and specialties are all strictly local, such as *beuscherl mit knödel* or *saure niernderl* with roast potatoes, the first being cooked cow's lung, cut into strips, the second roast pigs' kidneys, both cooked and served with vinegar sauce (78 schillings, $4.21, each). From personal experience, I can tell you they taste better than they sound. The things I do for readers!

The wine houses are, of course, much cheaper. You'll spot them all over town (particularly outside the inner city), and you'll find that virtually all of them have blackboard menus listing the classic Austrian dishes. They are not for our more fastidious or timid readers, and one should not be wearing one's best clothes, but after you've overcome the initial hesitation, you may form such an attachment that you'll eat in one every day. Sample sit-down meal in one of the better neighborhood wine houses: a Bauernschmaus (sausages and sauerkraut), cucumber salad, and beer for me; a beef goulash, and one Coke for Hope; total for both of us: 215 schillings ($11.62).

THE HOTEL RESTAURANTS: Surprisingly enough, some of these can be inexpensive, even though elegant in decor. The most surprising of all is the "second-class" dining room of the First Class **Hotel Regina,** 15

Rooseveltplatz (across from the Votivkirche and the University), which offers a daily three-course lunch or dinner for only 85 schillings ($4.59), including service, a more elaborate one for 130 schillings, and individual courses that can range from 60 to 100 schillings. It's easy to spend sparingly in this tall, airy dining area with vaulted ceilings, mammoth brass chandeliers, and colorful Tyrolean paintings of farmers in native costumes. Stay away, though, from the first-class dining room, where the brass chandeliers change to crystal ones, and also avoid the left side of the outdoor terrace area; in both these latter spots, prices rise sharply. The second-class room is open seven days a week, from 11:30 a.m. to 10 p.m.

Another of these restaurant surprises is provided by the **Hotel Graben,** in the heart of the inner city at 3 Dorotheergasse, which charges 55 schillings ($2.97) for a two-course meal, 95 schillings ($5.13) for a gargantuan three courses. On my last visit there, I began with a rich cream of mushroom soup, which had fresh sliced mushrooms floating in it; then went on to a tender serving of smoked pork with dumplings and sauerkraut, accompanied by a salad plate of tiny tomatoes, sweet and sour cabbage, lettuce, and potato salad; and then barely managed to finish a dessert of fruit and ice cream—the whole meal for $5.13. Open seven days a week, it keeps serving until 11 p.m.

OTHER CHEAP RESTAURANTS: If you like fish, you will like **Nordsee,** 84 Kärntnerstrasse (and at four other central locations), where fishburgers cost 18 schillings, steamed cod filet with vegetables 47, and a Coke 15 schillings. . . . One of the most popular self-service restaurants in town is the **Duran-Superimbiss,** at 14 Alserstrasse, in the University area, where you can choose between at least a dozen plate dinners averaging 40 schillings. There are also at least 25 varieties of open-face sandwiches, from 7 to 11 schillings each. . . . The **Wienerwald** chain operates fourteen chicken restaurants in Vienna. The two easiest to find are at 3 Annagasse and 12 Bellariastrasse. Half a roast bird will cost you 61 schillings, but they also serve less expensive dishes, like Hungarian goulash (55 schillings), ham and three eggs (39 schillings), and a remarkable portion of pommes frites (over the counter) for 20 schillings. . . . The self-service snack bar (Imbiss) at the **Steffl** (only large department store on the Kärntnerstrasse) serves a filling two-course menu, Monday through Saturday, for 43 schillings ($2.32), and many other moderately priced items, including goulash with dumplings ($3), a pair of frankfurters for $1.75, bean soup for $1.50, beer for either $1.20 (medium glass), 80¢ (small glass), or 40¢ (tiny glass—a so-called *pfiff*). After entering the Steffl, turn left and roll down the escalator to the basement where the Imbiss is found and if you are a Mozart fan, take the elevator to the fifth floor. Here tucked behind the sports department you'll find a bust of Mozart and pictures related to the last years of his life. Why? Because Mozart lived, composed the *Magic Flute* and died here on 5 December 1791, in a building located on this spot that was demolished in 1849.

THE UNIVERSITY MENSA: By far the least expensive meals in town are served at the **University Mensa,** 7 Universitätsstrasse, open Monday to Friday year round, except for two weeks during the Christmas holidays. You don't have to have a student ID card. At lunch time (from 11:45 a.m.

to 2 p.m.), it charges 36 schillings ($1.94) for a two-course, 48 schillings ($2.59) for a three-course meal, consisting of, for example, minestrone soup, fried fish filet or goulash with potatoes or vegetables, and salad, plus (for the 48-schilling variety) fruit or sweet. The seventh-floor self-service dining room, seats 600, and is reached by taking a slow Paternoster-type elevator to the sixth floor, and walking up one flight of stairs. Next to the Mensa (same floor) is a cafeteria, open Monday to Friday from 7:30 a.m. to 7:30 p.m., Saturday from 11 a.m. to 2 p.m., serving goulash for 30 schillings ($1.62), salads for 35 ($1.89), two wieners with mustard or ketchup and a roll for 18 (97¢), soups for 12 (64¢), beer 17 (91¢), pommes frites for 10 (54¢). It's located between the Rathaus and Roosevelt Square, five minutes by foot from the Hofburg. Nearest subway stop is Schottentor; from there it's a two-minute walk. Warning: the Paternoster stops once in a while—don't panic, just wait a few minutes until it runs again.

ORDERING IN "AUSTRIAN": Several readers have taken me to task for failing to provide a translation of Austrian menu terms, claiming that our German menu guide, at the back of the book, just isn't sufficient for Vienna. There may be some merit to that claim, and to fill the gap, we'll now set forth a few of the items that recur with particular frequency on an Austrian menu.

Among the soups, you'll most often find *griessnockerlsuppe* or *suppe mit griessnockerl* (which both refer to a clear soup with semolina dumplings), *leberknödlsuppe* or *suppe mit leberknödeln* (both referring to soup with liver dumplings), *rindsuppe* (beef broth), and *gulaschsuppe* (a liquidy Hungarian goulash).

The fish dishes carry designations almost identical to the ones you'll find in Germany. But among the meat plates, there's *bauernschmaus* (a combination of many varied sausages and pork items with sauerkraut and dumplings) or *tafelspitz* (boiled beef with vegetables), or simply *rindfleisch* or *beinfleisch* (boiled beef). You'll also encounter *backhendl* (fried and breaded chicken) with some frequency, as well as the omnipresent *wiener schnitzel* (breaded veal cutlet) and *natur schnitzel* (plain veal cutlet). And finally there's *gulasch* (stew), which comes either Hungarian-style *(Ungarisches gulasch)* or plain.

In the vegetable area, the item to remember is *nockerln,* which are little dumplings, usually served with a marvelous sauce, and altogether delicious. For dessert, you'll be offered the world's best *apfelstrudel* (which is apple strudel) or *palatschinken* (which are light, sugared pancakes), or *Salzburger nockerln* (a soufflé), or finally, *Kaiserschmarren* (a diced omelette, served with heaps of jam and sprinkled with sugar).

A word, finally, about Viennese coffee. It was brought here 300 years ago by the Turks, who had sought unsuccessfully to conquer Vienna and left this exotic souvenir, much in use by the anti-alcoholic Moslems but unknown until then in central Europe. Like tea to the British, coffee soon became an institution to the Viennese, who proceeded to create more than 20 varieties. You'll need to recognize the *kleiner schwarzer* (small cup without milk), the *kleiner brauner* (small cup with a little milk), the *melange* (large cup with milk), the *melange mit schlag* (same as above with whipped cream on top), the *einspänner* (glass of coffee topped by whipped cream), the *Türkischer* (black coffee boiled in a copper pot and served in tiny cups)—and there are endless others. But puzzlingly enough (to me, at least), the coffee you order is often accompanied by a glass of excellent

Viennese water—piped in from the Alps, and perhaps intended as a gesture of courtesy to the customer. Anybody heard another explanation?

READERS' EXPLANATIONS OF THE GLASS OF WATER SERVED WITH COFFEE: "Here is an article from the *Los Angeles Times* (June 1980) that will solve the mystery for you: 'The coffee is served on a small silver tray, always accompanied by a glass of water. The serving of water is said to stem from the right in the Middle Ages of every traveler to refresh himself from the town well'" (Kurt Friedberg, Palos Verdes Estates, California). . . . "I cannot pretend the answer to this, but I thought I would drop you a line to say that, in my experience, it is always the practice through the Balkans for a cup of coffee to be accompanied by a glass of water, usually mineral water. I think that I recollect from years spent in the Middle East in the fifties that the same practice applies there. I have always assumed that the glass of water was intended both as a kind of antidote to the bitterness of the coffee—true Arab coffee in particular is very bitter—and as a means of washing one's mouth of the coffee grounds that are always so much a part of coffee in this region. The Viennese, having taken over the coffee supplies from the vanquished Turkish army, probably also took over the custom" (B. G. Dexter, Australian Ambassador, Belgrade, Yugoslavia). . . . "I am able to solve the mystery for you. It is well known that coffee is invigorating and after a good cup one feels more awake and lively, but coffee also has a different effect on the body: it also is dehydrating, and shortly after one feels very tired again. This is where the glass of water comes in" (Walter Brank, Weipa, Queensland, Australia).

THE BALKAN RESTAURANTS (A MINOR SPLURGE): The influence of the Eastern European countries on the Viennese cuisine and the existence of numerous Balkan-style restaurants are an important aspect of the restaurant scene of this city. At the very atmospheric (gypsy music in the evening) and centrally located **Restaurant Budva,** 1 Naglergasse, off the Graben, a memorable garlic soup is 30 schillings ($1.62), green peppers cooked in olive oil 29 schillings ($1.56) per, beef goulash with polenta (corn mash) ($3.70), and a Hungarian-style dish called Csikos tokanj (meat cubes stewed with tomatoes, peppers and spices) 90 schillings ($4.86)—a hearty meal for about $8, including beer. Open seven days a week from 11:30 a.m. to 2:30 p.m. and 6:30 p.m. to 2:30 a.m. . . . And for an amazing combination of Greek and Viennese cuisine, the **Restaurant Der Grieche,** 5 Barnabitengasse (off the Mariahilferstrasse, about half-a-block from the Gerngross department store), gets a resounding recommendation. Panos Tsatsaris (he's Greek) is owner-chef, and how he can cook! For two persons who are both very hungry, I'd suggest, first, the Hellas-platte, which costs 200 schillings for two ($10.81) and includes several cutlets, pork chops, shish-kebab, cevapcici, all on a bed of rice with french-fried potatoes and vegetables, accompanied by a large Greek salad. The lamb chops (lammkotelett) for 100 schillings are as crisp and well-spiced as any I've ever tasted, and for a special treat, you can try either the tarama salat (red caviar mixed with goat's cheese, oils and spices) for 33 schillings ($1.78) or a mammoth Griechischer bauernsalat (green salad) with olives, onions, tomatoes, cucumbers, pieces of goat's cheese, and spiced rice in vine leaves) at 35 schillings ($1.89). This is a simple and quite unadorned restaurant to which you should go just for the personal attention and quality of the food. Open seven days a week from 11:30 a.m. to 2:30 p.m. and from 6 p.m. to midnight.

THE BIG SPLURGE: For 130 schillings ($7.02) per person, you can eat magnificently in Vienna—as, for example, in the spectacular setting of the

Wiener Rathauskeller, on Rathausplatz, where it's even possible to keep costs below that figure by ordering simpler dishes. Usually, however, you should plan to spend around 150 to 170 schillings or so for a thoroughly Viennese meal in this stunning vaulted cellar, with colorful ribbons and murals, which should be seen. A four-man band plays Viennese music every night. Closed Sunday. For outdoor dining, the **Restaurant Leopold Hauswirt,** 20 Otto Bauergasse, has a beautiful dining garden, replete with striped awning, and serves a daily, three-course lunch for exactly 160 schillings ($8.64). Dinner will run close to 200 schillings per person. Closed Sunday.

And finally for that special evening out, you'll want to know about the **Gösser Bierklinik,** at 4 Steindlgasse, just off the Central Graben. Before Christ it was the site of a Roman legionnaires' field camp, but since 1566 it has been a popular restaurant, consisting of eight adjoining rooms, each historically decorated. One room even displays a Turkish cannon ball that hit the place 300 years ago when Sultan Mustapha besieged the city. It's famous for its lengthy menu, listing, for example, broiled ribs of beef in radish sauce and roast potatoes (110 schillings, $5.94), roast wild boar filet with cranberry sauce and potato dumplings (155 schillings, $8.37), 18 salad varieties costing 35 schillings ($1.89) per serving, and, for children, a baby wiener schnitzel with french fries for 66 schillings ($3.56). Open daily from 9 a.m. to 11:30 p.m., but closed on Sundays.

READERS-WHO-HAVE-SPLURGED: "If you really want to splurge, try **Demels,** located at 14 Kohlmarkt (which is between the end of the Graben and Michaelerplatz); it's the most exclusive pastry shop in Vienna. Just to sit in this elegant atmosphere among the Viennese aristocracy sipping coffee is worth it! Pastry and coffee add up to about 80 schillings" (Robert L. Borland, East Rockaway, New York; note by AF: at Demel's nothing has changed since 1888, and you can have the ($2.70) culinary experience of a lifetime by ordering a sacher torte with whipped cream on the side, 50 schillings). . . . "This will seem like pure heresy, of course, but for my money Sachertorte is not at the Sacher Hotel, nor at Demel's but at Smutny's, located one block from the opera house. Cross the Ringstrasse facing the opera house, go down the first street on your left, then take the first right. If Smutny's appears full, go on in anyway; there's a cavernous upstairs, which can accommodate several hundred more guests" (Robert Markow, Montreal, Canada).

MEALS (STUDENT VARIETY): For youthful companionship: the **Mensa** of the Technische Hochschule Wien, a cafeteria on the ground floor of the famous school, 13 Karlsplatz, which serves a filling two-course lunch on weekdays only for only 36 schillings ($1.94). The school is only a short walk from the Opera; if you're elsewhere in Vienna, take the Stadtbahn to the Karlsplatz station.

READERS' RESTAURANT SELECTIONS: "**Alte Schmiede,** 1010 Wien, 9 Schönlaterngasse, is a cultural as well as a gastronomic experience. Traditional Viennese meals are served in a vaulted cellar restaurant (115 schillings will buy a two-course meal), and on the premises you'll find a blacksmith, pottery workshop, a library and literary meeting place where you can attend free readings by well-known writers. Open daily from 10 a.m. to midnight" (Susan Mulhern, Los Angeles, California). . . . "Have your breakfast at a confectionery (*konditorei*) shop in Vienna; superb pastry and cocoa for only about 65 schillings" (Myles Silberstein, Philadelphia, Pennsylvania). . . . "The basement cafeteria of **Gerngross'** department store at #48 Maria-hilferstrasse (15 minutes walk from the Westbahnhof) is a best buy for tasty lunches. A generous portion of cevapcici (a Balkan meat specialty) with vegetables costs only

48 schillings; (about $2.59). A giant sausage plate costs even less while chops are priced slightly higher" (T. K. Moy, Woodhaven, New York; note by AF: at Gerngross, the giant sausage is 28 schillings ($1.51), the daily menu only 54 schillings ($2.91). . . . "A student-type Mensa (card not necessary), serving three-course meals for 32 schillings, is located near the crossroads in Schwarzspanierstrasse. Another Mensa charging 30 schillings is in the New University at 7 Universität-strasse" (Mary Corcoran, Cologne, Germany; note by AF: the first of these establishments is the **Mensa des Afro-Asiatischen Instituts**, 15 Schwarzspanierstrasse —the building, incidentally, in which Beethoven died—which seats 100, is open only between 11:30 a.m. and 2 p.m. Monday to Friday, and serves typical three-course meals—like bean soup, fried fish fillet with potato salad and sweet pudding—for 32 schillings, about $1.72). . . . "Please add the **Schnitzelwirt** at 52 Neubaugasse. Although we were only in Vienna for three days, this place was such a hit that we ate there twice! For 63 schillings we had the most scrumptious wiener schnitzel we had ever experienced. We were served so much that it was literally more than the plate could hold and certainly more than we could eat" (Tom and Eileen Culligan, Fairfax, Virginia; note from AF: Neubaugasse is a side street off Mariahilferstrasse, halfway between Westbahnhof and Opernring). . . . "We had a delicious Italian dinner at the **Grotta Azzurra**, 5 Babenbergerstrasse, just off Mariahilferstrasse and about three blocks up from the Ring. I had a salad and pasta dish, my husband had cannelloni, and we each had Cokes. Our bill came to 236 schillings ($12.75). The service was excellent. For a minor splurge we felt it was well worth it!" (Amy and Mike Jablonovsky, APO New York; note by AF: Grotta Azzurra restaurant closes Saturday and Sunday).

READERS' SNACK SELECTIONS: "Whenever we felt like a cheap, light meal—or even just a snack—in Vienna, we went to **Trzesniewski's Buffet.** It is very centrally situated, in the Dorotheergasse, only two doors up from the Graben (which of course is right by St. Stephen's). Here you get delicious pieces of fresh bread, liberally topped with various spreads, such as pimiento with egg, cucumber, spiced egg, cheese spread, or tomato and pepper. The spreads are made, so we were told, from old and closely guarded family recipes. Certainly they are better than anything we had elsewhere. And the price? 5 Austrian schillings (27¢) per piece. There is also beer or apple juice for 7 schillings. So a light meal, with a drink, can cost you less than 25 schillings. There is only one problem—the place is well-known among the Viennese, and is usually packed out. Incidentally, the sandwiches can also be obtained in a box to take away" (Peter and Renata Singer, Oxford, England).

READERS-ON-THE-STARVATION-BUDGET (MEALS): "One afternoon I went to the produce market, where I put together a sausage, bread and raisin lunch for less than $1.50" (Victor Weisskopf, Frankfurt, Germany). . . . "A delicious moneysaver is to 'do as the Viennese do'—walk along with half a pound of incomparable Viennese delicatessen (*Aufschnitt*) in one hand and crispy Austrian 'Salzstangerl' in the other, happily munching away. The Viennese eat constantly, in all places, at all times" (Lisa Fellner, Wayne, New Jersey).

7. The Sights of Vienna

And now that you've unpacked in a budget room, and have marked out the nearest beisel for lunch, you'll turn to the visual glories of this magnificent city—once the hub of Europe—whose sights are associated with many of the most colorful, dramatic events of European history. It's thrilling to realize that such personages as Maria Theresa, Franz Josef, Haydn, Beethoven, Metternich, Brahms, Mozart, Liszt, Franz Lehar, Strauss, Madame de Stael, all lived and worked in buildings in Vienna which remain untouched to this day.

As a prelude to all your touring, go to a bookstore (or else to the Tourist Information Office in the Opernpassage) and pick up a thick

30-schilling brochure called "Vienna From A to Z," which was published by the city government, and whose pages are keyed to the unique, numbered plaques that are affixed to the front of every building of historical interest in Vienna. You'll spot these plaques everywhere: they sport four little red-and-white flags in summer and carry a number which corresponds to a similarly numbered explanation and description, in English, in the "Vienna from A to Z" booklet.

You may, of course, want to take an introductory guided tour, and for that, a number of tour operators—a typical one is **Vienna Sightseeing, 4** Stelzhamergasse, near the Hilton Hotel and Bahnhof Landstrasse, phone 72-46-83—offers three-hour trips through Vienna, which depart in summer at 9:30 and 10:30 a.m., and at 2:30 p.m., daily, from in front of the Opera House, cost 280 schillings ($15.13), and are an almost indispensable way to learn the arrangement, and chief sights, of the city. Another popular bus tour (350 schillings—$18.91; 9:30 a.m. and 2:30 p.m.), conducted by the same company, among others, goes through the romantic Vienna Forest to **Mayerling,** where Crown Prince Rudolph and Maria Vetsera committed suicide. But don't expect to see the hunting lodge where all this happened; it's been replaced by a chapel, housing an order of nuns. The trip takes four hours and departs daily at 9:30 a.m. and 2:30 p.m.

For a more extended visit to the incomparable **Schönbrunn Palace,** you can take tram #58 from along Mariahilferstrasse to Schönbrunn (a 15-minute ride, 18 schillings per person). That lets you off at the entrance to the palace grounds, which are open from 8 a.m. to 8 p.m. The Palace itself closes at 5 p.m. Its former occupants, the Habsburgs, who were once prohibited from entering Austria, are now allowed to return as private citizens.

If you're a summer traveler, you won't, unfortunately, be able to see the great **Spanish Riding School** (*Spanische Hofreitschule,* in the Hofburg), whose performances, in 1985 take place on Sundays at 10:45 a.m., and on designated Wednesdays at 7 p.m., from September to December, and from March to June. During the same period, however, you can watch rehearsals of the school Tuesday through Saturday from 10 a.m. to noon, and throughout the year you can take tours of the stables (sometimes including the riding arena as well) from 2 to 4 p.m. on Wednesdays and Saturdays, from 10 a.m. to noon on Sundays. Tickets can be purchased either next to the stable entrance at 2 Reitschulgasse, or at the main entrance of the Hofburg (1 Michaelerplatz, first door on the left, under the cupola) from 9 a.m. to 3 p.m. Tuesday through Friday, from 9 a.m. to noon on Saturday, cost 95 schillings for training sessions and tours, from 100 schillings (standing room) all the way up to 450 schillings for performances—the latter often being booked up as much as a year ahead. . . . The famous **Vienna Boys' Choir** (*Wiener Sängerknaben*) performs during Catholic high mass in the Chapel of the Imperial Palace (Hofburgkapelle) on Sundays at 9:15 a.m., from the second Sunday in September to the end of June. Tickets can sometimes be purchased at the booking office of the Burgkapelle on Friday at 5 p.m., but are more safely obtained by writing well in advance (at least eight weeks) to **Verwaltung Hofmusikkapelle,** attention Herr Leopold Rupp, Schweizerhof, Vienna 1; they cost 50 to 150 schillings, but the money need not be enclosed with your reservation requests; rather, you pay upon picking up your tickets at the booking office on Sunday before mass. The Burgkapelle itself is open to visitors on Tuesday and Thursday from 2:30 to 3:30 p.m.; entrance fee being 10 schillings (54¢). Vienna's **Prater** (amuse-

VIENNA:
THE INNER CITY

ment park) is best known for its ferris wheel (the Riesenrad, built in 1896), on which a ride will cost 30 schillings for adults, 15 for children. There is no admission charge at all to the grounds; only small fees for the various games, sports, and other rides; and at least four cheap beer-garden restaurants scattered throughout the park.

MUSEUMS: There are more than 40 important ones. Some you might consider are the enormous **Kunsthistorisches Museum,** on the Maria-Theresien-Platz (paintings, sculpture, antiquities); the **Albertina,** at 1 Augustinerstrasse (world's largest collection of engravings and prints); the **Beethoven Museum,** 8 Moelkerbastei (home of the composer); the **Haydn Museum,** 19 Haydngasse (home of the composer); the **Schubert Museum,** 54 Nussdorferstrasse (birthplace of the composer); the **Schubert-Sterbezimmer,** 6 Kettenbrückengasse (room where he died); the state rooms and private apartments of **Schönbrunn Castle;** the **Hofburg** (apartments of the Emperor Franz Joseph); the **Kapuzinergruft,** 2 Tegetthoff-strasse (crypt of the Habsburgs); the **Schatzkammer,** in the Hofburg (the imperial treasure); the **Mozart Memorial Rooms,** 5 Domgasse (relics of the composer); the **Academy of Art**, 3 Schillerplatz (classic paintings). And for a report in depth on the outstanding Viennese sights, here's Hope:

HOPE IN VIENNA: "In this remarkable city, everything, from the people themselves to the sacher torte, seems mature and cultivated. Nowhere else do you feel so deeply the manners and mores of days gone by—all the romance, grace and civilization of Old Europe sticks to Vienna through the memories of its residents who have seen better days and understand so well that this is the way of the world. And the cultivated character of the Viennese is illustrated in part by their interest in the arts and in good living. The Royal Palaces are charming, the theatre and opera are old and popular traditions, and fine museums and interesting monuments abound in such profusion that one is faced with an embarrassment of riches. Here are only a few among many interesting things to do and see in Vienna:

The Kunsthistorisches Museum

"Head first for the **Kunsthistorisches Museum** (Museum of Fine Arts), 1 Maria-Theresien-Platz (across the street from The Hofburg), which is another of the world's great museums. Go directly to the second floor where the gallery is. The collection, which by anybody's standards is a good one, becomes absolutely fabulous at many points, and is sensibly arranged chronologically and by country. To your right at the top of the staircase, under the dome, are Dutch painters—*Holländer and Flamen;* off the room, #15, is Jan Vermeer's renowned 'Artist in His Studio.' Just off the first Rubens Room are two smaller rooms of Rembrandts, including the wonderful painting of his mother and three self-portraits. But the high point of the entire museum is a shattering room full of Breughels, including 'The Hunters in the Snow' (you can hardly believe it's not real), 'The Tower of Babel,' 'Peasant Dance,' and many others of equal renown. In the side rooms are excellent Holbeins and paintings from the 15th and 16th centuries, some very important Dürers, Van Eycks, and Memling's famous 'Adam and Eve.' Then, on the other side of the staircase, are Italian, French and Spanish painters, with important works by Titian, Giorgione, Tintoretto, Caravaggio and Velazquez, among many others. Downstairs (first floor), to the right of the entrance, there's a collection of Egyptian, Greek and Roman antiquities (many uninspired Roman copies of Greek originals, but also a famous assemblage of cameos); and to the left, medieval, renaissance and baroque works, including the world's largest collection of tapestries (nearly 800 pieces)—the most important, must-see piece being Benvenuto Cellini's gold 'Saltcellar for King Francis I,' the very height of ornate mannerism. For 20 schillings ($1.08), you can have this experience of great art every day, except Monday, from 10 a.m. to 6 p.m., Saturday and Sunday from 9 a.m. to 6 p.m., as well as Tuesday and Friday evenings from 7 to 9 p.m.

Schönbrunn

"To visit Vienna and not to see the lovely 'summer palace,' **Schönbrunn**, is like not visiting Vienna at all. The glorious grounds of Schönbrunn, which were transformed into a formal baroque garden, have belonged to the Habsburgs since 1569. The present palace was begun in 1695 by Emperor Leopold I, but it was really Empress Maria Theresa who left the greatest imprint on Schönbrunn: in the course of having 16 children, running the country (with quite an able hand), and fighting a war for her right to sit on the Austrian throne, she still found time to decorate and redesign Schönbrunn (1743 to 1749) and it has remained virtually as she left it. To see the inside of the predominantly white and gilt rococo palace, you must wait for an English guide to take you through from 9 a.m. to noon and 1 to 5 p.m. (till 4 p.m. in the winter), or during special summer evening guided visits on Wednesday, Thursday and Saturday at 7:30 and 9:15 p.m.; the charge will be 40 schillings (20 schillings if you're a student), but the guide tells you everything about the palace, and usually throws in some historical commentary, too. Outstanding among many ornate rooms are the exotic 'Chinese Rooms'; the Large and Small Galleries; Napoleon's Room (where he stayed when at Schönbrunn); all the Guest Rooms, but especially the cunning 'Porcelain Room,' all in blue and white with inlaid drawings on the walls; and the stunning 'Millions Room' in the most highly ornate rococo, with its gold-framed mirrors and Indian paintings on rich wood-paneled walls. When you finish with the palace, you can take a delightful walk around the park where you'll see The Gloriette, an enormous classical stone arch which is directly opposite the Palace on the highest point in Schönbrunn, with excellent views of the surrounding countryside; the lovely Neptune fountain; artificial Roman ruins; followed by a zoo and the largest hothouse in Europe, the 'Palmenhaus.' Close to the main entrance is the lovely rococo **Schönbrunn Theatre,** the oldest in Vienna, but the only way (and the best way) to see the theatre is to attend a summer opera performance here—try to schedule one during your stay. Finally, to the right of the main entrance, closer to the palace, there's a **Carriage Museum** called the **Wagenburg,** containing imperial stage coaches, including a children's phaeton constructed for Napoleon's son, the Duke of Reichstatt. Closed Monday.

"To get to Schönbrunn, take street car #58 from anywhere along Mariahilferstrasse; it'll cost 18 schillings (97¢), and the trip requires about 15 minutes.

St. Stephen's

"Back in the city, every foreign visitor must pay tribute to **St. Stephen's Cathedral,** which is the focal point of Vienna—it has the highest steeple and is at the heartbeat of one of the busiest intersections in town (close to the Graben, the elegant shopping street with the famous baroque 'Plague Column' built by Leopold I to commemorate the end of a terrible epidemic of plague in Vienna in 1679). The church was founded in the 12th century, but what you'll see today is mostly from the 14th century—it's a handsome grey stone Gothic church with some Romanesque elements, and the interior decorations have just enough baroque gilt to add flavor. The old woodwork of the roof went up in flames in the last days of World War II (April 1945) but has now been completely rebuilt in steel. You can visit St. Stephen's daily from 8 a.m. to 5 p.m. And for 25 schillings you can take an elevator to the north tower for an excellent view, while for 20 schillings ($1.08) you can visit the crypt.

The Hofburg

"**The Hofburg,** which was the official residence of the Habsburgs and was built between the 13th and 20th centuries in every conceivable architectural style, is an enormous complex of buildings bounded by vast

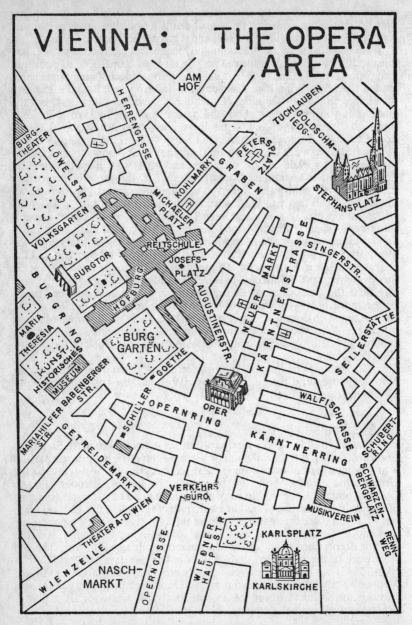

parks and open spaces. It's more like a small city than a palace, and you can easily spend days here getting lost looking for what you came to see (in several trips to Vienna I have not yet managed to see all of The Hofburg!). The Swiss Court is the oldest part of the palace, and in the oldest building is the Gothic Royal Chapel where the Vienna Boys' Choir sings. Not far away is St. Augustine's Church (best approached from Augustinerstrasse), which has the Loreto Chapel with its famous 'Heart Crypt'—a room containing 54 urns with the hearts of the Habsburgs in them! (This same church also made some pretty good matches: Empress Maria Theresa was married to Franz Stephen here, Marie Louise by proxy to Napoleon, and Emperor Franz Josef to Elisabeth). Close by (off Josefplatz) is the National Library with its celebrated baroque State Room. Actually located in the Old Castle is **The Schatzkammer,** which contains imperial and religious treasures: the museum is divided into two sections—The Crown Jewels and the Ecclesiastical Treasure Chamber. Among the items you'll find inside are christening robes of the imperial family; swords, imperial crosses; Coronation robes from the 12th through the 13th centuries; two prized Habsburg heirlooms with strange mystical and religious significance ('The Agate Bowl,' mistakenly thought to be the Holy Grail, and 'The Ainkhurn,' associated with Christ and also with sovereignty); the silver-pearl-gilt Empire cradle given to Napoleon (and his Austrian wife Marie Louise) by the city of Paris in honor of the birth of his son, who was immediately dubbed 'The King of Rome'; 'The Insignia and Regalia of The Holy Roman Empire' including the Sabre of Charlemagne; the Imperial Crown made in 962 (highlight of the collection); and The Imperial Book of Gospels, to mention a few. The Ecclesiastical section contains relics, paintings, statuary, vestments, altars, crosses, prayer books, etc.—and a wooden cupboard with a black and ivory crucifix which holds the keys to the Habsburg coffins. Though not nearly as sumptuous as the Bavarian Treasure House in Munich, this collection should be visited because of its great historical significance. Open Monday to Saturday from 8:30 a.m. to 4:30 p.m., Sunday from 8:30 a.m. to 1 p.m., for 20 schillings. . . . Then, to see the **Imperial Rooms** (which, while historically evocative, seem a little plain after the splendor of Schönbrunn), walk through the courtyard to the Reichskanzleitrakt (Chancellery of the Empire Building). You'll pay 20 schillings for a guided tour through the apartments of Franz Josef, Elisabeth, Czar Alexander I of Russia (a prominent guest at the Congress of Vienna), and the last Emperor of the Habsburgs, Charles I. Tours (which are occasionally conducted in German only) leave every 15 minutes from 8:30 a.m. to 4:30 p.m. weekdays, 8:30 a.m. to 1 p.m. Sundays. The predominant feeling of the rooms is Victorian for Franz Josef, baroque and rococo for Elisabeth, Alexander I and Charles I. Elisabeth was a beautiful and vain woman—she decreed that she would sit for no more portraits after the age of 30—and here you see her personal gymnasium where she kept in shape. The family portraits are interesting, so is the history: Franz Josef and Elisabeth lived apart because she had a morbid fear that a strain of family insanity would manifest itself in her; later she was assassinated in Geneva. . . . Another wing of the Burg (the one next to the Burgtor) worth a visit is the **Neue Hofburg:** it houses the world's second largest collection of armor (largest is in the Metropolitan Museum of Art in New York), and a unique assortment of ancient musical instruments, including the pianos of Beethoven, Schubert and Gustav Mahler. Open Tuesday to Friday 10 a.m. to 4 p.m., Saturday and Sunday 9 a.m. to 4 p.m.; entrance fee 20 schillings; closed Monday. . . . Next a walk through the lovely St. Michael's Gate and turn right to get to the **Spanish Riding School and Stallburg (Stable Castle).** In July and August, the famous Lippizaner horses don't perform, but they can be seen (20 of them) in their stables at the Lainzer Tiergarten in the Schönbrunn area. The Spanish Riding School (so-called because only Spanish stallions were used) is directly across the street from The Stallburg, which was built in 1565 by Ferdinand I. The Lippizaner horses are surely the most famous classical-style equestrian performers in the world (state owned, they've been doing the same act for nearly 400 years), but even without the spectacular show it's worthwhile to take a look at the beautiful baroque Riding Hall, which was built in 1735 by Fischer von Erlach for Charles VI, and which was also used as a ballroom during the Congress of Vienna (that epic conference in 1814 at which the wily Metternich was a principal character, as was Talleyrand, and where the great nations tried to reconstitute Europe after Napoleon's defeat).

Belvedere

"If I were in the market for palaces, I'd buy the lovely grey stone **Belvedere Palace,** with its unbelievably gorgeous sculpture garden, rather than Schönbrunn. True, you don't get the space you have at Schönbrunn and some of the rooms are not as lavish, but Belvedere, a light airy baroque palace built by Hildebrandt between 1714 and 1723, has a grace and unity about it that I like very much. It was built as a summer residence for Austria's beloved Prince Eugene (from Savoy), who successfully protected his adopted country from a couple of Turkish invasions, and was rewarded for his service and devotion by being made Minister of War, then later Prime Minister, by Emperor Charles VI. The elegant Belvedere is now the home of **The Austrian Gallery** (Österreichische Galerie), which has collections in three parts. Upper Belvedere Palace, the more formal and lavish palace, was used for state occasions and for guests (it was here in the Great Hall that the 'liberation' or 'State Treaty' was signed on May 15, 1955, ten years after World War II and the Occupation); it's now a gallery for 19th and 20th century art. The moderns are on the top floors of the museum, and there are interesting paintings by Wilhelm Thöny, Richard Gerstl, Herbert Boeckl and Egon Schiele. But look especially for the pictures of the now famous Oskar Kokoschka, and also for Gustav Klimt (1862–1918), whose Tiffany-like style and use of gold and fancy design is very exciting: be sure to see the rooms devoted to his work, including 'The Kiss' and 'Judith,' among others. Upper Belvedere is host to changing exhibitions, too, and there are wonderful views of Vienna from the top floor. Across the garden is the Lower Belvedere, the summer palace where Prince Eugene actually lived, now the Museum of Austrian Baroque; there are some fine frescoes, an elaborate gold Chinese room with a statue of Prince Eugene. The Museum of Medieval Austrian Art is in the Orangerie and has an interesting collection from the Middle Ages, comprised mostly of Church art or Biblical subjects—don't miss the Flügelaltar by the Donauschule in the last room. Belvedere is located at 27 Prinz Eugen Strasse, and is open Tuesday, Wednesday, Thursday and Saturday from 10 a.m. to 4 p.m.; Friday from 10 a.m. to 1 p.m.; and Sunday from 9 a.m. to noon; the Baroque and Medieval Museums are a good buy for 10 schillings, and the same ticket entitles you to visit the Upper Belvedere Gallery of 19th and 20th century art. All three collections are free on Saturday and Sunday in winter.

Crypts of the Habsburgs

"Most visitors feel themselves duty bound to make an historical pilgrimage to the Kapuziner Church (located close to the Albertina, behind the Opera House, on the little Tegetthoffstrasse 2—a street which becomes Neuer Markt), where the **Kaisergruft** or **Imperial Crypts** are located. This has been the burial place of the Habsburgs for the last 300 years, with some very elaborate funeral biers next to relatively simple ones—the coffin of Franz Josef is particularly plain and tasteful (Franz Josef's son Rudolf, who died at Mayerling, is buried here too): notice the bronze plaques above the lights reading 'Pax.' The crypt is open in summer from 10 a.m. to 4 p.m. (closed between noon and 1 p.m. for lunch) for 15 schillings. Most of the year (October 1 until May 1), open only from 10 a.m. until noon.

Composers' Homes

"Music lovers can have a field day in Vienna, the city that nurtured and inspired some of the greatest European composers. There are monuments to the musical giants everywhere—one of the loveliest is the airy, romantic, white stone circle of figures with Johann Strauss playing in its center in the Stadtpark (there are monuments to Franz Schubert, Franz Lehar and Anton Bruckner in the same park). Memorial rooms of Mozart, Beethoven, Schubert, Haydn and Johann Strauss can also be visited (all open Tuesday to Friday from 10 a.m. to 4 p.m., Saturday 2 to 6 p.m., Sunday and holidays from 9 a.m. to 1 p.m., closed Monday), but are recommended only for devotees, because all are plain and unadorned and only for someone who gets a kick out of just knowing that a great musical genius lived and composed in these very rooms (the Schubert Museum is in the actual birthplace of the composer, and the Haydn Museum is located in the house where Haydn died). For instance, at **Figarohaus** (5 Domgasse), which was Mozart's home from 1784 to 1787, *The Marriage of Figaro* was composed in the small baroque room in the back—in the salon he played chamber music concerts with Haydn, and accepted the 17-year-old Beethoven as a pupil. But aside from a scattering of pictures, letters, and scores written in his hand, there is little else to see. The house is located in a quaint old section (from the back of St. Stephen's Cathedral, walk to Domgasse—through the wooden doors and the arcade), which at that time was a wealthy neighborhood (he spent his prosperous days here); but later Mozart lived in poverty and died in poverty—Wolfgang was usually one step ahead of the gang of wolves at his door: a blight on Vienna and on all of us who persistently refuse to recognize and reward great artists while they're alive. . . . The moody and rebellious Beethoven fared much better than Mozart did. Rich men vied to become his patron. But he was such a stormy personality and his habits were so irregular (he sometimes played and composed in the middle of the night), that he was constantly being evicted from apartments all over Vienna. There was one landlord who loved him, however: Mr. Pasqualati, who owned **Pasqualati Haus** at 8 Moelkerbastei, and always kept Beethoven's apartment free—no one else was allowed to live in it, even when the restless Beethoven was not there. As a result, Beethoven lived there, on and off for 11 years, from 1804 to 1815, and the Fourth, Fifth and Seventh Symphonies as well as his violin concerto and some chamber music were written here. It's a long four-flight climb to see such personal effects as Beethoven's sugar box, a few portraits (including one of Beethoven's grandfather), and his scores. . . . And, last but not least, the **Johann Strauss Wohnung** (54 Praterstrasse), the apartment where the 'waltz-king' lived from 1863 to 1870, and where he composed the famous 'Blue Danube Waltz,' which many Austrians consider their unofficial national anthem."

READERS' SIGHTSEEING SUGGESTIONS: "Take the train to Melk from Vienna (free to Eurailpass holders) and visit the famous monastery. Return via the downstream boat on the Danube at 4 p.m. (free for Eurailpass holders). Get off at the Nussdorf stop, have a glass of wine at a Heurige and listen to music. Then take the D streetcar back to Vienna" (Mr. and Mrs. David Arnold, Falls Church, Virginia). . . . "Persons sympathetic to music should not leave Vienna without visiting the central cemetery (**Zentralfriedhof**, 234 Simmeringer Hauptstrasse) where, within feet of each other, are the graves of Beethoven, Brahms, Schubert, Johann Strauss, Franz von Suppe, Hugo Wolf and Arnold Schönbrunn, along with a memorial to Mozart. This section of the cemetery contains some of the most exquisitely beautiful gravestones I have ever seen, many of them true works of art in their simplicity and eloquence. To get to the cemetery, take tram 71 from Schwarzenberg Platz and get off at the next to the last stop" (Milton Schulman, Bronx, New York). . . . "To see the best of the **Danube River,** begin at the Franz Josef Bahnhof in Vienna, take the train to Krems, and from there the bus that passes the boat landing. Then take the boat as far as Melk. The total one-way trip, from the Franz Josef Bahnhof to the Melk station, takes four hours. Check in advance for schedules" (Robert Hajek, Big Timber, Montana; note from AF: This is quite a worthwhile excursion, costing about $18 second class, round-trip. Best train from the Franz Josef station departs at 9:34 a.m., with return trains arriving in Vienna at 6:35 and 8:20 p.m.). . . . "To see the Viennese at leisure, spend Sunday afternoon strolling at Schönbrunn. . . . This is a gorgeous city, the highlight of our trip" (Christie J. Bentham, Scarborough, Ontario, Canada). . . . "By the time we reached Vienna, we were accomplished 'standers' so we suffered no discomfort or inconvenience in buying standing room to the performance of the Spanish Riding School. Standing room can be bought only on the morning of the performance at the box office, which is located in the cupola of the Hofburg. The office opens at 9 a.m., but be there an hour or so early. We bought 70 schilling tickets for the upper balcony, and, as it turned out, the people who had seats up there had to stand anyway so they could see everything" (Margaret Kendrick, Davis, California, and Cheryl Riggins, Woodland, California). . . . "Did you know that for a very small fee one may visit the stables of the famed Spanish Riding School and gaze close range at the horses to one's heart's content?" (Mrs. Harcourt M. Stebbins, APO, New York). . . . "If you want to see the Spanish Riding School, I advise you to go during a morning practice session. You can watch from 10 until noon and it only costs 50 schillings. Come early and wait in line. It is worthwhile because by 9:30 the line is two blocks long. I was in line at 9 and had an excellent seat and was not in the mob" (Stephen A. Singer, Chicago, Illinois). . . . "Nearly every large city in Europe boasts a church or cathedral which is well-publicized and visited, but in Vienna I would also recommend a visit to the **Synagogue,** at 4 Seitenstettengasse, near Judengasse, which opens at 4:40 p.m. on Fridays and Saturdays, 5 p.m. Sunday through Thursday. The area alone takes one back to a period of from 50 to 100 years ago. The synagogue, recently rebuilt within the walls of the old building, is a stark contrast between old and new and a beautiful symbol of faith and courage. The members, justly proud of their building, are friendly and interesting (however, only German or Hebrew is spoken). This, to me, will be a long cherished memory" (Mrs. Harcourt M. Stebbins, APO, New York); note from AF: for more specific information on visiting hours, phone Rabbi Chaim Eisenberg at 36-16-55. . . . "No Vienna visitor who is even mildly interested in Austria's past can afford to miss the **Austrian Museum of Military History.** It is, in my opinion, the best thing of its kind in Europe—surpassing even the Musée de l'Armée in Paris. Among its exhibits is the automobile in which Archduke Francis Ferdinand and his wife were riding when they were assassinated on June 28, 1914—the spark that ignited World War I. Francis Ferdinand's blood-stained uniform is also on display. There are, additionally, countless mementos of Austria's great generals: Prince Eugene, Archduke Charles, Radetzky. This is quite in addition to the usual large collection of guns, uniforms, and sabres, all of which the museum exhibits very skillfully. I sincerely hope you will see fit to mention the museum in next year's edition of your book. The location is the Arsenal, Objekt 18, reached by taking a tram to the Südbahnhof, then walking a few blocks. You can probably pinpoint it better by consulting a city map" (Bill Murchison, Jr., Corsicana, Texas). . . . "If you would like to visit the **Vienna Woods**

on your own, take trolley #1 near the Opera House to Schottenring, where you change from tram 38 (use same ticket) to Grinzing. At Grinzing take the bus via the Vienna Woods to Kahlenberg. The round trip costs 36 schillings and takes an hour each way. Much cheaper than the regular tour, which costs 350 schillings. There is a panoramic view of all Vienna from Kahlenberg" (Morton I. Moskowitz, Brooklyn, New York). . . . "To reach the far more attractive area of the **Vienna Woods,** take the Baden bus across the street from the Opera House (Opernring and Operngasse) —36 schillings, ½ hour. Once in Baden, walk up through the Kurpark to Rudolhof, for a beer there. The park melts into the Vienna Woods, and this is the elegant Vienna Woods that Strauss' music describes" (Arthur E. Banta, Imperial Beach, California). . . . "While in Vienna, no one should miss a delightful boat ride on the Danube. We took a train to Melk (fare 138 schillings per person), visited the famous Monastery there, and caught the downstream boat back to Vienna at 4 p.m., arriving about 8 p.m. (cost 204 schillings per person). The scenery is breathtaking, the boats are charming and have wonderful food, delicious Rhine wine and good Bavarian beer at very cheap prices. If you prefer, you can take the boat all the way to Linz, stay overnight, and come back the following day, thus enjoying two complete days on the Danube at extremely reasonable fares" (William H. Read, Los Angeles, California). . . . "A 30-schilling ($1.62) tour of the Opera House, including a visit to the Theatre Museum, which shouldn't be missed, is conducted at 3 p.m. daily during most of the year, daily at 9, 10, and 11 a.m., at 1, 2 and 3 p.m. in summer" (Jay Wolf, New York City). . . . "The most complete and panoramic view of Vienna is from the Kahlenberg hill; buses will take you up there. In the twilight, Vienna surrounded by the Vienna Woods, with the blue Danube making a path around the city, is a sight not to be missed" (Grete and Charles Schwarz, New York City). . . . "When you take the tour to the catacombs of St. Stephen's Cathedral, be sure to ask the guide what language the tour is conducted in. It's easy to descend into the catacombs and commence the tour before you realize it's in German (as we did). The tour is very interesting, though" (Tricia A. Reeson, Tempe, Arizona). . . . "One of the most significant works of architecture and sculpture that came out of the post-World War II period seems to be hidden in Mauer, a suburb of Vienna: **Die Kirche in Wien-Mauer.** Fritz Wotruba (1907–1975), who designed the church, was honored with an exhibition at the Smithsonian Institution in Washington, D.C., and has sculptures shown all over the U.S. The church, however, is hardly known to the average Viennese. It is not mentioned in any of the many pamphlets on Vienna, nor are there signs directing cars, buses or pedestrians to it. When we went by private bus recently, we were lucky to find a lady who happened to live near the church and who graciously guided us to it. I think it's a most impressive church" (Lucy Anne McCluer, P.O. Box, Due West, South Carolina; note from AF: Sculptures by Fritz Wotruba are on display in the large Hofburg Courtyard. To reach the Wotruba-built church, take the S train from Südbahnhof to Atzgersdorf-Mauer—the 5th stop).

8. Evening Entertainment

The primary night-time attraction here is theatre—particularly musical theatre. In summer, the **Theater an der Wien,** 6 Linke Wienzeile, which witnessed the premiere of *Die Fledermaus,* remains open for nightly performances at seat prices ranging from 60 to 380 schillings, but also presents Broadway and London musicals for a considerably higher minimum of 250 schillings ($13.51). In the non-summer months, performances of the renowned **Staatsoper** (Austrian State Opera)—ensconced in the world's most resplendent opera house—are a major experience for which seat prices range as high as $50, but locations several tiers up provide perfectly adequate views and sell for 240 schillings ($12.97). The season lasts from September 1 to the end of June, and the best place to purchase tickets is at the Opera House box office, open weekdays from 9 a.m. to 5 p.m., and Sundays from 9 a.m. to noon. Standing room (which starts at 25 schillings) is superb here, because standees are lined up on a graded floor, behind railings on which they can lean. . . . Again in summer, the jewel-like **Kammeroper** at Schönbrunn Palace, presents operettas and comic operas for $5 to $12 per seat, while much lower prices are charged at the **Burgtheater** (as little as 50 schillings, $2.70, closed July and August), located across from the Rathaus, and showing the classic works (Schiller, Goethe) as well as modern plays; the **Akademie Theater** (contemporary playwrights) at 1 Lisztstrasse (tickets from 50 schillings, $2.70); and at the **Volksoper** (spectacular operettas and light operas), which charges as little as 60 schillings ($3.24) for fairly remote locations. . . . In July and August, when many theaters are closed, Vienna's **English Theater** at 12 Josefsgasse in the Rathaus area, presents highly professional productions of both classic and contemporary plays; phone 42-12-16 or 42-82-84 for further information.

DANCING: For the very young and student-age, there are the two popular and adjoining discotheques on Annagasse (off Kärntnerstrasse) in the inner city: **Tenne**, at #3, and **Take Five**, at #3A. Tenne charges a 30-schilling entrance fee, Take Five charges only 25 schillings (but a Coke is 60 schillings). Personally, I see little to choose between them—except that Tenne has live, modern groups, while the other relies on records.

While the already described dance spots are excellent for lone visitors who want to make contact with the inhabitants, **Scotch Dancing**, at 10 Parkring, is a good place to go once you have—most of the people there are coupled. One of the nicest dancehalls in the city, Scotch is a discotheque (some rock music, mostly slow and romantic) in a dark, candlelit cellar that's popular with the 23-to-30 crowd. Dancing from 8 p.m. on; there's no admission, but a Coke costs 60 schillings once inside.

OTHER $$$-A-DAY BOOKS: Europe on $25 a Day has now been supplemented by five other $$$-a-day guides dealing with individual European countries or areas: **Ireland on $25 a Day, Greece on $25 a Day, Spain and Morocco (plus the Canary Islands) on $25 a Day, England and Scotland on $25 a Day,** and **Scandinavia on $25 a Day.** In contrast with the book you are now reading, which deals primarily with 21 major European cities, each of the above guides treats in depth one particular country or area, and sets forth hotel, restaurant and sightseeing suggestions for literally scores of individual cities and tourist destinations in that country or area. The $$$-a-Day Books can be obtained at most bookstores, or by mailing the appropriate amount (see list on last page of this book) for each book to: Frommer/Pasmantier Publishers, 1230 Avenue of the Americas, New York, New York 10020.

SOME SPECIAL SPOTS: The **Alte Backstube**, 34 Lange Gasse, is the most unusual cafe in the entire city. Set in a 17th-century house which operated for two centuries as a bakery, it has been restored into a combination cafe and museum, illustrating the history of baking. Walk through the front room, which looks just like any pastry shop, and through the narrow corridors into the back, where you will see the original ovens and old-style implements. Then, in the candlelit cafe at the rear, you can sit in comfortable chairs and sip coffee for 26 schillings or a glass of wine for 27 schillings.

The **Griechenbeisl,** in the historic center of the city at 11 Fleischmarkt, is one of the oldest restaurants and beer parlors in Vienna, dating back to the 15th century. Food here is too expensive for us, but go late at night for a 35-schilling beer (a smaller glass, called a Seidl, costs only 24 schillings) and to listen to the zither and accordion music. Fantastically picturesque, this seven-room spot is located off an old crooked alley. The walls are yellowed; there are medieval mottoes printed over the mantelpieces and inside the bays of windows; and a "signature room" contains the autographs of Beethoven, Richard Wagner, Count Zeppelin and Mark Twain on wall and ceiling. Simply poke through all the rooms until you find one whose atmosphere suits your mood.

AN EVENING STROLL: And one evening, equipped with your "Vienna From A to Z" brochure, you ought merely to wander through the Inner City (*Innere Stadt*), into the Am Hof—to me, the most picturesque square of Vienna, which houses the oldest and most picturesque cellar of Vienna at the **Urbanikeller,** 12 Am Hof, where there's recorded music, vaulted brick ceilings and medieval furniture, a somewhat cool temperature, but also warming glasses of fiery Slivovitz (the almost tasteless Yugoslavian liqueur, that has a faint apple-like aftertaste) for 45 schillings per large shot, or a 28-schilling glass of Vienna's best white wine (*ein Viertel Gumpoldskirchner*). Entrance is free.

But don't go home yet. For another Viennese experience, have an 11 p.m. (it closes at 12:30 a.m.) glass of wine at the famous, old **Augustiner Keller,** 1 Augustinerstrasse, in the Albertina Building, behind the Opera, where *ein Viertel* (quarter-liter) of cold, white wine costs 18 to 30 schillings, and where there's much Viennese flavor to the entire establishment. After 6:30 p.m., when a small Heurigenmusik band plays, there's a 6-schilling entertainment charge.

And then, for a budget midnight snack, stop at one of the mobile hot dog stands of Vienna (there's always one next to St. Stephen's Cathedral, another at the corner of Mariahilferstrasse and Neubaugasse) and order not frankfurters (which are just frankfurters), but a *Bauernwurst*—a big fat sausage, bursting with flavor, for which the price is 25 schillings, including a roll and mustard.

And after such an evening of strolling and dreaming and drinking, you may burst into song as one American girl we overheard did, to the tune of the Vienna Waltz: "Oh, we are in Wien, da dum, da dum, Yes we are in Wien, da dum, da dum . . ."

GRINZING: One other night of your stay should be reserved for this attraction—Grinzing being the generic term for an entire area of open-air wine houses on the northwestern edge of the city, about five miles from the center; it can be reached by direct tram line, #38, from the University for a fare of 18 schillings. You'll quickly find that drinking in Grinzing is a unique Viennese experience and, rather than being a tourist activity, is engaged in mainly by the Viennese themselves; you're bound to end up talking to the locals and getting happily involved in the sentimental music and interna-

tional gossip that characterizes these beflowered wine gardens, where everybody drinks and sings. Even during the winter and fall seasons, there's action: accordionists wander through the wine halls and everyone joins in the soft Viennese airs. None of the establishments charges a minimum or cover; you can buy a quarter-liter mug of wine for 40 schillings ($2.16) and spend as long as you wish over it.

CAFE LIFE: The **Cafe Leopold Hawelka**, 6 Dorotheergasse (right off the Graben), is the one definitive meeting place of Viennese bohemians, attracting an intense-talking crowd of young (and older) intellectuals. Crowded tables, a hodge-podge of chairs, assorted caricatures and commentary art upon the walls, English and American newspapers to read; you can sit all night over an 18-schilling cup of coffee (small) or a large one for 26 schillings. Specialty of the house is *buchteln* (sort of a doughnut) baked fresh daily by Mrs. Hawelka and sold for 8 schillings apiece. Closed Tuesday.

READERS' ENTERTAINMENT SUGGESTIONS: "The first stop any visitor to Vienna should make is at the **Opernpassage.** Located under the intersection of the Opernring, the Kärntnerring, the Kärntner Strasse, and the Wiedner Hauptstrasse, it houses a small, moderate restaurant and the principal office of the city tourist office. You can buy your 'Vienna from A to Z' booklet here, pick up a map of the city, get advice on things to see and how to get there, and check the weekly schedule of theatre performances. If anything at the state theatres interests you, ascend to the Staatsoper and proceed to the box-office (on the other side of the Operngasse) where tickets are available to the Staatsoper, the Volksoper, the Burgtheater and the Akademie-Theater. Tickets go on sale one week before the day of performance: I had no trouble getting tickets for a performance at the Volksoper for the night I arrived (Saturday) and a performance at the Staatsoper Sunday. Unlike Italy, where tickets are available for opera almost to curtain time, tickets in Vienna should be obtained in advance, especially for the Staatsoper" (Robert L. Guenther, Mt. Marion, New York). . . . "For about $2, you can buy standing room for the **Volksoper.** We tried it both ways—we had $10 tickets one night and we stood there the next night—and we could see and hear much better from the standing room section. And anyway, you can sit during the intermission in the empty seats" (Mrs. Jack Gordon, Collingswood, New Jersey). . . . "The **Vienna Symphony** conducts concerts during the summer at least twice a week beginning at 8 p.m. in the city Rathaus (city hall), which is on Dr. Karl Lueger Ring, I believe. You see, the Rathaus is like a hollow square, the symphony playing within the walls and at the same time under the moon and stars. It is a thoroughly enchanting experience. Tickets may be obtained at the Rathaus earlier in the day, and cost 40 Austrian schillings ($2.16)" (Michael D. Colman, Huntington Woods, Mich.). . . . "There is a literally huge weinkeller called the **Zwölf Apostelkeller,** at 3 Sonnenfelsgasse, two or three streets beyond St. Stephen's on the right along Rotenturmstrasse, walking into the Innenstadt from the Ring. It is about a block off Rotenturmstrasse. This place has three or four levels, jammed on Saturday and other nights with students. Our party of three shared a quart of the 'heuriger' wine, and this cost us 90 schillings. The keller also serves light snacks, which we didn't try. I would especially recommend this place for students" (Victor C. Weisskopf, Frankfurt/Main, Germany). . . . "Tickets for the evening's performance at the **Staatsoper** are often unobtainable anywhere. Fortunately, there's nearly always a medical convention in Vienna, and where there are doctors, there are opera tickets. A well-dressed American can walk up to the registration desk at any of these conventions, urbanely say 'I did not order my tickets in advance, but do you have any?' and usually get the finest seats available, in all price ranges. Alternatively, try the concierge at any splurge-priced hotel" (Pauline Rissman, New York, New York). . . . "It is almost impossible to get seats for the Opera in season. If you know exactly when you will be in Vienna, you should write ahead for tickets or deal with a ticket agency and pay the 20% fee. Otherwise, you will have to line up for standing room. In that case, go very early, take food along, and follow this procedure: If you are near the head of the line, get **Parterrestehplatz** (orchestra standing room). If you cannot get this, get Galerie (upper balcony) standing room for 25 schillings. You will then line up on the stairs, and when the signal is given, dash upstairs with the mob and run for the Mitte section of the Galerie. Your 'seat' is reserved by tying a scarf or handkerchief to the rail. (We were friendly with an English couple—the husband was a basso studying in Vienna on scholarship and knew all the ins and outs of where to sit and stand, as they went every night). If you can get seats, the best ones are Mitte Balcony. Remember, if you get tickets ahead, you can nearly always sell them if you can't make the performance, as the Staatsoper is completely sold out most of the time and there are usually more people wanting tickets than there are tickets available, for any and all performances" (Sara and Peter Cleveland, Sharon, Massachusetts; note from AF: at each performance, 550 standing-room places are sold, a number so large that nearly everyone lining up for such tickets is able to obtain one). . . . "One of the best aspects of Vienna is its music (of course), and you can hear a free concert every night in the **Stadtpark**—outdoors in good weather, indoors in bad. For a seat, one must sit at a cafe there, but one drink will last all night, and it can be a cheap apfelsaft, if you wish" (Charles M. Super, New Haven, Connecticut; note by AF: this is a romantic (and cheap) evening activity, presented in the park adjoining the Hübner Kursalon Restaurant at 33 Johannesgasse. There is no admission. Go only to the inexpensive lower level, where you can sit over a Coke or beer all night. From April to November, concerts are presented from 8 to 11 p.m. nightly, and Strauss concerts are given inside the restaurants during tea-time, from 4 to 6 p.m. Standard price for a soft drink or coffee or tea, when the music plays, is 35 schillings ($1.89) in the afternoon, 60 schillings ($3.24) in the evening. . . . "From May to October, there are free organ recitals every Wednesday night from 7 to 8 p.m. on the new organ in **St. Stephen's Cathedral,** the sound of the instrument played by the resident organist is a treat which no music lover should miss" (Theodora and John Austen, Sandringham, Australia).

9. Miscellaneous Tips

For picnic ingredients, snacks and exciting atmosphere, the open-air meat-and-vegetable market of Vienna (the Naschmarkt), located on the Wienzeile, three blocks from the Opera (see our map of the Opera Area), should definitely be given an hour or two. Here you'll find the Theatre an der Wien (operettas), and across the marketlined street, one of the cheapest restaurants in Vienna (probably because it's so close to its food suppliers): **Naschmarkt Beisel,** at 14 Linke Wienzeile, where soup is 18 schillings and most plates range from 32 to 65 schillings . . . Vienna's major bicycle rental firm is **Werner Barl,** with branches at Salztorbrücke/Donaukanal, near Schwedenplatz, phone 66-34-22; at 8 Vivariumstrasse, near the Prater amusement park, phone 26-66-44; and at 47 Waldgasse, neuer Reumannplatz, roughly in the Südbahnhof area, phone 64-10-113, all charging 140 schillings ($7.56) per day, plus a refundable 500 schillings deposit . . . Laundromats in Vienna? There's great news: a new Westinghouse Automatic has opened in center city at 12 Tuchlauben, about 1½ blocks from the Hotel Wandl, and also near the Hoher Markt. And there's an equally convenient establishment at 59 Josefstädterstrasse, called Miele Selbstbedienung Münzautomaten. Both charge 80 schillings ($4.32) for a wash of up to 5 kilograms, 25 schillings to dry. . . . Best way to obtain definite reservations to various spectacles and performances in Vienna: write first to the Vienna Tourist Board, 5 Kinderspitalgasse, A-1090 Vienna, for a program of what will be playing during your stay in Vienna, then write directly for seats (do not enclose money) to the following: (for performances of the Spanish Riding School) **Spanische Reitschule,**

Hofburg, Michaelerplatz 1, A 1010 Vienna. Write at least three months in advance. They'll send to you by return mail brochures and a ticket order form; (for the Vienna Boys' Choir) **Hofmusikkapelle,** Hofburg-Schweizerhof, A 1010 Vienna—at least two months before your visit; (for the Opera, Volksoper Burg and Akademe Theater) **Bundestheaterverband,** 1 Goethegasse, Vienna 1. As luck would have it, nearly all these are closed throughout July and August. . . . Although there's not much to see beyond various items of furniture and books, his beige velour hat and black walking stick with ivory handle, his personal collection of antiquities, you may feel a thrill and certainly awe and respect (as I did) in visiting the former study and waiting room of **Sigmund Freud,** at 19 Berggasse, now a museum open to the public, Monday through Friday from 9 a.m. to 1 p.m., and on Saturday and Sunday from 9 a.m. to 3 p.m. Entrance is 20 schillings, 10 for students. Recently, a large lending-library of up-to-date psychoanalytic literature was installed, and it is available to any interested visitor. Freud lived and worked in this typical, old Viennese apartment house from 1891 to 1938, when he moved to London after the Nazi occupation of Austria. . . . For babysitters in Vienna, phone 95-11-35, the offices of **Baby Sitter Zentrale,** whose sitters charge 70 schillings an hour, plus transportation. . . . And for the most delicious pastries of your life, make a definite effort to stop at a Viennese konditorei at 4 p.m. of an afternoon.

READERS' SHOPPING SELECTIONS: "I'm sure there are many stores in Vienna, but this one captured our attention and enabled us to buy gifts for discriminating friends who never guessed our small capital outlay: **Ernst Sramek,** 66 Mariahilferstrasse. It is a small jewelry store, at which we bought the tiny petit point brooches for about 120 schillings ($6.48) each, and the authentic rosebuds and leaves dipped in gold for only 110 schillings ($5.94) each. We ordered more after coming home and received prompt and accurate attention" (Reba June Green, Bristol, Virginia). . . . **"Wiener Emailstudio Steinböck,** 24 Bauernmarkt, manufactures some of the most lovely enamel bracelets, pins, plates and bowls you see from Switzerland to Austria. They have seconds with flaws you need a magnifying glass to find, at less than half price, and firsts at a substantial reduction. It is located on the fifth floor of a nondescript building a block behind St. Stephen's and you need a schilling for the elevator (which only goes up!), but the bargains are great. The salesgirl has enough English to be helpful. Hope other travelers find this useful" (Rev. John Paul Carter, Ellcott City, Maryland).

WEEKEND IN BUDAPEST:

It may be a shock, upon arriving in Vienna, to learn that you've come so far East that you're almost next door to Budapest—and you can go there! All the Viennese travel agencies sell tickets for a weekend bus tour to Budapest, which departs from Vienna early every Tuesday, Thursday and Saturday morning and returns late the next night, with occasional additional departures in summer. But you'll pay less for the tour if you buy a ticket directly from the Vienna branch of the official Hungarian tourist bureau, called **Ibusz,** 26 Kärntnerstrasse (three blocks from the Opera). There, payment of 1500 schillings ($81.08) in summer, 1200 schillings ($64.86) off-season, takes care of everything but your visa (an additional 100 schillings) and booking fee (80 schillings more); transportation both ways, meals, lodgings, a four-hour city tour of Budapest, an evening of wine-tasting with gypsy music, and enough free time to do some worthwhile poking around on your own. For more detailed information phone Frau Rosenauer at 53-26-86.

You'll need to check in at Ibusz at least a few days in advance to reserve a place on this tour, and *must* turn in your passport two days before

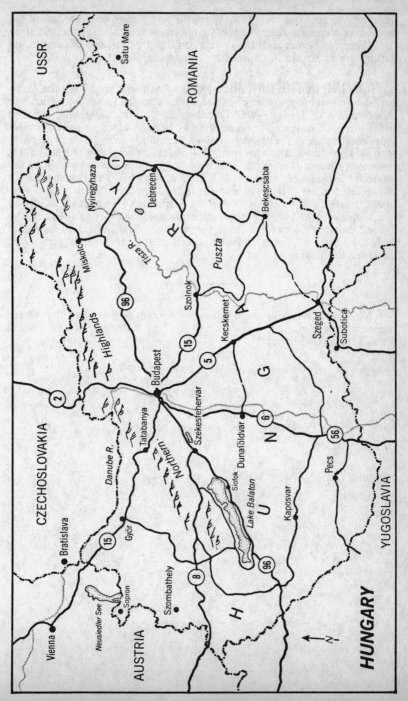

departure to get your visa (the passport is returned to you just before the bus leaves Vienna). A multilingual guide then accompanies the bus from the Hungarian border to Budapest and on the city tour, and the accommodations are at a good Budapest hotel. Amazing, nicht?

SWIMMING IN THE DANUBE: This is a final, wait-until-I-tell-the-folks-back-home experience. You can dunk in the Danube (actually, a tributary called the Alte Donau—Old Danube) either informally, and without benefit of bathhouses, at numerous public beaches along its banks; or else more elaborately at the **Gänsehäufel**—a beautifully scenic swimming park, with a segregated area for nudists—where lockers cost 30 schillings, low-cost restaurants abound, and Ping Pong tables are strewn about the grounds. To do either, take the U-Bahn (subway) No. 1 to Donauinsel (an 18-schilling ticket), then follow the crowd to this Coney Island-type establishment, and buy your locker key. Earlier, as you cross the bridge to the swimming park, you'll enjoy a panoramic view of Vienna's skyline, the United Nations' skyscraper complex, and the Kahlenberg Hill, where Prince Eugene of Savoy defeated the Turks in 1683, thus preserving Christian civilization.

No trip to Austria is complete without a stay in the city where incomparable mountain scenery provides the backdrop for the world famous music of Salzburg.

Chapter XV

SALZBURG

Urban Beauty, Rural Rates

1. Orientation and Getting Around
2. The Cheap, Cheap Budget Accommodations of Salzburg
3. Low-Cost Dining
4. The Enthralling Sights of Salzburg
5. Sightseeing Notes & Tours
6. Evening Activities
7. Salzburg Miscellany

SOME OF YOU saw it as many as five and six times! *The Sound of Music*—among the most successful films of all time—introduced an entire generation to the city of Salzburg, scene of the frolicsome Von Trapp family, home of the imposing convent that housed nun Julie (Maria) Andrews, site of the green-topped mountains on which she and they cavorted and sang, unforgettable vista of giant churches and university buildings dating back many hundreds of years. So indelible are these impressions and memories that when we first arrive in Salzburg, we feel we have been there before! Universally acknowledged to be one of the most awesomely beautiful cities on earth, its perfectly preserved old city with its baroque structures, its 17th century streets, its gaily beflowered horsecarts, its strolling female shoppers in colorful dirndls (they still wear them), all create an enthralling setting and mood, made more magical by the surrounding Alpine scenery that flanks every side of a city so filled with architectural wonders that it is known, to some, as the Austrian Rome. That title alone ought to be recommendation enough for a visit to Salzburg. Add the fact that Salzburg's accommodations—especially those offered in Alpine-styled private homes throughout the city—are (with those of Innsbruck) the cheapest in all of Austria, and you have compelling reasons for an immediate trip!

1. Orientation and Getting Around

How do you see the sights of Salzburg? You walk. You take glorious strolls, themselves a key activity, along the magical lanes and boulevards of a city in which nothing of importance (except Hellbrunn Castle and the Hallein salt mines) is more than 15 minutes away. Although it is the fourth largest urban center of under-populated Austria (after Vienna, Graz and Linz), Salzburg has a population of only 140,000 persons, and everything is human-scaled, close at hand, intimate and near. When you do take a streetcar or bus (usually from their main terminals at the Bahnhofplatz—the square facing the railway station—or at the Hanuschplatz in the old city), you pay only 43 U.S. cents a ride (by purchasing a ten-ticket block for 80 schillings), or else 54 U.S. cents (10 schillings) for a single ride, or $2.70 (50 schillings) for a full 24 hours of unlimited travel. Tickets are sold by conductors or at the tobacco shops around town carrying the sign "Tabak Trafik."

Arriving in Salzburg by air, you simply take a shuttle bus marked "S" to the railway station in town, for a one-way fare of only 9 schillings (54 U.S. cents). Arriving by train (after a trip of only 2½ hours from Munich, 3 hours from Vienna), you're again deposited at the Central Railway Station, in the so-called new city. From there by taxi to a hotel in the old city costs an average of 60 schillings ($3.24), and that's about the only occasion on which you'll desire a cab in the course of your stay; we've provided walking, streetcar or bus instructions for everything else.

LAYOUT: The city is split in half by the **Salzach River,** conveniently dividing the town into two distinct sections: "new city," or right bank, possessing the central railway station, most of the large hotels and nearly all the shops; and "old city," or left bank, the heart of historic Salzburg, site of Mozart's birthplace, all the churches and museums, and the Festival Hall complex. Each side of the city is itself dominated by a large hill which juts out from its midst: the **Kapuzinerberg** on the right bank, the **Mönchsberg** on the left bank. Both sides are connected by 10 bridges across the Salzach, which you'll have frequent occasion to use.

A VITAL NOTE: If your stay in Salzburg is scheduled for between July 15 and August 31, period of the Salzburg Musical Festival, then you must make advance reservations, at least three days prior to arrival, by phoning the main **City Tourist Information** office (phone 74620 or 71511) in the new city. And if you encounter difficulties in the course of the call, then ask to speak with Frau Ilse Korhonen, who is patient and friendly beyond measure, and knows more about budget accommodations than anyone else in town. Apart from the Festival period, your best course is to seek out your own preferred lodgings, from the recommendations which I now set forth below.

2. The Cheap, Cheap Budget Accommodations of Salzburg

What makes the prospect of a Salzburg stay so particularly pleasant and inexpensive is the tradition, among large numbers of Salzburgers, of making rooms in their homes available to tourists. As in Innsbruck, the other private-home capital of Austria, the people doing this are normal, middle-class citizens who rent their rooms, in my secret opinion, as much for the variety and interest of meeting foreign travelers, as for enhancing their incomes. Nothing beats staying in a private home in Salzburg, both

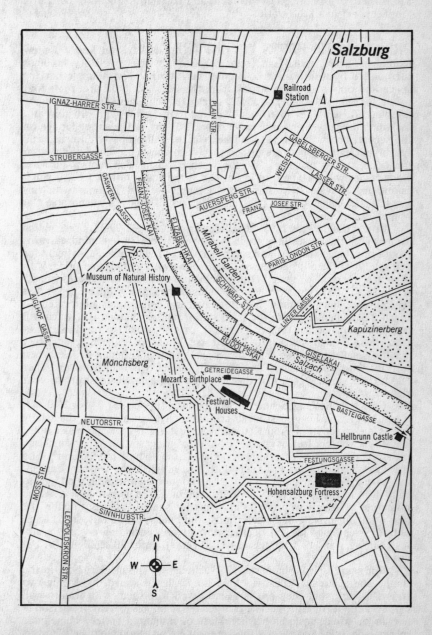

Salzburg

Railroad
Station

IGNAZ-HARRER STR.

STRUBERGASSE

GASWERK GASSE

FRANZ-JOSEF-KAI

ELIZABETHKAI

PLAIN STR.

AUERSPERG STR.

Mirabell Garden

SCHWARZ STR.

GABELSBERGER STR.

WEISER

LASSER STR.

FRANZ   JOSEF STR.

PARIS-LONDON STR.

LINZER GASSE

Kapuzinerberg

Museum of Natural History

AIGLHOF GASSE

Mönchsberg

RUDOLFSKAI

GISELAKAI

Salzach

GETREIDEGASSE

Mozart's Birthplace

Festival
Houses

BASTEIGASSE

Hellbrunn Castle

NEUTORSTR.

FESTUNGSGASSE

MOSS STR.

LEOPOLDSKRON STR.

SINNHUBSTR.

Hohensalzburg Fortress

N
W   E
S

within the city and on its outskirts. In both areas, you'll pay only $8.64 to $10.81 per person, breakfast included, and you'll meet the most delightful "innkeepers" in all the world.

PRIVATE HOME HOSTS WITHIN THE CITY: Frau Maria Rader-
bauer, 65 Schiesstattstrasse (phone 39-363), whose two-story home is surrounded by rose bushes, in a quiet neighborhood with ample parking space and only a 15-minute walk from the center of Salzburg, rents four rooms for only 180 schillings ($9.72) single, 160 schillings ($8.64) per person double, 170 schillings ($10) per person for the triple with private bath, including breakfast served between 8 and 10 a.m. in the sitting lounge on the second floor. Rooms, as you'd expect, are all properly furnished and sparkling clean; slippers are provided to each guest (they're placed next to the door); a bar of soap is on the wash basin in each room; and Mrs. Raderbauer will pick you up in her car at the train station, free, if you'll phone on arrival. If you're lucky enough to find a room with this English-speaking lady, as I did in 1984, you'll enjoy a memorable "at home" experience.

Frau Hilde Radisch, 5 Scheibenweg (phone 32-99-32), resembling Tootsie's mother, lives in a small, ivy-covered home a few hundred yards from Frau Raderbauer, where she rents a large four-bedded apartment for 160 schillings ($8.64) per person, a smaller twin for the same price, with breakfast (served to your bedroom) included in the rate. Baths are 25 schillings ($1.35) extra. While Frau Radisch speaks very little English, her teacher-daughter, Rainhild, is multilingual and helps out as interpreter. To reach 5 Scheibenweg from the train station, either take a taxi (which will cost around $3.50 for four passengers), or else walk first up Kaiserschützenstrasse, which leads into Jahnstrasse, then cross the Salzach River via the small (compared with the other bridges) Lehener Brücke, then turn into the second street heading right (called Schiesstattstrasse). After 300 further yards, you'll find the Scheibenweg, a small sidestreet to your right.

Frau Brigitte Lenglachher, 8 Scheibenweg (phone 351-042 or 38-0-44), a traditionalist who wears dirndl costumes, lives in a cottage diagonally across the street from Frau Radisch; and just like Frau Raderbauer does, she'll pick you up, free of charge, from the railway station in her small car, provided she's not busy serving breakfast (from about 8 to 9:30 a.m.). She speaks enough English to understand you; supplies you with an English-language "Welcome to our House" sheet containing instructions on how to walk to the old city, new city, etc.; maintains a guestbook in which numerous visitors have praised the hospitality she provides; is probably the best of all our private home selections; and finally, for all this, she charges only 175 schillings ($9.45) per person in twins, including a good breakfast. Showers are 10 schillings (54 U.S. cents), baths 20 schillings ($1.08) more.

Rudy and Friedl Simmerle, 13 Wachtelgasse (phone 356-795), in the same general area as the first three homes listed above, have only two rooms to rent, but they are large and well furnished, with wall-to-wall carpets and lots of mirrors. The charge: 170 schillings ($9.18) per person in a twin or triple, including a breakfast of unlimited coffee, homemade marmalade, juice and cheese, the latter served on a wooden plate. Showers are 15 schillings extra; use of the washing machine 25 schillings ($1.35) for a load; and this time it is Mr. Simmerle, fluent in English, who will pick you up and return you to the railway station or airport, provided only that you phone him about two days in advance.

PRIVATE HOME HOSTS ON THE OUTSKIRTS: Amid breathtaking mountain scenery, and never more than a 15-minute bus ride from the center of Salzburg, you'll want to consider:

Frau Germana Kapeller, 44 Berg (phone 533-214), rents four rooms furnished in Salzburg style, and with gleaming parquet floors. Rates for 1985: 180 schillings ($9.72) single, 165 schillings ($8.91) per person twin, 150 schillings ($8.10) triple, including breakfast served in a tastefully decorated basement room. And location is but a short walk from the small Maria Plain railroad station, from which the round-trip fare to the central railway station in Salzburg is 22 schillings ($1.18), free to Eurailpass holders. Frau Kapeller's is the first house to your left on Berg, walking up from the station.

THE AUSTRIAN SCHILLING: In this chapter on Salzburg, we've assumed the exchange rate of the Austrian schilling to be approximately 18.50 to the dollar, thus making each schilling worth about 5.4 U.S. cents.

Frau Mathilde Lindner, 64 Berg (phone 533-254), 200 yards up from number 44, offers four rooms, of which three are with balcony looking out onto a garden with deck chairs for sunbathing and a beautiful Alpine view. Inside, the rooms are furnished with new, unpainted-wood beds, wardrobes, tables and chairs, and one features a handcarved ceiling, all made by Herr Lindner, whose profession is that of a skilled carpenter. For all this, the rate is only 160 schillings ($8.64) per person, breakfast included, and Mr. Lindner offers free pick-up service from the station in Salzburg. To reach Salzburg from here, you either take the train from the Maria Plain station a short walk away, or bus G to the Kasern stop, the latter for a one-way fare of 10 schillings (54 U.S. cents).

Frau Christl, 57 Berg (phone 51187), is the English-speaking proprietress of the ten-room Pension Christl at that address, largest of the homes in this area, and possessing room both with and without private bath, which range in price from 150 schillings ($8.10) to 200 schillings ($10.81) per person; that includes a super continental breakfast that supplements the usual items with cheese, sausage or egg, and permits unlimited helpings of coffee or tea. Extra features of the Christl: a supplementary charge of only 100 schillings ($5.40) for the third or fourth person in a room; a well-kept garden for relaxing and sunbathing; free use of a small swimming pool; a laundromat service (50 schillings, or $2.70, per load, washed and dried); and the charming presence of Frau Christl, who freely proffers advice about Salzburg, and lives in the house with her poodle, Blacky. The breathtaking panorama of the Untersberg Mountain and the surrounding scenery that you can enjoy from the Pension Christl is a travel experience you'll long remember. Finally, Frau Christl will pick you up on arrival, and deliver you back to the Salzburg station when you depart, by private car, free.

Gästehaus Gassner, 126b Moosstrasse (phone 843-4-67), is a remarkably well-furnished and kept, three-story home with six guest rooms, in the southern section of Salzburg called Leopoldskron, all owned and managed singlehandedly by the kindly Frau Gassner, whose motto is "My Guest Is My King." You'll pay 160 schillings ($8.64) per person for the rooms without bath, 180 schillings ($9.72) per person for rooms with private shower and w.c., receiving large rooms with wall-to-wall carpets, ample wardrobe space (with plenty of hangers), French or twin beds, and the best bathrooms of any I've seen in a European guesthouse. Showers are free; breakfast, with juice, cheese, sausage, is included in the price and served at any time from 5:30 a.m. to noon (see Mrs. Gassner's motto, above) in a vast, parquet-floored dining room or, during summer, on an outdoor terrace; and Frau Gassner will drive you, free, from the railway station in Salzburg to her home. Altogether, one of the best values in town.

Haus Steiner, 156b Moosstrasse (phone 842-83-63), a short distance from Gästehaus Gassner, also rents six rooms on three floors, and provides the same free railway pick-up service as does Frau Gassner, but charges slightly lower rates: 160 schillings ($8.64) single, 150 schillings ($8.10) per person for twins, triples or quads, always for adequately furnished, spotlessly clean rooms that enjoy a nearby, small TV lounge; showers are free. To reach downtown Salzburg from Moosstrasse, take the M bus from the Kaserer stop, 200 yards away, to Hanuschplatz. Buses run every half hour, take 15 minutes for the ride, and charge 10 schillings (54 U.S. cents) one way.

Frau Elfriede Kernstock, 29 Karolingerstrasse (phone 43-94-15), in the airport area, rents three beautifully furnished (hand-painted cabinets, tables and chairs, wall-to-wall carpeting) but bathless twins and one apartment of her spotlessly clean, modern bungalow. The twins rent for 350 schillings ($18.91), the apartment for 400 schillings ($21.62) for two, 600 schillings ($32.43) for four, including breakfast for all. Third and fourth beds in the twin rooms cost 150 schillings ($8.10) per, again including breakfast. Phone the above number and Frau Kernstock will pick you up, free of charge, from the train station of Salzburg.

READERS' PRIVATE HOME SELECTIONS: "We stayed at the private home of **Frau Rosa Strobl,** 3 Pfaffingerweg (phone 238-242), about 10 minutes from the old city center in a quiet neighborhood where you have a fantastic view of the mountains in the area. Per person, bed-and-breakfast rates are 160 schillings ($8.64); location is about a mile and a half southeast of the inner city, and the atmosphere warm and friendly" (Dean Brown, APO, New York). . . . "My wife and I spent a night at the home of the **Auböck family,** 3 Emanuel-Schikanedergasse (phone 419-490). Herr Auböck and his lovely wife gave us an immaculate room with a great mountain view, and an excellent breakfast; they proudly maintain a guestbook in which prior visitors have expressed ecstatic opinions about their house. The price: only 150 schillings ($8.10) per person per night" (John R. Crosby, Fort Wayne, Indiana; note by AF: this is in that south-Salzburg section called Leopoldskron; to reach, take bus 5 from the railroad station to the Santnergasse stop, and walk only a few minutes from there). . . . "We were two adults and two children in two rooms for three nights at the private home of **Traude Moser,** 59 Berg, Salzburg-Kasern (phone 533-233), and paid only 1200 schillings, including hot showers. In 1985, Frau Moser will be charging 250 schillings ($13.51) for bathless twins, 280 schillings ($15.13) for the only twin with private shower (she has four rooms in all); and she will pick you up free from Salzburg station if you phone her first. Breakfast, included in the price, was served in a room overlooking Salzburg and the mountains, and all in all, this was the highlight of our trip" (Janice Davis, Flor, Missouri). . . . "We were lucky enough to find the private home of **Christa and Otto Gruber,** 76 Kendlerstrasse (phone 41-88-14), where twin rooms will be renting for only 220 schillings ($11.89), believe it or not, in 1985. This is in the Leopoldskron district of Salzburg, an exceedingly friendly establishment" (Betsy and Kevin Scallon, Cottage Grove, Wisconsin). . . ."The private home of **Frau Maria Bamberger,** 10 Gerhart-Hauptmann-Strasse (phone 42-98-53 or 42-96-53), was beautiful. We had a large room with balcony, but without private bath (which was directly across the hall), which included a phenomenal breakfast of cold cuts, cheese, basket of rolls, homemade jam, an egg, and a whole pot of hot chocolate; and yet the price for each of three available rooms (two doubles and a family room) is only 150 schillings ($8.10) per person for a long stay, 160 schillings ($8.64) for overnight" (Paul and Donna Dougherty, Pickering, Ontario, Canada; note from A.F.: the Bambergers' home is about two miles south of the city center, in the Leopoldskron district).

BUDGET HOTELS OF SALZBURG: For slightly more than the private
homes charge, and in far less personal a setting, you'll find an ample selection of budget hotels, in this city that's one of the lowest-priced of Austria, and one of the cheapest in Europe. They're located as follows:

Near the Railroad Station

Hotel Jahn, 31 Elisabethstrasse (phone 71405), is a small hotel of about 20 rooms, located less than five minutes on foot from the station, and distinguished chiefly for its low rates: 230 schillings ($12.43) for bathless singles, 360 schillings ($19.45) for bathless twins, a lowered 340 schillings ($18.37) for a bathless triple on the top (third) floor (because there is no elevator here!). All rates include breakfast served in the ground-floor restaurant above which is the hotel; showers are free; and while the Jahn is nothing to get excited about, it provides a clean and perfect location, especially for very short stays.

Pension Adlerhof, next door at 25 Elisabethstrasse (phone 75236), again with 20 rooms, is of slightly better quality and standards; its owners, the Pregartbauer family, take pride in preserving local customs and traditions, furnish all their rooms in Salzburg style, and host a folklore group in their downstairs restaurant every Saturday evening from 8 p.m. to midnight for the presentation of an Alpine music and dance program, complete with lederhosen, dirndl, yodeling and schuhplatteln. Their 1985 bed-and-breakfast rates: 210 schillings ($11.35) single, 360 schillings ($19.45) twin.

Gasthof Auerhahn, 15 Bahnhofstrasse (phone 51052), is a small but surprisingly well-furnished hotel, eighteen of whose 21 rooms are equipped with private shower and w.c. And although it is located across the street from secondary railroad tracks, they're used but once or twice a day and cause no noise whatsoever at night—of that I've been assured by the daughter of owner Herr Löcker, who works at the Salzburg tourist office, is fluent in English, competent on all matters having to do with Salzburg, and agreeable to answering questions in her father's hotel (he speaks a little English). Rates for room and breakfast (the latter served in the ground floor restaurant or, during summer, in the garden) are 480 schillings ($25.94) for a twin with private shower, 380 schillings ($20.54) for a twin without, 580 schillings ($31.35) for a triple with private shower. From the station, walk straight into Kaiserschützenstrasse, then turn right into Fanny-von-Lehnertstrasse which, after a few hundred yards, leads directly into the Bahnhofstrasse. Total walking time: 10 minutes.

Gasthof Dietmann, 13 Jgnaz-Harrer-Strasse (phone 31364), is a plain but clean hotel located 10 minutes on foot from the station, but in a somewhat noisy area; try to book the rooms on the courtyard which avoid the clamor of the street. Sixty-two beds in all, renting for 180 schillings ($9.72) single, 280 schillings ($15.13) for bathless twins, 350 schillings ($18.91) for twins with shower. Quickest way to get here from the station: turn left into Rainerstrasse, then right into St. Julien Strasse, cross the bridge (Lehener Brücke), and there's the Jgnaz-Harrer-Strasse.

Hotel Zum Hirschen, 21 St.-Julien-Strasse (phone 72403 or 71765), five minutes from the station and close to a highly popular beergarden restaurant where folklore musicians play light music in the evenings, is our splurge-priced selection around here: 610 schillings ($32.97) for doubles without bath, breakfast included, 770 schillings ($41.62) for doubles with bath, w.c. and breakfast. Turn left after leaving the station, and the second street turning right is the St.-Julien-Strasse.

In the Old City

Hotel Trumer Stüberl, 6 Bergstrasse (phone 74776), an easy walk from the birthplace of Mozart, American Express, and the Staatsbrücke, is a stand-out in Salzburg. Managed by a young, energetic and English-speaking couple, Hermann and Marianne Hirschbichler, this 22-room, 55-bed, five-floor house, built hundreds of years ago, has been completely refurbished inside, and now offers rooms with new mattresses on the beds, wall-to-wall carpeting, wood-beam-ceilings, hot water 24 hours a day, and delightful furnishings, for only 400 to 490 schillings per room ($21.62 to $26.48), including breakfast served in the ground-floor dining room. On the top floor: a particularly striking four-bedded apartment with inclined ceiling, private shower and w.c., renting for only 200 schillings ($10.81) per person, breakfast included—four happy backpackers were staying there at the time of my visit in summer, 1984. You'll spot the Trumer Stüberl easily by the eight small flags atop the main door, the red geranium flowers placed profusely in street windows.

Nearby, the **Hotel Goldene Krone,** 48 Linzergasse (phone 72300), a 55-bed establishment in another old, old building, is managed by the friendly Egger family, and charges (breakfast included) 285 schillings ($15.40) for bathless singles, 380 schillings ($20.54) for singles with bath, 420 schillings ($22.70) for bathless doubles, 520 schillings ($28.10) for doubles with bath, 700 schillings ($37.83) for triples with bath or private shower. **Hotel Zum Touristen** at 45 Linzergasse (phone 71401), across the street, is an alternate possibility, at 390 schillings for singles with private shower, 490 schillings for twins without shower, 600 schillings ($32.43) for twins equipped with private shower, breakfast included.

Hotel Wolf, 7 Kaigasse (phone 43453), in a quiet pedestrian zone at the very foot of the Hohensalzburg, is our Big Splurge in the Old City: housed in a 14th century building rated as a National Monument, it has ten rooms on three floors, all with private shower or bath and w.c., and antique furniture, a breakfast room with heavy oak chairs and tables, and is owned and managed by English-speaking Frau Erentraud Rottensteiner, who always wears dirndl costumes, and charges 380 to 450 schillings ($20.54 to $24.32) for singles with breakfast, 640 to 750 schillings ($34.59 to $40.54) for doubles with breakfast, the lower rates applying to the smaller rooms or to those on the top floor. Add a 20% supplement for stays from July 15 to September 30; and try to book rooms 5 or 7, especially attractive. (Incidentally, that strange object on the blue door behind the reception desk on the first floor is not an abacus, but an old Austrian *Türgeige,* a sort of medieval doorbell.)

Some Scattered Choices

Pension Bergland, 15 Rupertgasse (phone 72318), 20 minutes on foot from the central station, in Salzburg's Schallmoos district on the slopes of the Kapuzinerberg, is a most reasonably priced place with English-speaking owner (Herr Peter Kuhn), who rents 20 rooms on three floors for only 340 schillings ($18.37) per twin-bedded room, breakfast for two included, only 150 schillings ($8.10) per person for triple rooms with breakfast. From the station, turn left, cross under the train tunnel into Gabelsbergerstrasse, then turn into Bayerhamerstrasse; Rupertgasse is the first road turning left.

Pension Ganslhof, 6 Vogelweiderstrasse (phone 73853), about 200 yards from the Bergland, is a plain, no-frills, 35-bed establishment charging only 160 schillings ($8.64) per person for bathless twins, 130 schillings ($7.02) per person for triples, breakfast included, but plus 20 schillings ($1.08) for showers down the hall. To find it, either follow the same walking instructions as those given for the Bergland; or take bus 1 from the station to Mirabellplatz, changing there for a #4 bus to the Vogelweiderstrasse stop.

Pension Helmhof, 29 Kirchengasse (phone 33079), is a bit on the outskirts, in the northwestern part of town called Liefering, but it may have vacancies on days when the centrally located hotels are full. A 15-room pension in a typical Salzburg country house with red roof, green shutters and flowers on the window sills and balconies, it charges only 400 schillings ($21.62) for bathless twins, breakfast included, 550 schillings ($29.72) for twins with private bath and w.c. You can either take a taxi from the station for around 80 schillings ($4.32), or board bus 2 from the station to the Jgnaz-Harrer-Strasse stop, changing there into bus 4 to the Hafnermühlweg stop, from which the pension is a five-minute walk.

Four final possibilities: **Gasthof Römerwirt,** 47 Nonntaler Hauptstrasse (phone 43391), in a quiet location behind the Mönchsberg hill, charging 200 schillings ($10.81) for bathless singles, 300 schillings ($16.21) for bathless twins, breakfast included (take bus 5 from the station to the Nonntal stop); the **Salzburger Motel,** 48 Alpenstrasse (phone 20871), roughly in the same area as the Römerwirt, and best for tourists with cars (as it offers ample parking space): 320 schillings ($17.29) for singles with private shower and breakfast, 600 schillings ($32.43) for doubles with private shower and breakfast; **Gasthof Überführ,** 43 Ignaz-Rieder Kai (phone 23010), behind the Kapuzinerberg near the Salzach River, charging 350 schillings ($18.91) for singles with private shower and breakfast, 450 schillings ($24.32) for similarly equipped twins, and best reached by bus 7 from the station to the Überführ stop; and **Pension Jussy,** 11 Maxglaner Hauptstrasse (phone 44297), in the Maxglan district, where all rooms are without private facilities, and therefore rent for a low 170 schillings ($9.18) single, 350 schillings ($18.91) double, with breakfast; take bus 2 from the station, which stops near the Jussy.

READERS' BUDGET HOTEL SELECTIONS: "Please squeeze in a mention for **Gasthof Wallner,** 15 Aiglhofstrasse (phone 45-023)—it was our best accommodation value in nearly two months through Europe and England. Located at the bottom of a pleasant garden, it was absolutely quiet (rare for itself), and offered large double rooms with shower and toilet for 440 schillings ($23.78) per couple, including continental breakfast that was fresh and delicious. It is so good we really should keep it to ourselves—but the secret's out!" (Michael Randle, Rose Park, South Australia; note from AF: location is rather central, behind the Hohensalzberg Castle hill). . . ."We enjoyed a beautiful double room with private bath and large breakfast at the **Gasthof Grüner Wald,** 24 Landstrasse (phone 50-6-14), for only 520 schillings ($28.10). This is right off the highway only a mile or so north of the Salzburg railway station. It also has a swimming pool" (Charles P. Holzer, Emerson, New Jersey). . . ."We'd recommend **Hotel Itzlingerhof,** 11 Itzlinger Hauptstrasse (phone 51-2-10), to travelers with an automobile; they have a small area for off-street parking. Location is only six blocks north of the train station, and double rooms are only 400 schillings ($2.62)" (Paul V. Malven, West Lafayette, Indiana).

SALZBURG'S YOUTH HOSTELS:

There's both an official youth hostel a half-hour walk from the station, and an unofficial hostel only ten minutes on foot from the station, as well as four supplementary hostels that open in the summer months. The official establishment, which asks for a Youth Hostel card, but permits non-members to stay anyway for a 30-schilling ($1.62) surcharge per night, is the 360-bed **Jugendgästehaus Nonntal** at 18 Josef-Preis-Allee (phone 42670 or 46857), open all year, at a charge of 100 schillings ($5.40) per person per night, breakfast, sheets and showers included, the price unaffected by whether you occupy the several twin rooms or the 8-to-22-bed dormitories. Facilities include a TV room, a smokers room, kitchenettes with hot plates, a small disco, table tennis room, steel lockers, a coin laundry, and a restaurant serving three-course meals—mine consisted of cauliflower soup, roast beef with onion sauce, noodles, salad and apple pie—for 45 schillings ($2.59). There's also a midnight curfew. From the station, take bus 5 to the Justizgebaude stop (after crossing the Salzach bridge), then walk straight ahead, following the signs. Or you can walk all the way there in about 30 minutes.

The non-official hostel, requiring no hostel card, is the 150-bed **International Youth Hostel,** in a former school building at 9 Paracelsustrasse (phone 79649 or 73460), charging 80 schillings ($4.32) per night in eight-bedded dorms, 100 schillings ($5.40) per person in twins, 25 schillings ($1.35) for breakfast, with showers for free, and no curfew at all; it, too, is open all year. From the station, turn left, then, after about 200 yards, turn left again, pass the railway tunnel, and you'll find Paracelsustrasse to be the second street turning right.

In the unlikely event that both the major hostels are full, you can try the summer-only establishments, charging 90 schillings ($4.86) person: **Jugendherberge Aigen,** 34 Aigner Strasse (phone 23248); **Jugendherberge Glockengasse,** 8 Glockengasse (phone 76241); **Jugendherberge Eduard-Heinrich-Haus,** 2 Eduard-Heinrich-Strasse (phone 25976); or **Jugendherberge Haunspergstrasse,** 27 Haunspergstrasse (phone 75030).

3. Low-Cost Dining

The pleasures of low-cost Salzburg are just as abundant in the field of food. And Salzburg's particular contribution to budget living takes the form of exciting, and virtually unique, beergarden restaurants—three of them, all on the left bank, all attached to the breweries that make up much of the commercial life of Salzburg, and all of them refreshingly inexpensive. You can sit either indoors or out, stay till as late as midnight, and hear local bands playing marches and "evergreens" on Sundays during summer.

BEERGARDENS: You might even want to patronize a beergarden each night of your stay, in which case I'd start with the largest and most easily found (near the birthplace of Mozart), the 1800 seat **Sternbräu** at 23 Griesgasse, where there is both table service and a cafeteria line. Either way, you'll spend as little as 65 schillings ($3.51) for a typically Austrian, giant-portioned platter of, say, *beuscherl mit knödel* (calves liver cut in strips, cooked in a spicy sauce, served with a large, round, juicy dumpling, and accompanied by half a liter of beer and a roll). Soups are a dollar, salad bowls 42 schillings ($2.48), and only a few quality items—like a massive wiener schnitzel with mounds of fried potatoes and mixed salad—rise to a level of 96 schillings ($5.18).

The 1000-seat **Augustinerbräu** at 4 Augustinergasse near the railway bridge crossing the Salzach River, comes next; it features, in addition to its garden and prices similar to those of the Sternbräu, an enormous cellar restaurant heavily favored by students who bring their own food along to have with the beer (a full liter of cool, brown Augustinerbräu beer, brewed by the monks of the nearby St. Augustin monastery, and served in a stein, is only 32 schillings ($1.72). Or else these same students purchase their picnic-style ingredients at one of 12 stands in the hallway next to the cellar, selling cheese, cold cuts, bread, sausage, hamburgers, roast chicken, pretzels and the like. (The City Hospital is next door for fast medical treatment).

A similarly priced alternative: the 1200-seat **Stieglkeller,** partly carved into the hard rocks of the Mönchsberg mountain at 8 Festungsgasse, and best visited for its memorable folklore evenings, announced in the display posters and newspapers of Salzburg.

THE NON-BEERGARDENS: In the more traditional vein, the **Podium Restaurant** at 1 Gsättengasse near Museumplatz, in the old city, is a student-catering restaurant open seven days a week for both lunch and dinner, at which various two-course menus are priced at only 36 to 65 schillings ($1.94 to $3.51), wiener schnitzels with potatoes and salad are only 50 schillings ($2.70), salads are 20 schillings (mixed) to 40 schillings (Greek), and a great many other large dishes are considerably less than $3: *Tiroler knödel mit kraut* (potato-meat dumplings with sauerkraut), 37 schillings ($2), *gebratener leberkäse mit salat* (roast liver-meatloaf with salad), the same 37 schillings ($2), various omelettes only 32 schillings ($1.72). You may want to attend the literary matinees held at the restaurant on Sundays, the weekly, live jazz evenings scheduled for dates ascertained by phoning 44666.

The **Stiftskeller Sankt Peter,** 1 St. Peters Bezirk near the Dom (cathedral) at the foot of the Mönchsberg, and divided into eight separate dining rooms (the Haydnkeller, Pralatenstube, Barocker Festsalle, etc.), is of a higher standard than those we've just named, and tangibly more expensive (although still moderate)—95 schillings ($5.13), for instance, for river trout with caper sauce, rice and salad. But there are cheaper dishes, and among these are the popular *teller,* cold items served on wooden plates, such as the *kutschersalat* (coachman's salad) consisting of tomatoes, green peppers, onions and sausages in vinegar and sunflower oil, for 48 schillings

($2.59), or *innviertler jause,* a choice of smoked meats, roast pork, sour pickles and black bread, for 66 schillings ($3.56)—each of the massive plates is the equivalent of a full meal.

In the new city, **Stiegl-Eck,** at 10 Kaiserschützenstrasse, is found across the square from the central railway station, and enjoys large plate-glass windows facing both the station and the Forum department store. A 100-seat restaurant heavily patronized by local shop people, it features large, two-course menus—like *lebernockerlsuppe, schweinebraten mit semmelknödel und salat*—for 48 schillings ($2.59); a large-sized wiener schnitzel with mixed salad for 67 schillings ($3.62), *leberkäse mit spiegelei und salat* for 40 schillings ($2.16), half a liter of beer for 22 schillings ($1.18)—and there are always free salted pretzels in the bread basket on your table.

And finally, those old budget standbys, the chicken-serving **Wienerwald** chain, maintain branches in Salzburg at 31 Griesgasse (in the old city, near Mozart's birthplace) and at 46 Ygnaz-Harrer-Strasse (in the city's northern district), where they serve a full half-a-grilled-chicken for 57 schillings ($3.08), half a *grillhendl* (baked in breadcrumbs) for 71 schillings ($3.83), half a liter of beer for 22 schillings ($1.18), fried potatoes for 25 schillings, green or potato salad for 20 schillings.

SELF-SERVICE CAFETERIAS: These are a bit less expensive than the traditional restaurants, and of course they permit you to see first what you'll be tasting later. Biggest of all (and better than you'd expect from a railway station restaurant) is the self-service **Schnellimbissbuffet Hauptbahnhof** in the central railroad station at 1 Südtiroler Platz, open every day of the week from 6 a.m. to midnight, for the mass-market delivery of dishes averaging 45 schillings ($2.43) apiece; they include such filling ingredients as Austrian goulash with steamed potatoes, knockwurst with sauerkraut and cabbage, spaghetti with meat sauce and salad, accompanied by beer for 22 schillings ($1.18) more.

On the second floor of Salzburg's largest department store, the **Forum Restaurant,** 11 Südtiroler Platz, next to the central station, is open weekdays only, 9 a.m. to 5:30 p.m., when it serves up an exciting budget meal of two courses for only 44 and 60 schillings ($2.37 and $3.24). Or you can simply select a one-dish meal of goulash with a large dumpling *(knödel)* for 40 schillings ($2.16), a pair of franks with a roll and mustard for 21 schillings ($1.13), or various, tastily cooked (as everything in Salzburg is) 50-schilling plates, which include roast pork with steamed potatoes and vegetables, a rare beefsteak with roast potatoes and onion sauce.

And the final major cafeteria is found on the ground floor of the city's second largest department store, the **Interspar,** a bit far from the center at 15 Schumacherstrasse, near Salzburg's soccer stadium, in the Lehen district. It serves the city's cheapest wiener schnitzel (in all my wanderings), priced at only 49 schillings ($2.64), salad included; as well as three different two-course menus each day for only 40 schillings ($2.16): soup, followed by boiled beef with spinach and roast potatoes, in one combination, soup followed by fishburger with potato salad, in another. Open Monday through Friday from 9 a.m. to 6 p.m., Saturdays from 9 a.m. to 1 p.m.

THE STUDENT "MENSA": As you've seen, the cost of meals in Salzburg is so low that it scarcely is required that you patronize the institutional establishments. Still, if you'd like to spend as little as $1.08 for a two-course meal, lunchtime only, you can try the official student restaurant of Salzburg University, the **Mensa Aicherpassage,** 1 Mirabellplatz (basement), where persons of all ages, students or no, are usually admitted without hesitation—as, for example, me, in the summer of 1984! From 11:30 a.m. to 1:30 p.m., Mondays through Fridays only, it offers three, daily changing, two-course meals for the astonishing rates of 20, 24 and 30 schillings ($1.08, $1.29 and $1.62, respectively.)

4. The Enthralling Sights of Salzburg

The **birthplace of Mozart** comes first. The most heavily visited attraction in Salzburg, it is the third-floor apartment at 9 Getreidegasse where Wolfgang Amadeus Mozart was born on January 27, 1756, and where he lived for the first seven years of his prodigal life. He began to compose in this very apartment when he was five years old, and went on to create such extraordinary operas—the *Magic Flute, Marriage of Figaro, Don Giovanni, Idomeneo*—symphonies, chamber music, and piano concerti that he is today regarded as one of the greatest musical geniuses of all time; naturally, he died in poverty, in Vienna in 1791. On this, your pilgrimage to his birthplace, you should be greatly affected to see the crib of his first years, the original furnishings of the apartment. It is open Monday through Saturday from 10 a.m. to 4 p.m., and charges admission of 25 schillings ($1.35) for adults, 12 schillings (64¢) for children.

The **Hohensalzburg Fortress** is the next supreme sight of Salzburg. Built from 1077 to 1681 as a residence for those religious leaders with secular powers (the Fürsterzbischof) who ruled over Salzburg for more than 500 years, it is impressive not simply as a perfectly preserved medieval fortress, one of Europe's most important, but for the panoramic view it affords of virtually all of Salzburg. And stop to think: this entire enormous castle, with walls, turrets and fortifications, was built exclusively by hand, without assistance of machinery or external power. Today, a funicular on the Mönchsberg, the hill dominating Salzburg, brings you to the main entrance (from the Festungsgasse, near the Neptune Fountain) for a round-trip charge of 20 schillings, $1.08) to join conducted tours that leave every 15 minutes from 9 a.m. to 5:30 p.m.; the admission charge is 25 schillings ($1.35) for adults, 12 schillings (64¢) for students and 7 schillings (37¢) for children under 15. You'll be guided throughout the fortress, up and down many steps and along creaky wooden corridors, stopping to admire and hear explanations of every major feature, including the Royal Suite with its stone pillars, beautiful ceramic stove and medieval cylinder organ.

THE FESTIVAL HOUSES: Music is of course the highlight of Salzburg, and musical events are spectacularly presented and magnificently heard in the awesome **Festival Houses** of Salzburg, which can be visited on guided tours conducted at 11 a.m. and 3 p.m. on weekdays, except during the period of the Summer Festival (mid-July to the end of August); tour admission is 25 schillings ($1.35) for adults, 20 schillings ($1.08) for students and children, and may I note that a visit to these musical theatres is not to be missed. Though they are primarily booked during the Festival period, they present performances all year around—a series of 17 Advent Singing

Concerts in June of 1984 was practically sold out during the period of my own recent visit.

The Festival Houses, at 1 Hofstallgasse, consist of three separate but interconnected theatres: the Small House, Large House, and the Felsenreitschule.

The **Small House** *(Kleines Haus)*, seating 1,324 persons, boasts a stage as large as that of the Vienna State Opera, and is noted, too, for its interesting frescoes depicting the drama of life from birth to death, and scenes from the *Jedermann* (Everyman) play performed each year in the open air on the Domplatz of Salzburg.

The **Large House** *(Grosses Haus)*, seating 2,170 persons, and inaugurated in 1960 with a gala performance of *Der Rosenkavalier* conducted by Herbert von Karajan, is famous for its superb acoustics and a light-effect organ that can compose 1,600 shades of color. Don't fail to miss, in the modern foyer hallways, the white marble sculpture by Bertoni, the mosaic floors with equine motifs that recall the medieval ducal horse stables once maintained in this area, the cast-iron wall reliefs representing atonal music, the enormous Oscar Kokoschka Gobelin.

The **Felsenreitschule** is the open air theatre partially cut into solid rock, where the legendary Max Reinhardt launched Salzburg's fame as a theatre city in the 1920s with his production of *Das Grosse Salzburger Welttheater* by Hugo von Hofmannsthal; a suspension roof covers the entire theater, stage and all, in bad weather.

Immediately upon arriving in Salzburg, you'll want to seek out information on performances scheduled then for the Festival Houses, by consulting brochures distributed to all hotels or available from the small tourist office located near track 10 in the main hall of the central railway station. But you'll want to take the conducted tour of the Festival Houses, in any event.

HAUS DER NATUR: The **Museum of Natural History,** 5 Museumplatz, open daily except Sunday from 9 a.m. to noon and 2 to 5 p.m., is one of the most modern of its kind in Europe, and not only worth visiting on rainy days. On five floors and in 80 exhibition rooms, practically everything that lives or grows on our planet is brilliantly displayed, from stuffed rhinoceros to prehistoric animals to the twin roots of a fir tree hundreds of years old, from living tarantulas to a rock-crystal weighing 618 kilos, not to mention such abnormalities as a calf with two heads, a chicken with four legs and a deer with three, a giant DNA molecule, models of the *Saturn V* rocket, a moon landing scene and tiny piece of moon rock donated by President Nixon in 1973. Admission is 25 schillings ($1.35) for adults, 15 schillings (81¢) for children, and there's a snack bar to satisfy other needs on the third floor.

HELLBRUNN PALACE: Now for the excursions. **Hellbrunn Palace,** three miles south of Salzburg, was built in the 17th century as a hunting lodge and summer residence for the archbishops of Salzburg, who exercised secular powers as well. In addition to being an impressive example of the wealth and comforts afforded to absolute rulers at that time, it features—like the palace of the czars in Leningrad—hidden trick fountains and water sprays in its large garden grounds; on one marble chair, the archbishop could, by a wink of the eye to a servant, cause a water spout to jolt the serenity of whoever occupied the chair at that time. To see all this, you'll pay an admission charge of 35 schillings ($1.89), children and students only 17 schillings (91¢), and you'll be taken to visit various grottos, a 17th century toy theatre and a collection of imposing statues and sculptures, as you pass numerous other spots, corners and steps from which well-hidden outlets spit water—probably the only conducted tour of Europe in which laughing, running and hiding is expected of the tourist. To reach the palace from Salzburg, take bus H from the railway station (they depart every 30 minutes) directly to a stop in front of the palace ticket office; the fare is 10 schillings (54¢), one way. After the tour, which lasts half an hour only, you can then wander around (free) in the remaining part of the park, a pleasant interlude, or have a drink or snack in the *Schloss* (Palace) Restaurant.

THE SALT MINES NEAR HALLEIN: This excursion can be one of the highlights of your European trip. Hallein, ten miles south of Salzburg, is a small town of 14,000 residents that has become famous, in these parts, for its huge salt mines in the nearby Durrnstein Mountain, in active operation from Roman times to this very day (300 tons of salt are in fact produced each day). On an early train from the Salzburg central station (the schedule is posted on the window of the tourist information booth near track 10), the trip to Hallein will take only 15 minutes and is priced at 50 schillings ($2.70) round trip, with Eurailpass holders going free. In Hallein, you then walk to the Salzach River, cross it, and, following signs, reach the ground station of a funicular to the top of the Durrnstein Mountain (round-trip ride, also 50 schillings); then, from the mountaintop, you follow a footpath to the salt mine entrance, at which point you pay 75 schillings ($4.05) for the one-hour salt mine tour conducted by a uniformed miner. He'll place you in white coveralls (to protect from cold, humidity and dirt), seat you on the bench of a small electric railway car—and away you'll go! First you drive along a lengthy, cool, narrow, tunnel. Then you walk for nearly a mile underground, passing a huge salt-water lake, crossing the Austrian-German border, sliding down twice on wooden rails, listening to lectures on salt production, salt history, and salt mine safety, then emerging outdoors, after a long escalator ride and a return trip on the tiny electric train. You may well want to linger on in one of the three restaurants near the mine entrance, because the view is magnificent, and the food and drink prices reasonable—as everything is in this region of Salzburg.

5. Sightseeing Notes & Tours

OTHER SIGHTS: For readers with special interests, we'll quickly review the other sights and activities of Salzburg in alphabetical order:

The Cable Car to Untersberg

It operates daily, from 8:30 a.m. to 5 p.m., from St. Leonhard, seven miles from Salzburg on the road to Berchtesgaden, to the summit of the Untersberg Mountain. Round-trip ticket: 120 schillings ($6.48) adults, 60 schillings ($3.24) children. Direct bus service from the central station in Salzburg brings you to St. Leonhard.

The Carillon at Mozartplatz

Daily at 7 a.m., 11 a.m. and 5:30 p.m., the 35-bell chime, cast in Antwerp in the 17th century, plays its tunes.

Cathedral Museum and Excavations

The Cathedral itself, on Residenzplatz, and famed for its three bronze doors, is open to all, and free. The Cathedral Museum, inside, is open Monday through Saturday from 10 a.m. to 5 p.m., Sundays from 11 a.m. to 5 p.m., for an admission charge of 20 schillings for adults, 5 schillings for children. The excavations are available to visitors only from Easter to October.

Hellbrunn Zoo

Next to Hellbrunn Castle, which makes for a good combination visit, it's open from 8:30 a.m. to 5 p.m., for an entrance charge of 30 schillings ($1.62) for adults, 5 to 15 schillings (27¢ to 81¢) for children (according to age).

Mönchsberg Elevator

At the in-city mountain of the same name, it leads from the Anton Neumayer Platz to a panoramic platform, just below the Café Winkler, and operates daily from 7 a.m. to 3 p.m., for a round trip fare of 15 schillings (81¢) for adults, 7 schillings for children.

Mozart's Residence

At 8 Makartplatz (and not to be confused with the birthplace of Mozart at 9 Getreidegasse), it was here that Mozart lived as an adult, from 1773 to 1787. It is open throughout the year, at least until 6 p.m., and charges an entrance fee of 25 schillings ($1.35) for adults, 10 schillings (54¢) for students, only 5 schillings (27¢) for children under 14.

Museum Carolino Augusteum

Also known as the City Museum, it contains a collection of art exhibits ranging from ancient to present times. Open Tuesday through Sunday, 9 a.m. to 5 p.m., for admission of 20 schillings ($1.08) adults, 5 schillings children.

National Costume Museum

At 23 Griesgasse, second floor. It's where ladies planning to buy a dirndl should first go for inspiration; the exhibits are of traditional Salzburgian female dress, past and present. Open Monday through Saturday from 10 a.m. to noon and 2 to 5 p.m.; admission 25 schillings ($1.35) for adults, 15 schillings for children.

Residence Gallery

An art gallery of 16th to 19th century paintings, at 1 Residenzplatz, open daily from 10 a.m. to 5 p.m., 15 schillings (81¢) for adults, 10 for children.

The Catacombs of St. Peter

At 1 Sankt Peter Bezirk, where the church itself charges no admission, and has a quite lovely rococo interior. Price for the frequent conducted tours of the catacombs—relatives of Mozart and Haydn are among those buried here—is 10 schillings (54¢).

Toy Museum

Though it displays every conceivable sort of toy—from a hand-carved Noah's Ark to a merry-go-round, from model trains to tin soldiers, dating from the 16th century to now—more adults than children are in evidence! You go to 2 Bürgerspitalplatz, which is open daily except Mondays from 9 a.m. to 5 p.m., for an admission charge of 20 schillings ($1.08) adults, 5 schillings (27¢) children—that includes attendance at the Punch-and-Judy show presented every Wednesday and Friday at 3 p.m. in a special theatre room.

READERS' SIGHTSEEING COMMENTS: "Well worth a visit is the **Mozarteum,** which combines a library and museum of Mozart's scores and letters and an international music academy. A tour, including library, cottage that inspired *The Magic Flute,* a giant linden tree planted by Lilli Lehmann, concludes with a noontime organ concert of Mozart's music in his second residence, all for 40 schillings ($2.16). . . . Salzburg's **Cathedral** has a gleaming white interior with lovely dome and paintings, all in blue and terracotta" (Mrs. George J. Flynn, Washington, D.C.). . . ."My nomination for the most beautiful sight in Europe is the view of the colorful little town of Salzburg from the **Hohensalzburg Castle.** Try it at sunset! To offset the Austrian cuisine and the hours sitting at Festival performances, we took an hour's walk along the outskirts of the city, which brought us to a wooded mountain called the Gaisberg. A chair lift took us up the Gaisberg for a marvelous panorama of Salzburg's mountainous surroundings" (Joan Abel, New York, New York). . . ."Perhaps my most vivid recollection was of something that cost nothing at all. There are crowds of swans, ducks, moorhens and gulls on the Salzach River. We begged stale bread from cafés to feed them, and one evening walked along the river when the swans were flying off to higher reaches where they spend the night. The sight of five enormous swans flying wingtip to wingtip along the river at evening will remain with me for a long time." (Mrs. D.B. Craig, Rome, Italy). . . ."The salt mine tour is a must! The Disneyland-like ride into the mountain, the descent by wooden slide, and the underground lake, are all marvelous" (Gerry Buccini, Alberta, Canada).

ESCORTED TOURS: In a city as small as Salzburg, and as pleasurably covered on foot, it really isn't necessary to book a motorcoach tour unless you're desirous of visiting out-of-town sights and haven't the transportation to accomplish such excursions on your own. For readers planning more than a two-day stay in the Salzburg area, here's a quick list of the motorcoach tours you might consider:

Half-Day Salzkammergut (4½ hours), leaving daily at 2 p.m., April to September only, is a circular tour through Salzburg's lake district, a relaxing ride with breathtaking Alpine scenery that goes to Fuschlsee, Mondsee and Wolfgangsee, stopping at the famous Weisses Rössl hotel. The cost is 220 schillings ($11.89) per person.

Full-Day Salzkammergut (9 hours), leaving daily at 9 a.m., returning at 6 p.m., April to September only, and costing 280 schillings ($15.13), visits Fuschl, Wolfgangsee, Bad Ischl and Hallstadt (where a stop is made for lunch, not included in the price, and an inside tour of an archaeological museum with excavated relics from pre-Celtic times), then heads to lovely Gosau, where the Dachstein glacier reflects in the lake.

Full-Day Grossglockner Excursion, every Wednesday and Saturday at 7:30 a.m., returning at 7 p.m., from June 15 to September 30 only, and costing 380 schillings ($20.54), is a Grand Alpine Tour to Austria's highest peak, the Grossglockner (3,796 meters above sea level), up in serpentines and through tunnels, to the Franz-Josephs-Höhe (2,451 meters), where a two-hour stop is made for lunch, again not included in the price.

Half-Day Berchtesgaden, leaving daily at 2 p.m., returning at 6:30 p.m., and costing 180 schillings ($9.72), April to October only, is a trip on which you'll need your passport, as the border with Germany is crossed twice. The tour proceeds via Hellbrunn and Anif to Berchtesgaden and Königsee, and you'll see Hitler's former residence from your bus window.

Phone 71-733 to book aboard the desired tours, all of which depart from the central Mirabellplatz.

Bob's Bavarian Mountain and Picnic Tour

My own preferred alternative to the standard tours, operated in large 48-seater motorcoaches, is an eight-person trip by van, called **Bob's Bavarian Mountain and Picnic Tour,** which costs only 220 schillings ($11.89)—a price guaranteed to readers till the end of 1985—and combines a number of interesting Alpine visits. Operated not by a person named Bob, but by Frau Eveline Höringer (phone 72484 or 06246-3377), it leaves daily at 9 a.m. and 2 p.m. all year around, lasts four hours, will pick you up at your guesthouse or hotel, goes to all the major *Sound of Music* filming locations, including Leopoldskron, and also throws in a one-hour stop at Berchtesgaden (passport required) with its view of Hitler's *Eagle's Nest* (weather permitting). During the 50-mile trip, the English-speaking driver lectures on the history of Salzburg, and pithily describes the sights and scenery, the entire experience resembling the kind of trip you'd make in your own car, more than a commercial, group experience. But this is only a personal preference. If you agree, you might also want to consider Bob's two-hour evening tour of Salzburg, operated at 7 p.m., and the "Sound of Music" excursion, which substitutes the awesome Salzkammergut lakes for the drive through Bavaria and Berchtesgaden.

6. Evening Activities

Concerts, recitals, performances by noted musicians, evenings of classical music, operas—those are the stuff and substances of the evening nightlife of Salzburg, a city where discos and jazz clubs are barely tolerated, scarcely found. And since these activities change with the week, and are rarely announced long ahead, you'll have to rely on newspapers, posters, handouts, and not on this once-a-year guidebook to Europe. We've already referred to the outstanding musical events at the three structures of the Festival Houses. Let us now draw your attention to two other Salzburg institutions that provide balm for the evening hours:

The unusual, 300-seat **Marionette Theater,** 24 Schwarzstrasse next door to the Mozarteum, near Mirabellplatz, surely the largest marionette theatre in Europe, presents operas performed by nearly life-sized marionettes, from a repertoire of seven classic works, including Mozart's *Magic Flute* (all seven acts) and *Don Giovanni,* Rossini's *Barbiere di Siviglia,* and Johann Strauss's *Die Fledermaus;* you'll be astonished at the quality of the singing, the enveloping aura of the music presented in this small house. Seats range from 200 to 320 schillings ($10.81 to $17.29), performances begin at 8 p.m. (and in summer, at 4 p.m., too), and bookings can be made by phoning 72-406.

And then there's the equally unique, considerably cheaper **Salzburger Abend,** a 2½-hour evening of schuhplattlen dances, yodeling, zither solos and brass band music performed by a group of 50 Salzburgers in traditional costume, all of them members of a folklore club called Alpinia, a nonprofit organization formed in 1891. They perform twice a week, on Wednesdays and Saturdays, at 8:15 p.m., in the largest restaurant room of the Stieglkeller at 8 Festungsgasse, near the Domplatz; you eat or drink (see our restaurant discussion, earlier) while watching the colorful scenes. This is all such a typical Austrian happening, performed by such idealistic amateurs, that you'll learn far more here about Salzburg than from the *Sound of Music!* Phone Herr Langlechner at 351-042 or 38-0-44 for tickets, or else ask your guesthouse or hotel to book you a seat for 100 schillings ($5.40).

A READER'S ENTERTAINMENT TIP: "Don't despair if you hear that music festival performances are sold out. We were referred to a central ticket agency (called 'Polzer's,' I believe), where we were easily able to pick up seats for an important concert of Brahms" (Gerry Buccini, Alberta, Canada).

7. Salzburg Miscellany

Of the self-service laundromats, easiest to find is the **Constructa** at 10 Kaiserschützenstrasse, across from the central railroad station. It's open weekdays till 6:30 p.m., Saturdays till noon, and charges only 78 schillings ($4.21) for six kilos of laundry washed and dried. Elsewhere in town, the **Norge** at 16 Paris-Loudron-Strasse, between Mirabell and Makart Platz; and the **Waschanstalt Scharler** at 43 Schiesstattstrasse near the corner of Fasanenstrasse, in the Lehen district, maintain similar hours, and the Waschanstalt Scharler charges only 65 schillings ($3.51) for *six* kilos washed and dried. . . . Babysitters are obtained by phoning **Student Service** (phone 44511, extension 291), weekdays between 9 a.m. and 4 p.m. Their fee is 50 schillings ($2.70) per hour, plus carfare. . . . Bicycles? You get them at **Krois-Schmidler,** 88 Jgnaz-Harrer-Strasse (phone 32263), open weekdays from 8 a.m. to 6 p.m. Daily rental rate: 80 schillings, weekly 160 schillings, monthly 350 schillings, provided you leave a refundable deposit of 800 schillings. . . . The restful **Public Reading Room** *(Lesesaal)* of Salzburg University, 4 Hofstallgasse, across the street from the Festspielhaus, open weekdays from 9 a.m. to 7 p.m., Saturdays till noon, stocks a great many English and American magazines and newspapers, admits you free to its premises (on the second floor) for a relaxed perusal of them.

_____

And now we'll stop in another scenically beautiful Austrian city— Innsbruck—chosen site of two recent Winter Olympics.

Chapter XVI

INNSBRUCK

Crossroads of Austria

MOUNTAIN-SURROUNDED INNSBRUCK is not an especially important European city. Its population is a mere 120,000, its museums and other structures are of the second rank, but it is one of the most scenically attractive cities in all of Europe, for reasons similar to those which caused it to be chosen as site of the 1964 and 1976 Winter Olympics. And it is a transit city—a familiar sight—for nearly everyone traveling between Munich and Italy, or between Vienna and Switzerland; somehow, every highway and railway track seems to pass through. So many readers have found Innsbruck to be a convenient stopover point on their journeys through the Austrian Alps that I've been repeatedly urged to provide at least a brief discussion of its low-cost lodgings and meals, its evening activities, its unusually active train station, one of the busiest in Europe. Here goes:

1. Orientation and Getting Around

Like so many other notable cities of Europe, Innsbruck (which means "Inn Bridge") is divided by a river into a right and a left bank. The Inn River, which originates in Switzerland and flows, via the Danube, into the Black Sea, gave Innsbruck its name, and forms the natural barrier between the old town of the "right bank" (with its train station, museums, Hofkirche, University and most other places of importance) and the new city of the "left bank." The two "banks" are connected by eight bridges. It is difficult to get lost in Innsbruck: all main streets from the train station lead to the Inn.

Public transportation is provided by both buses and trams, all charging 12 schillings (64¢) for a one-way fare, which reduces to 9 schillings (48¢) if you purchase five tickets at a time. All trams and buses start from and end at the busy railway station, next door to which you'll find the highly efficient Tourist Information Office known as the Zimmernachweis. A small airport located two miles west of the city is used only for fairly infrequent commuter flights to and from Vienna and Zurich.

THE AUSTRIAN SCHILLING: In this chapter on Innsbruck, we've assumed the exchange value of the Austrian schilling to be approximately 18.50 to the dollar, making each schilling worth about 5.4 U.S. cents. As this edition goes to press, the dollar actually purchases more schillings than the above figure, and if it remains at its high levels, life in Innsbruck will be even cheaper than we've described.

---

2. Budget Lodgings in Town and Out

Because the surrounding scenery is so very picturesque, Innsbruck's hoteliers have placed as many establishments on the outskirts of town as in the center. But even the in-city lodgings possess breathtaking mountain views, and yet a low, low level of costs more frequently associated with countryside locations. I have six preferences in the center-city category:

Lydia Prantl, 7 Hörmannstrasse (phone 41-91-95), lives on the 4th floor of a modern, elevator-equipped apartment building in which she's been renting two rooms for over 20 years, largely to an Australian clientele (to judge from guestbook entries). One is a single renting for only 200 schillings ($10.81), breakfast included, the other a double costing only 260 shillings ($14.05), breakfast included, probably the best price deal in town. Third bed in the double room: 120 schillings ($6.48); showers down the hall: 20 schillings ($1.08) per. Turn right on leaving the station, then right again, crossing under the railway tunnel, then once more right after the covered swimming pool ("Städtisches Hallenbad") into Hörmannstrasse, all 10 minutes' walking distance from the station.

Gasthof Innbrücke, 1 Innstrasse (phone 81-9-34), occupies three floors of an ancient building whose foundations date to the year 1425; it has also been managed by the same family for four generations, and their price needs are refreshingly cheap: 200 schillings ($10.81) single, 280 schillings ($15.13) twin, including breakfast served in a ground-floor restaurant/dining room. From the station, walk up Museumstrasse, continue into Burggraben and Marktgraben (the old city) and then cross the Inn River (on the "Alte Innbrücke"), from which you'll spot the hotel.

Gästehaus Rosina Tautermann, 5 Stamser Feld (phone 83-7-15), consists of 23 simple but clean rooms on three floors of an apartment building in a quiet area on the other side of the Inn River: cross the Alte Innbrücke, walk up Höttinger Gasse, then turn left into Stamser Feld, a 25-minute walk from the station or five minutes by Bus B. Rooms are only 180 schillings ($9.72) single, 150 schillings ($8.10) per person in twins or triples, breakfast included, and with showers for free.

Pension Paula, 15 Weiherburggasse (phone 37-795), on an in-town hillside overlooking Innsbruck, is a graceful, country-style chalet managed by the charming Frau Hannelore Steidl (who acquired her fluent English

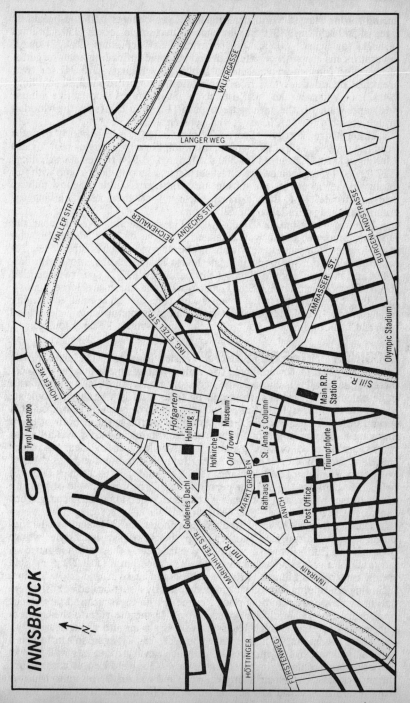

INNSBRUCK

←N→

during a long stay in Windsor, England). She charges bed-and-breakfast rates of 200 schillings ($10.81) for each of two single rooms, 350 schillings ($18.91) for twins, 460 ($24.86) for triples, 550 schillings ($29.72) quad. Several rooms are with private bath and balconies affording an unforgettable view of Innsbruck, yet rent for only 480 schillings ($25.94) for two, breakfast included. A taxi from the station will cost around 80 schillings ($4.32); or you can take the K-bus to the St. Nikolaus stop (a five-minute ride) and walk up the rather steep path (10 minutes) from the wooden bridge crossing the Inn River to the pension.

Hotel Bistro, 2 Pradler Strasse (phone 46-3-19), is less than 10 minutes from the station, a tiny, nine-room, mini hotel in which singles rent for 220 schillings ($11.89), doubles for 380 schillings ($20.54), triples 500 schillings ($27.02). All rates include breakfast served in a second-floor room with full mountain view. Leaving the station, turn right, cross under the low railway bridge, turn left into König-Laurin-Strasse, and then keep walking for about 300 yards parallel to the Sill River.

Pension Menghini, 29 Beda-Weber-Gasse (phone 41-243), near the Olympic Stadium, is the well-managed preserve of Herr Menghini, who also provides free pick-up service from the station (which is otherwise a 20-minute walk from the pension). His house has 18 rooms, most with balcony, and they will rent in 1985 for 410 schillings ($22.16) per twin-bedded room, for 660 schillings ($35.67) per quad (and these are large quads), including breakfast for all, showers, and free use of a small swimming pool outside. Herr Menghini's establishment is picturesquely decorated with old farming implements, and by an aquarium in the cozy lounge.

LODGINGS ON THE OUTSKIRTS: **Pension Rimml,** at 82 Harterhofweg

(phone 84-726), in Kranebitten, two miles west of Innsbruck, is the most picturesque of all our choices: the two-story house, built on a slope, has a huge balcony terrace, is surrounded by trees, and is a beauty to look at; rooms are in rural style, with heavy featherbed covers on beds; breakfast is served either in a glassed-in dining room or in the garden, both of them enjoying a unique panoramic view over mountains and city; and all guest rooms are located on the ground floor, making them ideal for older travelers. Herr Walter and Frau Anni Rimml (both fluent in English) rent 16 rooms, at rates of 240 schillings ($12.97) single, 360 schillings ($19.45) twin, 165 schillings ($8.91) per person in family rooms capable of housing either three or four; and breakfast is always included at no extra charge (but showers are 15 schillings—81¢—extra).

Haus Schwarz, 12 Lindenbuhelweg (phone 85-535), again in Kranebitten near the airport, is another lovely house of Tyrolean style, whose owner, Frau Edith Schwarz, will pick you up free at the station in her own car, and then proceed to charge you only 190 schillings ($10.27) per single room, only 190 schillings ($10.27) per person in twin and triple rooms, including continental breakfast supplemented by a soft-boiled egg; showers and use of a small swimming pool are free. From the station, if you're not picked up, Bus H should be boarded for a 15-minute ride to the Schneeburggasse stop, from which Haus Schwarz is a 5-minute walk.

Haus Rossmann, 13 Schulgasse (phone 27-25-02), again in Mutters, is a spotlessly clean, five-room guesthouse whose every room has wall-to-wall carpeting and a balcony for remarkable views. Toni and Leni Rossmann are the proprietors; Leni speaks English well, and will drive you up to Mutters from the Innsbruck railway station on arrival (free); and the charge for all this excellent hospitality is exactly 160 schillings ($8.64) per person in twins and triples, breakfast included. Showers are free—provided they're short ones!

Gasthof Traube, at 8 Vill (near Igls), phone 77-252, is another picture-book, Tyrolean building, this time managed by Frau Erika Mayer, fluent in English, friendly and accommodating; among other things, she lets you use her dining room for consuming picnic-style meals you've brought into the house. Her 24 rooms on two floors, all beautifully furnished, are priced at 165 schillings ($8.91) per person twin, 155 schillings ($8.37) per person triple, breakfast included. The village of Vill, near Igls, is three miles to the southeast of Innsbruck, and connected to the larger city by Bus J, charging 20 schillings for the one-way trip; be sure to leave at the stop called "Vill." From this quiet location, very near to a church, one can reach an open-air swimming pool by walking for ten minutes through a forest, opening onto a spectacular view of Innsbruck below.

Finally, **Haus Maria,** 9 Bilgeristrasse in Igls itself (phone 77-186), near the Patscherkofel cable car station, is only a minute's walk from the Igls tram stop. It's an 11-room house managed by Frau Margit Zettinig and her English-speaking son, Rudi, in which the charge is 350 schillings ($18.91) per twin-bedded room, only 150 schillings ($8.10) per person for quad-room 8, a beauty. All rooms sport Tyrolean feather-stuffed coverlets over their beds. And breakfast and free showers are included in all charges. From the train station in Innsbruck, take tram 6 to the Igls terminal—a 20-minute, 20-schilling trip.

READERS' PENSION AND PRIVATE HOME SELECTIONS: "We stumbled onto **Pension Glockenhaus,** 3 Weiherburggasse (phone 85-563), where singles are 180 schillings ($9.72), doubles 340 schillings ($18.37), including breakfast with unlimited coffee, and free showers. This pension, operated by Reinhard and Traudl Jahn, both English-speaking and extremely helpful, is in a remodeled, quaint, 300-year-old building, a ten-minute walk from the city center. It offers a real Austrian family atmosphere, because breakfast is served in a private kitchen. And finally, Herr Jahn also rents two dorms, with 9 and 12 cots apiece, for the astonishing rate of only 100 schillings ($5.40) per person—ideal for backpackers" (Agnes and Chris Lehn, Minneapolis, Minnesota; seconding recommendation from R. J. Gander, Llandrindod, Wales). . . . "**Frau Maria Rauschgatt,** at 6 Karwendelstrasse (phone 232-834), will no longer pick up tourists at the train station, but her apartment is only five minutes from the station by bus C, or a 25-minute walk, and the two rooms she rents provide excellent value at 130 schillings ($7.02) per bed in a twin-bedded room, 120 schillings ($6.48) per bed in a quad, breakfast included. The apartment is a second floor walk-up; showers are free" (Alan Reisner, Jamaica, New York). . . . "Our suggestion for Mutters, near Innsbruck, is **Haus Toni Wieshaber,** 2 Schulgasse (phone 22-950): super clean, super hospitable, and we were even able to enlist her daughter's babysitting service for a night away from our two small sons. Breakfast was plentiful (Kaiser rolls, cheese or sliced meats, coffee, cocoa or milk), and the rate only $35 for two rooms with a total of four beds. Clean air, and such friendly people!" (Mr. and Mrs. Dwight M. Fruge, Bellevue, Washington).

YOUTH HOSTELS AND STUDENT HOTELS: The 190-bed **Jugendherberge** at 147 Reichenaustrasse (phone 46-1-79 or 46-1-80), is the official youth hostel of Innsbruck, open all year around, and charging 120 schillings ($6.48) per person for the first night, 100 schillings ($5.40) for all successive nights, in six-bedded dorms, with breakfast and linen thrown in free. This is easily reached in five minutes from the train station, on Bus O, which stops directly in front of the hostel.

The private youth hostels of Innsbruck are two in number: **MK-Jugendzentrum,** 8a Sillgasse (phone 31-311), five minutes on foot from the station, consists of 120 beds in dorms of from 6 to 14 persons apiece, charges only 90 schillings ($4.86) per night, breakfast included, but is not open all year around, and varies its months of operation: phone first the **Schwedenhaus,** 17b Rennweg (phone 25-814), which is also called "Torsten-Arneus Haus" after a Swedish sponsor, is a modern, bungalow-like, two-story structure that accepts up to 80 guests in dorms holding 6 to 15 beds apiece. Daily rate, breakfast included, is again 90 schillings ($4.86). This one is open July and August only, and may be reached from the train station by taking Bus C to the Handelsakademie stop and walking 300 yards (straight ahead towards the wooden bridge) from there.

The costlier student hotel of Innsbruck is a tall, Hilton-like construction known as the **Internationale Studentenhaus,** 64 Innrain (phone 21-794), which houses local university students throughout all periods of the year other than from July 1 to September 30, when it's made available to tourists. It offers 500 beds, all in singles and twins, at a bed-and-breakfast rate of 220 schillings ($11.89) and 300 schillings ($16.21) respectively, including free showers. There's no curfew here. From the train station, walk into Meraner Strasse, then (after crossing Maria-Theresia-Strasse) into Anichstrasse, from which Innrain soon turns left; the walk requires all of ten minutes.

3. Low-Cost Food

The most exciting dining opportunity of Innsbruck is its **University Mensa,** 15 Herzog-Sigmund-Ufer, because it serves persons of any age, and requires no membership credentials or student identification; it also charges only 30 schillings ($1.62) for a two-course meal served in its self-service section (soup, pork chops and vegetable were on during a recent visit), only 65 schillings ($3.51) for a better two courses (soup, then wiener schnitzel, with salad) in a slightly tonier, smaller, table-service section adjoining the cafeteria. Hours are 9 to 7 p.m. on weekdays, 11 a.m. to 1 p.m. only on Saturdays, closed Sundays; and the Mensa is easily reached from the train station by walking up the Salurner Strasse and Maximilian Strasse into Kaiser-Franz-Joseph-Strasse, then turning left into the Huebnerstrasse until you reach the Universitätsbrücke (University Bridge crossing the Inn River: the Mensa is immediately there, facing the river.

Though some budget tourists take all their meals at the University Mensa, some spend slightly more for the Austrian specialties of six scattered Innsbruck cafes:

Nordsee, 11 Maria-Theresia-Strasse, open seven days a week, is a remarkably inexpensive, self-service fish restaurant selling fried sole and potato salad for 45 schillings ($2.43), salad bowls called "Fitnessteller" for 47 schillings ($2.54).

Hörtnagel 4 Burggraben, shares the premises of a butcher shop, where it offers a two-course "menu" (soup, roast pork and salad, let's say) for 60 schillings ($3.24), a splurgey alternative (with roast lamb or venison as the entree) for 100 schillings ($5.40). Open weekdays until 6:30 p.m., open Saturdays until 1 p.m. only.

Wienerwald, 24 Museumstrasse, half way between the station and the Inn River, is Innsbruck's branch of the chicken specialist: quarter grilled chicken (with accompaniments) for 55 schillings ($2.97), a filling chicken soup with noodles for 16 schillings (86¢). Open daily until 1 a.m., its best feature.

Uni-Snack, 1 Rechengasse, off the Innrain in the university area, is a student hangout featuring cheap, two-course student meals (soup, veal cutlet, salad) for only 42 schillings ($2.27), a heavy goulash soup for 20 schillings ($1.08).

Siesta Snackbar, in the same area, one flight up (over the supermarket) at 100 Innrain, lists three different two-course meals at 30 schillings, 45 schillings, and 60 schillings (the latter, $3.18), respectively.

And **Adambräu,** 16 Heiliggeiststrasse, two minutes from the train station and in a slightly higher category, is a brewery restaurant of heavy oaken tables and chairs, specializing—at a highly reasonable cost—in such Austrian classics as "beuscherl" (calves' lungs stewed in vinegar) with a large "semmelknödel" (dumpling) for 60 schillings ($3.24), wiener schnitzel with roast potatoes and salad for 80 schillings ($4.32), and, best of all, beer brewed in the same building, fresh from the barrel, for 22 schillings ($1.18) per cool half liter. Open daily except Sundays until 10 p.m.

4. Sights & Excursions

Though the city's main attractions are its surrounding mountains, in which tourists gambol about with glee, it maintains a number of lesser draws for those rainy days when you won't go wandering. Among the possibilities are:

The Alpenzoo, at Weiherburg, Innsbruck's most popular in-city visit, is Europe's only Alpine Zoo, a collection of all animals living in Austria's mountain regions including a number of otherwise-extinct species: you see bison, wildcats, wolves, bears, otters, beavers, griffons, vultures, owls, eagles and buzzards, all roaming or flying about in well-maintained settings. This is open seven days a week, from 9 a.m. to 6 p.m., for an admission charge of 32 schillings ($1.72) for adults, 16 schillings (86¢) for children under 15, and is reached in 30 minutes on foot from the station, or by taking Bus Z.

Hofkirche and **Volksmuseum,** 2 Universitätstrasse. The former is a large royal chapel adorned with unusual, over-life-sized bronze statues, and is the burial place of the Emperor Maximilian and Andreas Hofer, the Tyrol's national hero. The Volksmuseum, Innsbruck's second most popular sight, displays Tyrolean farmhouse furniture, tools, costumes and wood-carved Christmas cribs. Combined entrance fee for both institutions is 15 schillings (81¢) for adults, 7 schillings (37¢) for children, and hours are 9 a.m. to noon and 2 to 5 p.m., daily except Sundays, on Sundays until noon only.

The **Hofburg,** 1 Rennweg, a royal residence originally constructed by the Emperor Maximilian in the early 1500s, is to Innsbruck what Versailles is to Paris, Schönbrunn to Vienna—but pocket-sized. It was reconstructed in rococo style by the Empress Maria Theresia in the early 18th century. Open every day from 9 a.m. to 4 p.m., for an admission charge of 20 schillings ($1.08) for adults, 5 schillings (27¢) for children.

The **Goldenes Dachl,** at the upper end of Maria-Theresia-Strasse (near the Inn River), is a large "balcony" whose top is formed by a roof of 2,657 gold-plated tiles. It was constructed by Maximilian in the year 1500 to serve as a "royal box" for watching armor-clad knights riding armor-clad horses as they fought in tournaments in the square below. In the structure is now an "Olympiamuseum" showing video-films of the two Olympic Winter

Games that took place in Innsbruck in 1964 and 1976. Open daily, 9:30 a.m. to noon, 2 to 5 p.m., for an entrance fee of 20 schillings ($1.08) for adults, 10 schillings (54¢) for children.

The **Stadtturm** (City Tower), near the Goldenes Dachl, in the old town, is a favorite spot for taking photographs of Innsbruck and the surrounding mountains. Built in the early 14th century as a Gothic tower and reconstructed in 1560, it was also a medieval prison in those ancient times. Open March to October only, from 10 a.m. to 5 p.m. daily, for an admission of 15 schillings (81¢) for adults, 7 schillings (37¢) for children.

Tiroler Zeughaus, Zeughausgasse, originally Maximilian's armory, is today a museum for such diverse subjects as minerology, cartography, mountain stream and avalanche control, lumbering, fire fighting, coaches and old locomotives. Open May through September only, from 10 a.m. to 5 p.m. (Sundays from 9 to noon), for an admission charge of 15 schillings (81¢) for adults, 7 schillings (37¢) children.

Tiroler Landesmuseum, 15 Museumstrasse, is Innsbruck's museum of paintings, both ancient and modern, and is open all year from 9 a.m. to 5 p.m., Sundays to noon; 15 schillings for adults, 7 for children.

EXCURSIONS, TOURS AND MOUNTAIN HIKING: You haven't been

to Innsbruck until you've gone up into the surrounding mountains, and the best of the peaks—Innsbruck's "house mountain," in fact—is the **"Hafelekar,"** 2334 meters above sea level and three miles north of the city center. If you have the time and the weather is clear, you'll want to climb at least to the Seegrube stop half-way up on the great peak, via a funicular reached from the train station by taking tram 1 to the Hungerburg stop. From there, a round-trip by cable car to the Seegrube (1905 meters) is 157 schillings ($8.84), to the top of Hafelekar and return 189 schillings ($10.21). Eurailpass holders receive a 20% reduction. The panoramic view from either Seegrube or the peak of Hafelekar of the entire mountain chain is something you'll not forget.

A second cable car service is operated from Igls, three miles to the southeast of Innsbruck (near the Winter Olympic Ski Jump), to the top of the **Patscherkofel** mountain (2,247 meters). Take tram 6 to Igls (last stop), from which a round-trip cable car ticket costs 124 schillings ($6.70). But Hafelekar is your better choice.

Summers only, the city operates a two-hour escorted motorcoach sightseeing tour of Innsbruck and vicinity, focusing on the Olympic sites, for a cost of 110 schillings ($5.94), both mornings and afternoons. Tickets are sold at the "Zimmernachweis" office outside the train station, which will also advise you on departure hours, which vary. Departure point is the train station.

From the same "Zimmernachweis" office (see above), you'll be advised about a fascinating and entirely *free* day-long walking tour of the mountains, which the city also offers from June through September, leaving from the Kongresshaus at 8:30 a.m. daily, but available only to persons who can prove to the tourist office that they are planning a stay in Innsbruck of at least three days. Provided you're "repaying" the municipality in that fashion, you'll be transported by bus (with your group) to a nearby mountain—and off you'll go! Hiking time is four to six hours, the return to Innsbruck is between 4 and 6 p.m., and your only expense is for refreshments taken at a "gasthaus" up atop the mountain, where you stop at some point for rest and relaxation. If you survive, you're then given a

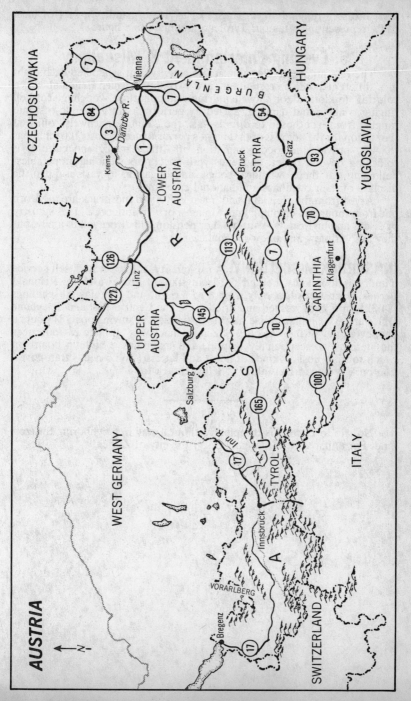

free, bronze "remembrance badge" of a "Kasermandl," a sort of local E.T., representing a famous Tyrolean mountain tale figure.

5. Evening Entertainment & Miscellany

The one unforgettable, unmissable activity, but scheduled each night in a different hotel or restaurant, is a two-hour **Tiroler Heimatabend,** a colorful, folkloric floor show featuring schuhplattling, yodeling, cowbell ringing, singing and dancing, all led by performers in authentic costume ranging from lederhosen to dirndls—ask the "Zimmernachweis" office at the station for the address of that night's performance. It costs 100 schillings ($5.40), provides a good summation of Alpine music and culture, is rollicking beyond belief, and ends with spectators standing atop tables, bellowing out their own local songs, and engaging in various jingoistic displays of their own flags and national emblems.

Apart from the Heimatabend, most visitors to Innsbruck are too worn out from mountain-climbing and Alpine sports to support a large industry of discos and nightspots. Your hotel or pension will direct you to a few, but they are very few and unexceptional.

INNSBRUCK MISCELLANY: A top-quality, coin-operated, self-service laundry is found just behind the train station: **Münzwascherei Reinhold Berger,** open weekdays only from 8 to 6 p.m., and charging 80 schillings ($4.32) for 5 kilos washed and dried. . . . The **Central Post and Telephone Office** at 2 Maximilianstrasse has the distinction of staying open 24 hours a day, every day of the week. . . . "Zimmernachweis" (phone 23-766), near the station, is exceptionally helpful, and maintains a bulletin board on which tourists post all kinds of notes and letters ("Who needs transportation on VW bus to Helsinki?", "Sell rucksack for $4").

No trip to Europe is complete without a stay in neighboring Switzerland. For a first visit to that nation, try the city of Zurich.

ZURICH

Accounting in the Alps

IMAGINE A BOULEVARD lined at one end with banks and squat department stores, which suddenly opens into a lake of the brightest blue, covered with sailboats and swans. Consider a city of enormous commercial fame, where stock markets and brokers' houses stand a five-minute walk from brooding forests and mountain chateaux. Think of efficient business activity carried on amid sidewalk cafés and tea-room conversations.

Zurich, the locale of these contrasts, is the city I'd choose for a first introduction to the land of contrasts, Switzerland. It is, to begin with, a functioning Swiss city, and not a single-minded resort center like Lucerne or St. Moritz. And yet it enjoys all the better attributes of a Swiss tourist attraction: heartstopping scenery; the restful calm that comes from an atmosphere of cleanliness and honest dealing; the variety and interest to be found in the multilingual, multinational character of the country; and finally, costs that, if not low, are at least moderate enough to remove the fear of over-expense from your vacation thoughts.

1. A Quick Orientation

If your trip to Europe is a summer one, try to schedule your Zurich stay for August 1, the national independence day of the country, when bonfires are burned on the mountain tops, bands play on every city square, and cafés stay open all night. The holiday is lovingly celebrated by the Swiss; every home in Zurich puts out a Swiss flag, and the banners of the 23 Swiss cantons are displayed round the lake. During this period, the hotel situation in Zurich becomes very tight (although not desperate), and you'd do well to stop in at the *Verkehrsbureau* (city tourist office) in the railroad station building, to the right as you leave the main entrance, and request their aid in finding a room (booking fees of 2 francs for one person, 3 francs for two, 4 francs for three). At all other times in Zurich, you can do it without official aid by simply consulting the recommendations that follow below.

GETTING AROUND: But first a warning: the taxis here are (except for those of Stockholm) the most expensive in all of Europe; it's therefore vital that you quickly master the bus and streetcar system (there are no subways), considered to be one of the finest of Europe (free transportation maps are available from the tourist office in the Central Station).

If you plan to do a great deal of traveling, you'll want to purchase a 4-franc ($1.90) "day ticket" good for unlimited rides on both the buses and streetcars within a 24-hour period. Otherwise, the cost for a single ride is one franc (47¢) for up to five stops, 1.40 francs (66¢) for from six stops to the city limits; single ride tickets can be purchased only from dispensing machines located at the trolley and bus stops themselves. If you'll be spending several days in Zurich, it will pay to purchase one of two different discount booklets available at major newsstands: the first, for 9 short rides, costs 6 francs ($2.85); the other, for 12 long rides, 12 francs.

The **airport** is connected with the center of Zurich by a modern train that goes right to an underground station underneath the arrival terminal. The **Central Railroad Station** of Zurich, built over 100 years ago in the very heart of the city, houses the city tourist office *(Verkehrsbureau),* where maps and many helpful brochures are available for the asking.

And now let's quickly seek a hotel. Though not as cheap as those in lower-cost Geneva, they can still be found in budget categories.

2. Hotels

There is no such thing as a bad Swiss hotel. This is the "nation of hotel-keepers," the training ground for aspiring hotel managers of every land. The standards taught at the famous Swiss hotel schools are so very impeccable as to be downright ridiculous. I visited a class in Lausanne where aspiring hôteliers were being taught which of six glasses to use for serving Bordeaux wine.

The difference, therefore, between a low-cost and a deluxe Swiss hotel is in decoration, not in comfort, and not in service. The budget hotels could not possibly be any cleaner than they already are; and the service could not be more polite. Because of that, and to be perfectly frank, you need have no qualms about staying at virtually any budget hotel in Zurich. But we'll set forth the chief qualities of a few outstanding choices. Unless otherwise stated, all the following hotels have elevators, and most of them provide a free breakfast for the price of a room (all also include service and taxes in their rates, which makes their prices not quite as high as they might first appear). Those in our first category are listed in ascending order of preference, beginning with three rather basic spots, then moving on to two normal budget hotels—the Bristol and the Limmathof—and then continuing with the type of Swiss hostelry about which we can wax rhapsodic.

ZURICH'S LEAST EXPENSIVE HOTELS: Hotel St. Georg, 11 Weberstrasse (phone 241-11-44), one of the cheapest we've found, is a five-minute

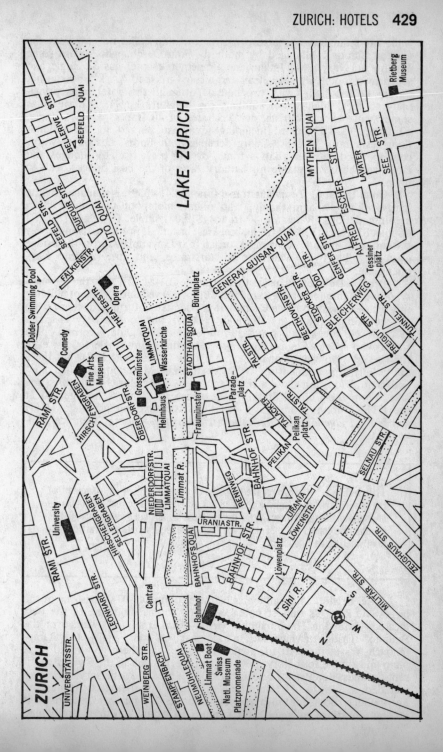

ZURICH

LAKE ZURICH

Rietberg Museum

BELLERIVE STR.
SEEFELD QUAI
SEEFELD STR.
DUFOUR STR.
FALKENSTR.
UTO QUAI

MYTHEN QUAI
ESCHER STR.
LAVATER STR.
SEE STR.
ALFRED ESCHER STR.
Tessiner platz

GENERAL·GUISAN·QUAI
Bürkliplatz
LIMMATQUAI
Wasserkirche
STADTHAUSQUAI
BEETHOVENSTR.
STOCKER STR.
TÖDI STR.
GENFER STR.
BLEICHERWEG
FREIGUT STR.
TUNNEL STR.

Dolder Swimming Pool
Comedy
Fine Arts Museum
THEATERSTR.
Opera
RAMI STR.
HIRSCHENGRABEN
OBERDORFSTR.
Grossmünster
Helmhaus
Fraumünster
Parade-platz
TALSTR.
TALACKER
PELIKAN
Pelikan platz
SELNAU STR.

University
RAMI STR.
LEONHARD STR.
HIRSCHENGRABEN
SELLERGRABEN
NIEDERDORFSTR.
LIMMATQUAI
Limmat R.
RENNWEG
BAHNHOF STR.
URANIA
URANIASTR.
LÖWENSTR.
ZEUGHAUS STR.

UNIVERSITÄTSSTR.
WEINBERG STR.
Central
BAHNHOFS QUAI
BAHNHOF STR.
Löwenplatz
Sihl R.
MILITÄR STR.

STAMPFENBACH
NEUMÜHLEQUAI
Limmat Boat.
Swiss Natl. Museum
Platzpromenade
Bahnhof

N W S E

walk from the Stauffacherstrasse streetcar stop (take no. 14 from the Central Station). Managed by motherly Frau Oesch, who speaks some English but very good Italian and French, the hotel has 30 single and seven twin rooms, all very clean and nicely furnished. (Ask for room no. 54 on the top floor, with two beds.) Although the hotel rents principally to local high-school students for long-term stays, it always has some available for tourists, at 1985 rates of 40 francs ($19.04) single, 60 francs ($28.57) twin, including breakfast, served in the ground-floor restaurant. The St. Georg occupies four floors, has an elevator, coin-operated showers (half a franc, or 23¢ per), two TV-lounges and large washbasins available for laundry. One of the best budget deals in town.

Hotel Italia, 61 Zeughausstrasse (phone 241-4339), is managed by the hard-working Papagni family, who offer simple but thoroughly clean accommodations. Rates are 40 francs ($19.04) single, 60 francs ($28.57) double, 82 francs ($39.04) triple, breakfast included. From the main railway station, walk up to Löwenstrasse, turn left at Löwenplatz, cross the bridge over the Sihl River, walk into Militärstrasse, and turn left into Kanonengasse.

Pension Dula, 50 Clausiusstrasse (phone 251-24-22), near the university, occupies three floors of an old but well-preserved and well-kept building in which 20 guest rooms are simply but adequately furnished; there is no elevator. Single rooms are 30 francs ($14.28), but doubles only 44 francs ($20.95). No breakfast is served. Proprietress Hilde Dula, a retired opera singer who speaks English well, also rents three tiny single rooms, each the size of a railway compartment, for only 20 francs ($9.52), but these are usually in permanent use by Swiss students. Most rooms in this quiet and central location have a panoramic view over Zurich, including the lake. From the Central Station, take streetcars 10 or 6, and get off at the ETH Station, from which the Dula is a five-minute walk. (ETH stands for *Eidgenössische Technische Hochschule—*Federal Technical University).

THE SWISS FRANC: For the purposes of this chapter, we've assumed that the worth of the Swiss franc is about 48 U.S. ¢, reflecting a current exchange rate of approximately 2.10 francs to the dollar. Prices set forth in Swiss francs, in this chapter, are correct for 1985; however, their dollar equivalents may vary slightly from what we've calculated.

Hotel Bristol, 34 Stampfenbachstrasse (phone 47-07-00), is one of the largest of Zurich's budget hotels, with 60 rooms, and one of the best located—from the Hauptbahnhof (main railroad station) walk over the Bahnhof Bridge (which doesn't appear on our map) to Stampfenbachstrasse, turn left for about 100 yards, and there you'll find it. A plain and simple four-story grey building, very much in the Swiss style, it rents bathless doubles for 65 francs ($30.95), breakfast and service charges included; singles for 45 francs (and there are lots of singles); triples and four-bedded rooms for much less per person; caters mainly to students, but accepts guests of all ages, and families to whom it offers family-plan arrangements permitting children to sleep free in the room of their parents, sharing a parent's bed.

Hotel Limmathof, 142 Limmatquai (phone 47-42-20), always one of our best-recommended budget hotels in Zurich, has been working through a long-term renovation project and has surfaced as an attractive, well-kept and beautifully located small hotel (55 rooms) that is excellent value for the money. Situated on the Limmat River, directly across the Bahnhof Bridge from the railroad station, the Limmathof has retained its charming turn-of-the-century façade while updating its interior. All rooms now have shiny parquet floors, most have modern suites of furniture and bright Persian throw rugs. The breakfast room, with its Swiss chairs and open balcony, is charming. And on the ground floor, there's a rustic Weinstube that provides a meeting-place for locals and guests, as well as three-course meals for only 11 Swiss francs ($5.23). All in all, a good buy at the uniform charge of 38 francs ($18.09) per person in bathless rooms, double, breakfast and service charge included, 35 francs per person in triples, 45 francs single.

Pension Fontana, 57 Gloriastrasse (phone 251-34-53), in the university area, has been in business for more than 100 years, enjoys 40 beds, four floors, no elevator, and charges 35 francs ($16.66) single, 52 francs ($24.76) double, 65 francs ($30.95) triple, for adequately furnished rooms inclusive of breakfast. Its present owner, the energetic and charming Frau Rosa Evelyn Bircher, keeps the establishment clean and shining with the aid of numerous Spanish and Italian chambermaids and charwomen whom you will constantly see washing up and waxing floors, dusting and polishing. From the Central Station, take streetcar 6 and get off at the Voltastrasse stop, which is directly in front of the Fontana.

The alcohol-free **Burma Hotel** (phone 361-10-08), a 5-minute tramride (11 or 14) from the station, at 26 Schindlerstrasse (corner of Stampfenbach), has singles at 42 francs ($20) and doubles for 65 francs ($30.95), including breakfast, service and taxes. Friendly and cheerful, although somewhat less personal than others we've named, it is a fine budget establishment, with a sober-style restaurant downstairs where substantial hot plates start at a low 6 francs.

Hotel Seefeld, at 11 Seehofstrasse (phone 252-25-70), near the Opera House and the lake, is heavily patronized by Swiss businessmen who praise its quiet and central location. Manager Herr Platten charges 45 francs ($21.42) for a single, 66 francs ($31.42) for a double, breakfast included. To find the hotel, walk to the lakeside end of Bahnhofstrasse, cross the Quai-Bridge, and turn into Uto-Quai (the street facing the lake); Seehofstrasse is the third street turning left.

Pension Titlis, named after a mountain peak near Lucerne, is in the central but quiet section of town called Hottingen, at 44 Rütistrasse (phone 252-73-59), and can be reached by streetcar 3 from the station (get off at Römerhof). Multilingual Frau Hulda Züsli keeps everything spotless and pleasant, at reasonable rates: 27 to 33 francs single, 50 to 54 francs double, 62 francs triple, breakfast included.

ZURICH'S MODERATELY PRICED HOTELS: Hotel Limmathaus, 118

Limmatstrasse (phone 42-52-40), less than ten minutes on foot from the station, is a big and highly recommended tourist-class establishment, and probably the most recently built (but the highest-priced) of all the hotels in this chapter. The 100-bed building looks as if it had been designed by Walter Gropius; the rooms are furnished in Scandinavian style, with all-new furniture; there's an exceedingly helpful and friendly staff; and prices are 53 francs ($25.23) single, 105 francs ($50) for a double, with breakfast, showers, service and taxes always included. A top find. Take trams 4 or 13 to Limmatplatz—a four minute ride from the station (third stop).

Hotel Rothus, 17 Marktgasse (phone 252-15-30), another big hotel, is located in the most interesting area of Zurich—the Niederdorf, just a block or two from the river, in the center of the city, but in a quaint, medieval section of the town, filled with narrow streets for walkers only, statues and fountains at every small plaza, and packed also with the cafés and night-spots of Zurich—the Rothus (whose lobby is one flight up) is above a nightclub, whose activity and noise may disturb, but may delight, you. It is, as I have said, a large place, with 50 rooms, all with private shower, neat and proper in the clean, woodsy, old-fashioned Swiss-style (there are big feather blankets on each bed), and the prices are fairly good for high-priced Zurich: 50 francs for one of 14 single rooms, with breakfast, 85 francs for a double with two breakfasts, 125 triple, 145 quadruple, with service charge included. Don't be deterred by the appearance of the downstairs exterior; upstairs is a large and attractive lobby, and excellent budget rooms. In the vicinity of the Rothus, and with similar prices: **Hotel Splendid** at 5 Rosengasse (phone 252-58-50), recently modernized and redecorated by two young new owners—singles for 38 francs, doubles for 66 francs, including service, taxes and free showers. Generally speaking, the latter establishment is a bit more conservative than the Rothus and therefore might be preferred by readers way of the sometimes boisterous life that can erupt after 10 p.m. on the Niederdorfstrasse.

A relative newcomer to this book is **Hotel Ascona,** 17 Meinrad-Lienert Strasse (phone 35-27-23), in a five-floor building that lacks an elevator. Because of that, 1985 rates are only 44 francs ($20.95) single, 62 francs ($29.52) double or twin, 78 francs ($37.14) triple, 88 francs ($41.90) quad, breakfast included, showers for free, and English-speaking Frau Bergwerf, the proprietress, will also wash your laundry for free (in her machine), her time permitting. The hotel restaurant serves three-course menus for 10 francs ($4.76), and the small disco in the basement doesn't cause a problem as it closes at midnight. Ascona is reached by taking streetcar 3 from the Central Station, to the sixth stop, Lochergut; the hotel is less than 50 yards away. Not far away, at 121 Langstrasse, **Hotel Rothaus** (phone 241-24-51), is an unusually well run (even by Swiss standards), newly redecorated hotel. The Ender family, who operate it, have managed hotels for many years, speak English fluently, try hard to please their customers, take pains in maintaining virtually soundproof conditions (through double-glazed windows), and charge only 50 francs ($23.80) single, 85 francs ($40.47) double, always including breakfast. A restaurant on the ground floor serves various daily menus ranging from 8 to 16 francs. From the Central Station, take bus 31 and get off at the fourth stop, called Militär-Langstrasse.

Hotel Sternen Oerlikon, 335 Schaffhauserstrasse (phone 311-77-77), is less central than any we've named (only ten minutes, however, by trams 7 or 14 from the train station; the stop is Sternen), but good value for moderate prices; a large, but restful and quiet, old-fashioned hotel, with a particularly distinguished restaurant and wine cellar. It charges 48 francs ($22.86) for a single room with breakfast, 80 francs ($38.09) double with breakfasts—including the service charge.

Those are the best individual budget hotels. The best *area* for moderately priced (not cheap) rooms is along the side of the lake, next to the Opernhaus of Zurich, where there's a lovely little section, jammed with small hotels and pensions that normally cater to somewhat older and more relaxed tourists (the area is located precisely where the word "Opera" appears on our map of Zurich). To reach it, simply take your luggage and board a streetcar to the Kreuzstrasse, whose lakeside location you should love. There, just behind the nearby Opernhaus, you'll find the modest **Pension Beau-Site,** 40 Dufourstrasse (phone 251-11-47), a converted townhouse whose appearance is like that of a 19th-century Victorian home: it's only 40 francs ($19.04) for bed-breakfast-and-service in a single room, 66 francs ($31.42) for a double; reservations are probably needed in high season, since the capacity is only 24 beds, but you can try phoning.

HOTELS FOR THE BIG SPLURGE: Hotel Goldenes Schwert, 14 Markt-

gasse (phone 252-59-40), in an old, four-story, two-elevator building ideally located in the very heart of the old town within easy walking distance of the station, the lake and the museums, accommodates its 65-or-so guests in singles with private bath for 60 francs ($28.57), in doubles or twins with private bath for 90 francs ($42.85), and in triples so equipped for 115 francs ($54.76), always including breakfast. In the same area but closer to Bellevueplatz, the smaller **Hotel Villette** at 4 Kruggasse (phone 32-23-35), with its reception room on the second floor, was completely modernized in 1982, and now charges 47 francs ($22.34) for singles without bath, 90 francs ($42.85) for twins with shower and w.c., inclusive of breakfast, and for rooms with radio, telephone and TV, in an elevator-equipped building, no less. Restaurant on the street level, decorated very much in the Swiss style, serves raclette (you'll be reading about it in later pages) for 6 francs ($2.85), farmer's sausages with leeks and beans (superbly delicious) for 10 francs ($4.76), and a vast assortment of Swiss wines. The latter establishment is closed on Sundays. In the very same area, **Hotel Rössli,** at 7 Rössligasse (phone 251-71-66), on mediaeval horse stable grounds (Rössli means horses in Swiss German), managed by Herr Walser, and **Hotel Krone,** at 88 Limmatquai (facing the Limmat River), phone 251-42-22, operated by the friendly Amon family (husband and wife team), both charge 44 francs ($20.95) for bathless singles, 75 francs ($35.71) for bathless twins, 90 francs ($42.85) for doubles with bath, including breakfast, and are highly recommended by me.

A BUDGET-PRICED RESORT HOTEL: For a change of scene, the

influential, long-established Women's Temperance Union of Zurich operates a moderately priced resort hotel on the high-altitude outskirts of the city, spectacular in terms of both rates (by Zurich standards) and setting, particularly suitable for families with children. Imagine checking into a beautiful mountainside resort in Aspen or Vail, Colorado, and paying only $15 per person for room, breakfast and service! The hotel that provides just that, **Hotel Zürichberg,** at 21 Orellistrasse (phone 252-38-48), is located on the hills that surround Zurich, and from its flowered terrace you have a panoramic view of the town, the lake and the mountains. Room charges are 38 to 58 francs ($18.09 to $27.61) single (the higher rates for the rooms with better views), 63 to 88 francs ($30 to $41.90) for doubles, 110 francs ($52.38) for triples, 133 francs ($63.33) for quads, inclusive of breakfast for all, with no service charge added and no tipping expected. The 100-bed hotel is located four minutes walking distance from the Allmend Fluntern streetcar terminus. To reach it from the Central Station, take streetcar 6 to the end of the line, then change to streetcar 5, which goes to the Allmend Fluntern stop, high overlooking Zurich. And make reservations well in advance in summertime.

INTO THE SUBURBS:
If everything we've listed is full, there's still no reason to despair; head instead for the Zurich Railway Station and look for an automatic hotel telephone booking service near the escalators leading downstairs to the underground shopping center; then, push the button marked "Thalwilerhof," lift the receiver, wait a few seconds, and soon you'll be talking without charge to a Heidi-type hostelry that can put you up in summer for as little as 32.50 francs ($15.47) per person, including breakfast.

Herr Roduner's **Hotel Thalwilerhof** (phone 720-0603), subject of these complex instructions, is located directly in front of the train station (but in a Swiss-pretty lakeside setting) of Zurich-Thalwil, six miles southeast of town, near the lake shore. No fewer than 80 trains a day make the 15-minute trip from 5 a.m. to midnight from the Zurich train station, 80 other trains a day make the 15-minute trip from 5 a.m. to midnight from the Zurich train station, 80 other trains return from Thalwil to Zurich, and round-trip fare is 5.20 francs ($2.47)—the same ticket being valid in summer for a lake steamer which cruises every hour between Zurich and Thalwil, but for a 1-franc supplement. What makes the Thalwilerhof such a find are its dozen-or-so rooms without private bath (about half the rooms in the hotel), which rent at only 65 francs ($30.95) per twin, 90 francs ($42.85) triple, 110 francs ($52.38) quad, breakfast included, and free showers down the hall. The hotel also operates a large terrace restaurant serving two-course prix fixe menus for only 8 francs ($3.80). Even if you do find accommodations in Zurich, you may want to travel to Thalwil by train, eat on the 60-seat terrace while watching the sailing boats, surfers and steamers, then return to Zurich by boat (using your rail ticket, plus the 1-franc surcharge)—a perfect way to spend half a day, weather permitting.

An alternate to the Thalwilherhof, especially in September when fairs, exhibitions and conferences can cause a severe bed-shortage in Zurich itself, is the suburban **Hotel Bahnhof,** at 1 Neue Dorfstrasse (phone 713-31-31), in Langnau am Albis, again about six miles outside Zurich. At this small and intimate hotel, managed by Frau Barmettler, singles are only 25 francs ($11.90), doubles 50 francs ($23.80), triples 75 francs ($35.71), always including a hearty breakfast. From Zurich's Selnau Station, trains to Langnau run hourly, take 20 minutes, cost 2.80 francs one way, and the hotel is directly across the street from Langnau station.

READERS' PENSION SELECTIONS: "**Hotel Poly**, 63 Universitätstrasse (phone 362-94-40), operates an Annex where I recently obtained a bathless single room for only 46 francs ($21.90), including breakfast in the main house" (D.I. Wardle, Riverdale, New York; note by AF: 1985 rates are, for rooms without bath: 60 francs double, 80 francs triple; for rooms with private shower: 50 francs single; 80 francs double. Take streetcar 10 from Central Station directly to the hotel, which you can see if you sit on the left side of the streetcar. Location is excellent, near the Technical University, just a ten-minute walk to Central Station. One of the nicest economy hotels of Zurich, with very friendly, English-speaking owner and staff). . . . "**Justinus Heim** at 146 Freudenbergstrasse (20 minutes from the station; take tram 10 and the Seilbahn) is usually the residence of students from four and five continents. I paid $14 for a spacious single room with breakfast, and free use of the showers downstairs" (Joseph Kaposi, Willowdale, Ontario, Canada; note by AF: this is a modern, nonprofit hotel, which specializes in accommodating students from developing countries, but accepts everyone, provided space is available. It's well managed by Herr Max Giger, an idealist in the best sense of the term, and will charge, in 1985, 28 francs, $13.33, for a single, 48 francs, $22.86, double, 65 francs, $30.95, triple, including breakfast. No curfew; free showers; 5 floors of rooms serviced by a lift; and free use of a large kitchen with 12 hot plates automatically switched off after 15 minutes, a clever energy-saving device. When I last visited in mid-1984, students from 32 nations (and 9 religions) were in attendance, including representatives from Peru, Uganda, Cyprus, Poland, Chile and Macao, most of them studying at the Technical University. Phone 361-38-06). . . . . "At the **Pension Peyer,** 39 Feldeggstrasse (phone 252-30-03), on a quiet street near the lake, our double room for 65 francs ($30.95), including breakfast, was large and sunny, well furnished, had a TV set and elegant balcony with turn-of-the-century, art nouveau, stained-glass windows. And guests could use the refrigerator and washing facilities" (Charles Dicken, San Diego, California).

READERS' HOTEL SELECTIONS: "Hotel Otter, in the old district of Munster, 7 Oberdorfstrasse (phone 251-22-07), has outstandingly clean double rooms for 70 francs a night. The hotel is quiet, but in the center of everything" (CDR J.B. Farrell, Ewa Beach, Hawaii). . . . "The OASE at 38 Freiestrasse, 8032 Zurich, is maintained by a Protestant religious organization that accepts all creeds, offers free use of a community kitchen (fully equipped with pots, dishes and cutlery), imposes no curfew, rents double rooms only to married couples, and charges only 33 francs ($15.71) for singles, 50 francs ($23.80) for doubles, breakfast included. While most rooms are rented on a monthly basis to residents of Zurich, a few are available to transients; phone first (252-39-81). These are clean, modern rooms, which enjoy excellent side facilities—laundry, TV room, music room, small gym. And if you're lucky enough to get in (the vacancies are few), take tram 3 from the Central Station to Hottingerplatz" (Beth Kelsey, Pedora, North Dakota). . . . "Hotel Rütli at 43 Zähringerstrasse (phone 251-54-26), not far from the station, is a brand-new little hotel of the Women's Temperance Organization (Frauenverein), located over their restaurant of the same name. Price is 37.50 francs per person in double rooms, singles 48 francs, not including breakfast, and showers on each floor are free. A particularly good choice for single girls" (Ingeborg Söderlund, Stockholm, Sweden).

FOR WOMEN, FAMILIES AND COUPLES ONLY: Zurich's accommo-

dations for female and family travelers are among the best in Europe: they include, first, the big and recently built **Foyer Hottingen,** 31 Hottingerstrasse (phone 47-93-15), whose most attractive feature—apart from its phenomenal (for Switzerland) prices of between 15 and 27 francs per person, including breakfast and free showers—is the exceptional warmth, charm, and efficiency of a dedicated staff, headed by a remarkable Mother Superior, Joseph-Marie. Open the entire year, and operated by a Catholic organization, the receptionist here is a nun, and the only inconvenience is a strict midnight curfew, after which the front door is locked. The Foyer will take not only young women, but older ones, as well as families with children and mature couples. Take tram 3 from the main station to Hottingerplatz. Even more modern than the Foyer, but for women and married couples only, is Zurich's **Y.W.C.A.,** located in an impressive recent construction called the **Martahaus,** at 36 Zähringerstrasse (phone 251-45-50), directly across the river from the main railroad station (walk across the bridge in front of the station, not shown on our map). Both the building and its interior furnishings could win an architectural award, and the prices win our $25-a-day award: exactly 30 francs ($14.28) per person in twin rooms without private bath, only 20 francs ($9.52) for a cot in one of two six-bedded dorms, always including breakfast and free showers; there are no singles. Write well in advance for summer reservations, and address your letters to the Martahaus. A close runner-up to the superb Martahaus is the smaller (80 beds) **Pension St. Josef** at 64 Hirschengraben (phone 251-27-57), five minutes on foot from the station. A modern, Catholic institution managed by an English-speaking nun, Sister Michel, it prices singles at 35 francs, doubles at 28 francs per person, triples and four-bedded rooms at 24 francs per bed per night, including breakfast and free showers. While there's a 12:30 a.m. curfew here, that regulation isn't strictly observed during the three summer months, provided you inform Sister Michel in advance of your late homecoming. Atmosphere is pleasant, location ideal, and the Josefsheim even provides supper for 6 francs.

FOR MEN ONLY: The center city **Y.M.C.A.** (also called Vereinshaus) at 33 Sihlstrasse (phone 221-36-73), between the Central Station and Paradeplatz, rents a few rooms (three twins and two singles, the other 20 are permanently occupied by locals) to transients in its large and rather modern building at the price of 25 francs ($11.90) per day, 155 francs ($73.80) per week, per person, service included. Low-cost food is available in a second-floor self-service cafeteria, open Monday to Friday from 7:45 a.m. to 7:45 p.m., Saturday 10 a.m. to 1:45 p.m., and serving breakfast for 4 francs ($1.90), two-course meals for 7.50 francs ($3.57), soup-sandwich-and-coffee for 6.50 francs ($3.09). . . . Secret of secrets: two *notbetten* (emergency beds) in a corridor on the sixth floor of the Martahaus (see above) are rented to men only for 20 francs ($9.52), including breakfast and showers. How's that for condescension!

3. Restaurants & Meals

CAFÉS: The cafés of Zurich are in a class by themselves. They're meeting halls, trysting spots, employment centers—and each of them caters to a specialized conversational group. The citizens of Zurich relax in cafés for hours on end. Their waiters would no sooner ask you to move on than they would criticize the sacred Swiss Army.

The venerable **Odeon Café,** on the corner of Limmatquai and Torgasse, where Lenin sat out the First World War, is the most famous and sophisticated of the Zurich cafés, an historic spot, but one charging only 2 francs (95¢) for coffee. The much more slickly modern **Select Café,** at 16 Limmatquai, corner of Schifflände Platz, is today heavily patronized by tourists, and it's a pleasant though no longer very European spot. Alcohol is not served, but coffee is—the best coffee in Zurich—and you can sit here all day and evening on a single cup (2 francs). **Café Litteraire** at 19 Schützenstrasse, corner of Lintheschergasse, popular with a talky and attractive crowd of Swiss, is a personal favorite of mine, as is the **Gran Café** at 66 Limmatquai, near the river.

MEALS: Fondue—melted cheese with wine and Kirsch, lapped up with chunks of bread—is the food specialty of Switzerland, and you ought to head immediately for a place that serves it. Try, for instance, the well-managed **Restaurant Walliser Kanne,** a block from the railroad station at 21 Lintheschergasse, corner of Schützengasse. This is a relatively high-priced steakhouse, but it dishes up a huge portion of fondue Valaisienne for 13.50 Swiss francs ($6.42). The more moderately priced **Blockhaus**, on 4 Schifflände, serves a similar fondue, and this time for only 8.50 francs (Fondue Neuchâteloise), with other inexpensive items to round off the meal. Order, however, only one serving of fondue for two persons—it comes in quantities much too massive for a single $25-a-day'er —but don't specifically advise the restaurant of your intention. Let one of you order the fondue, the other a cheaper item; it is served in such a way (small squares of bread, a metal bowl of melted cheese) as to make it easy for both of you to dip away together. Rösti—a specially made, Swiss type of fried potatoes—is another dish found only in this country. It's usually served with sausages and salad, costs about 7.50 francs ($3.57) in that plate combination. If ordered separately, order again only one portion for two persons; the plate of rösti I had last summer in Zurich was as big as a pizza pie. Where to find it? Try the **Olivenbaum**, at 10 Stadelhoferstrasse, where various plates are priced at 6.50 to 7.50 francs and are served all day. Open daily, from 6:30 a.m. till 8:30 p.m. on weekdays, to 7:30 p.m. weekends.

And a Bit About Raclette

The **Restaurant Raclette-Stube**, at 16 Zähringerstrasse, is the only fulltime raclette stube in Zurich. And raclette consists of a large platter of melted cheese accompanied by a boiled potato, pickled onion, and pickle; you spice the cheese with paprika, salt and pepper, then eat it with the chunks of potato and pickle (one uses forks and knives for this, unlike fondue). Each platter costs only 5.80 francs and the idea is to eat one platter, then request another and go on like that until you are full. In some parts of Switzerland, they even have raclette-eating contests to see who can get down the most platters (on a very hungry evening, I only managed to polish off three). Closed Wednesdays.

THE FRAUENVEREIN RESTAURANTS: The most phenomenal budget

eating spots in Zurich are a somber chain of restaurants operated by the city's Women's Temperance Union (*Zürcher Frauenverein für Alkoholfreie Wirtschaften*), which are generally known either as Frauenverein restaurants or simply Alkoholfreie restaurants, and where the strongest drink served is cider; they're often filled with hard-eyed, pinch-mouthed people who look eternally suspicious that somebody, somewhere, is enjoying himself or herself. I'd go there for most of my meals, nevertheless, because they're moderately priced and typically Swiss.

There are nine such places in Zurich, each bearing a separate name. Hope and I last ate at the **Restaurant Rütli**, at 43 Zähringerstrasse, a clean, woodsy-looking and austerely joyless place (like all the Alkoholfreie restaurants), where Hope had, for 10 francs ($4.76), a big bowl of mushroom soup and black bread, followed by a huge plate of Hungarian goulash and rice, and salad. For the same 10 francs, I had soup, a small mixed grill, cauliflower and potatoes. Not only was there no service charge, but better yet, tipping is absolutely prohibited throughout the Frauenverein chain.

A larger Frauenverein restaurant, and one I'd more strongly recommend, is the previously mentioned **Olivenbaum,** 10 Stadelhoferstrasse, in the building next to the Zurich-Stadelhofen Railroad Station, in the area of the Stadttheater, near the lake. It's open every day of the week, and if you'll order from the German-language menu—never the English one—you'll find two-course meals priced at not more than 7.80 francs, plus two francs for dessert, with the service charge always included in the price. Simply look for a sign reading "Alkoholfreies Restaurant," which designates the Olivenbaum. Prices here are slightly higher on Sundays.

A smaller Frauenverein restaurant is known as the **Restaurant Seidenhof,** and is found in the same building that houses the popular Seidenhof Hotel (which is also owned by the ubiquitous Frauenverein) at 7 Sihlstrasse, just a block from the Jelmoli Department Store, off the Bahnhofstrasse.

THE FABULOUS RESTAURANT URANIA LÖWENBRÄU: The larg-

est budget restaurant in Zurich, and the most consistently satisfying (although a bit higher in price than the Frauenvereins), is the **Urania Löwenbräu** at 9 Uraniastrasse (one block off Bahnhofstrasse)—which you reach from the station by walking down Bahnhofstrasse and turning left at the second traffic light. Actually, there are several Urania Restaurants in the same building. The one you're looking for is the Laube—a 200-person room, light, bright, and without tablecloths, but with plate meals (to be ordered only from the daily, typed tageskarte) averaging 7 and 11 francs, some of which are preceded by soup. Every day after 3 p.m., Laube serves its famous *Wädli* for 5 francs: salted and cooked pork pieces—rib, leg, and tongue—which provide reason enough for paying it a visit. Evenings a three-piece band plays music for dancing—at a small extra charge to you.

SELF-SERVICE CAFETERIAS: Though there aren't many, two accepta-

ble serve-yourself establishments are found in or near the two train stations of Zurich: the **Hauptbahnhof** (main station), where the simply titled Cafeteria Self-Service offers plates for 5.80 francs ($2.76) to 6.50 francs ($3.09); and the **Enge Station,** at whose Tessiner Platz you'll find the huge Hippo Self-Service, offering half a roast chicken with steamed potatoes for 7.50 francs ($3.57), Berner sausage with noodles for 6.70 francs ($3.19). Generally, I'd favor the normal restaurants in Zurich.

THE SILBERKUGELS: A Chock Full O'Nuts in Zurich? This may come

as a great surprise to visiting New Yorkers, but the **Silberkugels** are almost an exact copy (Swiss translation) of that venerable budget institution. There are nine such restaurants in the city and they all feature the familiar quick counter service, a limited, low-cost menu, and "Absolutely No Tipping Allowed." All are new, bright, modern and friendly and well frequented by Swiss lunchers-in-a-hurry. Even the bill of fare is Americanized. Here you can get a "Beefy" hamburger for from 2.30 to 5 francs. But you'll eat more cheaply by choosing one of the two daily hot plates, priced from 3 francs up, and augmenting that with a delicious bowl of yogurt mixed with fresh fruits for 1.60 francs. The most convenient Silberkugel to the main railway station is at 14 Bahnhofplatz—across from the front entrance and to the right. The other branches are located in the subway passage under the Bahnhofplatz (this one stays open late), at 120 Badenerstrasse, 7 Löwenstrasse, 46

Limmatstrasse, 33 Bleicherweg, 11 Franklinstrasse, 124 Altstetterstrasse, and 48 Stampfenbachstrasse. All nine also have take-out sections.

OTHERS: A good, typical, moderately priced restaurant? Across the Limmat River from the railroad station side, walk up Kirchgasse until you reach Oberdorfstrasse. Turn right and walk to 20 Oberdorfstrasse. You'll come upon the **Restaurant Weisser Wind,** a large, but quaint, and absolutely authentic Swiss restaurant, where for 10 francs ($4.76), you can have *Kässchnitte mit Ei und Schinken*—melted cheese on bread, with a fried egg on top, and cooked ham on the side. There are one or two cheaper plates than this, and two-course meals for as little as 9 francs ($4.28). Closed Sundays.

And, for natural-food lovers, **Vegetarian Restaurant Gleich,** 9 Seefeldstrasse, in the opera house area near Stadelhofer Platz, can be highly recommended: choice of 15 salads (including bean-and-onion) costing from 3.80 to 6 francs ($1.80 to $2.85). For larger appetites: an enormous cooked-vegetable bowl for 6.75 ($3.21), zucchini-and-tomato stew for 6.30 ($3), and two daily two-course menus, rather high at 15 francs ($7.14), but large enough to feed two (example: a plate of cannelloni—noodles with tomato sauce—followed by a delicious, gargantuan corn-and-cheese dish). All this is served in a tastefully furnished inside dining room and on an open-air, roof-covered terrace. It's a place where the eating and the surroundings are equally pleasant.

A highly atmospheric restaurant, well worth a stop-in for lunch or a Swiss specialty, is the relatively new **Zur Kantorei** on the ground floor of a picturesque 18th-century building in the tiny square of Neumarkt. Up above the restaurant is a long-established and well-known school for voice students, and therefore it's become a gathering place for singers and other people in the performing arts. The interior, with its hanging lamps of green glass, soaring windows and leather-covered seats, is an imaginative and comfortable setting for dining and conversation. Lunchtime is the best time to go, as set two-course lunches are priced from 9 to 13 francs. Throughout the day you can order cheese toast for 8 francs. There are some costly items on the menu, but the majority are reasonably priced and the quality high.

A SNACK OF ST. GALLER BRATWURSTS: Snack stands all over Zurich sell these famous white wursts, which are made from veal, not pork, but I'd buy mine at the renowned **Bell's,** 102 Bahnhofstrasse (one block from the station), which is undoubtedly the world's most beautiful butcher shop—even the lowly hamburger here has tastefully arranged cloves stuck in it. Hot grilled bratwursts sell at Bell's for 2.40 francs without bread, for 2.80 francs with, and there are attractive open sandwiches en gelée for 2 francs, as well as other picnic ingredients and salads.

DINING WITH THE SWISS ARMY: A short walk from Zurich's central railway station at 3 Militärstrasse, the Swiss Army serves civilians and soldiers alike at its **Militär-Kantine,** open Monday through Saturday from early in the morning until late at night. And while the civilian price for a two-course meal of 9.50 francs ($4.75) isn't exactly cheap (an example is a piquant vegetable soup, followed by a large and crisp cordon bleu with cauliflower and fried potatoes), the portions are huge and quality as good as in any far-more-expensive Swiss restaurant. Interesting as an oddity and for top quality at moderate cost; naturally, the military pay considerably less than you for the same meal.

DEPARTMENT STORE DINING: Jelmoli, Zurich's largest department store, on the Bahnhofstrasse near Paradeplatz, serves a continental break fast, but all you can eat, weekdays from 9 to 11 a.m., for 4 francs ($1.90). From 8 to 11 a.m., Saturdays only, buffet breakfast is served for 8 francs ($3.80); and there are three kinds of two-course lunches, ranging from 7 to 18 francs ($3.33 to $8.57), plus à la carte dishes. In the autumn of 1984, I tried *wurst à la diavolo* (cold veal salad with spicy salads), for 7.50 francs ($3.57), and found it filling and tasty. The enormous 300-seat dining room is on the top floor. If you are in a hurry, Jelmoli's ground-floor self-service cafeteria, with 60 seats inside and 60 on the street, called "Treff," is a good alternative choice, with quick lunches costing 6.50 francs ($3.09) for two choices daily. **Vilan,** next door to Jelmoli, with a 200-seat dining room on the upper floor—one-half of which is decorated and furnished like a Swiss chalet—sells three varieties of lunches, costing 7, 8 and 9 francs ($3.33, $3.80 and $4.29); you might choose curried lamb with rice and salad, beefsteak with steamed potatoes and vegetables, or veal stew in cream sauce with champignons, noodles and green salad. A typical Swiss dish, *rösti mit speck* (fried potatoes with bacon and two fried eggs) costs 6 francs ($2.85), large salad bowls 6.90 francs ($3.28), a glass of local wine (yes, Switzerland has excellent domestic wines) 2.10 francs ($1), beer 2.60 francs ($1.23), and a bottle of non-alcoholic beer (tastes like lemonade) 2 francs (95¢).

Finally, **Globus,** also on Bahnhofstrasse but nearer to the Central Station, in its top-floor restaurant called Le Pavillon, lists on the menu dishes not obtainable in the other department stores, such as *Basler mehlsuppe mit brotli* (soup made with flour, served with a roll) costing 3.75 francs ($1.78), quiche Lorraine for 7.50 francs ($3.57), and *geschnetzeltes rindfleisch mit spätzle* (a delicious beef stew with potato dumplings) for 9 francs ($4.28). There is a vast outdoor terrace, too, where coffee is served for 1.80 francs, croissants for 0.70 francs, beer for 2.50 francs, and Coke for 1.60 francs.

THE BIG SPLURGE: For the sake of your travel memories, shoot the wad at least once for a dinner consisting of fondue Bourguignon, that renowned Swiss specialty which is more a method of serving than a specific food item. What happens is that flaming braziers topped with bowls of boiling oil are placed on your table, along with trays of raw steak cut into one-inch squares. You stick long toothpicks into the squares, dip them each into the bowls of oil until they're cooked as you desire, then immerse the chunks in any of nine superb sauces placed on your table. If the chunks of meat are good, red beef, and if the sauces are well concocted (they usually are), then you'll have a memorable feast, and you'll run right out to Jemoli's Department Store the next day to buy a brazier for serving fondue Bourguignon to your astonished guests at home.

At several of the restaurants of Zurich, you'll be able to get a fondue

Bourguignon dinner for from 27.50 to 38 francs, but that's too much, even for a splurge. There's a 24.50-francs-per-person fondue Bourguignon ($11.66) at the Walliser Keller of the **Hotel Zürcherhof,** 21 Zähringerstrasse (a well-known restaurant to Zurich's gourmets, but with a surprisingly low-priced all-beef fondue, which must be purchased by at least two persons; closed Sundays)

READERS' RESTAURANT SELECTIONS: "The **Rheinfelder Bierhalle,** 76 Niederdorf Str., was our discovery. We ate there several times: the food is good and plentiful and very inexpensive. We had vegetable soup, beef goulash, boiled potatoes, lettuce and radish salad, all for 10 francs" (William A. Hagemann, Forest Hills, New York; note by AF: somewhat cheaper is the **Rheinfelder Bierhaus** at 19 Marktgasse, where the average price for a two-course menu—say, soup, weiner schnitzel with pommes frites and salad, is 9.50 francs). . . . "Our **Hürlimann Braustube,** directly opposite the Central Station at 9 Bahnhofplatz, offers a self-service cafeteria on the ground floor were complete meals may be had for from 8 to 10 francs" (Dominik Betschart, Manager, Hürlimann Braustube). . . . "The **Kosher Restaurant Schalom** in the Jewish Center Building at 33 Lavaterstrasse, near the Rietberg Museum and Enge Train Station, serves a filling daily menu for 18 francs (example: soup, beef rolls filled with sour cucumbers, stewed tomatoes and mashed potatoes). It's open Sunday through Friday from 11:30 a.m. to 2:30 p.m., and 6 to 10 p.m; Saturday from 11:30 a.m. to 2 p.m." (Pauline Rissman, Chicago, Illinois). . . . "We had a difficult time trying to find restaurants offering something other than omelettes and pizza. We did, however, find two vegetarian restaurants in Zurich which I feel would be very welcome by anyone reading your book, not to mention the vegetarians! The first, **Hiltl Vegi,** 28 Sihlstrasse, is really two restaurants in one. On the first floor it serves fast food, like McDonald's, ranging from vegetarian burgers to frozen yogurt, but with some prices on the high side. On the second floor is a sit-down dress-up restaurant, a great place for lunch after walking around the city. However, it did not compare to the second restaurant we found, **Vier Linden,** 48 Gemeindestrasse. We were so pleased with it we almost extended our stay in Zurich. The waitress and part-owner, Angelika, has a name to match her personality. I cannot recall enjoying a meal in the States as much as I did in her place; the atmosphere was wonderful and the food sheer ambrosia. A must is her 'rose-elixier,' a juice made from roses. Meals and desserts are very gratifying, at reasonable prices, and the place is easy to reach by bus and tram, which stops just nearby. We drove, so I do not remember the number of bus or tram. It is definitely worthwhile to go to Vier Linden" (Lori R. Fries, Forest Hills, New York; note by A. F.: Hiltl Vegi is Zurich's leading vegetarian restaurant, selling a huge chef's salad for 9 francs—carrots, tomatoes, cucumbers, onions, and various greens with Thousand Island dressing—and 13 kinds of tea for 2 francs. Other salads average 6.50 francs, and there are four varieties of vegetable platters ranging from 6 to 10 francs. Vier Linden, also called Bio-Restaurant, serves an excellent onion soup for 6 francs, two-egg omelettes for 7, Birchermüsli for 4.20 francs, daily platters for 7.50 francs, and porridge soup for 3 francs. And across the street from Vier Linden is a bakery specializing in fruit-, nut-, rice-, cinnamon-, barley-, cumin-, and other-spiced bread, selling for 60 centimes for rolls to 3.50 francs for loaves).

4. Starvation Budget

For lower-priced rooms and meals, you'll find that Zurich offers unusual rock-bottom facilities: a pair of Salvation Army hostels for normal tourists, and a series of "City Kitchens."

SALVATION ARMY (HEILSARMEE) HOSTELS: Right off, be reassured that Zurich's Salvation Army Hostels—one for men, one for women

—aren't maintained for down-and-out'ers, but for normally employed, if somewhat low income, single men and women; they also are entirely accustomed to accepting starvation-budget-style tourists. In fact, the male hostel—the 90-bed **Männerheim der Heilsarmee**, at 14 Magnusstrasse corner of Dienerstrasse (phone 242-48-11)—sets aside its entire third-floor dorm for male travelers, for whom the charge is an unbelievable 7 francs ($3.33) per night; Herr Stäheli is the friendly, English-speaking manager. The smaller female hostel, the **Frauenheim der Heilsarmee** at 6 Molkenstrasse (phone 242-48-00), supervised by Frau Bossart, also English-speaking, accommodates women tourists in very simple, very clean, twin rooms for 8 francs ($3.80) per person, including a simple breakfast. Both hostels are centrally located in the Helvetiaplatz area; both are rigidly segregated by sex and impose a 10 p.m. curfew; but both men and women can use the mensa-type restaurant at the Männerheim, where a two-course hot meal for 7 francs ($3.33) is served from noon to one, and from 6 to 7 p.m., seven days a week. Warning: the Frauenheim may close for reconstruction during part of 1985; phone first.

CITY KITCHENS: The next low-cost boom: at various residential locations throughout this city, the Zurich government maintains **Stadtküche Zürich**—Kitchens of the City of Zurich, a subsidized chain of cheery, little flower-bedecked restaurants, open only on weekdays, and for lunch (11:30 a.m. to 1 p.m.) only, that serve full meals for less than 6 francs. These are not charitable establishments, for the reason that no one in Switzerland is really poor; they are simply municipal restaurants, and tourists whose funds have faded should keep them in mind.

There are Stadtküche at 27 Luggwegstrasse (the **Alstetten**), at 332 Rohr Sihlquai (the **Rohr**), at 16 Schipfe (the **Schipfe**), at 34 Zentralstrasse (the **Zentral**) and elsewhere in town. The most centrally located of these is the Schipfe branch (64 seats) housed in a long low building on the Limmat River, on the railroad station side between the Rudolph Brun and the Rathaus Bridges, directly across the river from a large shoe store. Cross the Rathaus Bridge, then turn immediately right along the river and walk through a tunnel marked "Zum Bahnhof"—this will lead you to the proper riverside stretch of Schipfe, which is not to be confused with another segment of the Schipfe that goes uphill. The building housing the Schipfe Stadtküche is variously marked "Limmat-Club Zurich" and "Möbel-Wittwer," and is situated directly on the water. Hope and I recently ate at one of these Stadtküche, which turned out to be a wooden, chalet-like building, in a rustic setting, replete with oilcloth-covered tables and little vases of flowers, and a self-service counter. For 3.40 francs ($1.61) apiece, we each had a huge plateful of bratwurst and *rösti* (roast potatoes) and a lettuce salad; and for 90 centimes more, we had tea. More costly three-course meals cost all of 5 Swiss francs!

MIGROS: Something less expensive? In one of my worst penny-pinching periods, I was often able to keep lunch costs in Zurich to about $1.50. How is it done? At least 45 A&P-type supermarkets called **Migros** are spotted throughout Zurich—two of them in each district. The counters at Migros offer up the following items, among others: a cellophane-wrapped package of sharp cheddar cheese; a package of cellophane-wrapped rolls; and a banana. Take them to the check-out counter, and you'll be charged 2.80 Swiss francs ($1.33) for the lot. With your paper bag of groceries, you can then amble over to the banks of the Limmat, and munch away while the river flows by. Oh, happy days!

More recently, as an added bonus, 15 of the Migros Markets have installed self-service, sit-down Imbiss sections which may be the cheapest places to eat in all Zurich: breakfast for 2.80 francs, hot and cold platters for between 3.50 and 12 francs, a "Day's Menu" for only 5 francs. There are more Migros Markets in the residential districts than in the heart of the city, but you'll find one located about four blocks from the Bahnhof at Löwenplatz; another conveniently placed on Limmatplatz near the Limmathaus Hotel; and a brand-new one in the center of Altstetten (the old town).

PICNICS AT THE TAVERNA CATALANA: Another picnic-type place: the **Taverna Catalana,** at 8 Glockengasse, near the Bahnhofstrasse (from which you walk down Augustinergasse to find this on the first corner). With its distinguished waiters, polished oak tables, and parquet floors, you'll swear you stumbled by mistake into a big, big splurge; yet this is a thoroughly middle-class restaurant of Zurich that actually encourages patrons to bring their own food, provided they order a drink, such as a large bottle of beer for 2 francs. With half a chicken bought at Jelmoli's or Bell's for 4 francs, you'll dine in splendor among a crowd of Zürchers that includes not a single other tourist. Open daily except Sundays from 11 a. m. to 11:30 p.m. and until 7 p.m. on Saturdays.

THE SPECTACULAR UNIVERSITY MENSA RESTAURANT: A remarkable futuristic structure seating 750 persons (500 inside, 250 on the terrace), with terrace view overlooking all of Zurich, the seven-year-old **University Mensa** at 33 Leonhardstrasse serves anybody at all, student or not, at rates that start as low as 6 francs ($2.85) for, say, hamburger steak with sauce, noodles or salad, and ascend to 9 francs ($4.28) for fried filet of sole with boiled potatoes, mayonnaise and salad; actual students eat for about 30% less. Open Monday through Friday from 11:15 a.m. to 1:30 p.m., and from 5:30 to 7:15 p.m., the Mensa (whose actual affiliation is with the Swiss Federal Institute of Technology; Albert Einstein once taught there) is most easily reached by taking the Seilbahn cable car (Polybahn)— 50 centimes up, 50 down—from Centralplatz, then turning right at the top, across the large panoramic terrace into the underground mensa. Atop the terrace, students operate an auxiliary, weekday cafeteria selling open sandwiches and a glass of grapefruit juice for as little as 4.20 francs ($2).

READERS-ON-THE-STARVATION-BUDGET (BY ZURICH STANDARDS): "Another cheap place to eat is at the cafeteria of the **Y.M.C.A.,** 33 Sihlstrasse, *upstairs,* where two-course meals are 6 to 7 francs. There is a sign outside saying 'Cafe I. Stock.' This is *not* to be confused with the main floor restaurant of the Glockenhof Hotel next door. Clean, cheap and no tips. I always go here because it's *quiet*. Between 2 and 5 p.m. it is so peaceful, you can write letters there" (Mrs. S. C. Juillerat, Jura Bernois, Switzerland). . . . "A perfect picnic: Start with a loaf of French bread (one over a yard long costs 1.40 francs). Then buy a *whole* roast chicken. You can 'splurge' for this item at Bell's, where such a chicken costs 7 francs ($3.33), but numerous nearby snack stores charge only 6 francs for a chicken, and you can buy one in the delicatessen of the Globus Department Store for only 6.75 francs ($3.21). Buy a bottle of mineral water, in any store, for about 1.80 francs (85¢), and you have easily enough for two meals for a couple or four meals for one person—for $4.52. Top that!" (Mark Estren, Middletown, Connecticut).

SUB-STARVATION BUDGET: The ultramodern, stunningly designed Youth Hostel **Jugendherberge** of Zurich, is at 114 Mutschellenstrasse (phone 482-35-44), a 20-minute ride from the main station abroad tram no. 7 to Morgental. From there it's a seven-minute walk (Mutschellenstrasse starts next to the Migros Market). Or you can take a two-minute ride from the Morgental stop on bus 33, which stops in front of the hostel. Rates here are 13 francs ($6.19) per person in eight-bedded dorms, 18.50 francs ($8.80) per person in double and triple-bedded family rooms, including breakfast. And while membership in the International Youth Association is required, it's sold on the spot for 27 francs; if you plan to hostel elsewhere (validity of the membership card is one year), or to stay for a relatively long time in Zurich, it might pay to join up. Total capacity is 400 beds, on five floors. There is a 1 a.m. curfew, and if you return after 10:30 p.m., there is an extra fee of 1 franc, for the night porter. A self-service restaurant sells meals for 7 francs ($3.33), soft drinks (Coke, 1.50 francs), sandwiches (1.50 francs), fresh fruit, postage stamps, and the like; it operates from 2 to 10 p.m.; and for relaxation there are TV, games (table tennis, billiards, etc.) and lounge rooms available.

STUDENT IN ZURICH: Since there are no student hotels in the technical sense, in Zurich (there are Ys, hostels and the like), students arriving in Zurich should first obtain their own accommodations at one of the recommendations appearing earlier in this chapter. But then they should quickly head to the **SSR** (Schweizerischer Studentenreisedienst), the Swiss Student Travel Office, at 40 Bäckerstrasse (main office), or at 10 Leonhardstrasse, which offers several important services and products: among them, student charter flights, student train tickets at reductions up to 30% off standard fares, student hotels in resort cities other than Zurich: in Klosters, Davos, St. Moritz, Lucerne, Leysin, and Wengen, for instance. SSR also maintains offices in Geneva at 3 Rue Vignier (phone 299-733); in Basel at 10 Theaterstrasse (phone 228-868); and in Lausanne at 8 Rue de la Barre (phone 233-423). To get to the main office, take streetcar 14 from the Central Station to Stauffacherplatz (third stop), then turn right into Bäckerstrasse. To get to the Leonhardstrasse branch, simply walk out the front exit of the main station, turn left, cross the bridge, then walk diagonally across the central square and take the tiny **Polybahn** cable car to the top of the hill (50 centimes going up, 50 coming down). Turn left when you leave the cable car and walk about three blocks to the address. . . . Summer hours for SSR are: 9 a.m. to 5 p.m. on weekdays, from 10 a.m. to noon on Saturday and the phone is 242-30-00. . . . Incidentally, the city of Zurich gives considerable discounts to holders of student I.D. cards: 25% off on theater tickets, a lesser reduction on other scattered facilities. And you can take city sightseeing tour "A," which operates throughout the year, for half-price or 8 francs. . . . Finally, international students (show your cards) are welcomed as guests at the members-only **International Students' Club,** 1 Augustinerhof, where there are dances on Wednesday, Friday and Saturday nights; discussions and musical programs throughout the week.

5. Tours & Sightseeing

MUSEUMS AND TOURS: Hope has done the survey of Zurich's museums and sights in her section, "Hope in Zurich," appearing later in this chapter. But I'd merely add a suggestion that you do visit, while here, an especially beautiful museum of art, with a stunning collection of 19th and 20th century moderns. That's the **Kunsthaus**, on Heimplatz, just a block away from the Schauspielhaus. There's a Shavian drama behind the construction of this architectural masterpiece. An unsuccessful art student named Bührle went into the munitions-making business in Zurich, made a fortune, and then gave over the whole of his ill-gotten gains to build a new wing of this museum, which was finished just after his death in 1958. Entrance is 2 francs (95¢), except during special exhibitions periods, when the charge is from 5 to 7 francs. Open Tuesday through Friday from 10 a.m. to 9 p.m., Saturday and Sunday 10 a.m. to 5 p.m., Monday from 2 to 5 p.m.

Tours of Zurich cost 17 francs ($8.09), last two hours, and leave at 9 a.m., noon and 4 p.m. in the summertime only and at 10 a.m. and 2 p.m. the rest of the year, from in front of the railroad station. Excursions outside of Zurich leave from the railroad station too, and the best of these is a 5½-hour trip to Lucerne and alongside the Lake of Lucerne that leaves daily at 1 p.m., costs 44 francs ($2.09), returns at 6:30 p.m., and takes you into the William Tell country on the fringe of the Alps. Other full-day bus tours—primarily to Alpine villages and other woodsy mountain attractions —leave from the same spot at 8 and 9 a.m., via a cluster of buses that advertise their destinations and prices on sidewalk signs at the side of the Opera House. Nor should you forget the magnificent Swiss Railways, whose frequent and on-the-minute departures from the main railroad station offer countless opportunities for cheap, do-it-yourself excursions. It's often fun, and instructive, simply to take a train to a nearby Swiss location, and then to roam through the towns or countryside, independent and relaxed. There are specific train excursions that go to the high-altitude Jungfraujoch peak in the Alps and to the Bernese Oberland, to Lugano and Locarno (and then through the Gotthard tunnel into Italian Switzerland), to Montreux and the Castle of Chillon, to Lausanne and Geneva. For general sightseeing in Zurich, concentrate along the banks of the Limmat, where everything is older and more interesting; that's also where most of the specific sightseeing attractions are located.

HOPE IN ZURICH: "A trip to Zurich is like going home to Mother—to that secure haven where everything works properly, where you are cared for fondly in impeccably clean surroundings, and where your schedule—in keeping with the atmosphere—is orderly and moderate. Add to this the natural beauty of the city, and you'll realize that the best way to spend your time in Zurich is unwinding from the tumult of your earlier European stops. And the best places to unravel in Zurich (if weather permits) are on the lake, on excursions to nearby natural wonders, in window shopping on the remarkably attractive Bahnhofstrasse, or on strolls through the picturesque streets that jut off from Niederdorfstrasse (on one side of the Limmat) and from the Schipfe (on the other).

"And you can lounge about without a guilty conscience, because there are, in my opinion, only four 'must see' sights in Zurich. The rest, which we have also described, are strictly elective.

The Big Four

"The **Landesmuseum** or **Swiss National Museum,** located directly behind the main railway station on Museum Strasse, charges no admission, is open every day except Monday from 10 a.m. to noon and 2 to 5 p.m. and is one of the most interesting museums I've ever seen. Housed in a grey stone Victorian building that looks like Ronald Searle's St. Trinians, the museum is gigantic in both size and intention. To quote the Swiss National Museum's booklet (which you can buy for 1.50 francs, to guide yourself through the exhibitions): 'The museum collects Swiss antiquities of considerable historic, industrial or artistic importance, from primitive times until 1920. Its aim is to provide a systematic survey of our past, embracing all aspects of life, cultural epochs and regions of the country.' Here you have a kaleidoscope of Swiss life through the ages, from many aspects, all arranged neatly in chronological order. The story is told through church art (a fine collection); through magnificent model rooms from various periods, including the cloisters from the Blackfriars Monastery, several rooms from the Fraumünster Abbey, and representations of wealthy homes (all the furniture is authentic); through costumes; silverware; furniture; weapons; military uniforms; musical instruments and, of course, through an exhibition tracing Swiss clockmaking from the 16th to the 18th century. Viewing the exhibit is like standing on a Swiss mountain top—you get a panoramic view, with reflections of other European nations. Don't miss the historical handicraft shops (corn mill, shoemaker, cartwright, winepress, all from the 19th century) in Rooms 11 to 13; the magnificent furniture, including a coal stove dating back to 1620, in Room 29; the Mint, Room 75; or the Helmet and Sword of Zwingli (more about him later) in Room 50, the Weapons Hall. Free guided tours in English are offered in summer, usually at 10 a.m. on Thursdays. For information, ask at the entrance desk, or phone 221-10-10.

"The **Kunsthaus,** previously mentioned by Arthur, and located at 1 Heimplatz, directly across from the Schauspielhaus, is open Tuesday through Friday from 10 a.m. to 9 p.m., Saturday and Sunday from 10 a.m. to 5 p.m., Monday from 2 to 5 p.m., and is a superbly designed art gallery, with near-perfect lighting: daylight is used whenever possible, but even artificial lighting is employed without glare (at last!). The museum has a vast collection, but is well planned and pleasant to wander through, with two sculpture gardens in the center (which you'll see from outside). One wing accommodates changing exhibitions (usually very exciting fare); the older part of the museum has the permanent collection, which includes Swiss painting, but can also boast of ancient art; early church art; paintings by Rubens, Hals and Rembrandt; French impressionists, and a broad collection of modern sculpture and painting, including works by Picasso, Rodin, Arp, Lipschitz, Giacometti (100 works by Giacometti), Marini, Maillol, Munch, Kandinsky, Mondrian, Chagall, Miro, Rauschenberg, Bonnard, Segal, and others too numerous to mention. Entrance fee is 2 Swiss francs, but goes up to 5 to 8 francs when a special exhibition is in progress.

"The **Rietberg Museum,** entrance free, open Tuesday through Sunday from 10 a.m. to 5 p.m. (closed Monday), additionally on Wednesday evenings from 8 to 10 p.m., and located in the Rieterpark (a green, pine-treed place with a lovely view of the lake and the town) at 15 Gablerstrasse, is about a 10-minute ride from the center of Zurich; take the 7 streetcar to the Rietberg museum stop. The loosest definition best describes the famous collection of Baron von der Heydt which is housed here: it is an art gallery of non-European art. There's a bit of everything, including ancient art; works of the Indians from North, Central, and South America; Indian and South East Asian art; a Chinese and Japanese collection including sculpture, painting, ceramics and works in bronze; and so-called 'primitive' African art. But always the emphasis is on art, for the Rietberg Museum is an art gallery, not an anthropological or ethnological collection. There are many beautiful things to see here, all delightfully displayed, but particularly fascinating are the most famous Indian treasures of the museum, 'The Dancing Shiva,' upstairs in Room 12; the enormous votive stelae from the archaic Buddhist period of the Wei dynasty, in Room 9; the beautiful Chinese and Japenese paintings in Rooms 13 to 15; and the highly interesting African section, with its outstanding collection of African masks in Rooms 17, 18 and 19 (look for wooden 'puffy-cheeks,' my favorite).

"**The Grossmünster Church,** located a block or two from the City Hall just above the Limmatquai (you can't miss it—it dominates the area), may be visited from 9 a.m. to 6 p.m. (winters 10 a.m. to 4 p.m.; afternoons only on Sunday), and is an enormous Romanesque church whose present structure was begun in 1100 over the ruins of two former buildings: an earlier church and a convent. The oldest parts of the existing church are the crypt and the choir; the murals in the choir date from the 14th and 15th centuries. In the crypt is a large, primitive-looking statue of Charlemagne (built between 1450 and 1475), who is said to have founded the church when his horse bowed down here, on the very spot where the Zurich martyrs were buried; there is a stone relief inside the church on the north wall celebrating the event. Grossmünster is the Church of Zurich, and the home of the Swiss Reformation, for this was Huldrych Zwingli's pulpit from 1519 until his death in 1531. Here he preached zealously for the Gospel against the sale of church dispensations; rebelled against the church hierarchy and some of its mysticism; urged priests and nuns to marry openly (as he himself had done); persuaded the Swiss that it was a sin to hire themselves out as mercenaries; and took up the sword against those Swiss cantons that disagreed with him. He was killed in the battle of Kappel and his body was torn apart and set on fire. Grossmünster bears the mark of these troubled times: it was stripped of all religious ornamentation, and to this day looks bare and austere. But perhaps it's the presence of so much light in the Swiss church (especially after the semi-dark, romantic, mysterious cathedrals of France and Italy) that makes it look so stark. It's as though church officials decided that the Reformation was a matter of letting in more light.

The Six Electives

"The **Wasserkirche** or Waterside Church, on Limmatquai (with a statue of Zwingli on the square in back), was built between 1479 and 1488, supposedly on the spot where the three Zurich martyrs were beheaded. The church is pure Gothic but so spare and simple it looks almost modern.

"The **Helmhaus,** at the same location as the Wasserkirche, 31 Limmatquai, second and third floors, is a city-run gallery which hosts changing art exhibits (usually pretty good fare), for which there is no admission charge. Open every day, except Monday, from 10 a.m. to 6 p.m., Thursday evenings from 8 to 10 p.m.

"Diagonally across the bridge from the Wasserkirche is the **Meisen Guild House,** one of eight exquisite Guild Halls in Zurich. Most of the lovely old Guild Houses have today been converted into private clubs or public restaurants; but this one, built in 1757 and formerly the Wine Merchants Guild, contains the permanent exhibition of the Swiss National Museum's 18th-century porcelain and furniture. It provides a good way to see the inside of a Guild House for free (and without having to take a meal). Open daily, except holidays, from 10 a.m. to noon and 2 to 5 p.m., Mondays 2 to 5 p.m. only.

"Located directly opposite the Wasserkirche is the **Fraumünster Cathedral,** which was founded in 853 and used to be the Fraumünster Abbey, some of whose rooms you've already seen at the Landesmuseum. The present edifice was begun in 1170 and is a grey stone Gothic church with impressive stained glass windows (including five by Chagall and one by Giacometti), an impressive organ, and some remains of frescoes in the late Romanesque choir which date back to the 13th century; the cloisters have modern murals depicting Zurich's religious history. You may visit the church daily, except Sunday mornings, from 9 a.m. to noon and from 2 to 6 p.m.; winters, from 10 a.m. to 4 p.m.

"**St. Peter's Church** is the oldest parish church in Zurich, and stands in the heart of the oldest section of town. Its tower can be seen from the Fraumünster (and from practically anywhere else in Zurich), but the best way to get here is to cross the bridge opposite the Rathaus and then walk up the street off the right of the bridge, Weggen-Gasse (this avoids a long flight of stairs leading to the back door, which is locked anyway). It's a handsome church in modified Baroque style done in dark woods against decorated white walls. One of the church's pastors was Goethe's friend, John Kasper Lavater. The clock in the tower has the largest face in Europe (its minute hand is four yards long), but this is no surprise—we're in Switzerland, after all.

"**The Rathaus,** on Limmatquai, built between 1694 and 1698 in late Renaissance style with touches of Baroque, is a handsome grey stone City Hall with dark wood interiors and antique porcelain heating stoves. The large meeting hall upstairs has a tapestry which shows the heraldry of all the villages in the canton of Zurich, and glass-paintings showing the heraldry of all the Swiss cantons. It's about as interesting as any city hall could be, but it's free (just tip the concierge who shows you around) and open to the public Tuesdays, Thursdays, and Fridays from 10 to 11:30 a.m."

READERS-ON-AN-OUTING: "Take an express train to Lucerne, and you'll get there from Zurich in 50 minutes. Avoid the locals, which go by an entirely different route and take, believe it or not, a full hour and fifty minutes for the trip. At the Lucerne railroad station, get bus 1, marked Kriens, give the ticket-dispenser 1 franc, and ask to be let out at the stop nearest the Pilatus Railway. Walk up the hill at which you get out, and you'll find the station from which cable cars leave for the trip up Mount Pilatus. Sad to say, the trip to the top is far too expensive for the likes of us—40 francs, or $19.04 per person, round trip—but you can afford a round-trip ticket for the first station on the way up, called Krienseregg. That costs 10 francs ($4.76) per person, and allows you to spend as long as you like wandering around the mountain before taking your cable car back down. The air is brisk and bracing, the ride itself thrilling and a little overwhelming, and the whole outing an experience not to be missed" (Mark Estren, Middletown, Connecticut). . . . "From Zurich, take the very beautiful excursion to **Rheinfall**—the waterfall of the River Rhein—which is the greatest waterfall in Europe. You can go to Rheinfall by train from the central railroad station in Zurich to the Neuhausen and Rheinfall stop. The round-trip ticket for 2nd class seats costs 19 francs ($9.04) per person. It is about 50 minutes from Zurich to Neuhausen by train and from the station in Neuhausen to the waterfall about 15 minutes by foot. The boat fare under the waterfall is approximately two francs" (Dr. Z. and M. Palikan, Brno, Czechoslovakia). . . . "Make a side trip from Zurich to Interlaken, and then up to Grindelwald. It is along the same run as the train to Jungfrau, but is one of the earlier stops. Jungfrau is hardly in the price range of most budget tourists since it costs about $45 per person to make it all the way up. But Grindelwald is quite pretty, gives a great view of some very high peaks (the Eiger and Fiescherhörner), and is more affordable (about $8). And mention that the steamer-ride on the Zürchersee is free to those with Eurailpasses. It is also possible to ride on the boat one-way and hop on the train for a quick ride back to Zurich" (Lorna M. Rosenblith, Little Neck, New York).

6. Evening Entertainment

THEATRE: The **Zurich Schauspielhaus,** 34 Rämistrasse, is a highly regarded European theatre, whose repertory ranges from classic to modern, from old Greek tragedy and comedy to contemporary playwrights of all countries, all for seat prices as low as 10 francs ($4.76), as much as 45 francs ($21.42). Regrettably, the Schauspielhaus remains closed from July to early September. . . . You won't understand the farce comedies presented at some of the more local theatres, particularly those in which the star hams it up in *Schwyzerdütsch* while the rest of the company speaks German. Schwyzerdütsch is the local lingo that's been called not a language, but a throat disease. . . . Tickets for the opera, at the **Opernhaus** (phone 251-69-22; they speak English), start as low as 6 francs, which may be the world's lowest price for such; again, closed July and August. . . . Movies are a particularly good bet for Americans in Zurich, because they're subtitled in the multiple languages of Switzerland, rather than being dubbed with new voices, as in Italy and France. Several of Zurich's motion picture houses specialize in the American and English classics: *Rebecca, Odd Man Out, Brief Encounter.*

DISCOS, JAZZ AND DANCING: We'll deal with these in ascending order of age groups. University-age people go, first, to the **International Student Club,** at 1 Augustinerhof, near Paradeplatz, where the admission is five francs; dances take place on Wednesday, Friday and Saturday nights, and you'll have the best of chance of meeting other singles and stags, but you must have your international student card to enter; or, alternatively, to the larger and relatively expensive **Mascotte Discotheque,** 10 Theaterstrasse, which offers the city's best dance floor and dance-band for an entrance fee of from 5 to 9 francs, depending on the night of the week (women are admitted free Sunday to Tuesday), with drink prices pegged at a minimum 10 francs. A sophisticated young crowd (mainly in their 20s, some in their early 30s) attend. And then, at 13 Stadthausquai, near the Fraumünster Cathedral, there's **La Ferme,** a popular discotheque for the 21-to-30 age group, decorated like a rustic farm scene, with leaf-sprouting trees, wooden fences, a large mill wheel against one wall. There's also a large dance floor and the usual American-British discotheque music, for which you pay 5.50 francs to enter on Monday (folklore night), 4.50 francs Tuesday to Thursday, 8 francs on Friday, 8 on Saturday, 6 francs on Sunday afternoon, 4.50 francs on Sunday night. Americans are made to feel very welcome;

there are lots of stags; and you are not required to wear a tie (men) or a skirt (women). A slightly older group patronizes the **Red House** at 17 Marktgasse, open daily except Sundays from 9 p.m. to 2 a.m., to view both a floorshow and a striptease at an admission price of 8.80 francs, with drinks costing 10 to 16 francs. Interesting, Las Vegas-type attractions, including, on my 1984 visit, a magician who walked through a solid glass window, changed a dog into a canary, and conjured up 12-or-so lighted candles from the nose of a guest.

SWISS-STYLE GEMÜTLICHKEIT: The **Schäfli Restaurant**, at 6 Badergasse, just off the Limmatquai, next to the Rudolf-Brun Bridge, offers country shows to complement its two-course menus priced at only 8, 9 and 10 francs. Every evening in summer, from 8 p.m. to midnight, five musicians (accordion, trumpet, horn, clarinet and guitar) play Swiss, German, Austrian and Yugoslav folk music; but every evening also, there's a daily attraction which, when I was last there, was a Japanese yodler, whose skilled voice, combined with the frenetic applause from the enthusiastic audience, caused windows, glasses (and my eardrums) to vibrate close to the breaking point. There is no entrance fee, but the price of drinks contains a special music supplement, which brings beer to 4.20 francs, local wine to 6 francs. The restaurant is in the same building as the Hotel Schäfli, mentioned above, under "Zurich's least expensive hotels."

During the afternoon and at night, you can stop into the very central **Bierhalle Wolf** at 132 Limmatquai, a few doors down from the Seilbahn cable car, where a hearty Swiss "oompah" band in native costume performs at frequent intervals. This is an Alpine-inn sort of a place, very relaxed and friendly, where the band jokes with each other and the audience, and where you're likely to catch some genuine Swiss folk songs and a bit of that famous Swiss yodelling. There's no admission in the afternoon, a charge of only 2.50 francs in the evening, and beer is priced as low as 3 francs, soft drinks at 3.50. Here, the food is moderately priced and you can have a three-course meal for about 8 francs. Elsewhere on the cowbell scene, the recently opened **Swiss Chälet** at 14 Marktgasse claims that it provides real Swiss folklore (a colorful floorshow with yodelers, flag swingers, alphorn blowers), and also promises not to charge an entrance fee to bearers of this book. Here's a chance, in pleasant fashion, to learn about old Swiss traditions, surrounded as you'll be by farmhouse tools, harnesses and pitchforks, all the while imbibing soft drinks for just 5 francs, the hard stuff for 7.50 francs.

7. Excursions

A SHOPPING EXCURSION: You can't leave Europe without seizing the opportunity to buy a Swiss watch. But the most exciting store for a budget-priced watch is not in Zurich, but in Lucerne, 30 miles away. Take the train to Lucerne (45 minutes) and go to **Birnbaum's**, 34 Pilatusstrasse, where every member of the staff is a gracious human being, anxious to help you. Keep asking for the cheaper varieties, until they haul out the $25 and $30 trays. These are superb examples of the Swiss art. They would cost $40 to $50 in the U.S. My own favorites are the brands which have black faces, and severely modern, stripped-of-icing designs. Although many other watch shops in Lucerne offer similar values, Birnbaum's is included here because of their exceptional kindness to readers: they will act as a mail-drop, provide information on hotels and restaurants, even make occasional reservations for you!

DAY IN THE COUNTRY: Carved into a hillside overlooking the city, the **Dolder Schwimmbad** (swimming pool) offers a full day of bathing and lolling in the grass for an admission fee of 4.50 francs. It's a remarkable pool: for ten minutes each hour, electric motors create artificial waves— huge, high breakers simulating the roughest surf. The summer days in Zurich are apt to be surprisingly warm and a day at the Dolder, in a spectacular outdoor setting, is a treat that rivals the Riviera. You can merely observe (with no swimming) by paying a 3.50-franc ($1.66) admission charge to the open-air restaurant, to which you can also bring your own food (as long as you order a drink).

To get to the Dolder, take trolley 3 from the railroad station to the Römerhof stop and change there to the Dolderbahn, a cable car, for a six-minutes ride to the final (fourth) stop. From there it's a five-minute walk, simply following the "Dolder Wellenbad" signs. Even if you do not intend to swim, the trip on the Adlisberg (that's the name of the hill where the Dolder Pool is located) is worth the effort: you'll see one of the loveliest forests of Europe and enjoy a panoramic view of Zurich.

OTHER SWIMMING OPPORTUNITIES: Why it is, I can't explain, but swimming always seems to be an especially pleasant and appropriate activity in Zurich, whatever season I'm there. In addition to the spectacular outdoor Dolder Pool, there's a swimming area—**Badeanstalt Utoquai**—in the Lake of Zurich at the Utoquai, where you can swim among the swans every day of the week from 8 in the morning until 7 p.m., for 1.50 francs. Bathing suits are available for rental. And for indoor swimming throughout the year, you ought not to miss the vast **Hallenbad City,** a huge, glass-sided building just off the Sihlstrasse (between the Sihl Square and the Sihl River), which houses one of the most imposing swimming pools—more than 50 yards in length—that I for one have ever seen. You can rent a suit at a little shop opposite the ticket window, and your entire afternoon, including swimming suit, should cost no more than 3.80 to 4.50 francs, only 2 francs if you bring your own suit. Closed on Monday mornings.

BOATING: On sunny days, the green waters of the *Zürchersee* (Lake of Zurich) are the place to be, either for a tour of the lakeside towns, or for an hour of boating, among the swans (250 of them) and the many little ships that dot the lake. For either activity, go to the end of the Bahnhofstrasse, where you'll find a pier from which the lake ferries depart at nearly half-hour intervals. To the right of the main pier, as you face the lake, you'll then find a smaller pier at which boats are rented.

From the big pier, a boat departs at frequent intervals on a grand tour of the lake taking you to Rapperswil at the far end, near the foothills of the Alps. The trip lasts 2½ hours in either direction, and costs 23.50 Swiss francs, round-trip, second class.

From the smaller pier, however, a 1½-hour tour of the lake costs only 7.50 francs, or you can rent a row-boat for two to four persons (10 francs per hour for the boat), or a pedal boat for two to three persons (3.50 francs *per person* per hour). You might also rent a sailboat (24 francs per hour for two persons, one franc extra for each additional person, up to a maximum of five; 50 francs deposit). The same rates are available at the *Boots-vermietung* (Boat Rental) pier located just off the Bellevue Platz, at the Limmat River.

8. Zurich Miscellany

Laundromats abound. I particularly like **Speed Wash** at 55 Müller-strasse, near Helvetia Platz and Stauffacherstrasse, open seven days a week, until 8 p.m. on Sundays, until 10 p.m. all other days, and managed by English-speaking Herr Carlos Meyer, who replaces zippers for 14 francs ($6.66) and performs such other general repair work as the sewing on of buttons for 6.30 francs ($3) per 15 minutes of actual working time. And, oh yes, his laundromat charges only 9 francs ($4.28) for five kilos of laundry washed and dried. Closer to the Central Station (simply walk over the Brun-Bridge), the **Waschanstalt,** 11 Mühlegasse, is open weekdays only until 6 p.m., charges 11 francs ($5.23) for five kilos washed and dried. It's in the building of a post office. And a 10-minute uphill walk from the Central Station, 100 yards from the Kronenstrasse streetcar stop, **Reinigung Terlinden** at 148 Stampfenbachstrasse, also charges 11 francs ($5.23) for five kilos, and also performs dry cleaning and related functions. Open weekdays until 6.30 p.m., Saturdays till noon, closed Sundays. . . . A popular shopping center for people in a hurry is **Shopville,** located in the under-passage leading from the central railroad station to the Bahnhofstrasse. You can find practically everything there for your daily needs, and to help you in locating the various shops, there's an electronic shop finder near the bank. If you're hungry, stop in at the **Milchbar** for inexpensive milk shakes, and ham and cheese sandwiches, and at the **Gourmetbar,** for weiners, soups, mini-pizzas, all inexpensive. . . . Star-gazing in Zurich is the lastest game in town, with budget-minded astronomers flocking to the **Urania Observatory Tower** at 9 Uraniastrasse, in the same building as the popular Restaurant Urania-Löwenbräu, where they can gaze through a Zeiss telescope with a 30-centimeter lens (largest in Switzerland) at the moon, Saturn (see its engirdling rings) and other celestial bodies, provided weather conditions permit. Hours are 8:30 to 11 p.m. from April through September, 8 to 10 p.m. at all other times, and charge is 3 francs for adults, 1 franc for children. . . . For English-speaking babysitters in Zurich: phone 211-37-86 . . . A pharmacy (chemist) open 24 hours a day: at 14 Theaterstrasse, near Bellevueplatz . . . And a cozy reading room with English newspapers and magazines, all for free, can be found in the Pestalozzihaus, 17 Zäh-ringerstrasse near the main train station (cross the Bahnhofbrücke and turn right into Zähringerstrasse). It's open Monday to Friday from 9 a.m. to 8 p.m., Saturday to 6 p.m. . . . Restroom, shower, or toilet? You'll find all three in the underground shopping center known as **Shopville,** in front of the central railway station. . . . Best, and highest, daytime view of Zurich (and the nearby Alps) is from the **Uetliberg Hill;** trains costing 7.20 francs roundtrip go there from the Selnau Station. Best medium-altitude view of Zurich is from the plaza at 33 Leonhardstrasse, in front of the main university building. Walk up Rämistrasse to Künstlergasse, turn left on Künstlergasse for one short block. Or take the tiny Limmatquai cable car called the Polybahn (which you should learn to use), from the side of the Limmathof Hotel, which brings you up here for 50 centimes. And for an evening view, wander to the St. Peterhofstatt, with its illuminated clock

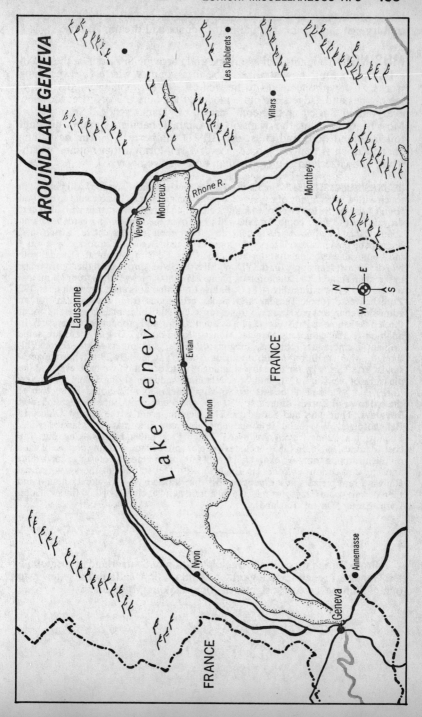

AROUND LAKE GENEVA

Les Diablerets

Villars

Monthey

Rhone R.

Montreux

Vevey

Lausanne

Lake Geneva

Evian

Thonon

FRANCE

N
W — E
S

Nyon

Annemasse

Geneva

FRANCE

tower of St. Peter's—Europe's largest clock face. This is the Europe of a century ago, and you can stand in the square and dream.

MUSINGS: Thoughts that assail one upon arriving in Zurich at the end of a European tour: how strange to be in a country where (a) everything works, (b) everyone seems to be well-off, (c) all appliances, machinery, telephones and gadgets are more modern than ours. . . . Notice, too, how everyone in Zurich says "merci" instead of "Danke schön." Strange. . . . Most beautiful sight: the swans on the Limmat; handiest store for discount toiletries and odds and ends: the EPA at Sihlporte. . . . The best thing about Zurich is that it's a base, so very well-located that nothing worthwhile in Switzerland is more than an hour or two away.

READERS' SUGGESTIONS: "Contact the Zurich Tourist Office, and they will put you in touch with a Swiss family of equal age, occupation and family background so that you **'Don't Miss the Swiss.'** We got to know a charming family who met us with their car, drove us out to their home, and showed us all over their house and garden, talking about Canada and Switzerland generally. They then gave us coffee, Kirsch, and homemade cream cakes. If they ever come to Canada, we will reciprocate, as it was a most enjoyable evening after our hotel life" (Mrs. G. Bird, Montreal, Canada; note by AF: Tourists can apply for the "Don't Miss the Swiss" program at the tourist office in the main station, 15 Bahnhofplatz, phone 211-40-00, on weekdays from 8 a.m. to 2 p.m.). . . . "The extraordinary **E. G. Bührle Collection** of French impressionists, 172 Zollikerstrasse (open Tuesday and Friday afternoons from 2 to 5 p.m. for an admission charge of 6.60 francs, 3 francs for students), while not as large as the one at the Jeu de Paume in Paris, is every bit as breathtaking and probably more unusual. In addition to the numerous Manets, Monets, Renoirs, and Degas, there are some brilliant Rembrandts, Rubens, Fragonards, Hals, and others—and sections, although rather small, on medieval religious statuary, and early 20th-century expressionist art. This is by far the most stunning private collection we have ever had the pleasure of viewing" (Mr. and Mrs. Vladimir Padunov, Long Island City, New York). . . . "Please call the attention of your readers to a 2½-hour walking tour of the old town of Zurich, offered at 9:30 a.m. and 3 p.m. from June to September on Tuesdays, Thursdays and Saturdays. The meeting point is the Tourist Office, 15 Bahnhofplatz. We found it to be enjoyable and informative" (Samuel Katz, Philadelphia, Pennsylvania; note by AF: I highly recommend this walking tour. The cost 10 francs, $4.76, in 1985—includes a cup of coffee in the morning or glass of wine on the afternoon tour. An expert guide will tell you the most interesting, important, amusing and curious episodes, in English). . . . "All stations of the Swiss Federal Railways rent bicycles at inexpensive cost (like 9 francs—$4.28—for 12 hours) and then permit you to transport the bike on a train at a flat charge of 2.50 francs" (John Case, Exeter, Devon, England).

From Zurich we continue our exploration of Switzerland in cosmopolitan Geneva, French-speaking center of international affairs and gateway to one of Europe's greatest sights, the breathtaking Mont Blanc.

Chapter XVIII

GENEVA

The Swiss Enchantress, Budget-Priced

FOR ANYONE WHO has ever dreamed of a world without poverty, filled with shining cities of beauty and comfort, Geneva is the place! One of the richest spots on earth, it is a cloud-cuckoo, never-never land, its streets so clean that you could (proverbially) eat off them, its residents well dressed (and a bit smug!), its boulevards lined with the shops of renowned couturiers and jewelers. Always in view: the gleaming, blue lake of Geneva (Lac Leman), its centerpiece a soaring, single jet fountain shooting a stream of foaming, white water more than 100 yards into the air. Behind the lake: the imposing Mont Blanc massif. Later in your tour of Europe, in other cities, you can return to reality; here you enjoy a sybaritic interlude of pastries and chocolate, of sparkling-pure, invigorating air, of other-worldly delights in a city that approaches utopian perfections, and yet feeds the mind as well: Voltaire, Rousseau, John Calvin, are among the Genevans or part-Genevans whose associations with the city are fascinating to encounter.

Like the *philosophes* of a prior time, there are current-day emigrés who have also found Geneva a good thing. The United Nations, for one, whose European headquarters are found here in an imposing palace that we'll be visiting in later pages of this chapter. And Geneva is the seat of untold other international organizations with passionately dedicated staffs: the World Council of Churches, the International Red Cross, groups promoting nuclear disarmament, groups seeking to end famine in underdeveloped lands. Their presence adds intellectual ferment to the mood of Geneva, an already agreeable combination of French *savoir faire,* Swiss stolidity, Italian vitality.

Finally, as you'd expect to learn in this budget-oriented guide, Geneva is outstanding in the moderately priced nature of its accommodations, cheapest of those in all the cities of Switzerland. Conclusion: the renowned city of Geneva is definitely a place to consider in the planning of your European itinerary!

1. Getting Around

GETTING AROUND TOWN: Though it's relatively large by European standards (340,000 people, including the outskirts), Geneva is an easily understood, easily navigated, city in which most sights and tourist activities can be accomplished on foot: from the railroad station to Lake Leman takes all of five minutes to walk, while the stroll to the Old City, across the Pont du Mont Blanc, takes ten minutes at most. The main railroad station, **Cornavin,** opens onto Cornavin Square and Rue du Mont Blanc, leading straight to Lake Leman, 300 yards away.

The lake and the Rhône River cut Geneva in half, creating a "right bank" (location of Cornavin Station and the imposing headquarters buildings of the international organizations), and a "left bank" (where most of the museums and sights, most of the shops, are found). Six bridges cross the Rhône, and most of these are traversed by the buses and streetcars that constitute the main means of public transportation in Geneva for those who don't simply stroll from place to place. Geneva's price structure for buses and streetcars is the easiest to understand in all of Europe: a flat 70 centimes (or 33 U.S. cents) for three stops, with all other trips (unlimited, any direction, with unlimited changes for one hour) priced at 1.20 francs (or 57 U.S. cents). Tickets are sold at slickly modern, automatic and very Swiss vending machines posted near every stop, or at the city transportation booth inside the Cornavin Station shopping center (and it is from the station that many of Geneva's 20 bus and streetcar lines depart). Taxis are fiendishly expensive ($7.50 the average trip), and should be avoided at all cost.

Arriving in Geneva by air, at **Cointrin Airport,** you can reduce the 5-franc ($2.38) cost of the Swissair bus from airport to Cornavin Station by simply taking public bus 33 instead; it performs the very same function for only 1.20 francs (57 U.S. cents), but departs from a point 100 yards from the airport entrance—follow the air cabin attendants and airport employees to the proper place.

And would you care to cross between right and left banks of Geneva by romantic ferry ships? Small motorboats, called *Mouettes Genevoises,* shuttle between old and new city every ten minutes for 1.20 francs (57 U.S. cents). And larger, lake-cruising ships (Compagnie Générale de Navigation sur le Lac Leman; phone 21-25-21) perform the lengthier excursions to such enchanting spots as Montreux (five hours, round trip), as you'll read in our sightseeing section, further on.

2. Budget Hotels and Pensions

They are found here in greater profusion, and at lower cost, than in any other city of Switzerland; and they are distributed, in almost equal quantities, on both the left and the right banks of the Rhône.

NEW CITY, RIGHT BANK: We start with an old favorite. In all the years that the **Hotel des Tourelles,** 2 Blvd. James-Fazy (phone 32-44-23), has been recommended in this book, I have never received a single complaint about it, but rather praise for its owner-manager, Mme. Christine Meier-Schürmann; its ideal location; its clean, large and nicely furnished rooms, most of which enjoy a view of the Rhône River; and of the old city on the other side. Twin rooms here are only 58 francs ($27.61), breakfast and free showers included, singles 42 francs ($20), triples 75 ($35.71), a solitary quad room 90 francs ($42.85), and those rates make of the des Tourelles one of the best budget choices in town. To reach it, turn right after leaving the Cornavin Station, and follow the Boulevard James-Fazy for about 300 yards until you pass the Rhône bridge; the des Tourelles is on the left corner.

Need to spend less? **Pension de la Servette,** 31 Rue de la Prairie (phone 34-02-30), is 500 yards to the rear of the Cornavin Station, a plain but Swiss-clean collection of about 20 rooms on four floors renting at only 42 francs ($20) for a twin with breakfast, 5 francs ($2.38) extra for showers. And you can get there in a few seconds by taking bus 33 going north (toward the airport); the second stop, Servette, is 50 yards from the pension. **Hotel Meublé la Cloche,** at 6 Rue de la Cloche (phone 32-94-81), is also cheap—48 francs ($22.85) for twins, 30 francs ($14.28) single, 66 francs ($31.42) triple, 80 francs ($38.09) quad, breakfast and showers included—for very large, high-ceilinged rooms, simply but adequately furnished, with carpets on the floor (unfortunately, there are only nine such rooms). Found on the second floor of an apartment building across the street from the elegant Noga Hilton Hotel, its English-speaking owners are M. et Mme Chabbey, who advise that from the Cornavin Station you walk down Rue du Mont Blanc to the lake, then turn left into Quai du Mont Blanc; Rue de la Cloche is the third street turning left from there.

Slightly higher-priced, but so very conveniently located only two blocks from Cornavin station **Hotel des 4 Nations,** 43 Rue de Zurich (phone 32-20-40), has singles for 42 francs ($20), twins or doubles 62 francs ($29.52), with breakfast. To find the chalet-like, 20-room hotel, walk up Rue de Lausanne (main exit, underground passage) to Rue de Zurich, second street going right. Perfect location, reasonable prices, and the restaurant at street level (same name, same owner) serves excellent meals in the budget range.

Two hundred yards from Cornavin Station, and again in this slightly higher-priced category, the **Hotel St. Gervais,** 20 Rue des Corps Saints (phone 32-45-72), rents 30 rooms on seven floors, at prices that average 65 francs ($30.95) per twin or double, 42 francs ($20) single, including breakfast and free showers, for rooms that are small but clean, and in a building where there is always hot water, where the elevator works perfectly (you'd expect nothing else in Switzerland), and where the desk clerk speaks English well. Only three minutes on foot from the station; simply turn right into Rue Cornavin, which leads into the Rue des Corps Saints.

A last right-bank hotel, long recommended in this guide, and only 250 yards from the station, is the **Hotel Tor,** 3 Rue Levrier (phone 31-72-74), and you who knew it when will not recognize it now! Modernized throughout, covered with wall-to-wall carpets, bestrewn with new furniture, and enjoying a new elevator, its rates have also increased, but to a still moderate 70 francs ($33.33) twin, 45 francs ($21.42) single, breakfast and

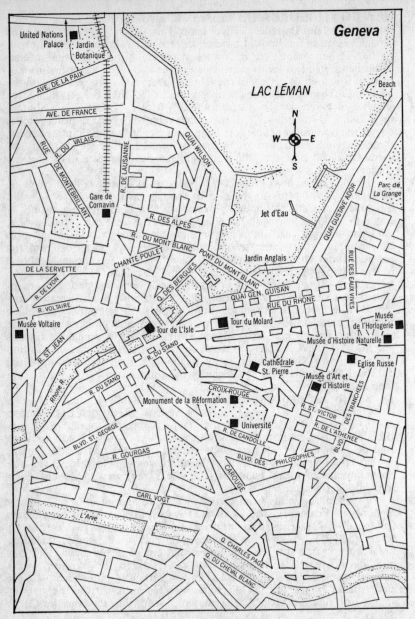

free showers thrown in, for bathless rooms. A few twins with private bath rent for an also-moderate 80 francs ($38.09). And a single disappointing feature is that owner Eray Salim, who comes from Turkey, continues to speak very little English. Location is perfect: from the station, walk down

Rue du Mont Blanc, passing the big Post Office building, then turn left to find the Rue Levrier on the small square used as a departure point for city sightseeing tours.

THE SWISS FRANC: Although the value of the once-mighty Swiss franc has recently fallen to an even lower level with respect to the U.S. dollar, we've assumed an exchange of 2.10 Swiss francs for $1 U.S. in the conversions appearing in this chapter; thus, each Swiss franc has been shown as worth about 47¢. The Swiss franc prices set forth in this chapter are correct for 1985, but their dollar equivalents will change by the time of your own trip.

OLD CITY, LEFT BANK: Generally lower-priced than their counterparts on the other side of the Rhône, these are led in value by a particularly happy choice, the **Hotel du Lac,** 15 Rue des Eaux-Vives (phone 35-45-80), managed by a Swiss-Italian couple, Cagnoli-Spiess (he's fluent in English), who polish, scrub, wax and dust their rooms to such a gleaming level of cleanliness that one hesitates to sully their perfection with one's own dirty shoes. Switzerland supreme: This is all on the sixth floor of an elevator-equipped building five minutes from the station by bus 1 (get off at Place des Eaux-Vives) or 25 minutes on foot. Double rooms (they come with one large French bed only) rent for 60 francs ($28.57), breakfast and showers-down-the-hall included, while singles are 40 francs ($19.04), triples 85 francs ($40.47).

Hotel Central Meublé, 2 Rue de la Rotisserie (phone 21-45-94), off Rue du Marché, a 15-minute walk from the station, charges only 54 francs ($25.71) per twin, 72 francs ($34.28) per triple, 90 francs ($42.85) per quad, and 100 francs ($47.61) for an immense five-bedded room, breakfast and showers included; does not mind that its guests are back-packers; and is generally a rather welcoming place, with a warm atmosphere. Its office is on the fourth floor, its 27 rooms on the fifth and sixth floors, and you must be careful to take not the first elevator to your left, but the one to the right, after first walking eight steps up; I didn't.

Hotel le Prince, 16 Rue des Voisins (phone 29-85-44), in the Plain Palais district, near the university, occupies a quiet location and usually has vacancies during high season when other more central hotels are tight. Twenty rooms, on four floors, renting at 44 francs ($20.95) for a single, 60 francs ($28.57) twin, 82 francs ($39.04) triple, 92 francs ($43.80) quad, bed and breakfast. Mr. Metrailler, English-speaking, is the manager; best travel option is to take bus 11 from the station to the Rue de Carouge stop, from which the hotel is a two-minute walk.

The large, seven-floor **Hotel le Grenil,** 7 Ave. Sainte-Clotilde (phone 28-30-55), is sponsored by the YMCA and YWCA of Geneva, and offers not simply traditional rooms (some of which have special facilities for handicapped guests), but two 8-bedded dorms renting for only 18 francs ($8.57) per person per night, with breakfast and showers included. Modern, bathless, single rooms are 45 francs ($21.42), bathless twins 62 francs ($29.52), twins with private shower 90 francs ($42.85), bathless triples only 70 francs ($33.33), bathless quads only 80 ($38.09), breakfast included. All this is found in quiet surroundings either 15 minutes from the station on foot, or 5 minutes with bus 11 (to the Place du Cirque stop, from which you walk up the Boulevard St. Georges to the Avenue St. Clothilde).

Hotel Beau Site, at 3 Place du Cirque (phone 28-10-08), is a kindly but otherwise unexceptional spot that remains in my memory for its cozy TV lounge with large red sofa on which guests squeeze themselves to watch the multi-lingual offerings of Swiss television. Denise Ray is the warm-hearted (and English-speaking) manager, and charges 44 francs ($20.95) for bathless singles, 65 francs ($30.95) for bathless doubles or twins, 82 francs ($39.52) triple, without bath, 105 francs ($50) for bathless quads, including breakfast with orange juice, and free showers. This is a 15-minute walk from the station; three stops with bus 11.

And when everything named above is unavailable, phone first (because half its rooms are taken by long-staying guests) to the **Hotel Pax** at 68 Rue du XXXI Decembre (phone 35-44-40), where bathless, "grand lit" doubles are 55 francs ($26.19) without private shower, 65 francs ($30.95) with private shower, but plus 5 francs ($2.38) per person for the usual (in Switzerland) continental breakfast. The walk there, from the station, is a long 30 minutes; take bus 1 to Place des Eaux-Vives, changing there to bus 12 for two stops.

READER'S HOTEL SELECTIONS: "On the outskirts of Geneva, but only a ten-minute tram ride from downtown, the **Hotel du Cheval Blanc,** 78 Rue de Geneve (phone 48-88-11), is clean, comfortable and reasonably priced: 54 francs for a double, 60 francs for a twin ($25.71 and $28.57, respectively), 42 francs ($20) single, 78 francs ($37.14) triple, including breakfast, but without bath. There are free showers down the hall" (Vincent Jolivet, Seattle, Washington).

3. Youth Accommodations, Youth-Style Meals

Among several youth facilities, one in particular—the 13-story **Cité Universitaire,** 46 Ave. Miremont (phone 46-23-55)—offers especial comfort, requires no student card and often fudges the definition of who constitutes a "youth"—I've seen people in their 30s and 40s quite easily obtain lodgings in this skyscraper, summer hotel. Best course is to phone the reception office between 10 a.m. and noon, or from 2 to 4 p.m., and you'll be assigned to one of 31 twin rooms (renting for 18 francs, $8.57, per person), or, more often, a bunk in the dormitory for only 12 francs $5.71 per night. In the same building: an excellent student *mensa* (cafeteria), open to persons of any age, that serves breakfast for only 4 francs ($1.90); large lunch platters—such as spaghetti bolognese with a salad, or ground steak with Swiss-style potatoes—for an average of 6.50 francs ($3.09); and permits you, on sunny days, to take the meal in an adjoining garden. About the only thing wrong with the Cité Universitaire is a 10:30 p.m. curfew! From the station, take bus 33 (1.20 francs) to the last stop, then walk back 200 yards to the easily spotted structure. An alternative to it, but far more costly, is the **Centre Universitaire Zofingien,** 6 Rue des Voisins (phone 29-11-40), in the university area, which rents a few of its summer vacancies to the young and nearly-young for 36 francs ($17.14) single, 54 francs ($25.71) double, 69 francs ($32.85) triple, breakfast and free showers included. A cafeteria in the same building serves spaghetti or omelettes for

4.50 francs ($2.14), soup for 2 francs (95¢), big platters of meat, vegetables and salad for 9 francs ($4.28). This time, take bus 11 or streetcar 12 to Pont d'Arve.

The standard youth hostel, open all year and unusually cheap, is actually called the **Official Youth Hostel** and is at 1 Rue des Plantaporrets (phone 29-06-19), and charges only 9 francs ($4.28) for a cot in its several large dormitories, provided you possess a hostel card (which they'll sell on the spot for 25 francs); your 9-franc payment brings you sheets and free showers as well, but neither breakfast nor other meals are served. There is, of course, a midnight curfew, in the standard youth hostel tradition, and manager Robert Heritier closes the hostel from 10 a.m. to 4 p.m. for cleaning. From the station, it's a 20-minute walk: turn right into the Avenue James-Fazy, cross the Rhône Bridge, then continue into the Quai de la Poste and Quai du Rhône, until you reach the Pont de Sous-Terre. Rue des Plantaporrets turns left from there, and the hostel is a short walk up the street, on your left, in a small park.

One final establishment—the **Centre Herbèrgement,** 37 Rue du Nant, corner of Rue des Vollandes, in the Eaux-Vives district on the left bank—becomes a youth hostel from July 1 to September 15 only, when it converts the basement of a school into six large dorms holding as many as 42 beds apiece. For this, you'll pay 12 francs ($5.71) a night. The curious booking procedure is to go to an old bus, now converted into an office and called CAR (Centre Accueil et Renseignements), at the corner of the Place Cornavin and Rue du Mont Blanc, near the underground exit of the railway station. Daily from 8 a.m. to 11 p.m., but summer only, they'll reserve a cot for you at the Centre Herbèrgement, and charge no booking fee for the service. Then, to reach the hostel, you'll take bus 22 (following directions supplied by the CAR hostesses); it's a large, grey building with a tall rectangular tower and lightning rod atop, and you take the entrance where the steps lead downstairs.

4. Eating Well at Moderate Cost

While the budget hotels are fairly evenly distributed between left and right banks, the low-priced restaurants aren't! Except for one big self-service cafeteria on the right bank, you must head for your low-cost needs to "la rive gauche."

RIGHT BANK: Restaurant Manora, 6 Rue Cornavin, is the aforementioned right-bank stand-out. Largest self-service restaurant in all of Geneva, it's found about 300 yards to the right of Cornavin Station (as you leave it), and is open seven days a week until 9:30 p.m. Offerings include at least 20 large main plates with salad, ranging in price from as little as 5.20 francs ($2.47) for roast turkey with risotto maison and salad, to 13 francs ($6.19) for entrecôte steak with french fries and salad; and a cup of coffee (1.20 francs) or beer (1.70 francs) adds only a bit more; special children's menus are only 3.50 francs ($1.66). You can eat well here at budget levels, and savor the food in a separate non-smokers section, if you wish!

If all you crave is a snack, and you're on the right bank, you can do fairly well at an Italian fast-food cafe called **Mac Spag,** 15 Rue Sismondi (corner of Rue Rossi), where the more simple pasta dishes, like spaghetti bolognese, are 5.50 francs ($2.61), while the exotic ones (cannelloni carbonara, lasagne al forno, tortellini with cheese) are 6.60 francs ($3.14). And again the restaurant is open seven days a week, until late at night.

Finally, if you're willing to eat standing up, on the right bank, lunchtime only but seven days a week, the familiar **Migros** shops, found almost everywhere, fit the bill at the cheapest rates in town. Easiest of all to find, and very central on the Rue Chantepoulet off the Rue Cornavin near the station, is the Migros at 5 Rue Chantepoulet. Here at the counter, a quarter roast chicken with french fries is only 4.90 francs ($2.33), ground steak *(steak haché)* with salad 5.60 francs ($2.66), spaghetti with meat sauce 4.90 francs ($2.33), coffee, tea or milk 1.20 francs.

There are two memorable restaurants on the right bank where you can eat for $10, but we've saved those for our "big, big splurge" section later on.

LEFT BANK: Just as in Paris, the better budget selections are on the left bank.

The picturesque Place du Molard near the lake, a colorful, cool and traffic-free spot, with flower market and fountain, is my own preferred spot for dining in Geneva, especially on a day when you can use one of the dozens of sidewalk tables placed in the square. Two restaurants, **Le Centre** at number 5, and **Le Commerce** at number 7, serve three-course menus, tax and tip included, for only 12 francs ($5.71), one-dish *plats du jour* for 10 francs ($4.76), large pizzas for 7 francs ($3.33) to 10 francs ($4.76) (the latter called a Super-Molard, which literally overlaps the large platter on which it's served). On the same square, you can sit at a table to consume the picnic-style meal you've purchased elsewhere, provided only that you buy a beer (2 francs) or coffee (1.80 francs) from one of the cafes.

A bit farther from the lake, **Taverne de la Madeleine,** at 20 Rue Toutes-Ames, nestled on a terrace against the old city wall, below the St. Pierre Cathedral and across from the Madeleine Church, is another quiet but popular restaurant in quiet surroundings, but one that serves no alcohol, not even that which you've brought yourself. Open every day except Sunday, it offers a series of unusually filling one-platter meals for 10 francs ($4.76), like a full half-a-chicken with roast potatoes covered by a creamy white sauce, or stewed hare with noodles, or piccata milanese with salad. If you're ravenously hungry, you can precede all this with a giant, heavy bowl of minestrone soup for 3.50 francs ($1.66), and you can end the meal with a pot of tea (chosen from eight different varieties) for 2.50 francs ($1.19). In the same area, less than 100 yards away, the Italian **Restaurant Romantica** at 3 Rue des Trois Perdix, and the Greek **Restaurant Dionysos** at 13 Rue de la Fontaine, both with open-air sections, and this time serving wine and beer (a relief), charge only 2 francs more for their plats du jour—a total of 12 francs ($5.71)—and offer exotic ingredients, a refreshing change of pace, like fried sardines with curry sauce (at the Dionysos) or veal cutlet milanese, slathered with melted cheese and topped with anchovies with an accompanying salad at no extra charge (at the Romantica).

Elsewhere on the left bank, **Le Zofage** at 6 Rue des Voisins near the university, heavily patronized by student-age folk, is a popular bistro with local atmosphere, seven-day-a-week hours of operation, and extremely reasonable prices for Switzerland: soup for 2 francs (95¢), spaghetti with butter sauce for 4.50 francs ($2.14), veal steaks with rice or potatoes, and salad, for 8 francs ($3.80). And Le Zofage is open till midnight.

And again on the left bank, in a familiar area, **Dente de Lion,** at 25 Rue des Eaux-Vives, is a small, budget-priced, vegetarian restaurant selling a large and filling three-course vegetable meal for 14 francs ($6.66)—like mozzarella, super salad bowl, and ice cream; or if you prefer, simply a daily platter for 9 francs ($4.28), or a big, thick bowl of vegetable soup, in quantities large enough for a meal, for 6 francs ($2.85). But this one is open weekdays only, from noon to 10 p.m.

RESTAURANTS (THE BIG, BIG SPLURGE): Two right-bank restaurants offer unusual meals of quality for about $10 to $11. The one where you'll eat to bursting is the **Cafe de Paris,** 14 Rue du Mont Blanc (150 yards from Cornavin Station), which for years has specialized in only one dish: entrecôte, served with french fries and green salad, in virtually unlimited quantities, and all for precisely 22 francs ($10.47). The steak is of the best quality, tender and cooked exactly to order, the sauce exquisite, the french fries are indeed unlimited, and the entrecôte itself is so large that the waitress leaves a portion on a hot plate, to be served later in the meal, when you get your second wind! Coffee, wine and beer (about $1.50) are available at the sidewalk tables, but the places inside are reserved for entrecôteurs only.

A famous name in Switzerland, the restaurant chain called **Mövenpick** maintains its Geneva branch at 17 Rue du Cendrier, one escalator flight up in the modern Cendrier Center, off the Rue du Mont Blanc, between the Cornavin Station and Lake Leman. An extremely professional, high quality, carefully managed restaurant using the very finest and freshest foods, Mövenpick is easily a place where you might spend $20 per person, but by choosing carefully from the four menu cards at each table, you can also eat for half that. Every day, for instance, there's a large plat du jour for 12.50 francs ($5.95)—like meat-filled lasagne, cooked al dente, with a giant salad—or you can carefully choose, as I did in the summer of 1984, a juicy hamburger steak (150 grams, rare) with mixed salad (cucumbers, radishes, carrots and tomatoes, with dressing), soft baked potato with butter and sour cream on the side, all accompanied by white wine (a *dezi,* or one-tenth of a liter), and all for an à la carte total of only 22.50 francs ($10.71), service included. And that's consumed in a cultivated atmosphere, with punctilious service, all very European and a refreshing change of pace.

5. The Major Sights

Rousseau, Voltaire, John Calvin—those are the violently different individuals about whom I'd plan the sequence of my sightseeing in Geneva. You do this by visiting several important museums, preferably by yourself and on your own, to freely associate with, to fantasize about, the thoughts and movements provoked by three great citizens or residents of historic Geneva.

The **Jean-Jacques Rousseau Museum,** on the ground floor of the University Library Building in the Promenade des Bastions, displays books, documents, letters, original handwritten pages of the epochal *Contrat Social,* and the death mask of one of Geneva's greatest sons—he was born here in 1712 and died in France in 1778, but always considered himself to be a citizen of free Geneva. His three major literary works—*La Nouvelle Héloise, Du Contrat Social,* and *Émile*—criticize social conventions and state religions, argue that man is good by nature but spoiled by society, cry out against the absolute rule of monarchs, stress the natural democratic rights of the people, and thereby lay the foundations for the French Revolution, of which he, posthumously, was perhaps the single major source. It is thrilling to see the documents and relics of one of the greatest social thinkers and reformers of recent times, in rooms that are open to the public, free, from 9 a.m. to noon and 2 to 5 p.m., closed Saturday afternoons and Sundays.

L'Institut et Musée Voltaire, 25 Rue des Délices, the only museum on the right bank of Geneva, is where the equally great Voltaire actually lived from 1755 to 1765, where he wrote part of *Candide* in rooms still furnished with their original pieces, and in which a full-sized model of Voltaire, wearing his actual clothes, sits near his original studio desk. That setting, together with the terra-cotta bust of Voltaire seen famously in dozens of books, and the many documents and letters displayed in showcases, makes for a memorable visit, every weekday afternoon (from 2 to 5 p.m.), for no charge at all. Voltaire, the sarcastic, witty and utterly clear-minded rationalist, led the historical movement now known as the Enlightenment, in which he questioned traditional doctrines and values, criticized the dominating role of the Catholic church, and preached tolerance, thereby attracting the enmity of kings and clerics alike. He was ultimately to be honored by being entombed in the Pantheon of Paris, where his remains now rest alongside those of Rousseau, Victor Hugo, and Emile Zola.

From your visits to these museums, and to the Monument of the information discussed below, you ought now to proceed to that symbol of world peace, attracting hundreds of visitors each day, that is the European headquarters of the **United Nations** in its **Geneva Palace,** two miles north of the city, and open to the public daily from noon to 4:45 p.m., for a five-franc ($2.38) admission charge. From the Cornavin Station of Geneva, take bus 0; get off one stop after the official UNO stop (which is for delegates and staff only); purchase your ticket at the guard's window; stick the small, round, blue tag on your lapel, walk then for about 200 yards to entrance no. 39 in the new, curved building, and wait for the next conducted tour to start, usually at 20-minute interals. Led by blue-uniformed, multilingual hostesses, the tours last an hour, take you through meeting rooms and past the rich displays donated by member nations, and include commentary on the history of the United Nations and its predecesesor, the League of Nations (the latter accounting for such artifacts as a bronze world globe donated by President Woodrow Wilson and a 750,000-volume library donated in 1920 by the late John D. Rockefellerm, Jr. The U.N. in Geneva employs a permanent staff of nearly 5,000 persons, and should very definitely be seen.

Other important sights of Geneva: the **Museum of Natural History,** 1 Route de Malagnou, open 10 a.m. to 5 p.m., Tuesday through Sunday, entrance free, one of the most modern of its kind in Europe, with fascinating, elaborate displays of animals, both living and stuffed, including two very energetic and productive ant families carrying leaves and other loads up and down transparent plastic tubes resembling the moving escalators at Charles de Gaulle Airport. Minerals are also displayed; various courses of instruction and lectures are presented (phone 35-91-30 for the schedules); and the institution is an important one, as well as comfortable and relaxing: a spacious cafeteria on the second floor serves good plats du jour for 9 francs ($4.28).

Only 100 yards away, and appropriately maintained in this clock-capital city, is the interesting **Watch-and-Clock Museum** *(Musée de l'Horlogerie et de l'Emaillerie),* 15 Route de Malagnon, open Tuesday through Sunday from 10 a.m. to noon and 2 to 6 p.m., Monday from 2 to 6 p.m. only, entrance free, displaying every sort of time-keeping piece, including tower, church, console, tambour and cross-shaped clocks, astronomical and sun-dial clocks, one moved by oil, sand and water, and hundreds of watches, from the simplest to the Omega Oyster, including one worn by Auguste Picard in 1960 on deep sea expeditions into the South there are historic clocks and watches made as far back as the well displayed in the lovely, small palais that houses the museum.

And incidentally, if your stay in Geneva is for three days or more, then an excursion to **Chamonix** and the imposing **Mont Blanc** region, clear weather permitting, should also be considered an indispensable (but unfortunately, not inexpensive) activity of your Geneva stay. We'll discuss such jaunts at a later point of this chapter.

6. More Sights

Now return to your hotel, pick up your camera and comfortable walking shoes, and wander quietly among the sights that supplement the major ones just discussed; while none of these is worth a special trip, they all partake of that special charm that envelops the visitor to Geneva.

THE "EAUX-VIVES JETTY" (OR JET D'EAU): An engineering wonder when it was built in 1886, and still unchallenged (as far as I know) in other cities, the giant, 145-meter-high water fountain in the midst of the lake off the Quai Gustave Ador (Old City), is Geneva's summer landmark, for it operates only from Ascension Day to the 30th of September, from 11 a.m. to 11 p.m. It leaves seven tons of water constantly suspended in the air, using two immense electric pumps to suck the water from the lake and shoot it upward into the cloudy blue sky above, an unforgettable sight, and one that should be photographed with you standing before it.

THE FLOWER CLOCK: An appropriate curiosity for a country so associated with time-keeping, watches and clocks, the **Flower Clock** (or *Horloge Fleurie*) in the English Garden (or *Jardin Anglais*), near the left-bank side of the Pont du Mont Blanc, is made of 6,300 flowers over a circumference area of 16 meters, was planted in 1955 to symbolize Geneva's eminence in the world of clock and watch manufacturing, and vies with the water jetty as a particularly popular spot for photo-taking by visiting tourists.

THE OLD CITY: Best visited on foot, clambering up and down cobblestoned alleys, steps and tunnels, the Old City of Geneva is 2,000 years of history and more than 20 important sights, including the Cathedral, St. Peter's Church, the Town Hall, Calvin's House, the Old Barracks and the Place du Bourg-de-Four (which, 2,000 years ago, was a Roman forum).

And now, an underground secret of Genevan travel: if you will hie yourself to the City Tourist Office (at the Tour de l'Ile), and place the request politely, those efficient Swiss who have thought of everything will provide you, free, with a Sony Walkman-type of apparatus, a portable, recorded cassette walking tour, and a detailed map, for do-it-yourself sightseeing throughout the Old City and its 2,000 years of sights. (But you will need to show your passport and leave a completely refundable 50-franc ($23.80) deposit, repaid to you when you return the recorder within four hours).

EGLISE RUSSE: The **Russian Orthodox Church,** built in traditional style in 1865, with nine gilded, onion-shaped cupolas, is the seat of the Russian-Orthodox Bishop in Western Europe; his home is across the street. That's at the Rue Lefort, near the Cours de Rive square.

MONUMENT INTERNATIONAL DE LA REFORMATION: On the Promenade des Bastions, near the Place Neuve, and also called the **Mur des Reformateurs,** this is an immensely impressive, detailed and complex memorial to the Protestant revolt against orthodoxy, built in 1917 to commemorate the 400th anniversary of the birth of churchman John Calvin. One hundred meters long, and carrying ten large statues and eight bas reliefs, all in stone and marble, it proclaims Geneva as the source and bulwark of the 16th and 17th century Reformation. Here you see the three most prominent Genevan reformers: Calvin, Farel and Beze, placed next to John Knox, the Scottish rebel and religious statesman, all flanked by lesser patrons of the violent movement that rejected Catholic doctrines and led to formation of the major, current-day Protestant religious bodies. The inscription *Post Tenebras Lux* (Light after Dark) recalls Calvin's battle-cry, and evokes the zealous attitudes of that era in Geneva.

MUSEUM OF ART AND HISTORY: Le Musée d'Art et d'Histoire, 2 Rue Charles-Galland, near the Russian-Orthodox Church, is somewhat different from most such museums in its emphasis on archaeological collections, including restorations of prehistoric pile dwellings found in Lake Leman, and Greek, Roman and Egyptian ceramics, statues and cult objects. There is, in addition, a fine display of paintings by Veronese, Corot, Rousseau (this time the painter not the philosopher-writer), Arp, Ernst and Picasso, and sculptures by Rodin and Giacometti. Open Tuesday through Sunday from 10 a.m. to 5 p.m., with no entrance charge.

COLLECTIONS BAUR: A small museum at 8 Rue Munier-Romilly, in the same area as the Russian Church and the Museum of Art and History, it will delight admirers of Oriental art with its ceramics of the Far East dating from the 7th to the 17th century, and its jades from China and lacquered objects from Japan, among many other treasures. Open Tuesday through Sunday, but only from 2 to 6 p.m.; admission of 3 francs to most, 1.50 francs to students.

GLORIOUS PARKS: Of 15 municipal parks, at least three are worth visiting: the **Parc de la Grange** and adjoining **Parc des Eaux-Vives** (both on the left bank) and the **Parc du Jardin Botanique** (on the right bank). The first two are famed for their old trees, including giant sycamores imported from California, and for the 250 varieties of roses cultivated in their gardens, some even growing on trees. The palace on the grounds of the **Parc de la Grange,** used as an official reception villa by the government of Geneva, is adorned by two renowned statues: "Venus and Adonis" by Canova and "Ganymede" by Thorwaldsen. Nearby excavation work has begun on a Roman house dating from the first century A.D. The Parc du Jardin Botanique (Park of the Botanical Gardens), between the United Nations Palace and the lake, is ideal for long walks under old, shady trees, all of which, together with plants and flowers, are marked with name tags. After your conducted visit to the United Nations, you'll find that a walk back to town through this park, the lake in full view, is most relaxing.

7. Excursions and Tours

COLOGNY: A small village on the French shores of the lake (you'll need your passport), 2½ miles northeast of the city and reached by public motorboat or bus 9, it enjoys an enthralling view of Lake Leman, the United Nations and the Jura Mountains, and became famous throughout the world for the sojourn there by Lord Byron, in Villa Diodati, in 1816. There he met Shelley, had tempestuous reunions with other friends and generally scandalized the burghers of Geneva.

CAROUGE: A mile and a half south of Geneva, and easily reached via streetcar 12, this is a small village of 10,000 inhabitants on the Arve River, popular for its picturesque streets, houses, bistros and open markets. A strategic road-crossing in Roman times, then property of the King of Sardinia, then of the French during the French Revolution, and of the Swiss since the Congress of Vienna in 1815, it has an atmosphere even more cultivated and international than that of Geneva, and is worthwhile visiting to lunch in one of its many restaurants, or to sip a glass of cool, white Fendant wine in an open-air cafe or bistro. Try especially to go on Wednesday or Saturday mornings, market days when vegetable and fruit stands, colorful beyond compare, blossom forth on the Place du Marché near the baroque Eglise de la Sainte-Croix built in 1780.

THE ASCENT TO THE SWISS ALPS: Perhaps the highlight of your stay in Geneva, and indeed one of the great sights of Europe, is a trip to nearby **Chamonix** in France, reached via a complicated train trip (you change three times) from Geneva's Eaux-Vives train station (take streetcar 12 from the center of town to reach the station) at 7:04 a.m. and 9:32 a.m., or by escorted motorcoach tour. The former costs 34 francs ($16.19) round trip (but is free to Eurailpass holders), while the full-day motorcoach tour, leaving daily at 8:30 a.m. from the Place Dorcière, is 50 francs ($23.80).

Either way, go only on a clear day, or else clouds or mists will obscure your view.

The main purpose of your trip to this Alpine village of 10,000 residents is the unforgettable view of the snow, glaciers and ice-covered peaks of the Mont Blanc massif. That can be had simply from the center of Chamonix, 1000 meters above sea level, but the enthralling view becomes an overwhelming one if you'll spend 22 francs ($10.47) more for the funicular that takes you from Chamonix to Le Brévent, a 2,500-meter-high peak far better for viewing these unique sights than the Aiguille du Midi, another promontory reached by funicular (this time, a costlier 34 francs, $16.19) from Chamonix. Budget travelers will content themselves with Le Brévent, or with a smaller funicular (26 francs, $12.38) that shuttles over three miles of the snow and ice of the Vallée Blanche to and from a station on Italian territory (in the Aosta region).

Do not—repeat, do not—neglect to take your passport for the trip to Chamonix, as the bus or train crosses the French/Swiss border at a minimum of two points.

Other escorted tours from Geneva of the remarkable mountain scenery all around include a four-hour **Jura Mountain Tour** by bus, but also including a chair-lift ascent to the Barilette mountain (it departs afternoons, three times a week, and is priced at 36 francs, $17.14), and a half-day trip that merely wanders through various countryside locations of the Geneva district, again for 36 francs, and is simply called the **Tour de la Campagne Genevoise.** Departure point for both is the bus terminal at Place Dorcière, where you can pick up a detailed, descriptive brochure. And then there are the lake cruises advertised all around, of which the cheapest is a 40-minute, 6-franc ($2.85) ride past various celebrated lakefront residences, such as the Chateau Rothschild, the villa of the Empress Josephine, the Villa Diodati (where Byron lived while in Geneva). Other cruises range in price and duration from 24 francs and 5 hours (to Nyon and Yvoire) to 47 francs for a grand, all-day (7 hours) traverse of the entire lake and to Montreux and Chillon.

Easiest-to-reach mountain near Geneva for the do-it-yourself method is **Le Salève,** 1347 meters tall, a kind of baby Mont Blanc, popular in winter for skiing and in summer and autumn for Delta glider fans. To reach it, simply take bus 8 (1.20 francs, 57 cents) to Veyrier, but take your passport, as Le Salève is on French territory. Once in Veyrier, walk to Le Pas-de-l'Echelle (10 minutes, including border-crossing), from where a super-modern funicular, constructed in 1984, transports you, in three minutes, to the top of Le Salève. From there a magnificent view is had over Geneva, the lake and the imposing Mont Blanc massif, weather permitting. The funicular costs 50 French francs ($6.25) roundtrip, 33 francs ($2.75) for children between 6 and 12, and operates from 8:30 a.m. to 10:30 p.m. in summer, to 5:30 p.m. winters.

Believing, as I firmly do, in the advantages of do-it-yourself sightseeing, I do not recommend the standard, two-hour **Tour de Ville** (city tour) of Geneva, going to many of the spots we've described earlier on, all best visited on-your-own, in the privacy of your own thoughts, and unaccompanied by 40 other chattering tourists. But if you're addicted to the escorted form of sightseeing, then you'll want to know that the two-hour tour starts from the Place Dorcière, which is about 200 yards from the station, off the Rue du Mont Blanc and near the Eglise Anglaise. It costs 19 francs ($9.04), stops for about 45 minutes in the old town for explorations on foot of the Cathedral, Town Hall, Calvin's house, and Reformation Monument, then boards you onto the bus again for a drive through the international district, on the right bank, passing the United Nations Palace, the headquarters of the World Health Organization, World Council of Churches, and International Red Cross, and allowing for a particularly tantalizing glimpse of the palace-residence in Geneva (he knows a good thing) of the Sheik of Kuwait; it could have been lifted from a dream of the *Thousand and One Nights.*

8. Evening Entertainment

You would not expect to find brassy nightclubs, strip joints and exotic performers in the town of John Calvin, and your expectations are borne out by the reality of Geneva's nightlife scene. It is a quiet and unusually sophisticated scene, marked by concerts and recitals, of which the summer variety are often in the open air and free to the public. But because the offerings are large, varied and constantly changing, it would be foolish to attempt a listing in this yearly published book; such notices are available free from the Geneva Tourist Office at Tour de l'Ile (phone 28-72-33), which you'll want to visit for all sorts of literature and maps, in any event; the location is on one of the bridges over the Rhône (the same one crossed by Julius Caesar in ancient days).

Among the evening activities of a permanent nature, those of interest to English-speaking visitors include, first, the **Folk Club International,** Maison des Jeunes, Villa Tardy at 6 Chemin du Bout du Monde (phone 47-34-64), which meets on the second Tuesday of every month for free performances by anybody who cares to act, sing, read, mime, jest or otherwise perform. Nonperformers pay 3 francs ($1.42) admission, while performers are admitted free and are even given drinks on the house. . . . **Radio Suisse Romande,** 66 Blvd. Carl Vogt (phone 29-23-33), located near the Official Youth Hostel, presents classical concerts, usually on Wednesday and Saturday evenings, for an entrance fee of 5 francs ($2.38). . . . And finally, the **Picwick Pub,** 80 Rue du Lausanne near the station (ten minutes from there on foot, or by taking bus 5 to the Butin stop) seems to be the unofficial headquarters for the large English-speaking community of Geneva, mainly members of international organizations like the U.N., who gather to imbibe English beer (2.50 francs), play darts and listen to jazz. Open Monday to Saturday from 10:30 a.m. to 1 a.m., Sundays from 4 p.m. to 1 a.m.

9. Geneva Miscellany

As in Zurich, everything here is fresh, new, efficient and reliable, and you might even consider a medical check-up by one of those wonder-working Swiss doctors, surely among the best in the world! For the name and address of an English-speaking physician, phone **Association des Médecins de Geneve,** 14 Blvd. de la Tour, at phone number 20-84-20. . . . Slick, self-service laundromats are abundant, and charge from 10 to 12 francs ($4.76 to $5.71) for five kilos washed and dried. Try, in ascending order of cost: **Salon Lavoir,** 61 Blvd. St. Georges (300 yards off the Place du Cirque—that's in the old city, left bank—open seven days a week until 10 p.m.); **La Lavandière,** 8 Rue de Lyon (behind Cornavin Station, New City, right bank); **Lavomat,** at 5 Rue Blanvalet, off Rue de la Mairie (Old City, left bank, near the Place des Eaux-Vives; English-speaking manageress); and **Self-Lavoir,** 4 Rue Montbrillant, again behind Cornavin Station (New

City, right bank), the last-named open weekdays only, and only until 6:30 p.m.. . . . Rue des Alpes (across from the huge Central Post Office) and Rue du Mont Blanc are lined with watch shops displaying numerous makes in the $25 to $30 range. . . . Babysitters charge 7 francs ($3.33) an hour, plus carfare, and can be hired by phoning fairly well in advance to **Bureau de Placement de l'Université,** at 20-93-33. . . . Bicycle rentals are most cheaply had at the Central Station near the luggage deposit. Six francs ($2.85) for four hours, 9 francs ($4.28) for 12 hours, 12 francs ($5.71) for 24 hours, with no requirement of a deposit (but you must show your passport). Alternately, the shop called **Procycle,** 17 Place Montbrillant (phone 34-26-22), charges 15 francs for a day, only 25 francs ($11.90) for the weekend, and an exciting 60 francs ($28.20) for a week, plus a refundable 100-franc ($47.61) deposit. There are plenty of nearby, flat places in which to cycle, and don't attempt Mont Blanc! . . . A last, relaxing interlude in Geneva: poring over the wide selection of good, English-language periodicals *(New Statesman, New Republic, Punch)* in the free reading room **(Salle Moynier)** of the Bibliothèque Publique in the University Library Building on the Promenade des Bastions, three flights upstairs from the Jean-Jacques Rousseau Museum. It's open weekdays from 9 a.m. to noon, from 2 to 6 p.m., Saturdays from 9 a.m. to noon only, and Rousseau would have approved.

From the carefully ordered grace and charm of Geneva, we travel now over the border to a different type of European city, Munich, in the heart of the Bavarian Alps, and experience again the rapid and dizzying changes in culture, cuisine, language and outlook that constitute the fascination of Europe.

Chapter XIX

MUNICH

Beer and Wurst at Bargain Rates

1. A Quick Orientation
2. Where to Stay
3. Restaurants & Meals
4. Evening Entertainment
5. Sightseeing
6. Tours & Excursions
7. Munich Miscellany

THE NORTH AND CENTRAL parts of Germany are often industrial and grim. Unless you've studied German, or have a profound knowledge of the culture of that nation, you probably won't want to include these areas on a first-time European vacation. The south of Germany is another matter. This is Bavaria, and its capital is Munich—a light-hearted, fun-loving city, whose residents look upon the pursuit of pleasure as nearly a full-time profession. If you want to imbibe something of the atmosphere of 19th-century Europe—go to Munich.

Munich has the best beer in Germany and the best food. Its avenues are broad, its theatres and nightspots numerous, and the low rates of its restaurants tend to offset the rising rates of its popular hotels. Can you live in Munich on a budget? Here's how:

1. A Quick Orientation

AIRPORT INFORMATION: Munich's airport, at Riem, five miles outside the city, is connected with the city air terminal at Central Station (*Hauptbahnhof*) by a bus that runs every 20 minutes and charges only 6 marks ($2.30), one way. If you take a taxi instead, you'll pay about $15, luggage included, to your hotel.

TRAINS: Munich's modern main railway station, the **Hauptbahnhof,** is located in the heart of the inner city. Numerous streetcar lines stop here, and you can take escalators to the *U-Bahn* (subway) or the *S-Bahn* (metropolitan railway). Rail travel times to some important European cities are: Rome 14 hours, Florence 11, Venice nine, Salzburg two, Vienna five, Paris or Amsterdam ten, Milan nine and Zurich five hours. The train information office, opposite track 21, is open Monday to Saturday from 6 a.m. to 11:30 p.m., Sunday from 6:30 a.m. to 11:30 p.m. For general train information phone, day or night, 59-29-91 or 59-33-21.

GETTING AROUND MUNICH: The subway (U-Bahn) is the key, and Munich's subway system is a marvel: it utilizes every sort of up-to-date electronic feature, and whisks you about almost soundlessly at an average fare of 1.80 marks. Criss-crossing the U-Bahn is the more extensive S-Bahn (*Stadtbahn*, or metropolitan railway), servicing the suburban locations. Since the S-Bahn is a state railway, it accepts Eurailpass! If you aren't equipped with one, purchase a *Mehrfahrtenkarte* (Multiple Journey Ticket) for 9 marks ($3.46), at one of the blue vending machines; they come in ten segments worth 90 pfennigs each. You fold up two segments for an average city ride and stick them in to be stamped by little blue machines at the entrance to the track. Or buy a 24-hour ticket, allowing unlimited travel on the U-Bahn, S-Bahn, streetcars and buses, for 6.50 marks ($2.50) for rides within city limits, and 12 marks ($4.61) for trips in the surrounding areas (about a 50-mile radius). These 24-hour tickets are also sold at the blue vending machines, and at most hotel desks, newspaper booths and travel agencies all over town. You'll soon acquire the hang of it (and if you don't, you can obtain a free, descriptive, English-language brochure at the information offices of the U- and S-trains in the underground passage at the Central Railway Station).

Taxis in Munich are never to be taken—they average as much as $6 for even the most simple in-city trip!

2. Where to Stay

PENSIONS: Apart from staying at the large Hotel-Pension Beck (where doubles, including service and tax, rent for only $9.23 per person; see our "super budget" section for details), the cheapest way to live in Munich is to take a room in a private home renting to tourists, or else to seek out one of its many pensions—which invariably turn out to be large apartments, occupying one or two floors of an apartment house or large, two-family home. Although many of these lack elevators, they are remarkably comfortable and homey, old-fashioned places, with homey, old-fashioned German hausfraus as their proprietresses; and many are quite centrally located, one block or so from the main shopping streets of Kaufingerstrasse and Neuhauser Strasse.

We'll group the pensions by geographical area, and discuss them in generally ascending order of cost within each area.

In the Area of the Bahnhof (Railroad Station)

No more than seven, personally measured minutes of walking time from the *Hauptbahnhof* (main railway station) of Munich are three initial opportunities for low-cost lodging, and of these, one—the 45-room **Pension Flora** at 49 Karlstrasse (phone 59-70-67)—is less than five, personally

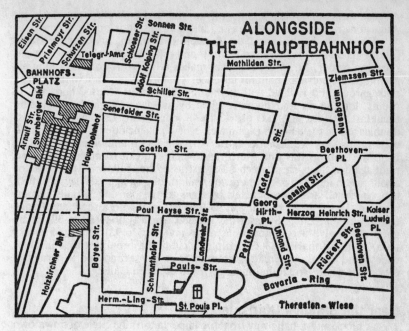

ALONGSIDE THE HAUPTBAHNHOF

measured minutes from the station. Operated by 84-year-old Adolf Baumgartner and his 47-year-old son, it offers small, but very clean, rooms, all with good furniture and wall-to-wall carpeting, at rates of 44 marks ($16.92) single, 60 marks ($23.07) twin, 2 marks (76¢) extra for showers. From the station, walk into Dachauerstrasse, from which Karlstrasse turns left; the Flora is at the intersection of these two streets. **Pension Marion,** at 25 Luisenstrasse (phone 59-25-54), is smaller (only seven rooms) but almost equally central, charges 38 marks ($14.61) for its only single room, 68 marks ($26.15) for twin rooms, all large, with modern furniture. This time, you simply walk up the Luisenstrasse (for about seven minutes) directly from the station. **Pension Armin,** five minutes from the station at 5 Augustenstrasse (phone 59-31-97), is an equally suitable place for backpackers and families alike, to whom it charges 42 marks ($16.15) single, 68 marks ($26.15) twin, only 30 marks ($11.53) per person for triples and quads. An extra 2.50 marks (96¢), handed to English-speaking Herr Mansouri, will bring you a token for the hot-water boiler, good for a ten-minute shower. From the station, walk into Dachauerstrasse, then turn into Augustenstrasse—the first street turning right.

Somewhat farther from the station, but still within ten minutes of it, is an even better low-cost value—the **Pension Hungaria,** 42 Briennerstrasse (phone 52-15-58)—whose owner, the cultivated, English-speaking Dr. Erika Wolff, charges a low 32 marks ($12.30) per person, including breakfast, service and tax, in a double room, 39 marks in a single, and is happy to take families with children, for whom special rates are often offered. Breakfast, to repeat a point, is included; the beds are modern and comfortable and the rooms attractive. To reach the Hungaria, turn left upon leaving the station and follow Dachauerstrasse several blocks to

Augustenstrasse, which shoots off to the right. Walk one block up Augustenstrasse to Briennerstrasse, and the pension is on the corner.

Elsewhere in this area, the **Pension Jedermann,** at 95 Bayerstrasse (phone 53-32-67), is quite a delightful and different place whose English-speaking owner, Mr. Werner Jenke, makes a hobby out of decorating his premises: the entrance hall, for instance, is colorfully papered to resemble a rock garden and is filled with plants and bowers of vines. There are 32 rooms, located on four floors reached by an elevator; singles (including breakfast, service and tax) are 42 to 48 marks ($16.15 to $18.46), most doubles are 58 to 78 marks (again with everything included), triples 75 to 85 marks. Showers are 3 marks extra. And the Jedermann is easily reached from the station: this time, turn right when you exit from the front, and right again at the corner, which is Bayerstrasse; then follow Bayerstrasse for about five minutes to #95, where you walk through a lighted alleyway into a courtyard and are then directed by signs to the pension. Highly recommended. In the same building at 95 Bayerstrasse, with a second entrance from Hermann Lingg Strasse, the **Pension Isaria** (phone 53-36-39) offers good alternative accommodations at 44 marks ($16.92) single, 65 marks ($25) twin, 80 marks ($30.76) triple, including a breakfast that includes cheese and a sausage spread. Reception is on the second floor (there is an elevator), where you'll find manager Frau Gertrud Bullinger.

Near the Stachus (Karlsplatz)

A block-and-a-half away from the important traffic circle of downtown Munich, whose formal name is Karlsplatz, the **Pension Zöllner,** 10 Sonnenstrasse (phone 55-40-35), is undoubtedly the best for the price (31 to 36 marks—$11.92 to $13.84—single, 53 to 65 marks—$20.38 to $25—for double rooms, breakfast, service and tax included) in Munich—a cleanly modernized apartment-type dwelling that has recently installed an efficient elevator. Frau Eleonore Geiger is fluent in English, and serves a generous breakfast that includes cold cuts and cheese.

THE MARK AND THE DOLLAR: As we write this Munich chapter, the German mark has declined to the point where its exchange rate is 2.60 marks to the dollar. Thus, one mark is presently worth 38 U.S. cents, but keep in mind that the figures may change by the time of your own trip to Munich.

In "Pre-War" Munich

And now we move to an area largely untouched by World War II bombs and still marked by the stately grey-stucco buildings associated with pre-1940 Germany. To the left of the train station (as you face it) is the important Goethestrasse. Walk down Goethestrasse for five blocks and the area becomes almost entirely pre-war, residential in character and extremely pleasant. At 51 Goethestrasse, above a small Bavarian-style restaurant, in a building with vaulted stone entrance, old tile floor, wrought iron banisters along stairs, the **Pension Tirol** (phone 53-46-90), managed by

English-speaking Maria Schmitzberger, is an old-fashioned, quiet apartment featuring feather blankets on comfortable, new beds and rates of 48 marks single, 70 marks ($26.92) double, 100 marks triple, 130 marks ($50) quad. Showers are free. The **Hotel-Pension Mariandl** (phone 53-41-08), in the same building, offers more or less the same (45 marks single, 68 marks double, 90 marks triple, 115 marks for a four-bedded room, including breakfast), and owners Hans and Judith Brugger have promised a 10% discount off the above to bearers of this book. (They also operate a flourishing budget restaurant in the same building, mentioned in the restaurant section of this chapter).

In a vaguely similar area, ten minutes on foot from the colorful Viktualienmarkt—Munich's central fruit, meat and vegetable market—an oddity and a bargain is the 50-bed **Gasthof Vietnam** (owned by a refugee Vietnamese professor who also operates a Vietnamese restaurant downstairs at which readers showing this book will receive a 20% discount), 14 Utzschneiderstrasse (phone 268-537), where doubles with breakfast are 48 to 54 marks ($18.46 to $20.76) and showers are free (from the Hauptbahnhof, take streetcar 19 or 20 and get off at Reichenbachplatz). It's really worth staying here simply to view the Viktualienmarkt and especially the sauerkraut stand (in the middle of the market) near the blue and white pole of sauerkraut king Ludwig Freisinger, whose deftness in scooping the sauerkraut (2 marks per pound) out of large wooden barrels is something to see. Nearly as delicious are his sour cucumbers (60 to 100 pfennigs per), which you munch on the spot, like the dozen or so other workaday gourmets around you.

Near the Octoberfest Meadow (A Short Walk from the Train Station)

Pension Westfalia, 23 Mozartstrasse (phone 53-03-77), on the third floor of a handsome, elevator-equipped, four-story house near Goetheplatz, just two blocks from the Octoberfest meadow (take bus 58, or U-Bahn 3 or 6 to Goetheplatz), is one of the city's outstanding pensions. The rooms are spotless, all with shiny wooden floors and bright print drapes; and Herr Bertram Hoos, owner of this budget house, received his training at the Berlin Hilton! I'm usually chary about using the word "excellent," but this one is. Singles are 40 marks ($15.38), doubles with private bath only 78 marks ($30), including breakfast, service and tax.

In this same broadly defined area (because the pensions here are quite scattered), you'll find two higher priced establishments, of which my own preferred choice would be the **Hotel Uhland,** 1 Uhlandstrasse (phone 53-92-77), on the top four stories of a baroque old building, whose wide and polished stairway is usually lined with pots of flowers, making more enjoyable the climb to the top floor (there is, however, an elevator). Here the inclusive charge (room, breakfast, service, tax) is a costly 78 marks ($30) single, 105 marks ($40.38) double, 125 marks ($48.07) triple, but the rooms are exceptionally good and large, and all are with private shower! From the right side of the Bahnhof (as you leave), walk down either Goethestrasse (to Pettenkoferstrasse, turning then into Georg-Hirth Platz) or down Paul Heyse Strasse directly to Georg-Hirth-Platz; or take tram 17 from behind the station, two stops to Georg-Hirth Platz; the pension is just off the Platz, on a short, tree-lined, quiet street. If I could take my pick of any pension in the city, I think I would stay at either the Westfalia (see above) or the Uhland, where there are phones and sinks in all rooms, and gleaming wooden floors; at the end of the street is the meadow that hosts the Octoberfest, and on clear nights you can see the Bavaria Statue shining across the field.

In Schwabing

The Greenwich Village of Munich, Schwabing is a district of artists and scholars, students and drop-outs, sidewalk cafes and galleries—but of very, very few moderately priced lodgings for transients. So far, the single low-cost oasis in my wanderings through here has been the **Pension Doria** on the fourth floor of the elevator-equipped 12 Hohenstaufenstrasse (phone 33-38-72), with seven rooms, of which three singles rent for 45 marks ($17.30), twins for 68 marks ($26.15), triples and quads for 20 marks ($7.69) per person, always with breakfast included; showers are 4 marks, baths 6 marks, extra. Owner Frau Rose-Marie Mäser is fluent in English. This is best reached by streetcar 18 from Karlsplatz to the Kurfürstenplatz stop, a quiet and pleasant location, from which the pension is a two-minute walk. Slightly more expensive, but also a bit more comfortable, is **Pension Schwabinus,** on the ground floor of an apartment house at 2 Georgenstrasse (phone 39-59-28), within an easy stroll of Schwabing's youthful nightlife. Its 19 rooms are tastefully furnished and the lounge-breakfast room has a TV. Rates, with breakfast, service and tax always included, are 59 marks ($22.69) single, 79 marks ($30.38) double, 120 marks ($46.15) quad; buffet breakfast and free showers included. The pension is easily reached from the Giselastrasse subway stop. Simply walk into Georgenstrasse from Leopold-strasse, to the second house on your right.

HOTELS: The budget hotels of Munich are generally more expensive than the pensions ($18 to $22 per person, when breakfast, service and taxes are included), but most of them have elevators, and nearly all are in relatively modern buildings, of post-World War II construction (when much of the central area of Munich was devastated by bombs). And where do you find the $18 to $22 hotels? They are located in every section of Munich, both near and far from the railroad station, but my advice is to walk no more than a block or two for yours. That's because Munich is one of the several cities in Europe whose railroad area is no dark and depressing place, but a fairly decent center of town. When you arrive by train in Munich, you can pick up your bags and find several recommended hotels just a short walk away.

Bayerstrasse and Senefelderstrasse

For example, as you step out the side entrance of the Munich Hauptbahnhof (the central railroad station) onto the Bayerstrasse, you'll be looking directly at the **Hotel Europäischer Hof,** 31 Bayer Strasse, corner of Senefelderstrasse (phone 55-46-21). By any standard—courtesy, cleanliness, extra services—this is now the top "big splurge" of Munich. The hotel literally shines. It has hospital-clean rooms, an elevator and unusually attractive dining hall, a reasonable price structure for bathless double rooms of 105 marks ($40.38), including breakfast, service and tax; and there are a great many rooms without private bath. Singles rent for 60 marks, again including breakfast, service and tax. What's all the more surprising about the Europäischer Hof is that it's a modernistic, seven-story

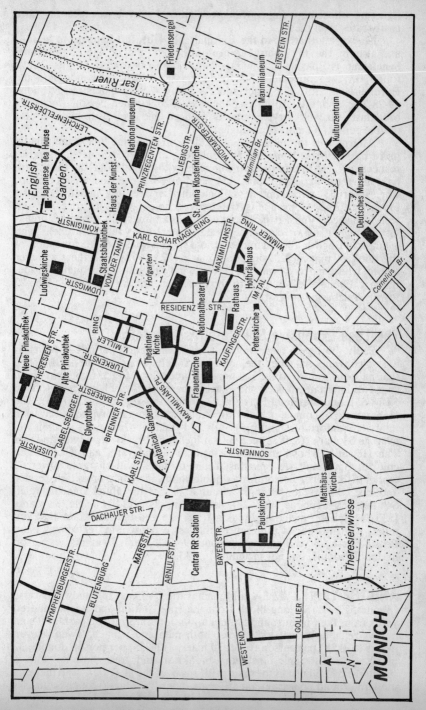

structure whose appearance would ordinarily lead you to expect far more costly rates than these.

Nearby alternatives to the Europäischer Hof, if it happens to be full, are also in the big splurge range—although one of these, the **Hotel Senefelder,** is a particular value that's just barely beyond our limits. That's found on the convenient Senefelderstrasse, which runs alongside the Europäischer Hof, the exact address being 4 Senefelderstrasse (phone 59-28-27); and the charge is 54 marks ($20.76) per person (*including* breakfast, tax and service) for its modern and well-furnished bathless double rooms, 62 marks for singles.

Alternatives to the Hotel Senefelder, on the same block: the slightly more basic Hotels **Monachia** and **Salzburg** at 3 and 1 Senefelderstrasse, respectively. Neither of the two compares with the former—but then, both have numerous double rooms that rent for 88 marks and less per night, singles for 53 marks and less, including service, tax and a generous breakfast. The Monachia is the better choice, with its spacious and well-furnished rooms. It sports, in addition, an unusually attractive breakfast room, and is owned and operated by Frau Irene von Mazzucchelli, who is fluent in English. She guarantees these special rates for 1985 to readers of this book: 52 marks ($20) singles, 88 marks ($33.84) twins. If there was ever a hotel whose narrow, cramped entrance gave no hint of the quality inside, this is it. Phone 55-52-81 to learn about vacancies at the Monachia, 59-56-27 for the Salzburg.

The Less Expensive Schillerstrasse hotels

Sadly, however, there will be times (convention periods—Munich is big on conventions) when the hotels on Senefelderstrasse are filled. When that happens, return to the Bahnhof entrance, look to the right, and you'll spot two alternate choices: the **Hotel Haberstock,** 4 Schillerstrasse (phone 55-78-55), and the **Hotel Helvetia,** 6 Schillerstrasse (phone 55-47-45). The Haberstock, of course, is by far the superior of the two: typically Bavarian in style, comfortable, and pleasantly old-fashioned. Its rates in 1985 will average 53 marks ($20.38) per person including breakfast, service and tax. The Helvetia, whose entrance is through a courtyard, and which has a colorful Bavarian-style breakfast room upstairs, will charge a lower 42 marks ($16.15) per person for a double room, including breakfast, service and tax. Down the street by about a block, the **Hotel Daheim** at 20 Schillerstrasse (phone 59-39-24), asks 60 marks ($23.07) single, 88 marks ($33.84) double, including breakfast, service and tax; and after that you might try (in order of preference) the less expensive but extremely plain **Pension Rose,** 24 Schillerstrasse (phone 59-43-47), only 26 marks per person in double rooms, but not including breakfast.

AND THE Ys: The YMCA in Munich is the **CVJM** at 13 Landwehrstrasse (phone 555-941), a long block from the train station and a few hundred yards from the Stachus, and although its rooms are rather spartan, it's an always reliable budget lodging for both men and women. Twenty-seven marks ($10.38) per person triple, 30 marks ($11.53) per person double, 32 marks ($12.30) single, including breakfast and free showers, with a surcharge of 3.50 marks for senior citizens over the age of 27. And there's a modern ground floor cafeteria (50 seats, open Tuesdays through Saturdays from 6 to 9 p.m. only) serving one-plate meals for 8 marks ($3.07), like grilled cheeseburgers with rice and salad, and offering half a liter of Löwenbräu beer for 2 marks (76¢).

SUPER BUDGET (BY MUNICH STANDARDS): Single rooms for as little as $10.76? Double for $9.23 per person? Hustle over to 36 Thierschstrasse, near the central Isartorplatz, to the 100-year-old apartment house converted into a budget hotel known as **Hotel-Pension Beck** (phone 22-07-08 or 22-57-68). It offers perfectly respectable rooms with modern furniture, wall-to-wall carpets, brightly colored wallpaper, for 20 to 25 marks ($7.69 to $9.61) per person in three-to-five-bedded dorms, 24 to 30 marks ($9.23 to $11.53) per person in bathless doubles, 28 to 36 marks ($10.76 to $13.84) single, with breakfast optional at 5 marks; free showers. Exact amount you'll pay within each range depends on floor number (there are five of them, and no elevator) and size of room, a determination judiciously made by energetic Frau Beck, who offers a special welcome to families with children, and a fully equipped kitchen on each floor, for free use by all guests. From the main station, take the S-Bahn (on which you can use your Eurailpass, free) three stops along to Isartorplatz, and walk about two hundred yards from there, or take streetcar 14, 19 or 20 from the station to the Max-Monument stop. If the Beck can't take you, walk ten minutes from the Hauptbahnhof to the astonishingly low-priced **Fremdenheim Weigl**, 32 Pettenkoferstrasse (second floor, phone 53-24-53), charging 25 to 30 marks single, 40 to 45 marks ($15.38 to $17.30) double, including service and tax. Herr Heinrich Dorsch is the sixtyish owner, a kind and helpful gentleman. The **Pension Spranger,** downstairs in the same building (phone 53-20-46), charges 28 to 35 marks ($10.76 to $13.46) single, 50 to 60 marks double, including service and tax, and its owner speaks fluent English. . . . Or try phoning the highly recommended **Pension Utzelmann,** 6 Pettenkoferstrasse (phone 59-48-89); singles for 50 marks, doubles for 70 marks, including breakfast, service and tax.

PRIVATE HOMES—FOR $8.46 TO $14.61 PER PERSON: If you'd prefer a family-type atmosphere, or a closer contact with local residents, you'll want to consider one of the following eight private homes in Munich, all visited as recently as late 1984.

    Frau Roswitha Wolfer, at 42 Blutenburgstrasse, third floor, rear building (phone 184-618), offers a single and a double room, each with hot and cold running water, for 30 marks ($11.53) per person, not including breakfast (which you can prepare yourself in her kitchen). That's in a fairly central location, near Rotkreuzplatz, reached from the central station by subway. Frau Wolfer speaks excellent English, and there's a coffee shop around the corner, for breakfast, at 4 marks.

    Herr Raimund Wagner and Mr. Lars Strong (the latter an American), 6 Hildegardstrasse (phone 22-62-55), offer 11 beds in single and double rooms for a rather high 45 marks ($17.30) for singles, but only 75 marks ($28.84) for doubles, with breakfast and free showers included; the location could not be more convenient, only five minutes on foot from the Marienplatz. While backpackers may not feel at home here, readers seeking a cultivated atmosphere in a setting of antiques will be thoroughly delighted. Some rooms are occupied by actors and actresses working in nearby theatres. The two gentlemen also own a country-house near

Chiemsee, Bavaria's largest lake (between Munich and Salzburg), where they rent rooms for weekends, or in winter for ski vacations. And Lars Strong spends about half an hour with arriving guests, delivering an orientation lecture on what to do and see in Munich. From the central station, take streetcars 14 or 19 to the Schauspielhaus stop, or the subway to Isartorplatz.

Frau Theresa Schramm, 25 Residenzstrasse, fourth floor, elevator (phone 220-198), is the unquestioned star of all private-room-renting people in Munich, for three reasons: her rates are economical, the location could not be better, and Frau Schramm offers free showers and use of her pressing iron. Each room is large and airy (one has the only balcony on the entire Residenzstrasse), and furnished with taste, and while three of the rooms are without running water and two have cold running water only, use of the bathroom is, of course, free. As I've said, this amazing landlady will permit you to use her pressing iron, and she will keep your perishable food in the fridge for no extra charge. And how much for all this largesse? Twenty-two marks ($8.46) per person in either two twin or three triple rooms! This poor man's Shangri-la is located between Marienplatz and Odeonsplatz but nearer to Odeonsplatz. Look for a famous confiserie—the Konditorei und Café Hag—in the same building.

Frau Katharina Mörtlbauer is a friendly, fast-talking woman who speaks some English and lives in a grey apartment block at 14 Passauerstrasse, third floor, 49 steps up (phone 760-7891), where she rents two double rooms—very nicely furnished—at 30 marks ($11.53) per bed, with breakfast optional at 5 marks more, and showers for free. Take the U-Bahn to the Harras station (the location is central), and walk about two minutes from there.

Frau Sophie Decker, whose residence at 19 Am Brombeerschlag (phone 714-97-96), is in a quiet residential area where buildings more than two stories high aren't permitted, rents a single room for 42 marks ($16.15), a double for 38 marks ($14.61) per person, including breakfast and free showers. Best for readers with cars, Mrs. Decker's is only 20 minutes by public transportation from the center of Munich, but you have to change twice. A taxi, for your initial trip there, will run about 20 marks.

Herr and Frau Friedrich and Theresa Boiger, at 9 Hans-Sachs-Strasse (phone 260-38-35), a couple in their 80s, rent two twins and a four-bedded room to backpackers and families alike, at 54 marks ($20.76) per twin, 100 marks ($38.46) per quad, with free use of a kitchen, free showers, but no breakfast. While the rooms are somewhat overladen with old furniture, the price is acceptable and the location good, almost in the very center of the city. From the Hauptbahnhof, take streetcar 27 to Fraunhofer-Müllerstrasse (four stops away), walk three minutes from there, and then ascend to the second floor. Frau Boiger speaks some English.

Frau Rosa Braun, at 37 Raintalerstrasse (phone 69-21-603), sister of Frau Mörtlbauer (see above), lives on the ground floor of a new apartment block, where she rents a nicely furnished, very clean room, with a bed that folds to the wall during the day to provide more space, the floor covered by a homespun sheep's wool carpet, for 30 marks ($11.53) per night, complete with breakfast. Take streetcar 15 or 25 from the center to Tegernseer Landstrasse (a trip of about ten minutes), walk from there into Wirtstrasse (not in the direction where the trees are, but where the bank is), then turn into the first street turning left, which is Raintalerstrasse, and you'll see a row of modern, brown and grey, seven-story buildings—Frau Braun lives in

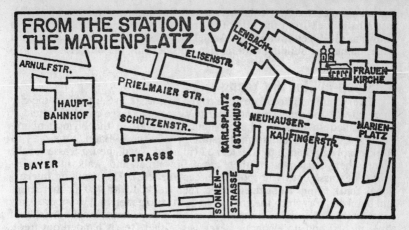

the first (you guessed right) brown house. Walking distance from Tegernseer Landstrasse streetcar-stop to her address is two minutes. Very little English spoken, but this is no great handicap, as Frau Braun understands the basic words.

Frau Katharina Ohde, 64 Nordendstrasse (phone 37-87-89), offers two rooms with two beds per, free use of her kitchen, free showers, and a separate, private w.c., for 30 marks ($11.53) per bed per night, but without breakfast; she occupies the fifth floor, reached by elevator, of a new apartment block built in 1977. Location is excellent: in the central Schwabing area, easily reached from the Central Railway Station by taking U-Bahn 8, the line going to Olympiazentrum, to the Hohenzollernplatz stop; or by boarding streetcar 18 at Stachus to the Kurfürstenplatz stop—from there it's a five-minute walk.

Frau Elke Hübner, 15 Bethmannstrasse (phone 96-88-37), rents a nicely furnished small apartment with two beds and kitchenette for a daily rate of 64 marks ($27.82), including breakfast, or for a weekly rate of 185 marks ($71.15), without breakfast. Frau Hübner speaks fairly fluent English, lives on the second floor of a modern building constructed in 1970. Take the S-Bahn from the Hauptbahnhof to Ismaning (a lovely residential district, north of the Englischer Garten, near the Isar River), a 15-minute trip; from the Ismaning station, Bethmannstrasse is five minutes by foot. An ideal home for longer stays.

STUDENT ACCOMMODATIONS: The only true "student hotel" of Munich is the large (420 beds) and bright, three-story **Haus International,** 87 Elisabethstrasse (phone 18-50-81), in Schwabing, whose facilities include a sauna and indoor swimming pool. It accepts both sexes, imposes no age limits, requires no student card, is open all year around, and charges only 30 marks ($11.53) per person in a five-bedded room, 32 marks in a quad, 34 marks per in a triple, 36 marks twin and 40 marks ($15.38) single. Take subway 8 from the Hauptbahnhof to Hohenzollernplatz (fourth stop), and walk five minutes from there. The female-only counterpart of the above establishment, charging 26 marks ($10) per person per night in its double and triple rooms, 28 marks in single rooms, always with breakfast included, is the nun-operated **Marienherberge,** at 9 Goethestrasse (phone 55-58-91), just a half-block from the side of the railroad station, which sometimes is known as the **Jugendwohnheim.** Actual lodgings at 9 Goethestrasse are in a huge, unmarked building with no sign outside; ring the buzzer.

A "Sleep-in" for the Young

Every summer from late June to the first week in September, the city augments its student accommodations by erecting a large circus-type tent at a site called In den Kirschen (phone 14-14-300) in the Nymphenburg-Botanical Garden area (from the station, take the U-Bahn, subway, 1 to Rotkreuzplatz, change to streetcar 12 (marked Amalienburgstrasse) to the Botanischer Garten stop, then cross the street and walk into Franz-Schrank-Strasse until you spot the circus-like tent). The resulting **International Youth Camp Kapuzinerhölzl** is then stocked with 400 air mattresses and blankets, for which the charge, to both young men and women, is only 5 marks ($1.92) a night. No curfew; no official age limit; maximum stay of three nights; and no alcoholic beverages, either (tea is handed out free). Phone first to inquire about space.

Youth Hostels and Camp Sites

Munich's largest youth hostel, the **Jugendherberge** at 20 Wendl-Dietrichstrasse (phone 72-36-50), near Rotkreuzplatz, can accommodate up to 550 guests in six- to 40-bed dorms with doubledecker beds, at a charge of 11 marks ($4.23) per night for "juniors" (under the age of 26), 13 marks ($5) for "seniors" (over 26), plus a one-time charge of 2 marks (76¢) for sheets. Breakfast is included; hot showers are free; and a canteen serves two-course meals for 5 marks ($1.92) from 5:45 to 7 p.m. Take subway 1 from Central Station to Rotkreuzplatz, then walk into Wendl-Dietrichstrasse. Munich's slightly classier youth hostel, the **Jugend-gästehaus** at 4 Miesingstrasse (phone 723-65-50), near the Hellabrunn Zoo, accommodates up to 344 persons, some in single and twin-bedded rooms, most in dorms with three to six cots, at a charge per person, including breakfast, of 23 marks ($8.84) single, 19 marks ($7.30) twin, 17 marks ($6.53) triple or quad, 14 marks ($5.38) in six-bedded dorms. Showers, meals, and other policies identical to those at the Jugendherberge. Take subway 8 from the Central Station to Sendlinger Tor Platz, then board bus 57 to the Thalkirchen (Zoo) stop. Both hostels, unfortunately, require an International Hostel Card.

Munich's largest camping site, the **Campingplatz Thalkirchen,** at 49 Zentralländstrasse (phone 723-17-07), open from mid-March through October, is located in picturesque, park-like surroundings along the Isar River, in a setting spacious enough for 2,500 guests and their caravans, cars, bikes and tents, for whom it provides washrooms, kitchens, self-service cafeterias, and even a bank. The per-person per-night charge is only 6 marks ($2.30), plus 6 marks per trailer (caravan, here), 3.50 marks per tent, 4 marks per car, 1 mark per motorbike. If you're on foot, take the U-Bahn to the Implerstrasse Station and change there to bus 57, which stops but two minutes away from the camping site. If you're with car or bike, simply ask for the Zoo area.

READERS' HOTEL SELECTIONS: "At the **Hotel Lisa,** 51 Herzogstrasse (phone 33-38-08), rooms have Kleenex in the bathrooms, featherbeds, and are well decorated, as in a home; breakfast, included in the price, is like a huge Dutch breakfast, not the German continental-style: cheese, ham, sausage, jelly, honey, egg, orange juice; older travelers will love it. A single costs 60 marks, 90 marks double—higher than the hotels *you* recommend in Munich, but worth it, in my view. This is in Schwabing, an easy subway ride four stops from the Hauptbahnhof to the Hohenzollernplatz, and then a three-block walk along Herzogstrasse. Although only limited English is spoken here, they understand 'single', 'double', 'do you have a room?', 'for two nights', 'three nights', etc." (John McGee, San Diego, California). . . . **"Pension am Karlstor,** 34 Neuhauser Strasse (phone 59-35-96), on a 'walking street' near the central Karlsplatz—right off it, in fact—next to a movie house, provided us with a lovely, large room with six beds, no bath, at a cost of 110 marks for the four of us, breakfast included" (Janet Lee, Transvaal, South Africa). . . . **"Hotel Bayernland** at 73 Bayerstrasse, phone 533-153 or 539-478, just three minutes from the Munich train station by turning right at the Bayerstrasse exit and walking one block, was our best find in three months of travel. This large, modern, elevator-equipped hotel offers spacious rooms, even with 15-foot ceilings, at prices lower than many nearby pensions. Singles are 55 to 70 marks, doubles 80 to 95 marks, including breakfast, and showers are free" (Jim Fuhrman, Beverly Hills, California). . . . **"Please include Hotel Grafinger Hof,** at 7 Zenettistrasse; it is a few short blocks from the Oktoberfest park, directly across the street from a laundromat and Catholic church. Gerhard Meyer, the English-speaking proprietor, was more than a host. He even offered to walk several blocks to pick up our rental car. His immaculate twin-bedded rooms rent for 67 marks ($25.76) nightly, including breakfast. Showers are 2.50 marks extra. . . . Enough cannot be said for the friendliness, good times, good food and drink in Munich" (Tom and Michelle Flesser, Evergreen Park, Illinois).

READERS' PENSION SELECTIONS: "Pension Süzer at 1 Mittererstrasse (phone 53-35-21), near the station, is operated by the very friendly Errol Süzer. Rooms were well appointed and spotless, and for a change there was toast for breakfast! Seventy-two marks ($27.69) for a double room, including breakfast" (P. Sheriff, Belmont, New South Wales, Australia; with an additional recommendation from Dr. George Sandusky, Thornville, Ohio; note by AF: owned by an English-speaking Turkish family, the Süzer reduces its rates to 30 marks, $11.53, per person in a 4-bedded room, with breakfast included. Very clean, and on the third floor of an elevator-equipped apartment building). . . . "A truly budget-priced find: **Hotel-Pension Erika,** 8 Landwehrstrasse (phone 554-327), one very long block from the station, where a large, clean single room in summer was had for 39 marks ($15), including a huge breakfast (both black and white bread kept fresh in glass receptacles, butter, jam, coffee, and an egg), modern plumbing in each room, a parking lot for guests, an elevator. Frau Kassner speaks 'not too good English,' but it's not at all needed. Truly, I feel, a buy in this 'not-so-inexpensive-for-singles' Bavarian capital" (Michael J. Romano, Staten Island, New York). . . . **"Pension Schmellergarten,** 20 Schmellerstrasse (phone 77-31-57), is only a five-minute U-Bahn ride from the Marienplatz to Poccistrasse. Here are spacious rooms renting for only 45 marks single, 68 double, 96 marks triple (the latter with private bath), including breakfast, service and tax, which is quite a bargain for Munich. I haven't words enough to praise the proprietors, Herr and Frau Ambie!" (Carolyn Planutis, Chicago, Illinois; note by A.F.: made suspicious by the name, I've checked the Munich phone book, and sure enough, the Schmellergarten exists!). . . . "Frau Gebhardt, owner of the **Pension Gebhardt,** 38 Goethestrasse (phone 539-446), is warm, friendly and outgoing, and speaks enough English to assist non-German-speaking tourists. She also loves children, as our son Kevin can attest. Rates, including breakfast, are 57 marks single, 83 marks double, 108 marks triple, 120 marks for a four-bedded room, children 4 to 12 half price, baths 2.50 marks" (Carol Conklin, Canton, Ohio; and strong recent seconding recommendations from Patricia A. Kennedy, Brooklyn, New York, and others). . . . "During the most heavily booked period of the Octoberfest, a bystander whom we met by chance directed us to the **Pension Luna,** on the second floor of 5 Landwehrstrasse (phone 59-78-33), about three blocks from the station. There, owner Frau Elfriede Schewe, who speaks English, charges only 45 marks ($17.30) single, 71 marks ($27.30) twin, 94 marks ($36.15) triple, inclusive of breakfast. Some other lucky reader might also try it at a time when Munich is packed" (Lorna Reid, Islington, Ontario, Canada). . . . "For the longer term visitor to Munich, Herr Rudolph Keis rents efficiency apartments in his **Pension Welti** at 45 Uhdestrasse (phone 791-15-42) in the quiet residential neighborhood of Solln. Each apartment consists of a bedroom/livingroom, bathroom, fully equipped kitchen, and included are television, telephone, all linens, and daily maid service, all for a 1985 price of 70 marks ($26.92) per apartment per night. Take the U-Bahn to Harras, and then bus 66 to Herterich-strasse, from which it's only a short walk to Uhdestrasse" (James A. Pope, Greensboro, North Carolina; note by AF: Rudolph Keis was born in Germany, emigrated to the U.S., served 12 years in the U.S. Army, and then returned to Germany, from New York City in 1963; motoring tourists can park in his under-ground garage for an optional charge. Singles cost 48 marks and doubles 70 marks in 1985).

3. Restaurants & Meals

I envy anyone their first trip to Munich. Even now, the memory of Bavarian cooking lingers in both my mind and taste buds. And what a thrill it was to obtain these feasts for a sum that would buy a mere snack at home. Have you got $4? With that in your pocket, you'll never go hungry in Munich. For instance:

MEALS FOR $4 AND UNDER: Even the department stores serve surprisingly tasty, noninstitutional dishes, and for proof of that I recom-mend, first, the enormously popular, crowded, stand-up, basement restau-rant called "Klause" of the **Kaufhof Department Store** on the Stachus (Karlsplatz), 400 yards from the train station, where there's always an attractive, copiously portioned *sonderangebot* (special, daily, one-platter meal) such as stuffed roast veal with dumplings and stringbeans for 8.50 marks ($3.26). In the same downstairs area, liver dumpling soup is 2.80 marks ($1.07), spaghetti with parmesan cheese 4.50 marks ($1.73), fried haddock with mixed salad 5 marks ($1.92), potato salad or french fries 1.80 marks (69¢) each, half a liter of tap beer 2.50 marks (96¢), coffee 1.50 marks (57¢) a cup, and a large assortment of pastries (try the Schwarz-wälder kirschtorte, a delight) average 2.50 marks (96¢) per slice. A general rule for budget living in any German city is to search out the major department store and then head for its **basement** restaurant, which is always half as costly as the already inexpensive upstairs restaurant that most German department stores maintain. The basement of the **Kaufhof** is a prime example.

A less-than-$4 meal outside the department store district can be had at the **Restaurant Mariandl,** 51 Goethestrasse, not far from the train station in the area of the Munich medical school. Here, weekdays only, and from 11:30 a.m. to 2:30 p.m. only, a home-cooked mensa-menu of two courses (example: a creamy cauliflower soup followed by roast leberkäs with mixed salad) is offered in a large, 150-seat dining room for only 8 marks ($3.07), service included. While officially for medical students only, the restaurant admits everyone, and the location is quite easily found from the train station, in the upper area of Goethestrasse, near the trees.

The cheaper sit-down meals in Munich are to be had at the restaurants of Munich's famous beer companies, which operate these places as much for prestige as for profit. There are eight such restaurants in Munich, huge establishments offering Bavarian specialties at extremely low prices. Two of the best are found on one of Munich's main streets—Neuhauser Strasse, which becomes Kaufingerstrasse just before it approaches the Munich Rathaus. The biggest, best and least expensive of these is the **Augustiner Grossgaststätten,** 16 Neuhauser Strasse, which is also the most typically Bavarian in decor, with tremendous vaulted arches and scrubbed oak tables. Here the price for a half liter of Augustiner beer is among the cheapest in town (2.60 marks), and the prices for solid food (all Bavarian) are correspondingly low: 3.50 marks for Munich's famous bread soup with brown onions, 8.50 marks for a stew of chicken and giblets (*geflügelreis*) and light, fluffy dumplings. Important—order only from the typed menu headed *Tagesspezialitäten* (which lists numerous main plates for less than 12 marks ($4.61), numerous wurst dishes for 4 and 6 marks; and go only into the blue-tableclothed room on the left (it bears the sign "Augustiner Bierhalle"), and not into the better-furnished, white-tableclothed area on the right, where the prices rise by 10% and more. A few doors up, the more modern **Pschorrbräu-Bierhallen,** 11 Neuhauser Strasse (operated by the company that produces Pschorrbräu beer), is somewhat more expensive unless you know how to order Munich's cheap wurst specialties from the typewritten menu, but I was still recently able to have bouillon with liver dumplings (3.50 marks), a main plate of Bavarian sausage with mixed salad (10.50 marks), and of course a huge glass (half liter) of Pschorrbräu beer, all for less than 17 marks.

When, by the way, you've completed the walk down Neuhauser Strasse, into Kaufinger Strasse, you'll eventually arrive at the Munich Rathaus (city hall), at which this pedestrians' thoroughfare widens into a small square in front of the city building. The street just before the Rathaus is called Weinstrasse, and at the corner (1 Weinstrasse) is the famous, old **Donisl Restaurant,** formerly a guard-house, and now the city's oldest restaurant, with a Bavarian-type skylight, held aloft by wooden walls garlanded with green leaves and blue-and-white ribbons. It is, despite these charms, one of the more moderate restaurants in Munich, serving daily platters (large portions) for 9 marks; and it opens as early as 9 a.m., when it specializes in the famous white sausage (*weisswürste*—5 marks for two of them, accompanied by sweet mustard) of Munich—something you should try. Specializing entirely in sausage dishes (including weisswürste) is the nearby **Bratwurst-Herzl** at 3 Heiliggeiststrasse, only a few yards from Marienplatz, near the huge Viktualienmarkt. Here, if you arrive as early as 7:30 or 8 a.m., you'll already find tables crowded with Muncheners merrily munching away on weisswürste, which are produced fresh on the premises each day. Average price for a dish of sausages (posted on blackboard menus) is 6 marks ($2.30), and you can choose among eight different brands of beer costing 2.70 marks ($1.03) per half liter. At the Donisl, a great many customers are tourists; at the Bratwurst-Herzl, you'll be among the very few outsiders. Closed Sundays.

IN AND NEAR THE RAILROAD STATION: In Munich's railroad station (Hauptbahnhof), you'll be happy to learn, there is now a **cafeteria** facing track 17, which stays open daily from 6 a.m. to 11 p.m. Its offerings are tasty and inexpensive. I recently had a good Deutsches Beefsteak, mashed potatoes and gravy, vegetables, salad and really excellent coffee (1.50 marks), for a total of 9 marks ($3.46). The selection is not large (about six entrees a day), but you don't have to wrestle with the language here, and can simply point to what looks good.

A bit of a splurge: the less modern and more typically Bavarian dinery (waitresses in dirndls, yellow-and-brown tablecloths, birch chairs) in the railroad station area, known as the **Badische Weinstuben,** 3 Lammerstrasse (in the rear of the Hotel Württemberger Hof; from the front entrance of the station, turn left along Dachauerstrasse, then left at Marsstrasse to Lammerstrasse). This is a choice for our more adventurous readers in search of truly typical Bavarian fare (liver dumplings, blood sausages, and all the rest). While everything here is à la carte, dishes are all reasonably priced and marvelously varied: gravy-colored noodles cooked with ham and served with mixed vegetables, for 11.50 marks ($4.42), grilled heart of beef with dumplings and salad for 13.50 marks ($5.19). And although the liver dumpling soup at 4 marks ($1.53) is priced higher than elsewhere in Munich, it's of top quality. You'll enjoy a good meal at the Badische Weinstuben for $7, a feast for $10 if you include the *leberknödelsuppe* (liver dumpling soup)—worthy of a Michelin star. Closed Sundays.

Back to the budget level: Probably the most popular restaurant in the station area, famous for its large portions, is the **Gaststätte Grüner Hof,** at 35 Bayerstrasse, in front of the side entrance to the station, which offers five two-course menus daily ranging in price from 8.50 to 14 marks ($3.26 to $5.38); à la carte plates from 3.80 to 14 marks ($1.46 to $5.38). Their schweinebraten with semmelknödel and kraut-salat for 10 marks ($3.84) is unique in Munich for size, price and quality (they have their own butcher shop). Open every day, from 7:30 a.m. until midnight.

NEAR CITY HALL: The **Murr Stube,** at the rear of the Vinzenz Murr butcher and delicatessen shop at 7 Rosenstrasse, one block from Marienplatz (and the Town Hall), is a delightful place tucked away at the back of a butcher/grocery shop, and serves a daily self-service *gedeck* (table d'hôte meal) for 5.90 marks ($2.26), sometimes for less, that usually consists of something like a meat platter with fried egg, salad, and a fruit salad. The Murr also serves marvelous leberkäse (made on the premises and therefore very fresh) for 2.60 marks the portion, as well as a large variety of sandwiches from 1.60 to 2.50 marks. The Rosenstrasse, where all this is found, is the street directly opposite the City Hall; go there at 11 a.m. to see the famous bellringing figurines, then head for lunch to Mr. Murr's remarkable butcher shop!

In the very same area, the **Weisses Bräuhaus,** 10 Tal (just off the Marienplatz—walk through the archway near the Beck store), a typical, old, Bavarian restaurant with a fortress-like arched dining room, serves large platter meals for 12 marks ($4.61), a mammoth schweineschnitzel with mixed salad at 11.50 marks ($4.42) that is more than enough for two, and is especially known for its unusual Weizenbier or Weissbier, a bittersweet-tasting white beer brewed with wheat and served in an over-sized champagne glass, with a slice of lemon on top: 3 marks ($1.15) per half liter. Note how the waitresses, all middle-aged, keep leather money bags under their tiny white aprons.

IN SCHWABING: In **Schwabing,** the Greenwich Village of Munich, budget restaurants are fairly numerous, but certainly one of the most popular is the **Gaststätte Weinbauer** at 5 Fendstrasse, off the Leopoldstrasse, where the day's menu ranges from 7.80 to 13.50 marks, and the servings are huge. Almost painfully plain in appearance, it is jammed with customers who crowd around large tables, and pack away the most massive plates of meat in gravy, mounds of potatoes and vegetables. Closed Wednesdays.

The broad **Leopoldstrasse,** from which the Weinbauer is just a short walk, is generally considered to constitute the heart of Schwabing (the small streets at the end are actually far less commercial and more truly Bohemian). On the Leopoldstrasse itself, the budget champion in **Gaststätte Zur Brez'n,** at 72 Leopoldstrasse, corner Fendstrasse, a typical Bavarian-style restaurant, with three dining rooms on three levels. Daily platters for 8 marks ($3.07) might include broad noodles with ham or an egg and green salad. Large salad bowls are 8 marks ($3.07), spare ribs 13 marks ($5), apfelstrudel mit schlagsahne 5.50 marks ($2.11), coffee 2.40 marks (92¢), half a liter of beer from the barrel 2.70 marks ($1.03). In summer 1984, my preferred choice here was the Münchner Sauerkrautteller—three meats and two sausages, served with lots of kraut and mashed potatoes—a highlight (for 11 marks, $4.23) of the Munich visit.

A final Leopoldstrasse restaurant is the large (80 tables) and usually jammed **Hahnhof** at 32 Leopoldstrasse, corner Giselastrasse on that stretch of the wide boulevard where sidewalk artists and sellers of handicrafts station themselves in summer. Here, on weekdays in summer only, the typewritten menu lists two-course dinners for 11 and 14 marks, service and tax included, and the meals are consumed in a vast sidewalk-café area of the restaurant.

NEAR THE BAVARIA RING: At the end of the Schwanthalerstrasse (where some of you may be staying), at 85, you next find: the good, brown and very prewar **Gasthof zur Festwiese,** plain, all of wood, and with no tablecloths, but with hearty two-course meals for 8, 9 and 10 marks (the latter including dessert).

IN THE UNIVERSITY AREA: Schellingstrasse, which runs off Ludwig Strasse, just below the Siegestor and the university buildings, is the classic budget restaurant street in the university area. One block down Schelling, at the corner of Amalienstrasse: the Bavarian-style **Gaststätte Atzinger,** at 9 Schellingstrasse, serves two-course meals for 7.50 and 8.50 marks, all included; big platters for 6 and 8 marks. Not far from Schellingstrasse, at 33 Türkenstrasse, **Gaststätte Allotria** is only slightly higher priced, but also offers nightly jazz starting at 9 p.m., for which there is no extra charge.

ELSEWHERE: And always remember that meals at the **Mathäser Bierstadt,** 5 Bayerstrasse, which you'll be visiting later in this chapter, are highly favored by the Bavarian citizenry, far more so than at the Hofbräuhaus. Sausages and sauerkraut for 7 marks ($2.69); two eggs with ham and roast potatoes for 7.50 marks ($2.88); complete dinners are priced at 15 marks. The "Beer City" has a cheap sausage stand out front and various large rooms; many platters are priced under 7 marks, and I find the food pretty good for a mass-produced operation.

The least expensive area of the Mathäser is the corridor-like restaurant through which you'll first pass on entering, on your way to the main rooms. There you'll be given a special small menu (it bears the designation, at the bottom, *Schnellgaststätte*) offering unusually good prices for Munich—soup for 2.60 marks, wurst plates for 4.50 and 6 marks, main courses for 6.50 to 12 marks—unavailable in the large, noncorridor-like areas. One budget tip here is to order half a roast chicken (½ *Brathuhn;* 7.50 marks) for two persons and share it; it's more than enough. Then, after gorging at unusually low cost, you can head upstairs to the mammoth Bierhalle with its brass band and "Zum Prosit" songs, or to any of the several other dining rooms in this veritable "beer city."

Something lighter? Thousands of Munich's working people walk every day through the underground shopping center of Stachus, where many make a short detour to the **Sandwich Buffet** (between the escalators) to munch one of 50 varieties of sandwiches, priced from 2.50 to 3.50 marks, and all named after cities; the "London," consisting of a Zeppelin-shaped roll stuffed with butter, roast beef, salami, lettuce and cucumbers, and spiced with paprika, is the Bavarian version of our hero sandwich. Half a liter of beer adds 2.50 marks more, but a glass of milk is only 1.20 marks. Other highly popular shops in this underground center are **Sieber,** a butcher shop with a small Imbiss-counter, selling, for an average price of 2.70 marks, all kinds of sausages, leberkäse, goulash soup and hamburgers, eaten on the spot. Everything Sieber sells, except bread, comes from his own butcher shop and is of top quality. Finally, next to Sieber, in an underground passage leading to the Hertie Department Store, called **Schmankerlgasse** (treat-street), you'll find a very tempting line of 20 tiny booth-like shops selling, among other items, meats, sausages, bread, pastries, brioches, fish, wine, coffee, ice cream, vegetable juices, fruit and pizza, and, just in case, at the end of this line, to your right, are very clean, and free, public toilets.

A BUDGET RECAP: To single out the top budget values from the foregoing list: they're the **Gaststätte Grüner Hof** alongside the station; the restaurant of the Vinzenz Murr butcher shop (**Murr Stube**), near the Town Hall; the basement of the **Kaufhof Department Store;** the corridor-like Schnellgaststätte of the **Mathäser Bier Stadt;** the **Augustiner Bierhalle;** and the **Weinbauer** in Schwabing.

SOME FINAL THOUGHTS: An important food tip: never order coffee with your meals in Germany. It has a foul taste, and it's liable to cost as much as 3 marks ($1.15) a cup. Order beer, Coca-Cola or an apfelsaft (cider)—uniformly good, and uniformly priced at about 85¢ a glass.

I can't end this section without urging you, strenuously, to taste the *Leberkäs* (literally, liver-cheese) at the **Imbiss Café** in the railroad station— for what may turn out to be the most delicious snack of your life. You'll find this sort of Leberkäs only in Munich, and in its best form at the aforementioned spot. Walk along the inner portion of the railroad station (next to where you go out to the trains, in front of track 16) until you see a counter surrounded by twelve upturned beer kegs—that's the Imbiss, which is also on the other side of the station's Schäffler-Saal Restaurant (you eat the Leberkäs standing up, at one of the kegs). A portion of Leberkäs, with *eine semmel* (a roll) and a small glass of beer will cost 5.25 marks. Douse it well with your serving of mild mustard, eat it, and you'll not only reorder another portion (2.20 marks per 100 grams, bread is 40 pfennigs, and the ethereal mustard *senf* is free), but you'll dream of it later—as I presently am doing—in other cities, and at other times, when Munich-style Leberkäs isn't attainable at four times the price.

THE BEER GARDENS: If it's a sunny day between May and October, and you're tired of sights and craving simple relaxation, you head—in Munich—for any of a dozen *biergarten* (beer gardens), which are open-air restaurants under shady trees (usually chestnut), serving beer and a small variety of such cold food items as sausages with black bread, cheese, roast chicken. These are found in every location, but my favorites are the **Augustinerkeller** at 52 Arnulfstrasse (near the Starnberger Bahnhof at the side of the main station); the **Chinesischer Turm** in the *Englischer Garten* (English Gardens) —take the subway to the Giselastrasse stop in Schwabing and walk from there; and the **Aumeister** at 1 Sondermeierstrasse, reached by taking the subway (U-Bahn) to the Studentenstadt stop in Schwabing, and walking for about 15 minutes into the English Gardens. In the beer gardens, price for a *mass* (liter) of beer served either in a large glass (big enough for raising a couple of goldfish) or earthen mug or stein is 5.50 marks, including a tip earned by the middle-aged waitress (some looking like Olympic discus champions) who carries up to 12 steins at a time (the world's record, held by a Munich waitress, naturally, is 21 steins). Buying a mass is your admission ticket, and nobody casts a dirty look if you bring along your own food (thereby saving money) and start cutting up bread and meat on the wooden table, like everyone else is doing. Here's a thoroughly gemütlich experience.

THE BIG SPLURGE: For this, the **Nürnberger Bratwurstglöckl am Dom,** 9 Frauenplatz, next to the distinctive two-tower cathedral of Munich, a short walk from the City Hall, is the place to go. An atmospheric old restaurant, with an Albrecht Dürer room upstairs, it is so very traditional that it serves in traditional tin dishes! Hot plates average 11 to 17 marks, but you might possibly like to order the cheaper and renowned Schweinswürst specialty—tiny sausages, about as large as your little finger. Four of these served with sauerkraut make a very tasty lunch at 6 marks. With soup at 3.50 marks and salad for 4, you'll be riotously stuffed for less than 14 marks. The normal meals, however, will run around 20 marks ($7.69), and this time are almost as memorable for the setting (Hansel and Gretel-type chairs, old oak tables, etchings and flowers) as for the food. Location, once again, is directly at the back of the *Dom* (Cathedral).

STARVATION BUDGET MEALS: A word of cheer for young folks: the **University Mensa,** at 13 Leopoldstrasse (subway station is Giselastrasse), officially for students with student cards only, is so busy serving an average of 7,500 meals per day that spot-checks are very rare, and practically any student-age person, whether enrolled at the university or not, can get a two-course, soup-and-main course plate meal for either 2.20 marks (84¢) (Stamm) or 3 marks ($1.15) (Auswahlessen), Monday through Friday from 11 a.m. to 2 p.m. Get there early, buy a yellow chip for Stamm or a blue one for Auswahlessen at one of the ground-floor booths, then walk up to the first-floor dining rooms. The menus (listing, by the way, the number of calories next to each item), are posted on the walls. Similar meals, rates and hours are available at the **Mensa** of the **Technische Universität,** 17 Arcisstrasse, ten minutes by foot from the railway station. And still another

Mensa can be found in the Olympic Village area (now partly used as student quarters and dorms), at 9 Helene-Mayer-Ring. This is **Mensa Oberwiesenfeld,** which serves lunch only, Monday through Friday, from 11 a.m. to 1:45 p.m. Take the subway to Olympiastadion. On my last trip to Munich in the summer of 1984, I also found that the lunch counters in Munich's dime stores (such as the Woolworth-Imbiss at 27 Kaufingerstrasse) still serve a mountainous plate lunch (bratwurst, potatoes and sauerkraut) for exactly 5.40 marks ($2.07). The town is studded, as well, with the German equivalent of hot dog stands, serving Bavarian sausages-on-a-bun that would please a gourmet at three times the price. At one of these, nearly a half-pound of sausage on a large roll, with mustard, costs 4 marks ($1.53), and it's a meal in itself. And shashlik (chunks of meat, interspersed with onions, served on a stick) is yours for exactly 4 marks ($1.53).

READERS' FOOD COMMENTS: "We'd like to vigorously dispute one point with you: You say never order coffee in Germany—that it's bad tasting and very expensive. Germany is the first place after almost seven weeks of touring where we found honest-to-goodness, good, American-type coffee . . . *everywhere.* And we found it cheaper than beer in many places" (Jess and Alice Brewis, Taylor, Michigan). . . . "I have insufficient words to praise the Munich beer. It was wonderful. The food, too, was excellent, although I found the sausage skins a little too tough for my teeth" (H.R. Baker, Rockhampton, Queensland, Australia). . . . "A night at the Hofbräuhaus or Mathäser Bierstadt is not complete without sampling German white radishes (about the size of a cucumber), served spiraled and salted" (E. M. Swan, Alexandria, Virginia).

READERS' BREAKFAST SELECTIONS: "One can eat breakfast for about 1.20 marks if, in the morning, one walks up the Sendlingerstrasse from Marienplatz. On the right side of the street, about two or three blocks from Marienplatz, is a bakery; stop there and grab a few breakfast rolls. Continue in the same direction, and on the left is the **Tschibo Coffee Store,** where a full cup of good coffee is 80 pfennigs" (Lynn A. Davis, Munich, Germany). . . . "A cheap cup of coffee? At the numerous Tschibo coffee stores, coffee is sold at 80 pfennigs (30¢) a cup. You drink it standing up, but it is about as good as anywhere else here. Where to find one? Try **Rosental,** near the Viktualienmarkt (the open-air green-grocery market)—also near the Rathaus" (Dr. L.K. Wynston, Long Beach, California). . . . "For people like me who are still hungry after a continental breakfast, Munich's **Kaufhalle Department Store** on Neuhauser Strasse's mall, offers an inexpensive treat from 9 a.m. to 11 a.m. at its basement snack counter. For 2.50 marks (96¢) you are served a boiled egg, two rolls, butter, jam and coffee or tea; for 3.20 marks (.$1.23), you get the same with coldmeats" (Mary Cummings, Minneapolis, Minnesota).

READERS' RESTAURANT SELECTIONS: "For cheap eats and entertainment in Munich, the **Weinkeller Sankt Michael,** in the basement of the Pschorrbräu Restaurant, about 200 yards off the Marienplatz, opposite St. Michael's Church at Neuhauser Strasse, is a find. You pay the equivalent of about $5 for your choice of meats, salads and bread from an excellent buffet. And the price includes a glass of wine, while a band plays polka and waltz music as you dine. Open evenings only, starting at 5 p.m." (Janet Levy, Bethesda, Maryland). . . . "At the closest streetcar stop to Nymphenburg Castle, next to a canal, the **Zum Metzgerwirt** serves refreshing meals for 9 marks; it has a shady beergarden, too" (Letha Lenhart, Wichita, Kansas).

4. Evening Entertainment

Munich is a city where you can, and should, indulge in a heavy dose of night-lifing. The cafés, dance halls, and night clubs here are as varied and numerous as in any major capital, but at a price level so low as to make you blink. Germans, you see, rarely entertain at home. Every evening in Munich, vast numbers of the citizenry descend on cafés and dance halls—and they expect to be received in a relaxed, non-gouging manner. The tourist benefits from the fact that night-clubbing in Munich is not a once-a-year activity for most of the populace.

The place where they most frequently go, and the spot that you can't miss, is the boisterous **Hofbräuhaus**, at 9 Platzl, Germany's largest beer hall, where literally thousands of gallons of the foamy stuff are consumed each night. This is your choice for an inexpensive evening full of Teutonic hanky-panky. On the ground floor, called the *Schwemme,* you drink beer costing only 5.40 marks for a full liter at long benches, and listen to a little brass band. On the second floor, there's a restaurant serving enormous German sausage meals for 7 marks (or you can order soup, 2.80 marks, followed by wienerwurst mit sauerkraut, 6 marks). Don't go downstairs unless you're willing to link arms and bellow out a song with your tablemates. . . . Across the street from the Hofbräuhaus is the **Platzl,** another large beer hall, with a daily 8 p.m. floor show of topical skits on Bavarian life, and performers who yodel and do *schuhplatteln*—the foot-stomping, thigh-slapping dance of the Alps. Entrance fee here, however, is 10 marks ($3.84), whereas the Hofbräuhaus is free.

The chief competitor of the Hofbräuhaus is the more modern—but equally mammoth—**Mathäser Bier Stadt** (Mathäser Beer City), at Bayer5 strasse (near the Stachus), which advertises that it has 5,000 seats. A slightly more refined (but equally cheap) version of the Hofbräuhaus, and perhaps patronized by fewer tourists and more local residents, it features a small brass band on its top floor, plus the usual camaraderie and beer guzzling (a full liter for 5.40 marks), plus several different restaurants in the same building (the quieter Kleiner Saal on the ground floor, where you eat; the upstairs Festsaal, where you dance on special holiday occasions; and most exciting of all, the mammoth Bierhalle, half a flight up on the mezzanine, where a center bandstand—like a boxing ring—blares music, and all the patrons drink and sing). While this Beer City doesn't approach the atmosphere of the Hofbräuhaus, which it is obviously trying to emulate, it does offer better food, served in far cleaner and tidier surroundings, and at moderate prices; a number of different *wurst* (sausage) dishes with potatoes for 7 marks; sauerbraten with *knödel* (dumplings) for 15 marks; the city's specialty—*kassler rippchen* (smoked pork chops)—for 17 marks, including sauerkraut and mashed potatoes; leberkäse and potato salad for 7.50 marks ($2.88); a half liter of beer for 2.80 marks. Most Germans make an entire evening out of the dining and the endless quaffing of beer here, surrounded by thousands of their compatriots.

FOR DANCING: That famous mecca for shy bachelors in Munich—the Ring Café—has been torn down, and we'll therefore have to limit our low-cost dancing recommendations to the following two almost-as-good establishments: First, the gigantic cellar-dancehall of the **Hackerkeller,** 4 Theresienhöhe, open seven days a week from 6:30 p.m. to 11 p.m., where a dance band in Bavarian costume alternates between modern and folk music, while up to 250 couples dance. There's no entrance fee, but you're expected at least to drink (beer for 3.80 marks per half liter) or earlier in the evening to eat (various menus from 7.50 to 18 marks, or a 22-mark portion of beef cut before your eyes from a whole steer rotating on a spit). Take streetcar 2, 19 or 20 from the station to the Theresienhöhe stop; the

Hackerkeller is in the futuristic block of buildings overlooking the October-fest meadow. Second, the **Park Cafe**, 7 Sophienstrasse (in the Alter Botanischer Garten), recently renovated, which consists of a restaurant section (daily platters from 8 marks up) and a large dance establishment open daily from 4 to 6 p.m. for afternoon waltzes and the like, very conservative, and again from 8 p.m. to 1 a.m., this time with rock music, a large dance floor and good bands playing. There's no entrance fee, but you'll be asked to purchase a 16.50-mark ($6.34) gedeck consisting of a small bottle of champagne and accompanying bottle of beer or orange juice; and all of this is but a five-minute walk from the railway station: turn left into Luitpoldstrasse (site of the large Hertie Department Store), cross the Luisenstrasse, and you're at the door. Closed Mondays.

FOR BOHEMIANS: The Greenwich Village area of Munich is **Schwabing** —and in some respects, it's zanier and more colorful than anything New York offers.

Schwabing is made up of two distinct sections, however, and only one of the two is really "far out": the northernmost district of Schwabing, at the end of the big Leopoldstrasse, where a number of little streets—**Occam Strasse, Feilitzschstrasse,** and **Ursula Strasse**—are literally jammed with cheap coffee houses and bars that cater to the rather sophisticated university life of Munich. The most candle-lit, cave-like, dark, and popular spot is the **Nachteule,** at 7 Occam Strasse, where beer (3.50 marks per half liter) is all you'll have to buy. That's followed by the **Schwabinger Brettl,** at 11 Occam Strasse. At the Brettl, the attempt is to recapture the atmosphere of Munich in the 1920s. On many nights, young artists present old German folk songs, poems, or little philosophical talks, as was the custom in Schwabing in former years. Lively and interesting. No admission; the singing starts around 10 p.m.; a half liter of beer costs 4.50 marks, but the first glass must be accompanied by a shot of schnapps, for a total price of 7 marks.

IN LOWER SCHWABING: A much more conventional area, and with much larger dance floors than the district described above, is the stretch of Schwabing that proceeds along the wide **Leopoldstrasse,** above the Sie-gestor; it's flanked, in summer, by sidewalk cafés and artists sketching caricatures, etc. Here you'll find, in quick succession, the famous **Domicile,** 19 Leopoldstrasse, a huge basement nightclub with no admission—a bottle of wine is 25 marks, the average hard drink 8 marks; the **Piné,** 25 Leopoldstrasse, with an admission charge of 3 marks; and the **Country Keller** at 29 Leopoldstrasse, the latter a western-style, basement nightclub restaurant featuring country music, "rancher stews" (mainly beans) for 8 marks, spare ribs for 17 marks, beer for 3.50 marks. Open daily from 8 p.m. to 3 a.m. . . . Catering to a very, very young crowd is the **Rum-pelkammer,** at 1 Trautenwolfstrasse, corner Leopoldstrasse, where the dancing is to records, there's no entrance fee, and a beer costs 3.50 marks.

FOR THEATER: Like London, Munich has a magnificent selection of theaters, with wonderfully cheap entrance prices. Contemporary plays are shown at the **Münchner Kammerspiele,** 26 Maximilianstrasse; at the theater **Die Kleine Freiheit,** 31 Maximilianstrasse, and in at least a dozen lesser playhouses. Seats are available at all the foregoing spots for as little as $4, sometimes less. Operettas (Strauss, Zeller, Offenbach), operas (Mozart, Rossini, Puccini, Handel, and Bizet) and ballets (Delibes, Egk, Henze), are beautifully performed in a gem-like setting at the **Staatstheater am Gärtnerplatz** 3 Gärtnerplatz, a 12-mark taxi ride from the Bahnhof. Ticket window is open here from 10 a.m. to 12:30 p.m. and from 3:30 to 5:30 p.m.; you must go in advance for tickets, but you can always buy standing room at the time of the performance for a little over 6 marks ($2.30). Seats range from 10 marks ($3.84) to a high of 65 marks ($25). Don't miss this place: spectacular scenery on three revolving stages, a spirited chorus and principals, an adequate corps de ballet. Their performance of *Die Fledermaus* put our Met to shame. Opera is presented nightly at the superb **Nationaltheater** (Bayerische Staatsoper), on Max-Joseph-Platz, famed for its progressive versions of the standard classics. Unfortunately, tickets— while standard in price—are hard to get: give serious thought to standing room. Somewhat lesser operatic productions, but still of a high order, are done at the **Cuvilliéstheater,** 1 Residenzstrasse. For theatrical classics (Goethe, Schiller), go to the **Bayerisches Staatsschauspiel,** in the **Residenztheater,** 1 Max-Joseph-Platz, where again you can obtain perfectly adequate seats for 15 marks.

READERS' TIPS: "Tickets for the opera and for operettas are hard to get but can be obtained best by standing in line at the theater the night you wish to go. If you are a student, show the identity card for your university—you'll get a discount. This goes for museums in Munich, as well" (Peter W. Bailey, Washington, D.C.). . . . "Students with international identity cards can line up an hour before opera time during the Summer 'Festspiele' (July and August) to see the international stars who perform during this time for about 7 marks. Surprisingly, tickets can run as high as 50 marks for the best seats and most operas are completely sold out months in advance" (Edward H. Pietraszek, Chicago, Illinois). . . . "In the **Gaststätte zum Grünen Inn,** 38 Turkenstrasse, there meets every Tuesday evening a society called the 'Columbus Gesellschaft,' a German-American society, over beer. No membership is required for Americans in transit, and proceedings are as informal as they can be. Further information can be obtained from the Amerikahaus, Munich, or by phoning 59-56-72 on Tuesdays and Thursdays between 11 a.m. and 1 p.m. This Gaststätte is also one of the cheapest in Munich" (G.O. Piper, A.P.O., New York). . . . "North of the Löwenbräu Brewery on Nymphenburgerstrasse is the **Dantebad Swimming Pool,** open until 4 p.m., and charging only 3 marks for adults, 2 marks for children" (Jeff and Barbara Wasserman, Oakdale, New York). . . . "Largest outdoor restaurant in Munich is the 6,500-seat **Hirschgarten Biergarten.** Take the S-Bahn to the Laim stop, or the streetcar to Romanplatz" (Michael Gaertner, Munich).

5. Sightseeing

THE TOP SIGHTS: After you've sampled the entertainment of Munich, your remaining schedule should at least include a long visit to the city's top attraction: the great **Deutsches Museum,** on an island in the Isar River (the *Isarinsel;* open daily from 9 a.m. to 5 p.m.; admission 4 marks, students 1.50 marks). This is the largest scientific and technical museum in Europe, with displays brilliantly arranged to show you the inner workings of man's finest machines and engineering feats. And to give you a theoretical grounding in science, the museum maintains a physics department on its first floor, made up of glass display cases with protruding handles and levers that you operate, and that illustrate the basic laws of physics.

It would take days to wander through the entire museum; if you have only a brief time available, go first to the aviation hall on the second floor, where actual aircraft—dating back to World War I—are preserved for you to clamber over and into. Then watch for the actual casting of aluminum on the ground floor at 10:30 a.m. and 2:30 p.m., the processing of plastics on the second floor at 11:30 a.m. and 3:30 p.m., other daily events listed on the wall opposite the information booth at the entrance.

The **Frauenkirche** is the distinctive, two-domed cathedral (Dom) of Munich, built in the 15th century, from whose south tower one once had a panoramic view of the city, and—on clear days—of the foothills of the Bavarian Alps, about 40 miles away. Currently closed for repairs, we're hoping the towers will reopen for tourist use in late 1985, but can't guarantee the date.

There are, of course, numerous museums in Munich, of which the outstanding one is the **Alte Pinakothek,** at 27 Barer Strasse; but for more on that and Munich's other top attractions (including the Nymphenburg Palace and its associated sights), I give you my wife Hope:

SIGHTSEEING WITH HOPE: "The key to the charm of Munich is that it is a Bavarian city. And the citizens of Bavaria, almost by definition, are simple, warm, friendly (rural, if you like), and devoted to the principle that enjoying oneself is the highest goal in life. (The magnificent Alpine scenery in this part of the world must certainly contribute to the feeling that life is to be savored.) Although the people work as hard as any 'Prussian' (a local term for anyone born in another part of Germany), they retain a characteristic easy-going attitude—as witness their tolerance for the fascinating, infamous King Ludwig II. Bizarre and fanciful as his behavior always was, nobody really got upset, until he bankrupted the country building his story-book castles and then offered, as his solution to the collapse of the economy, a trade with France—all of Bavaria for a small islet in the Mediterranean!

"Add to this the fact that since World War II, Munich has become a center for the German intellectuals who used to gather only in Berlin, and you have a city with a rich and diversified appeal. Along with all the fun of beer-drinking, shoulder-clapping gemütlichkeit, and a rich peasant culture, Munich enjoys a lively, sophisticated, up-to-the-latest-moment climate in the arts, and some of the finest museums in the world. In short, Munich makes for unique and exciting sightseeing.

The Alte Pinakothek

"Head first for the Alte Pinakothek, which in my opinion is one of the world's greatest museums. And go when you have several hours to spend, for this is the longest gallery in West Germany, with over 900 paintings (140 termed 'masterpieces'), some so marvelous that you'll welcome the luxury to stop awhile and absorb what you're seeing. The collection ranges over painters from the 14th to 18th centuries, including some of the wildest and most wonderful religious allegorical paintings (in the West Gallery on the first floor); Albrecht Altdorfer's remarkable 'Battle of Issus,' which took

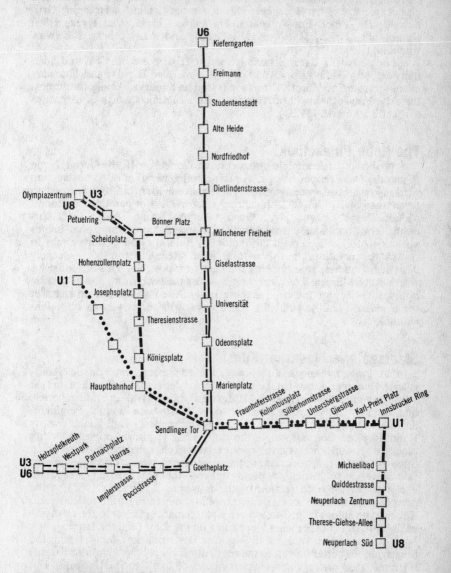

MUNICH SUBWAYS
(U-BAHN)

the artists 12 years to complete (Room III, upstairs); the largest collection of Rubens in the world (upstairs in Rooms VII, VIII, 8, 9 and 12); and elsewhere, works by Brueghel, Dürer, Cranach, Giotto, Holbein, Grünewald, Da Vinci, Fra Angelico, Fra Filippo Lippi, Van Dyck, Hals, Rembrandt, Titian, Velazquez, El Greco, and many others. It's overwhelming!

Located at 27 Barer Strasse (streetcar 18 or bus 53 or 55), and open daily except Mondays from 9 a.m. to 4:30 p.m., also Tuesday and Thursday evenings from 7 to 9 p.m. Admission is free on Sundays. At all other times, the Alte Pinakothek will provide you with a lifetime's worth of memories for just 3.50 marks ($1.34).

The Neue Pinakothek

"Following its complete destruction in World War II, the famous Neue Pinakothek was reopened in 1981 after a full generation of reconstruction work. Now it exists once again as an impressive modern building housing no fewer than 500 18th and 19th century masterworks of painting by Manet, Monet, Degas, Cezanne, Van Gogh, Gauguin, Klimt, Turner, Gainsborough, Goya and Canova, all exhibited along a sloping ramp that invites visitors to follow a certain chronological itinerary and permits them to regard the paintings in the natural light streaming through especially designed windows, guaranteeing the best view possible. This is a must for your visit to Munich. Location is right across the lawn from, and admission hours and prices are the same as those at, the Alte Pinakothek. And a ticket for 6 marks ($2.30), valid for seven days, will admit you to both Pinakotheks.

Staatsgalerie Moderner Kunst

"A long, five-block walk away, the enormous, modernistic **Staatsgalerie Moderner Kunst** (in the famous 'Haus der Kunst'—House of Art) at 1 Prinzregentenstrasse (near the Hofgarten), houses two separate galleries: one displays 20th-century classics (e.g., Kokoschka, Lionel Feininger, Salvador Dali, Andy Warhol, Robert Rauschenberg, Paul Klee, Wassily Kandinsky, de Chirico), while the other wing (entrance opposite, a city block away, walk east) is given over entirely to changing exhibitions, which often consist of the works of exciting new artists, whose canvases are on sale as well as on display. A disadvantage is that you must pay a separate entrance fee for each section of the museum: 2.50 marks (96¢) to the permanent exhibition, open daily except Monday from 9 a.m. to 4:30 p.m., Thursday evenings from 7 to 9 p.m.; a stiff 5 marks ($1.92) to the changing exhibitions in the other wing, depending on the show (and the latter wing is open seven days a week, until 7 p.m.). Best transport for reaching the Staatsgalerie (better known to the residents as simply the 'Haus der Kunst') is tram 20 (to Prinzregentenstrasse) or buses 53 or 55 (to Staatsgalerie). But this is a worthwhile museum experience and you can enter the West Wing galleries free on Sundays.

Nymphenburg

"Now, for a delightful day's outing, make an excursion to Munich's historic **Nymphenburg Palace,** the magnificent baroque-rococo (begun in

1664, but not completed till 1823) Wittelsbach summer residence. To get there, take subway 1 from the Hauptbahnhof, get off at the Rotkreuzplatz stop, and change there to streetcar 12 (total travel time: 15 minutes). Then, get off at Schloss Nymphenburg, look to your left—you can't miss it (from the streetcar stop, it's about a 10-minute walk along a small canal)—and you'll see a semicircle of buildings around the main villa, with a jet-water fountain and lovely green lawn in front. The moral of Nymphenburg is 'Never judge a palace by its cover.' From the front it looks pleasant enough (you could put up with it), but after a closer look at the grounds you'll be enchanted and never want to leave. There's a stunning park (about 500 acres!) sculptured with statues, lakes and waterfalls, and bordering the central formal gardens on both sides are forests of rustic splendor. For 4.50 marks ($1.73), you can buy an all-inclusive ticket which admits you to the Palace, Marstallmuseum, Amalienburg, Badenburg, Pagodenburg, and Magdalenenklause—there's so much that with time off for dreaming in the forest, you can easily spend an entire day at Nymphenburg, lunching in the exotic atmosphere of the palm house for fairly reasonable prices (bockwurst mit senf und brot, 6 marks; bouillon, 2 marks; beer, 3 marks; or a Coke for 2.80 marks)—but that's only if you have your repast at the self-service counter next door to the far more expensive Palmengarten restaurant. In a hurry? Then buy the 3-mark Kleine Karte which admits you simply to the three top sights of Nymphenburg: the Schloss, Amalienburg and the Marstallmuseum.

"Here's a plan for taking in all the sights; first, visit **Schloss Nymphenburg** itself (which is close to the ticket booth), an elegant French-style villa and the main abode for the royal summer residents; this was the first completed building and is the nucleus of the entire Nymphenburg complex. Inside, head in particular for the South Pavilion, also known as Queen Caroline's apartments, which has the bedroom (opposite the entrance, off the main drawing room) where Ludwig II was born on August 25, 1845. In the dining room is King Ludwig I's well-publicized 'Gallery of Beauties'—portraits of some very attractive court ladies, including Crown Princess Marie (Ludwig II's mother), and the fascinating Spanish dancer-courtesan (of Irish descent) Lola Montez, who ruined King Ludwig I's reputation in his declining years, and whose antics, politicking and complete dominance over the infatuated old man so annoyed the people that she became a contributing factor to the Revolution of 1848 and was banished from the country.

"The next stop is the **Marstallmuseum** (turn right as you leave the palace, last building in the immediate rectangle), which is one of the finest coach museums in all of Europe and houses Royal Bavarian carriages, sleighs and harness. And here, don't miss the sleigh or coach innovations of Ludwig II. In his attempt to bring back the grandeur of former days, he created a carriage that Cinderella would have blushed in, so heavily laden with gold it looks as if a 20-mule team couldn't pull it; the hub, the spokes of the wheels, every inch of it is sculptured gilt, curlicues, cherubs, lions and roses. And look for the elaborate display (with eight papier-mache horses) of Kaiser Karl VII's 'Krönungswagen,' a glass coronation coach made in Paris in 1740.

"Now to the park itself—and you'd best consult a plan of the grounds near the entrance so you won't get lost. Since I believe in saving the best for last, and the gem of the park is Amalienburg, I suggest a counter-clockwise tour. To the right of the entrance, and in a somewhat remote spot behind the hothouse and refreshment center, is the **Magdalenenklause,** a sort of religious retreat for royalty, where half the building is a chapel, with an imitation grotto. Continue way up the road on the same side of the lagoon to the **Pagodenburg,** built in 1716–19 by Max Emanuel, who wanted to create a Chinese tea house, but couldn't resist decorating the first floor and staircase in Dutch tiles. He was more successful on the upper story, but the place is tiny, somewhat disappointing though richly decorated and a charming playhouse in total effect. Directly opposite, but on the other side of the park, across the lagoon (follow the signs), is Max Emanuel's **Badenburg** (or bath house)—a swimming pool two stories high, the upper half in blue and white Delft tiles.

"Now walk back toward the palace (passing a small 'village' on the grounds) to the treat of Nymphenburg, the little **Amalienburg**—in the very height of rococo fashion. Built in 1734–39 as a hunting lodge for Electress Amalia (note the Diana over the front doorway), the first two rooms carry out the hunting and country theme, and then suddenly the remainder of the house takes on a highly decorative silver rococo style that surpasses anything found in the main palace, including a hall of mirrors that is as splendid a room as you're likely to find anywhere. The detailed sculptured silver reflected in the mirrors is breathtaking. And how's that for roughing it in a 'hunting lodge'!

"Finally, on this tour of Nymphenburg, china lovers can also visit the **Royal Porcelain Factory,** which is in a small guest house (#8) in the block of buildings opposite the Marstallmuseum. Entrance is free, but buying prices are high (35 marks for a small white ashtray) though the figurines are wonderfully real and done with some sense of humor. Castle hours are generally from 9 a.m. to 5 p.m. daily, except Mondays, with all the park pavilions (except Amalienburg) taking a one-hour lunch break at noon.

Residenzmuseum and Schatzkammer

"Back in town but still in royal company, the **Residenzmuseum,** which was the official palace, and the **Schatzkammer,** or Treasure House, are both located at 3 Max-Joseph-Platz (from the Bahnhof take the S-Bahn to Marienplatz, or take streetcars 1, 4 or 21, and get off at the Opera—it's behind the Rathaus, near the theatre) and share the same hours (except that the Residenzmuseum closes for lunch from 12:30 to 1:30 p.m.): Tuesdays through Saturdays from 10 a.m. to 4:30 p.m., Sundays from 10 a.m. to 1 p.m.

"The Schatzkammer has to be seen to be believed: it is an inconceivably splendid collection of jewelry and riches, including diamonds as big as hubcaps, rubies and emeralds in such profusion you'd think they were on sale at Woolworth's, plus silver, gold, ivory and pearls—all reflecting the vast wealth of the Bavarian royalty. There are jewelled crowns and crosses, goblets, medals, scepters, swords, dishware, personal items, and—in the third room—a stunning necklace and a magnificent statue of 'St. George Slaying the Dragon,' made in 1590 and all inlaid with precious stones—a bit ostentatious but quite beautiful. The Residenzmuseum, in the same building, contains court rooms from practically every period (Renaissance, Baroque, Rococo and Classic); it was badly damaged in World War II, but has now been totally restored to its former splendor. Among the many formal rooms, cabinets, audience chambers and bedrooms in the enormous place, I find most interesting the gold and glitter of the Ancestors Gallery with its portraits of all the Bavarian kings, dukes and related royalty; the lavishly frescoed Antiquarium (Antiques Hall: entrance off the Grottenhof), one of the earliest museums; and the Elector's bedroom (Paradeschlafzimmer), with the traditional railing around the bed in gold and white. It will cost you 2.50 marks to visit the Schatzkammer, the same at the Residenzmuseum.

Städtische Galerie im Lenbachhaus

"Located at 33 Luisenstrasse, just off Königsplatz, and not far from the Alte Pinakothek, the **Municipal Gallery** is devoted to Munich artists, whose work is displayed in an imitation Italian villa with a small garden in front. Though painters are represented from the 15th through the 20th centuries, the real impact of this gallery is felt from its more recent works. In fact, the main reason for a visit is to see the comprehensive collection of Vassily Kandinsky, whom some people call 'the father of abstract art.' The sheer number of Kandinsky's works amounts to an in-depth retrospective (it's the largest collection from his early period anywhere in the world), and it's fascinating to be able to trace the artist's development—from landscape painter to the abstraction of his 'Der Blaue Reiter' stage ('The Blue Rider' is the name of a group that Kandinsky started with Paul Klee). And in The Blue Rider section of the museum, there are also on view works by intimate friends of Kandinsky's including his devoted mistress Gabriele Münter (there's a study of Kandinsky by her); and some very interesting early Paul Klees, among others. The work of The Blue Rider group slowly casts a spell over you, taking you into a world of mutual friends until you feel you know all of them almost as well as you'd know the characters in a good novel. Be sure to view the Kandinsky paintings upstairs at a distance, as well as close up—and you'll see how they change. (Kandinsky and friends are housed in a separate wing—the older part of the villa containing the home, studio, work and collections of Germany's most famous 19th-century portrait painter, Franz Lenbach.) The museum is open daily except Monday from 10 a.m. to 6 p.m., Tuesdays until 8 p.m., for a 3-mark entrance fee (students: 1.50 marks), but is free on Sundays.

The Antikensammlungen and the Glyptothek

"The **Museum of Ancient Arts and Crafts** and the **Glyptothek** are both located directly across the street from the Lenbach Galerie on **Königsplatz** —a vast and startlingly impressive square designed à la Grecque, and featuring imitation Greek temples facing each other across acres of white stone. All this was built in the first half of the 19th century by King Ludwig I to house his enormous and precious collection of ancient Greek and Roman works. Ludwig was a great patron of the arts, and a dedicated Munich builder, especially fond of the classical period; you'll spot numerous plazas, squares and buildings sponsored by him. The **Staatliche Antikensammlungen,** open Tuesdays through Sundays from 10 a.m. to 4:30 p.m., on Wednesdays from noon to 8:30 p.m., closed Mondays, focuses on small sculpture (Greek and Etruscan statuettes and bronze tripods); pottery, glassware, and jewelry (intricate gold and silver work, in the basement). But the museum's star attraction is Ludwig's collection of Greek vases (mainly from the 5th and 6th centuries B.C.), all in excellent condition, quite beautifully cleaned and restored: seeing them is like walking through 'an art gallery in which the paintings' are on vases, pitchers and serving dishes.

"The **Glyptothek,** which suffered extensive damage in World War II, is now completely (except for the original neo-classical interior decoration) and, most tastefully restored in plain white brick, high ceilinged, 'Roman Bath' style. It's an impressive collection of Greek and Roman statuary, mosaics, busts and grave reliefs (Greek works to the left, Roman to the right), of which the outstanding pieces are the exquisite 'Barberini Faun' (Room II, to your left as you enter the museum), a Greek work from 220 B.C.; and the famous 'Warriors from the Temple of Aphaea at Aegina' (at the back of the museum, Rooms VII-IX), which are ancient sculptures (around 500 B.C.) that once decorated a pediment of the temple, depicting scenes from the Trojan War. You may also be quite smitten with a tiny Peloponnesian Zeus from 520 B.C. (Room I, in a lighted case), and by rooms full of Roman busts placed on almost eye-level stands—they give you the feeling you're walking through the Forum meeting Romans. The Glyptothek is open Wednesdays, Thursdays, and Fridays from 10 a.m. to 4:30 p.m., Tuesdays from noon to 8:30 p.m., Sundays again from 10 a.m. to 4:30 p.m., closed Mondays, and a 4-mark entrance fee (except on Sundays, when admission is free) will admit you to both museums.

The Bayerisches Nationalmuseum

"The **Bavarian National Museum,** at 3 Prinzregentenstrasse (a few steps down the street from the Staatsgalerie [Haus der Kunst] and also serviced by buses 53 and 55), has a vast and outstanding collection, emphasizing the historical and cultural development of Europe and Bavaria, from the Middle Ages through the 19th century. Here you'll see French ivories, Limoges enamels, church art, statuary, special craft exhibitions, armor, jewelry and costumes, textiles and tapestries, ceramics, furniture, stained glass, many other items, all gorgeously displayed. Outstanding are the famous Christmas Krippen (Nativity Scenes), and the Folk Art section —both in the basement, the Augsburg Weavers Room with its painted ceiling (room 9), the Passau Room with Gothic furniture (room 10), the recently opened armory room, and the Late Gothic Church Art Room—a particular joy because the setting provides such a perfect background for what it contains (room 15). Admission to the museum is 3 marks (students and scholars free), free on Sundays and hours are from 9:30 a.m. to 4:30 p.m. (Saturdays and Sundays 10 a.m. to 4 p.m.), daily except Mondays.

Münchner Stadtmuseum

"The title of the **Munich Municipal Museum,** at 1 St. Jakob's Platz (just two blocks from Marienplatz and the Rathaus; follow Rindermarkt, the street on which St. Peter's Church stands, into Oberanger, then look for an orange corner building with a tower and a red roof), would gull one into believing that here was a collection illustrating the history of Munich. Not altogether so—the Bavarian National Museum is older, larger, more important and more impressive historically—but, while there *are* some historical exhibitions to be found here, the general tone of the establishment is much like that of the Museum of Modern Art in New York: lively and sophisticated, human-sized and fun.

"The museum is divided into several departments: Munich City Planning (including a model of Olympic City); a German Beer Brewing Museum; a Photo and Film Museum; Model Rooms and 'The Children's World' (second floor, these *are* historical displays—the rooms are designed to show how residents lived in Munich in the 17th, 18th and 19th centuries—and the Children's World is filled with antique cribs, furniture, toys and games which kids love to see; Textiles and Costumes; a Puppet Theatre and Musical Instrument Collection. Outstanding, and not to be missed are the Morisco Dancers and the Puppet Theatre Collection. The famous Moriska-Tänzer (on the ground floor), fashioned in 1480 by Erasmus Grasser for the Dance-Hall of the old Rathaus, are small (about two feet high) statuettes, all caught in motion, dancing, with bizarre, individualistic, unforgettable faces—ten of them, richly decorated in red and gold: they couldn't be more alive. The Puppet Theatre Collection is truly a marvel and the most comprehensive display of everything to do with puppets (not simply the dolls themselves but paper scenery, stages, etc.) that I've ever seen—it traces the history of puppetry from its beginnings and in all countries. And, irresistible—there's a good-sized theatre where you or the kids can try your hand at being puppeteers. Open every day except Monday from 9 a.m. to 4:30 p.m. for a 1.50-mark entrance fee; free on Sundays.

The Deutsches Museum

"An additional word on the important **Deutsches Museum,** already described by Arthur: it's fascinating and completely absorbing (as 1.3 million visitors a year will attest), but overwhelming, with nearly 16 kilometers of corridors, endless demonstrations and shows; you must be selective, gearing your visit to where your own interests lie. Among the major departments are Marine Navigation, Aeronautics, Mining (in which you walk through model mines), Land Transport (every kind of vehicle imaginable, including another one of King Ludwig II's ornate chariots), Chemistry, Physics, Musical Instruments and Salon (where demonstrators play precious keyboard instruments from the 16th, 17th and 18th centuries), Astronautics (where one can trace the historical development of the rocket, and peruse all manner of space vehicles), and dozens of others. So that you can plan your day, you'll want to know that the major demonstrations are scheduled as follows: Casting of Metals (ground floor), 10:30 a.m. and 2:30 p.m.; High Voltage Plant (ground floor), 11 a.m., 2, and 4 p.m.; Model Railway (ground floor), every hour on the hour, starting at 10; and Zeiss Planetarium (sixth floor), 10 a.m., noon, 2 and 4 p.m. Summing up in its own words, the museum seeks 'to present visually the historic development of scientific and technical knowledge . . . by the display of originals and reproductions of historic apparatus and machinery and by means of models and demonstrations.' Here is a highlight of your European museum-going (and note the student-style, self-service cafeteria on the first floor).

And Finally

"Want some more? Just off Marienplatz near the Rathaus is **St. Peter's Church** (known to Munchners as 'Alter Peter'), the oldest parish church in Munich, begun in 1050 and finished in 1294. Very few of the original trappings remain in the interior of the church, which is now gleaming white and gilt rococo; but the church possesses a grisly visit-worthy relic that rivals any Alfred Hitchcock creation: a thoroughly gilded and bejeweled whole skeleton of a martyr (Saint Munditia, patron saint of lonely women), with fake eyes stuck into the skull and gems where the teeth should be, and a jeweled coronet on its head of fake hair (in a case on your left, at the back of the church). . . . The **Theatinerkirche,** across the square from the Residence Theater on Odeon Platz, with its great white, ornate interior, is widely regarded as the most beautiful Baroque church in Munich. . . . The Old Residence Theatre, or **Cuvilliés Theatre,** around the corner from the Residence Museum, is named for the architect who was commissioned by Max II Joseph to design it in 1753. Cuvilliés, a dwarf, began his career at court at the age of 11 as a king's jester, then later became one of Munich's foremost architects—another of his rococo masterpieces is the Amalienburg at Nymphenburg Palace. The breathtakingly beautiful and ornate 'candy box' auditorium, done in gilt, white and red, can be seen daily between 2 and 5 p.m. (Sundays from 10 a.m. to 5 p.m.) for 1 mark; and perhaps you'll also be one of the lucky few able to purchase a ticket to see an opera here."

READERS' SIGHTSEEING SELECTIONS: "Please urge your readers to take a day to visit the fantastic, fairytale-like castle of Neuschwanstein, in the Bavarian Alps near Füssen. It can be seen in a one-day tour from Munich, and it is an unforgettable sight perched on the summit of its own mountain with a mirror-like lake at its foot. Don't miss it" (Ronald A. Audet, Portsmouth, Virginia). . . . "The bus ride from Garmisch to **Neuschwanstein Castle** is completely free with a Eurailpass" (Casey Hern, Madison, Wisconsin). . . . "A Saturday afternoon trip out of Munich to Prien by train, then boat to Chiemsee Island to Herrenchiemsee, a tour through the castle, and then a 40-minute concert by candlelight (May to September only), is a must. Your Eurailpass takes you there and back. Concerts are at 7:30 and 8:30, Saturday evenings only. Be sure to start early in the afternoon as the last tour through the castle is at 4 p.m." (Lilly G. Doerre, St. Louis, Missouri). . . . "Visitors to Munich should be advised to visit the still-standing **Olympic Village,** which is easily reached by subway. You'll be amazed at the architecture of the stadium, the hall, swimming pool and tower, all of which can also be viewed on English-speaking tours for 4 marks ($1.53) at 11 a.m., and 2:30 p.m., March to October. Take the U-Bahn to Olympiazentrum" (Dave Shribman, Swampscott, Massachusetts). . . . "A fun and inexpensive day in Munich begins by taking tram 7 to the northern end of the line. Spend the morning exploring the Olympic Village; then at about noon go to the BMW factory, sign up for a free tour (which is given in German, English, French or Italian as needed), and visit the museum until the tour begins. The BMW factory has the best and most thorough industrial tour we've ever seen and should not be missed by anyone who is even the least bit interested in cars, motorcycles and/or industrial tours in general" (Larry and Trudy Phelps, Jacksonville, Florida). . . . "Don't miss swimming in the **Olympic Schwimmhalle** at the Olympic site, open daily from 7 a.m. to 10:30 p.m. Admission, including free use of a locker, is 4 marks." (Barry Bloom, Bronx, New York).

6. Tours & Excursions

TOURS: You needn't, in Munich, take any of the three-hour expensive variety. A perfectly adequate view of this medium-size city can be had on a one-hour nonstop city drive, costing 15 marks ($5.76). The city sightseeing buses that make these curtailed trips leave from the foot of Prielmayerstrasse (near the railroad station), right at the Hertie Department Store, at 10 a.m. and 2:30 p.m. Look for a parked bus marked "Müncher Fremdenrundfahrten." For more elaborate tours of Munich and vicinity, you'll be best off with the services of the prestigious **Deutsche Touring Office** (Europabus) inside the Starnberger Bahnhof next to the airport bus terminal side of the central railway station (ask for Herr Kerbl, whose phone is 59-18-24). Among their full-day offerings: a Bavarian Alps Tour (daily at 8:30 a.m.; 40 marks); one of Berchtesgaden (8 a.m.; 41 marks);

another to the Bavarian Royal Castles (8:30 a.m.; 41 marks), the last named being justifiably tops in popularity.

THE BLITZ BUS: No one should pass through Munich without using the opportunity to make a fast foray in the incredibly picturesque villages of the Bavarian Alps, which lie about 60 miles south of the city. There are scores of outstanding towns here—Mittenwald, Oberammergau, Oberstdorf, Berchtesgaden—but the city I'd pick for a first visit is Garmisch-Partenkirchen, site of the 1936 Winter Olympics, which lies just below the towering Zugspitze, Germany's highest mountain. As a G.I., I once was stationed for several months just twenty miles from Garmisch, and I can tell you it is magnificent. But another reason for traveling from Munich to Garmisch is the fabulous **Blitz Bus** of the Garmisch Casino, which takes you there and back for the extremely low price of 10 marks ($3.84).

The normal round-trip fare from Munich to Garmisch is 23 marks. To cut this cost, and thereby attract visitors to its roulette wheels, the Garmisch Casino (one of the most sophisticated in Europe) recently decided to operate its own bus, at a reduced fare, departing weekdays at 5:15 p.m., Saturdays and Sundays at 2 p.m., from a point at the right side of the Munich railroad station (as you face it), next to the air terminal (look for a sign marked "Bahnbuslinien," stop 11). Get to the station around 5 p.m., wear only your best clothes (tie and jacket are required of men), and start looking for a bus marked **"Casino Garmisch"** (which is not to be confused with another bus marked "Casino Express" that drives on weekends to a lesser-known gambling den in the town of Bad Reichenhall.) The bus makes the trip to Garmisch Casino, nonstop, in exactly one hour and 25 minutes. The 10-mark ticket permits you to enter the casino, right away. You can stroll around Garmisch for a couple of hours, although you must then eventually put in an appearance at the casino to have your ticket stamped valid for the return trip (no one, however, twists your arm to spend anything at the casino). The bus then returns to Munich, punctually at 10:55 p.m., and the return ride at night is an even quicker trip, bringing you to the center of Munich at half past midnight.

I think you'll like this fast evening-excursion to Garmisch. For the first hour of the ride, you'll pass through rolling countryside of great beauty. But then, gradually, the land will become hillier, and suddenly, looming through the mist, you see—an Alp! And then another and another, until you're in one of the most breathtaking mountain areas of Europe.

PILGRIMAGE TO DACHAU: "An important side trip from Munich is a trip to the concentration camp and memorial at **Dachau.** Trains leave the Munich Hauptbahnhof approximately every 20 minutes (except Saturdays when they run every two hours) for the town of Dachau, and a bus from the railroad station goes to the camp which is virtually untouched—a shocking reminder of recent history" (Ronald Kluger, Irvington, New Jersey). . . . "The pilgrimage to **Dachau Concentration Camp,** about ten miles from Munich, is heartbreaking but a must; trains run every 20 minutes, a round-trip ticket costs only 6 marks, and from the Dachau railroad station one can go straight to the camp for 80 pfennigs on the bus marked 'Dachau Ost' (Alan Schwartz, Detroit, Michigan). . . . "Consider a possible sidetrip to **Dachau,** which you reach from Munich by first taking the train to Dachau (6 DM, round-trip) and then the Dachau Ost bus (80 pfennigs) which meets the train. The camp is the next to last stop. This is not a pleasant trip, but worthwhile if it causes the traveler to remember what actually happened in the past and to determine that it shall never happen again" (John M. Littlewood, Champaign, Illinois; note from AF: Dachau is an obligatory visit for persons of conscience, a searing reminder of the sufferings of more than 200,000 so-called "undesirable elements"—mainly Jews, socialists and clergymen—incarcerated here by the Nazi regime between 1933 and 1945. The camp on the outskirts of this city of 30,000 people, 12 miles northwest of Munich, is now a permanent museum called the "Gedenkstätte" (or Memorial Site), where several barracks of the time, the morgue, the crematorium, the unspeakable *brausebad*, have been preserved, alongside photos, displays and a documentary film theatre of the Holocaust era, all open daily except Mondays from 9 a.m. to 5 p.m., entrance free. To reach Dachau from Munich, it's best to take S-Bahn 2 (the one marked "Petershausen") from the Hauptbahnhof, using three stubs of your "Streifenkarte," free for Eurailpass holders, to the Dachau station, then walk through the underpassage and either take bus 722 from the station square to the Gedenkstätte, or walk there in 45 minutes. Bus 722 (two stubs, or 1.50 marks, 57¢, not valid for Eurailpass) leaves Dachau station square at 11:22 a.m., 12:42 p.m., 2:02 and 3:22 p.m., and returns, from the camp to Dachau station, at 2:29, 3:49, 4:09, 4:21, 4:49 and 5:10 p.m. If you prefer to walk: turn right, after leaving Dachau station, into Frühlingstrasse, then after about 300 yards right again into Schleissheimer Strasse (crossing under the railway tracks), walk all the way up Schleissheimerstrasse for about a mile, to Alte Römerstrasse, then walk up Alte Römerstrasse for another mile, until you see the camp on your left).

READERS' EXCURSIONS: "A very interesting trip north from Munich is the 86-mark **Europabus** ride over the so-called 'Romantische Strasse,' passing two fantastic towns—Dinkelsbühl and especially Rothenburg—whose beauty is something I still can't get over; eventually, the bus heads for Frankfurt and Wiesbaden" (John M. Littlewood, Champaign, Illinois; note by A.F.: The Europabus departure, "über die Romantische Strasse"—is at 9 a.m. from the right side of the Munich Railroad Station, as you face it, arriving Wiesbaden at 8:40 p.m.). . . . "Holders of the Eurailpass should know of a way to approach Munich that is really fantastic. Although the fact is not often advertised, you can purchase a Europabus 'rider' for the 'Romantic Road' route, operated from May through October. I took the trip from Frankfurt to Munich, a 12-hour jaunt. The bus has an English-speaking guide who pointed out all the sights as we passed them, and we were given a lengthy sightseeing stop in Rothenburg-ob-der-Tauber, a perfect gem of a walled medieval town that has not changed in hundreds of years. This trip is a marvelous way to get to see more of Germany than the large towns, and its ready availability to Eurailpass holders makes it a real find" (Ronald A. Audet, Portsmouth, Virginia). . . . "The normal price for a trip up the **Zugspitze,** Germany's highest mountain, is 38 marks from Garmisch to the top and back down. The German Railroad offers special fares of 50 marks, however, from Munich to Garmisch, up the Zugspitze, and return to Munich. This makes the Munich-Garmisch trip cost only 12 marks ($4.61)" (Dr. L. K. Wynston, Long Beach, California).

7. Munich Miscellany

One of the key rules of budget travel is to eat what the locals eat. In Munich, it's readily apparent that the cheapest—and, at the same time, most expertly cooked—main courses are the popular local pork dishes—particularly those that come in the form of *wurst* (sausage). There are as many different varieties of sausage in Munich—weisswürste, bratwurst, Pfälzer fleischwurst, Griebenwurst, and so on and on—as there are cheeses or wines in Paris. . . . The student travel bureau of Munich is **Studentenreisen,** 47 Türkenstrasse (at the corner of Schellingstrasse, about 300 yards from the main building of the university), phone 28-36-83, open weekdays from 9 a.m. to 5:30 p.m.; they'll get you cheap intra-Europe flights, trains, buses and ships. . . . But if you are looking for more personal assistance on travel, Munich, shopping, theater tickets, eating, charter flights and sightseeing, the office you should visit is **Weichlein's International Travel Service,** on the third floor (walk-up) at 44 Land-

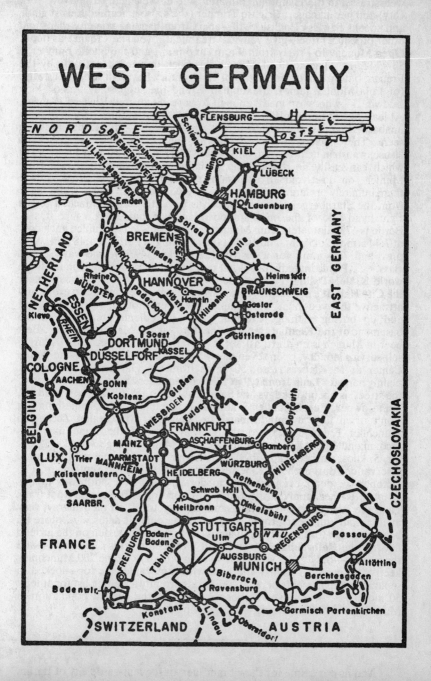

wehrstrasse, in the Hauptbahnhof area. Violet Weichlein (from New York City) and her manager, Brigitte Trenner (she's also a licensed tourist guide and speaks flawless English) will—apart from handing you city maps and other brochures free—give you VIP treatment if you show them this book. Open Monday to Friday from 9 a.m. to 6 p.m., and the phone number is 53-95-83. . . . The spirit of Munich has been influenced not only by the French, but by that eccentric trio of 19th century Bavarian Kings: Ludwig I (of Lola Montez fame), Maximilian I, and the supposedly "mad" king Ludwig II—who was "mad" enough to have discovered Richard Wagner. At least one of Ludwig II's extravagant castles near Munich—some of them unabashed copies of Versailles (to a smaller scale)—should definitely be seen. They include **Schloss Linderhof** near Oberammergau, **Schloss Neuschwanstein** near Füssen, and **Schloss Herrenchiemsee** near Prien, all of which can easily be reached via a simple second-class train ride from Munich, on do-it-yourself excursions whose freedom and privacy make them infinitely preferable, in my view, to escorted group tours. Trains leave from the Starnberger Bahnhof, which is the little station attached to the right hand side of the main station (Hauptbahnhof) as you face it. . . . Berlin is 675 kilometers from Munich. Three trains leave Munich each day, at 7:44 a.m., 12:45 p.m. and 10:27 p.m., arriving in Berlin at 4:48 p.m., 9:52 p.m. and 7:44 a.m., for a cost of 128 marks ($49.23), one-way, second class. . . . Picnic ingredients? What may be the finest delicatessen in all the world is **Alois Dallmayr's** world-renowned shop at 14 Dienerstrasse, near the City Hall. It's not entirely inexpensive, but its offerings are so exotic and attractive that you might wish simply to wander through, even if you don't end up buying a thing. Cheaper picnic ingredients are found in the basement of the **Kaufhof** department store, at the Marienplatz. . . . Best beer in Munich is on draft; ask for it, therefore, "vom Fass." . . . A large, self-service laundry, open seven days a week around the clock, is the **Wasch Center** at 18 Klenzestrasse, 50 yards from the Gärtnerplatztheater. A plainly named **"Laundromat,"** at 129 Schwanthalerstrasse, at the far end of the street, is open weekdays and Saturdays till 6 p.m., till noon on Sundays, but its owner, Herr Schaufler, is absolutely fluent in English, something you won't often find at laundromats. In Schwabing **Waschsalon Zoche,** 26 Münchner Freiheit, next to the subway stop of the same name, is recommendable. All such establishments in Munich charge 7 marks ($2.69) for 5 kilos washed and dried. . . . Arriving in Munich without hotel reservations during the Octoberfest period of 1985 (from September 21 to October 6), don't even attempt to find a bed at the addresses in this chapter. Rather, apply at the Tourist Information Office across from track 11 in the central railway station, and throw yourself on their mercy; they maintain an emergency room service for the difficult dates. . . . More on beer: that cast-iron construction across from the delicatessen on the ground floor of the **Hofbräuhaus** (to your left after entering) is Germany's—and the world's—only "beer stein safe"—a *Bierkrugsafe.* Some 200 Munchners keep their personal steins—the kind with a movable zinc top—locked in separate compartments here, and there is currently a waiting list for at least 50 more! . . . In case you've been wondering, the current population of Munich is 1,300,000 persons—and growing fast.

And now it's time for the vibrant, nervous, avant-garde city of Berlin.

Chapter XX

BERLIN

Threepenny Opera

1. Orientation & Transportation
2. Budget Hotels
3. Low-Cost Restaurants and Meals
4. Entertainment
5. Tours
6. Berlin Miscellany
7. Hope's Berlin

THE "BELEAGUERED ISLAND," the "enclave behind the Iron Curtain," the "bastion of democracy"—those are the terms that have frightened a great many persons from attempting a trip to Berlin. The result is that prices in West Berlin are slightly below those of West Germany. But that isn't the only reason for going to Berlin.

Berlin possesses a kind of sophistication that will not be found in the rest of Europe. The city lives on the brink of danger; its citizens live from day to day. And yet, this insecurity has resulted in alertness rather than resignation. There's a lively, electric feel to the city; a drink-and-be-merry-for-tomorrow-we-die mood; an urge to experience the new and the different. To some extent, these attitudes account for the highly esoteric and intense nightlife of the city—for clubs like **Metropol,** perhaps the largest discotheque in Germany, where 3,000 Berliners dance each night, or the **Riverboat,** which features the most frenetic jazz this side of New Orleans.

To witness all this on a visit to Berlin is a strange, and exciting, experience. It's also exciting, but depressing as well, to see the hideous wall that separates West Berlin from the unhappy Eastern sector of the city. You can feel the monotony of an authoritarian state by simply staring across the street into the Soviet zone near high vantage points at Potsdamer Platz or the Brandenburg Gate. The contrast between the relative bleakness of that area and the life of West Berlin is startling.

But that's the only depressing feature of a trip to Berlin. The rest couldn't be more contrasting, for Berlin has an amazing variety of entertainment attractions, sights to look at, places to tour, theatre to watch. Many persons regard Berlin as the most advanced cultural center in the world. But whether you come for that reason, or simply to see history-in-the-making, you'll be thrilled to your marrow by even a short visit to this key European city.

THE GERMAN MARK: At the time this chapter on Berlin was prepared, the German mark was worth about 38 U.S.¢ ($1 = DM2.60), and we've converted local prices into dollars at that approximate exchange. Rates set forth in marks should remain at the figures we've used, but their dollar equivalents may vary—perhaps in your favor—by the time of your own stay in Berlin.

---

1. Orientation & Transportation

Arriving by train, you come into the famous **Bahnhof Zoo** (the only train station in West Berlin), after first passing through East German border checks performed by the grim soldiers of the Volkspolizei. The experience is today utterly safe, but still a bit exciting, and numerous tourists now make the trip by rail between Munich or Frankfurt and West Berlin.

Arriving by plane, you land at **Tegel Airport,** from which city bus 9, charging only 2 marks (76¢), departs every ten minutes into town, and makes most of the trip along nearly the entire length of the Kurfürstendamm, that key boulevard where most of our hotel choices are concentrated.

Once in town, you move about from place to place by subway—the **U-Bahn**—operating from 4 a.m. to 1 a.m. Tickets, valid for 90 minutes, cost 2 marks (76¢) per trip and permit you to change as often as you like or transfer to buses to reach your destination. If you plan heavy use of the subways, you're well advised to purchase a *sammelkarte* good for five rides (8.50 marks), or a *touristenkarte* allowing unlimited travel for either two days (15 marks) or four days (30 marks). These can be had at the small **BVG** (Berliner Verkehrs Gesellschaft) ticket booth in front of Bahnhof Zoo. A second Berlin subway line—the **S-Bahn**—is primarily found in East Berlin, but also runs from Bahnhof Zoo to Bahnhof Friedrichstrasse, a border checkpoint for visiting East Berlin.

Boat trips along the canals and lakes of West Berlin permit you to discover the "unknown Berlin," a region extending from vast industrial suburbs to forests, beaches and lakes dotted in summer with hundreds of sail boats and surf boards. The water-bus ride from Wildenbruchbrücke (next to U-Bahn station Rathaus Neukölln) to the romantic Pfaueninsel at Wannsee Lake costs 5.50 marks, takes over three hours and is a most worthwhile sightseeing excursion. From the Pfaueninsel (Peacock Island), you can then catch a bus back to Bahnhof Zoo for only 2 marks (76¢). For further information on this relaxing (weather permitting) tour, phone 691-37-82.

Back, now, to the task of finding a room:

2. Budget Hotels

For the budgeteer, they're in the heart of the city. The main street of Berlin—the **Kurfürstendamm,** which the Berliners call "Ku-Damm"—and the small side streets heading off it, are literally crammed with small pensions and hotels. There is thus no need to leave the center of all activity in Berlin to find budget-priced rooms. We'll deal, first, with the least costly ones, then with the moderately priced variety.

DOUBLES FROM 48 TO 66 MARKS ($18.46 TO $25.38) PER ROOM, NOT INCLUDING BREAKFAST: The **Pension Knesebeck,** 86 Knesebeckstrasse (phone 31-72-55), owned and managed by English-speaking Frau Regina Kahlert, is a good choice if you prefer quiet surroundings, as 14 of the 16 rooms face a courtyard. Twins sell for 66 marks ($25.38); there's one single room for 45 marks ($17.30); a large family room with four beds, priced at 27 marks ($10.38) per person; and all rates include breakfast. Located between Savignyplatz and Ernst Reuter Platz, the pension is a ten-minute walk from Bahnhof Zoo, three minutes from the Kurfürstendamm.

Gästehaus Kronsbein, 12 Kalckreuthstrasse (phone 241-087), with 120 beds on four floors (no elevator), is owned and managed by a retired German soccer coach, Fiffi Kronsbein, who charges, in 1985, 32 marks ($12.30) for singles, only 60 marks ($23.07) for doubles or twins, 28 marks ($10.76) per person for rooms with three to five beds each, breakfast and free showers included. On weekends, as you'd expect, when soccer matches are played, this *Gästehaus* (guesthouse) is always fully booked with one of the teams and their fans, but there are numerous vacancies on weekdays. Though basic in furnishings and comforts, it is easygoing in atmosphere, very clean and excellently well-located between Nollendorf and Witten-bergplatz.

Hotel Stadt Tilsit, at 9 Stuttgarter Platz (phone 323-1027), is actually a pension occupying the first and second floors of an old apartment house furnished with pre-war beds, chairs and other pieces—they're adequate and comfortable. Frau Dams, the Tilsit's current owner, charges 38 marks ($14.61) single, 48 marks ($18.46) double, 26 marks ($10) for additional beds, and 6 marks ($2.30) for optional breakfasts, served in an unusually large breakfast room. From Tegel Airport, take bus 9 to the Kaiser-Friedrichstrasse stop.

Pension Centrum, at 31 Kantstrasse (phone 31-61-53), is a tiny, ten-bed boarding house in the convenient Savignyplatz area (take bus 9 to Leibniz-strasse), managed by a friendly couple, Herr and Frau Schmücker, who charge 33 marks ($12.69) single, 48 marks ($18.46) for a twin or double, plus 7 marks ($2.69) more for an egg-with-sausage breakfast served in a cozy dining room. While the Schmückers don't speak English, their daughters living elsewhere in the city are happy to act as interpreters over the phone.

Pension Hagera, on the third floor of 3 Giesebrechtstrasse (phone 883-58-06), a side street off Kurfürstendamm near Adenauerplatz, is in an old house with large rooms and heavy, stolid, Teutonic-type furniture. Mr. Kreutz, the English-speaking owner, charges 40 marks ($15.38) single, 58 marks ($22.30) double, 81 marks ($31.15) triple, plus 5 for an optional breakfast of cheese, cold cuts and rolls, with virtually unlimited—well, two cups at least—coffee.

At **Pension Viola,** 146 Kantstrasse (phone 31-64-57), near Bahnhof Zoo, single rooms are larger than the doubles in most other Berlin pensions, and rent for 35 marks ($13.46) single, 50 marks ($19.23) double.

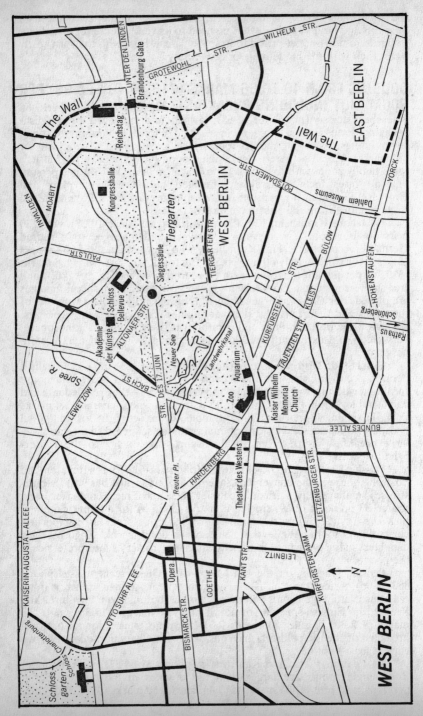

This is a quiet establishment, well run by Frau Carls, who speaks some English.

Budget rates for rooms with private shower? If you're lucky, you'll find a vacancy at the tiny **Pension Ursula,** 63 Sybelstrasse (phone 882-62-04), where all the rooms (all seven of them) are so equipped, and yet rent for only 44 marks ($16.92) single, 75 marks ($28.84) double, 90 marks ($34.61) triple, 105 marks ($40.38) for a very large, airy room with four beds. Breakfast, served to the room by owner Frau Werrmann, consists of rolls with butter and jam, cold cuts, cheese, coffee or tea, and is included in the price. Location, central but quiet: a three-minute walk from Adenauerplatz, reached by bus or subway.

And still another suitable accommodation in this price range is the **Pension Cortina,** 140 Kantstrasse (phone 313-9059), whose Italian owner and blonde German wife charge only 57 marks ($21.92) double, 70 ($28.46) triple, 81 ($31.14) quadruple, and 6.50 marks for breakfast. You'll have to walk up 42 steep steps before reaching the elevator landing (I did), but once upstairs, you'll be well pleased with an efficient, pleasant operation. Take bus 9 from Tegel Airport to Bahnhof Zoo, and get off at the Bleibtreustrasse stop.

Pension Majesty, on the third floor of 55 Mommsenstrasse (phone 323-20-61), near Olivaer Platz and Kurfürstendamm, is a rather large establishment that is popular with back-packers because of its many multi-bedded rooms. Owner, Herr Schassberger, charges 35 marks ($13.46) single, 49 marks ($18.84) twin, and 22 marks ($8.46) per person in rooms with four to five beds. Breakfast 6 marks ($2.30); showers 2 marks (76¢) extra. You'll enjoy the automatic Coke and beer dispenser in the lobby; keys are given to clients who plan to return late.

DOUBLES FROM 60 TO 86 MARKS ($23.07 TO $33.07) PER ROOM, NOT INCLUDING BREAKFAST:

Pension Lenz, at 8 Xantener Strasse (phone 881-51-58), is a choice selection for traveling families. That's because six of its 24 rooms are large "family" rooms—each spacious enough to sleep a family of four. Herr Karl Schröter is a friendly host who speaks English well and takes great pride in making guests feel at home. (If you want to strike up a conversation quickly, admire his chow-chow, Simba—a pride and joy.) All rooms have both hot-and-cold running water and telephones and are furnished in overstuffed German fashion, with big chairs and couches and heavy dressers. Prices are specially slanted toward budget-minded Americans (mention this book when you check in), with singles at 60 marks ($23.07), doubles for 85 marks ($32.69), triples at 110 marks ($42.30), plus 7 marks for breakfast, all including service. To get to the Lenz from Tegel airport, take bus 9 down Kurfürstendamm and step off at Olivaer Platz.

Pension Wittelsbach, 22 Wittelsbacherstrasse (four blocks from the Ku-Damm via Konstanzerstrasse, near the intersection of Brandenburgische and Konstanzer, phone 87-63-45), is a somewhat plain and old-fashioned establishment but with large and comfortable rooms and beds. It is owned by Frau Arzt, who speaks perfect English and whose homey, antique breakfast room is so typically Old Germany that I could barely suppress a grin when I last saw it. 1985 rates are: 55 to 60 marks (depending on size) single, 68 to 105 marks double, 26 marks for a third or fourth bed, all including a superb buffet-breakfast (whose ingredients change daily).

Readers have also been pleased with the **Pension Alster** at 10 Eisenacherstrasse (phone 246-952), managed by Frau Ingeborg Viebahn, who has a big shepherd dog that barks but does not bite. Singles are 43 marks, doubles 78 marks, breakfast included, and Frau Viebahn provides showers (with a large towel) for 4 marks extra.

For "big splurgers" desiring a top-quality pension—and willing to pay the price—there's the exceptionally attractive **Pension Pariser Eck,** Pariser Strasse 19 (phone 881-21-45), with 13 rooms, all huge and lovely, and with sitting areas in each. Frau Ingrid Grams, a gracious hostess, makes a point of keeping the surroundings "quiet and comfortable." Walls are painted tastefully off-white, the baths tiled, and every room has its own sink and telephone. Rates in 1985 are 42 marks ($16.15) single, 80 marks ($30.76) double, with service and tax included. A large breakfast, with egg, is 7.50 marks; an extra bed costs 27 marks. Take the #9 bus to the corner of Kurfürstendamm and Bleibtreustrasse and walk two blocks down Bleibtreustrasse and Sächsische Strasse to the pension on the corner of Pariser Strasse.

At 7 Motzstrasse, a serviceable 130-bed businessmen's-type-hotel, called the **Sachsenhof** (phone 216-2074), charges 46 marks for a bathless single, 86 marks double, 108 marks for a four-bedded room, plus 6.50 marks per person for breakfast. Owner Klaus Manzke operates a restaurant in the same building, where you can have a good two-course meal for 12 marks.

And now we arrive at the marvelously located **Pension Fasanenhaus,** which is a half-block off Kurfürstendamm at Fasanenstrasse 73 (the famous, deluxe Hotel Kempinski is located diagonally across the street), phone 881-6713. While singles here are as high as 50 marks ($19.23), doubles rent for as little as 80 marks ($30.76) and never for more than 85 ($32.69), triples 100, quads for 125, with breakfast and service included. The Fasanenhaus is run by an "old Berliner," Herr Dieter Rahn, who knows his beloved city well, is generous with information and maintains a marvelous "at home" atmosphere in his pension. Take the bus to the Uhlandstrasse stop. . . . Not far away, the **Hotel-Pension Dittberner,** 26 Wielandstrasse (phone 881-64-85), with its wall-to-wall carpeting in guest rooms, its lounge decorated with Japanese prints, an elevator, offers unusual comfort at a relatively moderate price: 90 marks ($34.61) for double rooms, including breakfast. Just off the Ku-Damm, it's reached by taking bus 19 to the Leibnizstrasse stop.

Another excellent value, in this price category, is the recently redecorated **Pension Finck** at 54 Güntzelstrasse (phone 861-2940), ten minutes' walk from Bahnhof Zoo, where pleasant Frau Finck charges 40 marks ($15.38) for a single, 85 marks ($32.69) double, 25 marks for a third or fourth bed, always including breakfast, and throws in hot baths for free. That's on the third floor of an elevator building.

Or try the nearby **Pension Royal,** Bleibtreustrasse 34 (phone 883-1800), charging 40 marks ($15.38) single, 85 marks ($32.69) double, breakfast included. Owner Renate Otto speaks English, and carefully advises that you receive a key to the lift after you've checked in. Thus, you need walk to the second-floor office only once, upon your first visit to the Royal.

The tiny seven-room **Pension Brinn,** Schillerstrasse 10 (phone 312-

1605), just a five-minute walk from the Zoo station, is popular with actors from the nearby Schiller Theatre. Well-furnished and well-cared-for rooms rent for 50 marks ($19.23) single, 85 marks ($32.69) double, plus 7 marks ($2.69) for breakfast.

And finally, **Pension Molthan** at 76 Lietzenburgerstrasse (phone 881-4717), offers 72 beds on three floors, charges 40 marks ($15.38) for singles, 60 marks ($23.07) for twins, 25 marks ($9.61) per person in rooms with three to five beds, 2.50 marks (96¢) for a shower and 7.50 marks ($2.88) for what they call an "American breakfast" but which consists of continental breakfast with eggs any style. Excellently located near Kurfürstendamm, Rankeplatz and Bahnhof Zoo.

DOUBLES FROM 88 TO 110 MARKS ($33.84 TO $42.30) PER ROOM, BUT THIS TIME WITH BREAKFAST INCLUDED (USUAL-LY):

Directly on the Kurfürstendamm, at 62, you'll now discover, in a large, substantial building, the 20-room **Hotel-Pension Leibniz-Eck** (phone 883-5055 or 883-1550), whose heavy oak furniture and old-fashioned decor is the kind you might have found in a pre-World War II, middle-class German home. The proprietor is the genial Rudi Jacubke, who very literally treats his clients as if they were guests in his own home. Special rates to readers of this book are 68 marks ($26.15) for a single, but only 95 marks ($36.53) double, including breakfast, service and tax.

In a slightly more expensive category, the big **Hotel Europa** (112 beds), about two blocks south of the Kurfürstendamm at Konstanzerstrasse 60 (phone 882-1091), is a modern, elevator-equipped building whose office is on the first floor. 1985 rates here, for modern but bathless rooms, are 68 marks ($26.15) single, 110 marks ($42.30) double, 44 marks per person in triples (with breakfast, service and tax included). Best bet for budget travelers are the rooms on the fifth floor—all of which come with small dormer windows and bright red eiderdown covers. Several of these are triples and quite charming indeed for three girls or a family. . . . Alternatively, try the pleasant, small, 42-room **Hotel les Nations** at 6 Zinzendorfstrasse (phone 392-20-26), whose English-speaking proprietress, Frau Spitzley, charges 68 marks single, 110 marks twin, 135 marks triple, for clean rooms with totally new furniture, and all in a quiet location 20 minutes' walk from the Kurfürstendamm. Breakfast is included in the price! Take bus 23 from Bahnhof Zoo, or else go by subway (U-Bahn) to the Turmstrasse stop.

A top-quality pension is the **Hotel-Pension Funk,** Fasanenstrasse 69 (phone 882-71-93), with its sweeping white marble staircase in the entrance-way and huge double-bedded rooms done in French provincial furnishings. Herr Groth, the proprietor, speaks English, and will fill you in on what's happening at the theater, opera and nightspots, in addition to providing hints for shopping and sightseeing. His rates for 1985 are 78 marks ($30) for doubles without bath, 89 marks ($34.23) for doubles with private shower, 45 marks ($17.30) for singles without bath, 50 marks ($19.23) for singles with shower, 100 marks ($38.46) triple and 120 marks ($46.15) quad rooms, with breakfast included, and free showers down the hall. Take bus 9 down the Ku-Damm to the corner of Fasanenstrasse.

Not far away, the 30-bed **Pension Modena** at 26 Wielandstrasse (phone 881-5294), kept spotlessly clean by manager Frau Brigitte Kreutz, charges

60 marks ($23.07) single, 99 marks ($38.07) double, including a hearty breakfast. . . . Similarly priced, and only a few minutes' walking distance from Bahnhof Zoo, is the tiny, 16-bed **Pension Chilcott,** 16 Meinekestrasse (phone 881-1297), charging 70 marks single, 94 marks double, 7.50 marks for breakfast. Frau Scharfling is the lady to see.

And finally, the **Hotel Burckschat** in the center of the inexpensive shopping street, Wilmersdorfer Strasse, at #67 (phone 323-4245), is for those who prefer modern but strictly impersonal surroundings, and who mainly want a private shower at a reasonable price. The large, straight-walled Burckschat has 114 rooms, all with private shower (but not toilet)—the majority of the rooms singles. Rooms are identically furnished in spare contemporary style. Singles in 1985 will be priced at 55 marks ($21.15), doubles at 88 marks ($33.84).

READERS' PENSION SELECTIONS "**Pension Bamberg**, 58 Bambergerstrasse (phone 211-78-77), charges just 30 marks for a single, 58 marks for a double, not including breakfast. These lodgings are clean and quiet, yet less than six minutes from the Kurfürstendamm" (Marty Hallinan, New York, New York). . . . "An excellent place to stay is **Pension Central**, on the first floor of 185 Kurfürstendamm, at the corner of Wielandstrasse, near Adenauerplatz U-Bahn (phone 881-63-43). I was charged 55 marks single for a 66 mark double room. It was very clean and warm (I was there in winter). There's a bar in the large dining room, the staff are friendly, and English is spoken" (Peter Hill, Sydney, Australia); note by AF: 1985 rates at Pension Central are: single 55 marks ($21.15), single with shower 60 marks ($23.07), twin 66 marks ($23.38), twin with shower 88 marks ($33.84), twin with shower and private w.c. 92 marks, all rates including breakfast). . . . "**Pension Brandies,** 27 Kaiser-damm (phone 302-7249 or 301-7195), charges only 68 marks ($26.15) for a twin room with breakfast, 110 marks ($42.30) for a triple with breakfast, and 135 marks ($50.85) for a football-field-sized quad. Showers are free, and breakfast is served in an impressive room equipped with color tv that also serves as a reading, writing and lounge area. I especially liked the two attic rooms reached by internal stairway. And last but not least, the owners, English-speaking women, really care for their guests, a rare quality nowadays" (G.A.O. Sieweke, Mayville, South Africa). . . . "At the **Pension Dorothee,** 14 Nurnberger Strasse (phone 211-43-85), close to the zoo station, Europa Center and the Kurfürstendamm, the atmosphere is extremely friendly, the rooms large, the beds with new mattresses, boiling hot water available all the time, and the location perfect. Herr Siegfried Munder and his mother insist that you treat their large tv lounge as your own. Rates are 40 marks ($15.38) for a single, 60 marks ($23) for a twin, 24 marks ($9.23) per person in a large triple or quad room. And optional breakfast is 5 marks ($1.92) extra, with free helpings of coffee. Showers are free. Arriving from Tegel Airport, take bus 9 to the Budapester Strasse stop, then walk into Nurnberger Strasse, cross the Kurfürstendamm, and the pension is the third house after the crossing (look for the green sign above the door)" (Ian Markley and Jackie Bell, Sydney, Australia).

READER'S PRIVATE ROOM RECOMMENDATION: "I found a real gem of a private room in the apartment of **Frau I. Zimmerman** at 69 Bergstrasse Steglitz (phone 796-13-12), who has a special fondness for Americans—offering hospitality and friendship that make you feel like a guest, not a customer. Our double room costing only 66 marks ($25.38) a night was wonderfully comfortable, clean, spacious, the bathroom modern, with free baths and oceans of hot water, and included in the rate was breakfast with meat, cheese, bread, egg, coffee or tea. From the Zoo, take the U-Bahn, line 9, in the direction of Steglitz, get off at Walter-Schreiber-Platz, and from there take bus 2 or 81 to Bergstrasse (4 stops); she lives right at that corner" (Thomas T. Tenenhaus, Binghamton, New York; note from AF: having zipped past briefly in the fall of 1984, I can report only that Mrs. Zimmerman's apartment is in a small, red-brick house facing a cemetery, in ultra-quiet surroundings).

READERS' HOTEL SELECTIONS (BIG SPLURGE VARIETY): "Just around the corner from your recommended Hotel-Pension Fasanenhaus, at Kurfürstendamm 217 (phone 881-6400), we found the **Pension Adler,** which has most luxurious double rooms, spacious as in a palace, at 120 marks ($46.15) per day for two people, with bath. Breakfast is extra, served by polite and helpful maids—one of them accompanied us to the Dahlem Museum, just to show us the way" (Robert S. Milne, Yonkers, New York, note by AF: 1985 rates are 85 marks single, 120 double, including breakfast). . . . "The **Hotel Juwel,** at 26 Meinekestrasse, just off the Ku-Damm (phone 882-7141), is a little steep for the $25 a day budget, but really is excellent. We paid 120 marks ($46.15) for a beautiful clean double room with a balcony. The price included a delicious breakfast (with a soft-boiled egg) served by the delightful lady owner, taxes, service and all the baths we wanted to take. The location can't be beat" (Sandra and James Risser, Des Moines, Iowa; note by AF: at the Juwel, normal singles will rent in 1985 for 65 marks, doubles for 120 marks, service and breakfast included).

PRIVATE HOMES ON THE OUTSKIRTS: These charge only 24 marks ($9.23) per person, breakfast included, and they may provide your only lodgings opportunity during those random periods when international fairs or important soccer matches cause all of Berlin to be jammed to capacity. The four establishments that follow can all be reached by buses running every 20 minutes from 5 a.m. to 1 a.m., all for a one-way-ticket cost of only 2 marks (76¢), and all provide off-the-beaten-track settings and scenery that the average Berlin visitor does not see. Thus:

Gerhard Alpers, 26A Zingerleweg (phone 365-33-83), rents two singles and two twins for 24 marks ($9.23) per person.

Herman Jahn, next door at #26 (phone 365-43-54), rents two twins and a single also for 24 marks ($9.23) per person per night, breakfast included. They're situated near clear, unpolluted Glienecke Lake, famous for its bridge leading to East Berlin, on the middle of which spies of both sides used to be exchanged during the 1950s. Both families like children, who can use the gardens for playing.

Astrid Stegmann, 111D Sakrower Kirchweg (phone 365-62-43 or 753-89-87), resides in a super-modern, three-story, red brick house where she offers a large apartment with private kitchen and bathroom for 50 marks ($19.23) a day for two persons, and a double room (including free use of her bathroom and kitchen) for 20 marks ($7.69) per person; additional beds can be placed in both the apartment and the double room. Optional hearty breakfast for 5 marks, and children are especially welcome. Location is next to the Wannsee, just across from the Pfaueninsel ("Peacock Island").

Siegfried Sternsdorf, 105 Selbitzerstrasse (phone 365-41-47), owns an old country house in the midst of a small park, where he can accommodate as many as 12 guests in three guest rooms at a per person rate of 24 marks ($9.23), including breakfast. Don't be put off by the lack of a name on the garden door, or by the dog, Konsar, who is quite friendly.

All four of these private quarters are in a residential district called Kladow, in the British sector of Berlin, one hour by public transportation from the center. Take bus 92 or 94 from the Zoo Station on a 25-minute trip to the Pichelsdorfer Strasse stop, where you'll change to bus 34 ("Glienicke"). Another 25 minutes, through parks and gardens, crossing the Havel River and passing a turkey farm, and you get off for Frau Stegmann's house at the Alt Kladow stop, for the other three homes at the

Waldallee stop. Of course, phone first. Price for the one-way bus ticket is 2 marks.

For private home accommodations closer to the center of Berlin, see the "Reader's Selection" for Frau J. Zimmerman, appearing on the preceding page. Her home has now been endorsed by several other readers as well.

STARVATION BUDGET: The youth hostels of West Berlin are open throughout the year, charge an all-inclusive rate for bed-and-breakfast of only 14 marks ($5.38), which ascends to 17 marks ($6.53) for persons over the age of 24. Those rather amazing prices are available, for instance, at **Jugendherberge "Ernst Reuter,"** Hermsdorfer Damm 48 (phone 404-16-10), in Berlin Hermsdorf (a huge, interesting hostel); at **Jugendherberge Bayernallee**, 36 Bayernallee (phone 305-3055), in Berlin-Charlottenburg; and at the completely new **Jugendgästehaus am Wannsee**, #1 Badeweg (phone 803-2034), whose 288 beds rent for 17.90 marks ($6.88), including breakfast. Largest and perhaps most comfortable of the youth hostels is the **Jugendgästehaus Berlin** at 3 Kluckstrasse (phone 261-1097), whose 421 beds rent for 16 marks ($6.08) including breakfast. This one's in the center of town, near the Kurfürstenstrasse U-Bahn station, and while it lacks the grounds and hearty outdoor flavor of the Bayernallee, Ernst Reuter, and Wannsee hostels, it's probably better suited to sightseeing young tourists, interested in the downtown life of West Berlin. There's a midnight curfew at all four hostels, as well as a requirement that you hold a Youth Hostel card, which, however, can be purchased on-the-spot for 30 marks ($13.04).

STUDENT IN BERLIN: Student headquarters in Berlin is the **ARTU** at 9 Hardenbergstrasse (near Amerika Haus), open weekdays from 9:30 a.m. to 6 p.m. (phone 31-07-71), and providing information on student charter flights, student discounts, and the like. For student meals, head directly across the street to the **Student Mensa** at 34 Hardenberg-strasse, where the lunchtime menu features soup at a mark, and main plates with vegetables from 1.80 to 2.80 marks. I.D. card needed. Both these outfits are located a short three blocks from the main Zoo railroad station. High-quality student lodgings are provided by the centrally located **Studentenhotel Berlin** at Meininger Strasse 10 (phone 784-67-20), near the Rathaus Schöneberg (City Hall) on John F. Kennedy Platz. Rates there for accommodations in four-bedded room are 25 marks per person, 28 marks in a two-bedded room. Breakfast is included at no no extra charge. Take bus 4, 85 or 73; the U-Bahn station is Rathaus Schöneberg.

READERS ON THE SUB-STARVATION BUDGET: "For rock-rock bottom accommodations you don't even have to leave the station. There's a **Mission Dormitory** right inside the Zoo terminal. It charges 15 marks ($5.76) a night for hostel-type cubicles—with hot water and lockers, but not showers" (Nat Freedland, New York, N.Y.). . . . "At my price level (the lowest) I recommend the **Bahnhof Mission**—they have an office in the Bahnhof and the Mission is right downstairs. It's a spotless, dormitory-style place, and costs 15 marks" (Pete Wilford, Morris Plains, N.J.; note by AF: the central train station in West Berlin is known as "Bahnhof Zoo," and is located across from the large Berlin Zoo; entrance to the Bahnhof Mission—which has a midnight curfew, and literally kicks you out of bed at 7 a.m.—is in the ticket-selling portion of the station next to the post office; you'll see signs. An even larger **Mission Dormitory** for both men and women, of which the railroad station is an annex, is found at 27 Franklinstrasse in the Tiergarten district, near the Ernst-Reuter-Platz U-Bahn stop. Cost is 15 marks per person per night, including a spartan breakfast of coffee, bread and marmalade. Showers are free, curfew is at 1 a.m., and dinner served from 6 to 9 p.m. for 2.10 marks).

HOTEL BOOKING AND INFORMATION OFFICES: Berlin's modern **Tourist Information Office** in the Europa Center (enter from Budapester Strasse), open daily from 7:30 a.m. to 10:30 p.m., will book you into hotels and pensions for a modest fee of 2 marks (76¢) and hands out free city maps and other free brochures. The **Informationszentrum Berlin,** at 20 Hardenbergstrasse (second floor), near Bahnhof Zoo, open Monday to Friday 8 a.m. to 7 p.m., Saturday to 4 p.m., provides general information about Berlin's political situation, including up-to-date advice on how to visit the Eastern sector, and distributes a free 96-page booklet, in English, containing interesting data on history, local government, museums, exhibitions, religious communities, and the like.

3. Low-Cost Restaurants and Meals

Have your very first meal in Berlin at the domed third-floor restaurant of the **Bilka Department Store** (Germany's answer to Macy's) at Joachimstalerstrasse 5, near the Zoo station in the heart of town. The single most popular budget eatery in Berlin, the Bilka restaurant is a vast, glassed-in room housed in a futuristic world's fair type building. You can have an excellent three-course meal here for only 11.50 marks ($4.42), including tax and service, from 11:30 a.m. to 5:30 p.m. weekdays and till 2 p.m. Saturdays, and my own, recent (1984) Bilka banquet may give you some idea of the hearty offerings. I had onion soup, then fried Leberknödel (liver dumplings) with a spicy sauce, accompanied by sauerkraut and mashed potatoes, with cream cake for dessert. Eleven and a half marks ($4.42) for the lot.

Another excellent choice—possibly for your second meal in Berlin—is the smaller but almost equally popular **Cafe Riegler** at 9 Hardenbergstrasse (across the street from the university mensa described in our "starvation budget" section below); its portions are widely reputed to be among the largest served in town! Ten different groaning platters are served each day, ranging in price from only 4 marks (vegetable stew with wieners) to an absolute maximum of 9 marks (for wiener schnitzel with french fries), and an example at 6.50 marks (only $2.50) would be the permanently available *knödel* plate—a potato dumpling, ostrich-egg-sized, with a spicy, pickled caper sauce and a huge mound of mashed potatoes. Dieter's delight. Open weekdays only from noon till around 8 p.m.

Your third worthy budget Berliner—cheapest of the lot—is the student-frequented **Dicke Wirtin** at 9 Carmerstrasse, off the Kurfürstendamm near Savignyplatz. Here the offerings are uniformly *Eintopfgerichte* (stews) costing only 5 marks ($1.53)—a dozen varieties of hot stews, ranging from pea-sauerkraut-and-bean stew to sweet-and-sour vegetable stews, all with barely perceptible traces of meat, chicken or pork; at that price, it's hard to complain that you're not receiving large chunks of protein. Open weekdays from noon to 10, Saturdays from 5 p.m. to 10, closed Sundays.

And finally, don't miss **Tegernseer Tönnchen,** at 34 Mommsenstrasse (from the Kurfürstendamm, turn right on Wilmersdorferstrasse, then left on Mommsenstrasse), where the decor and atmosphere is pure Bavarian beer hall. Open daily until midnight, it offers hearty one-plate meals from 9.50 to 16 marks ($3.65 to $6.15), accompanied by Tegernseer beer from Bavaria, 4.50 marks for half a liter.

THE BUDGET-MINDED BALKANS: If at this point your system has been saturated with the flavors and fats of the classic German cuisine, you might like to search out the increasingly popular Balkan restaurants of West Berlin, whose lighter and spicier cuisine can sometimes provide a welcome change. We recommend three, in particular: the **Paprika Grill,** 73 Fasanenstrasse (near the Kudamm), where a large plate of stuffed peppers and potatoes costs 9.50 marks ($3.65); the **Belgrad-Grill,** 67 Uhlandstrasse near the Ku-damm, serving schaschlik for 6 marks ($2.30), a *puszta platte* (pork cutlets on curried rice, with salad) for 10 marks ($3.84), all of it accompanied by excellent Yugoslav red wine at 6 marks ($2.30) per quarter liter; and **Athener Grill,** Kurfürstendamm 156, corner Albrecht-Achilles-Strasse, open from noon to 4 a.m., serving lamb cutlets with french fries or salad for 6.50 marks ($2.50), Greek salad for 4.50 marks ($1.73), and a large selection of Balkan-style pizzas for 5 marks ($1.92). At some of the above, waiters and waitresses are colorfully attired in Yugoslav, Hungarian, or Greek costumes, and in the evenings musicians usually play and sing Balkan folk songs.

THE ITALIAN "SPAGHETTERIAS": Pasta provides an occasional alternative to the more elaborate meals featured by the restaurants of Berlin. At the large, three-level and self-service **Pizzeria Mamma,** 29 Hardenbergstrasse, between the Zoo Station and the Zoo Palast movie theatre, all varieties of spaghetti with differing sauces are served for only 5.50 and 6 marks ($2.11 and $2.30), every day of the week until 1 a.m. Sidewalk tables and benches are pleasant for viewing the passing parade. On the Kurfürstendamm, corner of Adenauerplatz (next to the subway stop), spaghetti, maccaroni and lasagne dishes with huge portions sell for a much higher 12 marks ($4.61) at **Restaurante Mamma Lucia,** because of the table service performed by an Italian staff. A middle course, in both location and price, is then pursued by **San Marino** and **Piazza,** two adjoining spaghetterias heavily patronized by students, about halfway in position between Pizzeria Mamma and Mamma Lucia at the Savignyplatz (#'s 12 and 13), in the Technical University area: 11 marks ($4.23) for a large glass of draft beer *and* spaghetti.

THE $5 TO $6.50 RESTAURANTS: Along the Kurfürstendamm, and on the side streets directly off it, are a host of other places where one can dine well for a higher $5 to $6.50. These include the long-established, well-known **Restaurant Schultheiss-Bräuhaus,** corner of Kurfürstendamm and Meinekestrasse. Look this time for the giant daily platters selling for 8 marks ($3.07, that's for pea stew with a pair of wieners), or for 5 marks ($1.92, bringing you three potato omelettes—*Kartoffelpuffer*—with apple sauce), or for 10.50 marks ($4.03) beef goulash with salad, or, if you're really famished, for 13 marks ($5) the price of the renowned Bräuhausteller, a huge plate stacked high with six different cold cuts and three varieties of cheese, bread included.

A short walk away, in the same Kurfürstendamm area, the self-service restaurant of the Wertheim Department Store, called **"Imbisstube,"** offers a large variety of popular dishes—including a delicious sauerbrauten platter with red cabbage and roast potatoes for 9.50 marks ($3.65), a mammoth dish of beef goulash with rice and mixed salad for 8.50 marks ($3.26)—and has, since its recent opening, become quite popular with Berliners. You could make a meal here out of two rolls (40 pfennig each) and a bowl of thick pea soup with slices of wiener sausage swimming in it, 5.50 marks ($2.11). The restaurant, in the basement of the department store, next to the food department (it's fully air conditioned), shares store hours: Monday to Friday from 9:30 a.m. to 6:30 p.m., Saturday until 2 p.m.

And finally, you might want to visit one of the several restaurants at the big **KaDeWe Department Store** (largest in Europe), Tauentzienstrasse, corner of Wittenbergplatz. These include the self-service **Zille-Stube** on the third floor (daily platters from 7.50 to 9.50 marks—$2.88 to $3.65), and adjoining, sitdown **"Restaurant"** with waitress service and three-course table d'hotes for 13 to 17 marks—$5 to $6.53. In the same "KaDeWe" (standing for "Kaufhaus des Westens"), top (sixth) floor, is a gigantic food department (largest in Europe) containing, among other features, a dozen stands selling wieners, sandwiches, roast chicken, wine, sweets, soups and fishburgers. All these are open Monday to Friday, from 10 a.m. to 6:30 p.m., Saturdays until 2 p.m.

ON WILMERSDORFERSTRASSE: The cheap shopping street of Berlin
is not the elegant Kurfürstendamm, but the pedestrians-only Wilmersdorferstrasse, where a stroll provides insight into the life of the average-income Berliner. Most of them are drawn to the bustling department stores here, including a low-cost **Hertie** (known for particular values in low-cost shoes), whose unusually cheap, second-floor cafeteria serves fixed-price, three-course meals for 12 marks. Across the street, the cafeteria of the **Quelle Department Store** offers lighter two-course menus, for 11 marks, while the fourth-floor restaurant of the **Karstadt** store asks a standard 13 marks for two courses. A constant price war. And there are countless small, inexpensive restaurants crammed between the shops. Try, for instance, at 106 Wilmersdorferstrasse, the simple—but popular—**Pohlmann,** featuring various forms of *eintopfgerichte* (literally: one-pot-meals), such as a meat-and-potatoes stew, or a bowl of pea-soup with sausage bits, all filling and all priced under 6 marks. Or try, at 58 Wilmersdorferstrasse, the fish-featuring **Nordsee Restaurant,** selling fishburgers for 1.80 marks (69¢), fried haddock with a mountain of incomparable German potato salad for 7.50 marks ($2.88), sour herring with steamed potatoes, all in a delicious marinade, for 5.50 marks ($2.11). Diagonally across the street, at 117 Wilmersdorferstrasse, **Joseph Langer** features a pair of wieners with a bowl of pea soup for 2.75 marks ($1.05), while **Pufferpfanne,** at the corner of Kantstrasse, specializes in a filling potato omelette served with apple sauce and

known as *kartoffelpuffer*—only 3 marks ($1.15). Guten Appetit, and keep the Alka Seltzer handy.

LORETTA'S GARDEN: Is a place to eat outdoor picnic meals, without anyone requiring that you buy a thing. Walk up the Kurfürstendamm from the Europa Center side, turn left into Knesebeckstrasse, walk on for a block, and there you'll see: **Loretta's Garden,** with 100 tables, open to the public, weather permitting, from noon on. If you haven't brought the fixings, you can obtain all you'll need from nearly a dozen shops in the area selling beer, soft drinks, sausages and the like (an average of 3 marks—$1.15—per). You can go there at night, too, when amateur bands play.

THE WIENERWALDS: There is also in Berlin a chain of restaurants serving spit-roasted chicken—the **Wienerwald Brathendlstationen**—which you ought to try at least once: they are one of the great success stories of postwar Germany. Their originator, a restaurant waiter, once visited the Oktoberfest in Munich, where he saw Germans by the thousands wolfing down huge quantities of roast chicken—then a relatively expensive luxury in Germany. Determined to make roast chicken a mass-market commodity, he traveled to the United States, studied our chicken-roasting methods, and then—on the merest of shoestrings—opened a restaurant that would serve only a single item, roast chicken, for under $4. He decorated the place in a crowd-pleasing cornball Vienna Woods fashion, called it the "Wiener-wald," and expanded so quickly that he was soon operating scores of Wienerwalds, of which 20 are in West Berlin.

The Wienerwalds now serve half a roast chicken, plus salad, for 12.50 marks ($4.80). They also serve thick chicken soup (with noodles and several chunks of chicken) for 3.75 marks, and a small beer for 2.50 marks. The one we last visited was at Tauentzien Strasse 16 (corner of Marburger Strasse), but there are other members of the chain at Schwedenstrasse 19, Neue Kantstrasse 17, Turmstrasse 26, Kurt-Schumacher-Platz, Tegel Schloss Strasse 1, Bayerischer Platz 2, and at 13 other locations throughout the city. It's a filling meal, and the mass production of the roast chickens should amuse you.

READERS' RESTAURANT SELECTIONS: "At **Novo Skopje,** 38 Kurfürstendamm, you can get terrific 'pola pola'—pork sausage, beef, vegetables and a delicious sauce—plus a beer, for 14 marks" (Peter Hrycenko, Fleetwood, Pennsylvania). . . . "The **Verena Vegetarian Restaurant,** located just off the Kurfürstendamm on Clausewitzstrasse, and open daily except Tuesdays, and except Saturday and Sunday evenings, is not only inexpensive, but quiet, dignified, clean and attractive, with an extensive menu of tastefully prepared food—vegetable soup, 3.50 marks; cinnamon rice with cooked apples, 6 marks; yogurt, 2.80 marks—which non-vegetarians like ourselves found an enjoyable change of pace" (Barbara S. Lesko, Oakland, California; note by AF: open daily except Tuesdays from noon to 9 p.m., exact address is 67 Kurfürsten-damm, and two-course menus are priced from 9 to 13 marks, but some content themselves with simply the cooked rice with stewed fruit for 6 marks).

READERS' FOOD-AND-DRINK TIPS: "The finest and cheapest cup of coffee in Berlin (and in many other large German cities) is served not in restaurants or lunch rooms, but in specialty stores selling coffee in packages or cans. The theory is that a possible customer looking for a package of coffee to take home, should be given a sample cup, fresh-made, at 80 pfennigs (about 30¢) a cup. In actual practice, the stores are crowded most of the day by people who only want a cup of coffee. I have seen a line of 20 or 30 persons being served at the rate of 12 to 15 per minute. Each is quickly given a cup of boiling hot coffee, a little cream, and two or three lumps of sugar. They drink it at a stand-up table where there is a pitcher of lukewarm water to stretch or weaken the coffee if they wish. Two of these places are located on the same street, Kurfürstendamm, each within a hundred feet of the famous ruined church that stands almost in the center of the main business section. One of them is on the same side of the street as the church and a few doors from American Express. You can't miss it, the shop is filled with customers drinking coffee. A sign on the shop window reads 'Tchibo.' These little shops are not old-fashioned second-rate places, but bright and shining and as up-to-the-minute as the best commercial establishments in the city" (Albert Gerlach, Miami, Florida).

STARVATION BUDGET MEALS: Because they're such exciting secrets, I almost hate to divulge that Berlin possesses two mensa-type restaurants (army-style messhalls), totally proper and attractive, yet practically unknown even to the average Berliner, where filling, two-course meals can be had at lunchtime for less than $2.70!

The immense, 1,400-seat **Mensa der Technischen Universität** at 34 Hardenbergstrasse, easily found less than 250 yards from Bahnhof Zoo (it's the modern, low construction with red windows), is theoretically maintained for students. But if you'll walk through the student area, and then up the stairs, you'll find a public, non-student dining room where waitresses serve three daily dishes for only 2.80 marks ($1.07), like vegetable stew with sausage; or two-course luncheons for only 4.50 to 7 marks ($1.73 to $2.69), like fish filet with salad and dessert, or goulasch with noodles, plus fruit. There are à la carte delights for 6.50 marks ($2.50), chicken stew with vegetables) and 9 marks ($3.46, sauerbraten with red cabbage and potatoes); coffee for 90 pfennigs (34¢); Cokes for 1.50 marks (57¢); beer for 1.60 marks (61¢). And hours are from Monday through Friday, 11:30 a.m. to 2:30 p.m. only.

Then there's the **Kasino im Haus des Senators Für Wirtschaft,** on the fifth floor (via elevator) of 105 Martin Luther Strasse, facing the Schöneberger Rathaus (take the subway to this stop). There, soup is 1.60 marks (61¢), two-course meals are 4.50 and 6.50 marks ($1.73 and $2.50), à la carte offerings range from 4 marks (grilled sausage with red cabbage) to 10.50 marks (rumpsteak), and hours are again on weekdays only, from 11:30 a.m. to 2:30 p.m. This is a large (200 seats), public-service-oriented place with a busy, English-speaking manager, Frau Zimmer.

4. Entertainment

NIGHTTIME ENTERTAINMENT: Now for the action. You ought not to miss the **Cafe Keese,** 108 Bismarckstrasse (a ten-minute walk from the Ku-Damm), a large, cheerful dance hall populated by singles and couples in the 25-to-40 age range, where the gimmick is the "Ball Paradox"—a system by which the woman asks the man to dance and it is against the house rules for the man to refuse! Only on the hourly "Men's Choice," can the man issue the invitation (those males wanting to sit it out retire to the bar; the rest are fair game). Cafe Keese claims 43,000 couples to date who have met and married under the auspices of three German branches. Clientele is well dressed and comparatively attractive; there's no admission charge; and reasonable drink prices (8 marks a beer, including tax and service); orchestra is live and the dances tend to be slow—with very little in the rock line. Open 8 p.m. to 4 a.m.; closed Mondays.

People of all ages might enjoy the lively dancing and beer-swigging at the **Munich Hofbräuhaus,** across from the bombed church on Hardenbergstrasse. Admission to the atmospheric upstairs room is free on weekdays, 3 marks on Friday and Saturday, 2 marks on Sundays. The band is brassy; the crowd happy and noisy; the cost of a half-liter of beer only 6 marks, a full liter, 9, and a giant stein of five liters, 35 marks.

For much younger readers, the major teen-age spot in Berlin is the **Big Apple,** on Bundesalle, where all the latest dance steps are frenetically practiced, against an ear-shattering din of noise. Entrance fee (which is all you need spend) is 2 marks from Monday through Thursday, 3 marks on weekends, a mark less for girls, and payment of entrance is considered to be a *Verzehrbon,* exchangeable for one free drink inside.

Crowds are always waiting to get into the **Big Eden** at 202 Kurfürstendam—a monstrous discotheque that holds up to 2,000 people and is bugged from one end to the other with zany electronic gimmicks. Lights flash, sounds swell, the record player is a masterpiece of electronic workmanship. Every sort and species of young Berlin swinger turns up at the Big Eden—most in costume—as well as all young internationals who hone in on the "sound." The Big Eden is specifically geared to the thin pocketbook. During the week, you need purchase only a 4-mark *Verzehrbon* at the door; on Friday, Saturday and Sunday there's an additional 2-mark entrance fee. Drinks are priced from 4 marks on, including tax, and if you sit in the booths along the wall where there is a sign reading *Selbstbedienung* (self-service), you won't be bothered by waitresses and can go up to the self-service counter and buy drinks as you please, without further service charge. At one circular counter, there's curry sausage for sale at 1.50 marks per serving, spaghetti at 2.50 marks, and veal schnitzel platter for 6.50 marks. And all around there are lone, young Berliners ready and willing to strike up conversation with lone, young tourists. Open until 2 a.m. weekdays, until 5 a.m. weekends. (And by the way, unescorted girls are never charged an admission here, nor is anyone—male or female—who shows this book or chapter at the door.)

The larger **Metropol,** at 5 Nollendorfplatz, housed in a former theatre building two U-Bahn stops from Bahnhof Zoo, is another hangout for the young set. Here you'll find up to 3,000 people dancing to electronic music supervised by Berlin's most popular disc jockey. Entrance is 10 marks ($3.84), but drinks are a reasonable 3 marks ($1.15) for a beer or Coke, for example. Open from 7 p.m., Wednesdays through Sundays only. Smaller, less expensive, and "in" is the **Sudhaus,** at 21 Stromstrasse, in the Tiergarten and Moabit area (near U-Bahn stop Turmstrasse), which features both a live band and disco sound. Admission is 5 marks ($1.92) and drinks are identical in price to those at the Metropol. Open 8 p.m. to 2 or 4 a.m., depending on attendance.

We've saved one of the most exciting spots for the last. Berlin—true to its wild, woolly, avant-garde tradition—has another of these weird, labyrinthine nightspots (patronized mainly by people under 30), in the 1,300-seat **Riverboat** (at 177 Hohenzollerndamm; take the subway to Fehrbelliner Platz), whose motif is that of a Mississippi riverboat, and whose layout is like the maze of a fun-house: there are seemingly endless galleyways with booths on either side, portholes, photostat blowups of famous riverboats, and four disc jockeys working overtime. Entrance is 3 marks on weekends, 2 marks on weekdays; a glass of beer is 4 marks; stags of both sexes are much in evidence; and the Riverboat is closed Sundays.

READER'S ENTERTAINMENT SUGGESTIONS: "Deutsche Oper begins its season towards the end of August and runs until mid-July. You can get a pretty good seat for 15 marks, but in order to be sure of obtaining a ticket, it's better to make an advance reservation at the opera house (take U-bahn to Deutsche Oper). The box office is open between 2 and 8 p.m. You can also make reservations at any ticket agency" (Vera Wongcruawal, Bangkok, Thailand).

READER'S DAYTIME SELECTIONS "No one visiting Berlin should fail to see the **Schöneberg Rathaus,** where the Freedom Bell is, and where President Kennedy made his famous 'Ich bin ein Berliner' speech. There is free admission to the public on Wednesdays and Sundays from 10 a.m. to 2 p.m." (I. Skolnik, Bronx, New York). . . . "Berlin can be very warm during the summer, and so visitors will find that the cafes on Kurfürstendamm are deserted and the sidewalks are lifeless. Where is everybody? You'll find hordes of Berliners at the outdoor swimming pools and lake areas, which in addition to being good places to cool off, are also the best spots for viewing the latest bathing outfits. The best ones are **Olympia Stadium** (take U-bahn to Olympia Stadium), **Sommerbad Wilmersdorf** (take S-bahn to Heidelberger Platz), and **Wannsee Strandbad** (take bus 66 to Wannsee). Admission to these pools is 2.50 marks. If you prefer lakes and woods, head for **Krumme Lanke.** Take the U-bahn to Krumme Lanke, and turn right in front of the station along Fischerhüttenstrasse" (Richard Strasslein, Wilmington, Delaware). . . . "An interesting self-guided tour of the Wall is as follows: take the subway to *Checkpoint Charlie.* Walk to the *Wall.* Turn left and walk along the small street that runs along the Wall. As you walk, you read the slogans written on the Wall and also look into East Berlin from several viewing stands. After one mile you will come to *Potsdamer Platz.* One mile further is the *Tiergarten,* where you watch Russian soldiers guarding the Soviet War Memorial. On the other side of Tiergarten is the *Reichstag* and memorial crosses for those who died while seeking to escape from East Germany. Then take double-decker bus 69 back to the Zoo" (Philip S. Meyer, Indianapolis, Indiana).

5. Tours

Three companies, all of whose buses leave from the Kurfürstendamm-Uhlandstrasse corner, operate escorted tours of Berlin. Oldest and largest is **Severin und Kühn,** open seven days a week at 216 Kurfürstendamm (opposite the Kempinski Hotel), phone 883-10-15, whose most popular tour goes into both West and East Berlin, lasts seven hours, costs 45 marks, plus 15 marks for the East Berlin guide, leaves daily at 10 a.m., is perfectly safe and shouldn't be missed; a condensed version of the same thing, confined almost entirely to East Berlin, leaves at 2 p.m., lasts only four hours, and costs 28 marks, plus the 15-mark East German fee and an additional mark for an optional visit to the Pergamon Museum. If you merely wish to tour West Berlin, you can take a three-hour tour at 10 a.m. or 2:30 p.m. for 28 marks, or a two-hour tour at 11 a.m., 2 p.m. and 4 p.m. for 20 marks. Definitely take the one that goes into both halves of the city—and then read about do-it-yourself tours of East Berlin, below. Finally, you might want to consider an excursion to historic Potsdam, which includes a visit to Sanssouci Castle, New Castle, and Cecilienhof Palace, in the last-named of which the Potsdam Agreement was signed in 1945. Departures are every Tuesday, Thursday and Saturday at 9:30 a.m. for this eight-hour trip, which costs 93 marks, and includes lunch in a Potsdam restaurant. Severin und Kühn also sells theatre tickets and acts as a general tourist information office; the company's general manager and his assistant, Herr du Plessis and Herr Schaube, have for many years been helpful to readers of this book.

A DO-IT-YOURSELF TOUR OF EAST BERLIN: The commercial tours

of East Berlin are good for orientation purposes, but they are limited, for the most part, to lifeless statues and memorials—such as the Soviet War Cemetery—and fail to give you a real picture of life in East Berlin.

Despite the Wall, visitors are permitted to enter East Berlin on their own, at designated crossing points. To do so is precisely like crossing a border, except that the process is dragged out to a half-hour of passport-checking and questionnaire-filling, which is particularly infuriating when you realize the illegality of the entire procedure. But if you will tolerate that 30 minutes of red tape, and refrain from making comments about it to the East German Volks-Polizei, the whole business becomes routine.

Once again, it is—at least at the time of writing—entirely safe to enter East Berlin on your own. If you have any qualms about it, then register your name with the American MP's at Checkpoint Charlie, tell them the time at which you plan to return, and if you're not there at that time, they'll take action. But no normal tourist is detained. On our most recent trip to Berlin, Hope and I met dozens of American G.I.'s who had made so many weekend jaunts into East Berlin that they were walking encyclopedias of the sights to be found across the Wall.

To get to Checkpoint Charlie—which is your best crossing point—take the U-Bahn from the Zoological Garden Station (near the Kurfür-stendamm) to the Hallesches Tor station, and change there for the train that goes to **Kochstrasse**, one stop further on. The Kochstrasse exit is a block from the wall-crossing point. Before actually entering, you'll need to change 25 marks into 25 East-marks—this is required—and then pay over 5 marks to the Volks-Polizei for your visa (valid until midnight).

Once in East Berlin, you can take a cab to the places you'd like to see, or better yet, you can simply wander on foot, which is the preferred way to absorb the atmosphere of this unusual city. After visiting East Berlin's incomparable Pergamon Museum, Hope and I recently walked to the Friedrichstrasse Station, entered a huge market-place where we ate what seemed like sawdust-filled sausages for a snack, then took a long, long walk along Unter den Linden, and finally headed over to the showplace street of East Berlin (past the new Palast der Republik), once the famous "Stalinallee," but now renamed "Karl-Marx-Allee."

There are three restaurants on the Karl-Marx-Allee—the relatively expensive **Moskwa,** which features Russian specialties such as chicken à la Tabaka (4.75 East German marks) and filet steak Minsk (7.50 marks); and the less costly **Budapest** (where roast duck with pineapple slices and french fries cost 6.60 marks) and the **Warschau**—both on opposite corners of the intersection made by Fruchstrasse. We had coffee at the Warschau, but could have had a meal for 7 East German marks (which are now the exact equivalent of 7 West German marks).

Several establishments serving lighter—and therefore lower-priced—meals are located nearby. At the rococo-style **Ermeler-Haus,** 10 Märkisches Ufer, you can sit in either the basement or garden and have beefsteak with mushrooms for 6 marks, or a large beer for 1.56 marks. At **Gastmahl Des Meeres,** on the corner of Spandauer-Liebknechtstrasse, you eat fish in a large (East Berlin's largest) and reasonably priced fish house (fish stew is 3.30 marks; the most expensive item on the menu is filet of sole with vegetables and french fries for 6 marks). And finally, in the impressive, new government building called **Palast der Republik,** at Marx-Engels-Platz, three restaurants (the Spree, Linden and Palast) lists a long assortment of traditional dishes, including franks with potato salad (1.80 marks), veal cutlet with mushrooms (3.50 marks). And then, having had enough, you can take a cab back to the crossing point, recross, and ride the S-Bahn to the Bahnhof Zoo, where you'll emerge to the neon-lit, bustling life of free West Berlin. It is only, I think, at the moment that you return that the contrast between West Berlin and the dull existence of East Berlin really begins to sink in.

It might, of course, be well to precede your own tour of East Berlin with one of the commercial, guided variety. But don't miss a tour on your own—it's your chance to see current history being lived around you.

READERS' SELECTIONS (EAST BERLIN): "The opera is good in East Berlin and is worth seeing. Another experience we would recommend is to attend church services some Sunday morning in East Berlin. For Protestants, we recommend the Marienkirche. You'll have to ask directions, but it is within walking distance of Checkpoint Charlie" (Alan and Marti Lata, Gersweiler/Saar, West Germany). . . . "Berliner Ensemble and East German Opera only get footnote mentions; they should be expanded in Hope's section, as cultural pearls of both Berlins. Also Piscator's Theatre in East Berlin; he and Leo Blech are buried there" (Delos V. Smith, Jr., Hutchinson, Kansas). . . . "I suggest that budget travelers try the **Automat** on the Alexanderplatz, near the Centrum Warenhaus, for it has good hot meals for 2 marks, delicious coffee, and a lively crowd" (Tom Craig, Moore, South Carolina; note by AF: to visit the "Centrum"—East Berlin's largest department store—take the underground from the Pergamon Museum (which should be the first stop on your East Berlin tour) to Alexanderplatz. After touring the store (which is quite an experience), take the underground to Schillingstrasse, where you can then walk down to the Karl Marx Allee; **Haus Berlin,** also called Grossgaststätte Haus Berlin, at 1 Straussberger Platz, just off Karl Marx Allee, is so big that you'll usually find a vacant seat. The average prices here are 7 marks for breakfast, 10 marks each for a 3-course lunch or supper, all listed on an unusually detailed menu card). . . . "We had a huge banquet (which included wine, very good and cheap in East Germany) in the medieval, intimate atmosphere of the **Ratskeller** in the basement of the Town Hall, 14 Rathausstrasse. We spent 55 East German marks for two, for a tasty, well-flavored meal" (Eduardo Vergara, Moncton, New Brunswick, Canada). . . . "Since the erection of the Wall, West Berliners seldom travel to East Berlin, and as they were in part the patrons of East Berlin theatres, there are usually tickets available. However, allow time for border crossing, as the guards sometimes get nasty about it, especially if you appear obviously in a hurry. Unlike Vienna, where tie and jacket are required, the Socialist paradise makes no such imposition on its theatre goers" (Burt Wolfson, New York; note by AF: a theatre service for international tourists is operated by **Reisebüro der Deutschen Demokratischen Republik** at 5 Alexanderplatz, phone 212-33-75, which also arranges tours and the like. The week's schedule of theatre performances and concerts is posted all over East Berlin. Tickets are not expensive—from 6 to 15 marks for the Berliner Ensemble, for instance—and seats are usually available). . . . "Here's an ideal excursion for any Berlin visitor who wants to experience what it means to live with 'the Wall': Although **Steinstücken** is part of the American sector, it is completely surrounded by East Germany and linked to West Berlin by an access road that is walled on both sides. To reach this enclave, take a #18 doubledecker bus (be sure it is labelled Steinstücken, most buses do not go to the end of the line). Sit on the top deck of the bus so that you can see over and beyond the wall. It will be on both sides during the last one or two kms of your trip. Bus fare is 2 marks each way. When you arrive at Steinstücken, cross the pedestrian bridge over the railroad tracks. Follow the footpath to a simple monument, consisting of two helicopter propellers mounted upright marking the site of the helicopter pad that was Steinstücken's only link with freedom before the access road was opened in 1972. Continue along the dirt road to a turn-around used by Allied military vehicles patrolling the wall. Poke your head through some bushes just beyond that and you will find yourself about 50 meters from an East German guard tower. The confrontation is particularly eerie because there is no wall at that point. Be assured that this trip is safe and totally legal as long as you keep the railroad tracks (and the wire fence on each side of them) between you and the East Germans" (Paul and Patty Cooligan, APO, New York).

6. Berlin Miscellany

You'll quickly discover that Berliners are an atypical breed of Germans —witty, sophisticated, and totally irreverent. For instance, they've named the chapel and bell-tower, adjacent to the ruined Kaiser-Wilhelm-Gedächtniskirche on Kurfürstendamm, "the lipstick case and the powder box." Take one look and you'll see why. . . . What makes for this great humor? The Berliners attribute it to the city's dry, stimulating air— "Berliner Luft." It supposedly renders one tolerant and open-hearted, energetic and creative. . . . Don't be confused by Kurfürstendamm addresses; the numbers on one side of the street bear no relation to those on the other. . . . For theatre enthusiasts, the point to remember is that the theatres in West Berlin are surprisingly tiny. Therefore, always get the cheapest seats—you'll see fine. And don't walk away if the theatre is sold out. Nearly always, a few extra seats come available several minutes before curtain time. West Berlin's most famous theatre, and one you should see, is the **Schiller** (tickets start at 8 marks). . . . Berlin's flea market, **Die Nolle,** open daily except Tuesdays from 11 a.m. to 7:30 p.m., is located in sixteen old subway trains at Nollendorfplatz, a ten-minute walk from Wittenbergplatz, which is the square near the large KaDeWe department store. Even if you don't plan to buy an old sewing machine, pictures, furniture, coins or antique dolls, you might want to relax after browsing at the small flea market restaurant, ordering a Berliner boulette (a hamburger without the bun) for 3 marks. . . . For students of the new math (readers under 12), that mysterious grouping of lights atop a steel pole at the corner of Kudamm and Uhlandstrasse is neither a traffic indicator nor a radar trap, but rather the world's largest (and only) clock based on the theory of sets. Top two rectangular rows show the hours, with lights in the uppermost row standing for five hours, those in the lower row for one hour (you add them together). The two orange rows mark the minutes: lights in the upper row each indicate five minutes, those below are one minute (and again you add them together). What's the reason for it? To slow traffic, as motorists laboriously figure the time? To confuse the Russians? To prove that even clocks can be avant garde? Only in Berlin. . . . Two centrally located, easily found laundromats are the **Münz Waschsalon** at 43 Leibnizstrasse (corner of Niebuhrstrasse, near Savignyplatz and a few hundred yards off the Kurfürstendamm), open weekdays from 9 a.m. to 1 p.m. and 2:30 to 6:30 p.m., Saturdays from 9 a.m. to 1 p.m.; and the **LAR Waschsalon** (corner of Uhlandstrasse and Hohenzollerndamm, near the Hohenzollernplatz subway station), open weekdays from 8 a.m. to 6:30 p.m., Saturdays to 1 p.m. Both charge 5 marks for 8 kilos, one mark for drying. . . . To make child care easy, call one of Berlin's student-managed **babysitting agencies:** TUSMA, 34 Hardenbergstrasse (phone 313-4054) or Heinzelmännchen, 319 Clayallee (phone 801-4023). . . . If you need emergency medical service, phone 310031 or 114 for dental emergency service. . . . Local phone calls can be made from street phone booths for two

10-pfennig coins. . . . If you need an English newspaper, you'll find the newsstand in the covered passage at 206 Kurfurstendamm open seven days a week from 7 a.m. to 11 p.m. . . . Major stores are open Monday to Friday, 9 a.m. to 6 p.m., Saturdays to 1 p.m. Do your banking early in the day—hours are 9 a.m. to 1 p.m., Monday to Friday. . . . But for those with emergency needs for late-night money, the Wechselstube (money exchange office) inside the Bahnhof Zoo is open every day except Sundays until 9 p.m., Sundays until 6 p.m. . . . Also in the Zoo, Berlin's main **Post and Telephone Office** stays open 24 hours a day. . . . Best way to orient yourself in Berlin—and best over-all view of the city—is from the top of **I-Punkt Berlin,** the 22-story skyscraper in the Europa Center. You'll pay 1.50 marks to go up to the viewing terrace, called **Zur Fernrohrstrasse,** or literally translated, "Viewing Street," and there you can use the telescopes for free. Walk all the way around the terrace to your right and look through the farthest telescope and you can see across the Wall into East Berlin and focus on the Brandenburg Gate and Alexanderplatz. . . . The leading art gallery of West Berlin, and one you should visit, is the **Dahlem Museum,** Armin-Allee 24, open every day except Monday, charging no admission, and containing the world's largest collection of Rembrandts—24 paintings in all. But for more on that institution, and for a description of (a) East Berlin's sights, and (b) the sights of the immense Charlottenburg Palace, I give you to Hope:

7. Hope's Berlin

"Berlin is as exciting as a frontier town. But it has its disappointments —it won't be anything like you expect it to be. For instance, there's not a shred of Old Berlin left: that was totally reduced to ashes in the last days of street fighting at the end of World War II. Unter den Linden will never be the same; Christopher Isherwood's Berlin no longer exists. And there is not even very much left to remind one of Hitler, or that World War II took place—only the Reichstag (near the border of the two Berlins), an empty hulk by the end of the war, but now reconstructed; the famous Brandenburg Gate where the Russians placed a Flag of Victory and which was once a local viewing point into East Berlin; Goering's Headquarters; the Plötzensee Memorial, in a steely grey courtyard of a government building, where a plaque commemorates the German patriots who sought to assassinate Hitler and were hanged here; and the bunker where Hitler and Eva Braun committed suicide. But perhaps the most sensible monument to World War II is the **Kaiser Wilhelm Memorial Church,** left standing in ruins in the center of West Berlin (at the bottom of the Kurfürstendamm) as a permanent reminder to the German people, and all peoples, of the horrors of war.

"The next thing one looks for in Berlin is evidence of the Cold War, the Air Lift, and of the heroes of the beginning of that period (like Ernst Reuter, the first mayor of free West Berlin). Of course in Berlin the Cold War is all around you in the shape of the hideous Wall, but don't expect to see any spies (if you spot one, he's not a very good spy), and the feeling of intrigue in the city has considerably diminished with time. Even the Eastern Sector has been built up and today looks fairly presentable. There is a monument to the Air Lift at the former Tempelhof Air Terminal, a modern piece of sculpture by Ludwig. And you may also visit the **Schöneberg City Hall** (Rathaus), on John F. Kennedy Platz, where the late president delivered his famous 'Ich bin ein Berliner' speech, and whose tower contains an American gift: the Freedom Bell, along with a document signed by 17 million American citizens in support of West Berlin (the tower is open to visitors on Wednesdays and Sundays from 10 a.m. to 3:30 p.m.; but it's advisable to phone 78-33-318 first). At Checkpoint Charlie, which is the route through which most tourists pass into East Berlin, there is the not-to-be-missed **Museum of the Wall,** which includes documented history of all the grisly events that have taken place around the Berlin Wall, and several actual devices (escape cars, mini-submarines, the gondola of a hot-air balloon) used to cross the shameful border.

"When all the reconstruction is finally completed, West Berlin may emerge looking like the City of the Future. In many ways it already does, with its handsome new Europa Center, Congress Center and Philharmonic Hall. Then there is the unique **Hansa Quarter** (near the Victory Column, off the Street of the 17th of June), which was built in 1957 as part of an architectural exhibit—all totally new, with each building having been created by an architect from a different nation. **Corbusier House** was designed for the Hansa exhibition but was too gigantic to fit in the Quarter and was therefore placed near the Olympic Stadium: it's Berlin's largest apartment house, with 530 dwellings, most of them with multi-colored balconies that create an interesting facade (the effect is old to our eyes now, but was undoubtedly another Corbusier breakthrough).

"Nearly 40 years after the war, the city still has the dispersed feeling of a displaced person. The situation in West Berlin is, after all, rather like trying to re-build Manhattan in the Bronx. And for your museum going, you'll find yourself traveling fairly far to see the best. (In all fairness to the exuberant and energetic Berliners, I must mention that an entire complex of modern new museums is being built around St. Matthew's Church near Philharmonic Hall to house their vast collections, but until these are completed. . . .)

THE DAHLEM: "Your first trip should be to **Dahlem,** a fantastic, exciting complex of galleries and museums: it's downright cultural gluttony—at closing time people have to be thrown out bodily. Dahlem's vast collections include **The Picture Gallery; The Department of Sculpture; The Department of Prints and Drawings; The Ethnographical Museum** and **The Museums of Far Eastern, Islamic and Indian Art** (the latter an addition of recent years).

"See the Gallery first (enter at 23/27 Arnimallee, then proceed to your right on the first and second floors), a vast and rich treasure house of paintings—600 in all—from the 13th to the 18th centuries. Since nearly everything shown is outstanding, I'll confine myself to what is merely fantastic. In the first rooms you'll encounter the marvelous early panel paintings, which should not be missed—notice especially Multscher's 'Wurzacher Altar.' There are a number of Dürers (also Giottos, Fra Angelicos, Ghirlandaios), and Titian's famous 'Venus with the Organ Player.' On a rather crowded wall you'll bump into some exquisite Botticellis, including the celebrated 'Venus'; while another room contains the equally renowned 'Merchant George Gisze,' a portrait by Hans Holbein, the Younger. In other rooms, the Flemish and Dutch masters are well represented with works by the prolific Rubens, Van Dyck, Frans Hals, Jan Steen and Vermeer. But the top attraction of the Dutch section is the world's largest collection of Rembrandts, 24 paintings in all, on the second floor. Rembrandt's overflowing humanity makes me weep in public places: there's a sweet portrait of Saskia, a sexy one of Hendrickje Stoffels, the gorgeous 'Der Mennonitenprediger Anslo und seine Frau.' And the gem, and the most famous, of this collection is the stunning 'Man with the Golden Helmet,' which is so three dimensional and so alive I refuse to believe it's only paint.

"Every one of the other numerous departments in this museum complex displays its own fabulous treasures (and will show more of their rich collections when they move to new quarters). Would you believe that what has been described is only a bare fragment of what's available to delight you at Dahlem?

"Admission to all of this is free; and the collections are open Tuesday through Sunday from 9 a.m. to 5 p.m. To get to Dahlem take bus 1, 10 or 68; or walk from the Dahlem-Dorf subway stop (right as you exit to Brummerstrasse, then take a left on Fabeckstrasse, and left again when you come to Arnimallee).

THE MUSEUMS OF EAST BERLIN: "In order of importance, your next trip must be to **East Berlin's Museum Island.** Museum Island, located in central East Berlin between Bahnhof Friedrichstrasse and Bahnhof Marx-Engels Platz (which is also a healthy but interesting walk from Checkpoint Charlie—head for Unter den Linden, then go past the Historical Museum and across a small bridge to your left), includes the **Pergamon Museum,** the **National Gallery,** the **Bode Museum,** the **Altes Museum,** and the **Neues Museum** (the last named may be closed in 1985). The entire trip is worthwhile (including any fuss at the border) just to see the Pergamon Altar. The entire museum was built around it, and it's a spectacular sight: picture an enormous white marble Hellenistic temple with about 30 steps, and virtually intact—not even in Greece itself does one get a more solid idea of the glory of Greek civilization. In addition to the Pergamon Altar, there are intricate and gorgeous mosaics, smaller temples, a stunning Roman Market (Attilos), Roman and Greek statues, the fabulous Triumphant Way of Nebuchadnezzar, the Islamic Museum, and fantastic collections from Egypt and Mesopotamia. The **Bode Museum** (named after the imaginative and energetic curator of the Prussian Cultural Foundation who was responsible for most of what is seen today in both East and West Berlin) is noteworthy for its Egyptian Museum and its early Christian and Byzantine art—there are also paintings and sculptures from medieval times to the 18th century. The **National Gallery** shows, primarily, recent German artists, romanticists, impressionists, expressionists, abstract art, and such special exhibits as 'Proletarian and Socialist-Realist Art.' There is also a unique collection of 30,000 drawings from the 19th and 20th centuries. You might then like to pay a visit to the aforementioned, and heavily political, **Museum of German History,** at Unter den Linden 2, which has permanent exhibits of Germany from 1789 to 1974. It's quite a fascinating place for many reasons, not the least of which is a heavy dose of propaganda, described as follows in the official booklet: 'The Museum approaches the arrangement of its exhibits in a new way. It demonstrates the laws by which German history has progressed, putting the spotlight on the masses, the people, as the creators of history. Many original objects and books, pictures and documents of the given periods, most of which are now accessible to the public for the first time, show which forces brought war and misery to the German nation and who represented the German nation's genuine peaceful and democratic interests.'

"On Museum Island the museums are open from 9 a.m. to 6 p.m. daily except on Mondays and Tuesdays for the Bode Museum and National Gallery, every day of the week at the Pergamon. The Museum of German History is open weekdays except Fridays from 9 a.m. to 7 p.m., Saturdays and Sundays from 9 a.m. to 4 p.m. You may find it ironic that while most of capitalistic West Berlin's museums are free, the people's museums of East Germany charge admission: it'll cost you 1.05 marks for the museums on Museum Island (half price to students), and 50 pfennigs for the Museum of German History (30 pfennigs for students).

CHARLOTTENBURG PALACE: "Back in West Berlin, you'll want to spend another day at **Charlottenburg Palace,** which in addition to being a lovely Garden Palace which you can visit, is now also the home of the **Museum of Pre-and Early History,** and the **Museum of Arts and Crafts;** while across the street in new headquarters is the **Museum of Greek and Roman Art,** and nearby, at 70 Schlosstrasse, the **Department of Egyptian Antiquities,** where you'll see the single most famous object of art that Berlin possesses: the painted limestone bust of Queen Nefertiti, created over 3,300 years ago. The beautiful Nefertiti is an ageless, serene beauty (who, in profile, does somewhat resemble Barbra Streisand!), perfect down to the shadows on her throat. She casts a spell of timelessness that makes one feel quite peaceful.

"Now you'll want to explore the museum of the Palace itself. Even after suffering considerable damage during the war, the **Museum of Pre-and Early History** displays a fine collection of objects illustrating the life of prehistoric man in Europe and the Near East, starting with the Early Stone Age (a great drawback is the frustration one feels trying to follow the written commentaries handicapped by the language barrier). Take special note of Schliemann's Trojan finds and the curious face urns from North-East Germany and Poland (6th and 7th century B.C.). . . . Directly across the street from the main courtyard is the **Antiken Museum,** or **Department of Greek and Roman Antiquities,** which contains half the treasures from the old Antiquarium (the rest are shown at the Pergamon Museum), including Greek vases, small statues and urns from Greek and Mediterranean cultures, a display of ancient glass and jewelry, and some outstanding Egyptian mummy portraits. To me, however, the most interesting of this second 'complex of culture' is the **Museum of Arts and Crafts,** devoted to a survey collection of European decorative arts from the Middle Ages to the 18th century. The organization of the exhibits allows you to compare kindred pieces of work from different countries, displayed in the same time slot. Among the items you'll see are such classics of medieval ecclesiastical art as the Guelph Treasure (don't miss 'Das Kuppelreliquiar aus Köln' from 1175), plus highly decorated Scandinavian ivory horns, an Austrian reliquary of St. George, Gothic tapestry, as well as watches, games, drafting instruments, pottery and silver and gold ware. There are also exhibits of porcelain, including Meissen, Berlin and Nymphenburg china (and more in Charlottenburg Park at **The Belvedere,** which houses the famous Berlin porcelain) and some wonderful Tiffany vases (this is the first place I've ever enjoyed looking at china). . . . You can take a tour of **The Historical Rooms of Charlottenburg Palace** Tuesday through Sunday from 9 a.m. to 5 p.m., for 4.50 marks, but the guide speaks only German. . . . And you can see **The Gallery of Frederick the Great** (it's his great-grandfather, the Great Elector, depicted in the equestrian statue by Schlüter, who stands in the courtyard in front of the Palace) during the same hours as the historical rooms. Downstairs there is Empire furniture and paintings, upstairs it's baroque; probably the only painting you'll recognize is J. L. David's portrait of Napoleon, which graces the Courvoisier Cognac bottle. . . . Back of the rambling Palace are lovely grounds with a lake. If you're strolling around behind the Museum of Pre- and Early History you'll find the **Charlottenburg Mausoleum** (open every day except Mondays from 9 a.m. to 5 p.m., 50 pfennigs to enter), which has the tombs of King Friedrich Wilhelm III and Queen Luise by Ch. D. Rauch. . . . All the museums are closed on Fridays (except the Palace rooms, which close on Mondays) and all remaining days they are open from 9 a.m. to 5 p.m. All the museums are free (except the Palace and Mausoleum, whose prices have already been listed). To get to Charlottenburg you may take buses 54, 62 or 74; or walk about three blocks from the Sophie-Charlotte-Platz subway stop (go up Schlosstrasse to Spandauer Damm).

AND ELSEWHERE: "Berlin's most heavily frequented museum is the **New National Gallery** at Potsdamer Strasse 50, an immense and starkly modern building set into a vast square and surrounded by a sculpture garden. To my mind, and on first impression, the building is all lines and angles; but exciting exhibitions of modern art are changed with some frequency, and the collection is quite a comprehensive one, spanning the 19th and 20th centuries, and such artists as Manet, Renoir, Monet, Courbet and Pissarro, as well as Munch, Klee, Kokoschka, Picasso and several of the newer German, European and American painters. Admission is free and the gallery is open Tuesdays through Sundays from 9 a.m. to 5 p.m., closed Mondays. Take bus 24, 29, 75, 48 or 83.

"For the most far-out modern art, you may finally want to visit the **Akademie der Künste (Academy of Art)** at 10 Hanseatenweg, in the Hansa Quarter. Housed in a handsome new building that rather reminds one of a ski-lodge, the museum hosts exhibitions from all over the world of the very latest in art. Summers they're usually open every day from 10 a.m. to 7 p.m., and sometimes have two exhibits going at the same time—downstairs is free, while upstairs in the larger exhibition quarters you'll pay 3 marks to have a look at what's new. (You may find lectures, performances of experimental music and theatre in the studio of the Akademie in the evenings.)"

READERS' SUGGESTIONS: "The easiest way to get to Berlin from West Germany (we went from Hannover) is by train. You can even get a visa on board" (Patricia Zavoina, Lakeland, Florida). . . . "A very cheap method of traveling to Berlin, and one that we highly advise to every American (one-way; both ways may be a bit too much) is from Copenhagen by East German train to East Berlin, and then over to West Berlin by the S-Bahn. This approach furnishes a fantastic contrast between the two German areas that we all should have" (Dr. and Mrs. Ben G. Burnett, Dept. of Political Science, Whittier College, Whittier, California). . . . "My suggestion may help some travelers going from Copenhagen to Berlin. Take a train to Gedser (from where the train crosses to Grossenbrode Kai and thence into West Germany) and get off. Walk over to the East German boat pier and take an East German boat to Warnemunde. Visas can be purchased on the boat. My brother and I went on a Sunday morning, and in addition to us, there were only seven passengers on a 250-passenger vessel. In Warnemunde you can get your money exchanged into East German marks, catch lunch, and then board a train for East Berlin via Rostock and Neu Brandenburg, no changes. Get off the train at the main building which is a checkpoint between East and West Berlin, then back upstairs to the S-Bahn and into West Berlin. We left Gedser at ten in the morning, got to Warnemunde at twelve, boarded the train at two, and were in East Berlin by six-thirty that evening. The tickets from Gedser to East Berlin can be purchased at the Copenhagen train station for about $32 per person" (Philip Perkins, Washington, D.C.). . . . "My wife and I drove to Berlin on the Autobahn Helmstedt-Marienborn. The cost of our visas, obtained at the East German Control Point, was 5 marks per person ($1.92). The charge for use of the Autobahn was 5 marks ($1.92) one way, and 5 marks return. It took us 40 minutes to check in, obtain the necessary documents, and so forth. Total elapsed time from border to the center of Berlin was 2 hours, 40 minutes, but this was under unusually good conditions with little traffic" (Henry Gassmann, Fresno, California). . . . "It's no longer necessary to fly to Berlin. Last summer, I went there by bus from Hanover, and could have gone by train. The trip is a bit of a nuisance because of the Latin-American style ruckus at the border. But the bus carries an interpreter to help foreigners through. I was the only American on the bus; they weren't getting many that way. Did I check with the American consul? No. I just went" (Thomas Morley, Botany Department, University of Minnesota, Minneapolis, Minnesota).

Time now to pep it up with the happiest people of Europe—the Danes. A flight from Berlin to Copenhagen takes one hour. The smiles on the faces are the first thing you'll see.

Chapter XXI

COPENHAGEN

**Where the Budget "Hotels"
Are Private Homes**

AFTER COPENHAGEN, Europe can become a footnote. For this city has everything: a populace with friendship in its very soul; an astonishing variety of sights and activities; the gaiety and charm of a continuing festival.

Want an example of some of these qualities? On the outskirts of Copenhagen, in a small wooded park, is a country-style nightclub and dance-hall of gigantic size. Over 300 Danes gather here each night to dance, to eat, and to witness a floor show that brims with the vitality and good humor of Denmark. I first came here on a first date in Copenhagen, during my penny-pinched years as a G.I. overseas.

Like almost every other establishment in Copenhagen, there was no cover charge, no minimum, no glares, no pressures—only merriment and warmth. We danced the entire evening; I had a beer, she had an orange squash. When the bill was presented, it came to 4 kroner 50 öre—at that time, 63¢—including service charge. I left 6 kroner on the table.

"You don't understand," said the waiter. "The service charge is already included." "Well," I stuttered, "I thought I'd leave a little more." "In that case," he answered, "thank you very much." He smiled broadly, shook my hand, escorted us to the door, and said he hoped we'd return.

That's Copenhagen—a near-perfect civilization.

1. Introduction

A BUDGET SURVEY: But now for the depressing part. In the wave of inflation that has battered the cities of northernmost Europe, Copenhagen has surfaced well near the top. It's less expensive than Stockholm and Oslo, but more on a par with prices in American cities than with those we've learned to expect in the rest of Europe.

But can you combat the high cost of Copenhagen? You most definitely can, if you acquire the know-how. The main job is to avoid the fantastic surcharges that pile up on almost every penny you spend in Denmark. Years ago, the Danish government was one of the first in Europe to levy an added value tax of 10%, called "Moms" (it's pronounced "mumps" and is every bit as painful), on almost every item sold and service rendered in the country. As new governments were successively ushered in, "Moms" went up to 22%. That means that when you rent a room or buy a meal in Copenhagen, you pay the price of the room or meal, plus 15% service charge, plus 22% government tax, and thereby up your total outlay by 37%.

Certain places, however, are exempt from these surcharges, and it is *these* you should frequent. Private citizens, for instance, who rent out rooms in their homes, do not charge either service or tax. Self-service restaurants (which are popping up all over the country) don't add a service charge. And if you should purchase something expensive in one of Copenhagen's superb shops, and have it shipped from the shop—even if it's only to the next country on your itinerary—you'll save the tax.

If you can't completely avoid the surcharges, you can at least be sure of what you're paying. When you check into a hotel, make the desk clerk (even if you have to twist his arm) quote you the full price of the room, *with* service and tax included. When reading a menu prior to deciding on a restaurant, look for the line *Alle priser incl. Moms,* meaning "all prices include tax." By now, virtually every price quoted to you in restaurants and hotels should be an all-inclusive one: that is, it will include service charge and tax.

In working out your basic expenses in Copenhagen, you should, of course, figure on spending more than you would in Southern European cities. In the following pages, we've compiled a list of rooms in private homes renting from $15 to $22 for two persons, of rooms in pensions and budget hotels for $28 to $39, double including breakfast, and of restaurants where hot meals cost from $4.50 to $6. Picnic places and dormitories are included for our rock-bottom budget travelers, but regular tourists should count on paying a minimum of $20 to $26 a day for the bed-and-three-meals basics.

Once you've got the basics squared away, though, you're home free. Because there's lots to do and see in Copenhagen that costs hardly a cent. There's free entertainment all evening at Tivoli, free drinks at the breweries, free admission to most of the museums and sights, and simply a freedom in the air that makes you want to stroll through the lanes and squares smiling back at all the Danes who are smiling—so freely—at you.

ORIENTATION: Let's first find where we are. The most important geographical fact is that nearly everything of interest to tourists is conve-

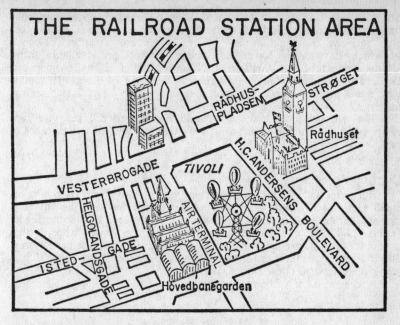

THE RAILROAD STATION AREA

niently grouped in the center of town. The two major downtown streets are H. C. Andersens Boulevard and Vesterbrogade. These intersect at one corner of the **Raadhuspladsen**—the Town Hall Square. Walking away from the Town Hall along Vesterbrogade, you first come to **Tivoli** on your left (Copenhagen's famous summer amusement center) and then the **Central Station.** In the streets that run alongside the Central Station are the majority of our recommended budget hotels, while along the Vesterbrogade there's an excellent selection of budget restaurants.

Buses, trams and sightseeing coaches all leave from the vicinity of, or pass through, the Town Hall Square (*Radhuspladsen*). On the opposite side of the square from Vesterbrogade, is the start of the **Strøget,** a fascinating mile-long shopping street maintained for pedestrians only—and which is a "must see" sight for tourists. The Strøget winds through **Old Copenhagen;** on either side are tiny lanes, antique buildings, churches and museums. It ends at **Kongens Nytorv,** the King's Square, where the Royal Theatre stands and where **Nyhavn,** the rowdy sailors' district, begins. There are parks, museums and sights in various parts of the city, but for a taste of Denmark, old and new, the sector from the Town Hall to the King's Square, along the Strøget, affords the most concentrated variety.

TRANSPORTATION: The **Centralstation** near the Tivoli grounds, is also the terminal of the *S-Tog* (S-Train), running to the suburbs within a 25-mile radius, while across the street is the S.A.S. city terminal, to which the airport bus delivers arriving passengers. The basic bus ticket (grundbillet), valid on both buses and S-Trains, costs only 6 kroner (60¢), but you're better off buying either a block of 9 tickets costing 50 kroner ($5), or special one-day tourist tickets, priced at 65 kroner (for the entire metropolitan area) which allow unlimited travel within the given areas. Within the city, you can easily get around by bus—there are no subways—most of which leave from Town Hall square. Tickets are available from all bus conductors. Ask the Tourist Office, located at 22 H.C. Andersens Boulevard at Town Hall square (in the building of Louis Tussaud's wax museum) for a free transportation map and helpful sightseeing folders.

The average local taxi fare should not exceed $5, but you can easily cover Copenhagen on foot, or by bus for 10% of the price of a taxi.

Cycling

But to really get around town during your stay, why not try a bike or small motorbike? That's what most of the Danes do—and the city is a cyclist's paradise, as a result. **København's Cyklebørs,** 157 Gothersgade (phone 14-07-17), near the parade grounds of Rosenborg Castle, is the cheapest of the bicycle firms. It rents standard, smooth-riding bikes for only 30 kroner a day, 50 kroner for two days and 100 kroner for a week, with a 100-kroner deposit. Closed Sundays.

And now, back to the task of finding a room.

2. Where to Stay

Whether you arrive in Copenhagen by plane or train, you'll ultimately be deposited near the railroad station. Inside the station are a number of booths bearing alphabetical signs. Walk over to the Kiosk marked "P," which is operated by the Copenhagen tourist association and open daily from 9 a.m. to midnight. This remarkable organization maintains a register of every hotel and guesthouse in or near Copenhagen, as well as the names of nearly 200 guest-accepting private homes; but more important, the organization stays in daily contact with these establishments to learn whether vacancies exist. As visitors approach the kiosk, they're given a form to complete, in which they designate the price range of the rooms they seek. Kiosk P then makes a few fast phone calls, and soon provides you with name, address, and bus instructions to an establishment willing to take you at that price. Their booking fee? Only 10 kroner ($1) per person.

ROOMS IN PRIVATE HOMES: During months other than June, July and August, Kiosk P will usually be able to find rooms in normal hotels or guesthouses for budget-minded tourists who check off the least expensive price category on the application form they're given. That's the category which prescribes a *maximum* room rent of 150 kroner ($15) per person, including service and tax. Therefore in these non-summer months, Kiosk P will usually be unwilling to book you into less expensive lodgings in a private home. These latter rooms normally rent for either 65 or 80 kroner ($6.50 or $8) per person, including service and tax but not breakfast, which is often available for 25 to 30 kroner ($2.50 to $3) extra. If such should be the case, then try placing your own phone calls to the private homes we've listed at the end of this section. Their names and phone num-

COPENHAGEN: ROOMS IN PRIVATE HOMES **537**

bers result from a visit to Copenhagen in mid 1984, and the accommodations and prices they offer provide the sure way—sometimes the only way in relatively high-priced Copenhagen—to live within a low, low budget.

In June, July and August, however, the attendants at Kiosk P make heavy use of their private home listings and will be happy to send you to such a residence. For then, if you check the least expensive category on the application form, you'll quite often find that all hotel rooms are booked. At that point, after first suggesting a higher priced category, these attendants will capitulate quite readily and phone a private home. Thus, you're back to living on a budget!

Amazingly enough, during certain short periods of the year, you may have no choice between a hotel in any price range and a private home. Copenhagen has become so popular that its hotel accommodations are occasionally overwhelmed by the tourist rush (sounds incredible, but it's true). In the last two weeks or so in July, and the first week in August, travelers arriving late in the day may be told by the attendants at Kiosk P—as I once was—that there simply isn't a vacant hotel room in all of Copenhagen.

That bit of news may turn out to be your greatest fortune. On the occasion just mentioned, Hope and I were given the address of a private home just ten minutes by bus from the heart of town. We arrived at a near-palatial estate, surrounded by grounds and flower gardens, and were greeted at the door by a gracious Danish lady who had patriotically responded to a broadcast appeal for additional private rooms. Our room cost $18 a night for the two of us. We were accorded the utmost privacy. We had breakfast at a neighborhood cafe, and then waited at the bus stop to go into town with Danes who were going to work. It was an experience that the $80-a-day tourists never know, and one we would not have missed.

On one recent crisis occasion, the Prime Minister of Denmark took foreign tourists into his home!

But let me not raise your expectations too high. The private room you rent will usually be simple (but clean and homey) and your hostess non-eminent (but just brimming with Danish good cheer and a warm-hearted concern for your comfort). Here's the list we promised, for do-it-yourself'ers seeking inexpensive lodgings in private homes:

Rooms in Private Homes—from $7.50 to $11.10 per Person

Arthur and Minna Allin, 49 Gammel Kongvej (phone 249-562), occupy an apartment at a central location, but five flights (and 72 steps) up; that's less than 15 minutes on foot from the central railway station, or a 25-kroner taxi ride. They rent two twin rooms, simply furnished, for 75 kroner ($7.50) per person; showers are free, and so is the use of their kitchen for preparing coffee or tea.

Mrs. Katja Schleisner, 8 Ved Lindevangen, Frederiksberg (phone 86-23-45), a retired secretary who speaks English well (she lived in London for a while), rents one room of her modern apartment just "for fun," not because she needs the money, but in order to meet and talk with people. Her charge is 110 kroner ($11) per day for a brightly furnished, single room whose floor is covered by a large black-and-white sheepskin carpet. Take bus 1 from the center of Copenhagen, getting off at the P. G. Ramms Alle stop after a 10-minute ride. Then turn right into the park with the children's playground; Mrs. Schleisner's apartment is in one of the red-brick buildings, a warm, relaxing and inviting home.

Mrs. Birgitte Randmets, 3 Hindegade, phone 15-39-99, owns a large apartment in which she rents a double room, well furnished, and with free use of a bathroom and kitchen, for 85 kroner ($8.50) per person, 30 kroner ($3) extra for a breakfast. She lived 15 years in Latin America, speaks fluent English, Spanish, and a few other languages, and enjoys meeting international guests. Location is near Kongens Nytorv square, where buses 1, 6, and 9 pass by her door.

Mrs. Ketty Andersen, 53 Saebyholmsvej, 2500 Frederiksberg (phone 714-599), is a widow in her sixties who years ago worked in the Chrysler Building in New York, and of course her English is perfect. She rents three rooms on the second floor of her grey house, at 110 kroner ($11) for a single, 160 kroner ($16) double, 240 kroner ($24) triple, plus 30 kroner for an optional breakfast. The double room, with two corner windows, is especially attractive; the furniture antique (in a positive sense); the walls decorated with oil paintings and old weapons (such as swords); the floors covered with oriental rugs; and baths are free. Take bus 1 to Frederiksberg from the main railroad station (on Vesterbrogade), show the address to the driver, and he'll stop there after a 15-minute ride.

Mr. and Mrs. Viggo and Gurli Hannibal, 2 Lighedsvej (Frederiksberg) (phone 861-310), both charming people, live in a small, spotlessly clean house in a quiet, residential section ten minutes by bus 1 from the central station. All they rent is one room with two single beds, at 100 kroner ($10) per bed, into which they can also place a third bed at a 70 kroner ($7) supplement. Breakfast, optional at 30 kroner, is a feast of cheese, a boiled egg, warm Danish pastry, juice, coffee or tea, marmalade and more. You'll find the Hannibals extremely anxious to please—as witness the small library of English-language books in your room, everything from *90 Minutes at Entebbe* to *The Brothers Karamazov*—and you'll especially like the garden with well-kept lawn, weeping willow, roses, rhododendrons, and (the Hannibals' pride) Chinese water pine tree.

Mrs. Daphne Paladini, 20 Dyrehavevej, 2930 Klampenborg (phone 64-07-44), who comes from Ireland and is fluent in six languages, rents four large double rooms and one small single, all of them furnished in superb, cultivated taste, on the first floor of her white brick bungalow; and all at a 1985 rate of only 110 kroner ($11) per bed in the two doubles, 120 kroner ($12) single, with breakfast for 35 kroner, and baths and showers for free. On your way to the free beach only three minutes away, you may meet a roaming reindeer in the nearby forest. From the central station, there are S-trains making the 15-minute trip to Klampenborg every 20 minutes or so, for 12 kroner, and from the Klampenborg station it's less than a five-minute walk to the refined atmosphere of Mrs. Paladini's lovely home.

Mr. Gregoire Sandler, 16 Laurids Bings Allee, 2000 Frederiksberg (phone 86-43-32 or 86-28-42), inhabits a former bishop's residence, a small palace of a house located in the midst of a beautiful park, where he rents the entire second floor consisting of two double and three twin-bedded rooms, all exquisitely furnished and with beige wall-to-wall carpeting, for 75 kroner ($7.50) per bed, with free showers and baths and a supplement of 50 kroner for additional beds, up to a total of four. No breakfast is served, but a small kitchen, amply equipped with pots and pans, cutlery and the like, is made available for your use. To reach this embassy-type address, take the S-train 5 stops to Peter Bangsvej station (from which it's a one-minute walk), or take bus 1 to Bangsvej, nine stops from the central station.

Mrs. Lillian Pretzsch, at 36 Christiansvej (phone 63-51-48), in the suburb of Charlottenlund, speaks English perfectly, likes receiving families with children (who can play in the garden with an Alsatian), and offers two doubles and a single renting for 195 kroner ($19.50) double, 90 kroner ($9) single, 70 kroner ($7) for a supplementary bed in the double rooms. Easily reached by S-train from Central Station (tracks 9 and 10) with departures every 20 minutes. Take the C-line for Klampenborg and get off at Charlottenlund, a 17-minute ride. Charlottenlund is a scenic, green and quiet area, close to town and beach.

And finally, **Mrs. Gerda Oslev,** 62 Bronshojvej, 2700 Bronshoj (phone 287-456), rents a single room (100 kroner) furnished like a ship's cabin, a double room (180 kroner for two) with balcony overlooking a garden, and charges 30 kroner for breakfast—all this in a charming, red-brick house in a quiet residential location. And baths are free.

Please bear in mind that these ten private homes possess a total of about 37 beds only, the capacity of one small pension, and some may be fully booked during the dates of your stay. Always *phone* before boarding taxi, bus or S-train!

PRIVATE HOMES THAT READERS HAVE LIKED: "Stay with a Danish family—ours was wonderful! At the home of **Mrs. Robert Hansen,** 57 Ellemosevej (phone 65-81-78), we paid 140 kroner ($14) a night for a large, extra-clean, double room; a bath-shower is also there for your use" (Marilyn and Mitchell Shapiro, New Orleans, Louisiana). . . . "A private home, with garden (which we were urged to use), quiet and clean, and only one block from the main street and bus line, is our recommendation. One double with our own toilet and basin for only 185 kroner ($18.50). Owner: **Mrs. Else Skovborg,** who speaks excellent English. Address: 29 Jyllandsvej (phone 462572)" (Mr. and Mrs. Michael Fleming, New York, New York). . . . "We stayed in the private home of **Mrs. Sorensen,** 18 Ceresvej (phone 31-68-14), a 15-minute walk from the station, where a large double room for the two of us cost 160 kroner ($16). Plenty of hot baths were available for nothing extra. Her home, which also has a triple room for rent, is situated in a lovely residential area of Copenhagen, very country-like. We were sorry to leave after only four nights" (Linda G. Lasker, Brooklyn, New York, strong seconding recommendation from Tom and Sheila Jones, Belmont, California, who received a "large and richly furnished room" in the "warm and casual home" of Mrs. Sorensen; note by A.F.: Triple rooms, in 1985, cost 225 kroner ($22.50). No breakfast served). . . . "We were sent to the residence of **Mr. Kurt Dahl,** 30 Hoejdedraget, 2500 Valby, phone 306090, who has been redecorating his house with unusual original ideas using delightful colors. He spoke excellent English and was a charming host, even bringing us fresh strawberries from his garden. Bus 6 or 41 will deliver you almost to his doorstep. The room per person was 70 kroner ($7)" (Mrs. L. I. Patterson, Indianapolis, Indiana; enthusiastic second from Walter Dotts, Richmond, Virginia). . . . "A really delightful double room was made available to us in nearby Virum for 145 kroner ($14.50), which included breakfast and baths, at the home of **Fay and Gyde Sorensen,** 97 Malmmesevej, 2830

Virum-Copenhagen (phone 02-85-2347). Fay is an American residing there for 20 years and is extremely helpful" (M. McCormick, Seattle, Washington). . . . "In Copenhagen, we stayed at the private home of **Mrs. Hanne Loye** (who was one of Denmark's finest actresses), 1 Ceresvej (phone 24-30-27), who rents three large rooms in her villa. No breakfast, but within three blocks are a bread shop serving famous open-faced sandwiches (we sampled them all—delicious!, a cheese shop (buy some of the world's tastiest yogurt), a fresh fruit and vegetable shop, a foreign-exchange bank, and a coin-operated laundromat (hope same kindly old man is there to help you!). We used (free) the world's largest bathtub—don't notice the naughty etchings!" (Ed Davies, Longview, Washington; note by A.F.: Hanne Love's rates in 1985 are 160 kroner ($16) twin, 230 kroner ($23) for a triple room. Her villa in the park is either reached on foot (15 minutes) from the Central Station (walk up Vesterbrogade, turn right into Bagerstraede, left into Gammel Kongevej, then right into Bulowsvej, and, finally, left into Grundtigsvej, from which Ceresvej goes right), or, if this sounds too complicated, by taking bus 1, from Central Station, five stops and a 6 kroner ticket to Frederiksberg city hall). . . . "We stayed with **Gregers and Mary Hansen** at 29 Ellemosevej (phone 69-14-29), 2900 Hellerup, who provided us with a lovely room, a breakfast of delightful breads, pastries, cheeses, sausages, ham, all served in what they call their winter room, a glassed-in solarium. It was a touch of heaven, and the Hansens delightful people. One hundred forty kroner ($14) per night for a double room, 70 kroner ($7) for an extra bed, 30 kroner ($3) for breakfast" (Doris C. Robinson, Portland, Oregon).

PRIVATE FAMILIES FARTHER OUT: "The best place we stayed anywhere in Europe was the home of **Nina Gertz** and family at 172 Lundevej (phone 531-028), Dragor, a 500-year-old fishing village only a short bus ride from Copenhagen. Not only do they make you a part of their warm and hospitable Danish family, but their village is a vacation in itself. In short, our stay with them was a rest within a vacation. Rates are 160 kroner ($16) per double room and for another 30 kroner each you get a breakfast which is delicious and enormous" (Mr. and Mrs. Richard Wein, Boston, Massachusetts). . . . "Best place to stay in the suburbs is at the private home of **Anna and Tage Petersen**, 7 Gentoftegade, 2820 Gentofte, phone 65-82-71, easily reached by S-train in 15 minutes, followed by a 5-minute walk from the Gentofte Station. We stayed there for a week, at $21 a day, including two wonderful breakfasts. The Petersens are reasonably fluent in English, and are exceedingly helpful; there are also excellent, inexpensive food and laundromat facilities nearby" (Laurie Rebas, Phoenix, Arizona). . . . "**Mrs. Birgitte Borgsmidt**, 6a Frisersvej, Charlottenlund (phone 63-70-20), is a former Pan Am flight purser, very friendly, with numerous stories to tell about her own travels. She also speaks English, German, French, Italian, and Spanish fluently, and, of course, Danish. She rents a single and a double room for about 80 kroner ($8) per person, including use of her kitchen facilities. I did much of my own cooking, which saved me a lot of money. Highly recommended to anyone who is budget-conscious and still wants to have a good time in Copenhagen." (Charlie Samra, Holland, Pennsylvania; note by AF: To reach Mrs. Borgsmidt's home, take the train to Klampenborg, get off at Charlottenlund, and walk ten minutes from there; or phone Mrs. Borgsmidt to pick you up at the station.

BUDGET HOTELS:
Back to the more standard beds and buildings. In Copenhagen, the most efficient way to rent a low-cost hotel room is through Kiosk P, of course. But if you'd rather avoid the booking fee or if you prefer to see what you're buying before putting up your cash, you'll want to consult our own recommendations below.

The majority of Copenhagen's cheaper hotels are arranged handily along two streets—the **Colbjornsensgade** and the **Helgolandsgade**—that run off Vesterbrogade, parallel to the side of the railroad station. They are all within a five-minute walk of the station, the airline bus terminal, Tivoli, and many of the best budget restaurants discussed further on. Their prices, however, are mixed, ranging anywhere from a hotel renting a bathless double for 290 kroner ($29), breakfast, service and taxes included, to another hotel renting a bathless double for a top 540 kroner ($54), inclusive. Instead of listing them by price, we've arranged the entire lot in the order in which you'd pass them walking along each street.

Along the Colbjornsensgade

Hotel Cosmopole, 11 Colbjornsensgade (phone 21-33-33), a 110-room hotel spread over five floors, and with no elevator, caters to a great many European tourists, and even gets some in the businessmen's bracket, to whom it offers small but comfortable rooms, many of which are completely equipped with new furniture. Room rates for 1985: 250 to 350 kroner ($25 to $35) single, 385 to 540 kroner ($38.50 to $54) double, including continental breakfast, 15% service charge and 22% government tax.

Hotel Union, next door at 7 Colbjornsensgade (phone 22-44-33), is an elevator-equipped structure whose 120 rooms all have new furniture and wall-to-wall carpets. Its rates are identical to the Cosmopole's, and both hotels are indeed owned and managed by Mr. Lars Thybo, a gentleman extremely helpful to readers on numerous occasions.

Our best-recommended choice on Colbjornsensgade, is the **Saga Hotel** at 20 (phone 24-45-59), managed by Ms. Ruth Bredwig and her son, Torben, who speaks excellent English and even accepts credit cards. Torben is a muscle-building enthusiast who will remind you of Arnold Schwarzenegger. Both try hard to create a friendly atmosphere. Rates in 1985 are: single without bath 200 to 220 kroner ($20 to $22); single with bath 320 to 350 kroner ($32 to $38); double without bath 330 to 380 kroner ($32 to $38); double with bath 460 to 510 kroner ($46 to $51); extra bed 160 kroner ($16). Lower rates apply to rooms on the top fourth floor —there is no elevator—and prices include breakfast served in a modern, nicely furnished and carpeted dining room. And if you show this book to Mrs. or Mr. Thorben when you arrive (the office is on the second floor) you'll be given an extra 5% discount on the above rates.

Along the Helgolandsgade

This, now, is the next parallel block over from the Colbjornsensgade. Note, first, the Missionhotel Hebron, at #4, mentioned below.

Hotel Triton, 7 Helgolandsgade (phone 31-32-66), is a big (275 beds) and lovely establishment with exceptionally good rooms, all with polished-wood floors and first-class hotel furnishings—but with big splurge prices only, even for its rooms without private bath. The latter rent for 245 kroner ($24.50) single, 400 kroner ($40) double, including breakfast, service and tax. Add about 120 kroner per room for private shower and toilet.

THE DANISH "CROWN": $1 currently buys approximately 10 Danish kroner, making each krone worth a little more than 10 U.S. cents. We've used that figure to convert kroner into dollars in this chapter, but should warn that the exchange rate fluctuates in Denmark and might differ by the time of your own trip there.

Hotel Selandia, 12 Helgolandsgade (phone 31-46-10), slightly more expensive, offers 81 rooms, 47 with private facilities, at the following 1985 rates: 250 to 300 kroner ($25 to $30) for singles, 380 to 460 kroner ($38 to $46) for twins, 500 to 600 kroner ($50 to $60) for triples, with the higher rates in each category being for rooms with bath and w.c. Buffet breakfast and showers are free. Although the entrance to this five-floor hotel is rather dark, it's a new place, with elevator, wall-to-wall carpets and modern furniture.

Hotel Absalon, 19 Helgolandsgade (phone 24-22-11), with 180 rooms, 23 bathrooms, hot and cold running water in each room, and no charge for showers, is the classic budget hotel in this area, and is my highest recommendation. Spread over four floors it has many assets—a brand-new elevator, cheerful breakfast room, little coffee shop off the entrance way, rooms furnished in Danish modern, hallways floored in simple, well-scrubbed linoleum, and exceptionally friendly proprietors—the young, much-traveled Nedergaard brothers, Eric and Mogens. Rates for 1985 are the same as for Hotel Selandia, above, which, by the way, is also owned by the Nedergaard brothers. Although somewhat beyond our limits, this is one of the best deals around. Across the street, at 16, the **Absalons Kaelder,** a restaurant under the same management, serves convenient two-course menus for 55 kroner ($5.50) in its cellar dining room.

The **Hotel Centrum,** 14 Helgolandsgade (phone 31-82-65), with 220 beds on four floors, specializes in group accommodations, but always has a few rooms for individual tourists, and charges, in 1985, 190 kroner ($19) for singles, 290 kroner ($29) for twins, 530 kroner for quads, and 600 kroner ($60) for a 5-bedded room, including breakfast. No elevator. The English-speaking owner-manager is a friendly resident from Rabat, Morocco, Mr. Beloued-Med.

While some of the Helgolandsgade hotels are a short stroll from red light activities, each of them was personally checked in the summer of 1984, and all the ones named are suitable and safe for any tourist, male or female, having no association with prostitution.

MISSION HOTELS: For some of the finest values, try the **Mission Hotels**—there are two of them in Copenhagen—and don't be frightened away by the name—these aren't for vagrants, but for ordinary tourists. Owned and operated by the Temperance Societies in Copenhagen, their main function is to foster the good life, which means that liquor isn't served on the premises and room rates are considerably lower than they would be in hotels of similar quality. Furthermore, their floors are so clean they shine and the linens are as fresh as from a family wash. While some of the missions are somewhat austere in appearance, who's going to quibble when the saving is that great?

Bathless, budget-worthy rooms are found in particular abundance at the **Missionshotellet Nebo,** 6 Istedgade (phone 21-12-17), next to the side entrance of the railroad station, a big (90 rooms), white-fronted hotel kept meticulously clean by an army of maids (most of them from Ireland) and well-managed by an efficient staff. Rates in 1985, including breakfast: 200 to 250 kroner ($20 to $25) single, 320 to 450 kroner ($32 to $45) double, 150 kroner ($15) for an extra bed in the room—and showers are free.

Missionshotellet Hebron, 4 Helgolandsgade (phone 31-69-06), two blocks from the railroad station, has 160 beds and, again, well-maintained, updated facilities. Rates for 1985, *breakfast,* service and taxes included, will be 200 to 250 kroner ($20 to $25) single, 310 to 400 kroner ($31 to $40) double, for bathless rooms, of course.

SOME SCATTERED BUDGET CHOICES: And then there are the

scattered choices—places renting double rooms for an average of 250 kroner ($25), service and taxes included, breakfast extra.

Most centrally located of these, less than a five-minute walk from the central railway station, is the **Hotel Carlton** at 14 Halmtorvet (phone 21-25-51), 100 beds on five floors, serviced by an old-fashioned elevator that was the second elevator ever to be installed in Copenhagen, 75 years ago. Rooms without bath, *including* breakfast, service and tax, are 180 kroner ($18) single, 310 kroner ($31) double, 145 kroner ($14.50) for a supplementary bed in a double room; the hotel is remarkably well-furnished for such low rates. Take the post office exit from the railroad station, turn left up Reventlowsgade, then right into Stampesgade, which continues into Halmtorvet.

The Y.M.C.A.-sponsored **K.F.U.M. Soldiers' Home,** 115 Gothers-gade (phone 15-40-44), gives priority to military guests, but always has a few available rooms for civilian tourists (it accepts both sexes) at a charge of 100 kroner ($10) single, 200 kroner ($20) double, only 45 kroner ($4.50) per bed in a six-bedded dorm. Clean, proper and sedate.

The 50-room, 70-bed **Soemannshjemmet Bethel,** at 22 Nyhavn (phone 13-0370), is a merchant-marine-sailors'-mission-hotel primarily, but is open to all, and charges 175 kroner ($17.50) for one of its 32 single rooms, 310 kroner ($31) for doubles, with breakfast (optional) at 20 kroner. Take bus 1, 6, 28 or 41 from the central station and get off at the Bethel stop.

Two blocks from the Kongens Nytorv, is a five-story modernistic structure maintained primarily for seamen and their families, which nevertheless manages to accommodate a great many tourists each summer. This is the hard-to-pronounce **Hotel Søfolkens Minde,** 19 Peder Skramsgade (phone 13-4882), whose prices for 1985 (including breakfast, service and tax) will be 190 kroner ($19) single, 290 kroner ($29) double, 420 kroner ($42) triple. Breakfast is served in the inexpensive cafeteria downstairs, which also offers hot plates from 16 to 35 kroner and a daily special of two courses for 36 kroner. The ferry to Sweden leaves from the docks one block away. Proper, quite respectable, and an excellent find—if you can get one of those few tourist openings.

Big Splurge Hotels

Finally, we consider the more expensive brand of Copenhagen hostelry: high quality hotels that nevertheless have some moderately priced rooms. Among them is a graceful, old, two-story building fronted by equally old trees, known as the **Hotel Capriole,** 7 Frederiksberg Allé (phone 21-64-64). Less than ten minutes on foot from the Central Station, it offers 22 rooms furnished in that now-timeless, unpainted-fir-wood style, for 220 kroner ($22) single, 350 kroner ($35) twin, 100 kroner ($10) for third and fourth beds, always including breakfast. From the station, walk up Vesterbrogade and turn left into Frederiksberg Allé. And ask for manager Ulrich Steen-Andreassen, who is comfortably fluent in English.

The 15-room, elevator-equipped **Hotel Sankt Joergen** (that means St. George), centrally located at 22 Julius Thomsensgade (phone 37-15-11), is owned and managed by the friendly Mrs. Brigitte Poulenard. Shiny brass door knobs, wall-to-wall carpets in all rooms, which rent for 240 kroner ($24) single, 380 kroner ($38) double, breakfast and free showers included. Take bus 2, 8 or 19 from Town Hall Square, two stops away.

The much larger (five-story, 160-bed) **Hotel City** at 24 Peder Skramsgade (phone 13-06-66), is around the corner from the hydrofoil to Malmö, Sweden (take bus 41 from the central station). Singles (there are 26 of them) rent for 240 kroner ($24), doubles for 290 to 400 kroner ($29 to $40, depending on size), again including breakfast and free showers.

Hotel Ibsen, 25 Vendersgade (phone 13-19-13), a typical, old-fashioned 100-bed family hotel where children are welcomed, is well managed by Mrs. Bertram and her daughter, Else-Maria, who both try hard to please their guests. A single costs 210 kroner, a double is 360 kroner ($36), 120 kroner extra for a third or fourth bed, always including breakfast and free showers. Take bus 16 from the station.

STUDENT HOSTELS AND DORMS:

The city's major non-profit hotel for the young-in-spirit is the **Copenhagen Hostel** at 55 Sjaellandsbroen (phone 52-29-08), consisting of nine bungalow-type buildings accommodating 448 guests, male and female, without age limit. Its remarkable price is 38 kroner ($3.80) per person per night, in normal twin or four-bedded rooms—and not in dorms! Twin rooms are reserved for couples. Rooms are so modern, and washroom and toilet facilities so up-to-date and kept so clean, that you'd do well to stay in this restaurant-equipped super-hostel (even though you'll need to purchase a youth hostel membership card for 120 kroner ($12) or a special visitor's card for 18 kroner ($2) per day, sold on the premises), in preference to several more expensive alternatives available to you. Located roughly halfway between the center of town and the airport, the hostel can be reached in 25 minutes by bus 37 (marked "Valby") from Holmens Bro near Christiansborg Palace, leaving every 20 minutes, from 6 a.m. to 1 a.m., or by bus 46 (marked "Bella Center") leaving from Vesterport station. The latter, however, operates only during

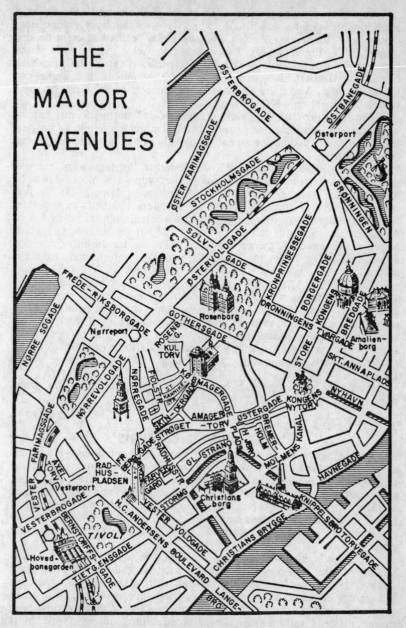

THE
MAJOR
AVENUES

peak hours. Ask the driver to let you off at the Copenhagen Hostel stop; the hostel is in a large, bare field with six white flagpoles at the entrance—it can't be missed—but you have to cross a small wooden bridge near the bus stop to reach it. No curfew, open 24 hours a day.

Copenhagen's second major hostel is the **Kobenhavns Vandrerhjem,** 8 Herbergsvejen (phone 28-97-15), which is open all year except from December 1 to January 2, has 344 beds. Price per bed in eight-bedded dorms, is 37 kroner ($3.70). Two minor drawbacks: the hostel is closed between 10 a.m. and noon for cleaning, and curfew is a strict 1:30 a.m. Take bus 2 from Town Hall Square for about 20 minutes (and 6 kroner) to Fuglesang Allé. And there's an open-air swimming pool (admission, with locker, 5 kroner) only 500 yards away.

The remainder of Copenhagen's hostels and dorms do not require either student identification or youth hostel membership. While they appeal mainly to young people, presumably anybody of any age who wishes can book into them.

The best-located of them all is the **Vesterbro Ungdomsgaard,** a large, white bungalow-type building set in a garden only a few blocks down the Vesterbrogade from the station at 8 Absalonsgade (phone 31-20-70). It is open from May 1 through September 1, offers 160 beds in separate, 6-to-50-bed dormitory rooms for men and women, imposes no curfew at night, and in 1985 will charge 75 kroner ($7.50) for bed-and-breakfast. Sheets are required and can be rented for 15 kroner, for the entire duration of your stay. Take buses 16, 28 or 41 if you don't care to walk from the station.

The modern **YMCA-YWCA Center,** 19 St. Kannikestraede (phone 11-30-31), off the central Amager pedestrian zone area, rents, between July 1 and August 15 only, 48 cots on two floors in dorms holding 2 to 14 male and female guests each, for an amazing low 48 kroner ($4.80) per person. A special desk, staffed by English-speaking volunteers, open daily from 8 a.m. to midnight, offers free advice and info on such topics as accommodations, restaurants, lost property and ways to meet young Danes.

And now to the open sandwiches, the superb beer, and the gravy-doused food:

3. Restaurants & Meals

Eating inexpensively in Copenhagen can take some doing—but let me assure you that the game is worth the flame. Denmark is much like France in the pride its people take in their cuisine. It's hard to find a really bad restaurant in Denmark, regardless of the price range, and often the tinier and less expensive the spot, the more care is lavished on the cookery. Most Danish restaurants post their menu outside the door and you can feel safe venturing into any one of them—after, of course, you've checked the prices.

Denmark's most distinguished delicacy is smørrebrod, which means literally "butter and bread." These are what we call Danish open-faced sandwiches; they are based on a simple slab of bread spread with butter, but the artistry comes in the construction of the super-structure, which can consist of anything from a single slice of cheese to a mass of tiny, pink shrimp to steak tartare (raw beef) topped with a raw egg yolk. Most restaurants have long lists of their special smørrebrod. The waitresses will bring you the list and you check with a pencil how many of each sandwich you want for your party. The Danes eat smørrebrod for lunch, for snacks, for appetizers and just for fun. And since one of the best budget travel rules is "When in a country eat what the natives eat," we trust you'll be piling into plates of smørrebrod yourself. These "sandwiches," by the way, are never picked up in the hand, but always eaten on the plate with a fork and knife.

Here, now, are some general tips on sticking to your food budget and the specific places that we like best. The categories and the establishments are set forth in generally *ascending* order of cost:

DO-IT-YOURSELF PICNICS: Very soon in your stay, you'll discover that Copenhagen is much like one enormous smorgasbord, with all the national delicacies laid out for your choice in pastry shop windows, smørrebrod stores and the most modern of magnificently stocked supermarkets. Choosing a meal from among all these tempting assortments can be the most delightful—and least expensive—way to eat in this city. On warm, sunny days, make it a picnic in Tivoli or alongside one of the mid-city canals or in the park on the harbor where the Little Mermaid sits. On chilly days or at night, take the food back to your hotel room. Your menu might consist of several open sandwiches, a side salad, a pastry and something to drink. Go to a supermarket—the **Irma** chain is one of the best—for the salad and beverage. Mixed salads packed into plastic containers cost around 14 kroner; a half liter of milk will cost 6 kroner; a bottle of Danish beer in a grocery shop will cost only 8 kroner, in contrast to the 18 kroner and more charged for the same beer in a restaurant. Pastries will cost from 4 to 6 kroner in one of the many pastry shops spotted about the city; and these shops also usually sell milk. Danish smørrebrod varies in price from 6 kroner to about 18 kroner, in the stores, depending on the ingredients. You can buy prewrapped picnic packs very cheaply from the white wagons on the Town Hall Square in the summer. After the smørrebrod shops have closed for the night, they often place their leftover sandwiches in vending machines outside the shops—insert 5 kroner and out pops a sandwich, just like in the Automat. One of the best shops in the city for smørrebrod—and one that stays open 24 hours a day—is **Favoriten's,** just opposite the central station at 6 Vesterbrogade. The variety is extensive, and prices range from 16 to 28 kroner (choose the cheaper ones, such as salami and onion, or cheese), and all are immediately well wrapped "to go." For a walk-away snack, purchase a polser, the Danish version of the hot dog, from one of the many mobile hot dog stands for 9 kroner, and follow that up with a rich "soft ice" for 8 kroner.

CHINESE (KINESISK) CAFETERIAS: Apart from the do-it-yourself method, the next least expensive means of eating well in Copenhagen is to patronize an absolutely unique collection of institutions known as "Chinese (Kinesisk, in Danish) Cafeterias." They are Chinese—but only in the sense that they're operated by Chinese residents—the food itself is Danish workingmen's variety, served with rice or noodles; and they are cafeterias, but only in the sense that you walk to a counter, order your dish, and carry it to be consumed at another counter or table. Totally nondescript in appearance, and less than dainty in their offerings of fried or roasted food items, the Chinese cafeterias undercut the prices of most other Danish restaurants by several kroner per dish, probably because an entire Chinese family usually works long hours in each cafeteria. Like the Chinese laundries at home, they provide exciting value.

The cheapest and most easily located of the Chinese cafeterias is probably the 60-seat **Mandarin Grill** at 1 Istedgade, immediately beside the railroad station, in the interesting (and perfectly safe) Copenhagen area of porno shops and budget hotels. Open from 11 a.m. to 1 a.m., seven days a week, the Mandarin has a staff of white-clad Chinese waiters and waitresses (supervised by the Cantonese owner, Mr. Cheung-Kau Fung) who serve you with amazing speed from a posted, English-language menu that lists all sorts of meat, rice and vegetable plates for only 26 to 34 kroner (extremely cheap for Copenhagen), and even less costly servings of "frikadeller" (two hot meat balls) with cold potato salad for 30 kroner, hamburgers for 13 kroner, french fries for 10 kroner. You can combine a smaller individual serving of meat balls (5 kroner) with french fries (10 kroner) for a perfectly adequate 15 kroner snack. Or try the delicious sweet-and-sour pork dish, for a high, but worth it, 34 kroner ($3.40), or half a roast chicken with french fries for 32 kroner ($3.20), or a spring roll for 9 kroner (90¢). Coffee with milk costs 8 kroner (80¢) a cup; nobody sells it cheaper in this area. Farther down at 23 Istegade near Viktoriagade, the higher quality but tiny **Kinesisk Grill Hus** charges 18 kroner for fillet of plaice with french fries and mayonnaise, 30 kroner for soya pork with bamboo shoots, 32 kroner for chicken and shrimp with fried rice or noodles, 30 kroner for chicken curry and rice, 12 kroner for lys pilsner (light, local beer—always the cheapest).

In other parts of Copenhagen, you might try the **Kina Grill** at 100 Norrebrogade (soup for 12 kroner, fried cod fillet with curry rice for 29 kroner; open Sundays), or the much larger **Mandarin Cafeteria** at 74 Osterbrogade, open every day of the week and with prices almost as low as those at the Mandarin Grill of Istedgade, described above.

Largest of all the Chinese cafeterias is the **Kinesisk Cafeteria** at 30 Dronningens Tvaergade, where a simple Scandinavian decor is accented by dragon-trimmed plates. Here the Danish specialties are varied with curries, spaghetti and chop suey, and you can order sharkfin soup (13 kroner) with your Danish frikadeller (meat balls) at 14.50 kroner. Or else a quarter of a roast chicken with rice for 27.50 kroner ($2.75). Famous for its large ham omelettes (23 kroner, or $2.30) and chicken soup bowls (12 kroner or $1.20) is **Grill Shanghai** at 141 Gammel Kongvej. And then there's the **China Garden Grill** at Vaernedamsvej 20 (a small side street off Gammel Kongevej, near Vesterbros Torv), a combination delicatessen and self-service restaurant open daily from noon to midnight, where various sandwiches go for 8.50 to 18 kroner, a hot dog for 9 kroner, and a quarter of a roast chicken with french fries for 25 kroner.

And thus those industrious Chinese do battle with inflation.

CAFETERIA MEALS: Serve yourself and save the service charge—it's as simple as that. Cafeteria dining is popular with the practical Danes and there are good cafeterias in every sector of the city. But the budget champ of them all—a veritable samaritan to low cost travelers—is the **Vista Self-Service Restaurant,** upstairs at 40 Vesterbrogade, a five-minute walk from the station.

The Vista serves the largest food portions I have ever seen in preparing this book. On a recent summer evening there, while Hope, daughter Pauline and I were vainly trying to finish two plates we had ordered for the three of us, a trio of British rock-and-roll types ordered one plate of fried potatoes with fried eggs on top (20 kroner), picked up the unlimited servings of fresh Danish bread that the Vista offers free, split the mound (it looked a foot high) among them, and still weren't able to finish their meal. Of the 28 vast platters offered on the menu, 14 are priced at from 24 to 36 kroner (\$2.40 to \$3.60), and the top price for veal steak with sauce béarnaise, potato dumplings and green peas is 52 kroner (\$5.20). By buying a seven-meal coupon for 200 kroner (\$20) you can eat seven meals regularly priced at 32 kroner per, with a saving of about 25¢ per serving. And the amazing thing is that each order is cooked especially for you! You walk to the serving counter, ask for the English-language menu (it's printed on yellow paper), place your order, receive a number, and then wait at a table until a loudspeaker announces (also in English) that the chefs have completed making your huge Danish repast. If you don't want to wait, you can choose from four immediately ready two-course dinners of the day, which are priced from 24 to 36 kroner. Be prepared, of course, to encounter large, lively crowds—including every itinerant hippie and aspiring Rolling Stone from across the continent, who seem drawn to the Vista by some ultrasonic homing device, and whose presence adds to the fun. The restaurant opens at 9 a.m. and closes punctually at 9 p.m.; get there early for dinner.

Other cafeterias? The increasingly popular vegetarian cafeteria, **City Helse Restaurant,** at 6 Vendersgade, sells filling daily platters for 42 kroner (\$4.20) that might consist of red peppers stuffed with rice and bean sprouts. On a recent Sunday afternoon, I ordered a second portion of the cooked rice with almonds and cherry sauce, only \$2. Open Monday to Friday from 11:30 a.m. to 7:30 p.m., closed on Saturday and Sunday. Cheaper is the cafeteria in Copenhagen's cheapest department store—**Daell's Varehus**—where 25 varieties of open sandwiches sell for 9.50 kroner each, and a pair of sausages with bread are 10 kroner. That's a 300-seat room on the sixth (top) floor of the bustling **Daell's,** on the Nørregade, down the "pedestrian street" from Town Hall Square.

Though most other department store cafeterias are considerably more expensive, you might also try the relatively moderate **Anva Cafeteria** at 2E Vesterbrogade, across from Tivoli. In the student quarter of Copenhagen, those busy streets near the university, the small **Bodega Cafe,** at 96 Norre Voldgade, a popular hangout for students, offers open sandwiches for 9 kroner each, which you can accompany with a beer for 12 kroner (\$1.20). Right across the street, at 27 Norre Voldgade, the larger **Cafe au Lait** is always crowded with students eating quick lunches for an average of \$4, or sipping a Coke for \$1. It's open seven days a week from 8 a.m. to 8 p.m., on Sundays from 10 a.m. Find a chair outside, so you can watch the busy traffic floating by.

STOCKING UP FOR THE DAY ON SMORGASBORD: Danish smorgasbord is a huge, all-you-can-eat buffet, where all the national specialties are trotted out for your enjoyment. Served traditionally at lunchtime only, it consists of multiple varieties of fish, salads, meats, usually a hot dish or two, cheese and fruits. There is a method to eating smorgasbord and it's not the pile-it-on-and-dig-in-to-your-elbows technique of the Western chuckwagon

that has possibly done more to alienate Danes from American tourists than any breach in international policy could ever do.

The rules are very simple. When you enter the restaurant, the buffet table will be in the center and all the tables around will be set up with plates and silverware. Sit down and wait for a waiter to approach you. Give him your beverage order. It is customary to drink "snaps" with the first course of herring and to follow that up with beer. But since both these drinks are rather expensive, don't be embarrassed to order an apple cider or a soft drink. After he has your order for drinks, pick up the plate before you, go over to the table and fill it up with as much herring and fish as you wish. The fish is always the first course and you never mix it with anything else. Go back to your table, eat the herring, then—leaving your plate behind you (the waiter will clear it off)—go back to the table, pick up a new plate and fill it up with any of the salad and meat dishes you want. One never uses the same plate for fish and meat. You can go back to the table as often as you wish and you can take a new plate each time if you prefer. You will notice that on all the large platters on the buffet table, the main dish is surrounded by such accessories as pickles and sauces. Let this be your guide as to what to eat with what (e.g., the steak tartare will be accompanied by horseradish, pickles, cucumber salad and raw egg yolk). Now, unlike the Swedish smorgasbord, the Danish dishes are not necessarily meant to be eaten as is, but are supposed to be laid out on slices of bread, smørrebord style, and eaten as open sandwiches. To the end, you will be provided with a basket of bread at your table. If you find your appetite failing, however, feel free to dispense with the bread as you work along. After attacking all the cold dishes, you follow up with the hot ones (of which there are seldom more than one or two) and then turn to the last course of fruit and cheese. At this point the waiter will approach you again and take your order for coffee.

Smorgasbord, eaten properly, can take the better part of an afternoon and it can certainly render you unwilling to eat again for hours. Thus, though it is usually a big splurge in price, it is an excellent investment in both quantity and enjoyment.

Largest, cheapest (by Copenhagen standards) and most conveniently found of the smorgasbord restaurants is the 160-seat **Bistro Buffet** in Copenhagen's main railroad station (Hovedbanegaard). Here, in attractive surroundings, you can choose among 100(!) different dishes for the all-inclusive price of 84 kroner ($8.40), plus beverage (beer, milk, coffee, soft drinks, or small vodka cost 15 kroner—$1.50—per glass or cup). This is the only place in town that serves smorgasbord every day from 11:30 a.m. to 9:30 p.m. Do try it, at least once.

And incidentally, the same railroad station offers an all-you-can-eat *breakfast* smorgasbord from 7 a.m. to 10 a.m., this time for 36 kroner ($3.60), including beverages; both meals are among the top values of Copenhagen. Look for the "Restaurant" sign at the head of the corridor leading to the Bistro Buffet, and don't confuse the Bistro with the large (100 seats) snackbar restaurant, alongside, open daily from 6:30 a.m. to 11:30 p.m. serving filling dishes such as two-course menus, for 46 kroner ($4.60).

THE BEST OF THE BUDGET RESTAURANTS: Practically unknown to tourists, but wildly popular among local residents, is the **Spisesalonen,** where the price is only 22 to 35 kroner ($2.20 to $3.50) for exceptionally large portions of a hearty, two-course meal, for example: soup, fish filet, goulash, or beefsteak with vegetables and potatoes. Drinks are reasonable, too: milk is 4 kroner, coffee costs 5, and a small Pilsner beer is 10 kroner. If you buy a coupon valid for five meals for 125 kroner ($12.50), you can eat five menus which would cost you 150 kroner ($15), if bought individually. The 16-table establishment, managed by Hans Hahn Petersen and Torben Schneller—one cooks, the other serves—is at 4 Sorgenfrigade, a side street off 177 Norrebrogade, reached by bus 5 or 16 from Town Hall Square. It's open Monday through Friday from 11:30 a.m. to 7 p.m. There is a coin laundry across the street, which you may wish to use while eating in the Spisesalonen.

Raadhuskroen at 12 Longangstraede near Town Hall Square charges either 35 or 40 kroner ($3.50 or $4) for each of its many large plate meals, each sufficient for many hours of hard touring.

Axelborg Bodega, 1 Axelborg, next to the Benneweis Circus, is an old "Vinstue" cafe that's a popular downtown eating place for Danes (in contrast to just tourists), who imbibe great platterloads of its Danish frikadeller and potato salad for 39.50 kroner, biksemad (see description below) for 42.50 kroner, a serving of three colorful open sandwiches for 22.50 kroner.

Pizza Mamma Rosa, 59 Ostergade, across from the Illum department store, is the best Italian budget restaurant I know in town, selling spaghetti for 34 kroner ($3.40), pizzas for 38 ($3.80), served on six long red tables in front. Quick service, top-quality food and large portions have made this place a very popular eatery.

EATING OUT IN TIVOLI: Inside the Tivoli Gardens (later described), the restaurants are almost all expensive—probably the most expensive in Copenhagen. And it hurts terribly to recommend that you stay away from them, because they are so flower-filled and breathtakingly lovely as to be reminiscent of another age—Renoir alone could capture their pastel hues. Their prices, however, are positively 20th century. You might try—and I am perfectly serious about this—ordering one of their dinners for two people, with extra plates. When Hope and I stopped in recently for a late snack at a Tivoli establishment, I ordered a simple bowl of soup, only to watch the waitress cart out a tureen large enough for an entire family. And Hope's plate of chicken livers, onion rings and cucumbers turned out to be a two-foot-long silver tray, again large enough to feed three.

There are, however, two moderately priced restaurants in Tivoli, where the atmosphere isn't as elegant but neither are the prices. **Groften** (immediately to the right of the Peacock Theatre, as you face it) serves a 62-kroner tourist's table d'hôte dinner of two courses, as well as individual plates for as little as 48 kroner (sausages with fried potatoes); but service and food have been somewhat disappointing on my latest visits there. **Paafuglen** (meaning Peacock), a spot with lots of outdoor seating, is owned by the management of a far more expensive downtown restaurant, and offers a large turisplatte of herring, salad, roast beef, salami, liverpaste and other items (you spread them all on bread) for 80 kroner. A nice touch here is the *Børneplatte* "children's plate" for 42, which consists of four small open sandwiches—flat and easy for the children to handle. Finally and fortunately for us, there is one cafeteria in Tivoli called the **Bix'en Self-Service Restaurant,** to the rear of the gardens near the rides (it's to one side of Det Mystiske Hus), which is probably the cheapest sit-down place in the area; it is basically utilitarian, but there are tables under the trees outside, and colorfully lit arches around the tables. Hot plates include such items as roast beef or fish, but don't go above 60 kroner ($6) in price, and average 35 kroner for the plainer dishes (fiskefilet, biksemad, frikadeller).

SOME FINAL FOOD AND DRINK TIPS: Go easy on the beer. Amazingly enough, those beer-loving Danes have loaded the sale of beer in restaurants and bars with so many taxes that it gets surprisingly expensive— as much as 20 kroner per bottle, as opposed to the 8 kroner you'd pay for the same bottle in a grocery store. To order draft beer, which is both better and cheaper, order "fadol." If you must have it bottled, ask for "Pilsner," not "Export," which costs only 17 kroner in most restaurants and is closer in taste to draft. Cheapest of all is the "Lys Pilsner," which has a low alcohol content and costs only 16 kroner in restaurants. . . . Milk is actually the least costly beverage to have with your meal, at a price considerably under the cost of tea, coffee or beer. . . . When in doubt over a Danish menu, ask for *biksemad,* or point out the word to your waiter, if you find it hard to pronounce. *Biksemad* is chopped meat fried with onion and potatoes, with a fried egg on top. It's always filling, always tasty, and always cheap. . . . Other reliables: *smorstegte hakkeboffer* ("hamburger beef-steak,") *sprodstegte fiskefiletter* ("fried filet of fish"). . . . What's the most popular open sandwich sold in Denmark? It's *leverpostej*—liver-paste and pickled cucumber, with a small chunk of meat jelly. . . . The real oddity: Danish pastry in Denmark is called "Wienerbrod," and must be ordered as such or you won't get it. . . . The best breakfasts in Copenhagen are the ones you can purchase in a bakery (Konditori or Bageri). They'll serve you a glass of milk, plus two luscious Danish pastries (Wienerbrod), for 16 kroner. . . . At least once, order the famous, unpronounceable Danish dessert—*rødgrød med fløde* (most K.A.R. restaurants serve it in summer) —whose taste is as delightful as the way it sounds (ask your waitress to speak the words aloud). . . . And finally, in reading Danish menus, don't confuse the abbreviation "kr" with "kl." The first stands for kroner, the second for the hour of the day. And thus, when a menu is headed with the words "Fra Kl. 12," it does *not* mean, as some non-Danish-speaking readers have supposed, that the meals cost 12 kroner, but instead that they are served starting at 12 noon.

4. Student in Copenhagen

STUDENT ASSISTANCE: For rock-bottom lodgings in Copenhagen, most student-age readers will make use of the hostels earlier described; for other facilities, and for student information, they should pay an early visit to the offices of **Use-It,** maintained as a student social and information center by the City of Copenhagen at 14 Magstraede (phone 15-65-18) less than five minutes on foot from Town Hall Square. From the Town Hall Square, stroll down the shopping street Strøget to Gammel Torv, then turn right along Radhusstraede, and use the entrance at 14 Magstraede. Use-It will help you with virtually everything except transportation; for that, go to the offices of D.I.S. on the Skindergade (see below).

Use-It is open from 10 a.m. to 7 p.m. throughout the year (until 8 p.m.

in summer), dispensing lists of student-style eating places, entertainment, medical and legal advice, maps of the city, personal offers (on a mammoth bulletin board), and inexpensive snacks at a cafeteria called "Spisehuset" in the same building. It will also direct you to still further hostels offering beds for between 35 and 70 kroner a night, including, in July and August only, a **Sleep-In** (phone 26-5059), at 6 Per Henrik Lings Allee (in an ice-skating hall in a park in the northern area of Copenhagen), charging 45 kroner ($4.50) for bed and breakfast, providing you bring your own sleeping bag.

Consistent with a 45-kroner bed is a 32-kroner meal, which, in Denmark, is had in the form of *lobescowes*—a potato stew that, in my experience, consists 70% of potatoes, 27% of water, and 3% of shredded beef—it resembles a similar item available in Hungary, is surprisingly tasty and sells for about 32 kroner ($3.20) at the Vista restaurant (mentioned earlier), for example.

After you've visited the Use-It reception area at 14 Magstraede, you'll also soon discover a youth-style restaurant known as "Spisehuset," a cafe named after socialist revolutionary Rosa Luxemburg (entrance from Radhusstraede), and many other constantly changing facilities and activities. Obviously, this is a key center for young people arriving in Copenhagen. For the price of a beer, you can meet fellow students at any of several other gathering spots in the city. At **Pilegaarden** on Pilestrade, just squeeze in wherever you can make a space and you'll be involved in conversation in no time. Crowded, noisy and candlelit, Pilegaarden is strictly for swilling and philosophizing. **Lille Apotek,** 15 Store Kannikestraede, has a bistro aura about it (it was originally an 18th-century pharmacy), as does **Laurits Betjent,** 16 Ved Stranden (the sign reads "Royal" in green neon), is for the serious talkers, although there's an occasional small combo and dancing. Located across the canal from the Royal Palace, this place pulls them in daily from 10 p.m. to 5 a.m., and charges an admission of 20 kroner. **Hviids Vinstue,** a remarkable cellar cafe—dark, smoky and dating atmospherically back to 1723—captures not just the students but theater folk from the Royal Theater across the square and a cross-section of Copenhagen's intelligentsia. Tradition makes this "the" spot for a before-dinner drink and for its famous hot, mulled wine served all day long during the Christmas season. . . . For information on student charter flights from Copenhagen to other European cities, stop at the modern offices of the **D.I.S.** (Danish International Student Committee), 28 Skindergade (phone 11-00-44), which offers breathtaking possibilities. Student railway fares? They're even cheaper. Check at the same D.I.S. office, which is best reached by walking up the Strøget from Town Hall Square, half a block past the Gammel Torv, then passing through Jorck's Passage to Skindergade, or else at the **Transalpino** travel office, one block away, at 6 Skoubogade (phone 14-46-33), open Monday to Friday from 9 a.m. to 5 p.m., Saturday to 1 p.m.

5. Tours & Sightseeing

THINGS TO DO, PLACES TO SEE: Good news, there's lots that's worth doing in Copenhagen that never costs a cent. You can prowl through the antique lanes of the old city. Tour a brewery and have a free beer. Stroll along the harbor and strike up a nodding acquaintance with Hans Christian Andersen's Little Mermaid. Visit the National Museum, where there is

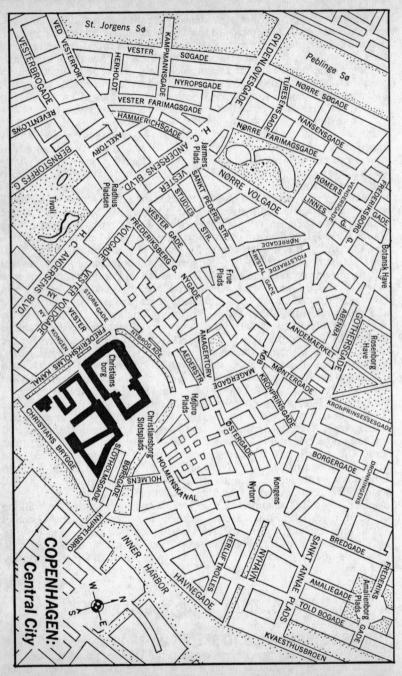

COPENHAGEN: Central City

never any admission charge, or the other museums on special free days. Explore the museum-like shops on the Strøget. Take a canal cruise to a small cluster of harborside shops and historic showplaces. And—above all—get to know personally some of the wonderful people that make up this "Wonderful Copenhagen."

TOURS: First we'll consider the free tours, then one for 60¢, and finally an assortment of bus tours that start at $9 and climb from there.

For Free

The stellar free attractions of Copenhagen are the tours of the city's famous big breweries, which produce what some people consider to be the world's greatest beer. You can visit either the **Carlsberg Breweries** (whose tours begin punctually at 8:30 a.m., 11 a.m. and 2:30 p.m., weekdays), or the **Tuborg Breweries** (which runs them continuously from 8:30 a.m. to 2:30 p.m., again weekdays only), and you ought to do it, first, because the beer-making procedure is a fascinating art—and second, because there's free beer for you to drink at the end of each visit. More interesting of the two is probably the Carlsberg visit because of the astonishing art gallery and photograph collection that adjoins its beer-drinking hall; but on the other hand, Tuborg seems to provide a more intimate tour. The guides at both plants deliver humorous and pun-laden spiels, which you should vastly enjoy. Take either the S-Tog to Enghave Station, or bus 6 to reach Carlsberg (whose address is 140 Ny Carlsbergvej); and take bus 1 from the center of town or bus 21 (ringline) to get to Tuborg (at 54 Strandvejen).

For 60¢

Summers only, you can ride out to the Langelinie, where the famous Copenhagen mermaid sits pensively on a rock, via special bus 50, whose round-trip fare is only 6 kroner (60¢) if you return within an hour. The city transport company operates this whimsical ride from the "bus port" at 12 Vestervolgade near City Hall Square in front of the King Frederik Hotel, at 10:30 a.m. and then at half-hour intervals until 5:30 p.m., but only from the first week in June to the end of August. Look for the yellow sign: "Mermaid No. 50," from which the bus sets off on its 10-minute ride. It then lingers at the statue for 10 minutes or so of picture taking, before returning to City Hall Square. Alternatively, you can make the same trip by sea (weather permitting) for 25 kroner ($2.50), round-trip, by boarding the Langelinie Boat Service at the Gammel Strand, across from Thorwaldsen's Museum. It departs every hour from 10 a.m. to 5 p.m., daily, and provides an especially pleasant experience.

For $9

The normal city tours are run by the organization called **Copenhagen Excursions,** whose buses leave from the statue of the Lure Horn Blowers —two men blowing curved horns—on the Town Hall Square. Best for openers is the **City Tour With a Visit to a Brewery,** which consists of a 1½-hour bus tour around all the most famed spots and concludes with a stop-off at one of the two Copenhagen breweries. These leave daily at 10 a.m., and cost 90 kroner ($9). The same city tour, without the brewery, is operated daily at noon, at the same price; go early and you'll save yourself the trouble of getting to the breweries on your own. (No brewery tours are ever included, however, on Saturdays or Sundays).

And Up

A unique **Industrial Art Tour,** which leaves at 1 p.m., Tuesdays and Thursdays only, lasting 2½ hours and costing 100 kroner ($10), includes an orientation visit to the famous Royal Copenhagen porcelain factory, the Museum of Decorative Art, (housed in a 200-year-old rococo building), and the center of Danish design, Den Permanente, will give you an insight to Danish creative arts and handicrafts. The **Royal Tour,** operated daily except Mondays at 10 a.m., lasting 2¾ hours, and costing 135 kroner ($13.50), includes visits to the Christiansborg, Rosenborg, and Amalienborg castles, with a stop at the last to watch the changing of the royal guards—though no trouping of the colors is performed when her majesty, the queen, is not in residence. The **Vikingland Tour,** departing Wednesdays and Sundays at 9 a.m., for a six-hour tour, goes to Roskilde, the ancient capital of Denmark, includes a visit to the spectacular Viking Ship Museum, where five restored ships, built 900 years ago, are on display. The price: 190 kroner ($19), lunch included.

TIVOLI: Step one foot inside, and you'll want to camp there for life. A vast amusement park in the heart of Copenhagen (between the central station and the Town Hall Square), this is one of Europe's top attractions—the lightest, loveliest, most refreshing area in the world, brimming with both goodhearted fun and culture! Go during the day to sit in the sunshine and have a picnic of smørrebrod in company with Danish mothers and their towheaded offspring, pretty secretaries and office-workers from the downtown firms. Go at night, when colored lights bathe the park in a fairytale glow and the entertainment schedule is packed. Admission is 16 kroner ($1.60), but children under 12 years of age are always admitted at half price.

If you'll arrive just slightly before 7 p.m., you'll be exactly in time for the action. **At 7 p.m.:** Danish variety acts (tight-rope walkers, trained seals) on the open-air stage in the center of the gardens; free. **7:30 and 9:30 p.m.:** top-name international stars entertain at the Concert Hall and Tivoli Theater, where the cheapest tickets are 20 kroner and every seat in both houses is good. **7:45 p.m.:** pantomime in the traditional Commedia dell'Arte style (Harlequin, Columbine, and all your friends) on the Peacock Stage to the left of the main entrance; free. **10 p.m.:** modern ballet on the Peacock Stage; free. **11:45 p.m.;** fireworks, twice a week, on Wednesdays and Saturdays.

Then there's dancing everywhere, fun houses and rides, and colorful parades of the Tivoli Boy Guards, every Saturday and Sunday at 6:30 and 8:30 p.m. (the Boy Guards consist of 106 youngsters from 9 to 16 years, who assemble before parading, near the Chinese Tower—the best spot to watch).

Tivoli stays open from May 1 to mid-September daily, from 10 a.m. to midnight. I don't want to appear blunt, but if you come to Copenhagen and miss this place, you are simply off your rocker!

BAKKEN: And there's another, even vaster, amusement park on the outskirts of Copenhagen—**Bakken**—which is supposed to be the oldest amusement park extant in the world. This is a far earthier place—very popular among the young Danes for dancing—with rides, restaurants and good-hearted, apple-cheeked Danish strip shows. There's no admission charge. Take the S-Tog marked "Klampenborg" from the central station at 4, 24 and 44 minutes past the hour. Round-trip fare is 24 kroner; riding-time to Klampenborg is 25 minutes; and upon arrival, you either turn left through the forest for the half-mile walk to Bakken, or (on hot days) right to a free public beach 250 yards away (and then to Bakken), where you'll be astonished at the percentage of topless female bathers. Bakken is usually open from mid-April till the end of August, starting at 3 p.m.

MUSEUMS AND CASTLES: To my mind, there are three which shouldn't be missed: the **Frihedsmuseet** (Museum of the Danish Resistance Movement, 1940-45), the important **National Museum** (Danish history is the subject matter), and the **Ny Carlsberg Glyptotek,** for classical antiquities and art of the 19th century. Then you'll want to take one of the hourly tours of the Royal Reception Rooms at **Christiansborg Palace.** For the details on these and many more interesting places, here's my Copenhagen-loving wife, Hope:

6. Hope's Copenhagen

"An independent and fascinating aspect of Copenhagen is the one associated with its royal history, and found today in the areas around its three major palaces: Amalienborg, Christiansborg and Rosenborg.

AMALIENBORG PALACE: "To the first of the three, you'll want to make only the briefest of visits. For, while the Queen of Denmark presently lives in one of the four palaces on Amalienborg Square, all you can see there is the Changing of the Guard (daily at 12 noon, but more colorful when the queen is in residence). Far more interesting, in my opinion, is the place where her predecessors lived, the great—

CHRISTIANSBORG PALACE: "Christiansborg Slot—on the Slotsholmen, the small island where the city was founded in 1167—was the official residence of the Danish kings until 1794, and with its spacious, cobblestoned courtyards and darkish grey buildings, it's a most impressive palace, which now houses the Royal Reception Rooms, the Danish Parliament, the Supreme Court and Prime Minister's Office—and a whole host of museums. You can take a 6-kroner conducted tour (departing daily in summer, daily except Saturdays at all other times, from a small office near the main gate from 10 a.m. to 4 p.m.) of the basement ruins of Absalon's Castle (he being the famous archbishop who founded Copenhagen in 1167).

"Now, look for signs that lead you to the Royal Reception Rooms, where you can take another tour—for 13 kroner, this time—departing at noon, 2 and 4 p.m., daily except Mondays in summer, and at 2 p.m. only, daily except Mondays and Saturdays in winter. Your guide will be a good-humored Dane who has quite a spiel prepared for your trip through the richly decorated rooms, including the famous quip about King Christian IX being the "father-in-law" of Europe (one of his daughters became Queen of England, another the Czarina of Russia, his son King George I of Greece). Another element of fun on the tours is provided by the soft overshoes you'll be asked to wear upon entering the palace. You'll fairly skate through the rooms—helping to polish the floors!

The Theatre Museum

"One of the grandest sights of Christiansborg Palace—but open only on Sundays and Wednesdays (Fridays too, June thru September) from 2 to 4 p.m.—is the Theatre Museum, at 10 Christiansborg Ridebane, in the palace's own Royal Court Theatre (from 1766). It's an old baroque court theatre, wood, gold and red velvet, in the style of 19th-century Old Europe, but still aristocratic and regal. You'll be able to wander through the orchestra, the loges, the steeply raked stage, the 200-year-old dressing rooms (each left with the trappings of a famous Danish actor), leisurely taking in the pictures and displays (which trace the development of almost three centuries of Danish Theatre); costumes and ballet shoes of Anna Pavlova, drawings of Sarah Bernhardt (who played in Denmark in 1880 and 1904), *Armida,* a ballet program, listing Hans Christian Andersen as an extra. Admission of only 5 kroner; don't miss it!

The Royal Danish Arsenal

"Not far from the Theatre Museum at 3 Tøjhusgade, is the admission-free Arsenal Museum (Tøjhusmuseet) located in one of the longest halls in all of Europe. Ordinarily, I am not a great one for arsenals, but this one is really quite interesting, with airplanes suspended from the ceiling and tanks in the middle of the floor, as well as the expected historical displays of cannons, cannon balls and the like. Even the guards in their colorful red, gold, and black uniforms seem part of the exhibition. Open in summer from 1 to 4 p.m. on weekdays, from 10 to 4 p.m. on Sunday; in other seasons, until only 3 p.m., Sundays 11 a.m. to 4 p.m.; don't fail to go upstairs, as well, to see the several thousand firearms of the Armory Hall. Free admission.

The National Museum

"If you'll now walk from the palace courtyard in the direction of the city hall, you'll cross a romantic little grey stone bridge which brings you to the National Museum, at 12 Frederiksholms Kanal—once the palace of the crown prince, now a gigantic museum housing what its own guidebook describes as a 'picture book of the cultural history of man.' The emphasis, of course, is on Danish history—with one of the most important items being the Bronze Age 'Sun Chariot from Trundholm,' Denmark's most famous find—but the exhibits deal with other cultures as well (an exposed Egyptian mummy, for instance), and the collection consists, in the main, not of mere paintings but of actual artifacts from bygone days—primitive tools, coins, structures, all else you can name. Admission is free, and the museum is open every day in summer from 10 a.m. to 4 p.m., and generally from 11 a.m. to 3 p.m. in other months. Skip Mondays, when all departments are closed.

ROSENBORG CASTLE: "Finally, the castles of Copenhagen include an ornate Renaissance palace—Rosenborg—which stands in the Kongens Have (King's Garden) at 4a Østervoldgade (from the central station, take the S-Tog to the Nørreport Station, from which the castle is only a short walk away). Built in 1606 by King Christian IV (a hard-drinking, hard-swearing, wenching young man who became one of Denmark's great improvers and builders, a man of culture and good taste), it now houses a chronological collection of the treasures of the Danish Royal Family, not the least of which are the Crown Jewels. You'll see the spectacular saddle and riding outfit of Christian IV, all studded with sapphires, diamonds, and pearls; the Crown Jewels in the Treasury in the cellar; the mirror room on the second floor; the Knights' Hall on the third floor. Hours at the castle (whose name means "Castle of the Roses") are from 11 a.m. to 3 p.m., daily, from May 1 to October 25; on Sundays, Tuesdays and Fridays from 11 a.m. to 1 p.m. in other months; and admission is 15 kroner for adults, 2 kroner for children.

THE ROYAL MUSEUM OF FINE ARTS: "Within walking distance of Rosenborg Castle (or take bus 40) is the vast **State Art Museum** (Statens Museum for Kunst) housing the world's largest collection of Danish art, as well as a small, but representative sampling of masterworks from other nations including an important collection of Matisse paintings. Admission is free, and the museum is open daily, except Monday, from 10 a.m. to 5 p.m. Engrossed as you may be in its collection of paintings, don't miss the Print Room and Library, where you will find Albrecht Dürers, many Rembrandts, Hogarths, Daumiers, Titians and Tintorettos.

ROYAL GIFTS FROM THE BEER KINGS: "Now we turn to another type of royalty. Denmark owes a large debt of gratitude to J. C. Jacobsen and his son Carl Jacobsen who, in addition to brewing a most delicious beer, in 1876 established the Carlsberg Foundation, which uses brewery profits for the advancement of art, science and Danish culture. Through their generosity, Copenhagen is graced with **The Ny Carlsberg Glyptotek** and **The Kunstindustrimuseet** or Museum of Applied Art (among other donations too numerous to mention here).

The Ny Carlsberg Glyptotek

"Located on Dantes Plads, off H. C. Andersens Blvd., the Glyptotek is directly across the street from the back entrance of the Tivoli Gardens, and is open May through September from 10 a.m. to 4 p.m. daily except Mondays, October through April from noon to 3 p.m. on weekdays (except Mondays) and from 10 a.m. to 4 p.m. Sundays, charging admission of 12 kroner, but none on Wednesdays and Sundays. The museum contains a vast collection of ancient art (Egyptian, Mesopotamian, Etruscan, Greek and Roman works), a large assortment of French painting and sculpture including numerous Impressionists, and finally a major selection of Danish artists of the 19th and early 20th century all displayed in a monumental building with a lovely winter garden in its center courtyard. Two recognized treasures of the Egyptian collection are the black stone 'Head of a King' (circa 400 B.C.) and the 5000-year-old miniature 'Hippopotamus' (in Room 3); be sure to see, as well, 'Gebu' or 'Lord Privy Seal,' whose image reaches out over the ages as the timeless incorruptible politician, and the ever-fascinating 'Anubis' the Keeper of the Dead, with his jackal's head on a human body. And don't miss Room 2, which contains a small but enthralling collection for mummy fanciers like me. One interesting sidelight of the French collection is the opportunity it affords to see some pre-Tahitian Gauguins: from them, you'll learn how Tahiti vivified and actually defined Gauguin as an artist.

Kunstindustrimuseet

"The **Kunstindustrimuseet,** or 'Museum of Decorative Art,' located between Amalienborg Palace and the Esplanaden at 68 Bredgade (if in doubt, start from Kongens Nytorv where Bredgade begins), charges no admission except on Sundays and holidays (when 7 kroner are asked), and is open daily except Mondays from 1 to 4 p.m. Housed in a graceful grey stone building with a small courtyard in front, this museum has large and pleasantly displayed collections of furniture, textiles, tapestries (the most famous being the Flemish Tournai from the 15th century), and all forms of decorative art; as well as a lovely large library which is open to the public weekdays (except Mondays) from 10 a.m. to 4 p.m. Modern design is not stinted: you'll see **Matisse** tapestries, as well as pieces from Georg Jensen, the Royal Porcelain factory, recent Danish furniture, design, etc.

ROYAL AND NON-ROYAL EXTRAS: "For a good panoramic view of the city, try the old **Round Tower,** built as an observatory in 1642, by our all-time Danish favorite Christian IV. It's located on Købmagergade (not too far from the 'Strøget'), is open in summer on weekdays from 10 a.m. to 5 p.m., Sundays and holidays from noon to 4 p.m. On weekdays you'll be charged 5 kroner to climb the long circular ramp to the top. . . . And if you have time, do try to see that marvelous antique in the midst of the city, the **Nyboder** section, which was also built by Christian IV. Only a short walk from the Esplanaden or the Resistance Museum: head for Gernersgade or Store Kongensgade, where you'll find a series of streets made up of tiny low-roofed orange doll houses, with short doors, small rooms, gas lamps on the streets: everything (except the cars parked out front) conspiring to transport you back 300 years. . . . **The Københaven Bymuseum** or City Museum, 59 Vesterbrogade, contains objects and paintings illustrating the history of the city, done in typically charming Danish fashion. There's a large model of Copenhagen in 1550 on the grass in front of the building (complete with water in the canals), peepshows inside, city models that light up, a huge model brewery, another model honoring the development of the Fire Brigade, and also a special room devoted to personal objects of Soren Kierkegaard. You can have all this, and more, for free; the museum's open daily, October to April, from 10 a.m. to 4 p.m., May to September from 1 to 4 p.m. (except Mondays, when it's closed). . . . **Thorvaldsen's Museum,** located near Christiansborg Castle (look for the most classy classical-looking building in the neighborhood, complete with friezes), opens every day from 10 a.m. to 4 p.m. in summer, until 3 p.m. in the winter, (when it closes on Tuesdays), with free admission, is a monument to Denmark's foremost sculptor, Bertel Thorvaldsen (1770-1844), and contains his statues and works, models and sketches for works in progress, his own private art collection (all of which he bequeathed to the city of Copenhagen), and his grave (he's buried in the courtyard). I find his work too conventionalized in the classic tradition for my tastes, but go and judge for yourself. . . . Last, but certainly not least, do visit **Denmark's Fight for Freedom Museum** (*Frihedsmuseet*), in Churchill Park, open daily except Monday in summer from 10 a.m. to 4 p.m. (Sunday til 5 p.m.), in winter from 11 a.m. to 3 p.m. (Sunday 11 to 4—closed Monday), which displays a chronological and graphic record of the German occupation of Denmark, and then shows you how the Danish resistance was set up (with illegal presses and radios, homemade rifles) and how the Germans reacted, with grisly exhibits of Nazi tortures, cases of material relating to the flight of Danish Jews to Sweden. Buy the 10-kroner guidebook in English (or ask for an automatic guide-tour) so that you can follow this inspiring exhibition of the courage, daring and determination of the Danish people to be free. Free admission."

OFFER FROM A SIGHTSEEING GUIDE: "I intend to quit my summer job as a guide on the ordinary bus tours, not only for the weekends like this year, but all the time next year. I am tired of having to speak two, three, or four languages on the same bus—which of course is completely unsatisfactory to the tourists, too—and of rushing by everything of interest in a hurry. The best way to see a city is definitely by foot. From 22 June to 8 September 1985, I therefore plan the following program:

"**Sunday at 4 p.m. and Wednesday at 5:30 p.m.:** A guided walking tour thru the heart of the old city. We meet at the Dragon & Bull Fountain in front of the Town Hall.

"**Monday and Thursday at 5:30 p.m.:** A guided walking tour to the old canals and the 'Castle Island.' Meeting point: same as above.

"**Saturday at 2 p.m.:** Meeting at the ramp of the Stock Exchange (Borsen), we'll go to Christianshavn ('Little Amsterdam').

"**Tuesday at 10:30 a.m.:** We meet at the corner of Gothersgade and Øster Voldgade to walk through the Botanical Gardens and visit the Royal Museum of Fine Arts.

"**Wednesdays at 10:30 a.m.:** A guided visit to the prehistorical section of the National Museum. Meet on the bridge of the Frederiksholm Canal.

"My charge will be 15 kroner per person per tour, but young people aged 14 to 25 pay 10 kroner, children under 14 are free. Duration of each tour: 2 hours. Language: English exclusively. Hope to see you!" (Mr. Helge Seidelin Jacobsen, **"The Guide Ring,"** 91 Kongelundsvej, 2300 Copenhagen, phone 51-25-90).

READERS ON EXCURSIONS: "An all-day trip by train from Copenhagen to **Odense** is fascinating, very easy, and can be done for less than half the cost of the conducted bus tour. The day before, provide yourself with a map of Odense at the Tourist Bureau in Copenhagen on Townhall Square, and buy a round-trip 2nd class rail ticket for 210 kroner ($21). Take the early morning Lyntog (lightning train) from the Central Station at 7:15 a.m. The entire train is put on the ferry from Korsør to Nyborg (a delightful 55-minute trip) and arrival in Odense is at 9:51 a.m. With your map of Odense, you will have no difficulty walking from the station through the park and the town to Hans Christian Andersen's house and museum on Hans Jensensstraede—it isn't far. Tours stay only a few minutes; we spent more than an hour here and enjoyed it thoroughly. There is also a delightful gift shop (Klods-Hans Kunsthaandvaerk) across the street, with superb and inexpensive Christmas items, among other delectable tidbits. Then go back one block to the bus stop on the 6-lane highway and, for 6 kroner, take local bus 2 going south, to *Den Fynske Landsby,* or 'The Funen Village'—the driver will let you off at the right place. This is a remarkable reconstruction of an Old Danish village, with farmhouses, a windmill, an inn, etc. Lunch at the Sortebro Kro (inn) here will cost about $7 (best bet is an omelet); it's a picturesque place with low beamed ceilings, rustic furniture, old pewter, candle molds, etc. Take the bus back to the center of town and have a look at the Town Hall. Then, if you have to wait for a train, spend the time by the pond in the beautiful park opposite the station. There are trains back to Copenhagen approximately every hour. We took the one at 4:16 p.m., arriving Copenhagen 7:13 p.m. It was the best excursion of our whole trip" (Mr. and Mrs. Paul Redin, Oklahoma City, Oklahoma). . . . "Anyone who visits the charming little town of **Dragør,** 8 miles southeast of Copenhagen, will want to stay several hours, taking pictures all of the time. Simply board bus 33 from the Bus Terminal in Copenhagen (across the street from the City Hall), and in 20 minutes you will be in Dragør, using your city bus-transfer as part of the fare. Buses run every 20 minutes back and forth from Copenhagen. You might also like to take the ferry to Sweden from Dragør, which will land you at Limhamn, not far south of Malmö. You can then come back to Copenhagen via ferry or hydrofoil" (Mrs. Calvin Smith, Clinton, Michigan). . . . "As wonderful as Copenhagen is, Denmark is really fun to visit, and about an hour away by train is **Krøge,** a small old harbor town that, like almost every place we visited, had its own tourist office which could provide friendly and informative assistance. The Saturday morning open air market is an especial treat" (Craig Nauman, Madison, Wisconsin). . . . "A must for those who visit Copenhagen is a trip to **Hillerød,** the home of Frederiksborg Slot. This was one of the most spectacular palaces in Europe (and we tried to see them all) and is virtually unknown to most tourists. Take the S-train from the central station (free to Eurail) and ask for directions to Frederiksborg Castle at the Hillerød station. It is located about 20 minutes' walk from the station. Admission is 10kr, or 5kr for students and 3kr for children" (John and Mary Banbury, Breckenridge, Colorado). . . . **"The Danish Open Air Museum** (Frilandsmuseet) situated on 90 acres in Lyngby, about 10 miles from downtown Copenhagen, consists of 50 authentic rural structures, completely unchanged, including several farms in simulated working condition, with horses, cows and chickens. Use your Eurailpass for the S-train to Sorgenfri, or take bus 84. Admission is 5 kroner and hours are from 10 to 5, Tuesday through Sunday, but only May through September" (Jeffrey Stanton, Marina del Rey, California; reminder from AF: since the Eurailpass is honored on all state railways, and since the subways and suburban railways (S-trains) in Copenhagen are state facilities, Eurailpass holders can travel free to many of the attractions listed above).

READERS-ON-BIKES: "I rode to the **Louisiana Museum** at Humlebaeck, 22 miles up the coast from Copenhagen. It's a beautiful ride—with Sweden right across the water. The suburbs north of Copenhagen are probably the most beautiful in the world, Arne Jacobsen's hand is everywhere. The Louisiana itself is a museum of contemporary art with a few pieces from the 30s, but almost all from the 50s and 60s including abstract, Pop, Op—the whole thing. It is also a beautiful building with fine sculpture around it and a view of the water. Hours are 10 a.m. to 5 p.m., daily, Wednesdays until 10 p.m., admission of 20 kroner, children under 16 free. Four miles beyond is Helsingor, which translates as Elsinore, Hamlet's home. I did not have the strength to go there, but it might be worthwhile" (B.L. Wendell, Baltimore, Maryland). . . . "We took a very enjoyable trip in one day from Copenhagen to **Elsinore**—an hour's train ride away. At the Elsinore train station, we then rented bikes (it's best to reserve them ahead of time) and pedaled to Kronberg Castle, where we had lunch. Afterward, we biked six kilometers to 'Louisiana,' the most beautiful modern art museum in all of Europe! It overlooks the sea and is worth visiting for its architecture alone! The entire trip—including train fares and bicycles for two persons—cost less than $13" (Deirdre Henderson and Mark Koplik, New Haven, Connecticut). . . .

A FAST BOAT TO SWEDEN: "An experience no one should miss is the hydrofoil or Flying Boat from Copenhagen to **Malmö,** Sweden. It leaves every hour, on the hour, from the corner of Nyhavn Canal and Havnegade (take bus 41 from Town Hall Square to end of line on Havnegade, or take any bus that goes to Kongens Nytorv and walk to the end of the Nyhavn Canal). Cost is 58 kroner ($5.80) one way, and no reduction for round-trip. Malmö itself is an interesting city, and one of the things not to be missed is its modern Municipal Theater, and the fountain on its grounds" (Mr. and Mrs. Paul Redin, Oklahoma City, Oklahoma). . . . "Travelers staying in Copenhagen would do well to take the early boat to **Malmö,** Sweden, look around for an hour, and then take the train to **Lund** ($2.10; I believe) to see a beautiful Gothic university town, very sophisticated, with quaint shops. Then one would do well to have lunch at **Staket** (I'm not sure of the spelling, but the railroad has a tourist booth that will help you), which is the oldest building in the city and a favorite mealtime gathering place of the students. (Dinner with over a pint of milk was $4). Lund is a beautiful city. I think anyone will be enchanted with its beautiful parks and buildings. You can still return to Copenhagen by a late ferry in time for the ballet/opera. We did!" (Karl Davis, New York, New York). . . . "We strongly recommend going to **Elsinore** by train, and then to **Helsingborg,** Sweden, by ferry, where you can have a walk around, and then return to Copenhagen by direct steamer" (Bruce Marschak, Chicago, Copenhagen, Illinois; note from AF: Elsinore-Helsinborg ferry is 28 kroner ($2.80), the Helsinborg Copenhagen steamer is 40 kroner ($4).

7. Evening Entertainment

In addition to what you'll find at the Tivoli, Copenhagen enjoys a 24-hour nightlife that roars on till morning in jazz clubs and dance halls, coffee houses and nightowl restaurants. Things don't start swinging until around 10 p.m., though. While the streets of Copenhagen may look absolutely deserted at that time, you'll be surprised at all the activity that's going on inside.

JAZZ: The city's major jazz club (music and dancing) is **Daddy's Dance Hall,** at 9 Axeltorv, near the famous Benneweis Circus, which looks like a white castle; you can't miss it. Entrance costs 20 to 40 kroner ($2 to $4), and festivities continue, unabated, until 4 a.m.

Jazzclub Vognporten, 14 Magstrade, specializes in traditional jazz, blues, and swing music. Admission is 20 to 40 kroner ($2 to $4), depending on the day of the week and whether you are a club member. Open daily from 9 p.m. to 2 a.m.

DANCING: This is a highly developed sport in Copenhagen, and seriously pursued. And since most Danes speak English, the prospects for a lonely single American tourist—male or female—are just great.

The choice of a dance hall is best made according to age-group. For those in the 18-to-30 range, **Dansetten** inside Tivoli is usually crowded to capacity, bright and noisy; it charges no admission except on Friday and Saturday nights (20 kroner). . . . People of all ages—in couples or stag— head for **Montmartre** at 41 Nørregade, open daily from 8 p.m. to 1 a.m. (Friday and Saturday to 4 a.m.), which features all kinds of jazz, blues, folk and funk music. Admission is 30 to 60 kroner ($3 to $6).

BEER HALLS: Our older and heartier readers will enjoy **Vin & Ølgod,** 45 Skindergade, a Danish beer hall where guests are presented with printed song pages and everybody joins in singing international rousers. A small band keeps the crowd singing and swilling; the result is very-Hofbräuhaus, and admission is 30 kroner on Friday and Saturday, 15 kroner on other days (with women admitted free on Tuesday nights). Closed Sundays.

Inside Tivoli, there's another such place and it's possibly the most popular summertime drinking-spot in all Copenhagen, for the Danes. Its name is **Faergekroen,** and it's a pink-painted wooden building on the Town Hall side of the lake. Everybody who can, squeezes around the tables inside where a man at a piano belts out Danish, American, English and German beer-drinking songs and whole benches of strangers link arms, singing and swaying, while pouring down mugs of beer at 26 kroner each. Those who can't fit are relegated to being mournful onlookers from the outdoor tables by the lake. There's no admission charge, but you'll want to drink.

NYHAVN: Now you're in the Greenwich Village of Copenhagen, a rowdy street of bars and cafes that parallels an often-pictured canal, located—amazingly enough—just a few steps from the plush Hotel d'Angleterre, near the big square called Kongens Nytorv. It's a rough-hewn, raucous area, but not dangerous (although women will be more comfortable with escorts), much frequented by Swedish sailors in search of the brew they can't purchase so easily across the sea. A hop from bar to bar makes for a modest "walk on the wild side." At **Cap Horn,** 21 Nyhavn, you'll find Dixieland jazz, a topless female disc jockey, and topless waitresses; **41 Nyhavn** features pop bands alternating with a free jukebox; **Sailor's Inn** at 17 Nyhavn collects an authentic crowd of old sea-dogs and their mates, all telling tales and acting frisky, often to the background strains of an accordion; the **Sailor's Inn** at 25 Nyhavn is much the same. At none of the clubs will you pay an entrance fee, although beer costs a stiff 15 to 18 kroner. All the clubs close down promptly at 2 a.m., in an obvious attempt to keep the lid on, and things aren't really roaring till about 11 p.m. It's an experience that shouldn't be missed. Items to note: the huge anchor at the head of the canal, memorial to Danish sailors who lost their lives in World War II; the small, white house at #67, where Hans Christian Andersen lived from 1845 to 1867; the 200-year-old Danish courtyard—a picture postcard sight—at #53 (walk in); the top of 11 **Nyhavn,** where you'll see the lit-up face of an astronomical clock, such as sailors use; and several real-life tattoo parlors, of which the main specimens are **Tattoo Ole and Arno** at 17, and **Tattoo Jack, Jorgen and Bimbo** between 37 and 39. Here you'll be adorned with up to 5,000 different motifs, ranging from a blue swallow or seagull for your bicep (for 100 to 300 kroner) to a butterfly or rose for your chest (for around 400 kroner). And if you have a month to spend in Copenhagen, plus a few thousand kroner, you can order a full-body job, including the Manhattan skyline, all known birds, animals and flowers, hearts, anchors, ships, and the Monster of Loch Ness.

COPENHAGEN'S GARDEN RESTAURANTS: For more than 125 years, Danes have been flocking to eat, drink, sing and dance until 1:30 a.m. at the eight wooden huts and buildings, surrounded by gaily colored lamps, benches and trees, that make up **Krogers Have** (*have* meaning "garden") at 18 Pileallee—Copenhagen's largest outdoor restaurant outside of Tivoli. A dance floor with continually playing band, strolling accordionists, and strategically situated pianists, completes the picture, and there's food in all price categories: 25 varieties of smørrebrod from 13 to 30 kroner, beer for 18 kroner, coffee for 10. If you can't find a vacancy among the 1,500 seats, then walk down the street to two similar but smaller establishments at 10 (Hansens Gamle Familiehave) or 16 (Petersens Familiehave), all of which are best reached by bus 28. Less ambitious than the Tivoli, the garden restaurants provide Danish families, and their friends, with simple, wholesome relaxation on warm summer days or nights, which may suit your own mood at the time of your visit.

THE CIRCUS: And lastly, schedule a performance at the 95-year-old **Cirkus Benneweis** on the Axeltorv, one block from Town Hall Square. One of our readers says, "This is the number one circus in all of Europe; the Benneweis horses are second only to those of the Spanish Riding School." We heartily concur, and add that this is probably the most exciting circus-going experience a big-city person will ever have! The theatre is small, and the performances are therefore closer and more real than they would be at, say, Madison Square Garden—if an aerialist were to fall, chances are good he might fall on you! Performances are scheduled weekdays at 8 p.m., weekends at 3 and 7 p.m., and prices range from 40 to 100 kroner; the average charge for a good seat is 60 kroner ($6). May through mid-October is the season.

8. Shopping

Copenhagen is one of the shopper's paradises of Europe. The designs of nearly every Danish article are fully ten years in advance of their American imitations, and prices are fully 20% less. Materials, looking as if they'd come from the hand-loom of Pablo Picasso, cost $4 and $5 a yard here, would cost $7 and $8 a yard in New York. Ceramic ashtrays, teakwood salad bowls and ice-buckets also go for a fraction of what they'd bring in the States.

SEEING THE SHOPS: The Danes, so famed for their interior design, arts and crafts, give to their shops such a museum-like quality that a few very pleasant hours can be spent poking through them, whether or not you intend to buy the wares. Take at least one long walk along the pedestrian street, Strøget (pronounced "Stroyet"), that runs from the Town Hall Square to Kongens Nytorv, where **Georg Jensen** peddles his silver, **Royal Copenhagen** their porcelain, and **Birger Christensen** his mink. Don't miss a tour of the famous **Illums Bolighus** or of **Illum's** department store, a brilliant showcase for the best in Danish furniture and household accessories.

Another—and the most important—showcase to visit: **Den Permanente** (The Permanent Exhibition), two blocks from the central railroad station, on Vesterbrogade, but on the other side of the street (and also in a smaller annex called Artium on Town Hall Square). Here on show (and for sale) are the highest-quality arts and crafts items in all Denmark, chosen for their merit by a special committee. The low-cost items are in the front section (near the windows) of the second floor; most popular of all: the teakwood pillboxes with silver inlay for only 60 kroner ($6); three-piece cutlery, in three different colors, Jensen-designed, for 100 kroner ($10) per set. And then there are teakwood candlesticks for under $11, worthy of a museum showing; wooden wastepaper baskets ($10), almost too lovely to use; ceramics and items of stainless steel; and, of course, the low-cost ice-buckets and salad bowls that are normally too expensive to purchase in the U.S. Every item is in perfect taste, because everything in Den Permanente has been judged to be the best of its type. For a relatively minor charge, Den Permanente then ships your purchases to the U.S., and takes care of all crating and customs details—but keep in mind that items which you ship home, as opposed to those you carry with you onto the plane, do not qualify for duty exemption under U.S. customs regulations. . . . After viewing the goods at Den Permanente, you can then head for the major department stores in Copenhagen (**Anva's,** for example, diagonally across from the railroad station and air terminal) for occasionally cheaper and almost-as-good equivalents. Finally, posters and reproductions are a good bet in this city. You'll pay about 40 kroner ($4) or less, per painting in any number of stores around Town Hall Square.

READERS' SELECTIONS: "Collectors of Royal Copenhagen china and porcelain who normally purchase from the Royal Copenhagen shop on the Strøget, should avoid the ground floor showroom and take the elevator to the 2nd floor, where the second and third 'sortings' (flawed goods) are displayed. Prices are 15% and 40% lower for minor differences in color and shading. And all such pieces are perfect, without chips or cracks. Stocks are changed daily" (F.H. Lambert, Worthing, England). . . . **"Chris Mollers Efte,** across the street from the Danish Resistance Museum at 49 Amaliengade, has the most exciting variety of things to buy. For example, there are specially made lambskin slippers (only available at this store) for $18 a pair; there are marvelous sheepskin rugs selling for $43 (I saw the same one that we bought for much more in New York); there are heavy Scandinavian sweaters and all kinds of other equipment for sports fans or just plain fans of fine quality goods. And the people who run this store are typical of all Copenhagen—warm, friendly and wonderful!" (Mr. & Mrs. R. S. Zimmerman, New York, N.Y.). . . . "Besides the famous Walk Street called 'Strøget' (a little expensive for $25-a-Day'ers), there are two other sections good for shopping. One is **Christianshavn** on the other side of the harbor. Take tram 2 from Radhuspladsen heading toward Tivoli, Christianborg, the harbor. After crossing the bridge you're in Christianshavn. Get off at the 1st or 2nd stop after the bridge and you'll be right in the middle of a shopping area (**Torvegade**) where the *Danes* shop. To buy leather goods—purses, jackets, etc.—go to **Ruskind og Nappahuset,** 36 Torvegade, cheaper because it is a factory outlet store. For stainless steel trays, flatware, wood trays, etc., go to **G. Lorich,** 55 Amagerbrogade. . . . The other section for shopping is on a street called **Norrebrogade,** reached by taking tram 16 from the railroad station to the stop beyond the Lakes. . . . Back in the center of town—a shop for gloves called **Gazelle,** 35 Vesterbrogade. . . . For men's clothing it is **Troelstrup,** 5 Vester Voldgade. . . . And, of course, **Anva,** Vesterbrogade, and **Magasin du Nord,** Kongens Nytorv, the two big department stores" (John W. Abrams, Reading, Pa.; note by AF: the very cheapest of the city's department stores—akin, let's say, to Alexander's in New York or Filene's basement in Boston—is **Daell's Varehus;** you'll enjoy a visit to it. The largest department store in Copenhagen—even the queen shops there—is **Magasin du Nord).**

9. Miscellaneous Tips

The Danes are great gagsters. Cartoon translated from a Danish newspaper shows one waiter yelling to another, "Hey, Povl, your Danish is better than mine. You'd better serve this Dane." Another depicts a tourist at Elsinore, asking: "If Hamlet never existed, then why did you build this castle?" . . . **Copenhagen Radio** (program 3) transmits world news in English from 8:15 to 8:20 a.m., every day except Sunday. . . . For a laundromat in the budget hotel area at the side of the central station, try the large **Quick Vask** at 45 Istedgade (corner of Absalonsgade), six short blocks from the station; a machine-load (7 kilos) costs 28 kroner, and the attendants are there from 6 a.m. to 10 p.m., 7 days a week. . . . Readers staying in the vicinity of the Kongens Nytorv can use instead the **Vaskomat** at 2 Borgergade, which is open from 6 a.m. to 10 p.m. six days a week, and charges 28 kroner for 7 kilos of wash. Directly across the street, **Rekord Rens** at 18 Borgergade, does same-day cleaning at reasonable rates. . . . Cheapest department store in Copenhagen, for that vital odd item: **Daell's Varehus,** 12 Nørregade. . . . A genuine, open-air flea market? One operates every Saturday from 9 a.m. to 2 p.m. on Israel Plads, a block west of the Norreport Station, on Frederiksborggade. And even though it's in dignified Scandinavia, you bargain. . . . Need a youth hostel card? You can buy one for 120 kroner (good all throughout Europe) at **Danmarks Vandrerhjem,** 39 Vesterbrogade. . . . A budget steam bath? The extremely pleasant, community-owned **Københavns Bad,** 12 Borgergade, offers *vapour* (steam) baths for 15 kroner, sunbaths for from 16 to 22 kroner. . . . Readers who will be driving to Copenhagen from the mainland of Europe should remember to buy a *round-trip* ticket on the auto ferry going there, which brings you a 30% savings over the cost of two one-way tickets; the round-trip reduction is applicable even if you are returning to the mainland by a different ferry than the one you took going over. . . . Want to return to England by boat? Or go to Oslo by boat? **D.F.D.S.** is the steamship line to consult at their offices (D.F.D.S. Travel Bureau) at 4A Vesterbrogade (phone 15-63-41), Copenhagen. And if you're in England, and want to come to Copenhagen by boat (via Harwich or Newcastle in England and Esbjerg in Denmark), consult **D.F.D.S. Seaways,** Latham House, 16 Minories (phone 481-3211), London. There are daily summer departures in both directions. Cost of the one-way trip is as little as $76, not including meals on ship. . . . Instant babysitters? Try **University Student Babysitters Minerva,** 52a Smallegade (phone 19-00-90), 22 to 27 kroner an hour plus cost of transportation. You can phone them from 1 to 8 on weekdays, 3 to 6 Saturdays, 5 to 7 p.m. Sundays.

READERS' SUGGESTIONS: "If you come to Denmark via the Puttgarden-Rodby ferry, then, no matter what the hour, go to one of the ship's restaurants and have the 'Kolde Bord'—cold table—all you can eat from a fabulous table of both hot and cold Scandinavian specialties—$6. The variety and attractiveness—and tastiness—of the dishes is almost overwhelming" (Jess and Alice Brewis, Taylor, Michigan). . . . "On the **Tuborg** tour, I was lucky enough to draw the public relations man as a guide, and there were only five of us on his tour. He treated us to some very interesting tales and some of the strong beer, which is rated 20% over here. It made my bike ride thru rush hour quite thrilling, to say the least. At the opera and ballet, I had seats in the gallery for $1.50, and I saw Rubinstein at the Tivoli Concert Hall for only $2" (Richard D. Gold, Los Altos, California). . . . "Five times I have been in Copenhagen, and I have always been able, despite contrary predictions, to pick up tickets for the **Royal Danish Ballet** on the day of performance, right at the box office" (Donna Cuervo, Richmond Hill, New York). . . . "Don't forget to mention the Copenhagen porn shops; you can browse, but you don't have to buy. Scents, inflatable erotica, smoking regalia and phallic gimmicks going back to Jungian archetypes are on display. I asked a rather haughty clerk about Chinese phantasies he had never heard of, but I'm sure they were on display two weeks later. If you use good old pearl-toothed American appreciation, you are welcomed, even if you're a menopausing browser and not a purchaser" (Delos V. Smith, Jr., Hutchinson, Kansas). . . . "We left Copenhagen for Oslo by the overnight **D.F.D.S.** 'ferry,' which was cheaper than airfare and much cleverer than by train since, for slightly more, we got an overnight 'hotel' room included in the deal. The second class cabin had running water, two berths and a porthole (a necessity for traveling since the ship got rather warm)" (Dr. and Mrs. S. M. Marcus, Keflavik, Iceland). . . . "There's free admission to the **Deer Park** next to Bakken, a beautiful, wild area where many deer wander unfenced. You can rent bikes at the train station for 28 kroner a day, and burn up some calories in the most wonderful way" (Bob and Chelly Gutin, Hartsdale, New York). . . . "Eurailpass owners should note that their passes are valid on the municipal S-Tog (S-Train), which is actually owned by the national railways" (Anthony Miller, Freehold, New Jersey). . . . "In the large central hall of the **Copenhagen Town Hall,** open to the public, stand four impressive statues, and although this is a public building, none are of political figures. Two of the four are of special interest to foreign visitors: Niels Bohr, the famous physicist who helped to give man so much physical power, and Hans Christian Andersen, whose wonderful stories may help to give us a little of the wisdom needed to use this power for good instead of harm. Perhaps this is a little beyond your subject of *Europe on $25 a Day,* but the combination of Bohr and Andersen seemed impressive to me in the same way as the World War II plaque which you wrote about seeing on the Palazzo Vecchio in Florence—and perhaps worthy of mention for the same reason" (Richard A. Givens, New York, New York).

Scandinavia only begins with Copenhagen, and a taste of this northern city should whet your appetite for more. The logical next step is a quick flight to Stockholm.

STOCKHOLM

Under 3 Crowns

STOCKHOLM, very simply stated, is like no other city you have ever seen. At times it resembles a Camelot, all surrounded by forests, laced with spires and turrets, very stately in its aspect and seemingly as conservative as a Ronald Reagan pep team. To think that this is the birthplace of cradle-to-grave security and experimental marriage is a shock that often takes a few hours to overcome.

Physically, the city is one of the loveliest of capitals. It spreads over 14 separate islands, each connected by vaulting bridges, under which the waters of Lake Mälaren—which flow into the Baltic Sea—are often covered with sailboats, cruising deep into the city. Some of the islands rise on steep cliffs from the water, and on these cliffs, high above, are the stern, dignified buildings of Sweden, untouched by the ravages of war for nearly two hundred years. Best yet, the city is surrounded by woodland and farms, never more than ten minutes away from any point in town.

Viewed from another aspect, the city is one of the most sophisticated in Europe, not only in the attainments of its art and culture, but in the social relationships of its citizens. There is no public graft in Sweden, no discernible poverty. If you probe deeply enough, you'll be constantly surprised by the projects and ideas erupting about you: the futuristic suburbs, all built within the past 30 years; the ingenious efforts to make life pleasant and full, within a framework of democracy. It may be a minor example, but it's typical of Sweden, that old-age pensioners are permitted to buy tickets on the Swedish Railways at half price.

For the tourist there's an endless variety of sights and activities: the unique open-air "museums," the Archipelago of Stockholm, the brilliant Royal Dramatic Theatre, the Milles Sculptures, the mysterious Flagship

Wasa. When Hope and I last had to depart this city, we felt we were being dragged away.

But how much, you now ask, does all of this cost? Well, despite all of Stockholm's very notable attractions, it has—by this book's standards—one major problem: it is Europe's most expensive city. Even the Stockholm tourist office, publishing a pamphlet of hints for penny-pinching tourists, had the grace to title it *See Stockholm at a MODERATE Price,* instead of *See Stockholm Cheaply.* "Moderate" is the accurate word. You will find meals in Stockholm selling at $5 to $6, but most likely you'll put out $7 to $8 for the average dinner. You can get a bed in a hostel for $8 or a room in a private home for $26 double, but if you plan to stay in a pension or a hotel, you will have to pay from $33 to $45 for a bathless double, including service charge.

As in our Copenhagen chapter, we'd suggest that you don't stay away—not by any means—Stockholm is far too fascinating to miss. But that you budget a little more for the daily necessities—about $25 or so—and consider Stockholm a "Big Splurge" city. With meals and lodgings under control, you'll find that low-cost sightseeing and entertainment abound, and much of it is covered in the pages to come.

Here, now, is how I'd organize a first visit:

1. Orientation

The very first thing to do upon arriving in Stockholm is to go to the hotel accommodations bureau (**Hotellcentralen**) in the Central Station and obtain a room (details appear in our section on accommodations below). Then, after depositing your bags, the very next thing to do is to take the subway *(Tunnelbana)* to the "Slussen" stop, where you'll find the great **Katarina Elevator** (one krona per person). It rises in an open lift to the roof of a tall building, from which you can see all the way to the Baltic and to the beginning of the Stockholm Archipelago. The city is spread out below you: the boats that go to Finland are on your left, the ships to nearby Russia are directly ahead.

From this vantage point, you'll first begin to understand the arrangement of the 14 islands that make up the city of Stockholm. But only five of them need concern you: Norrmalm, Södermalm, Gamla Stan, Kungsholmen and Djurgarden (the Deer Park).

The big northern island, which contains the shopping areas, the office buildings, the railroad station, air terminal, and almost all the hotels we'll recommend, is the **Norrmalm.** The major squares in the Norrmalm are the Norrmalmstorg, the Stureplan, and the Gustav Adolfs Torg (where the Opera is located).

Directly below the Norrmalm, and almost touching upon it, is the tiny island of **Gamla Stan**—the Old City—where the Royal Palace stands, and where the streets are narrow, twisting and incredibly picturesque. Although there are some cheap hotels here, they're mainly in centuries-old and somewhat damp-feeling buildings, and we've recommended only one of them. The Gamla Stan does have some of the best restaurants and nightspots of Stockholm, together with several bustling shopping streets so narrow that cars are excluded. It can't be missed.

Directly below the Gamla Stan is **Södermalm**—the Brooklyn of Stockholm—where the residents speak with a special argot all their own, and are fiercely proud of their island. This is almost entirely a residential area, and virtually no tourists—including us—go there. It's at the top of the

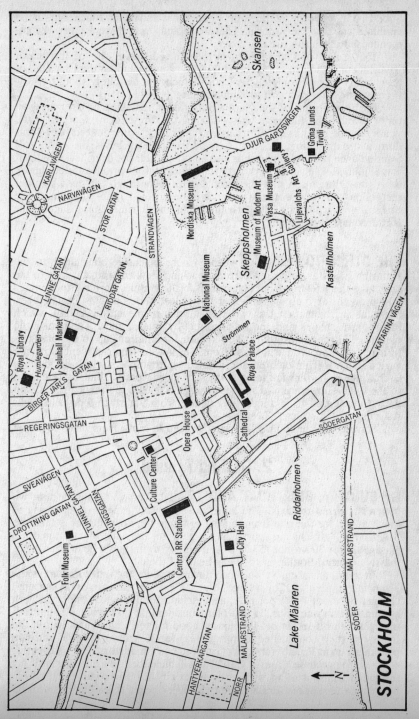

Skansen

DJUR GARDSVAGEN

Gröna Lunds
Tivoli

KARLAVAGEN

NARVAVAGEN

STOR GATAN

STRANDVAGEN

Nordiska Museum

Museum of Modern Art

Vasa Museum

Liljevalchs Art Gallery

Skeppsholmen

Kastellholmen

LINNE GATAN

RIDDAR GATAN

National Museum

Royal Library

Humlegarden

Saluhall Market

BIRGER JARLS GATAN

Strömmen

KATARINA VAGEN

Royal Palace

REGERINGSGATAN

Opera House

Cathedral

SODERGATAN

SVEAVAGEN

Culture Center

DROTTNING GATAN

TUNNEL GATAN

KUNGSGATAN

Central RR Station

City Hall

Riddarholmen

MALARSTRAND

Folk Museum

HANTVERKARGATAN

MALARSTRAND

SODER

MALARSTRAND

NORR

Lake Mälaren

N

STOCKHOLM

Södermalm, however, at the point where the island nearly touches upon the Gamla Stan, that the Katarina Elevator stands, and there are two recommended hotels in this area.

To the left of Gamla Stan is the **Kungsholmen,** site of the major government buildings of this capital of Sweden, including the City Hall of Stockholm. Except for the City Hall—which you definitely should visit—there's little to attract you to Kungsholmen.

But to the right of the Gamla Stan (after first skipping over an even tinier island—the **Skeppsholmen**—site of the Museum of Modern Art), you'll find the magnificent **Djurgarden** (Deer Park), pronounced yoor-gohr-dun, a breath-taking, wooded fairyland on whose lands the royalty of Sweden once rode to the hounds and let graze their pet deer. Even today it is maintained solely as a park with few residential or business buildings on it. It's to Djurgarden that the people of Stockholm go for their summer recreation—to the fascinating open-air museum and park of **Skansen,** to the carnival grounds of the **Tivoli Gröna Lund** and to the various dance halls scattered near both spots.

THE OTHER TOWER: As a slightly-more-expensive alternative to the Katarina Elevator, and for a farther-reaching view and introduction to the city, take the #69 bus from Nybroplan to the **Kaknäs Tower,** Stockholm's television tower built in 1967 and the tallest building (508 feet high) in Scandinavia. Note first the two wall murals in the entrance hall, which incorporate shapes and metals inspired by teletechnics. Then take the elevator (7 kronor for adults, 3.50 kronor for children) up to the observation room; there you can walk from window to window identifying the various islands from colored and labeled photographs set into the base of each window. If you want to scan any spot more closely, climb up one flight to the open-air terrace and view it through a telescope (one krona). Open daily from 9 a.m. to midnight in summer, from 9 a.m. to 6 p.m. in other seasons.

Having oriented yourself, you now need to move from place to place:

2. Getting Around

BY SUBWAY, BUS, BOAT AND TRAIN: And you'll notice that we haven't referred to taxis! The latter are fiendishly expensive, charging as much as $40 for the ride from airport to town. On arrival, simply take the S.A.S. bus, which transports passengers to the city air terminal on Vasagatan for 30 kronor ($3.75). Arriving by train, you'll be at the single, massive **Central Station** in the very heart of the city.

In town, an extensive bus and subway system (the latter known as the *Tunnelbana,* identified by a large, blue "T" at the entrance to all stations) charges 6 kronor (75¢) per ride, and includes unlimited transfers on both systems within one hour. If you plan considerable do-it-yourself sightseeing, you can buy a set of 20 coupons good for ten single rides within the inner city (two coupons equal one ticket) for 35 kronor ($4.37), and you pick these up at Pressbyran kiosks or from bus conductors. But a far better course is to purchase "Tourist Cards" available either on a one-day basis for unlimited transportation within the inner city for 16 kronor ($2), within both city and suburbs for 28 kronor ($3.50); or on a three-day basis for 55 kronor ($6.87) valid for both city and suburbs and including free entrance to both the Skansen and Grona Lund (Tivoli) amusement parks. On the same cards, children under 7 travel free, while children under 18 pay 50%; and note that the 28- and 55-kronor cards take you to such far-out places as Drottningholm Palace.

As you'd expect, there are numerous boat ferries starting and ending in Stockholm, linking the capital with other seaports of Sweden, with the other capitals of Scandinavia, and even with London; phone 22-70-00 for schedules and prices, or go to the Information Service at Sverigehuset, 200 yards from the central Sergelstorg (the square with the glass obelisk).

3. Affordable Accommodations

Just as in Copenhagen, the hotels of Stockholm are heavily booked in the summer months. That, however, doesn't mean that the city is crawling with tourists, but simply that there aren't enough hotels for the tourists who arrive in summer.

Again like Copenhagen, the city guarantees that it will eventually find you a room. To pick up their offer, go to the Central Railroad Station, where you'll find the office called **Hotellcentralen** on the station's lower level. Staffed with English-speaking aides, it maintains contact with a large and approved assortment of hotels and guesthouses (although not with every such establishment in Stockholm), and stays open Monday to Friday from 8 a.m. to 9 p.m., Saturday from 8 a.m. to 5 p.m., and Sunday from 1 to 9 p.m. to obtain a room for you. Charge for the service is 12 kronor ($1.50), for which you get a confirmed reservation together with travel instructions to the hotel you choose.

ROOMS IN PRIVATE HOUSES: The hotel price level of Stockholm is such that true budget tourists will want to obtain rooms in less expensive private homes (although there are some hostels and Ys within our budget range). But Hotellcentralen can often get a bit sticky about sending you to a private home if vacancies exist in higher-priced hotels. So what do *you* do if they refuse to give you the name of a private home? You walk out and walk over to the office of a commercial and slightly more expensive private room-finding service, of which a prime example is found within a short walk of the Central Railroad Station.

Room Rental Agencies

As you leave the station, turn left on Vasagatan and proceed to **Hotel Tjanst**, 38 Vasagatan (phone 10-44-37 or 10-44-57), whose plain and rather starkly lit office is on the second floor of an elderly building. Here you'll find Mr. Gustavsson, the owner and only employee of this one-man organization. He speaks fluent English and will, at your request, book you into a private home whose charges average 150 kronor ($18.75) single, 175 kronor ($21.87) double, including booking fee. Hotel Tjanst is open from 9 a.m. to noon and 1 to 5 p.m., Monday to Friday only.

(During the period from June 20 to August 15, Hotel Tjanst will often also be able to book you a 50% to 60% discount in several of Stockholm's major hotels. That's because hotel occupancies drop off sharply during that limited period, with the departure from town of seemingly half the population for summer vacation. Mr. Gustavsson asks that you avail yourself of these bargains, and of his year-round private home-finding facilities, only upon your arrival in Stockholm. Because he is so sure of being able to find you a room on the spot, from his secret list of several hundred private homes, he will not answer your reservation letters!)

Four actual private homes, charging 65 to 113 kronor per person ($8.13 to $14.13), without and with breakfast

If you'd rather go directly to one of my own recommendations, try:

Mrs. Eva Gisslar, 49 B Skeppargatan, second floor (phone 63-49-57). An English-speaking lady in her 40s, Mrs. Gisslar rents a spotlessly clean room with French double bed, parquet floor and green carpet for 225 kronor ($28.12) per night, including breakfast and free showers. Notice the original Miros in the living room. Centrally located, Mrs. Gisslar's is best reached via the T-bana to Östermalms, using the Sibyllegatan exit (from which the house is a five-minute walk).

Mr. Harold Jonasson, a friendly and always smiling, English-speaking gentleman, lives alone in a large apartment at 78 Asögatan (phone 84-70-08), in the Södermalm district of central Stockholm, where he rents three relatively small but adequately furnished rooms for 130 kronor ($16.25) per room (for two), including free use of the modern kitchen for preparing breakfast or other meals. And there's a bathroom and separate w.c. Take the T-bana to Stanstull, a short walk away.

Mrs. Lidia Sallström, at 8 Wittstocksgatan (phone 67-52-19; office phone: 21-95-19), is an "authorized tourist guide" who rents two double rooms (or, for larger families, her entire new flat) for 225 kronor ($28.12) per room (of two beds), including breakfast. Take the T-bana to Karlaplan (two stops from the Central Station), and walk three minutes from there.

On the outskirts of Stockholm:

Mrs. Kristina Brolin, at 16 Mariehällsvagen, 13147 Nacka (phone 716-3170), is known as much for her cooking as for the bungalow in which she rents two tastefully furnished rooms; on request, she'll prepare a superb supper for 30 kronor per guest. One hundred kronor ($12.50) for a single room, 200 kronor ($25) for a double, including breakfast for all.

As you'll note from the above, private homes in Stockholm charge up to 50% less than budget hotels, a refreshing differential that isn't found in such cities as Vienna or Amsterdam. But don't expect to find vacancies all the time, and always phone first.

BUDGET PENSIONS AND HOTELS: For a few dollars more (anywhere from $30 to $45 for a double room), you can stay in a hotel or pension. I've set forth my choices here, and it might be wise—especially if you are traveling in the peak of summer—to write ahead for reservations, making certain to enclose an international postal response coupon. The following suggestions are arranged by location, rather than by price, with $33 pensions next to $45 hotels, so you might read through the lot before picking those that appeal. Some of the best overall values for summer visitors are to be found at the summer "dorms" referred to below, where double rooms with full private showers rent for $16 to $38, including service charge. And if you're looking for the cheapest digs, turn now to our section on "Hotels" at the very end.

Near the Railroad Station

On leaving the railroad station turn left into Vasagatan, go past the huge red-stone Central Post Office building until you come to Bryggargatan street. At 12b you'll find the **Hotel Savoy** (phone 22-12-80), which caters to Swedish businessmen and prices its 50 rooms at 250 kronor ($31.25) single, 360 kronor ($45) double, 530 kronor ($66.25) triple, 620 kronor ($77.50) quad, breakfast and service included. The Savoy is actually the only budget hotel (by Swedish standards) in the immediate vicinity of the station—all others are far too expensive for this book.

SWEDISH KRONOR: As this chapter was prepared, the Swedish krona was selling at a rate of 8 to the dollar, making each krona worth, in our terms, about 13¢. That 8-to-1 conversion is the basis for dollar figures used in this chapter.

Returning now to Vasagatan and proceeding a few blocks farther up, you'll see a brown-and-green building with two towers and a clock; if you'll turn right before reaching this landmark, you'll be on Barnhusgatan where, at #4, English-speaking Mrs. Berglund manages the cheapish **Hotel Callmar,** third floor (phone 21-21-75). Six double rooms (and they can hold more), of which three are with running water, three without. Each has a stove reaching to the ceiling. For all this adventure, the charge is 280 kronor ($35) per double room, 120 kronor ($15) for a third or fourth bed, 20 kronor for a breakfast that includes cheese. Quiet location.

Another railroad station-area choice: the 40-bed **Hotel Sana,** 6B Upplandsgatan (phone 20-39-82), managed by an English-speaking former law student named Uvenbeck. He charges bargain rates (for Stockholm) of 180 kronor ($22.50) single, 275 kronor ($34.37) double, 85 kronor for a supplementary bed, 15 kronor for breakfast, nothing for showers, and places a TV set in the majority of rooms. Upplandsgatan is a continuation of Vasagatan, and the address is less than a five-minute walk from the station.

Your final railway station area option (10 minutes away by foot, next door to the Royal Dramatic Theatre) is the normally too expensive **Hotel Ornsköld** at 6 Nybrogatan (phone 67-02-85), where most rooms have costly private baths. There are, however, three small bathless singles (cubicles, really) and four large bathless quads, which owner Mr. Enstrand has promised to rent to readers of this book only for only 98 kronor ($12.25) in the cubicles, only 100 kronor ($12.50) per person in the quads, with use of nearby bathrooms and showers free.

Near the Odenplan

Families or groups of four traveling together will find accommodations for less than $14 per person at the 31-room **Hotel Gustav Vasa,** 61

Vastmannagatan (phone 34-38-01), off the Odenplan, four T-bana stops and 6 kronor from the Central Station. The Vasa, occupying three floors of an old apartment house, charges 210 kronor ($26.25) for singles, 290 kronor ($36.25) double or twin, 360 kronor ($45) for a large triple room, 440 kronor ($55) for quads the size of a tennis court. Amenities include a friendly, English-fluent, U.S.-liking owner, Mr. Orling, who offers free showers. The distinguished gentleman who lives in the same building, and frequently visits him—Mr. Lundquist—is one of Sweden's most famous landscape artists; make a polite request to see his studio and paintings, and he will usually show you around.

In the same area, at 1 St. Eriksplan (phone 34-02-85), the **Wasa Park Hotel,** owned by friendly English-speaking Mr. Andersson, has no running water in any of its 15 rooms on the second floor, but there are five very clean washrooms (as well as free showers). Rooms rent for 200 kronor ($25) single, 320 kronor ($40) twin, 400 kronor ($50) triple, including breakfast, and offer a very quiet location (all rooms face a backyard and garden). Two comfortable TV-lounges, and a phone in every room enhance the facilities. To find Wasa Park Hotel on the large St. Eriksplan: it's in the only building with a small turret on top.

Near the Hötorget

In the area of Stockholm's big skyscraper center (the Hötorget), we have three selections:

Hotel Resman, 77 Drottninggatan (phone 21-24-92), on the second floor of an old but well-preserved apartment building, rents 18 rooms, all with hot and cold running water (showers are free) for 190 kronor ($23.75) single, 320 kronor ($40) twin, and 620 kronor ($77.50) for a very large room with five beds. Breakfast is 25 kronor ($3.25) extra, but it's optional. At the lower end of the street, **Hotel Regent** at 10 Drottninggatan (phone 20-90-04), has 16 rooms, and rates slightly lower than those of the Resman. You'll have to walk up dark stairs to reach the office on the third floor. Although the hotel is rather dull and basic, it offers good value (for Stockholm).

Slightly more expensive in the same area: the recently modernized **Hotel Queen,** 71A Drottninggatan (phone 20-08-89), whose rates include a large, Scandinavian-style breakfast (with fresh fruit). Rates are 200 kronor ($25) single, 340 kronor ($42.50) double, 420 kronor ($52.50) triple, all for features and decor that make this surely among the most attractive of our Stockholm selections. Owner Christer Dahlberg, a graduate of Cornell, speaks English fluently.

Near Radmansgatan

In the area between Odenplan and the Hötorget, at 38 Odengatan, on the second floor (phone 30-63-49), a kindly gentleman named Chibba, who immigrated here from India many years ago, rents spotlessly clean rooms for 160 kronor ($20) single, 290 kronor ($36.25) double, 110 kronor ($13.75) per additional bed, in his **Pensionat Oden,** where showers are free. Since breakfast isn't served, guests are allowed use of the kitchen to prepare their own.

Not far away, at 31 Wallingatan (phone 11-10-76), a bearded Finnish artist named Anssi Aro owns and operates the **Pension Danielson** primarily for Finns (his reception room is covered with their photographs bearing effusive dedications), but he is happy to accept North Americans as well; his English is excellent. Rates are 170 kronor ($21.25) for a single without running water, 200 kronor ($25) with, 310 kronor ($41.33) for doubles, all of which are with running water. Showers are free, rooms spacious and well-furnished, and one (room 8) comes with three big windows.

Two short blocks from the Radmansgatan T-bana stop, **Hotel Svinhufud** at 51 Doebelnsgatan (phone 32-07-54), is ideal for small groups or large families, to whom owner Sassa Dorff (perfect English) offers special rates if they are readers of this book: 400 kronor ($50) for a room for four, 600 kronor ($75) for two connecting rooms with six beds. She'll also house backpackers possessing their own sleeping bags, space available, at the special rate (again for readers of this book only) of 70 kronor ($8.75) per night. What's the catch? There is none. And these are not dorm-style rooms, cots lined up as in a barracks, but comfortably furnished, airy and attractive bed chambers, whose rental will also entitle you to free additional cots for small children, free showers, free use of the semi-automatic washing machine, and free use of kitchen facilities (with large freezer). Mrs. Dorff is one of those remarkable European hostesses who, time permitting, will drive you free in her own private car, to the Milles Garden, City Hall and Drottningholm Court Theater, provided that you pay the cost of gasoline for the 30-mile trip. Why? Because, she explains, these three attractions are not properly covered on the standard sightseeing tours. Wait until you hear her expertly delivered descriptions!

On Södermalm

Just south of Gamla Stan on the island of Södermalm (where the Katarina Elevator is situated), you'll find an increasingly popular Stockholm choice, highly suitable for people who don't mind staying a bit out of the center for considerable savings in price. The 40-room **"Anno 1647"** Hotel, Mariagränd 3 (phone 44-04-80), opened in 1968, consists of two buildings dating back to the 17th century which have been completely renovated. Rooms are small, all with telephone and some with TV. Most have sinks only, but showers are free. The hotel itself is in a back alley, but the preferred rooms overlook Stockholm and offer a spectacular view. Singles cost 125 to 260 kronor ($15.62 to $32.50), twins 225 to 350 kronor ($28.12 to $43.75), triples (suites) 450 kronor ($56.25), and a super buffet breakfast is included. The subway stop is Slussen.

And Elsewhere

Hotel Hospits Elim at 25 Gamla Brogatan (off Vasagatan), about a five-minute walk from the Central Station (phone: 11-29-36), is a 27-room pension with interiors in Scandinavian decor featuring colorful rugs and potted plants—a homey, spotless lodging where singles are 175 kronor ($21.87), doubles 250 kronor ($31.25), breakfast 15 kronor, and showers are free.

Hotel Maria, at 38 St. Eriksgatan (phone 51-99-63), is a real bargain in expensive Stockholm, charging 180 kronor ($22.50) for singles, only 240 kronor ($30) for doubles or twins, 300 kronor ($37.50) for triples, 420 kronor ($52.50) for quads, including a rather remarkable buffet breakfast of cheese, sausages, rolls, corn flakes and pickled herring, with free use of showers. For this, you'll receive a room carpeted wall-to-wall, with modern furniture, and access to a TV lounge and washing machine. Reception is on the fifth floor, reached by elevator, where you'll meet a young, English-speaking couple, managers of the Maria, whose motto is "our guest is king." From the Central Station, take the subway (T-bana) to Fridhelm-splan (two stops); the hotel is near the subway exit in a modern building housing the St. Erik department store.

Stockholm's "Best Deal"—A $7.50 Summer Tourist Hostel

Nine months a year, from September through May, Stockholm's **Hostel Frescati**, 13 Professorsslingan (phone 15-79-96 or 15-50-90), is used exclusively by students of Stockholm's several universities. Three months a year, from June 1 to August 31, it becomes the best deal in town by renting its 166 twin and 12 triple rooms—all adequately furnished, with private shower and w.c.—to any room-seeking tourist, young or old, male or female, for only 60 kronor ($7.50) per bed per night, plus 25 kronor for breakfast, 36 kronor for main meals. The red-brick complex, which also houses a supermarket, various shops, and laundromat, imposes no curfew and is easily reached from the Central Station by T-bana to the Universitetet stop (6 kronor, four stops), changing there to bus 151; the T-bana ticket is valid also for the bus.

THE DELUXE DORMS: In summer only, you can also consider staying at one of the modern, new student hotels maintained by the University of Stockholm, which are open in summer to tourists of all ages. These are, of course, "dormitories"—but only in the sense that they are maintained on university grounds. They offer beautiful, modern, private rooms, not bunks; all the rooms are equipped with private toilet and most with shower, which makes them a trifle expensive, but still within reasonable limits. Each "dormitory" is also endowed with huge lounges and breakfast rooms, and each becomes a sort of international community in summer months.

Largest of these is the **Hotel Jerum**, Studentbacken 21 (phone 63-53-80), whose top rates for summer, 1985, will be 190 kronor ($23.75) for a single with private shower, 240 kronor ($30) for a similarly equipped double, breakfast included. It's open from June 1 until August 31 and is operated by hard-working students, who provide Waldorf-like service. To reach the hotel, simply take the subway to the Gärdet station, four minutes from center city. And to make advance reservations, write to **S.S.R.S.-Hotelservice**, Box 5903, Stockholm, 11489.

The second of the student hotels—again accepting tourists of all ages—is the equally modernistic **Domus**, 1 Körbärsvägen (phone 16-01-95), open all year. Rates here are higher: 280 kronor ($35) for singles with private bath, 330 kronor ($41.25) for doubles with private bath, with breakfast included. Underground #15 (Technical High School stop) links you to the heart of town.

HOSTELS AND DORMS: The hostel situation in Stockholm has its pluses and minuses. On the plus side, most hostels in the city are open to people of all ages and to families, and hostel cards are rarely required. On the minus side, many hostels—like the amazing hostel-ship **Af Chapman**—are fully booked months in advance and it's chancy to wait until you reach the city to do something about getting hostel space. The following prices are for ordinary tourists—members of youth hostel organizations are sometimes charged less.

The Amazing Af Chapman

For life in Stockholm on a starvation budget, let us first introduce you to the **Af Chapman,** a three-masted sailing ship and the most unusual youth hostel in the world. Years ago Af Chapman was a training ship for officer candidates of the Swedish navy. When the navy tired of the Af Chapman and announced it would scrap it, an idea came to the brilliant chief of the Stockholm Tourist Office. He bought the Af Chapman for exactly 5,000 kronor, moored it to a dock on the centrally located island of Skeppsholmen, and turned it into a youth hostel (which will also take families). There it has remained ever since—a fixture of the city to such an extent that all the maps of Stockholm now contain little drawings of the Af Chapman.

You can spot the Af Chapman from the verandah of the plush Grand Hotel (what a contrast!), and you can also easily walk to the dock from the Grand. There you'll board a real-life massive sailing ship—straight from an Errol Flynn movie—with crow's nests, portholes, towering masts, and sea gulls circling above. It's open from January 15 till December 15, charges exactly 57 kronor ($7.12) for a bunk (45 kronor, $5.63, if you're a card-carrying Youth Hostel member) and is so popular that it imposes a maximum stay of five nights. It has a phone number too: 10-37-15 or 20-57-05, and a female captain, Mrs. Birgit Meliha.

Incidentally, members of the public can visit the Af Chapman even if they don't plan to stay there. Hope and I recently did. And as we strolled on the weather-beaten deck, the ship's bells sounded!

More Hostels and Hostel Ships

Overflow from the Af Chapman is accommodated 100 yards away at a brand new (1983), 140-bed hostel called the **Vandrarhem,** at Handverkarhuset (phone 20-25-06) on Skeppsholmen, where, surprisingly, you'll need an official youth hostel card. Open all year, except from December 20 to January 10, it charges only 50 kronor ($6.25) per night for a bed in sparklingly new, beautifully furnished rooms with two to four beds apiece. Special charges: 22 kronor ($2.75) for breakfast, a one-time payment of 15 kronor ($1.88) for paper pillowcase and two sheets, 5 kronor (62¢) for towels. But showers are free. From the Central Station, take bus 59 to the Karl XII Torg, from which the hostel—a yellow, three-story building—is a short walk.

A former Swedish Navy marine chart survey ship called the **Gustaf Af Klint,** at Skepsbron quai, near Slussen, a ten-minute walk over the Central Bridge from the main railroad station, has now been converted into Stockholm's second floating hostel. In 1985, it will be offering 11 cabins with four bunks apiece, at 85 kronor ($10.62) per person per night, plus 26 kronor for an optional breakfast that includes an egg (served in the mess hall!). Midnight curfew; free showers; free use of a tiny sauna as well as free parking in front; and phone the young manager, Kaj Engdahl, well in advance (40-40-77 or 40-40-78), as there are already a great many advance bookings.

If neither ship can take you, then try alternative accommodations at the unusual 260-bed **Zinken** at 2 Pipmakargränd (phone 68-57-86). Seven lemon-yellow bungalow-type houses make up this 100-room youth and student hotel, where single and double rooms (no dorms) cost 55 kronor ($6.87) per person per night, plus 17 kronor for bedding and linens, while breakfast is 20 kronor extra, and showers, cooking facilities and use of the washing machine, are free. Off-season, rates are considerably lower in this congenial spot where guests seem to mingle and have a good time. Take subway 13, 14 or 15 to Hornstull, the fourth stop after the Central Railway Station and four stops after Gamla Stan. Leave at the exit marked Högalidsparken, cross the street, enter the pedestrian tunnel on the opposite end, go down the stairs on your right to Drakenbergsgatan. Then take the street to the left, walk to the end, go through the passage, turn to the right (where the rocks are), and you're at the Zinken.

And finally there's the **Columbus,** a privately owned hostel at 11 Tjärhovsgatan (phone 44-17-17), less than 250 yards from the Medborgarplatsen subway stop, where four-bedded rooms (mainly) rent for only 50 kronor ($6.25) per bed per night, free showers included. With its cooking and laundry facilities thrown in, its English-speaking managers, Robert Carlsson and Helena Hyvarinen, this is a top choice for you.

SUB-STARVATION BUDGET: A last resort. Although their facility is officially available only to persons traveling with car and tent, the management of the **Sätra,** an unusually scenic and well-equipped camping site located seven miles southwest of Stockholm, will occasionally accept up to six backpacker-type tourists, whom they permit to sleep in the locker room of the sauna for only 20 kronor ($2.50) per person. You also get to use the sauna. Considering the high costs of Stockholm, and the fact that summer days occur when every Stockholm hostel and ship is completely booked, I mention the possibility, but with some trepidation. From the Central Station, take subway 13 or 15 to the Bredäng stop (12 kronor, 20 minutes) and walk 15 minutes up the marked road to the camping entrance; nearby is one of the free sand beaches of Lake Mälaren. But always phone—97-70-71 —first, asking to speak with Yngre Karlsson, the friendly manager. Everyone there speaks fluent English.

READERS' ROOMS SELECTIONS: "We strongly recommend the 28-bed **Bema Hotel,** Upplandsgatan 13 (phone 10-23-81), whose proprietor speaks excellent English, helped with maps, etc. The charge for a single with hot and cold water in the room and a hall bath was 165 kronor ($20.62), 250 kronor ($31.25) double, 25 kronor per person for breakfast, nothing for showers. That is not at all bad by Swedish standards. Spotlessly clean, quiet and convenient to downtown and buses" (John G. Sindorf, Palmer, Alaska; note by AF: Take bus 59 from the Central Station and get off at the third stop called Tengnerlunden, or walk there in 15 minutes). . . . "The home of **Ms. Stina Lindström,** at 39 Danavägen in Bromma (phone 37-16-08), is a 25-minute ride on the Tunnelbana to Islandstorget, a pleasant, leafy suburb. She is a charming, elderly lady who made us feel welcome in her home, where she lets four rooms at a charge of only 160 kronor ($20) per double room, not including breakfast (which you make yourself in the kitchen). A 72-hour Tourist Ticket cost us 55 kronor each and is a definite money-saver for anyone staying in the suburbs. We felt we were extremely lucky to find Mrs. Lindström in high-priced Stockholm" (Josephine Addison, Tasmania, Australia).

4. Meals

Eating out in this city can be costly indeed. Count on a minimum of $4 for a light meal, $6.50 to $8 for a full dinner, and $13 for the "Big Splurge."

To keep within the bounds of even these generous allowances, study each menu carefully and try to choose from the least expensive main dishes offered, adding a non-alcoholic beverage and a low-cost dessert. As in many other European countries, it is often cheaper to have your main meal at lunchtime, when many restaurants offer an inexpensive price-fixed menu. Then eat a lighter supper at night in a self-service restaurant where you'll save the service charge. But having warned you, don't let us scare you. It is not necessary, when in Stockholm, to go either hungry or broke. Rather, you can keep your food costs cut to the bare minimum by reading and following these few simple tips.

1. EAT IN THE SPAGHETTI HOUSES: Italian immigrants to Sweden provide the city's tastiest, least expensive meals. Reason: they tend to work in family units, all members waiting on tables, washing the dishes, toiling long hours, and thus keeping costs down. A prime example is the 15-table **Leopardo** (also called the "Spaghetti House"), at 9 Riddargatan, corner of Nybrogatan, adjoining the Nybroplan-Square. Here the particular bargain is a 27 kronor ($3.37, service included) "snabblunch" served from 10:30 a.m. to 3:30 p.m., weekdays. It consists of a changing daily menu (such as tuna salad appetizer, followed by beef cutlet with boiled potato or risotto con carne, accompanied by bread, butter, milk or coffee—all included in the 27 kronor price! Weekends the emphasis shifts to costlier spaghetti dishes—12 different varieties—costing from 24 kronor apiece, ladled onto your plate from huge, steaming, copper pots. While the value isn't quite the same as the phenomenal "snabblunch," it's nevertheless quite a value for Stockholm. Closed Sundays.

Other recommended "spaghetti houses": **Pizzeria Bella Napoli** at 41 Odengatan, serving a large variety of spaghetti and pizza dishes for 29 kronor ($3.62), and open seven days a week until midnight.

The more centrally located **Lilla Bussola,** at 65 Master Samuelsgatan, is only a few steps from the central station. Pizzas, spaghetti, lasagne al forno, canelloni and risottos are 28 kronor ($3.50), and a delicious plate of tagliatelle boscailoa (green noodles with a ham-tomato-mushroom sauce) is 27 kronor ($3.37).

The one I like best of all, always crowded with Swedes fascinated by the Italian atmosphere and tasty food: **Osteria il Pozzo,** 16 Skeppergatan, near Östermalmstorg, open daily except Saturdays until 11 p.m., and serving seven daily platters for 25 to 34 kronor ($3.12 to $4.25). The friendly style and service of il Pozzo is not well reflected by the sign over the cash register which says (in Italian): "Credit is given only to clients over 90 accompanied by their parents."

2. EAT IN THE SELF-SERVICE "BARS": And don't think we're sending you into taverns; the Swedish word "bar," appearing alone or as the suffix of a word, refers to a cafeteria-type establishment where food is picked up by the diner either from a serving line or at a window opening to the kitchen where meals are prepared. Among the largest bars in Stockholm (although this one, and several others, don't actually use the word) is the **Clock,** 22 Sergelgatan, in the heart of the Hötorget skyscraper development, which serves soup and bread for 10 kronor ($1.25), hamburgers for 9 kronor ($1.12), french fries for 6 kronor (75¢). Other **Clocks** are at 56 Götagatan, next to the Medborgarpladsen T-bana stop (largest branch of the chain, with a separate section for non-smokers) and at 50 Kungsgatan, the latter again in the Hötorget skyscraper development. . . . This time in the Kunstradgarden—the central city park where free concerts are held on summer days—another bar is the similarly priced **7 Sekel Cafeteria** (across the street from the NK Department Store), where you can dine indoors in what looks like a botanical garden, or outdoors at one of the white tables right in front of a beautiful fountain. Daily platters (such as Swedish meatballs with potatoes, beetroot and salad) 27 kronor, a banana split 18 kronor, coffee 9 kronor.

Other recommended and popular bars include the **Olo** at 7 Olofsgatan, corner of Tunnelgatan in the Hötorget area; big hot platters for 22 to 28 kronor ($2.75 to $3.50), including bread, butter and a glass of milk. . . . **Carmen** at 22 Ostgötagatan, near Slussen, open weekdays only, when a spicy, filling meat-and-vegetable stew is sold there for only 30 kronor ($3.75). . . . **Oasen,** inside the Central Railway Station on its street level and open seven days a week until midnight, serving all manner of sandwiches, soups and drinks, as well as packed lunches for the onward trip by rail from this very station—the latter cost from 25 to 40 kronor.

Bars are scattered throughout the city—look for the magic three letters.

More "Bars" in Hötorget City

A word about the site of the Clock mentioned above: **Hötorget City** (also called Hötorgcity) is a project in the center of town that somewhat resembles our Rockefeller Center, except that it's years more modern. You'll spot the five gleaming white skyscrapers of the Hötorget (Haymarket) from almost any point in the city, but the "Star Wars" feeling they cause is most intensely felt on the elevated sidewalk on the plaza in front of the buildings, where several other inexpensive restaurants are located. To reach the plaza, walk up Kungsgatan until you see a big square on your left where the Concert Hall of Stockholm stands. That's the Hötorget. Turn left, walking in front of the Concert Hall (with its unusual Carl Milles statues), and you'll come to the Sergelgatan, with its new underground passage and shopping center and enormous fountain basin, illuminated at night by multicolored lights. A meal in one of the many "bars" (self-service cafeterias) in this area will make you think you're in an ultra-advanced civilization, full of people sprouting antennas from their heads—a literal world of tomorrow.

3. EAT IN THE DEPARTMENT STORE CAFETERIAS: The cheapest
and best of these is the Tobias Restaurangen (Tobias Restaurant) of the **Mauritz Department Store** at 14 Sergelstorg next to the skyscrapers of the Hötorget. Here a complete special lunch is 32 kronor ($4), most other hot plates are only 15 to 25 kronor, and—glory be—they're all openly displayed so that you can simply point to what you want. Or you can construct a massive salad bowl, do-it-yourself style, for 28 kronor ($3.50).

Higher in price is the second-floor cafeteria (walk through the children's section to find it) of **Ahlens** (corner of Klarabergsgatan and Drottninggatan), near the railroad station, where some main courses are 30 kronor ($3.75), and the posted menus are translated (thankfully) into English. (Incidentally, the sub-basement of Ahlens is one of the world's largest and most elegant grocery stores, and free samples are sometimes offered; it's also open every day including Sunday until 8 p.m. and sells a variety of ready-made picnic items—entrance is from T-Centralen subway station). You can skip the restaurant of the famous **P.U.B.** department store (a cooperative owned by its customers), and do the same at **NK.** While both serve weekday "snabb" (quick) lunches of two courses and milk, they charge an overly high 35 to 38 kronor for them.

4. EAT SMORGASBORD FOR BRUNCH OR LUNCH: Fill up once a day on an all-you-can-eat feast of Swedish specialties, and you can taper off eating for the rest of the day with minor snacks. If you like your big meal in the morning, get over to the **Centralens Restaurang** in the railroad station between 6:30 and 9:30 a.m., 8 to 10:30 a.m. on Sundays, where you can dive into a smorgasbord breakfast: juice, cereal, anchovies, jams, coffee, tea, chocolate milk, buttermilk, bread, rolls, eggs, smoked sausage and cheese—and all the servings you have the nerve to go back for!—at the reasonable price of 32 kronor ($4). The **Pub,** next door to the Centralens Restaurang, serves a "snabb lunch" (hot dish, salad buffet, coffee or milk) for 30 kronor ($3.75), including service, from 11 a.m. to 2 p.m., Monday through Friday. For not much more, you can have an all-you-can-eat lunch buffet at the **Ortagarden Restaurant,** at 31 Nybrogatan, near Oestermalmstorg, on the second floor of a public food market hall: for 38 kronor ($4.75) you can have hot soup, a choice of 25 salads, and four hot dishes, plus bread and butter, sitting on easy-chairs at large oval and round tables, under crystal chandeliers, in two large dining rooms. Beverages are extra, and usually average 85¢ for coffee, tea, milk, light beer and juices. Open Monday to Friday from 10:30 a.m. to 7 p.m. If you plan to lunch here, get there before 11:30 a.m.—you may not find seats later.

5. THE BEST OF THE BUDGET RESTAURANTS: The heavily patronized **Concorde Cafeteria** in the basement of the Central Station T-bana Station, Vasagatan entrance (underneath the Hotel Continental), charges only 28 kronor ($3.50) for a two-course "snabb" (quick) lunch of several varieties, of which one is always soup, followed by spaghetti with meat balls, accompanied by bread, butter, milk or coffee. By buying ten meal tickets at a time, for a total of 260 kronor, you can reduce the price per meal to $3.25—cheapest "snabb lunch" in town. The cafeteria is open daily until 7:30 p.m.

Stockholm's vegetarian restaurant—always a good bet for inexpensive eating—is **Grona Linjen,** at 10 Master Samuelsgatan (second floor), near the Norrmalmstorg. Here, the brightly garnished plates are mostly 28 kronor, soup and dessert are each 12 to 18 kronor, and the restaurant itself is a large, bright and airy place that sports a traditional green porcelain stove, of the sort you normally see at folk museums in Sweden. Open weekdays from 10:45 a.m. to 4 p.m. . . . To the left of the entrance to the Wasa ship exhibition (see farther on), the unusual, self-service **Cafe Bla Porten,** at 64 Djurgaresvägen, features salad dishes which you choose and mix yourself, and which range in price from 22 to 38 kronor, depending on the items you select. In a setting like that of a modern art gallery (abstract expressionist works adorn the walls), this is a fine place to eat either before or after visiting nearby Skansen or Gröna Lund. Open weekdays until 9 p.m., weekends until 5 p.m. . . . . The ground-floor level of the **Restaurant Pilen** at 12A Bryggargatan, two blocks from the railroad station, serves traditionally Swedish dishes in an informal atmosphere. Stop by on weekdays for the "Snabb-Lunch," a hot plate with bread, butter, milk or coffee, 28 kronor ($3.50). It's served from 11 a.m. to 2:30 p.m. on weekdays. Stop by during "Happy Hours"—between 3:30 p.m. and 7—and you'll obtain the same dishes at a considerable discount. The "Happy Hours" tradition is maintained by other Stockholm restaurants, too; watch for the signs.

Some Final Food Tips

The word "Korv" that you've been seeing on menus and signs all over town, means "sausage"—always a cheap, tasty dish. . . . A late night's snack? On the Norrmalmstorg side of the City Garden Park (Kungstradgarden), you'll find lines of late-night stands, in summer, serving waffles, fruit, hot sausages. . . . Swedish meatballs? They're called *Kottbullar* here, and are always marvelous. . . . The tastiest Swedish specialties? Try: blood pudding with lingonberries (blodpudding, lingonsylt), stuffed cabbage (kåldomar), delicious thick pea soup (artsoppa), and one dish which sounds like a children's game—pytt-i-panna—but turns out to be a simple but delicious hash. . . . On Thursday, it's traditional to eat pea soup followed by pancakes, washed down with hot punch. "When in Sweden . . . !"

And now, with rooms and meals behind us, we begin our tour of Stockholm.

5. Things to Do, Places to See

For some time now, Stockholm has maintained an entire complex of offices solely to service visitors who want to know "where to go and what to do." Called **Sverigehuset** (Sweden House), it is staffed by the Tourist Office of Stockholm and houses a **Tourist Center** for questions and aid, and the offices of the **Sweden at Home** program, through which you can meet and visit with a Swedish family in their home. Sweden House is located at Kungsträdgardan, opposite the NK Department Store. Stop by at least once to collect their free handouts on what's going on in town or to book any of the sightseeing tours offered in Stockholm (which include a full-day, archipelago fishing trip on a professional trawler, weekends only, from May to September). The staff is multilingual. And for 50 kronor ($6.25), you can purchase the **Stockholmskortet,** or **Key to Stockholm Card,** valid for 24 hours, which entitles you to use boats, buses and Tunnelbana (outskirts included), free admission to most of the museums and amusement parks, and various other discounts at restaurants and department stores. It can save you 500 kronor, or $62.50, if you take advantage of all the bargains offered. Cards valid 48 hours cost 80 kronor, 72 hours 120 kronor, 96 hours 160 kronor. With the card, you'll receive a special folder, containing a map of Stockholm and surroundings, and listing all the sights the Key will open to you free.

In addition to these services, Stockholm makes its English-speaking guests feel welcome in a variety of ways. Every weekday afternoon in summer at 6 p.m., the Stockholm radio station broadcasts an English-language *Calling All Tourists* program, announcing the events and activities scheduled in Stockholm that evening and following day. If you miss it simply dial 22-18-40, and an English-speaking "Miss Tourist" will give you recorded information on the day's events. Every day, there's an English news round-up in the Swedish papers. And special dances are always announced in both languages in the entertainment sections of the papers. Yet, despite all Sweden's efforts to let us know that we are welcome, there is probably no program that warms a tourist so totally as that which invites you to spend an evening with a Swedish family at home.

SWEDEN AT HOME: To apply for the "Sweden at Home" program, you must go in person to the Tourist Center at Sweden House (Kungsträdgartan) and fill out a form specifying your age, profession, hobbies and interests. The office will then contact a suitable host family who will invite you for a simple afternoon or evening of conversation. There are no rules as to age or sex on this program, and any interested visitor is welcome to apply. Nor is there any cost, of course, but it is customary to bring a little house gift—flowers, chocolates, a book or an attractive glass of after-dinner mints. Your hosts will speak fluent English and are usually as interested in talking about your country as you are about theirs. The program emphasizes that hosts cannot be expected to provide accommodation. My personal recommendation is to give it a try; Swedes seem somewhat standoffish and over-polite in public, but they relax and warm up quickly in the familiar setting of their own living-rooms.

TOURS: The cheapest, and, in some ways, most useful tour of Stockholm, is the 27 kronor, one-hour, *non-stop* "mini" tour, which leaves from the Karl XII-Torg, near the Opera House (you'll see signs and a ticket booth) at 11 a.m., noon, 2 and 3 p.m., daily from mid-June to mid-August. Despite its short duration, it's an amazingly far-ranging jaunt that passes through the most important sections of the town, and includes a short stop at **Fjällgatan,** where you'll enjoy a panoramic view of Stockholm.

I'd follow the city tour with a one-hour canal tour (it's called the **Royal Canal Tour),** which leaves every hour in summer from 10:30 a.m. to 7:30 p.m., from a dock (the *Strömkajen*) diagonally in front of the plush Grand Hotel (you ought to take this occasion to wander through the lobby of the Grand, simply to see old-time European elegance). But don't mistake this sightseeing boat for the larger archipelago boats (about which more later) moored directly in front of the Grand. The seagoing tour costs only 27 kronor, heads through the harbor of the city and around the Deer Garden, past the breathtaking "Embassy Row" of Stockholm, and under the bridges that vault over Mälaren Lake. Don't confuse this excursion with the more leisurely and costly (40 kronor) **Under the Bridges** canal ride offered by most sightseeing companies, which necessarily overlaps with portions of the shorter tour.

Then, if you wish an intensive escorted tour of the city (my suggestion is that you do it yourself, via 6 kronor subway rides and free or 10-kronor admission to the city's various museums and sights), you can consider the normal commercial offerings of the various sightseeing companies whose buses leave from a little ticket booth near the Royal Opera House at the Karl XII Torg. They offer three basic tours:

City Tour A, which costs 75 kronor ($9.37) for half a day, and leaves daily at 9:30 a.m., between March 1 and November 28, goes to the Royal Palace for a guided inside visit, then to the Riddarholm Church (burial place of the Swedish kings), and finally to the Old City.

City Tour B sets out at 1:30 p.m., also costs 75 kronor ($9.37), visits the Carl Milles Sculpture Garden, the City Hall (an inside visit), passes by the stately embassies of Stockholm, and onto the "Deer Garden" island.

On both these tours, the 75-kronor price includes admission charges to the various parks and exhibits, which lowers the relative cost of the tours somewhat.

Finally a trip through the **Archipelago of Stockholm**—the fantastic complex of over 24,000 islands leading out to the Baltic—is an absolute must at some point in your Stockholm stay. All the ships leave from in front of the Grand Hotel, make varying trips, the cheapest of which is a three-hour round-trip to Vaxholm for 60 kronor. But to do this one right, a five-hour round-trip—such as the one to Gustavsberg (75 kronor, and operated end of June to end of August only)—is more highly recommended. There's a restaurant on board, and the trip makes a fine outing. Check the schedules carefully.

SKANSEN: While organized tours are handy if you're cramped for time, as always in this book we'd suggest that you can save more money and see the city more thoroughly by touring on your own, possibly with a three-day tourist pass in hand for unlimited transportation.

For a trip to the past, schedule one of your early visits to this unique open-air "museum," located on the Djurgarden—which itself is a vast island-park. To Skansen, the Swedes have moved more than 150 of the ancient farmhouses and other buildings that once were scattered all over Sweden. Their purpose was to preserve and maintain these buildings as a heritage for the nation—a re-creation of what Sweden was like hundreds of years ago. You'll want to spend a full afternoon wandering over Skansen's peaceful grounds, riding in the little "children's" electric train (5 kronor) that goes past the chief buildings, gazing into the enclosures without bars where polar bears and oxen are kept, watching demonstrations of glass blowing, cheese-making, butter-churning and basketry. It's like no other park or museum in the world, with a wonderful *au naturel* quality about it, and while the admission charge is 14 kronor for adults, 4 kronor for children, the attractions are enough to keep you fascinated for hours.

To get to Skansen, take bus 44 to 47, which goes directly there (6 kronor per person), or take the seagoing ferry from the Slussen or the Nybroplan, which charges 7 kronor for the ride. But don't leave too late in the afternoon; the buildings at Skansen close at 5 p.m., although the park itself stays open until 11:30 p.m.

When dinnertime approaches, you can have a big-splurge meal without leaving Skansen at the famous but expensive **Solliden Restaurant,** directly in front of which is a large bandstand where folk dances and Swedish-language operas are performed on weekend evenings, free. The old-fashioned smorgasbord is 70 kronor ($8.75); ordering à la carte it's easy to spend $27 and up. . . . For a cheaper meal, you can try the **Värdhuset Cafeteria** at the rear side of the Restaurant Solliden building, where daily platters are 28 kronor ($3.50) and up. . . . Even cheaper selections are available at the numerous food stands in the old farmhouses (the ones with grass and flowers on their roofs) about a minute's walk from the cafeteria. There, hot pancakes—called "wafflors"—are 8 kronor ($1), sausages same price, and there are wooden benches and tables to sit at.

People-Watching

In the area around Skansen, you'll soon discover why the women of Sweden have become so legendary for their looks. Imagine, if you will, a number of dance halls where the women look like young versions of Ingrid Bergman, Greta Garbo, Anita Ekberg—this is the spot to witness that phenomenon.

The younger dance-seeking crowd goes to an open-air dancing area at the top of Skansen Hill. You enter through the main Skansen gate (fee is 15 kronor), take the escalator and then walk a few minutes until you see the dancing area, near the church on top of the hill. Here, Wednesday through Sunday evenings, in summer, large groups of young people take part in folk and similar dances. If you're in that age group, you might watch for a while to learn how it's done, then try for yourself.

Near Skansen, and still on the Djurgarden, is the huge amusement park of Stockholm, called **Gröna Lund,** and sometimes also referred to as the **Tivoli.** Open from 2 p.m. Monday to Saturday and from noon on Sunday, the admission charge is 15 kronor (5 kronor for children) throughout the day. As you walk in, you'll see two additional disco-style dance areas, where recently, within a period of six minutes, Hope and I spotted four stunners who would make Bo Derek look plain. Entrance fee of 15 kronor, with all drinks priced at 12 kronor thereafter.

THE WASA: The eeriest and most thrilling visit in Stockholm is to the **Wasa Museum** *(Wasavarvet),* on the Djurgarden, which houses the warship *Wasa,* resurrected from the bottom of Stockholm's harbor in 1961 after it had lain there for over 300 years! It has now rightfully become the most-visited tourist attraction in all of Scandinavia.

The history of the *Wasa* is a fascinating one. For years ocean archaeologists had hoped to recover one of the famous wooden warships of history, whose locations, on the ocean's floor, are generally well known. Anders Franzen, of Stockholm, surmised that such ships would still exist only in areas where the salt content of the water was insufficient to permit wood-devouring sea worms to exist. Subsequently, he learned that the harbor of Stockholm was one such place, and after searching through ancient naval archives, he discovered that a Swedish warship—the *Wasa*— had sunk in the Stockholm harbor, in 1628, just as it was leaving port on its maiden cruise.

Franzen proceeded to spend many summers crisscrossing the harbor of Stockholm in a one-man motorboat, dropping lines to dredge up objects from the deep. In 1956, he pulled up a wedge of centuries-old wood, and divers soon confirmed that he had found the *Wasa,* buried almost to the top of its hull in the muds below, and perfectly preserved! It took five years to raise the ship, until, on a thrilling day in April of 1961, with an enormous crowd headed by the King of Sweden in attendance, the *Wasa* broke surface. Fittingly, the first objects to appear were the sculpted figures of two Swedish sailors.

Because the *Wasa* would crumble if it were ever to dry out, it has been placed in a specially constructed museum where humidity is kept under constant control.

To see this, take bus 47 from Nybroplan, and ask the conductor to stop near the Wasa Museum, which is only a few hundred feet from the Gröna Lund amusement park. Entrance is 8 kronor ($1) for adults, 4 kronor for students with student identification, 2 kronor for children, and the building is open from 9:30 a.m. to 7 p.m. in July and August, 10 a.m. to 5 p.m. during the other ten months. There's a Technicolor movie about the raising of the Wasa which you ought to see before you view the ship, and there's a beautiful oakwood cafeteria just a few feet away. Don't miss it!

CITY HALL: William Butler Yeats said of Stockholm's **City Hall** that "no architectural work comparable to it has been accomplished since the Italian cities felt the excitement of the Renaissance." As you approach this unusual building, (it's built with 2 million red bricks), particularly as you stand within its inner court, you may agree. Its unique style is strikingly Scandinavian and utterly indigenous to its surroundings. You'll first enter into the famous "Blue Hall" which was originally meant to be painted blue, but remained red in motif when the architect decided not to paint over the bricks. From here, at the top of the stairs, is the Golden Hall, where the Nobel Prize Dinners are held each year. At the end of the Golden Hall, the Room of the 3 Crowns, and, elsewhere, the impressive legislative chamber, whose ceiling is decorated as in a Viking home. Multilingual guided tours of City Hall *(Stadshuset)* are operated weekdays at 10 a.m. sharp, Sundays at 10 and noon, costing 5 kronor on weekdays and at noon on Sunday. You can also make a non-guided visit to the Tower daily in summer from 11 a.m. to 3 p.m. for 5 kronor. Visitors are not permitted to tour the City Hall without a guide.

THE MILLES GARDEN: The great Swedish sculptor, Carl Milles (1875-1955), who created statues throughout the world, came home to Stockholm in 1906 to spend most of the last years of his life designing and building the **Milles Garden** on a hill on the island of Lidingo; it overlooks all of Stockholm. The resulting works, as you'll immediately see, are a sharp departure from every style of sculpture heretofore known, and are extremely moving in the fervor of their message. From the grounds of Milles' home, walk down the long flight of stairs into the gravel garden where the most exciting statues are placed. The Garden is open every day from May 1 through October 15 from 10 a.m. to 5 p.m. (in June and July on Tuesday and Friday evenings 7 to 9 p.m. as well), and admission is 10 kronor ($1.25). To get there, take subway line 13 or 14 to Ropsten (cost is 6 kronor from most points in town), then pick up the 221 bus from Ropsten to the gardens (6 kronor). To return to town, walk around the corner from the entrance to the gardens to the modern Foresta Hotel (expensive) where you'll see a stop for the bus to Ropsten.

From Ropsten, the Tunnelbana (subway) will bring you back into town—an easy trip.

STREAMLINED SUBURBS: Farsta, **Skärholmen** and **Vallingby** are the names of three suburbs of Stockholm constructed entirely within the last few decades (Vallingby dates back to 1954, Skärholmen was opened in 1968), according to rigid architectural plans laid down by Sweden's top city planners. They're entirely modern cities with futuristic buildings that look as though they were lifted from a World's Fair. To visit them, simply take the Tunnelbana to the stop of the suburb's name (each one is toward the end of a different line), and wander through each little city at your own pace.

THE STEAM BATHS: Even more so than in Denmark and Norway, the Swedes go in heavily for a combination of steam baths, sauna, showers, massages, and frigid immersions that's supposed to add ten years to your life. They claim, in Sweden, that two hours of sauna (here, it's sometimes also called *bastü*) equal eight hours of sleep—and that is, in fact, how a roistering Swede, who's been up until 4 a.m., revives himself to begin work the next day. I tried it on our last trip to Stockholm—and everything they say is true!

There's a steam bath in Stockholm for every purse. The most "luxurious" of the lot is the **Sturebadet,** on Sturegatan (#4) right at the Stureplan (the Sture Square), where a payment of 45 kronor will get you everything they have to offer except a sun-lamp treatment and a massage (it's 65 kronor for the entire works). Actually, however, you can go in for a quick swim and one steam room for only 20 kronor—even at the Sturebadet (which is open weekdays only). Slightly less expensive (10 to 15 kronor for a moderate treatment) are the **Kampementsbadet,** at Sandhamnsgatan in the Karlaplan area (take bus 41 to Osthammarsgatan), open weekdays from 8 a.m. to 7 p.m., on Saturday from 8 a.m. to noon; and the **Forsgrenska Badet** (closed in July), in the Civic House at Medborgarplatsen (take the T-bana to Medborgarplatsen), only 14 kronor for sauna and pool. Ask for either the *Herrbastu* (steam) or *Herrtuck* (dry heat) treatment at either.

One of the least expensive baths—and the spot where the young set gathers—is the **Vanadisbadet,** near the Domus Hotel at Vanadislunden, where there's also an enormous outdoor swimming pool. Take bus 52 or 515 to Vanadisvägan, and walk another five minutes; the sauna is free after you've paid 10 kronor for admission to the pool. **Erikdalsbadet,** near Skanstull, is even larger (two pools) and charges the same; take bus 48 or 54 to Skanstull.

WATER SPORTS, CYCLING AND ROLLER SKATING: For an afternoon of rowing, sailing and windsurfing on Lake Mälaren, which cuts into the heart of Stockholm, take the Tunnelbana to the Fridhemsplan stop, walk down the tree-lined Fridhemsgatan, cross the bridge over the highway and you'll be opposite a dock (called the Ralambshov). At the shore, rowboats, little sailboats and surfboards can be rented, for 20, 24 and 60 kronor ($2.50, $3 and $7.50), respectively. The rental operates from June to the end of August, usually from 9 a.m. to 4 p.m.; phone 43-13-13 for more information. The boat keepers can be found in the two green huts near the willow.

And right in the heart of the city, at the foot of Djurgardsbron, the bridge leading to the Deergarden, **Skepp and Hoj,** a rental company, leases (in summer only—May to first week in September) rowboats, canoes, bikes and roller skates. Rates for rowboats (maximum four persons) are 24 kronor ($3) the first hour, 16 kronor ($2) each following hour, 80 kronor ($10) per day, 250 kronor ($31.25) per week; canoes—same prices but maximum two persons; bikes 16, 8, 40 and 140 kronor ($2, $1, $5 and

$17.50), respectively, tandem 80 kronor ($10) per day; roller skates 16 kronor ($2) per hour, 8 kronor ($1) each consecutive hour and 40 kronor ($5) for a day. You'll need to leave your passport as the "deposit."

MUSEUMS: Here's a little-known fact about Stockholm: it has more museums than any European city other than London and Paris. Which ones to visit? Top priority goes to the **National Museum of Fine Arts,** the **Museum of Modern Art,** and the **Museum of Antiquities.** If you have time for only one, make it the Museum of Modern Art on the Skeppsholmen which is open every day from 11 a.m. to 9 p.m. for an admission charge of 10 kronor to the permanent collection. But now, here's Hope to go into more detail on Stockholm's best sights.

HOPE IN STOCKHOLM: "Maybe it's a personal quirk, but whenever I'm in Stockholm I always get a very 'resort town' feeling; and that's all the more astonishing because this is one of the most urbane and sophisticated of cities. Yet in the summer, when the sun is shining and people are strolling leisurely on the streets, with water everywhere, the air so crisp and clear, one's mood so tinglingly alive and healthy—where else could you be but at a spa? You'll catch this feeling at the places previously described by Arthur, but also—and in particular strength—at **Drottningholm Palace, Prins Eugens Waldemarsudde,** and **The Museum of Modern Art:**

Drottningholm

"Much of the excitement at Drottningholm Palace emanates from performances of opera, ballet and chamber music at the rococo **Court Theatre.** Built for Queen Lovisa Ulrika in 1766, this cream and blue auditorium with its painted-like-marble decorations (it's all plaster) is preserved exactly as it was the day it opened. In fact, it is probably the only place in the world where you can see an opera done just as it was in the 18th century: the settings, the stage effects, even most of the musical instruments, are the original ones (or from that time); the musicians and ushers wear powdered wigs; you may even find yourself sitting in the very chair that was once occupied by King Gustav III (Lovisa Ulrika's son), who wrote plays for this theatre and acted on its stage.

"If you're in Stockholm between May and September, make a special effort to see an opera at Drottningholm Palace Court Theatre. Performances begin at 8 p.m., tickets cost between 20 and 80 kronor ($2.50 and $10), and there are special Theatre Buses leaving from the Grand Hotel 45 minutes before curtain time (fare: 14 kronor). If you can't get tickets, then—during the day—at least see **The Court Theatre and Museum** (a collection of costumes, illustrations, and objects dealing with the history of European theatre in the 16th, 17th and 18th centuries, all located in the theatre). Also visit the French-inspired **Drottningholm Palace** (with its impressive sculptured gardens) and little **Chinese Pavilion.** Open any day in summer when the king is not in residence, from 11 a.m. to 4 p.m., Sundays from 1 to 4 (also during the months of April, September and October from 1 to 3 p.m. daily). There are guided tours (in English). Entrance fee to the Palace is 10 kronor, the Theatre Museum 10 kronor, and the Chinese Pavilion 10 kronor. The latter is located on the edge of the estate and is about a half-mile walk from the Palace. Known as the 'Queen's Play

House,' it's a charming little example of *chinoiserie,* which was so popular during the rococo period; Queen Lovisa Ulrika (for whom it was built between 1763 and 1769) was especially fond of this style.

"Drottningholm (literal translation is 'Queen's Island') is six miles west of Stockholm on an island in the Mälaren. To get there take the subway (T-bana) to Brommaplan, change to Mälarö-buses (all lines) for Drottningholm; in summer take the direct boat (50 minutes) from near City Hall.

Waldemarsudde

"Prins Eugen's Waldemarsudde, the former home of the 'Painter Prince' on Djurgarden, is in an idyllic setting—on the water, in the center of an enchanting green park, surrounded by beautiful landscaped gardens (which contain interesting pieces of sculpture). The Prince was a painter of some note (he did the murals in the Prince's Gallery at City Hall, and also the mural 'Rimfrost' in the Royal Foyer of the Dramatic Theatre, among others), and also a great collector of art. So he built a gallery connected to his home by a long underground passage to house his treasures, and bequeathed the lot to Sweden.

"The physical surroundings at Waldemarsudde are so luscious that you'll feel more as if you are going on a picnic than heading for a gallery. But an excellent selection of Scandinavian artists is displayed here, including works by Carl Milles, Anders Zorn, Ernst Josephson (don't miss his interesting portrait of Dr. Axel Munthe), and Edvard Munch. The 'Palace' itself, though quite modern, is elegantly decorated and, as per the Prince's instructions, it has remained practically untouched since his death. On the grounds you'll spot an Old Mill which is no longer working but contains industrial exhibitions that can be viewed in summer, and also 'Gamla Huset' (or Old House), which was the first house the prince lived in before his palace was built. On its first floor is a small museum of personal mementos—family photos, letters, early drawings, paint boxes and equipment, military swords, even his bowling ball and pins (the house is open in summer from noon to 5 p.m.). Fittingly enough, the romantic prince chose to be buried here in a grave of his own design (a simple stone plaque) in front of 'Gamla Huset,' overlooking the water at his beloved Waldemarsudde. To get to the grounds take bus 47, which practically stops at the front gate, or else simply walk (it's a pleasant stroll) from nearby Skansen. Waldemarsudde is open daily except Mondays, from 11 a.m. to 5 p.m. in summer, until 4 p.m. in winter, and may also be visited on Tuesday and Thursday evenings (7 to 9 p.m.) in summer; admission is 8 kronor.

Modern Art

"The Museum of Modern Art, on Skeppsholmen, was a major 'happening' years ago, mainly because of its display of the spectacular (and uniquely Swedish) sculpture-playland named 'She'—the brain-child and joint effort of Niki de Saint Phalle, Jean Tinguely and Per Olof Ultvedt. 'She' was tagged 'the biggest and best woman in the world' (82 feet long, 20 feet high and 30 feet wide), and was the one lady you got to know inside out. You entered the gigantic, colorfully decorated female (who was supine) through the womb (which caused some comment) and then discovered wit and amusement in every inside corner: a small cinema showing an early Garbo feature, a Coke bar inside one breast, a look-out point atop the navel, a slide, grinding machines, a lover's nest. I use the past tense because 'She,' who should have been a national monument, was later destroyed, and there's now only a book called 'She' to keep the memory green (15 kronor, on sale at the museum's bookshop). I still find it hard to believe that they really let 'She' go, but the Swedes will probably come up with something equally delightful to replace her, I mean 'she.' The permanent exhibit is also exceptional—in fact, it's regarded as one of the world's finest collections of 20th century art—with a broad selection of contemporary American artists (Andy Warhol, Roy Lichtenstein), together with dozens of famous cubist and surrealist paintings. Although the entrance charge is 15 kronor (free on Thursdays), a visit here is well worth it. The museum is open from 11 a.m. to 9 p.m. daily except Mondays throughout the year, and to get there you simply cross the Skeppsholmen Bridge, which is just opposite the National Museum (near the Grand Hotel), then walk past the church and the Museum of Far Eastern Antiquities until you spot a wild and jolly mobile by Alexander Calder, which stands directly in front of the Museum of Modern Art.

Some Other Sights

"The attractions remaining are of high caliber—any city would be proud to claim them—but for me they lack something of the air of gaiety and excitement so characteristic of the three major institutions described above. Still, if you have time, look in on the **Nationalmuseum,** near the Grand Hotel, which displays interesting decorative art from the Middle Ages to the present (some 25,000 items!), a number of very fine paintings—including a room full of Rembrandts and Rubens, some impressionists, Swedish art from all periods and, of course, a well-chosen exhibit of modern Scandinavian design (silver, jewelry, pottery, glass, rugs and furniture). Open Wednesday to Sunday from 10 a.m. to 4 p.m., also Tuesday from 10 a.m. to 9 p.m. Admission is a moderate 10 kronor.

"Also worth seeing is the vast **Nordic Museum** on Djurgarden, down the street from the Wasa Museum, displaying everything from soup to nuts on the development of Swedish culture from the 16th century to today—agriculture, fishing, folk art and handicrafts, textiles, costumes, furniture, even displays of table settings and food and drink. The entrance fee is 10 kronor (5 kronor for students). Hours are 10 a.m. to 4 p.m. weekdays, from noon to 5 p.m. Saturdays and Sundays (winters, closed Mondays). Take buses 47 or 44.

"Elsewhere the **Museum of National Antiquities** (Historiska Museet), 13 Narvavagen (corner of Linnegatan), is devoted to Sweden's history prior to the 16th century (stone and runic monuments, a Viking Room and Gold Treasury, medieval displays and Church Reliquaries, a Gothic Hall, a reconstructed Country Church, and the like). This is the principal museum in Sweden for studying the Viking Age, and it also contains the Royal Coin Cabinet. Open Tuesday to Sunday from 11 a.m. to 4 p.m.; admission is 15 kronor. The museum, incidentally, is within easy walking distance of the Karlaplan subway station and also the Nordic museum; after you cross the bridge, walk straight ahead on Narvavagen for about two blocks, until you come to the entrance at Narvavagen.

"For readers who feel uneasy unless they cover every Royal Palace, the **Stockholm Slott** (on the Slottsholmen Island in Gamla Stan; you'll see it from the Opera House) offers tours (every half hour) 10 a.m. to 1:30 p.m.

and Sunday at noon of the State Apartments, the Great Suite, and the Bernadotte Apartments, which are moderately interesting. The charge is 10 kronor for adults, 5 kronor for students, 5 for children, and everything is closed on Mondays. If you're willing to spend another krona, you can walk through the inner courtyard and visit the Hall of State where you'll see the silver throne that has been in use since Queen Christina's coronation in 1650, and the Chapel—that's on weekdays and Sundays from noon to 3 p.m. Changing of the Guard takes place in the courtyard, which is open to the public daily at noon in summer (1 on Sunday), and on Wednesdays, Saturdays and Sundays in winter.

"A few steps behind the Royal Palace is **Storkyrkan Church** (meaning The Great Church). Begun in the 13th century, it's the oldest church in Stockholm, and has provided the setting for royal weddings and coronations (Riddarholm Church is the Swedish Pantheon). There's no charge to enter, and the Church is officially open to tourists from 8 a.m. to 5:30 p.m.

"Finally, theatre buffs may wish to make a pilgrimage to the last home of the brooding Swedish playwright, August Strindberg. From 1908 until his death in 1912, Strindberg lived on the fourth floor of an apartment building at 85 Drottninggatan which he called The Blue Tower, describing his mood, not the color of the building. His third wife had left him, and Strindberg couldn't bear to have anything around that would remind him of her; so if the apartment seems sparsely furnished, that's the reason. In addition to the few furnishings, there are photos, first editions of his books and plays, personal mementos, and an especially touching series of pictures of Strindberg's funeral procession, surrounded by crowds, reflecting not only his position in the literary world, but also reminding us of his tremendous popularity as a writer of the people. The apartment is open from Tuesday through Saturday, 10 a.m. to 4 p.m., Sunday from noon to 5 p.m. Closed Monday. Admission is 5 kronor (children are free)."

6. Nighttime Entertainment

Sweden, until very recently, suffered under the strictest of liquor controls, with hardly a bar or non-membership club available for the refreshment of visitors. Now things are opening up a bit, and this year Stockholm can boast a number of "pubs" and a whole crop of discotheques where there may be an admission fee, but no membership requirement.

DANCING: First choice for dancing is in the area around Skansen (see above). The younger crowd goes to an open-air dancing area at the top of Skansen Hill. You enter through the main Skansen gate (fee is 15 kronor), take the escalator and then walk a few minutes until you see the dancing area, near the church on top of the hill. Here, from Wednesday through Sunday evenings, in summer, large groups of young people take part in folk and similar dances. You might watch for a while to learn how it's done, then try for yourself.

Near Skansen, and still on the Djurgarden, is the huge amusement park of Stockholm, called **Gröna Lund,** and sometimes also referred to as the **Tivoli.** Open from 2 p.m. Monday to Saturday and noon on Sunday, the admission charge is 15 kronor throughout the day. As you walk in, you'll see another outdoor dance floor, named **Dans Ut,** that caters to staid, older couples and features the traditional Swedish dances. I'd pass that by and keep walking to two livelier establishments, **Disco Fever** and **Jump In** (next to the ferris wheel). Entrance fee of 15 kronor, with all drinks priced at 12 kronor thereafter.

JAZZ: The "in" spot of Stockholm—unbelievably popular although open less than six years—is **Stampen** in Old Town at Stora Gramunkegrand 7 (near the Gamla Stan subway stop). Stampen looks much like an Old British pub. It's draped in Union Jacks and hung with an odd collection of baby carriages, stuffed animals and even one antique sleigh. At one end of the warm and overcrowded room, there's a bandstand upon which appear the finest jazz musicians presently in Sweden—many visiting from America and England. The crowd is enthusiastic, dropping the stolid Swedish mien to "go with" the music, and prices are moderate. Only beer is sold (starting at 24 kronor) and entrance fee is 30 kronor Sunday through Thursday, 35 kronor Friday and Saturday. Jazz begins at 9 p.m.

ROCK: **Engelen Steakhouse and Pub,** 59B Kornhamnstorg on Gamla Stan, a multi-roomed house with pop band upstairs, a discotheque downstairs, and two bars, is Stockholm's most popular pub at the moment of this writing. Entrance fee (applicable as a credit towards your dinner) is 25 to 35 kronor, depending on what bands are playing. The line stretches far from the door on Saturday nights.

Mosebacke, at Mosebacketorg, directly behind the Katarina elevator, is Stockholm's largest dance and rock music restaurant, seating up to 400 persons, of whom 200 choose the outdoor terrace overlooking the town. Entertainment is provided by traveling rock and folk musicians. Entrance fee ranges from 25 to 40 kronor, depending on the band or attraction, and one-plate meals can be had for 30 kronor ($3.75), beer for 24 kronor. Open daily from 6 p.m. to midnight.

THEATRE, MUSIC AND MOVIES: The **Royal Dramatic Theatre** of Stockholm is one of the great playhouses of Europe and prices its seats for as little as 10 to 50 kronor ($1.25 to $6.25). But it's closed in the tourist-heavy month of August. . . . The **Opera,** which has produced such stars as Jussi Bjoerling, Birgit Nilsson, Nicolai Gedda and Set Svanholm, vacations during the same month and offers tickets from an astonishing 22 kronor ($2.75) to a top of 55 kronor ($6.87)—a superb bargain. . . . American and English movies in Stockholm aren't dubbed—they're in English, and tickets are priced from 15 kronor. . . . Almost every day in summertime, free concerts or programs are presented in the **Kungstradgarden,** the City Garden Park. And during the daytime there are concerts, recorded and live, with everything from pop music to the Salvation Army on the docket. Musical and variety programs are often presented at night—always on Sunday. The poster at the park or in the nearby tourist office gives the list of events.

7. Miscellaneous Tips

STUDENTS IN STOCKHOLM: For you, the key name, and vital address, is the **Stockholm Student Reception Service** at #1 Körsbärsvägen, phone 15-03-40, next to T-bana (metro) stop "Tekniska Högskolan," which foreign students (and, for that matter, all youth under 30) are asked to make their very first stop for housing assistance, information, tickets to summer events and the like. And, of course, they also deal with the problems (housing, jobs) of students planning longer stays in Stockholm. . . . The key social center of Stockholm's student organization is the **Mocambo** in the Forum Hall, 2A Körsbärsvägen, which serves as a quiet club and pub, and it's open Thursday through Sunday from 9 p.m. to 2 a.m. . . . And for your travel arrangements (including those cheap charters) to other European cities, the organization to see is **SFS Resor,** at 89 Drottninggatan (phone 34-01-80).

THE MEAD-DRINKING, UNIVERSITY TOWN OF UPPSALA: "As you may know, several of the old English texts—for example, 'Beowulf' and the Arthurian legends, the Nordic and Icelandic sagas—are full of mention of the drinking of mead in the huge mead-halls of castles and palaces, for ceremonial purposes, welcomes, toasts, victory celebrations, etc. It served a multitude of uses, not least of which was simply getting plastered. Mead may be imbibed, in great style, just outside the famous city of Uppsala, a handy 45-minute train ride from Stockholm. . . . I spent the morning visiting the Uppsala Cathedral (largest in Scandinavia), the Carolina Rediviva (University Library) with its treasured Silver Codex, a Gothic Bible written in 500 A.D., Dag Hammarskjold's grave, and other sites. Then I took bus 24 (6 kronor) from the train station (to the left of the exit) and in ten minutes was in Gamla Uppsala, at the end of the line (a big parking lot). There are the Viking burial mounds, 1500 years old, a 12th-century church, and an old Uppland village. But behind the church is the Odinsborg Restaurant where one can get a steerhorn of mead for 24 kronor ($3). Mine was inscribed with the names of three of Sweden's royalty who, in 1866, 1879, and 1919, had drunk from that horn. The drink is excellent and, being made from honey and hops (a 14th-century recipe), tastes like a sweet beer. Drinking with both hands from the steerhorn is atmosphere enough, although the restaurant, especially upstairs, supplies more in abundance, with Viking relics, armor, battle weapons and old Swedish furniture. . . . For anyone interested in old Scandinavian or English history, this can be one way to touch an ancient and cherished part of it. Whether the mead is like that which satisfied Arthur's (no pun intended) throat after defending the realm, is a moot point. It's a fine way to round off an afternoon with the Vikings" (David L. Miles, Charlevoix, Michigan).

A STOCKHOLM SMORGASBORD (MISCELLANY): If you're as

curious as we were about the social and political structure of Sweden, then you may wish to read Marquis Childs' *Sweden: The Middle Way* before setting off for Stockholm. So comprehensive is the welfare program of Sweden that a cartoon in *Dagens Nyheter,* Stockholm's largest newspaper, showed an old man shocking an audience with the statement: "I retired on savings. I worked for years when they didn't take social security, health benefits, pension payments, union dues, and unemployment insurance out of your pay check." . . . Best way to say thank you in Swedish is *tack sa mycket* (pronounced tahk-sah-mick-it) . . . The kingdoms of Sweden, Norway and Denmark were once united, under a symbol of three crowns. Sweden kept the symbol (you'll see it atop the City Hall in Stockholm), uses it everywhere—the Swedish hockey team that beat the Russians was called "The Three Crowns." In this money-oriented book, three crowns means three kronor. . . . A walk along the Kungsgatan at night is a must, as is a stroll on the main street of Gamla Stan (Old Town)—the Vasterlanggatan—with its two-yard-wide side street at #81. Quieter moments: the **Public Reading Room** (Läsesalongen) in the Kulturhuset at 7 Sergelarkaden, is open Monday through Thursday from 9 a.m. until 8:30 p.m., Friday till 6 p.m., weekends from noon to 4 p.m., displays periodicals such as the *Times of London,* the *Guardian,* the *Economist,* lets you read them, free, sitting in one of 50 upholstered armchairs, listening to classical music via earphones next to your chair. . . . For late shopping, remember the **Servus Store,** located in the underground passage of the Tunnelbana at the Central Station, open every day from 9 a.m. to 9 p.m., and remember, too, the **Scheele Pharmacy** at 64 Klarabergsgatan (phone 21-89-34), near the Central Station, open 24 hours a day. . . . Stockholm's self-service laundromats include **Tvättomat** at 97 St. Eriksgatan, open Monday through Thursday only, until 6 p.m.; **Tvättomat** at 30 Hantverkargatan near the Radhuset subway stop, open weekdays only, and with early closing hours of 3 p.m. on Fridays; and **Albatrossvätt** at 81 Horsgatan (near the Zinkensdam subways stop), open weekdays from 8 a.m. to 7 p.m., Saturdays from 9 a.m. to 2 p.m. All charge 40 kronor ($5) for 5 kilos washed and dried.

READERS' SELECTIONS: "The finest organized tour I took in Europe was the 'life-seeing' tour offered in Stockholm, which leaves on weekdays in summer at 10 a.m. from the Karl XII Torg. This three-hour guided tour by bus investigates the Swedish social system by visiting diversified social institutions. There is a visit to a factory, a state-controlled hospital, Farsta, the newest Stockholm housing development (where we actually went into the home of a typical family and a pensioner and saw a recreation center) and a school building. The guide is so informative that when the tour is over, one feels one has really taken a close look at Swedish urban life. Such a tour is also offered in Copenhagen, but I found the Stockholm one far more fascinating" (Milton Schulman, Bronx, New York). . . . "Here's how to make your own personal visit to **Drottningholm Castle:** take subway T from Centralen to the Brommaplan (fare, 9 kronor); walk down to the square and take the blue bus that says Drottningholm Castle on it (fare, 5 kronor). Time: about 30 minutes. Castle admission is 10 kronor, Palace Theatre admission is 10 kronor, and the Chinese Pavilion is 10 kronor. Then, take a different and more interesting route back to town by getting on the ferry where the bus stops. Fare is 18 kronor, and you're back in town in 50 minutes" (Edward Pietraszek, Chicago, Illinois). . . . "For a day of complete relaxation, do as the outdoorsy Swedes do and take the Tunnelbana to the Fredhall stop. A short distance away, on lovely Lake Mälaren, is located the **Tranebergsbadet** where, for one krona, you can commune with Mother Nature to your heart's content. You may swim either in the Lake itself, or the heated pool, and there is space provided for tanning 'au naturel', although the latter occupation, unlike St. Tropez, is segregated! Sorry 'bout that" (Carma Bamber, San Francisco, California). . . . "A cheap and expedient way of going from Stockholm to Berlin for the more intrepid train traveler is via the city of Trelleborg, a ferry to the city of Sassnitz in E. Germany. From there a train straight to E. Berlin, which then goes to the Zoobahnhof in W. Berlin—total cost, second class, about $70 (depending on the rates of exchange), a saving of around $14 over the cost from Stockholm via Copenhagen and Hamburg to W. Berlin. If you can tolerate the military presence of the DDR for eight hours or so, the trip brings considerable savings of time and money" (R. Golden, New York, N.Y.). . . . "Balletomanes will certainly want to check out the new **Dance Museum** (Dansmuseet) which opened in Stockholm in the spring of 1981" (Delos V. Smith, Jr., Hutchinson, Kansas); note by AF: It's located at 10 Laboratoriegatan, in a plush residential area also called Embassy Row. Open Tuesday to Sunday from noon to 4 p.m., it features video shows, stage models, costumes, and masks, from Europe and Asia, claiming to be the first and only museum of this kind in the world. Entrance is free. Take bus 42, 44, 47 or 69 to reach it.

The last, the cheapest, and not the least of our three Scandinavian capitals, is Oslo—whose prices are slightly less than those you'll encounter in Stockholm. It's time—in the good-hearted phrase of the Oslo mayor—to "know the Norwegians."

Chapter XXIII

OSLO

The Fjord in Your Future

WHENEVER I THINK of Norway, I think of movies on the *Late Late Show,* featuring British Commandos joining Norwegian fishermen to blow up "a key installation." The heroism of Norway in World War II is typical of the sturdy nature of these people, and of the very sights that you will see in Oslo: the Kon-Tiki Raft of Thor Heyerdahl, the polar ship *Fram* in which the Norwegian explorer Nansen went to the North Pole.

As these feats indicate, the sea is very much a part of life in Norway. At noontime even in the capital city of Oslo, citizens stroll to the docks in front of City Hall and purchase little bags of freshly cooked shrimp that fishermen have caught in the night. And when you scan the menu of a budget restaurant here, chances are that fish will have rank over meat on the bill of fare.

Expect to see a city of nature-loving people whose resources (except for reserves of North Sea oil) are few, and whose prices are still reasonable by Scandinavian standards, though they have gone up considerably in recent years. There is a minimum of elegance or sophistication in this relatively small town (pop: approx. 500,000), and an emphasis instead upon clean, honest living, tinged with the outdoors. Norway is a paradise for sports lovers, and Oslo is a perfect starting point for the nature-viewing aspects of your European tour—a refreshing, tingling, frontier-type of city that lets you relax without ostentation, at moderate cost.

Although Norway (and Oslo in particular) has felt the impact of a general European inflation in the past several years, accommodations can still be had in a moderate range. In Oslo, rooms in a private home now rent for about $10 per person, $12 to $16 per person in a plain (but quite adequate) pension. Food will account for your major cash outlay, but if you follow the eating patterns of the country as described later in this chapter—a large breakfast, sandwich lunch and hot dinner between 4 and 6 p.m.—and eat at the restaurants suggested, you can keep your food costs to a reasonable level. Simply be careful not to wait too late for dinner, as the majority of budget restaurants close about 6 p.m., and the only ones left open thereafter are those geared—and priced—to the (affluent) tourist trade.

1. Orientation & Transportation

The city of Oslo occupies a magnificent physical site, with high hills on three sides and the great Oslo Fjord—60 miles long—in front. At some point in your stay, you'll want to see the town from one of its hillside vantage points, the tallest being the **Tryvanns Tower** on Tryvann Hill, from which you can scan the entire Oslo Fjord as it opens out into the sea (details later).

Directly on the Fjord is the **Oslo City Hall,** and it is from the waterfront street in front of this building that the tour buses leave, as well as the sightseeing launches that traverse the Fjord and the ferries that travel across to the peninsula of Bygdøy where the majority of Oslo's sightseeing attractions are located. It's here, too, that the famous shrimp boats of Oslo unload their wares.

The main street of Oslo is the **Karl Johans Gate,** a few blocks up from the City Hall. This is the congregating and strolling street for Oslo's citizens, and it serves as your major orientation point. At the top of the Karl Johans Gate is the **Royal Palace;** at the other end is the old **Central Station** (the main railroad terminal of Oslo) where you'll find the all important hotel accommodations bureau. Along the Karl Johans Gate, starting at the palace and continuing for a few hundred yards, is a narrow park called Student's Grove. As you walk from the palace towards the station, you'll first pass the famous **National Theatre,** with its statues of Ibsen and Bjornson, then the Parliament Building of Oslo, and finally you'll reach the station. Running parallel to the Karl Johans Gate, starting at the Royal Palace and continuing for several blocks, is the **Stortingsgate,** another important street; and now you're oriented in Oslo.

TRAINS, BUSES AND BOATS: The major trains all come in to the **Central Station** (formerly called the East Station), and only suburban lines use the secondary West Station. Still a third station, the popular **Holmenkollen,** next to the National Theatre, is used only for the pocket-sized electric trains that ascend winding, serpentine tracks to the tops of mountains overlooking Oslo, where you'll find much-patronized resorts. Because Oslo is such a small city, you'll rarely have need to use the buses, except to the Bygdøy peninsula, site of the Viking ships and the Kon-Tiki museum. Tickets are 9 kroner ($1.20), unless you wish to purchase an (unnecessary) all-day pass—the 24-hour Tourist Ticket —for 30 kroner ($4) adults, 15 kroner ($2) children under 16. From the harbor of Oslo, passenger ships and car ferries depart daily to Copenhagen, twice weekly to Newcastle, six times a week to Kiel, among other destinations; for ship schedules and prices, phone 41-50-70 or 20-50-50.

Arriving at the airport of Oslo (known as Fornebu), you have a choice of either city bus 31 ($2) or the S.A.S. bus ($3) for the five-mile ride to a terminal near the Central Station, both departing every twenty minutes.

2. Hotels

Of all the Scandinavian cities, Oslo has the tightest summer hotel situation—particularly in early June, and September, when the town is jammed (July and early August, aren't half as bad). But Oslo is also the only one of the major Scandinavian capitals whose tourist association will make advance reservations for you, thus sparing you the job of writing to possibly successive hotels. If you'll write a reasonable time in advance to the **Oslo Travel Association,** 19 Radhusgaten, specifying your requirements and the dates of your stay, they'll make all the arrangements. They will even, at your request, book you into a low-cost room in a private home, *whether or not* the hotels are filled. Thus, Oslo is the only one of the Scandinavian capitals to put the interests of its tourists ahead of its major hotels, and I for one say three cheers! Accompany your reservation request with a deposit (bank draft only) of $13.33 (100 kroner) *per person*. Of this, $10 (75 kroner) will be applied to your rent and $3.33 (25 kroner) deducted as a booking fee. In return, you will receive in the mail your confirmed reservations, plus a small map and tourist guide to Oslo.

But you'll suffer no catastrophe if you arrive without a reservation. For then, you simply go to the **Innkvartering** desk inside the Central Station, where attendants are on duty from 8 a.m. to 11 p.m. in summer (but from only 6 to 11 p.m. in winter) to find you a suitable room in your price range. Here, rooms in private homes will be arranged upon request. Prices range from 85 kroner ($11.33) double—and they are all thoroughly proper places that have been checked by the travel association. Booking fees at the accommodations desk are 12 kroner ($1.60) per adult, 6 kroner (80¢) per child.

A single warning: the young people who staff the Innkvartering service often make the typically Norwegian assumption that you'd prefer the rural outskirts of Oslo to the central, urban section of the city. They may, therefore, book you at a hotel located on a mountainside, two or three hundred yards from the last stop of the electric train that took 20 minutes to get you up there. Be sure to inquire about the *precise* location of the hotel they've chosen.

BUDGET PENSIONS AND HOTELS: Apart from rooming in a private home, the best way to stay on a budget in Oslo is to live in a "hospits" or pension charging $16 or less per person. What's the difference between a "hospits" and a pension? No one seems to know. Some Osloites claim that "hospits" is simply an older and now out-of-fashion word for "pension"; others will tell you that the owners of "hospits's" need not be licensed or know several languages, as must the operators of more formal establishments. Physically, the two species have always seemed identical to me—they're almost always a single floor of an office or apartment building with rooms for overnight guests—although the places with "hospits" in their title seem, often, to charge the lowest prices.

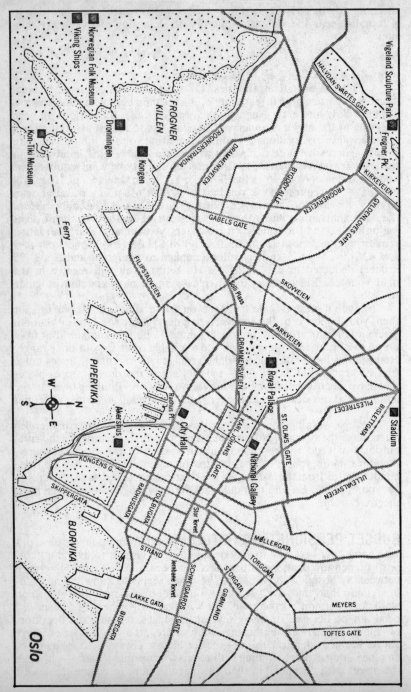

In the following listings, note that prices include service charge, unless otherwise mentioned, but not breakfast.

Double Rooms for $20 to $30

First, a cluster of inexpensive pensions, some of which are ultra-basic, some of which are quite charming but open only in summer.

Least expensive of all and suitable *only* for those who are willing to sacrifice amenities for convenience and price are an assortment of starvation-budget-quality spots near the railroad station. But equally cheap, and far better located *outside* the railroad station area, is the **Ellingsen Pensjonat** at 25 Holtegate (phone 60-03-59), near the Uranienborg streetcar stop behind the King's Palace, where 21 rooms on three floors rent—to readers of this book only—for 110 kroner ($14.66) single, including free showers (there are no doubles). Breakfast, however, is not served. The couple operating this pension are quite friendly and helpful, and will point the way to a nearby cafe where breakfast can be had for 30 kroner. To find their pension, look first for #25, then walk through a small garden to the main entrance where the name is posted at the door-bell.

Cochs Pensjonat, 25 Parkveien (phone 60-48-36), is an excellent value: a 72-room pension that keeps about 55 rooms for transients, it is located on the third floor of a very old building with ornately tiled hallways; rooms are high-ceilinged, spotless, newly painted and equipped with the usual narrow Norwegian beds. All rooms have hot-and-cold running water, and there are two bathrooms for the use of transients and no charge for baths. Singles (of which there are very few) cost 120 kroner ($16), doubles 185 kroner ($24.66), triples 225 kroner ($30), four-bedded rooms 280 kroner ($37.33). If you are booking ahead, you'll be requested to mail a 100 kroner per person deposit. Tram 11 or 7 connects you with the center of town.

Lindes Pensjonat, open all year at 41 Thomas Heftyesgate (phone 56-21-65), is a simple but clean establishment in the Vigeland Park area, easily reached by bus 72 or 73. Nine rooms, all on the third floor, are priced at 135 kroner ($18) single, 190 kroner ($25.33) double or twin, with showers and use of the family kitchen. Extra beds are 60 kroner ($8) a night. Owner Andvin Linde is fluent in English and will provide you with keys to the house if you plan to stay out late.

West Side Hotel at 13 Observatoriegate (phone 56-78-41), in a central but quiet location three blocks from the U.S. Embassy, is a very homey place operated by a Mr. Kittelson, who lived for many years in the United States, is obviously fluent in English, and likes to cook small dishes, like omelettes, for his guests. He rents seven doubles, all with modern furniture, for 200 kroner ($26.66) per room per night, two singles at 150 kroner ($20); charges 30 kroner ($4) extra for breakfast; permits free use of showers and free use of his own, five-kilo-capacity washing machine. Walking time from the Central Station: 15 minutes; or take bus 27 or trams 1 or 2 to the Slottsparken stop.

Helga Sylou-Creutz, a smiling Norwegian woman occupying a home at 100B Pilestrade (phone 69-29-22), rents three double and three triple rooms at a uniform price of 70 kroner ($9.33) per person per night. No breakfast, but free showers, and you're given a key to come and go as you please. Only five minutes from the center; take streetcar 7 to the Adamstuen stop, and you'll find the house in a garden with a white gate and lonely birch tree.

> **THE NORWEGIAN CURRENCY:** Presently selling at 7.50 kroner to the dollar, each krone has been valued by us at 13¢ for the conversion of kroner prices into dollars in this chapter.

Pension Sørå, centrally located at 3 Frognerveien (phone 56-58-47), offers 14 simple but adequately furnished rooms for 170 kroner ($22.66) single, 165 to 225 kroner ($22 to $30) twin, depending on size, 280 kroner ($37.33) triple, 340 kroner ($45.33) quad. Breakfast, on request only, is 30 kroner ($4), and showers are free. Why so cheap? Possibly because there's no elevator here, and office and rooms are on the fourth floor; entrance is around the corner at Oscars Gate. And best connection is streetcar 2 from Central Station to Solli Plass, a five-minute ride that costs 9 kroner.

Double Rooms for $25 to $32

A really excellent summer guesthouse is the **Sta. Katarinahjemmet Pension,** Majorstuveien 21B (phone 60-13-70 or 60-13-71), which is operated by the sisters of a Dominican convent and takes guests from June until the first of September. The guesthouse (which houses working girls in the winter) is set in the wooded convent grounds; the rooms are neat and modern. In the dining room you breakfast off three-centuries-old Norwegian tables. In the library you can choose from books in several languages. In the chapel with its multicolored windows you can even attend Mass daily in summer; guests are welcomed but never in any way urged. The guesthouse is non-sectarian and the white-robed nuns efficient but discreet. Highly recommended for both men and women. Singles are priced at 150 kroner ($20), doubles at 220 kroner ($29.33). Breakfast is an extra 40 kroner.

St. Hanshaugens Hospits, 31 Geitmyrsveien (phone 46-84-28), is an excellent 60-bedded guesthome in a big white house across from a lovely park and with a picturesque mountain backdrop. The rooms are spotless, spare and modern, the house comes equipped with a free, 16-car parking lot, and the proprietors—Mr. and Mrs. Rolf Berge—are English-speaking and friendly. All rooms are equipped with hot-and-cold running water, and the house itself has six showers (free) and two baths. Rates are 165 kroner ($22) single, 245 kroner ($32.66) double, 100 kroner for an extra bed in a double room. Take bus 17 to Louisenberg.

On the western outskirts of Oslo (15 minutes from the center by bus or train), is the **Holtekilen Summerhotel** (the educational center of the Baptist Union of Norway), 55 Micheletsvei, Stabekk/Oslo (phone 53-38-53), which operates as a hotel from June 1 through September 1. Here there are 30 rooms with running water, built-in closets, modern furnishings and large windows overlooking the surrounding lawns. Tubs and showers (free of charge) are available in the hallways. This is a superb place for people who are driving (unlimited parking), who have children (the lawns are for playing), or who prefer a rural setting with easy access to town. Singles are priced at 140 kroner ($18.66), doubles at 190 kroner ($25.33), triples at 225 kroner ($30), dorms at 40 kroner ($5.33) per bed, breakfast an extra 30 kroner. From University Square, take buses 32, 36 or 37; get off at Kveldsroveien and walk across the bridge to the school building. Highly recommended.

Trollvasshytta (it means house of the trolls), 1 Rodkleivfaret (phone 14-55-59), rents 16 rooms in a red and white wooden bungalow surrounded by trees. Accommodations are on the ground floor, and they're extremely well furnished, as is the lounge and dining room. It's a relaxing place. Twins are priced at 250 kroner ($33.33), triples at 300 kroner ($40), and two-family rooms, each with four beds, at 400 kroner ($53.33). A huge breakfast served from 8 to 10 a.m. is 35 kroner ($4.66) and an all-you-can-eat buffet lunch or dinner (prepared by English-speaking owner, Mr. Egli Nordli) is 80 kroner ($10.66), a bit high, but you can really stuff yourself. To get here take the Holmenkollen tram from the National Theatre 18 stops to Lillevann Station, cross the rails, walk down the street for 50 yards to Rodkleivfaret. The tram operates every 20 minutes from 6 a.m. to midnight and the fare is 9 kroner ($1.20).

Doubles for $32 to $40, breakfast included

Now for the costlier pensions and standard hotel rooms. In the very center of town and only three blocks from the Central Station, is the 97-bed **Hotel Fonix,** 19 Dronningensgate (phone 42-59-57), which charges precisely 290 kroner ($38.66) for one of their smaller double rooms (these are actually singles equipped with a supplementary single bed), 300 kroner ($40) for a normal double without bath, 190 kroner ($25.33) for a single, including an excellent breakfast featuring pickled herring, eggs, corn flakes, and apple jam homemade by the charming owner, Mrs. Betsy Kjelsberg. Clean, newly painted throughout, respectable, and moderately priced for its category.

In the peak summer period between June 20 and August 20, the **Y.W.C.A. Home (K.F.U.K. Hjemmet)** at 3B Neuberggaten (phone 44-17-87), near Frogner Park, houses both men and women in its 13 single and 13 double rooms for 150 kroner ($20) single, 240 kroner ($32) double, 270 kroner ($36) triple, including continental breakfast, free showers, and use of a pleasant lounge, sitting rooms, laundry room and garden. Unlike many establishments of this sort, there's no evening curfew, and a modern, mature atmosphere prevails.

HOSTELS AND DORMS: Oslo's youth hostel—and an excellent one it is—is the **Haraldsheim,** Haraldsheim 4, Grefsen/Oslo (phone 02-21-83-59). Situated in a countrified setting on the eastern outskirts of the city (on Grefsen Hill), it requires guests to have International Hostel cards or to purchase "guest cards" for 15 kroner ($2) per night. The overnight charge for bed-and-breakfast is 80 kroner ($10.66). Add 15 kroner ($2) for renting a sheet sleeping bag (which is required). While bedrooms are closed from 10 a.m. to 4 p.m., the outdoor picnic area (it offers a beautiful vista of the harbor of Oslo) is available all day, and the restaurant serving hot two-course meals for 30 kroner opens 5 to 7 p.m. Beds are in either six-bedded or eight-bedded rooms, and the hostel has a capacity (often filled in summer) of 260 persons. When it is filled, overflow goes to the modern **Bierke Student Home** (phone 64-87-87), charging similar rates, nearby. At both, curfew is a reasonable 1 a.m., and to reach both take trams 1 or 7 from the Central Station or National Theatre (look for the sign

"Sinsen" on the front of the tram) to the last stop. Or take the train (free to Eurailpass holders) from the Central Station to Grefsen, from which the Haraldsheim is a 150-yard walk.

Provided only that you have your own sleeping bag, and during the one-month period from July 15 to August 15 only, you can sleep overnight for only $4 in a temporary summer "Sleep-In" operated by the **Y.M.C.A.** (or **K.F.U.K.**) at 1 Mollergatan, with an entrance on Grubbegatan, five minutes walking distance from the Central Station; since the "Sleep-In" has no telephone, you'll need to inquire about vacancies first at the Innk-vartering desk in the Central Station. Sleeping quarters here consist of a thick carpet on which you place the sleeping bag, together with 50 other lucky male or female guests. The establishment is open from 7:30 a.m. to 10 a.m., and from 6:30 p.m. to 10 p.m., enforces an 11:30 p.m. curfew, and offers free showers included in its phenomenal 30 kroner price. From the Central Station, walk straight up Oslo's main street, the Karl Johans Gate, turn right next to the cathedral, and left on the other side of the market square, then walk up the second street to your right.

A HOUSING ODDITY: The hostel or "home" for members of the Norwegian navy and merchant marine, **Sjoemannshjem,** 4 Tollbugatan (phone 41-20-05), two minutes walk from the Central Station, also accepts non-seafaring tourists or families. Bathless singles there are 150 kroner ($20), twins or doubles 200 kroner ($26.66), and there are two large rooms with four beds apiece for which the charge is only 75 kroner ($10) per person. Buffet breakfast, enough to feed a horse, is 32 kroner ($4.26) extra; showers are free; and no evening curfew is ever imposed.

BOGSTAD CAMPING: Finally, if you're a group of four or more, you might consider renting one of the 20 little housekeeping chalets on the grounds of **Bogstad Camp and Turistsenter** in the Holmenkollen Sky-Jump area—largest campground in northern Europe, equipped with bank, restaurants, shops, laundries—on the grounds of a forest that could have served as the set for *Song of Norway.* Bus 41 from near the Central Station stops in front of the camp office. Each hut rents for 340 kroner ($45.33) per house per day, plus 50 kroner ($6.66) per person for rental of bed sheets. Fully equipped with stove, refrigerator and utensils, the chalets provide marvelously cheap but comfortable lodgings for mini-groups of four or five. Phone first (24-76-19) to manager Per Brun, or write to Bogstad Camp and Turistsenter, Oslo 7.

PRIVATE HOMES THAT READERS HAVE LIKED: "There is no better accommodation for families than at **Bella Vista Hospits,** at 11B Aarundveien, Arvoll (phone 22-72-17), six kilometers from the Central Station in Oslo, where there are English-speaking proprietors (Capt. and Mrs. J. A. Madsen). Large rooms cost 130 kroner ($17.33) per person, double occupancy, 150 kroner single, with breakfast for 30 kroner and showers for 5 kroner" (Dr. Anna Tollenaere-Blank, Warmond, Holland; note from AF: to reach the Bella Vista, take bus 31, which runs between airport and town; ask the driver to stop at the hospits—he knows it). . . . . "We recently traveled in Europe and found a good private room in Oslo at the picturesque home of **Mr. and Mrs. Solheim,** Doctor-Holms-vej 24 (phone 14-47-70). They made us feel at home, and their kindness was unforgettable. In a beautiful setting near the famous ski jump, their accommodations are reasonably priced and offer a refrigerator, stove, and free showers. English is spoken. Take the electric train behind the National Theatre to Holmenkollen; it's not too far to walk from the station" (J. Williams, Queensland,

Australia; note from AF: after leaving the train at Holmenkollen station walk up 200 yards to the restaurant, passing the monument of a soldier. Doctor-Holms-vej begins next to the restaurant's parking lot, but there is no sign. The Solheim's house is a red wooden loghouse. Price for a twin in 1985 is 225 kroner ($22.50).

3. Oslo Restaurants

On this subject, a preliminary and important note: the mealtime habits of Norwegians are somewhat unique, and you may be puzzled by the resulting restaurant situation unless you know them. The basic puzzle stems from the fact that very few Norwegians eat lunch—or at least lunch as we know it. How or why the custom began, no one seems to know, but the fact is that most people in Oslo work straight through the day without a lunch hour, and are thus able to knock off from work by 3:30 or 4 p.m.

How do they keep going? Around noontime, a Norwegian office worker will usually break out an open sandwich brought from home and eat it at his desk—working all the while. When he does leave the office, he then has an immediate big meal—inaccurately called a *middag,* which is really a dinner. That means that the evening eating hours are unusually early in Oslo—many of the less expensive restaurants have completed serving their evening meals and are entirely shut down by 6 p.m.

For the same reason, you'll often enter an Oslo restaurant around noontime, only to find sandwiches—and nothing else—being served. If you come again at 2 p.m., however, you'll find the staff first starting to prepare the really big meal—the *middag.* The lesson to learn from this is to schedule your evening meal for as early as 5 p.m.

But having absorbed this information, you can now proceed to forget most of it, because you won't be having lunch at your desk. I've sought out restaurants that do offer hot meals beginning at about 1 p.m., although again you're warned to return for supper no later than, say, 5:30.

THE KAFFISTOVAS: To get your cheapest but most filling meal, go to the **Stortorvet,** a big square with a church on one side, a flower market in the center, and a major department store—the **Christiania** (former name of Oslo) **Glasmagasin**—on the other. Overlooking the Square from a picture window on a second floor location, at #13 Karl Johans Gate, is one of the two **Kaffistova** restaurants—the plainest, most basic eateries in Oslo, owned and operated for country folk coming to town by an organization called The League of Country Youth. The prices here are low and the meals filling. Huge hunks of meat slathered with a thick gravy (the Norwegians go heavy on gravy), with a separate vast disk of potatoes accompanied by another tureen of gravy, and peas and carrots—for two such plates, along with two Cokes, Hope and I paid 100 kroner ($13.33) total. It is entirely possible to order one serving for two people, and even then you may not finish this "nourishing lunch."

There's an even better **Kaffistova** at Rosenkranzgate 8 (second floor), near the expensive Bristol Hotel and the Karl Johans Gate, where the food seems a little more delicately cooked. Don't confuse this establishment with the not-quite-as-cheap Grillstova downstairs at the same location.

Both Kaffistovas are self-service, cafeteria-style establishments, and both serve, in addition to their hot plates averaging 30 to 45 kroner ($4 to $6), fine shrimp appetizers (30 kroner the serving), a big bowl of soup for 18 kroner, a dessert for 18 kroner, and various open sandwiches starting at 14 kroner. Note the hours: the Karl Johans Gate Kaffistova is open weekdays only, from 7 a.m. to 8 p.m. The Rosenkrantzgate branch is open weekends as well, Saturdays until 3:30 p.m., Sundays until 7 p.m., weekdays also until 7 p.m.

FOUR VERY SPECIAL BUDGET RESTAURANTS: Norrona Cafeteria, up one flight of stairs at 19 Grensen in the heart of town, is our very top budget choice: clean, spacious, with moderate prices for top quality food, 300 comfortable chairs, wall-to-wall carpeting, white curtains on windows and a quiet and cultivated atmosphere. It's superbly supervised by Mr. Duggas, who also manages the mission hotel in the same building; he's fluent in English, and he maintains a separate dining room for non-smokers! Most patrons start with soup for 9.50 kroner ($1.26), and move on to Norwegian fishburgers for 28 kroner ($3.73), roast sausages with mashed potatoes or more elaborate meat plates with vegetables for 35 kroner ($4.66). Sandwiches range from 12 to 22 kroner ($1.60 to $2.93), desserts from 8 to 10 kroner ($1.06 to $1.33), the latter price for pudding with cranberry sauce; there's an English-language menu card which you can request. Mornings, the normal continental breakfast for 30 kroner ($4) is far exceeded in value by an all-you-can-eat buffet breakfast for 40 kroner ($5.33): as much as you want, filling up for the day on eggs, sausages, other cold cuts, four kinds of bread, cheeses, marmalades, corn flakes, milk, tea, coffee. Hours are Sunday to Friday from 8 a.m. to 5 p.m., Saturday to 3 p.m.

Cafe Moellhausen, at Viktoria Terrassen in central Oslo, is another modern self-service cafeteria operated, this time, by a gentleman from Korea, Mr. Chul Ho Lee, whose policy of moderate prices attracts employees and sales personnel of the surrounding business area; the restaurant is connected with a passageway to the Vika Department Store, to the rear of the building. At least ten daily platters sell for less than 35 kroner ($4.66), 15 types of open sandwiches go for 10 to 29 kroner ($1.20 to $3.86), fishburgers for 18 kroner ($2.40), beverages at appropriate levels. Open every day except Saturday from 10 a.m. to 6 p.m., it's reached by walking up Dronnings Maud Gate from Town Hall Square, and turning right just before reaching the two IBM office buildings.

Vegeta Vertshus, 3b Munkedamsvejen (corner of Stortingsgatan), is Oslo's major vegetarian restaurant, and offers some of the best values in town—like an all-you-can-eat buffet meal of soup, eight salads, soyburgers, potatoes, five other vegetables, bread, fresh fruit, cheese and coffee or tea for 55 kroner ($7.33). Daily platters cost 30 kroner ($4). The airy dining room is up a flight of stairs, and its 24 tables are usually crowded by noon, so it's best to get there either before noon or after 2 p.m. Open seven days a week until 11 p.m.

Cheaper—in fact, one of the budget standouts in Oslo—and much stricter and more intense in its vegetarian zeal, is the Kurbad Restaurant at 74 Akersgatan. Five minutes on foot from City Hall, it's owned by Seventh Day Adventists who prohibit the use of alcohol or cigarettes on the premises and dress their employees in neat orange-brown uniforms. A typical three-course "menu" might consist of carrot soup, lentil beef hash with vegetables, and figs with vanilla sauce for dessert, for only 33 kroner ($4.40). Open Monday to Thursday from noon to 6 p.m., Friday noon to 2 p.m., Sunday noon to 5:30 p.m., Saturday closed. Walking here (it's across from St. Olaf's Church), you'll pass a modern, gray post office building with a mural of fishermen with a net: this is a Picasso original.

THE OTHER BUDGET RESTAURANTS: A slightly less heavy meal
than those served at the Stovas is available at the very good (but also slightly more expensive) **Mamma Rosa Restaurant,** on the second floor at Övre Slottsgate 12, just off the Karl Johans Gate near the Parliament Building *(Storting)*. Here, in a very Italian atmosphere enhanced by guitar music from 7 to 9 p.m., Norwegian, Italian, and Viennese food is served at reasonable prices. Hope and I, in 1984, had a flavorsome Wiener schnitzel with anchovies for 38 kroner ($5.06) per person, and, the next day, an excellent pizza margherita for $3. Open Monday to Friday from 11 a.m. to 11:30 p.m., Sunday from 1 to 10:30 p.m.

At lunchtime, the large and brightly colored **Expressen Cafeteria** at 11 Fred Olsensgate, in front of the Central Station, offers bargain-rate dishes such as fishburger with a generous helping of salads for 24 kroner ($3.20), a vanilla pudding dessert for 8 kroner ($1.06), a daily soup (spinach cream, for example) for 9 kroner ($1.20). It's open seven days a week from 7 a.m. to 7 p.m.

Samson, diagonally across from the Mamma Rosa Restaurant, at Ö. Slottsgate 21 (corner Karl Johans Gate), is another cafeteria-style restaurant, where you order your food and pay for it at the counter and then a waitress brings it to your table when it is ready. An attractive upstairs room, with large windows overlooking the main street and lots of ornamental black wrought iron to divide the seating areas, it serves a choice of 12 hot plates starting at 32 kroner ($4.57). Open 8 a.m. to 7 p.m. on weekdays, to 4 p.m. on Saturday, closed Sunday.

THE SPECIALTIES: In observing your fellow diners, you'll find that
smoked salmon and scrambled eggs (with bread and butter) is particularly well liked by Norwegians, but it comes high—about 35 kroner for a serving. Nevertheless, the least expensive dishes in Oslo are generally those involving fish, which is always excellent. If you'd like a very inexpensive meat dish, the two Norwegian staples are *kjottkaker* (meat cakes) and *lapskaus* (hash). The latter dish looks like just plain hash, but somehow—in Oslo—it tastes better than our American variety. Always reasonably priced.

Some Oslo establishments serve *brun lapskaus* (hashed pork and potatoes, 34 kroner), or else such remarkable weirdies as reindeer hamburgers with cream sauce and red whortle-berries, 32 kroner (and if you think I'm making this up, then ask for *rensdyrkarbonader med fløtesaus og tyttebaer)!* Order milk with your meal, not beer. As in all the Scandinavian countries (even more so in Sweden), the cost of beer is increased by heavy, punitive taxes; in most restaurants, a half-liter is now 30 kroner ($4).

THE BIG SPLURGE: And now, when you're willing to spend upwards of
$10 per meal, try the following:

The Theatercafeen: Every day from 4 to 6 p.m. and from 8:15 to 11:15 p.m., four elderly musicians—a 96(!)(in 1984)-year-old pianist, two violinists and a bass fiddler, all professionals and serious—perform Strauss, Bach, Mozart and a few modern (but not too modern) composers from a balcony overlooking the large, tastefully furnished dining room of the **Theatercafeen** in the Hotel Continental building at 24 Stortingsgaten—one of the last remaining restaurants in Europe to offer such accompaniment. I'm told that 50 years ago, the restaurants of Vienna were famous for this sort of cultivated atmosphere. The menu is classic, too, with its roast leg of mutton with salad for 75 kroner ($10), Wiener schnitzel with vegetables for 70 kroner ($9.33), poached flounder for 65 kroner ($8.66), and Theatercafeen salad bowl—consisting mainly of cheese, shrimps and chicken at 52 kroner ($6.93).

Grand Cafe, in the large Grand Hotel building at 31 Karl Johansgate, patronized by a great many members of the Norwegian Parliament across the street, is both chic and traditional and slightly less expensive than the Theatercafeen. Three-course meals, in particular, sell for only 75 kroner ($10), and well-prepared daily platters—poached salmon with parsleyed potatoes (48 kroner, $6.40), beef and veal with whiskey sauce (45 kroner, $6)—are priced, as you see, at fairly moderate levels. Try to sit at the windows facing the busy and interesting square, and keep in mind the restaurant's closing day of Sunday.

READER'S RESTAURANT SELECTIONS: "**At Aulakjelleren,** a student cafeteria in the University at 47 Karl Johansgate, opposite the National Theatre, you may have not only hot dishes, but warm sandwiches—the latter a good substitute for dinner on the starvation budget. While the food isn't always the tastiest, it's cheap, and you will meet Norwegian and foreign students, without being asked for a student card" (Vegard Elvestrand, Oslo, Norway; note from AF: enter on the left side of the huge building with the four tall pillars, then down the steps next to the students' book store. Open weekdays 8 a.m. to 6 p.m., but closed during July and August; hot meals from 2 to 5 p.m. average 25 kroner, ($3.33), a plate).

4. Sights & Activities

You ought definitely to start with a trip up Tryvanns Hill for a view of the fjords, Norway's crowning glory. Then visit the shrimp boats, have a steam bath—and only then embark on the standard sightseeing.

A TRIP UP TRYVANNS HILL: It can be a full afternoon/evening's outing, which starts by your walking to the electric train behind the National Theatre and taking the Holmenkollen line to the Voksenkollen stop (9 kroner one-way). From there, hike up the hill to the **Tryvanns Tower,** a 15-minute walk. Then take the elevator to the observation gallery on top (10 kroner for adults, 5 kroner for children), and you will be standing at the highest point in Oslo, commanding—on a clear day—a view of 5,000 square miles, down the Oslo fjord and across to the Swedish border. Hours at the tower are 9:30 a.m. to 10 p.m. daily in June and July, from 10 a.m. to 8 p.m. in May and August, and from 10 a.m. to 6 p.m. in March, April, and September.

After leaving the tower, walk downhill until you come to the lodge-like **Frognerseteren Hovedrestaurant,** where you might next stop for a snack or a "Big Splurge" meal and take in the fabulous view. But be sure never to go inside (where meals start at $20). Rather, use the open-air, self-service, terrace cafeteria, commanding the most spectacular view imaginable of Oslo and the fjord. The photos you take here will be among the most memorable of your trip. Daily platters average 45 kroner ($6), sandwiches are 28 kroner ($3.73), and coffee 12 kroner ($1.60), with beer out of sight at

32 kroner ($4.26)—that curiously puritanical Scandinavian phenomenon. Although daylight lasts until 9 p.m. in summer, it's best to arrive no later than 5 or 6 for the best view and picture-taking possibilities. Independently visited, the Frognerseteren Restaurant is a ten-minute walk from the Frognerseteren electric train stop.

Leaving the restaurant, you can then walk down a marked path to the famous **Holmenkollen Ski Tower,** where annual ski jump contests in March attract champions from all over the world and huge crowds of spectators. You can take the lift to the top of the jump for still more amazing views, then visit the highly original **Ski Museum** at the foot of the jump. A combined ticket costs 18 kroner for adults, 10 kroner for children. Admission to the ski jump alone is 8 kroner for adults, 5 kroner for children. Hours are 10 a.m. to 9 p.m. daily in summer, but considerably more limited in winter. In the basement a cafeteria serves food and drinks for reasonable rates.

From the ski jump, it is just a short downhill walk to the Holmenkollen electric train station, where, refreshed and ready for city life again after your foray into the Oslo hills, you can catch a train back to the National Theatre.

SHRIMP BOATS ARE A'COMING: Throughout the night in the waters outside Oslo, local fishermen gather in vast quantities of tiny shrimp. At least three of these boats then sail to the dock that stands in front of the Oslo City Hall, cooking the shrimp as they go in vats on the decks of their boats. Starting at around 11 a.m., every day except Sunday and Monday, the citizens of Oslo wander to the docks, pay 12 kroner ($1.60) for a tin can full of freshly cooked shrimp, and chomp them down, sitting on the edge of the quay with feet dangling over the water, and throwing the husks of the shrimp into the bay where they're quickly gobbled up by the ever-present sea gulls. It's all great fun, and one can is more than enough for two people. But warning: the shrimp are so delicious that you're tempted to eat too many of them, thus spoiling your appetite for lunch!

STEAM BATHS: Yes, Oslo has them, too, and we'll list the three easiest to find. First, **Vestkantbadet,** 1 Sommerogaten, open to both sexes in separate areas, six days a week from 7:30 a.m. to 7:30 p.m. and on Sundays to 11:30 a.m. It costs 12 kroner ($1.60) for both sauna and swimming pool, 6 kroner (80¢) for children, and 36 kroner ($4.80) for the entire treatment —massage, steam room, rest cubicle, etc. From the National Theatre, walk up Drammensveien, pass the U.S. Embassy building to your left and keep on going for another 300 yards. You'll see a five-floor, red-brick building to your right (Oslo's public utilities administration has its offices there); Vestkantbadet is in the basement of it. Then there is the larger **Bislett Bath,** 60 Pilestredet (take streetcar 7 or 11, leave at Bislett Stadium stop, or walk 15 minutes from the center of town; closed in August). And, finally, **Toyen Bath,** 90 Helgensgate, next to the Munch Museum (bus 29 from City Hall will take you there). Opening times and prices of the Bislett and the Toyen are the same as of Vestkantbadet.

For no steam

The outdoor swimming pool of Oslo, whose temperature is maintained at a constant 70°, is the **Frognerbadet** in Frogner Park, near the Vigeland

Sculptures (the season is from May 20 to around September 10). Entrance is 10 kroner, and there are cafeterias, sunbathing areas and fine lawns. The beach of Oslo is the much-frequented **Ingierstrand Bad,** on the east side of the fjord, reached by bus 73 or 75 from Wessels Square; entrance is free.

RIDE A PLASTIC BIKE: Behind the Royal Palace, at 32 Oscarsgate (phone 44-18-80), a young Osloer with excellent knowledge of English, Lars Hotvedt, started, in 1982, a rental shop for plastic bikes, charging 45 kroner ($6) per day, and a 200-kroner ($26.66) refunded deposit. Except for the tires and transmission chain, these bikes (a Swedish invention, mentioned in *Time* magazine) are made entirely of plastic material, which makes them easier to maintain than conventional bikes, according to Lars. The shop is open Monday to Friday from 8 a.m. to 5 p.m., Saturday from 10 a.m. to 2 p.m., and also sells route maps of Oslo and surroundings, for 20 kroner ($2.66). Here is a unique way to explore the seashore and hills of this beautiful city.

INDISPENSABLE SIGHTS: The indispensable sights of Oslo are six in number, and they are all quite thrilling—a major highlight of your European tour. We'll first describe the sights themselves, and then discuss the best methods of seeing them.

THE VIKING SHIPS: It was as recently as 1904 that excavators found the last of the only three Viking ships to have survived the ten centuries since they were built. All three ships were apparently used as burial chambers for well-to-do Vikings, and all three have been magnificently restored and displayed in the **"Viking Ship Hall"** on the Bygdøy Peninsula, 15 minutes from the heart of Oslo. You'll see the Oseberg ship (reputedly the burial chamber of a lady of high rank), the Gokstad ship, and the smaller Tune ship, along with the relics that were found in each boat. It's thrilling to contemplate that the courageous Norwegian Vikings may actually have crossed the Atlantic in vessels of this sort. Open from 10 a.m. to 6 p.m. in summer, from 11 a.m. to 3 p.m. in winter; admission is 8 kroner, and the address is Huk Aveny 35, Bygdøy. Take bus 30 or, in summer, the ferry from Radhusplassen (City Hall Square), Pier 3.

THE POLAR SHIP "FRAM": This is the famous vessel that took Nansen to the Arctic in 1893 and Roald Amundsen to the South Pole in 1910. The entire ship has been hauled on land, and placed into a unique, pyramid-shaped building—mainly so that you can see the ingeniously designed round hull that enabled the ship to ride up and over the crushing masses of polar ice. The Norwegians are fiercely proud of their polar explorers, which accounts for their having made this unique building to cover the *Fram.* Again located on the Bygdøy Peninsula, with hours from 10 a.m. to 6 p.m. in summer, shorter hours in the fall/winter months and closed entirely from December 1 to April 15. Admission is 8 kroner for adults, 4 kroner for students and children.

THE KON-TIKI MUSEUM: This modern counterpart of the great polar feats of Norwegian sailors is only a few steps from the building housing the

Fram. Here you'll see the balsa-wood raft on which Thor Heyerdahl and his companions floated more than 4,000 miles, from Peru to Polynesia, to test the theory that South American Incas may have settled the South Pacific. Since the language of formal communication in the Norwegian navy is English, all the diaries and records are in English, and they're well displayed for your perusal. It's exciting to see this monument to a bit of history that occurred in our time. Available for viewing from 11 a.m. to 4 p.m., normally; from 10 to 6 in summer; admission is 8 kroner, 4 kroner for children. In 1979, a new wing was added to the museum to house the papyrus boat, *Ra II,* on which Heyerdahl and eight companions traveled 3,270 miles in 57 days from Morocco to Barbados to test the theory that Mediterranean vessels built before the time of Columbus could have made the trip.

THE VIGELAND SCULPTURES: Gustav Vigeland (1869-1943) was a Norwegian sculptor who created the controversial, sometimes depressing, but immensely impressive **Vigeland Sculptures,** which depict the human life-cycle, from birth to death. The statues are utterly explicit in their nudity and candor, and they are a major achievement that should be seen. Admission is free, and the park (which is also ideal for jogging) is open every day. In the **Vigeland's Museum,** 32 Nobelsgate, just to the left of the Park, you can see how this monumental work was created. Take tram 2 from the National Theatre to the main entrance at Kirkeveien. The museum is open daily except Monday from 1 to 7 p.m.

THE CITY HALL: This lavishly decorated building, which has become a symbol of Oslo, was completed in 1950. Its central hall contains the largest oil painting ever done, and the other rooms glitter with the best of Norway's art and crafts, including the painting "Life" by Edvard Munch, Norway's most famous artist. Despite the rich use of stone and woods in intricate designs employing a rainbow of colors, the overall effect is strong and peculiarly Scandinavian, a superb architectural feat. Open in summer from 10 a.m. to 2 p.m. weekdays, from noon to 3 p.m. on Sundays, and also from 6 to 8 p.m. on Mondays and Wednesdays, with no admission charge at any time. Winter hours are 11 a.m. to 2 p.m. daily, and noon to 3 on Sundays.

THE MUNCH MUSEUM: Last of the six, this is one of the world's greatest museums, containing virtually the entire life work (1,100 paintings, 4,500 sketches) of Edvard Munch, Norway's greatest contemporary artist; he bequeathed them to the city as a testamentary gift. They have now been arranged, chronologically, in a stunning, Scandinavian-style building at Toyengate 53, and it's fascinating to start with the artist's earliest works and watch him developing in power as he progresses to the macabre style for which he's most famous. Admission to the museum (open daily except Monday from 10 a.m. to 8 p.m., Sundays from noon) is free at all times, and you can get there via a 9-kroner ride on bus 29, which leaves from City Hall, or on bus 20 from Majorstua, or on the new subway from the Jerbanetorget Station to the Tøyen stop—9 kroner also.

GETTING TO THE SIGHTS: To visit five of these sites with a guide, you can take two half-day city tours described in our "tours" section, below.

The morning tour covers the City Hall, Holmenkollen and the Vigeland Sculptures; the afternoon trip goes to the Viking Hall, the *Fram,* the Kon-Tiki raft, and also takes in the interesting open-air Norwegian Folk Museum on the Bygdøy Peninsula. To get to Bygdøy on your own, simply take the Bygdøy ferry that leaves every half-hour in summer from Pier 3 in front of the City Hall, a ten-minute trip costing 9 kroner per person. To visit the Vigeland Sculptures, your best bet is tram 2, which passes directly in front of the main entrance to Frogner Park.

SIGHTSEEING TOURS: The buses all leave from in front of the City Hall *(Radhuset)* on a variety of differently priced trips. One excursion leaves at 10 a.m. (80 kroner, three hours), drives through the city, and then stops for visits to the Vigeland Sculptures in Frogner Park, the Holmenkollen ski jump, and City Hall. But the trip I prefer is the afternoon tour (2:30 p.m., 80 kroner for adults, 40 kroner for children, three hours) that passes through Oslo and its suburbs and includes full-fledged stops at the Viking Ships, the Kon-Tiki Raft, the Polar ship *Fram,* and the outdoor Norwegian Folk Museum. The tour is marvelously planned, it does not seem overly rushed, and yet it takes in a great deal. . . . There's also a sightseeing launch that leaves every hour in summer from a pier in front of the City Hall, and sails on a 50-minute cruise through the Oslo Fjord. Tickets are 30 kroner for adults, 15 kroner for children. From May 20 to August 27 the same sort of launch embarks (daily at 10:30 a.m., 1:30, 3:30 and 5:45 p.m.) on a longer two-hour trip through the islands and along the beaches and narrow sounds in the west part of the Fjord. Cost is 60 kroner for adults, 30 kroner for children; go to Pier 2 or 3, again in front of the City Hall. . . . For more ambitious tours of Norway, **Winge Travel Bureau,** at 33 Karl Johans Gate, offers escorted coach journeys that aren't too expensive.

OTHER SIGHTS: Remember the late Sonja Henie of the ice-skating movies? She was married to Norwegian shipping tycoon Niels Onstad, and, together, in the summer of 1968, they donated to Norway the Henie-Onstad **Art Center** at Hovikodden, Baerum, about 7½ miles from the center of Oslo. The Center is a unique concept in that it is both a museum exhibiting selections from the couple's private collection of over 300 works of art (none of which pre-date 1918), and a cultural foundation encouraging experimental work in the live arts of theatre, music, dance, film, literature, architecture, and arts and crafts. The building itself is worth the visit. Spread fan-like over the plateau on a promontory jutting into the Oslo Fjord, it consists of five "leaves" and a "stem." The "leaves" are the exhibition halls and concert rooms, while the "stem" is occupied with administrative offices. In order to keep the two experiences separate, the halls are windowless and shut off from the magnificent view. But between the rooms, and leading out from the cafeteria and restaurants, are terraces facing toward the fjord. Surrounding the museum is a 35-acre park and a walk through it will bring you to a small harbor and bathing beach. In the park is a sculpture garden and amphitheater. Getting to the Art Center is simple: take bus 32, 36 or 37, all of which leave from the University Square, take 25 minutes and cost 15 kroner one-way. The Center is open from 11 a.m. to 10 p.m. daily; admission 15 kroner for adults, 7 kroner for children. Ask at the Center or the Tourist Office for a copy of *Oslo This Week,* and keep your eye open for announcements of special programs to be held at the Center. Other activities in Oslo? **Oslo's Tourist Information Office** on the ground floor of the City Hall, waterfront entrance (phone 42-71-70), will provide you with maps, brochures, and every sort of advice, service and assistance except the sort relating to hotel bookings, which is the exclusive prerogative of the Innkvartering desk at the Central Station.

And now for some final comments on sightseeing in Oslo, here's Hope.

HOPE IN OSLO: "The Munch Museum, described earlier in this chapter, has rightfully become one of the city's top sights. But for his admirers, there's much more Munch in Oslo to meet the eye, and real aficionados will want to see his paintings at **The University Aula** (noon to 2 p.m. in summer, daily except Sundays); or in the canteen at the Freia Chocolate Factory, Johan Throne Holsts Plass 1. (There's also a Munch on the first floor of City Hall.) Most important, however, is the exciting collection of Munch at **The National Gallery**—a must!—where the best paintings are found in the Munch salen (others are in Room 28) on the second floor. Here, the air fairly vibrates with the bold color, direct force, and sheer unmitigated aliveness of this man's creations, and simply to stand in the center of the room is a breath-catching experience, like a punch in the stomach. Take special note of the eerie 'Dance of Life'; the very famous 'Shriek' (1893); 'White Night'; 'Moonlight' (1893); 'Ashes'; and the fantastic self-portraits. The rest of the gallery is also well worth seeing. Its emphasis is on 19th- and 20th-century Norwegian artists, scattered among a quite respectable collection of French impressionists and moderns, a few 16th- and 17th-century masterworks, and sculpture by Renoir, Vigeland, Rodin and Maillol. The museum is centrally located at Universitetsgaten 13 (just behind the University). Admission free, Monday through Friday 10 a.m. to 4 p.m., Wednesday and Thursday evenings from 6 to 8 p.m., Saturday 10 a.m. to 3 p.m., Sunday from noon to 3 p.m.

"If you liked the Viking Ships at Bygdøy and want to learn more about the culture that produced them, then pay a visit to the University's Collection of Antiquities at **The Historical Museum,** which houses Norwegian finds from the Stone Age through medieval times. Here you'll find Viking household articles, jewelry, art, tools, weapons, etc.; you'll also see the Treasure Room displaying valuables of silver and gold from all ages. In addition to the comprehensive Viking collection, there is also a fine display from the Middle Ages, including very impressive Stave Church facades (note especially the elaborate and intricately carved doors, almost pagan in appearance, with motifs of lions, snakes and dragons), and what is often referred to as Oslo's richest collection of art up to 1530. Open daily except Mondays, from noon to 3 p.m., admission free, the museum is situated just behind the National Gallery, at Frederiksgate 2.

"Only moderately interesting to visit, but of considerable historical significance, is **Akershus Castle** (for me the old castle has more mystery and atmosphere when its brooding presence is viewed from across the fjord in front of City Hall). Built in 1300 by King Haakon V Magnusson, it proved an impregnable fortress as well as a royal residence; but much of what you'll see today was the work of one of our favorite Danes, Christian IV, who transformed the fortress into a Renaissance Palace when he was king of both Denmark and Norway (1588 to 1648), and Oslo was known as Christiania. There's a touching monument on the castle grounds dedicated to Norwegian patriots who lost their lives here during World War II when the Nazis used Akershus as a prison and execution area, and next to the monument is Norway's **Resistance Museum (1940 to 1945),** open daily from 10 a.m. to 3 p.m., Sundays from 11 a.m. to 4 p.m., for an adult admission charge of 5 kroner. From the castle grounds there are beautiful views of Oslo and of the Oslo fjord. The castle is open in summer from 10 a.m. to 4 p.m., Sundays from 12:30 to 4 p.m. (spring, fall and winter open Sundays only), with guided tours at 11 a.m., 1 p.m. and 3 p.m. for a 5 kroner entrance fee; the best approach is from Radhusgate.

"If you happen to be in the Market Place on Stortorvet (one of Oslo's main shopping streets), you should take a look at the **Dom Church** or Oslo Cathedral, which was consecrated in 1697 but has been restored many times since then, most recently in 1950. Today, the inside of the cathedral is new, bright, clean and cheery, with the most wildly colorful ceiling I've ever seen in a church. Though the style of painting is nouveau-moderne (like Radio City Music Hall in New York), somehow the effect is luminescent and uplifting. The cathedral may be visited weekdays except on Monday from 9 a.m. to 3 p.m., Saturdays till noon in mid-summer, from 10 a.m. to 1 p.m. winter weekdays. Services are on Sundays at 11 a.m. and 6 p.m.

"There is, finally, an interesting and well-displayed collection at **The Oslo Museum of Applied Art,** St. Olavs Gate 1, of Norwegian and various foreign decorative art from the Middle Ages to the present day, which includes tapestry, furniture, metalwork, carved woodwork, glass, ceramics, costumes, etc. The Norwegian tapestry collection is especially good, and the most prized possession of the museum is the very rare and treasured Baldishol Tapestry, which was made at the end of the 12th century (there are only five tapestries from this period left in the world). The third floor houses a new permanent exhibition of modern Scandinavian design. Admission is free from 11 a.m. to 3 p.m. (also Tuesday evenings from 7 to 9 p.m.), closed Mondays."

5. Oslo Nights

There's little organized nightlife in nature-loving Oslo. Best thing in summer is simply to stroll along the Karl Johans Gate, stopping for beer or hot chocolate at one of the cafes in the "Student Grove" at the head of the street. But if you prefer something livelier, try the following.

DANCING: In central Oslo, the undisputed favorite among dance halls is the **Ridderhallen** (meaning medieval knights' hall), at 5 Torgatan, near the Oslo Cathedral, where the motif is swords, suits of armor and heraldry, but most of the waiters hail from Tunisia. They serve up beer at 30 kroner ($4), three sizes of pizza from 30 to 42 kroner ($4 to $5.60), and more expensive à la carte plates to the more than 600 guests of all ages attracted by modern dance music supplied by high-quality bands. Free admission on Mondays and Tuesdays, 10 kroner on Wednesdays and Thursdays, 20 kroner on Fridays, Saturdays and Sundays. If Ridderhallen is sold out (and it often is), you might try a nearby discotheque called **Kroa,** at 22 Storgaten, but its appeal is mainly to the under-25 crowd, and it is closed on Sundays, Mondays and Tuesdays. It costs 10 kroner to enter, and only beer is served at 30 kroner ($4) per half liter.

If you're above the age of 25, you'll enjoy **El Toro** at 7 Kristian IVs

Gate in the heart of town. There's a nightclub show from 9 to 10 p.m. followed by dancing to a live combo Monday through Saturday; you can dance and see the show from the bar for admission of 30 kroner and a compulsory beer for 30 kroner.

A swinging disco next door, the **Leopard Club,** stays open until 3:30 a.m. Admission is 30 kroner, beer 30 kroner before 11:45 p.m., 32 kroner thereafter.

FOLKLORE EVENINGS: Some of the travel agencies in Oslo sell 90-kroner ($12) tickets for a Monday, Wednesday and Friday evening summer tour to the restaurant of the Norwegian Folk Museum (on the Bygdøy peninsula) for an exhibition of Norwegian folk dancing and a meal (the meal is $10—75 kroner—extra, making a grant total of $22 per person for this evening of lore). On the bus going to the museum, the guides wear colorful folk costumes, they play a violin as they lead you up the hill to the restaurant, and the resulting picture is so attractive that tourists unable to get on the bus (space being limited) usually gnash their teeth and wail. Few of them realize that the same tour can be made, *sans* guide and *sans* group, for a fraction of the commercial cost. This, indeed, is a rule of budget travel in Europe: whatever a guided tour can do, you can do better.

Here's how it's done. On weekdays in June, July and August, from the City Hall Pier, take the 6:15 or 6:45 p.m. boat to Bygdøy (9 kroner, $1.20), get off at the first stop, and walk uphill for 15 minutes to the museum where the entrance charge is 10 kroner ($1.33). Once inside, walk uphill again to the restaurant, where the one-hour folk dancing show starts weekdays at 8 p.m. (there is no extra charge). Eat not at the costly, candle lit restaurant, but at the ground-floor cafeteria serving various hot dishes for 25 to 35 kroner, coffee or tea for 9 kroner. Then take bus 30 back to City Hall square for 9 kroner; it leaves every 15 minutes from the right of the museum's entrance. And compare. The people on the sightseeing tour have paid about $22 for this combination of elements; you have paid a total (including round-trip transportation) of about $8.93, provided you order one of the cheaper meals (which is precisely what the people on the tour are getting).

THEATRE, MUSIC AND MOVIES: The **National Theatre,** on the Karl Johans Gate just before the palace, is the very building in which the plays of Henrik Ibsen were first presented to an outraged Oslo populace, who booed them roundly. Let that be a reassuring lesson to all early failures. Cheap ticket prices (15 to 40 kroner), but the plays are in Norwegian. . . . Movies are probably your best bet in Oslo, because they're subtitled, not dubbed, and American films are therefore in English. But the showings begin promptly at 5, 7 and 9 p.m., and no one is seated after that time—a rigid Oslo custom that spares early-arriving spectators from the bother of latecomers. The 5 p.m. movies are the cheapest (24 kroner) and require no reserved seats. . . . **Orchestra Concerts** are scheduled every Sunday in summer at 1 p.m. and every Wednesday at 7 p.m. at the Vigeland Museum for a 10 kroner entrance fee. . . . **Folk dancing** exhibitions are presented every Monday and Thursday evening in July and August by the Young Peasants' Association (that's their name), at the Oslo Concert Hall, 14 Munkedamsveien. Programs run from 9 to 10 p.m. and admission is 30 kroner. . . . And always watch, as noted before, for the programs at the **Henie-Onstad Art Center,** which has become a center of living arts in Oslo.

6. Miscellaneous Tips

Distinguished English newspapers and magazines, in great profusion, are available to you, free, from 9 a.m. to 5 p.m. on weekdays, in the second floor reading room of the **Deichman Library,** 1 Henrik Ibsens Gate, Norway's largest public library. . . . Self-service laundries are most easily found in the Bislett Stadium Area—as, for example, the **Myntvaskeri,** 15 Vibesgatan, where ten machines are available weekdays from 8 a.m. to 8 p.m., Saturdays from 9 a.m. to 3 p.m., at a cost of 40 kroner ($5.33) for seven kilos washed and dried. Or try, in the same general area, **Norge Vaskeautometer,** 40 Theresegatan, corner of Wilhelmsgate, open Monday to Friday from 8 a.m. to 5 p.m., Saturdays to 1 p.m., charging 28 kroner ($3.73) for five kilos washed and dried; at the latter, the manager speaks English! Finally, for a giant wash, the **Vasketeria** at 63 Bygdøyallee, open weekdays only from 10 a.m. to 6 p.m., charges 46 kroner ($6.13) for *nine* kilos washed and dried. . . . The pharmacy at **4B Jernbanetorget** (phone 41-24-82) is open 24 hours a day; and if you need emergency medical assistance, call **First Aid** at 20-10-90 (a 24-hour service) or the **Oslo Red Cross** at 44-39-80.

READERS' TIPS: "Add the Parliament Building (Stortinget) to your tour tips. Free 45-minute tours at 11 a.m., noon, and 1 p.m., from June 15 to September 15 (when Parliament does not meet except in emergencies). Rooms are beautifully decorated —guide speaks English, Norwegian, German & perhaps more. He didn't give just a memorized talk, but *knew* much of Norwegian history as well as about the Parliament, and he encouraged questions of all sorts. Even our children said 'That was good—we learned something'" (Mrs. George Wallach, APO 80, New York). . . . "We spent one afternoon at the beach, at **Ingierstrand,** via motor launch from the city hall piers. It costs 9 kroner going, and 9 kroner returning, for both of us. The 'beach' is mainly rocks, but is an experience not to be missed, for those who haven't been to Scandinavian beaches before" (Mrs. Randell C. Widner, St. Petersburg, Florida). . . . "In the new university campus situated at Blindern, you will find a students' travel bureau where, with a student card, you can buy tickets to London for about $65 one-way, or join group train transports in Europe for half the fare. Phone 46-68-80. You can reach the campus by tram 7—Ulleval Hageby—to the end of the line (9 kroner) or by taking the subway marked Sognsvannsbanen from the National Theatre to Blindernveien for 9 kroner" (Vegard Elvestrand, Oslo, Norway; note by AF: the agency in question is the Universitetenes Reisebyraa, Universitetssentret, Blindern, Oslo). . . . "There is boat transportation from Oslo to Copenhagen, daily throughout the year, on the *M.V. King Olav V* and *M.V. Prinsesse Margrethe,* for which space can be booked from any travel agency in Oslo" (Pauline Rissman, Chicago, Illinois). . . . "The 16-hour **ferry cruise** from Oslo to Copenhagen is a Big Splurge (about $55 per person for a double-occupancy cabin with bath, which is reasonable considering the distance involved, considerably less if you take deck passage or a couchette), but well worth whatever you spend. It leaves Oslo at 5 p.m., so the fjord and harbor are in full sight and light, and arrives in Copenhagen at 9 a.m. the next morning—you can see Elsinore Castle just before breakfast. There are excellent accommodations, with three restaurants, a duty-free shop, sun decks, a playroom for children, cocktail lounges, and dinner choices (included in the price) are either a Scandinavian smorgasbord or a sit-down meal. Upon arrival, a bus awaits to transport you to the train station of Copenhagen; and, of course, the same service is available in the other direction, from Copenhagen to Oslo" (Rick and Janye Purdy, Lake Jackson, Texas).

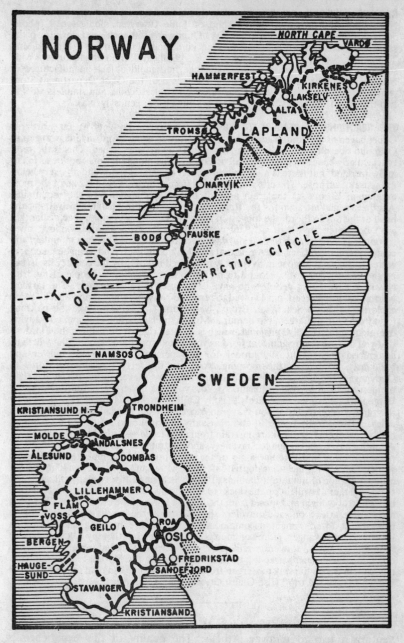

READERS' SHOPPING SELECTIONS: "We found a fantastic deal on hand-knitted Norwegian wool sweaters at the shop of **Lulle Otterstad,** Solligaten 2 (phone 56-27-00), near the American Embassy. Ours were $60 each, and downtown the same items were $85. She will ship sweaters home and fill mail orders" (Mr. and Mrs. Thomas G. Stoebe, London, England). . . . "**Stallen,** 8 Grensen, features a wide selection of inexpensive, better-than-average household objects manufactured in Norway and other Scandinavian countries. It is near the Glass Department Store which, by the way, has an enormous selection of glass, china and stainless steel at two-thirds of U.S. prices" (Jay R. Conley, Pittsburgh, Pennsylvania).

THE REACTIONS OF READERS TO NORWAY: "Anyone who gets as far north as Copenhagen or Stockholm and doesn't go to Norway is silly. And anyone who gets to Oslo and doesn't venture into the Norwegian countryside is mad. This is the most spectacularly beautiful country in all of Europe. The mountains may not be as tall as in Switzerland, but there is a far greater variety of natural sights and an overwhelming sense of surprise. The cross-country trip from Oslo to Bergen is one of the most exciting in Europe as the train ascends higher and higher into the mountains. Another special attraction is the train trip from Myrdal to Flaam, which lies at the head of the Sogne Fjord, the longest in Norway. This is a 48-minute spectacular that can't be beaten anywhere. A giant waterfall roaring away at your window, steep mountains leading down to peaceful valleys, a river that flows under a mountain and comes out on the other side. A ride that shouldn't be missed. And it can be taken free with a Eurailpass. My paean to Norway is inspired not only by the country itself, but by the Norwegians, who I found to be the most unforgettable people of my trip. Nowhere have I met people who gave of themselves so completely. The farthest North I got was Bergen, but I vowed to return to Norway someday and do a lot more exploring" (Milton Schulman, Bronx, New York). . . . "If you take the morning train from Oslo to Bergen, but detour at Myrdal to Flaam, then I recommend staying overnight at the **Heimly Pensjonat,** which is situated right at the head of the Fjord, so that you can see the magnificent fjord as you dine (supper is 60 kroner, but worth it: accommodations about 190 kroner for two persons, with private shower and breakfast). And if, in the morning, you take the ferry through the fjords to Gudvangen, the ascent by bus to Stalheim and Voss is even more spectacular than the descent from Myrdal to Flaam. At Voss you pick up an early afternoon train to Bergen—it's all timed very nicely" (Polly Chill, New York, New York). . . . "If by the time you reach Oslo, you crave an excursion from a steady diet of European cities, a fantastically beautiful and pleasantly informal mountain-fjord tour can be had by merely taking the morning train from Oslo to Bergen, the hydrofoil along the Atlantic coast from Bergen to Stavanger, and the train back again to Oslo. The train rides will bring you through some of the most breathtaking mountain and valley scenery anywhere, including tourist-infested Switzerland, with stops along the log cabins of colorful mountain hamlets. Bergen is a small town where villagers and seamen gather at twilight on the docks to sing hymns. The town and seaport can best be viewed at twilight and sunset from the hill just north of the train station. The train arrives late afternoon, and travelers should consult the tourist office three or so blocks east for overnight accommodations. There are morning and afternoon hydrofoils to Stavanger, more commercial than Bergen but thereby a better place to shop for sweaters, souvenirs and gifts" (Jay Evans, Colorado Springs, Colorado). . . . "Please emphasize the advisability of taking the Myrdal-Flaam train trip, but explain it's on the way to Bergen from Oslo, so people can plan to get off *before* Bergen to take the trip" (Ilse Gleestadt, Belmont, California).

Back now, to the mainland. If you're really ambitious, you'll now venture a trip to faraway Athens. The quality of this experience is something special—exotic, eastern and ancient. And it can be enjoyed at rock-bottom costs, because Greece ranks with Portugal as the least expensive of all the European nations.

Chapter XXIV

ATHENS

Dealing in Drachmas

TO RIDE FROM THE AIRPORT to Athens in a bus, and suddenly to see the stately Parthenon, on the Acropolis, high overlooking the city, is literally a thrill that comes once in a lifetime. Dazed by the sight, and deep in thought, you then plunge into the maws of Athens, a raucous and exotic town, and quickly you realize that this will be an experience wholly unlike the great part of your European tour.

Athens is a hybrid. The birthplace of Western civilization, with reminders everywhere of the great classic age, it is today the least Western of all European cities. In one moment, you'll tread where Demosthenes orated and Socrates taught, but in another, you'll pass pungent-smelling coffee houses where men alone—scores of them— sit chattering about the daily news—just as they do in Cairo or Casablanca.

There's nothing chic about Athens. It's a raw and a blunt place, with an unusually low price structure, and a hearty attitude toward life. If you'll enter into that mood, enjoying the low costs on which your stay there is possible, then you won't miss the minor comforts of other European capitals that are sometimes lacking in Athens. Instead you'll be able to focus clearly on the real aim of your trip: a first-hand experience of the great classic Greek civilization, which shaped our own.

At least one of three unforgettable books, *The Colossus of Maroussi* by Henry Miller, *The Bull of Minos* by Leonard Cottrell, and *The King Must Die* by Mary Renault, should be read either before or during your trip. All

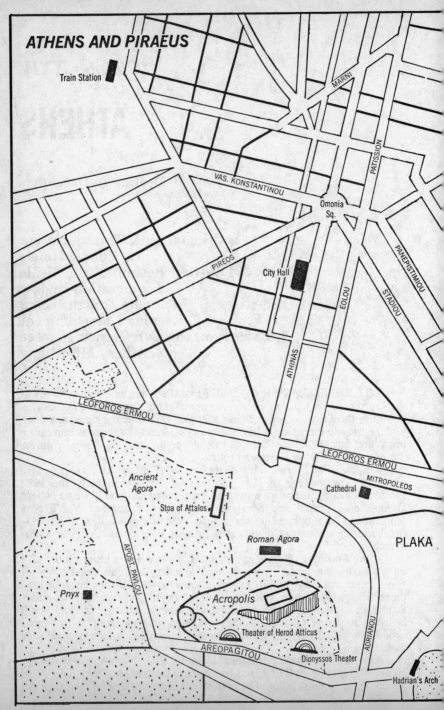

ATHENS AND PIRAEUS

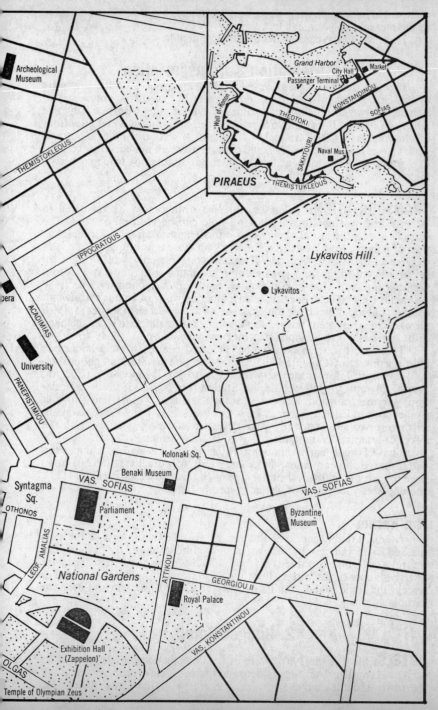

Archeological Museum

PIRAEUS

Grand Harbor

City Hall

Market

Passenger Terminal

Wall of Konon

THEOTOKI

KONSTANDINOU

SOFIAS

SAKHTOURI

Naval Mus.

THEMISTUKLEOUS

THEMISTOKLEOUS

IPPOCRATOUS

Lykavitos Hill.

Lykavitos

pera

ACADIMIAS

University

PANEPISTIMIOU

Kolonaki Sq.

Benaki Museum

VAS. SOFIAS

VAS. SOFIAS

Syntagma Sq.

OTHONOS

Parliament

Byzantine Museum

LEOF. AMALIAS

ATTIKOU

National Gardens

GEORGIOU II

Royal Palace

VAS. KONSTANTINOU

Exhibition Hall (Zappelon)

OLGAS

Temple of Olympian Zeus

three are in paperback, they weigh very little, and they'll add immeasurably to the pleasure of your stay in Greece.

First, we'll take care of the mechanical details:

1. Orientation & Transportation

If you're flying to Athens, you'll arrive at an airport six miles southeast of the city, between the Faliro and Glyfada beaches. It is connected to Athens by two airport-bus companies: Olympic runs from the Olympic Airlines City Air Terminal, 96 Syngrou Ave., and International goes from the International City Terminal, 4 Amalias St., just off Syntagma Square. Both charge 100 drachmas ($1), and operate every 20 minutes, from 6 a.m. to 9 p.m., or, for earlier or later flights, one hour prior to departure of flight.

TRANSPORTATION: There are no vast distances to be traversed in Athens, and just about everything of note can be reached on foot. The subway is of interest only because it offers transportation to Piraeus, the port of Athens, from which you'll embark on those adventures to "the Isles of Greece, the Isles of Greece." It operates one line only, which originates in suburban Kiffisia, and passes through Athens with stops at Victoria, Omonia Square, Monastiraki Square, and Piraeus; one-way fare is 30 drachmas (30¢). Buses service an extensive network of routes throughout the city, but are difficult for tourists because of the Greek alphabet in which all signs are presented; nevertheless, some visitors ultimately get the hang of it, especially if they phone first for bus information to 512-4910.

There are two train stations, both located near each other about one mile northwest of Omonia Square. The Peloponnes Station (phone 516-1601 for train information) services trains to the Peloponnese (Corinth, Patras, Olympia), while the Larissa Station (phone 821-3882 for information) services northern Greece (Larissa, Saloniki, Volos) and provides connections to Zurich, Vienna, Paris. It's advisable, in my view, always to make reservations or to buy your tickets in advance, possibly from the discount-granting **Transalpino** office at 28 Nikis Street.

Taxis? Forget 'em. Although they're relatively cheap by comparison with other European cities, and charge only 650 drachmas ($6.50) or so from the airport to town, their average in-city ride costs 300 drachmas ($3), and depletes your purse or wallet in speedy fashion.

The Harbor

Athens's main seaport is Piraeus, seven miles southwest of the city, reached in 15 minutes by subway from Omonia Square. By phoning the Information Office of Piraeus Harbor, 451-1311, you can verify departure or arrival times of the various lines and ships to and from the Greek Islands (except the Ionic islands, via Patras only), and for European and overseas harbors.

2. Budget Hotels

HOTELS: Most readers are aware of the demarcation that exists in cities such as Hong Kong or Algiers between the so-called European section of the town and the native quarters. Something of the same sort exists, amazingly enough, in Athens. The tourists, for the most part, stay in a single, confined area around Constitution Square (*Plateia Syntagmatos*), which has tall buildings and is modern and unexciting. The Greeks live elsewhere. A meeting of the two worlds occurs in the area around Omonia Square, which combines a little of both.

If you're adventurous enough to plunge into the very heart of things, away from the tourists, in a noisy neighborhood filled with bazaars and crowds, then you'll stay at the rather modern (1966) and really quite spectacular, 10-story **Hotel Alkistis,** on the Place du Théâtre (18 Plateia Theatrou), several short blocks from Omonia Square, phone 3219-811, where nearly every room has a view of the Acropolis and a pleasant little balcony, and all rooms have private bath or shower. Singles with breakfast run to a maximum of 1,500 drachmas ($15), everything included; doubles with two breakfasts are fixed at a top of 2150 drachmas ($21.50), and those prices, once again, are for rooms with private facilities. All this makes for an extremely comfortable stay, and one that is highly recommended, provided you're game for perfectly safe, but Eastern-style, surroundings.

If you'd rather stay in the more sedate Constitution Square section, then about the best you can do is at the smaller, 40-bed and much less pretentious, **Hotel Imperial,** at 46 Mitropoleos St. (phone 322-7617), which is only two short blocks from the downhill end of *Syntagma* (Constitution Square), almost directly opposite the Athens Cathedral. Here, the lobby is upstairs, but the manager (Mr. Klissouris) is English-speaking and extremely helpful, the rooms all come equipped with private shower, and the rates, with breakfast, service and tax included, are 1,850 drachmas ($18.50) single, 2,250 drachmas ($22.50) double. Alternatively, if you crave a higher-category hotel, and are willing to pay up to 3,600 drachmas ($36) for a double room with private bath and air conditioning, again with breakfast for two, service and taxes included, you can try to get into the superb **Hotel Plaka,** six short blocks from the bottom end of Constitution Square, at 7 Kapnikareas and Deka Sts. (phone 322-2096). This modern, seven-story building, which has a marble-lined lobby, a snack bar decorated as an old Athens tavern, and a roof garden restaurant with a magnificent view of the Acropolis, is undoubtedly among the best of the moderately priced hotels of Athens in terms of comfort and service, but certainly not the best bargain; in addition, demi-pension arrangements are sometimes required. Much cheaper (though simpler) in the same area is the tiny, 23-room **Cryst Hostel,** atop a grocery store at 11 Apollonos St., only three blocks from Syntagma Square, where singles are 900 drachmas ($9), doubles or twins 1,500 drachmas ($15), with shower 1,800 drachmas ($18), triples 2,000 drachmas ($20), an optional breakfast 150 drachmas per person. Phone 323-4581.

It's simply foolish, though, in a town as inexpensive as Athens, to pay as much as the Plaka asks, merely because of the sedate character of its street. Just a few blocks away, in the semi-tourist, semi-Greek area of Omonia Square, new hotels approaching the quality of the Plaka are springing up at the rate of two and three a year, offering clean, modern rooms with private bath or shower for only $15 to $29 double—all because they lack the favored Constitution Square location. Indeed, as you begin to walk from Constitution to Omonia Square, and even before you reach the latter, you'll encounter lower prices in a whole host of modern, good hotels.

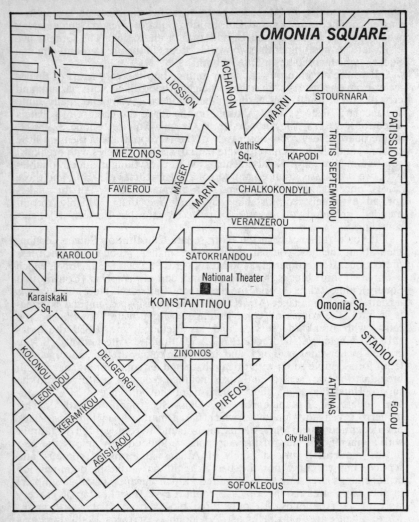

On and Near Omonia Square

Best of these, to my mind, is the cordial **Carolina Hotel,** 55 Kolokotroni St., corner of Kalamiotou (phone 322-0837), which was founded by two brothers, Gus and Lou, from South Carolina, of all places—and how they got here, no one seems to know. Last year they sold out to two Greek brothers, the easily-pronounced Athanassios and George Papayiannoulos. But like Gus and Lou before them, the new team is constantly cheerful, constantly helpful beyond call, and while their 35-room hotel is not the most comfortable in this area (although it's fairly new), it has all the amenities you'll need (elevator, lounge, snack bar, etc.) and fabulous rates. There are 10 double rooms with private bath that rent for a total of 1,900 drachmas ($19), service and taxes included; seven singles with bath for

1,500 drachmas ($15); thirteen doubles without bath for 1,525 drachmas ($15.25); three triples with bath for 2,250 drachmas ($22.50); and breakfast (optional) is 165 drachmas ($1.65). Europe on $15 a day! Location is on a segment of Kolokotroni Street (a bustling thoroughfare of retail stores) roughly halfway between Omonia and Constitution Squares.

Closer to Omonia Square, yet more comfortable and perhaps better suited to older tourists, is the splurge-priced **Hotel Acadimos,** 58 Acadimias St. (phone 362-92-21), near the National Library of Greece and a short walk from Omonia Square, whose slick, balconied appearance is like that of a Hilton. The hotel has two elevators, a large lobby with restaurant and bar, and eight floors; yet it charges only 2,950 drachmas ($29.50), including service and tax, for a double room with breakfast, private bath, telephone, and balcony facing either on the Acropolis or on Lycabettus Hill.

One tiny block off Omonia Square, the 64-room, third-class **Hotel Alma,** fairly recently built at 5 Dorou St. (phone 522-2833), charges 2,000 drachmas ($20) for a double room with private bath or shower (breakfast and service included); only 1,600 drachmas ($16) for a bathless double and breakfast, as does its nearby sister hotel, the **Amaryllis,** at 45 Veranzerou (phone 523-8738). Singles with breakfast are 1,300 drachmas ($13) at the Alma, 1,700 drachmas ($17) at the Amaryllis—the latter with private bath. Neither, however, is as well-recommended by me as the Acadimos or the hotels that follow.

Even cheaper—but still modern—hotels are found on the Agiou Constantinou, an avenue which runs into Omonia Square. Five blocks off Omonia Square, the **Hotel Kronos,** 18 Agiou Dimitriou St. (phone 3211-601), with 120 rooms on seven floors (there is an elevator), charges 1,500 drachmas ($15) for a twin with bath, 1,300 drachmas ($13) for a twin without bath, 1,800 drachmas ($18) triple with bath, 1,600 drachmas ($16) triple without bath—but breakfast is not included in any of these rates. **Hotel Neon-Kronos,** under different management, charges just slightly more (about 10% more) a few hundred yards away from the Kronos, at 12 Agion Asmaton St. (phone 3251-106); it has three floors, 100 beds, and an elevator. Both do look rather dull from the outside and have unimpressive reception lounges, but the area is quiet and the rooms simple but clean. Since their location is away from the center city, the chance of getting a room is high when budget hotels elsewhere are sold out. Nearer to Omonia Square, at 32 Agiou Constantinou, the big-splurge-priced **Hotel Achillion** (phone 523-0971), charges 2,400 drachmas ($24) for doubles with private bath, including breakfast and service. It is deservedly popular with tourists, as is the **Hotel Nestor,** two blocks away, at 58 Agiou Constantinou (phone 523-5576), which prices a well-furnished double room with private bath and breakfast at 2,500 drachmas ($25), service and tax included, a single with same at 2,100 drachmas ($21). Danish and Swedish tourists stay in this latter spot, in great numbers. To increase their American clientele, the owners of the Nestor, Messrs. D. Tsemberas and E. Apostolou, have offered a 10% discount to guests who display a copy of this book upon registering.

Elsewhere in the same area, the recently built and quite modern **Hotel El Greco,** one block to the south of the Square, at 65 Athinas St. (phone 324-4554), charges a splurgey 3,350 drachmas ($33.50) for a double with private shower and breakfast, including the 15% service charge (singles are too high for this book). But this is a rather imposing eight-story building with two elevators, three lounges, a bar and balconies—and altogether quite plush. Back in our range, to the west of the square, the cheaper but almost equally suitable **Hotel Arcadia,** 46 Marni St. (phone 522-6571), charges only 1,900 drachmas ($19) for a bathless double, service included, 2,250 drachmas ($22.50) for a double with private shower; 1,200 drachmas ($12) for singles without showers, 1,800 drachmas for a single with private shower. Breakfast is always included.

All of these hotels are superbly situated for touring. The main station of the subway that runs between Athens and Piraeus (where *Never on Sunday* was filmed) sits smack in the center of Omonia Square; while the bus to the Archaeological Museum stops only one short block from the Alma Hotel.

THE MODERN SIGNIFICANCE OF ATHENS: Out of a total Greek population of 9.7 million persons, 3.1 million or 32% live in Athens. Compared with that, only 5% of all Italians live in Rome, 15% of the British in London, 20% of the French in Paris.

THE LESS COSTLY GUESTHOUSES AND PENSIONS: This alternate sort of accommodation in Athens is more personal and intimate than the typical, large Athenian hotel. And one of the best of these establishments is **Tony's Pension,** 26 Zacharitsa St. (phone 923-63-70), where singles are a high 1,400 drachmas ($14), but twins or doubles only 1,700 drachmas ($17), triples 2,000 drachmas ($20), and all rooms are with private shower, w.c., and breakfast. Tony Nicolaidis, the jolly owner-manager who sometimes wears blue silk pyjamas while working at his second-floor reception desk, loves his job and will even pick you up on your arrival in town, free of charge, in his small car, if you give him a call and he is free. His pension is well-operated, invariably clean, and located at the foot of Philopappos Hill, five minutes on foot from the Olympic Airways Terminal.

Two alternate possibilities in the Plaka Area: **Guest House Kouros,** 11 Kodrou St. (phone: 322-7431), whose owner, Mr. Lambros Katsimbri, offers singles for a far more acceptable 800 drachmas ($8), doubles for 1,400 drachmas ($14), triples for 1,800 drachmas ($18), showers for free. And, still in Plaka, the 40-bed **Dioskouros Hotel,** 6 Pittakou St. (phone 3248-165), managed by English-speaking Peter Katsimpras, is another recommended choice, provided you're not squeamish about utterly bare but clean quarters. Rates for 1985 are: single room, 1,100 drachmas ($11); twin, 1,800 drachmas ($18); triple 2,100 drachmas ($21); and 2,400 drachmas ($24) for the only available family room with four beds. Showers are free.

Pension Marble House, at 35 Zinni St. (phone 2934-058), near the Olympic Airways building at Sygrou Avenue, is a nicely furnished 21-room guesthouse on four floors (no elevator), charging 1,100 drachmas ($11) for bathless singles, 1,400 drachmas ($14) for bathless twins, with showers, in the corridors, free. Optional breakfast is 190 drachmas ($1.90). Owned and managed by the English-speaking Tsiranis family (he works for TWA), this guest house can be reached by bus no. 5 or 7 from Syntagma Square (30-drachma ticket) to Zinni Street (fifth stop). Marble House is actually located in a tiny, quiet, blind alley, off Zinni; it's the building with the plants and flowers in front. Walking distance from Syntagma Square is ten minutes.

Clare's Apartment Hotel, at 24 Sorvolou St. in the Olympic Stadium area, 500 yards from the Royal Olympic Hotel (phone 9222-288), is an almost brand new (1982) lodging on four floors. Reached by elevator, the 12 two-room apartments, furnished with unpainted-pine beds, tables, chairs and wardrobes, and equipped with private shower, w.c., kitchen and Frigidaire, are priced at 1,750 drachmas ($17.50) per apartment (when occupied by two), or, if you are in a group of four, for $7 per person. This is an ideal choice for families or small university groups that plan longer stays in Athens but cannot afford restaurant meals. They pay only a 1,000-drachma deposit on the kitchen equipment—pots, pans, cutlery, etc.—fully refunded if nothing is missing or broken upon departure; they enjoy a panoramic roof garden for sunbathing and general relaxation, looking out over the Acropolis and Lycabettus Hill. But public transportation to Clare's Apartment Hotel is somewhat complicated, and it is advisable to take a taxi (from Syntagma Square about 200 drachmas, or $2) when you first arrive.

READERS' HOTEL SELECTIONS (OMONIA SQUARE): "New Athenian hotels, as a method of attracting business, offer unusually good rates during their first several years of operation. The C-category **Hotel Keramikos** at 30 Keramikou St. (phone 524-7631), near Omonia Square, where every room has private bath, will rent (in 1985) for only 1,500 drachmas ($15) per person in double rooms, 1,200 drachmas per person in triples, 1,000 drachmas per person in quad rooms, not including breakfast, which is 140 drachmas per person" (Pauline Rissman, New York, New York). . . . "At the **Hotel Epidauros,** 14 Koumoundourou St. (phone 523-0421), near Omonia Square, we paid 1,900 drachmas ($19) for a double room, breakfast, service and tax included, and received free use of showers, lots of hot water and fresh linens, the cleanest room we had in Greece" (Mrs. Charles Szumski, Arbuckle, California). . . . "We highly recommended the **Hotel Pythagorion** at 28 Agiou Constantinou St. (phone 524-2811) near Omonia Square. For 2,300 drachmas ($23), my husband and I had an attractive, spacious room with a modern desk, a huge clothing closet, a balcony, and a private bath with all facilities, with breakfast (which included croissants, a kaiser roll and fruitcake) included in the price of the room" (Mrs. Michael Popkin, New York, New York; seconding recommendations from Ruth Sussles, Alhambra, California, and Sharon Todd, Norfolk, Virginia).

READER'S HOTEL SELECTIONS (CONSTITUTION SQUARE): "**Hotel Nefeli,** 16A Iperidou St. (phone 32-28-044), was one of the best finds of our trip. It's a small, intimate hotel, newly built, at a street corner in the picturesque Plaka district, though only a few minutes walk to Syntagma Square, and not far from the Acropolis. The manager, Napoleon, went out of his way to be helpful to us, and we stayed ten days longer than planned" (Henry G. Blau, New York, NY; note by AF: 1985 rates are 2,400 drachmas ($24) for twins, 2,000 drachmas ($20) for singles, with shower and private w.c., breakfast included).

READERS' HOTEL SELECTIONS (PLAKA): "**Hotel Tempi,** 29 Aeolou St. (phone 321-31-75), is a small and cozy, clean, and wonderful, D-class hotel in the Plaka area operated by Mr. Dmitris Kanakis, a warm, friendly and English-speaking gentleman who offers an outdoor, rooftop lounge, a little coffee bar on the first floor, and a lending library of used books. The price is right—1,200 drachmas ($12) for bathless singles, 1,600 drachmas ($16) for bathless doubles, 160 ($1.60) for breakfast—the atmosphere terrific" (Judy Kinis, Hollywood, Florida). . . . "At the **Adonis Hotel,** 3 Kodrou, in Plaka (phone 324-9737), where we had a double room with private shower and huge balcony for 2,250 drachmas ($22.50), the best feature is the roof garden containing both a bar and dining area. Breakfast (coffee and rolls) is served

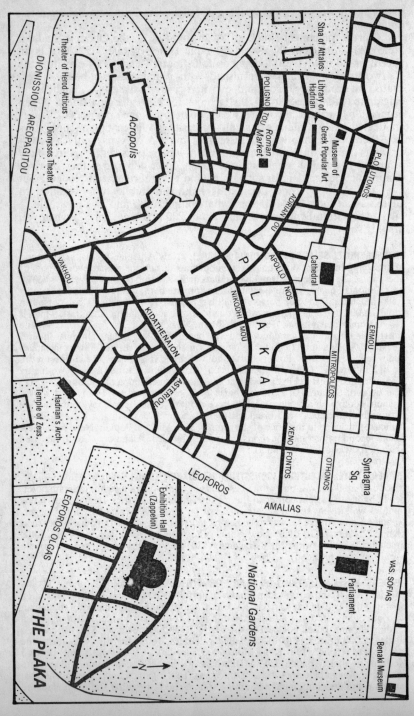

THE PLAKA

there and is eaten as you view the Acropolis and Lycabettus Hill. A real find!" (Michael and Juliette Hedger, Cremorne, Australia; note from AF: singles with private shower and breakfast, in 1985, are 1,650 drachmas ($16.50), doubles the same as above) . . . "**Attalos Hotel,** 29 Athinas St., next to Monasteraki and the Plaka, is category C, but we found the rooms good or better than the class B hotels we experienced all throughout Greece. The hotel has 80 rooms and the back rooms, which are very quiet, all have terraces with a view on the Acropolis. Rates for next year are 1500 drachmas ($15) single, 2400 drachmas ($24) double, 2900 drachmas ($29) triple, 3600 drachmas ($36) for a four-bedded family room, always including breakfast for all. Phone number is 321-28-01. Best reason for recommending the Attalos is its owner, Kostas Zisis, extremely friendly and helpful—the nicest man we met in Greece" (William Megalos, New York, New York). . . . "Most of the budget hotels in Plaka have closed, and remaining ones are hard to find. We were therefore fortunate to chance upon the **Hotel Delos,** 12 Makri Street (phone 9220-106), where Mr. Michael Spanoudakis, English-speaking, will be offering the following high-season rates in 1985 for rooms with private shower and w.c.: 1,850 drachmas ($18.50) for twins, 2,250 drachmas ($22.50) for triples, 3,700 drachmas ($37) for quads, ideal for families. Off-season prices are about 20% less; location is a quiet one" (Al and Norma Maffei, Pleasant Hill, California; note from AF: having recently seen the Delos, I can confirm Mr. and Mrs. Maffei's quite remarkable discovery, and can also report that Mr. Spanoudakis has guaranteed the above dollar equivalents, to readers of this book only, through the end of 1985).

3. Low-Cost Restaurants & Meals

FOOD AND DRINK: Virtually all the Athenian restaurants we discuss are tourist restaurants, equipped with menus printed in English or French. Because of that, and because few of our readers (including your author) can read Greek, we have not included a translation of Greek menu terms in our menu chapter, appearing farther on in this book. But we do have some menu comments:

When in doubt, ask your waiter for *moussaka*—a staple dish served in many of the Athenian restaurants and in all of the *tavernas* (smaller and totally unpretentious restaurants). Moussaka consists of baked, ground meat, covered with vegetables and spices, and sometimes topped with a layer of dough or mashed potatoes. Its quality varies from place to place, but if you're lucky you'll make a wonderfully tasty meal of it. And it's filling: you'll be more than stuffed if you have, for dinner, a plate of moussaka, a tomato salad, bread and wine. Eaten in the normal taverna, that combination should rarely cost more than 400 drachmas ($4).

Another staple entree in many Athenian restaurants is *dolmothakia* (rice and meat in vine leaves). For a lighter snack, ask for *souvlakia,* which are roasted and spitted chunks of lamb, flavored with oregano.

The Greek table wine is *retsina*—a red wine flavored with resin (pine sap)—and it's death to American tastes. To get it without the resin, specify that you want your wine *aresinato.*

The Greek aperitif—a before-meal drink—is *ouzo,* which is cheap (about $1 a shot), and taken either straight or in water (which it turns cloudy white). A Seven-Up-type drink, which Hope very much likes, is "gazoza" (or at least that's how it's pronounced!).

RESTAURANTS: The best street for budget restaurants serving palatable food is Kolokotroni Street, which juts off Venizelou Street, only a few steps

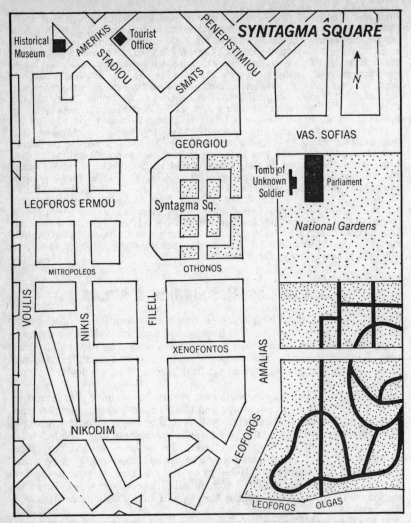

from the top of Constitution Square. There are, of course, many much cheaper restaurants than these in Athens, most of them, however, serving dishes that simply aren't acceptable to Western tastes. Because there's a vast difference between the meals a Greek workingman eats (heavily oiled, often sour) and those we're accustomed to, Athens is the only city in Europe in which I've specifically sought out the *tourist* restaurants. But don't expect corned-beef-and-cabbage; these are moderately priced tourist restaurants, and therefore the food is still Greek, although a few concessions are made.

Most popular of all (though a bit on the high side) is the **Restaurant Kentrikon,** 3 Kolokotroni St., near Constitution Square (you'll see the same Greeks and foreigners eating there over and over again), where the spicy lentil soup at 100 drachmas ($1) is almost a meal in itself, where the stuffed peppers plate is 220 drachmas ($2.20), and the cream custard (100 drachmas) is like the finest Mexican flan. Most chicken specialties here are 450 drachmas, roast lamb with cheese-flavored macaroni is 450 drachmas, and the highest item on the menu is a plate of wine-soaked shish kebab—and that comes to 550 drachmas ($5.50), including service charge. To compare these rates with the more normal prices of Athenian restaurants, stroll over to the popular **Taverna Platanos**, on a quiet, shady square at the foot of the Acropolis hill, 4 Diogenes St., where moussaka is only 250 drachmas ($2.50), macaroni 180 drachmas ($1.80), roast veal with french fries 380 drachmas ($3.80), feta cheese 70 drachmas (70¢), half a liter of retsina wine 80 drachmas (80¢). In business since 1932, the Platanos is only 200 yards from the Cathedral (Mitropolis Church), between Adrianou and Mnissikleos Streets in the heart of Plaka and is open daily except Sundays from noon to 3:45 p.m., and from 8:15 p.m. to midnight; its rates are Greek, and not tourist-oriented.

But you'll still want to try the now "high-priced" Kentrikon at least once. And if it's overly crowded on the occasion of your visit, you can simply walk two short blocks over to 6 Kriezotou Street, where you'll find the **Restaurant Corfu** (next door to the King's Palace Hotel), a much slicker and more modern restaurant than Kentrikon, and with slightly higher prices: 160 drachmas for a tomato salad, 380-or-so drachmas for a plate of moussaka (a ground-meat-and-potatoes casserole). The Corfu is usually uncrowded, which Kentrikon isn't, and it is open seven days a week, from noon to 1 a.m.

Rather than go to the Corfu, however, I'd take a longer walk to Omonia Square, where the **Restaurant Nea Olympia** (at 3 Emmanuel Benaki, just off Stadiou Street, two short blocks from the square) is to that area what Kentrikon is to Constitution Square. It's larger than Kentrikon, almost equally known, and actually less expensive than either Kentrikon or the Corfu: 120 drachmas for tomato salads, 280 drachmas for moussaka, 550 drachmas for roast lamb. Hope and I, on our last visit, had two tomato and cucumber salads, two moussakas, one glass of beer, one orangeade—and the total bill came to 1,100 drachmas, about $11, including tip. The Nea Olympia, by the way, sometimes lists the Athenian specialty—dolmothakia—a concoction of rice and meat served in vine leaves, for 140 drachmas ($1.40), which you ought to try. A good second choice, directly off Omonia Square (behind the large Omonia Restaurant and next door to the Hotel Europe (ten marble steps below street level) is the **Galaxias Restaurant** at 5 Satovriandou St., open seven days a week until midnight. At this popular, family-operated establishment, I was the only non-Greek client in the summer of 1984, when I enjoyed a tasty, lamb-and-green-beans stew with chicory salad, half a bottle of retsina wine, and a juicy orange for dessert, for only $3 then, $3.50 in 1985. Request their English menu card—they have one.

Other tourist restaurants? Near Constitution (Syntagma) Square, the really superb and quite cheap **Syntrivani,** a large (500 seats) open-air garden restaurant at 5 Filellinon St. (a few steps from the square), has an English-speaking owner—the eager-to-please Spanos Thanossos, an English menu, prices somewhat lower than those at our foregoing selections, and is open seven days a week, from noon to midnight. Simply to obtain a price comparison with the other restaurants we've named, I had my standard Athenian meal in this quite comfortable place—cucumber salad, moussaka (can't get enough of that stuff), a small beer, and a large slice of watermelon—for a total charge, including service, of 450 drachmas ($4.50).

But if you'll limit yourself to the main course, with salad, feta cheese and retsina wine, you can keep the bill to 350 drachmas ($3.50). . . . Remember this street: **Filellinon.** It is directly off Constitution Square, and crams budget restaurants such as the Syntrivani and budget travel agencies —Viking's and Lotus—along its length. Just off Filellinon, the rather new **Restaurant Diros,** at 10 Xenophontos St., serves good, home-cooking-type food at budget rates: 90 drachmas for a filling platter of bean soup, 180 drachmas for a large spaghetti dish, 260 drachmas for a quarter roast chicken lavishly garnished.

Near Monastiraki (much cheaper)

In the area of the flea market (in front of the church), at 2 Platia Monastiraki, the **Restaurant Sigalas** is one of those typical Greek eateries where you walk into the kitchen, peek at bubbling pots and pans, and then point to what you wish to have. At this popular restaurant with its straw padded chairs, à la carte prices are so reasonable that you can feast for less than 350 drachmas ($3.50); moussaka is 200 drachmas ($2), Greek salad 130 drachmas ($1.30), a garlic soup called "Patsas" 150 drachmas ($1.50), "Psarri"—stewed fish with tomatoes, a house specialty for 200 drachmas. And an excellent retsina wine, stored in five large barrels in the back, is 80 drachmas (80¢) per liter, all items including service charge (although it's customary to tip the young waiters 20 drachmas). Everything can be bought to take out for picnic purposes for 10% less. Open every day of the week from 8 a.m. to 11:30 p.m., and supervised by English-speaking Spiros Bairataris. If he is not there, ask for Andreos, the waiter who looks like Oliver Hardy.

In Plaka

Two final selections, for the Plaka area, always popular for its cheap (but tasty) food and cool local wines, begin with the **Taverna Byron,** at 1 Vakhou St., in the very center of Plaka, where you'll be sitting among many more Greeks than tourists. Stuffed vine leaves for 120 drachmas, french fries 70, Greek salad 160, souvlaki 160, and half a liter of open white, red or rosé wine, served in colored aluminum pitchers, for 85 drachmas. Look for a green glass roof in front, and try for a seat on the roof garden, from which the Acropolis is in full view. . . . Or seek out my own Plaka favorite: the big **Taverna Poulakis** at 6 Panos St., next to the Roman Agora, peaceful and relaxing. Costliest dish there is lamb chops with fried potatoes for 430 drachmas, but almost everything else is cheaper: moussaka for only 200 drachmas, a large stuffed tomato for 160 drachmas, french fries for 50, a liter of retsina wine for 80, black olives 20, feta cheese 35, and so on. From Monastiraki Square, walk up Areos Street, turn into the first street that goes left (the one with the basket shops), pass the stone wall, and the second street turning right (you cannot turn left) is the short Panos Street, lined on both sides with the 100 tables and the 350 chairs of the Taverna Poulakis.

A vegetarian restaurant, **Eden,** 3 Flessa St., in the Plaka area, is one of Athen's best budget restaurants, open seven days a week from 11 a.m. to 1 a.m., 59 tables in three ground-floor and second-floor dining rooms, and on a small terrace, with lots of space to sit and move around. The large menu lists various vegetable soups for 100 drachmas ($1), moussaka with mushrooms for 190 drachmas ($1.90), spinach balls, two big ones, for 140 drachmas ($1.40), large salad bowl 200 drachmas ($2)—a full meal by itself—carrott or lettuce salads 80 drachmas (80¢) each, and a specialty of the house which you should try, it's not served any other place, a zucchini-potato-feta-cheese pie, spiced with mint and oregano, called "bureki," for 160 drachmas ($1.60). Try to sit at one of the round tables in the second-floor dining room, the one with the high ceiling and the black-and-white-checkered floor. It's coolest there. From Syntagma Square: walk down Mitropoleus Street, turn left into Voulis Street, then right into Mikodimou Street, and you'll see the Eden sign.

DINING IN DROSIA—A DAY IN THE SUBURBS: On hot summer days, in-the-know Athenians take to the northern suburbs, where the air is cooler and open-air restaurants serve good food at reasonable prices. Such a one is the **Taverna Mitsos** in Drosia, phone 81-31-212 (about 20 miles north—take bus numbers 134, 135, 136 or 137 from Kaningos Square), where you can dine al fresco under tall pines. (Menu in Greek only, but waiters will take you to the kitchen and let you point, if need be.) Large steak with french fries, 380 drachmas ($3.80); meatballs with vegetables and french fries, 160 drachmas ($1.60); Greek salad, 90 drachmas (90¢); penerli—the local answer to pizza—200 drachmas ($2). A liter of retsina accompanying the meal, 90 drachmas (90¢), is a must.

READERS' RESTAURANT SELECTIONS: "I usually ate at the cheap and friendly **Taverna Psarra** (meaning "fisherman") at 16 Erechteos Street in the Plaka, filled with Greeks all eating together like one big family; usually someone has a guitar, and then everyone sings, and some even leap onto a table for a Zorba-like dance. A big salad is 110 drachmas, cheese 70 drachmas, moussaka or fish 200 drachmas, a half liter of retsina wine only 80 drachmas" (Sigrun Oladottir, Rejkjavik, Iceland; note from AF: in Plaka, look for the large signs pointing to the Taverna Attalos, walk 22 steps up, and you'll find Taverna Psarra in the corner with the three trees). . . . "My wife and I recommend **Gianakis**, 15 Agiou Konstantinou, just two blocks from Omonia Square. The atmosphere is friendly and the surroundings clean. Chicken with rice, potatoes, macaroni, pumpkin or okra is 180 drachmas, a side order of tomato or cucumber salad, 100 drachmas, feta cheese, 40 drachmas, coffee 50 drachmas, and a dessert of crème caramel, 70 drachmas—all of which adds up to quite a large meal for just a little under $4, service included" (Don & Shirley Ward, Unionville, Ontario, Canada). . . . "Consider the **Ideal Restaurant**, 46 Panepistimiou St. It's a clean, inexpensive place near Omonia Square. Dinners are delicious, the menu is varied, and selections can be made from samples in the front window. A full meal can be had for 650 drachmas, and vegetarians can feast for about 500. It's right next to the Ideal Cinema" (James L. Damewood, Dayton, Ohio). . . . "The best high quality food we found in Athens was at the **Delfi Restaurant**, 13 Nikis St., only two blocks from Syntagma (Constitution) Square, where the tzatziki was 120 drachmas, moussaka 280. But the best values in enjoyable food were a few blocks further into Plaka, where there are two adjacent, outdoor, budget-priced restaurants, of which the better is **Piccolino** at 26 Sotiris St., corner of Kidathineon, somewhat misnamed as a pizzeria. There we had tzatziki for 60 drachmas, moussaka for 180, octopus for 200 drachmas, plus french fries, salad, coffee and a half bottle of wine, resulting in a total price of 800 drachmas—$4 per person—for the two of us" (J. Norman MacLeod, Edmonton, Alberta, Canada).

READER'S BIG SPLURGE SELECTION: "**Seven Boats**, at 371 Sygrou Ave., serves fresh seafood that you select yourself from a large tank, and provides excellent service as well as moderate prices averaging about $7.50 per meal" (Jo Anne Lavely, Fremont, California).

CURRENCY: In this chapter, the drachma has been converted into dollars at the rate of approximately 100 drachmas per dollar, which makes each drachma worth about one U.S. cent. That rate, of course, fluctuates, but should not swing too far from the 100:1 ratio by the time of your own trip to Athens.

READERS' SELF-SERVICE SELECTIONS: "In Athens, the food problem is a lot nearer solution with the brand-new **Floca Self-Service** at 16 Emanuel Benaki, about 3 blocks from Omonia Square. It's one of the few U.S.-type cafeterias in Greece. I ate there at least once a day and ordinarily spent just about 400 drachmas, usually for something like a macaroni moussaka, spinach-cheese pie, beer, ice cream and coffee. The big wall menu is in English, and most of the counter girls are English-speaking coeds at the university and very helpful. I understand the management is planning more cafeterias directly on Omonia and Constitution Squares" (Nat Friedland, New York, N.Y.). . . . "The extremely inexpensive **Rodeo Self Service** at 17 Satobriandou, half a block from the back corner of the Omonia Hotel on Omonia Square, serves a large plate of delicious Greek-style lima beans for 90 drachmas, a plate of french fries for 60 drachmas, macaroni in sauce 65 drachmas, tomato salad 80 drachmas, moussaka 140 drachmas, fried eggs for 45 drachmas each. Particularly good when you are in a hurry, as there is no waiting" (John Bennett, Houston, Texas; note from AF: at the Rodeo, there are seats upstairs, and waiter service, without service charge. Closed Sundays).

4. Starvation Budget

The **YWCA** in Athens (its Greek initials are XEN) is housed in a big, modern, clean and beautifully located building at 11 Amerikis St. (phone 362-4291). Its very highest-priced twin rooms with bath go for 700 drachmas ($7); descend to 600 drachmas ($6), without bath; descend to 500 drachmas ($5) per person if you take a triple room. No young lady should pass it up.

A "Y" for men? The **YMCA** of Athens (whose initials here are XAN) is at 28 Omirou (phone 362-5960) corner of Acadimias, three-or-so short blocks from Constitution Square, in a relatively modern but utterly bare stone building in which rooms rent for the same prices as at the **YMCA**, above.

Athens possesses one official youth hostel, charging 400 drachmas ($4) per dormitory accommodation: **Athens Youth Hostel No. 1**, at 57 Kypselis St. (phone 822-5860), about five blocks behind the National Archaeological Museum. The dorms, on three floors, have from six to 20 double-decker beds each, with four washrooms and five toilets on every floor, and at the 400 drachma price they're an excellent bargain, available however only to possessors of a Youth Hostel Card, sold on the premises for $15. From Syntagma Square, take buses 2, 4 or 9 (30-drachma ticket) to the Zakynthon stop, and there's the official youth hostel, friendly, clean, and well managed by the English-speaking Angelos Vazaios.

Athens' *unofficial* youth hostel, simply called the **Athens Hostel**, is at 20 Ioulianou Street (phone 8213-940), three blocks up from the National Archaeological Museum, in a six-story building containing dormitories with four to eight beds apiece. Here the charge is 400 drachmas ($4) per person, but no youth hostel card is required, no curfew imposed, and showers and storage facilities (left luggage) are free. English-speaking manager Anastasios Spertalis is assisted by five or six young helpers, male and female, who work part-time for free meals and lodging, which might put a few ideas into your mind. How would you like to stay in Athens, say, for a few months?

READERS' SELECTIONS (STARVATION BUDGET): "The Student Inn is located in the heart of the Plaka, only a short distance from the Acropolis at 16 Kidathineon St. (phone 32-44-808). Rooms are clean, and a three-bedded room was just 550 drachmas ($5.50) per person. Hot showers are free 24 hours a day, and you may also use the washing machine at no charge. Owner Spiro is extremely friendly and helpful, and speaks fluent American; he lived 25 years in Manhattan before returning to Athens" (Craig Gross, Yale, South Dakota). . . . **"Pension Argo** at 25 Victoros Ougo (Victor Hugo) St. (phone 522-5939), ten minutes from the station, and almost half-way between Larissa train station and Omonia Square, is extremely basic but perfectly acceptable for backpackers eager to find an immediate pad upon arrival at the station; perhaps later one could search further in the Plaka area. Rooms are only 550 drachmas ($5.50) per person in twins, 450 drachmas ($4.50) in triples, 400 drachmas ($4) per person in quads, 300 drachmas ($3) per in a ten-cot dorm, with breakfast an additional 130 drachmas ($1.30), free showers, no curfew, and free use of a laundromat in the basement. Owner Kostas Pappaianni speaks excellent English, too" (Tony Delport and Merryl Gillmer, Durban, South Africa).

STUDENT DISCOUNTS ON TRAVEL AND TOURS: Discount-offering "student travel agencies" are found on practically every second street corner in central Athens, and many hotels, especially the small ones, will also claim to offer youth travel facilities at a discount. By far the best source, however, is the **Transalpino Office** at 28 Nikis St. (phone 322-0503 or 323-8177), 100 yards off Syntagma Square, specializing in student and youth travel. If you're under 26 years of age (student or not), Transalpino Express will sell you train, coach, air and ship tickets to everywhere in the world, from Amsterdam to Tokyo and London to Sydney, at up to 40% off published rates. And even if you are older than 26, Transalpino will sell you tickets, sometimes at special discount rates. Open Monday to Friday from 8 a.m. to 7 p.m., Saturday from 8 a.m. to 1:30 p.m.

For discounts off the cost of standard sightseeing tours in and from Athens, you'll want to make use of a unique budget-oriented travel agency called **Viking's Travel Bureau,** headed by a trio of English-speaking Greeks—the Cocconi brothers—whose office is at 3 Filellinon St. (phone 3229-383), just off Constitution Square. They offer to all readers of this book an up to 20% discount on local sightseeing tours and one-day cruises. Thus, the morning or afternoon Athens sightseeing tour, normally priced at 2,000 drachmas ($20), will cost you 1,600 drachmas ($16) instead; the one-day tour to Delphi 2,480 ($24.80) instead of 3,100 drachmas ($31); the popular one-day cruise to Aegina, Poros and Hydra 2,480 drachmas ($24.80) instead of 3,100 drachmas ($31)—by booking the latter cruise, you'll save almost as much as you paid for this book! Viking also operates the unusual "Do-As-You-Like-Tours" of Greece, described in a later section of this chapter, and my advice is to visit this stalwart institution the moment you set foot in Athens.

5. Tours & Sightseeing

DAYTIME: There's so much to know and learn about Athens that it's best to take, first, a guided half-day tour, and then retrace your steps with lesser speed and greater deliberation. Best bet for this is the complete four-hour tour (9 a.m. to 1 p.m., and 3 to 7 p.m.), which all the tour companies (the best one is Chat) offer for 2,000 drachmas ($20), and which is much to be preferred to the exhausting day-long variety or the insufficient (it omits the Acropolis) morning three-hour tour. By the end of four hours, you'll be aching to be let out to examine these thrilling spots at your own pace. All the tour companies of Athens run the same three standardized city tours, and all charge similar rates.

The tours devote a big thirty minutes to the exciting **Archaeological Museum,** 44 Patission St. (admission: 150 drachmas), which, in its own way is as absorbing as the Acropolis. The "Golden Mask of Agamemnon" is here, as well as the statue of the "Child Jockey," the "Thundering Zeus," and all the other works of classic sculpture at which we used to gaze, as kids, in the *National Geographic*. Here, too, are the recently added frescoes from the island of Santorini—alone justifying a visit. Schedule a full morning for this (and remember that the museum is closed Mondays, while there's free admission on Sundays). **The Benaki Museum** at 1 Koumbari (70 drachmas except on Sundays when it's free; closed Tuesdays), deals with a more recent Greek age, is interesting only for its basement of Greek costumes and clothing on life-sized models.

The Acropolis (150 drachmas) charges no admission on Sundays, and here, of course, you'll want to wander for hours. Remember that this site, on the dramatic hill overlooking Athens, is revered by all Greeks. There's a guard present to prevent you from forming human pyramids, standing on your head, etc., for picture-taking purposes, just as we'd prevent tourists from sitting on the lap of Lincoln, at the Memorial in Washington, D.C. If you're of student age, be sure to claim the reduced price student admission fee to the Acropolis of only 80 drachmas.

Two other visits should be coupled with your trip to the Acropolis. Behind the hills is the magnificently reconstructed **Stoa of Attalos** in the ancient Agora, the main market place and gathering spot of ancient Athens (admission: 70 drachmas for the site, 50 drachmas extra for the museum). Again no charge on Sundays. And carved into the side of the Acropolis is the **Theater of Dionysus** (free admission on Sundays, 50 drachmas all other days), which stands today almost exactly as it stood 20 centuries ago, when the comedies of Aristophanes were performed on this very stage and to these very same stone seats; a profound experience, especially for those knowledgeable in the theatre, who will know the names, as I'm proud to say Hope does, of the various portions of the stage and anterior stage.

HOPE IN ATHENS: And now, for a more intensive look at the sights of Athens, I give you Hope, who has had, on each one of our trips, a more rapturous reaction to the city than before. Here's her report:

"There's a message whistling round the ancient stones of Greece—prepare for it, listen for it. It's like the song of the Lorelei: once you hear it, you are changed forever. And in days to come, whenever petty, temporal irritations enter your life, you need only think of the stones of Greece to dispel them forthwith.

The Parthenon

"This jewel of 'The Golden Age of Pericles' (built in honor of Athena, patroness of Athens) should be the focus of your stay: it's considered by experts to be the most perfect building ever created by man. And it's deceptive: although, at first glance, a normal, rectangular, Doric structure, every one of its lines is subtly tapered to optically correct a straight line (which would otherwise recede or advance in viewing) into a graceful and slender perspective. There are 'curves' everywhere. Take, for example, the columns, which are not straight, as they appear to be, but gently tapered, and convex in their middle portions, thus making the top part appear more slender. For proof that the curves do exist, try this simple experiment: stoop down to the eye-level of one of the steps at the side of the Parthenon. You will immediately see a 'bulge' in the center of the step! . . . And this mathematical and aesthetic masterpiece becomes an even greater testament to the builders' art when one remembers that no mortar or cement of any kind was used in its construction; rather, each piece was carefully ground, chiseled and polished to make a perfect fit with the preceding piece. It staggers the imagination!

Temple of Athena Nike and the Erechtheum

"While you're atop the Acropolis (to which the entrance fee is 150 drachmas, with free entrance on Sundays), look carefully for the delicate, little Ionic **Temple of Athena Nike** (to your right as you approach the main entrance to the Acropolis, located almost over the stairs), which still has some of its original friezes depicting battles with the Persians and the Gods of Olympus; the temple is dedicated to the 'Wingless Victory'—wingless, else victory can fly away. . . . Then, walk to the **Erechtheum,** a larger Ionic temple perched on the original site of the even older Temple of Athena, which is supposed to have stood on the plot of land where Athena and Poseidon battled it out for God-supremacy of Athens. Athena brought forth an olive tree (there is still a little tree in front of the temple!) and Poseidon smote the earth and brought forth sea water. You'll probably remember the temple best for its Caryatides (or Maidens), six of them easily and gracefully supporting a heavy porch ceiling on their heads.

The Acropolis Museum

"And for heaven's sake, don't miss the tucked-away, easy-to-overlook **Acropolis Museum** (behind, to the right, and a bit downhill from the Parthenon; and for which there is no additional entrance charge), which contains some of the relics and pieces of statuary found on the Acropolis. You'll find some violent sculptures here (lions and lionesses tearing bulls and calves to pieces), the wonderful, Egyptian-looking Korai, parts of friezes that adorned the Acropolis temples (look for the ones that decorated the balustrade of the Athena Nike Temple), and the breathtaking, famous bas-relief of 'Athena Nike Adjusting Her Sandal'—a show stopper! The museum is open daily except Tuesdays from 9 a.m. to 3:30 p.m. (summers from 8 a.m. til 7 p.m.), Sundays from 10 a.m. to 6:30 p.m. The Acropolis itself is open every day: summers from 8 a.m. to 7 p.m., winters from 9 a.m. to 5 p.m., and charges admission of 150 drachmas ($1.50).

Elsewhere on and near the Acropolis

"No scholar would leave this area without also exploring the **Hills of the Pnyx and the Aeropagus** (both former assembly meeting places) and the **Hill of Philopappus,** with its monument of the same name at the top, built in the second century A.D. by the Roman consul, Philopappus, in honor of his two sons. It has an excellent view. And to be thorough you'll also want to clamber along the side of the Acropolis (on Dionysiou Aeropagitou Street) to see the **Theatre of Herod Atticus** (built in the second century A.D.), the **Temple of Asclepius** (he was the god of medicine; his daughter was Hygeia), the **Stoa of Eumenes,** and the grand, oldest theatre in Greece, the **Theatre of Dionysus,** described earlier in this chapter.

The Agora and the Stoa of Attalos

"Just a word about these other two Acropolis sights, referred to earlier by Arthur. As you walk through the ruins of the **Agora** (market place), keep in mind that this was the magnificent city-center of Athens, where Socrates and his disciples came daily for discourse. One of the first buildings you'll see is the **Temple of Hephaistos** (the **Theseion),** named after the god who shared with Athena the honor of being a patron deity of the arts and crafts. The temple was built around 450 B.C., and is the best preserved of all the Greek temples. Between the Theseiom and the Stoa of Attalos, you'll simply have to imagine that you are walking between other now-demolished temples, government buildings, a gymnasium and stoas (colonnades). On the way, you'll note a fragment of a colossal statue of the Emperor Hadrian (benevolent Roman ruler of Athens from 117 to 138 A.D.); sculptured on the torso is a small Romulus and Remus suckling at the Wolf of Rome. The **Stoa of Attalos,** your eventual destination, is a marvelous re-creation of the original, done by the American School of Classical Studies, and now a fascinating museum (open daily except Tuesdays from 9 a.m. to 7 p.m., Sundays from 10 a.m. to 6:30 p.m.) housing all the other relics of the Agora.

The National Archaelogical Museum

"With what you've now seen, you'll be ready to take on the National Archaeological Museum—the second (after the Acropolis) indispensable visit of your Athens stay (open from 8:30 a.m. to 7 p.m., Sundays 10 a.m. to 4:30 p.m., closed Mondays; admission of 150 drachmas, $1.50). And then, you'll want to wander farther afield to the astonishing—

Cemetery of Keramikos

"Located in the Monastiraki section (entrance at 148 Ermou St.), a 15-minute walk from Constitution Square, this is an ancient burial ground (sometimes also called the Dipylon Cemetery), some of whose relics date back as far as the Mycenaean era. It's an exciting place to visit because the excavations bring you the same sense of discovery that an archaeologist has—although there's a small museum on the site (with interesting grave findings), and a pamphlet-guide available, nothing outside is tagged, and you can simply walk around, finding things! You'll see the most unusual (and most ancient) gravestones in Greece, including a reproduction of the renowned monument that bears a bas-relief of a woman whose maid is bringing her jewels to gaze upon for one last time before death—a scene that has been an inspiration to so many poets (the original is at the Archaeological Museum). Excavations have recently unearthed an aqueduct here, as well, which is, in its own way, equally as remarkable as the statuary and fine arts. And the digging continues. Who knows what may be found next year? Admission of 50 drachmas (Sundays are free); open seven days a week from 8 a.m. to 4 p.m. (although the small museum closes on Tuesdays).

The Temple of Olympian Zeus and Hadrian's Arch

"Before you part from the ancient sights of Athens, see the **Temple of Olympian Zeus** (admission of 30 drachmas, free on Sundays), begun in the 6th century B.C., but not completed until Hadrian came to Athens. People of that time described it as the most splendid building they had ever seen; only 16 Corinthian columns now remain. Hadrian not only finished the building, but also built the **Arch of Hadrian** next to it, which served as the marker between two cities; on one side, the Arch carries the inscription: 'This is Athens, the Ancient City of Theseus'; on the other, 'This is the City of Hadrian, and not of Theseus.'

The Byzantine Museum

"For a direct contact with Byzantine art, the Greek-Orthodox art of the Middle Ages, you might also want to visit the **Byzantine Museum** (22 Vassilissis Sophias Ave.), which contains a world-famous collection of Byzantine artifacts; free entrance on Sundays, 150 drachmas at all other times; hours are 7:30 a.m. to 7:30 p.m., Sundays from 10 a.m. to 4 p.m., closed Mondays.

A Byzantine Church

"Then take in the seventh-century Greek Orthodox church of **St. Eleftherios**, next door to the Mitropoleos Church (or Cathedral of Athens).

"And on all your tours in Athens, wear rubber-soled shoes with low heels—particularly for the climb on the Acropolis!"

READERS' SIGHTSEEING SUGGESTIONS: "Strongly suggest you add superb view from the top of **Lykabettus Hill,** the highest point in Athens. You can take a funicular train to the top for 50 drachmas round-trip, 30 drachmas one-way, or walk up the path. A judicious compromise is to take the funicular up, and walk down. There is a small white church on the top of the hill (a clearly visible landmark from many parts of the city), and a cafeteria just below. Dusk is a good time to go up there, as the sun goes down into the sea beyond Piraeus harbor, and the light comes up all around—an unforgettable sight. I've been there twice" (J. H. E. Case, Exeter, Devon, England; note from AF: To find the "funicular," or *teleferik,* as it is known to the Greeks, walk from Syntagma Square along Leoforos Vasilissis Sofias Street—Embassy Row. Pass the modern war museum, with the four aeroplanes outside, turn left after the British Embassy into Plutarchou Street, and the funicular station is at the end of this street, as you will see. Once on top, you'll discover the cafeteria-restaurant is rather expensive for eating, but espresso or a Coke costs only 100 drachmas, $1, and the view is breathtaking. Walking down along the winding path with the wide steps that look like a trail of collapsed dominoes takes about 20 minutes, until you reach the asphalt road, from where bus no. 50—30 drachmas—will bring you back to the center—Kolonaki Square—in a few minutes).

6. Evening Entertainment

The **"Sound and Light"** presentation in Athens is a wonder, and shouldn't be missed. It's shown every night of the spring, summer and early fall months from a location on the **Pnyx,** a little hill that stands in front of the Acropolis (taxi from Constitution Square shouldn't cost more than 200 drachmas—$2), starting at 9 p.m. for the English-language performance. I won't describe any part of the show, except to say that it's done in sound and light, and that the ruins of ancient Athens are the performers. Take nothing better than the 250 drachmas seats (which sell for 150 drachmas to students); the spectacle lasts only 50 minutes.

And after Sound and Light? Head then for either the **Plaka** (see below) or visit the nearby Greek folk dances (nightly at 10:25 p.m., Wednesdays and Sundays at 8:15 p.m. and 10:25 p.m., from May to September) in an open air theatre at the foot of Philopappos hill. Two hundred drachmas for backless chairs, 300 and 400 drachmas for the more supportive ones. And keep in mind that on nights when Sound and Light isn't showing—because of the full moon—the Acropolis is available to visitors in all its glory—and until late in the evening. Go for one of the great sights of our world.

PLAKA: This is the most ancient residential section of Athens, on a hillside directly below the Acropolis, best known today for its outdoor taverns, which feature guitar music and folk-singing. Nearly a score of such places are crammed into the area, all varying widely in price, but none of them expensive—particularly if you stick to a single plate (with wine) as your late night snack. The best of the streets in Plaka, with the most action, is **Mnisikleos** (and that's not a typographical error), where you might look in on a rather expensive taverna called **Mostros** (22 Mnisikleos), which sometimes has a tiny floor show to supplement the usual trio of guitar players. But there are many less costly places on the side streets intersecting the Mnisikleos (such as the marvelously cheap **Taverna Attalos,** at 16 Erechteos, where prices for typical Greek dishes range from 450 to 800 drachmas), or the **Taverna Seven Brothers** at 39 Iperidou St., which features an orchestra and six dancers whom you can watch while devouring an 800-drachma fixed price meal consisting of appetizer (stuffed vine leaves, fish-egg salad, *tsatziki*—made of yogurt, garlic and cucumbers), a main dish such as souvlaki or shish kebab with Greek salad, accompanied by half a bottle of white domestic wine (alternately, you can limit your order to half a bottle of white or Cambas wine for 500 drachmas, which is served with fresh fruit at no extra cost—lowering the tab to about $6 for a pretty remarkable folkloric evening). . . . And there are other such buys all up and down the Plaka. Wander first, then choose.

7. Excursions through Glorious Greece

By the following comment, I certainly don't mean to downgrade Athens. This city is part of everyone's heritage, and should be seen. But in three days, you can see about everything you'll want to see in Athens, whose sights are magnificent but few. Utilize your remaining time to travel in the outlying islands and provinces of Greece, which are spectacularly beautiful and astonishingly cheap.

ROCK-BOTTOM TOURS: The very least costly way to do this is by using the facilities of **Viking's Travel Bureau,** 3 Filellinon St. (phone 322-9383), off Constitution Square, whose student services have already been described in an earlier portion of this chapter. Viking's deals with tourists of all ages, not merely with students, and their most popular program is a series of wonderfully planned "Do-As-You-Like" tours, for which they furnish the transportation, guides, and fairly basic lodgings, but you find your own meals (advised by the guide) in the towns where you stay overnight. I've known readers who have kept their food costs to under $3 a day on these tours, by eating the typical Greek shepherd's meal—ingredients are available at local markets for a few pennies—of olives, goat cheese *(feta),* bread, the Greek country wine *(retsina)* and yogurt.

The four-day "Do-As-You-Like" tour to Thebes, Delphi, Olympia (the most superb site in Greece), Tripolis, Argos, Epidauros, Mycenae, Corinth and Eleusis costs $195 for students and teachers, $225 for all others, leaves every Saturday from April to October. That price works out to not much more than you'd pay for a simple bus fare to these spots, and yet you receive, for no extra price, the services of a trained guide who comments on the sights, as well as your accommodations. It's an unparalleled value, the likes of which is offered in no other European country.

Other "Do-As-You-Like" tours that Viking's will operate in 1985: a unique, new one-day tour to Delphi leaving every Thursday from April through October for $30, including transportation and guides; and a spectacular Seven Day Discovery Cruise by yacht to Mykonos, Santorini and the Cyclades, costing $695 per person in two-berth cabins, $595 in four-berth cabins, including breakfast, light lunch, accommodation for seven nights, taxes, port fees and assistance by an English-speaking tour guide; the cruise departs every Friday from April to October. Lest there be any misunderstanding, let us repeat again that these are not limited to students or student-age people, but only to the young in spirit, which can include oldsters (who receive student reductions if they're over the age of 65!) and youngsters alike. Finally, Viking's Travel offers stand-by rates for all "Do-As-You-Like" tours with a 15% to 25% reduction. Contact the office one day prior to departure dates for these special bargains.

THE NORMAL TOURS: Readers who aren't up to the "Do-As-You-Like Tour" of the classic sites outside of Athens can obtain a less strenuous, but still inexpensive, alternative by visiting any travel agency other than Viking. All the companies in Athens offer the very same tour for the very same price: $275 for four days and three nights, on an itinerary that includes Delphi, Olympia, Epidauris, Mycenae and Corinth. That includes room, board, guide and bus; and many of the guides are remarkably well informed on the vast sweep of ancient Greek history.

The Greek Islands? To make a fairly full circuit of both the Cyclades and the Dodecanese groups, your least expensive bet will be the four-day cruises of the M/S *Neptune* or M/S *Apollo* of the Epirotiki Lines, which embarks from Piraeus (the port of Athens) at noon every Monday from April to October in 1985, goes to Mykonos, then to Kusadasi in Turkey, from where Ephesus and Patmos are visited, then to Rhodes, then on to Herakleion on Crete and to the volcanic island of Santorini, and back to Piraeus, with fairly lengthy daytime stops at each island. Charge per berth in a three- or four-person cabin is $570, including transportation, three meals a day and a midnight buffet over the four-day period. The ship returns to Piraeus on Friday morning at 7 a.m.

Believe me, though, an almost equally good glimpse of what the islands are like can be had by taking the simple trip on the afternoon steamer from Piraeus (check the days) to the wonderful island of Mykonos, seven hours away; followed by a couple of days in Mykonos. And to get the ferry to Mykonos, simply take the subway to Piraeus, then walk two short blocks to the dock.

BEACHES: Most beautiful of all is at Sounion, which is, however, a two-hour ride by public bus from Athens. Sounion is a peninsula on the southeast tip of Attica (the province in which Athens is located). The beach is set next to the quite stunning Ruins of Poseidon, and the swimming is excellent.

Much closer to town are four other renowned beach areas, of which **Varkiza** beach (entrance fee of 140 drachmas) is probably the best; it features modern bathing facilities set amidst palm trees, flower beds, and soft sands cleaned each day by special machines; very spiffy. Runner-up: the often crowded **Vouliagmeni** beach, where 180 drachmas brings you private locker, beach chair, umbrella and showers—and nearby is a natural open-air swimming pool in an extinct volcano crater which obtains its sweet water supply from (reputedly curative) underground warm springs; known as "Limni Lake," it's open from 8 a.m. to 5 p.m., for an entrance fee of only 200 drachmas ($2). And then there's the much less crowded Asteria Beach at **Glyfada** (next to the airport) charging a surprisingly high, for Athens, 200 drachmas ($2) to enter. All three beaches can be reached by bus no. 116 (30 drachmas) from outside the Zappion in downtown Athens.

READERS IN THE SUBURBS: "We hope that anyone who is in Greece from July to September will go to the town of Daphne, just outside of Athens, to the huge wine festival, which lasts for three summer months. Buses to Daphne leave Athens from all over the town at frequent intervals; stations can be located by the crowds of flagon-bearing Greeks who disembark from the buses, singing and laughing. The festival is held in a pine grove, enclosed and surrounded by oleander bushes. There is an open-air restaurant, folk-dancing displays, a dance floor where anyone can dance, a cafeteria, and 52 different wines in booths attended by girls in regional dress. The entrance fee is 250 drachmas and after that, all the wine you can drink is on the house—and you can drink all 52! The grove is open until about 1 a.m. every night, children are entirely welcome, and the atmosphere is gay and friendly" (David and Elizabeth Garin, Bloomington, Indiana). . . . "On the return trip from Piraeus to Athens, take green bus no. 165 (for 60 drachmas) instead of the subway, and you'll be able to see, on the half-hour ride, several residential commercial, industrial areas of Athens-Piraeus, thus glimpsing how the Greeks live and work, away from the tourists. It's better than any guided 'tour'" (Joel E. Abramson, Washington, D.C.).

READERS IN THE ISLANDS: "If you have only a short time to spend in Greece, and want to see a Greek island, you can take a boat from Piraeus (one block from the subway) to nearby **Hydra**. Deck class costs about 400 drachmas one way, takes about four hours. Go for the day or stay overnight (we did for about $6 per person). The harbor and town are beautifully picturesque, although the beaches are very small" (Elaine Mura, Clifton, New Jersey). . . . "Please advise readers that boats to Mykonos do not sail daily, and not to visit the closer islands—Aegina, Poros, Hydra—on weekends, when they are more crowded than Constitution Square" (L. Bernstein, Haifa, Israel). . . . "Having only a short time in Athens and wanting to take a look at a Greek island, we asked at the port of Piraeus if there was any boat which would take us for a quick trip to an island. We were directed to a ferry which, for 150 drachmas, took us on a beautiful 35-minute trip to the island of **Salamis** (12 miles from Piraeus). Upon debarking, we discovered a typical 'Zorba-type' island where they seldom see a tourist. They have a Tourist Directory, though, in which was listed a museum, monastery, and beach. We wandered around and it was just like a Greek movie" (Mrs. H. Brautman, North Miami Beach, Florida). . . . "If you haven't time to go to the famous Greek Islands, taste the real ethnicity of Greece by going from Athens to the nearby island of **Selinia**. Take the Metro to Piraeus and from Piraeus pay 150 drachmas to travel 30 minutes to Selinia. Sunning on the cliffs to the background music of a Greek inn will prove to be most exciting. Buy your lunch or dinner at the local grocery store where not a word of English is spoken but where a woman is more than glad to assist you with what you may want. Our one and only side trip from Athens, Salinia offered us the true Greek ethnicity that was lacking in Athens" (Rosalyn A. Paul, Chicago, Illinois). . . . "A lengthy but worthwhile one-day excursion from Athens is a public bus trip to **Cape Sounion** and the **Temple of Poseidon.** If you go early in the day you can even take a swim in the Aegean. The people at most travel agencies will tell you where to catch the public bus" (Deirdre Henderson and M. Koplik, New Haven, Connecticut).

SOUTH FROM GREECE: "For your readers who get as far as Athens, it is just a short flight to Cairo, the capital of the Arab world. Cairo, on both banks of the immortal Nile, is quite fascinating with its mosques, bazaars, modern section along the Nile, the panorama from the Cairo tower, and of course the Egyptian Museum housing a collection of treasures that is worthy of several visits. The people are extremely friendly and most do speak English well.

"Just outside of Cairo are Sakkara with its tombs and step Pyramid of King Zoser, Memphis with the colossal statue of Ramses II, and of course the pyramids and sphinx of Giza—don't miss the Son et Lumiere!

"For those with more time—and by all means find it—trains and inexpensive flights whisk you down to Luxor, ancient Thebes, with relics that will make the trip up the Nile one you'll never forget. The temples of Luxor, Karnak and the tombs on the west bank, the feluccas sailing by on the Nile, all contribute to a scene as tranquil as one could imagine. South of Luxor is Aswan, famous for its new high dam. The Nile is quite lovely here with monuments, Nubian villages and botanic islands. Hydrofoils leave Aswan for the temples of Abu Simbel which have miraculously been saved by engineers who lifted them from the reach of the rising Lake Nasser."

8. Athens Miscellany

IT'S GREEK TO ME: The fact that few tourists learn to speak a single word of Greek is really shameful. The words for "please" and "thank you" should at least be tried. "Please" is pronounced "Pah-rah-kah-loh." "Thank you" is: "eff-hah-ree-stow." For both words the emphasis is on the last syllable. You'll get a big reaction when you mispronounce these words, as you always will; most Greeks fail to suppress a broad smile, when I do.

Some other useful Greek words: "nero" (accent on the second syllable)—water; "kalimera"—how do you do, or good day.

ATHENS POTPOURRI: The 20-minute subway ride from Omonia Square to Piraeus costs 30 drachmas (30¢). . . . Ask for Constitution Square as Syntagma Square and the local residents will understand you. . . . From Constitution Square, catch bus 230 to the Acropolis and the Stoa of Attalos; bus 12 or the yellow trolley 12 (going in the opposite direction) brings you to the Archaeological Museum. . . . While most museums are open and free on Sundays, their Sunday hours are only from 10 a.m. to 2 p.m.—beware. . . . Monastiraki, site of the daily flea market in Athens, is the first subway stop after Omonia Square. The flea market is open every day. . . . Next to the last stop is Phaleron, where there are swimming beaches and seaside resorts. . . . It's probably best, however, not to swim at Phaleron, where there have been reports of serious pollution. In fact, it's best not to swim at any point closer to the city than Asteria Beach; and of course, after Asteria, you'll reach the ethereal, magnificent beach of Vouliagmeni. . . . There are virtually no drunks in Greece, and no drug problem. That's because, says a Greek friend, the Greeks have too much energy to be in need of such pick-me-ups. . . . A shoeshine in Athens costs 100 drachmas; so does a charcoal-roasted ear of corn, sold by various sidewalk vendors. A portion of that delicious skewered meat *(souvlaki)* which you'll see at numerous open barbeque-type places around Omonia Square, costs only 100 drachmas, and wrapped in a doughy piece of bread, with relish, it makes a perfect snack. . . . Most centrally located of the self-service laundromats is the **Omega** at 24 Kidathineon St. (phone 322-16-88), in Plaka, which is the third street turning right from Fillelinon Street, coming from Syntagma (Constitution) Square. The energetic lady who manages the laundromat speaks some English, and charges 300 drachmas ($3) for 5 kilos washed and dried. Hours are from 7:30 a.m. to 4:30 p.m., Monday to Saturday; closed Sundays. Try, alternately, the **Maytag** self-service laundry at 46 Didotou St. near Omonia Square, whose charges are about the same. . . . Care to ship a parcel home? The **Parcel Post Office** is at 29 Odos Koumondourou St., near Omonia Square, and is open weekdays only, from 7:30 a.m. to 7:30 p.m. At no. 25 on the same street, a small shop specializes in packing parcels, and will also sell all sizes of cardboard and wooden boxes (for $2 and up). . . . Embassy addresses in Athens are: **U.S.A.,** 91 Vassillissis Sofias (phone 721-2951); **Australia,** 10 Annou Gennadiou (phone 723-9511); **Canada,** 15 Messogion Street (phone 360-4611); **Great Britain,** 1 Ploutarchou Street (phone 723-6211). Whether or not you plan to stay at the Hotel Alkistis, schedule a visit to the wholesale marketplace behind the hotel, where you'll see mountains of olives, oceans of olive oil, and hills of coffee. . . . If you're in Athens in August, don't fail to get tickets (some cost as little as 100 drachmas) to the **Athens Festival,** in the Herod Atticus Theatre that's carved into the side of the Acropolis. The setting alone is a memorable experience, and if the National Theatre of Greece is doing a classic (a comedy by Aristophanes, a drama by Euripides), you'll have an evening of theatre that you will never forget. And take standing room (which means that you'll sit on mountain-side rocks, above the last row of seats) if all seats have been sold.

READER'S SHOPPING SELECTION: "The antique shop of **Dionisios Panu,** which is located at 24 Ifestou, near the flea market, offers the greatest selection of antiques at prices so low that my friend and I nearly purchased the entire shop. Cost for a wine set, tray, and six handmade brass cups, was $10 to $25. Other items were even lower" (Allan A. Armour, Brooklyn, New York; note by AF: Ifestou Street is, in reality, the heart of the Athens flea market, although the shops along it stay open throughout the week, and not merely on the flea market's one day—Sunday—of operation. I like the **Curiosity Shop** at no. 17, which seems to carry the most tasteful collection of ikons, samovars, cow bells, wood paintings—the items featured by the Ifestou Street stores. The subway station here is Monastiraki, one stop from Omonia Square on the way to Piraeus; don't miss the Sunday flea market, in any event). . . . "The leather sandal and handbag shop of **K.J. Prifitis** at 62 Adrianou St. in the Plaka district, sells the best and least expensive ($3 to $9) sandals in Athens, including extra large men's sizes (#12). Its owner speaks little English, his son a bit more, but both are very friendly" (Roxann Filaseta, Modesto, California.

OTHER TIPS: If you want American coffee in a Greek restaurant, ask for Nescafe (this is not a commercial). If you ask for coffee, they'll bring you Greek coffee, which could power an automobile. Ask for Nescafe, and they'll bring you instant Nescafe, which, by some feat of salesmanship, seems to be the only American coffee stocked by the budget restaurants. . . . Scarcely any theatre in Athens charges more than 350 drachmas, and you might take a look. . . . Motion-picture houses in Athens show a great many American and British films in English, with subtitles. Often, the Greeks attend a showing from 10 p.m. to 12, and then go out for dancing and music—a custom that will explain the deserted appearance of most tavernas in the pre-midnight hours. . . . Virtually all the museums, exhibits and monuments of Athens charge no admission on Thursdays, and some are free on Sundays as well. . . . How to Ingratiate Yourself Among the Greeks: complain vehemently about the British refusal to return the Elgin Marbles to Athens. Those are the magnificent bas-relief sculptures that once adorned the front of the Parthenon. In 1800, the British ambassador, Lord Elgin, shipped the "marbles" to the British Museum in London, purportedly to protect them from Turkish vandalism. The Greeks want them back, and they should be back (advt)! . . . If you'd like to have a map of Athens, or brochures on the Greek islands, the best place to go is the Tourist Information Office at Syntagma Square, corner Karageorgi Street, in the ground floor of the National Bank of Greece. It's open Monday to Friday from 8 a.m. to 8 p.m. (shorter hours off season), and from 8 a.m. to 2 p.m. Saturday. To find it, look for the modern ten-story building, six of which are decorated with green plants.

READERS' TRANSPORTATION SUGGESTIONS: "A cheap way to get to Greece (there are several alternate methods) is to take the train to Brindisi from Paris, Bologna or Rome and then take the 18-hour overnight ferry to Patras; the fare is $45 (but students get a 30% discount), meals extra. From Patras, drive or take the bus to Athens for an additional $6." (Alexander Sterne, New York, New York; note by AF: from Rome to Brindisi is 7 to 10 hours by train, and costs $21 second class; from Brindisi to Patras by ferry is a 20-hour trip, costing $45 minimum; apart from flying there, this is the quickest way to get to Athens from Western Europe). . . . "Although it takes 24 hours, the cheapest and easiest way to go to Greece from Europe, or vice-versa, is to take the ferry between Brindisi, Italy, and Patras, Greece. It's a beautiful ferry, equipped with an outdoor swimming pool, bar, lounge and restaurant; the price of $45 makes it very popular with Europeans. Food is expensive aboard, so buy your own before leaving. Of the two ships, the *Appia* is newer and prettier than her sister ship, the *Egnatia;* contact the Hellenic-Mediterranean Line if interested" (Linda Blum, Buffalo, New York). . . . "A word of warning! Get to Brindisi at least three hours before the boat leaves if you can; they have no idea what 'organization' is there. If you are a Eurailpasser, don't let them try to tell you there is no place for you—they have only arbitrary law there. And be prepared to shell out a 6,000-lire debarkation tax. However, no problems at Patras in Greece, going in the other direction. They have figured it all out, like clockwork. You walk down the street to the left from the station (you'll see boats docked there), stop in the Hellenic Mediterranean office on the way, get your ticket, pay your tax, go through customs on the dock, and jump on the boat. I would recommend you stock up on food and drink before getting on—the bar and meals on board are rather steep" (Danielle Rappaport, A.P.O., New York). . . . "We returned via a Yugoslavian cruise ship for under $90 each. It left from Piraeus, went to Venice, and also afforded us the opportunity to see different parts of Yugoslavia, as well as Delphi. This was one of the highlights of our trip, a very clean boat, good service, good food, a good rest, and the price was only slightly more than the cost of the train to Brindisi from Rome and then the boat to Piraeus from Brindisi!" (Mr. and Mrs. Victor A. Lobree, San Lorenzo, California). . . . "One day I went from Athens to **Porto Rafti** by bus, for 80 drachmas (80¢) each way. Porto Rafti is on the other side of the Greek peninsula which Athens is on. It has a little harbor on the Aegean Sea, and is just a little fishing village where Greeks go to bathe and spend the day on picnics. Tourists never seem to go there. But the ride up over the mountains and through the groves of olives, vineyards and fig orchards was lovely, and so very interesting. It took a little more than an hour each way. The buses run every hour and leave from just past the Polytechnic Institute on a square (many of the out-of-town buses start from this special square). Pack your lunch and make a day of it at this little village so quiet and beautiful. There are many small sandy beaches, and one rather large one" (Madelin L. Lawler, Mt. Prospect, Illinois). . . . "Try the Greek buses. From Athens, one may take a bus to Corinth. From Corinth, a bus to Mycenae. From there a bus to Argos and Tripolis (of little interest), but from there a 4½ hour ride to Olympia. From Olympia, ride the bus to Pyrgos, Patras and Aeghion. Take the ferry to Itea, and Delphi is a short ride away. Then a bus back to Athens. This do-it-yourself tour lasted five days (with overnight stays in Mycenae, Olympia, Patras and Delphi), cost less than $50 for transportation" (Raymond Ginn, Hermosa Beach, California).

We'll move next to the country whose accommodations are even less expensive than those of Greece. At some point in your trip, you'll want to be in the price paradise of all—Spain.

MADRID

Bullfights and Bargains

A TRIP TO SPAIN is like an intense session of daydreaming—except that it's real. Those three medieval horsemen who ride across the bullring at the start of a *corrida* in Madrid, aren't putting on a show for tourists—they're for real, and no one smiles. The farmers tossing grain into the air to rid it of chaff; the women drawing water from a village well—these are scenes that can be found ten minutes from Madrid, and they are as real as if the 20th century had never occurred. In no other land will you feel, so much, that you have stepped through a time machine into the past. There are plains in Spain where you needn't even shut your eyes to imagine that Don Quixote and Sancho Panza are riding on the scrubby, bare land that stretches into the distance, unmarred by billboards or smokestacks.

Against such a background, your visit to Spain will be a joy, because the Spanish people are honest, dignified, friendly and helpful. Since it's so easy to live among them on the lowest of costs, we'll engage in only the briefest survey of accommodations in Madrid. Remember that if you avoid only the obviously deluxe establishments, you'll automatically be on a budget standard; and if you then choose well, you'll find surprisingly pleasant rooms for those low rates.

1. Orientation & Transportation

Let's first get you settled. Budget tourists arriving in Madrid by air take the yellow airport bus into town, only 300 pesetas ($2), and never a taxi, 2,000 pesetas ($13.33). The pleasantly low-cost bus service runs every 20 minutes from Barajas Airport to the Plaza Colón underground air terminal. Once there, you rely on the rather antique but thoroughly reliable and very cheap—50 pesetas (33¢) for a one-way fare, 400 pesetas ($2.66) for ten tickets—subway system of Madrid (the Metro), operating from 6:30 a.m. to 1 a.m. Maps at each station show you the routes, and we've also listed the nearest stations for many of our hotel recommendations appearing below. City buses, 50 pesetas (33¢) per ride, are extensive in their routes, but too difficult to master in the course of a short stay; and taxis, while relatively cheap, 400 pesetas ($2.66), for the average ride, are not for cost-conscious tourists.

For trips from Madrid to other Spanish cities, you'll need to know about the several—

RAILWAY STATIONS: There are three of them, and it's important to distinguish the cities they serve. Largest and most important is **Atocha Station,** whose trains go to suburban points, such as Toledo (1½ hours driving time), as well as to the south, including Granada (seven hours), Malaga (seven hours), Sevilla (six hours), Cadiz (eight hours), Algeciras (13 hours), Lisbon (nine hours). **Chamartin Station,** more modern, is the terminal for trains to and from the northwest, including Valladolid (three hours), Barcelona (eight hours) and Paris (18 hours). The smallest, **Principe Pio Station,** services the west of Spain: Salamanca (3½ hours), Vigo (nine hours) and La Coruña (ten hours). All three stations are best reached via Metro to these stops: Atocha for Atocha, Chamartin for Chamartin, Norte for Principe Pio. Train information for all three stations can be had by phoning 733-30-00 or 733-22-00. To purchase tickets and for reservations, including sleeper accommodations, one can go either to the train stations or, better, to the centrally located office of the Spanish Railways, called **Recife,** at 44 Alcalà (phone 247-00-00), a short distance from Puerta del Sol, and open Monday to Friday from 8 a.m. to 2 p.m. and 4 to 6 p.m., from 8 a.m. to 1:30 p.m. on Saturday.

ADDITIONAL AIDS: If, before seeking a hotel, you'd like literature, maps, and more detailed advice, you're best off to head for the city's best organized tourist information office, operated by the National Ministry of Tourism, and called **Turismo.** It's found at street level in the 40-story Torre de Madrid building, in the Plaza de España, and is open weekdays from 9 a.m. to 7 p.m., Saturdays from 9:30 a.m. to 1:30 p.m., but closed Sundays. While the people here will not book hotels, they'll tell you about restaurants, museums, local festivals and the like, and all in flawless English. A second municipal information office, **Oficina de Turismo,** at 3 Plaza Mayor, closes for lunch, in the Spanish fashion, from 1:30 to 4 p.m., but is reasonably helpful during their short hours of business. Equipped with their glossy brochures, encouraged and impressed by their Spanish dignity, you now embark on the quite pleasant task, in Spain, of finding a remarkably high quality hotel within the price range we recommend:

2. Where to Stay

HOTELS: For one startling example of the remarkably low hotel costs of Spain, we'll begin with an establishment—The Francisco I—that is located in the very center of the city.

Whenever I argue with an anti-$25-a-day'er, I use the **Hotel Francisco I** as a case in point—not because it's an inexpensive hotel (it's not), but because it reveals how sharply the cost of hotels descends when one ventures to the lesser-known establishments, and how moderate is the price level of even quality hotels in Spain. For this tastefully furnished hotel, done in classic Spanish style, and situated at 15 Arenal (phone 248-02-04), just off the Puerta del Sol—the central-most square of Madrid—charges only 4,000 pesetas ($26.66) for an immaculate double room with private bath and breakfast for two, 2,800 pesetas ($18.66) single. Just a few hundred yards away, at the Plaza de España, the four-star-and-famous **Hotel Plaza** charges more than twice as much. I defy anyone to shuttle back and forth between the two hotels, and then assert that the Plaza is *that* much better.

IN THE CENTER OF TOWN: Nor is this an isolated example. In the very center of Madrid are numerous, almost elegant, hotels offering double rooms with private bath for $35, $29, or even $23 and under. We'll begin with the highest priced of the lot, and then descend to the more simple—but still attractive—establishments that charge $12 and less for a bathless double.

Doubles with private bath for $23 to $35 a night

The best-located (because it's central, yet in a quiet area) of the moderately priced hotels is the **Hotel Carlos V,** 5 Maestro Vitoria (phone 231-41-00), a block from the Puerta del Sol (center of the city), where the highest-priced double room with private bath costs 5,350 pesetas ($35.66), service included. That outlay brings you a well-appointed bedchamber with crystal chandeliers, in a hotel that the Spanish government ranks as three star, and in a seven-story, air-conditioned, 70-room building filled with marble and brass that is constantly being polished by an army of maids. Such are the values of Spain.

Even better finds are located on the Gran Via, which is the main street of Madrid and one of the best of these (although it won't initially seem that way from the appearance of its downstairs lobby) is the **Hotel Lope de Vega,** 59 Gran Via (phone 247-70-00), with an unprepossessing entrance, but a stunning interior of paneled lounges and red velvet chairs, and large, tastefully decorated bedrooms. Singles with private bath are 2,100 pesetas ($14), doubles 4,000 pesetas ($26.66), all with breakfast, service and tax included. And all 50 rooms are on the ninth, tenth and eleventh floors of a 12-story building, with superb views over Madrid. . . . Nearby, on a side street off Gran Via, at 29-31 Calle San Bernardo, the modern **Hotel Alexandra** (phone 242-04-00) charges a fairly similar 2,900 pesetas ($19.33) single, 4,400 pesetas ($29.33) for a twin or double room, again with bath and breakfast. . . . If all three of these initial choices are packed, then walk to the **Hotel Europa** 4 Calle de Carmen (phone 221-29-00), just off the Puerta del Sol (by 20 feet), in the very heart of Madrid, where doubles with private bath are 4,300 pesetas ($28.66), singles with bath 2,500 pesetas ($16.66), breakfast included. The staff at this remarkably low-priced, well-located, 60-room hotel is a particularly courteous one, by any standard, although the Europa isn't nearly of the same quality as the Lope de Vega or Carlos V, our two top choices.

Two other hotels with private-bath-doubles for $24 to $33 a night are located near the important Atocha Railroad Station in Madrid. Cheaper of the two is the fairly modern **Hotel Mediodia,** 8 Plaza Emperador Carlos V (phone 227-30-60), directly across from the Atocha station, charging 2,250 pesetas ($15) for a single with private bath, 3,500 pesetas ($23.33) for a double with bath and breakfast. A few steps away, the spanking-new and much better **Hotel Mercator,** 123 Atocha (phone 429-05-00), has now equipped each of its 90 rooms with private bath, yet charges only 4,800 pesetas ($32) double, 3,250 pesetas ($21.66) single, for a room so equipped. While the avenue on which it stands is not a terribly interesting one, it is quite close to the Prado and might be considered by tourists planning extensive and frequent visits to that renowned museum.

Finally, a number of $19 a night doubles (with private bath) are to be found on the street that runs alongside American Express, in the well-located, pleasant area of Madrid near the important Cortes (parliament) building. In the corner structure at 3 Plaza de las Cortes, are several of these, of which by far the best is the strikingly lovely **Residencia Trianon** (phone 429-3926), which takes up the building's third floor (there's an elevator), and also offers doubles with bath and breakfast for 2,850 pesetas ($19), singles without bath for a remarkable 1,250 pesetas ($8.33). Next door, a category higher, and English-speaking, is the **Hostal Florida** (phone 429-8068), in the building at 25 Marques de Cubas, across from the side entrance to American Express, where doubles with private bath and breakfast are 2,800 pesetas ($18.66). Phone first to each of these popular pensions.

THE SPANISH PESETA: Just so you'll know, we've converted pesetas into dollars at the rate of 150 pesetas to the dollar, which should be the amount you'll receive in 1985.

Doubles for $17 to $28 a night

Back in the center of town, a romantic-sounding street called the "Mesonero Romanos," which is right off the important Gran Via, is the site of the huge, ten-story **Hotel Regente,** Mesonero Romanos 9 (phone 221-29-41), which charges 2,500 pesetas ($16.66) for a single with shower, 4,000 pesetas ($26.66) for a double with shower; has plenty of these rooms available; and keeps them spare but well-maintained; most budgeteers seem to like the Regente less for its hotel aspects than for its nearby flamenco nightclub, the Torre Bermejas, to which guests of the hotel are admitted at a 10% discount. But it's a thoroughly proper, desirable hotel, that has facilities for families and some English-speaking personnel well-supervised by an energetic, owner-manager, Señor Villar Sanchez. You may want to comparison shop between the Regente and the more intimate **Hotel Negresco,** Mesonero Romanos 12 (phone 222-65-30), which offers air-conditioned doubles with bath but without breakfast for 4,250 pesetas ($28.33), and is a top-rated budget choice, although its rooms are fairly compact in size. Or try, again in the very heart of Madrid, the small **Hostal Maria Christina** on the second floor of 20 Fuencarral (phone 231-63-00), where doubles with private shower and w.c. are 2,500 pesetas ($16.66), singles 1,700 pesetas ($11.33), again with private shower; breakfast 200 pesetas—and optional.

Doubles for $13 to $25 a Night

Cheaper than these, but also in a central location, is the fine **Hotel Continental**, at 44 Gran Via (phone 221-46-40). Singles here rent for a reasonable 2,000 pesetas ($13.33) including breakfast, doubles with private shower and breakfast for 2,750 pesetas ($18.33), doubles with bath and breakfast for 3,200 pesetas ($21.33). There's an unusually friendly management, and a kitchen and cook so good that I would enthusiastically recommend you take demi-pension terms (room without bath, breakfast and one other meal, if they're offered to guests at the time of your stay). Highly recommended.

In the same building that houses the Continental (44 Gran Via) are no fewer than five other budget hotels—one per floor—of which my own preference would be for the cozy, 29-room **Hostel Valencia** on the fifth floor (phone 222-11-15), operated by Antonio Ramirez, and his charming, San Diego-born, American wife, Laurie. Their 1985 rates are 1,600 pesetas ($10.66) single, 2,650 pesetas ($17.66) twin, 3,600 pesetas ($24) triple, always with breakfast and private shower included—and no language problem! It's in the same building that you'll find the Restaurant Valencia, recommended in our "big splurge" restaurant section ahead. But if everything is full at the time of your visit, then walk over to a somewhat higher-priced, hotel-filled structure at 34-38 Gran Via, housing the **Hotel California** (phone 222-47-03), a 27-room pension with a friendly atmosphere, whose proprietors—a charming family—will offer the following in 1985: singles with shower and w.c., 2,700 pesetas ($18) with breakfast, doubles with shower, and w.c., 4,100 pesetas ($27.33) with breakfast.

A final and much cheaper selection in this low-priced category is found in the old section of Madrid, directly opposite the colorful café Las Cuevas de Luis Candelas (whose doorman is dressed as an 18th-century Spanish bandit). That's the **Hostal La Macarena**, Cava de San Miguel 8 (second floor), phone 265-9221, a friendly and fairly spacious, two-floor pension whose owners, Mr. Antonio and Mrs. Julia, charge a low 1,200 pesetas ($8) for a single with breakfast, 1,600 pesetas ($10.66) for a double with shower and two breakfasts. From the train station, ask a cab driver to take you to the "Plaza Mayor—frente Cuchilleros" (it'll cost 500 pesetas, if you have suitcases with you), and then point to the above address, which is best recommended for our younger readers, for its colorful location, its largely student clientele, and the large number of rooms of which it disposes. To the many readers who have asked, "Macarena" refers to the "Holy Virgin of Sevilla," and triple rooms here are 2,200 pesetas ($14.66), including breakfast with an egg and bacon! If, improbably, La Macarena is full, then try the "costlier" **Hostal Roma,** nearby in a quieter location at 1 Travesia de Trujillos (phone 231-19-06), and occupying an entire old apartment building with enormous staircase. In 1985, the Roma will be charging 2,000 pesetas ($13.33) for singles with breakfast and free showers, 3,100 pesetas ($20.66) for doubles on the same basis, all for simply furnished, but large and clean, rooms with parquet floors.

Additional clusters of $13-a-night doubles? See our "Starvation Budget" section, below, for a dozen or so selections; and see "Readers' Selections," below, for additional doubles charging less than $18 a night.

READERS' HOTEL SELECTIONS: "**Hostal Lisboa,** 17 Ventura de la Vega (phone 222-83-45), is nothing on the outside, but elegant inside, located just a few blocks from American Express and within easy walking distance of virtually everything worth seeing in the downtown area; spotlessly clean; and offers double rooms with private bath for 2,750 pesetas ($18.33)" (John Wilcock, New York City). . . . "**Hostal Cosme,** on the third floor of 1 Calle del Principe, two blocks from the Puerta del Sol (phone 232-3307), is a brand-new hostal run by a charming (but non-English-speaking) woman and her young son. We had the cleanest room we'd ever seen, including a sink and brand-new shower unit, for 2,000 pesetas ($13.33) a night. There is a telephone and a TV set for guests, and the entire establishment is like a large, extremely well-kept home, carpets and all" (Mrs. Ray Fisher, New York, New York; hearty and second endorsement from Mr. and Mrs. Peter Young, West Hempstead, New York). . . . "**Hostal Matute,** 11 Plaza Matute (phone 228-6904), was excellent—double room with private bath and shower for only 3,300 pesetas ($22), with breakfast. Owner speaks English very well—has spent some time in the U.S.A." (R. J. Scheurenberg, London, England, and also endorsed by Luis Sanchez, Hialeah, Florida, and John G. Sindorf, Palmer, Alaska, who both report that owner Alberto Gutierrez has been especially kind to readers of this book). . . . "**Hostal-Residencia Almanzor,** 11 Carrera de San Jeronimo (phone 429-3801), is an 11-room lodging on the second floor of an old apartment building only 200 yards off the Puerta del Sol. All rooms are with shower and private w.c., and yet rent for only 1,250 pesetas ($8.33) single, 2,250 pesetas ($15) double, 3,000 pesetas ($20) triple, no breakfast. We can highly recommend it." (Max and Mary Zoche, Peoria, Illinois).

ROOMS—THE STARVATION BUDGET: The first-class pensions (as rated by the Spanish government) of Madrid charge about $6.50 per person for double rooms, and two of the best located of these, both on the broad Paseo del Prado, a few steps from the Prado and a short walk from the Atocha Station, are the well-furnished and quite lovely **Hostal Residencia Sud Americana,** 12 Paseo del Prado (phone 429-25-64), 1,900 pesetas ($12.66) for a bathless double; and, in the same building the simpler, second-class **Hostal Residencia Coruña,** 12 Paseo del Prado (phone 429-25-43), charging 1,800 pesetas ($12) for a bathless double, 1,200 pesetas ($8) single, owner of the Coruña, Señor Luis Justo, possesses an excellent command of English. He also offers several multi-bedded rooms (four beds and up), for which the price is only 700 pesetas ($4.66) per person per night! Another building housing four such pensions, on a small side street just off the mid-point of the important Gran Via, is at 6 Calle Concepcion Arenal, where you'll find the **Hostal Concepcion Arenal** (phone 222-6883), the slightly higher-priced (by pennies) **Pension Fenix** (phone 231-4120), the **Hostal Rias Atlas** (phone 231-9101), and the cheaper **Hostal Regional** (phone 222-6127), at the last named of which there are free hot showers, as well as the right (gratis) to use the owner's ironing board and iron. Double rooms without bath are 1,800 pesetas at the Conception, 2,000 pesetas at the Fenix, 1,300 at the Rias Atlas, 1,400 pesetas at the Hostal Regional.

Star of all the starvation budget pensions is the marvelously well-located (only a few steps from the Puerta del Sol) **Hostal Rifer,** 5 Calle Mayor (phone 232-3197), offering 12 sparkling clean rooms, beds with the whitest sheets you have ever seen, new wallpaper, large shining mirrors everywhere, and the following spectacular 1985 rates: 2,100 pesetas ($14) for twins with shower, 2,250 pesetas ($15) with shower and private w.c., 1,000 pesetas ($6.66) per person in a quad with shower and w.c., but all without breakfast, there being several coffee shops next door. Take the elevator to the fourth floor, where owner-manager Sra. Yulia y Miguel—some French, very little English, spoken—will herself open the door. An alternate choice, again well-located, and especially appropriate for single travelers (because 10 of its 20 rooms are singles), is the **Hostal Residencia Piquio,** at 21 Calle San Mateo (phone 445-21-16), where rates for rooms with private shower are 800 pesetas single, 1,400 pesetas ($9.33) double. The friendly dueña: Señora Paquita Barba Rodriguez.

Among the best streets for finding starvation-budget hotels in Madrid (rooms for $6 and less, per person) are the **Calle del Principe** (which runs off the Plaza de Canalejas) and the **Calle de Echegaray,** one block away, where you'll discover several such places. Try the Calle del Principe first, and don't be deterred by the entrance appearance of the hotels; such choices as the excellent **Hostal Regional,** 18 Calle del Principe, phone 222-33-73 (1,000 pesetas single, $6.66, 1,400 pesetas, $9.33, double) may have an utterly plain stairway "lobby," but many of their rooms face onto the pleasant Plaza St. Ana, around the corner, and although fairly spartan, they're clean and attended by a friendly staff and management.

The single official youth hostel of Madrid (requiring a membership card, which they'll sell you on the spot for $15) is the 75-bed **Youth Hostel** at 28 Calle Santa Cruz de Mercenado (phone 247-4532), on two floors of an apartment building. It takes both men and women, in dormitory accommodations priced at only 500 pesetas ($3.33) per night, breakfast included, or for 600 pesetas ($4) to people over 26. Subway stop is Arguelles, or simply walk 10 minutes from the Plaza de España (behind the plush Princesa Plaza Hotel). And if you don't initially spot the tiny youth hostel placard at 28, then look for the Maltese red cross pharmacy sign next door.

The official student travel agency in Madrid is **Tive,** at 88 Calle Fernando el Catolico (phone 449-68-00), directly opposite the main entrance to the University, and only one block from the Moncloa subway station (buses 61 and 16 also stop just outside). It's open weekdays from 9 a.m. to 1:30 p.m. and from 4:30 to 6:30 p.m., Saturdays from 9 a.m. to 1 p.m., for information on student charter flights and the like. It also issues the International Student Identity Card, whose cost you'll recoup on your first visit to the Prado—to which I.D. holders are admitted free!

READERS-ON-THE-STARVATION-BUDGET: "For the three of us—myself, my wife, and our 2½-year-old-son—we paid only 2,000 pesetas ($13.33) a night at the **Hostal Residencia Carreras,** 18 Calle del Principe (phone 222-00-36), in a large room, with unlimited hot showers free" (Tom Webber, Newport Beach, California). . . . "Please mention the night watchman or *Serenos* of Madrid. There's one of these for each block, and if you arrive home after 10:30 you just clap your hands and he comes and opens the door. A tip of 10 pesetas is customary" (Mark Evrett, Vancouver, B.C., Canada). . . . "By far the best accommodation we encountered throughout Europe was the **Hostal Buelta,** 4 Calle del Doctor Drumen (phone 239-98-07); tariff was an unbelievable 1,500 pesetas for a double room, and location was across the Plaza del Emperador from Atocha railway station, convenient for visits to El Retiro park (directly opposite) and the Prado. The genial manager is keen to show rooms to prospective guests before bookings are confirmed" (George Wilson, Box Hill, Australia); note from AF: Hostal Buelta is ideal for single travelers: of its 100 rooms on six floors; there's an elevator; 60 are singles selling, in 1985, for 1,200 pesetas ($8); that's without breakfast, but at least four coffee shops around the corner fill the gap.

READERS-ON-THE-SUB-STARVATION-BUDGET: "An extraordinarily cheap and clean pension lies within five minutes of American Express. It's **Huespedes Fucar,** Calle Fucar 6 (phone 230-3418). Friendly owner, shower, immaculate rooms, all for only 700 pesetas ($4.66) per night per person" (Herb Kestenbaum, Maplewood, New Jersey; note from AF: Calle Fucar is off the Calle de Atocha, two blocks from the Paseo del Prado). . . . "I shared a double for only 700 pesetas ($4.66) a night at the **Hostal**

Residencia Benamar, in the heart of the city at 20 Calle de San Mateo (phone 419-0222), and could have had a single for 850 pesetas ($5.66). A shower or bath located down the hall is free of charge. Large and comfortable, with a pleasant sitting room where you get acquainted with other guests" (Glenn Moses, Georgetown University, Washington, D.C.; strong second from Paul Forchione, Northlake, Illinois, who adds that "the Tribunal station of the metro is just one block from the Benamar, and the important Gran Via is within easy walking distance. The extremely friendly and helpful English-speaking proprietor, Mr. Benjamin Viñuela, makes this a pleasurable and convenient place to stay"; note from AF: from the Gran Via, walk up the Calle Fuencarral for seven short blocks and then right; or take the subway to the Tribunal stop).

3. Where to Eat

RESTAURANTS: Madrid is where you'll discover miracles in the pricing of meals, ranging downwards to a restaurant charging 300 pesetas ($2) for a three-course dinner, including service—we've described it further on in this chapter. You'll also encounter a regulation requiring that every restaurant in Madrid offer a fixed price Tourist Menu (also known as the *Menu del Dia*) consisting of three courses, bread, wine and service—all at a sum appropriate to the official classification of the restaurant. And for each course served on that meal, there must be at least three available choices (i.e., at least three different appetizers, three different main courses, and so on) carrying no supplement to the fixed price, although other choices can be priced a few pesetas higher.

Such is the proud independence of many Spanish restaurateurs, however, and their dislike of the Menu del Dia rule, that numerous restaurants in Madrid offer an even lower-priced meal—called a *cubierto* or a *cubierto de la casa*—which again consists of several courses, but offers no choice within each course. These cubiertos are what the budget tourist will seek out. They're found in restaurants that cluster in four particular areas, as follows:

On the Calle del Barco

Currently the best street for budget restaurants in Madrid, the Calle del Barco is found behind the Sepu department store, which is on the Gran Via; from the store, walk down the Calle Gonzalo Jimenez de Quesada, which leads directly to the del Barco. And there you'll find, in quick order, four pleasant and quiet restaurants—the **Restaurant Pagasarri,** at 7 Calle del Barco; the **Restaurant Nuevo Barco,** at 6 Calle del Barco; the **Restaurant Archanda,** at Calle del Barco 8; and the **Restaurant Copatisan** at 18—all serving either cubiertos or Menus del Dia for 450 to 600 pesetas (that's as little as $3 to $4) for three courses, beverage and service, remember), and offering à la carte selections for much less. The Pagassari, for instance, serves a one-egg tortilla española (an omelette mixed with potatoes, a Spanish mainstay, but a dish that many Americans don't like) for 200 pesetas ($1.33), a two-egg tortilla española for 250 pesetas. The Nuevo Barco serves the thrilling gazpacho (the cold, summer vegetable soup, flavored with garlic, a Spanish classic that you must try at least once) for 220 pesetas on Thursdays and Sundays in summer. All the restaurants also serve *platos combinados*—combined plates, increasingly popular in Madrid, and consisting of large, single-dish meals, with several different items on them for only 125 to 220 pesetas, a high of $1.46. Last summer at the Restaurante Archanda, I had gazpacho (which was thick, creamy and bland, not thin, oily and tart as sometimes is the case in U.S. Spanish-style restaurants), followed by a two-egg tortilla española, with flan for dessert, bread and beer on the side, and my total check, including service, came to 600 pesetas ($4). . . . For *platos combinados* (150 to 200 pesetas) and one-plate dishes (120 to 200 pesetas), the Copatisan seems most popular in the area; but watch its late dining hours: 1 to 4 p.m. for lunch, 8:30 to 11:30 p.m. for dinner, daily.

Across from the Atocha Station

Directly across the wide boulevard from the front of Atocha Station, the **Restaurant La Viña de Atocha,** at 11 Plaza del Emperador Carlos V, charges 600 pesetas for its tourist menu, but only 500 pesetas for its cubierto—the cubierto consisting of soup, roast veal with vegetables, bread, wine, dessert and service charge. Fairly regional in character, and less tourist-oriented than our Calle del Barco choices, this will repay the intrepid tourist who steps inside with a meal entirely typical of Spain. Closed Wednesdays. Along the right side of Atocha Station (as you face the front of the station), the **Restaurante Conidas Pepe,** 12 Calle de Mendez Alvano, is a smaller and more simple place serving a menu del dia (three courses) for 450 pesetas ($3), while around the corner from the Viña de Atocha, the **Restaurante Dorna,** at 118 Calle de Atocha, corner of Calle Drumen, offers à la carte dining at prices that total well under 600 pesetas for a full meal. Conidas Pepe is closed Wednesdays.

On the Ventura de la Vega

Now you're in the area of American Express. As you walk past AmEx, uphill on San Jeronimo, you'll see a statue of Cervantes in a small square. Behind the statue there begins a street called Calle del Prado. Walk up this street until you pass a side street called Ventura de la Vega on your right; here you'll find the largest number of budget restaurants in Madrid, with rates entirely similar to those on the Calle del Barco.

You'll want to stroll along the Ventura de la Vega, comparing menus and interiors. The **Restaurante Bilbaino** at 11 on the street, charges 450 pesetas for its three-course-with-wine menu del dia, as does the **Restaurante El Santuario** at 13. And both restaurants offer *platos del dia* (daily specials) at remarkable prices; Spanish omelettes *(tortilla española)* for 140 pesetas (93¢); fish soup for 180 pesetas; string beans with ham *(judias verdes)* for 180 pesetas; the famous flan dessert for 120 pesetas (80¢). Cheaper still is the **Restaurante Ballestreros** at 6 Ventura de la Vega, whose tourist menu is only 400 pesetas, and which frequently puts on a special cubierto—again three courses in size—for only 350 pesetas—a starvation budget wonder! There are at least two other budget finds on the street, including the well-recommended **Restaurante Hylogui** at 3 Ventura de la Vega (450 pesetas for the set menu), and the **Restaurante Los Motivos** at 10 (also 450 pesetas).

For variety, you might also like the **Restaurante La Choza** at 11 Calle Echegaray, one block from the Ventura de la Vega and parallel to it, where a three-course cubierto (but without wine) is 500 pesetas. Don't be distressed by the outward appearance of this self-styled "restaurante economico"; push aside the curtains at the door, walk inside, and you'll find a pleasant interior, with a motherly white-haired cashier at the desk. Sundays for lunch (La Choza is closed on Sunday evenings), you'll receive

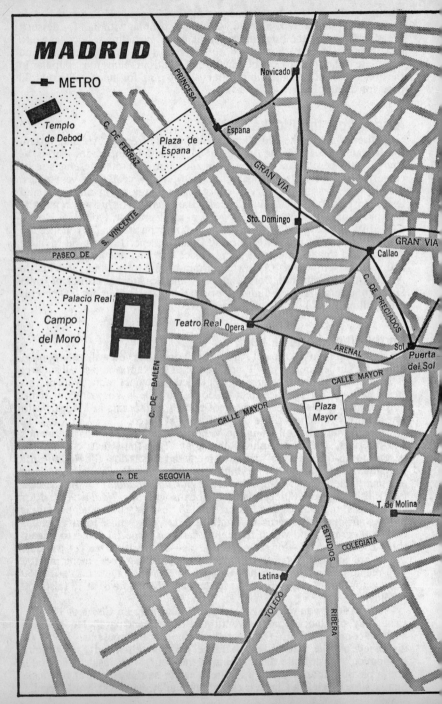

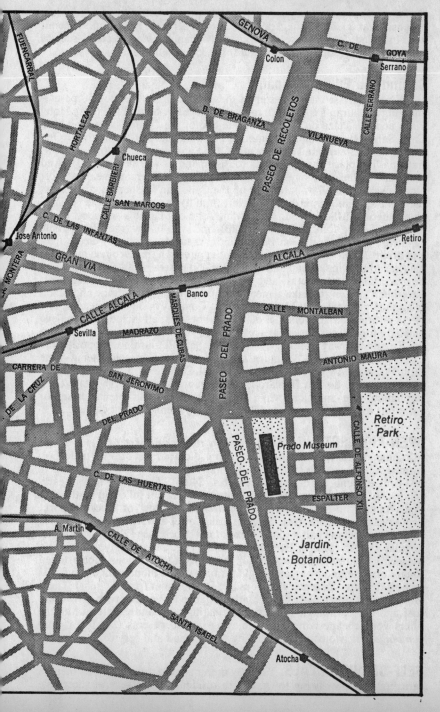

paella as the main course on the 400 peseta cubierto. Slightly less expensive, at 3 Calle Echegaray, **La Casonas** serves a three-course menu, wine included, for 450 pesetas ($3), a daily-changing *plato del dia*—such as fried calamares (superb, crispy squid) for 350 pesetas ($2.33).

Behind the Edificio España

Finally, a last major cluster of these "one fork," 450 to 550 peseta-charging restaurants is located, rather surprisingly, behind the plush Hotel Plaza and the Plaza de España, at one end of the Gran Via, on the little Calle San Leonardo and the intersecting Calle de San Bernardino. One such is the **Restaurante Veracruz** at 5 Calle San Leonardo, a long, narrow, trattoria-like place that prices its tourist menu at 450 pesetas ($3). And there are higher category, but still refreshingly moderate, meals a short block away. If you'll walk that far up the Calle San Leonardo, you'll cross the Calle de San Bernardino; look left (uphill) and you'll see the remarkable **Cafeteria Milo** at 9 San Bernardino (one of Madrid's very best in the low-cost field); look right (downhill) and you'll spy the **Restaurante Comicay,** at 1 Calle de San Bernardino. At the antiseptically clean, light and bright **Milo,** where waiters outnumber guests, a three-course menu del dia (including wine, bread and service) is 450 pesetas ($3), fish soup *(sopa de pescado)* is 160 pesetas, and some young things, weak from the heat, have been known to make a meal out of the tomatoes, lettuce and onion salad (145 pesetas). The Moorish-looking Comicay is slightly cheaper, and offers a three-course menu del dia for 450 pesetas, all included, a one-egg omelette for 130 pesetas. That's less than 20 yards from an exit of the Plaza de España subway station. At 6 Calle San Bernardino, opposite the Comicay, **Restaurante Aranjuez** serves a good 550-peseta menu, wine included, while two short blocks away, at 4 Calle de Antonio Grilo at the corner of Calle de San Bernardo, the **Restaurante Las Burgas** stays open throughout the summer (when some nearby establishments close for vacation) to offer its excellent 450 peseta ($3) menu, wine included.

OPEN-AIR RESTAURANTS: Two, in the very heart of Madrid, are recommendable: **Restaurante El Club,** at 4 Victoria, just off Puerta del Sol, with 60 seats at outside tables, plus 100 more inside, serves a daily changing two-course menu averaging 700 pesetas ($4.66). The one I had in early summer of 1984 consisted of thick, tasty noodle soup, followed by the dish that's unique to Madrid, *cocido madrileno* (a stew of chicken, pork, pepper-sausage, beans, mixed pickles, cauliflower and strips of bacon). A la carte offers include half a roast chicken for 425 pesetas ($2.83), two-person tortillas for 375 ($2.50). Even more central, at 22 Plaza Mayor, **Cafeteria Magerit** is splurgey but worth it for the view of this famous cobblestoned square ornamented by arcades and four turrets, the monument of Philip III on horseback in the center (he looks like Darth Vader from the rear). There are very few other places (St. Mark's Square in Venice, perhaps) where past and present mingle in such a fascinating way, and Cafeteria Magerit offers your cheapest means of enjoying it: 600 pesetas ($4) for a *plato combinado* of two courses, including wine, bread and service.

SELF-SERVICE MEALS: You may prefer a more quickly served meal (a rarity in this slow-living town, where residents order several successive courses and spend hours consuming them). Throughout Madrid are restaurants calling themselves cafeterias; but they're not—at least in our sense of the term. A cafeteria in Spain is more akin to a counter-style snack-bar, and in Madrid some of them seem to combine, in my experience, the worst aspects of American and Spanish snacks. They're also not particularly inexpensive, and I'd pass them up. Among the few true self-service cafeterias in Madrid, a major establishment which you should visit, is the **Tobogán,** at 1 Calle Mayor, just off the big Puerta del Sol, which many consider to be the center of Madrid. Its sign is almost indistinguishable and it's confusingly situated next door to the Nebraska Cafeteria (i.e., a Spanish non-cafeteria), but it's a phenomenal place inside—clean, air-conditioned, fairly cheap—and fast. Offerings range from cubiertos at 400 pesetas (here taking the form of a single tray on which are three courses and a flask of the Tobogán's own brand of wine) to individual meat-and-vegetable plates at 300 pesetas. Sunday is paella day, when a little iron skillet of the fabulous stuff goes for 240 pesetas. Open from 12:30 to 4 p.m. and from 7:30 to 11:30 p.m.; take care lest you choose more plates than you can finish.

THE CHEAPEST RESTAURANT IN THE TOWN: Two short blocks to the side of the Gran Via (at the end near to the big Plaza Cibeles) is a restaurant-and-bar street called the Calle Barbieri, off which runs the Calle de San Marco. I walked down these streets one year, passed a restaurant sign offering a three-course meal for 300 pesetas ($2), walked on a few steps, froze, and suddenly wondered if the work of doing this book had permanently addled my senses. But the **Restaurante El Criollo,** at 21 Calle Barbieri, actually does serve a three-course, meat-for-the-main-course meal for only 300 pesetas ($2). Its owner, a determined gentleman named Alejandre Yubero, candidly admits that *mi familia no queria que me dedicase a negocios*—and how right they were! *Cual es el secreto?"* (How do you do it?), I asked Sr. Yubero. *"uno sencillo,"* he answered firmly. *"Aprovechar todo"* (Very simple, I waste nothing). Open daily, except Sunday evening, from 1:15 to 4:30 p.m. for lunch, from 8:15 p.m. to 11:30 p.m. for dinner.

THE BIG SPLURGE: A restaurant in Madrid where budget-living French tourists go, is the **Valencia,** at 44 Gran Via (one flight up), in the heart of the city. And that's a far better recommendation than mine for the quality of the Spanish food served there. Several different three-course prix fixe menus are offered: I'd take the 800-peseta ($5.33) cubierto, although it is possible to eat cheaper, if you are less than ravenously hungry. And for your beverage, I'd pass up the wine in favor of a big pitcher of sangria—a milder, ices wine-and-fruit drink—which comes with the cubierto. Lunch is the most carefully prepared meal of the day; pechuga valenciana (a baked chicken dish is the specialty of the house.

A super splurge: for outdoor dining in the summertime, **Restaurante El Pulpito** at 9 Plaza Mayor, affords an exciting view of the majestic Plaza Mayor with its 17th-century façades, and serves the most typical of Spanish food items, well prepared and flavored, but not in the more expensive fashion of Madrid's best restaurants. Although this is a "Four Fork" restaurant with high à la carte prices, it serves a three-course-and-wine menu del dia every day (top of the menu) for exactly 1,200 pesetas ($8), service and tax included, and if you'll stay with the set meal—choosing pechugas en bechamel (breast of chicken with sauce bechamel) as your

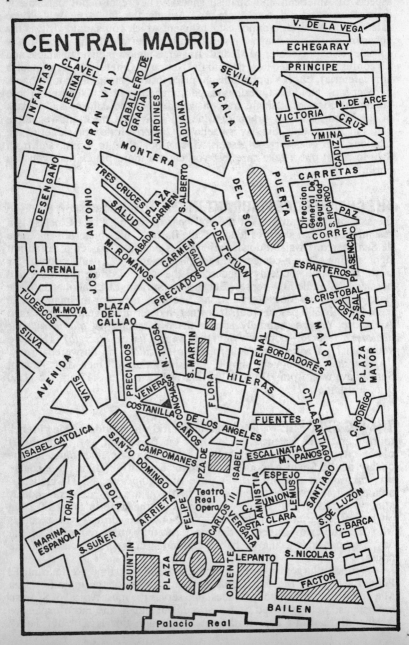

CENTRAL MADRID

main course—you'll be delighted with both the culinary and financial results.

And lastly, in the American Express area, the most popular tourist restaurant of them all—the **Edelweiss** (corner of Calle de Jovellanos and Calle de Zorilla, directly behind the Cortes building)— charges 1,500 pesetas ($10) for a three-course menu, wine included, consisting mainly of German specialties, served by a dozen whitecoated waiters, two of whom speak English. Turn right at the corner as you leave American Express, walk in one block, then up. Best thing about the Edelweiss? It opens for dinner at 7 p.m., much earlier than most other restaurants in Madrid. Hours are from 1 to 4 p.m. and 7 p.m. to midnight, Monday through Saturday, closed Sundays.

(Which reminds me to mention that dining hours in Spain are unusually late: some restaurants in Madrid aren't open until 1:30 or 2 p.m. for lunch, until 8 p.m. or even 8:30 p.m. for dinner.)

READERS' RESTAURANT SELECTIONS: "In my opinion, the restaurant in Madrid that offers the most good food for the least money is the **Restaurante las Arenas,** at 28 Calle de Embajadores at the corner of the Calle de Fray Ceferino Gonzalez (right around the corner from the 'Jumble Market'). For 500 pesetas ($3.33), I received a half-bottle of wine, bread, a small dish of the best paella I've ever had, a main course of steak and french fries, and my choice of any dessert on the regular menu (e.g., an ice cream sundae worth about 80 pesetas). For an extra 100 pesetas, one can have an enormous green salad. In addition, each table has a large pitcher of ice water—a welcome 'extra' on hot Spanish afternoons" (J. David Murphy, Barrie, Ontario, Canada; note from AF: Restaurante las Arenas is open daily except Sunday evenings, from 1 to 4 p.m. and 9 to midnight, and several other readers have rhapsodized about owner Elias Ferrero's gazpacho soup for 120 pesetas. Best way to reach las Arenas is by subway to Tirso de Molina, one stop from the Puerta del Sol, and then by walking from there up Calle Duque de Alba, which leads to Calle de Embajadores). . . . "**Terra a Nosa,** at Cava San Miguel 3, is just behind Plaza Mayor, across from the big Mercado. A 900 peseta fixed price dinner is available, but if one watches what the locals eat, a better choice for less can be made from the à la carte menu. The atmosphere is typical and friendly, and the food is delicious. Closed Wednesdays. We came back three times to be able to sample different items from the menu" (Malcolm and Karla Lansky, Los Angeles, California).

4. What to See & Do

DAYTIME SIGHTSEEING: Toledo and Aranjuez, El Escorial and the Valley of the Fallen, Segovia and La Granja—these cities and sites, all an hour-or-so from Madrid, are what's important in this area of Spain, and each of them can best be reached on do-it-yourself excursions by bus or train, or by renting a car for the day if you're three or more. There's scarcely a valid sightseeing attraction in the world that's limited only to persons on a commercial tour, or that can't be reached simply by means of public transportation—as all of the above can. As one reader recently commented: "Take the public bus from Madrid to Toledo; it's not only money you save, it's the fun and depth of the experience you have. Get a taxi in Toledo to take you to the lookout at the other side of the river and then to drop you off at one of the city gates. Then get lost on your own and you won't soon forget Toledo. The State Tourist brochure is all you need to guide you around the city; the patter of a commercial guide is silly."

Best of the bus stations for Toledo is the **Estacion Sur de Autobuses** at 17 Calle Canarias (subway station is Palos de Moguer), from which coaches leave at frequent intervals on the one-hour trip to Toledo, charging 320 pesetas, one-way. Or you can take (for 450 pesetas) the "Ferrobus"—a self-propelled, four-coach electric train—from tracks *(vias)* 7, 8, 9, 10 or 11 of the Atocha railroad station, as early as 7:20 a.m.

If you're determined, nevertheless, to take a commercial tour, keep in mind that most of the above attractions are visited both on half-day and full-day excursions, and that often the major difference between the cheaper half-day tour and the costlier full-day tour is that you don't waste endless time, on the former, waiting for lunch in the tourist restaurant (they invariably serve boiled pork on a 95° day) to which the full-day tour takes you; the half-day tour also leaves an hour earlier in the morning, and often covers almost the very same ground as the latter. And finally, if you must take a tour (2,400 pesetas for the "Artistic Morning Tour" starting at 9:30 a.m., 1,800 pesetas for the "Panoramic Afternoon Tour" starting at 3:30 p.m.), then buy it from **Mundicolor-Pullmantour,** 8 Plaza de Oriente (phone 241-18-07), next to the Royal Palace, whose booking clerks give a 10% discount to bearers of this book.

In town, the major sights are of course the **Prado Museum** (see below), the **Royal Palace** (on the Plaza de Oriente, nearest subway stop is Plaza de España), a **bullfight** on late Sunday afternoons (subway is Ventas); and then secondly, **El Retiro Park,** the **Museum Lazaro Galdiano,** the **Royal Tapestry Factory,** the tiny **Panteon de Goya,** all with normal viewing hours and either free or nominal admission, except for the Royal Palace, which charges 120 pesetas. Most of the above are closed on Sunday afternoons, when it's time to buy that paperback edition of *Death in the Afternoon* and prepare for the bullfight.

THE PRADO: Surely, this is the greatest museum in the world. It is smaller and better arranged than the Louvre; it is far more selective and would never think of accepting the trivia (murals by David) with which the Louvre fills its halls; and it has a greater concentration of masterpieces than even the Uffizi in Florence—works by El Greco, Goya, Velasquez, Titian, Tintoretto, Rubens, Van Dyck, Murillo, Ribera, Breughel—you will reel from the impact of this great art collected in one spot. The Prado is open daily except Mondays from 10 a.m. to 6 p.m., Sundays from 10 a.m. to 2 p.m. only, and charges admission of 250 pesetas, which includes entrance to the new Picasso exhibition at the Cason del Buen Retiro, a 300-yard walk from the Prado, next to the end of Calle Felipe IV, and facing Retiro Park. Highlight of this annex is Picasso's famous "Guernica," protected by an enormous, illuminated glass cage, which has become a sort of national shrine, witnessed by the hundreds of Spaniards pilgrimaging there daily. . . . High spot of the museum, in my poor opinion, is the room of sketches by Goya on the first floor, which make fierce, passionate commentaries on the themes of war, death, poverty, tyranny. The Velasquez rooms are another indispensable stop. . . . For lunch-time visitors, the Prado maintains a modern, new cafeteria next to its basement room of Goyas, selling quite excellent sandwiches for 100 to 175 pesetas, red wine for 100 pesetas. . . . Schedule the Prado for the beginning of your Madrid stay; you'll want to shoot yourself if you find only a few hours available for this profound experience at the end of your visit.

BULLFIGHTS: They're presented in the famous **Plaza de Toros** of Madrid every Sunday and on holidays from Easter Sunday till the end of October, beginning late in the afternoon—often as late as 6 p.m. Tickets can be obtained either through your hotel (usually) or by going directly to the mid-town ticket center for the bullfights, at 3 Calle de la Victoria (just off the Puerta del Sol; walk one short block up the Carrera de San Jeronimo, and then turn right on Victoria), which is open on Saturdays from 10 a.m. to 1 and from 5 to 9 p.m., and on Sundays (the day of the fights) from 10 a.m. to 5 p.m. Tickets for normal fights—that is, those not involving the most celebrated matadors—start as low as 500 pesetas for the worst *sol* (in the sunlight) seats, ascend to a high of 2,500 pesetas for the best *sombra* (in the shadow) locations, and it's my recommendation that you buy the 1,600-peseta variety *(tendidos bajos, filas* 1-14, *sombra)* which are perfectly adequate, and will cost you 1,840 pesetas when the ticket broker's 15% fee is added on. The subway station for the Plaza de Toros is Ventas, seven stops from the Puerta del Sol.

When you arrive at the ring, be sure to rent a leather cushion (only 50 pesetas) from the vendors under the stands—that's to place on the concrete seats. If you don't you'll wish you had! And to get back to town after the fights are over (when every cab is taken), simply walk into the subway on the corner of the Plaza de Toros, and take the first train that comes along to the Puerta del Sol stop; you're thus back in the center of everything.

If there isn't a bullfight during the days of your stay in Madrid, then at least visit the bullfight museum (Museo Taurino) next to the rear entrance of the Plaza de Toros arena. Here, memorabilia of the great bullfighter, Manolete, are revered like religious relics. And by looking down from the inside windows on the second floor, you can see the open-air stables where black bulls stand or lie on sawdust and straw, stoically awaiting their performance and last glorious moments. Open Monday through Saturday from 10 a.m. to 1 p.m. and from 3:30 to 6 p.m., for a 50-peseta admission fee.

For non-violent sightseeing, here now is Hope:

HOPE IN MADRID: "The spirit of Madrid is elusive. And filled with contradictions. And not what one expects. Perhaps because our heads are filled with dreams of castles in Spain, we come to Madrid expecting an immediate impact transporting us into passionate, mantillas-to-the-wind, roses-between-the-teeth, sunny Iberia! Instead, on a first glimpse of Madrid, one is disappointed to find a bustling, 'moderne' city—a lingering flavor of the 20's and 30's in decay—with broad boulevards, chunky stone monuments, and tall buildings.

"Ernest Hemingway rushed to the defense of Madrid in his classic work on bullfighting, *Death in the Afternoon* (as he also did during the Spanish Civil War). He acknowledges that Madrid has been accused of being the 'least Spanish' of all the cities of Spain. But he proclaims that since Madrid is a large melting pot for all of Spain, and offers the visitor a variety of life-styles to observe and enjoy, it is actually the *most* Spanish of cities.

"I can only recommend that you relax and let the Spain in Madrid unfold itself to you bit by bit.

Sightseeing in Madrid

"Go to **The Prado** first. It's the most important gallery in Madrid, the city's number one sightseeing attraction. If you can spend a couple of days there, you're to be envied.

"The second most interesting 'sight,' in my view, is the **Plaza Mayor,** a large formal 17th-century square built by Philip aII, whose cobblestones have seen bullfights, tournaments, and the most severe punishments of the Spanish Inquisition. Today, you'll find shops, markets, restaurants, outdoor musicales on summer evenings, and the most intriguing surrounding neighborhood in all of Madrid for wandering and explorations.

The Outskirts

"Before probing Madrid in any greater depth, take the more important excursions outside the city (by bus or train). An hour out of Madrid, and a real must, is El Greco's town—**Toledo**—looking exactly as he painted it. Once there, try to see the **Cathedral; El Greco's House and Museum;** the **Tránsito Synagogue;** the **Church of Santo Tomé; Museum of Santa Cruz;** the **Alcázar;** and more (hours mostly from 10 a.m. to 2 p.m. and 3:30 to 7 p.m., admission of 150 pesetas per visit, except at Santa Cruz where it's 175 pesetas). . . . And then, you won't want to miss **El Escorial,** Philip II's 16th-century monastic retreat—an enormous, square, granite pile of stones, quite accurately described by all who see it as 'the penal institution.' Nonetheless, there's a famous library here, as well as important collections of paintings and tapestries; the Royal Pantheon; the King's Apartments; the Church; the Prince's Cottage; and again much more—depending on your time and durability. An all-inclusive ticket costs 225 pesetas, and the hours are from 10 a.m. to 1 p.m. and 3:30 to 6:30 p.m. . . . Farther from Madrid (and well worth the trip) is the typically Castilian town of **Segovia.** There, among many treasures, the outstanding sights are the splendid, eerie, almost perfectly preserved **Roman Aqueduct** (which is still in use!), and the **Alcázar,** a pink-shimmering, real fairyland castle in the clouds. Begun in the 11th century and added to by each succeeding generation, this has, among several layers of history, the Throne Room where Isabella was proclaimed Queen of Castile, a chapel, and adjacent 'retablo' with 15th-century decorations. Open daily from 10:30 a.m. until sun-down for a 50-peseta entrance fee. . . . But as far as I'm concerned, and unless you've a taste for the macabre, you can skip that 'eighth wonder of the world,' the **Valle de los Caidos** (Valley of the Fallen), a monument to the dead of the Spanish Civil War, and burial place of Spain's long-time dictator, General-issimo Franco, as well as of José Antonio, father of the Falangist Party. Essentially, this is a huge cathedral carved into the center of a mountain, and a monumental bore.

Back In Town—The Royal Palace

"The **Palacio Real** (built on the site of the old Alcázar Real; sometimes referred to as the 'Palacio de Oriente' and located on Plaza de Oriente, nearest subway stop is Plaza de España), begun around two hundred years ago, but completed only a hundred years ago, is no less lavish because of its relative youth. Conceived on a grand scale, it has some 2,800 rooms! But you will probably walk through only 50 of them if you take the combination Palace and Private Apartments Tour for 150 pesetas (a 200-peseta entrance fee includes a visit to the adjoining gallery of Gothic tapestries—a rich collection from the 15th and 16th centuries). The Private Apartments here are every bit as ornate as the Palace proper. In the private Royal Chapel, a focal point is a glass case displaying what appears to be a strange over-sized doll. Actually, it's bones of a Roman Christian Martyr (St. Felix), wrapped in wax and silk and made to look like a small person (a gift to Queen Isabella II from the Pope).

"If you're so inclined, you can also tour the antique **Royal Library,** with over 300,000 books (impressive-looking in mahogany, with priceless early 15th-century books, rich book bindings; engravings; Queen Isabella's prayer book; rare manuscripts); **The Museum of Coins and Musical Instruments**—including five violins by Stradivarius made for the Spanish Court (admission is 120 pesetas); the **Royal Pharmacy** (with 18th-century documents and pieces on display; this pharmacy serviced the royal family: admission, 25 pesetas); the **Royal Armory** (an interesting collection which ranges from the 15th to the 18th century, all pieces belonging to Spanish monarchs; Charles V's armor, ornate saddles, bows, guns, etc., children's armor—to get the little tykes accustomed to the weight of war: admission 60 pesetas); and finally, through a lovely, cool green garden, in Campo del Moro (directly behind the Palace), **The Carriage Museum** (antique carriages and harness: entrance, 75 pesetas). The Royal Palace is open from 10 a.m. to 12:45 p.m. and 4 to 5:45 p.m., Sundays from 10 a.m. to 1:30 p.m.; a 385-peseta ticket admits you to everything, but that's quite a lot to see.

Lázaro Galdiano Museum

"Very much out of the way (at Calle de Serrano 122—from Puerta del Sol take bus #51), but a perfect little gem of a museum, is the **Museo Lázaro Galdiano,** open daily except Mondays from 10 a.m. to 2 p.m.; admission is 50 pesetas, Sundays 25 pesetas. Housed in a small mansion, its four floors and 37 odd rooms are chock full of treasure—objects d'art, furniture, paintings, all vying for your attention. For instance, on the first floor there are small art objects and ecclesiastical art from all over the world (Spanish altar pieces, Maltese crosses), gold, silver and glassware; cases of charming antique jewelry (medieval, Renaissance and baroque); Celtic and Iberian pre-historic bronze pieces, as well as Roman and medieval bronzes. And to top off the ground floor, there is, tucked casually in a corner (on your right at the end of the floor, off a room with mini-copies of Roman statuary) in a green velvet niche, a portrait by Leonardo da Vinci of a winsomely sad young lady—the Gioconda in reverse. I now suggest you take the elevator to the top floor (fourth, that is) and work your way down. Along the route you'll see famed tapestries and textiles (some pieces from the 15th and 16th centuries), embroidered ecclesiastical robes, a display of fans, collections of weapons and armor, pottery, clocks, ornate and interesting furniture, paintings by Bosch, Dürer, Memling, Rembrandt, Van der Meer, Breughel, Van Dyck, El Greco, Valásquez, Lucas Cranach, and a room-full of Goyas. And my listing of what's to be seen here is by no means complete!

The Royal Tapestry Factory

"The **Real Fábrica de Tapices,** at Fuenterrabia 2 (in the neighborhood of the Atocha Railway Station) is a fully operational tapestry-making plant (of the highest order), which still uses antique hand looms from the mid-eighteenth century. You'll tour the factory and be given a complete demonstration of how tapestries are made; the employees are quite accustomed to being interrupted by rubber-neckers and seem to take great pride in showing off various stitches, and happily gossiping about the wealthy buyers of their current work. It is, in sum, a jolly tour (more so if you speak Spanish), and available to you weekdays only from 9:30 a.m. to 12:30 p.m. for an admission fee of only 25 pesetas. But closed weekends and the entire month of August.

The Army Museum

"Just a few blocks from The Prado, at Méndez Núñez 1, is the **Museo Del Ejercito,** which is open from 10 a.m. to 5 p.m. every day except Monday for a recently-reduced 50 peseta entrance fee; children under 14 are admitted free of charge. Located in a former royal palace (built during King Felipe IV's reign—the frescoed ceilings inside were designed by Velásquez), this long red-brick building is immediately recognizable as an Army Museum—the porch is littered with dozens of cannons. At the door, there's a model of the Alcázar of Toledo showing the damage it sustained during the Spanish Civil War. Inside, the museum contains well-displayed exhibits of uniforms, armor, flags, medals, coins, guns, swords (including those of Boabdil, the last Moorish king of Granada; El Cid Campeador; and one attributed to Cervantes), etc.; a vast collection of historical objects from all eras, up to the Civil War. Of special interest to me is the room dedicated to historical mementos of the age of Spanish colonization including Pizarro's flag, a Moorish-style campaign tent of Carlos V, and a letter signed by Admiral Nelson; the tiny uniforms for royal infants; the model of Madrid under siege during the Civil War; and (downstairs) a room devoted to military medicine, and another to the Civil Guard, with a gruesome album of pictures supposedly honoring the National Guard.

The Pantheon of Goya

"In an isolated, somewhat difficult to find spot (beyond the North Station on Paseo de la Florida) is the **Panteón de Goya** in the **Ermita San Antonio de la Florida,** a tiny church which is the burial place of the artist and contains a famous and very fine ceiling fresco by him, painted on the dome of the church. It's worth a visit if you have the time, but don't be confused by the identical church across the street which is used for services. The church you're looking for is on your right, and is exclusively a memorial to Goya. Open daily except Wednesdays and Sundays from 10 a.m. to 1 p.m. and from 4 to 5 p.m. (winters 11 a.m. to 1 p.m. and 3 to 6 p.m.), and the entrance fee is 50 pesetas.

The Convent of Las Descalzas Reales

"Would a 'Royal Nunnery' interest you? Then go to the **Museum of the Convento-Monasterio de las Descalzas Reales,** located at 3 Plaza de las Descalzas (off the Gran Via's Plaza de Callao—take the small street called Postigo de San Martin; the Convent's to your left), open daily from 10:30 a.m. to 12:45 p.m., for a 100-peseta entrance fee. This medieval (15th century) mansion which was turned into a convent by Princess Juana of Austria in the 16th century, was always closely associated with the Palace (as a royal retreat), and aristocratic ladies who were so inclined took the veil here. Since it is still a working convent (of the very strict Franciscan Clarissas Order), you must wait for a guide to take you through. The old building itself is interesting, with a magnificent frescoed hall and staircase (the beginning of the ancient palace). Inside you'll see priceless antique tapestries (two rooms contain 'El Triunfo de la Eucaristia,' made from cartoons by Rubens), priests' robes and vestments gorgeously embroidered with gold thread and jewels (like matadors' capes), a small art gallery which includes Flemish primitives, a Breughel, a Titian, and a Caravaggio, as well as 15th- and 16th-century sacred and religious relics.

The Cerralbo Museum

"This is not an 'important' museum, but it possesses a certain charm and gives you a peep into the inner sanctum of the Spanish nobility in days of yore. The mansion, located at 17 Ventura Rodriguez (behind the Plaza de España), was built during the last half of the 19th century, and the house with its collections was donated to the state by the last childless Marquis of Cerralbo. The collection includes some good paintings and drawings: an El Greco (in the home's private chapel), other works by Ribera, Zurbarán, Veronese, Titian, Tintoretto, Tiepolo, Van Dyck (one or two works from each); an upstairs gallery of the family's armor; and porcelain and china. But the real interest remains the house itself; though somewhat faded now, it's still like a miniature, but very homey, palace. These nobles provided themselves with a billiards room, a beautiful library, and their own little ballroom, with a special balcony for the orchestra and a gilded ceiling decorated with cupids. You'll find murals and ceiling frescoes in many of the larger, more public salons, but even in the cozier family-only rooms the decor is rich and elaborate running to garish (note, for the latter quality, the Venetian chandelier in the music room downstairs). Open daily, except Monday, from 10 a.m. to 2 p.m., for an entrance fee of 200 pesetas. Closed during the month of August.

Recent Additions

"Recently reopened after extensive renovations, the **Museo Nacional de Artes Decorativas** at Montalbán 12, off the Plaza de las Cibeles (walk past the Post Office, then left), offers a rich collection of ceramics, furniture, and other decorative art objects from all the regions of Spain, displayed in 62 rooms ranging over five floors; exhibits are organized chronologically (as far as possible), so that each floor (starting with the second) represents a different century—one can practically trace the history of furniture in Spain. Among many riches (including examples of pre-

Christian glass) on the ground floor, Room 8, a chapel with leather tapestries and an elaborately worked leather altar, is a knock-out; on the next floor, in Rooms 12, 13, and 14, ceilings and arches are Gothic with a distinctly Moorish influence, and there are large tapestries, delicately carved statues, beautifully worked chests. Upstairs again, one finds *the* most baroque bed, two types of 17th-century kitchens, an 18th-century collection of dolls and dolls' houses, a room-full of fans, opera glasses, and walking sticks, and much more to intrigue and delight you. Leave enough time to enjoy it. Open daily except Sundays and Mondays from 10 a.m. to 5 p.m., for a 150-peseta entrance fee. . . . A few years back, Madrid opened its new **zoo** at Casa de Campo, and it's a beauty, one of the most modern, well-organized, attractive zoos I've seen. It's divided by continents, and currently on display is wildlife (2,500 animals) from Africa, Europe, and China (including two giant pandas presented to Spain upon the occasion of the King's visit to Peking in 1978). Most animals are in the open (without cages), separated from the public by moats, and children are permitted to pet the accessible ones (like the little beavers romping on the grass). To get to the zoo, take the Metro to the Batan Station, and exit at the right side of the Parque, then bear left for the healthy walk to the zoo; or take the bus (Linea 33, cost 50 pesetas), which you can pick up at Plaza de España directly to the zoo. Hours are from 10 a.m. to sunset, and admission is 315 pesetas, 160 pesetas for children up to 8 years, free for those under 3. . . . Madrid's newest attraction is the **Museo de Cera Colón** (The Wax Museum), on an underground floor of the new modern skyscraper ('Centro Colón') on Plaza Colón, open daily from 10:30 a.m. to 2 p.m. and 4 to 9 p.m. While admission charges, at 350 pesetas for adults and 150 pesetas for children, are overly high, the museum is tremendous fun. There are interesting historical tableaux (some with films); wax representations of distinguished people in the arts (Cervantes is the feature of a wonderful panorama of scenes from *Don Quixote,* accompanied by music from *Man of La Mancha),* sciences, sports (bull-fighters receive special treatment with a slide-show and a grisly representation of the hospital room in which Manolete died); a collection of the famous and the infamous. Some of the living come off not so well (Taylor and Burton look terrible, as do Churchill and Kennedy), but there are so many good tricks—a room of mirrors, magic and monsters; Anthony Quinn 'breathing' (look for him on a bed, covered with a Mexican blanket, right behind Golda Meir!); Rasputin pushing open a door; and a wax guard planted next to one of the exhibits (I won't tell you where), who looks so alive you feel he's about to tell you not to touch.

Miscellany

"All galleries pale in the aura of The Prado. But, if you're in Madrid for some time, you might want to look in on the **Museo Real Academia de Bellas Artes de San Fernando.** Located at 13 Alcalá (the broad boulevard between Puerta del Sol and the Plaza de las Cibeles), this rather badly lit museum contains Spanish painters from every era (some non-Spaniards as well: Van Dyck, Correggio, Bellini, Rubens' *'Susannah and the Elders',* plus Velázquez, Murillo, Sorollo, Vincente Lopez, Ribera and Zurbarán, and is, for the most part, not really a first-rate collection. One star attraction, however, is a fine room full of Goyas (the first room you'll see), including his famous festival scene *'El Entierro de la Sardina.'* The museum, which may close for repairs for a short while in 1985, is ordinarily open daily except Sundays, from 10 a.m. to 2 p.m., for an entrance fee of 50 pesetas. . . . The **Spanish Museum of Contemporary Art** (open weekdays except Mondays, from 10 a.m. to 6 p.m. and 10 a.m. to 3 p.m. on weekends, for an entrance fee of 150 pesetas) is currently housed in a modern glass and steel building at Ciudad Universitario (look for the black tower) displaying paintings, sculpture, designs and other works of contemporary Spanish artists. The **Museo de America,** also on the university campus, deals with the civilizations of the people of the Americas, including the Philippines, who were touched by Spanish colonization; open daily except Mondays from 10 a.m. to 2 p.m., for a 50-peseta entrance fee—but not really worth the excursion at present, unless you'd like to see University City; nearest Metro is Moncloa. The **Archaeological Museum** (at Serrano 13, open daily except Mondays and Thursdays from 9:30 a.m. to 1:30 p.m., and charging 150 pesetas) has been redecorated and exhibits are now so attractively displayed that a visit becomes not only intellectually stimulating, but a real treat. The collection ranges over prehistoric and ancient to medieval times: Greek and Roman displays, ancient Iberian sculptures, 10th-century bronze pieces; a 12th-century choir stall; tapestries, furniture and church trappings from the 15th and 16th centuries; Visigothic jewelry, including a gorgeous crown from the 7th century; and a small masterpiece sculptured in ivory, the Fernando Crucifix (Isidoro de Leon, 1063). If you can't get to Altamira, you can see a reproduction here of the important 15,000-year-old Altamira cave paintings (viewed via an entrance in the garden to the left of the main gate). Your 150-peseta ticket will also admit you to the Altamira Pinturas, provided you use it immediately; otherwise you'll pay an additional 50 peseta entrance fee. Tip: once inside the cave, sit down—you'll see better."

READERS' DAYTIME SUGGESTIONS: "On an August day, nothing beats a trip to the pool. A fantastically large, inexpensive one (125 pesetas per person) is found at the **Parque Sindical.** Take the metro to Moncloa, where tickets are sold for the bus trip to the park, which also features other sports facilities and serves inexpensive refreshments" (Jill and Randy Freese, Erie, Pennsylvania). . . . "On my last trip, I found an inexpensive way to go to **El Escorial.** First, take the Madrid subway (50 pesetas) to the Atocha Station. Trains leave for El Escorial nearly every hour and the travel time is one hour. All trains carry uniformly priced coaches, and the fare roundtrip is 565 pesetas. At the station one can take a bus for 50 pesetas or walk to El Escorial and see Phillip II's cottage en route. An entrance ticket for all the places of interest may be purchased for 100 pesetas. A side trip by local bus to The Valley of the Fallen can then easily be arranged in El Escorial, but leave Madrid early to do all of this in a day" (Edward J. Walsh, Riverdale, New York). . . . "We spent a couple of pleasant days in Madrid cooling off at the **Casa de Campo** municipal swimming pool, which costs 125 pesetas for the whole day and is a great way to meet young Spaniards. Just take the Metro to the El Lago stop" (Muriel Feiner, Brooklyn, N.Y.). . . . "Don't miss the **Archaeological Museum.** Its Roman mosaics, prehistoric cave paintings and Visigoth crowns are among the finest in the world" (Dr. James Gould, Tampa, Florida). . . . "So pleased were we with the directions for going to El Escorial via public transportation that we found our way to **Toledo** the same way! As we do not speak Spanish, we had someone write down our destination and off we went to the railway station with paper in hand, bought our tickets and took the train. After a day in Toledo we found there is a bus that runs back to Madrid every hour, and with great ease we took the public bus back. We had a grand day traveling with Spanish families and we were amazed that it was so very much cheaper than taking a 'tourist tour' for the day. . . . and I might add, more enjoyable" (Anne Brown, Port Washington, New York). . . . "Here is an easy and economical way to get to Toledo from Madrid. Just take the Southbound #3 Metro Subway to the Palos de Moguer stop (third stop beyond Puerta del Sol), where you'll find an exit going directly into the bus station. Step to Window 24 where for 640 pesetas you can buy a round-trip bus ticket to Toledo. Summertime, there is a 12 noon bus leaving Madrid for the one-hour ride, giving you five full hours in Toledo before catching the bus which leaves Toledo at 6 p.m. for Madrid" (Raymond Holbrook, Dallas, Texas). . . . "When I visited Toledo, I looked at the train schedule. One train left for Madrid at 6:45 p.m., the last departed at 8:20 and was marked 'Fiesta.' This meant that the train traveled at this time only on Sundays and holidays. Because of this quixotic labeling, I missed my train to Madrid. The day that this mishap occurred was August 14, the event of the Assumption, which is Toledo's special holiday. As the hotels were filled, I wandered about all night long, and I left at 6:35 a.m. On one of the pages of your book, a reader says, '. . . Then get lost on your own and you soon won't forget Toledo.' I did just that, perhaps more so than this reader had intended" (Charles W. McDonald, Memphis, Tennessee). . . . "A one-day trip to Toledo has to be planned very carefully from the time standpoint. The 9 a.m. bus arrives at 10:30 a.m., and you must then immediately proceed to the cathedral, for it closes at 1 p.m. and does not reopen till 4 p.m. The last bus to Madrid leaves at 7 p.m. From the bus station near the Atocha Railroad Station, the buses leave at 9 a.m., 12, 3:30, 6, 7, and 8 p.m. going. Apply at ticket window Number 12; there are dozens of windows with no labels, and if you wait in line at the wrong window you will miss the 9 a.m. bus. . . . In Toledo don't get off at the bottom of the hill where the walls are. Stay on to the last stop at the Alcazar. . . . Spend the morning at the Cathedral—one of the great treasure houses of Christianity. It will take all your time until 1 p.m. Then, after lunch, get down to the Church of Santo Tome, where El Greco's greatest painting, 'The Burial of the Count of Orgaz,' is on view (a terrific experience). Do not go to El Greco's so-called house, for it is a terrible disappointment. Head along the street by San Tome below near the river to the Synagogue of El Transito, which has been beautifully restored. Next, rush to the Museum of Santa Cruz, which is across from the Alcazar, before it closes. Then go to the bus station by the Alcazar to catch the 7 p.m. bus" (Lester B. Bridaham, Denver, Colorado; note from AF: one-way bus fare, Madrid/Toledo, is 320 pesetas, round-trip 640 pesetas).

5. Evening Entertainment

Flamenco dancing—that and bullfighting are the two major art forms of Spain, as far as I'm concerned—and the "tablaos" of Madrid (the flamenco nightclubs) can keep me rooted to the spot for hours. To attend a tablao requires only the purchase of a single drink, which you can nurse all evening, but the drink, quite naturally, comes high: 2,000 pesetas ($13.33) at the **Torres Bermejas** on the Mesonero Romanos (just off the Gran Via); or at the **Arco de Cuchilleros,** 7 Cuchilleros, at the bottom of the steps leading to the Plaza Mayor, and directly across the street from our recommended budget lodging at the Hostal La Macarena. At these, the show is a near-continuous one (from 10:30 p.m. to 3 a.m.), and you ought not to feel distressed if a singer is performing at the moment of your entrance—the foot-stomping dancers will come on soon.

If the flamenco clubs are still too costly for your budget, you might be able to see a bit of flamenco at one of the two major music halls of Madrid (usually, but not always, presenting an evening of variety acts—be sure to check). These are the **Teatro de la Zarzuela,** at 2 Jovellanos, a block behind

American Express (where most seats range from 300 to 650 pesetas, with only a few choice orchestra locations costing 500 and more), and the **Teatro Calderon** at 18 Atocha (where most seats are 350 to 600 pesetas). At both, shows go on twice nightly, at 7 and 10:30 p.m.

Anc if it's Saturday night when you're in Madrid, inquire about the possible scheduling of a special Saturday evening (11 p.m.) bull-fight (by apprentice matadors) at the Plaza de Toros. That's become an important new evening activity in Madrid, although some Madrileños are so repelled by the awkwardness of most apprentice bullfighters that they do all possible to prevent publicity about these fights. The seats, in any event, are cheaper than for Sunday afternoon corridas, and kids under 14 years of age are permitted to attend—the only time they can.

MADRID'S TIVOLI:
Just recently, Madrid opened its answer to Copenhagen's Tivoli and Los Angeles's Disneyland, and—can you believe it?—they've come up with an entertainment that quite respectably compares. The **Parque de Atracciones,** in the Casa de Campo, is a combination carnival-park, pleasure-garden, World's Fair and restaurant-dancehall complex, that has quickly become a nighttime must on a visit to Madrid. A 50-peseta entrance fee (25 pesetas for children), admits you to the festival grounds laced with Venetian-type canals—a park area where it's cool on even the hottest of nights—and 50 pesetas is the charge for most of the rides, which are creative and unique. From the Plaza de España, take the suburban subway to Batan, and from there it's but a short stroll to the Parque.

DISCOS AND TASCAS:
Yes, traditional Madrid has the most modern form of nighttime entertainment, too. Sophisticated discotheques for Madrileños in their 20s and 30s: the **Victor III Club** on the third floor of the Hotel Sanvy (first drink charge to men is 500 pesetas weekdays, 700 to 900 pesetas weekends; women pay half); the super-modern **Benasur**, 3 Princesa off the Plaza España, open until 5 a.m. and charging 800 pesetas for entrance . . . Currently the most popular discos in Madrid (as of late 1984), but strictly for the under-25 set only, are: **Teatro Pacha** at 11 Barcelo (Tribunal subway stop), open daily from 7 p.m., capacity 400; **Rock Ola** near the America metro stop, where three bands play to 250 guests nightly; and—claiming to be the largest in Europe—the 3,500-person **Macumba** inside the Chamartin railroad station, but not open every day (phone 733-35-05 for information). All charge about $5 for entrance, but that includes the first drink. . . . Early evening (7 to 10 p.m.) entertainment in Madrid is primarily devoted to "tasca-hopping"—making the rounds of one bar (tasca) after another to sample "tapas" (tidbits and hors d'oeuvres), 60 pesetas apiece, washed down by "chatos" (small glasses) of wine (50 pesetas per glass). The Plaza St. Ana is one area for tascas, as is the Calle Echegaray and the Calle Barbieri, the latter the location of the largest and best tasca I've found: **Valderas** (1 Calle Barbieri, corner of Calle de las Infantas), which has a ten-yard-long bar lined with exotic tapas. Unless you choose the varieties involving fresh shrimp, most tapas should cost you no more than the 60 pesetas referred to above.

MORE NIGHTLIFE IN MADRID: We should expand a bit on **Teatro Calderon,** 18 Atocha, which charges 400 to 1,200 pesetas for seats; it's the variety music hall of the working folk of Madrid, with pop singers, acrobats, spicy skits that are not for children. **La Latina,** at 2 Plaza de la Cebada, is somewhat similar, and charges 500 to 800 pesetas for seats. . . . Most of the film theatres of Madrid are dreary places showing hackneyed, Latin-American comedies, but one—the **Cine Bellas Artes,** next door to the Teatro Bellas Artes on the Calle del Marques de Casa Riera, which is just off the downhill end of the Gran Via—shines forth like a diamond among the dross, showing films by Losey, Kurosawa, Truffaut, Schlesinger, and attracting Madrid's brightest set, who line up as early as 3:45 p.m. to see the day's feature that begins at 4:30 p.m. Seats *(butacas)* are 400 pesetas, and just as on New York's Third Avenue, the lines are almost as interesting as the films.

6. Madrid Miscellany

SHOPPING TIPS: In this cheapest-of-all capital cities, you'll find the world's cheapest shoe store, the huge **Los Guerrilleros,** directly on the Puerta del Sol at 5. The area to the left (as you face the store) contains the $9 and $11 varieties, the one to the right goes higher in price. You take down the number of the shoes you want from the window display, write the number on a slip of paper, and hand it to one of the sales girls, who will eventually fit you. There are both men's and women's styles, and the pair of well-worn white loafers I bought a year ago for $9 are still on my feet, intact, as I type these words. Directly across the Puerta del Sol, at 12, the **Casa de Diego** sells nothing but ladies' fans—some for as little as 250 pesetas ($1.66). Bullfighters hats? Authentic ones? Try any of the hat shops on the Plaza Mayor.

READERS' SHOPPING SELECTIONS: "A good starting place for shopping is the large department store, **Galerias Preciados,** where you can establish a price base for comparison with small shops. The **Oportunidades,** just across the street, is the bargain basement of this large store, where we picked up such buys as men's leather-palmed knit-back driving gloves for $5 a pair, good quality leather pumps for my wife at $9, and leather children's shoes at comparable prices" (W. W. Woodmansee, Santa Monica, California). . . . "Saffron, a spice used in Spanish cooking, can be purchased in cartons of 10 packages each for 300 pesetas ($2), and the equivalent would cost $15 in the States for the same quantity. Wonderful buy to bring back to friends who use this spice in cooking. . . . Spain also manufactures a very famous toilet soap called **Maja Jabon,** which sells for 150 pesetas a bar ($1). Three of these bars sell for about $4.50 in the States in better department stores. They make wonderful gifts for women back home" (Edward Pietraszek, Chicago, Illinois; note by AF: a convenient shop for purchasing Maja soap is **Arjona** at 33 Fuencarral, off the Gran Via).

USEFUL INFORMATION: Recommended parking place for your car: the underground "Estacionamiento de Coches" at **Plaza de las Descalzas,** which charges 70 pesetas per hour for the first three hours, 75 pesetas each subsequent hour; a similar establishment in **Plaza Santo Domingo** (look for a large "P" on a blue-background sign) charges about the same. . . . The real Madrid, where streets look like Spanish streets are supposed to look, is located behind the Plaza Mayor, and a daytime stroll there can be fascinating. From one corner of the Plaza Mayor, walk down the steps into Cuchilleros (tourist Madrid), walk to the end of Cuchilleros into the ancient street called Cava Baja, then walk to the end of the Cava Baja and you'll find the Mercado (Market) de la Cebada (fresh fish, rabbits, much exotica) and next to it, the Piscina de la Latina, a 140-peseta swimming pool. If this ten-minute stroll is too much of a chore, then at least walk from another end of the Plaza Mayor along the Cava de San Miguel, which at night resembles a set from Carmen. . . . When in doubt, order *pechuga,* the famous breaded breast of chicken dish of Madrid, always tasty, or *merluza* (hake), the always fresh, always inexpensive and popular fish specialty of Spain. . . . Open seven days a week until midnight, the **OK Drugstore** at 25 Gran Via, corner of the Calle de la Montera, carries everything a tourist needs (newspapers, books, toothpaste, aspirins, batteries). . . . Across the street, at 3 Calle Fuencarral (look for the tall building with the clock and antennas), the **International Telephone Office,** open daily from 9 a.m. to 1 p.m. and from 5 to 9 p.m., charges $11 for a three-minute call to New York. If you want to send a letter, head for the cathedral-like **Main Post Office,** on Plaza de Cibeles (Metro: Banco), which is open from 8 a.m. to 6 p.m. weekdays, until 1 p.m. Sundays. Although the **Parcel Post Office** is in the same building, you'll have to use the entrance from Calle de Montalban (hours are Monday to Friday only from 10 a.m. to 2 p.m. and from 4 to 6 p.m.). . . . On the subject of **hours,** most stores open Monday to Saturday from 9:30 a.m. to 6 p.m.—banks from 9:30 a.m. to 2 p.m. weekdays. . . . **Embassies: USA,** 75 Calle de Serrano (phone 276-3600); **Canada,** 35 Calle Nunez de Balboa (phone 431-4300); **Australia,** 143 Paseo de la Castellana (phone 279-8501); **U.K.,** 16 Calle Fernando el Santo (phone 419-0202). . . . A cheap and almost-constantly-open laundromat: the **Miele Coin Laundry,** corner Calla del Conde Duque and Travesia del Conde Duque, a block behind the Plaza Hotel at Plaza de España, charging 450 pesetas ($3) for 11 pounds—5 kilos—washed and dried. . . . A life-saving tip: don't assume that Madrid's taxi drivers will stop for traffic lights. Look, and await an absence of traffic, before you cross the street. . . . The Sunday morning visit (9 a.m. to 2 p.m.) to the famous flea market of Madrid (**El Rastro**) is indispensable. Take the subway to Tirso de Molina, then walk to Plaza de Cascorro. . . . As earlier noted, **Tive,** 88 Calle de Fernando El Catolico, one short block from the Moncloa subway stop, and open from 9 a.m. to 1:30 p.m. and 4:30 to 6:30 p.m. only, is the official student travel agency of Madrid. It concentrates on student charter flights and trains, but occasionally assists with accommodations and sells city sightseeing tours at a discount. . . . **Tourist police:** phone 091 for help. Babysitters: phone 449-68-00 (they speak English). **Doctors or dentists:** phone the Anglo-American Hospital, 1 Paseo de Juan XXIII, 234-67-00. . . . Madrid's newspaper of entertainment activities and attractions is a tiny weekly called *Guia del Ocio,* (50 pesetas), but I prefer to use one of the two major daily newspapers: *Ya,* or better yet *ABC,* whose listings are extensive and designate the non-dubbed films with the initials "V.O.". . . . Swimming pools throughout Madrid charge as little as 85 to 125 pesetas, but an outlay of 2,000 pesetas ($13.33) will entitle you not simply to admission, but also to unlimited buffet snacks and unlimited wine, at the swank roof-top pool (open June to September, daily from 11 a.m. to 7:30 p.m.) of the **Hotel Emperador** in the heart of the city at 53 Gran Via (take the self-service elevator to "Piscina"). A fine pool, which provides an added sociological insight into how Madrid's upper crust spend their day; how vou'll react is up to you.

———

Where to from Madrid? Lisbon, of course, a longtime budget favorite in close-by Portugal.

LISBON

**Price Paradise
of Europe**

ALTHOUGH IT IS the capital of a nation, Lisbon has the atmosphere and attitude of a lighthearted resort, and it's easy to see why. It is on the sea—or just two miles or so from it—and the stretch of beach that begins at its outskirts is a Riviera, a place of casinos and brightly striped umbrellas, of great seafood restaurants and boating docks. The climate is balmy and mild, the people easygoing and affable, the bulls of the *corridas* allowed to survive! Best of all, it is the cheapest city of Western Europe, a price paradise of inexpensive lodgings, remarkably low-cost restaurant meals, stunning shopping values.

And yet, from this easygoing, sunny, slow-paced city, half the world was explored! At the great seaside embarkation points for the Portuguese navigators, impressive monuments tell of voyages in the 1500s to India and to Brazil. From the wealth of those conquests came the monumental royal palaces of Portugal, the royal coaches that fill one of the world's most fascinating museums, the collections of intricate tapestries and jewels that so delightfully assault the senses. Yet again, although Portugal possesses a history and culture second to few, it presents its sightseeing wonders in simple, and non-overwhelming, fashion. There is no Eiffel Tower-type structure here, no Grand' Place or Piazza San Marco. Rather, there are jumbled narrow streets and picturesquely beflowered squares; scores of informal small restaurants with sidewalk tables; steep hillside neighborhoods—the historic Alfama is the prime example—of quaint, ancient structures housing a lively and colorful workingclass population; small museums and shops; taverns and cafés. There is no air or water pollution, scarcely any cloverleaf highways, hardly a single center-city skyscraper. For a refreshing change from urban pressures, at the lowest of costs, you'll want to include Lisbon on your European trip!

1. Orientation & Getting Around

The heart of the city extends for about two miles from the **Praca do Commercio** (the Square of Commerce), near the Tagus waterfront, to the **Praca do Marques de Pombal** (named after the prime minister who rebuilt the town after a major earthquake destroyed it in 1755; this is also called the **Rotunda**). The first mile of this area, from Square of Commerce to the **Rossio Square,** is crisscrossed by small shopping streets; the second mile, from Rossio to Pombal Square, is dominated by the **Avenida da Liberdade,** Lisbon's Champs Elysées. To the right and left of the Square of Commerce, as viewed from the waterfront, are two fascinating "old town" districts, the **Alfama** and the **Barrio Alto,** the first topped by **Saint George's Castle,** the other an inner-city business district. All other parts of Lisbon, with few exceptions, are of little interest to tourists, because everything else is relatively new and rarely older than a hundred years.

GETTING AROUND: It's scarcely necessary to brief you about transportation in a city where even the taxis (average ride: $2) are cheap. From **Portela Airport** to your hotel is, in fact, only a $4 ride (and that's for six miles of distance) by taxi, only 50¢ by public Green Line bus. A fairly limited subway system of only 20 stations charges the lowest fares in Europe (25¢ per ticket if you buy ten at a time, 35¢ otherwise), and there's a far more extensive bus and trolley network on which tickets are 19¢ apiece if you purchase a block (module) of 10 tickets for 250 escudos, at booths located on most major squares (such as the Rossio). If you'll be staying in Lisbon for at least a week, a seven-day pass priced at $5.50 can reduce costs even further.

Arriving by train from Madrid or Paris, you'll debark at the **Santa Apolonia Station,** Lisbon's major terminus, named after a nearby church; but you'll also need to know about three subsidiary stations: **Rossio** (for local trains to Sintra), **Cais de Sodre** (to and from Estoril and Cascais), and **Sul e Sueste** (reached by first crossing the Tagus River, for trains to and from the Algarve). There are tourist information booths at the airport (phone 725-974) and at Santa Apolonia Railway Station (phone 864-181), but the main such office is at **Palacio Foz,** Praca dos Restauradores (across from the Central Post Office), open daily from 9 a.m. to 8 p.m. (phone 363-314).

2. Low-Cost Lodgings

The budget accommodations here are legendary in the quality they provide for the price they charge, and your only real problem will be choosing a location for your stay from the following alternatives:

NEAR THE ROTUNDA AND PARQUE: Residencia Caravela, 38 Rua Ferreira Lapa (phone 539-011), off the Avenida de Loule, 100 yards from the U.S. Embassy and the Centro Cultural Americano (where you can peruse U.S. newspapers and magazines, free, most afternoons), is an excellent first choice, in a quiet, central, three-story, elevator-equipped building, with English-speaking manager (Eduardo Silva) and receptionist (Señor Abel). For rooms with private bath and shower, in 1985, they'll be charging only 1500 escudos ($11.53) single, 2200 escudos ($16.92) twin, 3000 escudos ($23.07) triple, 3500 escudos ($26.92) quad, always including continental breakfast; and of their 45 rooms, one in particular—#203—has a football-field-sized bathroom; try to get it. From the airport, take bus 22; from Santa Apolonia Station bus 12; and in both instances, ask the driver for the American Embassy stop.

Residencia Astoria, 10 Rua Braakamp (phone 544-800), just off the Rotunda, with 60 rooms on four floors, all with private bath and w.c., is not among our more outstanding choices, but the location is perfect, the (rather small) rooms are clean and proper, both the owner and manager are friendly and English-speaking, and rates, including breakfast served in a mensa-type dining room on the third floor, are 2100 escudos ($16.15) single, 2500 escudos ($19.23) twin, 3500 escudos ($26.92) triple.

Residencia Horizonte, 42 Avenida Antonio Augusto de Aguiar (phone 539-526), next to the Parque Metro stop, five minutes on foot from the Rotunda, and another of these multi-floor, elevator establishments, is highly recommended by me, and charges 2200 escudos ($16.92) for singles with private bath and breakfast, 2500 escudos ($19.23) for double rooms with private bath and two breakfasts. Señor Antonio is this time the fluent-in-English manager.

Residencia Nazareth, diagonally across the street at 25 Avenida Antonio Augusto de Aguiar (phone 542-016), fourth and fifth floors (there's an elevator), is amply endowed with large, multi-bedded rooms, and therefore ideal for both families, small groups and backpackers. It offers a full 32 rooms, all with private shower and wc; includes breakfast in its moderate rates; and charges only 2200 escudos ($16.92) single with private shower and breakfast, 3500 escudos ($26.92) for twins with breakfast and shower, 4500 escudos ($34.61) for triples so equipped and supplied, 5500 escudos ($42.30) quad. Both the owner (Senhor Nazir—he's from India) and the manager (Senhor Rais—he's Portuguese) are fluent in English, and both quite proud of their dorm-like values.

Residencia Aleluia, 32 Rua Luciano Cordeiro (phone 57-37-02), again less than five minutes on foot from the Rotunda, operates 12 rooms on the second floor of an apartment house, all of them with shower, w.c. and TV set, and all at attractive (for 1985) rates: 1900 escudos ($14.61) for twins, 2300 escudos ($17.69) for triples, 2600 escudos ($20) for a four-bedded family room, with optional breakfast at 200 escudos ($1.53) extra. Senhor Antonio Morais da Costa, the English-speaking manager who encourages you to call him "Tony," will pick you up at the station or air terminal if you'll phone in on arrival

ON AND OFF THE AVENIDA DE LIBERDADE: This is a broad and (in spots) rather elegant avenue, quiet and refined. On or near it you'll find:

Hotel Lis, 180 Avenida de Liberdade (phone 563-434), about half-way between the Rotunda and the Praca dos Restauradores, a popular hotel long recommended in this book and friendly to our readers (manageress

Camila Ramos is the architect of that policy). There are 63 rooms on five floors, all with bath and private w.c., and all reached by elevator. Rates, including breakfast: 2400 escudos ($18.46) single, 2800 escudos ($21.53) double.

Hotel Dom Sancho I, 202 Avenida de Liberdade (phone 548-648), two blocks from the Lis and across the avenue from the deluxe Tivoli Hotel, is of a slightly lower standard than the Lis but also considerably cheaper: singles with private bath and breakfast 1500 escudos ($11.53), twins or doubles on the same basis 2000 escudos ($15.38). The Avenida Metro stop is nearby (it also services the Lis Hotel); the reception desk is on the third floor, reached by a cage-like elevator.

Hotel Jorge V, 3 Rua Silveira (phone 562-525), on a quiet side street off the Avenida de Liberdade, is surely one of the finest and best-managed standard-class hotels of Lisbon. Fifty rooms on two floors, two elevators, modern furnishings, and these 1985 rates: 3100 escudos ($23.84) single, 3750 escudos ($28.84) twin, 4400 escudos ($33.84) for suites resembling two-room apartments, 4700 escudos ($36.15) for such a suite occupied by four persons, all rates including breakfast, bath, bidet. Owner Antonio Ribeiro and receptionist Señor Vasquis both speak English perfectly, and will assist and advise you on matters related to your Lisbon stay.

The rock-bottom **Pensao Sevilha,** 11 Placa da Alegria (literally: Fun Square), phone 369-579, two minutes from Avenida de Liberdade, near the Praca dos Restauradores, is definitely no-frills, but perfectly acceptable if all you are seeking is a clean room in a central area at bargain rates. There are 42 rooms, priced at 700 escudos ($5.38, no mistake) for a single without shower, 800 escudos ($6.15) with shower, and at 1100 and 1300 escudos ($8.46 and $10) for twin rooms without and with shower, respectively, including breakfast (and that's no mistake either). You'll need to walk up 42 steps to the reception office in this elevator-lacking building, where a kind lady with some basic knowledge of English will show you to a room, some with antique white-and-gold ornamented furniture (like room 206), some with brand-new unpainted wooden beds, tables, chairs and wardrobes (like 212). Most of the gigantic rooms look out onto a park with a fountain and goldfish-filled pool. While the Sevilha is not for the more fastidious travelers, it is ideal for experienced budget types, and a particular Shangri-La for backpackers.

NEAR THE ROSSIO: Residencia Insulana, 52 Rua da Assuncao (phone 323-131), is another favorite of mine, centrally located in the very heart of town, above a ladies' fashion shop (take the elevator to a reception room on the second floor). For remarkable guest rooms with wall-to-wall carpeting, small writing desks, large bathtubs, private w.c., bidet, telephone and many extras, and for use of a modern public lounge and cozy breakfast room (breakfast is included in the price), you'll pay 2800 escudos ($21.53) for singles, 3600 escudos ($27.69) twins or doubles. Manager Diamantino Carvalho de Castro and his reception manager, Señor Abel, create such satisfaction that a Brazilian couple I met here in the summer of 1984 went out of their way to tell me it was their fourth stay!

Residencia Roma, 22a Travessa da Gloria (phone 360-557), next to the Rossio railway station, is a less costly, highly recommended establishment of 24 rooms on the second and third floors of an apartment house.

All rooms are with private bath and breakfast, and rent in 1985 for a reasonable 2000 escudos ($15.38) for singles, 2800 escudos ($21.53) for twins, with breakfast served in your room, if you wish. Reception, you'll note, is on the second floor, where you'll meet charming Señorita Manuela.

Residencia do Sul, 59 Praca Dom Pedro, in the very center of the Rossio district (phone 322-511 or 847-259), is the most basic of our Rossio area choices, but with its 120 rooms (some located in three annexes—*filials* —in the same area), you may find accommodations here in peak season (July and August) when Lisbon vacancies are occasionally difficult to discover. Rooms are simply furnished but adequate and clean, and rent for a breathtaking 1000 escudos ($7.69) single, 1300 escudos ($10) twin or double, without breakfast. To find the hotel, look for the big National Theatre building; the do Sul, at 59, is diagonally across from it, sharing the same entrance with a tobacco shop.

NINE SCATTERED CHOICES: **York House Hotel,** 32 Rua das Janelas Verdes (phone 662-4535), and **York House Hotel Annex,** half a block away at 47 (phone 668-143), are two unique establishments whose rates are mainly, but not always, in a splurgey category, but with remarkable rooms furnished with exquisite antiques. Entering, you'll think yourself in a ceramic-tile factory, while later you'll delight to tiny courtyards filled with acacia, pepper and palm trees, and to patios lined with extraordinarily beautiful plants. Originally a convent, the house or complex was bought many years later by two ladies from York (hence the name), who later sold it to the present owners, Dr. Telles and Senhor Hespanha, both comfortably fluent in English. Seventy-five percent of the guests are still British. For very special amenities and atmosphere, you'll pay a high (for Lisbon) 3750 escudos ($28.84) for a single with private bath and breakfast, 4500 escudos ($34.61) for a twin or double with private bath and breakfast, the latter meal served in a glassed-in verandah in winter, in a garden in summer. But here's a budget tip: six single rooms without private bath rent for only 2000 escudos ($15.38) in summer, when their long-stay winter residents are on vacation, and one particular suite, consisting of a large sitting room and adjoining bedroom with four beds, all lavishly yet tastefully furnished, rents for only 6250 escudos ($48.07) for four persons. If you're a family of four or a small group, a stay in that room will be among the highlights of your European trip. All this is within the city limits, roughly half-way between Rossio and the suspension bridge (Ponte 25 de Abril), best reached on arrival via a $4 taxi ride from Portela Airport, a $2.50 fare from Santa Apollonia Railway Station. Public buses and streetcars stop directly in front of York House, whose receptionist will supply you with the transport details.

Hotel Berna, 13 Avenida Antonio Serpa (phone 774-642 or 774-741), near metro stop Campo Pequeno (itself three stops from the Rotunda), is three-star quality for one-star prices (compared, let's say, with hotels in Rome or London). Modern (it opened in 1983), with comfortable contemporary furniture in rooms all equipped with private bath and w.c., direct dial phone and radio; 10 floors in size (serviced by two elevators); with spacious lounge and garage for free parking, it nevertheless charges only 2800 escudos ($21.53) for a single with bath and breakfast, only 3375 escudos for twins or doubles with private bath and breakfasts (that's

$25.96 for the two of you), 4000 escudos ($30.76) triple—less expensive than York House, and more centrally located; an excellent value. And walking to and from the metro station, you'll pass the imposing bull-fight area of Lisbon, with its onion-shaped turrets resembling a Russian church.

If Lisbon is sold out during the period of your stay, your chances of finding a vacancy are good at one of three hotels totaling 180 rooms, all on the same street and next to one another, adjacent to the San Sebastiao Metro stop: **Hotel Dom Manuel I,** 187 Avenida Duque d'Avila (phone 562-340); **Hotel do Reno,** 195 Avenida Duque d'Avila (phone 548-181); and **Hotel Principe** at 199 Avenida Duque d'Avila (phone 536-151). All three charge an average of 2500 escudos ($19.23) for singles with bath and breakfast, 3400 escudos ($26.15) for twins with bath and breakfast, all three are tourist class in category (the Principe being the slightly superior establishment), and one—the do Reno—offers a number of four-bedded rooms for 4500 escudos ($34.61).

On the same street, but five blocks up, the 25-room **Pensao Patria** at 42 Avenida Duque d'Avila (phone 530-620), is of much lower standard and accordingly far less expensive: 1500 escudos ($11.53) for a twin-bedded room with hot and cold running water but without private bath, with breakfast included. Basic, but clean and friendly; its reception lobby is on the sixth floor, reached by elevator.

Residencia Capital, 87 Avenida Elias Garcia (phone 767-330), near the Campo Pequeno Metro stop (three stops from Rotunda), rents 22 rooms on six floors serviced by two tiny elevators. Each room is with bath, bidet and w.c., and yet rents for only 1750 escudos ($13.46) single, 2250 escudos ($17.30) double or twin, 2800 escudos ($21.53) triple, 3200 escudos ($24.61) quad, breakfast included.

Equally cheap: the **Residencia Lisboniense,** 1 Rua Pinhero Chagas (phone 544-628), near the Lisbon Sheraton and next to the Saldanha Metro stop. Half of its 30 rooms (on five floors) are without private bath, all are rather small, but all are clean and utterly acceptable, especially at these rates: 1200 escudos ($9.23) for singles without bath, 1350 escudos ($10.38) for singles with private shower, 1300 escudos singles with private bath (and that's only $10), 1700 escudos ($13.07) for twins without bath, 1950 escudos ($15) with private shower, 2100 escudos ($16.15) twins with private bath. Manager, Señor Nunes, can be found on the third floor (reached by elevator) and speaks some English; he's promised to do everything possible to assure you a pleasant stay.

Lisbon's Youth Hostel

There's only one, open all year around to both sexes, provided they'll accept non-private accommodations (the dorms hold 8 to 30 cots apiece), a daytime curfew from noon to 6 p.m. (meaning only that they close the hostel for cleaning during those hours), and a later midnight curfew, and the absolute necessity to hold a Youth Hostel card (sold on the spot, however, for 1700 escudos, or $13.07). If you do comply, you'll enjoy bed-and-breakfast rates of only 500 escudos ($3.84) per night in the 133-bed **Pousada de Juventude,** 46 Rua Andrade Corvo (phone 57-10-54), in a central location, next to the Picoas Metro stop (one stop after Rotunda). In leaving the subway station, make sure you take the "R. Virato" exit, which practically leads to the hostel 30 yards away.

THE PORTUGUESE ESCUDO: Prices in this chapter have been converted into dollars at the rather conservative rate of 130 escudos to one dollar. If that rate should change by the time of your own stay in Lisbon (and it probably will, in your favor), then dollar equivalents in this chapter will be slightly off, although prices set forth in escudos will remain the same.

3. Lisbon's Remarkable Restaurants

They feature the cheapest meals in all of Europe, built around a number of classic dishes that you'll want to burn into your memory. There is, first, *caldo verde* soup (made with mashed potatoes, finely shredded cabbage and small pieces of peppery sausage, usually served with olives, and all cooked in a beef broth); spectacular. And then there's the ubiquitous *bacalhau assado* (grilled, dried and salted codfish—Portugal's national dish—prepared in over 200 different fashions, and served with steamed potatoes, salad and onion sauce); superb. There is *bife na frigideira* (not a deep-frozen dish—*frigideira* stands for frying pan—but a beefsteak served with potatoes and wine sauce); *carne de porco à alentejana* (pork stewed in a mussel sauce spiced with five herbs; a prize winner); an egg dish called *barrigas de freira*—literally translated, "nuns' tummies"—a delight worth its name); and *pudim molotov,* a foamy, sweet dessert, served with creme caramel, resembling a cross between a sponge cake and a pudding, and out-of-this-world in taste. And the wines! More than 50% of the agricultural production of Lisbon's coast consists of wines: sweet wines (like the muscatel), white wines *(bucelas)* and reds *(colares* and *tintos),* scores of different brands; when in doubt, simply request the local wine *de casa* (of the house), and you won't be disappointed. Cheese is taken for dessert, any of dozens of types, and one, a creamy, smoked, sheep cheese called *serra da estrela,* is a delicacy scarcely found elsewhere in Europe. A portion of this cheese, a bottle of local wine, and chunks of dark bread, a feast equivalent to a light meal, will cost less than $2.50 in any second or third-class restaurant (we'll explain these categories in a moment). In the same sort of restaurant, a three-course meal of soup, main dish, dessert, half a bottle of wine, and a cup of Brazilian coffee totals to a mighty $4, and can be had for as little as $3.50!

Restaurants in Lisbon are officially classified into four categories— luxury, first, second and third—and the only difference, believe me, between the top two and the bottom two are in service and physical setting, not in the quality of the food offered or in its tastiness. Naturally, we'll limit ourselves to recommendations of third and fourth class establishments, most of which maintain an English-language menu to hand you; if not, feel free to enter the kitchen and point to what you'd like—a traditional and perfectly acceptable custom in Portugal, as it is in Greece. Like their higher-priced colleagues, the third and fourth class restaurants open late for dinner, around 8 p.m. Here are some good ones:

Tasca do Marinheiro, 38 Rua da Conceiao da Gloria, a narrow, uphill street off the Avenida de Liberdade, near Restauradores, is for readers craving inexpensive seafood. Do Marinheiro, a seafood specialist, offers fresh grilled sardines with salad for only 200 escudos ($1.53), eight other

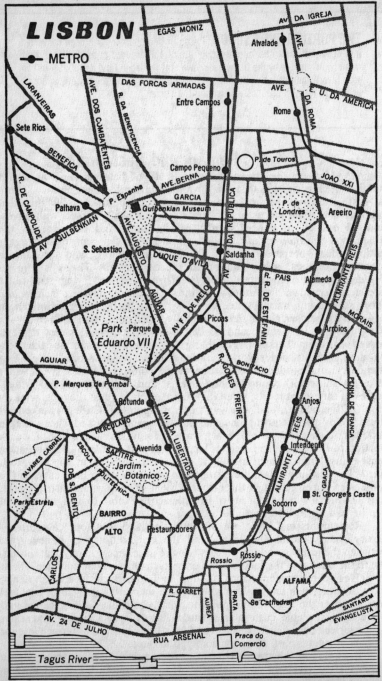

fish dishes and 10 meat dishes for an average of 300 escudos ($2.30), four daily platters—one apiece of veal, fish, pork and chicken—for 180 to 300 escudos ($1.38 to $2.30), spinach soup (a specialty of the house) for 30¢ (repeat, 30 U.S. cents). You can eat like a king here for $4, *including* wine and dessert.

Restaurante Estrella, 14a Rua de Santa Marta, on a parallel street to the Avenida de Liberdade, lists five multi-course menus of the day, each for only 400 escudos ($3.07). The one I sampled in the summer of 1984, from an English menu card that must be specifically requested, began with a thick vegetable soup (spinach, carrots, some garlic) in a large tin cup, followed by steamed white fish with boiled potatoes, salad, and a bottle of local red wine (enough for three full glasses); it was unusually tasty and filling. The restaurant, a bit off the beaten track, can be spotted by its window display of sausages and wine bottles, strings of garlic and glasses of mixed pickles and fish.

Casa Geraldinos, 3 Rua de Santo Antonio dos Capuchos, on a steep uphill street off Restauradores (walk first up Rua Talhal), is the smallest of our selections, frequented only by locals and students of the nearby medical faculty, and always crowded at lunchtime. Home-cooked meals, plain Portuguese dishes, nothing fancy, are the bill of fare, and your meal of *soupa do carne* (beef broth with rice and vegetables), followed by *cozido à Portuguesa* (a potpourri of pork, beef, sausages, cabbage, rice, carrots—enough to fill two stomachs, followed by a *sobremesa* (say, a chocolate mousse dessert), and accompanied by the house wine served in a little ceramic pitcher, will cost less than four U.S. dollars.

Restaurante Andorra, at 82 Rua das Portas San Antao, off the Restauradores, behind the Central Post Office building, is only slightly more expensive, and creates a more cultivated atmosphere by, for example, serving bread and butter automatically, without request, with your meal, the waiter using a pincer-like instrument to place the bread next to your plate. Average table d'hote meal *(menu),* of which there are more than a dozen varieties, will cost you around $5, an example being: tomato-and-fish soup as a starter, fried swordfish with steamed potatoes and salad as your main course, a sweet for dessert, all accompanied by a small bottle of *vinho tinato da casa* (local red wine). The upstairs portion of the restaurant is the more comfortable place in which to sit.

Restaurante Cubata, 133 Rua dos Bacalhoeiros, about 250 yards from the Antinel, just off the Praca do Comercio (and therefore a fine place at which to eat either before or after climbing to Saint George's Castle, 200 yards up), is especially unpretentious in appearance, in fact alarmingly so (from the outside), but the dishes served at 20 inside tables are delicious, first class, and very reasonably priced. Soups 50¢ (try the *caldo verde),* 25 main plates (such as haddock filet with steamed tomatoes) average $2.75, grilled shrimps are $4, salads 45¢; by staying with the moderate main plates, you can eat easily for under $4.50.

Restaurante Casa de Lampreia, 271 Rua da Madalena, is a popular small eatery just off the Da Fugueira Square in the Rossio district, with English-speaking waiter and a choice of ten multi-course *menus,* none costing more than 400 escudos ($3.07). Consider, as one example: *soupa alentejana* (prepared with garlic, a fresh egg, and white bread), roast rabbit with fried potatoes, mixed salad, cheese for dessert, a half bottle of auburn-colored local wine, a cup of coffee at the end, and your tip (included in the price), all for a total of $4.

READERS' RESTAURANT SELECTION: "**Restaurant da Trinidade,** 10 Rua Nova da Trinidade (off the central Rua Garrett, near the Rossio), is one of the best in Lisbon, with its excellent seafood and incredibly inexpensive menu. We each had mixed salad, grilled fresh red snapper with potatoes and vegetables, a big bottle of their best white wine (we shared the wine), dessert and coffee, which cost in total only 1000 escudos, less than $8, for both of us. It was amazing" (Arto and Zabel Khrimian, Long Island City, New York; note from AF: closed Sundays).

CAFETERIAS AND COFFEE SHOPS: Located in the basement of
Lisbon's largest (and only) department store, **Cafeteria Grandes Armazens do Chido,** at the corner of Barrett and 1 Dizembro Streets near the "Eiffel Tower" in the Rossio district, is certainly among the best of the city's self-service restaurants, displaying its dishes for your choice. Four different one-plate meals are offered for only 200 escudos ($1.53), a dozen classier dishes for from 200 to 300 escudos ($1.53 to $2.30), soup for 40 escudos, wine or a Coke for 30 escudos.

Of the city's numerous coffee shops (serving coffee from Portugal's former colonial possession, Brazil), the **Pastelaria Suica** (better known as the Swiss Cafe) is easily the most popular, probably because of its location at 105 Dom Pedro Square, in the heart of Rossio, where coffee drinkers gaze out upon the busy, clattering life that passes in front of the National Theater to their right, a fountain and monument in front, the ruins of a convent destroyed in the great earthquake of 1755 to their left, on the hill. Here, coffee served in a glass is 45 escudos (34¢), a glass of quality Madeira wine 100 escudos (76¢), omelettes and salads $1, toasted sandwiches with cheese or ham $1.80, a selection of daily platters $3 to $3.50. At lunchtime, a waiter may ask you to move inside from the sidewalk tables, unless you've ordered a platter.

The city's oldest coffee shop is the **Brasileira** at 12 Rua Garrett, in the shopping area of Rossio, next door to the Hotel Borges, one block from the Praca de Camoes. Here, black Brazilian coffee, strong and aromatic, is sold for only 20¢ standing up, or for 30¢ sitting, while quick lunches average $3. It's a typical business coffee house where deals are made, conversations and political discussions had, cards and chess played, and constant coffee breaks enjoyed.

A VERY SPECIAL VEGETARIAN RESTAURANT: Not a single tourist,
to my knowledge, has yet entered the precincts of an excellent, budget-priced vegetarian restaurant of Lisbon, where you can have bountiful, three-course meals including beverage (carrot juice and the like) for around $3. The probable reason: it has no name, and it's almost impossible to find at its second floor, 110 Rua de Emenda address, unless you have precise instructions: from Praca Camoes (just off busy Garrett Street in the shopping district), walk up Rua da Horta Seca (passing the post office with prominent CORREIO letters on the wall), then turn into the first street to your right, which is Rua de Emenda. Then walk upstairs to the second floor (there are no signs) passing the newspaper distribution office on the first floor, and there you'll see the famous, unmarked vegetarian restaurant of three rooms, the kitchen in full sight, displaying every classic vegetable dish on a posted blackboard. In addition to its three-course, $3 meal, individual plates (like a colorful vegetable hash, or a soja bean hamburger) sell for as little as $1.50 to $2.20, a maximum of 280 escudos, and the specialty of the

house—soja bean cottage cheese, found nowhere else in Europe—is only 100 escudos (77¢) per portion. Open Monday to Friday from noon to 3 p.m., and from 6 to 8 p.m., Saturday for lunch only, closed Sundays.

PORT-WINE TASTING: Portugal is world renowned for its Madeira, vinho verde and Port wines, of which 148 varieties are available for tasting, at about 40¢ per drink, at the **Solar do Vinho do Porto,** 45 Rua de San Pedro de Alcantara, open seven days a week from 10 a.m. to 11 p.m. Either walk or take the yellow streetcar going uphill from the Calcada da Gloria (a small side street off the Avenida da Liberdade, across from the Pan Am office) for a two-minute, 10¢ ascent to the unmarked, large green wooden door that is #45 on the Rua. Then pass through a second glass door, and you'll find yourself in a lounge resembling that of a luxury hotel, with cozy leather chairs, wall tapestries, artistic lamps, an English-speaking waiter, and a long list of wines (some can be priced at several dollars, so be careful in restricting yourself to the 40¢ choices). If, at the end, you can still stand, you'll want next to cross the street to an observation platform where you'll enjoy a panoramic view over the city and Saint George's Castle.

4. Sights of Lisbon

Some are within easy walking distance, others are miles away or atop steep hills, and you might want to consider a conducted, 2000-escudo ($15.38), three-hour conducted tour, on which you'll save 10% by simply flashing this book to one of the desk clerks at **Star Travel Agency,** 4 Avenida Sidonio Pais (phone 539-871), near the Rotunda. (If you have any problem about this, ask for Mr. Fernando Caldeira, who has direct knowledge of the discount). Two tours are offered: "Panoramic Lisbon" (Saint George's Castle, the old Alfama district, Belem in the outskirts), leaving daily at 9:30 a.m.; and "Tourist Lisbon" (Royal Coach Museum in Belem, the Cristo Re monument across the suspension bridge, the Jeronimos Monastery), leaving daily at 2:30 p.m. While departure point is always the Rotunda, buses will pick you up and deliver you back to your hotel if a timely request is made.

The major sights of Lisbon are the Gulbenkian Museum, the Coach Museum, the Monastery of Jeronimos, and Saint George's Castle, all of which can be visited sans conducted tour, sans major expenditure. If that's your own style of sightseeing, you may be aided by the following details:

GULBENKIAN MUSEUM: Opened in 1969, it has quickly become one of Europe's great art treasures, the repository of perhaps the largest privately owned collection of paintings, furniture, ceramics, sculptures, tapestries and coins in the world, covering over 5,000 years of cultural history. You travel through time, through this wonderfully arranged museum, passing Egyptian artifacts of the third millenium before Christ; Chinese porcelain of the 14th-century Ming dynasty; Japanese prints of the 17th century Ukio-e School; Greek gold coins from 500 B.C.; stone cylinder seals of Mesopotamia, 3000 B.C.; silk carpets from Armenia; and, quite as you'd expect, paintings by Rubens, Rembrandt, Gainsborough, Renoir, Turner, Ghirlandaio, Watteau. Quite centrally located at 45 Avenida de Berna near Metro Station Palhava, two stops after Rotunda, the museum is open daily except Mondays, charges 10 escudos (that's 8 U.S. cents) on weekdays, is free Saturdays and Sundays.

THE COACH MUSEUM: Originally a riding school for the royal family, this is today a remarkable museum drawing coach aficionados from all over the world who gravely study yesteryears' counterpart to our Cadillacs and Rolls Royces. More than 60 royal, papal, ducal, and other state and parade coaches are on display, the oldest dating from the year 1581, the newest an 1824-model actually used by Queen Elizabeth II of England during her 1958 state visit to Lisbon. Location is at Praca Alfonso da Albuquerque in Belem, three miles from the center of Lisbon; and the museum, an unexpectedly riveting spot, is open daily except Mondays for an entrance fee of 50 escudos on weekdays (42¢), but is free on Saturdays and Sundays.

THE MONASTERY OF SAN JERONIMOS: An enormous palace and church built by Portuguese kings in thanksgiving for the discoveries of Vasco da Gama (buried here) and other Portuguese navigators of the world. The giant Gothic-Renaissance Church of Santa Maria, which forms part of the monastery, is famed for the stone lace-work of its adjoining cloisters; don't miss them. Besides Vasco da Gama, there is also buried here Portugal's "Shakespeare," the immortal Luis da Camoes, as well as three Portuguese kings, their sarcophagi decorated with elephants, in vogue at the time of India's discovery. The monastery is open free to visitors, daily, from 8 a.m. to 7 p.m., and best way to reach it is via bus 12 from the Rotunda—the same bus that also serves the Coach Museum.

SAINT GEORGE'S CASTLE: Over 2000 years ago this strategic hill overlooking Lisbon was the site of important Roman fortifications. Having changed hands many times since, it is today what Hyde Park is to London: simply a place for relaxation and picnics, enjoying a unique photographable view over and beyond Lisbon. There are gardens with artificial lakes, a children's playground, peacocks, swans, ducks and geese, a great many stone benches and tables, a great many people enjoying packed lunches in the open air. Open daily until sunset, and with no entrance charge at all.

OTHER INTERESTING VISITS: The **National Art Gallery Museum,** 95 Rua das Janelas Verdes, open Tuesdays through Sundays from 10 a.m. to 5 p.m. for an entrance fee of 50 escudos (38¢) on weekdays, none on weekends, exhibits paintings by Portuguese masters, items of gold imported by Vasco da Gama from the Far East, several interesting works of Lucas Cranach, Velazquez, Pieter Brueghel, Hans Holbein, Albrecht Durer, and an absolute "must-see" masterpiece by Hieronymus Bosch, the "Temptations of St. Anthony." An intriguing oddity is an enormous silver platter, weighing 2,000 pounds, made in the 17th century for a Portuguese king. . . . The **Centro de Arte Moderna** (Museum of Modern Art) near the Gulbenkian Museum, less than two years old, is primarily devoted to works (not simply paintings but tapestries and furniture as well) by Portuguese artists, but also displays a number of "names": Henry Moore, Fernand

Leger, Vasarely. Open daily except Mondays from 10 a.m. to 5 p.m. for an entrance fee of 50 escudos (38¢); nearest Metro station is San Sebastao. . . . **Se Cathedral,** uphill behind the central Praca dos Restauradores, was built in the 13th century in Romanesque style by the first king of Portugal, Alfonso Henriquez, allegedly on the foundations of a mosque; it was heavily damaged by the great earthquake of 1755, but remains the oldest surviving church of Lisbon. Free entrance, open daily from 9 a.m. to 6 p.m. . . . **Tower of Belem** was built in the 16th century as a watch-tower protecting or defending Portuguese ships importing spices from the East, from pirates; it now houses a small museum, open Tuesdays to Sundays from 10 a.m. to 5 p.m., entrance 50 escudos (38¢), and enjoys a worthwhile panoramic view over the Tagus from its top platform. . . . The **Monument of the Discoveries,** several hundred yards from the Tower of Belem (Belem means Bethlehem), was constructed in 1960 to commemorate the 500th anniversary of the death of Henry the Navigator, who founded Portugal's first observatory and discovered Madeira, the Azores and Senegambia, the West African region around the Senegal and Gambia Rivers; from here, bus #12 takes you back to the center of Lisbon in less than ten minutes. . . . **Ponte 25 de Abril,** longest suspension bridge in Europe (more than a mile), connects Lisbon with Setubal across the Tagus, was inaugurated in 1966 as the Salazar Bridge, and then renamed "25th of April" after the revolution which deposed the Salazar dictatorship. Across the bridge is the **Christo Re Statue,** a memorial to Portuguese soldiers who have died in numerous wars, offering an elevator ascent to the 300-foot-high platform on top, for 50 escudos (38¢). . . . The **Aguas Livres Viaduct,** ten miles long, with 109 arches, looks Roman but was built in the 18th century, and to this day feeds the many fountains of Lisbon. . . . The **Santa Justa Elevator** in the heart of Rossio was built by none other than Monsieur Alexandre Gustave Eiffel of Paris fame, in 1910, and is therefore called the "Eiffel Tower." A grey-painted, Gothic-style steel campanile with broad viewing platform on top, reached by a slow but spacious elevator that takes you up for 10¢, it is today Lisbon's major observation tower, with a fine view, especially of the adjoining Bairro Alto district and the ruins of its Carmo Church, a 14th-century structure destroyed in the 1755 earthquake and now an open-air archaeological museum. . . . The **Army Museum,** in front of the Santa Apollonia Railway Station, houses a large collection of weapons from crossbow to tanks, including Vasco da Gama's sword, the kind you can lift with two arms only. It is not a "must" but handy for killing time while waiting to catch a train for Madrid at the station. Open Tuesdays through Sundays from 11 a.m. to 5 p.m., for an admission fee of 30 escudos on weekdays, none on Sundays.

5. Lisbon for Students

Tagus Turismo Juvenil, occupying two offices—a main one at 20 Rua Camilo Castelo Branco (phone 548-685), just off the central Rotunda, a smaller one at 9 Praca de Londres (phone 884-957), between the Campo Pequeno and Areeiro Metro stops—is Lisbon's youth-and-student travel agency, bringing you major savings (from 20% to 40%) on flights, train tickets, tours, theatres, concerts and bullfights. It is closed, at both locations, on weekends, but is otherwise the most professionally run organization of this sort that I've encountered in southern Europe, a contrast to the charmingly provincial style one sometimes encounters in Lisbon. Use it!

6. Entertainment, Both Night and Day

You are now in the land of the fado, that hauntingly nostalgic, strangely wailing sound of the Portuguese chanteuse, and it is required of every visitor to visit a fado nightclub, at the peril of being judged not to have seen Lisbon! Fado restaurants, which are simply normal restaurants that feature fado after 10 p.m., are found primarily in the Alfama or Barrio Alto districts; late at night, they introduce the featured fado singer, dressed in black, accompanied by guitarist, and the songs of fado (which means "fate") continue until early in the morning. A typical establishment of the moderately priced category is **Restaurante Sr. Vinho** at 18 Rua do Meio a Lapa, at Barrio Alto, which opens at 8:30 p.m. and closes at 3:30 a.m., and which you can visit simply by ordering drinks totaling less than $10; it is not necessary also to eat there. Your hotel desk clerk may recommend others closer to your hotel's location.

About the only recommendable disco in a largely disco-less city, and for the young only, is **Banana Power** at 53 Rua Cascais (phone 631-815 or 647-302) in the Alcantara district between Lisbon and Belem, at the foot of the suspension bridge. It is an old factory building with only a small sign outside, capable of receiving as many as 500 guests, who listen to two alternating bands, and pay a minimum consumption fee of $5. Open seven days a week from 11 p.m. to 6 a.m., it can be reached by streetcar 17 from the Praca do Comercio in about 15 minutes, and for 19¢, but the better course might be to take a taxi for $2, one way. Look for the large Jumbo Supermarket next door; and phone before going.

While bullfights are as popular here as in Madrid, there is one crucial difference between the two national sports: in Portugal, the bull is not killed, but rather out-maneuvered by a horseback-rider, the Cavaleiro, or by three men, the Os Forcados, who fight the bull in far more sporting fashion with their bare hands. Bullfights take place in the July-September period only, last about four hours per fight, involve eight bulls on each occasion, cost about $2.50 for entrance, and are to be found in the **Praca de Touros,** next to Metro stop Campo Pequeno.

Cheapest entertainment of Lisbon (about 300 escudos, $2.30) is the cinema, of which about ten theatres are found along the Avenida da Liberdade. Smaller houses, such as the **Animatografo do Rossio,** 25 Rua dos Sapateiros off the Rossio (pass through the archway on Rossio Square, across the square from the National Theatre), charge only 50 cents, often show English-language classics in their original versions, with Portuguese subtitles.

7. Bargains in Shopping

In this area, as in so many others, Lisbon is Europe's cheapest city. At the big department store, **Grandes Armazens de Chido,** corner of Rua Barrett and Rua 1 Dezembro, in the "Eiffel Tower" area, umbrellas cost $4.50 as opposed to, say, $10 in Paris. Cork, one of the main export articles of Portugal (of ten bottle cork stoppers in the world, nine come from Portugal's coast), is best purchased at **Casa das Corticas,** 4 Rua da Escola Politecnica. Until recently also known as Mr. Cork's Shop, it is today managed by his widow, who speaks some English, and will aid you in selecting a cigarette box, board, bottle or puppet, all made of cork, easily packed in a suitcase, and all at reasonable cost: a stunning cigarette box costs all of $3. Location is a five-minute walk from the uphill stop of the yellow streetcar at Calcada da Gloria, off Restauradores. For original

Portuguese fishermen's sweaters, the classic source is **Correa and Rodriguez** at 10 Praca San Paulo; they expect you to try on sweaters and be perfectly satisfied before you buy, at prices per sweater ranging from $10 to $25. Location: near the central Praca do Comercio. For original oil paintings of typical Portuguese scenes, selling for an average of only $30, a good address is **Livraria Ferin,** 72 Rua Nova do Almada, next to the Grande Armazens department store mentioned earlier; they'll remove the painting from its stretch frame and roll it for easy packing. And don't miss the **Lisbon Flea Market,** called the Thieves Market, uphill from Santa Apolonia Station and held twice weekly on Tuesdays and Saturdays. Shoes for $5, belts for 50¢, leather bottles $2, hats for $3, as well as jewelry, keys, toys, sunglasses, books, are scattered about in great quantity and sometimes conceal a real gem among the dross.

8. Lisbon Miscellany

We conclude by pointing out that babysitters are to be hired by phoning **Hospedeiras** at 604-353; that English-speaking doctors can be found at the **British Hospital,** 49 Rua Saraiva de Carvalho (phone 602-020 or 603-785); and that a good self-service laundromat is the **La vimpa,** open weekdays only, at 22a Avenida de Paris, next to Metro stop Areeiro.

A REMINDER: Several thousands of the readers of this book are now members of a unique travel "co-operative," the **$25-a-Day Travel Club.** Because other readers have said they missed seeing the description of the club appearing in Chapter I, we've decided to repeat the description here, just ahead of our "Tale of Many Cities" chapter that virtually all readers consult.

The **$25-a-Day Travel Club** is now in its 22d successful year of operation. It was formed at the urging of numerous readers of the $$$-a-Day and Dollarwise Guides, who felt that such an organization could provide continuing travel information and a sense of community to value-minded travelers in all parts of the world. And so it does!

In keeping with the budget concept, the annual membership fee is low and is immediately exceeded by the value of your benefits. Upon receipt of $15 (U.S. residents), or $18 (Canadian, Mexican, and other foreign residents) in U.S. currency to cover one year's membership, we will send all new members the following items:

1) Any Two of the Following Books

Please designate in your letter which two you wish to receive:

Europe on $25 a Day
Australia on $25 a Day
England and Scotland on $25 a Day
Greece on $25 a Day (including Istanbul and Turkey's Aegean Coast)
Hawaii on $35 a Day
Ireland on $25 a Day
India on $15 & $25 a Day
Israel on $30 & $35 a Day
Mexico on $25 a Day

New York on $35 a Day
New Zealand on $20 & $25 a Day
Scandinavia on $35 a Day
South America on $25 a Day
Spain and Morocco (plus the Canary Is.) on $25 a Day
Washington, D.C. on $35 a Day

Dollarwise Guide to Austria & Hungary
Dollarwise Guide to Canada
Dollarwise Guide to the Caribbean (including Bermuda and The Bahamas)
Dollarwise Guide to Egypt
Dollarwise Guide to England & Scotland
Dollarwise Guide to Florida
Dollarwise Guide to France
Dollarwise Guide to Germany
Dollarwise Guide to Italy
Dollarwise Guide to Portugal (plus Madeira and the Azores)
Dollarwise Guide to Switzerland and Liechtenstein
Dollarwise Guide to California and Las Vegas
Dollarwise Guide to Cruises from the United States
Dollarwise Guide to New England
Dollarwise Guide to the Northwest
Dollarwise Guide to the Southeast and New Orleans
Dollarwise Guide to the Southwest
(Dollarwise Guides discuss accommodations and facilities in all price ranges, with emphasis on the medium-priced).

Dollarwise Guide to Cruises
(This complete guide covers all the basics of cruising—ports of call, costs, fly-cruise package bargains, cabin selection booking, embarkation and debarkation and describes in detail over 60 or so ships cruising in Alaska, the Caribbean, Mexico, Hawaii, Panama, Canada, and the United States.)

How to Beat the High Cost of Travel
(This useful guide will help you save money and enjoy a more creative travel experience. It's filled with tips on everything from packing, when to see the sights, and how to avoid taxes, to special advice for students and senior citizens budget travel.)

The New York Urban Athlete
(The ultimate guide to all the sports facilities in New York City for jocks and novices).

Museums in New York
(A complete guide to all the museums, historic houses, gardens, zoos, and more in the five boroughs. Illustrated with over 200 photographs).

Fast 'n' Easy Phrase Book
(The four most useful languages—French, German, Spanish, and Italian—all in one convenient, easy-to-use phrase guide.)

Where to Stay USA
(By the Council on International Educational Exchange, this extraordinary

PORTUGAL

VALENÇA
MONÇÃO
P DA BARCA
VIANA DO CASTELO
BRAGANÇA
CHAVES
BRAGA
GUIMARAES
VILA REAL
PORTO
T. DE MONCORVO
VIZEU
AVEIRO
VILAR FORMOSO
CURIA
BUSSACO
GUARDA
FIGUEIRA DA FOZ
COIMBRA
COVILHÃ
CASTELO BRANCO
LEIRIA
SEGURA
NAZARÉ
BATALHA
S. MARTINHO DO PORTO
TOMAR
FÁTIMA
ALCOBAÇA
C. DA RAINHA
MARVÃO
PORTALEGRE
SANTAREM
T. VERDAS
ELVAS
MAFRA
SINTRA
V. FRANCA DE XIRA
ESTREMOZ
CASCAIS
LISBON
MONTEMOR O NOVO
ESTORIL
CACILHAS
SETUBAL
ÉVORA
ALCACER DO SAL
S. LEONARDO
FERREIRA DO ALENTEJO
S. TIAGO DO CACEM
BEJA
V. VERDE DE FICALHO
ODEMIRA
S. BRAZ DE ALPORTEL
LAGOS
SAGRES
V. REAL DE STO ANTONIO
PRAIA DA ROCHA
FARO

guide is the first to list accommodations in all 50 states that cost anywhere from $3 to $25 per night.)

A Guide for the Disabled Traveler
(A guide to the best destinations for wheelchair travelers and other disabled vacationers in Europe, the United States, and Canada by an experienced wheelchair traveler. Includes detailed information about accommodations, restaurants, sights, transportation, and their accessibility.)

Marilyn Wood's Wonderful Weekends
(This very selective guide covers the best mini-vacation destinations within a 175-mile radius of New York City. It describes special country inns and other accommodations, restaurants, picnic spots, sights, and activities—all the information needed for a two- or three-day stay.)

Bed & Breakfast—North America
(This guide lists over 150 organizations of bed & breakfast homes and referral agencies in the U.S. and Canada, along with the scenic attractions, businesses, and major schools and universities nearby each.)

2) A One-Year Subscription to *The Wonderful World of Budget Travel*

This quarterly eight-page tabloid newspaper keeps you up to date on fast-breaking developments in low-cost travel in all parts of the world bringing you the latest money-saving information—the kind of information you'd have to pay $25 a year to obtain elsewhere. This consumer-conscious publication also features columns of special interest to readers: The Traveler's Directory (members all over the world who are willing to provide hospitality to other members as they pass through their home cities); Share-a-Trip (offers and requests from members for travel companions who can share costs and help avoid the burdensome single supplement); and Readers Ask . . . Readers Reply (travel questions from members to which other members reply with authentic firsthand information).

3) A Copy of *Arthur Frommer's Guide to New York*

This is a pocket-size guide to hotels, restaurants, nightspots, and sightseeing attractions in all price ranges throughout the New York area.

4) Your Personal Membership Card

This entitles you to purchase through the Club all Arthur Frommer publications for a third to a half off their regular retail prices during the term of your membership.

So why not join this hardy band of international budgeteers and participate in its exchange of travel information and hospitality? Simply send your name and address, together with your membership fee of U.S. $15 (U.S. residents) or U.S. $18 (Canadian, Mexican, and other foreign residents), in U.S. currency to: $25-A-Day Travel Club, Inc., Frommer/ Pasmantier Publishers, 1230 Avenue of the Americas, New York, NY 10020. And please remember to specify which *two* of the books in section (1) above you wish to receive in your initial package of members' benefits. Or, if you prefer, use the last page of this book, simply checking off the two books you select and enclosing $15 or $18 in U.S. currency.

Chapter XXVII

A TALE OF MANY CITIES

Low-Cost Living in
One Hundred Towns

EVENTUALLY, *Europe on $25 a Day* hopes to give the full budget treatment to at least forty major European cities—a chapter on each. But that takes time—and a lot of shoe leather.

In the interval, our notebooks are continually growing with observations on cities only briefly viewed. And, in addition, each day's mail brings tips from readers on hotels and restaurants they've liked in dozens of other European cities.

These finds are too good to waste. As an interim step towards an encyclopedic *Europe on $25 a Day*, this chapter of lists and quick observations has been temporarily inserted into this book. Where a statement is in quotation marks, followed by a name, it represents only the opinion of the reader who mailed it in. I stand by every other statement made. The information is set forth alphabetically by country and then by city, as follows:

AUSTRIA

Bregenz
"**Frau Anni Findler** at Kaiserstrasse 31 (phone 23-85-03), opposite the Central Hotel, and only three minutes from the train station, rents spotlessly clean double rooms for 230 schillings per night, and, if requested, will serve a continental breakfast for 25 schillings. She is a charming person who speaks English and does everything to make her guests comfortable. Fresh flowers in our room the two weeks we stayed with her made us feel very welcome. Anyone who has stayed with Frau Findler wants to return" (Frances H. Sterns, Willimantic, Connecticut).

Klagenfurt
"**Pension Wachau**, 19 Wilfriedgasse, phone 04222-21717, is highly recommendable. Rooms with hot and cold water, washbasins, central heating, free bathing. Cheap, very good food in the pension. We paid $58 for *two* rooms for the night. Lots of parking" (Dr. and Mrs. J.A.A. Engelbrecht and sons, Port Elizabeth, South Africa); note by AF: Klagenfurt is capital of the Austrian province of Carinthia (Kärnten), and is located about half-way between Venice and Vienna).

A NOTE ABOUT READERS' SELECTIONS: Sharp-eyed readers of earlier editions of this book may notice that some readers' selections, appearing in the "Tale of Many Cities" chapter of those earlier editions, are repeated in this edition—but often with minor changes in the prices or other details appearing in them. Because some readers' selections seem too good to be dropped from a new edition, we mail a questionnaire—in November of every year—to every particularly intriguing hotel or restaurant listed in this chapter, requesting that those establishments confirm in writing the prices they intend to charge, and the policies they plan to follow, for the *next year*—in this case, 1985. If they fail to answer, we drop the reader's selection. If they do answer, and their answers show them to be a budget establishment, we re-write the reader's selection to make it accurate and up-to-date for the coming year (or maintain it unchanged if the response shows it should not be changed). Thus, a reader who has earlier written in that he "spent $14 for a double room" at a particular hotel, may find his reader's selection stating, this year, that he "spent $16 for a double room" at that hotel. He may even find a phone number added to the address of his find, or some other bit of technical information that we have gleaned from the hotel's response to our questionnaire.

We hope our readers will forgive this slight tampering with their letters, because its purpose is to ensure that every detail, every price, every item of information in this book shall be absolutely accurate and up-to-date for the year in which the book is published. The furnishing of responsible, useful information is the primary aim of this book, requiring a massive amount of research and inspection each year, and warranting—we hope you'll agree—these minor liberties with your letters (which, by the way, we treasure and read with the greatest care and attention).

Velden am Wörthersee

"We highly recommend a stay in Velden am Wörthersee, a charming little Austrian resort, set amongst gardens, parks, mountains and a lake. After seeing Rome, Florence and Venice and on our way to Vienna (by Eurailpass), we took the advice of a friend and left the train at Velden station (most express trains stop here, coming and going from and to Italy, Munich, Zurich and Vienna), then booked ourselves for 3 days into **Pension Haus Brigitte,** 5 Koschatpromenade, phone 04274-2088, for a daily bed-and-breakfast rate of 270 schillings ($14.60). We were here in July; in June and September the rates go down to 200 and 230 schillings ($10.81 and $12.43). Our room was clean and nicely furnished, with shower and private w.c. After Vatican City, the Uffizi and Doges' Palace, Velden was an ideal place to relax from museums and enjoy nature. Haus Brigitte is managed by a charming and helpful, English-speaking couple, Brigitte and Lienhart Gfrerrer—he drove the Duke and Duchess of Windsor around Velden, when they were vacationing in Velden in 1956—and will expertly advise you what walks, excursions, boat rides and other worthwhile visits to make, including to the houses where Alban Berg composed 'Lulu,' and Gustav Mahler some of his symphonies, or to Roman excavation sites. For us, Velden was a vacation within a vacation" (Bob and Sally Ross, Bloomington, Indiana).

BELGIUM

Antwerp

"At the **'Old Tom Hotel',** in the heart of the city, only half a block from the central station, we had a room which slept four people and for breakfast each morning we were served two eggs, two slices of bacon, coffee, bread and butter, all for the price of about $38 for all four of us" (Oscar E. Plummer, Maroa, Illinois; note from AF: Old Tom Hotel is at 53 de Keyzerlei Street (phone 233-07-17). Its 1985 rates are Bf800 ($14.59) single, Bf 1,200 ($21.81) twin without bath). . . . "For a real treat, go to the center of town, at 6 Carnotstraat, where, on the first floor, the **Sarma Restaurant,** serves steak with mushroom sauce for 200 Bfr ($3.63), tomato salad for 45 (81¢). The quality and taste are outstanding. Beer is the big drink in Antwerp, and whoever comes here must try the mussels casseroles, eel in herb sauce, and just about any kind of seafood you can name. Sarma is near the Central Station" (H.P. Koenig, New York, New York). . . . "Antwerp happens to be one of the real undiscovered finds on the international travel beat. Great food, friendly people, just about everyone speaks English. A whole string of restaurants along Suikerrui, running right to the river, only a block from Fabiola, feature such specials as all the mussels and French fried potatoes you can eat for about $6. And you can get a steak platter for $5" (Ellen Kaye, New York, N.Y.). . . . "This city's **Royal Museum of Art** deserves prominent mention somewhere in your book as possessing one of the best collections of Flemish art in Europe, from the 14th to the 20th centuries. Entrance free; closed Mondays" (Michael R. Stein, Wauwatosa, Wisconsin).

Bruges

"We stayed at the very picturesque **Hotel Rembrandt-Rubens,** 38 Walplaats (phone 336439), for 1000 Bfr ($18.18), including breakfast and service for two. Right on the recommended tourist route" (Evelyn Lakott, Cambridge, Massachusetts). . . . **"Hotel Cosmopolite,** 18 Kuipersstraat (phone 33-20-96), was full of gracious hospitality and friendliness. The rooms are clean and large, and the dining room attractive. Rates are 650 Belgian francs single, 1600 francs quad, 950 francs double, including breakfast" (R. Dahlquist, Michigan City, Indiana). . . . "The **Huyse Elckerlyc,** Hauwerstraat 23 (phone 050/336226), offered the best accommodations and finest breakfast I had in three months in Europe. Open to tourists in July and August only, these modern rooms go for 450 Belgian francs ($8.18) single and 800 francs ($14.54) double. An all-you-can-eat breakfast is included (bread, jam, cheese and a special gingery cake-like bread). And it's only ten minutes from the train station" (Randy Mink, Elgin, Illinois). . . . "In Bruges (which, by the way, is the city in Belgium most worthy of visiting), we happened upon the **Hotel St. Christophe** (Nieuwe Gentweg 76, phone 331176), which is a bit pricy (1200 francs ($21.81) for two, including breakfast) but *great!* It has a garden out back where you can have breakfast. In addition to the nice hotel, there are rooms out back, beyond the gardens, which are . . . well, just fun to stay in. The service is good, as was the breakfast. We highly recommend both the Hotel St. Christophe and the city of Bruges!" (Richard and Eleanor Leary, Springfield, Illinois). . . . "Bruges is indeed a lovely city, well worth the visit. I discovered the **Hotel Suffolk Punch,** t'Zand 24, phone 33-51-73. The proprietor, Frans Vercammen, and especially his wife, are friendly, very hospitable and ready to please. Double rooms for 1000 francs with breakfast, singles 600" (Mrs. Ellen Landa, Tucson, Arizona).

Ghent

"For those of student age, the best bargain in Europe is **Home A. Vermeylen,** Stalhofstraat 6 (phone 22-09-11), which gives you a private room with sink, bedside light controls, your choice of four radio stations on the intercom, all in a very modern and clean building, and all (including continental breakfast) for under $10. Lunch, if you want it, is an extra 150 francs, dinner 150 francs. In addition there's a library, modern *hot* showers, and a bar and lounge where you can meet the other student inhabitants. The Vermeylen home is open only from July 15 to the end of September" (Pauline Hadley, New York City). . . . "Please encourage your readers not to pass through Belgium without stopping to see Van Eyck's painting, 'The

Mystic Lamb,' in Saint Bavon's church in Ghent. (You can take one of the railroad's 'Beau Jour' excursions from Brussels to Bruges, with a stop at Ghent to see the painting.) The admission is 30 francs to see this magnificent work in its authentic setting. One of the panels has been stolen, but a copy has replaced it, so you will get the full effect. If you ask him, the guard will shut the painting so that the outside of the altar panels can also be studied" (Luella Boddewyn, New York, New York).

CZECHOSLOVAKIA

Prague

"Prague is surely one of the most beautiful cities in the world and should be seen by anyone who is in nearby Vienna. One spends not more than $12 a day while staying there with a private family. The **Pragotour Tourist Agency,** Obecniho 2 (phone 231-72-81 or 231-59-9), close to the downtown air terminal building, will make the booking for you. By eating in the simple restaurants one avoids a 10% service charge. Transport on buses and trams and in the very clean and modern subway is 10 cents. But U.S. newspapers are available only at the American Embassy, and a visa is needed" (Lewis G. Phillips, Rootstown, Ohio). . . . "We were awed by some of the sightseeing in Prague. Specifically, the Hradcin with the Cathedral of St. Vitus and the Treasury, then St. Nicholas Church, Charles Bridge and the Old Town . . . Visas must be obtained at a Czech consulate before going to Prague. It takes about 2 hours to get one, and you will need photographs. If driving in Czechoslovakia, be sure to buckle up your seat, and slow down near construction sites, as the police enforce these two laws very well" (Elaine Berger, Oakland, California).

ENGLAND

Bath

"We ate at the **Edwardian** Hotel, at 38 Westgate Street, very close to the Roman Baths (for economy eat downstairs). Informal atmosphere, but a wide selection of excellent food at reasonable prices. I had beef bourguignonne with wine sauce and mushrooms, a large portion of broccoli, carrots and baked potatoes, all well seasoned, and half a pint of beer, for about £6.50 ($9.10), VAT and service included" (Stephen Lepore, Venice, California). . . . "The **Huntsman,** 1 Terrace Walk, North Parade, serves delicious food from one kitchen to a tearoom, pub and dining room. You choose the location according to style and price. We ate several meals there and it is the one place I would go back to after eight ʌ ⁊ks of 'eating out'" (Mrs. Kenneth V. Crow, Tracyton, Washington).

Brighton

"We've lived in Brighton for 5 months and find it a most delightful town, worthy of space in your book. It's only an hour from London by train, but it's off the beaten path for American tourists, and offers many insights into British social customs, since it was one of the very first seaside resorts. We can recommend **Le Flemings Hotel,** 15 Regency Square, phone Brighton 27-539, £13.50 per person including full English breakfast and color TV in your room, a block from the seafront, and close to the central entertainment area. Brighton is also a treat for architecture hounds —the Regency squares and crescents are famous throughout England, and the Royal Pavilion is something out of the 'Arabian Nights' by the Nash Brothers—a pseudo-Indian exterior and a romantic Chinese interior" (Diane Stanfield, Brighton, England). . . . **"Stanway House,** 19 Broad Street (phone 0304-602-439), owned by Mr. and Mrs. Miszuro, was immaculately clean and attractive, and the Smiths are eager to please. It is within sight of the palace pier and beach. A delicious full

English breakfast is served in an attractive, cheery dining room, and 1985 bed-and-breakfast rates will be only 8 pounds per person" (Dorothy Long, El Toro, California).

Cambridge

"The absolutely spotless **Ellensleigh Guest House** of Jo and Denis Marchant, 37 Tenison Road (phone 64888), is located near the train station, about a fifteen minute walk from the center of town. They are delightful proprietors and charge only £8 ($11.20) per person, including a fantastic, huge breakfast" (Fred Baskind, New York, New York). . . . "Punting on the Cam is a must, and it's even more pleasurable with a handsome college man doing the punting. On Silver Street, at the river, is **Chauffeur-Punt,** where for just 2 pounds one can sit back as straw-hatted punters do the hard work. As they expertly pole their way, dodging the helpless novices, they are happy to elaborate on the historic bridges and colleges, while you lie back in the pillows" (Annie Gebeaux, New York City).

Canterbury

"Excellent accommodations are available at the **Pilgrims Guest House,** 18 The Friars (phone 64531), around the corner from the Cathedral and the river Stour; this guest house offers very light, spotlessly-clean rooms with hot and cold water, efficient heat, electric outlets specially designed for shavers on 220 volt current, and rates in 1985 of only 8.50 pounds per person twin, 9.50 pounds single, 8 pounds triple, breakfast included" (Howard Kissel, Milwaukee, Wisconsin, as well as Robert B. Lawrence, Schenectady, New York). . . . "At **York House,** 22 Old Dover Road (phone 65-743), the charge is £7.50 per person, and Mrs. Bone's breakfast of mushrooms and bacon cannot be beaten. A house full of works of art, and clean in every way" (Lester B. Bridaham, Denver, Colorado; note from AF: Mrs. Bone also serves a free pot of tea on the arrival of new guests). . . . "We want to enthusiastically endorse a bed-and-breakfast house which we happened upon in Canterbury: **Mrs. K. Sylvester,** St. Jude, 11 Nunnery Road, phone 68-665. It's run by an extremely warm, gregarious English couple who recently returned after several years of living in South Africa. Mrs. Sylvester drove to the train station, from where we had called, to pick us up. When we arrived, she, her husband and their 12-year-old son served us tea in their living room. We paid $20 for a double, with a large and very well prepared breakfast" (Harold and Judy Ziesat, Rochester, New York; note by AF: 1985 rates are £9, $12.60, per person with English breakfast naturally).

Chester

"A city that should be included in your "Tale of Many Cities" is Chester, an historic site with the complete circuit of medieval walls still preserved. (Behind the medieval fronts of the old buildings are modern shopping centers and convenient parking garages.) One of the nicest places to stay here is with Mrs. N. Cowie, who calls her place **Elgin;** it's located at 2 Princes Avenue off Queens Road (which is off City Road, just a block from the R.R. station). Mrs. Cowie will charge from £6.50 in 1985, no service charge or value added tax. This will include a very satisfactory English breakfast and space to park your car. The city center and main attractions are easily reached by walking and Mrs. Cowie will do all she can to make you feel at home. Telephone number is 23372. Chester is a good touring center for Cheshire, the moors of Derbyshire, and Wales" (James and Yvonne Bunting, Woonsocket, Rhode Island). . . . "Chester is one of the most delightful towns anywhere in the world and you should hasten to add the **Hamilton Guest House,** whose 1985 charge is £9 per person. Located at 5–7 Hamilton Street in the Hoole area of town, it is neat and outstandingly warm. The hosts make you feel comfortable and 'at home'" (The Stratings, Colorado Springs, Colorado).

Dover

"As many people come from the continent to Dover in the late afternoon and wish to remain there overnight, we think that the address of **Linden Guest House**—Bed and Breakfast, Mr. and Mrs. D. Bowles, 231 Folkestone Road, Dover, Kent, tel: Dover 205-449, would be helpful. Mr. and Mrs. Bowles are charming and kind. Their home is spotlessly clean, with running hot water and heat in each room. Excellent breakfast. No trouble parking car. Bus stops at the corner. Price £8 per person. One should not pass through Dover without visiting the great Norman castle" (Mr. and Mrs. Wm. T. Halstead, Los Gatos, California). . . . "At a bed-and-breakfast house called **'The Dell,'** at 233 Folkestone Road, phone 0304/20-24-22, the tariff was £8 a night, with a real English breakfast of bacon and eggs, etc. Mr. and Mrs. Robbins, the owners, are delightful people" (Anne Baker, Western Australia).

Folkestone

"We have a guesthouse on the South Coast and last week we had no fewer than 7 persons from Canada and the U.S. stay with us. We do bed and breakfast, for which they can have cereal, fruit juice, one egg, two rashers (slices of bacon) and three sausages, tea or coffee, toast and marmalade. A bath or shower can be taken at no extra cost. Early morning tea is an extra 12p. The guests we had suggested we write, as our terms for 1985 are only £7 per head. Thank you, yours faithfully" (Mr. and Mrs. A. North, 3 East Cliff Gardens, phone 0303/53313, Folkestone, Kent).

Lake District

"**Anworth House,** just off the main thoroughfare in Keswick, Cumbria, heart of the Lake District, is operated by Jean and Norman Gallagher, and charges only £9 per person, in 1985, for bed-and-breakfast. Their address: 27 Eskin Street, Keswick, phone Keswick 0596-74009. Mr. Gallagher is a Cumbrian climbing enthusiast and most helpful in directing guests to interesting walks in the area. This is certainly good value, in a picturesque setting" (Gerry Kath, Minneapolis, Minnesota). . . . "My **Rockside Guest House,** Ambleside Road, Windermere, Cumbria, phone Windermere 09662-5343, is 200 yards from the railroad station, 50 yards from the main bus stop. We offer single, twin, double and family rooms, with a total of 20 beds. Three of our rooms are on the ground floor, ideal for elderly visitors. The tariff is £10 per person, with breakfast. Bath and showers are free. We are open all year" (Mavis Fowles, Proprietor).

Leeds

"My wife and I stayed at the **Cardigan Guest House,** 36 Cardigan Road, Headingley, Leeds, at £9 per night per person for bed and breakfast. TV lounge, tea and biscuits served in the evening. A friendly proprietress, Mrs. Jackson. Highly recommendable" (G. G. Boyce, Thornton, Cape Town, South Africa; note from AF: the phone number is 0532 784301).

Liverpool

"I note that the city of Liverpool is not mentioned. Liverpool is visited by many thousands of overseas tourists each year, including large numbers from the United States. The city's reasonably priced accommodations allow visitors the opportunity to enjoy the area's many attractions, including a wide range of shops, two Cathedrals and other fine buildings, and a variety of excellent facilities in leisure and the arts. Liverpool is also an ideal base for wider travel to places such as Chester, North

Wales, or the Lancashire Coast" (Peter Heaton, Publicity and Information Officer, City of Liverpool; note from AF: Readers visiting Liverpool in 1985 are kindly requested to mail in comments on hotels, restaurants, noteworthy personal experiences).

Oxford

"**Westgate Hotel,** 1 Botley Road (phone 72-67-21, is a small private hotel, containing about 30 beds in single, double and twin rooms, situated approximately 8 minutes from the railroad station by foot. We were very lucky to find rooms in this model clean house. Madame proprietor was very accommodating. The price for a double room, bed and breakfast, is £20 ($28)" (Dr. Z. and M. Pelikan, Brno, Czechoslovakia). . . . "On St. John Street, I rang the bell at #58 (phone 55454), and stayed at the guest home of **Mrs. R. M. Old.** For £8 ($11.20), I had one of the largest rooms and breakfasts of my journey. The cozy on my morning teapot will illustrate the type of comfort strived for" (Carma Bamber, San Francisco, California). . . . "We recently returned from visiting my home town of Oxford, where we stayed at **Becket House,** 5 Becket Street, phone 72-46-75, two minutes from the railroad station and ten from the city center. Proprietors are very friendly, always ready to oblige; rooms are clean and comfortable; and price a reasonable £16 a night for two, bed and breakfast" (Mrs. Pamela Bailberg, Holyoke, Massachusetts). . . . "Don't miss dinner at a pub called **Dudley's Lamb and Flag,** about eleven miles out of Oxford on the road to Kingston Bagpuize (but check these directions with an Oxonian!). It's worth the trip, even if you are only spending one night in Oxford. The place is beloved by the natives of the area. They say there is no pub in England quite like it, and I can believe it. The proprietor is straight out of Dickens. When I asked him if he had grouse, he replied, 'If I did serve it, I'd have to charge 30 bob a plate, and that's a little above my station in life, sir—though I'm sure it's not above yours.' We settled for an excellent roast duck, and the bill—which the *diner himself* computes at Dudley's—came to an admittedly steepish £10.50 ($14.70) for the two of us. But this included an after-dinner nectar called 'Monk's Coffee,' which is made with B&B. It was easily worth twice the price" (James Hefferman, Charlottesville, Va.). . . . "Don't miss a walk through Christ Church (College) Meadow to River to watch student crews work out and see their unique boating clubhouses. Herds of cattle—cows, sheep—throughout the meadows. Trees, flowers—all very beautiful against a backdrop of college buildings and spires in the background" (Rex Coffin, New York, N.Y.). . . . "Don't miss a performance at the **Oxford Playhouse,** also known as the University Theatre, where I saw an excellent production of Shakespeare's 'The Winter's Tale' for £5.50 ($7.70). And it's such fun to sit amongst the students, of all races, and listen to their animated conversations" (Carma Bamber, San Francisco, California).

Plymouth

"We found Plymouth a convenient place from which to make trips into other parts of Devon and into Cornwall. We stayed in the clean and delightful **Staffordshire Guest House,** 34 Pier Street, West Hoe, phone 66-79-17, whose owners, Reg and Sylvia Bawden, are very nice people. They made us feel very much at home. Price, including a full English breakfast, with a little added touch each day by Sylvia, was 7 pounds each" (Julie and Jane and Homer Cline, Clearwater, Florida).

Salisbury

"We highly recommend the **Warren Guest House,** owned by Mrs. Baxter, 15 High Street, Downton, Salisbury, Wiltshire, phone 0725-20-263. She was a charming hostess and eager to please. When I commented idly on the beautiful church behind her house, she immediately rang up the vicar and arranged a personalized tour for us, which included clambering up to the bell tower itself. We paid £10.50 per person in a double *with* private bath, and with breakfast" (Connie Woulf, no address). . . . "We have never stayed with people kinder or more helpful than Mr. and Mrs.

Marks, owners of the **Hayburn Wyke Guest House,** 72 Castle Road, Salisbury, phone 24-141, charging £9 per person per night, breakfast included, in 1985. The stay was exceptional for several reasons: 1. The Marks told us about a seafood restaurant, the Wheat Sherf, a very special inn, with incredibly low prices: 2. The Marks' home was so clean it sparkled. The mattress on our bed was the best I slept on all summer. The food was very good. 3. Mr. Marks gave us tips on routes and advice on driving in England. Finally: When we left, our car did not start. Mr. Marks took over, called Avis, the local mechanic (who fixed it), and while the men dealt with the car, Mrs. Marks invited me to tea" (Betsy and James Vardaman, McGregor, Texas; note by AF: Mr. Marks also operates private car service to and from the railway station, airports, ferry terminals and to places of historical interest).

Southampton

"For anyone using Southampton as a port-point, we feel that **Beacon Guest House,** 49 Archers Road (phone 25910), is the find of the year. Only ten minutes by taxi from the docks, in a semi-suburban area, this comfortable, clean home is entirely focused on its guests' convenience by the Scottish and Irish ladies who run it. Not a sideline with them, these two people devote their energies to any needs of the traveler. For £9, they supply room with hot and cold water, breakfast (copious), evening tea. Dinner was also superbly cooked and cost only £4.75" (Mrs. Theodora Wilbur, Haverford, Pennsylvania). . . . "While in Southampton, we took quite a few little trips to surrounding areas which were very interesting. We spent one day at Bournemouth—a lively resort which was only an 84-mile round trip by bus. One day we took the bus to a town called Beaulieu to see Lord Montague's castle and his vintage car display. Another day we took the ferry to the Isle of Wight (one hour each way) and the local bus tour on this isle lasted from 1 p.m. to 6 p.m.—very enjoyable. We were quite surprised to find so many interesting places nearby, as we'd been told there was nothing to do there" (Mr. and Mrs. Orbin H. Giles, Cathedral City, California).

Stratford-on-Avon

"Alcester Road, about a mile from the center of Stratford, is lined with bed-and-breakfast guesthouses, each charging about £7.50 per person" (Ellen Liman, New York City). . . . "Shipston Road (coming from Oxford) is [also] lined with bed-and-breakfast places, most of which have hot and cold water in the rooms. We stayed at **Craig House** (Sheila and Bill Giles, proprietors), #69 Shipston Road (phone 29-74-73). Very clean, and costing £7.50 per person" (Mr. and Mrs. Stephen Zeluck, Bayside, New York). . . . "Stratford-on-Avon is on everyone's itinerary, and therefore often overcrowded and impersonal. But there we found the friendliest welcome of our whole trip (and also the cheapest bed-and-breakfast) at the charming home of **Ray and Nancy Strong** at 217 Evesham Road, phone 0789/29-78-74. The Strongs have just three rooms, each modern and well furnished, and they offer them with a generous breakfast for just £7.50 per person. That may be the cheapest room rate in Stratford, but the charm and friendliness of the Strong's home would make it a bargain at twice the price. They seem especially to like students and foreign tourists, and Mrs. Strong is the sort of person who says a sincere goodbye at the door and then stands waving at the window. It took away all the commercialism which we had been told to excuse in that tourist-filled town" (Mr. and Mrs. Loren L. Wyss, Portland, Oregon). . . . **"Meg and Bob Morton,** Grove Farm, Ettington, Stratford-on-Avon, phone 0789/74-02-28, charged us £7.50 pounds per person in 1984. This is a lovely farm at the roundabout junction of A422 and A429, just 5 miles from town. It's a large, 200-year-old home surrounded by farm and forest land. In the morning, we heard a cuckoo bird outside our window. The best part, however, are the Mortons. They are gracious and interesting people and made our evening with them one of the most memorable of our trip" (Jan and Tim Howard, Marathon, Florida). . . . **"Salamander Guesthouse,** 40 Grove Road, phone 0789-20-57-28, proprietress Mrs. J.

Copestick, in a very nice row home, three-story, just 2 blocks from the center, charges £9 ($12.60) for accommodations. We recommend it" (Patricia C. Moretti, Norristown, Pennsylvania). . . . "Be sure to check and see if the Royal Shakespeare Company's Stratford Theatre is continuing its policy of holding rear seats and standing room locations open until the day of the performance. They were doing this during my stay, and the result was that I got tickets on the day of the performance to plays which had been sold out for weeks. These seats cost £2 ($2.80) to stand, and they were excellent values. . . . The theatre-goer trying to pass the day waiting for the evening performance would be well advised to take the Midland Red Bus to Coventry for the day to see the glorious new cathedral that has risen out of the ashes of the ancient one which was destroyed during the war. The new cathedral is an architectural masterpiece; and the ruins of the old are still standing. Its cross is made of the shattered beams of the original building, and it will bring tears to the eyes of all but the most iron-hearted. Inscribed in the remnants of what was once the support for beautiful stained glass windows is the prayer, 'Father Forgive,' roughly carved out with the bayonet of a captured German prisoner" (Burt Wolfson, New York, New York).

Winchester

"A fine bed-and-breakfast home in Winchester, which was once the capital of England, is **Mrs. Petty's** home at 9A Magdalen Hill, (phone 63-802), two minutes from Chesil Street. Price for room and breakfast at Mrs. Petty's is £8.50—and that's in 1985" (Caroline Strachan, Monterey Park, California).

York

"Maureen and Albert Bond are proprietors of **Green View**, 5 Clifton Green, telephone York 21-964, which has accommodations for nine guests, and one could not wish for better or more comfortable rooms at the current rate of £8.50 per person per night, which includes a most generous full English breakfast" (Con and Jack Richards, Victoria, Australia). . . . "I have a family guest house in York and throughout the last year have had countless Americans stay with me. I rent single, double and family rooms, at these rates per person per day, inclusive breakfast: one day £9. Evening dinner, served on request, is £6.50. The name is **Annjoa House,** 34 Millfield Road (phone 53-731). We are 10 minutes' walk from the railway station and 5 minutes from the city center. There is hot and cold water in all rooms, and the guest's lounge has a color TV" (Mrs. Sylvia Graham, Proprietress). . . . "We stayed at the **Montclare Guest House,** 32 Claremont Terrace, Gillygate, York. The proprietress is a fantastically friendly person, she opened her home to us and made our stay so enjoyable we couldn't thank her enough. She even served us fresh strawberries and cream with tea one afternoon. You can't always expect that nicety, but at the Montclare you can count on clean rooms, friendly hospitality, good varied cooking—something other than that old English staple of fried eggs for breakfast—and very reasonable rates: 8 pounds per person, bed and breakfast" (Tricia A. Reeson, Tempe, Arizona; note from AF: phone number is 0904 27054).

FINLAND

Helsinki

"We moved to a 'summer hotel' (open only May 20 to September 10) which we recommend very highly. It is the **Satakuntatalo,** Lapinrinne 1 (phone 90-694-0311), where lovely double rooms are 150 to 190 Finnish marks, 55 more for an extra bed, breakfast and service included, private lavatory adjoining. Showers were down the hall and a sauna was available for about $1! This summer hotel was run by very gracious and helpful students" (Haskell and Margaret Rothstein, East Detroit, Michigan). . . . "In Finland, no one should miss a sauna bath. I had one every day, and I never felt so clean in my life! The energetic old lady scrubs you, rubs you, pummels you, beats you, boils you, rinses you and splashes you. It's like going through an automatic washer but more pleasant. In the luxury hotel **Vaakuna,** next to the station (which I don't think is so magnificent!), you may use the sauna, and receive a diploma for going through the ordeal! . . . A good way to see Finland, I think, is by ship from Stockholm. It's an overnight trip and the Smörgasbord on board is fabulous. My round-trip ticket cost $50, and I sailed from Stockholm to Helsinki; went by train to Turku; and sailed back to Stockholm. If I'd had time, I'd have gone up into the Finnish lake district. Perhaps next year" (J. R. Reid, New York). . . . "I settled for the **Youth Hostel** in the Olympic Stadium. It was clean and pleasant and has various prices ranging from singles for $10 to dorm beds at $5. To find the Hostel, take tram 3 (from the Silja Line or the Central Post Office); there is a stop immediately after it turns out of the Mannerheimintie, but for the Hostel you get off at the next one. The **Rose Room Discotheque,** in a passage at the side of the Seurahuone Hotel, opposite the station, also served self-service lunch from 11 a.m. to 2 p.m., Monday to Saturday, for about $4. You can load your tray as high as you like with meat, potatoes and a salad, but you may go to the table only once. The price includes a glass of milk (which Finns drink the way Germans drink beer) and a cup of coffee. Self-service here means you clear your own table, too. Major sights are the Cathedrals, the National Museum, Mannerheim's home, the Rock Church, Parliament House, the Suomenlinna islands, Finlandia Hall, the Imperial-style district around Senate Square. There are 3 things a tourist should have in Helsinki: the Helsinki Guide and the Helsinki Route Map, obtainable from the Finnish Tourist Bureau, and the Helsinki Transport Card directory, which you got with the card; they are all free. The Cards cost 45 Finnmarks for one day, 60 for 2 and 70 Finnmarks for 3 days, and are just like the Stockholm Cards described in your Stockholm chapter" (G. Agnew, Munich, Germany).

FRANCE

Amiens

"We were directed to the **Hotel Spatial,** near Monument General LeClerq, which turned out to be our best hotel in Europe. Address: 15 Rue Alexandre-Fatton (phone 91-53-23), a block or two from the railroad station. It charges only 100 francs for a bathless double, or 140 francs for a double with bath, taxes and service included. No charge for parking car in rear. Frequented by French travelers. Very comfortable" (Evelyn Lakott, Cambridge, Massachusetts). . . . "To see the cathedral, the most grand, high-flown and triumphant of them all, is to understand how hard men can try (and succeed). Amiens *is* Gothic" (Mrs. Peter Diller, Los Angeles, California).

Arles

"The **Hotel Terminus & Van Gogh,** 5 Place Lamartine (phone 96-12-32), combines modern comfort with a 19th century Van Gogh atmosphere. Run by a gray-haired French couple, the hotel offers double rooms for 100 francs, singles for 75 francs, with service charge (but not breakfast—an extra 15 francs) included. Our room had Van-Gogh-style wooden chairs with reed seats, flaming red curtains and sunflower-yellow shutters. The dining room is 19th century in design and Van Gogh prints decorate the lobby. Other pluses: new plumbing, thin gray carpeting, good heating, even a sewing kit in the closet. The Terminus & Van Gogh is three minutes from the train station" (Randy Mink, Elgin, Illinois). . . . "Arles is a most pleasant place to walk around, especially on Saturday when the huge market takes place. We stayed at **Hotel Gaugin,** 3 Place Voltaire, phone 96-14-35, for 145 francs for bed and breakfast for two. It is an eight minute walk from the station, close to all the scenic things and happenings in town" (Tom and Nance O'Connell, Aldgate, South Australia). . . . "This surprising town, where Van Gogh worked for two years, was also an ancient Roman city, built by Caesar some years BC. Many beautiful Roman buildings and ruins remain, including an Arena (where bullfights sometimes take place), an Amphitheatre and many very interesting museums and mosaics. A week here is not really enough to take in all the many sights, including the biggest market we've ever seen selling everything from magician's kits to antiques to live animals! HOTEL: the **Moderne** (phone 960-821), on the Place du Forum, is friendly, clean, and charges 85 francs for single, 110 for double rooms, without bath. RESTAU-RANT: The **L'Arlaten**, 7 Rue de la Cavalerie, offers gargantuan and delicious three-course meals for 52, 68 and 90 francs ($6.50, $8.50 and $11.25) on its fixed-price menu. It was the biggest and the best-cooked and served meal we've had. SIDETRIPS: Stay in Arles and take a trip to **Nimes** (½-hour away), a city with fantastic Roman monuments including a colosseum almost as big as the one in Rome and perfectly preserved, and some amazing gardens and fountains, with sunken pools and swans. **Les Baux,** a tiny village perched in the mountains, with its fantastic Dead City of the Caves, is half-an-hour from Arles, reachable only by taxi or car, but worth renting either to get to see their unforgettable place" (Mr. and Mrs. Harold Carlton, London, England). . . . "I had a delicious provençal meal at **Le Criquet Restaurant,** 21 Rue Porte de Laure; its prix fix menu (the only menu) offers four filling courses, including bread and wine, for 38 francs, not including service—that's left to the customer's discretion. The cheapest restaurant in town" (Lyle Brown, Victoria, B.C., Canada; note from AF: several favorable letters on the husband-and-wife-operated Le Criquet, which is closed Fridays). . . . "It's easy to assume, incorrectly, that the town and its hotels are located just off the area of the RR station. That is only the edge of the city. Proceeding beyond the station, you can go over the hill to many other fine places for rooms and food. . . . By appropriately juggling buses and trains, we managed to see some of Arles, all of Nimes, the Pont du Gard, and return to Arles, all in one day" (Helene Kansas, Satellite Beach, Florida).

Avignon

"Avignon, an hour from Marseilles, one of the great art cities of France, was the home of the Popes in the 14th century, and is rich in relics and monuments. Exceptional museum there is the **Calvet Musée,** with an extraordinary collection of art, sculpture and besides this, a charming garden with peacocks roaming about where visitors may wander too" (Loretta Spanover, Fresh Meadows, New York; note from AF: see also the **Musée du Petit Palais,** exhibiting over 400 paintings and pieces of sculpture from the Middle Ages; entrance fee is 12 francs). . . . "A superb find was the **Hotel du Parc,** 18 Rue Agricol Perdiguier (phone 82-71-55) about 4 blocks from the station, where we had a spotless, spacious double for 160 francs ($20), breakfast in bed included. The exceedingly helpful proprietress told us of an inexpensive restaurant—La Marmite—around the corner, where for 48 francs ($6) we had the 'menu conseillé,' with choice of hors d'oeuvre, entree and dessert" (Ida Tirone, West Seneca, New York).

Bayeux

"Visiting the impressive and touching Normandy Beaches, a starting point six miles away is Bayeux, France, where you might like to try the **Hotel du Luxembourg,** 25 Rue des Bouchers. It's clean and worthwhile; a bathless double in 1985 will be 150 francs, service included; also eat in their restaurant" (Marilyn and Mitchell Shapiro, New Orleans, Louisiana). . . . "We found the **Hotel du Luxembourg** recommended by one of your readers quite comfortable. We paid 260 francs ($32.50) for a triple room with bath and breakfast. . . . The famed Bayeux Tapestry—an 11th century embroidery recounting Duke William's conquest of Britain in 1066—is as impressive as it is made out to be. Entrance is 10 francs per person, 5 francs for students, with children under 10 admitted free, and we recommend that visitors invest an additional franc in the 'teleguide' or recorded commentary which points out many an interesting detail one might otherwise overlook. Visitors to the Normandy Beaches would do well to stop for an hour at Arromanches (6 miles from Bayeux) to see ruins of the 'Mulberry' floating harbours designed by Winston Churchill for the Allied landings in 1944. The D-Day Museum at Port Winston (Arromanches) has an interesting film of D-Day operations as well as touching mementos" (Mr. and Mrs. P. K. Pal, Calcutta, India).

Bordeaux

"Try the **Hotel des Pyrenees,** 12 Rue Saint Remi (phone 81-66-58), which is a five-minute ride on Bus #1 from the Bordeaux rail station. The hotel is spotless, with large rooms, and run by the most courteous French couple I've met. Their son speaks English and is most helpful. The cost of a bathless double room is about 140 francs ($17.50) in this hotel recommended by a number of Touring Associations, and is well worth the money. I highly recommend this hotel and restaurant" (Harvey G. Lockhart, Brooklyn, New York). . . . "We were in Bordeaux to look at the wines, but on a Sunday we made a pilgrimage to the **Toulouse-Lautrec Museum** at Albi (the painter's birthplace and gallery). With our Eurailpass, we took a train for Toulouse at about 6 a.m., were at Toulouse about 9 a.m., waited about half an hour for a railcar which runs about every 2 hours the 50 miles to Albi. There were many students there, and the collection is interesting not only for the originals of old favorites, but the sketches and work behind those masterpieces. The return trip Toulouse-Bordeaux on the Turbotrain was in itself an exciting experience" (M. Cooper, Mt. Barker W.A., Australia).

Calais

"We found a good place to eat and a hotel at reasonable prices in Calais, which I would like to share with you. First, **Creperie La Cremaillere,** 14 Rue Jean de Vienne. My husband here had a full meal of crêpes: fried egg crêpe, ground meat and ratatouille crêpe and a dessert crêpe, all for 36 francs. I had a delicious shrimp, tomato and crab crêpe for 24 francs. With a cup of coffee and a salad (equally good), we had a delicious, light but filling meal. It's a casual restaurant with very friendly attendants. We stayed in the **Bellevue Hotel.** I regret I do not have the address or phone number. However, you can find it very near a large, main square of Calais. It's small with some rooms facing the water. Our room with private shower and sink, toilet in the hallway, was 140 francs. Breakfast was not included and cost 16 francs per person" (Karen M. Kimbrough; note by AF: Address and phone number of the Bellevue Hotel are 23 Place d'Armes, 34-53-75).

Cannes

"We give a high recommendation to the **Hotel de France,** 85 Rue dAntibes (phone 39-23-34), located two blocks from the public beach, and a really charming splurge-hotel; singles with shower and breakfast are 185 to 260 francs ($23.12 to $32.50), doubles with shower-bath and breakfast 220 to 290 francs ($27.50 to $36.25). The rooms are large, clean, and very inviting, and the management is exceedingly friendly" (Marilyn and Mitchell Shapiro, New Orleans, Louisiana; strong second from Caron Smith, San Francisco, California). . . . "After much searching, we located the **Hotel Pullman,** at 9 Rue Jean Daumas. While the proprietress there speaks no English, she is quite charming and makes sure guests do not forget their keys. Rooms are large and immaculate. Located 2 blocks from a public beach. 160 francs tout compris for a bathless double" (Pauline Hadley Maud, New York, New York). . . . "We found good accommodations at **Hotel du Nord,** 6 Rue Jean Jaures (phone 38-48-79), right opposite the station, and paid 175 francs for four per night sharing a large spacious room.

Cannes was delightful, and also a stopping-off place for a launch cruise to the islands of Ste. Marguerite and Ste. Honorat, a real treat!" (M. Phillips, Tasmania, Australia).

Carcassonne

"We stayed at **Hotel Astoria,** 18 Rue Tourtel, phone 25-31-38, just a short walk from the station (follow the arrows on the left as you cross the canal bridge in front of the station; walking time is about 5 minutes). A double room with shower cost us only 115 francs, a real bargain. No English spoken, but the elderly couple who run the hotel are so nice it is not necessary" (J.A. Bissell, Victoria, Australia). . . . "Carcassonne is the most breathtaking city we have walked into, awe-inspiring in a different sense than Rome's Ancient Forum or Chamonix's Mont Blanc massif. For as you walk through the city from the station, looking for a nice restaurant, you wonder where the mediaeval part is that you've heard so much about. And then, through an alley, with few buildings, you see it, the city upon a hill, ramparts and towers, a fortress. When you get there, having walked across the beautiful Pont Vieux, with its suspended, cast-iron lanterns, you stand on the cobblestone waiting to see Chaucer's miller. The **Hotel Central,** five blocks from the station, on 27 Boulevard Jean-Jaurès, is where we stayed. A sunny, light-colored room with a view on the street and trees, with toilet and bathroom, cost us 120 francs a night for two. The phone number is 25-03-84. All the restaurants in the ancient city were good and cheap. We ate at one called **Cafe du Comte Roger,** for the equivalent of five dollars per person (order the omelette aux fines herbes). Do recommend this stop to your readers. History gushes here" (Peter B. Kaufman, Karen S. Makoff, Ithaca, New York).

Chamonix

"At the **Chalet Ski Station,** Chamonix Mont Blanc 74400, phone (50) 53-20-25, a dormitory-like establishment with separate rooms for men and women, the charge is only 28 francs per bed" (Lori Clark, San Rafael, California). . . . "In expensive Chamonix, we found a pension, the **Hotel Du Grépon** (phone 53-13-03), owned by A. Bossonney, a Chamonix guide, serving a 55-franc meal which outclassed anything we found in some of the more expensive restaurants in the main part of the village. The hotel (which charges 105 francs per person for overnight lodgings) is located on the Impasse du Rhodendrons, and a menu is placed at the intersection of this street and the main street" (Ronald Korman, Los Angeles, California).

Chartres

"After leaving the chateaux of the Loire River, we decided to spend the night in Chartres to visit the city's famous and beautiful cathedral; we stayed at the **Hotel Jehan-de-Beauce,** 19 Avenue Jehan-de-Beauce (phone 21-01-41), very close to the train station. For 210 francs we had a large, clean, warm room with showers and toilet, and with three single beds, breakfast and all taxes and services included; normal doubles with private bath are 185 francs, breakfast and all else included. This was our best find in three months of European travel" (Mrs. Sandra Hunt, Poughkeepsie, New York). . . . "There is a youth hostel here with beds for 50 francs ($6.25) a night, and from its windows you see the Cathedral sitting on the hill. To get there, walk to the Cathedral and behind it down to the river, then look for signs that say **"Auberge de Jeunesse"**. . . . I suggest instead of enduring the high prices of Paris, to commute from Chartres, it's only an hour by train. And there are enchanting, free organ concerts every Sunday evening at 5 p.m." (Danielle Jehanne Rappaport, APO New York). . . . "Be sure not to miss the English language tour of Chartres, which is presented by a volunteer named Malcolm Miller. He has been giving these tours twice a day, at noon and 2:45 p.m., seven days a week, for 28 years. He is the world's number one expert on Chartres and will bring the stained glass windows and sculptures alive for you. Plan to take more than one tour, because each one is different. Best of all, admission to this tour is absolutely free!" (Richard J. Waksman, Tarrytown, New York).

Cherbourg

"I had a single room for 80 francs a night at the **Hotel Tabac Toulorge,** 10 Place Jean Jaurés (phone 53-06-03). This is right across the street from the Cher-bourg Gare—not the Cherbourg Maritime Gare which lets you out by the ship. A few people sometimes like to arrive at a port a day before leaving, so this little hotel (where doubles are only 115 francs) can be very convenient. Just make sure the train stops at Cherbourg Gare, and not Cherbourg Maritime" (Adrian Allen, Miami Beach, Florida; note by AF: this hotel is also called "De la Gare").

Le Havre

"For inexpensive accommodations in Le Havre, I shared a large double room with a fellow passenger at the newly-decorated **Hotel d'Yport,** 27 Cours de la Republique (phone 25-21-08), near the railway station, paying 65 francs ($8.12) each, including breakfast; this was for a double with running water. Doubles with w.c. are 178 francs; singles with w.c. are 145, with running water 91 francs. I discovered that the YMCA at 153 Boulevard Strasbourg (phone 42-47-86) has a few single rooms for men at only 50 francs per night. The Y also issues temporary passes that allow travelers to use their cafeteria, and adequate full-course meals can be had there for 30 francs" (Henry S. Sloan, New York, New York).

Lourdes

"The **Estival Hotel** (5 Rue Alsace Lorraine, phone 94-05-86), a three-minute walk from the Grotto, is a wonderful big splurge selection for a visit to Lourdes. The nice room and three complete meals cost 180 francs per day per person. Demi-pension is 150 francs (Al Silva, Tulare, California). . . . "We stayed at the very inexpensive **Bearn Hotel,** 23 Avenue de la Gare (phone 94-25-40), where the rooms go for 50 to 105 francs, pension from 120 to 160 francs" (Pauline H. Maude, New York, New York). . . . "A suggestion for anyone intending to visit Lourdes: the **Hotel Terminus,** 31 Avenue de la Gare (phone 94-68-00) across from the R/R station where accommodations are 120 francs ($15) each" (Bob Gaughan, Camillus, New York).

Lyon

"**Hotel de Geneve,** 10 Quai Perrache, tel. Lyon 37-11-59, was very clean, has pleasant owners. My room was in fact a double, normally costing 95 francs for two, petit dejeuner 14 fr. It is only five minutes from the station. Turn right, go down steps to Rue Belier, which then turns left to the Quai. Then turn right and hotel is 100 yards away to your right" (Angela Wear, England). . . . **"Pension Le Baudelaire** is but a 5-minute walk from the ultra modern transport complex of the Lyon-Perrache railway station, at 6 rue d'Auvergne, a street that runs parallel to the modern pedestrian shopping mall, rue Victor Hugo. Its proprietors don't speak English but are so kind and patient that communication is no problem. We paid 130 francs ($16.25) for a double room, basin and bidet, including breakfast. From the station, follow the path to the left corner of the park (Place Carnot) as you leave the escalator. Cross the rue de Condé and walk up rue Henri IV, which becomes rue d'Auvergne after a couple of blocks. Pension Le Baudelaire will be on your left. Telephone is 837-85-34" (Melanie Pearce and Kaz Bluhm, Yinnar, Victoria, Australia).

Marseille

"Here is one that no economy traveler can afford to miss. Right across from the St. Charles railway station (as you exit from the left), you will see a whole block of hotels, among them the **Hotel de France** at 1 Bd. Maurice Bourdet (phone 39-18-82). This charming and tiny hotel will give you a double room, without bath but with plenty of hot water and a breakfast of hot chocolate (or coffee) and croissants, all for 120 francs ($15)! The rooms are tiny, but spotlessly clean, and we liked it so well we stayed there on two occasions. There is one man who speaks English, but if you will try out whatever meager French you possess (and mine was really meager!) you will be given a send-off like a family member when you do decide to leave" (Neva and Don Kaiser, Miami, Florida). . . . "As two students traveling on the common limited budget, we were pleased to find the recently established **Hôtel Pilote,** 9 Rue du Théatre Française (phone 48-73-74), in central Marseille, where we had a room for two (costing 125 francs), shower or bath (12 francs), continental breakfast (18 francs). We found the proprietor to be a pleasant young man speaking, besides French, English, German and Spanish. He has created a charming and very up-to-date atmosphere with a certain 'freshness' that other hotels in the same price category definitely lack. One who is aware of the cost to stay at this hotel will be pleasantly surprised upon entering" (Leone Crackorowski, Montclair, New Jersey, and Barbara Neisman, Philadelphia, Pennsylvania; note by AF: owner of the Pilote has offered a 10% reduction to readers of this book).

Reims

"Reims, whose history dates back to the baptism of Clovis in 496 A.D., is famous for its beautiful cathedral, begun in 1211, the coronation site of French kings, as well as for the numerous underground caverns which house storage facilities for the world-renowned products of the surrounding province, Champagne. Reims is also the place where the Germans surrendered to the Allies in 1945. For $22, the three of us (dad, mom, 15-year-old son) stayed in the attractive and clean **Hotel des Arcades,** at 31 Rue de L'Etape (phone 47-42-39). Our room was bathless, but had a sink and bidet. Breakfast was an additional $8 for the 3 of us. Although restaurants were often higher than our $20 a day budget would allow, we had a good dinner at the **Self-Service Talleyrand,** which is part of a department store of the same name, on the corner of Rue de Talleyrand and Rue de Vesle, the main shopping street. Steak and pommes frites were $3.60, sausage and pommes frites $2.50" (Mr. and Mrs. Victor Malzahn, Colfax, California).

Strasbourg

"**Grand Hotel de Paris,** 13 Rue de la Mesange, tel. 321-550, two blocks from the station, was a "grand hotel" once, is now considerably less than grand, but still very adequate. Rooms were clean and comfortable; Strasbourg Cathedral a short walk away and most interesting to visit. For two doubles and one single we paid 450 French francs, which included 17 francs per person for breakfast" (Virginia Gillette, Roxbury, Connecticut). . . . "**Hotel des Princes,** 33 Rue Geiler, tel. 615519, a two-star hotel, is without question the best hotel value we have found in five months to date of European travel; rooms are large, clean and fresh, service excellent, and location in a quiet neighborhood, a 15-minute walk from the Cathedral and center of town. 1985 rates will be: double with shower 190 francs, with bath 207 francs, continental breakfast an additional 18 francs per person, served in the breakfast room or in bed" (Carl and Jean Auer, Hillsborough California). . . . "We encountered a fabulous experience at the restaurant in the **Hotel au Cycliste,** 8 Rue des Bateliers (phone 36-20-01), 50 meters off the Quai des Bateliers. Not much charm, in fact, it looks almost suspicious, old walls, dingy lighting, a few locals scattered around, but the food is perhaps only one or two notches below the finest cuisine for an absolute fraction of the cost. We had a carafe of Alsatian red wine, two salads, one pepper steak in creme sauce, one entrecote provencale (steak in an incredible garlic-tomato sauce), *mounds* of pommes frites (whoops, forgot 6 snails), 1 coffee and the most scrumptious custard rhubarb pie the likes of which only my mother made in my experience. The bill was about $20 to $25. I don't think you can miss this one" (Peter and Lana Knudsvig, Paris).

Tours

"The **Hotel des Capucines,** 6 Rue Blaise-Pascal (phone 05-20-41), is my recommendation for Tours, which I am sure most tourists visit at some time, on their way to chateaus. It is a good place for older people, for there are rooms on the ground floor, without any stairs. A small, new hotel just a 'stone's throw' from the buses that take you to the chateaus, every room has a shower, and yet the charge is only 70 francs for ground floor rooms without bath, 115 francs for rooms with bath on the upper floors—18 rooms in all. Breakfast is 13 francs. Mr. Gaudron, the owner-manager, does not speak English, but he is a helpful, kindly man. On leaving the depot turn left, walk past a dead end street about a block to Blaise-Pascal, turn left to number 6. It is that easy!" (Nellie Hull, Chicago, Illinois; strong seconding recommendation from Elsie Lee, New York, New York). . . . "**Hotel Français,** at 11 Rue de Nantes (phone 05-59-12), across from the train station's left side, was no Ritz, but it was decent, homey and very clean. The 118 francs we paid for a double room included hot water in the room, though no shower. This is still a fantastic deal in expensive and often-booked-up Tours" (Bram Fine, Oak Park, Illinois).

GERMANY

Augsburg

"A visitor to Augsburg ought not miss seeing the still-inhabited 'Fuggerei,' founded in 1519 by the fabulously rich Jakob Fugger, banker and financier to the Habsburgs. What is the 'Fuggerei'? A section of homes for the town's poor people. That's 1519, not 1919" (David and Francie Robertson, Los Angeles, California). . . . "**Hotel Thalia,** 5 Obstmarkt (phone 313-037), was the gem of our trip to Europe. Located in the heart of the old city, only a few steps from the main Maximilian-strasse, it's an older building, completely and very tastefully modernized and decorated in the interior. Five floors, with elevator service to the first four, free showers, good breakfast. A single cost 40 marks" (Henry Elsner, Jr., Philadelphia, Pennsylvania).

Baden-Baden

"We stayed in the **Hotel Geroldsauer Mühle,** on the borderline of the towns of Baden-Baden and Geroldsau (the location is in the Black Forest, on the bank of the Oos River, only a couple of minutes by car or bus from the center of Baden-Baden). Owned by Herr Heinrich Diringer, telephone Baden-Baden 74-08, it was our best find in nearly a month's travelling in Germany and the Benelux countries. We paid 110 marks per night for a triple room with a shower and refrigerator, and included in this price was breakfast for 3, plus a "kurkarte" entitling us to use the Kurhaus facilities, and drink the mineral water of Baden-Baden, during our stay of seven days. A private parking lot and use of garden chairs are further pluses" (N. Kataczynski, Natanya, Israel).

Berchtesgaden

"It was late at night and we were in need of somewhere to stay, when we came across the **Gasthaus zur Hobelbank,** (phone 43-63), managed by Werner Brunner. There we enjoyed a magnificent meal with some of the best onion soup I've ever had, and the house specialty, toast dishes. We also stayed at the Gasthaus and paid 68 marks ($26.15) for two double rooms without breakfast. The rooms and bathroom were so clean it was a delight to use them" (R. F. Cameron, Vaucluse, Australia). . . . "My best European bargain is, admittedly, in a very touristy area: Berchtesgaden, site of Hitler's home, 20 miles from Salzburg, with its nearby salt mines and skiing. **Gästehaus Panorama,** at Königseestrasse 27 (phone 22-04), one block from the train station, is where I've stayed on three occasions. Cross the street from the train station, walk to the traffic light 100 yards away (you can only see this light—no others), turn the corner, go across the bridge, walk one block, it's left up the steps. The cost is only 27 marks ($10.38), including breakfast! Can't believe it isn't yet in your book" (John Holland, APO, New York).

Bingen

"An absolutely delightful pension in Bingen, which is located on the Rhine, just shortly after the steamer leaves Koblenz on the way to Mainz: **Hotel Goldener Kochlöffel** 22 Rheinstrasse, phone 13944. The double we had was quiet and comfortable, with w.c. in it; the bath was across the hall. We paid 39 marks each, inclusive a lovely continental breakfast with boiled egg. The hotel has a history going back to 1450 when it was a cloister for nuns, and the name Goldener Kochlöffel means the 'golden cooking spoon,' which was derived from the tasty food the nuns prepared and fed the poor who came knocking on their doors" (Mr. and Mrs. Robert K. McKnight, Hayward, California).

Bremen

"Grouped around the Marktplatz are most of the worthwhile old buildings in Bremen. The **Cathedral** (currently closed for repairs) is a harmonious mixture of Romanesque and Gothic styles, built in the 11th, 13th, and 16th centuries. A crypt in the Cathedral has the curious property of preserving bodies placed in it; they dry to a black parchment stretched over the bones. For one mark you can see for yourself. The **Rathaus** is well-worth a visit, as you would expect from old whalebones and what-not collected from all over the globe. As the building is still in official use, it can be seen only by guided tour, which takes place Mondays to Fridays at 10 a.m., 11 a.m., and at noon, on Saturdays and Sundays at 11 a.m. and noon. The lore is in German, however. Star exhibit is an eight-foot 1500 lb. model of a warship hung from the ceiling. It used to hang in the Guildhall, on pulleys. When the merchants were good and tanked at one of their feasts, they would lower it to the floor, load its cannons, about 40¼-inch bore cannons, hoist the ship to their ceiling again, and fire away. They shot out most of the windows in the place every time they did it, quite aside from disturbing the neighbors. The **Ratskeller,** in the cellar of the Rathaus, is an excellent restaurant and stocks 600 different German wines. Also on the Marktplatz is the **Guildhall,** the meeting place of the powerful Merchants' Guild, and well worth a visit. Except for the very modern parliament building, the rest of the marktplatz is bounded by fine old patrician houses. The most charming part of Bremen is the **Schnoor Quarter,** not far from the Marktplatz, a medieval district of narrow streets and tiny houses, dating back as far as the 14th century. The city has turned these houses over to artists, rent-free, on condition that they restore and preserve them. Besides living quarters and studios for the artists, the district is filled with interesting little shops: art galleries, antique shops, etc.; everything from hand-painted fabrics to organ grinders. I did not visit the museums, but the city art museum is said to have particularly good and important collections of Dutch paintings and of modern German Realists. The best thing about sight-seeing in Bremen is that practically all the sights are concentrated in the old part of Bremen, within easy walking distance of each other. This is just as well as parking is practically impossible in the center. There is plenty to do at night in Bremen. The theater is considered one of the most progressive in Germany. Tickets, between DM 10 and DM 35, are easy to get, and the best tickets still available on the night of the performance can be had for 5 marks by those who can show student identification."

Cologne

"We were quite satisfied with the **Hotel Heinzelmännchen,** 5-7 Hohe Pforte (phone 21-12-17), which charged 60 marks ($23.07) for a double without bath, breakfast and service included" (William Lydecker, St. Peter, Minnesota). . . . "At least 95 points must go to the spic and span, brightly wall-papered **Hotel Brandenburger Hof.** Only about five minutes from the 'Bahnhof' and near the massively impressive Dom Cathedral, the Brandenburger's rates are 35 to 38 marks single, 50 to 55 marks ($19.23 to $21.15) double, 78 marks ($30) triple, which includes service and breakfast. The people are just lovely too. Address is Brandenburger Strasse 2-4, and the telephone number is 12-28-89" (Carma Bamber, San Francisco, California; note by AF: Frau Alvano, the kind owner of Brandenburger Hof, has promised to guarantee these rates to holders of the book until the end of 1985. To reach the hotel, leave the Central Station at the Breslauer Platz exit—Brandenburger Strasse is the third small street turning left). . . . "Readers should make an effort to travel the short distance from Cologne to the former capital of the Holy Roman Empire, Aachen. The cathedral, part of which dates from before Charlemagne, is the most unusual I have seen, and contains the actual throne of Charlemagne. In addition, the area surrounding the cathedral is a delightful maze of twisting, medieval streets with sidewalk markets, and ancient homes. The trip from Cologne and back can easily be made in a day, or even less" (Ronald A. Audet, Portsmouth, Virginia). . . . "From mid-April to mid-October, the Rhine steamer leaves Cologne at 7 a.m. daily and arrives at Mainz at 9 p.m., 14 hours later and a long ride. The fare is 127 marks ($48.84). From Mainz it leaves at 8:45 a.m. and arrives Cologne at 6 p.m., less than 10 hours. I took the 14-hour ride but to anyone considering this interesting trip to old castles, may I suggest either getting on at Rüdesheim or Koblenz and traveling the distance between those two cities, because it's between those cities that the most spectacular scenery and castles are to be found; and both cities are served by connecting trains taking you either to Cologne or Frankfurt, depending upon which direction you happen to be traveling. The food on the steamer is excellent and not really too expensive and the service is incomparable" (Edward H. Pietraszek, Cicero, Illinois). . . . "The **Opera** in Cologne is housed in a very beautiful, modern building which is itself one of the chief tourist sights of the city. What many tourists do not realize is that the performances there are excellent and the price absurdly low, from 13 to 60 marks. For 15 DM, I had an excellent seat for a beautifully sung performance of Verdi's 'Don Carlos.' The auditorium is so well designed that there are no really bad seats; you can, therefore, buy the cheapest tickets. . . . Perhaps the most beautiful view in Europe is of Cologne with its cathedral and medieval houses bathed in floodlights as seen from across the Rhine. The best way is to walk across the Deutzer Bridge, just behind the cathedral" (Ronald A. Audet, Portsmouth, Virginia).

Frankfurt

"**Pension Lohmann,** Stuttgarter Strasse 31 (phone 232-534), charged us 27 marks ($10.38) per person for a double overnight and breakfast the following morning. Singles with breakfast are 32 marks ($12.30)" (Mrs. Gilbert S. Brown, Dallas, Texas). . . . "**Hotel Wiesbaden,** Baseler Strasse 52 (phone 23-23-47), is just off the Bahnhof Platz, a few hundred yards from where the airport trains arrive and depart. A double without bath, breakfast not included nor required, cost 65 marks, including service and tax. Extremely friendly staff" (William Lydecker, St. Peter, Minnesota). . . . "We discovered the ultra-modern, 530-bed **Jugendherberge,** 12 Am Deutschherrnufer (phone 61-90-58), which charges a mere 11 marks per night, including breakfast. To get there from the train station, just take a left after crossing the Alte Brücke, and walk 100 yards" (Michael Mollod, Kinnelon, New Jersey). . . . "We recommend **Hotel Europa,** 17 Baseler Strasse, phone 23-6013, 3 minutes off the Central Station, for big splurgers. All rooms are with shower and w.c. and cost 80 marks single, 95 double, 120 marks twin, including breakfast. The overflow is sent to **Hotel Tourist,** next door, 23 Baseler Strasse, phone 23-30-95, with rates about 20% lower. Both hotels have a lot of 3- and 4-bedded rooms and seem ideal for students or family groups. Nearby, **DEMA Reisen,** a travel agency managed by the owner of Hotel Europa, operates sightseeing tours of the city, as well as daily excursions on the Rhine, to Heidelberg and Rothenburg" (Theodore Zoche, Peoria, Illinois; Note from AF: Owner of Dema Reisen Travel Office, 7 Mannheimerstrasse, phone 23-10-91, Mr. Gonzalez-Nache has promised to grant a 20% reduction on sightseeing and excursions to readers who show a copy of this guidebook to him). . . . "I stayed at **Hotel Weisses Haus,** 18 Jahnstrasse, phone 55-46-05. The family who runs it is most friendly and helpful, charging only $22 for a single with bath and breakfast!" (Stephanie Congrave, North Delta, B.C., Canada). . . . "Don't miss the opera in Frankfurt. The opera house is less than 13 years old, every seat is a good one, and the productions are top quality. . . . For other evening enjoyment, head for **Sachsenhausen,** just across the Main River. This is the old section of the city, and the streets are lined with gasthouses where you can sing, link arms and drink apple wine (the 'national drink' of Frankfurt), all very inexpensively. A large glass of apple wine costs 2.50 marks (96¢), and at that price, you'll be unconscious before too long" (Bill Buck, APO 57, New York, New York). . . . "You can't visit Frankfurt without seeing **Sachsenhausen,** the area of town reached by crossing the Main on the Alte Brücke (Old Bridge). First you will see the modern, 120 meter silo-tower of **Henninger Brewery,** with the two revolving restaurants on top; the area all around contains outdoor applewine inns, and, as in Vienna's Grinzing district, one can spot these places by the lanterns bedecked with green boughs. The people are warm and friendly and invite you to link arms and sing, whether you know the songs or not" (Marcia Hanf, Urbana, Illinois).

Füssen

"Here, in the Bavarian Alps, we found a hotel room near the Neuschwanstein Castle that was the nicest we enjoyed anywhere in Europe: **Schlossrestaurant Neuschwanstein,** Hohenschwangau, phone 08362-81110. It was located on the hillside in the woods, and was very quiet. At night, a spotlight lit up the Neuschwanstein Castle—a beautiful sight! The rooms were furnished exquisitely, and the staff was most accommodating. A huge breakfast with cheese and meat was included in the room price, which was as follows: single 30 marks, double 55, double with shower 65, and double with shower and private w.c. 70 marks" (Betsy and Kevin Scallon, Cottage Grove, Wisconsin).

Garmisch

"The **Pension Haus Mirabell,** Hindenburgstrasse 20 (phone 4826), had a spotlessly clean double room for us for about 35 marks ($13.46) per person including breakfast" (Paul Simon, Troy, Ill.). . . . "We found the **Gästehaus Kornmüller,** Höllentalstr. 36, to be superb, and extended our stay there because of the excellent arrangements. Frau Kornmüller could not have been pleasanter or more helpful in responding to our needs. We paid 28 marks per person, including breakfast served in the garden; and were advised by her to dine at the Restaurant Frauendorfer in Partenkirchen (corner Ludwig-Mittenwaldstrasse), where the food was reasonable, excellent, with a Bavarian band playing—it is well worth a visit" (Virginia Gillette, Roxbury, Connecticut). . . . "I heartily recommend the **'Gästehaus Kornmüller',** Höllentalstrasse 36, phone 3557. Excellent rooms in a typically Bavarian home, range from 25 to 34 marks ($9.61 to $13.07) per person, including breakfast" (Edwin C. Carlson, D.D.S., St. Petersburg, Florida). . . . "At the **Gästehaus Jocher,** St-Martin-Strasse 19 (phone 3642), we were well received, had a room with balcony for 20 marks ($7.69) per person, including a good breakfast in our room or on the balcony, and the entire house was well painted, clean and well landscaped" (Name withheld, Costa Mesa, California). . . . "We highly recommend you add **Haus Herzogsheim,** 20A Griesgartenstrasse, phone 21-37, our favorite small hotel in Europe. It is delightful, spotlessly clean, with painted furniture, geraniums on balconies, and located near the heart of Garmisch. Frau Maria Herzog, owner-operator, is a charming lady who speaks beautiful English. Our double room, with breakfast, cost 60 marks, a great bargain" (Dr. John and Dr. Julia Hall, Arkadelphia, Arkansas). . . . "We suggest **Hotel Pension Therese,** 41 Wettersteinstrasse (phone 2773), charging 50 marks for a double with shower in the hall and breakfast. Turn right three blocks from the station. From Garmisch, we went to Neuschwanstein Castle; from Garmisch, buses leave in front of the train station at 8 a.m. and 12:10 p.m. Eurailpass is valid on bus. It's about a two-hour drive to Hohenschwangau, where the castle is. If we did it again, we would go to Füssen, there being several trains a day from Munich to Füssen. The castle is about a 10 minute bus ride from Füssen, or you can walk from Füssen on a pleasant, marked hiking trail" (Philip S. Mayer, Indianapolis, Indiana). . . . "The most memorable place we stayed in Europe was **Gästehaus Royal,** 10 Sankt-Martin-Strasse, phone 4820. Turn left as you exit the train station, turn left at the first street (Sankt-Martin-Strasse), go down the steps to street level, walk under the train tracks and after about 100 yards you'll find the Royal, on your right. Frau Steiner is a gracious host, and our room was large and well arranged, beautifully decorated with a balcony that faced the snow-capped mountains (it was in October). Our cost of 25 marks each for our double room was inexpensive, the breakfast delicious. We actually felt we were guests in someone's home" (James E. Dorough, Birmingham, Alabama).

Hamburg

"Go to the **Hotel-Pension Adina,** at 63 Johnsallee (phone 44-29-59), near the University. 50 marks ($19.23) for a single room big enough for a football game, 75 marks double, including breakfast" (Joel Kerbel, Toronto, Ontario, Canada). . . . "The 100-bed **Hotel-Pension Amsterdam,** Moorweidenstrasse 34 (one block from the University), tel: 44-27-01, proved to have one of the nicest rooms of our trip. A large pleasant double room with balcony overlooking a garden came to 85 DM (taxes, a large Dutch breakfast and service included). There were a number of other pensions in this building so that it probably would be a good place to go to be assured of obtaining a room" (Robert S. Kaplan, Ithaca, New York). . . . **"Hotel-Pension Gertrud Meyn,** Hansaplatz 2, phone 24-53-09; we obtained this room (a large double with inexhaustible hot water) located on the second floor (as are very many of the pensions of this variety) of a building about two blocks from the main rail station. The room, breakfast included, cost DM 65" (Charles T. Morello, Jr., Norwood, New Jersey). . . . "The delightful pension called **Elite,** 24 Binderstrasse, phone 45-46-27, is operated by Frau Carla Feld, a charming hostess who went to no end of trouble to make us feel at home during our 10-day stay. Situated near the university, in walking distance from the Dammtor Bahnhof, spotlessly clean rooms, excellent breakfast, very reasonable prices: 60 marks single, 80 marks double, including breakfast and free showers" (Elizabeth and Sid Aron, Victoria, Australia).

Harz Mountains

"Untouched by war and nestled in the Harz Mountains (of birdseed fame) is **Bad Harzburg,** about 40 miles southeast of Hanover. **Goslar** is another 'jewel' town on the way there, where the finest singing canaries have been raised for over 700 years. The freshness and beauty of these places can hardly be described. In a fairy tale setting—so perfectly undisturbed that you arrive by chugging steam-engine-pulled train—is a town but a few minutes from East Germany. There are mountain rails through forests that have a perfect Hansel and Gretel atmosphere" (Mrs. Peter Diller, Los Angeles, California). . . . "Quite by chance I found a family accommodation in the "Harz Mountains" which can only be described as absolutely tops. First of all, your brief mention of the Harz mountains in your book does not do the area any justice. It is very beautiful, and Braunlage health resort is right in the middle of it: **Frau Inge Winkelsesser,** 11 Dr Vogeler Strasse, 3389 Braunlage, phone 05520-2060, charges 22 marks per person per night. She is very friendly and helpful. On the week-end they even took us on a tour through the mountains and neighboring towns in their car and generally could not do enough for us. In fact, from the moment we met them, we felt like long lost relatives returning home, not like strangers. Our week there can only be described as the crowning of our holiday" (Mr. and Mrs. Joachim Kohr, Woodridge, Queensland, Australia).

Heidelberg

"We found a delightful place to eat called **Zum Güldenen Schaf.** It's near the Club 1900, which is at 115 Hauptstrasse. A large plate of sausage, kraut and potatoes, with beer, was both excellent and cheap—under $6!" (Tali & Lynn Petersons, Hollis, New York). . . . "The **Gasthaus zur Backmulde,** Schiffgasse 11 (phone 22-551), is beside the old University. One enters a courtyard from Schiff-gasse, a narrow street leading up from the river. The window where rooms are booked overlooks the courtyard from the kitchen of the restaurant which is also part of the establishment. Double rooms are 65 to 85 marks a night, including breakfast and service charge, singles are 48 to 54 marks, and there's an inexpensive 10 mark restaurant in the basement. The building has been newly furnished and decorated and is extremely clean and attractive. Bathrooms may be used for only a slight extra charge and with the use of large and abundant towels. Beside our twin beds were a couple of delicious chocolates and a card wishing us a good night. On the table were fresh flowers. Outside was an ancient tower which housed many doves, and below was a part of the Heidelberg University. Delightful" (Mrs. J. Paul Boushelle, Las Cruces, New Mexico). . . . "**Hotel Goldener Falke,** on Haupt Strasse, 204 (phone 26474) is in the old city, near the University. A room with bathtub and sink (no toilet) is 58 marks ($22.30) for two, but no breakfast. Floors tilt slightly, but room was very clean. Another hotel we inspected (and it was a toss-up where we stayed) was **Hotel Zum Pfalzgrafen,** Kettengasse 21 (phone 20489), charging 80 DM double, 50 DM single, breakfast included, with toilet and bath, 1 DM extra, on the same floor" (Nat and Inge Frankel, Oakland, California). . . . "The charming old home of **Erika Jeske** has been converted into a seven-room guesthouse, at 2 Mittelbadgasse, phone 23-733, half a block off the market square, a few minutes from the university. For only 32 marks ($12.30) per day for two, we had a cozy third-floor room with window-boxes of geraniums, and overlooking the quiet street. Frau Jeske speaks fluent English and is most helpful. We recommend her to you" (Mr. and Mrs. John B. Stokes, Jr., Moorestown New Jersey). . . . "In four months of travel in Europe, we found no hotel more gracious than **Hotel-Pension Elite,** 15 Bunsenstrasse (phone 25-734). 10 minutes from the Hauptbahnhof, quiet, beautifully-furnished, spotless clean, charming proprietor—Herr Helmut Knorzer—who speaks English fluently. Then, of course, there are the extra touches, like fresh flowers on the breakfast table, exquisite china cups and a beautiful little patio garden. A real find in Heidelberg!" (Lorna and Aubrey McTaggart, San Diego, California; note from AF: 1985 rates here are 40 marks ($15.38) single, 65 marks ($25) double, breakfast included). . . . "A must if you're in Heidelberg is the Student Prison (Karzer) in the old university. You have to ring a bell marked 'Karzer,' hidden to the left of the tall doors which front the building (one block off University Square), then you wander alone up a flight of stairs, but at that point a clerk greets you and collects a tiny fee (50 pfennigs each). The five rooms were used for well over a century (until the early 1900's), are decorated from floor to, and including, ceiling with whimsical drawings and writings (done entirely by means such as charcoal and candlewax) on the minds of the students who were detained there for such things as drinking or rowdy behavior. Closed Sundays" (Jess and Alice Brewis, Taylor, Michigan). . . . "Heidelberg is the students' paradise and you can eat a very filling meal for 12 marks ($4.61) if you choose your spot. There are several places in the University area where you select your food at long counters, eat it standing up if you are in a hurry, or carry it to wooden tables in the back. Try, in particular, the **Zum Roten Ochsen** or **Zum Seppl**" (Renee Calipert, Montreal, Canada). . . . "For a slight foray off the beaten track into the scenic surroundings of Heidelberg, by rail or car, there is **Weinheim,** a small picturesque town with 2 castles, Europe's largest botanical forest ("Exotenwald"), park and medieval market square. It's a 25 mark taxi ride from the Heidelberg railroad station, or a 15 kilometer trip by car on the Heidelberg-Frankfurt Autobahn. In Weinheim, Hotel Schmittberger Hof, phone 06201-5-25-37, with 35 rooms, averaging 40 marks per person, with breakfast, private shower and w.c., is an ideal place to stay" (Klaus Gemming, New Haven, Connecticut).

Koblenz

"If you are considering a trip on the Rhine by boat, it's especially right to start at Koblenz, ending your trip at Bingen. You will see the greatest number of castles and the most beautiful scenery that way, and the trip is still short enough not to be boring. Eurailpasses are valid for your trip" (J. Thomas Renfrow, Tulsa, Oklahoma). . . . **"Gasthaus Christ,** Schürtzenstrasse 32 (phone 37702), has a very friendly proprietor who charges 43 marks single, 65 marks double, for a clean room with hot and cold running water, breakfast included" (Ronald M. Greenberg, Los Angeles, California). . . . "You failed to mention **Hotel Kramer,** at 12 Kardinal Krementz Strasse, some 5 minutes from the railway station. It offers excellent accommodation with private facilities and full breakfast for 38 to 55 marks single and 65-100 marks double, with the added bonus of a likeable and helpful proprietor" (W. Butterfield, Cronulla, Australia).

Nürnberg
"I strongly recommend **Pension Fischer,** 11 Brunnengasse, phone 0911-22-61-89, run by Charlotte and Gustl Widtmann. Singles 32, doubles 62 marks, with an egg-breakfast cheerfully served by Frau Widtmann. Pension Fischer is only 5 minutes away from the rail station in the so-called Old-Town, beautifully restored after the destruction in the last war. Nürnberg should be a MUST for anyone interested in Germany: it is the home town of Albrecht Dürer, Veit Stoss worked here, it houses the famous Germanisches Museum, and in mid-September there is the Old Town Festival, with parades in mediaeval costumes, new wine, onion pie and lots of different sausages" (Christa Kabitz-Sommer, Washington, D.C.).

Oberammergau
"We stayed with a friendly German family, who rent out four upstairs rooms in their home. The two of us had a double bed and sink, in a clean and nice room, with a beautiful view of the Alps from our window. The charge is 25 marks ($9.61) per person per night, including breakfast, and the address is: **Karl Bierling,** St. Gregor 5, tel. 08822/4579. That's about a block from the start of the cable car, and a ten-minute walk from the center of town" (Mr. and Mrs. Tom Curry, St. Peter, Illinois). . . . "We stayed in over 30 different places during our three months in Europe, but nowhere was our reception better than at the **Pension Wiedemann** (phone 4680) at 34 Herrnpoint. We arrived at their home after dark one snowy evening, without having called first, and Herr Wiedemann simply opened the door and said, 'Herein!' His price? 35 marks for a double! We felt, and still feel, that we experienced with the Wiedemanns the *spirit* of hospitality itself" (James Hoggard, Wichita Falls, Texas; seconded by Maria Schumer, Bloomfield, New Jersey). . . . "Our find here was the **Pension Schnitzlerstube,** 4 Turnerweg, phone 861, operated by the Rutz family. Despite its rustic, chalet-style exterior, the pension is only about three years old, so it has excellent modern fittings. When we were there, a double with shower cost 65 marks for the two of us. It has a swimming pool, and is a ten minutes walk from the center of Oberammergau. The next road to the right, after the Turnerweg, is the route to Linderhof Castle" (R.D. Richardson, Lane Cove, Australia). . . . "Instead of staying in expensive and commercial Oberammergau, we drove to Unterammergau. Our most pleasant experience came from our stay there with the Heirgeist family at **Fremdenheim Welfenhof.** The family purchased the house in 1918, but it was built in 910 and rebuilt in 1554. We paid 40 marks for a double with breakfast. No bath facilities were available" (Darrell and Carol Falen, Lawrence, Kansas).

Rothenburg
"While visiting Rothenburg, my wife and I and our 10-year-old son spent a night at the home of **Mr. & Mrs. Barbl Pfliegl,** Eichenweg 4 (phone 09861-4185). I can wholeheartedly recommend them to your readers. Price for a single room is 22 marks

($8.46), a double is 38 marks ($14.61), and there's a 2 mark discount for those staying more than one night. Included in the price is a delicious breakfast" (Peter Admiraal, Marion, New York). . . . "For the unsuspecting traveller visiting Rothenburg, it smacks of Alice's apocalyptic journey into Wonderland; it truly defies description. Once you've adjusted, however, take at least one of your repasts at the enchanting, ivy-covered **Baumeisterhaus,** located at Obere Schmiedgasse 3. Built in 1596, it offers mouth-watering menus and excellent 'rotwein'—excellent white wine, too" (Pauline Hadley, New York City). . . . "We visited many cities and stayed at many places, and none was nicer or more reasonable in prices of their food or rooms than the **Gasthof Zur Schranne** located at Schrannenplatz 6 (phone 09861/2258). Although the owner could speak no English, she could understand some, and was more than helpful. Our large, newly-furnished, bright, airy room for two cost us 56 marks a day including tax, service and breakfast. Some rooms have showers and w.c., yet rent for only 75 marks per day" (Art Rastetter, Massillon, Ohio). . . . "I was lucky enough to stumble upon the residence of **George and Frida Ohr,** 6 Untere Schmiedgasse, phone 4966, where a double room with shower and breakfast cost only 38 marks ($14.61). A wonderful couple, they did everything possible to make my stay a pleasant one. They live just down the street from the market square above a beauty parlor. The Herr speaks English. Also, a few steps away is the Criminal Museum which contains a wide variety of torture chamber devices and legal documents of the middle ages. The town itself was perhaps the most photographic of any in Germany" (Robert Ryan, Oak Harbor, Washington). . . . "A narrow street directly across from the town hall leads into the Kapellenplatz where stands the **Gasthof Butz** (phone 2201). A room (clean and spacious and cozy) for two costs DM 50, breakfast included. Dinner runs DM 8.50 and offers good bratwurst, potatoes, salad and beer. The building is fairly new (post W.W. II, we believe) but built with all the 16th-century charm that prevades this fairy-tale town. We cannot imagine a traveller who seeks to discover the soul and spirit of pre-industrial Germany not spending hours exploring and photographing Rothenburg. English spoken at the Gasthaus Butz" (David and Francie Robertson, Los Angeles, California). . . . "Found a lovely Fremdenzimmer owned by **Frau Pöschel,** at 22 Wenggasse. For 36 marks ($13.84) had a clean, comfortable double room, including breakfast" (Mr. and Mrs. Randall C. Williams, Tempe, Arizona). . . . "I stayed at an excellent guesthouse in Rothenburg, the beautiful walled mediaeval city, that should definitely be in your readers' selection: **Willi Then Guesthouse,** 8a Johannitergasse, phone 5177, in a very quiet street two minutes' walk from the railway station and five minutes from the town center. The rooms are big, modern, clean and fresh, with showers, and we paid 22 marks per person, including a huge breakfast. Mr Then speaks English, both he and his wife are delightful, he even carries information all in Japanese. To get there, leave the station, walk to Ansbacherstrasse, then walk one block to Johannitergasse, then turn right. It's one of the finest places we stayed in Europe" (Paul Bergman, Los Angeles, California). . . . "We found a delightful private house at 4 Schumannstrasse, phone 4217, where **Frau R. Götz** rented us a room with three beds for 55 marks, inclusive breakfast! She also let us wash clothes in the bathtub and hang them in the back yard, even got us a dental appointment" (Jo Ann Royce, North Fork, California). . . . "We found a wonderful place to stay near Rothenburg, probably best for those readers with a car or bicycle: the farm of **Erwin Knoll,** 8801 Bockenfeld near Rothenburg, phone 09861-4817. They charge 38 marks for a double room with breakfast, which was a feast, everything fresh from their farm. And in the evening they entertained us with organ and accordion music" (Cheryl and Bill Bennett, Englewood, Colorado).

Trier

"Your book omits mention of the city of Trier in Germany, a 50-minute train ride from Luxembourg (for **Icelandic** passengers headed for Germany). It's a place well worth visiting for a variety of reasons. The oldest city in Germany, it has absolutely everything for historians, fascinating Roman ruins (the most spectacular, the Porta Negra, a 10 minute-walk from the train station). It has Roman artifacts and excavations in a marvelous collection, the oldest (Romanesque) cathedral in Germany, of aesthetic as well as historic interest, a lovely medieval collection, and, for historians more interested in modern times, the (well-restored) house in which Karl Marx was born. Walking down from the train station, I found the **Hotel Kurfürst Balduin,** about one or two blocks along, in the Theodor Heuss Allee 22 (phone [0651] 25-610). It turned out to be a real find. For 38 marks ($14.61), I had a very comfortable, quiet, clean room, and a generous breakfast measured against the usual inclusive continental breakfast, i.e., a fresh egg as well as fresh rolls and coffee. Had I been willing to spend 55 DM for the night (no longer considered more than very modest), I could have had a quite large beautiful double room, with lounge, private bath and w.c. The hotel was a bit old-fashioned (no elevator), but very charmingly appointed, good-sized rooms, a lounge-coffee-room with TV for the guests, and a very amiable proprietress who speaks excellent English, and keeps a schedule of train connections to Luxembourg" (Lore J. Wagner, Geneva, New York). . . . "Coming back into Germany we wanted to visit the sights of Trier. But accommodations there were scarce and expensive, so we back-tracked a little to the suburb of Igel, between Trier and the Luxembourg border. Here, the **Gasthaus Zum Löwen,** 30 Trierer Strasse, phone 06501-2536, cost us 54 marks ($20.76) a night for two with 2 breakfasts. The kind proprietor knew that our children were with us and agreed to let them sleep in our room. Please remind anyone staying in Igel to view the ancient Roman column there, just a half block up on the left from the Gasthaus Zum Löwen" (Priscilla G. Bornmann, APO New York). . . . "Readers visiting Tier, Germany's oldest city and one of its most enchanting, should try to stay at the **Central Hotel,** 32 Sichelstrasse, phone 74077. It was a real find. The location itself is incredible: 2 blocks from the cathedral, 2 from the main train station, 2 from the central Theodor Heuss Allee. We paid 70 marks for a twin with bath and w.c., plus a huge breakfast" (Margie Wilhelm, Wehrheim, West Germany).

Wiesbaden

"We found a most attractive hotel, **Hotel Nassau,** Rheingaustrasse 148, Biebrich (a suburb of Wiesbaden), tel. 66007. Take Bus No. 4 from the Wiesbaden Railway Station to the Biebrich Terminus (about 10 minutes) and the Hotel is situated on the opposite side of the road, and to the left. This point is the Boat Terminus for Rhine River Steamers, and is extremely useful for Eurailpass holders, who can travel 'free' on the Europabus between Munich and Wiesbaden along the 'Romantic Road,' and wish to connect with a Rhine River Steamer for the Wiesbaden-Köln trip, which is also 'free' on Eurail. The rooms of the hotel are very attractive and comfortable and the manageress charming. Double rooms are 80 DM, singles 45 DM, including breakfast. We felt this was very good value as we were advised we would have to pay far more at the Railway Station tourist office" (Roslyn and Cynthia Arnold, Woolahra, N.S.W., Australia). . . . "I recommend **Hotel Singer,** 9 Albrechtstrasse, phone 37-37-28, just 10 minutes from the Bahnhof, down Bahnhofstrasse, then left. Very large, bright, cheery room, comfortable beds. Good breakfast. Without bath, double 70 marks" (G. Harchal, Frankfurt, Germany).

Würzburg

"I would like to see you include a note on Würzburg. The Europabus from Füssen ends here, and the one from Munich let us off there when we asked. The main sight is the lovely Baroque Residence, which Napoleon called the most spectacular provincial court in Europe. Across the river is the Marienburg castle with a fabulous view over the city and a museum with the best collection anywhere of Tilman Riemenschneider's works. With its parks and churches, Würzburg is a gracious city and a relief if you have only been seeing big cities on your trip" (Catherine Balliet, Bloomington, Indiana).

GREECE

Corfu

"If you should ultimately find space to include the increasingly popular Island of Corfu in your book, you can recommend the **Hotel Avra** (phone 39-269) in Benitsa (a fishing village nine miles outside the town of Corfu) for persons seeking a comfortable, clean country inn completely unspoiled by commercial greed. Run by the truly hospitable Spinoula family, who treat clients as if they were guests in their own home, it offers a simple but clean room with private shower and full pension of three big, good meals for 1,700 drachmas per day single, only 2,800 drachmas double; at least demi-pension is obligatory, at a cost of 1,300 drachmas for a single room, 2,400 for a double. It also has its own beach and is in a beautiful situation, 30 minutes by bus from town. A favorite with discriminating British travelers, many of whom return annually to the Avra for their holidays" (Bernard K. Schram, Ste. Genevieve, Missouri; note by AF: The same Spinoula family who operates the Avra recently in 1982 opened a new hotel nearby, called **Benitsa,** phone 92-424, with the same rates, in 1985, as mentioned above for the Avra). . . . "In Corfu, we recommend **Hotel Bretagne,** 27 National Stadium Street, tel. 30724, where a double with shower and breakfast was only 2,600 drachmas ($26). The owner of the hotel will pick you up from the ferry wharf and return you there on your departure. This is away from the center of town, but delightfully located near the beachfront" (Michael and Juliette Hudger, Cremorne, Australia).

Crete

"I would like to highly recommend the **Vines Pension** in Iraklion, run by the Katsirdakis family. The address is Korytsas 13 (phone 28-57-51), and is actually in Poros, a suburb of Iraklion, but it is only a short walk from where the boats from Piraeus dock. We had a double room, with bath, for 1400 drachmas ($14). Rooms are large, airy and very clean, and a full bath is just a few steps down the hall" (Ed and Betty Quinn, Skokie, Illinois).

Delphi

"We recommend both the **Hotel Hermes** (phone 82-318), and **E. Zinelis House** (otherwise known as the **Hotel Athina,** phone 82-239). Both were very attractive, had views beyond description, and most pleasant management. We planned to stay a day and we remained a week. At E. Zinelis House, doubles were 1,400 drachmas, triples 2,000 drachmas, singles 900 drachmas. We ate and visited at the Hotel Hermes (1,200 drachmas for a single with private bath, 1,800 drachmas double with bath, plus breakfast at 115 drachmas per person, and service), which was full the day we arrived" (Frank L. Esterquest, Oxford, Ohio).

Olympia

"The 'D' class **Hotel Pelops** is an exceptional bargain (1,300 drachmas single, 1,580 drachmas double), but more than that, I wish to commend the gracious owners of the hotel. In two and a-half months of travel, we found the Hotel Pelops (phone 22-543 or 22-792) the one to which we would most like to return because of the warmth, the hospitality, and the consideration shown us. We went to Olympia for two days but stayed a week, and in our proposed trip this summer, we must return to Olympia—not so much for the ruins—but for Hotel Pelops. For example, when we erroneously thought we could not have our car washed in Olympia, the owners unhesitatingly let us use their hose and water; when we had used all of the hotel's supply of ice for our drinks, the owner wordlessly drove away and obtained additional ice" (Mildred Liles, Houston, Texas). . . . "At the 60-bed **Youth Hostel** in the center of town (18 Praxitelis Kondilis, phone 22580), rates are as little as 275 drachmas per person, and youth hostel membership is not required" (Nikolaus

Lorey, Velden, Austria). . . . "Museums in Olympia close on Tuesdays" (Elsie McGillicuddy, Pasadena, California).

Patras

"A new **International Youth Hostel** has opened in 1981 in Patras, near the ferry terminal, operated by Theodoros Vazouras and his wife Donna. Both very friendly and English-speaking. Their charge is 250 drachmas ($2.50) per night and their establishment makes an excellent alternative, in my view, to boarding the crowded night train to Athens and attempting to find a place in Athens at a late hour. Trains run in the morning to Athens. I took one at 8:19 a.m., arriving in Athens early that afternoon. By the way the Brindisi-Patras ferry is a very popular one, despite the 20 hour trip" (Mike Weston, Richmond, Virginia; note from AF: exact address here is 62 Iroon Politheniou Street, phone 061-427-278).

Rhodes

"This is a greatly favored summer location for Europeans, with wonderful Crusader walls, beautiful scenery, fine trips. Hotels apt to be expensive, but in the center of the town, there is the less expensive **Hotel Spartalis,** Rue Nic. Plastiras (phone 24371), which made a very good impression. Someone staying there liked it very much, and we had lunch and dinner there several times. The charges: 2,800 drachmas for double with bath" (Mrs. Walter Stuber, Great Barrington, Massachusetts; note by AF: single rooms here are 1900 drachmas; all rates plummet in low season, prior to July 1). . . . "This is fast becoming the Miami of the Mediterranean, and it's so full of Swedes that in August, one cannot believe there could be anyone left in Stockholm" (Hanns Ebenstein, London, England).

HUNGARY

Budapest

"In this most beautiful of Eastern European cities, one can easily avoid the high priced hotels assigned by the state travel agency, for if requested, the **Budapest Tourist Agency** at #5 Roosevelt Square (phone 173-555) and ask for the helpful Josef Banfalvi), will provide accommodations in private homes at around $10 per night. This offers a unique opportunity to 'live' in a Communist city" (Mrs. Lorraine DeR. Hedlund, Ardmore, Oklahoma). . . . "While in Vienna, my husband, my son and I decided to go to Budapest. Ibusz, the Hungarian Tourist Office, got us our visas. When I remarked, tongue in cheek, it was too bad that we could not use our Eurailpass on this phase of our wanderings, we were told that the pass was good as far as the Hungarian border, and we would just have to pay from there to Budapest. We took advantage of that both coming and going. As we had been warned, all Budapest hotels were sold out due to an international soccer game, but the Hungarian Travel Office got us a private room for the night in a "government approved" apartment of a widow who must have known much better days, for much of her furniture was magnificent. The owner spoke adequate English. The charge was the equivalent of $10 for the three of us" (Mrs. Elmer S. Zweig, Fort Wayne, Indiana). . . . "A must for all travellers is a step back into the past, with a visit to the **Turkish Bath,** situated near the Erzsebet Bridge, on Szt. Gellert Rakpart. For 80 U.S. cents, you can enjoy a 16th century atmosphere, including two steam rooms, ice-water pool, and a dimly-lit central pool with surrounding smaller pools of varying temperatures. On completion of one's bathing you can relax on a comfortable bed until you are ready to face the outside 20th century world again" (Michael Lemits, Sydney, Australia). . . . "Budapest is a low-cost budget tourist's heaven. I had a lovely dinner at the **Mata Pince Restaurant,** including mushroom soup (the best mushroom soups I've ever tasted seemed to be available in every restaurant in Budapest), an excellent veal gulash with potatoes, and mineral water, for under $6. An equivalent meal in Western Europe would have cost at least twice that. Good restaurants are abundant in this lovely city. In addition, the music here is as fine as in any city in the world, at low prices. I went twice to the opera here, paying less than $1 for sitting in the center of the sixth orchestra row. Hungarians are friendly and helpful people whose good manners will overcome any language difficulties. Records are fantastic buys: 70 U.S. cents for Hungarian pressings, $1.40 for Deutsche Grammophon" (Paul Grimes, San Francisco, California).

IRELAND

Cork

"May I suggest to your readers the Ring of Kerry tour. This is a one-day excursion leaving at 10 a.m. and returning at 10 p.m. You see some of the most marvelous scenery, including the Lakes of Killarney and Dingle Bay. There are two stops along the way for meals and several photo stops. You are never rushed, but can eat a leisurely meal. Definitely not to be missed" (Erika J. Papp, Jackson Heights, New York). . . . "The charge for a clean, attractive room at **York Guest House,** phone 50-10-55, operated by friendly Mary McQuillan, was 8 pounds (Irish) each, including a big breakfast. From the station, turn left, then walk along Lower Glanmire Road to York Street. The address is 3 York Street" (Mr. and Mrs. A. Farmer, Burnaby, B.C., Canada).

Dublin

"For £8.50 ($8.50) per day (including a most generous and delicious breakfast, too!), I stayed with a Mrs. C. Drain of 265 Clontarf Road, in a home rightly called **'Bayview,'** as it looks directly across the bay of the Irish Sea. Great view, very nice people—a real "buy" for the money. Mrs. Drain's establishment is but five minutes' bus ride from the center of Dublin. The phone number is 339-870. Whereas your book doesn't have much in it regarding Dublin, I certainly hope that your next edition includes this lovely little place called Bayview—your readers simply can't go wrong" (Robert M. Sullivan, Chicago, Illinois). . . . "We highly recommend a bed-and-breakfast place called **'San Vista,'** at 237 Clontarf Road, phone 339-582. Mrs. O'Connell, the proprietress, was lovely to us. Breakfasts were excellent and served at a time to fit *our* schedule. Her rates for 1985 will be £9 ($9) inclusive (no extra charge for tax, baths, etc.), and her home, reached by bus #30, is located right on the main bus line to downtown; just cross the road for the bus! Mrs. O'Connell has taken in guests for 15 years and the comments in her guest book attest to the fact that our wonderful stay was similar to the satisfaction of previous guests" (Marcia Stimatz and Kathleen Gallagher, Butte, Montana). . . . "Please mention the bed-and-breakfast establishment operated by Mrs. P. Doody in the suburbs of Dublin, **'San Anton's,'** on the bay of the Irish Sea, near the beach, yacht club, and the city bus line which runs until 11 p.m. each night. For 9 pounds a night you receive a lovely room with a sink and a hearty Irish breakfast. The address: 286 Clontarf Road, phone 33-34-70. While in this country whose people are so outgoing and friendly, I think that staying with a family such as this one is the greatest of travel experiences" (Kathleen M. Buekley, Tours, France). . . . "Dublin is the town of *Ulysses,* and some visitors will want to view the various major sections of Dublin that are referred to in Joyce's epic novel. It takes a day to walk the path of Leopold Bloom's 24 hour journey, but the experience is unrivalled, even though one must depend on his imagination and memory of the book to supplement the direct visual appreciation, due to the changes that have taken place since 1904" (Tom Burnett, Washington, D.C.). . . . "The one-hour visit to the **Guinness Brewery,** St. James Gate, is free and is followed by an opportunity to sample the product at no cost. This trip should be a must for people staying in Dublin, but, in addition, it is a delightful way to pass the time for anyone with a few hours between planes at Dublin Airport. The route is below; take the airport bus to Dublin bus station (£2.20, $2.20), walk across the River Liffey to Fleet Street, and take a No. 78 bus to the Guinness Brewery (cost 40p), take in the one-hour visit and film show, one or two glasses of free Guinness and then board any bus to O'Connell Street. Walk from there, five to ten minutes, to the bus station and return to the airport via the airport bus, total cost, $6.50. Time required is about four hours. I landed at 9:20 a.m., visited the brewery, returned to the airport, had lunch, and went out at 2:05 p.m." (F.J. Spencer, Richmond, Virginia). . . . "In Dublin, I found that you could rent a bicycle for a day for about $7.50, by far the cheapest means of sightseeing transportation. The name of the big shop was **Fagans,** and it is located on Capel Street" (Matthew S. Watson, London, England). . . . "Let me offer the following cultural footnote to Dublin for the benefit of tourists interested in literature. Any admirer of James Joyce must not fail to see his museum at the **Martello Tower** in Sandycove. It houses photographs, manuscripts, and memorabilia, and there's a great view from the top. Take the #8 bus from Eden Quay in Dublin to Sandycove Harbour in Dun Laoghaire. It's about a thirty-minute ride; fare each way is 75p. When you arrive, a short walk to the left of the bus stop will bring you to the tower. It's open for summer tourists from 10 a.m. to 1 p.m., from 2 to 5:15 p.m., Sundays only from 2:30 to 6 p.m. Admission 60 pence, students 45 pence and children 30 pence" (James R. Paris, Weehawken, New Jersey). . . . "Take a bus trip (either public service or tour) to **Glendaloch** and its ruins. Another interesting trip is to *Wexford,* especially the free walking tour of the city conducted by Mr. Paddy Doran, a member of the local historical society" (Vincent Garvy, Annapolis, Maryland). . . . "May I recommend to you a bed and breakfast in Dublin which my wife and I found superb? It is run by a wonderfully hospitable Irish lady named **Mrs. Myra O'Flaherty,** the address is 312 Clontarf Road, phone 332-787. Her lovely home overlooks Dublin bay and is only 15 minutes from central Dublin on bus 30. Her breakfasts are lovely and she is the soul of Irish charm. Since Dublin I think deserves a bit more space than you give it, I hope you will tell people about Mrs. O'Flaherty, whose rate, with breakfast, will be £9 in 1985" (Alan Hausman, Columbus, Ohio). . . . "There is a pleasant bed and breakfast establishment called **Inishowen Guest House,** 199 South Circular Road, Dublin, phone 780-272, run by Mrs. K. Logue, ten minutes by bus from downtown. The rates are £9.50 for a single, £17 for a double, but the shower is extra. I also want to recommend highly the **Gaiety Theater,** South King Street, in Dublin. For £2 I heard a musical revue of top quality featuring excellent Irish talent" (David Fourney, Takoma Park, Maryland). . . . "We enjoyed five days' b&b at the home of **Mrs. Bird,** 25a Oakley Road, Ranelagh, phone 97-22-86. She has a brick Edwardian house, two bathrooms for guests, and six bedrooms, with sinks in each. It is newly decorated, centrally heated and spotlessly clean. Ranelagh is a district of lovely privately owned homes, near shopping centers with delis, take-aways, restaurants and good pubs. Our truly Irish breakfast of bacon and eggs, sausage, tomato, toast and Irish bread was served in a lovely dining room, on Irish bone china. Buses 11, 11a, 12, 13 and 13a are all near and take you into central Dublin. The price is 9 Irish pounds per person" (A.H. Rowley, Calgary, Alberta, Canada).

Killarney

"One mile out of Killarney, on the Cork Road, **Mr. and Mrs. Denis O'Donoghue** (pronounced O'Dunahoo) operate an immaculately clean B and B. They call their home **Cum A Ciste,** which means Valley of the Treasure. It has eight neat rooms, each with two double beds and a sink as well as other furniture, of course. For 8 pounds per person we had a good night's rest and a very filling breakfast of our choice, which included porridge, toast, eggs, bacon and coffee. Don't stay anywhere else in Killarney!" (Tom and Michelle Flessor, Evergreen Park, Illinois). . . . "The most delightful stay I had in any pension or hotel in Europe was at **Aisling House** (phone 064-31112) on Countess Road, which runs parallel to the train station, but can only be reached by leaving the station and turning right. Take the first left onto the large road. Pass the cinema and take another left, passing a church. Walk for about 3-5 minutes more. Proprietors are extremely nice and the price was terrific— £8.50 ($8.50) for bed and breakfast" (Sue Ulloa, Bainbridge Island, Washington). . . . **"St. Enda's Guest House** (phone 064-31994), owned by Mrs. Joan M. Mahon, near the Tore Hotel, serves excellent breakfast, is clean. We paid £8 each for a double room with breakfast" (Ted Johnson, San Francisco, California). . . . "I kept asking what was the attraction of Killarney that caused it to expand in population so greatly during July and August? Some of the reasons are: 1. An easy town to walk in, with shops and accommodations centrally located; 2. Friendly people, the Irish; 3. Abundant restaurants, pubs and entertainment spots; 4. Many excellent tourist accommodations to satisfy every taste; 5. The picturesque scenery surrounding Killarney, the primary reason why so many visit this area of the Emerald Isle" (Al Uher, Delmar, California).

Limerick

"My **St. Rita's Guest House** is on the main road from Limerick to Shannon Airport and also on the road from Galway to Killarney that passes Limerick City. The exact address is St. Rita's, Ennis Road, Limerick (tel: Limerick 55809). The house is Regency architecture and has eight bedrooms, all large and spacious and with hot and cold running water in each. I have a large lounge and dining room so it is quite a home away from home. My terms for Bed and Breakfast usually run around £9.50 each person or roughly $9.50. I have adequate toilet and bathroom requirements" (Mrs. Bernadette Clancy, Limerick, Ireland). . . . **"Mrs. Evelyn Murphy,** at 8 Davis Street (phone 47227), is straight down from the train station, very handy to town, buses and train. Good bed and breakfast—single £9, double £7 each per night. Very nice lady" (Woodrow and Letress Berryhill, Phoenix, Arizona).

ITALY

Amalfi

"Touring the Sorrento area, the best find of our entire trip was in Amalfi, where we spent a week-end in a lovely pension called **Pensione Sole** (phone (871-147), a few feet from the beach. In season, a bathless double room is 30,000 lire, not including breakfast" (Jacques and Magdeleine Tremblay, Quebec City, Canada; seconding recommendation from Maria Zilzer, New York City). . . . **Hotel D'Italie et Suisse** (phone 871-444), just beside the sea, is cheap and good. They have a few single rooms for 34,000 lire, during high season and with private shower" (Agneta Palme, Stockholm, Sweden). . . . **"Pensione Amalfi,** at 10 Via San Giacomo (phone 089-87-24-40), operated by the eight-member Salvatore Lucibello family, and centrally located, is highly recommended. In the main building are one single and 23 twin rooms, some with 3 beds, all with private bath. In the rear is a pleasant garden, wall-enclosed, with tables and chairs. Cost: 16,000 lire per person, with breakfast. Each of the Lucibellos is friendly, helpful, pleasant; and several speak English" (Charlotte Scott, Elmira, New York).

Assisi

"I should very much like to recommend the **Monastero S. Colette,** 3 Borgo S. Pietro, Assisi (takes men and women), phone 812-345, where I had an extremely comfortable room (with wash basin) and breakfast for 19,000 lire ($11.87). The French nuns, although they speak only a little English, are expert at making themselves understood, and understanding all nationalities, and hot water is available. You are given a latch-key on arrival. Incidentally, the station at Assisi is some distance from the town, and a taxi costs at least 12,000 lire. The bus, though only moderately frequent (½ to 1 hourly according to time of day, perhaps more in season), is only 500 lire—quite a worthwhile saving" (Mollie Boyle, Bramcote, Warwickshire, Wales). . . . "A great many tourists come to this beautiful, peaceful town, the birthplace of St. Francis and of St. Claire. The hotels are always full and we stumbled upon a medieval villa, now a Guest House, which turned out to be another Graymoor Sisters', like the one in Rome. It is known in town as the 'American Sisters,' technically **St. Anthony's Guest House,** Via Galeazzo Alessi 10. Telephone 812-542. Full pension is 30,000 lire ($18.75) a day per person. The food is excellent; the service is perfect; a lovely garden overlooks the Umbrian Hills; and all the sisters are most accommodating and speak English. The place is so serene and restful that we stayed four days instead of only two" (Mr. and Mrs. Stanley P. Cooper, Temple City, California). . . . **"The Hostel of the Swedish Sisters of St. Birgitta** in Assisi (Suore svedesi di S. Brigida, Via Moiano 1, tel. (075) 812693) is situated on a hillside approximately four minutes' walk from the upper town and overlooking the lower city. The Sisters in attendance at the inn were most pleasant and cordial. Suggest you look this one over as we thought it to be one of the best (including first class hotels) we found in all our travels. The rooms were immaculate, though simply furnished, and the food superb (Italian cuisine, of course). Room and meals (continental breakfast, noon meal and dinner) all inclusive for 32,000 lire ($20) per day per person" (Bernard R. Higgins, Cleveland, Ohio). . . . "Besides the Basilica of Saint Francis with its grotto frescoes, also worth visiting is the crypt, as well as the legendary crucifix that spoke to St. Francis. See, too, the Basilica of Santa Maria degli Angeli in the valley near the station: the Portiuncula is inside, as well as the spot where Francis died, and the rooms where he and his first followers lived and worked" (Danielle Jehanne Rappaport, APO, New York).

Capri

"Try the **Hotel Maresca,** on the Marina Grande (phone 837-0442). One can't miss it. It's the only good-looking hotel in the port area. Unbelievable how clean it is. The owner speaks English, German and French. We had a good-sized double with terrace. Even from the bed, you could see the Bay of Naples (Naples, the Vesuvio, Sorrento). Free swimming possibilities. We paid 23,500 lire ($14.68) per person, but breakfast was included. One of the best buys in Europe" (Dr. George Ballun, Woodside, New York, with numerous seconding recommendations from other readers as well). . . . "I found, in the upper town of Capri ('Anacapri'), a modestly-priced pension called **Albergo Loreley,** tel: 837-1440. On Capri, which is to my mind the most beautiful island in the world (I've made 10 trips to Europe and 4 trips around the world), hotels can be quite expensive. This is a fairly new place (10 years old), small and intimate, very clean. The owner, Sr. D'Angiola, and his family, are extremely courteous and genuinely friendly and helpful. One feels as if in a friendly home. Rates are very reasonable; single rooms with breakfast are 25,000 lire ($15.62), and doubles with two meals are from 23,000 lire ($14.37) per person" (Jerome Siegel, Bronx, New York). . . . "Most of the restaurants in Capri are rather expensive. We stood outside one such costly place and were almost tempted to splurge. Fortunately, my wife smelled a roasting chicken across the street in a modest delicatessen with a few tables. We ordered two platters of fish/vegetables or chicken/pasta, including fresh olives and bread, full meals for some ridiculous price like $6 each. The food couldn't have been better at any price. Our find was **Scialapopolo,** at 31 Via le Botteghe. It's opposite Cappannino, a tourist-type restaurant. To find it, take the funicular to the top, to the main piazza, turn left, and enter the archway just to the side of the Vuotto store" (George Velsey, Port Washington, New York). . . . "For an excursion to Capri, it is far cheaper and certainly more enjoyable to do it on your own, rather than on an organized tour" (Paul Rorovsky, Johannesburg, South Africa). . . . "We found a nice and cozy ristorante-pizzeria-trattoria one night wandering through the charming streets of Capri: **La Cisterna,** 5 Via M. Serafina. The suggestions of the waiter, who was most friendly, welcoming and sincerely interested in pleasing his customers, added that extra touch to our visit to Capri. Among them: home-made ravioli made with fresh pasta, a bottle of crisp white Capri wine made on the waiter's own vineyard on the island, and a Grappa digestivo distilled from the same native wine. Pizzas were 4 to 5,000, pasta dishes around 3,000, and main courses of fish and meat between 5 and 7,000 lire. A note about the trip to the Blue Grotto on Capri: the motor launch from Marina Grande cost at the time 4,000 lire, plus the additional fees for the entrance and the rowboat that takes you into the grotto itself, which costs another 3,000 lire. If you plan to visit Anacapri on the other side of the island, you could take the pathway down to the grotto entrance and save yourself the motorlaunch fee" (Rodney Chonka, Vineyard Haven, Massachusetts).

Genoa

"I was booked at the **Hotel Pension Lausanne,** 33a via Balbi (phone 261-634), just to the left of Columbus' statue of Piazza Stazione. I paid 15,000 lire for a single for one night, plus 3,500 lire for breakfast. Doubles are 26,000 lire" (J. Raymond Reid, Soest, Germany). . . . "I was quite lucky to find a comfortable, nicely furnished, quiet room with running hot and cold water at the **Pensione Della Posta,** Via Balbi 15, tel: 280-103, on the top floor of an elevator building, about 500 yards from the railway station and 200 from American Express. The English-speaking owner himself will serve your breakfast in your room, for which he charges 23,000 lire ($14.37) single" (Peter N. Abbot, New York, New York). . . . . . . **"Pensione Bel Soggiorno,** Via XX Settembre 19 (phone 581-418), in the center of town, is operated by a lovely couple, Ingrid and Sergio Possio. She is German, he Italian. Both speak excellent English. A bathless single was 24,000 lire (Helen Hasler, Kent, England; note from AF: for better orientation, note that the Bel Soggiorno is located next door to the Genoa Brignole Railroad Station).

Ischia

"After Paris we made our way to Ischia, a small island off the coast of Italy, and there we ran into a gold-mine of a hotel—the **Pensione Villa Panoramica** at 11 Via Mirabella (tel. 991-414)—where a double room with two meals (breakfast and one other) ran us 42,000 lire per person. The rooms are immaculate and the service out of this world, i.e., a maid takes dirty laundry, cleans and irons it, then lays it out for us. The villa is a stone's throw from a beach—sand, not gravel—and a leisurely after-dinner walk brings you to the main shopping centers on the island. One of the rooms we had, had a breathtaking view of the ocean, distant islands, and an island fortress" (Howard Passe, Richard Kelsey, Bob Beccarelli, Charlie Czeupak, Union, New Jersey).

Lake Como

"Four kilometers west of Lago Como, in the town of Cernobbio, we found high up on the hill (a car is needed here) the **Hotel Asnigo** (phone 510062), with a superb view of the lake. We stayed here two days, paying 24,000 lire per person per day for bed and breakfast. I cannot recommend this place enough to your readers" (Jacques and Magdeleine Tremblay, Quebec City, Canada). . . . "We can recommend **Hotel Plinio,** Laglio-Torriggia, Lago di Como, phone 031-400-135, a few kilometers north of the city of Como. For $13 per person per day (1982) we had a nice room with large balcony and breathtaking view on the lake and the opposite shore. Showers are free. The next day, we drove to Cadenabbia to visit the beautiful Villa Carlotta (unforgettable gardens) and from there we took the boat to Bellagio, which is the loveliest spot on Lake Como" (Mr. and Mrs. J. G. Nawar, Ottawa, Canada; note from AF: this hotel was completely modernized and charges in 1985 $38 for a twin with bath and buffet breakfast).

Milan

"**The Hotel-Pension Londra,** Piazza Argentina 4 (phone 228-400), is quite close to the station, charges 34,000 lire ($21.25) for a double (including service and taxes). Clean and well-furnished" (Henry B. Coons, A.P.O., New York; note from AF:

owner Gianfranco Volante has promised a 10% discount to readers, on these rates, in 1985). . . . "I think Hotel-Pensione Londra deserves more than the 4 lines in small print. Both husband and wife who run the place were extremely helpful. One morning we found our car gone. I thought it was stolen. The street cleaners had removed it to another spot. After many phone calls and calming words from the owners, we found it" (Rose Swensen, New York City). . . . "We lived for six weeks at the **Pensione Parva Domus** on Piazza Argentina 4 (downstairs from the Pension Londra), phone 273-915. Its owner, Mr. Rodolfo, speaks English and was helpful to us. The price of a clean, spacious room for two (without bath) was 40,000 lire per night" (Dr. Paul W. Mosler, Seattle, Washington; note by A.F.; numerous other enthusiastic recommendations for the Parva Domus, and for its friendly, helpful Mr. Rodolfo Begni, who is apparently happy to answer telephoned inquiries for assistance and will grant a 10% discount to readers of this book; but try for a room facing away from the street—according to reader Carlo Gurunlian, Montreal, "it sounds like the Indianapolis 500 for 24 hours a day"). . . . **"Motta** is a large and famous quick-service food bar as well as a sit-down restaurant complete with a section that sells specialty foods of the region. It is directly across from the tourist office and to the right as you leave the Duomo. For about $5 you can have a cold meat variety plate, vegetable plate, or your choice of a large salad—a filling meal" (Linda Lusardi, West Covina, California). . . . "To see a performance at **La Scala** for 10,000 lire, including tax, get standing room. We did this, and found the usher motioning us to front row balcony seats as soon as the lights went down. We saw perfectly. The cheapest seats, incidentally, go for 12,000 lire, including tax" (Frank and Linda Peterson, McLean, Virginia). . . . "Scala: When no concierge or 'private contact' could get me a ticket because it was SOLD OUT, I walked to Scala and got one at the box office" (Lida Van Zahn, Johannesburg, South Africa). . . . "The roof of the Duomo is fascinating. You can clamber all over it for a couple of hundred lire (more if you use the elevator) amid a forest of saints and gargoyles, and look over the city through the telescopes. . . . I found the shops in the **Vittorio Emanuele Gallery** a refuge from the rain, and I loved just to sit out at a table in front of the Biffi at the intersection of the walkways with a Cinzano and soda (that's the way everybody drinks it now) and just watch the people go by. Frankly, I enjoyed that more than the Via Veneto in Rome, because there were more people going by in the Galleria in Milan" (J. Raymond Reid, Soest, Germany). . . . "Strong recommendation for Milano. It's part of the new emerging Italy, and it's a city which runs for the Italian, not for the tourist. Be sure to visit the **Sforza Castle** and the **Museum of Science & Technology,** which contains models of Leonardo da Vinci's scientific inventions. They are free throughout the week, but closed on Mondays" (Bette & Paul Wood, Cambridge, Massachusetts). . . . "In addition to the Duomo, visit the Church of Santa Maria delle Grazie, where, on a wall in a room off the church, is painted Leonardo da Vinci's 'The Last Supper.' Closed Mondays" (Danielle Jehanne Rappaport, Munich, Germany).

Naples

"I have been commuting to Naples for two years on a regular basis of three to four times a month. I feel the **Pensione Suisse** is still the best buy in Naples. It is centrally located, yet situated in the better part of Naples in the Santa Lucia cinema building. Several years ago, Tino Hausner and his wife took over the pensione and moved it from the fourth to the second floor. The move was most beneficial to the customer, as the rooms are larger, in excellent condition, and with convenient bathrooms. The price is 30,000 lire ($18.75) per day for two persons, including shower. And that's at Via Raffaele de Cesare 7, phone 425-162" (LCDR R. W. Martowski, U.S.N., FPO, New York; note from A.F.: Of all the pensions in Naples described on this page, Pensione Suisse is the one to which I would give preference—mainly because Tino Hausner and his Italian wife try really hard to make your stay a pleasant one, and their standards of cleanliness and sanitation are above the local level). . . . "The **Hotel Rex,** Via Palepoli 12 (phone 41-61-02), not far from the American Express office, charged 70,000 lire for a family of five adults. Perhaps we got a special price for an immense family room, but the rates were certainly under those of other hotels we considered. A very satisfactory stop" (Frank L. Esterquest, Oxford, Ohio). . . . "The **Hotel Rex** has clean, good, large, second class rooms, renting—for a bathless double—at 49,000 lire, including tax and service (34,000 lire single). The address is Via Palepoli #12, two blocks from the American Express office in the popular tourists' Santa Lucia area. Take bus #106 or 150 from the train station" (L.F. Ivanhoe, Rome, Italy). . . . "Don't let your readers buy a tour to **Capri.**. . . . it's a simple matter to take the steamer from the main docks, for 7,800 lire round trip. A beautifully-engineered funicular then brings you to the main tourist area, and if you wish you may make bus excursions from there up to Anacapri. The whole island is a bit commercial, but too beautiful to miss. Many tempting boutique shops for the ladies. Hotels looked quite inviting too, if you were planning to stay. The trip to the Blue Grotto costs 7,000 lire by motor launch, *but* you must pay an additional 3,000 lire when you get there to transfer into a rowboat and be towed around inside the Grotto. It would be nice to know this in advance, instead of feeling you've been 'had' " (Mr. and Mrs. Randell C. Widner, St. Petersburg, Florida). . . . "No visitor to Naples should miss a bus ride on the fantastic Amalfi-Sorrento road" (Dr. Jindrick Fantl, Prague, Czechoslovakia).

Palermo

"**The Hotel Sausele,** Via V. Errante 12 (phone 23-75-24), is near the station. It is Swiss owned and operated, with typical Swiss standards of impeccable cleanliness, honesty and efficiency. We had a delightful double room without bath but with breakfast included for 43,000 lire ($26.87)" (Dr. Augustus H. Fenn, Portsmouth, New Hampshire; note by AF: there have been numerous other recommendations for the 40-room Sausele, whose roof garden and air-conditioned lounge are apparently standouts).

Perugia

"The **Mensa Popolare** (patronized by students and workers alike) is off the famous Via Maestra della Volte (ask the traffic controller near the Duomo) and serves only the noonday meal (three courses) for 3,500 lire. The precise address is 16 Via Antonio Fratti. A snack can be had in a little pizzeria on Via di Priori (off Corso Vanucci), where a pizza costs 3,000 lire a portion. If one gets tired of talking to oneself in Perugia, he need only go to the Università per Stranieri, where he will find many Anglo-Saxons in the bar" (C. K. Hunter, Munich, Germany). . . . "The **Albergo Aurora,** 21 Viale Indipendenza (phone 24819) is right on the main street coming into the center of town off the autostrada. We had a nice double room away from the street with two single beds and right next to the bath, for 23,000 lire per night. We kept our room in Perugia while visiting Assisi, as hotels in the latter can become very crowded" (Walt Keirlle, San Diego, California).

Pescara

"We would like to mention the city of Pescara as an excellent stopover place for people heading down the Adriatic Coast of Italy to Brindisi. We had planned on stopping at Ancona but it looked so awful that we hopped right back on the train and continued to Pescara—a very good choice. It is a modern resort town with a large, pleasant beach. We stayed at the **Hotel Bologna,** near the station for 33,500 lire for three. It was clean and satisfactory though not outstanding. We did, however, have an excellent dinner at a newish little place nearby called **La Bianca Oca.** It cost 24,000 lire for three and included four courses and wine" (Jan and Asbjorg Clemson, White Rock, B.C.)

Pisa

"Just one block from the leaning tower was the **Albergo Gronchi,** 1 Piazza Archivescovado (phone 23-626), with a large room for the two of us for just 30,000 lire ($18.75), not including breakfast. The ceiling was decoratively hand-painted and when we left the next morning, the proprietor came running after us with our little traveling clock which we had left behind" (Paul Simon, Troy, Illinois). . . . **"Hotel Di Stefano,** 35 Via S. Apollonia (phone 26359), was our cleanest and most comfortable hotel in Italy, and charged only 32,000 lire ($20) for a double room without bath, with breakfast an extra 4,500 lire per person" (Robin Harper, Augsburg, Germany). . . . "The railway workers' restaurant, **DLF Tavola Calda,** to the left as you leave the station, is also open to the public, at prices about 20% higher. Still, with pasta for 2,200 lire, meat dishes for 5,000, a quarter liter of wine for 600, and 800 lire for bread and cover, a meal can be put together for about 9,000 lire ($5.62)" (Norriss, Edith and Elizabeth Hetherington, Berkeley, California).

Positano

"In Positano we found our best bargain, **Casa Celeste,** recommended by some Australians sitting behind us on the bus, who had lived in Positano ten years. Celeste is a delightful Italian woman who speaks Italian very clearly and succinctly and can be understood by those who know a little Italian. She charged us 31,000 lire for a beautiful double room with shower and a balcony overlooking Positano and the Amalfi coast. Breakfast was included, featuring homemade grape jam served on a terrace over the ocean. I unfortunately do not know the address, but know she is listed in the phone book" (Sylvia Sensiper and Bill Borden, Santa Monica, California).

Rapallo

"Try the **Pensione Elvezia,** 12 Via Ferraretto (phone 50564), where the friendly English-speaking proprietress charges 35,000 lire ($21.87) per person in high season for room and full pension (huge, well-cooked meals)" (Gerald J. Veverka, Westchester, Illinois). . . . "In Rapallo we found a very well-placed hotel called **Cavour,** in an arcade half-way between the station and the sea. We had a quiet, beautiful room with full bathroom for 32,000 lire for two people. No food was included but all sorts of cafés and shops were near and the owners were marvellous to us, including their pet-restaurant, Da Giorgio, quite near, where we had a good three-course meal with wine for 10,000 lire" (L. Phillips, Adelaide, South Australia; note from AF: the address is 20 Galleria Raggio; phone 54-040).

Rimini

"A real find was the **Ciotti Hotel,** 98 Viale Regina Elena (phone 80055, in Rimini). This Adriatic beach resort is a great favorite of the Swiss, Germans and Austrians, so everyone speaks German and some English. The hotel cost 38,000 lire (in May-June and September), 48,000 lire (in July and August), for full pension per person, and the three meals per day were equal to five elsewhere, and were the best in Italy that we came across. All this for a very clean modern hotel (showers in all the rooms) facing a lovely beach. This would be an excellent break in the travel routine between Rome or Florence and Venice. Rimini is also the place to stop and visit San Marino, which is only a couple of miles away" (Dr. Alex Weiskopf, San Mateo, California). . . . "A city official found us a room at the **Pensione Villa Erika,** 11 Viale Marino (phone 81522), for 29,000 lire per person full pension, 19,000 for our three-year-old son. The pension is ultra modern, ultra-clean, right on the beach, and would be first class in the U.S. Let me stress that the Erika is the *rule,* not the exception" (Frank and Sara Sharp, Fayetteville, Arkansas).

Siena

"The **Villa Terraia,** 3 km. from Siena at 13 Via del Ascarello (phone 22-11-08), charged 59,000 lire ($36.87) for a bathless double room. This was the villa where

Garibaldi lived and one can see the 12 huge California redwoods he brought around the Horn as seedlings and planted here. After capital-hopping, a few days in a villa in Tuscany are a delight. The villa is clean and filled with art treasures and has a superb view of Siena" (Virginia Ryder, Sausalito, California). . . . "The Albergo Villa Terraia is somewhat difficult to find, being located on a hill to the north-northeast of the Old City. Albergo la Toscana is located downtown, within the city walls, but a nightmare to find with a car. We finally settled on staying at the **Hotel Moderno,** a second-class hotel, and paid 36,000 lire ($22.50) for a twin without bath. The address: 19 Via Baldassare Peruzzi. A big plus: they have parking in a locked garage for the car" (Dan Else, FPO, NY; note from AF: the phone number is 288-453). . . . "A superb hunting-ground for the Italian Mediaevalist, Siena rivalled Florence in battle and art during the 13th century. Its cathedral is perhaps more imposing— inside and outside—than Florence's. It should be a 'must' for all visitors to Florence. And here is an excellent hotel find: **Albergo Chiusarelli,** 9 Via Curtatone, phone 280-562, across from San Domenico Church, almost at the limit of car traffic and therefore very convenient. Just modernized (1983), they charged 60,000 lire for a 3-bedded room with bath and free parking" (Mr. and Mrs. P.K. Pal, Montreal, Canada).

Sorrento

"At the **Hotel Girasole,** 302 Corso Italia, phone 878-13-71, owned and operated by a friendly Italian family, the Ruoccos, who spoke some English, we found a home away from home! The rooms were clean, spacious and offered a beautiful view. A double with private bath and shower and breakfast was 37,000 lire, a single 20,000. It is a twelve minute walk from the station" (Harry Sarno, Michigan). . . . "We stayed at the **Hotel Apollo Meublé,** Via Luigi De Maio 13 (phone 878-3701), which is new, modern, clean and centrally located on a street between the two main squares of town. It is convenient to buses, tourist offices, railway station and the port. Our neatly furnished room has a large balcony overlooking the street, was equipped with heating facilities, and can be air conditioned for 2,500 lire a day. The proprietors are very friendly and understand English. Single with bath, 26,000 lire; double with bath, 36,000 lire; breakfast is 4,500 lire per person." (Margie Greenberg, Brooklyn, New York). . . . "Stayed at the **Hotel Schweizerhof,** where I had a single with private shower for 22,000 lire ($13.75). From the Circumvesuviana station, head down a block, turn left, and walk to the main square. Then ask the travel agency there where it is—it's just a stone's throw away" (Danielle Jehanne Rappaport, Munich, Germany). . . . "A most exceptional find was the **Hotel Loreley et Londres,** Via Valifano 2, tel. 878-15-08, only 8 minutes' walk from the train station, and well worth it. Although it shares the grand view of the entire coastal area there—Capri, Ischia, Vesuvius, Harbor, etc.—with the nearby plush hotels, it provided a single room, with bath and balcony, for only 19,000 lire ($11.87)" (Embry L. Riebel, Miami, Florida; note by AF: Reader P.G.W.A. Lommerse, Killarney, Manitoba, Canada, praises the fact that Hotel Loreley has an elevator going down to a beach which can be used for swimming in summer. Both swimming and sunbathing there are free). . . . "On my return from Pompeii, I passed by Sorrento and took a bus to Amalfi. The scenery is wonderful and exuberant. No one should miss the trip Sorrento-Amalfi by bus. It's much better to stay in Sorrento in order to visit Pompeii, Ercolano and Capri than in Naples, which is a noisy and crowded city" (Carlos Humberto Machado, Minas, Brazil).

Taormina, Sicily

"Taormina, in Sicily, is one of Europe's most famous resorts (Churchill wintered here), high on the slopes of Mt. Tauro, with Mt. Etna (a still active volcano) rising majestically in the distance. The climate is incredible and is comparable only to that of Waikiki Beach in Hawaii. Just as in Waikiki, it almost never rains here, and when it does it is a sprinkling, a 'blessing.' I had planned to spend only two days, but have been so impressed with the beautiful weather that I am extending my stay to a week.

Taormina seems to be a favorite with the English, Germans, *and* Italians from the other areas of Italy, and there are accommodations to suit everyone. Your budgeteers would have no difficulty finding a room at reasonable rates. Being captivated by the beauty of the city I wanted a room with a view. I found one with private bath in the moderately expensive (40,000 lire single, 65,000 lire double, breakfast included) **Hotel Belvedere,** at 79 Via Bagnoli Croce (phone 23791), which has been owned and run by the same family since it was built 'by grandfather' in 1906. I opened two huge door-windows, step onto the balcony, and there before me is a spectacular view. I am about 300 feet above sea level, at my feet are terraces and patios, rich with palms and other tropical plants and flowers, gleaming in the sunlight. Directly ahead is the blue Mediterranean and just off to the right is the gently curving shoreline of the bay. The water is calm and the only ripples visible are those made by slowly moving sailboats. In the distance at the right is the huge cone of Mt. Etna, with periodic bursts of smoke puffing at the peak" (John W. Scheifele, Bronx, New York). . . . "I shared a room with a friend at the **Pensione Svizzera** on the Via Pirandello, no. 26, phone 23790. The price for our room—a large room with a private bath—was 36,000 lire a day for two, breakfast included. A large window in our room overlooked the sea and Isola Bella—a spectacular view. The pension is owned and operated by a young Italian and his German wife and their staff; English, Italian and German are spoken. The funicular that goes down to the beach at Mazzarro is just a few steps from the pension. The congenial atmosphere of the pension, plus the Sicilian sun, made for a marvelous stay in Taormina" (Todd W. Lehman, New York, New York). . . . "During our stay in Taormina we discovered several places of good value. The town itself is beautiful, set high on a mountainside over a sandy coastline, the perfect spot to relax and enjoy the sun and the beach. First, we found spotless accommodation at **Pensione Villa Sirena,** 36 Via Pirandello, phone 23773, which is well situated, especially for travelers without a car. The friendly proprietress speaks English. We had a double room with private w.c. and shower, continental breakfast and a Million Dollar view, for 38,000 lire. Visitors should be sure to try the first class food at **Trattoria da Dino,** also on Via Pirandello, near the head of the "funivia." Try the fresh seafood, reasonably priced. Another find was the home-made pasta and pizza at **L'Angolo** ("the corner"), just off Corso Umberto, at 17 Via Damiano Rosso. Prices at both restaurants are around 3,500 lire for a meatless pasta dish, 7,000 for meat and fish dishes" (Morna Russell and Maureen Ciarniello, Vancouver, B.C., Canada).

Verona

"We found a lovely older hotel just 2 blocks from the Arena which forms the center of Verona: **Hotel Bra,** 6 Piazza Pradaval, 35,000 lire for a twin which also included breakfast. The folks there didn't speak a word of English and we didn't speak any Italian, but we managed nonetheless. After the hustle and bustle of Venice, Verona was a nice contrast: magnificent churches throughout the city, each with marvelous interiors and paintings by well-known artists, and of course we also had to see the famous balcony of Juliet" (Richard Bowen, Munich, Germany). . . . "At the **Hotel Siena,** 41 Via Marconi, phone 23-074, I paid 24,000 lire for a room with single bed, private bath, no breakfast. It's small, family run, and 10 to 15 minutes' walk from the railway station. Good restaurant around the corner; close to the Roman forum and all other attractions" (Mrs. B. Bagnell, Whitby, Ontario, Canada).

Vicenza

"My daughter is stationed at the American Army hospital in Vicenza, about an hour by train to the west of Venice, near Padova and Verona. She reserved a room for the weekend for the three of us at the **Albergo Due Mori,** on 26, Via due Ruote, phone 21-886. This is right in the heart of the city: take bus #1 from the railway station, down Viale Roma. Outside, the hotel looks ancient, but inside all is modern, spotless, and beautifully furnished, and for 3 of us, the cost was only 42,000 lire

($26.25) for the room with shower and toilet. Everyone was helpful, kind and sympathetic. I almost felt like one of the family. This is the loveliest hotel of our travels" (Edith M. Gauthier, Buffalo, New York). . . . **"Tre Visi Restaurant,** was the best I found in Vicenza, serving the finest northern Italian cuisine for less than $20 for a couple for a 4-5 course dinner. Their grilled specialties, such as veal steaks and tortellini, are the best I have found in my travels. This is close to the Central Piazza and most every native of Vicenza can tell the visitor how to find it. I would also urge a bus trip from the train station (500 lire) to Monte Berico, which provides a magnificent hilltop view of the city. The civil museum and Teatro Olimpico in downtown Vicenza are marvelous examples of the architecture of Palladio and well worth the stopover" (Dr. Allen W. Parks, Frankfurt, Germany).

LIECHTENSTEIN

"Hotel Meierhof (tel. 075-21836) is in Triesen, near Vaduz on the road to Malbun, fairly new, clean, and offers a marvelous view. Double room with bath costs approximately 72 Swiss francs" (Eugene S. Quillen, Anacortes, Washington). . . . "Malbun-Triesberg, near Liechtenstein, is a lovely ski resort, the starting point for many mountain hikes through meadows of alpine flowers (it's a flower-protected area) and tinkling cow bells. We had nice rooms at **Hotel Hubertushof,** phone 075-2-46-27, next to the chair lift, for 25 Swiss francs per person including breakfast and private shower. A chance stop, Malbun became our favorite place during our family's vacation in the German, Austrian and Swiss Alps" (Nancy Johnson, McLean, Virginia).

LUXEMBOURG

"We found the **Carlton Hotel,** 9 Rue de Strasbourg (phone 48-48-02), to be quite pleasant, yet reasonable. For 1,600 Bfr ($29.09), we had a double room, breakfast, free shower and service. English is spoken" (Tom and Mary Wagner, Monroeville, Pennsylvania). . . . "Since many budget readers fly Icelandic Airlines to Luxembourg, they may be interested in how to get from downtown to the airport. Bus number 9 leaves frequently from just outside the train station and costs 20 francs instead of 100 francs for the regular airline buses. Do not confuse Bus 9 with Bus 9A. From the airport to town, walk south out to a parking lot. Look for a bus stop marked Arret Ligne 9" (David W. Smith, Carbondale, Illinois). . . . "I liked the **Luxembourg City Hostel.** From the airport bus 9 goes near it. For an adult, the fees at the large hostel are 175 Bfr for a bed, 150 Bfr for a great supper with seconds, 75 Bfr for breakfast. They also pack lunch if requested" (Pat Diehnelt, Ashippun, Wisconsin; note by AF: Correct address and phone number of this youth hostel (310 beds) are 2 Rue du Fort Olisy, 26-889. In 1985 the rates are 175 Bfr if you are over 18, 150 if you are under. Youth Hostel card is required, it's sold on the premises for 660 Bfr.). . . . "We found a wonderful place, **Hotel Delta,** 76 Rue Ad. Fischer, phone 48-02-79; owners speak English and are very friendly. A single room without a shower is 900 Belgian Francs, with shower 1,200. Doubles are 1,300 without, 1,600 with shower, all rates including breakfast. Rooms are beautiful and clean, and if you go, don't forget to look up, the ceilings are a sight" (Malena Didenko, New York City). . . . "For slightly over $3, I had a one-day Luxembourg rail pass. I took a one hour ride to Clervaux, stayed there for two hours hiking around the scenic town, returned to Kautenbach briefly and took the waiting train to Wiltz for three hours in the uptown-downtown town, and then returned to Luxembourg City about 5:30 p.m. I liked the Hostel in Luxembourg City and stayed there at the beginning and end of the trip. From the airport, bus #9 goes near the hostel on its way to the old area and then on to the station, 20 francs per person and 20 more for luggage. The airport bus is more expensive. The Hostel serves a great supper for 120 francs, with second helpings on some dishes. They also pack a lunch if requested" (Pat Diehnelt, Ashippun, Wisconsin).

MONACO

"I discovered the **Hotel de la Poste,** 5 Rue des Oliviers (phone 30-70-56), only two blocks from all the action and the Hotel de Paris, and convenient to the Old Beach Club and other beaches. At the height of the season M. and Mme. Ernest Heidl, the proprietors, gave me a single room with a view of the sea, breakfast included, for 90 francs a day (doubles are 125 francs, all included)" (Barron Polan, New York, New York). . . . "I can suggest the **Hotel Helvetia,** at 1 bis Rue Grimaldi (phone 30-21-71), at the head of Rue Princess Caroline, and only one block from the railroad station, maybe one and one-half blocks. In late July we walked in there at 9 p.m., with no reservations, and found a room for three, with a private bath (and bath tub) and balcony for 325 francs ($40.62), including three breakfasts. There is an elevator, and breakfast is served in a large, pleasant room overlooking Rue Princesse Caroline and the sea at the foot of the hill. This is a good thing, especially in the heavy season of an expensive area" (Zollene Bennett, La Jolla, California). . . . **"Hotel de France,** near the Station at 6 Rue de la Turbie (phone 30-24-64), charges only 105 francs for bathless doubles, 85 francs for singles. Students receive a considerable reduction, plus free showers" (Kathy Pasmantier, West Orange, New Jersey). . . . "If you find yourself in Monaco at lunch time, and can't find a budget restaurant, may I suggest that you go to the market, which is inside a large hall at the bottom of the road that goes up to the Palace and expensive Oceanographic Museum. Here you can buy milk, wine, fruits, vegetables, bread, meat, pizza, cheese, etc., which you can then take up the hill, and sit on one of the benches in the little parks on the cliffs (on each side of the museum) and have lunch while looking down at the Mediterranean" (David McCaughna, Northants, England).

MOROCCO

"Considering the current popularity of travel in Spain, you should tell your readers to take a side trip into Morocco. Tangier is only a half-hour by jet from Málaga, or a delightful 2½-hour steamer crossing from Gibraltar or Algeciras. We found this trip to be one of the most exciting aspects of our journey, what with all the veiled women, robed Bedouins, camels, mosques, Arab tea houses, snake charmers, etc. Morocco might be on the African continent but you *ought* to give it a mention. It's out of this world" (Mrs. L. Lauler, Los Altos, California; for specific recommendations, see under "Tangier," below).

Tangier

"Anyone visiting the Iberian peninsula should make it a point to cross over to Tangier, so close to Europe, and yet an entirely different world. Tangier is 2½ hours from Algeciras, Spain, via boat. Tourist class fares are 1,800 pesetas one way, 2,400 pesetas first class. Fares to the Spanish port of Ceuta, on the coast of Morocco, are only 900 pesetas tourist class, 1,300 pesetas first class. . . . I had a clean and comfortable room with private shower at the **Mamora Hotel,** 19 Rue des Postes (phone 341-05), located just inside the old section of town; a double with bath was 80 dirhams. We had dinner at the posh **Marhaba Palace** restaurant, Porte de la Casbah, where a native orchestra and dancers entertained us throughout a five-course dinner that featured couscous and included wine. But several other spots around here are genuine clip joints, with very sexy but also very thirsty B-girls. Tangier is teeming with all manner of con men, money changers, pimps, junk peddlers, etc.; especially to be avoided are the ones who call themselves 'Charlie'" (Henry S. Sloan, New York, New York; note: current exchange rate is about 7.60 dirhams to the dollar; further note from AF: owner of the Hotel Mamora has promised readers of this book who display a copy of 10% discount on the above prices. Arriving in Tangier by boat, train or bus, steer clear of the many unofficial self-appointed guides seeking to recommend shady hotels or pensions. The official guides, whom you can trust, wear an oval metal badge bearing a government registration number). . . . "You can go from Algeciras to Tangier via **Cia Transmediterranea** (office about one block from the dock) for about 1,800 pesetas each way. Don't miss seeing **The Casbah,** but several friends living in Tangier tell me you can really get better buys in the European quarters of the city; they added that if you really feel obliged to buy in the Casbah, ask for recommendations. And by all means try mint tea in a native restaurant. In the evening, go to the Petit Socco and sit at a cafe; it's in the Casbah, but perfectly safe and reeks of atmosphere" (Elaine Mura, Clifton, New Jersey). . . . "Tangier remains the biggest bargain resort in the Mediterranean, especially for those who want to give the appearance of living in luxury on very limited means. There are dozens and dozens of low-priced hotels in the Medina, and even in the town itself, but my recommendation is the **Hotel Mamora,** 19 Rue des Postes (phone 341-05). In 1985, the daily charge for a room with a big double bed is 80 dirhams ($10.52), a single 55 dirhams ($7.23). The place is perfectly clean, decent and respectable" (Hanns Ebensten, London, England). . . . "For travelers going to Tangier, we suggest leaving from Algeciras, just across the bay from Gibraltar. The price is almost half of that from the British port. Tangier is another world, completely different from Europe, and anyone who gets this far south should not miss it. Moroccan leather is unbeatable and dirt cheap, although it takes an expert bargainer to get the good buys. By this time, we qualified, and we filled our suitcases with leather goods" (Barry Saunders, Victoria, Canada). . . . "I ended up at a pleasant little hotel, also close to the dock: **Pension Tantan** (33 Rue de Poste—Petit Socco—tel. 326-41), where I had a very pleasant room under the roof with a nice view of the harbour and lots of sun for about $5. There were a great many young people there as well. It is run by a very pleasant young man, who doesn't speak English (only French and Arabic) but his friendliness makes up for it" (Charles Reynolds, London, England).

THE NETHERLANDS

Haarlem
"Haarlem, only 15 minutes from Amsterdam by train, is also much less expensive, as the city tourist office there is using private homes to take care of tourists. We were fortunate to be given the home of **Mr. and Mrs. J. Brands,** Santpoorterplein 12, tel. 023-26-13-78. The price was 28 guilders ($9.33) per person, including a huge breakfast" (Roger Capps, Portland, Oregon).

The Hague
"For travelers on a rigid budget, let me suggest a student guest house called the **Haus Grüno,** at Sweelinckstraat 49 (phone 63-22-77). We arrived late on an afternoon and were shown an attic room, small yet comfortable, with a gabled window and cots and a sink. The proprietor seemed so elderly that I feared he'd never make it to the top of the stairs and I wouldn't let him tote our bags. But he was a nice, old gentleman, and he included a breakfast in the 29 guilders each he charged us—the lowest rate we paid in Holland. By the bye, The Hague has *two* great collections: don't go only to the **Mauritshuis** in the center of town with its Rembrandts and Vermeers, but be sure to see the **Haags Gemeentemuseum** on the outskirts, with *inter alia,* the greatest Mondrian collection in the world, tracing the development from his post-Impressionist period up to his characteristic later geometric-abstract style" (Richard M. Koffler, Philadelphia, Pennsylvania).

NORWAY

Bergen
"If, by the time you reach Oslo, you crave a respite from a steady diet of European cities, a fantastically beautiful and pleasantly informal mountain-fjord tour

can be had by merely taking the morning train from Oslo to Bergen, the hydrofoil along the Atlantic Coast from Bergen to Stavanger, and the train back again to Oslo. The train rides will bring you through some of the most breathtaking mountain and valley scenery anywhere, including tourist-infested Switzerland, with stops along the log cabins of colorful mountain hamlets. **Bergen** is a city where townsfolk and seamen gather at twilight on the docks to sing hymns. The town and seaport can best be viewed at twilight and sunset from the hill just north of the train station. The train arrives late afternoon and travelers should consult the tourist office three or so blocks east for overnight accommodations. There are morning and afternoon hydrofoils to Stavanger, more commercial than Bergen but thereby a better place to shop for sweaters, souvenirs, and gifts" (Jay Evans, Colorado Springs, Colorado). . . . "We found a pleasant pension owned by **Edel and Sven,** at 11 Blaansvei—135 kroner a double with a very good bathroom with one of the best showers in Europe; phone 311-527" (Peter and Sally Francis, Victoria, Australia). . . . "We recommend a brief excursion (sans guide, of course) from Bergen to Oslo, which will incorporate a representative selection of scenic grandeur, and yet take only an extra day out of a busy tourist's schedule. Take the 8 a.m. train out of Bergen to Voss. At Voss, a bus will be waiting for the train, which arrives about 10 a.m. The bus proceeds through scenic mountainous countryside to Vangsnes, a hamlet-sized ferry stop. The bus' arrival is timed to meet the ferry which crosses the Sognefjord at that point in 35 minutes. Get off at the next port-of-call, which is a small village called Balestrand, where you overnight. Before leaving in the morning, a walk to a 900-year-old Stave church provides a good diversion from the natural beauties which abound. At 10 a.m., a boat leaves from the dock in front of the hotel for a 4-hour cruise on the Sognefjord to Flam. This is probably the most magnificent cruise in the world, passing through high-walled and majestic fjord after fjord. The mail boat's last stop (cost: 45 kroner per person) was Flam, the terminal stop of the Flam-Myrdal spur line. The electric railway winds its way through and up the mountainside past hundreds of waterfalls of all sizes, lazy valleys and jagged peaks. At Myrdal, the electric train arrives just in time to meet the express to Oslo" (Mr. and Mrs. Richard D. Greenfield, Lynbrook, New York).

SCOTLAND

Isle of Arran

"Please find space for inclusion of the **Allandale Guest House,** Brodick Pier, Isle of Arran (telephone Brodick 2278). Mr. and Mrs. Small took a personal interest in all the guests who stayed there, and during the summer months, took them tramping. For £16 one got dinner, bed and breakfast, with your own bathroom, shower, TV and toilet. Tea, coffee, sugar and milk were at your disposal day and night (hot-water-machine stood in the hallway), and one helped oneself to coffee, etc. . . . The evening meal is a 3-courser, with coffee taken in the lounge, while for breakfast we had fruit juice, hot cereal, bacon and eggs, loads of toast, and the choice of tea or coffee" (Lecia Katherine Boyd and Robert Terrell Price, Waikeria, Teawamutu, New Zealand; note from AF: Arran is for active and adventurous sorts, who don't mind walking up and down for miles).

Edinburgh

This is the capital of Scotland, the home of Robert Burns and Robert Louis Stevenson, and one of the most beautiful cities on earth, boasting a breathtaking boulevard—Princess Street, with its famous Princess Gardens. Prices increase during the first two weeks of the Edinburgh Music and Drama Festival—in 1985 from late August to mid-September—but are quite reasonable at all other times. Even during the Festival period, however, young women arriving in Edinburgh may find accommodations by going to the office of the Edinburgh Central Council of the

YWCA, 7 Randolph Place (phone 225-4379), where there's a booking desk and an inexpensive coffee house, open weekdays, 9:30 a.m. to 5, on Saturdays until 1 p.m.

Older readers and couples will want to try the normal bed-and-breakfast houses, whose reader recommendations now follow: "We have been meaning to strongly recommend the **Clifton Hotel,** at 18 Hopetown Crescent (off MacDonald Road), which has a charming owner, an amusing Victorian decor, and charges £8.50 per person for bed and breakfast. Telephone number 556-1180" (Lynn & Sandy Comesky, Palo Alto, California; numerous recommendations for the Clifton from other readers as well). . . . "We stayed at **St. Valery Guest House,** 36 Coates Gardens (phone 337-1893), operated by Mr. and Mrs. R. Shannon. They are just charming, and truthfully, we have never seen a more spotless home—it just shines! Here, for a lovely room overlooking several pretty backyards, plus a huge and beautifully served breakfast, we paid just £8 per person per night. We give this the highest recommendation" (Mrs. Robert Wade Hughey, Lafayette, California). . . . "My find in Europe was the **Rosehall Hotel,** 101 Dalkeith Road in the Newington section of Edinburgh (phone 667-5952). Spotlessly clean, convenient and inexpensive for Edinburgh (£13 per person in either single or twin bedded rooms, breakfast and service included); the biggest surprise of all was the breakfast, one of the best I have ever had in my whole life; it must be seen to be believed. Ron and Ray Michel are the cordial hosts" (Michael Hirsch, Albany, New York; note by A.F.: numerous seconding recommendations for the Rosehall Hotel from other readers). . . . "My husband and I would like to recommend the **Kiloran Guest House,** 17 Leamington Terrace, phone 229-1789, run by John and Gina Haldane in Edinburgh. This delightful couple went out of their way to make us feel at home. They gave us tea after we came from the show and a delicious breakfast in the morning. I'll sum up our stay at Kiloran Guest House by using Mrs. Haldane's own words: 'Even though you are staying for one night, that doesn't mean that I have to treat you like strangers.' Bed and breakfast for one was only £7" (Mr. and Mrs. W.F. Payne, CFPO, C.A.F.E.). . . . "For a comfortable stay in Edinburgh, I'd recommend Mrs. Milne's guest house, **Arlington,** 11 Eyre Place. For £8.50 per person we had an excellent twin bed room with hot and cold water and a breakfast you should see to believe. Juice or grapefruit segments, cereals or two eggs and bacon or sausage, milk, coffee, butter, jam, etc., served on tables laid with pure linen and china. Flowers on every table. The lady is most helpful and the service impeccable. A good find" (Efi Vicka, Athens, Greece). . . . "I would be much obliged if you would list my **Gifford Guest House,** at 103 Dalkeith Road (phone 667-4688). The price is from £7.50 per person per night, including breakfast" (H. M. Bride, Edinburgh). . . . "I paid 8 pounds per night for a very comfortable room, with full English breakfast, at **Kariba Guest House,** 10 Granville Terrace, phone 229-37-73. Its owner, Mrs. Dorothy Walls, is warm and friendly and the house is quite tastefully furnished and decorated. Some rooms have private showers. Each room has a black-and-white TV set, and there is a color TV in the lounge. I strongly recommend this lodging to anybody visiting Edinburgh" (Val Lloyd, Parkville, Victoria, Australia). . . . "I recommend **Boxers Restaurant,** 18 Hower Street, phone 225-72-25, an 8 minute walk from Princes Street. From Princes Street, walk up Frederick Street, cross over George Street and Queen Street, and Boxers is another 2 blocks further down on the left. You can eat really well at lunch time for less than $5. For example, quiche for $1.50, hot savouries $2.30, salads all 60 cents, smoked mackerel $1.75. And everything is made fresh daily on the premises. Opening hours are Monday to Saturday from 11 a.m. to 6 p.m., closed Sunday" (Alexander Cox, Tokyo, Japan).

Glasgow

"At **Mrs. Mary Auld's Guesthouse,** 8 Belgrave Terrace (phone 339-8668), the rate is very reasonable—about £8 per person, for clean and comfortable rooms, and Mrs. Auld does a wonderful job of making everyone feel at home. She served a good breakfast and every evening had a big pot of tea and refreshments set out" (R.N. Palmer, Vancouver, British Columbia). . . . "Glasgow is probably the most overlooked and underrated tourist center in Britain. It may not be the most beautiful city in the world, but it has many outstanding attractions, including the Kelvingrove Art Gallery, the Pollock House, and the Museum of Transport. Nearly all the city's museums offer free admission—not the least of Glasgow's attractions for the budget traveller" (John Warrick, Dardanelle, Arkansas). . . . "We have only a 2-bedroom here in Glasgow, at 11 Balmoral Drive, Bearsden, but would be delighted to have guests, for which the charge would be only £8 for the double, per person, with breakfast" (**The Cowans,** 11 Balmoral Drive, Bearsden, Glasgow)

Inverness

"If you're in the mood to do a bit of exhilarating hiking and enjoy some of Scotland's most spectacular scenery, then take a bus from Inverness to Fort Augustus and Loch Ness (yes, home of the fabled 'beastie'). From there you can 'head for the hills.' Good hiking paths" (Carma Bamber, San Francisco, California). . . . "An unbelievable guesthouse is **Leinster Lodge** at 27 Southside Road (phone 233-311), where the rooms are large and beautiful, the proprietress (Mrs. Sime) friendly and helpful, and the charge (including the usual delicious breakfast) is £8 per person" (Fred Baskind, New York, New York). . . . "My recommendation is **MacDonald House Hotel** (phone Inverness 32878), at 1 Ardoss Terrace, on the West bank of the River Ness across the way from the castle. For £7.50 per person, the proprietress, Mrs. J.K. Allan, provides clean, spacious rooms (most of them with individual color TV sets), plenty of hot water (a rarity in budget Britain), and a cosy television lounge in which tea and biscuits are served before bedtime, and a hearty breakfast (bacon, sausage and eggs, etc.) in the morning. The house is fully carpeted with tartan runners and is quite charming" (Norman Rosenthal, Johannesburg, South Africa). . . . "Stayed at a delightful little hotel, **The Crown Hotel,** 19 Ardconnel Street, phone 231-135, just moments from the station. £8.50 gets you a single room and full English breakfast, prepared with lots of T.L.C. by proprietress Mrs. M. McLeod. The whole place was immaculate, clean, freshly painted (1981), modern. One of the nicest, if not the nicest, places I've stayed" (Scott Fisher, Washington, D.C.). . . . "Inverness is not to be missed, as it is near Loch Ness and has a fantastic Scottish review six nights a week called 'The Kilt is Our Delight', complete with pipes, dancers and all the trimmings" (Connie Nelsen, Tacoma, Washington). . . . "In 1984 I traveled to Inverness and came across a bed-and-breakfast lodging so far overlooked in your book. It's within walking distance of the railroad station, and owned by a most delightful hostess, **Mrs. K. MacKenzie.** The address is Lochewe, 5 Abertarff Road, and it cost us 7 pounds per person. The breakfast includes porridge, if requested" (Mrs. Ann E. Childers, Houston, Texas). . . . "While in Inverness, anyone would be foolish not to spend a day on **Gordon's Mini Bus.** It was 6 pounds for students, £7.50 for adults for the whole day, including morning coffee and a lunch of sausage rolls and haggis. Although the tours always include Loch Ness (Nessie comes along in the bus and poses for pictures), Gordon gears the rest of the day to the interests, age, and footwear of his customers. We went for a magnificent hike in the hills above Loch Ness, with historical tales of Bonnie Prince Charlie and Robbie Burns poetry. Other days may include Culloden, Cawdor, a distillery, or a highland cattle auction. Gordon has a way about him that guarantees you a dozen new friends from all over the world at the end of the day. Because the size of the tour is limited to 12, one would be wise to book ahead, either at the Tourist Office, or by contacting Dr Gordon Williamson, Heather Cottage, Kessock, Inverness, phone 046373 (Kessock) 202" (Jamie Newland, Leamington, Ontario, Canada).

SPAIN

Barcelona

SPLURGE-PRICED HOTELS: "At the beautiful modern **Hotel Gaudi,** Conde de Asalto, 12, tel: 232-57-06, we paid 3,700 pesetas for twin bed room #520 with bath and balcony, tax and service included. Lift, English spoken" (Mr. and Mrs. Anthony

Yourevich, San Francisco, California; note from A.F: owner José Mestres Blanch has offered a 10% discount off these rates to readers.)

BUDGET HOTELS: "We went to the desk of the **Hotel Internacional,** 78 Ramblas (on the corner of Boqueria and the Ramblas, phone 302-2566) and found that we could have a double with complete bathroom with balcony overlooking the Ramblas for 3,100 pesetas ($20.66). Location was perfect, only several blocks from the Plaza de Cataluna, with the bustling Ramblas to walk up and down just outside our hotel door" (Raoul and Linda Weinstein, St. Thomas, Virgin Islands).

STARVATION BUDGET PENSIONS: "While working in Barcelona this past year, I've been living at **Hostal Residencia Lesseps,** Mayor de Gracia 239 (tel: 218-4434). Recently opened, it charges 500 pesetas ($3.33) per person in a double room, 750 pesetas ($5) for a single. The rooms are well-lighted, modernly furnished, and quite comfortable. Breakfast is the only meal given, costing 150 pesetas (coffee and croissant); cold baths and showers are free, but hot ones will cost another 125 pesetas. Only Spanish is spoken, but the management is a pleasure to deal with, in any case. Calle Mayor de Gracia is quite centrally located, as it is merely a continuation of Paseo de Gracia on the other side of Avenida Diagonal" (Roberta Carr, Barcelona, Spain; note by A.F.: numerous other letters from readers, all enthusiastic; some claim English *is* spoken). . . . **"Pension Lepanto** (302-0081), 10 Raurich off Calle Fernando (near the Ramblas), charges only 950 pts. for a single with a double bed, 1,300 pts. for a double room with a single and a double bed. Cold water sink. Exceedingly comfortable, a great place to congratulate yourself on living so cheaply after Copenhagen. Breakfast is 150 pts., and a bath is 150 pts. extra" (Alan C. Feuer, Oak Park, Michigan). . . . **"Pension Pintor,** 25 Calle Gignas, in Barcelona, phone 315-47-08, is a lovely place on the fringe of the Gothic quarter. Its prices were extraordinary: only 1,250 pesetas for a double without breakfast, with free hot showers included. The owner and his wife speak German and French so we communicated in a combination of both. The pension has our recommendation for its cleanliness, friendliness and convenient location to most of the wonderful sights" (Karen L. Gregory, Seattle, Washington).

RESTAURANTS: "Our prize find of our whole trip was a tiny, knotty-pine-paneled restaurant in the old quarter of Barcelona. They have—believe it or not—a 280 pesetas ($1.86) menu, an alternate 360 pesetas ($2.40) feast. Our meal (very well prepared): vegetable soup, then a tremendous platter of vermicelli (thread-like noodles) and spaghetti in a delicious meat and tomato sauce, then breaded veal cutlet and green beans, a green tossed salad, bread, and a banana for dessert. We forked over a total of 550 pesetas, or ($3.66) each, plus service. Where is this find? It's the **Restaurante Casa José,** 10 Plaza San José Oriol, which is 2-3 blocks off the Ramblas, and hidden just behind a large Cathedral which dominates the Plaza. Closed Saturdays" (Jess and Alice Brewis, Taylor, Michigan; note from AF: Casa José is highly recommendable. Its owner, Señor Jesus Ruiz, does everything imaginable to please readers of this book. Ask for the typewritten, English-language menu). . . . **"Los Torreros,** 408 Avenida José Antonio Primo de Rivera, two blocks from the Plaza de España, serves excellent cubiertos for 300 and 380 pesetas—three courses and wine. Only open for lunch. The food was the best we had in Barcelona and we went back several times" (James Welch, New Orleans, Louisiana). . . . "We visited the new **Picasso Museum** (open 9 to 1:45 and 4 to 8:30) which is on Calle Montcada 15, off Calle de Fernando (which is one block north of the Plaza Real)." (Mrs. Lee Weisman, Los Angeles, California). . . . "Barcelona is a special treat in food, ambience and price. The word for Barcelona's restaurants from kitchen staff to waiters is *pride.* Most of the meals I had were generous, tasty and artistically assembled on the platter. One terrific restaurant is **La Taverna,** just off the Ramblas, at 10 Calle de Escudellers. Order the 'plata del dia' at 320 pesetas. Ours consisted of half a baked chicken, fried potatoes, fresh tomatoes, bread, vino de la casa, dessert (fresh fruit salad) and coffee. Another good restaurant is the **Cosmos,** corner Ramblas and Calle de Escudellers. Its dining room overlooks the Ramblas (the colorful main shopping, strolling and meeting street, very active day and night). It's clean, modern and has a menu card in four languages. I would recommend *butifanna,* a typical Spanish sausage served with white beans and bread, 165 to 280 pesetas; it's traditional, tasty and filling. While in Barcelona treat yourself to a bottle of Ventura, an excellent domestic brandy for a mere 200 pesetas per bottle. And walk to the end of the Ramblas at the foot of the Christopher Columbus monument and board the two-decker boat for a trip to the harbour lighthouse and back, only 50 pesetas. It provides a great view of this important port. With a replica of the *Santa Maria* tied up near the port authority building, you can imagine a scene not too different from the day Columbus sailed for America" (J.R. McNalis, Orlando, Florida).

SIGHTSEEING, NIGHTSPOTS AND TRIPS: "The **'Pueblo Español'** was built in Barcelona as part of an international exposition in the twenties, and is a fascinating Spanish 'village' where every house is in the style of a different region of the country. Craftsmen make and sell all sorts of articles in the houses, and the prices are quite reasonable. We even got a copy of a medieval saint's statue for $6 after having seen the same thing in town for $9" (Mrs. Thomas E. Carnell, Trotwood, Ohio). . . . "Fifty cents will buy you a view of the most fantastic architectural sight in all Europe: the Cathedral of the Sacred Family, the masterpiece of the Barcelona architect Gaudi, not to be missed" (Mr. & Mrs. Loring Eutemey, New York, New York). . . . "Head for **Montjuich Park,** for the best of Barcelona. To get there, take bus #8 from the Plaza de España. The fare is 50 pesetas, or 33¢. First, there is Pueblo Español (Spanish Village) from 9 a.m. on, where you see typical Spanish towns. The price is 80¢ for admission. But the very best of all—and it is free—is a fabulous water play and illumination display of the famous fountains of Montjuich Park on Saturday and Sunday evenings from 10 p.m. to 12 p.m. This is not to be missed" (C. Fieldman, Bronx, New York). . . . "Take the electric Catalana RR to **Montserrat,** that spectacular sawtoothed mountain an hour and a half by train from Barcelona. The 900 peseta round trip includes thrilling four-minute aerial tram rides to and from the monastery built upon the high sides of this mountain. Plan to go there in time for the 1:00 p.m. music by the Montserrat Escolania boys choir. Food may be purchased at the self-service restaurant, and splurgers may wish to stay overnight at the Hostal Abat Cisneros (2 persons, max. price 3,100 pesetas for overnight. Breakfast 400 pesetas). There are funicular rides and posted walking trips providing panoramic view. The RR trip costs a fraction of the conducted tour price" (Faith C. Callihan, Caldwell, Idaho). . . . "Even if Barcelona were covered only as a jumping-off point to Mallorca, it would be deserved. Boats leave every night but Sunday at 10 p.m. for the eight-hour trip. The cost 3rd class (four to a cabin) is approximately 2,100 pesetas each way, 2nd class is 2,400 pesetas" (Bill Slagle, Montlake Terrace, Washington). . . . "To get to Palma by boat, turn left out of Francia Station, walk down to Via Leyatana, and a boat company is just down on the right. During summer months, get there early to insure a seat on the deck. During nice weather, most everyone travels deck class" (Barry Glen, Cedarhurst, New York).

SHOPPING: "My wife is a real guitar fan and found a small 'Fabrica de Guitarras' called **Los Flamencos** at San Pablo 28 (just off the Ramblas), half a block from Plaza San Agustin, where she had all manner of beautifully hand-made guitars to choose from. She got one of the lighter models for 5,000 pesetas ($33)" (Steven Otto, Apapa, Nigeria).

Costa Brava (not a city, but the stretch of seashore along the Mediterranean, where Spain joins France)

"We'd like to recommend the **Hotel Diana** (phone 34-03-04) in Tossa de Mar (the most beautiful town on the Costa Brava in Spain). This is a renovated villa right on the beach; we paid 3,500 pesetas ($23.33) apiece for all three meals, and a beautiful double room with private modern bath and balcony" (Arnold Friedman, Flushing, New York; seconding recommendation from Rochelle Seiden, Brooklyn, New York). . . . "I realize that there are many real bargains along this beautiful stretch, but I hardly think the **Cap d'Or** (phone 340081), at 14 Apartado in Tossa de Mar, can be surpassed. Family-run, good food, directly on the Mediterranean, all for 3,260 pesetas ($21.73) single, 3,160 pesetas ($21.06) per person double (full pension). Clientele mostly British and French" (Dr. James T. Vail, Jr., A.P.O., New York). . . . "We spent three weeks at the **Hotel Casa Delgado,** 7 Pola (phone

34-02-91), Tossa de Mar/Gerona, Spain, and we recommend it highly. A single with shower is 850 pesetas; double with shower 1,300 pesetas per person; double with bath 1,900 pesetas per person, all including breakfast. It's just a few steps from the door to a beautiful beach, and that is free" (Muriel Pierce, St. Petersburg, Florida, with recent seconding recommendations from other readers as well). . . . "One block away from the Cap d'Or, up a picturesque little street, at 13 Pont Vell, we found **Hostal Maria-Rosa,** phone 340-285. Mama Maria is the owner, assisted by daughter Rosa, who speaks English. Rooms were clean and pleasant; meals were excellent; and 1985 rates are 750 pesetas ($5) single, 1300 ($8.66) double, 200 ($1.33) breakfast, and 300 ($2) per lunch or supper" (George P. Jullion, Mukilteo, Washington).

Granada

"At the **Hostal California,** Cuesta de Gomerey 37 (phone 22-40-56), I had a beautifully clean and spacious double room with bath for only 1,600 pesetas. Meals are also very cheap and very fine food, and, oh, so filling! The owner, Sr. Miguel Quijada, is a wonderful host. I do hope you will include this amazing hotel in your book, so that others can enjoy a very warm and pleasant few days at what must be the very best value in town" (Philip Wolanski, Sydney, Australia). . . . "I wish to share with you and your readers the greatest bargain in restaurants I found in Europe (1984) this time: **Restaurant Bar Leon,** 4 Calle Pau, downtown, near Plaza Nueva, on the first floor. It offers the following 'Menu de Dia' for 380 pesetas: 'gazpacho o ensalada del tiempo, ternera estofada o calamares, com patatas o ensalada, pano, vino y fruta.' Unbelievably delicious, filling, inexpensive. I ate there three times" (Françisco De Sousa, Rio de Janeiro, Brazil). . . . "Perhaps the most pleasant budget hotel I ever found is the **Hostal Ganivet,** 5 Calle Angel Ganivet, Granada, on the second floor. My single room was beautiful! Heavy Spanish oak furniture, even an armoire with full-length mirror, marble floors, an easy chair, all this for only 850 pesetas per night, or 650 per person in a double. Showers and breakfast are 130 pesetas extra. There was plenty of hot water, immaculate bathrooms. I also found a wonderful cafeteria in Granada, **Kardonah,** on Plaza de la Trinidad: pleasant decor, counter or booths, where I had soup, salad, the biggest breaded pork chop I've ever seen, potatoes, flan and beer, all for only 375 pesetas. Truly a find!" (Stuart Brooks, New York, NY).

Ibiza, Balearic Islands

"My choice is the **Hostal Mar Blau,** Apartado 127, Los Molinos (phone 301284), where my single room and three meals came to 2,400 pesetas ($16) per day; it is perched atop a hill overlooking the sea, is very clean, features good food served by the friendly owners, and is located so that one can swim off the nearby rocks" (Marilyn Ramey, London, England). . . . "This is paradise—a lovely, pine-wooded island edged with beaches, where a double room with a view of the Mediterranean and a private swimming pool lined with flowering oleander trees cost me only $10 a day. When you finally climb out of the pool, just clap your hands and a waiter will appear with a small bottle of iced champagne. This will cost you the staggering sum of $3. There is absolutely nothing to do in this tiny fishing village except swim, fish, relax, read, write, and eat the best seafood east of Maine. Warning to all dieters: don't come here; we all put on so much weight that we can't get into our clothes and have to run around in muumuus" (Ruth Ivor, Siena, Italy). . . . "From Valencia I took a night boat to Ibiza. My ticket cost 1,000 pesetas ($6.66) third class. I strongly recommend that whenever anyone takes a boat to one of the Balearic Islands during the summer months, they buy only a third class ticket. There is first and second as well as third class, but they are all unbearably hot and stuffy and by morning everyone has thrown pretense overboard and is asleep on the decks. And sleeping under the warm Mediterranean skies is an experience that shouldn't be missed! In Ibiza I have stayed at a new hotel '**Hotel Internacional,**' Apartado 351, Jesus, Ibiza (phone 30-24-92), in a double room (with bath and breakfast) for 3,000 pesetas ($20) a night. The very helpful owner is Hans Anink" (Gloria A. Boyd, Brookline,

Massachusetts; note from AF: the night boat from Valencia to Ibiza leaves Mondays and Fridays at midnight, arrives Ibiza at 8 a.m., tickets range from 1,000 to 2,200 pesetas, depending on class of accommodation).

Málaga

"Málaga is a pleasant city (pop. 300,000) with an atmosphere of quiet gaity, on the South Coast. Although it is quite a tourist attraction, it is not dominated nor ruined by the tourist, as I understand nearby Torremolinos has been. I stayed in the **Hostal Andalucia,** Alarcón Luján 8 (phone 211-960), just a few steps from the Plaza Queipo de Llano, the main Plaza, and I recommend it highly. Singles are 900 pesetas, double 1,600" (Robert M. Stanton, Madison, Wisconsin).

Mallorca (Balearic Islands)

"If one wants sheer pleasure rather than just another inexpensive place to stay, try the **Juan Bernadell** (Calle San Elias No. 11, 20, Palma, tel: 215867). A private house, not a hotel, this place has wonderful food, good rooms with large sunny balconies and views, and very personable, friendly owners. Juan, who speaks English very well, offers rapid Spanish courses, and his wife serves the best food in Mallorca. Rooms at $18 a day, rooms and full board $28" (D.E. Kone, Oakland, California). . . . "Getting off the boat in Mallorca, one should cross the bridge in front of the building, and take the bus to **Plaza Gomilla,** where any hotel should not cost more than $15 a day per person. There are tourists galore there, but never mind. I took the bus to Illetas Beach, which wasn't crowded at all, and in a nice cove" (Barry Glen, Cedarhurst, New York). . . . "**Hostal Versalles,** 27 Rafaletas, Porto-Pi, Mallorca (phone 400-311), was the delight of our three-week stay in Mallorca. Away from the busy Palma, but near the beaches and town activities, we enjoyed the best of both worlds. A 'football' game on television, a drink at the bar, or a swim in the pool, could occupy a cloudy day. For a double room with bath (in October) and full pension we paid only 2,500 pesetas. The personnel were friendly and many spoke English" (L. Kern, Kingston, Ont., Canada). . . . "Palma Nova, a beautiful beach, can be reached by taking a #25 bus for 50 pesetas; it's too far to walk. Rent a Vespa for $12 to see the island; I rented one and drove to Playa Formentor, a lovely beach about an hour and a half from Palma and worth the trip, especially since you see quite a bit along the way. Stay on the left side of the island, which is prettier, and wander over to the Victoria Hotel after 10 any night if you're looking for company" (Elaine Mura, Clifton, New Jersey).

Seville

"Please tell your readers that anyone who misses Spain, misses Europe. And anyone who misses Seville, misses Spain. While Madrid is big and bustling, it does not hold the country's top attractions as do Paris in France and Rome in Italy. After the Prado in Madrid, turn South. The traveler must visit Andalusia for the real Spain. Seville is the 'Florence of Spain,' having a wealth of the nation's finest art and architecture. The Sevillians are dignified as are all Spaniards, but they seem to have even a further refinement, as do the Florentines over their countrymen" (Ray F. Allen, Upper Nyack, New York). . . . "Fantastic, fantastic find for true Spanish flavor, yet modern conveniences; **Hotel Murillo,** 9, Calle Lope de Rueda (phone 21-60-95), 3,000 pesetas ($20) for a double with private bath. Breakfast is included; it's served in the hotel lobby which is filled with old Spanish relics and is charming and lovely. This hotel is in the Santa Cruz district of old, narrow streets. A perfect place to imbibe the spirit of old and glorious Spain" (Judy Ellison, Syracuse, New York, and Jane Glaubinger, Mt. Vernon, New York). . . . "The **Hotel Lyon,** on Vidrio #17, charges 2,100 pesetas single, 2,800 pesetas double, including breakfast and one other meal. I had a charming room, with beautiful massive furniture and private bath. Walking distance to the center of Seville, i.e., the Alcazar, Giralda, etc." (Teresa de la Barrera, La Jolla, California). . . . "In Spain, the **Hostal Atenas** in Seville (Calle Caballerizas 1; telephone 21-80-47) was our greatest find, even though to get there we did exactly what we were told *not* to do—we listened to a wizened little man who accosted us at the railroad station. The rate for two persons, breakfast included, but for a bathless room, was 1,600 pesetas ($10.66). The atmosphere was great—tiles, interior patio and greenery, and 'family' more than 'staff.' The food was excellent, and we were given numerous choices. English is understood but little; however, we observed one visitor being led smilingly to the kitchen to point to what he wanted, and he returned a witness to a clean kitchen. . . . Seville is a delight, with its horsedrawn carriages; its ancient Santa Cruz district; its beautiful Maria Luisa Park; the Alcázar; the ornate cathedral, third largest in the world and containing the supposed tomb of Columbus; the adjacent Giralda tower, built by the Moors in the 12th century, and from which one can inspect at close view the gargoyles and flying buttresses of the cathedral. For nine cents each, we took a city bus westward to the end of the line at Santiponce (not Aljarafe, as claimed by the Ministerio de Información y Turismo folder on Seville), and walked about a block to the ruins of the Roman city of Itálica, birthplace of the emperors Hadrian and Trajan. Its amphitheater and mosaics are impressive" (Prof. Robert R. Morrison, Collegedale, Tennessee).

Valencia

"There is an entire long block of hotels and hostals on Avd. Neptuno, right on the sea, a 50 pts. bus ride or 240 pts. cab ride from the main train station. We splurged for the last days of our vacation, and stayed at the two-star **Hotel La Marcelina** (phone 371-32-90). Our room, facing the sea, with private shower, was 2,700 pesetas (twin). The hotel was spotlessly clean, and the hosts delightful, a family one of whom spoke excellent English. We looked at a room at the **Hostal La Barraca** at Avd. Neptuno 36 (phone 371-61-11); it was also nice, though smaller, and went for about 2,600 pesetas with shower and breakfast for two people. At least four or five other hostals were in the same block, along with over a dozen restaurants" (Joseph F. O'Donnell, Portsmouth, Virginia).

SWEDEN

Helsingborg

"**Bengt and Anita Rosengren** have at least 2 rooms for rent in a beautiful part of Helsingborg. We paid less than $50 for my family of five, for 2 rooms and breakfast that were super. Their address is Ostra Vallgatan 16, phone 13-21-08. I told them I would tell you about them. They do not speak English" (Jack Hantalman, Fort Collins, Colorado).

Malmö

"The **Hotel Hembygden** is a small and centrally situated hotel where you pay 145 kronor ($18.12) for a single room. It is old but clean. Address: Isak Slaktaregatan 7 (phone 10-49-50), just off Stortorget" (Agenta Palme, Stockholm, Sweden).

SWITZERLAND

Basel

"We think the best bargain hotel in all of Basel is the **Hotel-Hospiz Engelhof** at 1 Stiftsgasse (corner of Nadelberg), phone 25-22-44 (60 to 71 francs for a double room, breakfast included); if it happens to be full, try the **Hotel Rochat** (same rates), half a block away at 23 Petersgraben (phone 25-8140). Both are Christian hospices" (Mr. and Mrs. James Hester, Binningen, Switzerland). . . . "The totally modern **Pension Steinenschanze,** 69 Steinengraben (phone 23-53-53), is the local Y.W.C.A., takes women and men, too, and charges 80 francs ($38.09) for a double room, 50 francs in a single" (Jeanne Pasmantier, West Orange, New Jersey; note from AF: readers possessing a valid student card will be charged only 25 francs ($11.90) per person, single or double, breakfast included, at the Steinenschanze). . . . "Anyone can stay in university housing in Basel for 18-22 francs, with private bath, and bedding all furnished. However, only July through September" (Walter and Josephine Magnolia, Lynhook, New York).

"Cheapest in town is the **Youth Hostel (Jugendherberge),** a centrally located, modern building, situated near the Rhine River in the idyllic St. Alban Valley at 10 St. Albankirchrain (phone 23-05-72), with 220 beds priced at 13.50 francs ($6.42) in 6-8 bedded dorms. A cafeteria in the house sells breakfast for 4.50 and dinner for 6.50 francs. You'll need a hostel card, but you can also buy one on the spot for 25 francs ($11.90). From the Central Station (Bahnhof), take streetcar number 2 to Kunstmuseum—third stop—then walk into the second street turning right, for about 200 yards, keep on walking downhill until you reach a small park with a church. You'll find the hostel just behind this park" (Adam Slote, New York City, New York, note from AF: the Basel youth hostel is managed by English-speaking Leo Hetschel, who is eager to have Americans as guests). . . . "Our find in restaurants is the **Schuhmachernzunft** on 6 Hutgasse, a small street between the Basler and EPA stores on the Marktplatz. In this delightful hangout for the Swiss, we've had enormous meals at moderate cost. The food is excellent, the atmosphere unmatched in warmth and hospitality in Basel, and the portions of food unbelievable. There's a menu card in English. Be prepared to share your table with delightful people, from flower peddlers to old gentlemen playing chess. . . . For those people who are taking a quick tour of the city and want a good, cheap, fast, filling meal, one of the two large department stores (the **Rheinbrücke,** at 22 Greifengasse), would be a good choice. Avoid the restaurant area and head for the grocery section to get a variety of meals at a stand-up counter; one can then be content until time for a late European dinner. . . . One should also make it a point to see the Zoo. Admission 6 SF (children pay 2.50 SF). You can spend hours wandering around. I am quite sure I got closer to some animals than any African hunter. They attempt to put all the animals they can in open spaces surrounded by deep moats. Terrific afternoon for less than $4. . . . The **Museum of Fine Arts** (Kunstmuseum) in Basel, closed Mondays, has the best Holbein collection in Europe, plus a very good modern art section and free entrance on Wednesday afternoons from 2 to 5 and weekends" (Mr. & Mrs. James Hester, Binningen, Switzerland). . . . "We ate in a charming little restaurant located near the historic center: **Die Brasserie mit Pfiff,** 35 Falknerstrasse. Reasonable native dinners for 10.50 francs, ($5) and reduced prices on regular meals after 9 p.m. Daily specials are offered. Strictly local atmosphere and typical Swiss decor. Large portions of tasty and attractively prepared food. A winner!" (Jeff Karp and H. Levinson, Montreal, Quebec, Canada).

Berne

Hotel Kreuz, 41 Zeughausgasse (phone 22-11-62), (37 francs per person, single or double, including breakfast, service and taxes) is an excellent choice, and as you have noted in so many other cities, it is a part of the cluster of good reasonable hotels usually found in a central area" (George W. Crowley, Beverly, Massachusetts; note by AF: major per person reductions are available here for persons occupying triple or 4-bedded rooms). . . . "Berne is charming. A Valium for the soul! Kind people, clean and sunny rooms at the **Hotel Zum Goldenen Schlüssel,** Rathausgasse 72, telephone 220-216, near the railroad station and close to the center of town. Double room with breakfast for 72 francs. Good rate for Berne" (Shirley Karpf, Durdas, Ontario, Canada). . . . "We discovered **Marthahaus,** at Wyttenbachstrasse 22a (phone 42-41-35), a clean simple place with a very good continental breakfast. We had a room for four for 92 francs" (Mrs. Carolyn Baker, Fayetteville, Georgia). . . . "Unlike many hostels, the **Youth Hostel** in Berne is not a 40-minute walk from the center of town, but only 10 minutes from the train station. Nor does it require guests to take the standard youth hostel breakfast. 10 francs is the charge for a bed in an 8-person dorm. A youth hostel card is required. Check-in starts at 5 p.m." (Cheryl Johnson, Bowie, Maryland; note from AF: street address is 4 Weihergasse, phone 22-63-16. Total capacity: 260 beds). . . . "I discovered, right in the center of town, an admirable and very cheap restaurant called **Gfeller am Bärenplatz;** right at 21 Bärenplatz (as its name implies—don't confuse it with the Bärengraben) and only about two minutes from the station. On the ground floor, lunch and dinner are listed at 8.60 francs each—2 courses, service included; that's $4.09. But I preferred to eat upstairs, where from 11 to 3 and from 6 to 8 (including Sundays) there is a self-service, offering a wide choice, and with the great advantage (especially for foreigners) that you can see exactly what you are getting. Roomy, comfortable, spotlessly clean, good food. . . . There is another place in Berne for quick lunches: upstairs in the **EPA** Marktgasse 24. This place is a department store, and so, of course, open only during shopping hours. The Bernese flock into it to get modest-priced meals at a self-service counter." (Charles Wrong, Providence, Rhode Island).

Interlaken

"Outside of expensive Interlaken, on the road from Brienz, numerous 'Zimmer frei' signs announce spacious single rooms without breakfast for $10 and doubles for $16 in private homes" (Joseph Gibson, Lufkin, Texas). . . . "When we first arrived in Interlaken, we could not find a room for less than $12 a person. Finally, we discovered a wonderful student hostel—a chalet—called **Balmer's Hostel in Matten,** phone 22-19-61. Doubles there are 40 francs ($19.04) per night, but for $7 per person, we slept in one of the four-person dorms, a huge double-decker bed, and received a continental breakfast. This clean, but unluxurious, place has a recreation room with a jukebox, where students of different nations congregate; and there are no curfew hours and no requirements of a youth hostel card. About three blocks away from the hostel is the meadow where Schiller's Pastoral Play, 'William Tell,' is presented in a natural setting (they actually use real houses, horses, etc.). The play is in German, but there is also an English 'libretto.' It's worth seeing for the setting, and seats can be obtained for 8 francs" (Susan Miller, Flushing, New York; note from AF: the 80-bed Balmer's Hostel, operated by the jolly Herr Eric Balmer, is a ten minute walk from the station, permits use of the washing machine for 4 francs, offers space in a 8-bedded dorm for only 11 francs ($5.23) per night, and provides as many cups of hot chocolate as you wish in its continental breakfast. Take bus #5 from the West Station). . . . "I returned to Interlaken West and the **Helvetia Hotel** (at Bahnhofstrasse, phone 228-383) this year and it's just as delightful as it was last year. It is located 1½ blocks from the R.R. station and charges 26 Swiss Francs single, breakfast and service included. The bath is on the first floor of the hotel. The coffee is delicious, the hotel immaculate, the view of the Alps from the bedroom is fabulous and the price is only 26 francs per night single, 44 francs double, including breakfast. Let's hope you pass this information on to your 1985 readers" (Mrs. Leatrice Reid, Ottawa, Ontario). . . . "Four easy blocks from the West Station on a quiet, residential street is the clean and delightful **Hotel Beyeler Garni** run by the Beyeler family at Bernastrasse 37 (phone 22-90-30). All rooms large and airy with hot and cold water and wall-to-wall carpeting. Doubles without bath 23 S.F. per person, doubles with shower 26 S.F. per person, and with complete bath 32 S.F. in winter, with summer rates 5 S.F. more. Breakfast, service and taxes included and English spoken. Open all year. You may even watch Swiss color TV in the breakfast room" (Mr. and Mrs. D. C. Gillette, Lake Placid, Florida). . . . "A true find, stumbled upon during a Christmas visit to Interlaken, is the charming **Swiss Inn** (tel 22-36-26), which is a refurbished Victorian house at 23 General-Guisan-Strasse, a 5-minute walk from the West Station. For 36 francs, I had a beautiful room with antique furniture, lace curtains and featherbed. Breakfast, which is included, is served by the proprietor, Herr Müller, and features homemade bread, if you can believe it. He speaks fluent English" (J.W. Shank, Denver, Colorado, note by AF: 1985 rates at the Inn are 56 to 68 francs for bathless doubles, including breakfast served by Frau Vreny). . . . "We had a beautiful room in the home of **Frau Kammer,** 30 Brienzstrasse (phone 22-67-67), with full use of a kitchen and a free shower, for the equivalent of $7.50 a day per person. Even when the stores were closed (we arrived on New Year's Day), the landlady gave us food. The house has an incredible view of the Jungfrau and is an easy five minutes' walk from town. On leaving, we were asked to please recommend her house to your book. We do so gladly!" (Lee Steppacher, Canton, New York). . . . "While at Interlaken, we stumbled across a genuine family hotel, five minutes' walk from the train station: **Hotel Lötschberg,** General Guisan Strasse (phone 22-25-45), owned and operated by the Hutmacher family. First class comfort in immaculate surroundings, a good breakfast, friendly, pleasant service, all for 54 francs ($25.71) for double room" (L. N. Chanaryk, Manitoba, Canada). . . . "Without doubt my best bargain on a recent holiday in Europe was **Motel Marti,** Brienzstrasse, phone 22-26-02, situated a 12-minute walk from the east station. I stayed in a large, comfortable room with private shower and toilet, breakfast included, all for 36 francs. Had I stayed in a smaller room, without shower and w.c., but with running water, the cost would have been 27 francs. Frau Eggler, the proprietress, is a very charming and helpful lady" (Miss E. Cameron, Salisbury, Zimbabwe).

"My advice is to visit the Ost railroad station (there are 2 stations in town, only 3 minutes apart) and check the pictographs on the wall in the ticket office foyer. There will be at least a dozen 4 x 6 card notices for "zimmers," all self-explanatory, including whether they'll pick you up in a car or not. Our 'expensive' lodgings with the **Ritschard family,** 38 Oberst Boningstrasse, phone 22-52-23, consisted of a double with an overhead shower, refrigerator, range, kitchenette—but no breakfast—at 28 francs per day! Stocking up at the Migros Supermarket, across from the other Interlaken solved our nutritional needs for the length of our 4 day stay. And note that Eurailpasses are accepted on the lake steamers" (Stewart Kovacs, Ypsilanti, Michigan). . . . At the **Alfa Garni,** 7 Bernastrasse, phone 22-69-22, only two minutes from the railroad station, we had an upstairs room with shower and toilet, and grand views of the Swiss mountains. The hotel is operated by two sisters, Hedy Kopp-Scharz and Edith Schaub-Scharz, who put on a good breakfast and charge 64 to 72 francs a night per couple. This may be a little high for some of your readers, but is well justified by atmosphere and amenities" (William Ross, Western Australia). . . . "The **Raclette Tavern** at the Hotel Metropole in Interlaken offered delightful atmosphere and a new eating experience for only 5.50 francs" (Patricia Wilson and Diane Larson, Los Angeles, California). . . . "Readers traveling in the Jungfrau region of the Swiss Alps should stay with the warm, friendly Knöpfli family—**Jack and Christine Knöpfli,** Bella Vista, 3855 Brienz, telephone 036-512213—who live in the beautiful lakeside village of Brienz, across the lake from Interlaken. Our happy stay was inexpensive, only 40 francs per night for a double which included baths and an excellent continental breakfast on their patio overlooking the Brienzersee. And our Eurail ticket held valid also for the ferry service to the Interlaken East Station from which leave the private railways for Murren and the Jungfraujoch" (Keith and Jess Parker, Capetown, South Africa; note from AF: the Knöpflis will fetch you free from the station if you phone them in advance).

Lausanne

"We stayed at the **Hotel Alagare Transit,** 14 Avenue du Simplon (phone 279-252), located on the same block as the railroad station. Our small, but clean and airy, double room cost 60 francs ($28.57) including taxes but not breakfast. The hotel had several dining rooms serving different-priced meals. We ate in the moderately-priced room for about 12 francs ($5.71) each" (Mrs. Bernard Greenberg, Brooklyn, New York). . . . **"Logements des Prés-de-Vidy,** 1007 Lausanne, 36 Chemin du Bois de Vaux (phone 24-24-79), is really a *great* place, with free showers, and is brand new, with a good breakfast, for 19 Sw. francs per person all together; twin-bedded rooms but so many of them that I had mine as a single the whole time. Just a four-minute walk from Lac Leman and it's beautiful and clean. Take Bus #1 at the train station, ask for street address. This place is really fantastic" (Margaret Bratsenis, Branford, Connecticut). . . . "For less than $14 a night, per person, we had a triple room in a charming pension, located 6 minutes' walking distance from the railway station. The address is 11 rue de la Gare, and the name of the establishment is **"The Old Inn"** (Pension des Etudiants), phone 23-62-21 or 23-91-83. Our room was absolutely huge and lavishly furnished, the proprietress charming and most helpful" (Diane Neaven, Montreal, Canada; note from AF: 1985 rates at the Old Inn, for rooms with private shower, are 40 francs ($19.04) single, 65 francs ($30.95) double, 85 francs ($40.47) triple, including breakfast). . . . "In Lausanne, Eurailpasses can be used on the metro" (Diane Larson, Los Angeles, California).

Leysin

"Nestled high in the Alps in Leysin, near Lake Geneva, is the **Club Vagabond** (phone 025-341321), open November through April only. As the name implies, it's a haven for vagabonds and vagabonds-at-heart. The chalet is more of a friendly club than a hotel, and the proprietors, Dave and Johanne Smith (of Canada), take great pains to keep it that way. Atmosphere and attire are refreshingly informal, and accommodations are mostly in rooms bunking two to four persons. The rooms are basic, but spotless, and most have balconies overlooking the grandeur of the Alps. Their rates are fantastic: a double room with breakfast is 22 francs ($10.47) per person; three and four-bedded rooms 19 francs ($9.04) per person. Winter is the ski season, so prices go up then to 28 francs per person for a double room, 24 francs per person in the three- and four-bedded rooms. Here's a real swingin' place with a young international atmosphere" (Jules Klar, New York City; note by A.F.: the Club Vagabond is a five-minute walk from the Leysin-Feyday railway station, highest in the village).

Lucerne

"A true Godsend to us in Lucerne was the self-service restaurant in the **Hotel Krone,** on the Weinmarkt Platz. It is unmarked, and is located on the ground floor, to the left of the entrance. Be careful not to go upstairs to the more traditional restaurant. Soup was only 1.80 francs, a full dinner, complete with soup and salad, was only 8.50 francs ($4.04). A must for all $25-a-Day'ers!" (Nikko and Ron Parry, Inglewood, California). . . . "A fellow passenger gave us the name of **Pension Panorama** at Kapuzinerweg 9 (phone 36-67-01 or 36-22-98), a quiet street on a hill about 10 walking minutes from the Lion monument. It is operated by the delightful Theresa von Euw, a friendly, English speaking (and singing) lady. We paid 28 francs ($13.33) per person for a gorgeous double overlooking Lucerne and the lake. Mrs. von Euw is a superb and funny lady, and her pension definitely deserves to be listed" (Glenn and Deborah Rifkin, Watertown, Massachusetts). . . . "A necessary trip from Lucerne is to the summit of **Mt. Pilatus,** which can be reached by steamer (free to Eurailpass users) to Alpnachstad, from where you use a *train* to get to the top. The train both ways is 28.50 SF or you can take the circular tour (down the other side of the mountain) via exciting cable cars to Kriens for 4 additional Swiss Francs, if you present your first train tickets. From Kriens there is a trolley-bus (one franc, a 15-minute ride) back to Lucerne. Don't miss it! The total cost came to about $18 with lunch at a self-service restaurant on the summit, as opposed to the $25 commercial tour. Readers can save money by going down by train, which is exciting in itself: the steepest gradient in the world—it seemed nearly vertical" (Wendy E. Peppin and Helen Davis, Elmhurst, New York). . . . "A must is a visit to the **Swiss Transport Museum.** Trolley bus no. 2 will take you there from the Bahnhof. The visit should also include seeing the "Kosmorama" and the Longines Planetarium" (Anthony Healy, Crows Nest, Australia). . . . "At the end of May we spent a few days in Lucerne and from there took a wonderful day trip by paddle steamer to Weggis, a charming town full of flowers. Walking to the right from the dock along the lake, away from the expensive restaurants, we came upon **Seerestaurant Buhlegg,** where we enjoyed a delicious lunch at a very moderate price on a deck with a great view of lake and mountains. Then we took the cable car to the Rigi, stopping at Kaltbad, as the summit was in the clouds. Walking down the little road away from the hotels, we soon found ourselves on paths in woods and idyllic Alpine pastures. There were numerous flowers, but the highlight was a meadow of crocus blooming just at the edge of melting snow. The cable car fare was about $10 round trip, but half of that for Eurailpass holders" (Amy Bush, Berkeley, California). . . . "You can purchase excursion tickets for a trip up **Mount Pilatus** that includes a lake steamer from Lucerne to Alpnachstad, the Clog railway (steepest in the world, 45 degrees average slope) up the mountain, then cable car down the opposite side of Pilatus to Frakmuntegg, and from there to Kriens. From Kriens take the trolley back to Lucerne. The entire trip costs 46 francs. One can spend the day on Pilatus, a trip well worth the money" (Philip Schrodt, Skokie, Illinois). . . . "I have been using the Arthur Frommer books for years. In fact before starting to make plans for any trip abroad the first stop is the bookstore for a copy of the appropriate book. However this is the first time I have written to recommend a place I found to be outstanding. Purely by luck my sister and I happened on a small guest house located just five minutes from Lucerne. It's called **Landgasthaus Clarida,** Meggen (phone 37-12-87). What made our stop so outstanding was the food. The first night there we were served dinner on an open patio. The veal dish we chose was superbly prepared and served. The second night we had calf's liver that was absolutely delicious. It seems on any trip there is at least one place that lingers in your memory, but this one is well worth making a five-minute jog in your travels" (Kathleen Rice, Cheshire, Connecticut; note by AF: 1985 rates are 37 francs for rooms without, 42 for rooms with, bath, and meals (lunch or supper) are 13 francs extra). . . . "Visitors to Lucerne should definitely bypass the highly advertised tours to Mt. Pilatus or Rigi and head instead for nearby **Mt. Titlis.** Easily visited in a half-day from Lucerne, Titlis is ascended by a combination of cog-wheel railway and cable cars. At the top one can walk through passages inside the glacier and can ski throughout most of the summer. We even got caught in a snowstorm in July! Desk clerks in any hotel can provide details on the quickest and cheapest ways to reach Titlis. And are you looking for a Swiss music box? Avoid the shops in or near Lucerne's covered bridges and head instead for the larger showrooms on and near Löwenplatz, adjacent to the Lion Monument, these places have identical boxes at 20% to 50% less than those nearer the lake front" (Ronald A. Audet, Portsmouth, Virginia). . . . "If you intend to buy a Swiss watch, go to **Birnbaum's,** 34 Pilatusstrasse, where every member of the staff is a gracious human being, anxious to help you. Keep asking for the cheaper varieties, until they haul out the $25 to $30 trays. Although many other watch shops in Lucerne offer similar values, Birnbaum's kindness is exceptional" (Yetta Reich, New York City). . . . "In Lucerne, we stayed at the **Pension Wirth,** 68 Brukstrasse (phone 22-67-65). Our bathless single room was clean and spacious and cost only 30 francs a night, breakfast included" (Mr. and Mrs. Mark Buckbee, Roseburg, Oregon).

Lugano

"The one reasonably-priced eating place is the **Hotel Pestalozzi** restaurant on Pestalozzi Street, close to the lake. Price for a complete meal amounts to 7 to 8 Swiss francs, which comes to $3.33 to $3.80. Two seating rooms are available, one with tablecloths" (Hans Hagen, Sunnyvale, California). . . . "A restaurant worthy of mention is one situated in a department store called **Epa-Unip** at 22 Via Nassa, three minutes from the main square (Piazza della Reforma). Between 11 and 2 o'clock you can have a fixed price meal (pasta, meat, salad) for 4.50 to 6 francs. Or one can choose several fine specialties for well under 8 francs. The restaurant is operated cafeteria style, the chef speaks English well. The other waitresses are most friendly" (Ronald Murdock, Nova Scotia, Canada). . . . **"Hotel Sport Garni,** 20 Via P. Regazzoni, has big, well furnished rooms, with 2 beds. Nice view for most of them, a lovely garden with trees and lots of flowers. Only 300 meters' walk from the train station. Mr. Pelican, the manager, is friendly, polite and speaks English well. Prices with breakfast are 45 francs for single, 80 for double. Shower and a big w.c. at floor (every 5 rooms), very tidy and clean" (Nick Demertzis, Thessaloniki, Greece).

Montreux

"The charming pension named below is situated on a hill, with a view of the Swiss mountains. The rooms are comfortable, and there is excellent cuisine at very moderate rates: approximately Sw. Fr. 30 per person for bed and breakfast, without private bath. I can recommend the **Hotel-Pension Wilhelm** (tel: 631-431), Rue du Marché 13, Montreux, very highly. Also, it is located a short walk from the railroad station, which is convenient" (Rose J. Glukes, Los Angeles, California). . . . **"Villa Tilda,** Quai Vernex, tel. 633-814, is a small house right on the side of Lake Geneva, as good as all the big, expensive hotels next door. Pleasant lady runs this. Rooms a little old-fashioned, but may appeal especially to American readers. Very comfort-able and clean, breakfast served in cheerful dining room. Single room costs 35 fr., doubles with private shower are from 65 francs, including breakfast of course. About 10 minutes from station" (Angela Wear, England).

Zermatt

"A must for readers going to Zermatt is the **Hotel Alphubel** (phone 67-30-03). It's a five-minute walk from the train station, right off the main street. A double room with knotty pine paneling, a balcony and a beautiful view of Zermatt's mountains costs from 62 francs ($29.52) up, including breakfast" (Barbara Pilarcyzk and J.R. Ford, Laguna Beach, California). . . . "Right across from the railway station is the **Hotel Bahnhof** (appropriately named) with large dorms (not over-crowded even when full) for 17 francs ($8.09) per person. It's the cheapest you'll find in Zermatt and you get full use of a large kitchen with all the pots, dishes and utensils you'll need. Buy your food at the Coop a block away. Plentiful hot showers are provided at no extra charge" (Richard Krimsky, Los Angeles, California; note: phone 67-24-06 for the remarkable Bahnhof Hotel). . . . "For anyone who loves the outdoors, this has to be as close to heaven as one can find on earth. It is reached only by train and therefore there are no cars in the town. Horse-and-buggies meet tourists at the station. There must be at least twenty different cable cars, cog trains, chair lifts, etc., that can be taken *up* from Zermatt which is already very high—and literally hundreds of trails in the area. It is from this town and its trails that the Matterhorn can be seen. We took cable cars up to where they were skiing" (Norbert H. Roihl, M.D., Fort Lauderdale, Florida). . . . "If any of your readers should consider a trip to Zermatt (a gorgeous village high in the Swiss Alps)—it is not on the Eurailpass but definitely worth going to—you can hitch a ride from Brig or Visp to Täsch and then walk from there to Zermatt. Otherwise the cost is 29 Swiss Francs from Visp, which is still on the Eurailpass. Even paying this amount is worth it, for Zermatt is fantastic. You can go hiking, summer skiing or climb the Matterhorn" (Mona Sajous, New York, New York). . . . "We happened upon the lovely **Hotel Mischabel** (phone 67-11-31), where we had a double with breakfast for 58 SF. The people on the staff were among the nicest we met anywhere in Europe. Our room was done entirely in knotty pine and French doors led onto a balcony with a breath-taking view of the Matterhorn. Highly recommended" (Gail Redmond, Jersey City, New Jersey). . . . "Noting that Zermatt was quite expensive, we made use of a hotel in Taesch: **Hotel Täscherhof,** phone 028/67-18-18. This was by far the best we have encountered so far in Europe. They charged us 130 francs ($61.90) for a double plus a triple room for my family of five, breakfast included. From Tasch, you can take the first train to Zermatt, a 10-minute trip. The hotel is opposite the station" (Dr. L.A. Oelofse, Capetown, South Africa).

TURKEY

Ankara

"Prices in the Middle East are really a joy. A fine example is the **Hotel Baykal,** 26 Hukumet Caddesi (phone 117-249), in Ankara, where a brand-new single comparing well with the very best German second-class room, goes for 1,300 T.L. a night, complete with private balcony. In Turkey, it is impossible to spend more than $4 for a meal, unless one is really stupid; and the food is wonderful" (David D. Morrison, Cambridge, Massachusetts). . . . "In Ankara, the **Yeni Hotel,** at 5 Sanayii Caddesi (phone 24-32-20), is the largest hotel in town, yet reasonable in price: 3,000 lira ($9.37) for singles, 5,000 lira ($15.62) for twins or doubles, always including private bath and breakfast. The **Piknik** (180 T.L. for the average meal) was our choice for lunch" (Ted & Lynn Kotzin, Los Angeles, Calif.).

Istanbul

Note from AF: As a preface to what follows, bear in mind that the current exchange rate (as of December, 1984) of the Turkish currency is 350 Turkish lira to one U.S. dollar: "I've been staying at the **Hotel Güngör,** 4 Divanyolu Cad., Sultanahmet (phone 26-23-19), a student-type hotel only five blocks from the enormous covered bazaar, near the beautiful Blue Mosque, the famed Topkapi Palace, and St. Sophia. There are dormitory and double rooms. For the dormitory, the charge is 500 lire per person, for double rooms it's 750 lira, 850 lira for triples. Everyone there is quite friendly" (Tricia Bobnar, Madison, Pennsylvania; plus numerous other endorsements). . . . "Better than the Güngör, in my view, is the **Hotel Pirlanta,** Divanyolu Cad., Sultanahmet (phone 277-085), about 180 yards from the Güngör and equally popular with students. Dorm without shower 600 lira, with shower 1100 lira; bathless single 800 lira, bathless double 1300 lira" (Christina Lorey, Bonn, Germany). . . . "The **Yücelt Youth Hostel,** Caferiye Sokak No. 6 (phone 22-47-90), was a good home for the week I spent in Istanbul. We had a simple, but clean, triple room with balcony for only 600 lira apiece. A dormitory bed is 500 lira. Hot showers and an outdoor cafeteria downstairs. The desk personnel speak English. Catering mostly to students, the Yücelt stands minutes away from such grand sights as the Hagia Sophia, Blue Mosque and Topkapi Palace" (Randy Mink, Elgin, Illinois). . . . "The **Hotel Kapitol,** at Asmali Mescit Caddesi 54 (phone 44-45-72), is the place to stay. For $13 per person, you get a very clean room with sink and just down the hall is a shower and rest room. It is located one block from the American Embassy and within five blocks of Taksim Square, along the Istiklal Caddesi" (Bruce A. Winters, Fresno, California). . . . **"Hotel Kavak** in the Tepebasi section, phone 44-58-44, across from the old Pera Palace Hotel, has English-speakers on the staff, is modest and comfortable. A double with bath and breakfast costs 7,500 lire ($23.43)" (Dr. and Mrs. John W. Hernández, Las Cruces, New Mexico). . . . "A must trip for anyone in or near Istanbul is a ferry boat ride up the Bosporus; they run frequently. We left at 10:25 a.m., on the trip to Saniyer, taking one and a half hours from pier no. 3, with the boat criss-crossing from Europe to Asia; it touches six Asian ports and one in Europe. Upon arrival in Saniyer at 12 noon, you will have plenty of time to stroll through the town and return to a picturesque restaurant at the pier for lunch before catching the return boat to Istanbul, which leaves at 1:30 p.m. and arrives back in Istanbul at 3:30 p.m. Believe it or not, the cost is 200 T.L. for the round trip, so be sure to buy a round trip before leaving. This three-and-a-half hour ride is the longest we have ever had for the money. Avoid the advertised tours of the Bosporus, but be sure to take the above ferry used by the local residents" (William H. Read, Hollywood, California). . . . "A two-and-a-half hour ferry trip from pier no. 4 at the foot of the **Galata Bridge** (old Istanbul side) through the Prince's Islands to Pendik in Asia Minor costs 200 T.L. second class (the sun deck is open to both first and second class). A fantastic ride back to Kadikoy in a Dolmus (Turkish combination of a taxi and a bus at fixed fare and no tip) cost 200 T.L., and a ferry back across the Bosporus to Istanbul was 31¢. Round trip cost was $1.87 per person for relaxation, outstanding scenery on an 'island cruise,' and a lesson in the Turkish language and hospitality from scores of curious, friendly commuters. Here is a place where an American is really helped to feel at home" (Lt. and Mrs. William E. Peterson, Portland, Oregon). . . . "Bus #84, #86 or #34 from Yeni Camii (old city end of Galata) goes to the **Archaeological Museum,** Topkapi Saray (the best sight in Turkey—perfect gem of the decadent grandeur that was the Ottoman Empire—admission 160 T.L.), **Aya Sofia** and the **Blue Mosques.** . . . Don't miss the **Karye Museum,** the most beautiful Byzantine mosaics we've seen. It's hard to find, though. Take the Edirne Kapa bus to the end of the line, and then ask. . . . Covered bazaar prices are lower in the morning, because the guided tours come by in the afternoon" (Mrs. Barbara Papesch, Switzerland). . . . "For the student traveler to Istanbul, **VIP Youth Travel** at Cumhuriet Cad. Harbiye, phone 41-65-14 (with a branch office in New York City at 3 East 54th Street, phone 421-5400), is a must. It is staffed by students on a voluntary basis and directs its work in the area of youth and student tourism, but in addition provides services for adults and other education personnel. In a country where French and German are practically useless, a traveler needs advice because of language and cultural difficulties, and I found these university students particularly adept at conveying the flavor of the New Turkey both in politics, art and interpretation of values. They will suggest restaurants like the **Sofra** (a particularly good Turkish Kebab), and the **Cinar,** where a reasonable meal can be had for less than $8. They will also suggest good restaurants that supply Turkish and European food in all price ranges. I found Istanbul a beautiful city, perhaps the most colorful in Europe. The Blue Mosque, Topkapi Palace, St.Sophia, a cruise in the Bosporus, Turkish folk dancing with the Eastern overtones not found elsewhere in Europe, and a lovely climate (70 degrees F); the six days I spent there were a completely enjoyable time" (Jeremid Slattery, New York, New York; note from AF: don't, whatever you do, miss Topkapi Palace). . . . "Train fare, 2nd class, round trip from Ankara to Istanbul, is approximately 900 T.L. ($2.81) (only 450 T.L. ($1.40) for students). A train leaves each city for the other around 8 to 9 p.m. each day. The compartments are quite comfortable, as are the beds. On arriving in Istanbul, do not let a porter take your bag. They meet you at the train and then carry it onto the ferry that goes from the railway station across the Bosporus and stops just under the Ataturk Bridge. They take the ferry with you and then charge 100 T.L. when you disembark! The ferry is the greatest bargain in Eurasia: 31¢ for the entire trip!" (James E. Kennington, Jr., APO, New York). . . . "Be sure to visit **Dolmabahce Palace** in Istanbul. The memory of the excerpt from 'Thousand Nights and a Night' will last longer than any of the photographs I took" (James E. Kennington, Jr., APO, New York). . . . "There are three ways to travel in Istanbul and Ankara—by taxi, bus, and dolmuc (pronounced dole-moosh). Taxi drivers should be questioned about their price to a certain point and always prior to entering the vehicle. Never accept the originally quoted price; arguing for 30 seconds will lower it to what it should be—1/2 to 2/3rds of the original. Dolmuces charge a set fee, an average of 100 T.L. for travelling along a set, major route; they are usually a large automobile or a microbus. Bus prices in Istanbul usually run about 50 T.L. To distinguish between taxis and dolmuces is sometimes difficult. In Ankara, dolmuces have a solid yellow line around the car body and usually have a plaque on top, listing the sections of the city that are travelled. The word 'Dolmuc' is lettered on the trunk or rear window. Taxis have a black and yellow checkered border around them. In Istanbul, the story is different. There is no obvious difference between taxis and dolmuces; all of them have a solid yellow line around the body. To catch a dolmuc, stand on a major intersection, or the corner of a street, and when a cab stops, say, 'Dolmuc—(then give the area you are trying to reach)—?" (James E. Kennington, Jr., APO, New York). . . . "All European marketplaces, bargaining, and goods pale before Istanbul's 'Grand Bazaar,' a labyrinth of tunnels, arcades, and courtyards which could take a most demanding shopper days to go through. Luckily there are some good, cheap and rather clean restaurants in the Bazaar. Suede coats, made to measure, for $40 to $75 . . . quite matchless gold and silver jewelry at all prices . . . $4 could buy a brilliantly colored woven cloth, dinnertable size . . . antique finds of every type . . . sigh" (Mrs. Barbara Papesch, Switzerland). . . . "Anyone can enter the famous mosques, free, but there is a fee for the museums, ranging from 50¢ to $1. The boat trips up the Bosporus and to the Princes' Islands are also inexpensive and highly worthwhile" (Ted & Lynn Kotzin, Los Angeles, Calif.). . . . "The fare from Istanbul to Haifa with **Turkish Maritime Lines** is about $85 (payable in U.S. currency), third class, off-season, ships leave once every two weeks, on alternating Wednesdays, and the trip takes four to five days, including a one-day stop at Izmir. Although third class dormitory conditions are a bit cramped, the food is quite good and plentiful, and all passengers are free to use the decks and lounges" (Henry S. Sloan, New York, New York). . . . "Muzaffer Vyanik, who calls himself 'Muzo,' has a shop in the covered bazaar which sells suede and leather coats and jackets at rock-bottom prices. The workmanship is of the highest quality and 'John' has a great deal of pride in his tailors. We bought a full-length green suede lady's coat from him; the identical coat was more than twice as much at the leather shop in one of the leading hotels. This is the covered bazaar at Stalls #s 21, 23 and 25, under the name Stil Suet Export" (Mr. and Mrs. Richard D. Greenfield, Hartsdale, New York).

WALES

Aberystwyth

"Our best find in England was the **Glan-Y-Mor Guesthouse** at 62 Marine Terrace, Aberystwyth, Dyfed, Wales, tel. 615-312, operated by Mr. and Mrs. George, who are friendly people. Most rooms overlook the water, the whole house has tasteful wallpaper and old furniture, and the meals there are the best I have ever eaten. Price per person, single, double or twin: £9. Dinner: £5 extra, and is excellent. I'd like other readers to share my good luck finding it" (J. Myers, London, England).

Cardiff

"Although you do not include Cardiff, Wales, in your book, it is a beautiful, fascinating city with very friendly people and certainly deserving of mention. We stayed in the **Coleshill Hotel** (Bed & Breakfast), 142 Newport Road, phone Cardiff 491-798. Our host was absolutely delightful, serving us a delicious breakfast and giving us the nicest and definitely the cleanest double room that we had in three months of travel in Europe. The bus from the train station stops right at the front door (I don't remember the number), and the cost was only £7 per person. There was parking, too, and do be sure to recommend a visit to the unique Cardiff Castle. It is like no other in Europe and well worth visiting" (Mr. and Mrs. Mark C. Lee, Modesto, California). . . . "At **Mrs. Ostanek's Guest House,** 1 Despenser Gardens (phone 33-400), I had a spacious single room with breakfast, bath, service, VAT, all inclusive, for £7.50. It's right next to the Despenser Gardens and eight minutes' walk from the RR station" (Lecia Katherine Boyd, Waikeria, Teawamutu, New Zealand).

YUGOSLAVIA

Dubrovnik

"For the tourist who wants to swim and wants to be assured of sun; for the tourist who likes a warm sea; for the tourist who wants to pass his evenings at first-rate concerts and plays—I'd like to recommend Dubrovnik, on the Dalmatian Coast. . . . One can get a charming room with bath in a private home for as little as $10 and can eat in town quite easily for $5. . . . Every night in July and August, when the Summer Festival is on, there are several events to choose from. These include operas, a fantastic production of *Hamlet* performed in the courtyard and on the battlements of 13th-century Fort Lovrjenac, concerts by visiting soloists and Yugoslavians, folk dancing, etc. The most expensive ticket to *Hamlet* costs $8 and scales down; the best tickets to hear Anton Dermota in a magnificent lieder concert in the Rector's Palace, cost $6.50" (Jay Wolf, New York City). . . . "Dubrovnik, a beautiful city on the Dalmatian Coast of Yugoslavia, is the capital of the ancient Republic of Ragusa, with a wonderful summer festival. When the periodic ships arrive in Dubrovnik, local women descend on them like vultures to offer rooms in their homes to tourists. We took a chance and went with a young girl who spoke some English. The home turned out to be on the top of a very high hill, a literally breathtaking walk, but a magnificent view of the harbor. The family was friendly, and we had a comfortable accommodation for two for $10 a night. Not everyone on the boat made such a good connection, but it's worth a try. If you don't like the first room you choose, there are dozens of women in the streets ready to offer you something else. The lingua franca between room-renters and tourists seems to be German, so the women will follow you asking 'Zimmer.' We had to summon all our broken German and their broken English to say that we already had a room. This

gets to be a drag, unfortunately" (Phyllis and Steve Wilson, Chicago, Illinois). . . .
"I have seen the coastline of Mexico, both east and west, the coastline all down the western side of South America, and of many parts of the Mediterranean, but I think I shall never see islands and coastline more beautiful and beckoning than those of the Dalmatian coastline. Such terraced fields and vineyards with ramparts of ancient rock, like multifortresses of a disappearing rural existence! The little coves and inlets sheltering pink-roofed fishing villages have a dreamy verdancy, and the rocky shoreline deceptively gives the appearance of roughly packed ancient yellow sand drying in the sun and gently bleaching over the centuries. A coast of history, of fortresses and centuries of battle—right and wrong. The mountains are spaced to blend from a deep blue-green thru the spectrum to a misty blue-grey lost in the horizon. Particularly pleasing to the eye in beauty and strangeness was the island of **Korcula.** If I have lots of money some day and six months I don't know what to do with, I would go to this land and soak up the mystery and beauty of it. It is Yugoslavia" (Madelin L. Lawler, Mt. Prospect, Illinois). . . . "We have an absolutely great suggestion for readers looking for a room in a private home within the walls of the old city. English-speaking **Mr. Mihocevic** has two bright, cheerful double-bedded and one twin-bedded room to let for stays of several days (Strosmajerova 1, Dubrovnik; telephone 26-172). The house is in a three-floor walk-up in an ancient, but spotless building on a narrow quiet street only one block from the morning open market (great for quick snacks) and a short walk from access to the seaward sunbathing rocks beyond the city walls. Rates are $10 for a double in July and August, less the rest of the year, and include touches like Turkish coffee in the morning, slippers at the doorstep of each room, free showers, and an occasional nightcap. The magnificent bathroom right down the hall (with a picture-window overlooking the ancient city, no less) is fully equipped and has plenty of hot water (free showers)" (David C. Brezic, New York, New York).

Split

"The best guesthouse we found was the one run by **Mr. Ivan and Mrs. Katica Sanic,** Koncareva 351, 58000 Split (phone 058-46-404). It's on the main road as you enter the outskirts from the south, and public transportation is available to the city center. Their service and hospitality were unsurpassed, and furnishings and baths were all immaculate. A double room cost $18 a night, including a large breakfast with eggs and fresh fruit from their trees" (Christine & Carl Haas, San Jose, California).

Chapter XXVIII

CAPSULE VOCABULARIES

For the Essentials of Life

**French, German,
Italian, Spanish,
Portuguese, Dutch,
Danish & Swedish**

THE MOST FAMOUS last words of the American tourist are: "They speak English everywhere."

Well, they don't. You can, with luck, be stranded in a European town among people who will simply shrug their shoulders to an English-uttered request.

But necessity is not the only reason for studying a foreign tongue—half of the fun of a European vacation comes from trying out the local language! It brings amazing dividends in better service and treatment, too. Europeans, like most persons, are sensitive and proud. They react best to tourists who show some regard for the language and culture of their host country.

To do that, you needn't become a full-time scholar. In any language, a very small group of words and phrases can be shifted and rearranged to fulfill almost any need. If you can learn the foreign equivalents of such terms as "where is," "do you have," "how much is this"—then you can travel comfortably in Europe and make your wants known. Half an hour of study, packed in as your train or plane approaches a particular country, ought to do the job.

What follows below are eight capsule vocabularies—for French, German, Italian, Spanish, Portuguese, Dutch, Danish and Swedish—containing those absolutely essential phrases which you'll use time and again in your tour of Europe. The column at the right-hand side of each page provides phonetic pronunciations of these terms as they'd sound in English. Pronounce the phonetic syllable "ay" as in "play" or "day," never as in "aye, aye, sir."

FRENCH

		Pronounced
Hello	**Bonjour**	bohn-zhoor
How are you?	**Comment allez-vous?**	koh-mawh-tah-lay-voo
Very well	**Très bien**	tray-byanh
Thank you	**Merci**	mayr-see
Goodbye	**Au revoir**	aw-ruh-vwahr
Please	**S'il vous plaît**	sill-voo-play
Yes	**Oui**	wee
No	**Non**	nawh
Excuse me	**Pardon**	par-dawh
Give me	**Donnez-moi**	duh-nay-mwah
Where is?	**Où est?**	oo ay
the station	**la gare**	lah-gar
a hotel	**un hôtel**	uh-no-tel
a restaurant	**un restaurant**	uh-res-tow-rawh
the toilet	**le lavabo**	luh-lah-vah-bo
To the right	**A droite**	ah-drwaht
To the left	**A gauche**	ah-gohsh
Straight ahead	**Tout droit**	too-drwah
I would like	**Je voudrais**	zhuh-voo-dray
to eat	**manger**	mawh-zhay
a room	**une chambre**	ewn-shawm-bruh
for one night	**pour une nuit**	poor-ewn-nwee
How much is it?	**Combien ça coute?**	kawm-byanh-sah-koot
The check, please	**L'addition, s.v.p.**	lah-dee-syohnh
When?	**Quand?**	kawnh
Yesterday	**Hier**	yayr
Today	**Aujourd'hui**	oh-zhoor-dwee
Tomorrow	**Demain**	duh-manh
Breakfast	**Le petit déjeuner**	luh puh-tee day-zhuh-nay
Lunch	**Déjeuner**	day-zhuh-nay
Dinner	**Dîner**	dee-nay

1 **un** (uhnh)	**10** **dix** (deess)	**19** **dix-neuf** (deez-nuff)
2 **deux** (duh)	**11** **onze** (ohnze)	**20** **vingt** (vanh)
3 **trois** (trwa)	**12** **douze** (dooze)	**30** **trente** (trawnt)
4 **quatre** (kahtr)	**13** **treize** (trezz)	**40** **quarante** (ka-rawnt)
5 **cinq** (sank)	**14** **quatorze** (ka-torze)	**50** **cinquante** (san-kawnt)
6 **six** (seess)	**15** **quinze** (kanze)	**100** **cent** (sawnh)
7 **sept** (set)	**16** **seize** (sezz)	**200** **deux** (duh-sawn)
8 **huit** (weet)	**17** **dix-sept** (dee-set)	**1000** **mille** (meel)
9 **neuf** (nuff)	**18** **dix-huit** (deez-weet)	

GERMAN

		Pronounced
Hello	**Guten Tag**	goo-ten-tahk
How are you?	**Wie geht es Ihnen?**	vee gayt ess ee-nen
Very well	**Sehr gut**	zayr goot
Thank you	**Danke schön**	dahn-keh-shern
Goodbye	**Auf Wiedersehen**	owf vee dayr-zayn
Please	**Bitte**	bit-tuh
Yes	**Ja**	yah
No	**Nein**	nine
Excuse me	**Entschuldigen Sie**	en-shool-di-gen zee
Give me	**Geben Sie mir**	gay-ben zee meer
Where is?	**Wo ist?**	voh eest
the station	**der Bahnhof**	dayr bahn-hoft
a hotel	**ein Hotel**	ain hotel
a restaurant	**ein Restaurant**	ain res-tow-rahng
the toilet	**die Toilette**	dee twah-let-tuh
To the right	**Nach rechts**	nakh reshts
To the left	**Nach links**	nakh leenks
Straight ahead	**Geradeaus**	geh-rah-deh-ows
I would like	**Ich möchte**	ikh mersh-ta
to eat	**essen**	ess-en
a room	**ein Zimmer**	ain tzim-mer
for one night	**für eine Nacht**	feer ai-neh nakht
How much is it?	**Wieviel kostet?**	vee-feel kaw-stet
The check, please	**Zahlen, bitte**	tzah-len bit-tuh
When?	**Wann?**	vahn
Yesterday	**Gestern**	geh-stern
Today	**Heute**	hoy-tuh
Tomorrow	**Morgen**	more-gen
Breakfast	**Frühstück**	free-shtick
Lunch	**Mittagessen**	mi-tahg-gess-en
Dinner	**Abendessen**	ah-bend-ess-en

1 **eins** (aintz)	**11** **elf** (ellf)	**20** **zwanzig** (tzvahn-tzig)
2 **zwei** (tzvai)	**12** **zwölf** (tzvuhlf)	**30** **dreissig** (dry-tzik)
3 **drei** (dry)	**13** **dreizehn** (dry-tzayn)	**40** **vierzig** (feer-tzik)
4 **vier** (feer)	**14** **vierzehn** (feer-tzayn)	**50** **fünfzig** (fewnf-tzik)
5 **fünf** (fewnf)	**15** **fünfzehn** (fewnf-tzayn)	**60** **sechzig** (zex-tzik)
6 **sechs** (zex)	**16** **sechzehn** (sex-tzayn)	**70** **siebzig** (zeeb-tzik)
7 **sieben** (zee-ben)	**17** **siebzehn** (zeeb-tzayn)	**80** **achtzig** (akht-tzik)
8 **acht** (ahkht)	**18** **achtzehn** (akh-tzayn)	**90** **neunzig** (noyn-tzik)
9 **neun** (noyn)	**19** **neunzehn** (noyn-tzayn)	**100** **hundert** (hoon-dert)
10 **zehn** (tzayn)		

ITALIAN

Pronounced

Hello	**Buon giorno**	bwohn djor-noh
How are you?	**Come sta?**	koh-may stah
Very well	**Molto bene**	mohl-toh bay-nay
Thank you	**Grazie**	grah-tzyeh
Goodbye	**A rivederla**	ah ree-vay-dehr lah
Please	**Per piacere**	payr pee-ya-chay-ray
Yes	**Si**	see
No	**No**	noh
Excuse me	**Scusi**	skoo-zee
Give me	**Mi dia**	mee-dee-ah
Where is?	**Dov'é**	doh-vay
the station	**la stazione**	la stah-tzyonay
a hotel	**un albergo**	oon ahl-bayr-goh
a restaurant	**un ristorante**	oon rees-to-rahn-tay
the toilet	**il gabinetto**	eel ga-bee-naytoh
To the right	**A destra**	ah dess-trah
To the left	**A sinistra**	ah see-nee-strah
Straight ahead	**Avanti**	ah-vahn-tee
I would like	**Vorrei**	vohr-ray
to eat	**mangiare**	mahn-djah-ray
a room	**una camera**	oona kah-may-rah
for one night	**per una notte**	payr oona noh-tay
How much is it?	**Quanto costa?**	kwan-toh kaw-stah
The check, please	**Il conto, per piacere**	eel kohn-toh
When?	**Quando?**	kwahn-doh
Yesterday	**Ieri**	ee-yay-ree
Today	**Oggi**	aw-djee
Tomorrow	**Domani**	doh-mah-nee
Breakfast	**Colazione**	koh-lah-tzyoh-nay
Lunch	**Pranzo**	prahn-tzoh
Dinner	**Cena**	chay-nah

1 **uno** (oo-noh)	**11** **undici** (oon-dee-chee)	**18** **diciotto** (dee-chah-toh) toh)
2 **due** (doo-ay)	**12** **dodici** (doh-dee-chee)	
3 **tre** (tray)	**13** **tredici** (tray-dee-chee)	**19** **dicianove** (dee-chay-novay)
4 **quattro** (kwah-troh)	**14** **quattordici** (kawh-tohr-dee-chee)	**20** **venti** (vayn-tee)
5 **cinque** (cheen-kway)		**30** **trenta** (trayn-tah)
6 **sei** (say)	**15** **quindici** (kween-dee-chee)	**40** **quaranta** (kwah-rahn-tah)
7 **sette** (set-tay)	**16** **sedici** (say-dee-chee)	**100** **cento** (chayn-toh)
8 **otto** (aw-toh)	**17** **diciasette** (dee-chay-se-tay)	**1000** **mille** (mee-lay)
9 **nove** (noh-vay)		
10 **dieci** (dee-ah-chee)		

SPANISH

		Pronounced
Hello	**Buenos dias**	bway-noss dee-ahss
How are you?	**Cómo está usted?**	koh-moh ess-tah oo-steth
Very well	**Muy bien**	mwee-byen
Thank you	**Gracias**	grah-thee-ahss
Goodbye	**Adios**	ah-dyohss
Please	**Por favor**	pohr fah-bohr
Yes	**Si**	see
No	**No**	noh
Excuse me	**Perdóneme**	pehr-doh-nehmay
Give me	**Déme**	day-may
Where is?	**Dónde esta?**	dohn-day ess-tah
the station	**la estación**	la ess-tah-thyohn
a hotel	**un hotel**	oon-oh-tel
a restaurant	**un restaurante**	oon res-tow-rahn-tay
the toilet	**el retrete**	el ray-tray-tay
To the right	**A la derecha**	ah lay day-ray-chuh
To the left	**A la izquierda**	ah lay eeth-kyayr-duh
Straight ahead	**Adelante**	ah-day-lahn-tay
I would like	**Quiero**	kyehr-oh
to eat	**comer**	koh-mayr
a room	**una habitacion**	oo-nah ah-bee-tah-thyon
How much is it?	**Cuánto?**	kwahn-toh
The check, please	**La cuenta**	lah kwen-tah
When?	**Cuándo?**	kwan-doh?
Yesterday	**Ayer**	ah-yayr
Today	**Hoy**	oy
Tomorrow	**Mañana**	mahn-yah-nah
Breakfast	**Desayuno**	deh-sai-yoo-noh
Lunch	**Almuerzo**	ahl-mwayr-thoh
Dinner	**Cena**	thay-nah

1	**uno** (oo-noh)	13	**trece** (tray-thay)	30	**treinta** (trayn-tah)
2	**dos** (dose)	14	**catorce** (kah-tor-thay)	40	**cuarenta** (kwah-ren-tah)
3	**tres** (trayss)	15	**quince** (keen-thay)	50	**cincuenta** (theen-kwen-tah)
4	**cuatro** (kwah-troh)	16	**dieciséis** (dyeth-ee-sayss)	60	**sesenta** (say-sen-tah)
5	**cinco** (theen-koh)	17	**diecisieto** (dyeth-ee-sye-tay)	70	**setenta** (say-ten-tah)
6	**seis** (sayss)	18	**dieciocho** (dyeth-ee-oh-choh)	80	**ochenta** (oh-chen-tah)
7	**siete** (syeh-tay)	19	**diecinueve** (dyeth-ee-nwaybay)	90	**noventa** (noh-ben-tah)
8	**ocho** (oh-choh)	20	**veinte** (bayn-tay)	100	**cien** (thyen)
9	**nueve** (nway-bay)				
10	**diez** (dyeth)				
11	**once** (ohn-thay)				
12	**doce** (doh-thay)				

PORTUGUESE

English	Portuguese	Pronounced
Hello	olá	oh-lah
How are you?	como está?	como esh-tah
Very well	muito bem	muy-toh bym
Thank you	muito obrigado	muy-toh obree-gah-do
Good-bye	adeus	adeush
Please	faça favor	fassa fah-vohr
Yes	sim	seem
No	não	naion
Excuse me	desculpe-me	dash-culpa-meh
Give me	dê-me	deh-meh
Where is?	onde fiça?	ondeh feecah
the station	a estaçao	a aish-tassaion
a hotel	um hotel	oom hotel
a restaurant	um restaurante	oom rash-tauranteh
the toilet	a casa de banho	ah cahzah de bahnhoo
To the right	á direita	aah deeraitah
To the left	á esquerda	aah ash-kerdah
Straight ahead	em frente	ym fraintah
I would like—	gostaria de	goosh-tareeah de
to eat	comer	coh-mere
a room	um quarto	oom quarr-toh
How much is it?	quanto custa	quahnto coosh-tah
The check, please	a conta se faz, favor	ah cohnta sa fahsh, fah-vohr
When	quando	quandoh
Yesterday	ontem	ohntym
Today	hoje	hoyhje
Tomorrow	amanha	ahmain-hayh
Breakfast	pequeno almoc	paikainoh aahimohssoh
Lunch	almoço	aahlmohssoh
Dinner	jantar	jain-taah

1	**um** oom	13	**trêze** traihzeh	40	**quarenta** quaraintah
2	**dois** doysh	14	**catorze** cahtohrzeh	50	**cinquenta** sseenquaintah
3	**três** traishe	15	**quinze** keenzeh	60	**sessenta** ssaissaihntah
4	**quatro** quaahtroh	16	**dezasseis** dehzaissaish	70	**setenta** ssaitaintah
5	**cinco** sseencoh	17	**dezassete** dehrzassaihteh	80	**otenta** oyhtaintah
6	**seis** ssaish	18	**dezoito** dehzoytoh	90	**noventa** nohvaintah
7	**sete** ssaiteh	19	**dezanove** dehzanohveh	100	**cem** sym
8	**oito** oytoh	20	**vinte** veenteh		
9	**nove** nohveh	30	**trinta** treehntah		
10	**dez** daish				
11	**onze** onzeh				
12	**dôze** doze				

DUTCH

English	Dutch	Pronounced
Hello	**Hallo**	ha-loh
How are you?	**Hoe gaat het met U?**	hoo-haht-ut-met-oo
Very well	**Uitstekend**	out-stayk-end
Thank you	**Dank U**	dahnk-ew
Goodbye	**Goeden dag**	hoo-dun dahk
Please	**Alstublieft**	ah-stoo-bleeft
Yes	**Ja**	yah
No	**Neen**	nay
Excuse me	**Pardon**	par-dawn
Give me	**Geeft U mij**	hayft oo may
Where is?	**Waar is?**	vahr iz
the station	**het station**	het stah-ssyonh
a hotel	**een hotel**	uhn ho-tel
a restaurant	**een restaurant**	uhn res-to-rahng
the toilet	**het toilet**	het twah-let
To the right	**Rechts**	rekhts
To the left	**Links**	links
Straight ahead	**Rechtdoor**	rekht-dour
I would like	**Ik zou graag**	ik zow hrah
to eat	**eten**	ay-ten
a room	**een kamer**	uhn kah-mer
for one night	**voor een nacht**	voor ayn nakht
How much is it?	**Hoe veel kost het?**	hoo fayl kawst het
The check, please	**De rekening**	duh ray-ken-ing
When?	**Wanneer?**	vah-neer
Yesterday	**Gisteren**	his-ter-en
Today	**Vandaag**	van-dahkh
Tomorrow	**Morgen**	mor-hen
Breakfast	**Ontbijt**	ohnt-bayt
Lunch	**Lunch**	lunch
Dinner	**Diner**	dee-nay

1	**een** (ayn)	11	**elf** (elf)	20	**twintig** (twin-tukh)
2	**twee** (tway)	12	**twaalf** (tvahlf)	30	**dertig** (dayr-tukh)
3	**drie** (dree)	13	**dertien** (dayr-teen)	40	**veertig** (vayr-tukh)
4	**vier** (veer)	14	**veertien** (vayr-teen)	50	**vijftig** (vahf-tukh)
5	**vijf** (vayf)	15	**vijftien** (vayf-teen)	60	**zestig** (zes-tukh)
6	**zes** (zes)	16	**zestien** (zes-teen)	70	**zeventig** (zay-vun-tukh)
7	**zeven** (zay-vun)	17	**zeventien** (zay-vun-teen)	80	**tachtig** (takh-tukh)
8	**acht** (akht)	18	**achtien** (akh-teen)	90	**negentig** (nay-hen-tukh)
9	**negen** (nay-hen)	19	**negentien** (nay-hen-teen)	100	**honderd** (hon-dayrt)
10	**tien** (teen)				

DANISH

		Prounounced
Hello	God Dag	go da
How are you?	Hvordan har De det?	vohr-dan hahr dee day
Very well	Tak, godt	tak gaht
Thank you	Tak	tak
Goodbye	Farvel	fahr-vel
Please	Vaer saa venlig	vayr saw venlee
Yes	Ja	ya
No	Nej	nai
Excuse me	Unkskyld	own-skeel
I don't understand	Jeg forstaar ikke	vai fawr-star ik-uh
Give me	Giv mig	Gee-mai
Where is?	Hvor er der?	vohr ayr der
the station	jernbanestationen	yayrn-ban-uh-sta-sh-onun
a hotel	et hotel	it ho-tel
a restaurant	en restaurant	in rest-oh-rahng
the toilet	toilettet	twah-let-tud
To the right	Til hojre	til hoi-ruh
To the left	Til venstre	till ven-struh
I would like	Jeg vilde gerne have	yai-vil-luh gayr-nuh-ha
to eat	noget at spise	noh-ud ah spee-suh
a room	et Vaerelse	it vay-rul-suh
How much is it?	Hvor meget?	vohr ma-yud
When?	Hvornaar?	vohr-nawr
Yesterday	i Gaar	ee gawr
Today	i Dag	ee da
Tomorrow	i Morgen	ee mawrn
Write it out	Skriv det	skreev day

1	en (ayn)	11	elve (el-vuh)	30	tredive (tred-vuh)
2	to (toh)	12	tolv (tahll)	40	fyrre (fer-raw)
3	tre (tray)	13	tretten (tret-un)	50	halvtreds (hal-tress)
4	fire (fee-rah)	14	fjorten (fyawr-tun)	60	tres (tress)
5	fem (fem)	15	femten (fem-tun)	70	halvfjerds (half-yayrss)
6	seks (sex)	16	seksten (saiss-tun)	80	firs (feerss)
7	syv (syee)	17	sytten (ser-tun)	90	halvfems (hal-femss)
8	otte (oh-tuh)	18	atten (a-tun)	100	hundrede (hoon-rud-uh)
9	ni (nee)	19	nitten (nitun)		
10	ti (tee)	20	tyve (tee-vuh)		

SWEDISH

		Pronounced
Hello	God dag	goo dah
How are you?	Hur står det till?	hoor store det till
Very well	Tack, bra	tahk brah
Thank you	Tack	tahk
Goodbye	Adjö	ah-yer
Please	Var snäll och	vahr snell oh
Yes	Ja	yah
No	Nej	nay
Excuse me	Ursäkta	oor-sek-tah
I don't understand	Jag förstår inte	yah fur-tore in tuh
Give me	Ge mig	yay may
Where is?	Var finns det?	vahr finss det
the station	stationen	stah-shoo-nen
a hotel	ett hotell	et ho-tel
a restaurant	en restaurang	en rest-oh-rahng
a toilet	toaletten	twah-let-ten
To the right	At höger	oht her-ger
To the left	At vänster	oht yen-ster
Straight ahead	Rakt fram	rahkt-frahm
I would like	Jag vill ha	ya vill hah
to eat	mat	maht
a room	ett rum	et ruhm
How much is it?	Vad kostar det?	vahd kaw-stahr dayt
That's too expensive	Det är för mycket	dayt ayr fer mik-ket
Something cheaper	Inte så mycket	in-tuh so mik-ket
When?	Nä?	nayr
Yesterday	I går	ee gore
Today	I dag	ee dah
Tomorrow	I morgon	ee mawr-rawn

1	ett (et)	11	elva (el-vah)	21	tjugoetti (chew-goo-et)
2	tva (tvoh)	12	tolv (tawlv)		
3	tre (tray)	13	tretton (tret-tawn)	22	tijugotvØ (chew-goo-tvo)
4	fyra (fee-rah)	14	fjorton (fyoor-tawn)		
5	fem (fem)	15	femton (fem-tawn)	30	trettio (tret-tee)
6	sex (sex)	16	sexton (sex-tawn)	40	fyrtio (fur-tee)
7	sju (shew)	17	sjutton (shuht-tawn)	50	femtio (fem-tee)
8	ätta (awt-tah)	18	aderton (ahr-tawn)	60	sextio (sex-tee)
9	nio (nee-joh)	19	nitton (nit-tawn)	70	sjuttio (shut-tee)
10	tio (tee-yoo)	20	tjugo (chew-goo)	100	hundra (huhn-drah)

Chapter XXIX

MENU TRANSLATIONS

In Eight Languages

SOMEHOW, there are few words to describe the sinking feeling in the pit of your stomach caused by a Barcelona menu that lists *alcachofas, angulas y lletados con acelgas* as the choice you face for supper. Absent a translation of these exotic phrases, dinner becomes The Big Surprise. You stab blindly at the bill of fare, hope for the best, and usually end up with "octopus soup" or some similar delicacy.

Obviously, you'll need translations of European menus. They follow below, arranged for seven European languages in the same groupings that you'll find on a menu: soups, meats, vegetables, desserts, and so forth. Pronunciations are omitted; in this area, it usually pays simply to point to what you want.

A preliminary warning: in using these lists, don't be intimidated by the seemingly large number of menu terms that you won't find listed in them. Your bewilderment results from the common practice in European restaurants of adorning menus with fanciful, but totally meaningless, adjectives. Thus, a simple *wienerschnitzel* (breaded veal cutlet) is rarely described as such in a Munich restaurant: it's called a *wienerschnitzel Münchner art* (breaded veal cutlet Munich style), but at heart, it's a simple breaded veal cutlet. The same literary touches are often indulged in by American restaurants, whose menus offer "Shenandoah County Tomato Juice" or "Special Prime-Tested Kansas City Steaks." Just look for the basic root of the menu terms, which is all you're getting, in any event. Bon Appetit!

FRENCH MENU TERMS

SOUPS

bouillabaisse	fish soup	potage au vermicelle	noodle soup
consommé	clear soup		
potage (or)soupe	soup	potage aux lentilles	lentil soup
potage à la reine	cream of chicken	potage portugais	tomato soup
		potage Saint-Germain	pea soup
soupe à l'oignon	onion soup	potage de volaille	chicken broth

MEATS

agneau	lamb	gigot ragout de mouton	leg of mutton stew
ailerons	chicken wings		
aloyan	sirloin	grenouille	frog
bifteck	steak	jambon	ham
boeuf	beef	lapin	rabbit
canard	duck	mouton	mutton
caneton	duckling	oie	goose
cerf	venison	pot au feu	beef stew
cervelles	brains	poulet	chicken
charcuterie	cold cuts	poussin	squab chicken
chateaubriand	filet steak	ris de veau	sweetbreads
coq au vin	chicken in wine	rognons	kidneys
côtelette d'agneau	lamb chop	rôti	roast
dindonneau farci	stuffed turkey	saucisse grillé	fried sausage
dinde	turkey	tournedos	small filet steaks
foie	liver	veau	veal
foie gras	goose liver	volaille	poultry

FISH

aigrefin	haddock	huîtres	oysters
anguille	eel	maquereau	mackerel
brochet	pike	moule	mussel
crevette	shrimp	poissons	fish
escargots	snails	saumon fumé	smoked salmon
hareng	herring	thon	tuna
homard	lobster	truite	trout

EGGS

oeufs brouillés	scrambled eggs	oeufs frits	fried eggs
oeufs à la coque	soft boiled eggs	oeufs frits au jambon	ham and eggs
oeufs durs	hard boiled eggs	oeufs pochés	poached eggs

SALADS

crudités	vegetable salad	salade de laitue	lettuce salad
salade de concombres	cucumber salad	salade niçoise	tuna salad
		salade variée	mixed salad

VEGETABLES

asperge	asparagus	navets	turnips
aubergines	eggplant	petits pois	green peas
choucroute	sauerkraut	pommes frites	French fried
choux	cabbage		potatoes
cornichon	pickle	purée de pommes	mashed
épinards	spinach		potatoes
haricots verts	green beans	radis	radish
légumes	vegetables	riz	rice

BEVERAGES, CONDIMENTS, AND OTHERS

beurre	butter	moutarde	mustard
bière	beer	patisserie	pastry
café	coffee	petit pain	a roll
citron	lemon	poivre	pepper
cognac	brandy	sel	salt
crème	cream	sucre	sugar
croissants	breakfast rolls	thé	tea
de l'eau	water	vin	wine
jus d'orange	orange juice	vin blanc	white wine
jus de tomates	tomato juice	vin rouge	red wine
lait	milk	vinaigre	vinegar

DESSERTS

ananas	pineapple	fruits frais	fresh fruit
compotes de fruits	stewed	gateau	cake
	fruits	glace à la vanille	vanilla ice
crème a la vanille	vanilla		cream
	custard	macedoine de fruits	fruit salad
fraises	strawberries	oranges	oranges
framboises	raspberries	pamplemousse	grapefruit
fromage	cheese	petits fours	tea cakes
fromage à la crème	cream	raisins	grapes
	cheese	tartes	pastries

COOKING TERMS

à point	medium	meunière (or) au beurre	buttered
bien cuit	well done	rôti	roast
farci	stuffed	saignant	rare
frit	fried		

GERMAN MENU TERMS

SOUPS

Erbsensuppe	pea soup	**Kraftbrühe**	consomme
Gemüsesuppe	vegetable soup	**Linsensuppe**	lentil soup
Hühnerbrühe	chicken soup	**Nudelsuppe**	noodle soup
Kartoffelsuppe	potato soup	**Ochsenschwanzsuppe**	oxtail
Königinsuppe	cream of chicken		soup

MEATS

Aufschnitt	cold cuts	**Kassler Rippchen**	pork chops
Brathuhn	roast chicken	**Lamm**	lamb
Bratwurst	grilled sausage	**Leber**	liver
Deutsches Beefsteak	hamburger	**Nieren**	kidneys
	steak	**Ragout**	stew
Eisbein	pig's knuckles	**Rinderbraten**	roast beef
Ente	duck	**Rindfleisch**	beef
Gans	goose	**Sauerbraten**	sauerbraten
Gefüllte Kalbsbrust	stuffed	**Schinken**	ham
	breast of veal	**Schweinebraten**	roast pork
Hammel	mutton	**Taube**	pigeon
Hirn	brains	**Truthahn**	turkey
Kalb	veal	**Wiener Schnitzel**	veal cutlet
Kaltes Geflügel	cold poultry	**Wurst**	sausage

FISH

Aal	eel	**Lachs**	salmon
Forelle	trout	**Makrele**	mackerel
Hecht	pike	**Rheinsalm**	Rhine salmon
Karpfen	carp	**Schellfisch**	haddock
Krebs	crawfish	**Seezunge**	sole

EGGS

Eier in Schale	boiled eggs	**mit Speck**	with bacon
Rühreier	scrambled eggs	**Verlorene Eier**	poached eggs
Spiegeleier	fried eggs		

SANDWICHES

Käsebrot	cheese sandwich	Schwarzbrot mit Butter	
Schinkenbrot	ham sandwich		rye bread and butter
		Wurstbrot	sausage sandwich

SALADS

Gemischter Salat	mixed salad	Kopfsalat	lettuce salad
Gurkensalat	cucumber salad	Rohkostplatte	vegetable salad

VEGETABLES

Artischocken	artichokes	Reis	rice
Blumenkohl	cauliflower	Rote Rüben	beets
Bohnen	beans	Rotkraut	red cabbage
Bratkartoffeln	fried potatoes	Salat	lettuce
Erbsen	peas	Salzkartoffeln	boiled potatoes
Grüne Bohnen	string beans	Sauerkraut	sauerkraut
Gurken	cucumbers	Spargel	asparagus
Karotten	carrots	Spinat	spinach
Kartoffelbrei	mashed potatoes	Steinpilze	mushrooms
Kartoffelsalat	potato salad	Tomaten	tomatoes
Knödel	dumplings	Vorspeisen	hors d'oeuvres
Kohl	cabbage	Weisse Rüben	turnips

DESSERTS

Blätterteiggebäck	puff pastry	Obstsalat	fruit salad
Bratapfel	baked apple	Pfannkuchen	sugared pancakes
Käse	cheese	Pflaumenkompott	stewed plums
Klösse	dumplings	Teegebäck	tea cakes
Kompott	stewed fruit	Torten	pastries
Obstkuchen	fruit tart		

FRUITS

Ananas	pineapples	Kirschen	cherries
Apfel	apples	Pfirsiche	peaches
Apfelsinen	oranges	Weintrauben	grapes
Bananen	bananas	Zitronen	lemons
Birnen	pears		

BEVERAGES

Bier	beer	Eine Tasse Kaffee	a cup of
Ein Dunkles	a dark beer		coffee
Ein Helles	a light beer	Eine Tasse Tee	a cup of tea
Milch	milk	Tomatensaft	tomato juice
Rotwein	red wine	Wasser	water
Sahne	cream	Weinbrand	brandy
Schokolade	chocolate		

CONDIMENTS AND OTHERS

Brot	bread	Pfeffer	pepper
Brötchen	rolls	Salz	salt
Butter	butter	Senf	mustard
Eis	ice	Zitrone	lemon
Essig	vinegar	Zucker	sugar

COOKING TERMS

gebacken	baked	geröstet	broiled
gebraten	fried	gut durchgebraten	well done
gefüllt	stuffed	nicht durchgebraten	rare
gekocht	boiled	paniert	breaded

SPANISH MENU TERMS

SOUPS

caldo de gallina	chicken soup	sopa espesa	thick soup
gazpacho	cold soup	sopa de fideos	noodle soup
sopa	soup	sopa de guisantes	pea soup
sopa de cebolla	onion soup	sopa de lentejas	lentil soup
sopa clara	consomme	sopa de tortuga	turtle soup

MEATS

albóndigas	meat balls	conejo	rabbit
aves	poultry	cordero	lamb
cabeza de ternera	calf's head	faisan	pheasant
carne	meat	filete de ternera	filet of veal
carne fría	cold cuts	ganso	goose
cerdo	pork	higado	liver

chuleta	chop	jamón	ham
chuleta de carnero	mutton chop	lengua	tongue
ciervo	venison	paloma	pigeon
pato	duck	riñones	kidneys
pavo	turkey	salchicha	sausage
perdiz	partridge	ternera	veal
pollo	chicken	tocino	bacon
ragout	ragout	vaca	beef

FISH

almejas	clams	ostras	oysters
anchoas	anchovies	paella	assorted sea food and
arenque	herring		rice
bonito	tunny	pescado	fish
callos	tripe	salmon	salmon
caracoles	snails	salmón ahumado	smoked
caviare	caviar		salmon
gambas	shrimp	sardinas	sardines
langosta	lobster	sollo	pike
lenguado	sole	trucha	trout

VEGETABLES

aceitunas	olives	judias verdes	string beans
arroz	rice	lechuga	lettuce
berenjena	eggplant	legumbres	vegetables
cebolla	onion	pasta italiana	spaghetti
col	cabbage	patatas	potatoes
col fermentada	sauerkraut	pepino	cucumber
coliflor	cauliflower	rábanos	radishes
entremeses	hors d'oeuvres	remolachas	beets
esparragos	asparagus	setas	mushrooms
espinaca	spinach	tomate	tomato
guisantes	peas	zanahorias	carrots

SALADS

ensalada de apio	celery salad	ensalada varias	mixed salad
ensalada de pepinos	cucumber salad	lechuga	lettuce salad

EGGS

huevos	eggs	huevos fritos	fried eggs
huevos duros	hard-boiled eggs	huevos pasados	boiled eggs
huevos escalfados	poached eggs	huevos y tochino	bacon and eggs

FRUITS

albaricoques	apricots	manzanas	apples
cerezas	cherries	melocoton	peach
ciruelas	plums	naranjas	oranges
ciruelas con nata	with cream	pera	pear
frambuesas	raspberries	piña	pineapple
fruta	fruit	plátanos	bananas
fresas	strawberries	uvas	grapes
limon	lemon		

DESSERTS

buñuelos	doughnuts	helado	ice cream
bruñelos de fruta	fruit tart	macedonia	fruit salad
compota	stewed fruit	el postre	dessert
flan	caramel custard	queso	cheese
galletas	tea cakes	torta	cake

BEVERAGES

agua	water	jugo de tomate	tomato juice
aguardiente	brandy	leche	milk
café	coffee	licor	liqueur
cerveza	beer	sidra	cidar
ginebra	gin	sifon	soda
jerez	sherry	té	tea
jugo de naranjas	orange juice	vino	wine

CONDIMENTS AND OTHERS

aceite	oil	pan	bread
ajo	garlic	panecillo	roll
azúcar	sugar	pimienta	pepper
hielo	ice	sal	salt
manteca	butter	tostada	toast
mostaza	mustard	vinagre	vinegar

COOKING TERMS

asado	roast	**frito**	fried
cocido	broiled	**muy hecho**	well done
empanado	breaded	**poco hecho**	rare

RECURRING ITEMS: Among the classic dishes of Spain, which you'll find on nearly every menu, are *arroz con pollo* (chicken and rice), *paella* (sea food and rice), and *guisado* or *caldo gallego,* which both refer to various types of meat stews. The word *chuletas* refers to cutlets (like *chuletas de ternera*—veal cutlets), *costillas* are chops (costillas de . . .) and *relleno* is chopped meat. In addition to wine, a favorite summertime beverage is *sangria,* a punch drink made of fruit juices and vermouth, nearly always served in a big iced pitcher, and quite mild.

PORTUGUESE MENU TERMS

SOUPS (SOPAS)

caldo verde	potato and cabbage	sopa à alentejana	Alentejo soup
Canja de galinha	chicken soup	sopa de cebola	onion
crème de camarão	cream of shrimp	sopa de mariscos	shellfish
		sopa de queijo	cheese
crème de legumes	cream of vegetable	sopa de tomato	tomato

EGGS (OVOS)

com presunto	with ham	mexidos	scrambled
cozidos	hard boiled	omeleta	omelet
escalfados	poached	quentes	soft boiled
estrelados	fried	tortilha	Spanish omelet

FISH

ameijoas	clams	ostras	oysters
atum	tuna	peixe	fish
bacalhau	salted codfish	peixe espada	swordfish
cherne	turbot	percebes	barnacles
camarãos	shrimps	pescada	hake
eiró	eel	robalo	bass
lagosta	lobster	sardinhas	sardines
linguado	sole	salmonete	red mullet
lulas	squid	santola	crab

SPECIALTIES

bife na frigideira	steak with mustard sauce	**porco Alentejano**	pork in a sauce of tomatoes and clams
cladeirada	fishermen's stew		
cozido à portuguesa	Portuguese stew		

MEAT (CARNE)

bife	steak	**iscas**	liver
borrego	lamb	**lingua**	tongue
cabrito	kid	**porco**	pork
carne	meat	**presunto**	ham
carneiro	mutton	**rim**	kidney
coelho	rabbit	**salchichas**	sausages
costeletas	chops	**vaca**	beef
dobrada	tripe	**vitela**	veal

POULTRY

aves	poultry	**ganso**	goose
borracho	pigeon	**pato**	duck
frango	chicken	**perdiz**	partridge
galinha	fowl	**perú**	turkey

VEGETABLES

aipo	celery	**couves**	cabbage
alcachôfra	artichoke	**ervilhas**	peas
arroz	rice	**espargos**	asparagus
azeitonas	olives	**espinafres**	spinach
batatas	potatoes	**favas**	broad beans
berinjela	eggplant	**feijão**	bean
beterrabas	beets	**legumes**	vegetables
cebola	onion	**nabo**	turnip
cenouras	carrots	**pepino**	cucumber
congumelo	mushroom	**tomate**	tomato
couve-flor	cauliflower		

SALAD

agrioes	watercress	**salada verde**	green salad
alface	lettuce	**Russa**	Russian
salada mista	mixed salad		

DESSERTS

arroz doce	rice pudding	pêssego Melba	peach Melba
bolo	cake	pudim flan	egg custard
gelados diversos	mixed ice cream	pudim de pao	bread pudding
		salada de frutas	fruit salad
maca assada	baked apple	sobremesa	dessert
pastelaria	pastry	sorvetes	sherbets
		queijo	cheese

FRUIT

abacate	avocado	melancia	watermelon
alperches	apricots	melao	melon
ameixa	plum	morangos	strawberries
ananas	pineapple	peras	pears
cerajas	cherries	pêssegos	peaches
figos	figs	roma	pomegranate
framboesa	raspberry	tâmara	date
frutas	fruits	toronja	grapefruit
laranjas	oranges	uvas	grapes
limao	lemon	macas	apples

BEVERAGES

água	water	leite	milk
água mineral	mineral water	sumo de fruta	fruit juice
café	coffee	sumo de laranja	orange juice
chá	tea	sumo de tomate	tomato juice
cerveja	beer	vinho branco	white wine
com gelo	with ice	vinho tinto	red wine
laranjada	orangeade	vinho verde	"young" wine

CONDIMENTS

açúcar	sugar	mostarda	mustard
alho	garlic	compota	jam
azeite	olive oil	pimenta	pepper
caril	curry	sal	salt
manteiga	butter	vinagre	vinegar

MISCELLANEOUS

chocolate	chocolate	pão	bread
biscoito	cracker	pão torrado	toast
gelo	ice		

COOKING TERMS

assado no forno	baked	frito	fried
cozido	boiled	mal passado	rare
estufada	braised	bem passado	well done

ITALIAN MENU TERMS

SOUPS

brodo	consomme	riso in brodo	rice soup
minestra	soup	zuppa alla Pavese	egg soup
minestrone	vegetable soup	zuppa di fagioli	bean soup
pastina in brodo	noodle soup	zuppa di pesce	fish soup

FISH

acciugh	anchovies	merluzzo	cod
aragosta	lobster	ostriche	oysters
aringhe	herrings	pesce	fish
filetto di sogliola	filet of sole	sardine	sardine
fritto di pesce	assorted fried fish	scampi fritti	fried shrimps
		sgombro	mackerel
frutta di mare	assorted sea foods	sogliola	sole
		tonno	tuna fish
gamberi	shrimps	trota	trout

MEATS

abbachio	baby lamb	lingua	tongue
agnello	lamb	maiale	pork
anitra	duck	manzo lesso	boiled beef
bistecca	steak	pancetta	bacon
carne	meat	pollo	chicken
carne fredda assortita	cold cuts	pollo alla diavolo	deviled chicken
cervello	brains		

cotoletta alla Bolognese	veal cutlet with melted cheese	prosciutto	ham
		reni	kidney
cotoletta alla Milanese	breaded veal cutlet	rosbif	roast beef
		salsicce	sausages
		saltimbocca	veal and ham
fagiano	pheasant	tacchino	turkey
fegatini	chicken livers	tournedo	beef
fegato	liver	vitello	veal
lepre	rabbit		

EGGS

omelette or frittata	omelette	strapazzate al pomodoro	tomato omelette
omelette alla parmigiana	cheese omelette	uova	eggs
		uova affogate	poached eggs
omelette di fegatini	omelette w/chicken livers	uova a la coque	boiled eggs
		uova fritte	fried eggs
omelette di funghi	mushroom omelette	uova strapazzate	scrambled eggs
pan dorato	French fried toast		

VEGETABLES

antipasto	hors d'oeuvres	olive	olives
asparagi	asparagus	patate	potatoes
cannelloni	pasta with meat filling	peperoni	green, red or yellow peppers
carciofi	artichokes	piselli	peas
carrote	carrots	pizza	you know this one
cavolfiore	cauliflower	pomodori	tomatoes
cavolo	cabbage	ravioli alla Fiorentina	cheese ravioli
cetrioli	cucumbers		
cipolle	onions	ravioli alla vegetariana	ravioli with tomato sauce
fagiolini	string beans		
fettuccine	noodles	riso	rice
funghi	mushrooms	risotto	rice dish
insalata mista	mixed salad	sedano	celery
insalata verde	lettuce salad	spinaci	spinach
lattuga	lettuce	verdura	vegetables
melanzana	eggplant	zucchini	squash

FRUITS

ananasso	pineapple	frutta cotta	stewed fruit
aranci	oranges	limoni	lemons

banane	bananas	**mele**	apples
ciliegie	cherries	**pere**	pears
frutta	fruit	**uva**	grape

BEVERAGES

acqua	water	**caffè**	coffee
acqua minerale	mineral water	**latte**	milk
aranciata	orangeade	**limonata**	lemonade
bibite	beverages	**thè**	tea
birra	beer	**vino**	wine

DESSERTS

budino	pudding	**macedonia di frutta**	fruit salad
cassata	ice cream with fruit	**pasticceria**	pastry
dolci	dessert	**pesca alla Melba**	peach melba
formaggio	cheese	**torta**	cake
gelato	ice cream		

CONDIMENTS AND OTHERS

aceto	vinegar	**olio**	oil
biscotti	crackers	**pane**	bread
burro	butter	**pepe**	pepper
ghiaccio	ice	**sale**	salt
marmellata	jam	**sott'aceti**	pickles
mostarda	mustard	**zucchero**	sugar

COOKING TERMS

al sangue	rare	**ben cotto**	well done
arrosto	roast	**lesso (or) bollito**	broiled

ITALIAN STAPLES: You'll invariably find, at the start of the menu, a collection of soups including *pastina in brodo* or *tortellini in brodo* or some other *in brodo* combination, which merely refer to various types of pasta served in a soup broth. Into it you sprinkle grated cheese, and the resulting combination makes an always satisfying first course. The spaghetti dishes come next, either *al pomodoro* (with tomato sauce) or *alla Bolognese* or *con carne* (meat sauce) or *alle vongole* (with clam sauce) or, best yet, *alla carbonara* (cooked in egg, with bits of bacon—delicious). Among the main courses, the term *scallopine,* followed by various words, always refers to slices of veal, cooked in various ways; while *cotolette* is almost always a breaded veal cutlet. *Saltimbocca* is the famous veal-and-ham dish; *bistecca* is beefsteak; *maiale* indicates a pork dish; *manzo* a beef plate; *pollo* is chicken; *ossobuco* is shank of veal; *fegato* is liver. Among the other items, *risotto* indicates a rice dish, served alone or with various sauces; and *cassata* is the name for ice-cream-and-fruit. Among the adjectival food terms, *filetto* means filet (like *filetto di sogliole*—filet of sole); *involtini* indicates something that is rolled (like *involtini di manzo*—rolled beef); and *salsa* or *sugo* means sauce. Thus, *spaghetti al sugo di carne* is spaghetti with meat sauce.

Some recurring main courses include: *bracciola alla milanese* (fried veal chop), *manzo bollito* (boiled beef), *pollo alla cacciatora* (stewed chicken), *spezzatino di manzo* (beef stew), *vitello al forno* (roast veal).

SWEDISH MENU TERMS

SOUPS

ärtsoppa	pea soup	**kålsoppa**	cabbage soup
buljong	broth	**soppa**	soup

MEATS

anka	duck	**korv**	sausage
biffstek	steak	**kyckling**	chicken
fårkött	mutton	**lamm**	lamb
fläsk	port	**lever**	liver
gås	goose	**oxe**	beef
kalv	veal	**rostbiff**	roast beef
		skinka	ham

VEGETABLES

ärta	pea	**lök**	onion
ärwskocka	artichoke	**makaroner**	macaroni
blomkål	cauliflower	**morot**	carrot
bruna bönor	kidney beans	**potatis**	potatoes
gurka	cucumber	**rödbeta**	beet
kål	cabbage	**sparris**	asparagus

FISH

anjovis	anchovies	**torsk**	cod
fisk	fish	**makrill**	mackerel

hummer	lobster	**ostron**	oyster
karp	carp	**sill**	herring
kaviar	caviar	**stör**	sturgeon
kolja	haddock		

DESSERTS

sockerkaka	cake	**ost**	cheese
kakor	pastry	**russinkaka**	plumcake

FRUITS

apelsiner	oranges	**persika**	peach
körsbär	cherry	**plommon**	plum
avocado	avocado	**vindruva**	grape
päron	pear		

BEVERAGES

kaffe	coffee	**öl or pilsner**	beer
karnmjölk	buttermilk	**te**	tea
mjölk	milk	**vatten**	water
öl	ale		

CONDIMENTS AND OTHERS

ägg	egg	**salt**	salt
attika	vinegar	**senap**	mustard
bröd	bread	**smör**	butter
peppar	pepper	**socker**	sugar
pepparrot	horseradish	**vitlök**	garlic

DUTCH MENU TERMS

SOUPS

aardapplesoep	potato soup	**kippensoep**	chicken soup
bonensoep	bean soup	**soep**	soup
erwtensoep	pea soup	**tomatensoep**	tomato soup
groentesoep	vegetable soup	**uiensoep**	onion soup

MEATS

bief	beef	koude schotel	cold cuts
biefstuk	steak	lamscotelet	lamb chops
chateaubriand	filet steak	lamsvlees	lamb
eend	duck	lever	liver
gans	goose	niertjes	kidneys
gebraden worst	fried sausage	ragout	beef stew
gevogelte	poultry	spek	bacon
kalkoen	turkey	varkensvlees	pork
kip	chicken	worstjes	sausages
kohijn	rabbit		

FISH

forel	trout	makreel	mackerel
garnalen	shrimp	mosselen	mussels
gerookte zalm	smoked salmon	oesters	oysters
haring	herring	sardientjes	sardines
kabeljauw	haddock	vis	fish
kreeft	lobster	zalm	salmon

EGGS

eieren	eggs	spiegeleieren	fried eggs
hardgekookte eieren	hard-boiled eggs	zachtgekookte eieren	boiled eggs
roereieren	scrambled eggs		

VEGETABLES

aardappelen	potatoes	prinsesseboontjes	green beans
asperges	asparagus	purée	mashed potatoes
augurkjes	pickles	radijsjes	radishes
bonen	beans	rapen	turnips
bieten	beets	rijst	rice
erwtjes	peas	sla	lettuce
groente	vegetables	spinazie	spinach
kool	cabbage	tomaten	tomatoes
patates frites	French fried potatoes	worteltjes	carrots
		zuurkool	sauerkraut

SALADS

sla	salad	**komkommersla**	cucumber salad

FRUITS

appelen	apples	**fruit**	fruit
bananen	bananas	**kersen**	cherries
citroenen	lemons	**sinaasappelen**	oranges
druiven	grapes	**pruimen**	plums

DESSERTS

ananas	pineapple	**kaas**	cheese
cake	cake	**nagerecht**	dessert
frambozen	raspberries	**omelette**	omelette
ijs	ice cream	**compôte**	stewed fruits
jam	jam	**zwatre bessen**	blackberries

BEVERAGES, CONDIMENTS, AND OTHERS

azijn	vinegar	**peper**	pepper
bier	beer	**rode wijn**	red wine
boter	butter	**suiker**	sugar
broodje	a roll	**thee**	tea
cognac	brandy	**tomaten sap**	tomato juice
croissants	breakfast rolls	**water**	water
gebak	pastry	**wijn**	wine
koffie	coffee	**witte wijn**	white wine
melk	milk	**zout**	salt
mosterd	mustard		

COOKING TERMS

gebakken	fried	**niet doorgebakken**	rare
gekookt	boiled	**onder de vlam geroosterd**	
goed doorgebakken	well done		broiled

DANISH MENU TERMS

SOUPS AND APPETIZERS

aspargesuppe	asparagus soup	**koldt bord**	hors d'oeuvres
blomkaalsuppe	cauliflower soup	**smorrebrod**	open sandwiches
gule aerter	pea soup		

FISH

al	eel	**musslinger**	mussels
fiskerfrikadeller	fish cakes	**orred**	trout
helleflynder	halibut	**pighvarre**	turbot
hummer	lobster	**rejer**	shrimps
krabber	crabs	**rodspaette**	plaice
krebs	crayfish	**sild**	herring
laks	salmon	**torsk**	cod
makrel	mackerel		

MEATS AND EGGS

aeggekage	omelette	**kalvesteg**	roast veal
agerhons	partridge	**kylling**	chicken
and	duck	**lam**	lamb
andesteg	roast duck	**lammesteg**	roast lamb
blødkogt aeg	soft-boiled egg	**lever**	liver
bof	steak	**leverpostej**	liver paté
boller	meat balls	**okse**	beef
due	pigeon	**oksesteg**	roast beef
dyr	venison	**polser**	sausages
fasan	pheasant	**roraeg**	scrambled eggs
flaeskesteg	roast pork	**skinke**	ham
gaas	goose	**spegepolse**	salami
hakkebof	hamburger	**spejlaeg**	fried egg
hardkogt aeg	hard-boiled egg	**svin**	pork
kalkun	turkey	**tunge**	tongue
kalve	veal	**vildand**	wild duck

VEGETABLES

aerter	peas	**kartofler**	potatoes
agurk	cucumber	**log**	onions
asparges	asparagus	**ris**	rice
blomkaal	cauliflower	**rodkal**	red cabbage
bonner	string beans	**rosenkaal**	brussels sprouts

gulerodder	carrots	**tomater**	tomatoes
hvidkal	cabbage		

FRUITS

aebler	apples	**ferskner**	peaches
ananas	pineapple	**hindbaer**	raspberries
appelsiner	oranges	**jordbaer**	strawberries
blommer	plums	**paerer**	pears

DESSERTS

budding	pudding	**kompot**	stewed fruit
hindbaer med flode	raspberries	**kager**	pastry
	with cream	**ost**	cheese
is	ice cream		

BEVERAGES, CONDIMENTS, AND OTHERS

aeblemost	apple juice	**salt**	salt
brod	bread	**smor**	butter
flode	cream	**te**	tea
kaffe	coffee	**vand**	water
maelk	milk	**vin**	wine
ol	beer	**Wienerbrod**	Danish Pastry
ristet brod	toast		

COOKING TERMS

grilleret	grilled	**ristet**	fried
farseret	stuffed	**stegt**	roast
kogt	broiled		

Chapter XXX

MONEY RATES

The Cost of $25

THE SUBJECT of European currency was once enshrouded in a haze of black markets and mathematical formulas. By skillfully changing your dollars into foreign money at the right time, and in the right place, you could once increase your funds by as much as 20%.

In those days, every smart tourist carried hand-me-down lists of money-changers who performed this feat: a celebrated bartender in Paris, who gave you many more francs to the dollar; a bookseller in Barcelona, who offered half-again as many pesetas as you could obtain at the Spanish bank.

Those days, and those gentlemen, have—sad to relate—vanished with the increasing prosperity of Europe. Today, virtually every European currency is solid and stable. Excepting only the currencies of Turkey and Yugoslavia, there no longer exists any significant difference between the unofficial rates of exchange for all European currencies. You'll receive, for instance, almost as many francs for your dollar in Paris, as you will in New York or Switzerland. While, at certain periods of the year, a variance of 1% or so may creep into those rates, the difference just isn't worth the effort to obtain it.

We'll therefore eliminate any general discussion of money-changing from this chapter, and concentrate on bare essentials: the rates of exchange for the currencies of Western Europe, set forth in condensed, easy-to-use style:

AUSTRIA

The unit of Austrian currency is the schilling, divided into 100 groschen. Currently, one receives approximately 18.50 schillings for one dollar, and equivalencies are as follows:

Schillings	U.S.$	Schillings	U.S.$
1	.05	20	1.08
2	.11	25	1.35
5	.27	50	2.70
10	.54	100	5.40

BELGIUM

Basic unit is the franc, of which you get 55 for a dollar; the franc is further divided into 100 centimes.

Francs	U.S.$	Francs	U.S.$
1	.02	25	.45
5	.09	50	.91
10	.18	100	1.82

DENMARK

Kroner and ore are the units used. You'll receive approximately 10 kroner to the dollar, and 100 ore for each krone.

Ore	U.S.$	Kroner	U.S.$
1	.001	1	.10
5	.005	2	.20
10	.010	5	.50
25	.025	10	1.00
		50	5.00

FRANCE

Francs and centimes are the units used; there are 100 centimes to a franc. Current rate is approximately 8 francs for one dollar, making each franc worth about

Centimes	U.S.$	Francs	U.S.$
5	.006	1	.12
10	.012	2	.25
20	.025	5	.62
80	.10	10	1.25
		40	5.00

GERMANY

The basic monetary unit in Germany is the mark, which is further subdivided into 100 pfennigs. Current rate of exchange is approximately 2.60 marks to the dollar, which results in the following:

Pfennigs	U.S.$	Marks	U.S.$
1	.004	1	0.38
5	.02	5	1.92
10	.04	10	3.84
50	.19	20	7.69

GREECE

Drachmas and leptas (but you'll rarely see a lepta). Approximately 100 drachmas to the dollar, and 100 leptas to each drachma.

Drachmas	U.S.$	Drachmas	U.S.$
1	.010	15	.15
5	.050	20	.20
10	.10	30	.30
		100	1.00

HOLLAND

Monetary unit is the guilder, sometimes known as the florin or the gulden. Each guilder is divided into 100 "cents." As of the time we wrote this year's chapter on Amsterdam, the guilder was exchanged at a rate of 3 to the dollar, which made each guilder worth approximately 33 U.S. cents.

Dutch Cents	U.S.$	Guilders	U.S.$
1	.003	1	.33
5	.017	5	1.66
10	.03	10	3.33
25	.83	20	6.66

ITALY

The unit of Italian currency is the lira, spelled in the plural: lire. The exchange rate is about 1,600 lire to the dollar, which makes each lira worth .062 U.S. cents.

Lire	U.S.$	Lire	U.S.$
50	.031	1000	.62
100	.062	5000	3.12
500	.31	10,000	6.25

NORWAY

Norway, like Denmark, uses kroner and ore. You'll receive approximately 7.50 kroner for a dollar, and 100 ore for each krone.

Ore	U.S.$	Kroner	U.S.$
10	.013	1	.13
25	.033	5	.66
50	.066	10	1.33
		25	3.33
		50	6.66

PORTUGAL

The unit of currency is the escudo; approximately 130 to a dollar.

Escudos	U.S.$	Escudos	U.S.$
1	.007	20	.15
5	.038	50	.38
10	.077	100	.77

SPAIN

Spain uses pesetas and centimos (100 centimos to a peseta). At a bank or other exchange point, you'll usually receive 150 pesetas for one U.S. dollar.

Pesetas	U.S.$	Pesetas	U.S.$
1	.006	20	.13
5	.033	50	.33
10	.06	100	.66

SWEDEN

Sweden's basic money unit is the krona, spelled kronor in the plural. There are 100 ore per krona. You'll get 8 to a dollar.

Ore	U.S.$	Kronor	U.S.$
5	.006	1	.12
10	.012	2	.25
25	.031	5	.62
50	.062	10	1.25

SWITZERLAND

The Swiss currency, strongest in the world, uses francs and centimes. Following successive devaluations of the U.S. dollar, travelers now receive 2.10 francs to the dollar; and at that current rate of exchange, it's convenient to use 47¢ as the value of the franc.

Centimes	U.S.$	Francs	U.S.$
5	.023	1	.47
10	.047	5	2.38
20	.095	20	9.52
50	.23	50	23.80

UNITED KINGDOM
(England, Scotland, Wales and Northern Ireland)

Basic unit is the pound, divided into 100 new pence. The pound is now worth about $1.40.

Pence	U.S.$	Pounds	U.S.$
1	.014	1	1.40
5	.070	2	2.80
25	.35	5	7.00
50	.70	10	14.00

AND FINALLY

To round off the list: Yugoslavia, having devalued its currency considerably, now gives 140 dinars for one U.S. dollar. Finland exchanges approximately 5.80 Finnish marks (markka) for one dollar. In Turkey, the official rate is 320 pounds (lira) to a dollar and in Ireland one dollar is worth about 1 Irish pound.

And there you have it—*Europe on $25 a Day.*

About The Authors

Arthur Frommer is a graduate of the Yale University Law School, where he was an editor of the Yale Law Journal, and he is a member of the New York Bar. After service in Europe with U.S. Army Intelligence, he practiced law in New York until a growing involvement with this and other books required full-time attention to activities in the travel industry. He is the founder of Arthur Frommer, Inc., a travel publishing company; of Arthur Frommer Hotels, Inc., which created the Hotel Arthur Frommers in Amsterdam and Copenhagen; of the $25-a-Day Travel Club, Inc.; and of Arthur Frommer Holidays, Inc., a wholesale tour and charter operator. In addition to writing *Europe on $25 a Day*, he is the author of *A Dollarwise Guide to New York, Surprising Amsterdam,* and two books dealing with political and legal topics.

Hope Arthur (Mrs. Arthur Frommer) is a graduate of Northwestern University and of The Royal Academy of Dramatic Art in London. She has appeared on Broadway (as Maria in "The Best House in Naples") and in numerous Off-Broadway productions, and has directed plays for the Circle and Cherry Lane Theatres and for the National Academy of T.V. Arts & Sciences. Currently she is on the faculty of the Lee Strasberg Institute. In addition to her theatrical activities, she has written for national magazines.

NOW, SAVE MONEY ON ALL YOUR TRAVELS!
Join Arthur Frommer's $25-A-Day Travel Club

Saving money while traveling is never a simple matter, which is why, over 22 years ago, the **$25-A-Day Travel Club** was formed. Actually, the idea came from readers of the Arthur Frommer Publications who felt that such an organization could bring financial benefits, continuing travel information, and a sense of community to economy-minded travelers all over the world.

In keeping with the money-saving concept, the annual membership fee is low—$15 (U.S. residents) or $18 (Canadian, Mexican, and foreign residents)—and is immediately exceeded by the value of your benefits which include:

(1) The latest edition of any TWO of the books listed on the following page.

(2) An annual subscription to an 8-page quarterly newspaper *The Wonderful World of Budget Travel* which keeps you up-to-date on fastbreaking developments in low-cost travel in all parts of the world—bringing you the kind of information you'd have to pay over $25 a year to obtain elsewhere. This consumer-conscious publication also includes the following columns:

Travelers' Directory—members all over the world who are willing to provide hospitality to other members as they pass through their home cities.

Share-a-Trip—requests from members for travel companions who can share costs and help avoid the burdensome single supplement.

Readers Ask ... Readers Reply—travel questions from members to which other members reply with authentic firsthand information.

(3) A copy of *Arthur Frommer's Guide to New York.*

(4) Your personal membership card which entitles you to purchase through the Club all Arthur Frommer Publications for a third to a half off their regular retail prices during the term of your membership.

So why not join this hardy band of international budgeteers NOW and participate in its exchange of information and hospitality? Simply send $15 (U.S. residents) or $18 U.S. (Canadian, Mexican, and other foreign residents) along with your name and address to: $25-A-Day Travel Club, Inc., 1230 Avenue of the Americas, New York, NY 10020. Remember to specify which *two* of the books in section (1) above you wish to receive in your initial package of members' benefits. Or tear out this page, check off any two books on the opposite side and send it to us with your membership fee.